COLLECTIVE BARGAINING AND LABOR RELATIONS

COLLECTIVE BARGAINING AND LABOR RELATIONS

Terry L. Leap

Clemson University

Macmillan Publishing Company
New York

Collier Macmillan Canada
Toronto

Maxwell Macmillan International
New York   Oxford   Singapore   Sydney

Editor: Charles Stewart
Production Supervisor: John Travis
Production Manager: Sandra Moore
Text Designer: Jane Edelstein
Cover Designer: Jane Edelstein
Illustrations by Academy ArtWorks, Inc.

Copyright © 1991 by Macmillan Publishing Company, a division of Macmillan, Inc. Printed in the United States of America

All rights reserved. No part of this book may be reproduced or transmitted in any form or by any means, electronic or mechanical, including photocopying, recording, or any information storage and retrieval system, without permission in writing from the publisher.

Macmillan Publishing Company
866 Third Avenue, New York, New York 10022

Collier Macmillan Canada

1200 Eglinton Ave., E.
Suite 200
Don Mills, Ontario M3C 3N1

Library of Congress Cataloging in Publication Data

Leap, Terry L. (date)
    Collective bargaining and labor relations / Terry L. Leap.
       p.   cm.
    Includes bibliographical references and index.
    ISBN 0-02-369070-4
     1. Collective bargaining. 2. Industrial relations. I. Title.
HD6971.5.L43   1991
331.89—dc20
                                                                                                                                                      90-35862
                                                                                                                                                       CIP

Printing: 1   2   3   4   5   6   7   8   9   Year 1   2   3   4   5   6   7   8   9   0

To the memory of Vivian Johnson Coston

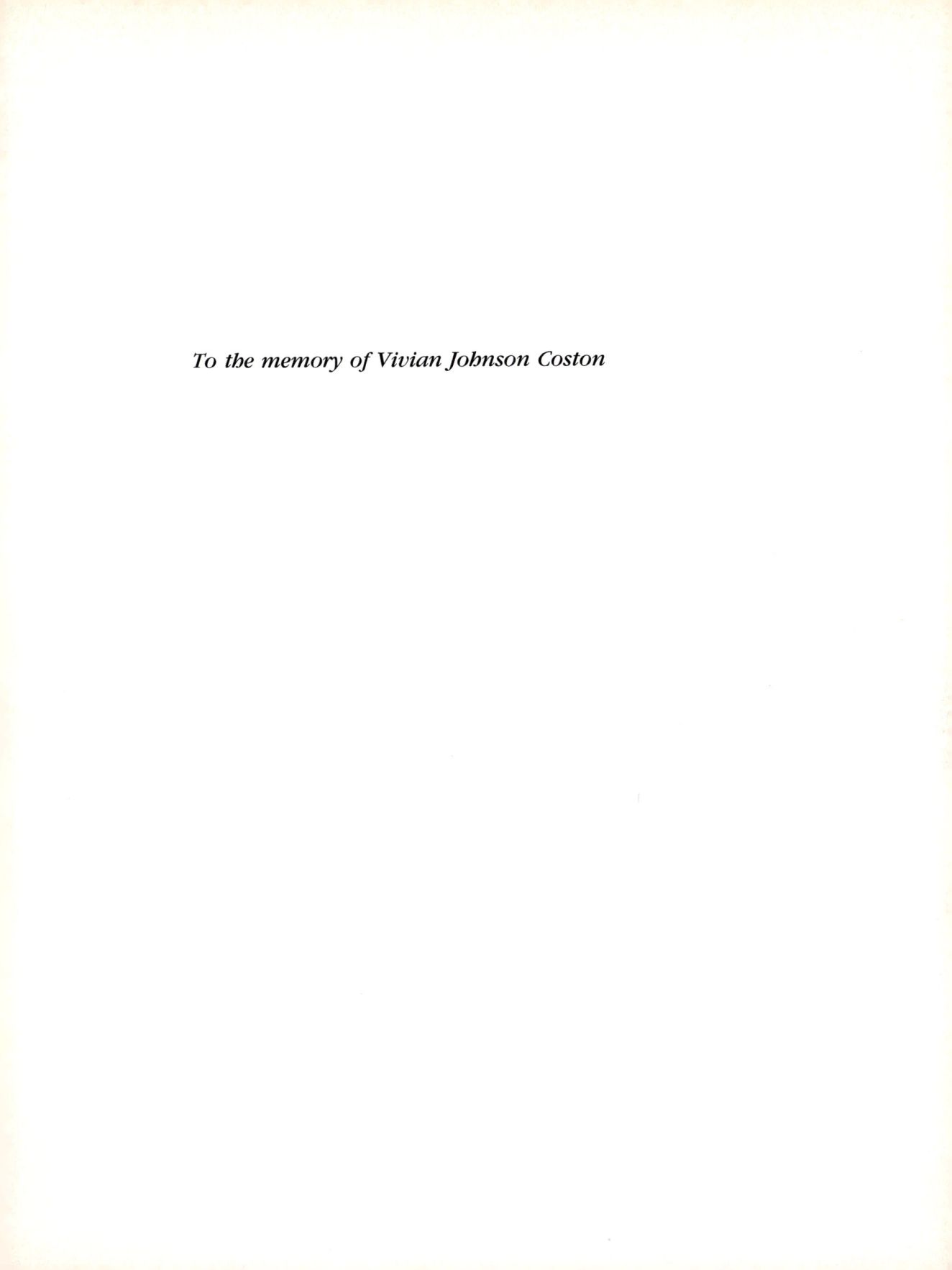

PREFACE

Collective bargaining and labor relations continues to be a subject of significant interest to many students in business, economics, education, health care administration, and other disciplines. Some students enrolled in a course on collective bargaining and labor relations have had some exposure to organized labor through their employment experiences (or the experiences of their friends and families). Other students have little knowledge of the field, but want to know more about it. Still others may want to learn about the field because they anticipate working in an organization whose employees are union members.

Collective Bargaining and Labor Relations examines the evolution, current state, and future of union–management relations in the United States. Having taught graduate and undergraduate courses in the field over the past 15 years, I have developed an appreciation for the rich history of the U.S. labor movement. Collective bargaining and labor relations is a fascinating subject at all organizational levels—the shop floor, the bargaining table, and the boardrooms of corporate and labor leaders. This claim is not based just on my personal biases, but also on the enthusiasm that students have exhibited toward the subject in my undergraduate and graduate classes.

As the plan for the book evolved, I decided that a successful addition to the collective bargaining and labor relations textbook market should have several characteristics.

First, the content should be thorough and comprehensive. *Collective Bargaining and Labor Relations* covers the traditional topics of labor history, labor law, union organizing campaigns, labor disputes, grievances and arbitration, substantive provisions of the collective bargaining agreement, and public-sector collective bargaining. The book also discusses emerging issues such as labor–management cooperation programs, the membership decline in U.S. labor unions, the impact of foreign competition and industry deregulation on the U.S. labor movement, and drug testing and AIDS in the workplace, to name a few.

Second, a successful textbook must be written in a style that is easy to understand without sacrificing important details. Every effort has been made to use a writing style that is both appealing and readable. Some college-level texts are written in such general terms that the student emerges from the course with little more than a vague idea as to what a particular discipline is all about. A textbook that fails to demonstrate the complexities of the field short-changes the student. Many of our students are prospective managers and supervisors. Others may serve as shop stewards, negotiators, or union officials. *Collective Bargaining and Labor Relations* provides details that should be understood by those who will be directly or indirectly involved with the field.

Third, a book on collective bargaining and labor relations needs realistic and timely examples. The chapters of this book provide numerous examples of recent vintage. Many of the latest developments have been covered by *The Wall Street Journal, Business Week*, various publications by The Bureau of National Affairs, Inc. (such as *Collective Bargaining Negotiations & Contracts*), and other business periodicals. In addition, a number of the chapters contain supplemental cases for student analysis. These include National Labor Relations Board unfair labor practice cases; summaries of recent labor disputes; and arbitration cases involving grievances over compensation, management rights, employee discipline and discharge, and other issues.

Fourth, a textbook needs a mechanism to encourage the student to critically evaluate the material from the chapters. To meet this objective, *Collective Bargaining and Labor Relations* contains discussion questions and short exercises at the end of each chapter.

Fifth, a book needs to be well-referenced and reflect the most current academic and professional literature in the field. *Collective Bargaining and Labor Relations* cites both the classic literature in the field as well as a large volume of material from the late 1980s and 1990.

Finally, a book should be able to accommodate a variety of pedagogical approaches. Instructors teaching collective bargaining and labor relations develop teaching styles that suit their personal preferences, level of student preparedness, and institutional norms. Some instructors emphasize the traditional lecture method, whereas others use case studies, simulation, supplemental readings on current topics, and other methods. *Collective Bargaining and Labor Relations* is written to support these alternative teaching methods. There is sufficient detail in the text to allow students to acquire a basic understanding of the major topics. Instructors can choose to expand on selected topics with lectures, confident that the student will have a basic understanding of the remaining topics. I believe that the book gives the instructor the latitude to use whatever pedagogical methods he or she desires to improve the student's mastery of topics in the field as well as to sharpen their decision-making skills.

ACKNOWLEDGMENTS

A number of people played an important role in the development and publication of *Collective Bargaining and Labor Relations*. Charles Stewart, Barbara Newman, and John Travis of Macmillan Publishing Company were always available to help me through the numerous decisions that are encountered in a project of this type. I am also indebted to a number of colleagues who reviewed all or part of this manuscript: Arthur Eliot Berkeley, Memphis State University; James A. Bitter, University of Northern Colorado; James B. Dworkin, Purdue University; Daniel G. Gallagher, James Madison University; Isadore B. Helburn, The University of Texas at Austin; Marvin S. Katzman, George Washington University; and Steven D. Maurer, Washington State University.

There are also a number of individuals who played an indirect, but important, role in helping me through this project. First and foremost, my wife Carolyn took over many of my domestic chores so that I could spend more time developing the text. To her I owe a debt of gratitude. My daughter Cathy, now a student at Indiana University, provided an incentive to finish this manuscript so that I could use the royalty income to help pay for her education. My son Christopher, however, made me realize that there are more important things in life than sitting hours on end in front of a personal computer. I would like to thank two colleagues, Michael D. Crino and Pete Nagele of Clemson University, for their suggestions on various parts of the book. I would also like to thank my graduate student assistant Melanie A. Wallace for her help during the final stages of manuscript preparation. Finally thanks go to William H. Hendrix, Head of the Department of Management, and Ryan C. Amacher, Dean of the College of Commerce and Industry at Clemson University for providing the administrative support for my work.

T.L.L.

CONTENTS

▲ ▲

▲ **PART I**
AN INTRODUCTION TO COLLECTIVE BARGAINING AND LABOR RELATIONS 1

1 *An Overview of Labor Relations* 2

    Introduction 3
    Why Unions Exist 4
        Managements' View of Labor Unions 5
        Are Labor Unions Good or Bad? 6
        Establishing the Union-Management Relationship 6
    The Three Levels of Union-Management Interaction 7
        Contract Negotiations 7
        Contract Administration 9
        Informal Joint Consultation 10
    Unionization Trends 11
    Collective Bargaining and the U.S. Labor Force 12
    The Impact of Collective Bargaining on Organizations and Society 15
        Impact of Collective Bargaining on Employees 17
        Impact of Collective Bargaining on Employers 18
        Impact of Collective Bargaining on Society 18
    The Academic Foundation of Labor Relations 19
    Plan for the Book 21
    Discussion Questions and Exercises 21

2 *The History of Collective Bargaining and Labor Relations in the United States* 23

    Introduction 24
    The Theory of Labor Movements 24
    Organized Labor: The First Unions 28
        From Farm to Factory: Early Labor Force Problems 28
    Labor Crises and Violence 30
        Violence on the Railroads 30
        The Haymarket Square Riot 32

Violence in Coal Mining and the Molly Maguires   32
The Role of Violence in the Labor Movement   33
The National Labor Union   34
The Knights of Labor   36
Political and Economic Perspectives of the Knights   36
The Rise and Fall of the Knights: What Happened?   37
The American Federation of Labor (AFL)   38
Political and Economic Perspectives of the AFL   39
The Industrial Workers of the World (IWW)   40
Political and Economic Perspective of the IWW   40
Downfall of the IWW   41
Trade Unionism in the 20th Century   42
1900–1920   42
The Roaring 1920s: Not A Roaring Time for Unionism   42
The 1930s: The Rise of the CIO and Labor Legislation   44
The 1940s: World War II and the Increasing Power of Unions   48
The 1950s: The AFL and CIO Unite   49
The Labor Movement Since 1960   50
An Historical Synthesis and Summary   51
Discussion Questions and Exercises   53

▲ PART II
ESTABLISHING THE COLLECTIVE BARGAINING RELATIONSHIP   57

3 *The Legal Foundation of Collective Bargaining*   58

Introduction   59
The Historical Roots of Labor Relations Law   60
The Conspiracy Doctrine Applied to Unions   60
The Use and Abuse of the Labor Injunction   61
Role of the Sherman Antitrust Act   62
Yellow-Dog Contracts   63
The Need for Labor Legislation   63
The Railway Labor Act   64
The Norris-LaGuardia Act   65
The Wagner Act: Employer Unfair Labor Practices and Union Impetus   66
Historical Background   66
Organizations and Employees Covered   67
Section 7: Cornerstone of the Wagner Act   68
Employer Unfair Labor Practices: Protecting Employee and Union Rights   68
The Taft-Hartley Act: Rebalancing the Scales of Power   72
Historical Background   72
Provisions and Coverage of the Taft-Hartley Act   73

The National Labor Relations Board   80
    Processing Unfair Labor Practice Complaints and Charges   80
    The Private Settlement of Unfair Labor Practices   82
    Conducting Certification Elections   82
    The Board as a Political, Social, and Economic Weather Vane   83
The Landrum-Griffin Act: An Attempt to Control Labor Corruption   84
    Historical Background   84
    Provisions of the Landrum-Griffin Act   85
    Enforcement of the Landrum-Griffin Act   88
Other Legislation Having an Impact on Collective Bargaining and Labor Relations   88
    Equal Employment Opportunity Laws   89
    Compensation and Employee Benefit Laws   90
    The Occupational Safety and Health Act of 1970   90
Private-Sector and Public-Sector Collective Bargaining: Basic Differences in the Legal Frameworks   91
Summary and Conclusions   92
Discussion Questions and Exercises   93

4 *The Bargaining Unit*   95

Introduction   96
The Doctrine of Exclusive Representation   96
The Importance of the Bargaining Unit Structure   98
NLRB Criteria for Determining the Appropriate Bargaining Unit   100
The Treatment of Specialized Employee Groups   103
    Employees Who May Warrant Separate Bargaining Units   103
    Employees Who are Excluded from Bargaining Units   107
Some Common Bargaining Unit Structures   114
    Single-Employer, Single-Location Units   115
    Single-Employer, Multi-Location Units   116
    Multi-Employer Bargaining Units   118
    Coordinated Bargaining   120
Bargaining Units in Expanding Organizations   121
    Accretions to the Bargaining Unit   121
    Successorship Employers   122
Presumptively Appropriate Bargaining Units   124
Summary and Conclusions   125
Bargaining Unit Cases   126
    Cooper Union   126
    Community Hospital at Glen Cove   128
    Futuramik Industries   130
    U.S. Pollution Control, Inc.   131

5 *Union Organization Campaigns and Certification Elections*   133

Introduction   134

The Organizing Atmosphere   135
    Factors That Affect Employee Interest in Unions   135
    Factors in the Work Environment   138
    Personal and Demographic Factors   139
Union and Management Tactics During Organizational Campaigns   141
    Union Organizing Strategies   141
    Measures Taken by Employers During the Organizing Campaign   148
The Certification Election   158
Post-Election Matters   161
    Challenged Election Ballots   161
    Unfair Labor Practices That Preclude a Fair Election   162
    When Members No Longer Support the Union: The Decertification Process   164
Summary and Conclusions   165
Discussion Questions and Exercises   166
Certification Election Cases   167

▲ **PART III**
UNION AND MANAGEMENT ORGANIZATIONAL STRUCTURES, GOALS, AND POLICIES FOR COLLECTIVE BARGAINING   173

6 *The Union Structure, Goals, and Policies for Collective Bargaining*   174

Introduction   175
The Major Levels of Unionism   176
The AFL-CIO   178
    The AFL-CIO Structure   179
    Financial Aspects of the AFL-CIO   181
    Major Areas of Concern for the AFL-CIO   181
    The AFL-CIO: A Summary   188
The International Unions   189
    The Size of International Unions   189
    International Union Functions   190
    The Governance of International Unions   191
    International Union Organizational Structures   194
    International Union Finances   195
    The Central Role of International Unions   196
The Local Unions   198
    Local Union Functions   199
    Local Union Governance and Politics   201
Merger Activities and Organized Labor   202
    Union Mergers   202
    The Impact of Unions on Corporate Mergers and Buyouts   204
Unions as Democratic Institutions   205
    Democracy Defined   205

Barriers to Union Democracy   206
Some Suggestions for Making Unions More Democratic   208
Labor Unions and Organized Crime   209
How Big Is the Problem of Labor Racketeering and Who Is Involved?   209
The Effects of Organized Crime on Unions, Business, and Society   212
Government Action Against Labor Racketeering   213
Union Goals in Collective Bargaining   214
Determinants of Union Goals   215
A Look at Some Typical Union Bargaining Goals   217
Summary and Conclusions   218
Discussion Questions and Exercises   219

7 *Management Structure, Goals, and Policies for Collective Bargaining*   220

Introduction   221
Management Goals and Strategies   221
The Personnel/Human Resource Management Function   222
Major Differences Between Unionized and Nonunionized Firms   226
Recruitment and Selection of Employees   226
Training and Development of Employees   228
Employee Performance Appraisal   229
Compensation and Employee Benefits   231
Work Rules and Job Security Measures   233
Employee Discipline and Control   234
Bargaining With the Union   234
Management Bargaining Goals   235
Factors Affecting Management Bargaining Goals   236
Recent Trends in Management Bargaining Objectives   241
Balancing Union and Management Power Structures   242
Multiemployer Bargaining   245
Union-Management Cooperative Efforts   245
Opportunities Created by Cooperative Efforts   246
Potential Fears and Drawbacks of Cooperative Programs   247
Summary and Conclusions   249
Discussion Questions and Exercises   250

▲ PART IV
COLLECTIVE BARGAINING AGREEMENT NEGOTIATIONS   253

8 *The Collective Bargaining Process: A Theoretical Overview*   254

Introduction   255
The Role and Spectrum of Bargaining Theories   255
Mathematical/Economic Bargaining Models   256

Behavioral Bargaining Models 257
Descriptive Approaches to Bargaining 257
Some Selected Bargaining Theories 258
Pigou's Original Bargaining Model 258
A Behavioral Theory of Labor Negotiations 261
The Hicks Bargaining Model 263
Similarities Among Bargaining Theories 264
Settlement Points and Ranges 264
Costs of Agreeing and Disagreeing 265
The Rationality Assumption 266
The Element of Timing 267
Communications Issues and Policies 267
Bargaining Tactics and Concessions 268
A Model of Collective Bargaining Power 268
Sources of Bargaining Power 269
Factors That Dilute Bargaining Power 271
Relative, Absolute, and Total Bargaining Power 272
Problems With the Bargaining Power Concept 272
Collective Bargaining Tactics and Outcomes 273
Reaching a Settlement 273
Work Stoppages: Strikes and Lockouts 274
Dissolution of the Bargaining Relationship 275
Assessing the Outcome of Collective Bargaining 276
Summary and Conclusions 276
Discussion Questions and Exercises 277

9 *The Collective Bargaining Process: Preparation, Tactics, and Issues* 278

Introduction 279
Stages of the Bargaining Process 280
Preparation for Collective Bargaining 282
Beginning Preparations 282
Selecting a Bargaining Team and Chief Negotiator 283
Reviewing Previous Negotiations 287
Examining the Current Contract with an Eye Toward Change 288
Gathering Data on the Firm and the Industry 289
Economic Data Relevant to Collective Bargaining 290
Input From Employees and Supervisors 291
Formulating Proposals, Priorities, and Bottom-Line Positions 292
Selecting the Bargaining Site 296
Organizing the Plethora of Bargaining Information 296
The Legal Requirements of Collective Bargaining 297
Notification of Intent to Bargain 297
The Concept of Good-Faith Bargaining 298
Strategies and Tactics at the Bargaining Table 303

The Initial Proposal Stage   303
The Primary Bargaining Stage   304
The Eleventh-Hour Bargaining Stage   312
Summary and Conclusions   316
Discussion Questions and Exercises   317

▲ PART V
RESOLVING INTEREST AND RIGHTS DISPUTES OVER THE COLLECTIVE BARGAINING AGREEMENT   319

10 *Negotiation Impasses and Labor Disputes*   320

Introduction   321
Conflict in Labor-Management Relations   321
The Role of Conflict   321
Sources of Conflict in Labor-Management Relations   322
The Role of Mediation in Preventing Labor Disputes   328
Federal and State Mediation Agencies   329
The Functions of Labor Mediators   330
Mediation Effectiveness   334
Strikes and Lockouts   335
The Economic Strike   337
The Unfair Labor Practice Strike   347
Sympathy Strikes   348
Wildcat Strikes and Slowdowns   349
Lockouts   351
National Emergency Disputes   353
Summary and Conclusions   354
Discussion Questions and Exercises   355
Selected Labor Disputes   355

11 *Contract Administration: The Grievance Procedure*   360

Introduction   361
The Role of Contract Administration in Labor Relations   361
Sources of Grievances in Union-Management Relations   363
Disciplinary Problems   363
Disputes Over Compensation Practices   364
Problems Associated with Working Conditions   364
Inconsistent Enforcement of Personnel Policies by Supervisors   365
Economic Conditions Leading to Layoffs and Reduced Working Hours   365
Ambiguous Contract Language   367
Conflicts Regarding Past Practices   368
The Effect of Individual Employee Characteristics on Grievance Filing   368

Components of Grievance Procedures 369
    Parties to a Grievance 369
    Defining the Grievance 370
    Time Limits Between Stages of the Grievance Procedure 372
    Persons Involved in Processing and Evaluating Grievances 373
    Resolving Grievances 375
Processing Grievances 377
    The Initial Stage 377
    Processing Grievances to Higher Stages 379
Abuse and Misuse of Grievance Procedures 384
The Union's Duty of Fair Representation in Grievance Administration 385
Criteria for Evaluating Grievance Procedures 389
Summary and Conclusions 391
Appendix: Boeing-International Association of Machinists and Aerospace Workers Grievance Procedure 392

12 Labor Arbitration 397

Introduction 398
Arbitrator Selection 398
    The Arbitration Tribunal 400
The Legal Status of Arbitration 402
    The Enforceability of Arbitration Clauses: The *Lincoln Mills* Decision 403
    The Arbitration Tribunal and the Courts: The Trilogy Cases 404
    Grievances and Unfair Labor Practices: NLRB Deferral Policies 406
    Civil Rights Grievances: *Alexander v. Gardner-Denver* 408
    Arbitration and the Law: A Summary 409
The Issue of Arbitrability 410
Preparing a Case for Arbitration 411
Conducting the Arbitration Hearing 412
    The Setting 412
    Stating the Issue to Be Heard by the Arbitrator 413
    Procedural Rules and Practices 414
Common Errors in Arbitration 422
Factors Affecting Arbitration Decisions and Awards 422
    Interpreting the Collective Bargaining Agreement 423
    Sifting Through the Evidence 424
    Evaluating the Testimony of Witnesses 425
    Considering the Role of Custom and Past Practice 426
    Incorporating External Law into Arbitration Decisions 429
    Assessing the Precedent Value of Arbitration Awards 431
Professional and Ethical Standards for Arbitrators 432
Summary and Conclusions 432
Discussion Questions and Exercises 433
Appendix: Code of Professional Responsibility for Arbitrators 434

▲ PART VI
SUBSTANTIVE PROVISIONS OF THE COLLECTIVE BARGAINING AGREEMENT   445

13 *Economic and Compensation Issues*   447

Introduction   448
Factors Influencing Compensation in Collective Bargaining   450
    Economic Influences and External Labor Markets   450
    Organizational Influences and Internal Labor Markets   452
    Financial Condition of the Organization and Industry   452
    Inflation and Cost-of-Living Considerations   454
    Pay Equity   455
    Laws Regulating Compensation and Employee Benefits   456
    The Impact of Unions on Pay Levels   458
The Pay Level Decision   461
    The Concept of External Equity   461
    Sources of Wage and Salary Data   461
    Using the Wage Salary Data   463
The Pay Structure Decision   465
    The Concept of Internal Equity   465
    Job Evaluation: The Major Steps   466
    Job Evaluation: Some Important Considerations   467
    Computerized Job Evaluation and Skill-Based Pay   468
Merging the Pay Level and Pay Structure   468
    Establishing the Pay Policy Line   468
    Determining the Number of Pay Grades or Job Classifications   470
    Determining the Range of Pay Grades   472
    Determining Overlap Between Pay Grades   472
    The Use of Seniority and Merit in Pay Increases   473
    Supplementary Pay   476
    Wage Adjustments During the Life of the Collective Bargaining Agreement   478
    Two-Tier Compensation Systems   479
    Wage Rates for Promotions, Demotions, and Transfers   480
Individual and Group Incentive Programs   480
    Individual Incentive Programs   481
    Examples of Individual Incentive Programs   483
    Group and Organizational Incentives   483
    Examples of Group Incentive Programs   484
Sex Discrimination in Compensation Programs   485
    Equal Pay for Equal Work   486
    Comparable Worth: The Unsettled Issue   487
Summary and Conclusions   490
Discussion Questions and Exercises   490
Cases in Compensation   491
Appendix: The Major Methods of Job Evaluation   494

The Ranking Method   494
The Classification Method   494
The Factor Comparison Method   495
The Point Method   495

14 *Employee Benefit Programs*   496

Introduction   497
The Role of Employee Benefit Programs in Collective Bargaining Agreements   498
The Government's Role in Employee Benefit Plans   500
    Mandatory and Government-Provided Employee Benefits   500
    Government Regulation of Employee Benefits   504
Collectively-Bargained Benefits   504
Group Life Insurance   505
Accidental Death and Dismemberment Insurance   507
Group Health Insurance   507
    Medical Expense Insurance   507
    Health Maintenance Organizations   510
    Disability Income Insurance   511
    Other Important Health Care Contract Provisions   513
    Health Care Cost Containment Measures   513
Retirement Programs   517
    The Concept of a Pension   517
    The Employee Retirement Income Security Act of 1974   518
    Retirement Plan Terminology and Provisions   519
Income Maintenance Benefits   522
Paid Vacations, Holidays, and Sick Leave   523
Childcare and Eldercare Benefits   525
Employee Assistance Programs   526
Other Employee Benefit Programs   527
Communicating Employee Benefits   528
Summary and Conclusions   529
Discussion Questions and Exercises   530
Cases in Employee Benefits   530
Appendix: Calculating the Cost of Compensation and Benefit Provisions   533

15 *Institutional Issues: Balancing Management Rights Against Union and Employee Security*   549

Introduction   550
Management Rights   550
    The Residualist and Implied Obligation Views of Management Rights   551
    Management Rights Clauses   552
    Legal Factors Affecting Management Rights   553
    Management Rights and Arbitration   554
Seniority Arrangements   554
    The Application of Seniority Provisions   555

Calculating Seniority   558
The Effect of Mergers, Acquisitions, and Plant Closings on Seniority   558
Seniority Systems and Discrimination   561
Technological Change and Worker Displacement   562
Work Rules   563
Robotics Technology   565
Plant Closings and Layoffs   566
Subcontracting   568
Health and Safety in the Workplace   571
Health and Safety Provisions in the Collective Bargaining Agreement   571
The Occupational Safety and Health Act of 1970   572
Health and Safety Grievances: Arbitrators, OSHA, and the Courts   574
Emerging Health and Safety Rules   578
Union Security Issues   582
Types of Union Security Arrangements   582
Checkoff Provisions   583
Arguments For and Against Union Security   584
Right-to-Work Laws   585
Summary and Conclusions   586
Discussion Questions and Exercises   586
Cases on Institutional Issues   586

16 *Employee Rights, Job Security, and Discipline*   590

Introduction   591
Management's Right to Discharge and Discipline Employees   592
Contractual Rights to Employment   592
Tenured Employees   593
At-Will Employees   593
The Quasi-Contractual Rights of Employees Under a Collective Bargaining Agreement   596
Causes of Employee Discipline Problems   597
Categories of Employee Discipline Problems   598
The Attendance Problem: Absenteeism and Tardiness   598
Rule Violations   599
Drug and Alcohol Problems   600
Dishonesty   603
Off-Duty Misconduct   606
Employee Insubordination and Abusive Behavior   610
Employee Incompetency   612
Carelessness, Negligent Actions, and Horseplay   613
Some Issues Affecting Disciplinary Measures   614
Use of Reasonable Rules and Standards   614
Burden of Proof, Due Process, and Equal Protection   614
The Concept of Just Cause   615
Discharge: The Ultimate Penalty   615

Corrective Disciplinary Policy and Procedures 617
    Categories of Violations 617
    The Penalty Structure 619
    Corrective Discipline: The Bottom Line 620
Arbitral Review and Modification of Disciplinary Sanctions 620
Arbitral Remedies in Discharge and Discipline Cases 622
Summary and Conclusions 623
Discussion Questions and Exercises 624
Cases on Employee Discipline 624

▲ PART VII
PUBLIC-SECTOR LABOR RELATIONS 631

17 Public-Sector Labor Relations 632

Introduction 633
The Growth of Public-Sector Unionism 635
    The Early Days 635
    The 1960s and Beyond 636
Types of Unions Representing Public Employees 638
Major Differences Between Public- and Private-Sector Collective Bargaining 641
    The Right of Public Employees to Bargain Collectively 641
    The Right of Public Employees to Engage in Work Stoppages 642
    Multilateral Bargaining 645
    Budgeting Issues and the Nonprofit Status of Governmental Agencies 646
    Unique Organizational Issues 649
Collective Bargaining Among Federal Government Employees 651
Collective Bargaining Among State and Local Employees 653
    Sources of Bargaining Rights for State and Local Employees 653
    Organizing and Bargaining in the Absence of Statutory Protections 654
    Components of State and Local Bargaining Laws 654
Discussion Questions and Exercises 672
Public-Sector Strike Case 673

▲ PART VIII
FUTURE DIRECTIONS 677

18 The Challenges Facing Collective Bargaining and Labor Relations 678

Introduction 679
Union Membership Losses 679
    The Decline in Union Strongholds 679
    The Deregulation of Certain Unionized Industries 681
    The Legalistic Encroachment on Collective Bargaining 683

    The Negative Image of Labor Unions   684
    The Antiunion Managerial and Political Environment   685
Strategic Choices for the Future   687
    The Continued Use of Adversarial Tactics or More Cooperation?   687
    Responding to Foreign Competition and the Specter of 1992 Europe   689
    Changing the Legal Structure   691
    Employee Ownership and Gainsharing   691
    Organized Labor's Use of Strategic Management Concepts   694
    Bargaining Innovations   695
Summary and Conclusions   697
Discussion Questions and Exercises   698

Glossary   699

Index   725

An Introduction to Collective Bargaining and Labor Relations

▲ ▲

Despite the well-publicized decline of organized labor in the United States, collective bargaining and labor relations continues to be an important force in both the private and public sectors. Publications ranging from The Wall Street Journal *and* Business Week *to local newspapers carry news on labor negotiations, strikes, and other events in organized labor. Collective bargaining also has a rich and colorful history. Labor leaders such as Samuel Gompers, John L. Lewis, George Meany, and many others have helped to create profound changes in workplaces throughout the United States.*

Part I sets the stage for understanding the field of collective bargaining and labor relations. Prominent concepts, trends, historical events, and labor leaders are discussed. Chapter 1 explains why labor unions exist, the three levels of union-management interaction, a statistical summary of collective bargaining and labor force trends, the academic foundation of labor relations, and a brief description of the general impact that collective bargaining has on society. Chapter 2 traces the historical evolution of the labor movement in the United States. Emphasis is placed on historical, economic, and social factors associated with the rise of unionism and collective bargaining.

1 An Overview of Labor Relations

- **Introduction**
- **Why Unions Exist**
  Management's View of Labor Unions
  Are Labor Unions Good or Bad?
  Establishing the Union-Management Relationship
- **The Three Levels of Union-Management Interaction**
  Contract Negotiations
  Contract Administration
  Informal Joint Consultation
- **Unionization Trends**
- **Collective Bargaining and the U.S. Labor Force**
- **The Impact of Collective Bargaining on Organizations and Society**
  Impact of Collective Bargaining on Employees
  Impact of Collective Bargaining on Employers
  Impact of Collective Bargaining on Society
- **The Academic Foundation of Labor Relations**
- **Plan for the Book**
- **Discussion Questions and Exercises**

▲ Introduction

Collective bargaining and labor relations is a dynamic, constantly changing field with a rich and colorful history. The terms "labor union" and "collective bargaining" conjure up images of tense negotiating sessions in smoke-filled rooms, work stoppages, picket lines, occasional violence, and powerful labor leaders who exert pressure on top corporate management. The news media has been responsible for overpublicizing some of the more controversial events and personalities. For example, a great deal of publicity has been generated by the labor strife at Eastern Airlines, the violence associated with the Greyhound Lines, Inc., labor dispute, the communications workers' strike in the Midwest and Northeast, and the labor-management turmoil in the coal fields of Virginia. However, the newsworthy events that catch the eye of the media and public do not typify the daily events in collective bargaining and labor relations. In fact, very little of the activity between labor and management provides fuel for bold headlines and front-page news.

Modern-day collective bargaining and labor relations is a complicated business that involves a myriad of federal and state laws, lengthy and legalistic contract provisions, elaborate structures for negotiating and administering the collective bargaining agreement, and numerous social, economic, and international forces that shape and affect the collective bargaining agreement. Much of what occurs in labor relations has an important impact on corporate strategy and performance and on the individual lives of employees. The brash and charismatic labor leaders who openly clashed with staunch corporate heads bent on defeating organized labor have gradually been replaced by a new and different breed who follow a less dramatic and more subtle approach at the bargaining table. The relationship between organized labor and the corporate community today requires a calculating, well-informed, and intelligent leadership. Professional negotiators often command large amounts of economic data and information germane to the workplace. They must understand compensation systems, employee benefit programs, safety and health regulations, and the latest developments in equal employment opportunity laws.

Many union-management relationships survive for years and even decades. Such relationships are typically marked by peace and cooperation, yet they can be occasionally checkered with hostility and even violence. Most union-management relations are characterized by calm periods followed by times of intense negotiating activity. Dealings between labor and management are governed by formal, legalistic rules as well as behind-the-scenes political behavior among key corporate and union officials. As is the case with a variety of relationships, arrangements between union and management involve considerable give-and-take in order to maintain harmony and peace in the workplace.

This book describes and analyzes the union-management relationship. It focuses primarily on the development, current state, and future of private-sector labor relations in the United States. Labor relations among federal, state, and local government employees are also discussed. The typical reader is generally better informed about management issues, but is less sophisticated when it comes to understanding the nature of U.S. labor unions. In order to achieve a balance, considerable attention is given to the leadership, organizational structures, and operations of labor unions.

▲ Why Unions Exist

A labor union is any organization that represents a group of employees with regard to compensation, hours, and other conditions of work. Unions act as agents for their members who are employed in a variety of occupations by private-sector firms and governmental agencies. Approximately 18 million workers in the United States are union members, belonging to more than 200 labor organizations representing various employee groups.

Some labor organizations use the term "union" as part of their official name (e.g., Aluminum Workers International Union, Amalgamated Clothing and Textile Workers Union, and Retail Clerks International Union). Others do not use the term in their title even though they function as labor unions (e.g., American Federation of Musicians, International Brotherhood of Teamsters[1] and Ohio Civil Service Employees Association). As long as a labor organization *behaves* like a union, it is regarded as one and comes under the jurisdiction of the various federal and state laws governing union-management relations and concerted labor activities.

Although labor unions have existed in the United States for nearly 200 years, they did not become a significant force in the United States until after 1935. At that time, protective federal legislation allowed unions to organize workers and bargain collectively with employers without undue interference by antiunion individuals and organizations. Protective legislation by itself, however, was not enough to generate the phenomenal growth that unions experienced in the 20 years following the passage of these laws. Nonunionized employees had to feel a need to join unions and were compelled to do so for a variety of reasons. The primary reason was the employee's desire to gain power and secure more favorable compensation and working conditions. With the possible exception of certain highly skilled employees, most workers are dispensable and have little individual bargaining power or leverage with their employers. If the worker is not satisfied with his or her pay level, benefits, or working conditions, many employers feel that it is not difficult to find someone who is more appreciative and willing to work for the going rate. Few employees have the ability, skills, or talent to force their employer into a precarious position by threatening to resign.

The balance of power is reversed, however, if a *group* of several hundred employees threaten simultaneously to withhold their services by way of an economic strike. Most companies are unable to replace large numbers of employees, even those who are unskilled. Unions provide a means by which employees can band together to equalize their bargaining power vis-a-vis the employer. The presence of a labor union no longer allows the company unilaterally to establish wage scales and benefits. These provisions must be negotiated with the union, thereby giving employees a voice in the way they are treated at work.

Unions have managed to flourish and survive simply because they have provided a service that millions of workers have found useful. In the United States, unions have obtained some of the highest wages and most extensive benefits in the

---

[1] The full name of the Teamsters Union is the International Brotherhood of Teamsters, Chauffeurs, Warehousemen, and Helpers of America.

world. These gains have spilled over into nonunionized sectors as well. For many workers, labor unions have spelled the difference between living on the edge of poverty and enjoying a middle-class lifestyle. Although it is difficult to measure the magnitude of the changes that unions have wrought, it is safe to say that they have been responsible for a significant redistribution of wealth in the United States.[2]

Politically, labor unions have sought to represent the interests of workers through the endorsement and voting support of candidates for public office and through the political lobbying activities of the AFL-CIO. The latter is a federation of unions (the AFL-CIO is not a union itself) whose main function is to persuade legislators to vote for or against proposed laws that affect labor and the workplace. Despite the fact that unions represent less than 20 percent of the United States labor force, the spillover effects into nonunionized sectors coupled with the unions' political lobbying efforts have given them a pervasive impact on society. Many important laws are largely the result of pressures exerted by organized labor. Primary examples are workers' compensation laws, welfare programs to reduce poverty, equal employment opportunity laws, health and safety laws, and even legislation to improve housing and health care.

Management's View of Labor Unions

Management generally does not welcome the interventions that unions impose on decision-making discretion and authority. If all or part of a company or plant becomes unionized, the personnel manager in that organization is suddenly faced with a "co-director" of personnel in the form of a labor organization. Nearly every decision with respect to pay, employee transfers and promotions, training programs, performance appraisal methods, and job design, among others, is scrutinized and often contested by union officials. In short, employers may relinquish their right to make many personnel decisions unilaterally. For example, if a personnel manager in a unionized company wanted to institute an incentive pay program for production employees, this issue would have to be negotiated with the union. The requirement to negotiate is especially important if installing the incentive pay program would change the letter or spirit of the current labor agreement. An employer's ability to switch employees from one job to another quickly or to request that one employee help another in a different job category during busy times is also restricted in many union-management settings.

Obviously, such encroachment on managerial autonomy is viewed with disdain by those who are antiunion. Opponents of unionism also note that unions attempt to destroy an employee's desire to work hard and advance because unions prefer the use of seniority rather than individual merit and initiative as the criteria for promotion. Unions are also accused of sheltering the unreliable and incompetent employee from disciplinary action and discharge. Persons with antiunion sentiments are also quick to point out that unions stifle technological improvements and foster inefficiencies in the workplace. Other opponents note that unions are responsible

---

[2] Alvin Schwartz, *The Unions* (New York: The Viking Press, 1972), p. 31.

for aggravating inflationary spirals and have driven up the cost of many goods and services because they force employers into paying artificially high wages.

Are Labor Unions Good or Bad?

The presence of labor unions in the workplace has both good and bad points insofar as business and society are concerned. Union leaders often accuse corporate heads and management of overemphasizing profits, return on equity, and earnings per share at the expense of the welfare and dignity of employees. Those on the management side believe that unions are bent on destroying free competition and enterprise. Neither statement is entirely accurate, although both contain some element of truth.

The relationship between union and management varies considerably from one situation to another. History is replete with stories of companies who abused employees through wage cuts, inhumane working conditions, and unfair disciplinary actions and firings. History also gives us examples of union behavior of dubious social value. It is not only inaccurate, but also probably unfair, to take either an extreme pro-management or pro-union position. Management tends to forget that unions gained a foothold and grew because of abuses and inequities in the workplace. Likewise, union leaders sometimes forget that management is in business to serve customers, make a profit, keep stockholders satisfied, and ensure the survival and growth of their organizations.

The belief that managers are prone to exploit and neglect employees whereas unions are the workers' savior is also inaccurate. Corporations such as IBM and Xerox, for example, have provided excellent pay and benefits and have done much to help employees manage their careers and fulfill their potential. Union leaders such as Sidney Hillman of the Clothing Workers and Walter Reuther of the Auto Workers exemplify the socially responsible side of the labor movement. However, other union leaders have been irresponsibly involved in pension plan scandals, embezzlement of union funds, and violence that have created serious financial and social repercussions for the very union members whose interests they were supposed to protect.

Any generalizations about unions or management's view on unions are likely to be misleading. Although individual biases inevitably arise, each union-management relationship must be examined and assessed on a case-by-case basis. Some union-management relations are relatively peaceful and even cordial, whereas others are marred by continual hostility. A number of factors contribute to the quality of a specific labor relationship. They are discussed in subsequent sections of this book.

Establishing the Union–Management Relationship

In order to become the exclusive bargaining representative for a group of employees, a labor union must follow a legally prescribed path. Unions employ professional organizers who attempt to persuade nonunionized employees to join their respective labor organizations. Professional organizers will try to target a group of employees for inclusion in a *bargaining unit*. A bargaining unit may, for example, only consist of employees in one department or it may be comprised of employees from several departments in a plant or organization. It is possible that the bargaining unit may be made up of employees across departmental lines who all come from the same occupational group (e.g., all registered nurses working in a large private hospital may be grouped into a single bargaining unit even though some work in the intensive care unit, whereas others work in pediatrics, radiology, or physical therapy). Ultimately, the National Labor Relations Board (NLRB), a federal agency that regulates much of the labor relations activity in the private sector, will decide which employees constitute the appropriate bargaining unit. Chapter 4 covers bargaining unit criteria and legal doctrines in greater detail.

Another major step in establishing the collective bargaining relationship between union and management is the *certification election* conducted under the supervision of the NLRB. Employees who are members of the bargaining unit are eligible to vote; a simple majority of those voting either for the union or against it determines the outcome. Chapter 5 covers the social, organizational, and legal aspects of union organizing campaigns and certification elections.

Once the certification is completed and the union becomes the exclusive representative of the bargaining-unit employees, the company and the union are legally obligated to bargain in good faith over wages, hours, and working conditions.

▲ The Three Levels of Union-Management Interaction

Most impressions of labor relations center on the *contract negotiations* process. However, contract negotiations represent only one level of interaction between labor and management. Once the contract is negotiated, the parties must live with it and deal with it on a daily basis. This process is known as *contract administration*. In addition, management and the labor union, through a process known as *informal joint consultation*, occasionally meet in a nonnegotiating setting to discuss complex matters of mutual concern.

Contract Negotiations

Contract negotiations between union and management center on the terms and provisions of the *collective bargaining agreement*, which provides a detailed description of the compensation package, hours, and working conditions affecting employees in a specific bargaining unit. Collective bargaining agreements are typically very detailed documents. Many are the size of a small book, containing fine print and legal terminology. They cover items such as wage rates, pay grades, group life and health insurance, seniority arrangements, overtime work, clothing allowances, and many more work-related issues and benefits. Examples of contract negotiations have included the following:

- ▲ Averting a threatened strike, the District of Columbia Nurses Association agreed with the Washington Hospital Center on a three-year contract providing 1,200 registered nurses with wage increases averaging 24 percent over the first two years of the contract.[3]

- A 15-week strike by some 10,000 workers at General Dynamics Corporation's Electric Boat Division shipyard in Groton, Connecticut ended on October 11, 1988 with the ratification of a 46-month collective bargaining agreement. Among other things, workers returning to work were slated to receive a $1,000 bonus and bonuses of 5 percent of annual pay in the first year, 4 percent the second year, 3 percent the third year, and a $600 bonus in the final year of the contract.[4]
- Chrysler Motors Corporation reached an agreement in May of 1988 with the United Auto Workers on two-year contracts that provided 64,000 plant and white-collar employees with job security measures, a profit-sharing plan, and other benefits. The Chrysler-UAW agreement was similar to earlier agreements negotiated by the UAW with Ford and General Motors.[5]

Because of the lengthy and complex nature of most collective bargaining agreements, the process of negotiating a contract can be quite long and difficult. Union and management negotiators spend months preparing for negotiations. The actual negotiation sessions span weeks and, in some cases, several months. A deadline for reaching an agreement is usually set with the understanding that a work stoppage will likely occur if a settlement is not reached by the stipulated time. Thus, the typical negotiation process starts rather slowly, builds in intensity, and may reach a frenzied pace as the deadline or contract expiration date draws near.

The vast majority of collective bargaining agreements are negotiated to the satisfaction of both union and management without a work stoppage. Occasionally the negotiations will break down and both sides begin to realize that further talks are useless. A situation such as this is known as an *impasse* or *interest dispute*. Impasses are often resolved with the help of a *labor mediator* who serves as a conduit or facilitator for helping the parties resume negotiations, resolve their differences, and avoid a work stoppage. Mediators have no legal power to force the parties to resume negotiations or reach a meeting of the minds; their function is much like that of a counselor or facilitator. Labor mediators encourage parties to discuss their differences. They make suggestions to help them reach a settlement, and try to eliminate feelings of ill will that sometimes arise during contract negotiations.

Despite the best efforts of negotiators and mediators, deadlines occasionally arrive before settlements are made. The negotiators may elect to continue talks if a settlement appears imminent. If a settlement does not appear in the offing, the union may decide to call an *economic strike*. In a few instances, management may elect to ban employees from work by way of a *lockout*. Both economic strikes and lockouts are designed to exert pressure on the opposing side to make bargaining

---

[3] The Bureau of National Affairs, Inc., *Collective Bargaining Negotiations & Contracts* (Washington, D.C.: The Bureau of National Affairs, Inc., October 6, 1988), p. 2.
[4] The Bureau of National Affairs, Inc., *Collective Bargaining Negotiations & Contracts* (Washington, D.C.: The Bureau of National Affairs, Inc., October 20, 1988), p. 1.
[5] The Bureau of National Affairs, Inc., *Collective Bargaining Negotiations & Contracts* (Washington, D.C.: The Bureau of National Affairs, Inc., May 19, 1988), p. 1.

concessions; management is pressured to settle because work stoppages result in production shutdowns and sales losses, whereas the union suffers because their members are out of jobs until an agreement is reached. Chapters 8, 9, and 10 cover the dynamics of negotiations, impasses, and work stoppages.

Contract Administration

Contract administration is the process by which union and management resolve *rights disputes* over the application of the collective bargaining agreement. The centerpiece of contract administration is a formal *grievance procedure*. When a party to the collective bargaining agreement believes that a provision of the agreement is not being properly interpreted or applied, a grievance is filed. The following cases are typical of those that arise under the process of contract administration:

- ▲ Two truck drivers employed by a retail grocery chain went on a drinking spree during a layover and assaulted two other drivers from the same firm. Their intoxication, coupled with the injuries that they inflicted on the other drivers, disrupted the company's delivery schedule. An arbitrator ruled that such conduct was adequate grounds for discharge.[6]
- ▲ An employee who was absent on an excused unpaid personal holiday was properly denied credit under the collective bargaining agreement for perfect attendance, according to an arbitrator.[7]
- ▲ An asbestos removal project was completed in the classrooms of a Westbury, Connecticut school. Upon returning to work, however, the teachers discovered that the rooms were still covered with dust. The Board of Education ordered the teachers to remain at work, but an arbitrator ruled that such an order violated the safety and health provisions of the teachers' collective bargaining agreement.[8]
- ▲ A police officer was suspended from his job for behaving in an unprofessional manner after he handcuffed and berated a man who threw rocks at the officer's barking dogs. An arbitrator ruled that the suspension was justified.[9]

Once a collective bargaining agreement has been negotiated, both the union and management are expected to abide by its terms and provisions. Regardless of how painstakingly, carefully, and skillfully a collective bargaining agreement is drafted during the negotiations process, there will always be terms and provisions whose meaning, intent, and application are unclear. For example, a classic problem area in contract administration is management's right to discharge an employee for "just cause." What do the parties mean by the phrase "discharge for just cause"? If an employee is fired after being discovered asleep on the job, the union may feel that the discharge was unfair, whereas the employer may believe the termination was justified. Given the enormous number of terms, provisions, and items contained

---

[6] *Lucky Stores, Inc.*, 83 LA 760 (1984).
[7] *H-N Advertising and Display Company*, 87 LA 776.
[8] 90 LA 442.
[9] *City of El Paso, Texas*, 76 LA 595 (1981).

in a collective bargaining agreement, it is almost inevitable that differences of opinion, weak areas, and loopholes will be uncovered.

Unless the grievance is minor and settled quickly and informally, it is usually put into writing. Most grievance procedures contain three to five stages; a grievance moves upward from the first to higher stages until it is resolved to the satisfaction of both parties. A minor grievance such as a dispute over whether a certain employee has accumulated 14 rather than 15 sick-leave days can be easily verified and resolved at the first stage. A more complex grievance such as an interpretation of the "just cause" discharge provision in a case involving numerous extenuating circumstances and conflicting evidence may proceed to the final stage. If a grievance procedure is functioning properly, most grievances can be resolved by union and management officials. However, the last stage in nearly all grievance procedures is *final and binding arbitration*. If union and management are unable to resolve the dispute among themselves, they place the final resolution in the hands of a labor arbitrator(s) whose decision is the final word.

There is generally no appeal that either party can make beyond arbitration. The National Labor Relations Board (NLRB) and federal courts have supported the institution of labor arbitration and normally will not reverse an arbitrator's award. Even though one side may vehemently disagree with an arbitrator's decision, it is expected to abide by whatever he or she rules. To disregard an arbitrator's ruling is to invite a breach of contract suit by the other party. For example, if an arbitrator agrees that a discharged employee was not fired for cause, management is obligated to reinstate the employee (often with back pay and restoration of seniority and lost benefits). Should management elect to ignore the reinstatement order, the union would likely resort to legal action to enforce the award.

Contract administration and labor arbitration allow union and management to settle differences of opinion over contract terms quickly and economically. Over a period of time, the "law of the shop" is fashioned and rights disputes are resolved without resorting to work stoppages and unnecessarily harsh feelings. Thus, the employer and union need only deal with the threat of strikes and lockouts every two or three years if contract negotiations fail. The process of contract administration helps immeasurably to maintain industrial peace between bargaining sessions. Chapters 11 and 12 deal with contract administration and labor arbitration.

Informal Joint Consultation

Unions and employers are not always adversaries. In fact, there are a number of issues of mutual concern to both organized labor and management. The following examples are illustrative:

▲ A joint union-management committee to study worker complaints of illness has been established by the Boeing Commercial Airplane Co. and the International Association of Machinists. Employee health problems began after Boeing began complying with federal regulations to build airplane interiors from fire-resistant materials.[10]

---

[10] The Bureau of National Affairs, Inc., *Collective Bargaining Negotiations & Contracts* (Washington, D.C.: The Bureau of National Affairs, Inc., October 20, 1988), p. 2.

▲ Under the guidance of the United Auto Workers-Chrysler Joint Committee on Health and Safety, an employee assistance program was designed to help Chrysler employees and their families with financial and domestic problems. The joint committee also established a separate mental health and substance abuse program for employees in Delaware and Michigan.[11]

▲ A clarification agreement on employee drug testing was reached in early 1988 between the International Association of Machinists and United Technologies Corp.'s Pratt & Whitney operations in Connecticut.[12]

Management and labor unions occasionally meet to discuss matters of mutual concern in a nonnegotiating session. Complex issues such as group insurance, retirement programs, job evaluation systems, employee health and safety programs, and comparable worth in the pay structure can be discussed when there is no settlement or strike deadline lurking on the horizon. Informal joint consultation can take place in a more relaxed atmosphere and either side can make use of consultants and experts for whatever issue is being discussed. Meetings of this nature may allow union and management officials to formulate bargaining proposals that can be easily negotiated because of the foundation laid during informal joint consultation sessions. Subsequent bargaining sessions may be more cordial and the chances of bargaining impasses, work stoppages, and grievances may be reduced. In addition, a number of union-management cooperation programs have arisen since the 1980s. These programs are sometimes viewed as a major development that will have a profound effect on the future of organized labor and corporate management. Union-management cooperative programs are discussed in Chapters 7 and 18.

▲ Unionization Trends

Labor unions have existed in the United States since the early part of the 19th century. Prior to the 1930s, they were not a significant force in our society because of repressive tactics by employers, judges, and legislators. These tactics were permissible because there were no federal or state laws prohibiting their use. With the passage of the Wagner Act in 1935, labor organizations received protection from antiunion employers and groups. The Wagner Act acted as a powerful catalyst that allowed unions to grow rapidly over the ensuing two decades. Union growth was so impressive between 1935 and the end of World War II that legislation curbing the power of labor organizations (the Taft-Hartley Act of 1947) had to be enacted to rebalance the labor-management power relationship. The growth of unionism, while phenomenal, was also uneven. Union organizers made their biggest inroads in the heavily industrialized Northeast and upper Midwest. Industries such as transportation, the skilled construction trades, steel, mining, and automobile manufacturing provided the most fertile grounds for unionization. Still remaining relatively union free were the South and Southwest and industries such as the white-collar

---

[11] The Bureau of National Affairs, Inc., *Collective Bargaining Negotiations & Contracts* (Washington, D.C.: The Bureau of National Affairs, Inc., August 11, 1988), p. 3.
[12] The Bureau of National Affairs, Inc., *Collective Bargaining Negotiations & Contracts* (Washington, D.C.: The Bureau of National Affairs, Inc., February 25, 1988), p. 3.

service organizations, textile mills, strip mining, and other nonmanufacturing concerns.

New York, West Virginia, Hawaii, and Pennsylvania are the most heavily unionized states, with approximately 35 percent of the nonagricultural employees in these states belonging to labor organizations. South Carolina, North Carolina, Mississippi, and South Dakota are the least unionized, with fewer than 13 percent of employees belonging to unions. A number of reasons are thought to determine the extent of unionization in a specific geographical area. Factors such as the types of industries located in a particular region, the racial composition of the labor force, urban-suburban-rural dimensions of an area, local economic conditions and wage levels, the extent to which businesses are willing to discourage unions, familiarity with unions by labor force members, education and skill levels within the labor force, the presence of right-to-work legislation,[13] among others, all influence the degree to which unions have made inroads.

▲ Collective Bargaining and the U.S. Labor Force

The size, composition, and changing nature of the labor force in the United States has a direct impact on collective bargaining and labor relations. First, the success of union organizers will hinge on factors such as the skill and education levels of the labor force, their degree of job satisfaction, their permanency (or mobility) in the labor market, as well as their age, race, sex, place of residence, and other demographic characteristics. Second, the ease or difficulty with which collective bargaining agreements are negotiated is, to some extent, affected by the composition of a firm's labor force. Even after union and management negotiators settle on contract terms, the bargaining unit members who will be covered by the agreement usually must approve (ratify) the new contract. As the labor force becomes more heterogeneous in terms of age, sex, race, educational composition, and family structure, the more diverse will be their demands and expectations. It has become increasingly difficult to please everyone who is to be covered by a single, uniform collective bargaining agreement. This lack of consensus may partially explain why the number of contract rejections by union members has increased over the years. Third, a more diverse labor force may make contract administration more difficult and could possibly increase the number of grievances filed.

The labor force is defined as all noninstitutionalized individuals over the age of 16 who are either working or seeking work. At the time of this writing, the U.S. labor force numbers approximately 120 million workers. Over the years, the labor force has been in a state of flux, changing in both size and composition. The following summarizes how the U.S. labor force has changed and discusses the implications of these changes on union-management relations.

---

[13] Right-to-work laws make it illegal for a union and employer to negotiate an agreement mandating that employees must join or financially support a labor union. Currently, 20 states have enacted right-to-work laws.

1. *The percentage of unionized employees has decreased since the 1950s.* In 1945, the percentage of nonagricultural employees who were unionized reached a peak of 35.8 percent.[14] By 1989, this percentage had decreased to approximately 16 percent. However, in absolute numbers of members, unions continued to grow until the mid-1970s because the size of the labor force continued to increase. However, it now appears that many unions are experiencing a decline in the absolute number of members.[15] Major reasons for this decline in union membership include the following: industrial shifts away from the union strongholds in the heavy manufacturing industries of the Northeast to the lighter service and manufacturing industries in the Sunbelt; the loss of jobs in unionized firms because of foreign competition, automation, and deregulation; and the increasing proportion of white-collar workers who are more resistant to union organizing campaigns; and the passage of legislation protecting employee rights and working conditions (e.g., laws concerning health and safety, equal employment opportunity, and pension reform). Whether a decline in union membership has also resulted in a concomitant decline in union influence is subject to debate. Organized labor is still an important political, social, and economic force in the United States. For the foreseeable future, employers will continue to respect the threat of union organizing efforts and strikes.

2. *The labor force participation rate for females has increased.* By the mid-1980s, 44.5 percent of females over age 16 were working. This percentage is expected to increase to 47 percent by the year 2000.[16] This trend has important implications for collective bargaining because females may desire different benefits and collective bargaining agreement provisions than their male counterparts. For example, a worker whose spouse also holds a job may not desire health insurance if the partner's employer already provides such coverage. Thus, married employees may wish to maximize take-home pay by eliminating deductions for duplicate benefits. Single parent, head-of-household employees might be interested in company-sponsored child-care centers and liberal sick-leave and absenteeism policies.

3. *Although segments of the labor force are highly educated, there is a growing problem with functional illiteracy and the lack of basic English, mathematical, and scientific skills.* The number of students in the United States who continued their education beyond high school rose dramatically after World War II. The greater exposure to radio, television, and the news media has also resulted in a better informed populace. If labor unions are to survive, they will have to pitch their organizational campaigns to employees who are more likely to view themselves as professionals. In the past, unions have been used primarily by unskilled workers and skilled craft workers in the construction trades. Professional and white-collar workers with more formal education have not felt

---

[14] Chester A. Morgan, *Labor Economics*, 3rd ed. (Austin, Texas: Business Publications, Inc., 1970), p. 354.
[15] The Bureau of National Affairs, Inc., "Union Organizing Outlook," *Collective Bargaining Negotiations & Contracts* (Washington, D.C.: The Bureau of National Affairs, Inc., February 28, 1988), p. 4.
[16] Howard N. Fullerton, Jr., "Labor Force Projections: 1986–2000," *Monthly Labor Review* (September 1987), p. 22.

compelled to join unions because of the blue-collar stigma associated with such organizations. This trend began to change in the 1960s as teachers looked to unions for bargaining power. Other professionals such as nurses followed suit. Furthermore, professionals are likely to demand contract provisions that are far different from what traditional blue-collar union members have desired. Problems of *underemployment*, where a person is overqualified for the job he or she holds, and issues of *job enrichment* may also receive greater attention at the bargaining table.

At the other extreme are the workers who have few marketable job skills. *Business Week*, in a series of articles, has pointed to an "underclass" of workers who lack the basic reading, writing, and other skills needed for successful employment.[17] Organized labor and management will ultimately have to deal with the problems faced by this segment of the labor force through special recruiting, training, and job-retention efforts.

4. *The median age of the workforce is increasing.* As the large cohort of post–World War II baby boomers ages, the overall age of the U.S. labor force will reach unprecedented levels. Contributing to this is the advent of age discrimination legislation that protects the employment rights of persons age 40 and above; it is conceivable that a person 100 years of age who is physically and mentally capable of work is protected by federal law from job discrimination!

    Older employees have concerns not shared by their younger counterparts. Greater emphasis on job security, group life and health insurance, pension programs, and technological advances to adapt the work routine to the gradual deterioration of physical and mental capabilities are prime examples. No doubt these and other issues relevant to the older employee will in the future receive more attention in collective negotiations, contract administration, and informal joint consultation.

5. *Minorities are occupying more prominent positions in the labor force.* Although minorities have always been active participants in the labor force, they have been relegated to undesirable, low-paying jobs. The passage of equal employment opportunity legislation has opened the doors for greater upward job mobility for blacks and other minorities. Blacks are now better sheltered against unfair, racially-motivated employment actions. These laws may reduce their dependency on labor unions to ensure protection in the workplace.

    Nonracial minorities, such as older employees and the handicapped, also enjoy greater protection. The latter group, because of the technological advances that lighten the physical burden of work, have access to more job opportunities now than they did in the past. A potential dilemma may exist in union-management relations because labor unions are sometimes threatened by technological changes that displace their members. Thus, advances that may prove beneficial to older or handicapped employees may adversely affect others

---

[17] See Bruce Nussbaum, "Needed: Human Capital," Aaron Bernstein, "Where the Jobs Are Is Where the Skills Aren't," Elizabeth Ehrlich and Susan B. Garland, "For American Business, A New World of Workers," Susan B. Garland, "Why the Underclass Can't Get Out From Under," Elizabeth Erlich, "America's Schools Still Aren't Making the Grade," and Karen Pennar, "It's Time to Put Our Money Where Our Future Is," *Business Week* (September 19, 1988), pp. 100–141.

covered by a collective bargaining agreement. These and other conflicts of interest will be faced by union and management officials who must negotiate and administer collective bargaining agreements affecting an increasingly heterogeneous labor force.

According to the U.S. Department of Labor's report, *Workforce 2000: Work and Workers for the 21st Century*, several important changes in the labor force will occur by the year 2000.[18] These will include the following:

- A "relatively healthy pace" of growth in the economy and an increasing need to improve employee productivity.
- A decline in the manufacturing sector's share of the economy. Unions will have to direct their organizing away from their traditional strongholds and attempt to attract workers who have not been unionized in the past.
- A significant expansion in the skill levels needed to fill jobs created by service industries. Labor-management relations will be forced to become increasingly concerned with employee training and development.

▲ The Impact of Collective Bargaining on Organizations and Society

Figure 1–1 paints a broad portrait of the collective bargaining process and its impact on employees, the organization, and society. Up to this point, we have briefly discussed the precursor conditions for unionism, the certification process, and the three levels of interaction between union and management (contract negotiations, contract administration, and informal joint consultation, together known as *collective bargaining*).

The process of collective bargaining is affected by a number of external factors and forces with which both management and labor unions must deal. One factor, already discussed is the *labor force. Technological forces* are also important to both sides. Companies characterized as high tech or capital intensive, for example, have less concern for the impact of unions than firms that are heavily dependent on unskilled or semiskilled labor. As a result, unions have frequently attempted to control technological change in order to protect job opportunities (see Chapter 15). Other prominent factors involve *international forces*. These may have a profound impact on labor-management relations, especially for firms that can take advantage of less expensive foreign labor. *Economic conditions* such as inflation rates, unemployment levels, as well as geographic differences in economic conditions, all affect the collective bargaining process. During periods of high inflation, unions will exert more pressure on management to keep wage levels in line with changes in the consumer price index. Periods of high unemployment may dilute the bargaining power of unions because the effectiveness of the strike as an economic weapon is lessened. During adverse economic times, bargaining concerns

---

[18] The Bureau of National Affairs, Inc., "Labor Projections For 2000," *Collective Bargaining Negotiations & Contracts* (Washington, D.C.: The Bureau of National Affairs, Inc., July 16, 1987), p. 4. *Workforce 2000: Work and Workers for the 21st Century* was prepared for the U.S. Labor Department by the Hudson Institute, a private research organization.

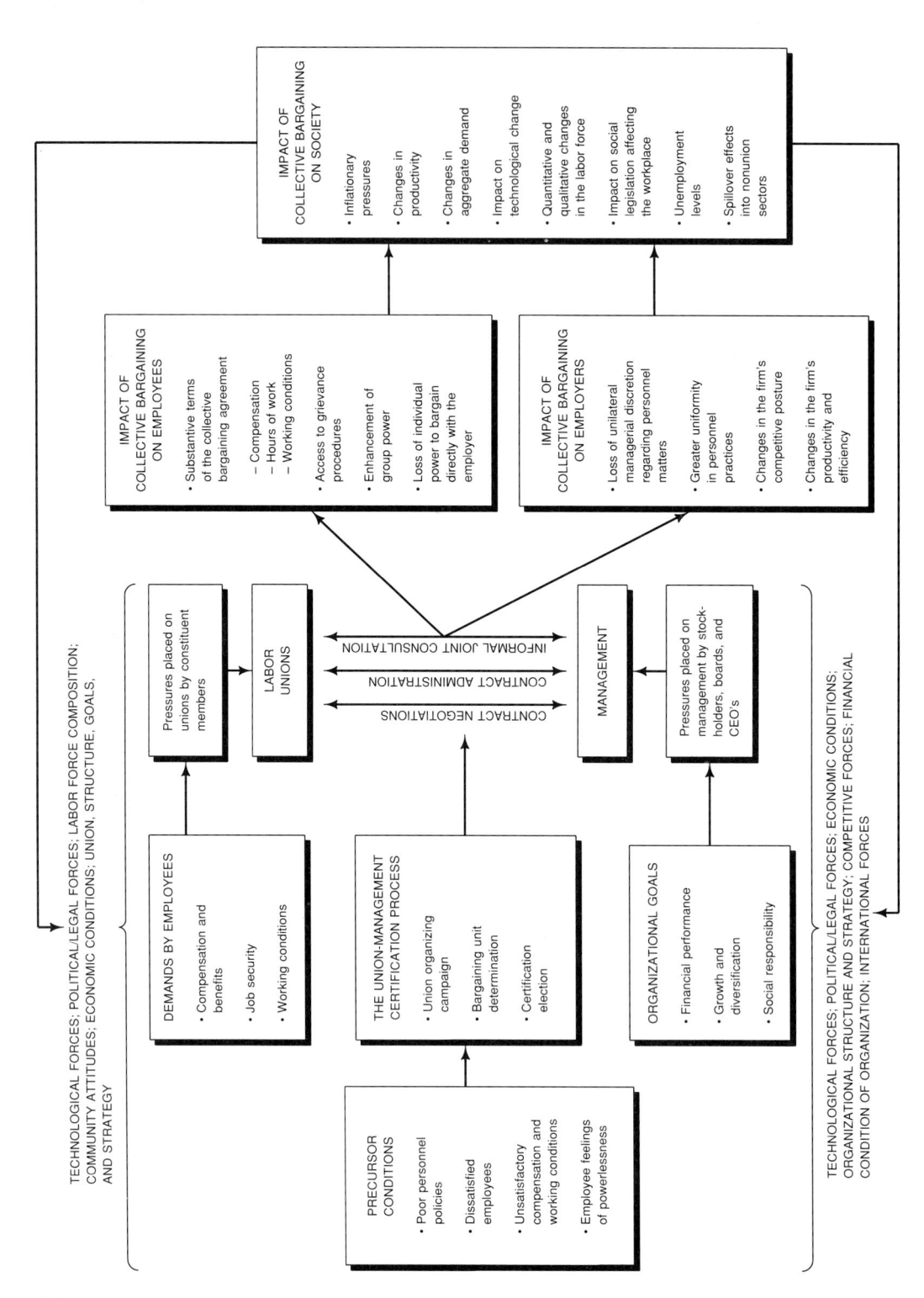

Figure 1–1 An Overview of Labor-Management Relations

may shift from higher wages and better benefits to job security issues such as demanding protection from layoffs. In extreme cases, employee concessions or "give-backs" may be necessary to bail the employer out of dire financial straits. Companies that have achieved high profits, good rates of return, and a bright economic outlook are challenged to "share the wealth" by unions through generous wage increases and liberalized benefits. Technological, international, and economic forces are discussed more extensively in subsequent chapters.

Collective bargaining in the United States is affected by *political and legal forces*, especially labor relations law. The extensive set of federal and state laws cover nearly every facet of union-management relations for both private-sector and governmental employees who are represented by labor unions. These laws are primarily *procedural*; that is, they dictate how the parties must deal with each other, but they generally do not regulate how many vacation days, holidays, or benefits workers receive. In addition, U.S. labor laws do not dictate employee hiring, performance, or retention standards (except to forbid discrimination by race, sex, age, and other factors). Chapter 3 discusses the major labor laws having a direct impact on collective bargaining as well as legislation that is peripheral to the collective bargaining process.

Management faces many of the same external factors as unions. Substantial attention has been given to the concept of *strategic management* in recent years.[19] Corporations formulate their respective strategies by determining their goals for product lines, market share, financial performance, and competitive emphasis. Managers must also assess environmental threats and opportunities such as the presence of certain competitors, economic conditions, and consumer tastes. The corporate strategy, in essence, is the roadmap by which companies chart their course toward fulfilling designated financial, product, market, and other organizational goals. One strategic roadblock that management must consider is the presence of a labor union that imposes constraints on managerial decision prerogatives. Executives in unionized corporations must therefore integrate the labor relations function into their strategic plans.

Impact of Collective Bargaining on Employees

Figure 1–1 lists four major effects that the collective bargaining process has on employees. First, a uniform set of substantive collective bargaining provisions applies to all bargaining-unit employees. A standard wage scale, seniority provisions, and benefit programs are common examples. Uniform provisions such as these ensure a more egalitarian atmosphere in the workplace and tend to reduce the uncertainty associated with personnel practices and procedures. Second, employees obtain access to a formal grievance procedure through which they can contest management's personnel decisions. Third, employee power is increased through the threat or use of unfair labor practice charges if the employer violates certain federal labor law provisions as well as through work stoppages via the economic

---

[19] See, for example, John Evansohn, "The Effects of Managerial Control on Unionization," *Industrial Relations* (Winter 1988), pp. 91–103.

strike. Finally, employees often lose their individual power to bargain with the employer. Instead of annually negotiating a salary or wage increase on an individual basis, employees are forced to accept a standardized wage scale or promotion system in which the roles of superior job performance, meritorious accomplishments, and exceptional initiative and reliability are largely ignored. Although an arrangement of this nature may be perfectly acceptable to many employees, the more ambitious and upwardly mobile worker may feel that such a system is both confining and frustrating.

Impact of Collective Bargaining on Employers

By now, the reader is cognizant of the fact that unionization has a potentially profound impact on the management and operational performance of a firm. Figure 1–1 shows that management typically loses much of its unilateral discretion on personnel matters. A by-product of this, however, is that unions have forced some organizations into renovating or refurbishing personnel practices and policies that had become antiquated and a source of employee morale problems. Greater uniformity in personnel practices and policies help to lighten the employers' burden when they are forced to make tough decisions on matters such as individual pay raises, promotions, and disciplinary matters.

For labor-intensive firms whose product price and competitive edge are heavily affected by the cost of labor, unionization can be an anathema. Take, for example, the problem facing private hospital administrators who allocate 50 to 70 percent of their budgets for personnel expenditures. Even a modest pay level increase could be financially devastating. Unionization poses a real threat to many private-sector hospitals already pressured by heavy competition and rising nonlabor costs.

Unions are also thought to hinder production and efficiency through the enforcement of certain work rules and procedures. Unions may protect less desirable employees whose performance is substandard.[20] The practice of featherbedding (a situation in which the employer is forced to pay a worker even when little or no work is performed) received wide publicity when the railroads shifted from steam to diesel-powered locomotives. The change eliminated the need for firemen whose primary job was to feed coal into the steam locomotive boilers. Because of union pressure, however, the railway fireman's job has survived. A number of other restrictive work rules are discussed in Chapter 15.

Impact of Collective Bargaining on Society

There is little doubt that unionization and collective bargaining have a pervasive effect on the economy and society. The magnitude of these effects present a series of questions that have not and probably will not be resolved with any certainty. Do unions cause inflation? Has collective bargaining hindered productivity in our economy? What effect has collective bargaining played in either stimulating or stifling

---

[20] See, for example, Steven G. Allen, "Productivity Levels and Productivity Change Under Unionism," *Industrial Relations* (Winter 1988), pp. 94–113.

aggregate demand for goods and services? How has the labor force been affected by the presence of unions? Has collective bargaining encouraged the passage of social legislation affecting the workplace? If so, has the labor movement worked itself out of usefulness by encouraging the passage of such legislation? To what extent has the threat of unionization caused nonunionized firms to fashion their compensation and personnel policies after unionized firms?

One major problem in assessing the impact of unionism and collective bargaining on society is that we do not know what the state of affairs would have been had unions never existed. For example, the effects of collective bargaining settlements on the economy are complex, only partly understood, and debated by economists. A related issue is the extent to which unions affect unemployment levels. Labor unions carefully guard the employment rights of their constituents whenever possible. However, there are some who believe that the high pay structures imposed by unions have forced employers to close plants and abandon labor-intensive production methods in favor of more capital-intensive methods. Although we know that wages, inflation, and unemployment levels are interrelated, it is difficult to hold constant a number of other economic variables (e.g., international forces, consumer tastes, and interest rates) that also affect wages and unemployment. Likewise, we can measure economic phenomena such as wages, unemployment, productivity, aggregate demand, and so on, but we have no way of knowing precisely how these measures might differ if collective bargaining and unionism did not exist.

The reader will have the opportunity to form opinions about the impact of collective bargaining as he or she moves through the text. A goal of this book is simply to make the reader aware of the complexities that arise in the union-management relationship. Some readers will reach the balanced understanding that neither the union nor the management view is always correct. Scholars who have attempted to measure the impact of unions have often been frustrated because there is no way rigorously to test, measure, and isolate social and economic phenomena in a complex and ever-changing environment. Nevertheless, it is safe to conclude that collective bargaining and labor relations do represent an important institution that has had a profound impact on business and society.

Figure 1–1 attempts to portray the proverbial forest of collective bargaining and labor relations. The development, process, and structure of collective bargaining both affect and are affected by our society and economy. The remainder of this book will examine the major components of collective bargaining in greater detail. However, the reader might be wise to glance back occasionally to Figure 1–1 to see how particular aspects of collective bargaining relate to each other.

▲ The Academic Foundation of Labor Relations

Contributing scholars to the broad field of labor relations have included individuals from broad disciplines such as law, economics, sociology, psychology, and history as well as from the more specialized disciplines such as labor law, labor economics, industrial psychology, and management. For a number of years, it has been possible to obtain specialized undergraduate and graduate degrees, including the Ph.D., in labor and industrial relations.

Much has been written about the changing role of work over the centuries. However, the genesis of labor and industrial relations, as we know it, lies in the repudiation of classical economics insofar as the treatment of labor is concerned. Early on in the British and U.S. industrial revolutions, labor was regarded in a cavalier fashion by employers who had few qualms about imposing deplorable working conditions and subsistence wages on workers. Labor was regarded as a "commodity" and was treated as any other factor of production, without regard to humanitarian considerations. Sidney and Beatrice Webb, two British economists, pointed to the need for abandoning the commodity approach to labor advocated by classical economists. The Webbs noted the poor working and living conditions of British workers and the unequal bargaining power between employees and employers. Later, John R. Commons, who is probably most deserving of the title "Father of U.S. Industrial Relations," called for "transactions and working rules of collective action."[21] Commons was an early part of the so-called institutional school of economics that emphasized the importance of negotiation and compromise among the divergent interests of labor, management, and the public.[22] The institutionalists felt that the primary problem in industrial society was the clash between the job security interests of workers and the organizational efficiency needs of employers. Both these interests were regarded as legitimate and it was purported that a means for continuous accommodation between workers and management was needed. In the field of labor relations, collective bargaining became the means for such accommodation.

As worklife in large organizations became commonplace, industrial psychologists and sociologists began to take a strong interest in issues such as worker motivation, group dynamics in the workplace, job satisfaction, leadership, and other issues grounded in the social sciences. Names such as Frederick Taylor, Frank and Lillian Gilbreth, Elton Mayo and the classic Hawthorne studies fell under the rubric of scientific management and the human relations school. Scientific management was primarily concerned with maximizing worker efficiency and productivity, whereas the human relations school's basic premise was worker-management cooperation.

Over the past four decades, scholars from a variety of disciplines have focused attention on issues related to collective bargaining and labor relations. Some scholars have been interested in the economic impact of unionism, whereas others concentrated on labor history, public policy, bargaining behavior, and labor market research. The presence of numerous labor relations publications bears witness to the proliferation of research activity in the field. Contributions from scholars from multiple disciplines has not only resulted in a wide range of research, but also in divergent opinions about labor relations, a result that is not surprising when one considers the size, complexity, and pervasive impact of the field.

[21] John R. Commons, *Institutional Economics: Its Place in the Political Economy*, (New York: Macmillan, 1934), p. 162.
[22] Thomas A. Kochan and Harry C. Katz, *Collective Bargaining and Industrial Relations*, 2nd ed. (Homewood, Illinois: Richard D. Irwin, Inc., 1988), p. 25.

Several common threads run through the literature on collective bargaining and labor relations. First, labor is not a factor of production in the same sense as capital and land; human beings are more than mere extensions of machines. Workers cannot be used, abused, depreciated, and discarded after they have lost their maximum productive potential. Second, there is a potential conflict of interest between the interests and goals of workers and those of management. Not all workers perceive such conflict. Some who do, still elect not to do anything about it. Third, there are a number of ways to deal with this conflict although collective bargaining is probably regarded as the most acceptable method by most labor relations experts. Alternative methods of resolving worker-employer conflict are through individual bargaining by employees, protective legislation, and mutual nonunion worker-company agreements. Fourth, most labor relations research takes or attempts to take a neutral stance favoring neither management nor labor unions.

▲ Plan for the Book

The book is divided into eight parts and each forms a foundation for subsequent sections. Part I, Introduction to Collective Bargaining and Industrial Relations, continues by covering the history of the U.S. labor movement. Part II, Establishing the Collective Bargaining Relationship, deals with the regulation of the labor-management relationship, bargaining-unit determination and structure, and union organizing campaigns. Part III, Union-Management Organization Structures for Collective Bargaining, describes the strategy and structure of labor unions and the corporate personnel-industrial relations function. Part IV, Collective Bargaining Agreement Negotiations, discusses bargaining theory, the practical aspects of bargaining preparations, and contract negotiations. Part V, Resolving Interest and Rights Disputes Over the Collective Bargaining Agreement, deals with the resolution of labor disputes, contract interpretation, grievance procedures, and the institution of labor arbitration. Part VI deals with the substantive provisions commonly found in collective bargaining agreements. These provisions include wages, premium pay, and employee benefit programs as well as important topics such as management rights, seniority, subcontracting, union security, and employee discipline. Part VII, Public-Sector Collective Bargaining, describes the unique aspects of labor-management relations in governmental agencies such as public schools, police and firefighting departments, and other public entities. Part VIII, Future Directions, analyzes the labor-management relationship at the dawn of the 21st century.

Table 1–1 illustrates the plan of the book.

▲ Discussion Questions and Exercises

1. Why do labor unions exist? How do you believe they help employees?
2. What are your current perceptions regarding the value of labor unions? How did your family, friends, and work experiences shape your opinion of organized labor?

Table 1–1 ▲ Plan for the Book

Part I: An Introduction to Collective Bargaining and Labor Relations
- ▲ Chapter 1–An Overview of Labor Relations
- ▲ Chapter 2–The History of Collective Bargaining and Labor Relations in the United States

Part II: Establishing the Collective Bargaining Relationship
- ▲ Chapter 3–The Legal Foundation of Collective Bargaining
- ▲ Chapter 4–The Bargaining Unit
- ▲ Chapter 5–Union Organization Campaigns and Certification Elections

Part III: Union and Management Organizational Structures, Goals, and Policies for Collective Bargaining
- ▲ Chapter 6–The Union Structure, Goals, and Policies for Collective Bargaining
- ▲ Chapter 7–Management Structure, Goals, and Policies for Collective Bargaining

Part IV: Negotiating the Collective Bargaining Agreement
- ▲ Chapter 8–The Collective Bargaining Process: A Theoretical Overview
- ▲ Chapter 9–The Collective Bargaining Process: Preparations, Tactics, and Issues

Part V: Resolving Interest and Rights Disputes Over the Collective Bargaining Agreement
- ▲ Chapter 10–Negotiation Impasses and Labor Disputes
- ▲ Chapter 11–Contract Administration: The Grievance Procedure
- ▲ Chapter 12–Labor Arbitration

Part VI: Substantive Provisions of the Collective Bargaining Agreement
- ▲ Chapter 13–Economic and Compensation Issues
- ▲ Chapter 14–Employee Benefit Programs
- ▲ Chapter 15–Institutional Issues: Balancing Management Rights Against Union and Employee Security
- ▲ Chapter 16–Employee Rights, Job Security, and Discipline

Part VII: Public-Sector Collective Bargaining
- ▲ Chapter 17–Public-Sector Collective Bargaining

Part VIII: Future Directions
- ▲ Chapter 18–The Challenges Facing Collective Bargaining and Labor Relations

3. If you were a manager in a firm that became unionized after you had been working there for several years, what changes might you expect in your job responsibilities?
4. Visit two local firms—one that is nonunion and one that is at least partially organized by a union. Interview a manager at each of these firms and ask how he or she believes a union affects a firm's personnel practices and operations. Compare the responses of these individuals. How do their perceptions compare with your answer to question 3 above?
5. What implications will changes in the U.S. labor force have on organized labor?
6. Do you believe that collective bargaining serves a useful social purpose? Why or why not?

2 The History of Collective Bargaining and Labor Relations in the United States

- **Introduction**
- **The Theory of Labor Movements**
- **Organized Labor: The First Unions**
  From Farm to Factory: Early Labor-Force Problems
- **Labor Crises and Violence**
  Violence on the Railroads
  The Haymarket Square Riot
  Violence in Coal Mining and the Molly Maguires
  The Role of Violence in the Labor Movement
- **The National Labor Union**
- **The Knights of Labor**
  Political and Economic Perspectives of the Knights
  The Rise and Fall of the Knights: What Happened?
- **The American Federation of Labor (AFL)**
  Political and Economic Perspectives of the AFL
- **The Industrial Workers of the World (IWW)**
  Political and Economic Perspective of the IWW
  Downfall of the IWW
- **Trade Unionism in the 20th Century**
  1900–1920
  The Roaring 1920s: Not A Roaring Time for Unionism
  The 1930s: The Rise of the CIO and Labor Legislation
  The 1940s: World War II and the Increasing Power of Unions
  The 1950s: The AFL and CIO Unite
  The Labor Movement since 1960
- **A Historical Synthesis and Summary**
- **Discussion Questions and Exercises**
  United States Labor History Timeline

▲ Introduction

Before analyzing present-day collective bargaining and labor relations, it is important to summarize several of the more important historical developments that have occurred over the past two centuries. The reader will thereby gain insights into some key social, political, legal, and economic factors shaping the course of unionism and labor relations in the United States. It is also important to note the names of prominent personalities, organizations, and events in labor history. The major contribution of this chapter, however, is to illustrate the origins and conditions under which the labor movement flourished. As is often the case with any type of long-term social change, the ebb and flow of the U.S. labor movement is affected by a number of factors, some of which are easy to discern and others of which are complex and often imponderable. This chapter traces the evolution of the U.S. labor movement by noting the central figures, events, time frames, and forces of major concern. Emphasis is placed on factors that both stimulated and discouraged the labor force's attraction to unionism and collective bargaining.

▲ The Theory of Labor Movements

The environment that has created labor unions as well as the institutional arrangements established by the government and corporations for dealing with unions is known as the *labor movement*. On the surface, the term "labor movement" somehow implies that a conscious, concerted, well-organized effort by workers and labor leaders must have taken place over the past 200 years. In reality, this was not the case. The U.S. labor movement can be best characterized by a series of disjointed efforts involving a multitude of persons and groups with differing ideologies and aspirations. Marxists, socialists, and communists who advocated overthrowing the existing capitalistic system, along with those who opted for working within the system, have all made their mark on the labor movement. Whereas some leaders advocated force and violence to achieve their goals, others felt that negotiation and compromise were the more suitable alternatives. A number of early labor leaders focused on philosophical issues and ideological reform, yet others felt that the American worker was more interested in "bread-and-butter" unionism that focused on improving working and living conditions.[1]

Labor movement theories vary considerably, depending on the personal background and historical reference of the particular theorist. For example, the classical economist Adam Smith viewed early union activity (around 1780) as "desperate, and [an] act with the folly and extravagance of desperate men who must either starve or frighten their masters into an immediate compliance with their demands."[2] Karl Marx, over a half century later, advanced a radically different labor movement theory that focused on eliminating class conflicts between workers and entrepreneurs (the bourgeoisie) by converting to a socialist industrial state.[3] Other so-

---

[1] See, for example, Melvin Dobofsky and Warren Van Tine, eds., *Labor Leaders in America* (Champaign, Illinois: University of Illinois Press, 1987).
[2] Adam Smith, *Wealth of Nations* (New York: Random House, 1937), pp. 66–67.
[3] Karl Marx, *The Communist Manifesto* (New York: Random House, 1937), pp. 66–67.

cialist theoreticians viewed labor unions as a temporary revolutionary institution whose major role was to aid in the overthrow of capitalism.[4] Fabian socialists Sidney and Beatrice Webb believed that labor movements are based on the desire of working-class members to elevate their economic and political status within an industrial society. According to the Webbs:

> If the democratic state is to attain its fullest and finest development, it is essential that the actual needs and desires of the human agents concerned should be the main considerations in determining the conditions of employment. Here we find the special function of the Trade Union in the administration of industry.[5]

Up to this point, the discussion has focused on European labor theorists. Between 1917 and 1928, several prominent American theorists set forth their ideas as the labor movement in the United States gained momentum. Professor Robert F. Hoxie focused his theory of the U.S. labor movement on the *function* of unions and he categorized five principal classes of unionism:[6]

1. *Business unionism* attempts to improve the economic status of the employee by working within the existing capitalistic, free-enterprise system. As we examine the evolution of labor unions in the United States, it will become apparent that business unionism is the mode that has dominated.
2. *Uplift unionism* assumes an idealistic posture in which unions raise both the economic *as well as* the cultural level of its membership. In addition to advocating collective bargaining, uplift unionism encourages the use of educational and recreational programs to develop a well-rounded worker.
3. *Revolutionary unionism* emphasizes long-run ideological goals and downplays the economic, short-run objectives of business unionism. A major goal of revolutionary unionism is to overthrow the existing capitalistic system. As a result, it was never a predominant form of unionism in the United States because most workers regarded it as too radical and of little use for providing immediate economic needs such as food, clothing, shelter, and better working conditions.
4. *Predatory unionism* best describes the seamy side of the labor movement. Here, the racketeering labor leaders prey upon their members rather than represent them. Bribes, strong-arm tactics, and collusive arrangements with employers characterize predatory unionism. Although most unions cannot be classified as predatory, there have been enough instances of internal corruption within the ranks of a few unions that Congress has enacted legislation to protect the rank-and-file union members against the very leaders who have been entrusted to represent and protect them.
5. *Dependent unionism* is unionism that is instigated and controlled by the employer. Commonly called a *company union*, dependent unionism may be undertaken by employers who wish to prevent outside, independent unions from organizing their workers. In essence, management literally negotiates wages, hours, and working conditions with itself. An arrangement of this nature

---
[4] Chester A. Morgan, *Labor Economics*, 3rd ed. (Austin, Texas: Business Publications, Inc., 1970), pp. 316–318.
[5] Sidney and Beatrice Webb, *Industrial Democracy* (New York: Longmans, Green & Co., Inc., 1920), p. 821.
[6] Robert F. Hoxie, *Trade Unionism in the United States* (New York: D. Appleton & Co., 1917).

usually short changes the employee. As a result, company unionism is illegal under federal labor law.

Hoxie viewed the labor movement in terms of union functions and objectives, but said little about the conditions that affect the growth or decline of unionism. John R. Commons, a professor of political economy at the University of Wisconsin during the first third of this century, painted a detailed portrait of the factors underlying the U.S. labor movement.[7] Commons theorized that labor movements originate and develop through a series of peculiar economic, social, political, and geographic forces. Factors such as the worker's ability to own land and vote, the rapid expansion of markets, our complex form of government, immigration laws, and business cycles have all played a part in the peaks, plateaus, and valleys of the U.S. labor movement. For example, the ability to own land and participate in the political process may have slowed the progress of the U.S. labor movement because employees could voice their concerns about worklife to legislators rather than unions. The rapid expansion of markets that resulted from the development of rail and water transportation stimulated the labor movement. On the other hand, an influx of immigrants into this country produced a loosely organized, culturally divided working class comprised of unskilled workers of diverse backgrounds who spoke different languages, all of which made a concerted labor movement develop more slowly. Union membership is also affected by business cycles. It increases during prosperity and declines during recessionary periods. Contrary to other theorists, Professor Commons felt that the labor movement preceded industrialization and was not tied to a working-class consciousness, as believed by the socialist theorists.

Frank Tannenbaum had yet a different conceptualization of the labor movement. He focused primarily on the power balance between the worker and employer. By combining a psychological with an economic approach, Tannenbaum theorized that industrial workers felt degraded, insecure, and helpless in the mass production-oriented factory. As a result, unionism was the vehicle by which workers could satisfy their desire to "belong" to something and increase their control over the labor market. By doing so, workers gained power and enhanced job security, whereas employers were forced to abdicate some of their unilateral decision-making power. Tannenbaum originally viewed unionism as a revolutionary device for allowing workers to overtake and dominate the managerial class. Thirty years later, he modified this view and held that unions were more of a conservative counter-revolutionary agency primarily concerned with wages, hours, and working conditions. As the labor movement matured, Tannenbaum felt that unions would protect workers against automation, eliminate the inferiority complex of the working class, and allow workers and employers to merge into a relationship of mutual respect and harmony.[8]

Perhaps the most general and flexible view of the labor movement was the *job-consciousness* or *scarcity-consciousness* theory of Selig Perlman, a colleague

---

[7] John R. Commons and Associates, *History of Labour in the United States*, 2 vols. (New York: Macmillan Co., 1918).

[8] Frank Tannenbaum, *The Labor Movement: Its Conservative Function and Social Consequences* (New York: G.P. Putnam's Sons, 1921); and idem, *A Philosophy of Labor* (New York: Alfred A. Knopf, Inc., 1951). Cited in Chester A. Morgan, *Labor Economics,* 3rd ed. (Austin, Texas: Business Publications, Inc., 1970), p. 326.

of John Commons at the University of Wisconsin.[9] Professor Perlman believed that three basic factors play a key role in the development of a labor movement: (1) the resistance power of capitalism, (2) the degree of dominance over the labor movement by the intellectual's mentality, and (3) the maturity of the trade union mentality. History illustrates how the capitalist employer group has attempted to maintain itself as the ruling group by resisting and fighting unionization whenever possible. The staying power of the capitalist group is a function of their ability to counteract unionism through legal, political, and economic means as well as the degree to which the working class accepts the legitimacy of capitalism. Perlman's second factor, the intellectual's mentality, refers to the ability of the idealistic intellectual to influence or dominate the labor movement. In the United States, the intellectuals have played a limited role in the labor movement, as witnessed by the emphasis placed on pragmatic unionism rather than broad, sweeping ideological change. Finally, the trade union mentality factor refers to the preference of the workers and union leaders for the aforementioned short-run economic gains rather than revolutionary, ideological changes. The trade union mentality is concerned with joint control of jobs between the union and employer through collective bargaining.

Thus, labor attempts to establish a proprietary interest in the job through the promulgation of standardized work rules, grievance procedures, and the rationing of scarce job opportunities among union members. A significant percentage of the workers in this country have displayed a strong trade union mentality. Perlman concluded that the offsetting forces of the resistance power of capitalism and trade union mentality, coupled with the ineffective influence of the intellectual to shape and direct the labor movement, have resulted in a conservative, pragmatic brand of unionism in the United States.

Other theorists have also contributed to the body of knowledge surrounding labor movements. Some, such as Carlton H. Parker, focused on the psychological origins of worker discontent and unionism, whereas others, such as Professor Arthur M. Ross, viewed unions as political institutions whose mission is tied closely to the personal ambitions of union leaders.[10] The brief discussion of labor theorists presented here merely serves to acquaint the reader with the basic concept of the labor movement. Most labor movement theories to varying degrees account for the origins of unionism, the behavior of unions, the ideological orientation of unionism, and the effects of unions on society. In the United States, the more accurate theories portray unions as institutions whose primary concern is to enhance the economic welfare of the constituent worker group. Furthermore, unions in the United States also serve as social institutions that engender a sense of unity for their members. Against this backdrop, we will now examine the important events, organizations, and personalities that have shaped the U.S. labor movement.[11]

---

[9] Selig Perlman, *A Theory of the Labor Movement* (New York: Macmillan Co., 1928).
[10] Carlton H. Parker, *The Casual Laborer and Other Essays* (New York: Harcourt, Brace, and Howe, 1920) and Arthur M. Ross, *Trade Union Wage Policy* (Berkeley: University of California Press, 1948).
[11] Also see Richard A. Lester, *As Unions Mature: An Analysis of the Evolution of American Unionism* (Princeton, New Jersey: Princeton University Press, 1958), Mark Perlman, *Labor Union Theories in America* (White Plains, New York: Row, Peterson & Co., 1958), and Selig Perlman, *A Theory of the Labor Movement* (New York: Macmillan Co., 1928).

▲ Organized Labor: The First Unions

Our brief discussion of the U.S. labor movement alludes to a form of unionism whose genesis is based on the exploitation of the powerless workers by those in control of the capitalistic system. This view is not entirely accurate because the first workers to unionize in the United States were not the poor, unskilled, and illiterate factory workers, but rather the craft workers who possessed important skills. By most historical accounts, the shoemakers in Philadelphia made the first concerted efforts to unionize around the turn of the 19th century. A number of significant economic, social, and legal events surrounded the emergence of these embryonic labor organizations from their humble beginnings. However, labor unions originally surfaced at the beginning of the 19th century and experienced sporadic growth over the following 110 years. They became a significant economic, social, and political force after 1935 when protective legislation was enacted that fostered the growth in union membership.[12]

From Farm to Factory: Early Labor-Force Problems

During the colonial period, the economy was primarily agrarian. No widespread transportation or market distribution system yet existed. The labor force was comprised of free and unfree workers who often toiled side-by-side on farms and plantations. Black slaves, who were bound to a lifetime obligation of servitude, and white indentured servants, who were obligated to work for their land-owning masters for a stipulated period of time after which they were freed, made up the unfree component of the labor force. Owners and masters generally exercised total domination over unfree workers. The concept of unionism was obviously inappropriate and alien under such circumstances. However, the notion of unfree labor was unpopular in many quarters. There were those who thought that the institutions of slavery and indentured servitude were morally wrong. Others, more economically concerned, viewed the encroachment of such labor on the skilled trades with a great deal of disdain.

Early periods in the U.S. economy were plagued by shortages of skilled labor. Various methods of attracting and retaining skilled craftsmen, including training slaves in the skilled trades, had to be used. The scarcity of skilled labor required heavy reliance on importing such individuals from Europe through financial and other inducements. Skilled craftsmen thus had considerable leverage insofar as wages and working conditions were concerned.

Although agriculture remained the dominant segment of the economy, the factory system was beginning to arise in certain industries such as textiles and shipbuilding. Life in the early factories was, to put it mildly, very harsh. Adults and children worked long hours in dirty, monotonous, and unsafe conditions. The tide of immigrants from Europe increased the population, stimulated the demand for goods, and served as a source of labor for an economy that was making the transition from agriculture to mass production. By the end of the 19th century, immigrant labor accounted for roughly one-third of the labor force.

---

[12] See David Brody, ed., *The American Labor Movement* (New York: Harper and Row, 1971).

The rise of industrialism in the United States, the presence of unskilled and relatively powerless workers, and the often deplorable working conditions, undoubtedly aided and abetted the formation of labor unions. However, the actual causes of unions are still not easy to ascertain. Despite the unpleasantries of factory work, many members of the labor force were economically better off than they had previously been, especially skilled craft workers who, as noted previously, were among the first to organize. The labor movement was moving slowly and unmistakably.

Probably the prime ingredient underlying the formation of unions for craft workers such as shoemakers, printers, carpenters, and bricklayers was their desire to regulate wage rates and job opportunities. According to Reynolds:

> In the beginning, the union simply decided on its 'price' [wage rate], and the members pledged themselves not to work below this price. A little later, it became customary for a union committee to visit each employer and request his adherence to the union rate. Those who refused to agree were struck. . . . When nonconforming employers were struck, the *walking delegate*. . . went from shop to shop to make sure that all union members were out. Strikebreakers were termed *rats*, and later, *scabs*. The locals of the same trade in different cities exchanged lists of scabs and agreed not to admit them to membership. . . . Strikes were financed by levies on the membership. They were relatively peaceful, and, except in depression periods, most of them were successful.[13]

Reynolds' description of the behavior and tactics of the earliest unions are, to a large extent, illustrative of the strategies employed by today's labor organizations. In addition to regulating wages and engaging in strikes, unions attempted to ostracize nonunion workers socially. Union workers would often neither live in the same boarding house nor work alongside their nonunion counterparts. Members of the skilled trades further regulated job opportunities through apprenticeship programs by requiring that workers wishing to enter a specific trade such as carpentry be admitted to the program and serve an apprenticeship period that could last several years.

Despite their power at the local level, many of the early unions were vulnerable from two sides: employer-instigated legal action and downturns in the business cycle. The Philadelphia shoemakers union met its demise as a result of being adjudged guilty of *criminal conspiracy* because the union called a strike to force a wage increase. The trial involved, among other things, the issue of managerial prerogatives versus the rights of organized workers to have a say in determining their wages. Six similar trials involving craft unions in the clothing trades were also held during the 1820s with the unions losing four of the six. Each trial dealt with tactics employed by unions (strikes and demands for uniform wage rates) and not the legitimacy of a union's right to exist *per se*.[14]

Economic slowdowns also took their toll, as witnessed by the depressed conditions of the late 1820s, 1830s (the Panic of 1837), and 1840s. Similarly, the country experienced a post-Civil War depression between 1873 and 1878. Em-

---

[13] Lloyd G. Reynolds, *Labor Economics and Labor Relations*, 7th ed., (Englewood Cliffs, N.J.: Prentice-Hall, Inc., 1978), pp. 335–336.

[14] Christopher L. Tomlins, "Criminal Conspiracy and Early Labor Combinations: Massachusetts, 1824–1840," *Labor History* (Summer 1987), p. 370.

ployers simultaneously used various devices to destroy unions through strikebreakers, antiunion propaganda in the press, violence, and the labeling of unions as "foreign and unpatriotic." An attempt was made by early labor leaders to resort to political action, perhaps to offset some of the setbacks precipitated by hostile employers and depressed economic conditions. Workingmen's parties, as they were called, emerged with platforms usually including such items as the 10-hour work day, child labor legislation, abolition of convict labor competition, mechanics' lien laws, and the elimination of home and factory sweatshops. Although many of the ideas and beliefs of the workingmens' parties were adopted by other political parties (Democrats and Federalists), the United States has never had a true labor party like those found in Europe. Today, most of labor's political activities are restricted to lobbying and supporting candidates via worker support at the polls.

To summarize, the first unions had several common characteristics. First, their operations and sphere of influence were restricted to local areas. Second, they catered to the skilled craft worker, not to the unskilled mill hand or factory employee. Third, their existence was continually threatened by economic recessions. This lack of permanency seriously diluted the power of early unions. Fourth, they did not ordinarily use a written collective bargaining agreement, and they directed their efforts toward a very limited, although important, range of issues such as wage rates and job opportunities. Fifth, they were the constant targets of employers who were bent on their elimination.

▲ Labor Crises and Violence

The development of the labor movement in the United States involved a certain amount of bloodshed, loss of lives, brutality, and personal vendettas among union leaders, employers, and workers. Whether labor violence could have been avoided is hard to say. Nevertheless, several key events, groups, and personalities involving labor crises and violence serve to illustrate the personal sacrifices made by individuals who were involved with the early labor movement. Such events also illustrate the emotional fervor and commitment of both the labor leaders of late 19th century unions as well as employer groups who were equally aggressive in opposing and destroying unionism.

Violence on the Railroads

During the latter part of the 19th century, railroads were the chief mode of transportation and shipping. Thus, any disruption to rail service posed a potentially severe threat to the flow of commerce. Widespread riots permeated the railroad industry in 1877 as a result of an economic depression, substantial wage cuts, layoffs, and the subordination of worker interests in favor of stockholder dividends. Starting at Martinsburg, West Virginia, Baltimore and Ohio Railroad workers struck and halted the movement of freight trains. As the strike spread to other points along the line, the National Guard and federal troops were called into action. A three-day riot in Baltimore claimed 13 lives and created numerous casualties. In Pittsburgh, troops fired into a crowd of strikers, killing 20. Fires also destroyed several million dollars worth of railroad equipment.

Flare-ups occurred in other major Northeastern cities as well as in the large railway centers of Chicago and St. Louis. These actions involved the Pullman strike and Eugene Debs, leader of the American Railway Union (ARU).[15] The ARU was an *industrial union* comprised of unskilled workers and laborers (as opposed to a *craft union* of skilled workers). The Pullman Company, a railway passenger car manufacturer, laid off over half of its 5,800 employees and drastically cut the wages of its remaining employees. At this time (1894), the railroad industry was over expanded and over capitalized with miles of railroad lines that allegedly led nowhere. A circumstance peculiar to the Pullman Company, and to its president George Pullman, was that the firm controlled the town in which its operations were located. Workers were forced to live in Pullman-owned homes and buy from Pullman stores. In short, the company literally owned the town and, according to Eugene Debs, workers were human chattels or slaves of the paternalistic Pullman Company.[16]

The ARU presented a united front against Pullman by refusing to operate any train that contained cars manufactured by the company. This strategy actually expanded the impact of the strike well beyond Pullman's firm and placed a great deal of pressure on the railroads who, in turn, were expected to pressure Pullman into resolving the labor dispute. Debs initially ordered ARU members not to damage railroad property and, instead, instructed them to remove Pullman cars from passenger trains and place them on a side track. Because passenger service was the predominant mode of long-distance transportation, a strategy such as this was viewed quite seriously by the railroads and public officials. The railroads countered by hiring strikebreakers and obtaining a court order (injunction) to stop strike activities on the premise that strikes interfered with U.S. mail deliveries. President Grover Cleveland ordered federal troops to operate the trains to ensure unfettered movement of the mail. Striking workers responded by burning over 700 cars in the Chicago railway yards. A great deal of antiunion public sentiment was generated by the Pullman strike, and Debs earned a jail sentence for his efforts. This particular labor dispute demonstrated that a union could be thwarted by a powerful employer, court injunctions, and negative public opinion. While languishing in jail, Debs reflected on his defeat and became convinced that no form of business unionism could succeed. He adopted a more revolutionary view and in 1912 became a candidate for the U.S. presidency under the Socialist party.[17]

---

[15] Irving Stone, *Adversary in the House: The Life of Eugene V. Debs* (New York: Doubleday, 1947).
[16] Ray Ginger, *The Bending Cross: A Biography of Eugene Victor Debs* (New Brunswick, New Jersey: Rutgers University Press, 1949).
[17] Sanford Cohen, *Labor in the United States*, 5th ed., (Columbus, Ohio: Charles E. Merrill Publishing Company, 1979), pp. 54–56, and Chester A. Morgan, *Labor Economics*, 3rd ed. (Austin, Texas: Business Publications, Inc., 1970), p. 350.

The Haymarket Square Riot

Perhaps the single biggest blot on the reputation of labor unions was the infamous Haymarket Square riot in May of 1886.[18] Employees of the McCormick Harvester Machine Company were striking in an attempt to secure an eight-hour work day. What started as a mass rally of striking workers in Chicago's Haymarket Square ended in violence. Police ordered the crowd to disperse and an unknown person threw a bomb into the crowd, killing nine civilians and a police officer. Numerous others were injured, including 63 police. The incident generated tremendous anti-union sentiment, especially against the Knights of Labor.[19] Eight labor leaders were tried and convicted of murder under the assumption that they had conspired with or aided the anonymous bomb thrower. Of the eight, four were executed for the crime, one committed suicide while in prison, and the remaining three were eventually pardoned.[20]

Violence in Coal Mining and the Molly Maguires

Some of the worst labor violence in U.S. history, in terms of sheer brutality, occurred in the coal-mining regions of Colorado, Illinois, and Pennsylvania. Ludlow, Colorado, site of the Colorado Fuel and Iron Company mines, undoubtedly represented the bloodiest of the confrontations between miners who were trying to mobilize a union and a management who was willing to pull all of the stops to remain nonunion. According to the late Saul Alinsky, who wrote about the Ludlow Massacre in his biography of John L. Lewis:

> The management of the company was implacably hostile and extraordinarily intransigent on the subject of organized labor. They fought the union in every conceivable way, importing the Baldwin-Felts Detective Agency, which rode around in an armored car shooting down strikers on sight. They got injunctions and indictments against labor organizers. They evicted miners and their families from company homes into the freezing temperatures of a Colorado winter. To meet this forced exodus, the union set up tents, where soon hundreds of miners and their families were sheltered.[21]

The *New York Times* later described how the state militia attacked the tent community of miners and their families on the morning of April 20, 1914:

> The Ludlow Camp is a mass of charred debris and buried beneath is a story of horror unparalleled in the history of industrial warfare. In holes that had been

---

[18] The Haymarket riot occurred on May 1, 1886, and is the origin of May Day, a workers' holiday celebrated world-wide.
[19] See Lesley Wischmann, "Remembering the Haymarket Anarchists: A Hundred Years Later," *Monthly Labor Review* (October 1987), p. 17. Also see Frank Harris, *Bomb: The Haymarket Riot* (Chicago: University of Chicago Press, 1963) and Wendy Snyder, *Haymarket* (Cambridge, Massachusetts: MIT Press, 1970).
[20] Sidney Lens, *The Labor Wars: From the Molly Maguires to the Sitdowns* (Garden City, N.Y.: Doubleday, 1973) and Chester A. Morgan, *Labor Economics*, 3rd ed. (Austin, Texas: Business Publications, Inc., 1970), pp. 346–347.
[21] Saul Alinsky, *John L. Lewis: An Unauthorized Biography* (New York: G.P. Putnam's Sons, 1949), p. 9.

dug for their protection against rifle fire, the women and children died like rats when the flames swept over them. One pit uncovered this afternoon disclosed the bodies of ten children and two women.[22]

Undoubtedly, the outrage stemming from the violent and gruesome scene at Ludlow affected not only coal miners, but left other Americans hot with indignation. Unlike the Haymarket and Pullman episodes that worked to the detriment of organized labor, the Ludlow massacre served as a catalyst for unionism in the coal mining industry and perhaps other industries as well. The schism between coal miners and coal operators widened and provided a better opportunity for the union (later known as the United Mine Workers) to secure a foothold.

In Pennsylvania, the Molly Maguires created their own brand of violence. Originally members of an Irish secret society to protect farmers against eviction by English landlords, the Molly Maguires engaged in terrorist activities such as burning property, shooting at particularly hated foremen and superintendents, derailing mine cars, and beating up strikebreakers.[23] Their name stems from the fact that they sometimes disguised themselves as women while terrorizing the coal fields of Pennsylvania and West Virginia. The coal operators brought in Pinkerton's National Detective Agency to destroy this secret society. Knowing that most of the Molly Maguires were Irish Roman Catholics, Pinkerton assigned James McParland to infiltrate the group. McParland, a young and likeable Irish Catholic, soon gained acceptance by the leaders of the Molly Maguires and encouraged his new friends to even bloodier violence before he turned traitor and informed law enforcement officials and subsequently testified against them in court. As a result, 14 Molly Maguires were hanged for their crimes. The Pinkertons, with the help of McParland, had by 1876 broken the secret terrorist organization.

The Role of Violence in the Labor Movement

The above incidents are only a few, albeit a prominent few, of the examples of labor violence in the United States. Although the cases described here occurred while the labor movement was still in its infancy, numerous other instances have arisen in more recent years. Many of these stem from isolated strike-related skirmishes involving picket-line activities or post-strike personal vendettas. Others, such as the famous confrontation between the United Mine Worker's (UMW) John L. Lewis and Big Bill Hutcheson of the Carpenter's Union during the 1935 AFL convention (Lewis hit Hutcheson in the mouth) or the tragic death of Joseph Yablonski who, along with his wife and daughter, was murdered on the order of W.A. (Tony) Boyle over the disputed UMW presidential election, also represent well-publicized incidents of labor violence.

From the standpoint of public sentiment, labor violence represents a more serious blot to unions than to management. Yet there are numerous cases in which management instigated the trouble. The public is much less aware that most inter-

---
[22] Saul Alinsky, *John L. Lewis: An Unauthorized Biography* (New York: G.P. Putnam's Sons, 1949), p. 9.
[23] See Wayne G. Broehl, Jr., *The Molly Maguires* (Cambridge, Massachusetts: Harvard University Press, 1964).

action between labor and management has been and continues to be nonviolent and businesslike. Early workers and union leaders lacked legal protection and other legitimate means of airing their complaints. They resorted to violence because it was the only means of getting the attention that they felt was necessary. Of course, many union leaders and members came from rough-and-tumble environments where the use of physical force was an accepted means of dealing with the opposition. Jay Gould, the railroad magnate, once boasted that he could hire one half of the working class to kill the other half.[24] Although Gould never followed up on his statement, the economic and social plight of the early industrial labor force gives his opinion a truthful ring.

The cases of labor violence described here illustrate the personal sacrifices that individuals on both the union and management sides were willing to make to defend and further their respective causes. From the worker's standpoint, a steady job not only occupied most of his or her waking hours, but represented the essence of that individual's social and economic well being. It is of little wonder that the preservation and enhancement of employment rights could lead to aggressive and occasionally hostile action. For the employer, the union represented a major threat to business interests; the means used to thwart labor organizations were often brutal.

The Carnegie Steel Works in Homestead, Pennsylvania, was the site of a classic labor dispute (1892) that illustrated the willingness of workers, employers, and even townspeople to draw battle lines and fight to a bloody finish. A mini-war between steel workers and Pinkerton agents hired by Carnegie to protect the plant resulted in the agents' capture by townspeople who held them hostage until the National Guard intervened. Although the union "lost" this particular round, the incident helped publicize some of the abuses by management in provoking the hostility.[25] The Homestead incident also helped provide a sense of unity to the labor movement.[26]

▲ The National Labor Union

The end of the Civil War marked the beginning of broad-scale industrialization and big business in the United States. Large plantations were no longer the predominant employer in the economy and, of course, the emancipation of the slaves marked the end of the unfree segment of the labor force. Large-scale business growth ensued as the result of a developing national network of railroads and the leadership provided by industrialists such as John D. Rockefeller, Andrew Carnegie, and Jay Gould. The advent of mass production technologies and the corporate business structure resulted in an increasingly narrow and simple form of factory work for the approx-

---

[24] David H. Rosenbloom and Jay M. Shafritz, *Essentials of Labor Relations* (Reston, Virginia: Reston Publishing Co., 1985), p. 16.
[25] See R. I. Finch, "Unionism in the Iron and Steel Industry," *Political Science Quarterly*, Vol. 24 (1909) and Arthur C. Burgoyne, *Homestead* (New York: Augustus C. Kelly, 1893, reprinted 1969).
[26] See John A. Garraty, "The United States Steel Corporation Versus Labor: The Early Years," *Labor History* (Winter 1960).

imately 4.5 million persons employed in manufacturing. Many of the handicraft skills were no longer necessary for this new form of production. The influx of immigrants provided a large, unskilled, and submissive supply of labor that was seemingly ready-made for factory life.

Labor unions were forced to adapt to the national scope of the new and powerful corporate-industrial society by becoming more national as well. The formation of national unions, it was hoped, would allow labor to present a more united front and bring about greater uniformity with respect to wages, hours, and working conditions for a particular craft. Also, more political influence and financial stability would enable unions to weather better the downside of the business cycle. Although a number of "national" unions emerged prior to the Civil War (e.g., the typographers, carpenters, bricklayers, and locomotive engineers), the National Labor Union (1866–1872) represented the first serious attempt to amalgamate *all types* of labor on a national basis.[27]

The National Labor Union (NLU) was formed in Baltimore by William H. Sylvis. Despite its short life, it represented the first serious response to the changing economy and industrial expansion in the United States. As a loose federation, the NLU was torn by a certain degree of dissension, but finally focused its efforts on the eight-hour day and the greenback movement. The eight-hour day was the result of the zealous efforts of Ira Steward, a Boston machinist, who believed that if people worked a shorter day there would be a greater demand for goods and services as a result of the workers' greater amount of leisure time. Increased economic activity, in turn, would supposedly raise wages and improve the standard of living. On the surface, the NLU was successful in getting eight-hour laws passed in a number of states (and for federal employees). However, most of these laws were not enforced and employees could "agree" to work longer hours at the employer's request.

A second venture of the NLU was the support of greenbackism, a somewhat grandiose plan to help the less affluent raise capital so that they could compete with the wealthy. Labor leaders proposed that greenback currency be made convertible into low-interest government bonds in order to remove the bankers' monopoly on available capital. The ultimate aim of the greenback movement was to replace capitalism with a system of worker-owned cooperatives.

An unsuccessful foray into the political arena, a failure to fully understand the growing power of capitalism, and the distinctly utopian flavor of the NLU ultimately led to its downfall. However, the concept of a national labor federation was born and subsequent organizations such as the Knights of Labor, American Federation of Labor, and others would try their hand at nationalizing the labor movement in the United States.[28]

---

[27] For details on this stage of the American labor movement, see Lloyd Ulman, *The Rise of the National Union* (Cambridge, Massachusetts: Harvard University Press, 1956).
[28] See Sanford Cohen, *Labor in the United States*, 5th ed., (Columbus, Ohio: Charles E. Merrill Publishing Company, 1979), pp. 52–54 and Chester A. Morgan, *Labor Economics*, 3rd ed. (Austin, Texas: Business Publications, Inc., 1970), p. 345.

The Knights of Labor

Originally founded in Philadelphia in 1869 and initially led by Uriah Stephens, the Knights of Labor experienced a meteoric rise and sudden fall over a 12-year period (1881–1893). Because they feared employer persecution, the Noble Order of the Knights of Labor spent the first half of its life (1869–1881) shrouded in secrecy and even initially used an elaborate system of secret handshakes, passwords, and rituals. In 1879, Terence V. Powderly succeeded Stephens as the Knight's leader and subsequently brought the organization into public view. It was during Powderly's tenure that the Knights became a significant force on the American labor scene. The rise and fall of the organization provided some interesting lessons for the labor movement.[29]

Political and Economic Perspectives of the Knights

The Knights believed that the factory system with its mass-production technology was dehumanizing to workers because it destroyed the feeling of pride in their work, diminished their sense of accomplishment, and placed too much power in the hands of entrepreneurs and bankers who held the economy's purse strings. Unlike other leaders of labor organizations that existed before and after the Knights of Labor, Powderly emphasized the common goals between workers and employers. He downplayed the class struggle or inherent conflict upon which other labor leaders focused. The Knights also shunned the traditional goals regarding wages, hours, and working conditions in favor of more noble, idealistic, and philosophical goals. Their slogan became "An injury to one is the concern of all." Powderly envisioned one big union in which skilled workers would support the unskilled and the strong would protect the weak. Because the Knights of Labor emphasized the goals of "moral betterment" and felt that worker concerns should be on a higher ground than material and physical well-being, they welcomed a wide range of members, including both employees and employers. The Knights specifically excluded lawyers, bankers, professional gamblers, stockbrokers, and bootleggers from membership.[30]

To achieve their objectives, the Knights established several goals:

1. *Education of the general public.* The Knights felt that the existing industrial system did not promote the best interest of the worker or society. Hence, they were compelled to educate the general public. Specifically, the Knights felt that workers, employers, and politicians all acted primarily for their own selfish means rather than in the best interests of the citizenry. It was therefore up to organized labor to help change this situation.

---

[29] Terence V. Powderly, *Thirty Years of Labor: 1859–1889* (Columbus, Ohio: Excelsior Publishing House, 1889), Joseph G. Rayback, *A History of American Labor* (New York: Macmillan, 1968), and Norman J. Ware, *The Labor Movement in the United States, 1860–1895* (Gloucester, Mass.: Peter Smith, 1929, reprinted 1959).

[30] See Leon Fink, *Workingmen's Democracy: The Knights of Labor and American Politics* (Urbana, Illinois: University of Illinois Press, 1983).

2. *Consumer and producer cooperatives.* The Knights believed that the class conflict between the workers and employers would be eliminated if producer and consumer cooperatives were established. Cooperation would allow employees to own the factories and, in essence, become their own boss; no longer would the interests of employees be subordinate to those of shareholders and management.
3. *Strikes, boycotts, and other relatively violent labor tactics were de-emphasized.* Work stoppages were regarded with disdain by the Knights' leadership. Strikes were generally discouraged because they deprived workers of jobs and were not in the best interests of the employees' moral betterment.

The Knights of Labor, while not revolutionary, were most definitely a reform-oriented organization. They pushed for labor legislation such as health and safety laws, restriction on child labor under age 15, and the weekly payment of wages in money rather than in credit for purchases in company-owned stores. Broader objectives such as compulsory public education and free textbooks, the graduated income tax, and government ownership of public utilities were also advocated. Many of these "reforms" are taken for granted today, but they were considered quite radical for the 1880s.[31]

The Rise and Fall of the Knights: What Happened?

Between 1882 and 1886, the Knights of Labor membership increased from 42,000 members to 700,000. Although the Knights denounced the use of strikes, it was the success of the strike weapon in the railroad industry that had workers rushing to join the union ranks. When the organization forced Jay Gould to capitulate to the union's demands in the face of a threatened strike on the Wabash Railroad, the newspapers published accounts of the ordeal that made the Knights appear extremely formidable and capable of inflicting severe damage to any employer who stood in the way. Unskilled and otherwise powerless workers viewed the Knights as a savior who welcomed them with open arms. The Knights' willingness to accept unskilled workers was especially important because prior unions had admitted only skilled and craft employees.

The success of the Knights was short-lived. The overconfident attitude engendered by the victory over the Wabash Railroad led to other strikes whose outcomes were not so successful. Powderly's inept, naive, and vacillating leadership style was probably the primary reason behind the fall of the Knights. The Knights' organization structure was unwieldy and the local delegates often pulled in a different direction than the national headquarters desired. Employer opposition to unionism and strikes also helped to drive nails into the Knights' coffin. Another death knell was the Haymarket incident, for which the Knights were blamed. Notions such as the idea that skilled workers would support the unskilled masses; that workers were more interested in high ideals and lofty moral issues than in wages, hours, and daily

---

[31] See Leon Fink, "The New Labor History and the Powers of Historical Pessimism: Consensus, Hegemony, and the Case of the Knights of Labor," *Journal of American History* (June 1988), p. 15.

working conditions; that employers could be united with workers for the betterment of all; or that consumer cooperatives could be more efficiently run than other businesses were unrealistic for this period in labor history. By 1892, the Knights of Labor was virtually extinct, although it continued to function weakly until 1917.

▲ The American Federation of Labor (AFL)

The AFL emerged as an antithesis to the Knights of Labor. Formed by a discontented faction from within the Knights, the AFL was led by Samuel Gompers and Adolph Strasser of the cigarmakers' union. Under Samuel Gompers, the AFL ushered in the era of business unionism in this country, and there appears to have been a concerted effort to avoid the earlier pitfalls encountered by the Knights. In addition to learning from the mistakes of others, Gompers possessed an energetic and tenacious attitude as he launched the AFL into an environment that was to remain hostile to organized labor for the next 40 years. During his youth, Gompers had sided with the socialists. As he matured, he drifted away from socialism and later held socialists in contempt, viewing their doctrines as unsound, wrong, and unrealistic. Gompers believed that capitalism would endure and unions would have to exist within that system; as a result, it would behoove the intelligent union leader to focus on "pure and simple" unionism that measured achievement in terms of immediate economic gains such as higher wages, benefits, and a shorter working day.[32]

AFL leaders built a solid organizational structure that centered on the viability and autonomy of the craft union. The "one big union" idea set forth by the Knights had no place in the hearts of AFL leaders. Skilled craft workers were viewed as having the economic power; the endless stream of unskilled immigrant workers were left to fend for themselves. Craft workers at the local level were strongly affiliated with those at the national level who, in turn, were placed under the umbrella of the AFL. Emphasis was placed on unions that were stable and financially solvent. Since the number of craft workers was limited because of apprenticeship programs and entrance restrictions, their pay rates were high. Thus, scarce and highly trained craft workers could wield considerable bargaining power and would be difficult to replace during times of economic growth and low unemployment. The AFL also supported high union dues. Gompers worked diligently to promote

---

[32] See Samuel Gompers (Nick Salvatore, ed.) *Seventy Years of Life and Labor: An Autobiography* (Ithaca, New York: ILR Press, Cornell University, 1923, 1985), Samuel Gompers, *The American Labor Movement: Its Makeup, Achievements, and Inspirations* (Washington, D.C.: American Federation of Labor, 1914), Frank L. Grubbs, *The Struggle for Labor Loyalty: Gompers of the A.F. of L. and the Pacifists, 1917–1920* (Durham, North Carolina: Duke University Press, 1968), Stuart Bruce Kaufman, *Samuel Gompers and the Origins of the American Federation of Labor, 1848–1896,* (Westport, Connecticut: Greenwood Press, 1973), Harold G. Livesay, *Samuel Gompers and Organized Labor in America* (Boston: Little, Brown and Co., 1978), Philip Taft, *The A.F. of L. in the Time of Gompers* (New York: Harper and Row, 1957).

respectability and social acceptance of unions in the industrial community. He succeeded to a much greater degree than did earlier labor organizations.[33]

Political and Economic Perspectives of the AFL

As its name implies, the American Federation of Labor was not a union but a *federation* of autonomous craft unions. Each of these unions had its own leadership, constitution, by-laws, and dues structure because each represented its own specific craft. The AFL worked primarily as a coordinating body and political arm. In addition, the AFL helped resolve jurisdictional disputes among the various member unions.

Although the Knights of Labor philosophically shunned the use of the strike, the AFL embraced it enthusiastically. Gompers supported capitalism, but felt that the industrialist-capitalists, as a group, would try to pay the worker as little as possible. The strike was seen as the means by which the wage-earner could force the industrialist's hand and achieve a higher wage than would otherwise be granted.

Gompers recognized the need for involvement in the political arena even though he strongly believed that unions were not revolutionary political organizations. Unlike the labor movements in many European countries, the United States has never had a viable labor party. Instead, labor has endorsed political candidates who supported worker causes and concerns; more often than not, these candidates were Democrats. Gompers initiated this strategy because he believed that a three-party political system would be too divisive. Instead, Gompers' philosophy was to reward politicians who supported labor and punish those who did not. The AFL backed the Democratic presidential candidacy for Woodrow Wilson in 1912 as well as that of Robert LaFollette in 1924. LaFollette ran on the Independent ticket and the AFL's endorsement of his candidacy ran contrary to their normal strategy of supporting someone who was either GOP or Democrat.

Collective bargaining, as we know it today, was instituted by Gompers and the AFL. The 1890s heralded the use of written, signed labor contracts covering wages, hours, and working conditions. Although some skeptics claimed that the rhetoric of collective bargaining would surpass its performance, the precedent was set by Gompers. In the years to come, the institution of collective bargaining would provide sizeable material and economic gains for workers. Certainly the antiunion actions of employers are adequate proof that organizations such as the AFL were viewed as a formidable threat whose performance did indeed match their rhetoric.

By 1900, the AFL included 48 national unions, most of which were composed of workers from the skilled craft trades (the exceptions being the unskilled mine workers and garment workers). The early years of the AFL were marked by a steady, but not particularly rapid, growth. The unspectacular growth was attributable to the more exclusive nature of the AFL, a craft-dominated federation that ignored the needs of unskilled workers. Thus, there remained a great mass of workers who were

---

[33] See Philip Taft, *The AFL in the Time of Gompers* (New York: Harper and Row, 1957) and *The AFL from the Death of Gompers to the Merger* (New York: Harper and Row, 1959).

ripe for other union organizers. Various socialist sects appeared on the scene and offered hope for the unskilled. One in particular, the Industrial Workers of the World (IWW), posed the most significant attack from the left on the AFL.

▲ The Industrial Workers of the World (IWW)

The Industrial Workers of the World, also known as the Wobblies, represented a radical departure from both the Knights and the AFL. Under "Big Bill" Haywood,[34] a one-eyed leader of the ultraradical Western Federation of Miners, the IWW's chief objective was to overthrow capitalism and replace it with militant trade unionism whereby the workers controlled the economy. In his famous 1905 speech, Haywood commented:

> Fellow workers! This is the Continental Congress of the working class. We are here to confederate the workers of this country into a working class movement ... to put the whole working class in possession of economic power ... [and] in control of the machinery of production.... We are going down into the gutter... to get at the mass of workers and bring them up to a decent plane of living.[35]

The leadership of the IWW believed that labor was in a life-or-death class struggle and that the only hope of winning was through revolutionary political and economic action. Haywood and his charges also despised the AFL and regarded Gompers as a selfish and uncaring leader who failed to support Eugene Debs and the Pullman strikers in their time of need.

Political and Economic Perspective of the IWW

The IWW's preamble proclaimed that workers and capitalists had nothing in common. A declaration such as this had an enticing ring to the masses of unskilled and migrant farm workers who had not been effectively represented by a labor organization. As the AFL advocated bread-and-butter unionism, the IWW looked to the establishment of socialism as its ultimate goal. By 1912, seven years after the IWW's inception, their membership was approximately 100,000, consisting mainly of migrant workers, textile mill employees, lumberjacks, and dockworkers. According to Haywood, "every man that earns his livelihood either by his brain or his muscle" was eligible to join under the IWW's one big union.

It also appears that the IWW was willing to engage in sabotage and violence against employers, although this was legally difficult to prove at the time. Nevertheless, this image did little to endear the IWW to the general public. Newspapers inflamed negative public sentiment by publishing stories that painted a violent and almost insane caricature of IWW leaders as destroyers of property, murderers, and

---

[34] Haywood was jailed and released on bail. He fled to the Soviet Union where he died in 1928.
[35] Alvin Schwartz, *The Unions* (New York: The Viking Press, 1972), p. 45. Reprinted with permission, Curtis-Brown, Ltd., copyright, 1972 by Alvin Schwartz.

jailbirds. Many of the IWW members were itinerant and unemployed workers. A lax dues collection system kept the membership and financial base of the organization on unstable ground. Within four years of its founding, the IWW was in dire financial straits, probably due in part to the questionable integrity of some of the organization's officers:

> Nothing was more striking in the recent [IWW] convention than the stories of local financial losses. "All down the line" said one delegate, "we have had experience with secretaries who have absconded with funds." "No less than three have done the same thing [in our local]," was the testimony of another. This happened three times to one local in one year according to a third statement. Indeed so loose is the local financial control... that there appears to exist a body of circulating professional agitators who make it their business to go from locality to locality for the sole purpose of getting themselves elected to the treasurer's office and absconding with the funds.[36]

For members of a labor organization with such lofty and idealistic goals, the dishonest and undermining behavior of IWW officials must have been demoralizing.[37]

Downfall of the IWW

A discussion of the IWW's political and economic perspective dovetails nicely into the reasons for the organization's demise. As has been noted, the IWW suffered from a poor public image, an unstable membership, financial problems, and internal corruption. The IWW also repeated a mistake that had helped cripple the Knights of Labor—it was one big union attempting to achieve broad social reforms at the expense of more short-run material economic gains. Leaders in the IWW could never make up their minds as to how they should most effectively muster their forces to build a membership base; some wanted to raid the AFL, whereas others favored different tactics. Politically, the IWW never achieved significant power because many of their members were politically apathetic or were not registered voters. Rebellion, rather than political action and lobbying, best describes the IWW strategy.

Soon after World War I began, the government cracked down on the nation's radicals for fear that they would undermine the war effort. Wobblies were arrested, union halls were closed, and records and propaganda confiscated. Interestingly enough, 50 students at the University of California-Berkeley formed an IWW chapter in 1970. Even at that late date, the U.S. Attorney General still listed the IWW as a subversive organization.[38]

---

[36] Derek C. Bok and John T. Dunlop, *Labor and the American Community* (New York: Simon and Schuster, 1970), pp. 67–68.
[37] See Michael Irvin, "Wobblies Still," *The Progressive* (June 1985), p. 29.
[38] See Melvyn Dubofsky, *We Shall Be All: A History of the Industrial Workers of the World* (Westminster, Maryland: Quadrangle Books, 1969 and Patrick Renshaw, *Wobblies: The Story of Syndicalism in the United States* (Garden City, New York: Doubleday, 1967).

▲ Trade Unionism in the 20th Century

1900–1920

Labor unions of the late 19th century had their ups and downs in terms of membership numbers. As the 20th century dawned, unions began to experience less spectacular, but more stable, membership growth patterns. The AFL contributed to this growth and, between 1897 and 1904, they more than doubled the number of international unions under their wing from 58 to 120. Slowly, but surely, labor unions continued to grow until World War I. The World War I period (1914–1920) was one of rapid progress as union membership doubled from 2.5 million in 1914 to 5 million by 1920. Two factors attributed to this phenomenal growth during the war years: the encouragement of collective bargaining by the government and the high levels of employment.

The keen interest of the federal government in labor unions during World War I stemmed from the need to avoid work stoppages, especially in industries vital to the war effort. The War Labor Board was established to settle union-management disputes. The Board recognized the right of unions to organize and engage in collective bargaining. In addition, the high employment level supplied more candidates for unions. The AFL pledged their cooperation with the War Labor Board and the labor movement enjoyed unprecedented prosperity.

The Roaring 1920s: Not a Roaring Time for Unionism

The end of World War I marked the beginning of the exciting and economically rewarding decade of the 1920s. Conditions of economic prosperity usually represent good times for union organizers to sign up members and make successful inroads into nonunionized sectors. However, the 1920s was a notable exception to this rule; unions suffered serious setbacks despite the economic prosperity. Between 1920 and 1923, union membership declined from 5 million to 3.5 million. In the next 7 years, union membership slowly decreased (with the exception of 1927) so that by 1930, less than 3.4 million persons belonged to unions.[39]

What factors caused this decline? Some of the problems stemmed from the unions themselves, whereas others could be attributed to antiunion tactics. It is probable that many workers were lured into joining unions during World War I because of a perceived need for national unity in the face of a world war. Once the war ended, worker cohesiveness may have dissolved and union membership declined. Another possible explanation is that during the 1920s, wages kept up with price increases and economic prosperity improved the nation's quality of life. Thus, workers probably did not feel the need to use unions to help them achieve economic gains. Many potential union members remained unorganized because of the AFL's aversion to industrial unions comprised of unskilled workers.

Stubbornly, the AFL adhered to craft unionism. This strategy made it difficult to organize and bargain effectively with the industrial corporate giants (a classic

---

[39] Sanford Cohen, *Labor in the United States*, 5th ed., (Columbus, Ohio: Charles E. Merrill Publishing Company, 1979), p. 70.

example was the 1919 strike against the United States Steel Corporation; 24 craft unions were involved in what became an uncoordinated fiasco because of internal union difficulties). Unions continued to be plagued by a poor public image associated with the infiltration of political radicals, communists, and labor racketeers. Out of desperation, union leaders had accepted the help of these groups in the hope of building their membership base. Union officials also were betting that once these groups joined, they could somehow be controlled. Much to their chagrin, they realized too late that they were losing their bets in many cases.

Perhaps most devastating were the antiunion employer tactics that became increasingly popular during the 1920s. The following represented some of the more common methods:

- *Blacklisting* employees who were union members. Companies often shared these lists and banned union sympathizers from employment.
- *Industrial spies* were hired through the Pinkerton detective agency to observe union meetings and supply companies with the names of union sympathizers and members. Union members were often blackmailed into sabotaging their labor organizations (these individuals were called "hooked men" and the Pinkerton agents were called "hookers").
- *Physical violence* and a technique known as *roughshadowing* were used to intimidate union members. Roughshadowing is a tactic whereby a large and threatening-looking individual follows and "stalks" a union sympathizer. Unlike with the predatory stalking of a feline, the employee is aware that he or she is being followed. The intended result is to frighten the victim away from remaining in the union.
- *Strikebreaking tactics* designed to demoralize striking workers and inflame negative public sentiment against unions were used. The most notable was the *Mohawk Valley Formula*, which involved stirring up violence, labeling union leaders as outside agitators, organizing a back-to-work movement, employing a skeleton crew of strikebreakers to give the appearance that the plant was still operating during the strike, and using the press to slander union leaders.
- *Company-run unions* were formed in place of unions run by outsiders. Management was thus able to control the collective bargaining process by, in essence, negotiating its own labor contract. An arrangement such as this can undermine the interests of employees and make a sham out of the bargaining relationship.
- *Yellow dog contracts* were used to force employees into remaining union-free. Upon being hired, an employee signed the yellow dog contract, agreeing not to join a union. If the employee did so, this constituted a breach of contract and the individual could be discharged.
- *The Sherman Antitrust Act* was used against unions because they allegedly restricted the flow of commerce and established artificially high wage rates. Originally designed to control price-fixing arrangements and the monopoly power of large corporations, the Sherman Act was also found by employers to be an effective weapon against unions, primarily because the Act provided for triple damages against union officers and members who were judged to have disrupted

a company's business. The threat of such a huge legal liability undoubtedly frightened and discouraged those who would otherwise have supported unions.[40]

- *Paternalism* through company ownership of local stores, employee housing, and financial institutions gave management control over their employees' work lives as well as their private lives. Employees would often become heavily indebted to their employers, making it difficult for workers to sever ties with the company. Paternalism was most common in small mill and mining towns where the local economy was tied exclusively to one firm.
- *Sweetheart arrangements* between employers and union officials worked to the detriment of workers. For example, a company could bribe union negotiators or officials to avoid the discussion of certain issues at the bargaining table or to ignore enforcement of specific collective bargaining agreement provisions.
- *Court injunctions* were issued to suppress union organizing activities and collective bargaining under the premise that unions caused irreparable "property damage" to the firm. Since equity court judges were generally more sympathetic to the employer's view, injunctions were relatively easy to secure. Union officials and employees who violated the terms and conditions of an injunction could be held in contempt of court.

All of these tactics are now illegal (or highly restricted) under federal law. However, during the 1920s and early 1930s, antiunion measures such as these were not only legal, but were supported by the court system and the government. Two reasons can be cited for this lack of support for organized labor. First, the economic prosperity of the 1920s encouraged the government to adopt a hands-off policy with respect to economic and social conditions. The federal government was interested in supporting organized labor only when it was in the national interest; that is, the government adopted a cooperative posture with the union during World War I when labor peace was imperative. Second, Samuel Gompers began to suffer from poor health and died in 1924. His successor, William Green of the United Mine Workers, did little to revive labor's diminishing influence. Green attempted to develop a cooperative posture with employers who, needless to say, were not interested. As the 1920s drew to a close, 3.5 million or 6 percent of the work force was unionized. The labor movement was most certainly at a low ebb.

The 1930s: The Rise of the CIO and Labor Legislation

The economic prosperity of the 1920s came to a crushing halt in the following decade. October 24, 1929 (Black Thursday) marked the beginning of the Depression Era that stretched through the 1930s.[41] At first, the country went through a period of denial, but reluctantly began to realize that the great crash in late 1929

---

[40] The Clayton Act (1914) exempted unions from the coverage of the Sherman Antitrust Act and stated that labor organizations were not illegal combinations or conspiracies. However, various judicial interpretations continued to hold unions liable under the Sherman Act. In 1932, the Norris-LaGuardia Act was passed and it effectively relieved unions from antitrust liabilities.

[41] See Irving Bernstein, *The Lean Years, A History of the American Worker*, 1920–1933 (Boston: Houghton Mifflin, 1960).

was more than a shake-up in the securities market. Both the gross national product and wages fell to one half of their pre-Depression levels. The following paragraph presents a graphic illustration of life during the early 1930s:

> There were long breadlines in New York City, a municipal soup kitchen in Milwaukee, and parades of protest by growing armies of unemployed everywhere. The skies over Gary and Pittsburgh no longer had their dull red glow as furnaces went out. In Detroit, the automobile industry was grinding to a stop. A new business sprang up on every corner with a sign, "Unemployed. Buy apples, 5¢ each." Destitute people began to live in Hoovervilles or in tarpaper shacks, many of them built around garbage dumps. Americans laughed with bitterness as Will Rogers cracked, "We hold the distinction of being the only nation in the history of the world that went to the poor house in an automobile." Women were working for a maximum of 25¢ an hour and many for 10¢ an hour. Taxi drivers in New York were averaging fifteen dollars a week for a six-day week. The salaries and wages of 1925 were more than halved by 1931. The national income dove from eighty-one billion dollars in 1929 to forty-one billion in 1932. By that time there were approximately fifteen million Americans unemployed. The new world aged through those years. A plague was in the land as hundreds of thousands of people hungry, heartsick, and driven by fear took to the road seeking not security but just bread and shelter.
>
> The wave of unemployment engulfed the labor movement, and many of the 15,000,000 unemployed were union men and women. By 1931 the AF of L was losing more than 7,000 dues-paying members each week, and the situation was steadily getting worse. The impact of the depression smashed those standards the AF of L had so patiently and painfully achieved. Working conditions and wage-and-hour standards were gone with the tornado of the depression. The very life of organized labor was at stake. Millions of unemployed desperately walked the streets searching for any kind of job at any kind of pay.[42]

Hard times and poverty did not discriminate—they affected the professional, skilled, and unskilled alike. No longer could diligence, hard work, and intelligence ensure material well-being. Only after the Roosevelt Administration instituted New Deal legislation did the economy begin to regain life.[43] As we will see, labor unions were also benefactors of Roosevelt's new plan.[44]

The lethargic posture of unions, and the AFL in particular, continued into the 1930s. Distrustful of the government, battered by employers, and clinging tenaciously to the concept of craft unionism, the AFL failed to see that the world had changed. Industrial mass production technology now depended on the more specialized and less-skilled workers who, in the eyes of the AFL, were neither politically and economically powerful nor clamoring to join a union. Instead, AFL leadership focused on alleviating unemployment through reduced work weeks where everyone shared the work that was available. The AFL also took a stand against unemployment

---

[42] Saul Alinsky, *John L. Lewis: An Unauthorized Biography* (New York: G.P. Putnam's Sons, 1949), pp. 62–63.
[43] See Milton Derber and Edwin Young, *Labor and the New Deal* (Madison, Wisconsin: University of Wisconsin Press, 1957).
[44] See David Brody, "Labor and the Great Depression: The Interpretive Prospects," *Labor History* (Spring 1972).

compensation benefits for those who had lost their jobs. Clearly, the AFL was out of step with the times. By living in the past, they still believed that their previous successes in organizing skilled craft workers and their failures with industrial unions (between 1910 and 1920) should dictate organizational strategy during the 1930s.

The hopes of organized labor were temporarily raised by the passage of the National Industrial Recovery Act (NIRA) in 1933.[45] Among other things, section 7(a) of the Act provided that workers should have the right to organize and bargain collectively without coercion, interference, and restraint by employers. The Act, although declared unconstitutional in 1935, had two effects. First, it served as a catalyst for industrial unionism under the leadership of John L. Lewis, who was about to break away from the AFL to form his own organization designed to unionize the unskilled worker. Second, for the first time in history, the federal government officially recognized the right of workers to unionize and bargain with their employers. The downfall of the NIRA was the result of problems with other parts of the Act that dealt with codes of fair competition rather than with Section 7(a), which pertained to union-management relations. The failure of the NIRA set the stage for Congress to pass pro-union legislation that focused solely on labor.

The conflict over craft versus industrial unionism that had been brewing for over three decades finally reached a climax in 1935 when the Committee for Industrial Organization (CIO) was formed within the AFL by John L. Lewis.[46] Lewis was originally from the United Mine Workers and was supported by a number of other industrial unions. William Green, then head of the AFL, responded by suspending and later expelling some of the renegade members who supported industrial unionism. The emotionalism surrounding the issue of industrial unions was perhaps best illustrated when John L. Lewis hit William Hutcheson in the jaw in full view of the press and delegates at the AFL's 1935 convention. According to Saul Alinsky in his biography of Lewis,

> Lewis walked up the aisle and approached Hutcheson. As usual, the convention became quiet. Lewis in a low voice said something to Hutcheson that caused the leader of the Carpenters Union to reply profanely. First the word "bastard" was heard, then the crack of Lewis's fist on Hutcheson's face. A few more blows were exchanged and Hutcheson and Lewis grappled and went down amidst collapsing chairs and tables.
>
> Lewis knew that with one punch at Hutcheson he would be doing what thousands of workers wanted to do. By attacking Hutcheson, he was attacking the trade unionism these workers so bitterly hated. He knew that with one blow on Hutcheson's face he would rupture the uneasy peace within the Federation creating the revolt necessary for secession.[47]

The industrial unions that were expelled in 1938 reconstituted into a rival federation known as the Congress of Industrial Organizations (CIO). Thus the stage

---

[45] During the two-year life of the NIRA, union membership increased by 33 percent and therefore illustrated the powerful effect of the law on organized labor. See Florence Peterson, *American Labor Unions* (New York: Harper & Brothers, 1945), p. 56.
[46] See, for example, Robert H. Zieger, *John L. Lewis: Labor Leader* (Boston: Twayne, 1988).
[47] Saul Alinsky, *John L. Lewis: An Unauthorized Biography* (New York: G.P. Putnam's Sons, 1949), p. 76.

was set for incorporating into the the labor movement the unskilled masses who served as the backbone to modern industrialization. In their early years, industrial unions used the sit-down strike to gain leverage with employers. The CIO initially concentrated on organizing workers in the mass production industries such as rubber, autos, and steel. General Motors Corporation employees provided the best example of the sit-down strike. Considerable fervor in using this tactic was demonstrated by GM employees who managed to close the Atlanta, Kansas City, Cleveland, and Detroit plants by declaring, "When the boss won't talk, don't take a walk, sit down!, sit down!" In Flint, Michigan, sit-down strikes in Fisher Body Plants 1 and 2 resulted in a court order demanding that workers leave. When they refused, police pumped tear gas into the plants and the workers responded by throwing tools, pipes, car door hinges, and whatever else they could find. Later that night, the workers turned a firehose on the police and drove them back. Michigan governor Frank Murphy ordered 1,500 National Guardsmen to Flint to remove the strikers. Murphy, the grandson of an Irish revolutionary, knew that considerable bloodshed would likely ensue. He visited John L. Lewis and requested that he halt the strike before it was too late. Lewis replied:

> You want my answer sir? I shall give it to you. Tomorrow morning I shall personally enter General Motors plant Chevrolet No. 4. I shall then walk up to the largest window in the plant, open it, divest myself of my outer raiment, remove my shirt, and bare my bosom. Then, when you order your troops to fire, mine will be the first breast those bullets will strike. And as my body falls from that window to the ground, you listen to the voice of your grandfather as he whispers in your ear, "Frank, are you sure you are doing the right thing?"[48]

Governor Murphy did not order troops into the plant, and GM subsequently agreed to recognize the union. Later, the Ford Motor Company was targeted for union organization. In 1937, several steel firms, known collectively as Little Steel, under the leadership of Republic Steel became the focal point of a violent labor upheaval. On Memorial Day, 1937, South Chicago was the scene of the bloody Memorial Day Massacre. The dispute was precipitated by union-organizing campaigns that eventually resulted in Republic Steel and others coming to terms with the CIO. When John L. Lewis resigned his post as head of the CIO, Philip Murray, who had headed the Steel Workers Organizing Committee, took the CIO reins. The CIO had established a strong and successful foundation built on solid leadership, realistic business unionism goals, and the effective use of sit-down strikes.

Although the emergence of the CIO was a significant development as the labor movement progressed through the 1930s, it was not *the* most favorable development insofar as the long-run effect on labor was concerned. That distinction belongs to the passage of the Wagner Act in 1935, which rectified what had gone wrong under the National Industrial Recovery Act. Labor leaders called the Wagner Act their "Magna Carta" because it guaranteed workers the right to form, join, and assist labor organizations. The Act also required that employees bargain with unions in

---

[48] Alvin Schwartz, *The Unions* (New York: Viking Press, 1972), pp. 52–53. Reprinted with permission, Curtis-Brown, Ltd., copyright 1972 by Alvin Schwartz.

good faith. Nearly all of the antiunion employer tactics described earlier were deemed illegal under the Act, and the National Labor Relations Board (NLRB) was established to enforce the Act's provisions. The Wagner Act is discussed in greater detail in Chapter 3.

The passage of the Wagner Act and the establishment of the CIO had a tremendous effect on the membership levels of labor unions during the 1930s. By the end of the decade, the membership rolls had swollen to nearly 9 million workers. For the first time, labor organizations, their leaders, and their members had become a factor to be reckoned with within the economic and political arena.

▲ The 1940s: World War II and the Increasing Power of Unions

The inroads made in the steel and auto industries in the late 1930s began paying big dividends in 1940 and 1941 as successful organizing campaigns resulted in escalating membership trends. After experiencing the Great Depression, workers were ready to join unions for reasons of job and economic security. Successes enjoyed by the CIO also appear to have helped the AFL gain more members and the rivalry between the two organizations intensified.

With the attack on Pearl Harbor on December 7, 1941, the nation became involved in World War II. As in World War I, dominant labor organizations once again pledged their support to the war effort. Unsettled labor-management disputes were resolved by the National War Labor Board's compulsory arbitration tribunal as a means of avoiding strikes and work stoppages. An anti-inflation program was instituted to hold the line on prices in an economy that was suddenly experiencing high wages, high levels of productivity, and shortages of consumer goods. In stark contrast to the 1930s, the war economy meant virtually no unemployment. Economic insecurity was replaced by an even more frightening insecurity as the nation fought for survival. Labor shortages, longer working days, seven-day work weeks, and population shifts to areas where war goods were being produced characterized a war-charged economy of the early 1940s. Because of high levels of employment, unions experienced a very rapid growth rate. By the end of the war approximately 15 million workers belonged to labor organizations.

The post-war labor scene was beset with a number of problems. First, unrestrained collective bargaining, complete with strikes and lockouts was once again possible. The year following the war (1946) was the most strike-prone in labor history. Part of the 1946 strike wave was probably due to pent-up worker demands and frustrations created by war-time price controls and wage freezes as well as working conditions that were no longer acceptable once the war had ended. Also, many employer-union relationships were still in their infancy. This situation undoubtedly led to labor disputes that the more mature and seasoned negotiators, union officials, and managers would have avoided.

A second problem, at least from an employer's perspective, was the increasing power held by unions. Clearly, the period between 1935 and the end of World War II saw unparalleled growth in union membership and power. Yet the Wagner Act only tied the hands of employers; unions were subject to very little federal or state regulation. As employers had done in earlier decades, unions were now engaging in practices of dubious social value. Tactics such as secondary boycotts, intimidation of recalcitrant employees during union organizing campaigns, internal union corruption, and strikes of a questionable nature, to name a few, were coming to the attention of Congress. In 1947, the Taft-Hartley Act was passed to regulate union activities. Union unfair labor practices were written into the law and the National Labor Relations Board was given the authority to regulate the labor relations activities of both employers and labor organizations.

A third problem characterizing the labor movement was the constant feud between the AFL and CIO over craft-versus-industrial-unionism and organizational and jurisdictional issues. The two factions often spent more time fighting with each other than taking care of their members' interests. However, by the end of World War II the AFL-CIO conflict was gradually beginning to de-escalate as the craft and industrial union distinction became more blurred (because of technological changes). The old guard was gradually replaced by a new and less embattled leadership.

The 1950s: The AFL and CIO Unite

The 1950s brought about different sets of issues for the labor movement. With the passage of the Taft-Hartley Act, labor leaders were fearful that the power of unionism may have once again been on the decline. The presence of communists and internal corruption in the ranks of some unions also hurt labor's image. Communist infiltration in the CIO ranks presented a paradox. On one hand, the presence of communists was not good from a public relations standpoint, especially in the 1950s, when anticommunist feelings were especially intense. Yet, communists related well to many rank-and-file workers and they were tireless union organizers, a job that was often physically dangerous. While the CIO had to resolve the problem of what to do with the communists, the AFL had to deal with internal corruption within some of its member unions. These problems were compounded by AFL and CIO raids on each other's membership, which resulted in a lot of energy being expended for little net gain. Each side stole approximately 1,200 of the other side's members. All of these factors pointed toward a need for greater unity in the labor movement.

Several preliminary measures were taken to alleviate some problems. First, the CIO expelled 11 communist-dominated unions with almost 900,000 members. Second, the AFL expelled some of its more corrupt unions. Third, the AFL and CIO agreed to establish no-raiding pacts. All of these measures led to the eventual merger of the AFL and CIO in 1955. With the deaths of AFL president William Green[49] and CIO leader Philip Murray within 11 days in 1952 and the emergence of George Meany and Walter Reuther as leaders of the AFL and CIO, respectively, the level of animosity that had existed for years was suddenly reduced. George Meany was appointed president of the new AFL-CIO, the largest labor federation in the world, with over 15.5 million members. As an indication of how much times had changed,

---

[49] See Craig Phelan, *William Green: Biography of a Labor Leader* (Albany, New York: State University of New York Press, 1989).

the industrial union members outnumbered the craft union members by nearly 2 to 1 after the merger.[50]

All was not healed by the AFL-CIO merger, however. A U.S. Senate committee (the McClellan Committee) began investigating racketeering practices within the Teamsters Union and other labor organizations. This investigation resulted in the AFL-CIO Code of Ethical Practices. Both the Teamsters and the United Textile Workers Union were expelled from the AFL-CIO in 1957, costing the federation 1.5 million members.[51] In 1959, Congress passed the Labor-Management Reporting and Disclosure Act (also known as the Landrum-Griffin Act) designed to control and reduce internal corruption within the labor movement. This law is discussed in Chapter 3.

The Labor Movement since 1960

From 1960 to the present, labor unions have continued to undergo change. Union membership levels stabilized and then began declining in the 1980s. A number of social and legal changes have occurred that have had a significant impact on the labor movement.

First, the scope of the collective bargaining agreement has gradually widened as more provisions have been incorporated into labor contracts. Greater union and employee awareness of the smorgasbord of options available to them—such as prepaid legal plans, cost-of-living adjustments, supplemental unemployment benefits, and dozens of others—reflects the complexity and sophistication of union-management relations.

Second, unions are no longer strictly blue-collar organizations. Professionals such as teachers, professors, nurses, and even a few physicians have become unionized. Because of the shift toward white-collar employment and a decline in the number of blue-collar jobs relative to white-collar positions, unions have organized professional, administrative, and clerical employees in large numbers since the early 1960s.

Third, unions have actively and successfully organized public-sector employees. Police officers, firefighters, public school employees, and health-care workers have represented relatively new and abundant sources of union membership. As discussed in Chapter 17, public-sector collective bargaining presents a unique set of legal and economic issues.

Fourth, the passage of civil rights, compensation, health and safety, and other employment laws has altered the status of the labor movement. Federal and state legislation now protects workers from the abuses of racial, sex, and other forms of discrimination as well as unsafe working conditions. Before the enactment of such legislation, unions carried much of the protective burden.

Fifth, the political influence of labor over the past 25 years has been significant, but not overwhelmingly strong. Although political candidates often desire to have the support of labor during election years, they realize that labor does not vote in

---

[50] See Joseph C. Goulden, *Meany* (New York: Antheneum, 1972).
[51] The Teamsters were readmitted to the AFL-CIO on October 24, 1987.

a block. Union members differ in their political preferences and on the issues that they feel are important. Today, the AFL-CIO is an active political lobbying group and the fruits of its labors affect both union and nonunion workers. It should also be remembered that organized labor is still plagued by a negative public image that undoubtedly can be traced back to earlier days when violence, communist infiltration, and labor racketeering were more commonplace.

Sixth, a number of firms have begun using management consultants and union avoidance tactics designed to prevent unions from successfully organizing employees or to dilute the power of existing union representation. Concession bargaining and the use of bankruptcy laws to avoid the obligations imposed by a collective bargaining agreement have also been used by some employers. Organized labor has countered through innovations such as corporate campaigns that are designed to embarrass or place economic and public pressure on antiunion firms.[52] The trends and developments since the 1960s provide a focus for the remainder of this book.

▲ A Historical Synthesis and Summary

This chapter serves as a backdrop for the remainder of the book, which will focus on the labor relations scene of the early 1990s. A historical perspective such as the one presented here is important from three standpoints. First, students of labor relations should be aware of major labor personalities and events. Labor history is rich with interesting characters and occurrences that, because of time and space constraints, were not mentioned here. However, the reader with the time, energy, and interest can find a wealth of fascinating information—the history of the U.S. labor movement is indeed an exciting subject.

Second, the need to understand the factors shaping the direction and effects on the labor movement is probably even more important. Historical analyses allow us to uncover factors and trends. We may compare and contrast the development of various historical phenomena, and speculate about the nature of future developments.

Third, collective bargaining and labor relations in the United States differ from those found in other countries. Unions and employers in Western European countries bargain on a more centralized basis through the use of employer associations and union confederations. Collective bargaining agreements in many European countries do not cover employee benefits, such as health insurance, because such benefits are mandated by the government. In addition, Western European countries such as West Germany allow for greater worker participation in the personnel matters of a company through a process known as co-determination. Countries such as Great Britain have strong labor parties, a phenomenon that has never developed in the United States. Unions in the Soviet Union and Eastern European

---

[52] See Jonathan Grossman and William T. Moye, "Labor History in the 1970s: A Question of Identity," in Thomas A. Kochan, Daniel J. B. Mitchell, and Lee Dyer, eds., *Industrial Relations Research in the 1970s: Review and Appraisal* (Madison, Wisconsin: Industrial Relations Research Association, 1982), pp. 283–309.

countries are controlled almost entirely by their communist governments. However, the 1980s has witnessed uprisings in Poland under the Solidarity movement led by Lech Walesa. Major political upheavals in the Soviet Union and Eastern European countries that began occurring in 1989 may further change the role of organized labor in communist countries. In Japan, lifetime employment and enterprise unions are common (although there are indications that the practice of lifetime employment is diminishing). Lifetime employment means that unions have fewer concerns regarding employees job security. Enterprise unions have adopted a more cooperative stance with employers than is found in the United States. For example, Japanese government, business, and labor leaders meet each spring to discuss general economic and business trends for the upcoming year. They use this information as a basis for wage increases.[53] Thus, each labor movement is somewhat unique and develops through a different set of economic, social, and political forces.[54] Moreover, labor-management practices that work well in a particular country are not necessarily useful when applied to the unique social and economic context of another country's labor movement.

In summary, the labor movement in the United States has the following characteristics:[55]

▲ Unionization preceded industrialization in the United States, but the industrial revolution in the latter half of the 19th century fueled the growth of labor organizations.

▲ Prior to the passage of the Wagner Act in 1935, employers took whatever measures possible to hinder the growth of unions as a means of protecting their managerial autonomy and business interests. By the 1980s, more subtle anti-union tactics by employers had re-emerged (discussed in Chapter 5).

▲ Labor leaders who attempted to build unionization based on the short-range material goals of improving wages, hours, and working conditions ("bread-and-butter" unionism or business unionism) were more likely to be successful than those who tried to appeal to workers on an ideological level. Early labor leaders who have had a long-term effect on the American Labor movement, such as Samuel Gompers (AFL) and John L. Lewis (CIO) advocated concerns that had immediate economic and employment-related consequences for workers. Labor leaders such as Terence V. Powderly (Knights of Labor) and "Big Bill" Haywood (IWW) had a much less enduring impact on the labor movement because workers were either unable or unwilling to relate to long-term ideological goals of political, social, and economic reform.

▲ Until the 1930s, public policy was not conducive to a rapidly expanding labor movement. With the passage of protective legislation and the creation of a more

---

[53] Kazutoshi Kashiro, "Development of Collective Bargaining in Post-War Japan," in Taishiro Shirai, ed., *Contemporary Industrial Relations in Japan* (Madison, Wisconsin: University of Wisconsin Press, 1982), pp. 205–258. Cited in Thomas A. Kochan and Harry C. Katz, *Collective Bargaining and Industrial Relations*, 2nd ed. (Homewood, Illinois: Richard D. Irwin, Inc., 1988), p. 148.
[54] See Walter Galenson, ed. *Comparative Labor Movements* (New York: Russell & Russell, 1968).
[55] Also see Orley Ashenfelter and John Pencavel, "American Trade Union Growth: 1900–1960," *Quarterly Journal of Economics* (August 1969), pp. 434–448 and David Montgomery, *The Fall of the House of Labor* (New York: Cambridge University Press, 1987).

favorable legal environment, union membership increased. The federal government's need to obtain the cooperation of organized labor during World War I and World War II also facilitated union membership growth.
- Unions have attempted to enlarge their sphere of influence by organizing professional, white-collar, and governmental employees. They have also attempted to do this by expanding the number of items addressed at the bargaining table.
- Although union-management relations have a large adversarial element, the 1980s and 1990s are witnessing an increased number of cooperative efforts between corporations and organized labor.

A timeline diagram of the important historical events of the American labor movement is provided on pages 54–55.

▲ Discussion Questions and Exercises

1. Which of the labor movement theories discussed here do you believe most appropriately describes the developments associated with the U.S. labor movement?
2. What social, political, and economic factors allowed the U.S. labor movement to flourish? What factors curtailed the U.S. labor movement?
3. Suppose protective labor legislation such as the Railway Labor Act, the Norris-LaGuardia Act, and the Wagner Act had been passed around 1900 instead of in the late 1920s and 1930s. Do you believe that the course of labor history in the United States might have been significantly different?
4. Suppose you have the opportunity this evening to have dinner with Terence V. Powderly of the Knights of Labor and "Big Bill" Haywood of the IWW. Having the advantage of 20–20 historical hindsight, what advice would you give to these gentlemen?
5. Do you believe that the violence associated with the Haymarket Square incident, the railroad labor disputes, or the coal mines served any useful social purpose? Explain.
6. Labor organizations such as the AFL and the CIO were successful, whereas organizations such as the National Labor Union, the Knights of Labor, and the IWW were relatively unsuccessful. What contributions did the "unsuccessful" labor organizations make to the development of the U.S. labor movement?
7. What impact did the following developments have on the U.S. labor movement?
   a. Major wars
   b. Periods of economic recession
   c. Periods of economic prosperity
   d. Protective legislation such as the Wagner Act
8. Research the background and lives of one of the labor leaders discussed in this chapter. What factors compelled this individual to become involved in organized labor? What personality characteristics did this individual possess? What factors led to his or her success or failure?
9. What predictions would you make regarding the course of the U.S. labor movement over the next 25 years?

▲ United States Labor History Timeline

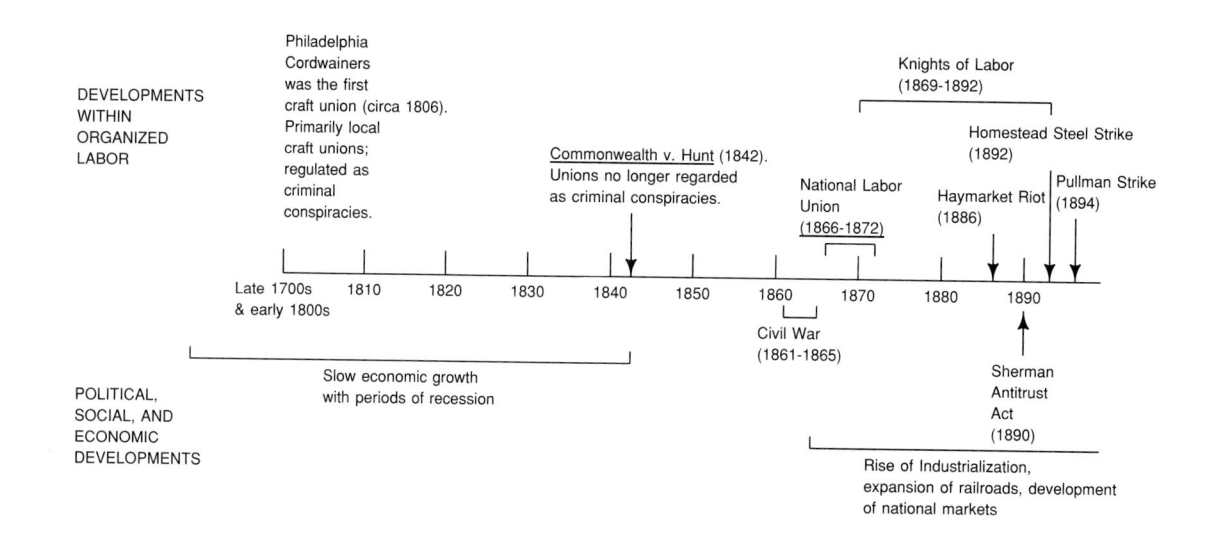

DEVELOPMENTS WITHIN ORGANIZED LABOR

- Philadelphia Cordwainers was the first craft union (circa 1806). Primarily local craft unions; regulated as criminal conspiracies.
- Commonwealth v. Hunt (1842). Unions no longer regarded as criminal conspiracies.
- National Labor Union (1866-1872)
- Knights of Labor (1869-1892)
- Haymarket Riot (1886)
- Homestead Steel Strike (1892)
- Pullman Strike (1894)

Timeline: Late 1700s & early 1800s — 1810 — 1820 — 1830 — 1840 — 1850 — 1860 — 1870 — 1880 — 1890

POLITICAL, SOCIAL, AND ECONOMIC DEVELOPMENTS

- Slow economic growth with periods of recession
- Civil War (1861-1865)
- Sherman Antitrust Act (1890)
- Rise of Industrialization, expansion of railroads, development of national markets

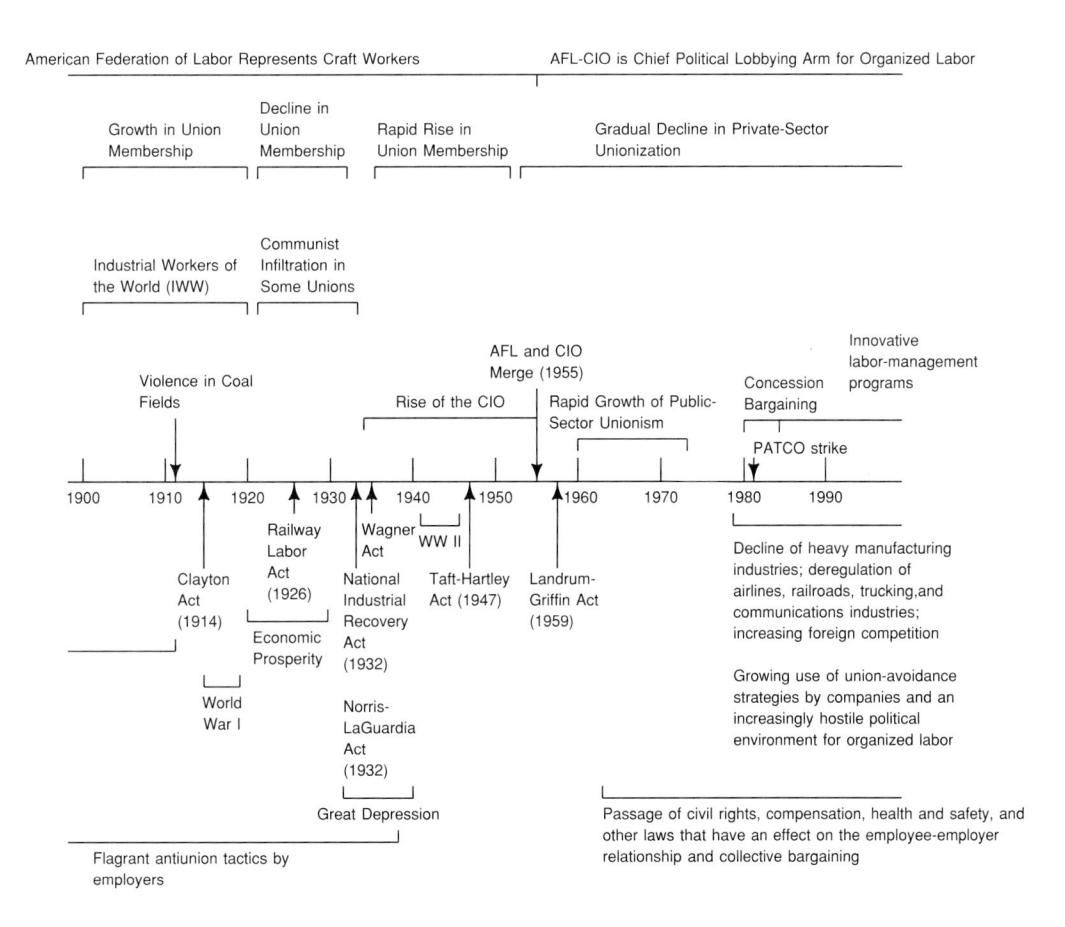

2 THE HISTORY OF COLLECTIVE BARGAINING AND LABOR RELATIONS IN THE UNITED STATES ▲ 55

American Federation of Labor Represents Craft Workers | AFL-CIO is Chief Political Lobbying Arm for Organized Labor

Growth in Union Membership | Decline in Union Membership | Rapid Rise in Union Membership | Gradual Decline in Private-Sector Unionization

Industrial Workers of the World (IWW) | Communist Infiltration in Some Unions

Violence in Coal Fields | AFL and CIO Merge (1955) | Innovative labor-management programs
Rise of the CIO | Rapid Growth of Public-Sector Unionism | Concession Bargaining
PATCO strike

1900 1910 1920 1930 1940 1950 1960 1970 1980 1990

Clayton Act (1914) | Railway Labor Act (1926) | Wagner Act | WW II | Taft-Hartley Act (1947) | Landrum-Griffin Act (1959)
National Industrial Recovery Act (1932)
Economic Prosperity
World War I
Norris-LaGuardia Act (1932)
Great Depression

Flagrant antiunion tactics by employers

Decline of heavy manufacturing industries; deregulation of airlines, railroads, trucking, and communications industries; increasing foreign competition

Growing use of union-avoidance strategies by companies and an increasingly hostile political environment for organized labor

Passage of civil rights, compensation, health and safety, and other laws that have an effect on the employee-employer relationship and collective bargaining

Part II

Establishing the Collective Bargaining Relationship

▲ ▲ ▲ ▲ ▲ ▲ ▲ ▲ ▲ ▲ ▲ ▲ ▲ ▲ ▲ ▲ ▲ ▲ ▲ ▲

The following three chapters discuss the legal basis of collective bargaining, bargaining unit structures, and union-organizing campaigns. These three areas form the foundation and establish the legal ground rules for the labor–management relationship.

Chapter 3 presents an overview of the major substantive and procedural laws affecting the union–management relationship. In addition to discussing the laws, the chapter also deals with enforcement agencies such as the National Labor Relations Board.

Chapter 4 covers the bargaining unit, an issue of central importance in labor–management relations. Also discussed are the concepts of exclusive representation, the criteria for establishing a bargaining unit, and the issue of employees who are excluded from the bargaining unit. Emphasis is given to the critical importance of the bargaining unit structure on the outcome of the certification election, the quality of union-management relations, and the bargaining power relationship between the two parties.

The tactics that professional organizers use in encouraging nonunion employees to join a union are outlined in Chapter 5. Employer responses to organizing campaigns are discussed, with emphasis on the effectiveness and legality of such responses. The certification election process is covered and includes a discussion of election procedures, runoff elections, decertification procedures, and other relevant topics.

3 The Legal Foundation of Collective Bargaining

- **Introduction**
- **The Historical Roots of Labor Relations Law**
  The Conspiracy Doctrine Applied to Unions
  The Use and Abuse of the Labor Injunction
  Role of the Sherman Antitrust Act
  Yellow-Dog Contracts
  The Need for Labor Legislation
- **The Railway Labor Act**
- **The Norris-LaGuardia Act**
- **The Wagner Act: Employer Unfair Labor Practices and Union Impetus**
  Historical Background
  Organizations and Employees Covered
  Section 7: Cornerstone of the Wagner Act
  Employer Unfair Labor Practices: Protecting Employee and Union Rights
    Employer Interference with Section 7 Rights
    Dominating or Illegally Assisting Labor Unions
    Employer Discrimination against Union Supporters
    Employer Retaliation for Filing Unfair Labor Practice Charges
    Employer Obligation to Bargain in Good Faith
  Results of the Wagner Act
- **The Taft-Hartley Act: Rebalancing the Scales of Power**
  Historical Background
  Provisions and Coverage of the Taft-Hartley Act
    Union Restraint and Coercion of Employees
    Union Restraint and Coercion of Employers
    A Union's Refusal to Bargain in Good Faith

Prohibited Strikes and Boycotts by Unions
Excessive and Discriminatory Union Fees and Dues
Antifeatherbedding Provisions
Organizational and Recognition Picketing by Noncertified Unions
Other Provisions

▲ **The National Labor Relations Board**
Processing Unfair Labor Practice Complaints and Charges
The Private Settlement of Unfair Labor Practices
Conducting Certification Elections
The Board as a Political, Social, and Economic Weather Vane

▲ **The Landrum-Griffin Act: An Attempt to Control Labor Corruption**
Historical Background
Provisions of the Landrum-Griffin Act
  The Union Members' "Bill of Rights"
  Election of Union Officers
  The Control of Trusteeships
  Fiduciary Standards
  Other Provisions of the Landrum-Griffin Act
Enforcement of the Landrum-Griffin Act

▲ **Other Legislation Having an Impact on Collective Bargaining and Labor Relations**
Equal Employment Opportunity Laws
Compensation and Employee Benefit Laws
The Occupational Safety and Health Act of 1970

▲ **Private-Sector and Public-Sector Collective Bargaining: Basic Differences in the Legal Frameworks**

▲ **Summary and Conclusions**

▲ **Discussion Questions and Exercises**

▲ Introduction

Labor-management relations in the United States is extensively regulated. Persons dealing with union-management relations must be knowledgeable about the legislation, executive orders, and court decisions that affect their particular situation. For example, the personnel director in a *private* university must deal with *federal* collective bargaining laws, whereas the personnel director in a *public* university must deal with whatever *state* laws apply to this particular institution. Airline and railway employees are covered by one set of laws and private manufacturing firms must adhere to *another* set of federal laws. For public employees in states not having collective bargaining laws, or for small private firms not eligible for coverage under federal law, there may be *no* applicable legislation to which unions, management, and employees can turn to for guidance in matters relating to collective bargaining. The quagmire is intensified when one considers other legislation such as equal employment opportunity laws, compensation and employee benefit legislation, and health and safety legislation, all of which affect the substance of collective bargaining.

This chapter discusses the major substantive and procedural legislation that has a bearing on labor relations activity in the United States. Emphasis is placed on labor laws that directly pertain to the private sector. Also summarized is legislation having a peripheral impact on collective bargaining and labor relations, as well as public-sector labor legislation.

A major purpose of this discussion is to acquaint the reader with the legal boundaries within which employers, unions, and others associated with labor relations must operate. Persons attempting to understand labor relations law must deal with several challenges. First, acquiring a basic content knowledge of the 20 or so federal laws affecting labor-management relations is no easy task when the myriad of provisions and sheer volume of such legislation are considered. Second, most of these laws have accompanying regulations that are written by the various governmental agencies whose task it is to administer and enforce the letter and spirit of the labor laws. Third, the interpretation of labor legislation differs among administrative agencies and the courts. The interpretation of a labor law depends on the officials responsible for adjudication, the circumstances surrounding each case, and the legal trends that are developing at a particular point in time.

Much of the discussion in this chapter is couched in general terms; it must be remembered that the field of labor relations law is in a state of flux and today's rule becomes changed and antiquated tomorrow. This chapter briefly analyzes the historical roots of labor relations law and then treats each of the major labor laws chronologically in the order of their passage. An overview of equal employment opportunity laws, compensation and employee benefit laws, and health and safety laws is provided to illustrate their impact on labor-management relations.

▲ The Historical Roots of Labor Relations Law

Chapter 2 illustrates the uphill battle that labor unions faced throughout the 19th century and the early part of the 20th century. Employers and others who were antiunion resorted to various legal tactics to thwart the organizing efforts of labor organizations. As a result, the growth of unionism was significantly hampered until protective legislation was enacted in the 1930s.

The Conspiracy Doctrine Applied to Unions

Employers initially attacked unions as criminal conspiracies whose control of wages was allegedly "an unnatural, artificial means of raising the price of work beyond its standard, and taking an undue advantage of the public".[1] Unions were regarded as

---
[1] Benjamin J. Taylor and Fred Witney, *Labor Relations Law*, 5th ed. (Englewood Cliffs, New Jersey: Prentice-Hall, Inc., 1987), p. 13.

conspiracies because they forced the prices of commodities to rise. It was argued that economic growth would suffer, unemployment would rise, and the rights of the public and nonunion employees would be compromised. The early conspiracy trials were decidedly biased against unions. Juries were often stacked with persons who were either employers themselves or who had strong allegiances toward management. Injunctions were often issued when union representatives and counsel were not present to defend their position. Despite vigorous and cogent arguments by defense counsels on the merits of collective bargaining, the courts remained unconvinced and frequently held unions to be unlawful. Interestingly, prosecutors in conspiracy trials presented no empirical evidence on the negative impact of unions; antiunion arguments were instead based primarily on speculation.

The tide turned somewhat in 1842, when labor unions were declared to be lawful organizations and were no longer regarded as criminal conspiracies. In *Commonwealth v. Hunt*, unions could no longer be indicted and convicted under the conspiracy doctrine unless either the *means* used by unions or the *objectives* of unions could be shown to be unlawful.[2] Union members were given the right not to work for an employer who did not hire members of their association. Furthermore, actions by workers to raise their wages through collective bargaining were not regarded as a conspiracy even though it forced employers to raise prices and suffer lower profits. Thus, union activities were no longer regarded as criminal. *Commonwealth v. Hunt* represented a first step toward recognizing the legitimacy of labor unions. Civil conspiracy cases against unions continued after 1842, but their effectiveness in curtailing union organizational activities was diminished. This turn of events forced employers to look for newer and more potent legal weapons.

The Use and Abuse of the Labor Injunction

When labor disputes and work stoppages occurred, employers began to secure injunctions to bring disputes to a halt and dilute the power of unions.[3] An injunction is an order issued by an *equity court* that prevents a person or organization from performing an action that will likely cause *irreparable* damage to another party. Injunctions are normally used when quick action is needed to protect property or prevent bodily injury. Unlike many court proceedings, courts of equity do not use juries to evaluate the facts of a specific case. Instead, a judge has sole responsibility for hearing the facts and issuing an injunction if the situation warrants.

Employers found the injunction to be an effective weapon against unions. A primary reason for this was that the "property damage" feared by employers who were affected by labor disputes was not confined solely to *physical* property damage. If an employer could demonstrate that a dispute with a union damaged business (e.g., a work stoppage curtailing production), then an injunction could be obtained. Judges were often more sympathetic to employers than they were to unions and

---

[2] 4 Metcalf 3 (1842).
[3] See Felix Frankfurter and Nathan Greene, *The Labor Injunction* (New York: The Macmillan Company, 1930).

would issue injunctions based on flimsy or questionable evidence. In certain instances, injunctions were worded to prevent persons or organizations not directly involved in a labor dispute from aiding union workers (such as forbidding churches from providing meals to striking employees). Even when it was later determined that a temporary injunction had been issued without just cause, it had already destroyed the union's bargaining position and dampened employee enthusiasm.

Labor injunctions proved to be an ideal method for stifling the effective operation of unions. Their widespread and indiscriminate use was fostered by the U.S. Supreme Court when the constitutionality of the labor injunction was upheld in the *Debs* case involving striking Pullman Company employees (see Chapter 2). The injunction remained as a prime legal weapon through the 19th century and the first 30 years of this century.

Role of the Sherman Antitrust Act

Although the labor injunction's purpose was to *restrain* the activities of unions, the Sherman Antitrust Act both restrained *and* punished unions whose activities disrupted the flow of commerce. The Sherman Act was enacted in 1890 to regulate the monopolistic and price-fixing powers of large corporations. Such practices were regarded as detrimental to free competition and endangered the traditional character of economic life in the United States.

The most noteworthy application of the Sherman Act against labor unions was the *Danbury Hatters* case.[4] In 1902, the United Hatters of North America attempted to organize the employees of Loewe and Company of Danbury, Connecticut. A strike ensued when the company refused to recognize the union, but the firm retained the upper hand by hiring strike replacements. The union countered by organizing a nationwide boycott of Loewe and Company's products and the AFL supported the United Hatters' efforts. As a result, the boycott caused an $85,000 loss in one year and, in 1903, the company sued the union for damages under the Sherman Act. After nearly 12 years of litigation, the Supreme Court sustained a judgment of $252,000 against the United Hatters (the Sherman Act provides for *treble* damages). Furthermore, not only was the union as an organization liable, but individual rank-and-file members were also responsible for the financial obligation imposed by the court judgment. Needless to say, such a threat had a chilling effect on unions, especially for the workers whose personal assets could be wiped out by an adverse decision against their union.

A double standard in the application of the Sherman Act began to emerge. One standard applied to large corporations and business combinations whose sheer size or price-fixing practices thwarted free competition. A second standard was applied to labor organizations engaging in strikes or boycotts of a firm's products. Labor unions at this juncture were not nearly as large and capable of significantly interrupting the flow of commerce as were major corporations. Yet, if the courts believed

---

[4] 208 U.S. 274 (1908).

that a union's activities could be adduced as intentionally restricting the flow of goods in interstate commerce, then the Sherman Act could be used to inhibit collective bargaining and other concerted action. The Sherman Act was applied to labor organizations even though most labor disputes had a miniscule impact on interstate commerce and the economy.

Yellow-Dog Contracts

A yellow-dog contract was used to prevent employees from forming or joining a labor union. As a condition of employment, a worker was required to sign an agreement stating that he or she did not currently belong to a union and would not join or form a union while employed by the firm. Yellow-dog contracts were used to ensure that the new employee completely understood the company's antiunion sentiments. Violations of the yellow-dog contract normally led to the offending employee's discharge.

Prior to 1932, when the Norris-LaGuardia Act was passed to control the use of injunctions and yellow-dog contracts, the courts were not sympathetic to the employee's plight. It was alleged that an employee "voluntarily" signed the yellow-dog contract. In reality, many employees were faced with bleak job alternatives and had little choice but to sign if they expected to be hired. In some instances, a worker had to sign to avoid employer blacklists.

The yellow-dog contract enjoyed its most widespread use in the coal mining industry of Pennsylvania and West Virginia. In 1917, the U.S. Supreme Court held that a labor injunction could be used to enforce a yellow-dog contract.[5] When an employer was faced with a union-organizing campaign, yellow-dog contracts were used to eliminate the threat. If a union organizer attempted to persuade employees who had signed the yellow-dog contract to join a union, the employer could apply for an injunction to stop further organizing efforts. Should union officials persist in their organizing efforts, they could be held in contempt of court and would face fines or imprisonment. Thus, the yellow-dog contract was a superlative antiunion weapon and was especially useful in deterring union organizers.[6]

The Need for Labor Legislation

A reading of Chapter 2, as well as the discussion presented so far in this chapter, illustrates the antiunion attitude held by both employers and the judiciary. Clearly, the rights of workers to join, form, or assist labor organizations was challenged and suppressed at nearly every turn. Concern for society and the economy was used to justify antilabor sentiments. In addition, the *laissez faire* teachings of classical economists (who felt that the forces of supply and demand, rather than labor unions, should establish the proper wage levels and working conditions) were used to bolster this position. The quest by employees to improve their wages and working

---

[5] *Hitchman Coal Co. v. Mitchell*, 245 U.S. 299 (1917).
[6] See Joel Seidman, *The Yellow Dog Contract* (Baltimore: Johns Hopkins Press, 1932).

conditions was largely ignored in the fray or, at best, was relegated to a lower priority.

Gradually, federal and state legislators became aware of the plight of employees who worked long and hard hours in unsafe, monotonous, and degrading jobs at subsistence wages. The need to balance the rights of labor and management grew increasingly apparent. Antiunion conduct of spying, threats of physical violence, and strike-breaking tactics of questionable value became more commonplace. Although employees had the right to bargain collectively, the use of labor injunctions, yellow-dog contracts, and industrial espionage effectively violated this right.

At the turn of the century, a number of states passed well-intentioned, but largely ineffective, laws designed to protect the organization and bargaining rights of workers. Certain laws were struck down as being unconstitutional, whereas others were poorly drafted and easily circumvented by those bent on suppressing unionism. Federal laws such as the Erdman Act (1898), the Clayton Act (1914), and the National Industrial Recovery Act (1933) were designed to promote a more equitable industrial relations policy, but these too were either of limited use or were declared unconstitutional.

World War I demonstrated that industrial peace was possible even when workers were allowed to organize and bargain collectively. The passage of the Railway Labor Act in 1926 provided a model example of legislation that reduced labor conflict and recognized the need to allow workers and employees to carve out their respective interests via collective bargaining without unnecessarily hindering the flow of interstate commerce.

In summary, several points emerged that pointed to the need for more extensive labor legislation:

1. Federal court decisions were aligned against unionism and collective bargaining.
2. Employers were often willing to take drastic action to destroy unionism.
3. Labor disputes and work stoppages had a detrimental impact on the economy.
4. Collective bargaining, if properly sanctioned, could lead to industrial peace, provide better employment conditions for workers, and stimulate economic growth.
5. Employee rights to unionize and bargain collectively did not necessarily conflict with an employer's right to conduct business in the best interests of the firm.

Against this backdrop, the following discussion focuses on the labor laws that have been enacted between 1926 and the present.

▲ The Railway Labor Act

The Railway Labor Act was enacted in 1926 to help reduce labor conflict on the railroads and to regulate the collective bargaining process.[7] Today, the Act covers both railroad employees and airline employees. Other transportation modes, such as trucking, bus lines, and maritime operations, are covered by different labor laws

[7] 44 Stat. 577, as amended (1926).

regulating private-sector organizations. Perhaps of greatest significance is that the Railway Labor Act represented the first comprehensive piece of labor legislation enacted by the federal government.

The National Mediation Board (NMB) was established by the Act's 1934 amendments and it is empowered to conduct certification elections to determine whether a union is desired by employees. The Board also helps union and management mediate labor disputes, interpret labor agreement provisions, and will arbitrate disputes over contract negotiations if the parties voluntarily submit them to the NMB. For example, in early 1989 a federal arbitrator granted Pan American World Airways $21 million a year in labor cost-savings over a 29-month period. Pan Am workers had earlier rejected a contract settlement between the airline and the Transport Workers Union. Although Pan Am's management asked for wage cuts of nearly 10 percent, the arbitrator cut labor costs through work-rule changes and reductions in employee benefits.[8]

Grievances arising out of the interpretation or application of a contract are handled by the National Railroad Adjustment Board (NRAB). The NMB focuses on adjusting labor disputes that arise *during* contract negotiations, whereas the NRAB deals with rights disputes over the interpretation of *existing* collective bargaining agreements.

The Railway Labor Act was regarded as a well-designed law. Work stoppages in the railroad industry potentially have serious nationwide repercussions; a mechanism was needed to promote collective bargaining and control labor disputes. The NMB is empowered to deal with work stoppages that pose a threat to national well-being. Considerable controversy has stemmed from the way in which some of these disputes have been handled. Several railroad strikes were outlawed in the 1960s and a system of compulsory arbitration was imposed. Some labor scholars and practitioners believe that compulsory interest arbitration, which forces union and management to accept contract provisions imposed by third parties (arbitrators), stifles meaningful collective bargaining. They believe that the economic strike is a useful weapon that encourages good-faith bargaining. Without the strike weapon, union and management may depend too heavily on the arbitration tribunal to fashion the terms of the labor agreement.

▲ The Norris-LaGuardia Act

The Norris-LaGuardia Act of 1932 sounded the death knell of the labor injunction and the yellow-dog contract.[9] Although neither of these weapons was outlawed under the Act, their effectiveness was diminished to the point where they no longer possessed the potency to destroy union-organizing efforts or to quell the use of economic strikes.

Labor injunctions could no longer be easily obtained by employers who desired to neutralize the power of unions. Procedural limitations were placed on the is-

---

[8] The Bureau of National Affairs, Inc., "Pan Am-TWU Award," *Collective Bargaining Negotiations & Contracts* (Washington, D.C.: The Bureau of National Affairs, Inc., February 23, 1989), p. 1.
[9] 47 Stat. 70 (1932).

suance of injunctions. For example, the standards of proof and quality of evidence and testimony were established under the Act, and unions were better protected from frivolous charges by employers. A person seeking a temporary injunction must post a bond; if it is later determined that the basis for the injunction is unfounded, then the union can be compensated for any damages that it might have suffered. The procurement of an injunction against a union is based on the premise that no other adequate legal remedies are available. For example, if striking workers engage in picket-line violence, an injunction will be issued to prevent picketing only if local law enforcement officers cannot handle the situation. Measures were also taken to ensure a speedy and complete hearing for the parties involved in the equity court's injunction proceedings. Should it prove necessary to issue a temporary injunction without a hearing, the injunction will automatically expire in five days. Blanket injunctions that prevent anyone remotely involved with the labor dispute from aiding the union (e.g., merchants lending credit to strikers) are prohibited under the Act. Only unlawful acts may be prevented through labor injunctions. An injunction cannot be issued to stop the activities of persons who lawfully support union members during a labor dispute.

The Norris-LaGuardia Act declared that yellow-dog contracts are not enforceable in a court of law. This measure eliminated what had once been a major threat to employee job security and labor unionism. Three years later, the yellow-dog contract was declared illegal under the Wagner Act.

In summary, the process of collective bargaining and the institution of labor unionism received the protection needed to develop and grow. Yellow-dog contracts could no longer be used to intimidate employees from joining unions. Picketing and strikes of a nonviolent nature cannot be halted by injunctions. Nevertheless, employers still had other weapons at their disposal for suppressing unionization in their firms. Although the Norris-LaGuardia Act was a major milestone in labor relations history, additional legislation was on the horizon to protect employee rights and to balance the power between employers and unions.

▲ The Wagner Act: Employer Unfair Labor Practices and Union Impetus

Historical Background

The Norris-LaGuardia Act gave unions an encouraging, but not totally adequate, start. Legal protection was needed to help employees join or form unions and bargain collectively without fear of reprisal by employers. There were no legal sanctions that prevented management from firing employees who supported unionization. Acts of industrial espionage and strike-breaking tactics still represented legitimate methods of breaking labor organizations and intimidating employees.[10] The future of the U.S. labor movement remained uncertain until protective legis-

---

[10] See Sidney Howard and Robert Dunn, *The Labor Spy* (New York: The Republican Publishing Company, 1921), Edward Levinson, *I Break Strikes: The Technique of Pearl L. Bergoff* (New York: R. M. McBride and Company, 1935), and Frank Palmer, *Spies in Steel: An Exposé of Industrial Warfare* (Denver, Colorado: The Labor Press, 1928).

lation could be passed that would allow workers to unionize and to engage in collective bargaining.

Several factors operated in favor of passing legislation designed to protect concerted activities by employees. First, World War I provided a proving ground for legally structuring the union-management relationship and protecting employee rights via the National War Labor Board. Second, the passage and successful implementation of the Railway Labor Act further illustrated that effective and sensible regulation of union-management relations was possible. Third, the earlier abortive legislative attempts to protect those interested in joining unions, such as the various state laws and the National Industrial Recovery Act, probably made supporters of such legislation even more determined to seek a democratic legal environment for employees and unions. Finally, and most important, the enactment of protective labor legislation was expected to act as an economic stimulus and stabilizer for the nation. The antiunion motives of employers allegedly deprived workers of their fair share of the economy and diluted their purchasing power. Thus, the engineers of the Roosevelt-era New Deal legislation viewed protective labor laws as a means of stimulating aggregate demand in a depression-ridden economy. The Wagner Act was passed to reduce work stoppages associated with union-recognition disputes and to encourage increased wages through the collective bargaining process, both of which were expected to have positive effects on the economy.[11]

Organizations and Employees Covered

The Wagner Act covers private-sector firms that are large enough to have an impact on commerce between the states.[12] When a firm buys or sells goods or services across state lines, it is generally considered to have an effect on interstate commerce. Because of the potentially large number of firms that operate in interstate commerce, the National Labor Relations Board has established standards by which it determines whether an organization should fall under its jurisdiction. These standards are based on the gross revenues of a firm and they vary, depending on the type of organization under consideration. For example, nonretail businesses must have direct sales of $50,000 per year, whereas retail enterprises must have at least $500,000 total annual business volume. Hotels must generate $500,000 in business, private universities and colleges are required to have an income of $1,000,000, and the list goes on for other types of businesses such as office buildings ($100,000), health care institutions ($250,000), and symphony orchestras ($1,000,000), to name a few.

The NLRB exercises jurisdiction over every conceivable type of private enterprise that meets these dollar guidelines. Under the 1970 Postal Reorganization Act, U.S. Postal Service employees are also covered. However, organizations whose revenues fall below the minimum levels prescribed by the NLRB are exempted, and may be covered by state laws in some instances. Furthermore, agricultural laborers,

---

[11] See Charles G. Morris, ed., *A Critical Appraisal of the National Labor Relations Act* (Washington, D.C.: The Bureau of National Affairs, Inc., 1986).
[12] 49 Stat. 449 (1935).

domestic servants, independent contractors, supervisors, and federal and state government employees are not protected under the Wagner Act.

Section 7: Cornerstone of the Wagner Act

The rights of employees to form, join, or assist labor unions engaged in legal concerted activities are explicitly guaranteed under Section 7 of the Wagner Act. In addition, Section 7 establishes the right of employees to engage in collective bargaining with employers over wages, hours, and working conditions. Should collective bargaining fail to achieve the desired results, Section 7 protects the workers' right to strike in order to secure better employment conditions. As a means of maximizing an employee's freedom of choice, Section 7 stipulates that an individual "shall have the right to *refrain* from any or all activities" noted above.

For the first time, private-sector employees had the legal right to associate (or not associate) with labor organizations without fear of reprisal or undue pressure by employers or others. Despite its brevity, the implications of Section 7 for organized labor were far-reaching. Although Section 7 does not give employees and unions unfettered freedom to do as they please, restrictions associated with labor union activities were kept to a minimum to protect workers from the many antiunion activities that had been so effectively used over the years.

Employer Unfair Labor Practices: Protecting Employee and Union Rights

In order to give specific meaning to the rights set forth in Section 7, Congress specified a series of unfair labor practices that prevented employers from interfering with or intimidating workers who desired to form, join, or assist a union. Five employer unfair labor practices were established under the Act. They are now known as Sections 8(a)(1) through 8(a)(5).[13]

Employer Interference with Section 7 Rights

Section 8(a)(1) forbids an employer from interfering with, restraining, or coercing employees in the exercise of the rights guaranteed under Section 7. Any employer conduct that discourages workers from joining or forming a union represents a potential violation of Section 8(a)(1). Whenever an employer violates Sections 8(a)(2) through 8(a)(5), a violation of 8(a)(1) is automatically added (this is known as a derivative violation). Examples of specific employer violations of Section 8(a)(1) include:

- ▲ Discharging or threatening to discharge employees who support or join a union.
- ▲ Spying or pretending to spy on union meetings.
- ▲ Questioning employees about their union activities in a manner that might be perceived as threatening.

---

[13] See Peter D. Walther, J. Freedley Hunsicker, and Jonathan A. Kane, *NLRB Remedies for Unfair Labor Practices*, revised ed. (Philadelphia: Industrial Research Unit, The Wharton School, University of Pennsylvania, 1986).

- Telling employees that a plant will be relocated or closed down if the union wins a certification election.
- Granting wage increases that are deliberately timed to coincide with union-organizing campaigns as a means of chilling employee enthusiasm for supporting a union.

Thus Section 8(a)(1) forbids negative employer behavior that interferes with employee Section 7 rights. It also prohibits positive behavior, such as granting wage increases, if the employer's motives are to discourage unionization.

Dominating or Illegally Assisting Labor Unions

Section 8(a)(2) makes it unlawful for an employer "to dominate or interfere with the formation or administration of any labor organization or contribute financial or other support to it." This provision makes *company unions* illegal. Employers can neither form a union nor contribute financial support to a union that represents or is attempting to represent their workers. An employer will "dominate" a union under the meaning of Section 8(a)(2) if it helps to get the organization started, formulates its bargaining agenda or mode of operation, takes part in union meetings, or otherwise influences union actions or policies. An employer "interferes" with a union through various *sweetheart arrangements* such as bribing union negotiators during contract talks, giving one union access to the workplace during an organizing campaign while denying access to rival unions, and providing direct or indirect financial aid to a labor organization. An employer normally violates Section 8(a)(2) by:[14]

- Taking an active part in establishing a union for its employees.
- Pressuring employees to join a certain union (except where a legal union-security agreement is in force).
- Using supervisors to help a specific union obtain authorization card signatures from employees.
- Requiring job applicants to sign authorization cards, union membership forms, or dues checkoff authorizations prior to being hired.

If the NLRB determines that a company is *dominating* a union, it will have the labor organization disbanded. Should the NLRB decide that the employer is *interfering* with, but not dominating, the operation of a union, it will issue a cease-and-desist order to prevent further employer interference. The essence of Section 8(a)(2) is to maintain a neutral, "hands-off" posture by employers insofar as union activities are concerned. A labor organization cannot function objectively and in the best interests of its members if an employer is able to control its operations and policies; the key is to preserve the company and union as *independent and autonomous* entities. However, it is legally permissible for shop stewards employed by the company to conduct union business and adjust employee grievances during

---

[14] Office of the General Counsel, National Labor Relations Board, *A Guide to Basic Law and Procedures Under the National Labor Relations Act* (Washington, D.C.: U.S. Government Printing Office, 1978), p. 20.

working hours. Likewise, actions by companies that constitute normal social courtesies or amenities, such as an employer picking up the restaurant tab for a union representative during a business luncheon, do not generally violate 8(a)(2). If an employer provides an unusually lavish meal or an all-expenses-paid trip for a union official to visit plants, offices, or attend meetings, then an 8(a)(2) violation is more likely.[15]

Employer Discrimination against Union Supporters

Section 8(a)(3) makes it an unfair labor practice for an employer to discriminate against employees "in regard to hire or tenure of employment or any term or condition of employment" for the purpose of encouraging or discouraging membership in a labor organization. The essence of 8(a)(3) is to disallow consideration of an employee's union status when taking personnel actions such as hiring, promoting, evaluating employee performance, granting pay raises, and disciplining employees. As previously noted, an employee can be discharged for failing to join a union or pay union dues *if* a valid union security agreement is in force. In addition, employers are free to discharge, transfer, or lay off workers for genuine economic or disciplinary reasons; the key is to avoid a union animus in personnel decisions.

Examples of illegal discrimination under Section 8(a)(3) include:

▲ Discharging an employee who has urged others to join a union.
▲ Refusing to hire qualified workers because they engaged in a lawful strike.
▲ Placing employees serving as permanent strike replacements at the top of the seniority list (superseniority).
▲ Discontinuing an operation at one plant, discharging its employees, and then reopening the plant with different employees at a new location because employees at the first plant joined a union (this is known as a "runaway plant").
▲ Rejecting qualified job applicants who are known to be favorably disposed toward unions or who have previously belonged to a union.
▲ Constructively discharging an employee engaged in union activities by making worklife so intolerable that the individual resigns.

A common misconception is that federal labor laws protect employees against *all* unjust discharges. This belief is not true. In fact, many persons not protected by individual contracts or collective bargaining agreements can be discharged for good cause, bad cause, or no cause at all. Legal recourse is often available to individuals who are dismissed in violation of employment contracts, or because of racial or sex discrimination or union activities. Employees who are discharged for other reasons may have no remedies to protect their employment status.

Section 8(a)(3) violations must be based on employer *intent* to encourage or discourage union activity or membership. Proving antiunion intent by an employer can be difficult. The NLRB will try to ascertain whether a personnel action such as discharge was done for a valid reason or was, perhaps, a subterfuge for discouraging union activity. That is, were the employer's reasons for discharging an employee simply a pretext for damaging the union? Did a union supporter receive harsher

---

[15] Bruce Feldacker, *Labor Guide to Labor Law*, 2nd ed. (Reston, Virginia: Reston Publishing Co., 1983), p. 137.

punishment than other nonunion employees who had committed similar transgressions? In summary, the NLRB must demonstrate that the employer was aware of union activity by certain employees *and* intentionally tried to thwart these activities through various unfair personnel actions.

Employer Retaliation for Filing Unfair Labor Practice Charges

Section 8(a)(4) makes it illegal for an employer "to discharge or otherwise discriminate against an employee because he has filed charges or given testimony under this Act." Employers are forbidden from discharging, laying off, or engaging in other forms of discrimination in working conditions against employees who have filed unfair labor practice charges, supplied affidavits, or testified before the NLRB. This provision protects persons who might otherwise be reluctant to assist the NLRB in prosecuting labor law violators.

Employer Obligation to Bargain in Good Faith

Perhaps the most significant of the employer unfair labor practice provisions is *Section 8(a)(5)*, which requires that management negotiators bargain in good faith with their union counterparts over items directly affecting wages, hours, and working conditions; these are known as *mandatory* bargaining items. Without a provision such as 8(a)(5), a company could elect to ignore union requests to bargain or they could simply go through the motions of negotiating with a labor organization without any intention of reaching an agreement. Such tactics would make a shambles of the collective bargaining process and would render meaningless the certification election and the union's role as the exclusive representative for bargaining unit employees. The good-faith bargaining concept legally requires that the employer:

1. Meet at a reasonable time and place with negotiators selected by the union for the purpose of collective bargaining.
2. Supply union negotiators with "relevant and necessary" information that will allow them to bargain intelligently and effectively with respect to wages, hours, and other conditions of employment.
3. Refrain from taking unilateral action on items that the employer is contractually obligated to negotiate with the union. Management would violate the good-faith bargaining concept if, for example, they made changes in a previously-negotiated wage scale without seeking approval from the union. A "take-it-or-leave-it" posture by management negotiators over terms and conditions of the collective bargaining agreement is also likely to be construed by the NLRB as bad-faith bargaining.

The NLRB is faced with a complex task when it attempts to evaluate negotiation behaviors and tactics in order to distinguish between good- and bad-faith bargaining. Generally speaking, employers are expected to listen to the union's demands and make proposals and counterproposals in an *attempt* to reach an agreement. However, as long as the employer bargains in good faith, it is under *no* obligation to reach an agreement or sign a contract with the labor organization. The discussion of good-faith bargaining is developed more extensively in Chapter 9.

Results of the Wagner Act

The passage of the Wagner Act had a profound impact on the U.S. labor movement. Previously unprotected private-sector employees were able to unionize and engage in meaningful collective bargaining; no longer were employers able unilaterally to dictate working conditions to millions of workers. Congress also created the National Labor Relations Board to enforce the Wagner Act's provisions (the structure of the NLRB was changed somewhat with the passage of the Taft-Hartley Act in 1947).

An element of uncertainty lingered over the Wagner Act, however, because certain groups questioned the law's constitutionality. The National Lawyer's Committee of the American Liberty League declared that the Act was unconstitutional. Soon thereafter, numerous attacks against the NLRB began. A great deal of the initial legal flurry stemmed from misunderstandings over the purpose and functions of the Wagner Act. Nevertheless, attacks on the law greatly diminished the NLRB's effectiveness during its first two years of operation.

The issue of constitutionality was finally resolved in April of 1937, when the U.S. Supreme Court (by a 5–4 margin) validated the legitimacy of the Wagner Act in the *Jones & Laughlin Steel Company* case.[16] A key point made by the Supreme Court justices holding the majority view was that it was proper for Congress to take action to prohibit employers from interfering with the right of workers to organize and bargain collectively because of the "catastrophic" effects that organizational strikes could have on interstate commerce and the economy. Thus, the stage was set for ushering in a new era in U.S. labor relations.

In the 12 years following passage of the Wagner Act (1935–1947), the NLRB reinstated 76,268 workers who had been discharged because of union activities and awarded $12.4 million in back pay. Over 1,700 company-dominated unions were disbanded during this period. Furthermore, the NLRB ordered employers to bargain with legally certified labor organizations on 5,070 occasions. As noted in Chapter 2, the membership rolls in many unions soared to unprecedented heights. Clearly, the substantive provisions of the Act and its enforcement mechanisms were taking effect.[17]

▲ The Taft-Hartley Act: Rebalancing the Scales of Power

Historical Background

The Wagner Act represented a major milestone in labor relations for those who supported unionism. However, employers and various interest groups who sided with management felt that they were short changed and placed at a disadvantage by a law that tied the hands of corporations, yet allowed labor unions unfettered rein in conducting their business. Feelings of indignation by employers, misunder-

---

[16] 301 U.S. 1 (1937).
[17] Benjamin J. Taylor and Fred Witney, *Labor Relations Law*, 5th ed. (Englewood Cliffs, New Jersey: Prentice-Hall, Inc., 1987), pp. 203–204.

standings surrounding the Wagner Act, and union practices that were viewed with disdain by certain public interest groups set the stage for the passage of additional labor legislation to counter the effects of the Wagner Act.

As unions began to grow and gain power, they too became guilty of practices that had potentially negative effects on society, employers, and workers. For example, strikes in the coal mining industry during World War II gave the United Mine Workers a negative public image and prompted a government seizure of the mines and passage of the War Labor Disputes Act. Unions also supported the closed-shop arrangement that forced employers to hire only union members. Secondary boycotts called by unions disrupted the businesses of neutral employers who were often innocent bystanders in labor disputes. Despite their egalitarian base, some unions discriminated against minority groups by forcing them into racially segregated locals. Labor organizations also received well-deserved negative press through the mishandling of member dues, work slowdowns, sit-down strikes, and output restrictions.

Misconceptions about the Wagner Act continued long after its passage. Despite beliefs to the contrary, the Act provided no mediation or conciliation functions. Rather, the NLRB served to regulate and punish employers who sometimes unwittingly violated the law. Other employers did not understand that NLRB decisions on unfair labor practice cases could be appealed in federal court. Apparently, some believed that the NLRB served as prosecutor, judge, and jury whose decisions were final and not subject to review. The inadequacies of the Wagner Act and the NLRB were further "evidenced" by the wave of strikes that engulfed the United States in 1946. Although a number of post-war factors such as a reduction in work hours, inflationary pressures, and shortages of certain goods exacerbated labor tensions and contributed to employer-employee disputes, the Wagner Act served as a convenient scapegoat and target for those who felt that the activities of labor organizations should be regulated.

The Taft-Hartley Act (also known as the Labor-Management Relations Act) amended the Wagner Act in 1947.[18] A series of union unfair labor practices were established, closed shops were outlawed (although other forms of union security were legalized), and a set of procedures for dealing with national emergency strikes was formulated. Employees *and* employers were protected from certain practices by labor organizations that could disrupt meaningful collective bargaining and contract administration. Thus, the Taft-Hartley Act represented an attempt to rebalance power and ensure fair play between employers, labor organizations, and employees.

Provisions and Coverage of the Taft-Hartley Act

Several union unfair labor practices were promulgated under the Taft-Hartley Act. The first three parallel those found in the Wagner Act; the basic difference being that they apply to unions rather than employers. However, the remaining unfair labor practice provisions are different and were tailored to prevent certain questionable practices by unions.

---

[18] 61 Stat. 136, as amended (1947).

Union Restraint and Coercion of Employees

Section 8(b)(1)(A) protects employees' Section 7 rights by making it an unfair labor practice for unions to restrain or coerce employees with regard to their joining or supporting labor organizations. As mentioned earlier, an employee has a right to *refrain* from union activities if he or she so desires. Some of the more flagrant union violations of Section 8(b)(1)(A) involve threats of violence or loss of jobs:

- Acts of picket-line violence that deter nonstriking employees from entering the workplace.
- Threats of bodily injury to nonstriking employees by the union.
- Statements to employees who oppose the union during an organizing campaign that they will lose their jobs if the union wins the certification election.
- Threats to employees that they will be discharged from their jobs if they do not support the union's activities or position on a certain matter.

Other violations of 8(b)(1)(A) include:

- Entering into an agreement with an employer that recognizes the union as the exclusive bargaining representative when, in fact, it lacks a majority of the employees' support.
- Fining or expelling union members for crossing an unlawful picket line (such as might occur during a secondary boycott).
- Refusing to process the meritorious grievance of a bargaining unit employee who has criticized union officers.
- Maintaining a seniority arrangement with an employer under which seniority is based on an employee's prior representation by the union at another place of employment.
- Basing job referrals on an employee's race, sex, or union status.

Union Restraint and Coercion of Employers

Section 8(b)(1)(B) prohibits a union from restraining or coercing an employer in the selection of a bargaining representative. Employers have the right to designate whomever they deem appropriate to bargain on their behalf with the union. Furthermore, the union cannot influence the employer in its selection of individuals who are responsible for helping to adjust employee grievances. Thus, 8(b)(1)(B) is violated by union conduct such as:[19]

- Insisting on meeting only with a company's owners and refusing to meet with the attorney that the firm has hired to represent it in contract negotiations. A union also creates an unfair labor practice if it threatens to strike in order to force the company to change bargaining representatives.
- Striking against several members of an employer association (where a *group* of

---

[19] Office of the General Counsel, National Labor Relations Board, *A Guide to Basic Labor Law and Procedures Under the National Labor Relations Act* (Washington, D.C.: U.S. Government Printing Office, 1978), p. 32.

employers negotiates a *single* labor contract with a union) in an attempt to "break" the association and obtain individual contracts from each firm.
- Forcing an employer during contract negotiations to accept working conditions that will be established by a bargaining group to which it does not belong.

Section 8(b)(2) makes it an unfair labor practice for a union to force an employer to discriminate against an employee in order to influence the employee's union membership. This unfair labor practice is similar to the previously-discussed 8(a)(3) violation by employers, the only difference being that a *union* is forcing an employer to discriminate in hiring or granting tenure to an employee who fails to join or support a union.[20] Examples of 8(b)(2) violations by unions include:

- Requiring an employer to hire only union members (closed shop) or giving hiring preference to union members (preferential shop).
- Operating a union hiring hall that fails to refer qualified union and nonunion applicants on an equal basis.
- Causing an employer to discharge employees because they circulated a petition urging a change in the union's method of selecting shop stewards or because they made speeches against a contract proposed by a union.
- Forcing an employer to reduce the seniority of an employee who engaged in antiunion acts.

A Union's Refusal to Bargain in Good Faith

Section 8(b)(3) imposes the same duty to bargain in good faith on unions that is imposed on employers. Unions are not likely to engage in stalling tactics or outright refusals to bargain with a company. They may, however, do things such as insisting on negotiating over permissive bargaining subjects or adopting a take-it-or-leave-it stance on certain issues. A legal requirement that applies exclusively to labor organizations is the duty to bargain fairly with respect to the employees it represents. This duty entails avoiding contract provisions that may be racially discriminatory or otherwise arbitrary and unfair to union members covered by a collective bargaining agreement. Specific violations of 8(b)(3) might include a union's

- Insisting on the inclusion of illegal provisions in a collective bargaining agreement (such as the closed shop).
- Refusing to process a legitimate grievance filed by a bargaining-unit employee because of the employee's antiunion activities or because of race or sex factors.
- Failing to notify the employer within 60 days (90 days for health care institutions) of the expiration date of the collective bargaining agreement if the union wishes to negotiate a new agreement.
- Refusing to put a bargaining agreement into writing even though the employer requests a written contract.

---

[20] A union can force the employer to terminate an employee who fails to join the union or pay union dues when a valid union security agreement is in effect.

Prohibited Strikes and Boycotts by Unions

Section 8(b)(4) consists of four subparts (A through D) and is one of the most complex provisions of the Taft-Hartley Act. It has been the basis of extensive debate and litigation. This section is designed to protect employers or individuals who are not *directly* or *primarily* involved in a labor dispute. If a union either *engages* in a strike or boycott or otherwise *threatens, coerces, or restrains* persons or organizations engaging in interstate commerce for any of the objects prohibited under 8(b)(4)(A-D), then the union has committed an unfair labor practice.

The first section of this unfair labor practice, Section 8(b)(4)(A), prohibits unions from *compelling* an employer to join a labor or employer organization or from entering into a *hot cargo agreement* (a firm agrees with a union not to handle products produced by another firm). Examples of 8(b)(4)(A) violations include:[21]

- In an attempt to compel a beer distributor to recognize a union, the union prevents the distributor from obtaining beer by inducing the supplying brewery's employees to refuse to fill the distributor's orders.
- A union pickets an employer (or threatens to picket it) to force that employer to do business only with companies who have an agreement with the union (or other unionized firms).

The second part of 8(b)(4) deals with the controversial *secondary boycott* provision. A secondary boycott occurs if a labor union has a dispute with Company A (the primary employer) and, in the furtherance of that dispute, causes employees of Company B (a secondary or neutral employer) to stop handling the products of or doing business with Company A. The secondary employer may supply the primary employer with parts, materials, or services (for example, a tire manufacturer supplies an automobile company with tires) or the secondary employer may purchase goods and services from the primary employer (such as an airline that purchases jet fuel from a fuel distributor). To constitute a secondary boycott, the neutral employer must be truly neutral and not subject to common ownership or management by the primary firm. In addition, a neutral employer becomes an ally with the primary employer if a substantial amount of work normally done by striking employees of the primary firm is subcontracted to the secondary employer. Specific examples of secondary boycott activities include:

- Picketing a neutral employer to stop doing business with another firm (the primary employer) while the union is having a dispute with the primary employer.
- Asking employees of a machine shop not to work on parts supplied by a nonunion firm that the union is trying to organize.
- Telling an employer that its plant will be picketed if it continues to do business with a company that the union has designated as "unfair."

---

[21] Office of the General Counsel, National Labor Relations Board, *A Guide to Basic Law and Procedures Under the National Labor Relations Act* (Washington, D.C.: U.S. Government Printing Office, 1978), pp. 37–38.

Some tough judgment calls must be made from time to time by the NLRB and federal courts about what constitutes secondary boycott activity.[22] For example, when does a secondary employer lose its neutral status? How much managerial control or ownership must the primary employer possess over a secondary employer before the latter becomes an ally? Likewise, how much work normally done by striking primary employees can be subcontracted to a neutral employer before an ally relationship exists? To complicate the issue further, a secondary employer is not protected from the *incidental effects* of union action that is taken directly against the primary employer. It is normally lawful for a union to *urge* employees of a neutral firm such as a supplier not to cross a picket line and make deliveries at the primary employer's plant. As long as a picket line does not prevent persons from entering or leaving a plant, building, or work site, then the union's actions are legitimate.

Normally, primary and secondary employers operate at different locations. However, there are situations in which employees of a primary employer and those of a secondary employer work on the same premises (known as a "common-situs" situation). A typical example of the common-situs or shared-site situation is where a subcontractor, such as an electrical firm, with whom the union has a dispute is performing work on a construction site along with other subcontractors (carpenters, masons, plumbers, etc.) who are not involved in a labor dispute with the union. In this case, the union representing the electricians can picket at the construction site if such picketing is directed solely at the electrical subcontractor (the primary employer). Should the electricians' union direct their picketing toward the various secondary employers who are also working on the site, then the picketing constitutes an illegal secondary boycott. The problem lies in determining where to draw the line between legal and illegal picketing. To assist parties in determining whether the objectives of picketing activities are primary or secondary, the NLRB and the courts have formulated guidelines known as the *Moore Dry Dock* standards.[23] Picketing is *primary* if the following conditions are met:

1. The picketing must occur when the primary employer is working on the premises and is conducting its customary business.
2. The picketing must be confined to places that are reasonably close to where the employees of the primary employer are working.
3. Picket signs or banners must clearly indicate that the dispute is with the primary employer and not with a secondary employer(s).

In order to clarify the issue and isolate the employees of the secondary employer, a *reserve gate* may be established. Per the above example, a special reserve gate could be established for the electrical workers. This arrangement would force the electricians' union to confine their picketing activities to the reserve gate only. All other employees would enter the workplace at another location and would avoid contact with the picket lines. Any attempt by the electricians' union to picket at a site other than the reserve gate would likely result in an 8(b)(4)(B) violation.

---

[22] See Samuel A. DiLullo, "Secondary Boycotts: Has the Court Gone Too Far or Maybe Not Far Enough?" *Labor Law Journal* (June 1989), pp. 376–381.
[23] 92 NLRB 547 (1950).

Section 8(b)(4)(B) also prohibits a union from engaging in a secondary strike or boycott to force a primary employer to recognize or bargain with it (when the union is not the certified bargaining representative for the primary employer's workers). Similarly, Section 8(b)(4)(C) is violated if a union applies pressure on an employer to recognize or bargain with it when the employees of the firm have already certified *another* union as its bargaining representative.[24]

Section 8(b)(4)(D) prohibits strikes, or a union threat to strike, over *jurisdictional* disputes. A jurisdictional dispute is a dispute between two or more unions over an employer's assignment of work to members of a specific union. For example, on a construction project, brick masons may have been assigned the task of building a brick retaining wall. In order to build the wall, it is necessary to construct a wooden support frame. The carpenters' union believes that the construction of the support frame should be assigned to them, although they have no quarrel about the masonry component of the job. The masons, however, desire to construct *both* the frame and the brick work. Should the carpenters' union strike over this dispute, they would violate Section 8(b)(4)(D). Section 10(k) of the Taft-Hartley Act requires that the NLRB resolve jurisdictional disputes if the parties cannot do so on their own or through arbitration within 10 days. There has been a strong predilection by the Board to honor the employer's *original* work assignment unless the assignment violates the terms of the collective bargaining agreement. The NLRB also considers the skills of the employees, company and industry practices, previous agreements between the employer and the union, and prior arbitration and joint board awards that are relevant to the case at hand.

Excessive and Discriminatory Union Fees and Dues

Section 8(b)(5) makes it illegal for a union to charge membership fees that are excessive or discriminatory. The NLRB considers factors such as the practices and customs of labor organizations in a particular industry as well as the compensation level of the employees who must pay the union initiation fees and monthly dues. A $500 initiation fee would be financially burdensome and excessive for a laborer earning the minimum wage, but quite reasonable for a skilled craft worker making $40,000 a year. Unions are more likely to run afoul of Section 8(b)(5) when they apply initiation fees and dues in a discriminatory fashion. If a union charges a significantly lower initiation fee for employees who join a union before a certification election and then raises the fee for those joining after the union wins the election, then an 8(b)(5) violation is probable. Unions whose fees and dues are unusually high in relation to other unions in the same area may also leave themselves open to an unfair labor practice charge. Any dues or fee differentials that are based on a member's race or sex would be illegal under both the Taft-Hartley Act as well as other civil rights laws.

---

[24] See Ralph M. Dereshinsky, Alan D. Berkowitz, and Philip A. Miscimarra, *The NLRB and Secondary Boycotts*, revised ed., (Philadelphia: Industrial Research Unit, The Wharton School, University of Pennsylvania, 1981).

Antifeatherbedding Provisions

An interesting but largely ineffective provision of the Taft-Hartley Act is *Section 8(b)(6)*, the *antifeatherbedding clause*. Section 8(b)(6) forbids a labor organization "to cause or attempt to cause an employer to pay or deliver any money or other thing of value... for services which are not performed." Featherbedding controversies often arise as the result of technological changes, the elimination of certain products or services by a firm, or the redesigning of a job. All of these make employee skills obsolete or eliminate the need for specific work. For example, some of the newer jet airliners no longer require flight engineers; the advent of diesel locomotives radically altered the role of the railroad fireman, and computer technology, automation, and robotics have totally eliminated the need for the human element in some jobs. Even when technological advances are not a factor, employers will occasionally find themselves overstaffed. Unions are mindful of the need to protect the job-security interests of their members. Thus, labor organizations often attempt to protect their constituents in the face of job obsolescence and cutbacks in staffing.

Two major questions arise insofar as featherbedding is concerned. Is the employer obligated to pay employees for work not performed? Can unions legally force a company to pay for work that is unnecessary and useless? The answer to both questions appears to be yes. As long as the employees are available and willing to perform work, then the union will not likely violate the antifeatherbedding provision. If a collective bargaining agreement stipulates that a two-person crew is needed to perform a job, but the work can be efficiently and safely performed by one person, the employer must still pay both employees. Similarly, employees who perform unnecessary work—such as following a painters union contract that requires the application of three coats of paint on a job when one coat is sufficient—does not violate 8(b)(6) because work, albeit needless work, is performed.

Organizational and Recognition Picketing by Noncertified Unions

Section 8(b)(7) regulates organizational and recognition picketing. *Organizational picketing* is done to induce employees to accept the union as their representative, whereas *recognition picketing* is directed at obtaining the employer's recognition of the union as its employees' bargaining representative. Under the Taft-Hartley Act, organizational and recognition picketing are prohibited under the following conditions:[25]

1. When the employer has lawfully recognized another union.
2. When a valid representation election has been held within the previous 12 months. This provision protects the employer from repeated certification attempts, especially by a union that was narrowly defeated in an earlier certification election.

---

[25] Office of the General Counsel, National Labor Relations Board, *A Guide to Basic Law and Procedures Under the National Labor Relations Act* (Washington, D.C.: U.S. Government Printing Office, 1978), pp. 42–43.

3. When a representation petition is not filed "within a reasonable period of time not to exceed thirty days from the commencement of such picketing." This section (8(b)(7)(C)) prevents a union from "hanging around" and disrupting work activities indefinitely while they attempt to secure an adequate number of authorization card signatures. An employer can file an 8(b)(7)(C) charge against a union and call for an immediate (expedited) election to force the union's hand in resolving the representation issue. Expedited elections are rarely used because the circumstances are usually such that the union realizes that it has little chance of winning; it agrees to cease picketing and disclaims further interest in representing the employees. However, a proviso to 8(b)(7)(C) allows *informational picketing* by a union to convey a specific message (such as informing the public of an employer's substandard wages and working conditions) provided that the picketing does not have the objective or significant effect of preventing employees, customers, or suppliers from entering the company's premises.[26]

Other Provisions

The Taft-Hartley Act contains additional provisions of importance that are discussed in other parts of this text. In addition to unfair labor practice charges and union certification procedures, the NLRA created the Federal Mediation and Conciliation Service, established procedures for dealing with national emergency strikes (see Chapter 10), and allowed civil suits between employers and unions for violations of labor contract terms (see Chapter 12). In 1974, special procedures were added to the NLRA to cover labor disputes in the health care industry.

▲ The National Labor Relations Board

The National Labor Relations Board consists of a five-member Board, an independent General Counsel (both located in Washington, D.C.), and a group of regional, subregional, and resident offices located throughout the United States. Members of the Board are appointed by the president, with Senate confirmation, for five-year terms. General Counsel members are appointed in a similar fashion to serve four-year terms. Each of the 33 regional offices has a director appointed by the Board and a staff of field examiners and attorneys who are career civil service employees.

Processing Unfair Labor Practice Complaints and Charges

The regional offices are the starting point for unfair labor practice charges. They process cases on behalf of the General Counsel, which serves as the prosecuting arm for the NLRB. An unfair labor practice charge (known as a "C" case) may be filed by an employer, employee, labor organization, or any other person by completing a charge form that must be signed and affirmed under oath. The complaint

---

[26] See Neal Orkin and Elizabeth Tirone, "Consumer Secondary Picketing, *Safeco*, and the Limits of Economic Jurisprudence," *Labor Law Journal* (January 1989), pp. 21–30.

is investigated by regional office staff members, and the charged party is notified of a hearing on the allegations if the investigation reveals that an unfair labor practice was possibly committed. An NLRB administrative law judge (ALJ) conducts the hearing, using rules of evidence and procedures that apply in U.S. District Courts. The ALJ makes a recommendation to the Board as to whether the charged party has committed an unfair labor practice and suggests appropriate sanctions. Any of the parties involved may appeal the ALJ's recommendations to the Board, who will then make a binding decision. This decision may be appealed to one of 11 U.S. Courts of Appeal which will affirm, deny, modify, or remand the Board's ruling. In a relatively few instances, an unfair labor practice charge may be appealed to the U.S. Supreme Court if the Court elects to hear the case by granting a *writ of certiorari*.

Once the unfair labor practice case has been decided, a compliance officer at the regional level has the responsibility of ensuring that the appropriate parties adhere to the Board's orders. In some instances, the Board secures a cease-and-desist order to prevent further unfair labor practices by a union or company. An order may be obtained to prevent a union from engaging in secondary boycott activities. Employers may be ordered to reinstate an employee, perhaps with back pay, who was discharged for assisting union organizers. The regional compliance officer routinely checks with the charging party approximately two months after the final resolution of a case. Appropriate action is taken by the Board to force compliance if the offending party has failed to live up to its obligations; usually noncompliance compels the Board to seek court-ordered enforcement or contempt of court charges.

A case may take anywhere from one to three years to process, depending on the complexity of the issues and the level to which the case is appealed. Unfortunately, some parties (usually employers) will attempt to circumvent the law and dilute its effectiveness by illegally delaying the process and intentionally ignoring contempt citations or Board orders.[27] Companies willing to pay fines for contempt charges pose a thorny dilemma for the NLRB. Probably the best examples of how the law fails to operate properly have arisen in the Southern textile industry. Unfair labor practice cases involving Milliken and Company and the J. P. Stevens Company spanned nearly a quarter of a century. Milliken, a firm whose annual revenues were believed to be $2 billion (at the time of the unfair labor practice case), eventually paid $5 million in back pay, whereas J. P. Stevens paid $1.3 million in back wages.

Even when legal expenses are added to these totals, it is obvious that there are instances when "crime does pay." First, the back pay settlements (estimated at $10,000 per worker) were scant compensation for those who lost their jobs or faced relocation because they could no longer find employment in their textile mill-dominated communities. Second, the settlements involving these two companies were, in all likelihood, less than what the companies would have paid in improved wages and benefits if the Textile Workers Union had won certification elections in

---

[27] The Bureau of National Affairs, Inc., "Delays in NLRB Operations Discussed by ULP Victims," *Labor Relations Reporter*, Vol. 127 (Washington, D.C.: The Bureau of National Affairs, Inc., February 15, 1988), pp. 205–207.

the late 1950s. Third, the amount of the back pay awards was small and imposed little financial burden on companies whose assets and revenues were so large. As noted by Gagla, "Unscrupulous employers view the penalties as the cost of a license to kill unions."[28] One might also argue that firms who elect to side-step federal labor laws by viewing the cost of breaking them as simply another business expense are acting in an economically rational manner. The blame, it may be argued, should not be placed on errant firms, but rather on those who enact and enforce the law. To deal with this predicament, the Labor Law Reform Act of 1977 was proposed to put more pressure and stiffer penalties on firms that frequently and flagrantly violate the NLRA. However, the bill succumbed to a Senate filibuster in the summer of 1978.[29]

The Private Settlement of Unfair Labor Practices

When parties to an unfair labor practice forego an NLRB hearing and negotiate a settlement, the NLRB will honor the agreement even if the remedies fall short of what the agency would have ordered. The NLRB has decided to support such settlements because agreement by the parties filing the unfair labor practice charge was voluntary and because the union found the settlement fair. Settlements of this nature represent a compromise designed to eliminate the time, expense, and uncertainties of litigation. The Board stated that the parties should not be deprived of "the opportunity to reach an early restoration of industrial peace."

In reviewing private settlements between employers and unions, the NLRB will examine the following factors:

- whether the employer, union, and individuals involved have agreed to a binding settlement;
- whether the NLRB supports the settlement;
- whether the settlement is reasonable in light of the nature of the violations alleged, the risks inherent in litigation, and the stage of litigation;
- whether there has been any fraud, coercion, or duress by any of the parties in reaching an agreement; and
- whether the employer has engaged in a history of violations of the NLRA or has breached previous settlement agreements involving unfair labor practices.[30]

Conducting Certification Elections

Under Section 9 of the Act, certification proceedings are conducted under the auspices of the NLRB, with the bulk of the certification election work being done by the regional offices. Labor organizations desiring to represent a group of employees must file a representation petition and document the workers' "show of interest" with at least 30 percent having signed authorization cards. The NLRB will

---

[28] Ken Gagla, *Union Organizing and Staying Organized* (Reston, Virginia: Reston Publishing Co., 1983), p. 5.
[29] Ken Gagla, *Union Organizing and Staying Organized* (Reston, Virginia: Reston Publishing Co., 1983), p. 7.
[30] *Independent Stove Co., Inc.*, 127 LRRM 1204 (1987). See The Bureau of National Affairs, Inc., *Collective Bargaining Negotiations & Contracts* (Washington, D.C.: The Bureau of National Affairs, Inc., March 24, 1988), p. 3.

then hold a representation hearing to resolve any disputes between the company and union regarding the appropriateness of the proposed bargaining unit. Using the criteria set forth in the NLRA (see Chapter 4), the regional officers recommend the final composition of the unit and a certification election is then held. Eligible bargaining unit employees who vote in the election are given a minimum of two choices (the union or no union) and the majority of the votes cast decides the outcome. If the union wins, then the employer becomes legally obligated to bargain in good faith with the newly elected labor organization. Should the "no-union" choice prevail, then another certification election by any union for this group of employees is forbidden for 12 months. Unless there are challenges by the union or employer regarding pre-election improprieties or disputes over the eligibility of certain employees who voted in the election, the NLRB will certify the results. Occasionally, disputes over employer or union actions that allegedly disrupted and biased the election will result in unfair labor practice charges that can complicate matters and delay final certification. A discussion of bargaining unit and certification issues is found in Chapters 4 and 5.

The Board as a Political, Social, and Economic Weather Vane

The NLRB is a quasi-judicial agency with the specialized mission of dealing with unfair labor practice cases and certification elections. Although NLRB decisions can be appealed in U.S. circuit court, nearly all cases are adjudicated without such appeals. The NLRB, in essence, acts as a buffer between litigants and the federal courts. As a result, the NLRB's decisions have shaped labor policy in the United States through its analysis, interpretation, and application of the National Labor Relations Act. Because of its profound impact on U.S. labor relations, the NLRB has been the subject of considerable and often severe controversy. Charges aimed at the NLRB have not been limited to specific interest groups; rather, groups from labor, management, and academic circles have all directed criticism at the Board. Several reasons lie behind such criticism. First, the Board and General Counsel appointments are made by the president of the United States. Unlike Supreme Court appointments, Board members do not have lifetime tenure. Board members appointed by Republican presidents have been criticized for their conservative, pro-management posture, whereas Democratic appointees have been accused of having a pro-labor bias. Less than a week after George Bush was elected president, Owen Bieber, president of the United Auto Workers offered this comment:

> The next president should put a stop to the open hostility toward unions that we've had from the past administration and the current National Labor Relations Board.
>
> The NLRB under President Reagan took very one-sided, antilabor positions that have crippled [union] organizing drives and made it difficult for unions to represent members effectively. Congress intended [the] NLRB to be a neutral agency, and the president should restore that.[31]

---

[31] The Associated Press, "Business Leaders Offer Advice for President Bush," *The Greenville News* (November 13, 1988), p. 4E, reprinted with permission. See The Bureau of National Affairs, Inc., "NLRB Assessment," *Collective Bargaining Contracts & Negotiations* (Washington, D.C.: The Bureau of National Affairs, Inc., May 4, 1989), p. 4.

A second reason for such criticism is that only three of the full five-member Board are required to hear a case. Thus, only two votes are needed to decide an important case, a fact that some find disconcerting. Third, there has been criticism that the Board has eroded the intent of Congress in its overly broad interpretation of the law.

As is the case with any agency charged with enforcing a federal statute, a certain amount of criticism is probably inevitable. Undoubtedly, political bias will creep into the thoughts and decisions of those whose task it is to interpret and apply public policy in a broad and ever-changing social and economic environment. Some of the alleged inconsistencies in Board decisions may also stem from their attempt to fashion decisions that are responsive to current needs in the workplace. Furthermore, statutory language is couched in general terms, yet it must be applied to a very specific set of circumstances, thereby leaving considerable leeway for differences in opinion. The point being made here is that the NLRB's decisions are both controversial and subject to change.

Some critics have suggested that the NLRB be abolished. If this should occur, what would take its place? Would, for example, labor courts be any less biased or more efficient than the NLRB? Is there any reason to believe that unfair labor practice charges and representation disputes could be handled with a greater degree of consistency or expertise if they could be submitted directly to the federal courts? Could the problem of political favoritism be eliminated if Board members were given lifetime appointments? If so, would labor policy become more stagnant and less responsive to industrial and societal needs? These are difficult questions to answer. In all probability, the NLRB will remain intact and continue to direct labor policy in the United States. The Board will also likely remain shrouded in controversy, especially when its rulings go against a large and vocal interest group. One of the difficulties encountered in evaluating the quality of Board rulings is that those doing the evaluating judge the NLRB using their personal standards and values.[32]

▲ The Landrum-Griffin Act: An Attempt to Control Labor Corruption

Historical Background

Corruption within certain labor organizations has existed since their inception, the most notable examples being in the building trades, longshoremen, and Teamsters unions. Although unions are supposed to protect and represent their members, they have, on occasion, been guilty of engaging in violence, extortion, mishandling of union funds, and sweetheart arrangements with employers. Some unions were infiltrated by members of organized crime. Others would not allow members to have a voice in union affairs. Initially, little was done to protect employees from the corrupt internal practices of union leaders because unions were not significant social institutions. The judicial posture prior to the 1930s was probably not sympathetic toward renegade employees who joined organizations.

---

[32] See Edward B. Miller, *An Administrative Appraisal of the NLRB*, revised ed. (Philadelphia: The Wharton School, University of Pennsylvania, 1980).

As labor organizations grew rapidly after 1935, corruption became more difficult to ignore. By the 1950s, Congress became involved and established a committee known as the Senate Select Committee on Improper Activities in the Labor or Management Field. The committee was better known as the McClellan Committee and it was charged with uncovering the widespread abuses that plagued certain labor unions. Most of the committee's efforts were focused on five unions: the Teamsters, Bakery and Confectionery Workers, United Textile Workers, Operating Engineers, and Allied Industrial Workers of America. After three years of hearings, the committee concluded that some unions denied rank-and-file members a voice in union matters, committed acts of violence against their members, extorted money from employers, raided local union treasuries under the guise of trusteeship arrangements, and accepted bribes from management. The end result of the McClellan Committee's investigation was the passage of the Labor-Management Reporting and Disclosure Act of 1959, known commonly as the Landrum-Griffin Act.[33]

Provisions of the Landrum-Griffin Act

The Union Members' "Bill of Rights"

Title I of the Act has been labelled the "bill of rights" because it attempts to guarantee that members will have a voice in union affairs. This section gives members the right to meet and assemble freely with other members and to express their opinions on union policies, leadership, and candidates for union office. These rights, however, are subject to the parliamentary rules of procedure normally used at meetings. Furthermore, unions have the right to adopt and enforce *reasonable* rules of conduct. Unions can also discipline members whose actions interfere with a union's legal or contractual obligations.

The "bill of rights" also provides that union members, through a democratic procedure, must have a say in whether union fees, dues, or assessments should be increased. Local union dues and fees cannot be increased unless local members approve by a majority vote; international assessments can also be increased if a group of union delegates or an executive board approves.

A labor organization cannot limit the right of any member to bring suit against it. This provision also includes a member's right to petition a legislature (or communicate with particular legislators) on labor matters without censorship by the union. The Act, however, requires that any such member exhaust reasonable union hearing procedure within four months and that no interested employer can finance, encourage, or participate in such proceedings (this latter provision has been declared unconstitutional).

Finally, a union is not allowed to fine, suspend, or otherwise discipline a member without *procedural due process*. If a union member's conduct violates the by-laws of a union (such as in failing to honor a legal picket line) and the union attempts

---

[33] See Janice R. Bellace and Alan D. Berkowitz, *The Landrum-Griffin Act: Twenty Years of Federal Protection of Union Members' Rights* (Philadelphia: Industrial Research Unit, The Wharton School, University of Pennsylvania, 1979).

to levy a fine on the member, then it must first serve a written notice containing specific charges. The member must be given a reasonable time to prepare a defense and the union is obligated to provide the member with a full and fair hearing.

Election of Union Officers

The Landrum-Griffin Act establishes requirements concerning the election of union officers. Title IV to the Act ensures that elections are conducted in a democratic manner. This provision also curtails incumbent union officers who usurp their power to thwart the challenges of rival candidates for union office. The Act regulates the frequency with which elections must be held and sets forth procedural standards for conducting an election. Labor organizations have the right to establish reasonable standards for candidates who wish to run for a union office. The law forbids most convicted felons from holding office within five years from the date that their prison sentence expires. Candidates for union offices must have the same degree of access to union members as current officers.

In short, the election procedures are designated to eliminate malpractices that have hindered democracy in unions. Not all of the blame can be placed on union officers and candidates, however. Other than caring about meetings held during contract negotiations or meetings regarding an important issue such as a troublesome grievance or threats of layoffs, most members are apathetic about union business. This apathy often spills over into the nomination and election of union officers, thereby opening the door to questionable election practices. As a result, Title IV of the Act not only protects union members from unscrupulous union officers and candidates, but to a certain extent also protects members from their own apathy and indifference.

The Control of Trusteeships

The term "trusteeship" in labor relations pertains to the seizure of a local union by its international. Trusteeships are normally used by international unions to clean up corruption or mismanagement on the local level. An international or national union has formal authority over its respective locals and its officers. Cases of misappropriated funds, unauthorized strikes, or internal corruption in a local union may prompt seizure by the parent union.

The McClellan Committee, in the course of its investigation, uncovered abuses in the trusteeship arrangement. Local treasuries were plundered and officers whose views conflicted with the international ruling body were censored or impeached. Title III of the Landrum-Griffin Act regulates trusteeships and allows the seizure of a local only if a legitimate reason exists for so doing. Major acceptable reasons for imposing a trusteeship include corruption, financial malpractice, lack of adherence to union contracts and good faith bargaining practices, restoring democratic practices, or carrying out the legitimate objectives of the union.

For example, the Service Employees International Union (SEIU) placed its San Francisco Local 250 in trusteeship. In response to member complaints, SEIU international officials conducted internal hearings on the operations of the 28,000 member health care local and then invoked the trusteeship. The union attributed some of the local's problems to a "long and draining strike" against the Kaiser Foundation Health Plan that depleted the union's treasury.[34]

When a trusteeship is imposed on a local union, the international union must file periodic reports on each trusteeship so that the U.S. Department of Labor can monitor developments. Special attention is paid to the financial condition of the local union during the trusteeship.

Fiduciary Standards

Labor organizations collect large sums of money through membership dues and fees, pension plans, and other employee benefit programs. Persons responsible for collecting, keeping, or investing funds are known as *fiduciaries*. Title V of the Act regulates the fiduciary responsibility of union officers and union employees. Fiduciaries must separate their personal financial interests from the union's financial interests. Specifically, a fiduciary cannot deal with its union as an adverse party; nor can a fiduciary hold a pecuniary or personal interest that conflicts with the union's interest.

The Act requires (under Title II) that fiduciaries report all expenditures of union funds. Information on the amount and purpose of such expenditures is made available to union members. All persons who receive or otherwise exercise control over union monies must be bonded. Fiduciaries who misuse or embezzle funds are guilty of a federal crime. It is permissible, however, for unions to make loans, not to exceed $2000, to their personnel. An interesting provision within Title V is that a union cannot grant amnesty to officers or personnel who violate their responsibilities as fiduciaries; otherwise, the union leadership could, in essence, forgive themselves for financial wrongdoing. Under the Act, an individual union member can file civil suit for appropriate relief if the union fails to do so. This provision is designed to allow union members to seek restitution for funds that were misappropriated by officers.

Other Provisions of the Landrum-Griffin Act

The Landrum-Griffin Act requires that both unions and employers file periodic reports. For example, Title II of the Act requires that each union have a constitution and set of by-laws, copies of which must be on file with the U.S. Secretary of Labor. Collective bargaining agreements and union financial statements must also be filed with the Secretary. Employers are also required to file information on certain activities such as financial dealings with unions and the use of labor-relations consultants.

Title VI of the Act added several miscellaneous provisions, the most notable being a ban on extortionate picketing against employers by individuals who seek to profit personally (as opposed to collectively) from such actions. Title VII of the

---

[34] The Bureau of National Affairs, Inc., "SEIU Trusteeship," *Collective Bargaining Negotiations & Contracts* (Washington, D.C.: The Bureau of National Affairs, Inc., February 26, 1987), p. 1.

Landrum-Griffin Act amended the Taft-Hartley Act and clarified federal-state jurisdictional issues that had arisen under the NLRA. In addition, the Act closed several loopholes in the secondary boycott provisions of the Taft-Hartley Act and added a seventh unfair labor practice on union picketing (discussed earlier in this chapter under Section 8(b)(7)). A form of closed shop was legalized under Title VII *only* for the building and construction industry.

Enforcement of the Landrum-Griffin Act

The U.S. Department of Labor has primary responsibility for enforcing the Act. However, union members whose Bill of Rights provisions (Title I) or financial safeguards provisions (Title V) have been violated file civil charges directly in federal or state court. Also, the Title VII amendments to the Taft-Hartley Act are enforced by the NLRB.

Criminal penalties are possible for those who violate the Landrum-Griffin Act. Fines up to $10,000 and sentences of up to one year in jail are possible for persons who either fail to file the required reports or who file false reports. Violations of union election procedures that are called to the attention of the Secretary of Labor may result in having the unfair election overturned and a new election held. More severe penalties are possible for those who violate financial fiduciary provisions; unions may be ordered to reimburse members for lost assets and fines up to $10,000 per person and jail sentences up to five years may be levied.

The preceding discussion of the Landrum-Griffin Act may leave the impression that corruption runs rampant in labor unions. Nothing could be further from the truth. Only a small fraction of 1 percent of all local unions are likely to be involved in serious violations of the Act, and most union officers carry out their duties in a professional and honest manner. Nevertheless, the seriousness and flagrant nature of the violations committed by some unions were deemed reprehensible enough to warrant restrictive legislation.

▲ Other Legislation Having an Impact on Collective Bargaining and Labor Relations

Thus far, the focus of this chapter has been on labor legislation that primarily regulates the manner in which unions, employers, and workers deal with each other in a unionized setting or during a union-organizing drive. However, parties responsible for the negotiation and administration of collective bargaining agreements must also be familiar with a number of federal laws that pertain to personnel management in both unionized and nonunionized organizations. These laws cover equal employment opportunity issues (also known as fair employment practice laws), compensation and employee benefits, and health and safety. Most states also have laws that apply to personnel practices in each of these areas and, in many instances, they provide for more comprehensive coverage than the federal laws. A brief description of the major federal laws is provided here; some are treated in more detail in subsequent chapters.

Equal Employment Opportunity Laws

The mid-1960s marked a major legal and social watershed as federal civil rights laws were enacted. These laws prohibited unfair discrimination in employment against protected groups. Some of the major federal equal employment opportunity (EEO) laws are the following:

- ▲ *Title VII of the 1964 Civil Rights Act*, as amended, provides protection against employment discrimination based on race, sex, religion, color, and national origin. The law applies to nearly all private and public organizations as well as to labor unions and employment agencies. Employment practices involving hiring, firing, promotions, compensation, and other employment conditions are covered under the Act. Title VII is enforced by the Equal Employment Opportunity Commission (EEOC), a federal administrative agency that functions much like the NLRB. EEOC decisions can be appealed in the federal court system.
- ▲ *Age Discrimination in Employment Act of 1967* (ADEA) protects persons age 40 and above from unfair employment decisions that are geared to age rather than ability and qualifications to perform the job. The ADEA is enforced by the EEOC and covers essentially the same practices and organizations as Title VII.
- ▲ *Federal Laws and Executive Orders Mandating Affirmative Action* apply to organizations that have business contracts with the federal government (e.g., a computer firm that supplies software to the Department of Defense) or that receives federal financial assistance (e.g., a university that receives a federally-subsidized grant to perform agriculture research). The concept of affirmative action goes beyond the nondiscrimination provisions of Title VII and the ADEA by requiring that organizations doing business with the federal government make a special good-faith effort to provide opportunities to qualified minorities who have traditionally been underutilized in certain job categories. *Executive Orders 11246 and 11375* primarily provide for race and sex affirmative action, whereas *Executive Order 11141* applies to age-related affirmative action. The *Rehabilitation Act of 1973* requires affirmative action for qualified physically and mentally handicapped persons and the *Vietnam Era Veterans' Readjustment Assistance Act of 1974* calls for affirmative action for qualified veterans of the Vietnam era as well as disabled veterans.
- ▲ *State EEO laws* often expand the coverage of federal laws. For example, Title VII does not cover firms with fewer than 15 employees, whereas many state laws do. In addition, state laws often include groups not covered by federal laws by prohibiting discrimination based on political affiliation, physical appearance, sexual preferences, and arrest and conviction records.

An understanding of EEO laws and the manner in which they are enforced is important for union and management officials involved in the collective bargaining process. Not only is intentional discrimination often illegal, but unwary negotiators, supervisors, and officials can encounter legal pitfalls even when there is no intent to discriminate. Some of the most troublesome areas include: promotion and seniority systems that place specific groups at a disadvantage; unequal pay, benefits, and working conditions between men and women; sexual and racial harassment at work; and failure to administer the collective bargaining agreement in an unbiased fashion.

Compensation and Employee Benefit Laws

Compensation and employee benefits (see Chapters 13 and 14) comprise an integral part of nearly all collective bargaining agreements. Persons responsible for negotiating and administering labor contracts must therefore understand the provisions of federal and state laws applicable to this area. The two most prominent laws are the Fair Labor Standards Act (FLSA), as amended, originally passed in 1938, and the Employment Retirement Income Security Act (ERISA) of 1974.

The *Fair Labor Standards Act* is probably best known as the federal minimum wage law. It also covers working hours, overtime compensation, and restrictions on the use of child labor. The Act contains numerous exemptions and restrictions. Managerial, professional, and salaried employees are not normally covered. Both public- and private-sector organizations fall under the purview of the Act, which is enforced by the Wage and Hour Division of the U.S. Department of Labor.

The *Employee Retirement Income Security Act* (ERISA) of 1974 regulates private-sector pension plans and is jointly enforced by the Department of Labor and the Department of the Treasury. The primary objective of ERISA is to ensure that workers who accumulate retirement benefits do not lose them through the dishonesty or mismanagement of pension plan administrators (fiduciaries), loopholes in the retirement program, or bankruptcy of the employer. A series of provisions covering such items as participation standards, vesting of the employer's contributions, funding standards, fiduciary responsibilities, federal insurance protecting employees from insolvent programs, and reporting requirements by fiduciaries are the major components of the Act.

Several other compensation laws are also of relevance to the collective bargaining process. The *Social Security Act of 1935*, as amended, regulates the myriad of retirement, survivorship, disability, and Medicare benefits that are provided by the federal government and financed through mandatory payroll taxes levied on workers and employers. Unfair pay differences that are geared to sex (and that usually work to the disadvantage of women) are illegal under the *Equal Pay Act of 1963*. The Equal Pay Act is enforced by the EEOC and prohibits pay discrimination in jobs involving equal work except for differences based on productivity, merit, or seniority. Employers receiving federal government contracts are required to abide by the *Walsh-Healey Act*, which sets minimum wage rates for specific industries and regulates work hours. The *Davis-Bacon Act* regulates wage rates, overtime, work hours, and benefits for private contractors engaged in public works construction. Nearly all states have passed *workers' compensation laws* that provide benefits for employees who are injured on the job. Finally, *state insurance codes* regulate group life and health insurance programs that are commonly contained in collective bargaining agreements.

The Occupational Safety and Health Act of 1970

Because of the high accident rates and job-related deaths in certain industries and the cavalier attitude on the part of some employers regarding worker safety, the *Occupational Health and Safety Act* (OSHA) was passed. OSHA contains a long list of specific safety and health standards for most private-sector employers and federal agencies. The Act is enforced by the Department of Labor (Occupational Safety and Health Administration) and requires inspections of the workplace by OSHA officials, recordkeeping by employers, the reporting of on-the-job accidents, and warnings to employees regarding safety hazards that are found during OSHA inspections.

Collective bargaining agreements may incorporate general safety standards and provisions that are similar to those found in the Act. Many contracts have provisions that cover safety equipment, first aid, physical examinations for employees, investigation of accidents, hazardous work, and safety committees. The presence of a labor union may also create pressure on the employer to abide by the standards and provisions established by OSHA.

▲ Private-Sector and Public-Sector Collective Bargaining: Basic Differences in the Legal Frameworks

The discussion up to this point has focused almost exclusively on labor legislation that covers union-management relations in the *private sector* (the Railway Labor Act, Wagner Act, Taft-Hartley Act, and Landrum-Griffin Act). Beginning in the early 1960s, federal, state, and municipal employees began to unionize and bargain collectively with their respective *public-sector* employers. The Wagner, Taft-Hartley, and other laws discussed earlier in this chapter generally do not apply to government employees who, instead, are covered by a patchwork quilt of federal, state, and local labor laws.

Federal employees are covered by the Civil Service Reform Act of 1978, whereas state and municipal workers may be covered by laws in their respective locales. For example, a public school teacher in Iowa is covered by a comprehensive collective bargaining statute that spells out certification procedures, unfair labor practices, impasse resolution mechanisms, and the role of the administrative agency (public employment relations board) that enforces the law. Other employees in different locations (primarily in the South) either have no laws or less comprehensive laws to define their collective bargaining rights.

Public-sector collective bargaining presents a unique set of legal issues that is addressed in Chapter 17. However, a primary distinction between the sectors involves the limited ability of government workers to engage legally in economic strikes. The inability of government employees to strike requires a different approach to resolving negotiation disputes and impasses. Furthermore, unfair labor practices, certification procedures, and the scope of bargaining issues may be more restricted in public-sector collective bargaining than in the private sector.

▲ Summary and Conclusions

This chapter and the previous chapter on labor history illustrate how the legal environment surrounding unionization has evolved from one of overt hostility and repression to a more even-handed approach that has attempted to balance the rights of workers, unions, employers, and society.[35] The 19th and early 20th century judicial system often sided with the employer and paved the way for the use of injunctions, yellow-dog contracts, the Sherman Antitrust Act, and strike-breaking tactics against unions. As a group, legislators were more sympathetic to the plight of employees and labor organizations. Congress enacted protective legislation designed to foster collective bargaining, regulate and control labor disputes (without restricting the employee's right to join a union and participate in nonviolent work stoppages), and stimulate the depression-ridden economy of the 1930s.[36]

The Railway Labor Act of 1926 marked the beginning of the *collective* rights era in which unions began to grow and exert influence in the industrial arena. Although the initial influence of the Railway Labor Act was confined to the railway industry, it paved the way for the Wagner Act whose effects were more pervasive and far-reaching. The period from 1935 (when the Wagner Act was passed) until 1959 (when the Landrum-Griffin Act became law) marked an era of changing power relations between labor and management, followed by legislative adjustment to these changes. When employers possessed the legal and economic advantage, the Wagner Act provided the counterweight that protected the rights of employees and labor organizations. As unions became powerful, the Taft-Hartley Act was promulgated to rebalance the scales of power. Subsequent legislation was necessary to thwart internal corruption within the ranks of labor unions (Landrum-Griffin Act). Thus, at 12-year intervals (1935, 1947, and 1959) major pieces of labor legislation were passed to form the basis of the collective rights era on which this chapter has focused.

As the 1960s dawned, concerns began to shift and the push for civil rights in all facets of social and economic life began to emerge. Employment discrimination against blacks and other racial minorities, women, older citizens, and certain religious groups resulted in the passage of civil rights legislation and ushered in the *group* rights era. The Civil Rights Act of 1964 (Title VII), the Age Discrimination in Employment Act of 1967, and other equal employment opportunity laws formed the nucleus of the group rights movement. Labor unions have generally been supportive of civil rights legislation. However, the passage of these laws may have eroded the usefulness of labor organizations since employees now have other ave-

---

[35] For an excellent outline of American labor law, see William B. Gould IV, *A Primer on American Labor Law* (Cambridge, Massachusetts: MIT Press, 1986).

[36] For a critique of U.S. labor policy see Theodore J. St. Antoine, "The Role of Law," in Jack Stieber, Robert B. McKersie, and D. Quinn Mills, *U.S. Industrial Relations 1950–1980: A Critical Assessment* (Madison, Wisconsin: Industrial Relations Research Association, 1981), pp. 159–197.

nues of relief and do not need to depend solely on unions to redress racial, sexist, or other injustices in the workplace.

The 1970s and 1980s witnessed yet another era in which the focus has shifted toward the protection of an employee's *individual rights*. It might be argued that ERISA protects individual employees and their pension rights and OSHA does the same with respect to health and safety in the workplace. A number of state courts have reversed the dismissals of *at-will employees* who have lost their jobs under questionable circumstances. An at-will employee has no individual employment contract or collective bargaining agreement to protect job security and can generally be discharged for good cause, bad cause, or no cause at all. In recent years, some courts have reversed such discharges, especially for terminations that are contrary to the public interest (e.g., an employee who is discharged for refusing to violate a law or falsify reports may be reinstated in some states, although there is no guarantee of reinstatement). The employment at-will issue is discussed in more depth in Chapter 16.

In summary, employees working in a unionized setting have acquired collective rights via the collective bargaining agreement. Added to this are the group rights that have emerged from the various equal employment opportunity laws and, finally, the individual rights stemming from ERISA, OSHA, and court decisions on the employment at-will issue. A number of labor law issues are discussed in more detail in subsequent chapters. The reader should bear in mind that U.S. labor law is both complex and rapidly changing. Any textbook discussion of legal matters in labor relations is therefore, at best, only a superficial snapshot of a dynamic field that is interesting to follow as the courts and various administrative agencies continue to interpret and apply the law.[37]

▲ Discussion Questions and Exercises

1. Although the wording and terminology of a labor law may remain unchanged for years, the NLRB and courts often change the way in which they view and interpret the law. What factors account for these changes?
2. Using the *Labor Relations Reference Manual* (unfair labor practice cases published by The Bureau of National Affairs, Inc. and found in most large libraries or law libraries), summarize a recent case involving one or more of the following unfair labor practices:
    a. Employer domination or interference with a union.
    b. Employer discrimination against union supporters.
    c. Employer failure to bargain in good faith.
    d. Union restraint and coercion of employees.
    e. A prohibited strike or boycott by a union.
    f. Illegal picketing by a union.
    g. Secondary boycott.
    h. Jurisdictional dispute.

---

[37] See Owen G. Herrnstadt, "Time Once Again to Climb the Industrial Mountain Top: A Call For Labor Law Reform," *Labor Law Journal* (March 1988), pp. 187–188.

How did the NLRB or court rule on the case(s) you analyzed? What justifications did the NLRB or court present to support their decision?
3. One of the more controversial NLRB chairpersons was Reagan-appointee Donald Dotson, who was notoriously pro-management. What suggestions would you make that might improve the manner in which the NLRB performs its function? How can either a management or labor bias be avoided when the president appoints members to the Board?
4. Contact the nearest NLRB office and obtain information on filing an unfair labor practice charge. What are the steps associated with filing a charge and what problems and delays are likely to be encountered?
5. Do you believe that the penalties for violating the NLRA are sufficient to deter labor-law violators? Why or why not? Research the debates surrounding the ill-fated Labor Reform Act of 1978. Why did this law fail to pass?
6. The Wagner and Taft-Hartley Acts were passed during a time when labor and management were clearly adversaries. Today, a number of labor organizations and corporations have developed cooperative programs designed to control labor costs, deal with technological changes, and address problems of common interest. What problems might the current legal structure present to such cooperative programs?

4 The Bargaining Unit

- **Introduction**
- **The Doctrine of Exclusive Representation**
- **The Importance of the Bargaining Unit Structure**
- **NLRB Criteria for Determining the Appropriate Bargaining Unit**
- **The Treatment of Specialized Employee Groups**
  Employees Who May Warrant Separate Bargaining Units
   Craft Workers
   Professional and Technical Employees
   Plant Guards and Security Personnel
  Employees Who Are Excluded from Bargaining Units
   Supervisors and Managers
   Confidential Employees
   Agricultural Laborers
   Part-Time, Dual Status, and Seasonal Employees
   Independent Contractors
   Individuals Employed by a Parent or Spouse
- **Some Common Bargaining Unit Structures**
  Single-Employer, Single-Location Units
  Single-Employer, Multi-Location Units
  Multi-Employer Bargaining Units
  Coordinated Bargaining
- **Bargaining Units in Expanding Organizations**
  Accretions to the Bargaining Unit
  Successorship Employers
- **Presumptively Appropriate Bargaining Units**
- **Summary and Conclusions**

- ▲ **Discussion Questions and Exercises**
- ▲ **Bargaining Unit Cases**
  Cooper Union
  Community Hospital at Glen Cove
  Futuramik Industries
  U.S. Pollution Control, Inc.

▲ Introduction

Prior to conducting a certification election to decide whether a union will win the right to represent a group of employees, the National Labor Relations Board must define the proper bargaining unit. The formal bargaining unit specifically determines which employees have the right to vote in the certification election and to be represented by the union (if the union wins the election). For example, a bargaining unit may consist of all nonsupervisory employees working on three production lines in a radio assembly plant. In another example, all security guards at a nuclear power facility may comprise a bargaining unit. Bargaining units may also be defined along departmental lines; workers in the manufacturing and shipping departments of a plant may be included, whereas those working in other departments such as sales, quality control, and administration may not be part of the unit. Employees who are not included in the bargaining unit are either represented under a different contract or not covered by a labor agreement.

Bargaining units can be found in all shapes and sizes. Some units are very small, consisting of fewer than five employees. Other bargaining units are large, multi-plant or multi-employer structures that contain several thousand members. Craft bargaining units are normally comprised of highly trained workers who possess a common set of skills, such as carpenters or brick masons. Industrial units are more heterogeneous, containing workers with a wide range of skills and a multitude of job descriptions.

▲ The Doctrine of Exclusive Representation

A union certified by the NLRB becomes the *exclusive bargaining representative* for all bargaining unit employees. Regardless of the structure of a particular bargaining unit, the union obtaining the bargaining rights for a group of workers must represent all members of the unit on a fair and equal basis. The union not only represents employees who supported the union during the organizational campaign, but also those who campaigned against the union. In right-to-work states, the union must also represent employees who elect not to join the union or pay union dues. The doctrine of exclusive representation provides both a benefit as well as an obligation for the union. On the one hand, the union does not have to share its bargaining rights with another labor organization. On the other hand, it must fully represent all employees in the bargaining unit, regardless of their individual views on unionism.

Not all countries adhere to the concept of exclusive bargaining representatives. Employees in Western European countries, for example, often work in bargaining units represented by several labor organizations. The exclusive representation status of labor organizations in the United States allows the union to present a united front for its members when it negotiates wages, hours, and working conditions. Management is less likely to undermine the power of the collective bargaining process by employing the divide-and-conquer strategy of negotiating with several unions or with employees on an individual basis.

Under the doctrine of exclusive representation, an employer cannot normally enter into contracts with individual workers if these contracts contain provisions different from the collective bargaining agreement.[1] The only notable exception to the doctrine of exclusive representation is the employee's right to present grievances directly to the employer without union assistance. When an employee deals directly with the employer, the settlement of the grievance cannot be inconsistent with the terms of the collective bargaining agreement. Furthermore, the employer is under no obligation to meet and confer with individual employees. The employer may refuse to deal directly with individual employee grievances and may insist that they be processed through the grievance procedure. According to the U.S. Supreme Court, to allow one or two employees or a dissident group to promote their special interests directly to the employer would undermine the concept of collective bargaining.[2] Thus, the Court's interpretation of an employee's ability to bypass the contractual grievance procedure is narrow because the doctrine of exclusive representation was designed to protect the union's ability to present a united front.

Employees, as a group, derive bargaining power from their membership in a bargaining unit. Individual membership in a union, *in the absence of employer recognition or NLRB certification*, carries little or no bargaining clout for an employee. Whether an employee is a bargaining unit member depends primarily on his or her job duties and work assignments. An employee working in a bargaining-unit job will generally lose whatever rights have accrued under a collective bargaining agreement if he or she is promoted or transferred to a job that is outside the bargaining unit. An employee who does not work in a bargaining unit may retain union membership, but such membership means little insofar as bargaining power with the employer is concerned. Thus, the key points with regard to the doctrine of exclusive representation and an employee's membership in the bargaining unit are the following:

1. The concept of exclusive representation enables the union to bargain more effectively with the employer and minimizes the problem of divisive factions within the bargaining unit.

---

[1] Bruce Feldacker, *Labor Guide to Labor Law*, 2nd ed. (Reston, Virginia: Reston Publishing Co., Inc., 1983), p. 134.
[2] *Emporium Capwell Co. v. Western Addition Community Organization*, 420 U.S. 50 (1975).

2. The union has a legal duty to represent fairly all bargaining unit employees (discussed in greater detail in Chapter 12).
3. The bargaining power of an individual employee is very limited. Collective bargaining power is obtained through one's membership in the bargaining unit. Bargaining unit membership, in turn, is a function of the employee's job assignment.
4. Individual union membership (through the payment of initiation fees and periodic dues) does not, by itself, create bargaining power for the employee. The key to an employee's bargaining power is membership in the bargaining unit.

The doctrine of exclusive representation and the concept of the bargaining unit are key features in U.S. labor relations. In some instances, the problem of where to draw bargaining unit lines is very difficult to resolve. There are also instances in which the structure of the appropriate bargaining unit becomes a more heated issue than the outcome of the certification election.

This chapter focuses on the importance of the bargaining unit concept. Attention is given to the NLRB criteria used in establishing bargaining units. Some of the more common bargaining unit structures are analyzed along with a discussion of the employee groups who are either excluded from bargaining units or are separated into units by themselves. Finally, the problems associated with bargaining-unit structures in expanding and changing organizations are covered. Selected NLRB cases are presented at the end of the chapter to illustrate the problems and issues that can arise in determining the appropriate bargaining unit structure.

▲ The Importance of the Bargaining Unit Structure

The bargaining unit structure is normally decided prior to the certification election and may therefore have a significant impact on its outcome. Although NLRB proceedings to determine the proper bargaining unit are supposed to be "nonadversarial," they can, in fact, be extremely adversarial. Political observers are well acquainted with the phenomenon of gerrymandering, a practice of arranging voting districts so that one political party gains an advantage in an election. A similar strategy can be employed in a certification election, by either the union or the employer, in an attempt to swing the election in its favor. For example, a union may wish to exclude certain technical workers from bargaining-unit membership, whereas the employer may wish to include them in the unit with unskilled workers. The employer's strategy is to include as many antiunion employees as possible in the election unit in order to increase the likelihood of defeating the union. If the union has reason to believe that the technical employees will vote "no union" in the election, it will try to persuade the NLRB to exclude this subgroup of employees from the election unit. In this case, there is a good chance that the NLRB will grant the union's request. In other cases, the NLRB may not be persuaded to drop or add specific employee groups. Their ruling can conceivably determine which side will emerge from the election victorious.

If the union wins the certification election, then the composition of the bargaining unit will determine which employees will be covered by the ensuing collective bargaining agreement. The composition of the bargaining unit will also determine the bargaining strategies of the union and the employer. A bargaining unit consisting of skilled craft workers in the construction trades will likely present a different set of demands than a group of white-collar clerical employees. Likewise, a unit comprised of unskilled workers will probably desire a different set of contract terms than a group of professional employees.

The composition of the bargaining unit can determine which side possesses superior bargaining power. One of the key determinants of collective bargaining power is a party's ability to withstand a work stoppage. For example, if a bargaining-unit structure in a manufacturing facility included *both* the production workers and employees of the shipping department, then the effect of a strike could be devastating to the employer. Management, in anticipation of an economic strike by production workers, may build up inventory levels in order to continue shipments during the work stoppage. However, a bargaining unit comprised of employees who produce as well as ship the finished product places the company in a precarious position, especially if strike replacements cannot be hired. On the other hand, management is in a better position to withstand an economic strike if the production and shipping departments are in separate bargaining units; normal plant operations could be maintained with fewer strike replacements. Consideration must occasionally be given to the impact of a work stoppage on the general public. A strike that cripples a large firm may pose an inconvenience to the public that could otherwise have been prevented under a different bargaining-unit arrangement.

Once the collective bargaining agreement has been negotiated, the structure of the bargaining unit will determine the ease or difficulty with which the agreement can be administered. A union may become discouraged from organizing a heterogeneous group of employees if it appears that the proposed unit is too diverse to maintain a harmonious relationship among various individuals and groups. Meaningful employee participation and industrial democracy may be hindered if the bargaining unit is too large and diversified. Problems with a union's ability to represent employees fairly, excessive use of the grievance procedure, employee threats of union decertification, and morale problems may result when too many diverse interests must be satisfied. For this reason, the NLRB considers the employees' "community of interest," among other factors, in drawing bargaining unit lines.

Finally, when the NLRB formulates a standard bargaining unit structure for a given industry, such as in the health care industry, the phenomenon of pattern bargaining is more likely to occur. Pattern bargaining is a situation in which the contract settlement in one firm sets the pattern for wages, hours, and working conditions for other firms in the same industry. Pattern bargaining tends to standardize compensation and benefits within an industry and, in some cases, can have an inflationary impact. Thus, the bargaining-unit structure may have important economic implications, especially in industries such as automobile manufacturing, where collective bargaining agreements among the "Big Three" (General Motors, Ford, and Chrysler) cover thousands of workers and affect the price of a major durable good.

This discussion is not intended to impart the notion that large, diverse bar-

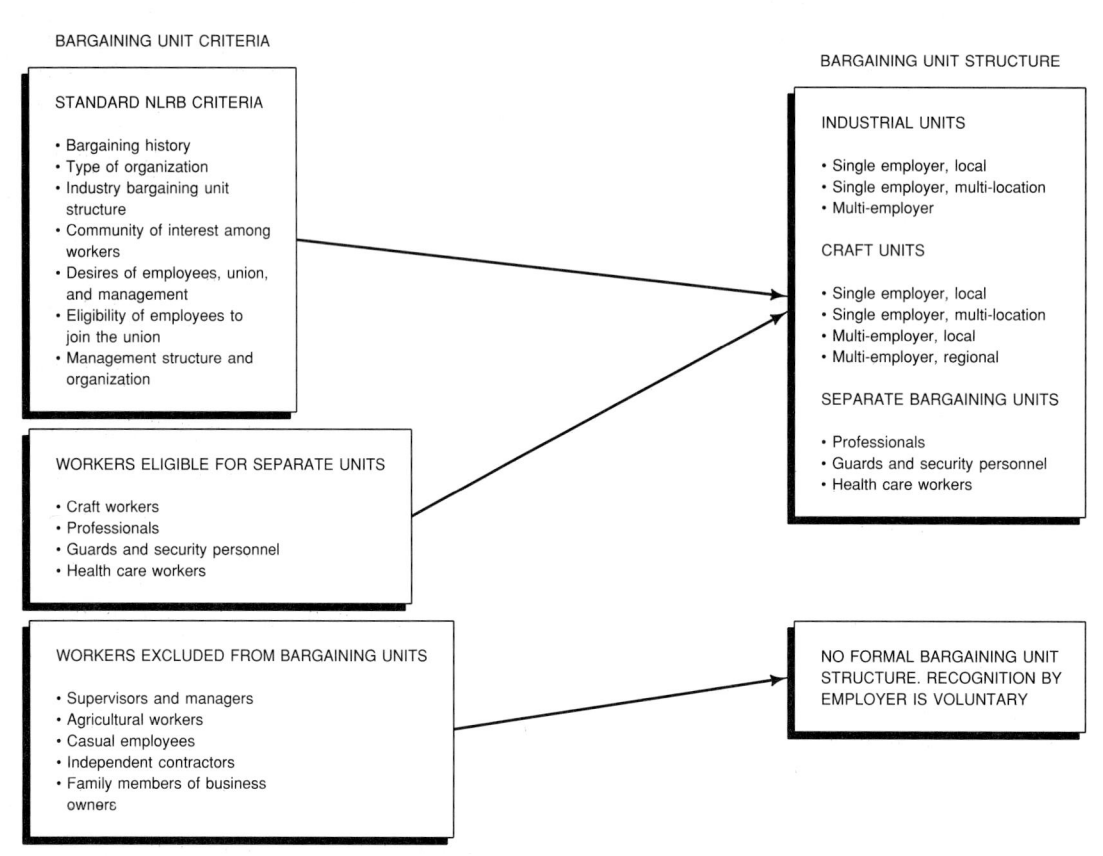

FIGURE 4–1

BARGAINING UNIT CRITERIA

STANDARD NLRB CRITERIA
- Bargaining history
- Type of organization
- Industry bargaining unit structure
- Community of interest among workers
- Desires of employees, union, and management
- Eligibility of employees to join the union
- Management structure and organization

WORKERS ELIGIBLE FOR SEPARATE UNITS
- Craft workers
- Professionals
- Guards and security personnel
- Health care workers

WORKERS EXCLUDED FROM BARGAINING UNITS
- Supervisors and managers
- Agricultural workers
- Casual employees
- Independent contractors
- Family members of business owners

BARGAINING UNIT STRUCTURE

INDUSTRIAL UNITS
- Single employer, local
- Single employer, multi-location
- Multi-employer

CRAFT UNITS
- Single employer, local
- Single employer, multi-location
- Multi-employer, local
- Multi-employer, regional

SEPARATE BARGAINING UNITS
- Professionals
- Guards and security personnel
- Health care workers

NO FORMAL BARGAINING UNIT STRUCTURE. RECOGNITION BY EMPLOYER IS VOLUNTARY

---

gaining units are undesirable. In fact, they may be very practical under certain conditions. The purpose of this segment of the chapter is to illustrate the potential impact that the bargaining unit structure can have on the entire collective bargaining process. Because the bargaining unit is central to collective bargaining, the NLRB devotes a great deal of attention to its proper construction. The following discussion examines the criteria used in determining the appropriate bargaining unit structure. Figure 4–1 summarizes the major factors that shape the composition of bargaining units. Some of these factors have evolved through a long line of NLRB decisions, whereas others are legally mandated under Section 9 of the National Labor Relations Act.

▲ NLRB Criteria for Determining the Appropriate Bargaining Unit

The NLRB is ultimately responsible for establishing the bargaining unit structure. In a large organization containing numerous departments and a variety of employees, the NLRB could conceivably select from a wide range of bargaining-unit options. The bargaining-unit structure has a crucial impact on the climate of labor relations in a particular firm; the determination of the most appropriate unit can involve the consideration of a host of complex factors. If both the employer and the union agree on the appropriateness of a bargaining unit structure, then the NLRB is likely to respect the parties' wishes unless there are overriding reasons for using a different structure. When the parties disagree about the composition of the bargaining unit, the NLRB will attempt to balance the rights of all concerned in constructing the bargaining unit.

Over the years, the NLRB has been involved with thousands of bargaining-unit determinations. In the United States, there are approximately 200,000 bargaining units. A series of guidelines has evolved to provide guidance and ensure a degree of uniformity in decision-making. Seven criteria are currently used by the NLRB to structure bargaining units:[3]

1. *The history, extent, and type of organization of employees in a plant.* Although this factor does not carry a great deal of weight during a unit determination hearing, it may merit consideration in some instances. For example, if a group of employees had previously decertified a labor organization and is now being organized by another union, the NLRB would likely consider the composition of the former unit. If the former unit was plagued with difficulties that stemmed from the unit structure, the NLRB might elect to alter the composition of the new unit. Issues such as the strike history of the previous bargaining unit, problems associated with negotiations and contract administration, and other events associated with the employees' bargaining history may prove helpful in determining the unit structure.

2. *The bargaining unit structure and nature of collective bargaining activities of other workers in the same firm or in the same industry.* To achieve a degree of consistency, the NLRB will attempt to construct bargaining units along similar lines under similar circumstances. For example, the NLRB attempts to standardize hospital bargaining units whenever possible. Industries such as steel and coal mining are characterized by multi-plant and multi-employer bargaining units. The petrochemical industry, on the other hand, contains single-plant units. When certain bargaining unit structures have proven to be workable in specific industries, the NLRB has often continued to use these units.

3. *The skills, wage levels and pay structure, job categories, and working conditions of the employees being organized.* These factors are commonly called the employees' "community of interest," and they carry a great deal of weight. Questions such as whether the employees are subject to the same personnel policies, have common supervision, are paid under similar pay scales or employee benefit programs, work in the same or similar job environments, have similar skill levels and job functions, and perform integrated work tasks are all community-of-interest considerations.

---

[3] Because social and economic conditions affecting the workplace change, it is likely that the NLRB's interpretation of the bargaining-unit criteria and definitions of special employee groups will gradually change. For example, an analysis of the treatment of supervisors and managers reveals considerable variation over the past 40 years. Also see Thomas A. Kochan and Harry C. Katz, *Collective Bargaining and Industrial Relations*, 2nd. ed. (Homewood, Illinois: Richard D. Irwin, Inc., 1988), pp. 102–148, and Benjamin J. Taylor and Fred Witney, *Labor Relations Law*, 5th ed. (Englewood Cliffs, New Jersey: Prentice-Hall, Inc., 1987), pp. 325–365.

4. *The desires of the employees and the union.* If possible, the NLRB will consider the wishes of the employees and the union if the unit is otherwise appropriate and there are no strong objections by the employer. The NLRB will not usually design a bargaining unit that includes only employees who have signed authorization cards while excluding those who have refused to sign. To do so could be detrimental to the interests of the employer and to others who are not in the bargaining unit. Suppose that a group of laboratory technicians in a large private hospital has signed authorization cards, whereas a group of X-ray technicians in the same hospital does not support the union. In this case, the NLRB will likely include the technicians from both departments in the bargaining unit because of their strong community of interest. To define the unit based on authorization card signatures would not only ensure a union victory, but would possibly disrupt the uniformity of the hospital's pay, benefit, and personnel policies. Most hospital administrators would object to a situation such as this and the NLRB would probably respect management's position.
5. *The eligibility of employees for membership in the union(s) involved in the certification proceedings.* The constitution and by-laws of some unions restrict the types of employees who are eligible to join. In a vast majority of instances, a union will avoid bargaining units containing workers who would not be eligible for membership. Occasionally, there are scattered groups of employees who "fall between the cracks" and are not included in any bargaining unit because, among other reasons, they do not qualify for membership in a specific union(s). Employees such as these may be formed into a *residual* bargaining unit. Residual bargaining units often represent a marked departure to the community-of-interest factor discussed earlier. The NLRB allows the creation of residual units, however, because some employees would otherwise have no opportunity to engage in and benefit from the process of collective bargaining.
6. *The relationship between the bargaining unit and the firm's organizational structure, management, and operations.* This factor overlaps somewhat with the community-of-interest factor. The NLRB may consider whether to restrict a bargaining unit to a single plant or allow a multi-plant unit consisting of a geographically dispersed group of employees. Employees who are involved in the same production process that spans several different plants may be included in the same unit because of community-of-interest considerations. Instances arise in which departments containing salaried employees may not be merged with a department consisting primarily of hourly-paid workers. The NLRB may be reluctant to split employees who report to the same supervisor into separate units because such an arrangement is incongruous with the firm's organizational structure.[4]

---

[4] Also see John E. Abodeely, Randi C. Hammer, and Andrew L. Sandler, *The NLRB and the Appropriate Bargaining Unit,* revised ed. (Philadelphia: Industrial Research Unit, The Wharton School, University of Pennsylvania, 1981), pp. 11–83.

▲ The Treatment of Specialized Employee Groups

Some employee groups are treated uniquely under the National Labor Relations Act and are afforded special consideration by the NLRB when bargaining-unit lines are drawn. The first category of employees discussed here (craft workers, professional employees and plant guards) is allowed to form a separate bargaining-unit that consists only of one type of worker. The second category of employees (supervisors and managers, confidential employees, agricultural workers, casual employees, independent contractors, and family members of business owners) receive no protection under the NLRA and, as a result, may find it difficult to unionize.

Employees Who May Warrant Separate Bargaining Units

Craft Workers

Craft workers are individuals who have acquired specialized skills and job knowledge. Persons who work in the construction trades, such as plumbers, carpenters, electricians, and masons, are examples of craft workers. They are usually represented by unions that cater to the needs of a particular craft. Many craft workers develop specialized skills through lengthy and demanding apprenticeship programs, which include both on-the-job and classroom training. In numerous locations throughout the United States, craft workers are employed at hourly rates that are considerably greater than the earnings of their less skilled counterparts; often the wages and benefits for a particular craft are standardized in a metropolitan area.

Because of their uniqueness, craft workers may believe that they have little in common with other workers who are covered under the same bargaining agreement. As a result, they may attempt to establish a separate unit that better represents their special interests. When a group of craft workers desires to break away from an existing unit and form its own bargaining unit, the issue of *craft severance* arises. Over the years, the craft severance problem has generated controversy among labor lawyers, management, and union officials. Questions arise such as: What constitutes a true craft? Under what conditions should a group of employees be granted permission to split from an existing bargaining unit? What impact will severance have on the bargaining power of employees who remain in the original unit and what are the rights of these employees? Some of the controversy and uncertainty surrounding craft severance was addressed in 1966 when the NLRB decided the *Mallinckrodt Chemical Works* case and two related cases.[5] The Board held that it would consider the following factors relevant in craft severance cases:

1. Whether the proposed unit consists of a distinct and homogeneous group of skilled craft workers or a group of employees in a functionally independent department for which a tradition of separate representation exists.

---

[5] *Mallinckrodt Chemical Works*, 64 LRRM 1011 (1966), *Holmberg, Inc.*, 64 LRRM 1025 (1966), and *E.I. du Pont de Nemours & Co.*, 64 LRRM 1021 (1966).

2. The employees' collective bargaining history as well as whether the stability of existing patterns of bargaining will be disrupted as a result of the severance.[6]
3. The extent to which the craft workers in the proposed bargaining unit have established and maintained their separate identity while being part of the broader unit. Along with this, the NLRB will consider the degree to which the craft workers can achieve improved participation and democracy if they form a new unit.
4. The history and pattern of collective bargaining in the industry involved.
5. The degree of integration of the employer's production processes, including the extent to which the employer's normal operations are dependent upon the employees who wish to break from the original unit.
6. The qualifications of the union seeking to establish a separate unit, including the union's experience in representing the type of employees desiring to sever from the unit.

Craft severance cases often occur as the result of organizational or technological changes that increase the number of skilled employees who work in bargaining-unit jobs. Such cases may also arise from poorly conceived bargaining-unit structures and in instances where a group of employees gradually discovers that it possesses a community of interest that is distinct from that of its fellow employees in the bargaining unit. Because of the doctrine established in *Mallinckrodt*, the NLRB has sparingly granted permission to craft workers to sever from the broader unit unless their interests are clearly different from other bargaining unit members. For example, the Board denied a petition for severance of three multi-craft units from the established production and maintenance unit because there was a substantial bargaining history on a plant-wide basis as well as a significant community of interest with other employees.[7] In fact, as a bargaining relationship becomes established, it is likely that the community of interest bonding a group of employees will become stronger and the chances of obtaining severance will decrease. However, severance was granted to a group of furniture sales personnel who desired to separate from a unit comprised of clerical and warehouse employees. The NLRB determined that the sales force was distinct from nonselling employees because they were not subject to the same supervision, spent the majority of their time on the selling floor, received sales commissions, and had little contact with warehouse employees. Based on this evidence, the Board determined that a separate sales unit was appropriate.[8]

Professional and Technical Employees

Professional employees have the option of either remaining in a bargaining unit with nonprofessional employees or forming a separate unit. Unlike with craft workers, who must demonstrate that their severance will not significantly destroy the effectiveness of the original (broader) unit, the NLRB has not required such strin-

---

[6] *National Tube Co.*, 76 NLRB 1199 (1948) and *American Potash & Chemical Corp.*, 107 NLRB 1418 (1954).
[7] *Bendix Corp.*, 94 LRRM 1596 (1977).
[8] *Levitz Furniture*, 92 LRRM 1069 (1976).

gent proof for professional employees. The major question facing professional employees who desire to remain separate from other employees is whether they conform with the definition of a "professional" under Section 2 (12) of the Labor Management Relations Act:

> The term "professional employee" means—(a) any employee in work (i) predominantly intellectual and varied in character as opposed to routine mental, manual, or physical work; (ii) involving the consistent exercise of discretion and judgment in its performance; (iii) of such character that the output produced or the result accomplished cannot be standardized in relation to a given period of time; (iv) requiring knowledge of an advanced type in a field of science or learning customarily acquired by a prolonged course of specialized intellectual instruction and study in an institution or a hospital, as distinguished from a general academic education or from an apprenticeship or from training in the performance of routine mental, manual, or physical processes; or (b) any employee, who (i) has completed the courses of specialized intellectual instruction and study described in clause (iv) of paragraph (a), and (ii) is performing related work under the supervision of a professional person to qualify himself to become a professional employee as defined in paragraph (a).

This definition sets up general standards for professional workers; it is left to the NLRB to decide whether a specific group of employees meets these guidelines and qualifies for a separate professional unit. Because professionals often have different job concerns from nonprofessionals, their employment interests could be subordinated if they were forced to remain in the bargaining unit with other employees. To qualify as a professional under Section 9 (d) of the Act, an employee must be working in a professional capacity. Possessing the credentials of a professional, by itself, does not necessarily warrant a separate unit. For example, a group of teachers who have been hired during the summer months to work as clerks in a resort hotel would not warrant separate consideration for a distinct bargaining unit because the job being performed does not conform to the professional definition set forth above. Routine clerical work does not normally require an advanced knowledge in a field of science nor does it involve predominantly intellectual work of a nonstandard nature.

Although professional work must be sufficiently complex and challenging, a person is not necessarily required to hold a college degree to qualify as a professional. However, technical employees who acquire specialized job knowledge and skills in a technical school, community college, or on the job generally do not qualify as professionals. In deciding whether to include technical employees such as welders, mechanics, or repair personnel in a bargaining unit with other employees, the NLRB will consider factors such as community of interest, bargaining history, and other factors mentioned earlier in this chapter.

The NLRB has considerable latitude in defining professionalism. An examination of Board decisions reveals that some critical *combination* of skills and job complexity appears necessary for attaining professional status. The professional qualifications of an employee are not the sole determinant nor is the complexity of the job always an overriding criterion. Rather, the NLRB examines both the person and the job attributes of a particular group of employees. Despite the guidelines set forth under the NLRA, the NLRB's determination of professional standing is an uncertain and sometimes controversial process. As a result, such decisions are made on a case-by-case basis and are often hard to predict.

The issue of whether a group of professionals will remain in a bargaining unit with nonprofessionals is usually determined during the certification election. First, the NLRB must rule that a subset of employees in the proposed unit constitutes a professional group. If the NLRB decides that the group conforms with the professional definition, the parties proceed with the certification election. The professional group must make two choices when casting its ballots: (1) Do the professionals wish to be included in the broad unit or form a separate unit? and (2) Do the professionals wish to be represented by the union petitioning for certification? If the professional group votes to remain in the larger unit with the nonprofessionals, then the ballots of the professionals are counted as part of the larger unit to determine whether the petitioning union wins the election. Should the professionals elect to form a separate bargaining unit, the majority of votes cast by the professional group only will decide whether the union will represent them. In the latter case, the union may represent employees in two bargaining units if it receives the majority of the votes from both the professional and nonprofessional groups.

Plant Guards and Security Personnel

Plant guards and security personnel enforce rules designed to protect the employer's property and the safety of persons on the company's premises. Section 9 (b)(3) of the Taft-Hartley Act requires that "any individual employed as a guard to enforce against employees and other persons rules to protect property of the employer or to protect the safety of persons on the employer's premises" must be included in a bargaining unit that is separate from other employees. Furthermore, plant guards and security personnel cannot be represented by a union that "admits to membership... employees other than guards." Thus, plant guards are not allowed to be included in a bargaining unit with, for example, production and maintenance employees. The NLRB will only certify as the exclusive bargaining representative those unions that are devoted exclusively to the collective bargaining interests of plant guards.

The rationale for treating plant guards differently under the NLRA is that such individuals have a daily responsibility for the safety of persons and property. Moreover, if they were included in the same bargaining unit with other personnel, a serious conflict of interest could occur during a strike. Work stoppages are occasionally characterized by vandalism and violence; employers have argued that plant guards must remain separate from other employees so that they will be available to protect property if the need arises. By allowing plant guards to be represented only by unions who cater to the needs of security personnel, the probability that a labor organization will be able to exert pressure on a group of plant guards is presumably minimized. For example, suppose that the Teamsters Union represents both a group of plant guards and a group of production workers (in separate bargaining units). If the production workers engaged in an economic strike, then the security of the plant could be jeopardized because of the Teamsters' influence over the guards.

The NLRB has also had to wrestle with the issue of what constitutes a plant guard. Any person, whether armed, uniformed, or deputized, is considered to be a guard if that person's job is to enforce rules to protect the safety of persons or property. Interestingly, this definition includes watchmen whose primary duty is to check for fires rather than enforce company security rules. Production employees who devote one-fourth of their working time to guard or watchmen activities have been regarded as plant guards by the NLRB. Janitors are not deemed to be plant guards even though they have access to production areas, warehouses, and offices and been given the right to limit the access of others to these areas. In 1966, the NLRB held that persons who work on or service electronic surveillance and security devices are not plant guards under the meaning of the Act.[9]

Some critics argue that plant guards have been unfairly restricted and, as a result, have had their collective bargaining power diluted. Plant guards who unionize and engage in collective bargaining generally do not pose a significant strike hazard to their employers because there are relatively few guards in most plants. It is possible to train replacement guards or to employ the services of a private security agency. The plight of plant guards is compounded because they are denied the right to affiliate with mainstream labor unions and the success of guard unions has been limited. As a result of Taft-Hartley restrictions on plant guards, the Supreme Court has stated that the collective bargaining rights of this group are "distinctly second class."[10]

Employees Who are Excluded from Bargaining Units

The preceding section dealt with employee groups who were protected under the National Labor Relations Act, but were required or allowed to form bargaining units that are separate from other employees. This section discusses several categories of employees whose rights to unionize and bargain collectively are not protected under federal law. Supervisors and managers, confidential employees, agricultural workers, casual employees, independent contractors, and relatives of business owners may not enjoy the same protection and bargaining rights as other employee groups. Although employers may recognize and bargain with such groups, they are not required to do so under the NLRA. If employers engage in unfair labor practices against these excluded groups, the employees do not have legal recourse through the National Labor Relations Board.

Supervisors and Managers

The treatment of supervisors and managers under the National Labor Relations Act has long been a subject of controversy. Under the original Wagner Act, supervisors were granted full protection to unionize and engage in collective bargaining. The subsequent passage of the Taft-Hartley Act radically changed the way supervisors were treated. In effect, supervisors were stripped of their protection under the

---

[9] *American District Telegraph Company*, 160 NLRB 1130 (1966).
[10] Benjamin J. Taylor and Fred Witney, *Labor Relations Law*, 5th ed. (Englewood Cliffs, New Jersey: Prentice-Hall, Inc., 1987), p. 354.

NLRA; this effectively negated their ability to engage in meaningful collective bargaining. The rationale of Congress in excluding supervisors from protection under the Act was that their allegiance to management would be impaired if supervisors could both make managerial decisions, yet negotiate with management over wages, hours, and working conditions. Although various interest groups have taken exception to this viewpoint, Congress has withstood pressures to alter the legal status of supervisors since the passage of the Taft-Hartley Act in 1947. The U.S. Constitution, because it allows freedom of association, protects the rights of supervisors to form or join a union. However, the employer has a legal right to refuse to recognize the supervisors' union and may even discharge or discipline supervisors for union activities.

Section 2 (11) of the NLRA defines a supervisor as:

> any individual having authority, in the interest of the employer, to hire, transfer, suspend, lay off, recall, promote, discharge, assign, reward, or discipline other employees, or responsibly to direct them, or to adjust their grievances, or effectively to recommend such action, if ... the exercise of such authority is not of a merely routine or clerical nature, but requires the use of independent judgment.

Although this definition outlines 12 supervisory duties, an employee does not need to perform all of these duties to be regarded as a supervisor under the Act. Furthermore, Section 2 (11) does not require that a supervisor have sole authority to take any of the 12 actions. If an employee's recommendations carry substantial weight in a personnel decision, then the NLRB will likely consider the individual to be a supervisor. For example, most supervisors are allowed to make the final recommendation as to whether an employee should be hired. Likewise, supervisors have traditionally had considerable influence regarding promotion, transfer, lay off, and disciplinary matters affecting employees under their direction.

The advancement of personnel management practices and the concern for controlling hiring, evaluation, and firing decisions has diffused many personnel decisions; supervisors now share these responsibilities with others such as personnel management specialists.[11] Nevertheless, when a person's recommendations on personnel matters carry significant weight, the person is acting in a supervisory capacity. This situation should be contrasted with one in which the employer, prior to taking a personnel action, polls a number of experienced and respected employees to solicit their views regarding a job applicant or employee. Management can either accept or ignore the opinions of these employees in making hiring, firing, or other decisions. Employees whose opinions are solicited prior to a personnel action are generally not regarded as supervisors because no single employee's opinion substantially influences the final decision. It should also be noted that an employee's job title carries little or no weight regarding supervisory status; the employee's authority, duties and responsibilities are the key factors. Otherwise, an astute employer could circumvent the National Labor Relations Act and avoid attendant col-

---

[11] See Leonard A. Schlesinger and Janice A. Klein, "The First-Line Supervisor: Past, Present, and Future," in J. Lorsch, *Handbook of Organizational Behavior* (Englewood Cliffs, New Jersey: Prentice-Hall, Inc., 1984).

lective bargaining obligations by conferring the title of "supervisor" on employees who are targets for union organizers.

Another important consideration in distinguishing between employees who are supervisors and those who are not is the extent to which they exercise independent judgment in their duties. A person who makes a hiring decision is a supervisor. The personnel specialist who informs the job applicant of the hiring decision, completes the paperwork, and instructs the new employee about where to report for orientation or work is not a supervisor under Section 2 (11) because the specialist is merely following a standardized procedure. However, personnel specialists who screen job applicants and reject those who are not suitable, or who otherwise have discretion as to where employees should be placed after hiring may be regarded as supervisors. The same is true for individuals who exercise discretion regarding the distribution of work, vacation time, or placement of employees on various jobs. However, employees who instruct or train other employees in the proper performance of their jobs are not regarded as supervisors unless they also influence hiring, promotion, retention, or other personnel decisions.

The term *supervisor* is normally applied to an individual who spends his or her work time directing the work of others, making job assignments, and influencing personnel actions affecting subordinates. However, there are *managerial employees* who do not supervise others. For example, an assistant to the president of a corporation is clearly a managerial employee, yet such an individual may not directly supervise other employees. Instead, the assistant to the president may serve as an advisor on policy-making matters. Many professional workers serve in a managerial capacity, but not in a supervisory capacity. Earlier in this chapter, it was noted that nonsupervisory professional workers are protected under the National Labor Relations Act. In 1974, the U.S. Supreme Court held that all managerial employees (both supervisory and nonsupervisory) are excluded from the scope of the NLRA.[12] Some employees are regarded as being managerial because their job interests are closely aligned with management. Based on the community of interest factor, the NLRB might decide that an administrative assistant who works closely with a firm's top executives and travels with executives on business trips is not protected under the NLRA.

Another type of managerial employee is a person who is involved in policy-making or decisions that involve discretion and individual judgment in carrying out company policies. A comptroller who formulates and monitors a company's budget would be an example of this type of manager, as would an individual responsible for making decisions on large purchases of supplies and equipment. An interesting U.S. Supreme Court decision involved the issue of whether college professors in a private university should be regarded as managers. The Court reversed an earlier NLRB ruling and held that full-time faculty were managers because they had policy-making authority over admissions standards, curriculum requirements, and other academic matters.[13]

Other professional employees working in a nonsupervisory, nonmanagerial ca-

---

[12] *NLRB v. Bell Aerospace Co.*, 416 U.S. 267 (1974).
[13] *NLRB v. Yeshiva University*, 103 LRRM 2526 (1980).

pacity enjoy the full protection of the National Labor Relations Act. A dilemma is created, however, for employees who serve as supervisors on a part-time basis and perform bargaining unit work at other times. In a situation such as this, the NLRB must make its determination on a case-by-case basis. Does an employee who occasionally serves in a supervisory capacity (when the full-time supervisors are on vacation or sick leave) lose his or her protection under the NLRA? The answer depends on how often the employee performs substitute supervisory work as well as the amount of discretion that the temporary supervisor is allowed. If the employee performs supervisory work at frequent intervals and is given considerable authority to direct the work of others (as opposed to simply following a detailed set of instructions from management), then he or she may be regarded as managerial.[14]

Confidential Employees

Confidential employees have access to crucial or sensitive information that management desires to protect. Employees with knowledge of a firm's production processes, financial dealings, corporate strategic plans, and personnel matters are often regarded as confidential employees. Such individuals are placed in a position of trust; the employer must rely on them not to divulge information that could place the company at a competitive disadvantage or in a precarious legal or financial position. Confidential employees are generally closely aligned with management and may be excluded from protection under the National Labor Relations Act. However, the only confidential employees excluded from protection under the Act are those who are involved with labor relations matters.

Examples of confidential employees who have been excluded under the Act include a secretary to a plant superintendent, personnel department employees, the secretary to a personnel manager, and the secretary of an office manager.[15] To include such confidential employees in the bargaining unit could create a conflict of interest when the union negotiates a collective bargaining agreement with management or administers an existing contract. A confidential employee could be placed in the uncompromising position of being pressured into divulging classified financial or personnel information that the union might find very useful during contract negotiations. By excluding confidential employees from bargaining units, potential industrial espionage problems are minimized.

Employees having access to other types of confidential information that have no bearing on labor-relations policy or activities are not excluded under the NLRA; they retain the right to join a union and bargain collectively. Accounting clerks, production records clerks, payroll clerks, telephone operators, timekeepers, a secretary to an industrial engineering manager, and telephone operators are examples of individuals who are not considered to be confidential employees because they do not work with someone who formulates labor-relations policy. Even employees

---

[14] See James P. Begin and Barbara A. Lee, "NLRA Exclusion Criteria and Professional Work," *Industrial Relations* (Winter 1987), pp. 83–95.
[15] Charles G. Morris, *The Developing Labor Law* (Washington, D.C.: The Bureau of National Affairs, Inc., 1971), p. 217.

working in the personnel department of a plant or corporate headquarters are not necessarily deemed to be confidential employees if they do not work with persons who effectuate personnel policy or have access to sensitive information.

Agricultural Laborers

Agricultural employees are excluded from protection under the National Labor Relations Act. However, not all persons who engage in farming-related work are agricultural employees. For example, an employee who harvests produce in the field is an agricultural employee. But the truck driver who transports the produce to a processing facility may not be an agricultural worker. Likewise, a person who processes the produce at a cannery is likely to be regarded as a commercial rather than an agricultural employee. In 1948, the NLRB established a standard to distinguish between agricultural operations (whose employees are excluded under the Act) and commercial business concerns (whose workers enjoy full legal protection and collective bargaining rights):

> If the practice involved is an integral part of ordinary production or farming operations, and is an essential step before the products can be marketed in normal outlets, it retains its agricultural characteristics. However, if the practice... is adopted in order to add greater value to the farm products, it acquires attributes of a commercial venture.[16]

The U.S. Supreme Court ruled, in 1977, that drivers who delivered poultry feed from their employer's feedmill to independently owned farms were not agricultural laborers and therefore were covered under the NLRA.[17] Along the same lines, the NLRB held that drivers who transported their employer's live poultry from the farm to a meat processing plant were not agricultural employees.[18] However, a dairy farm helper who spent the majority of his working time processing, handling, and delivering milk produced by his employer's farm was regarded as an agricultural employee. The rationale behind this decision was that the helper spent very little time working with commodities produced by other farmers and was not involved in any "value-added" commercial production process.[19]

A major reason for excluding agricultural laborers from protection under the NLRA is because of the seasonal and transient nature of their work. The plight of the migrant farm worker has received nationwide attention due primarily to the efforts of Cesar Chavez in California. Several states have passed laws to permit meaningful collective bargaining for agricultural workers. The most publicized state law is the 1975 California statute that establishes the procedures for certification elections and permits strikes during the harvest season, when work stoppages would have their most profound effect. However, agricultural workers in over 40 states do not receive any legal protection with regard to joining a union or bargaining collectively.

---

[16] *Di Giorgio Fruit Corp.*, 23 LRRM 1188 (1948).
[17] *Bayside Enterprise, Inc.*, 94 LRRM 2199 (1977).
[18] *Valmac Industries, Inc.*, 99 LRRM 1193 (1978).
[19] *NLRB v. Karl's Farm Dairy, Inc.*, 92 LRRM 1334 (1978).

Part-Time, Dual-Status, and Seasonal Employees

Part-time employees are included in bargaining units and receive protection under the National Labor Relations Act, whereas *casual employees* are generally excluded. If a part-time employee possesses a community of interest with other bargaining unit employees and works on a regular basis (for example, the employee works one evening per week and all day on Saturdays), then this individual will be included in the unit. Casual employees are scheduled to work on an "as needed" or intermittent basis. The NLRB may distinguish between part-time and casual employees by the number of hours worked. In a case involving a group of department store employees, the NLRB decided that those who worked at least 15 days during a 90-day period were regarded as part-time employees and could be included in the bargaining unit.[20] Seasonal workers, such as college students who are employed on summer jobs, may be included in a bargaining unit if there is a reasonable expectation of continued employment from one season to the next. For example, a cement plant hired a group of college students for summer employment. The student group was employed on a full-time basis for three summers and was included in the bargaining unit.

Dual-status employees work part time in the bargaining unit and spend the remainder of their work time in a job outside the unit. The difference between a part-time employee and a dual-status employee is that the latter works full time. A person who spends three working days per week in an office doing clerical work and two days outside making sales calls is an example of a dual-status employee. The NLRB has held that dual status employees must have a sufficient interest in conditions of employment in the bargaining unit in order to make their inclusion meaningful.[21] A grocery store employee who spent the majority of her time working in the produce department and a shorter amount of time in the meat department was excluded from membership in the latter bargaining unit because she did not have a sufficient community of interest with the meatcutters.[22] A different position was taken with respect to an employee who spent approximately 20 percent of his working time with dock workers and local drivers. In this case, the employee was included in the unit of drivers and dock workers because the employee shared a community of interest with this group based on duties, compensation, benefits, and working conditions.[23] A special case of the dual-status employee includes individuals known as driver-sales personnel. Persons who sell and deliver products to retail establishments often drive vans or trucks. Should such individuals be included in the same bargaining unit with truckers who drive company vehicles on a full-time basis? The answer is generally no, unless a community of interest between driver-sales personnel and professional drivers can be demonstrated.

---

[20] *Scoa, Inc.*, 52 LRRM 1244 (1963).
[21] *Berea Publishing Co.*, 52 LRRM 1051 (1963).
[22] *Bonanno Family Foods, Inc.*, 95 LRRM 1330 (1977).
[23] *NLRB v. Georgia, Florida, and Alabama Transportation Co.*, 97 LRRM 2500 (1978).

Independent Contractors

Independent contractors are excluded from protection under the National Labor Relations Act. As is the case with other excluded employees, issues arise as to whether certain employees should be regarded as independent contractors. An independent contractor is normally hired to perform a specific job and the employer does not attempt to control how the work is completed. For example, newspaper carriers, professional movers who own and operate vans and equipment under the auspices of a nationwide moving company, free-lance photographers, and sales personnel may be regarded as independent contractors. The NLRB and courts use the "right to control" test to determine whether individuals are employees or independent contractors. According to a Congressional report, independent contractors are defined as follows:

> "Independent contractors" undertake to do a job for a price, decide how the work will be done, usually hire others to do the work, and depend for their income not upon wages, but upon the difference between what they pay for goods ... and labor and what they receive for the end result, that is, upon profits.[24]

Persons whose work is directed by others, receive a salary or wage for services performed, and are not normally responsible for procuring materials needed to perform a job are likely to be regarded as employees entitled to protection under the NLRA. For example, a painter employed by a general contractor to paint the interior walls in an apartment complex would be regarded as an employee if the contractor established the schedule, work specifications, materials, and labor requirements for the job. If the painter were responsible for the above requirements, then he or she would likely be considered as an independent contractor unless employed routinely and exclusively by the general contractor. Some employers attempt to consider nearly all of their "employees" as independent contractors in order to avoid paying Social Security, workers' compensation, or other legally mandated benefits. However, the "right to control" test is the key consideration and the NLRB has stated that it will "carefully balance all factors bearing on the relationship" before deciding whether an individual meets the definition of an independent contractor.[25]

Individuals Employed by A Parent or Spouse

Because of the potential conflict of interest involved, individuals employed by their parents or spouse are excluded from protection under federal labor law. The NLRB also excludes the children and spouses of persons who hold a substantial stock interest in a corporation in which all corporate stock is held by a group of individuals or a family and is not traded on the stock market. As a general rule, the NLRB applies the rule primarily to members of the company owner's or stockholder's

---

[24] Charles G. Morris, *The Developing Labor Law* (Washington, D.C.: The Bureau of National Affairs, Inc., 1971) p. 207.
[25] *National Freight, Inc.*, 55 LRRM 1259 (1964).

immediate family. However, other family members, such as in-laws or cousins, may be excluded if they enjoy a privileged relationship with management.

A key point with regard to the employment of children or a spouse is the element of ownership. Ownership may be based on a sole proprietorship, partnership, or by the control of a majority of the corporate stock. Immediate or close family members of a company's owner are excluded from protection under the NLRA, but the spouse or child of a nonowner manager is covered under the Act. For example, the wife of a company manager "who is not at all an owner" was held eligible to vote in a union representation election.[26]

▲ Some Common Bargaining Unit Structures

The preceding discussion illustrates the importance of as well as the problems associated with determining the bargaining unit structure. In the United States, a variety of bargaining units exist and the National Labor Relations Board must attempt to balance the diverse interests of employers, workers, and labor organizations as they construct the appropriate unit. As noted earlier, bargaining units can be classified along a number of lines, such as craft units, industrial units, multi-plant units, and multi-employer units; they may range in size from fewer than five to over 1,000 members. A bargaining unit may include only workers of a specific craft or it may be an industrial unit containing both skilled and unskilled employees. Some bargaining units are confined to a single department within a large organization. Other units are broader and include all nonsupervisory employees who work in a plant. The broadest bargaining units are multi-plant or multi-employer units that cover a geographically dispersed group of workers.

Although a multitude of bargaining units exist, there are three basic dimensions that can be used to classify bargaining unit structures. First, bargaining units can be classified by *size*. Second, bargaining units vary by their *heterogeneity of membership*; craft units are homogeneous units, whereas industrial units are heterogeneous. Third, bargaining units can be distinguished by their *degree of centralization or decentralization*. For example, a bargaining unit comprised of 30 laborers employed by a small tool and die firm represents a decentralized bargaining unit structure; the laborers negotiate a collective bargaining agreement with the owners of the local firm. A more centralized structure would be one covering employees who work at several different plants owned by the same company. The most centralized bargaining unit is one covering workers employed by different companies within the same industry; the underground coal mining industry is characterized by bargaining units that are built along multi-employer lines. Small mining operations that normally compete with one another unite and bargain with the powerful United Mine Workers.

---

[26] *Pargas of Crescent City*, 78 LRRM 1712 (1971).

Single-Employer, Single-Location Units

One of the most decentralized or "localized" bargaining unit structures is the single-employer, single-location bargaining unit. A single location may be a plant, university, or department. Single-employer bargaining units may be homogeneous in nature (e.g., a group of registered nurses employed by a private community hospital) or heterogeneous (e.g., all production, maintenance, and general labor workers in a cement plant). Single-employer, single-location units are commonly found in the petrochemical, electrical machinery, ordinance, textile, and paper manufacturing industries. In fact, this type of bargaining unit is most commonly found in the manufacturing sector.[27]

Single-employer, single-location bargaining units pose certain advantages and disadvantages for effective collective bargaining. A major advantage is that the employees in such bargaining units may have more direct input into contract negotiations and administration of the collective bargaining agreement. Labor agreements can be tailored to the desires of a specific group of workers who may believe that the union has a better understanding of local concerns in a plant or department. However, single-location bargaining units may also become overly fragmented and specialized. When this occurs, the employer is forced to deal with a multitude of dissimilar units and conflicting local political interests. Such a climate not only decreases the quality of labor relations, but may also dilute the bargaining power of the employees and make them more vulnerable to technological and organizational changes. For example, the suspension of a product line in a manufacturing

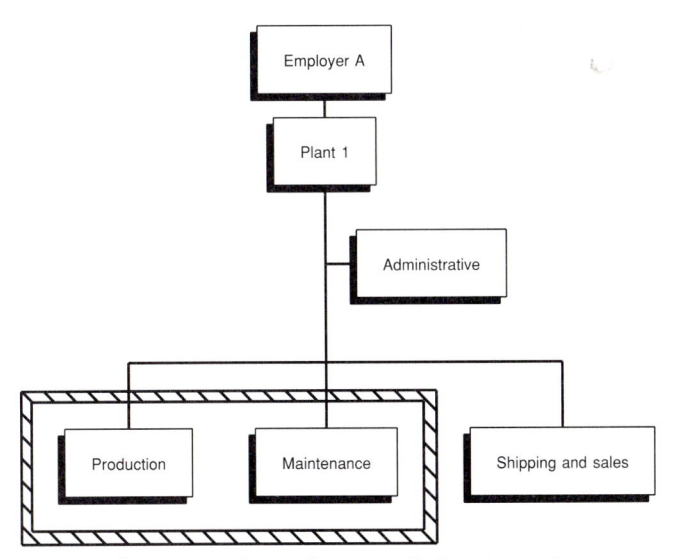

FIGURE 4–2A. Single employer, single location unit.

---

[27] Thomas A. Kochan and Harry C. Katz, *Collective Bargaining and Industrial Relations*, 2nd. ed. (Homewood, Illinois: Richard D. Irwin, Inc., 1988), p. 122.

facility could conceivably eliminate the need for an entire bargaining unit of employees who worked exclusively with that product line.

The railroads were a prime example of an industry plagued by a large number of fragmented bargaining units. At one time, the Consolidated Rail Corporation (CONRAIL) had to deal with 286 different collective bargaining agreements.[28] Although the number of agreements was later reduced, such an arrangement often creates a multitude of restrictive work rules, intensifies jurisdictional rivalries between unions, and increases the probability that the job skills of employees may be rendered obsolete because of technological changes. The latter characterized the plight of the railroad fireman whose job duties were nearly eliminated with the widespread introduction of electromotive diesel engines.

Decentralized, single-location bargaining units may also create imbalances in the bargaining power between employees and management, especially when employees can be easily replaced because of their meager job skills. Labor difficulties in a small bargaining unit may also have the opposite effect if the employees involved have specialized job skills that prevent easy replacement by management during a strike. Suppose that a group of hospital maintenance workers calls a strike. A hospital administrator could conceivably find strike replacements for a number of the less skilled maintenance or clerical employees, but it would be much more difficult to replace technical and professional workers.[29] Furthermore, inequities in the employment conditions of different workers may occur when there are multiple bargaining units within a single organization. If the production and maintenance employees have access to a grievance procedure while the technical employees do not, morale in the workplace may suffer. Finally, when management is forced to deal with numerous collective bargaining agreements, it is distracted from other managerial duties and obligations that are important to the survival and growth of the organization.

Single-Employer, Multi-Location Units

A more centralized bargaining-unit structure is one that covers multiple plants, stores, or offices owned by the same employer. Under the single-employer, multi-location bargaining unit, one collective bargaining agreement covers employees who work at different geographical sites. Before creating a multi-location bargaining unit, the National Labor Relations Board considers factors such as the integration of production facilities between plants, the degree of employee interchange, the geographical separation between the facilities, and the bargaining history of the employer. Single-employer, multi-location units are common in industries associated with automobiles, communications, rubber, and public utilities.[30]

---

[28] William F. Glueck and Lawrence R. Jauch, *Business Policy and Strategic Management*, 4th ed. (New York: McGraw-Hill Book Company, 1984), p. 795.

[29] Maintenance employees are regarded as "other nonprofessional employees" under the 1989 NLRB bargaining unit guidelines for health care institutions. See, The Bureau of National Affairs, Inc., "Health Care Bargaining Units Proposed," *Bulletin to Management* (Washington, D.C.: The Bureau of National Affairs, Inc., September 15, 1988), p. 296.

[30] Thomas A. Kochan and Harry C. Katz, *Collective Bargaining and Industrial Relations*, 2nd ed. (Homewood, Illinois: Richard D. Irwin, Inc., 1988) p. 121.

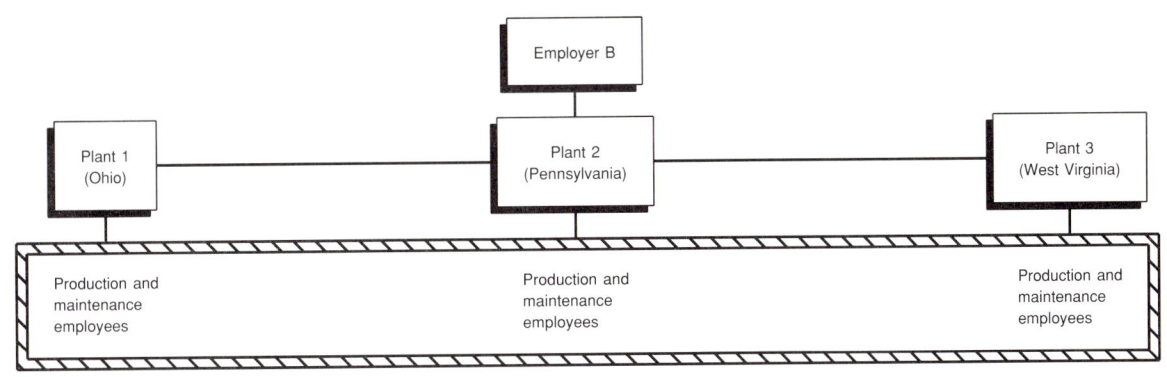

FIGURE 4–2B. Single employer, multi-location unit.

Multi-location units are most appropriate when there is a strong community of interest among employees at different plants, offices, or stores owned by a single firm. Uniform pay scales, employee benefits, job descriptions, and production and service facilities make the use of multi-plant bargaining units more feasible. For example, suppose that a retail food chain owns and operates 50 stores in a particular state. If the stores are similar in character with respect to merchandise sold, hours of operation, work duties of the employees, and pay and benefits, then a multi-store unit may be appropriate. Likewise, the U.S. Court of Appeals held that a multi-office bargaining unit was appropriate because the company maintained a centrally-determined labor policy, close supervision of employees from a district office, and uniform working conditions throughout the district.[31] However, the NLRB decided that a textile firm that operated two mills 20 miles apart should not form a multi-plant unit. The Board determined that a bargaining unit of one textile mill was appropriate. The NLRB based its decision on the degree of autonomy of the plant that the union petitioned to represent, the lack of employee interchange between the two plants, the geographical separation of the facilities, the absence of any bargaining history, and the fact that no union sought to represent a multi-plant unit.[32]

Centralized, multi-locational bargaining units allow the standardization of compensation and employee benefit programs within the same firm. A master collective bargaining agreement may be negotiated covering all production and maintenance workers employed by a manufacturer who operates plants in several different Midwest and Southeastern states. Such a master agreement would typically contain a standard wage scale, plant-wide seniority system, grievance procedure, and layoff policy, to name a few provisions. Local agreements may be negotiated to supplement the master contract and tailor it to local conditions. For example, employees working at a plant in Michigan may need a provision in the collective bargaining agreement that provides for compensation lost due to inclement winter weather, whereas their counterparts in New Orleans would have little need for such a provision.

---

[31] *NLRB v. Pinkerton's Inc.*, 74 LRRM 2355 (1970).
[32] *Dixie Belle Mills, Inc.*, 51 LRRM 1344 (1962).

However, workers in New Orleans would probably demand a holiday provision for the Mardi Gras celebration, an event of little interest to the firm's Michigan employees.

The multi-locational bargaining unit takes much of the collective bargaining power away from local plant and union officials and places it in the hands of full-time professional negotiators and administrators. Responsibility for negotiating and administering a master collective bargaining agreement is given to the international or national union officials and the company's vice-president for personnel or industrial relations. Generally speaking, the degree of sophistication, professionalism, and sense of responsibility is greater for these individuals than it is for local officials who may get emotionally involved in issues at a particular plant and take an overly narrow view of the bargaining process. Although most local union and management officials are well-informed and responsible administrators, the level of expertise needed to negotiate a complex collective bargaining agreement is more likely to be found among international union representatives and top management officials.

Multi-location bargaining units offer the advantages of standardizing personnel policies throughout a firm and providing greater responsibility and sophistication at the bargaining table. However, there are two significant drawbacks to this bargaining structure. First, intraorganizational conflicts may occur, especially if there are differences in the community of employee interests at various locations. Workers at one plant may not ratify or otherwise support a master collective bargaining agreement if they believe that it does not serve their interests or if local union officials have incited discontent among employees. Likewise, employees in one plant may elect not to support a strike called by a union, thereby creating a chasm in worker unity that could damage the union's bargaining power.

A second problem associated with multi-location bargaining units is the devastating impact that a strike can have on a company. Employers faced with a work stoppage at one plant can often transfer work to other locations and avoid major disruptions to production, shipping, and sales. However, when work stoppages occur simultaneously at a number of facilities owned by a single employer, they can have a crippling effect on the firm and may cause irreparable damage to its competitive position.

Multi-Employer Bargaining Units

The most centralized bargaining unit structure is the multi-employer unit. Under this arrangement, a group of firms within the same industry join together and negotiate a common collective bargaining agreement. For example, a group of general contractors in the construction industry may band together and bargain with the carpenters' union. The collective bargaining agreement negotiated between the general contractors and the union might cover a dozen firms within a metropolitan area. Other examples of multi-employer bargaining can be found in the coal mining, trucking, garment, retail trade, and hotel industries.

Many multi-employer bargaining units involve small firms that deal with large and powerful unions. Several small, competing trucking firms may join forces in order to present a united front when negotiating with the Teamsters Union. Simi-

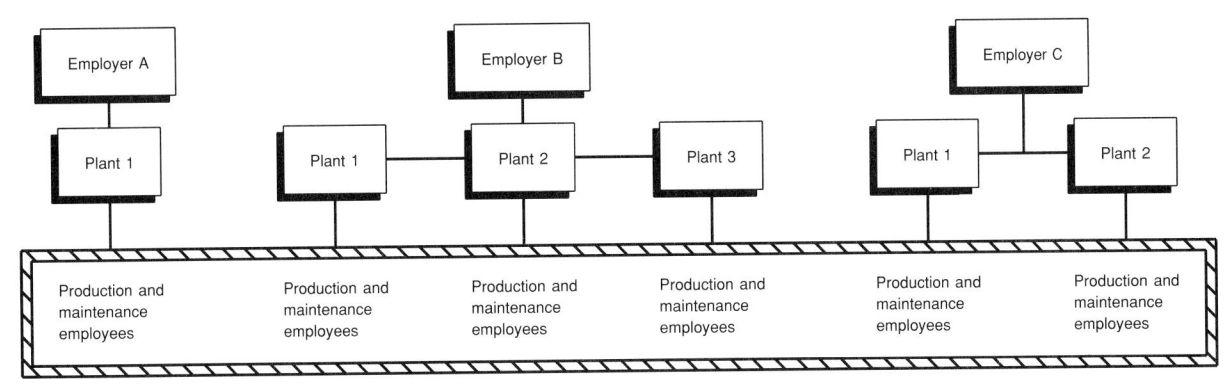

FIGURE 4–2C. Multi-employer unit.

larly, a group of coal operators may form a regional association and negotiate with the United Mine Workers. Although these firms are competitors, they feel that it is to their advantage to establish a common collective bargaining agreement with the union. By so doing, they standardize labor costs throughout a segment of the industry. Firms that unite their bargaining efforts will continue to compete with regard to factors other than labor costs. For example, trucking firms with the same wage and benefit structure can still compete on the basis of delivery speed, reliability, and other services.

Unlike other bargaining units, the multi-employer unit is based primarily on the consent of the firms involved. Companies that elect to join a multi-employer unit must adhere to the terms and conditions of the bargaining agreement regardless of the impact that such an agreement may have on one firm. If, for example, a financially weak firm is part of a multi-employer unit and cannot meet the wage obligations imposed by the collective bargaining agreement, it is not relieved of these obligations and may be forced into insolvency. What if a majority of the employees of a single firm in the unit no longer desire to be represented by the union? Does this relieve the firm of its bargaining obligations in the multi-employer unit? The answer to this question is usually no.[33] Thus, a company's participation in a multi-employer unit should be considered carefully. However, employers may opt to sever relations with a multi-employer unit after the collective bargaining agreement has expired.[34]

Multi-employer bargaining unit structures eliminate the need for multiple collective bargaining agreements in an industry and, as mentioned earlier, allow smaller firms to bargain on a more equal footing with the larger unions. Large and powerful unions are less likely to isolate small companies and threaten to strike and shut down their operations unless they acquiesce to the union's demands. Small firms could be vulnerable to such divide-and-conquer tactics, without a multi-employer

---

[33] *Retail Associates, Inc.*, 120 NLRB 395 (1958).
[34] Charles J. Morris, *The Developing Labor Law* (Washington, D.C.: The Bureau of National Affairs, Inc., 1971), pp. 241–244. Withdrawal from a multi-employer bargaining unit must be both timely and unequivocal.

unit. Once the union obtained wage and other concessions from one firm, it could then isolate the next firm and attempt the same tactic. Multi-employer bargaining units also allow small firms to pool their resources and obtain the services of professional negotiators who are knowledgeable about contract provisions and bargaining tactics. It is also possible that cost savings on employee benefit packages such as group life and health insurance can be obtained through multi-employer bargaining arrangements because of pooled administrative costs and economies of scale.

There are several problems associated with multi-employer bargaining units. First, bargaining may be more difficult if the firms within the unit vary in terms of size, products made, customers served, and financial condition. Outside of the collective bargaining context, these companies are still competitors and it is inevitable that some competition will surface at the bargaining table. During negotiations, financially strong firms may seize the opportunity to impose onerous wage- and employee-benefit structures on their less affluent industry competitors. Problems of contract administration may also arise as an attempt is made to apply a uniform collective bargaining agreement to several firms whose modes of operation and organizational culture differ. Professional negotiators hired from the outside as well as managers hired to police the agreement for all firms in the multi-employer unit may reduce these problems. A second major problem confronting multi-employer bargaining units is the widespread impact of work stoppages. An economic strike can cripple a significant segment of an industry and have a detrimental impact on the economy. This problem has arisen in the transportation industry, especially trucking, and can pose an inconvenience to the public.

Coordinated Bargaining

Occasionally two or more unions will band together in what is known as coordinated bargaining in order to negotiate with a large and powerful employer. Coordinated bargaining uses the same rationale of "equalizing bargaining power" that is found in multi-employer bargaining arrangements. For example, two unions, the Communications Workers of America (CWA) and the International Brotherhood of Electrical Workers (IBEW), agreed to coordinate bargaining with the American Telephone & Telegraph Company (AT&T) in 1989. The agreement is intended to help the unions avoid a repeat of the 1986 round of bargaining when 155,000 employees represented by the CWA struck for three weeks while the IBEW's 41,000 members reached an agreement and stayed on the job. The two unions agreed to identify national bargaining goals and then co-chair common bargaining tables for negotiations with AT&T.[35]

In an effort to avoid an erosion in bargaining power, six major unions agreed to develop a strategy for coordinated bargaining with newspaper industry employers. The Newspaper Guild, Graphic Communications Union, Communications

---

[35] The Bureau of National Affairs, Inc., "CWA-IBEW Coordinated Negotiating Program," *Collective Bargaining Negotiations & Contracts* (Washington, D.C.: The Bureau of National Affairs, Inc., January 28, 1988), p. 2.

Workers, Teamsters, Service Employees, and Machinists unions agreed to appoint staff members to a task force to work out a program for joint negotiations.[36]

▲ Bargaining Units In Expanding Organizations

Organizations are dynamic entities. Some businesses capitalize on growing consumer demand by increasing production and sales of their goods and services. Other organizations diversify and add new products and services to existing lines. Each year many firms expand through corporate mergers and acquisitions. Corporate growth leads to the addition of new production facilities, offices, plants, warehouses, and employees. In declining industries, firms are forced to retrench and delete product lines, close facilities, and sell all or part of a business to other corporations.[37]

Organizational changes create two major bargaining unit issues. First, the addition of employees may result in *bargaining-unit accretions.* Bargaining-unit accretions raise the question of whether to include the new employees in the original bargaining unit. If these employees are excluded from the original unit, then what procedure is available in the event that the new employees desire union representation? A second issue that may arise concerns *successorship employers.* The ownership, control, and character of a firm can change radically in the event that one firm is acquired by or merges with another. If a unionized company is purchased by another company, then what happens to the collective bargaining rights of the employees? Is the firm legally obligated to honor a bargaining-unit structure and collective bargaining agreement that was negotiated by another firm? If so, under what circumstances is an acquiring firm required to recognize a previously established exclusive bargaining representative?

Accretions to the Bargaining Unit

As a company grows and adds new employees, the issue of bargaining-unit accretions arises. When new employees are added to an existing bargaining unit, these individuals are automatically included in the unit regardless of their desires regarding union representation. For example, if a bargaining unit originally contained 200 production and maintenance employees and the company gradually has added 50 production workers to the unit over a two-year period, then the additional employees are included in the original unit. If a legal union security agreement is in effect, these employees would also be required to join the union. In this situation, the NLRB assumes that the 50 new production workers have the same community of interest as the original 200 production and maintenance workers.

The accretion issue becomes more complex when it appears that the community of interest between the employees of the original unit and the new em-

---

[36] The Bureau of National Affairs, Inc., *Collective Bargaining Negotiations & Contracts* (Washington, D.C.: The Bureau of National Affairs, Inc., March 26, 1987), p. 3.
[37] A *unit clarification petition* may be filed by a union or employer when the parties dispute a certain job classification or when additional employees have been added to the bargaining unit.

ployees differs. Suppose that a group of maintenance technicians are hired to service a firm's recently installed computer system. The employer may believe that employees hired to perform computer maintenance duties differ from those who work on other types of production machinery. Under these circumstances, the employer can file a clarification petition with the NLRB and request that they determine whether the computer maintenance workers possess a community of interest with other maintenance employees. If the NLRB rules that the community of interest does exist, then the computer maintenance technicians are added to the original bargaining unit and are not given the right to form a separate unit and vote in a certification election. Should the NLRB decide that the computer technicians possess a community of interest that is distinct from that of other maintenance workers, then any union desiring to represent this group must go through the complete certification process.

When a company establishes a new operation or facility, a question may arise as to whether the employees at the new facility are an accretion or a separate bargaining unit. A union representing a firm's employees may press to represent employees at the new facility automatically and may desire to extend the current collective bargaining agreement to these employees. By automatically gaining representation rights to the employees in the new facility, the union does not have to spend time and money on an organizational campaign, cope with the uncertainty of a certification election, or deal with a rival union that is also interested in organizing these employees. The United Auto Workers and General Motors agreed to such an arrangement in 1979. When GM opened a new plant that involved work traditionally performed by UAW members, GM agreed to an "accretion clause" that automatically included employees at the new facility in the bargaining unit.[38] In resolving such issues, the NLRB considers such factors as whether the new employees are separated physically or geographically from employees in the original unit, and whether they share the same supervision and have the same pay scales, hours, and working conditions.[39]

Successorship Employers

When two or more companies complete a merger or acquisition, the corporate identity of one employer is eliminated and a *successorship employer* is created. For example, if Company A is purchased by Company B, then Company B is the successorship employer and Company A is the predecessor. Or, Companies A and B may merge and create a new firm, Company C, which is a successorship employer. Because mergers, buy-outs, and corporate acquisitions are commonplace, the issue of what happens to the collective bargaining rights of employees who are caught up in these transactions is important. The U.S. Supreme Court, in the *Burns International Security Services, Inc.* case, outlined the following rights of predecessor

---

[38] See Thomas A. Kochan and Harry C. Katz, *Collective Bargaining and Industrial Relations*, 2nd ed. (Homewood, Illinois: Richard D. Irwin, Inc., 1988), pp. 118–119.
[39] *Consolidated Edison Co.*, 48 LRRM 1539 (1961), *Essex Wire Corp.*, 47 LRRM 1369 (1961), and *Texlite, Inc.*, 46 LRRM 1014 (1960).

employees, unions, and collective bargaining agreements involved in successorship situations:[40]

1. A successor employer is not obligated to accept the collective bargaining agreement established between the predecessor employer and the union.
2. The successor employer is under no obligation to hire employees of the predecessor firm. However, if the successor employer elects to hire the employees of the predecessor firm, then the hiring decisions cannot be influenced by an employee's previous union membership.
3. The successor employer is obligated to bargain with the union only if a majority of the successor's workforce is comprised of bargaining-unit employees from the predecessor firm. In addition, it is assumed that the successor employer is remaining in the same essential business as the predecessor. If the successor employer has maintained a substantial continuity of business operations, uses the same plant and equipment, and employs the same workforce under similar working conditions, then it is likely that the bargaining obligations established by the predecessor employer carry over to the successor.
4. Since the successor employer is not obligated to accept the terms and conditions of the predecessor's collective bargaining agreement, it has the right to establish a new set of wages, hours, and working conditions immediately upon assuming control of the predecessor's operations.[41] Thus, a successor may offer to hire employees of the predecessor at lower wage rates and with fewer benefits. Once the initial wages, hours, and working conditions are established, the successor is obligated to negotiate any further changes with the union. However, firms that go out of business and then re-open under a different name (but with the same management and line of business) cannot dodge obligations created by prior collective bargaining agreements. Such companies are known as *alter ego* employers and are not viewed in the same light as successorship employers.

Thus, a corporate realignment does not necessarily mean that the bargaining unit or the bargaining rights of the employees will be destroyed. If, however, the successor employer does not rehire the predecessor's employees or totally eliminates the predecessor's operations, then the bargaining unit will be eliminated and any subsequent collective bargaining will involve an entirely new certification campaign and an NLRB election.[42]

---

[40] *Burns International Security Services, Inc.*, 74 LRRM 1098 (1970). Also see Bruce Feldacker, *Labor Guide to Labor Law*, 2nd ed., (Reston, Virginia: Reston Publishing Company, 1983) pp. 196–199 and Charles J. Morris, ed., *The Developing Labor Law* (Washington, D.C.: The Bureau of National Affairs, Inc., 1971), pp. 359–372.

[41] In a 1987 U. S. Supreme Court decision, *Fall River Dyeing v. NLRB*, 107 S. Ct. 2225 (1987), it was held that three factors must be present for the successorship doctrine to apply: "(1) There is 'substantial continuity' in the new business operations of the new employer and the predecessor; (2) The bargaining unit remains appropriate after the change of employers; and (3) The predecessor employed a majority of the new employer's workers." In Robert F. Mace, "The Supreme Court's Labor Law Successorship Doctrine After *Fall River Dyeing*," *Labor Law Journal* (February 1988), reprinted in Craig T. Norback, ed. *The Human Resources Yearbook, 1989 Edition* (Englewood Cliffs, New Jersey: Prentice-Hall, Inc., 1989), p. 8.16.

[42] For a discussion of NLRB rulings on successorship obligations, see Betty Southard Murphy, Wayne E. Barlow, and D. Diane Hatch, "Successorship and Labor Obligations," *Personnel Journal* (November 1985), p. 26.

▲ Presumptively Appropriate Bargaining Units

Although the NLRB has delineated a number of factors that make the formulation of a bargaining unit somewhat easier, the case-by-case task of analyzing the relevant unit criteria can be difficult and time consuming. As a result, the NLRB has established a series of commonly accepted units for a number of industries known as *presumptively appropriate units*. As the name implies, the NLRB *presumes* that one bargaining unit structure will best serve the needs and community of interest for employees in a particular industry. For example, the NLRB favors eight different bargaining units for employees of health care institutions:[43]

1. registered nurses;
2. physicians;
3. other professionals, except for registered nurses and physicians;[44]
4. technical employees (medical laboratory, respiratory therapy, radiography, emergency medicine, and licensed practical nurses);
5. skilled maintenance employees;
6. business office clerical employees;
7. security guards; and
8. other nonprofessional employees.[45]

In automobile agencies, the appropriate unit will separate sales and office employees from service department employees.[46] As noted earlier, the NLRB has traditionally permitted employees in the construction trades to draw bargaining unit lines based on different crafts. The appropriate unit for department store employees includes both sales and nonsales personnel.[47] The NLRB has held that any unit of U.S. Postal Service employees that is "less-than-nationwide" in scope is not appropriate unless it encompasses all employees within a "district or sectional center."[48] Likewise, the NLRB favors a fleet-wide bargaining unit in the shipping industry and a system-wide unit for public utilities.[49]

The NLRB is willing to make exceptions to presumptively appropriate bargaining units if the employer or union can demonstrate that another unit would be more workable. Factors such as a company's unique organizational structure or a lack of the usual community of interest among a group of employees can influence

---

[43] The Bureau of National Affairs, Inc., "NLRB Health Care Unit Rules," *Collective Bargaining Negotiations & Contracts* (Washington, D.C.: The Bureau of National Affairs, Inc., September 8, 1988), p. 4, and The Bureau of National Affairs, Inc., "Health Care Bargaining Units Proposed," *Bulletin to Management* (Washington, D.C.: The Bureau of National Affairs, Inc., September 15, 1988), p. 296.

[44] See Barbara A. Lee and Joan Parker, "Supervisory Participation in Professional Associations: Implications of *North Shore University Hospital*," *Industrial and Labor Relations Review* (April 1987), pp. 364–381.

[45] See Thomas P. Brown, IV, "Appropriate Bargaining Units in Health-Care Institutions: The Disparity of Interests Test," *Employee Relations Law Journal* (Spring 1985), pp. 717–722, and John G. Kilgour, "The Health-Care Bargaining Unit Controversy: Community of Interest Versus Disparity of Interest," *Labor Law Journal* (February 1989), pp. 81–93.

[46] *Babb Motors*, 34 LRRM 1148 (1954).

[47] *Retail Store Union v. NLRB*, 66 LRRM (1967).

[48] *U.S. Postal Service*, 85 LRRM 1212 (1974).

[49] *Moore-McCormack Lines, Inc.*, 51 LRRM 1361 (1962) and *Pacific Gas & Electric Co.*, 29 LRRM 1256 (1952).

the NLRB to deviate from its standard unit. In drawing bargaining unit lines for single-location grocery stores, the NLRB regards a store-wide unit of all nonsupervisory employees as being appropriate. However, if meat department or produce department employees can demonstrate a distinct community of interest, then these groups may form a separate unit.[50]

▲ Summary and Conclusions

The bargaining-unit structure has important strategic implications to the entire collective bargaining process. Once the bargaining unit is determined, it will have a significant impact on how the union conducts its organizing campaign and the likelihood that it will win the certification election. The bargaining unit structure also dictates bargaining and contract administration strategies for the employer and union. Criteria used by the National Labor Relations Board in determining the proper bargaining unit were discussed. Employee groups who receive special consideration when bargaining unit lines are drawn were identified. Some of the more common bargaining unit structures were analyzed in terms of their advantages and disadvantages to collective bargaining efficiency. Finally, the issues of organizational change on bargaining units and presumptively appropriate bargaining units were treated.

A reading of this chapter illustrates that establishing the proper bargaining unit is a complex process that is fraught with potential problems. First, the NLRB must carefully examine the job tasks, organizational structure, personnel policies, bargaining history, and desires of the employer and union against the criteria that have evolved through years of bargaining-unit determinations. Second, the issue of whether to include or exclude employee groups from the bargaining unit must be addressed with an eye toward the effect that such decisions will have on the certification election and the collective bargaining process. Along with these considerations, special categories of employees such as craft workers, security guards, supervisors and managers, dual-status employees, and others must be considered. Occasionally, heated disputes arise over the inclusion or exclusion of these employees in a bargaining unit. An analysis of published NLRB cases reveals numerous instances where disputes over the composition of a bargaining unit are argued before the Board and even find their way into the federal courts. The number of such cases litigated is strong evidence of the importance attached to bargaining-unit structures by employers and unions. Four actual cases presented at the end of this chapter illustrate some of the complex issues that frequently arise in determining the appropriate bargaining unit.

Although this chapter focuses on the bargaining unit criteria that are routinely used by the NLRB, it should be emphasized that the application of these criteria are, to some extent, controlled by broader social and economic forces. There has been a gradual move toward more centralized bargaining unit structures in private-sector labor-management relations (such as multi-locational and multi-employer

---

[50] *Weis Markets, Inc.* 39 LRRM 1465 (1956).

units). The growth of large corporations and national and international product markets has played a role in the centralization process. Along with their corporate counterparts, many labor unions have merged in order to become stronger and better able to deal with big business. Public policies concerning health and safety, equal employment opportunity, and various compensation laws have standardized personnel practices and have summoned the need for a level of expertise that is more likely to be found in centralized bargaining structures where highly trained labor relations professionals are employed.

▲ Discussion Questions and Exercises

1. What is the doctrine of exclusive representation? Do you believe that the doctrine has merit in U.S. Labor relations?
2. Obtain recent articles on migrant agricultural workers. Do you believe that migrant workers are treated fairly under U.S. labor laws? If not, how should Congress amend current laws to help migrant workers?
3. What effect might the wave of corporate mergers, acquisitions, and hostile takeovers have on bargaining-unit structures and labor relations in the United States? Discuss.
4. Should supervisors and managers receive more protection under the National Labor Relations Act? Why or why not?
5. Determining the bargaining-unit structure has created some heated arguments between union and management officials. Why should bargaining-unit determination be such a critical issue?

▲ ▲ ▲ ▲ BARGAINING UNIT CASES

Cooper Union

Cooper Union is a private, nonprofit, tuition-free institution of higher education located in Manhattan (New York). The university consists of three schools: the Schools of Art, Architecture, and Engineering. Cooper Union has a student body of approximately 900 to 1,000 students and employs 55 to 60 full-time and 80 part-time faculty members. The Cooper Union Charter vests ultimate authority in a 16-member board of trustees that contains no faculty representatives.

In 1974, following an NLRB-supervised election, the Cooper Union Federation of College Teachers, AFT, NYSUT, AFL-CIO (known hereafter as "the union") was certified to represent a unit of full-time faculty members and librarians. Part-time (adjunct) faculty, deans, assistant deans, division heads, and the library head were excluded from the bargaining unit. The union and the university entered into their only collective bargaining agreement in 1978 and the agreement expired in August, 1980.

The U.S. Supreme Court made an important decision in 1980 regarding the managerial status of faculty members at another institution of higher learning, Yeshiva University. In *NLRB v. Yeshiva* (103 LRRM 2526), the Court held that college faculty members are managers and are not entitled to protection under the National Labor Relations Act if they "exercise discretion within, or even independently of, established employer policy." The Supreme Court added that faculty "must be aligned with management" and noted that Yeshiva faculty members exercised absolute authority in academic matters such as course offerings, scheduling, grading, matriculation, and admissions. Although the Court concluded that Yeshiva's faculty was managerial, it stated that there may be faculty at other institutions of higher learning that are nonmanagerial.

Following the *Yeshiva* decision, Cooper Union withdrew its recognition of the union. The university contended that faculty members were managerial employees who were not entitled to protection under the NLRA. Subsequently, the union filed an unfair labor practice charge under sections 8(a)(1) and 8(a)(5) of the Act. An administrative law judge at the NLRB regional level concluded that Cooper Union's full-time faculty members were managerial employees and dismissed the complaint. However, the Board (in Washington, D.C.) reversed and held that the faculty did not exercise sufficient authority over academic matters to be considered managerial employees; they were therefore protected under the NLRA. The case was then appealed to the U.S. Court of Appeals (Second Circuit, New York).

Evidence presented to the U.S. Court of Appeals indicated that Cooper Union's faculty had significant authority in certain core academic matters, but such authority was far from absolute. University financial matters were handled primarily by the trustees with minimal input from the faculty. A major restructuring of the organization had also been undertaken without faculty participation and over their strong opposition. Faculty input into the appointment, retention, or employment of nonteaching staff was nonexistent and their ability to strongly influence the hiring, promotion, and tenure decisions was questionable. In short, faculty governance at Cooper Union was almost nonexistent and, in 1978, an accreditation team visited the campus and noted that the deans at Cooper Union were unusually strong, whereas the faculty members were unusually weak.

Discussion Questions

1. Although the NLRA does not explicitly exclude managerial employees as it does supervisors, the Supreme Court has held that the Act implies such an exclusion. What are the differences between managerial and supervisory employees? Under what circumstances can an employee be a professional employee and receive protection under the Act and yet not be a supervisor or manager?
2. Based on your observations and knowledge of faculty members at your

college or university, do you believe that they should be included or excluded from protection under the NLRA?
3. Using the citation of the *Yeshiva* decision in the case narrative, read the case and compare the Yeshiva faculty's authority with that of Cooper Union. What differences do you note between the two faculties?
4. Based on your analysis of *Cooper Union*, how do you believe the U.S. Court of Appeals ruled on the managerial status of the faculty? Should part-time faculty members be included in the bargaining unit?

Community Hospital at Glen Cove

The Community Hospital at Glen Cove (New York) is a private institution with 279 beds and approximately 1100 employees. The hospital complex consists of four buildings connected by corridors and tunnels. Two additions built in 1983 give the physical plant a total of 250,000 square feet. A separate mansion on the grounds houses a drug program. The hospital's registered nurses are represented by the New York State Nurses Association. There is no history of collective bargaining for the institution's other employees.

Teamsters Union, Local 810, sought to represent a bargaining unit of all full-time and regular part-time skilled and plant maintenance employees at the hospital. The proposed unit included carpenters, painters, plumbers, electricians, refrigeration engineers, locksmiths, 11 helpers, and maintenance and utility employees, all of whom worked in the hospital's engineering department. Other employees such as supervisors, office employees, and guards were to be excluded from the proposed unit.

At the initial representation hearing, the hospital administration (also referred to as "the employer") contended that the bargaining unit proposed by the Teamsters union was inappropriate and argued that the only suitable unit was a broad service and maintenance unit. At a second meeting, the employer argued that the hospital is a small, functionally integrated facility, and the only appropriate unit is a unit of all nonprofessional employees. However, the employer contended that if a unit of maintenance employees is deemed appropriate, then the unit should include all such employees and not just those in the engineering department as suggested by the Teamsters.

The engineering department is one of 27 departments within the hospital and is supervised by a chief engineer who has the primary responsibility for making hiring, scheduling, disciplinary, and firing decisions involving departmental employees. Four shops are contained within the engineering department: plumbing/maintenance, electrical, paint, and carpentry. Employees within the department possess a wide range of skills and use various specialized tools and equipment. Pay for individual employees within the department varies considerably, depending on their respective experience, skills, and job functions. There are 14 pay grades for hospital employees and the majority of the engineering employees are in pay grades 7–10; the majority of other nonprofessional employees (service, general maintenance, technical, office clericals, and security personnel) are in pay grades 2–4. The engineering department employees are eligible for the same employee benefits as other professional and nonprofessional employees and are subject to a hospital-wide set of personnel policies.

The engineering office and shops are concentrated in the northwest section of the hospital complex and the painting shop is located in the south/central section. All employees in the engineering department report to the maintenance shop at the beginning of their respective shifts and all wear green uniforms while on duty. On each shift, a maintenance employee performs rounds and uses an extensive checklist to ensure the proper working order of various equipment such as heaters, pumps, converters, exhaust fans, and compressors. Maintenance employees also respond to work requests submitted by hospital employees. Engineering employees perform their duties throughout the hospital and come into contact with other employees. Some preventive maintenance tasks and repairs must be done in the various shops of the engineering department.

The following job classifications exist within the engineering department:

1. *Stationary Boiler Operators* operate, maintain, and repair the high pressure boilers and related pumps, motors, blowers, and compressors. Two stationary boiler operators also perform general maintenance/repair tasks.
2. *Painters* spend 95 percent of their time painting and plastering the interior of the hospital. They do a limited amount of exterior painting and wallpapering. The lead painter spends 80 to 90 percent of the time painting and also mixes paints and paints machinery.
3. *Electrical Shop Maintenance Employees* repair and replace equipment for the refrigeration and air conditioning systems. They also repair suction machines, cast saws, laundry machines and install electrical wiring, cables, and fixtures. These employees perform safety checks on housekeeping machines and biomedical equipment such as cardioscopes and defibrillators. Preventive maintenance and repairs on motorized beds and kitchen equipment is also performed by this employee group.
4. *Plumbing Maintenance Workers* install and repair plumbing and heating equipment or fixtures such as circulators, hot water heaters, tanks, sinks, and pumps. They do some soldering, brazing, pipe cutting, and threading.
5. *Carpenters* erect wood and steel partitions, walls, door frames, make and install shelves, and maintain doors and door frames.
6. *Clerk-typists* perform typing and filing duties and distribute work request forms to the lead workers in each of the above engineering subdivisions.

An examination of the job descriptions of employees in building services, laundry, dietary, central supply, and purchasing reveals that their work does not require the degree of skill and knowledge of employees in the engineering department. The work of the former group consists of simple tasks requiring basic skills and training. However, there are various other nonprofessional job classifications in the medical departments that require specialized skills and knowledge (such as EKG, laboratory, and X-ray technicians as well as licensed practical nurses).

Discussion Questions

1. Why does the Teamsters Union desire a more narrowly defined bargaining unit than the employer? How would the complexion of the collective bargaining process be affected with a narrow unit comprised only of engineering department employees?
2. One of the landmark cases involving bargaining unit determinations in the health care industry is the *St. Francis Hospital(II)* case (116 LRRM 1465). In *St. Francis Hospital (II)*, the Board stated that a sharp "disparity-of-interests" test that analyzes traditional community of interest factors must be used in health care institutions. Examine the *St. Francis II* case and apply its rulings to the Glen Cove Hospital case.
3. Based on the information presented in the *Glen Cove* case, would you favor the union's proposed bargaining unit or the employers proposed unit?

Futuramik Industries

The Ladies Garment Workers Union engaged in a certification election campaign at Futuramik Industries. It resulted in a 93 to 86 union victory. Futuramik Industries is a closely held corporation dominated by the Ramondetta family whose members together own 86 percent of the outstanding corporate stock. Daniel Trefethen, vice-president of the corporation, owns approximately 10 percent of Futuramik's stock and is actively engaged in the day-to-day operation of the firm. As plant manager, Mr. Trefethen is responsible for three production and maintenance shifts.

Gloria Trefethen, the vice-president's wife, works in the company's quality control department and reports directly to Paul Kasputis. Kasputis, in turn, reports to Daniel Trefethen or Ed Gianzenetti, vice-president and sales manager. The evidence shows that Gloria Trefethen resides with her husband and presumably is dependent on him.

An NLRB hearing officer recommended that Mrs. Trefethen's ballot and bargaining unit membership be challenged because of her relationship with the company's vice-president.

Discussion Questions

1. Does the fact that Mr. Trefethen holds 10 percent of Futuramik's stock have a bearing on his wife's status as a bargaining unit member? Note: the Trefethens are not related to the Ramondettas.

2. Why is the NLRB sensitive to the inclusion of family members of business owners in the bargaining unit of a closely held corporation? What do family members have in common with other excluded groups such as supervisors, managers, and security personnel?
3. Would Mrs. Trefethen's membership in the bargaining unit be less susceptible to challenge if her husband were a stockholder who either did not work in the firm or held a nonsupervisory position? What if Gloria Trefethen were a sister or cousin of Daniel Trefethen?
4. If you were a union official, would you feel comfortable knowing that the wife of the firm's vice-president was in the bargaining unit?
5. How should the NLRB rule on Mrs. Trefethen's inclusion in the bargaining unit?

U.S. Pollution Control, Inc.

Teamsters Union, Local 222 won a certification election involving 11 employees of U.S. Pollution Control, Inc. Three ballots were challenged by the employer. One of the challenged ballots pertained to the bargaining-unit eligibility of Mr. Randy Shephard.

Randy Shephard was employed by U.S. Pollution Control in Salt Lake City, Utah, as a pollution control specialist attached to its Special Services/Small Operator Program; he is the only such specialist employed at the Salt Lake City office. His job is to pick up, manifest, and transport small quantities of hazardous waste in Oklahoma, Idaho, Wyoming, and Utah, with most of his time being spent within 100 miles of Salt Lake City. When Shephard needs assistance in his work, his first option is to contact his immediate supervisor, Charles Soukup, who works out of the firm's Oklahoma City office. Soukup will then send employees to help Mr. Shephard, if they are available. Otherwise, Shephard is authorized to use two casual employees in Salt Lake City. Both casual employees were initially interviewed by Shephard, who then recommended to Soukup that they be hired. Soukup screened the two employees' applications and made the final hiring decision. Additionally, Shephard devotes approximately 50 percent of his time to sales-related duties. These duties include contacting existing and potential customers and responding to their inquiries about the company's services. Shephard also makes bids on work for prospective customers.

Shephard is paid a monthly salary. Unlike other employees at the Salt Lake City operation, he does not punch a time clock, is not paid overtime, and receives sick benefits. Shephard also differs from his fellow employees in that he has an assigned office area.

Discussion Questions

1. Shephard interviewed and recommended that two casual employees be hired to assist him on an "as-needed" basis. Does this fact make Shephard

a supervisor? Would the casual employees be entitled to membership in the bargaining unit?
2. Does the fact that Mr. Shephard bids on work for his employer make him a managerial employee? If so, what effect would his managerial status have on his eligibility to remain in the bargaining unit?
3. How does the NLRB regard dual-status employees? Since Mr. Shephard spends approximately 50 percent of his time doing nonunit sales work, how does this affect his community of interest with other bargaining unit members? What community of interest factors are relevant to this case?

5 Union Organization Campaigns and Certification Elections

- **Introduction**
- **The Organizing Atmosphere**
  Factors That Affect Employee Interest in Unions
  Factors in the Work Environment
  Personal and Demographic Factors
- **Union and Management Tactics during Organizational Campaigns**
  Union Organizing Strategies
    Establishing Organizational Targets
    Making the Initial Advances
    Obtaining the Critical Mass of Employee Support
  Measures Taken by Employers During the Organizing Campaign
    Proactive Measures by Management
    Legal Reactive Measures by Employers
    Illegal Reactive Measures by Management
- **The Certification Election**
- **Post-Election Matters**
  Challenged Election Ballots
  Unfair Labor Practices That Preclude a Fair Election
  When Members No Longer Support the Union: The Decertification Process
- **Summary and Conclusions**
- **Discussion Questions and Exercises**
- **Certification Election Cases**
  Westwood Horizons Hotel
  Metz Metallurgical Corp.
  Conair Corporation

Introduction

> But Nissan is pulling out all the stops. It airs slick messages over the plant's closed circuit television system, such as the one that blames the union [the United Auto Workers] for layoffs at GM and shows Mr. Benefield [Nissan, USA's president] noting that Nissan has never had a layoff. "Do you want job security at Nissan," he asks workers, "or do you want job security UAW style?"
>
> ... The union, for its part, has shipped in 30 professional organizers. They put ads in the local papers, hand out leaflets to workers as they enter and leave [the plant], and make housecalls. Some 1,700 of the 2,400 workers have received visits.
>
> The heated atmosphere has made the factory a house divided. In the cafeteria, "they sit at their own tables, and we sit at ours," says Stanley Tribble, 57, who opposes the UAW. "You don't eat with your enemies."
>
> Jerry C. Waldrop, another foe of the UAW, has a friend who favors the union. They don't discuss it. "I still consider the young man my friend," he says, "although sometimes I'd like to choke him."
>
> Workers wear their hearts on their sleeves. Pro-union forces in shirts that read "Vote Yes for a Safer Workplace" work alongside people wearing shirts saying "I Can Speak for Myself." Both sides try to appeal to patriotism: Antiunion workers have adopted the American flag as their symbol at rallies, while a pro-union T-shirt seemingly tries to tap anti-Japanese sentiment by proclaiming: "Unite! The 13 Colonies did it."[1]

The atmosphere surrounding the union organizing campaign and defeat of the United Auto Workers (by a 2-to-1 margin) in the certification election at Nissan's Smyrna, Tennessee plant captured nationwide attention in the summer of 1989. As the passage above suggests, union organizing campaigns are often accompanied by a great deal of campaign rhetoric, emotionalism, and legal pitfalls. Most employers view unions as an encroachment on managerial autonomy and regard a union organizing campaign as a serious matter that threatens the stability of the employer-employee relationship. A labor union will normally target a group of employees who work in a designated locale, plant, or department(s) and attempt to educate them on the merits of organized labor. Union organizers must often overcome strong objections and reluctance on the part of some employees as well as antiunion countermeasures by management. The dynamics of the union organizing campaign contain social, legal, and economic factors that are of interest to both labor practitioners and academicians. This chapter discusses union organizing tactics, factors that encourage or discourage employee interest in unions, permissible pre-election conduct by employers and unions, the NLRB certification process, methods used by management to deter unions, and post-election matters.

---

[1] Gregory A. Patterson, "The UAW's Chances at Japanese Plants Hinge on Nissan Vote," *The Wall Street Journal* (July 25, 1989), p. 1. Reprinted with permission of *The Wall Street Journal* © 1989 Dow Jones & Company, Inc. All rights reserved Worldwide.

▲ The Organizing Atmosphere

Labor unions organize and represent employees with regard to wages, hours, and working conditions. As is the case with any business entity, unions employ strategies for accomplishing their goals and they operate with finite resources. Some labor organizations, such as the craft unions, will only organize members of a skilled trade. Other unions, such as the American Federation of State, County, and Municipal Employees (AFSCME) primarily organize state and local governmental employees and are not concerned with private sector or federal government workers. Unions such as the meatcutters focus on one occupation, but are willing to represent other types of workers if the opportunity arises. Finally, unions such as the Teamsters are willing to organize nearly any occupational group.

Labor unions also differ in their degree of aggressiveness and methods of organizing. A union may expend a great deal of time and money in organizing the employees of a targeted firm. The same union, however, may make only a quick or half-hearted attempt to attract other workers. A union organizer who visits a city primarily to organize telecommunications workers may, while in town, make a superficial attempt to organize some radio station employees simply because they are convenient to reach. Unions also differ somewhat with respect to their organizational philosophies; some emphasize achieving immediate economic gains for their constituent members, whereas others use broader social issues, such as an unemployment problem or discrimination in the workplace, to attract attention and garner worker support. Regardless of their organizational philosophy or aggressiveness, a union will generally try to direct its efforts where the payoffs are greatest.

Labor unions are becoming increasingly sophisticated insofar as organizing strategies and tactics are concerned. Employers are also taking measures that are designed to negate legally the efforts of union organizers. Consulting firms that specialize in helping management avoid and defeat unions are becoming more commonplace.[2] Union organizers are learning to be more astute at distinguishing between employees who are ripe for unionization and those who are not receptive to organizational efforts. Both organized labor and management must be cognizant of the legal restrictions imposed on organizational campaigns and certification elections because the line between legal and illegal conduct is often thin and, at times, blurred.

Factors That Affect Employee Interest in Unions

An employee's decision to join and support a labor union during the organizing campaign is based on a number of factors, some of which are not well understood.[3] Figure 5–1 summarizes the major factors that affect the degree of employee attrac-

---

[2] See Kinsey Wilson and Steve Askin, "Secrets of a Union Buster," *The Nation* (June 13, 1981), p. 725.
[3] Attempts have been made to measure employee commitment to labor unions. See Michael E. Gordon, John W. Philpot, Robert E. Burt, Cynthia A. Thompson, and William E. Spiller, "Commitment to the Union: Development of a Measure and an Examination of its Correlates," *Journal of Applied Psychology*, Vol. 65, No. 4 (1980), pp. 479–499; Robert T. Ladd, Michael E. Gordon, Laura Beauvais, and Richard L. Morgan, "Union Commitment: Replication and Extension," *Journal of Applied Psychology*, Vol. 67, No. 5 (1982), pp. 640–644; and Clive Fulligar, "A Factor Analytic Study on the Validity of a Union Commitment Scale," *Journal of Applied Psychology*, Vol. 71, No. 1 (1986), pp. 129–136.

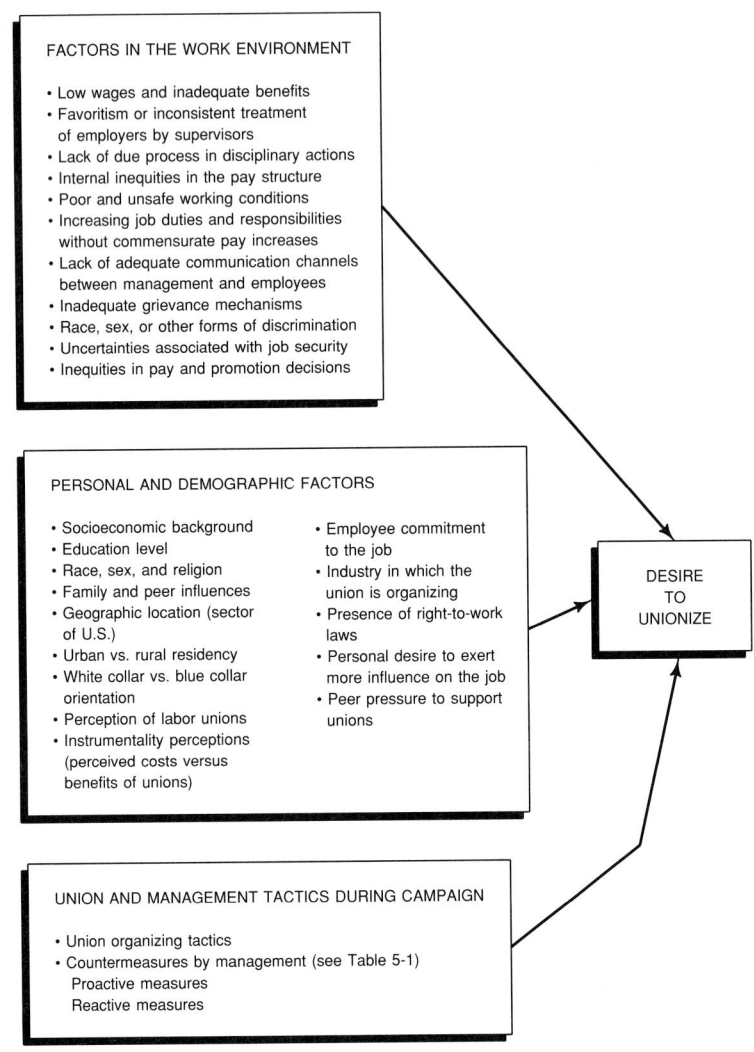

```
┌─────────────────────────────────────────┐
│ FACTORS IN THE WORK ENVIRONMENT         │
│                                         │
│ • Low wages and inadequate benefits     │
│ • Favoritism or inconsistent treatment  │
│   of employers by supervisors           │
│ • Lack of due process in disciplinary   │
│   actions                               │
│ • Internal inequities in the pay        │
│   structure                             │
│ • Poor and unsafe working conditions    │
│ • Increasing job duties and             │
│   responsibilities without commensurate │
│   pay increases                         │
│ • Lack of adequate communication        │
│   channels between management and       │
│   employees                             │
│ • Inadequate grievance mechanisms       │
│ • Race, sex, or other forms of          │
│   discrimination                        │
│ • Uncertainties associated with job     │
│   security                              │
│ • Inequities in pay and promotion       │
│   decisions                             │
└─────────────────────────────────────────┘

┌──────────────────────────────────────────────────┐
│ PERSONAL AND DEMOGRAPHIC FACTORS                 │
│                                                  │
│ • Socioeconomic background   • Employee          │
│ • Education level              commitment to     │
│ • Race, sex, and religion      the job           │
│ • Family and peer            • Industry in which │
│   influences                   the union is      │
│ • Geographic location          organizing        │
│   (sector of U.S.)           • Presence of       │
│ • Urban vs. rural              right-to-work     │
│   residency                    laws              │
│ • White collar vs. blue      • Personal desire   │
│   collar orientation           to exert more     │
│ • Perception of labor          influence on the  │
│   unions                       job               │
│ • Instrumentality            • Peer pressure to  │
│   perceptions (perceived       support unions    │
│   costs versus benefits                          │
│   of unions)                                     │
└──────────────────────────────────────────────────┘

            ┌──────────┐
            │ DESIRE   │
            │ TO       │
            │ UNIONIZE │
            └──────────┘

┌─────────────────────────────────────────────────┐
│ UNION AND MANAGEMENT TACTICS DURING CAMPAIGN    │
│                                                 │
│ • Union organizing tactics                      │
│ • Countermeasures by management (see Table 5-1) │
│     Proactive measures                          │
│     Reactive measures                           │
└─────────────────────────────────────────────────┘
```

FIGURE 5–1 Factors Affecting Employee Propensity to Join and Support Unions

tion to labor unions. Some factors have been empirically verified; others are based primarily on extrapolations or the anecdotal experiences of labor relations practitioners and scholars.[4] Although research has been done on worker tendencies to join unions, more is needed before we can fully understand the dynamics of union organization campaigns and certification elections. A number of prominent re-

---

[4] For examples of anecdotal accounts of union campaign activities, see James P. Swann, Jr., *NLRB Elections: A Guide for Employers*, (Washington, D.C.: The Bureau of National Affairs, Inc., 1980); Ken Gagla, *Union Organizing and Staying Organized*, (Reston, Virginia: Reston Publishing Company, Inc., 1983); and James W. Hunt, *Employer's Guide to Labor Relations* (Washington, D.C.: The Bureau of National Affairs, Inc., 1979).

searchers have analyzed employee propensities to unionize and have noted the following:[5]

1. Workers are more likely to join a union if there is a significant degree of dissatisfaction with the economic or "bread-and-butter" aspects of their job (wages, hours, and working conditions).
2. The primary impetus behind the unionization of white-collar workers is to obtain more influence over job-related conditions rather than to actually change these conditions.
3. Nonunionized blacks and other racial minorities are more willing to support unions than unorganized white workers.[6]
4. Female white-collar workers are more receptive to unions than their male counterparts.[7]
5. Blue-collar workers in the South are not significantly different from blue-collar workers in the Northeast insofar as their interest in joining unions is concerned. However, white-collar workers in the South are significantly less willing to join unions than Northeastern white-collar workers.

---

[5] Examples of empirical work on employee propensities to unionize include Herbert R. Northrup, "The AFL-CIO Blue Cross-Blue Shield Campaign: A Study of Organizational Failure," *Industrial and Labor Relations Review* (July 1990). pp. 525–541. Satish P. Deshpande and Jack Fiorito, "Specific and General Beliefs in Union Voting Models," *Academy of Management Journal* (December 1989), pp. 883–897; W. Clay Hamner and Frank J. Smith, "Worker Attitudes As Predictors of Unionization Activity," *Journal of Applied Psychology*, Vol. 63, No. 4 (1978), pp. 415–421; Henry S. Farber and Daniel H. Saks, "Why Workers Want Unions: The Role of Relative Wages and Job Characteristics," *Journal of Political Economy*, Vol. 88, No. 21 (1980), pp. 349–369; Richard B. Freeman, "Why Are Unions Faring Poorly in NLRB Representation Elections?", in Richard L. Rowan, *Readings in Labor Economics and Labor Relations* (Homewood, Illinois: Richard D. Irwin, Inc., 1985), pp. 129–141; Thomas A. Kochan and Harry C. Katz, *Collective Bargaining and Industrial Relations*, 2nd ed. (Homewood, Illinois: Richard D. Irwin, Inc., 1988), pp. 164–168; Richard B. Freeman and James L. Medoff, *What Do Unions Do?* (New York: Basic Books, Inc., 1984), pp. 26–33; Jeanne M. Brett, "Why Employees Want Unions," *Organizational Dynamics* (Spring 1980); Stuart A. Youngblood, Angelo S. DeNisi, Julie L. Molleston, and William H. Mobley, "The Impact of Work Environment, Instrumentality Beliefs, Perceived Labor Union Image, and Subjective Norms on Union Voting Intentions," *Academy of Management Journal*, Vol 27, No. 3 (September 1984), pp. 576–590; Herbert G. Heneman, III, and Marcus Sandver, "Predicting the Outcome of Union Certification Elections: A Review of the Literature," *Industrial and Labor Relations Review*, Vol. 36 (July 1983), pp. 537–559; Julius Getman, Stephen Goldberg, and Jeanne Herman, *Union Representation Elections: Law and Reality* (New York: Russell Sage Foundation, 1976); Arthur P. Brief and Dale E. Rude, "Voting in Union Certification Elections: A Conceptual Analysis," *Academy of Management Review*, Vol. 6, No. 2 (1981), pp. 261–267; William N. Cooke, "Determinants of the Outcomes of Union Certification Elections," *Industrial and Labor Relations Review* (April 1983), pp. 402–414; Thomas A. DeCotiis and Jean-Yves LeLouarn, "A Predictive Study of Voting Behavior in a Representation Election Using Union Instrumentality and Work Perceptions," *Organizational Behavior and Human Performance*, Vol. 27, No. 1 (1981), pp. 103–118; Michael E. Gordon and Larry E. Long, "Demographic and Attitudinal Correlates of Union Joining," *Industrial Relations* (Fall 1981), pp. 306–311; Thomas A. Kochan, "How American Workers View Labor Unions," *Monthly Labor Review* (April 1979), pp. 23–31; Joel Seidman, Jack London, and Bernard Karsh, "Why Workers Join Unions," *Annals of the American Academy of Political and Social Science* (March 1951), pp. 75–84; and Chester A. Schriesheim, "Job Satisfaction, Attitudes Toward Unions, and Voting in a Union Representation Election," *Journal of Applied Psychology*, Vol. 63, No. 5 (1978), pp. 548–552.

[6] However, one study has shown that black members felt less responsibility to the union than white members, perhaps because of the generally shorter tenure of blacks as union members. See Clive Fulligar, "A Factor Analytic Study on the Validity of a Union Commitment Scale," *Journal of Applied Psychology* (February 1986), p. 129.

[7] See M. F. Payson, "Wooing the Pink-Collar Work Force," *Personnel Journal* (January 1984), pp. 48–53.

6. Employees working in intermediate-size organizations are more receptive to unions than employees in very small or very large establishments.
7. No specific race, sex, or socioeconomic group was found to be uniformly hostile toward labor unions. A likely exception would be members of management who are normally not targets for union organizers.
8. An estimated one-third of the unorganized labor force is willing to join a labor union under the proper circumstances.
9. Workers generally do not remember a great deal about the substance of pre-election campaign statements by union organizers or management. When they do remember, however, they are more likely to vote for the side from whom the influential information was obtained.
10. Employees who are undecided about whether to support the union usually vote against certification.
11. The more an employer uses antiunion tactics (both legal and illegal), the greater the likelihood that the union will lose the certification election.

The reader is cautioned to accept these findings with a certain amount of reservation. Although the research was conducted carefully and systematically, there is a great deal of variation that can occur from one organizational setting to the next. Thus, any generalization about the outcome of a certification election is uncertain. The following discussion provides a closer look at union organizing campaigns as well as factors affecting the outcome of certification elections.

Factors in the Work Environment

An examination of the literature on union organizing campaigns, coupled with the opinions of those involved in such campaigns, leads to one fundamental conclusion: Employees in the United States are most attracted to unions when they become exceedingly displeased with life at work. Work-related factors are by far the most prominent reason given by employees who turn to labor unions as a means of achieving more equitable treatment on the job. Morton Bahr, president of the Communications Workers of America, described the conditions faced by cafeteria workers employed by ARA Services at Stephen F. Austin University in Nacogdoches, Texas:

> I have been exposed to the degradation of city poverty. I've been in the Harlems and the Bedford-Stuyvesants [communities in New York City] and in those apartments, in those basements, but I've never been exposed to rural poverty such as exists in east Texas. Shacks with two rooms, it was deplorable.
>
> I visited some of the cafeteria workers who lived under those conditions on the evening that I arrived in Nacogdoches, and one woman said to me, "Do I look like an animal? Do I walk on all fours? I'm a human being, I think I deserve to be treated with some dignity." None of those I visited said anything about earning a nickle more, all they talked about was being treated like a person.[8]

---

[8] Morton Bahr (interview), "Without Dialogue There Can Be No Cooperation," in Philip L. Quaglieri, *America's Labor Leaders* (Lexington, Massachusetts: Lexington Books, 1989), p. 26. Reprinted with permission.

Figure 5–1 lists a number of factors in the work environment that frequently become points of contention during a union organizing campaign. Union organizers often attempt to pinpoint specific areas of employee dissatisfaction *and* they may add fuel to the fire and create controversy by showing employees exactly how deplorable their compensation, benefits, and working conditions are relative to those found in unionized firms. Management consultants who specialize in helping firms maintain a nonunion environment also focus on the work-related factors depicted in Figure 5–1. Management may reduce the employees' desire to join a union by maintaining a work environment that provides adequate compensation, equitable treatment,[9] and reasonable job security. The preventive labor relations posture of many firms also includes a certain amount of public relations activity designed to remind employees periodically of their favorable working conditions and fair treatment.

The presence of favorable factors in the work environment does not necessarily guarantee that a firm will remain union-free. Likewise, subpar compensation or benefits as well as other inequities do not automatically mean that a union will solicit employee support and win the certification election. By addressing the work environment factors listed in Figure 5–1, employers reduce the probability that a union will gain a foothold in the organization. When employers fail to maintain reasonable working conditions, the odds may shift in favor of the union. Union organizers must first target a particular firm as a likely candidate for organization. Although an undesirable work environment may provide the bait for a union organizer, there are other factors that may either encourage or discourage further organizing attempts. For example, if the union does not feel that the employees can be organized into a workable bargaining unit, then it may decide to direct its organizing efforts elsewhere. Union organizers may feel that the number of employees involved is too small to warrant investing time and money into an organizing campaign. Furthermore, a union may decide not to make a serious attempt at organizing a group of employees if there is reason to believe that the chances of certification are marginal.[10]

Personal and Demographic Factors

Much has been said about individual propensities to accept or reject labor unions, although research on this topic is somewhat limited. Younger workers, women, and blacks seem more likely to vote for unions in certification elections than others. A possible explanation for these findings is that these workers have traditionally held lower-paying, less desirable jobs and they have exerted relatively little control over job-related matters. Moreover, blacks and women historically have experienced greater employment discrimination, which could lead to their seeking the protection of a labor union. Blue-collar workers have been more receptive to labor unions, although the white-collar sector has taken a much stronger interest over the past

---

[9] See Gerald E. Fryxell and Michael E. Gordon, "Workplace Justice and Job Satisfaction With Union and Management," *Academy of Management Journal* (December 1989), pp. 851–866.
[10] See C. L. Maranto, "Corporate Characteristics and Union Organizing," *Industrial Relations* (Fall 1988), pp. 352–370.

25 years.[11] Much of the white-collar membership in labor unions is among governmental employees (see Chapter 17).[12] There is, however, little difference in the propensity to unionize between persons of different educational levels. Regional labor-force differences (most notably North versus South) regarding employee willingness to join or support unions have also largely disappeared.[13]

Figure 5–1 lists other personal and demographic factors that probably affect employee propensity to unionize. For example, family influences and religious preferences undoubtedly affect voting choices for individual workers in a union certification election. Persons from white-collar families whose orientation is pro-management may exhibit an antiunion bias. Other individuals may have a negative image of organized labor that stems from publicized incidents of corruption and alleged connections with organized crime by union officials. However, a negative conception of unions may not prevent a worker from supporting them in a certification election when employment conditions are substandard. It is also possible that an employee may sign an authorization card because of peer pressure, yet vote against the union in the secret-ballot NLRB election.

Workers in the United States are pragmatic and normally have to be convinced that a union will provide greater pay, benefits, and improved quality of worklife before they are willing to vote for and financially support a labor organization. An employee is more likely to support a union if he or she believes that the perceived benefits of unionization will exceed the costs of membership. The most obvious costs of belonging to a union are the initiation fees and periodic dues assessments. There are also other, less obvious "costs" to union membership, such as acquiescing to the desires of the bargaining unit majority, attending union meetings, and possibly creating a rift between friends who are working in a supervisory or managerial role.

Some labor experts claim that an employee is more likely to support a union if he or she has a long-term commitment to remain at a particular firm. Employees who view a job as being temporary may be less likely to support a union during an organizational campaign. The presence of right-to-work legislation (currently existing in 20 states) may also reduce union support because these laws forbid compulsory union membership. Right-to-work laws allow an employee to refuse joining a union that has been certified as the exclusive bargaining representative; yet the nonunion employee remains in the bargaining unit and receives all of the benefits and protection afforded under the collective bargaining agreement.

This brief discussion on personal and demographic factors affecting the propensity of an employee to join a union is simplistic because it only analyzes one factor at a time and ignores the *combined* effects of several factors. For example, employee educational levels apparently have no strong impact on propensity to unionize, but what effect does the combination of education and the presence of right-to-work legislation have on union support? Likewise, how do peer influences

---

[11] In recent years, there appears to have been a decline in white-collar union organizing. See John G. Kilgour, "White-Collar Union Organizing: A Reappraisal," *Personnel* (August 1986), p. 14.
[12] See Kenneth L. Warner, Rupert F. Chisholm, and Robert F. Munzenrider, "Motives for Unionization Among State Social Service Employees," *Public Personnel Management* (May-June 1978), pp. 181–191.
[13] See, for example, B. Ruth Montgomery, "The Influence of Attitudes and Normative Pressures on Voting Decisions in a Union Certification Election," *Industrial and Labor Relations Review* (January 1989), pp. 262–279.

interact with organizational size to shape an employee's voting behavior? The combinations of factors that can be analyzed are nearly endless, and they serve to illustrate the need for more research.

▲ Union and Management Tactics during Organizational Campaigns

Union Organizing Strategies

Figure 5–2 outlines many of the measures taken by labor unions as they attempt to target and organize a group of employees.[14] Unions employ numerous tactics in their quest to become the exclusive bargaining representative for an election unit

```
┌─────────────────┐   ┌─────────────────┐   ┌─────────────────┐   ┌─────────────────┐
│  ESTABLISHING   │   │   MAKING THE    │   │  OBTAINING THE  │   │    THE NLRB     │
│ ORGANIZATIONAL  │──▶│ INITIAL ADVANCES│──▶│ "CRITICAL MASS" │──▶│  CERTIFICATION  │
│     TARGETS     │   │                 │   │   OF EMPLOYEE   │   │     PROCESS     │
│                 │   │                 │   │     SUPPORT     │   │                 │
└─────────────────┘   └─────────────────┘   └─────────────────┘   └─────────────────┘
```

- Identifying potential targets
  - AFL-CIO data on unorganized workers
  - type of employees and workers preferred by a particular union
  - financial and time constraints of the union
  - economic, social, and industrial factors
  - other factors

- Conducting telephone surveys directed at worker targets to obtain a more accurate measure of their desire to unionize

- Gathering data on the target group's compensation and working conditions

- Formulating an organizing platform and agenda

- Enlisting the support of prounion employees to assist in the organizational campaign

- Holding training sessions for organizing committee members

- Obtaining organization charts and diagrams of the workplace in order to better define employee contact points and the appropriate election unit

- Gaining access to the target group
  - personal visits to workers' homes
  - oral or written solicitation during working hours by employee organizers
  - small group meetings
  - mass meetings
  - use of news media

- Conveying the union's message to the target group

- Responding to employer counter-measures

- Obtaining employee authorization card signatures

- Clarifying the election unit

- Filing the certification election petition

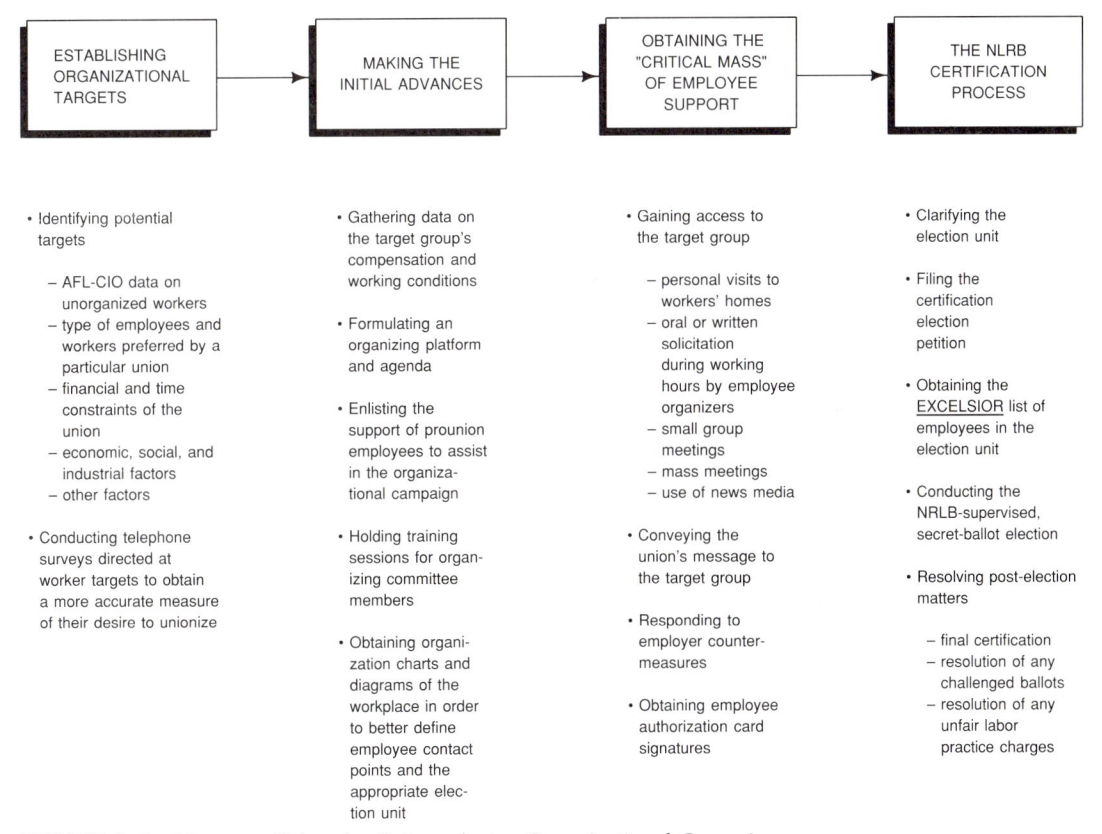

- Obtaining the EXCELSIOR list of employees in the election unit

- Conducting the NRLB-supervised, secret-ballot election

- Resolving post-election matters
  - final certification
  - resolution of any challenged ballots
  - resolution of any unfair labor practice charges

FIGURE 5–2 Measures Taken by Unions during Organizational Campaigns

---

[14] Also see William E. Fulmer, "Step by Step Through a Union Campaign," *Harvard Business Review* (July-August 1981), p. 94; Julius G. Getman, "Ruminations on Union Organizing in the Private Sector," *University of Chicago Law Review*, Vol. 53 (1986), pp. 45–77; Cheryl L. Maranto, "Corporate Characteristics and Union Organizing," *Industrial Relations*, Vol. 27, No. 3 (1988), pp. 352–370; and Cheryl L. Maranto and Jack Fiorito, "The Effect of Union Characteristics on the Outcome of NLRB Certification Elections," *Industrial and Labor Relations Review*, Vol. 40, No. 2 (1987), pp. 225–240.

of employees. Figure 5–2 depicts the general sequence of events. However, no two organizational campaigns are alike because of differences among union organizational philosophies, the employees being organized, and tactics used by employers to defeat union organizing efforts.

Establishing Organizational Targets

In a fashion similar to that of entrepreneurs who are looking for new business opportunities, labor unions generally seek to expand their membership rolls as a means of generating revenues and increasing their influence in the labor movement. When targeting an employee group, a labor union must select those that best suit its membership and financial objectives. Most unions establish organizational targets by performing all or some of the following activities:

1. Information on unorganized segments of the labor force is collected. Data on nonunionized employees may be obtained from the AFL-CIO or generated internally by the international union offices.
2. Information on unorganized sectors of the labor market is evaluated in light of the types of employees preferred by the union. At this point, the union must consider the financial and time constraints that it must face.[15] An attempt is usually made to narrow the search to those prospective bargaining-unit employees who appear to be most suitable for an organizing campaign.
3. The targeting process now shifts to determining the likelihood of successfully organizing a particular group of employees. Telephone surveys may be used to obtain an initial indication of how receptive the targeted group of employees would be toward unions. Some telephone surveys avoid direct questions about unions and instead focus on political preferences, employee views on various economic and social programs, and other questions whose responses can then be used to *infer* employee preferences about organized labor. In addition, the telephone survey may include direct questions about an employee's compensation and working conditions that can be used as a barometer of general employee satisfaction.
4. A union will also attempt to obtain information on how the employer will react to an organizational campaign. Factors such as the employer's financial condition, its reactions to previous organizational campaigns, and the extent to which other firms in the industry are unionized all merit consideration.
5. There will also be concern as to how easy or difficult it might be to service the bargaining unit if the union becomes the exclusive bargaining representative for a group of employees. A union may have serious doubts about initiating an organizational campaign (even if there is a high probability that the union may win) if the targeted group is comprised of a diverse mixture of skilled, unskilled, part-time, full-time, transient, and permanent employees. In such instances, union officials may believe that a collective bargaining agreement, which suits the needs of all employees, would be difficult to negotiate and administer.

---

[15] See Paula B. Voos, "Union Organizing Expenditures: Determinants and Their Implications for Union Growth," *Journal of Labor Research* (Winter 1987), p. 19.

Making the Initial Advances

Once the union has targeted an employee group, the next stage involves attracting the employees' attention and stimulating their interest in collective bargaining. The individual primarily responsible for making the initial advances and establishing face-to-face contact with the targeted employee group is the professional union organizer. Organizers are usually employed on a full-time basis by the international union and they have been trained (either formally or through on-the-job experience) to initiate and direct organizational campaigns. Professional union organizers possess an understanding of how to approach employees, how to enlist the support of pro-union workers to aid in the campaign, and how to deal with antiunion tactics by employers.[16] Although organizers employ their favorite techniques to accomplish the task of obtaining union certification, Figure 5–2 outlines the major functions of the organizer during the early stages of the campaign.[17]

The movie *Norma Rae* portrays the experiences of a union official who attempts to organize workers in a textile plant located in a small Southern mill town. Similarly, Gagla describes some of the pitfalls associated with being a union organizer who must travel to unfamiliar territory to perform a very delicate task, often in the face of severe hostility.

> Organizing is the most difficult job in unions. Rejection is nearly a daily occurrence and some prospects are belligerent and insulting. There is a strong likelihood that the organizer will be arrested and convicted for, at least, trespassing, and as a consequence, find it difficult to obtain personal credit. While not as prevalent as in the 1930s, there is still the danger of violence, enough so that some organizers feel compelled to carry a handgun. Frequent overnight travel is common. Organizing is very uncertain; there is no formula guaranteeing success. The organizer must become immune or, at least, accustomed to rejection and, more important, proceed to the next prospect with the same enthusiasm as he or she had the first day on the job.[18]

One of the first steps that a union organizer must take is to become familiar with the targeted employees' compensation, benefits, and working conditions. Since union organizers are not usually allowed on the employer's property, other (often ingenious) methods may be used to secure this information. The union organizer may obtain copies of pay scales as well as employee handbooks that outline work rules, benefits, and other items. Such information may be procured through employees who are supportive of the union organizing drive. In other instances, the union organizer may pose as a job applicant and even go so far as to accept a job with the firm in order to get a closer look at the workplace. Some organizers use a detailed checklist to ensure that nothing is overlooked in the process of obtaining as much information as possible. After sufficient information is collected, the union

---

[16] For an excellent analysis of union organizer characteristics, see Thomas F. Reed, "Do Union Organizers Matter? Individual Differences, Campaign Practices, and Representation Election Outcomes," *Industrial and Labor Relations Review* (October 1989), pp. 103–119.

[17] See, for example, Herbert G. Heneman, III and Marcus H. Sandver, "Union Characteristics and Organizing Success," *Journal of Labor Research* (Fall 1989), pp. 377–389.

[18] Ken Gagla, *Union Organizing and Staying Organized* (Reston, Virginia: Reston Publishing Company, 1983), p. 95.

organizer will formulate an agenda and platform as a means of selling the targeted group of employees on the benefits of organized labor and collective bargaining. According to recent research, union organizers tend to emphasize grievance procedures, job security, benefits, and higher pay.[19] The information is organized so that the employees will be convinced that they deserve better compensation and working conditions than they have currently. Generally speaking, a union organizer will emphasize one of the following themes in order to stimulate employee enthusiasm and support:

1. The pay, employee benefits, and working conditions of the targeted group are *compared* with those of other employees in the community or industry in order to illustrate problems that can be eliminated if the union is elected as the employees' exclusive bargaining representative. If the targeted employees' pay and working conditions are subpar relative to other workers in the community, then the union may use local conditions as the standard of comparison. On the other hand, organizers may emphasize industry-wide comparisons if these data lend themselves to better illustrating the union's point. Unions, as might be expected, will emphasize the information that best serves their purposes.[20] However, union organizers are cognizant of the fact that management will attempt to refute the union's contentions by citing the "apples versus oranges" comparison argument. For example, if the union is attempting to organize a group of relatively unskilled workers in a community whose economy contains many skilled and technical workers, management will insist that community-based comparisons are unrealistic. Likewise, the union that focuses on intraindustry differentials runs the risk of being accused of making unrealistic comparisons because of geographic variations in the cost of living (e.g., comparing the pay and benefits of computer programmers in Indianapolis with those in Boston).

2. Inequities and injustices in the workplace may be illustrated by the union as a means of persuading employees to take action and "fight back" against management. Under this strategy, the union will portray the employer as being unfair and uncaring. Specific instances of favoritism, invidious discrimination, capricious disciplinary actions, and employee discharges or layoffs without "just cause" are often cited to document and support the union's position. The union will normally emphasize that the employer does not have a grievance procedure or appeal mechanism to ensure equal protection and due process in the workplace. Examples of safety hazards will also be illustrated if they exist. In short, the union organizer(s) will emphasize that the quality of the employees' worklife is in need of substantial improvement and that the union is the vehicle by which such improvements can be made.

3. The company's income and profit picture may be used to convince the employees that they are not receiving their fair share of the profits. Union organizers generally have little difficulty in obtaining financial information on firms

---

[19] See Monty L. Lynn and Jozell Brister, "Trends in Union Organizing Issues and Tactics," *Industrial Relations* (Winter 1989), pp. 104-113.
[20] This tactic is known as "cherry picking."

that are publicly held (that is, they trade their stock through public exchanges). For firms whose profit picture is good, the union may claim that employees have been short changed in favor of stockholder dividends, capital improvements, or building retained earnings. The union will argue that the employees are directly responsible for the firm's favorable financial position, yet they are not being properly rewarded for their efforts and productivity. If the union is unable to obtain a firm's financial statements, then it may find other means for ascertaining the solvency of the employer. One unobtrusive measure of a firm's financial position may be the rate at which it invests in new equipment and facilities. An expanding firm is generally in a secure financial position and the union may emphasize this to encourage employees to press for improved compensation and employee benefits. In addition, an employer that makes substantial capital expenditures in a particular location is not as likely to relocate or close a facility if the union wins the certification election.

Many union organizers believe that it is critical to enlist the support of pro-union employees during the organizational campaign. There are several reasons for soliciting the assistance of such employees. First, union organizers are not usually allowed to enter the workplace. The law allows management to protect its property rights and minimize disruptions in the work routine that would arise if outsiders were allowed access to employees during business hours. Union organizers frequently attempt to circumvent this problem by contacting employees before or after work. In some cases, union organizers will patronize restaurants or bars where employees are known to congregate. In other instances, contact can be made by talking to employees as they enter or leave company property. The union organizer may also visit employees in their homes. When none of these alternatives are suitable, then the union may use the news media (or may use the media in combination with the aforementioned approaches). If the employees are inaccessible, then the NLRB may secure a court order that allows the organizers to solicit union membership on company property. This exception is rare and, as a result, the only way of spreading the union's message to a majority of the targeted employees is through pro-union workers who come into face-to-face contact with their co-workers.

A second reason for using pro-union employees during the campaign is that they are known personally to the employees, whereas the union organizer is an outsider. Sympathetic pro-union employees act as intermediaries for the union. Many employees may be reluctant to deal directly with union organizers because they are distrustful of strangers and are fearful that the employer will see them talking with the union representative and will take retaliatory action.

A less obvious third reason for obtaining the support of current employees in the organizing campaign is that they will form the foundation for local union leadership if the union wins the certification election. Once the NLRB election is completed, the union organizer will move to another location, and will no longer be involved in the daily affairs of the newly formed bargaining unit. Employees who assist the union during the organizing drive may subsequently become officers at the local union level. The experience and knowledge that they acquired during the campaign will be of benefit in their new leadership role.

Because pro-union employees often play an integral role in the success (or lack of success) in the union organizing campaign, union officials are generally careful to select and train workers who they believe will be most effective. A primary consideration is to use only those employees who command the respect of their fellow workers. Identifying and enlisting the support of such employees can be a difficult task. Most workplaces have a variety of employees, some of which are respected by their peers, whereas others are disliked and even despised. A particular employee may enjoy a great deal of respect and admiration within a specific social circle at work and yet be excluded from other social groups. The key is to find workers who are respected by all (or nearly all) workers. If this is not possible, then the next best alternative is to find someone who does not have a large number of enemies in any particular quarter. Unfortunately, a union organizer faces a serious dilemma when the most zealous union supporter is also a chronic malcontent who has earned an undying enmity from both management and fellow employees.

Pro-union employees must also have the endurance and fortitude to withstand the pressures of the organizing campaign. Many union organizers spend a great deal of time and effort educating and preparing union adherents to serve as persuasive labor advocates during the campaign. Union supporters must have a basic understanding of appropriate pre-election conduct, methods for approaching and convincing reluctant employees of the benefits of collective bargaining, and unfair labor practices and NLRB procedures.

In addition to carefully cultivating employees who will help with the campaign, the union organizer is usually interested in obtaining diagrams of the plant, facilities, and work areas occupied by the targeted employee group. Diagrams of the workplace are useful in helping the organizer decide on the structure of the appropriate bargaining unit. This information will also aid in establishing the solicitation areas for each employee who is assisting with the organizational drive. As discussed in a subsequent section of this chapter, there are different solicitation rules, depending on whether one is in a work or nonwork area. Workplace diagrams also ensure that no employee or group is overlooked in the campaign. Finally, precise knowledge of company property lines will determine those areas in which the organizer can solicit union support. For example, employees may park in a public lot rather than on the employer's premises, thereby allowing the union organizer to make direct contact with them as they enter and leave the workplace.

Obtaining the Critical Mass of Employee Support

Once the agenda for the organizing campaign is established, the focus shifts to selling the idea of unionization to the employee target group. Union organizers and employees who are union adherents normally use several techniques to convey their message. Most organizing efforts involve the use of written and verbal solicitation, both in the workplace and in locations away from work. In some cases, the union organizer may arrange to visit individually with each employee, whereas in other instances group meetings may be held.

Union organizers and their assistants may attempt to visit with employees in their homes. Employees have varied reactions to this practice. Some employees welcome the opportunity because it allows them to express their problems and concerns candidly without the fear of being overheard by a supervisor or fellow employees who side with management. Other employees resent being bothered during off-duty time and regard home visits by union organizers as an intrusion. In small communities that are dominated by one company, there is an added fear that the employer will learn about the visit, view it as a sign of union sympathy, and retaliate. Because of the time-consuming nature of housecalls, some union organizers either do not use this approach at all or they limit it to employees who are undecided about whether to support the union.

Nearly all union organizing campaigns involve the use of employee meetings. Mass meetings held in a local auditorium or convention center are designed to provide information on workplace problems and issues, with emphasis being placed on how the union will alleviate such conditions. Union organizers usually plan and advertise mass meetings so that attendance is good, thereby giving the impression that the union enjoys strong support. In addition, the union organizer will often make sure that the event has media coverage. Smaller meetings may be arranged to cater to certain employee groups, such as those working in a specific department or on a particular shift as well as those with unique problems at work (e.g., older employees who have experienced difficulties with the health insurance program or women who are facing pay discrimination). Unlike mass meetings, which employ speeches and campaign rhetoric, small group meetings are more conducive to question-and-answer sessions and may give the employee a greater sense of involvement.

Regardless of the media used to reach employees, messages about the union must be simple and understandable. A message that is complex and difficult to decipher is not as likely to impress employees as one that makes a point concisely and forcefully. For this reason, most campaign literature that is distributed by unions is straightforward, doing little to muddy the waters and obscure the intended message.

Once the organizing drive is underway, it will have the employer's undivided attention. Measures will be taken by the company to offset and rebut the actions and remarks of union organizers. Employer countermeasures designed to dilute the effectiveness of the campaign are addressed later in this chapter. The conflict between union and management will usually intensify once the employees are approached and union literature is distributed.

The primary objective of the union organizer at this stage of the campaign is to secure employee signatures on authorization cards (also called recognition cards). By signing an authorization card, the employee is expressing an interest in having the union as his or her exclusive bargaining representative. There is no obligation on the part of an employee to vote for the union in a certification election simply because he or she has signed an authorization card. Employees may sign the card because of peer pressure or because they believe that the issue of unionization should be put to a secret ballot vote. Furthermore, employees who initially sign an authorization card may later change their minds and vote against the union in the NLRB-supervised election. The National Labor Relations Act requires that a minimum of 30 percent of eligible employees sign authorization cards before the NLRB will hold a certification election. In practice, union organizers generally attempt to secure the signatures of at least 60 to 70 percent (and perhaps as many as 90 percent) of the eligible employees before proceeding to an election. The reason for obtaining substantially more than the necessary number of signatures needed for an election is to ensure that the union will have a safety margin to offset those employees who either do not participate in the election or who decide to vote against the union despite having signed the authorization card. If the organizer has difficulty in securing the minimum number of signatures, then the union may quietly allow the campaign to die rather than proceed with an ill-advised election that the union is likely to lose. It should be noted that an employer may recognize and bargain with a union based on a showing of authorization cards by the union. However, most employers refuse to accept this method of recognition and insist on a secret-ballot election. In fact, labor consultants may advise the employer not to examine signed authorization cards because they reveal the identity of union supporters; such knowledge may later help the union establish an antilabor intent by the employer if unfair labor practice charges are filed.[21]

Measures Taken by Employers during the Organizing Campaign

In recent years, there has been growing management opposition to unions before and during organizing campaigns. During the 1970s and 1980s, management became increasingly hostile toward organized labor. The goal of a union-free environment, once espoused only by a few militantly antiunion firms, has spread until perhaps the majority of U.S. corporations are now willing to fight union organizing attempts. Two labor researchers, Richard B. Freeman and Morris M. Kleiner, have found that firms with higher wages, better work conditions, and superior supervisory practices were less likely to commit unfair labor practices against unions and employees than were firms with lower wages and less favorable working conditions and supervisory practices. Freeman and Kleiner also found that firms with poor working conditions and supervisory practices were especially likely to campaign against the union. Opposition by supervisors was found to be particularly effective in defeating union organizing drives. Managers who either faced or lost union organizing campaigns were likely to suffer setbacks in their careers (firing, reassignment, retraining, or denied promotion).[22]

Table 5-1 outlines measures (and countermeasures) that may be taken by management during the organizing campaign in order to discourage employee support of the union.[23] Two categories of managerial antiunion actions are illustrated

---

[21] Some union organizers will suggest that authorization signatures be verified by a neutral, respected party like a local minister or some other person who is not connected with the employer or union. This procedure protects the identity of the card signees and avoids the bureaucratic involvement of the NLRB.

[22] Richard B. Freeman and Morris M. Kleiner, "Employer Behavior in the Face of Union Organizing Drives," *Industrial and Labor Relations Review* (April 1990), pp. 351–365.

[23] Also see John J. Lawler, "A Typology of Employer Counter-Organizing Tactics," (Industrial Relations Research Association 1986 Spring Meeting) *Labor Law Journal* (August 1986), pp. 549–554; and Thomas A. Kochan, Robert B. McKersie, and John Chalykoff, "The Effects of Corporate Strategy and Workplace Innovations on Union Representation," *Industrial and Labor Relations Review* (July 1986), pp. 487–501.

Table 5-1 ▲ Measures and Countermeasures by Management to Prevent Unionism

Prior to a Union Organizing Campaign	After a Union Organizing Campaign is Underway	
Proactive Measures	*Legal Reactive Measures*	*Illegal Reactive Measures*
Adequate and Equitable Wages and Salary Programs	Nonthreatening, Noncoercive, and Factual Antiunion Propaganda	Threatening to Discharge Employees Who Support the Union
Comprehensive Employee Benefits	▲ letters to employees	Threatening to Close or Relocate a Plant or Facilities if the Union Wins the Certification Election
Favorable Supervisory–Employee Relationships	▲ speeches to employees	
Open Channels of Communication	▲ information posted on bulletin boards	
	▲ lobby or cafeteria displays	Spying on Union Activities or Meetings
Safe Working Conditions	▲ film and slide shows	Making Job Assignments Based on Whether an Employee Supports a Union
Job Security Measures	"Vote No" Committees Comprised of Antiunion Employees	
Grievance Mechanisms which Afford Due Process and Equal Protection	Hiring Labor Consultants to Provide Advice During Union Organizing Campaigns	Circulating Antiunion Propaganda that:
Equitable Promotion and Transfer Policies		▲ emphasizes that it is futile to elect the union because compensation and working conditions will not change
Periodic Communications on the Organization's Success and Benefits in a Nonunion Environment	Forming Supervisory Committees to Ensure that Work Activities are not Disrupted	
Organizational Structure	Banning Union Organizers from Soliciting on Company Property (unless there are special circumstances)	▲ predicts strikes and turmoil in the workplace if the union is certified as the employee's bargaining representatives
▲ small plants (fewer than 200 employees)		
▲ establishing operations in rural Southern areas		
▲ designing facilities to limit access by union organizers	Forbidding Employees from Distributing Union Literature	▲ otherwise violates an employee's Sec. 7 right
Screening out Pro-Union Job Candidates During the Hiring Process (generally illegal)		Holding Captive Audience Speeches Within 24 Hours of the Certification Election
Employee Attitude Surveys		Providing Support to a Company-Dominated or Favored Union in order to Exclude an "Outside" Union

in Table 5–1: proactive measures and reactive measures. *Proactive measures* are used to prevent or discourage employee interest in unions by creating a work environment that makes unions unnecessary or by developing a workforce that is antiunion. Proactive measures taken *before* union organizers approach a firm's employees often focus on improving wages, hours, and working conditions or eliminating problems that might encourage employees to unionize. Other (potentially illegal) proactive measures that can be taken by management are discriminating against union adherents during the hiring process, indoctrinating employees via threats against organized labor soon after they are hired, and permanently replacing workers who engage in economic strikes. According to Richard Belous, a labor economist at the Conference Board:

> When firms are doing well they are willing to "play softball with unions." Now employers are insecure and they've "switched to hardball." Measures that might have been unthinkable a few years ago such as decertifications or the use of replacement workers during a strike are now standard operating procedures.[24]

Once the employer is aware that a union is interested in organizing a group of its employees, then *reactive measures* may be taken either to put a halt to the campaign or to defeat the union in the NLRB certification election.[25] Table 5–1 distinguishes between legal and illegal reactive measures. Legal reactive measures are those that the employer can use without violating the National Labor Relations Act or other laws. The legality of a specific reactive measure is often hard to determine, as witnessed by the plethora of NLRB and court cases stemming from employer practices during union organizing drives. Several of the more troublesome and controversial management actions, such as employer speeches prior to the certification election, threatening statements to employees, and union solicitation bans on company premises, are treated separately later in this chapter.

Proactive Measures by Management

An examination of Table 5–1 reveals that most of the proactive measures that can be taken by management focus on the traditional wages, hours, and working conditions typically embodied in collective bargaining agreements. The bottom line of such proactive measures is to eliminate the employees' need for organized labor by providing pay, benefits, and worklife that are equal to or better than those found in unionized firms. By taking this approach, management attempts to eliminate issues that a union could later use to generate worker enthusiasm and support. Employees who are satisfied with their compensation, benefits, and working conditions may be less influenced by the sales pitch of union organizers and less willing to attend organizing meetings, sign authorization cards, or vote affirmatively in a certification election. This line of reasoning leads many companies to establish personnel policies and practices that are progressive and equitable.

---

[24] The Bureau of National Affairs, Inc., "Union Organizing Outlook," *Collective Bargaining Negotiations & Contracts* (Washington, D.C.: The Bureau of National Affairs, Inc., February 28, 1988), p. 4.
[25] See Clemens P. Work, "Making It Clear Who's Boss," *U.S. News & World Report* (September 8, 1986), p. 43.

Compensation and employee benefits may be kept above industry or community norms in firms using proactive measures to discourage unionization. Greater care can be taken to handle promotion, transfer, and disciplinary decisions in a fair manner. Communication channels that provide timely and accurate information of concern to employees may help tremendously to dispel rumors and allay fears, especially during economic downturns, when layoffs or reduced working hours pose a threat. Some companies periodically survey employees to determine whether there are problems that need to be corrected before they create serious dissension and dissatisfaction. Surveys may be taken by either distributing questionnaires that can be completed and returned anonymously or by obtaining information from first-line supervisors who are in daily contact with employees.

One proactive measure that is sometimes taken by an employer is to screen out union sympathizers during the employment recruitment and selection process. By avoiding recruitment through union hiring halls, companies may eliminate workers who would be favorably disposed toward unions. This method is not illegal because an employer has the right to recruit employees from whatever source he or she desires. However, there are a number of NLRB and federal court cases that demonstrate the illegality (under section 8(a)(3) and 8(a)(1) of the National Labor Relations Act) of questioning job applicants about previous union membership or their feelings toward unions. Application blanks that ask prospective employees to supply information on union membership are generally viewed unfavorably by the NLRB and courts. Companies that warn job applicants that unions are not acceptable are usually in violation of the NLRA. Equally illegal are instances of job discrimination in which an otherwise qualified applicant is rejected because of the union activities of relatives. The only instances in which it may be permissible to discriminate against union adherents are when the employee is not qualified for the job (or other applicants are better qualified) or when the employee is applying for a supervisory position not protected under the NLRA.[26]

Legal Reactive Measures by Employers

Employers often walk a legal tightrope during an organizing campaign and they must exercise caution insofar as antiunion actions and statements to employees are concerned. Table 5–1 lists the legal reactive measures that management may take to defeat the union's campaign efforts. It should be noted that these seemingly legal measures may degenerate into illegal measures if they, in any way, become threatening to employees or otherwise jeopardize their Section 7 rights under the National Labor Relations Act.

Letters, speeches, or other information directed to employees are permissible under federal law as long as they do not explicitly or implicitly alter the terms or conditions of the employment relationship. One interesting line of NLRB decisions involves the issue of employer communications to workers during the union organizing campaign. Because of the legal dangers associated with antiunion statements made *directly* by management, an employer may encourage nonsupervisory

---

[26] Terry L. Leap, G. Stephen Taylor, William H. Hendrix, and Zhu Z. Wei, "Pre-employment Screening as a Means of Eliminating Union Adherents," *Labor Law Journal* (April 1988), pp. 208–219.

employees to speak out against the union. "Vote-no" committees comprised of workers who are against the union may be used to discourage fellow employees from signing authorization cards or voting affirmatively in the certification election. Statements that would be illegal if made by management may be legal when voiced by members of a "vote-no" committee. Management may even provide literature or coaching sessions for antiunion committee members. However, if an employer uses a "vote-no" committee as a conduit to threaten employees, then an unfair labor practice is likely. The key point regarding threatening statements is the *ability* of the party to make good on or carry through with the threat. Statements made by a group of employees of their own volition are not likely to be regarded as threats by the NLRB because fellow employees do not control wages, hours, and working conditions. An exception to this rule would be threats of bodily injury or property damage to coworkers by members of a "vote-no" committee. When a "vote-no" committee becomes a pawn of management, then threatening statements or promises of benefit are often illegal.

An increasingly popular method of combating unions in recent years is to use management consulting firms that specialize in maintaining union-free work environments.[27] Some management firms offer training programs for personnel managers and supervisors on topics such as "Defending the 'Union-Free' Status", "How to Decertify a Union", and "How to Conduct a Union Vulnerability Audit and Training Program."[28] Management consulting firms also help employers avoid violations under the National Labor Relations Act by providing advice during organizing campaigns. Employers who must deal with unions for the first time are often ill-prepared to withstand the tactics of a sophisticated and savvy organizer. Because of the thin line separating legal from illegal activity during union organizing drives, astute employers may seek the services of experts who possess the knowledge to help them steer clear of unfair labor practice violations.

Labor relations consultants also integrate psychological ploys into their antiunion programs. One manual distributed by a management consulting firm urges employers to properly indoctrinate new employees and "shape their attitudes in healthy and productive ways their first several months of employment and quickly discharge those who don't come around."[29] The basis for this approach, according to the consulting firm, is that newly hired employees are more impressionable than those who have worked with a firm for extended periods. Regardless of the tactics used, management consulting firms that help companies combat labor unions are on the rise. According to one observer:

> During the 1970s, the labor management consulting industry expanded an estimated 10 times over. Employing slick and effective new techniques, the consultants have created a growing market for their services. There may now be as many as 1,000 firms in the field, involved on management's behalf in two-thirds

---

[27] The Bureau of National Affairs, Inc., *Labor Relations Consultants: Issues, Trends, and Controversies* (Washington, D.C.: The Bureau of National Affairs, Inc., June 24, 1985); and Jules Bernstein, "The Evolution of the Use of Management Consultants in Labor Relations: A Labor Perspective," *Labor Law Journal* (May 1985), pp. 292–299.

[28] The author frequently receives advertisements for training programs on topics dealing with maintaining a union-free status.

[29] Steve Lagerfeld, "The Pop Psychologist as Union Buster," *AFL-CIO American Federationist* (November 1981), 4th page of article.

of all organizing drives. These are only estimates: a recent survey found that less than 3 percent of the consulting firms admitted engaging in the activities that require them to report to the Department of Labor.[30]

Although some management consultants openly advertise their programs, this statement indicates that many consulting activities are shrouded in behind-the-scenes secrecy. Because of their sophistication, antiunion consulting firms have skillfully avoided involving their clients in unfair labor practice cases and have had a high rate of success in helping to defeat unions in certification elections.

Employers may form supervisory committees to ensure that work activities are not disrupted by union organizing activities. Management retains the right to maintain an orderly working environment that is free of distractions and there is no violation of the federal labor laws if they ask union organizers to leave company property, forbid the distribution of union literature in work areas, or ban other organizing activities that directly encroach on work routines. Management cannot ban the distribution of union literature in nonworking areas, nor can they forbid discussions of union matters among employees on the company premises during breaks or free time.

The NLRB often has to balance the property and managerial rights of the employer against the rights of employees to engage in union activities. Although the employer does not have the right to ban union solicitation by pro-labor employees, actions that significantly disrupt the work routine are not permissible. In one case, a group of employees wore shirts emblazoned with a derogatory and suggestively obscene slogan. The employer gave the offending parties the option of either removing the shirts or leaving work (without pay). An unfair labor practice charge was filed by the union, but the NLRB ruled for the company and noted that management had a right to maintain discipline in the workplace. In this case, management prerogatives took precedence over the employees' right to free speech. Other instances in which employees wore union insignias on their clothing or placed controversial bumper stickers on their automobiles have been protected under free speech entitlements because there was no detrimental effect on the work environment.

Illegal Reactive Measures by Management

A number of illegal actions by the employer during a union organizing campaign are possible. Table 5–1 lists the more common violations that occur during the course of a certification drive and that usually result in charges being filed by the

---

[30] Steve Lagerfeld, "The Pop Psychologist as Union Buster," *AFL-CIO American Federationist*, (November 1981), no pages listed. Also see John J. Lawler and Robin West, "Impact of Union Avoidance Strategy in Representation Elections," *Industrial Relations* (Fall 1985), pp. 406–420; William N. Cooke, "The Rising Toll of Discrimination against Union Activists," *Industrial Relations*, Vol. 24, No. 3 (Fall 1985), pp. 421–442; William T. Dickens, "The Effect of Company Campaigns on Union Certification Elections: Law and Reality Once Again," *Industrial and Labor Relations Review*, Vol. 36, (July 1983), pp. 560–575; Robert Flanagan, "The Behavioral Foundations of Union Election Regulation," *Stanford Law Review*, XXVIII (July 1976), pp. 1195–1205; John J. Lawler, "The Influences of Management Consultants on the Outcome of Certification Elections," *Industrial and Labor Relations Review*, Vol. 38, (October 1984), pp. 335–348; Kent Murrman and Andrew Porter, "Employer Tactics and NLRB Election Outcomes: Some Preliminary Evidence," *Proceedings*, 35th Annual Meeting of the Industrial Relations Research Association (Madison, Wisconsin: IRRA 1983), pp. 67–72.

employees or union under Section 8(a) of the National Labor Relations Act. Although the focus here is on employer transgressions, unions may also violate federal laws by threatening, intimidating, or coercing employees in the exercise of their rights to join or refrain from joining a union under Section 7 of the Act (see Chapter 3).

Perhaps one of the most flagrant actions that an employer can take is to threaten to discharge workers or close (or relocate) a plant if the union wins the certification election. Employers are usually aware of the illegality of direct threats and adopt more subtle approaches for sending antiunion messages to their employees; in fact, some of the most chilling threats may be delivered in a very cordial manner. For example, a young union supporter who worked in a plant along with his grandfather was approached by a supervisor. After exchanging pleasantries, the supervisor smiled and asked: "How long has your grandfather worked here?" Although the supervisor did not directly threaten either the young man or his grandfather, the supervisor's seemingly innocent question was a thinly veiled threat that chilled the young employee's desire to remain a union advocate. Instances such as these require that the NLRB and federal courts carefully examine the actions of employers to determine what constitutes a threat. In so doing, they have attempted to reconcile the free speech rights of management against the employees' right to unionize and bargain collectively. The following guidelines have evolved through various NLRB and court cases and are useful in determining whether actions by management constitute a threat:

1. The party issuing a threat must have the ability or means to carry through with the threat. In most cases, an employer is in a position to act on threatening statements to employees. For example, if a supervisor tells an employee that he or she will be discharged, then the employee has a good reason to believe such statements because supervisors usually play a prominent role in disciplinary actions. Likewise, if a supervisor remarks that a plant or department will be shut down if a union wins representation rights, then a violation is likely because the supervisor represents management and is presumed to have "inside" information on the sentiments of management.

2. Employers generally do not have the legal right to question employees about union organizing activities. Questions such as "How do you (the employee) feel about unions?", "Which way will you vote in the certification election?", "Were you talking to a union organizer at the front gate this morning?", and "How many people in your department have signed authorization cards?" are all examples of potentially illegal questions. Employer inquiries such as these often have an intimidating effect on employees even though no threat was made.

    There may be instances when a first-line supervisor will ask about union activities out of idle curiosity with no intent to engage in retaliatory action. The NLRB may not regard such behavior to be illegal, especially if the supervisor confines questioning to a few close personal friends. However, if the questioning becomes repetitive and spreads beyond the supervisor's immediate social circle, then the NLRB is more likely to find a violation.

3. The social and organizational context in which an employer makes statements about unions also has an impact on whether a threat was made. Statements

made by supervisors or managers to *individual* employees are more likely to be viewed as threatening than would a similar statement made to a group of employees. Interestingly, it is perfectly legal for unions to make individual sales pitches and visit workers in their homes, but employers are forbidden from so doing. Employers should avoid speaking to workers in management authority areas such as company conference rooms, board rooms, or other locations on company property where employees do not normally work or visit. This guideline applies even in cases where the employer's statements are not coercive, the reason being that workers are more apt to be intimidated in a "foreign" managerial setting.

4. During an organizing campaign, management may make *predictions* about what will happen if the union wins the certification election. The NLRB tends to make a distinction between predictions that fall within the *control* of management versus those that are not directly controllable by the company. If a firm's president predicts that unionization will lead to factory closings and layoffs, then the NLRB will regard such statements as threats because the president has the power to turn such "predictions" into reality. However, what if the president voices concern that wage increases stemming from collective bargaining will raise prices for the firm's product and result in a loss of business? Speculation such as this is beyond management's control and does not constitute a threat.

   Another area of concern involves management statements about the outcome of collective bargaining. Management is on safe legal footing when it states that there are no guarantees that negotiations with a union will lead to improved compensation and benefits. As long as management bargains with the union in good faith, pay and benefits may be increased, decreased, or remain the same. However, employers who remark that "negotiations will assume zero pay and benefits" or will "start from scratch" may violate the law because they create the impression that employees are having their present compensation package eliminated *before* negotiations commence.

5. Employer statements indicating that it is futile for employees to vote for the union are also illegal in most circumstances. This limitation on employer speech is known as the *futility doctrine*. When management emphasizes that employees will be no better off after the union has been certified as the exclusive bargaining representative, then the NLRB is likely to invoke the futility doctrine. Statements such as these may be augmented with predictions of strikes, pay cuts, and layoffs. The futility doctrine *per se* may not constitute an unfair labor practice, although statements of futility may result in the NLRB's ordering a second certification election if the union loses the first. Remarks such as these, while containing no direct threat, interfere with the employees' free choice in selecting a bargaining representative.

The categories of employer statements discussed above deal primarily with direct and indirect threats to employees. Threats by employers that encroach on the rights of workers to vote as they see fit in a certification election conducted by the NLRB are illegal under federal law. However, this does not mean that management must remain silent and defenseless while the union conducts its campaign. In fact, Section 8(c) of the Taft-Hartley Act permits nonthreatening free speech by employers:

> The expressing of any views, argument, or opinion, or the dissemination thereof, whether in written, printed, graphic, or visual form shall not constitute or be evidence of an unfair labor practice under any of the provisions of the Act, if such expression contains no threat of reprisal or force or promise of benefit.

Employers may make speeches and distribute written information to employees urging them to vote against the union. Factual and truthful information about the employer's view on unions may be conveyed to workers as long as threats of reprisal or promises of benefit are not made.

The following are examples of legitimate, nonthreatening statements:[31]

1. The company believes that unions are not in the best interests of the employees.
2. Wages and benefits paid by the company are competitive with other firms in the local community or industry.
3. Superior employees may be handicapped by seniority and promotion clauses found in many union contracts.
4. The union that is attempting to secure certification has been involved in several lengthy strikes during the past year.
5. Union dues will average $25 per month for each employee.
6. Unions have the legal right to fine or expel members who work during a strike.
7. Employees do not have to sign authorization cards.
8. An employer can rebut or correct false information or statements made by union organizers.
9. The only guarantees of improved wages, benefits, and job security are good business conditions, not labor unions.
10. The company is required by law to bargain in good faith, but there is no guarantee that the union will be able to live up to all of its promises. Collective bargaining, rather than promises made during an organizing campaign, determines what the union will achieve.
11. A strike will not necessarily force the company to accede to union demands. In fact, the company has the right to continue operations during a work stoppage and may hire permanent replacements to fill jobs previously held by strikers.
12. An employee is not required to vote for the union in a secret ballot election even though he or she has signed an authorization card.

One of the most controversial issues surrounding pre-election conduct concerns statements that involve *substantial* misrepresentations of fact. As the organizing campaign becomes heated, accusations and erroneous comments are occasionally made by either the union or the employer. The NLRB recognizes that a broad range of campaign promises, tactics, propaganda, and rhetoric are permissible.

---

[31] Adapted from James W. Hunt, *Employer's Guide to Labor Relations* (Washington, D.C.: The Bureau of National Affairs, Inc., 1979), pp. 45–47.

A dilemma is created when nonthreatening, yet patently false, information is disseminated. Should substantial misrepresentations of important issues be grounds for setting aside a certification election? If a sufficient amount of time remains before an election, then the party damaged by erroneous statements will have an opportunity to respond and correct the misrepresentation. What happens, however, if damaging and false statements are made immediately preceding the election? Should mature and well-informed employees be expected to distinguish between reasonable and erroneous propaganda?

Apparently the NLRB has experienced considerable difficulty in answering these and other questions pertaining to pre-election statements. Originally (in 1962), the Board held that substantial misrepresentations of material facts made immediately before an election were grounds for setting aside an election.[32] This doctrine stood for 15 years before being reversed. In 1977, the Board decided that it would "no longer probe into the truth or falsity" of statements made during a certification campaign because "mature individuals....are capable of recognizing campaign propaganda for what it is and discounting it."[33] One year later, the NLRB reversed its position and returned to essentially the same position that it had held in 1962. Thus, the NLRB was once again willing to examine the impact of misrepresentations made prior to a certification election.[34] This decision was short-lived because, in 1982, the NLRB returned to its hands-off policy and ruled that an election would be set aside only for the abuse of Board processes or the use of fraudulent documents.[35] The indecisiveness of the NLRB was based primarily on changes in Board membership rather than changes in social, legal, or economic conditions. Because of union opposition to the current NLRB posture on free speech preceding certification elections, it is possible that we may see yet another reversal on this issue in the future.

A method frequently used by employers to counter the effects of union campaign activities involves *captive audience speeches*. Management may require that employees attend a mass meeting during work hours to hear nonthreatening speeches by employers (or their representatives) on the topic of unions and collective bargaining. It has been estimated that captive audience speeches are used in nearly two-thirds of employer antiunion campaigns.[36] As long as the employer does not engage in unfair labor practice violations, captive audience meetings are not only legal, but there is also no obligation on the part of management to allow union officials to attend and rebut what has been said. Except in unusual circumstances, the union must continue to hold its meetings off company property. Unions may be allowed to enter the workplace if there is no other reasonable access to employees or if the employer has committed an unfair labor practice (for example, making threatening remarks) during the course of a captive audience speech. The *24-hour rule* is a notable exception to the captive audience issue; it forbids mandatory mass meetings within 24 hours of the certification election. The basis for

---

[32] *Hollywood Ceramics*, 140 NLRB 221 (1962).
[33] *Shopping Cart Food Market, Inc.*, 228 NLRB 190 (1977).
[34] *General Knit of California*, 239 NLRB No. 101 (1978).
[35] *Midland National Life Insurance Co.*, 263 NLRB No. 24 (1982).
[36] John J. Lawler and Robin West, "Impact of Union Avoidance Strategy in Representation Elections," *Industrial Relations* (Fall 1985), p. 412.

this rule is to ensure that union officials have sufficient time to respond to employer speeches. However, the 24-hour rule does not prevent a supervisor from discussing the upcoming election with a small group of employees, nor does it forbid antiunion speeches at voluntary social events such as company picnics. The NLRB is adamant about enforcing the rule even to the point of setting aside an election because a meeting that began more than 24 hours before the election ended within the proscribed time frame.[37]

Employers who grant pay or benefit increases during the organizing drive as a means of subduing the workers' enthusiasm for the union usually are in violation of the NLRA. Although a strategy of this nature is more palatable than some of the previously discussed threats and actions by employers, the NLRB has held that such conduct violates the employees' Section 7 rights. Pay or benefit increases that were either regularly scheduled or planned prior to the campaign are not regarded as unfair labor practices.

A final reactive measure that has been used by a few unscrupulous employers is to undermine the union through racist appeals. Some union organizers have been abhorrently branded with racist names.[38] Employers may also tell white workers that the union will primarily benefit and protect blacks. Statements calculated to influence racial prejudice or inflame racial tensions may be grounds for setting aside a certification election. A 1962 election in Georgia was set aside when the employer mailed a photograph of an interracial couple dancing. The photo was designed to exacerbate the racial hostilities between black and white employees.[39]

▲ The Certification Election

The discussion up to this point has focused on the activities that occur *prior* to an NLRB-conducted certification election. The federal labor laws were written to protect the rights of employees to a free, unfettered selection of a bargaining representative. Simultaneously, unions must have the opportunity to contact employees and inform them of the merits of collective bargaining without unduly restricting the employer's right to maintain a productive work environment that is free of major disruptions. The responsibility for delicately balancing the rights of all concerned falls on the NLRB; not only must the Board ensure that the pre-election conduct of both parties is in compliance with the law, but it also must establish safeguards to guarantee that the certification election is conducted in a fair manner.

Representation matters are governed under Section 9 of the NLRA. Once the union obtains authorization card signatures from 30 percent of the employees in the proposed bargaining unit or election unit, then a "showing of interest" has been

---

[37] Suppose that a certification election is scheduled for 3 P.M. on October 15. The employer holds a captive-audience meeting that commences at 1:30 on October 14. During the meeting, management encourages employees (in a nonthreatening manner) to vote "no union." If, for example, the captive audience meeting is adjourned at 3:15 P.M., the employer may have violated the 24-hour rule.
[38] See Alvin Schwartz, *The Unions* (New York: The Viking Press, 1972), pp.169–170.
[39] Also see J. J. Lawler, "A Typology of Employer Counter-Organizing Tactics," *Proceedings of the Spring Meeting* (Madison, Wisconsin: Industrial Relations Research Association, 1986), pp. 549–554.

established. The union then files a representation petition with the NLRB. Before conducting an election, the Board will make an investigation to ascertain that the authorization cards presented by the union have been properly signed and that no dispute exists regarding the legitimacy of the bargaining unit. If there is controversy, a representation hearing is held to resolve the issue.

The NLRB will not conduct a certification election if another valid election has been held within the previous 12 months. The 12-month rule applies regardless of whether the union or the employer won the previous election; the key to this provision is to protect the employer from the constant disruptions associated with certification elections. However, a union is not prohibited from attempting to organize a different group of the firm's employees (not merely a subdivision of the group involved in the first election) and may legally press for another election within the 12-month period. In order to promote stability in collective bargaining relationships, the NLRB will protect an incumbent union from being unseated by a rival labor organization through a provision known as a *contract bar*. Once a collective bargaining agreement has been negotiated, the union is protected from the organizing efforts of another union for up to a maximum of three years. After three years (or less if the parties negotiate a shorter contract), another union may attempt to become the exclusive bargaining representative and petition for an election.

The least complicated certification election involves only one union in a situation where there is no dispute over the legitimacy of authorization card signatures, the composition of the bargaining unit, or the pre-election conduct of the parties. Problems arise when more than one union is vying for representation rights; a second runoff election may be needed to determine which union, if any, has exclusive representation status.[40] Should the voting rights of an employee or group of employees be challenged by either side, then the election process is further complicated. Perhaps the most difficult dilemma occurs when unfair labor practice charges are filed in conjunction with an election. In complex unfair labor practice cases that are appealed in the federal courts, there can be lengthy delays before the final election results are certified. Many labor relations observers (especially those who are pro-union) believe that such delays undermine the integrity of the National Labor Relations Act. William H. Wynn, president of the United Food and Commercial Workers' union, provides an example of the frustrations surrounding such delays:

> We organized SeaFirst, the big bank out in San Francisco, in 1977. And despite all the court decisions, including the one at the Supreme Court, and board decisions in our favor, SeaFirst, through delays and court actions, has not engaged in any sort of bargaining with us to this day. So, if an employer is willing to spend some dollars in legal fees, and break a few labor laws, which, by the way, have no financial penalties attached, they can keep a union out.[41]

---

[40] Although unions win fewer than 50 percent of the certification elections when only one union is on the ballot, the union win rate increases dramatically when more than one labor organization is vying to represent a group of bargaining unit employees. See James B. Dworkin and James R. Fain, "Success in Multiple Union Elections: Exclusive Jurisdiction vs. Competition," *Journal of Labor Research* (Winter 1989), pp. 91–101.

[41] William H. Wynn (interview), "Building On Diversity," in Philip L. Quaglieri, *America's Labor Leaders* (Lexington, Massachusetts: Lexington Books, 1989), p. 254. Reprinted with permission.

The voting eligibility of an employee must be resolved prior to the certification election. An employee is usually entitled to vote if he or she has worked in the bargaining unit during the eligibility period established by the NLRB. If a current employee was on the last payroll immediately before the election date, then there is little question regarding eligibility. Employees who are ill, on vacation, temporarily laid off, or on military leave are usually eligible to vote if they appear at the polls on election day. The NLRB also recognizes the irregular and seasonal nature of certain types of employment and will allow workers to vote if they have a continuing interest in their jobs. For example, the NLRB held that employees of a construction company were allowed to vote if they had worked for the employer at least 65 days during the year before the election. Employees in the television, film, motion picture, and recording industries have been held eligible to vote if they worked a mere two days during the year preceding the election.[42] Economic strikers retain their right to vote in a certification election for 12 months after the commencement of the strike. This rule is specifically spelled out in Section 9(c)(3) of the NLRA and it pertains to strikers who have been *permanently* replaced by nonstriking or newly hired employees. Section 9(c)(3) makes it more difficult for employers to "break" a union by allowing a strike to occur, hiring replacements, and then decertifying the union. Permanent replacements also have the right to vote in a certification or decertification election.

Once an election has been directed by the NLRB, it is usually held within 30 days. Employers must supply the union with a list of names and addresses of all eligible employees within seven days after an election has been directed so that there is ample time to contact those involved.[43] As a means of subverting the election, an employer will occasionally provide incomplete or inaccurate lists to the union. There have also been cases in which a company hires a large number of antiunion employees immediately before the election. Relatives of supervisors and others who have been coached to vote against the union are put on the payroll long enough to participate in the certification election and, immediately thereafter, are placed on layoff status. Under either of these circumstances, the NLRB may set aside the results of the first election and order a second.

NLRB representation elections use secret ballots and offer the employee a minimum of two alternatives. If only one union (e.g., the UAW) is attempting to gain representation rights, then the choice on the ballot is between the UAW and "no union." The outcome of the election is determined by the simple majority of the *votes cast*. As is the case with most elections, the desires of those who fail to vote are ignored. If there are 300 eligible voters and 250 actually vote, then 126 votes for the union means that the union wins the right to become the exclusive bargaining representative for the entire group of 300. It is conceivable that some of the 50 workers who abstained from voting did so because they opposed the union and erroneously concluded that a "non-vote" was tantamount to a "no vote". When an election is close, the non-voters (much to their chagrin) can make a

---

[42] Office of the General Counsel, National Labor Relations Board, *A Guide To Basic Law and Procedures Under the National Labor Relations Act* (Washington, D.C.: U.S. Government Printing Office, 1978), pp. 16–17.
[43] *Excelsior Underwear, Inc.*, 156 NLRB 1236 (1962).

difference in the outcome.[44] When more than one union is attempting to represent a group of employees, one choice must secure a majority of the votes cast. Otherwise, a second or runoff election may be necessary between the two top choices from the first election.

At the conclusion of the election, the NLRB will count the ballots and certify the results. Unless there are objections regarding pre-election conduct, improprieties during the election, or challenged ballots cast by allegedly ineligible voters, the election process is complete. If the union wins the election, then it becomes the exclusive representative for the bargaining unit employees. The next step for the victorious union is to prepare for contract negotiations with the firm (discussed in Chapter 9). If the union loses the election, neither they nor any other union can petition for another certification election for at least 12 months. But, as stated earlier, employees who were not part of the election unit in the first certification attempt are not covered by the 12-month rule.

▲ Post-Election Matters

The most straightforward certification process is one in which a representation petition is filed, the NLRB conducts the election and certifies the results, and the matter is closed. Unfortunately, problems arise that affect the integrity and outcome of the election. Challenged ballots and unfair labor practices by the company or the union during the campaign can prolong the proceedings. Even when there is no direct violation of a federal labor law, an election may be set aside if either the union or the employer engages in acts of fraud or incites racial hostilities that interfere with voting freedoms. Not only can controversies and legal proceedings arise after the representation election, but they may delay the final certification of election results for many months.

Challenged Election Ballots

The eligibility of a particular employee or group of employees is occasionally challenged by either the company or the union. A dispute may occur as to whether an employee is a full-fledged bargaining unit member (perhaps because the employee works 10 hours a week in a bargaining unit job and spends the rest of the work week outside the unit). Questions may arise regarding the status of employees on indefinite sick leave or military duty. There also may be concerns about employees who have been on layoff status. Should such employees be allowed to vote in a certification election if their chances of reinstatement are almost nonexistent? Because of these and other questions, the ballots cast by certain employees are subject to challenge.

The NLRB normally attempts to resolve voter eligibility problems *before* the election. When this is not possible, the ballots in question are not included in count.

---

[44] See Richard N. Block and Myron Roomkin, "Determinants of Voter Participation in Union Certification Elections," *Monthly Labor Review* (April 1982), p. 45.

If the election outcome is not affected by the challenged votes, then the NLRB will certify the results and not rule on the ballots in question. For example, if there are six challenged ballots and the company wins the election by a margin of 20 votes, then the challenged ballots are irrelevant. The NLRB would have to rule on the eligibility of the challenged voters if the outcome were decided by less than six votes.

Ballots must be challenged when the employee in question appears at the polls to vote. A union or employer cannot challenge an employee's eligibility after the voting has occurred. This "challenge now or forever hold your peace" policy prevents the losing side from prolonging the election process, especially when the outcome is decided by a narrow margin.

Unfair Labor Practices That Preclude a Fair Election

Unfair labor practices committed by either the employer or the union may, in some cases, disrupt a certification election to the point of rendering it useless. When unfair labor practices contaminate certification election results and deny employees their rights under Section 7, the NLRB may either order a second certification election or require that the employer bargain with the union even though the employer won the election. Because of its controversial nature, this discussion focuses on the second alternative of ordering the employer to bargain with the union. How does one explain the following scenario?

> After the union secured nearly 70 percent of the bargaining unit employees' signatures, an election was held. Much to the amazement of everyone, the union lost the election by a considerable margin.

Why did so many employees who signed authorization cards later vote against the union in the secret ballot election conducted by the NLRB? Perhaps some employees changed their minds about supporting the union after they signed the authorization cards. Others signed the cards knowing full well that they would later vote against the union; they may have signed simply to avoid further campaign pressure by union organizers and adherents. A third group of employees may have signed because they supported the union, but were later intimidated and threatened by the employer into voting against the union. Primarily because of the third group of employees, the NLRB may disregard the results of the certification election and order the employer to bargain with the union if it can be demonstrated that the union once had the majority of support from employees.[45]

The history of second-chance certification elections is not good; if the union is defeated in the first certification election because employees have been intimidated, then the probability of the union emerging victorious in the second election is low. When a union secures a majority of valid authorization card signatures and then loses the certification election because of the employer's unfair labor practices, the NLRB may decide that a second election would be futile and order the employer to bargain over wages, hours, and working conditions. In some cases, the NLRB may issue a bargaining order even though an election has not been held. If the union's card-based majority is destroyed by the employer's unfair labor practices, then the

---

[45] See, for example, Marcus H. Sandver, "The Validity of Union Authorization Cards as a Predictor of Success in NLRB Certification Elections," *Labor Law Journal*, Vol. 28, No. 11 (1977), pp. 696–702.

NLRB order to bargain may be justified without conducting a certification election.[46] The U.S. Supreme Court, in justifying bargaining orders, has stated the following:

> The language and history of the act clearly indicate that Congress intended to impose upon an employer the duty to bargain with a union that has presented convincing evidence of majority support, even though the union has not petitioned for and won a Board-supervised election.[47]

The "convincing evidence" noted here usually takes the form of valid signed authorization cards. An authorization card is normally considered valid if it clearly indicates that the employee is authorizing the union to represent him or her (and is not merely a call for an election), the cards are signed and dated, and the signatures were obtained without deception or fraud.

To summarize, the U.S. Supreme Court has established three categories of unfair labor practices that can be committed during an organizational campaign. The first category includes acts that are so "pervasive" and "atrocious" that a bargaining order may be issued in the absence of a card-based union majority. J.P. Stevens, a previously mentioned firm with a history of flagrant unfair labor practices against employees working in Southern textile mills, was ordered to bargain by the NLRB, although the union did not secure the required number of authorization card signatures. The order was predicated on J.P. Stevens's threats of layoffs and plant closings, blatant surveillance of employees, threatening interrogations, and promises of improved benefits, all of which were designed to undermine the union.[48]

A second category of unfair labor practices involves a milder form of misconduct in which an employer destroys the majority employee support for the union because of unfair labor practices. Unlike the first category of cases, it must be shown that the union had established a majority of employee support that was subsequently destroyed by the employer. The third category of violations are those that are minor and do not warrant a bargaining order.[49] For example, an employer who provides pay increases for employees during an organizing campaign without fully understanding the illegality of such a measure may be required to submit to a second certification after winning the first. Some violations by an employer, however, are relatively minor and do not warrant a bargaining order or a second election.

Despite the considerable amount of controversy surrounding NLRB bargaining orders against firms that commit unfair labor practices during organizational campaigns, relatively few such orders are made. Of all of the NLRB elections conducted, the union wins fewer than one half and bargaining orders are issued in only 1.2 percent of the total elections held.[50] The sparing use of bargaining orders by the NLRB implies that they are used primarily as drastic, last-resort measures. Nearly all of these orders occur only after it has been determined that a card-based majority has been established by the union (the second category of cases noted above).

---

[46] *J. P. Stevens v. NLRB*, 441 F. (2d) 514 (CA 5, 1971).
[47] *Summer and Co., Linden Lumber Division v. NLRB*, 419 U.S. 301 (1974).
[48] See "Union Wins Access, Vote at J. P. Stevens Plants," *Monthly Labor Review* (January 1980), p. 56.
[49] Benjamin J. Taylor and Fred Witney, *Labor Relations Law*, 5th ed. (Englewood Cliffs, New Jersey: Prentice-Hall, Inc., 1987), pp. 307–315.
[50] Unions won 48 percent of the certification elections held in 1987 and 46.3 percent for the first quarter of 1988. See The Bureau of National Affairs, Inc., "Union Success in NLRB Elections," *Labor Relations Reporter* (August 22, 1988), pp. 525–527.

However, the liability stemming from such orders can be great because a 1975 NLRB decision imposes a retroactive legal obligation that commences on the date that the unfair labor practice started.[51] Employers who attempt to defeat a union by tying up the final certification through lengthy NLRB and federal court proceedings run the risk of having to make pay and benefit increases that are retroactive for as much as several years.[52]

▲ When Members No Longer Support the Union: The Decertification Process

The certification process gives a union the exclusive right to represent bargaining unit employees for a minimum of 12 months and up to a maximum of three years, if a valid contract bar exists. What happens if the employees become disenchanted with the union's lack of success at the bargaining table? Promises made by union leaders during the heat of the certification campaign may not have been fulfilled. Administrative and political problems arise and create dissention among bargaining unit members. Normal employee attrition, layoffs, or the addition of new employees may erode the union's majority status in the bargaining unit. Rival unions occasionally emerge and claim that they can provide a set of wages, hours, and working conditions that is superior to what is currently available under the existing collective bargaining agreement.[53] In short, employees may perceive that they are either no longer effectively represented by the incumbent union or that they would be in a better position if they elected another union as their representative.[54]

The Taft-Hartley Act contains provisions by which employees may decertify their union. In fact, the decertification process is quite similar to the certification process in that 30 percent of the bargaining-unit employees must sign a decertification petition after which the NLRB will conduct a secret-ballot election. If the "no union" choice on the ballot receives the majority of the votes cast, then the union no longer represents the employees and another certification election is banned for 12 months. The employer is free from another election and has no collective bargaining obligations for the next year.

Employers must maintain a hands-off policy with regard to encouraging workers to go forth with decertification proceedings. The typical antiunion employer would be exceedingly pleased to assist employees in their efforts to get rid of a union. However, employers are not allowed to initiate a decertification petition, conduct an employee poll of union support, or otherwise plant the seeds for a

---

[51] *Trading Port*, 219 NLRB 298 (1975).
[52] See J. J. Lawler and R. West, "Impact of Union-Avoidance Strategy in Representation Elections," *Industrial Relations* (Fall 1985), pp. 406–420; and M. Goldfield, "The Decline of Organized Labor: NLRB Union Certification Election Results," *Politics and Society*, Vol. 11 (1982), pp. 167–209.
[53] When an "outside" union attempts to "raid" an incumbent union, the incumbent usually wins. See Charles Odewahn and Clyde Scott, "An Analysis of Multi-Union Elections Involving Incumbent Unions," *Journal of Labor Research* (Spring 1989), pp. 197–206; and Charles Odewahn and Clyde Scott, "Multi-Union Elections Involving Incumbents: The Legal Environment," *Labor Law Journal* (July 1989), pp. 404–410.
[54] The number of decertifications has been on the rise. See Francis T. Coleman, "Once a Union, Not Always a Union," *Personnel Journal* (March 1985), p. 42.

decertification movement. Except for answering questions about the proper procedures to follow in the decertification process, employers must remain neutral. Employers are usually expected to continue their bargaining and contract administration duties with the union despite the presence of a decertification movement; only after the decertification has taken place are employers no longer obligated to deal with the labor organization.[55]

What happens if the union loses its majority support in the bargaining unit? Does the employer have to sit by idly and wait for the employees to initiate a decertification campaign, or is it legally permissible for the employer to take action? An employer may withdraw union recognition after one year if the union no longer has the majority support of unit employees (unless a contract bar precludes such action). The union's loss of majority support must not stem from employer coercion. As long as a majority of the employees no longer support the union, the employer does not have to recognize or bargain with it. Determining whether a union has lost the majority support is not easy in many cases. The NLRB will usually not conclude that a union has lost its majority status even though there has been a high degree of employee turnover (resignations or discharges), general expressions of dissatisfaction with the union, resignations from the union, or permanent replacement of striking workers. Also, the NLRB does not assume that new employees (recent hires or strike replacements) are necessarily against the union. The most convincing proof that the union no longer enjoys adequate support is through a petition signed by the majority of the employees stating that they no longer wish to be represented by the incumbent labor organization.[56]

▲ Summary and Conclusions

Organizing campaigns and certification elections are serious matters, both to the union and the employer whose workers are the target of the campaign. Unions must organize new members in order to survive and grow. Management uses proactive and reactive measures to discourage employees from joining unions and to mount counterattacks against them. Employees involved in organizing campaigns must decide whether to support the union or remain loyal to their employer by examining their personal beliefs about unions and by sifting through a maze of confusing and often conflicting campaign propaganda. The NLRB must ensure that the National Labor Relations Act is not violated as a result of pre-election conduct. Both the campaign and the election must be conducted in a manner that protects the property and managerial rights of the employer, yet allows the union to have reasonable

---

[55] See William J. Bigoness and Ellen R. Pierce, "Responding to Union Decertification Elections," *Personnel Journal* (August 1988), pp. 49–50.

[56] See Trevor Bain, et. al., "Deauthorization Elections: An Early Warning Signal to Decertification?," *Labor Law Journal* (July 1988), pp. 432–436; Ellen R. Pierce and Richard Blackburn, "The Union Decertification Process: Employer Do's and Don'ts," *Employee Relations Law Journal* (August 1986), pp. 205–220; James B. Dworkin and Marian Extejt, "Why Workers Decertify Their Unions," presented at the 1979 Academy of Management national meeting; and Lisa M. Lynch and Marcus H. Sandver, "Determinants of the Decertification Process: Evidence from Employer-Initiated Elections," *Journal of Labor Research* (Winter 1987), p. 87.

access to the targeted employees. Employees must be free to make individual decisions about unionization and collective bargaining without being subjected to intimidating strong-arm tactics by the employer or the union. In short, the NLRB attempts to regulate organizing campaigns and conduct certification elections that protect employees' Section 7 rights (to form, join, or assist a labor organization). The major objective of the NLRB is to ensure that the "laboratory conditions" of the union certification or decertification process are not contaminated by employer or union unfair labor practices.

Even when the union wins a certification election, there is no guarantee that the parties will enjoy a constructive relationship. Approximately one-third of union-management bargaining relationships never achieve a collective bargaining agreement. As long as the employer bargains in good faith, then there is no legal obligation for the company to negotiate and sign a labor contract. If employees subsequently lose confidence in the union, then decertifications are possible. The number of decertifications is relatively small (less than 10 percent of all elections). However, decertifications rates have risen over the past decade and may be indicative of increasing dissatisfaction by some union members.[57]

▲ Discussion Questions and Exercises

1. Obtain newspaper and magazine articles on the 1989 certification election involving Nissan employees (Smyrna, Tennessee) and the United Auto Workers (UAW). What issues did the union raise in its organizing campaign? How would you explain the wide margin of defeat for the UAW?
2. Why has the National Labor Relations Act been ineffective in deterring firms that are willing to prevent the unionization of their employees at almost any cost? Discuss.
3. Obtain organizing literature from a local union in your community. What issues are raised in the literature and how is the message conveyed to prospective union members?
4. Evaluate the legality and effectiveness of the following antiunion tactics:
   a. A trucking company screens job applicants and eliminates those who indicate that they are former union members or who believe that unions serve a useful purpose in society.
   b. A large department store enlists the services of a marketing consultant who develops subliminal messages that convey an antiunion message in videotapes and recordings played to employees.
   c. A small steel manufacturer establishes "vote-no" committees comprised of employees whom management has identified as charismatic leaders in the workplace. These employees are paid a bonus for participating in "vote-no" committee activities.
   d. A grocery chain conducts annual attitude surveys to determine whether employees are satisfied with working conditions.

---

[57] See Marvin J. Levine, "Double-Digit Decertification Election Activity: Union Organizational Weaknesses in the 1980s," *Labor Law Journal* (May 1989), pp. 311–315.

e. A hospital administrator periodically discusses the disadvantages of unions with employees (even though a union organizing campaign is not underway).
5. What unfair labor practices might a union commit during an organizing campaign? Discuss.
6. You are a union organizer. Outline a training program that you would use to prepare employees to serve as union advocates during a certification election. What knowledge and skills should these employees obtain? What type of employee (in terms of personality, work experience, and other personal characteristics) would you prefer?
7. You are the corporate personnel/human resource manager of a manufacturing firm that currently has several nonunion plants in the southeastern section of the United States. Draft a set of guidelines that your first-line and departmental supervisors can refer to in the event that a union attempts to organize employees at one of your plants.

▲ ▲ ▲ ▲ CERTIFICATION ELECTION CASES

Westwood Horizons Hotel

The Culinary Workers and Bartenders, Local 814, (Los Angeles), commenced an organizing campaign among employees of the Westwood Horizons Hotel dining room, kitchen, housekeeping, and laundry. The union, an AFL-CIO affiliate, was the only labor organization involved in this particular certification attempt.

About two weeks before the NLRB secret-ballot election, Francisco Marcial, a pro-union employee, told a fellow employee, Jesus Luna, in the presence of three pro-union employees and several other employees whose union sympathies were unknown, that he would beat up Luna and other employees who did not vote for the union. Arthuro Naharo, another pro-union employee who was present, also threatened to beat up Luna and two other employees, Ignacio Garcia and Fernando Fuentes, and anyone else who did not vote for the union in the upcoming election. At this point, Luna replied that he was "with them" and would vote for the union "so they would not comply with their threats and beat [him] up."

On election day, Garcia was working in the hotel's kitchen when Marcial approached him and said "Let's go vote." When Garcia said that he would vote later, Marcial said that Garcia had to go with him immediately. Marcial then grabbed Garcia's upper right arm and held it during the five-minute walk to the voting area. Marcial continued to hold Garcia's arm as they entered the voting area located in the hotel garage. Naharo then told employee Ronnie Torres, one of 15 employees waiting to vote, that Marcial had used force to bring Garcia to the voting area. Word of Marcial's force against Garcia spread to others who were standing in the voting line. Marcial placed Garcia at the head of the voting line and both men subsequently entered the voting room together and cast their ballots.

After he voted, Marcial and three other pro-union employees went to the front desk of the hotel where Fuentes was using the public address system to release employees from work, by department, to vote in the election. Marcial, who had threatened Fuentes two weeks earlier, approached him and said, "Friend Fernando, you have to go vote now." When Fuentes, who had not planned to vote, objected and stated that he could not leave his work post because he was still announcing, Marcial replied, "If you don't go now, you'll go by force with us." Wilfredo Sanchez, one of the pro-union employees, told Fuentes: "Don't be stupid. You have to go with us."

While escorting Fuentes to the voting area, Marcial told him that he had to vote yes. Hector Huardo, another pro-union employee, also told Fuentes: "You have to vote yes. Don't be stupid." Then, as Fuentes stood in line to vote with Luna (the third employee threatened two weeks earlier) and 10 other employees, Marcial and six pro-union employees stood on both sides of the voting line and kept repeating, "Vote for the union." "Vote yes." "Vote yes." This activity continued for approximately three minutes until the NLRB agent came to the doorway of the voting room and told the pro-union employees to leave. Marcial and the others left, but returned momentarily and resumed their "Vote yes" chant for an additional ten minutes.

The Culinary Workers and Bartenders union won the certification election and the employer, Westwood Horizons Hotel, moved to have the election set aside because of the misconduct by Marcial and other employees on the day of the election. They also cited the general atmosphere of fear and reprisal that was created prior to the election.

Discussion Questions

1. What factors should the National Labor Relations Board consider in evaluating the seriousness of the pro-union employees' actions and the degree of intimidation that such actions could have on prospective voters?
2. Does it make any difference that the employees who made the threatening statements did so without union approval?
3. What constitutes the voting area? How can the NLRB agent conducting the election have control over employee conduct and statements while workers are waiting to vote in an area adjacent to the voting booth?
4. If the NLRB decides to set aside the election, what safeguards (if any) can be taken to ensure a democratic second election?

Metz Metallurgical Corp.

The Service Employees Union (AFL-CIO) was attempting to organize a group of 136 employees at the New Jersey firm of Metz Metallurgical Corporation. A certification election was scheduled for the first week of January, 1983.

An employee of the prospective bargaining unit, Robert Ciancimino, was working on December 20, 1982, when a company supervisor, Randy Van Lit, initiated a conversation by asking Ciancimino how he felt about the union. Ciancimino replied that the union had its good points and its bad points. Van Lit then predicted that the employees would lose certain fringe benefits if the union became their bargaining representative. Ciancimino told Van Lit that they would not lose any benefits. Later, Ciancimino discussed Van Lit's comments with a fellow employee, Wayne Tracey.

Two days later, Ciancimino had an on-the-job encounter with Charles Crincoli, his supervisor. Crincoli told Ciancimino to perform another employee's duties in the metallurgical department. Ciancimino, instead, went to a vault to get silver, a task unrelated to Crincoli's order. When Crincoli asked what Ciancimino was doing, the employee said that he had gone for silver. Crincoli replied that he didn't want any insubordination and that "when I tell you to go over there and do your job, go do it." In a parting remark, Crincoli added, "You don't need any union, your job is on the line."

The union subsequently lost the certification election and filed charges with the NLRB to have the election results set aside. It was alleged by the union that the comments of Van Lit and Crincoli prevented a fair election.

Discussion Questions

1. Did the remarks of Van Lit and Crincoli constitute a threat that conceivably violated Ciancimino's Section 7 rights?
2. Is it safe to assume that the supervisors' isolated remarks were spread among employees to the extent that a free election was no longer possible?
3. Where does one draw the line between a supervisor's threat to discipline an employee for legitimate reasons and the expression of anti-union sentiments? Did Crincoli's warning to Ciancimino fall in the latter category simply because of his offhand comment about the union?
4. The supervisor's remarks were made 17 days before the certification election. Would this time gap possibly affect the NLRB's decision to set aside the election?

Conair Corporation

Conair Corporation is engaged in the manufacturing, sale, and distribution of hair care and personal grooming products. The company maintains administrative offices, manufacturing operations, and distribution facilities in Edison, New Jersey. Over three-fourths of Conair's employees are Spanish-speaking.

In March of 1977, the International Ladies' Garment Workers' Union (ILGW) began an organizational campaign at Conair's Edison plant. Shortly after becoming aware of the union's efforts, the company conducted a series of management-employee meetings. Such meetings were unprecedented prior to this time and they were held in direct response to the organizational campaign. Conair vice presidents John Mayorek and Jerry Kampel held a meeting for all 300 bargaining-unit workers in the plant cafeteria on April 4. At that meeting, Mayorek indicated that the company knew of the organizational campaign. He then pointed out the benefits provided by the company in the past and cautioned that certain benefits would be lost with unionization. Mayorek also promised that, in the future, the company would provide a variety of new benefits, many of which were in response to employee complaints aired at the meeting. Vice president Mayorek further informed the group that the company had an "open-door" policy, a feature apparently unknown to most of the Conair workers. The open-door policy would allow employees to bring their complaints directly to management. Mayorek then cautioned the workers that direct access to management would be lost with unionization.

On April 6, Conair President Leandro Rizzuto addressed a second mass meeting of the employees, which was held in the firm's production area. Rizzuto reiterated the earlier comments of Mayorek and warned that if he had to pay the increased wages of the union, Conair would close the Edison plant. Later in the day, Rizzuto, Mayorek, and Kampel held several meetings with groups of 10 to 15 employees, during which they again spoke of current and future benefits and of the open-door policy. Rizzuto stated at the small group sessions that if a union came in, it would be cheaper to move the company to Hong Kong, where Conair was already involved in a joint venture.

In response to Conair's statements at these meetings, the union called an unfair labor practice strike on the morning of April 11. Approximately 125 to 140 of the 300 employees participated in the strike and over 100 remained at the plant to picket. The first two days of the strike were marred by incidents of picket line violence that included a physical assault on a trucking firm employee, the setting of several small fires, vandalism to company property, rock and bottle throwing, name-calling and threats to nonstriking employees, and minor bodily injury to nonstrikers and damage to their automobiles. Conair secured injunctions to contain further violence and filed unfair labor practice charges against the union.

On April 13, the union petitioned the NLRB for certification as the employees' bargaining representative and simultaneously filed an unfair labor practice charge against the company based on the early April meetings. An election was scheduled for May 6, but was postponed pending the outcome of the unfair labor practice charges. One week later, the company sent mailgrams to the striking workers announcing that they would assume that the workers had quit their jobs unless they returned to work by the 22nd of the month. Several months later, Conair sent another letter to the strikers indicating to them that their group medical and life insurance programs had been cancelled.

During the summer months, Conair hired a bilingual personnel director and instituted a number of improvements, such as a job bidding system, a systematic set of salary and performance evaluation standards, an employee credit union, hot food in the company cafeteria, formal termination and layoff procedures, and an employee newsletter, among other things. The union made an unconditional offer to return striking employees to work, effective September 28. Although most of the strikers were reinstated, the company required them to fill out job applications. Furthermore, 13 strikers were not reinstated and 5 others were offered jobs that were less desirable than the ones they had held prior to the strike.

The NLRB resolved the unfair labor practice charges filed by the company and then scheduled a certification election for December 7. During the two weeks prior to the election, Conair supervisory personnel repeatedly stated to various unit employees that the Edison plant would be closed and moved to Hong Kong if the union won the election. Supervisors also warned on several occasions that, in the event of a union victory, the employees would not receive their Christmas bonuses. "Raffle tickets" inundated the plant, warning that a vote for the union was a vote for plant closure. Conair distributed campaign literature (printed both in Spanish and in English) and "Statements of Account" declaring that the company's profit-sharing plan was for nonunion employees only.

The union lost the election by a vote of 136 to 69 (41 ballots were challenged). On March 8, 1978, the NLRB regional director filed a complaint in which he consolidated the union's previous unfair labor practice charges against Conair with the ILGW's later challenge to the December 7, 1977 election.

Discussion Questions

1. Did the employer's initial worker meetings and the statements made in connection with these meetings constitute "outrageous" and "pervasive" unfair labor practices that could warrant a bargaining order?
2. What is the legality of the employer's letter of ultimatum to the striking employees?
3. What impact would the picket line violence have on the employees' job reinstatement and the union's ability to secure a bargaining order?
4. Although it was not mentioned in the case, the union did not secure a majority of the bargaining unit authorization card signatures. Will this have an effect on whether the NLRB will issue a bargaining order? Why?
5. What factors could have contributed to the employer's substantial victory margin in the December 7 election? Do you believe that the employer jeopardized its cause by making threatening statements within two weeks prior to the election? Would Conair still have won the election in the absence of these threats?
6. In your opinion, what are the odds of the union's winning a second certification election, based on your knowledge of the facts presented here?

Part III

Union and Management Organizational Structures, Goals, and Policies for Collective Bargaining

▲ ▲

Part III of this book consists of two chapters. Chapter 6 provides an overview of labor unions. Emphasis is placed on the organizational structures and leadership of unions. The three major levels of unionism—the federation, the international unions, and the local unions—are discussed, along with their respective roles and modes of operation. Some of the major trends and statistics associated with labor unions are also analyzed. Although a number of similarities exist between profit-seeking business organizations and labor unions, the goals and bottom-line objectives of these two categories of organizations often differ. Likewise, there are leadership issues that make unions different from other organizations.

Chapter 7 focuses on management's organizational response to labor unions and collective bargaining. Most organizations place the responsibility for collective bargaining with the personnel and human resource management department or division. Some heavily unionized companies create a separate industrial relations department to deal with contract negotiations and administration. Regardless of the exact organizational structure used by management, most firms employ a full-time staff of professionals to deal with personnel and human resource matters. Functions of the personnel department in a unionized firm include preparing for contract negotiations, representing management at the bargaining table, and working with union officials on administering the contract and other matters of mutual concern. Chapter 7 provides an overview of the personnel/human resource management function and places special emphasis on how this function differs between unionized and nonunionized firms. A discussion of management's bargaining goals and a comparison of how management attempts to equalize collective bargaining power is also included. Finally, examples of recent cooperative efforts and concessions between business and labor organizations are provided.

6 | The Union Structure, Goals, and Policies for Collective Bargaining

- **Introduction**
- **The Major Levels of Unionism**
- **The AFL-CIO**
  The AFL-CIO Structure
  Financial Aspects of the AFL-CIO
  Major Areas of Concern for the AFL-CIO
    Organizing Nonunion Workers
    Legislative Concerns
    Political Influence
    Community Services
    International Affairs
    Civil Rights
    Employment Training and Education
    Worker Well-Being and Social Security
    Research and Public Relations
  The AFL-CIO: A Summary
- **The International Unions**
  The Size of International Unions
  International Union Functions
  The Governance of International Unions
  International Union Organizational Structures
  International Union Finances
  The Central Role of International Unions
- **The Local Unions**
  Local Union Functions
  Local Union Governance and Politics

- **Merger Activities and Organized Labor**
  Union Mergers
  The Impact of Unions on Corporate Mergers and Buyouts
- **Unions as Democratic Institutions**
  Democracy Defined
  Barriers to Union Democracy
  Some Suggestions for Making Unions More Democratic
- **Labor Unions and Organized Crime**
  How Big is the Problem of Labor Racketeering and Who is Involved?
  The Effects of Organized Crime on Unions, Business, and Society
  Government Action against Labor Racketeering
- **Union Goals in Collective Bargaining**
  Determinants of Union Goals
  A Look at Some Typical Union Bargaining Goals
- **Summary and Conclusions**
- **Discussion Questions and Exercises**

▲ Introduction

Unions are complex and dynamic organizations committed to advancing the economic and social interests of its members. Although labor unions focus their efforts on workplace issues, they also help workers deal with social and economic problems such as civil rights, poverty, and housing. During collective negotiations, unions assume an aggressive posture as they attempt to secure favorable contract terms for their constituents. Between rounds of contract negotiations, union officials serve in a watchdog capacity to ensure management compliance with the terms and conditions of the collective bargaining agreement. Labor unions in the United States are economically oriented and place heavy emphasis on obtaining contract settlements that have an immediate monetary benefit to their membership.

Labor organizations also have a broad political agenda. Union officials are elected by and serve at the pleasure of their members. Although many elected union officials remain in office for years or even decades, the Landrum-Griffin Act requires that they face re-election at specified intervals (for example, elections for local union officers must be held every three years). Occasionally, the election of union officers results in a heated campaign, especially when an upstart candidate challenges an entrenched incumbent officer. Union officials are cognizant of the need to please the membership and fulfill their expectations. In addition to securing an acceptable contract at the bargaining table, members expect the union to process their grievances in a timely and fair manner and to support them whenever problems arise at work. When union members feel that the leadership has failed to live up to their expectations, union officials may run the risk of not being re-elected or, worse, may face impeachment. If the political climate within the union deteriorates considerably, members may push for decertification.

Labor organizations are also political in a broader sense that goes beyond internal union politics. Primarily through the political lobbying efforts of the AFL-CIO, the labor movement in the United States attempts to secure the passage of legislation that benefits all workers, both unionized and nonunionized. Some legislation, such as health and safety laws, labor reform bills, and equal employment opportunity laws, have a direct impact on the worker. However, the efforts of the AFL-CIO are also directed at legislation involving tariffs, public housing, and the regulation of forestry activities—none of which appear to be directly related to wages, hours, and working conditions, although these laws have an indirect impact on the labor force.

▲ The Major Levels of Unionism

The basic structure of the U.S. labor movement consists of three levels of unionism: the local union, the international union, and the federation (for unions belonging to the AFL-CIO). Most labor organizations consist of an international union and a series of local unions that are geographically dispersed. The international is analogous to the corporate headquarters or home office of a large company, and the locals are scattered in various cities where the union has organized employee groups. International unions (also called national unions if they do not operate in Canada) control the activities of their local unions in a fashion similar to which a corporate home office might oversee the operations of a plant or subsidiary. For example, the Distillery, Rectifying, Wine and Allied Workers' International Union of America has its headquarters in Englewood, New Jersey and has 20,000 members and 58 locals. The International Association of Machinists and Aerospace Workers, with international offices in Washington, D.C., has 750,000 members in 1,500 locals. The 1.0 million member United Auto Workers has its headquarters in Detroit and has jurisdiction over 1,200 locals.[1]

The local unions are primarily responsible for dealing directly with the daily problems and concerns of union members who work in a specific region, city, or plant. For example, Teamsters Local No. 5 takes care of Teamsters members who work in Baton Rouge, Louisiana. Communications Workers Union members in Greenville, South Carolina are served by CWU Local 3710. The yellow pages of any metropolitan telephone directory (under "labor organizations") lists local affiliates for most major labor unions. There are an estimated 65,000 locals in the United States, most of which are controlled by an international union. They range in size from fewer than 10 members to several thousand. Local 32-B of the Service Employees International Union in New York City represents 56,000 building service employees and is larger than many international unions.[2]

At the apex of the United States labor pyramid is the federation, better known

---

[1] Based on Courtney D. Gifford, *Directory of U.S. Labor Organizations*, 1988–89 edition (Washington, D.C.: The Bureau of National Affairs, Inc., 1988), pp. 39, 42, and 47.
[2] Marten Estey, *The Unions: Structure, Development, and Management*, 3rd ed. (New York: Harcourt, Brace, and Jovanovich, 1981), p. 49.

as the American Federation of Labor and Congress of Industrial Organizations (AFL-CIO). Contrary to common misconception, the AFL-CIO is not a labor union; it does no bargaining or contract administration. Rather, the AFL-CIO is a confederation of 90 autonomous international and local unions. The affiliated unions created the federation in 1955 when the AFL and the CIO merged. Its primary functions are to promote the interests of labor through its influence on broad national and international policies and through coordinating a wide range of joint union activities involving AFL-CIO member unions. Despite occupying the top rung in the labor movement hierarchy, the AFL-CIO exercises little formal control over its affiliate unions. Most of the federation's power is informal and is confined to its ability to persuade labor leaders at the international level to adhere to the goals and objectives of the AFL-CIO.

Figure 6-1 summarizes the organizational structure of the U.S. labor movement and illustrates the basic relationship between its three major levels. However, Figure 6-1 is an oversimplification in that the actual structure within each of the three levels is complex and requires further elaboration.

American Federation of Labor–Congress of Industrial Organization

(AFL–CIO)

Washington, D.C.

AFL-CIO FUNCTIONS AND CONCERNS
- Political lobbying and education
- Organizing campaign assistance
- Community services
- International labor affairs
- Civil Rights
- Employment training and education
- Worker well being and social security
- Labor research
- Public relations

International unions

90 AFL–CIO affiliated unions

14.2 million workers

International unions not affiliated with the AFL-CIO

Approximately 90 national and international unions

4.0 million workers

INTERNATIONAL FUNCTIONS AND CONCERNS
- Union strategies and policies
- Contract negotiations
- Training union officers and shop stewards
- Communications to members on labor matters
- Administration of employee benefit program
- Political lobbying
- Labor research
- Contract administration
- Public relations

Independent local unions

Locals   Locals   Locals   Locals   Locals   Locals   Locals   Locals   Locals

60,000 locals

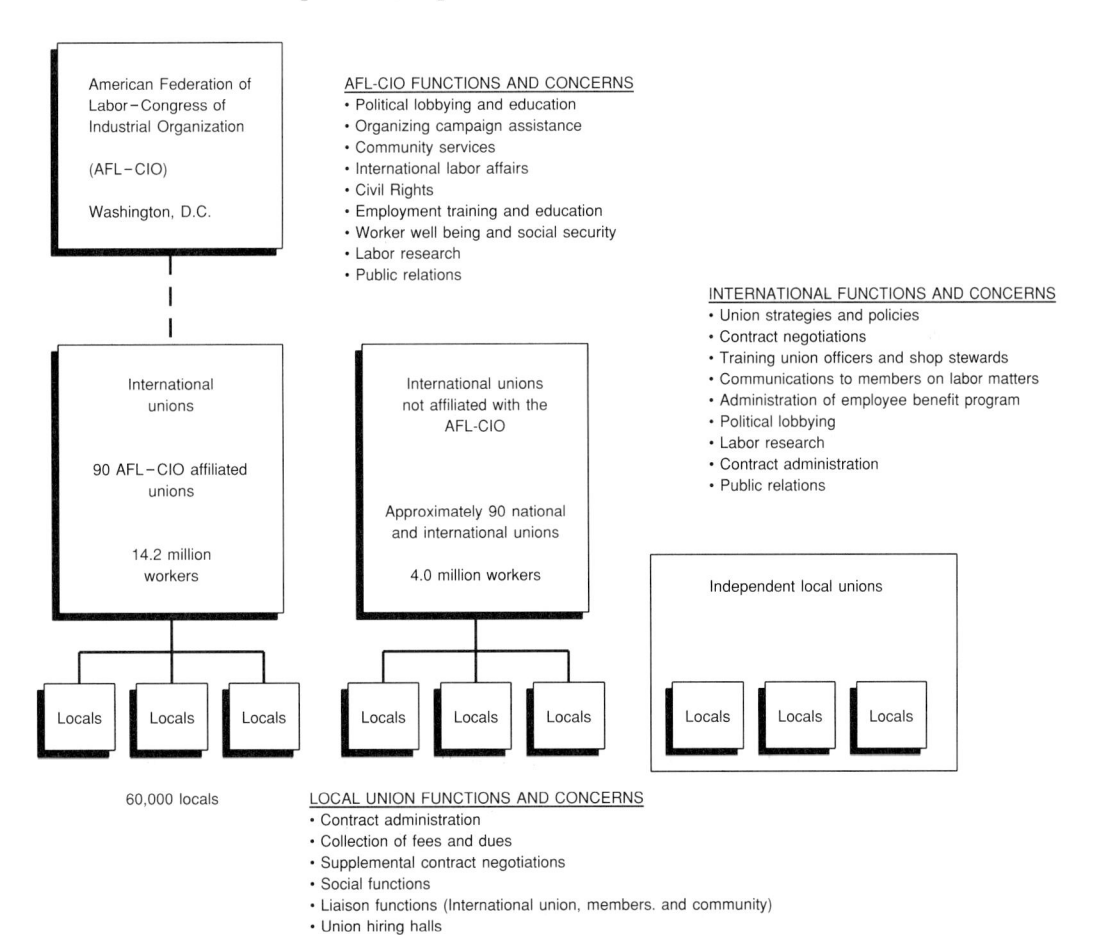

LOCAL UNION FUNCTIONS AND CONCERNS
- Contract administration
- Collection of fees and dues
- Supplemental contract negotiations
- Social functions
- Liaison functions (International union, members, and community)
- Union hiring halls
- Apprenticeship training programs

FIGURE 6–1 Structure of the United States Labor Movement

▲ The AFL-CIO

The AFL-CIO is a diverse organization that serves labor and society in a multitude of ways.[3] As mentioned previously, the AFL-CIO is a federation of 90 independent unions or, as the federation leadership states, "a union of unions." Approximately 14.2 million or 80 percent of all unionized workers belong to labor organizations that are affiliated with the AFL-CIO. These 90 unions contain more than 60,000 local unions, which engage in collective bargaining with several hundred thousand employers.[4]

Each union within the AFL-CIO remains autonomous and conducts its affairs in the manner prescribed by its respective leaders and members. Unions that are affiliated with the AFL-CIO usually include the federation's designation in the union title. Common examples include the Tobacco Workers International Union, AFL-CIO and the National Maritime Union of America, AFL-CIO. Until recently, some large unions were not affiliated with the AFL-CIO. The 1.6 million member Teamsters union was expelled in 1957 because of corruption found in the union's ranks by Robert Kennedy and the McClellan Committee. However, in October of 1987, the executive council of the AFL-CIO voted unanimously to allow the Teamsters to rejoin its ranks.[5] In October of 1989, the United Mine Workers (UMW) applied for reaffiliation with the AFL-CIO after a 40-year hiatus (the UMW formerly belonged to the AFL).[6] Both the Teamsters and the UMW reaffiliated with the AFL-CIO due to major threats to their existence: the Teamsters because of a federal investigation into corrupt practices, and the UMW because of dwindling membership.

Each AFL-CIO union is free to withdraw at any time and each formulates its own economic policies, conducts its own contract negotiations, sets dues and initiation fees, and provides whatever services that it desires for its members. Although member unions remain free to conduct their internal affairs as they see fit, they do cede authority to the AFL-CIO over the following matters:

1. Every affiliated union must comply with the AFL-CIO Ethical Practices Codes, which establish basic standards of union democracy and financial integrity.
2. No union controlled by communists, fascists, or other totalitarians can remain in the AFL-CIO.
3. Each union agrees to submit certain types of disputes (e.g., jurisdictional dis-

---

[3] The AFL-CIO's full organizational name is the American Federation of Labor and Congress of Industrial Organizations.
[4] AFL-CIO membership information as of November 1, 1989, and provided by AFL-CIO headquarters (via telephone) on December 28, 1989. The membership information does not include United Mine Worker members who applied for reaffiliation in October, 1989.
[5] "AFL-CIO, Teamsters Heal 30-Year-Old Rift," *The Greenville News* (syndicated by the *New York Times*), October 25, 1987, p. 1-A. The Teamsters' motivation to rejoin the AFL-CIO was based, in part, on the U.S. Justice Department's attempt to seize control of the union because of its domination by organized crime. Also see William A. Krupman, "The Teamsters: Far from a Toothless Tiger," *The Wall Street Journal* (July 14, 1988), p. 26; Aaron Bernstein, "The AFL-CIO: A Tougher Team with the Teamsters," *Business Week* (November 9, 1987), p. 110; and Norm Miller, "Teamsters Reentry: A Moral Problem," *Dissent* (Spring 1988), p. 134.
[6] See Alecia Swasy, "United Mine Workers Union Applies to Rejoin AFL-CIO After Long Absence," *The Wall Street Journal* (October 4, 1989).

putes) between affiliated unions to the mediating and judicial processes of the AFL-CIO.[7]

The AFL-CIO constitution spells out a number of objectives that the federation attempts to pursue. A prime objective is to encourage free collective bargaining for all workers so that they may enjoy improved wages, hours, and working conditions. Along with this, the AFL-CIO promotes legislation that benefits workers. For example, it works for increases in the minimum wage. It also lobbies against laws that reduce tariff barriers; these laws are perceived to be detrimental to both unionized and nonunionized employees. The AFL-CIO has long championed civil rights and the economic and social betterment of women and minorities. Some other stated objectives in the federation's constitution are protecting and strengthening democratic traditions and institutions, promoting world-wide peace and freedom, protecting the labor movement from corruption and racketeers, encouraging workers to vote in political elections, and promoting the sale of union-made goods through the union label.

The AFL-CIO Structure

Figure 6–2 outlines the organizational chart of the AFL-CIO. Every two years, the federation holds its national convention during which it sets general policies. Affiliated unions are represented at the convention in proportion to their membership sizes. The convention, which is the supreme governing body for the AFL-CIO, also elects the president, secretary-treasurer, and 34 vice presidents. These officers make up the AFL-CIO Executive Council, which governs federation affairs between conventions and supplements convention policies.

The General Board, comprised of the Executive Council and the chief executive officer of each member union, meets to discuss matters referred to it by the officers and Executive Council. For example, it traditionally has been the body that acts on recommendations to endorse, support, and raise funds for presidential and vice presidential candidates in election years.

The AFL-CIO is headquartered in Washington, D.C., so that close contact can be maintained with members of Congress and others in influential policy-making positions. In addition, the federation has offices throughout the United States. Each state has an AFL-CIO headquarters and a president who is responsible for political lobbying, public relations, and dealing with labor issues in their respective states. There are approximately 800 state and local AFL-CIO central bodies that serve the 60,000 affiliated locals and that carry on legislative, political, and community service activities.

The AFL-CIO also has eight constitutional departments constructed along trade and industrial groupings in order to serve unions having common interests. They are the Building and Construction Trades, Maritime Trades, Metal Trades, Industrial Union, Union and Service Trades, Public Employee, Food and Allied Service Trades, and Professional Employees departments. Each of these departments has its own executive body, holds its own conventions, and manages and finances its affairs

---

[7] *This is the AFL-CIO* (Washington, D.C.: The AFL-CIO, 1984).

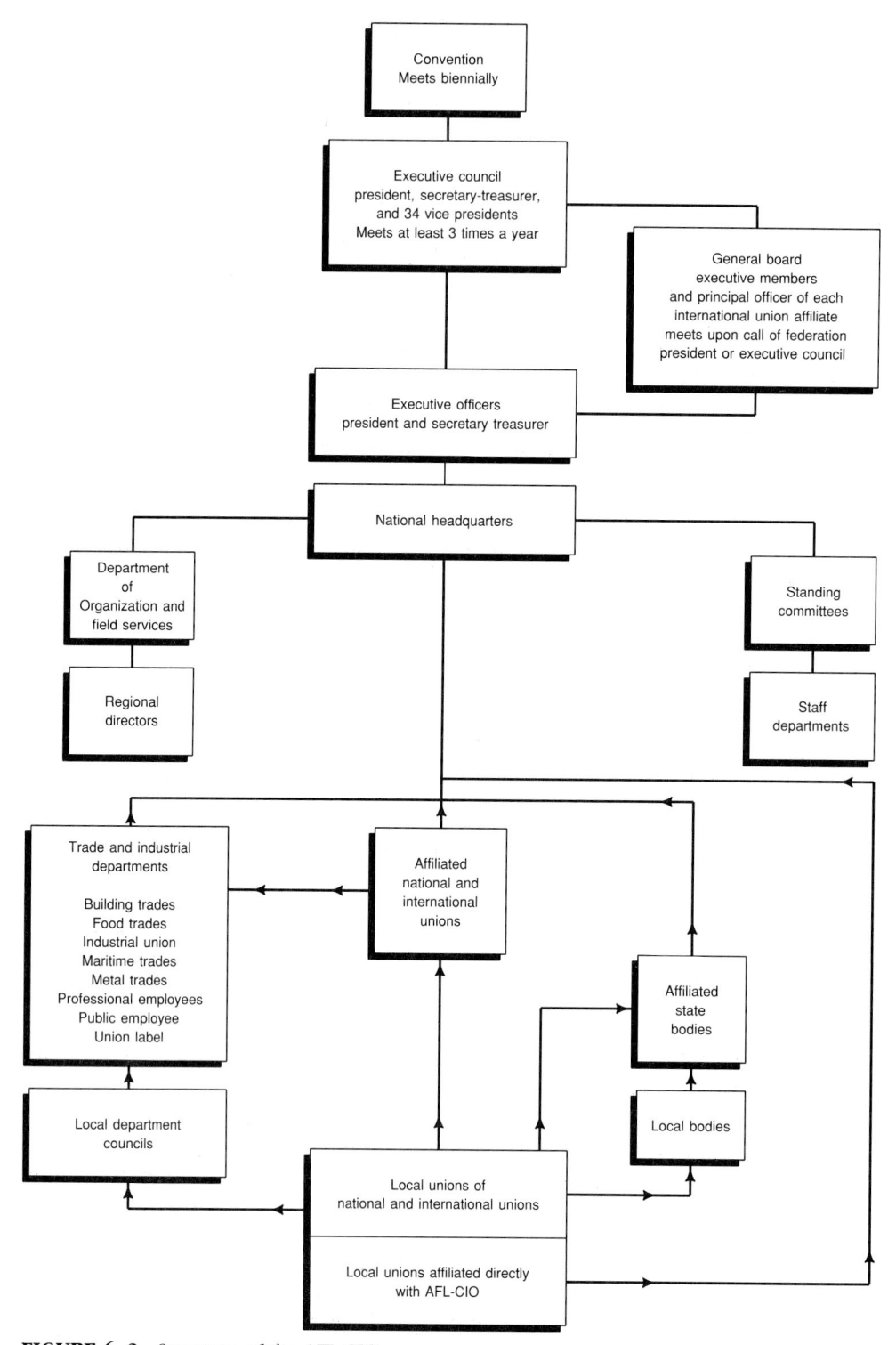

FIGURE 6–2 Structure of the AFL-CIO

within the framework of the AFL-CIO constitution. In addition, they function on state and local levels through more than 600 department councils. The eight departments are represented at the AFL-CIO conventions and on the General Board and help to shape AFL-CIO policy in their specialized areas.

Financial Aspects of the AFL-CIO

The AFL-CIO's operations are financed primarily through regular dues, known as a per capita tax.[8] Most of these funds are used to cover regular operating expenses. In addition, a small share of per capita payments is allocated to the special purposes fund from which the federation assists workers in other countries, worthy causes such as Red Cross disaster relief programs, and special programs of the Executive Council. A detailed accounting of the AFL-CIO's expenses is presented to members at the biennial convention.[9]

Major Areas of Concern for the AFL-CIO

A recent AFL-CIO publication lists several areas to which the federation devotes a substantial amount of attention and effort. Some of these areas have a direct impact on unions and the workplace, whereas others have a broader effect on society.[10]

Organizing Nonunion Workers

When the AFL and the CIO merged in 1955, it was stated that "the major unfinished task of the American Labor movement" is to organize the unorganized. Although each union is primarily responsible for organizing its own members, the AFL-CIO provides advice and assistance to its affiliates. The Department of Organization and Field Service directs a staff that coordinates the organizing efforts of member unions and provides supplementary personnel and guidance.

The federation is occasionally called upon to settle organizational disputes among member unions through the AFL-CIO's Organizing Responsibilities Procedures System. In March of 1988, the exclusive right to organize more than 3,000 brewery employees of the Adolph Coors Co., in Golden, Colorado, was awarded to the Teamsters union.[11] The Teamsters were vying with the International Association of Machinists to organize the Golden, Colorado, employees.[12] However, both unions

---

[8] The affiliated unions pay a fixed amount on behalf of their members. In 1986, the monthly per capita tax for national and international unions was 31 cents per member. Thus, each member of an affiliated union contributed $3.72 that year to support the AFL-CIO. The most recent Executive Council report indicates that 46 million dollars was contributed to the AFL-CIO by member unions in 1984.

[9] AFL-CIO, *30th Anniversary Report of the AFL-CIO Executive Council* (Anaheim, California: AFL-CIO, 1985), pp. 10–17.

[10] Much of the information in this section is derived from *This Is the AFL-CIO* (Washington, D.C.: AFL-CIO, 1984), pp. 8–20.

[11] In August of 1987, the AFL-CIO called off its 10-year boycott of Coors beer when a settlement agreement called for a union election at the Adolph Coors Company's brewery in Golden, Colorado, and the use of union contractors to complete construction of the firm's $70-million plant in Elkton, Virginia. See Sandra D. Atchison, "Will Labor's Joe Sixpack Come Back to Coors?," *Business Week* (September 7, 1987), p. 29; and The Bureau of National Affairs, Inc., *Collective Bargaining Negotiations & Contracts* (Washington, D.C.: The Bureau of National Affairs, Inc., August 27, 1987), p. 3.

[12] Sandra Atchison and Aaron Bernstein, "A Silver Bullet for the Union Drive at Coors: The Pact With the AFL-CIO Unravels as the Teamsters Step In," *Business Week* (July 1, 1988), p. 61.

were ordered to share organizing rights at a smaller Coors distributing and packaging operation in Elkton, Virginia.[13]

The AFL-CIO's Department of Organization and Field Service is also responsible for maintaining a liaison with the federation's community services, urban affairs, legislation, political education, and civil rights functions. The department serves the 800 state and local AFL-CIO central bodies and affiliated unions. Because the federation places a great deal of importance on the Department of Organization and Field Services, it consumes approximately one-fourth of the AFL-CIO's overall general fund expenses. For example, an organizing drive by the AFL-CIO that generated a great deal of public attention began in 1985 as 10 affiliated unions attempted to organize 28,000 Blue Cross-Blue Shield employees nationwide.[14] In addition, the AFL-CIO launched a drive to promote unionism and "extend labor's role from the workplace to the marketplace" by offering associate memberships and various employee benefits (legal services, life insurance, discount travel plans) for nonunion workers. The federation's associated memberships are for employees working in sectors where union organizing drives have not traditionally been successful and for formerly unionized workers who lost their jobs through plant closings.[15]

Legislative Concerns

The AFL-CIO believes that democracy in the workplace, economic gains, and individual rights are largely affected by federal and state legislation. Thus a primary function of the federation, as noted previously, is to serve as a legislative advocate for all workers. Representatives from the AFL-CIO present labor's viewpoint at each stage of the legislative process. Professional lobbyists attached to the AFL-CIO Department of Legislation and affiliated unions discuss pending bills with federal legislators on Capitol Hill. In the state legislatures, the task of political lobbying is carried out by AFL-CIO state federations. The state federations also back up the efforts of federal lobbyists when necessary.

The legislative agenda of the AFL-CIO is broad and is dictated by the policy resolutions set forth at the federation's biennial convention. Working by itself or in coalition with other public interest organizations, the AFL-CIO has historically pursued legislative issues that include taxes, civil rights, social security, international trade and economic policy, education, jobs legislation, and consumer and environmental protection. The AFL-CIO has claimed that "there is hardly a major law of consequence passed by Congress over the last three decades that doesn't have the union label stitched into the fabric of its legislative history."[16] President Lyndon B. Johnson called the AFL-CIO the "People's Lobby". Later Jimmy Carter claimed that a U.S. President had three major concerns: foreign affairs, national affairs, and George Meany (then the president of the AFL-CIO, who retired from office in 1979). The

---

[13] The Bureau of National Affairs, Inc., *Collective Bargaining Negotiations & Contracts* (Washington, D.C.: The Bureau of National Affairs, Inc., April 21, 1988), p. 3.
[14] The Bureau of National Affairs, Inc., *Collective Bargaining Negotiations & Contracts* (Washington, D.C.: The Bureau of National Affairs, Inc., January 28, 1988), p. 4.
[15] The Bureau of National Affairs, Inc., *Collective Bargaining Negotiations & Contracts* (Washington, D.C.: The Bureau of National Affairs, Inc., April 11, 1988), p. 4.
[16] *This Is the AFL-CIO* (Washington, D.C.: The AFL-CIO, 1984), p. 10.

following comment by Sol C. Chaikin, president of the International Ladies' Garment Workers' Union (ILGW), provides insight into Meany's influence:

> I was friendly with Jimmy Carter, friendly enough so that in 1980 he asked me to second his nomination for the presidency of the United States.... Well, he was having a difficult time with Meany and [he] asked me, "Chick, how do I deal with Meany? Why can't we be more compatible, more interacting and forthcoming?" My response was, "I'm going to tell you how to do it, but you will not like it, and you will not do it." I said, "You have to treat George Meany as a sovereign power."[17]

Political Influence

Labor movements throughout the world attempt to exercise political influence. In Western European countries, labor parties similar to the two major political parties in the United States represent workers. However, there has never been a viable labor party in the U.S.; instead, the labor movement in this country has attempted to exert political influence through lobbying efforts, support of political candidates whose platforms are favorable to labor, and educational efforts designed to encourage voter registration and worker participation in the political process.

The AFL-CIO's Committee on Political Education (COPE) provides programs of political education and conducts nationwide, nonpartisan registration and get-out-the-vote campaigns among union members. At the national level, COPE maintains a staff of field representatives and prepares leaflets, posters, and research materials. These materials include the voting records of all U.S. senators and representatives on key labor issues. In each of the 50 states, a state COPE functions under the direction of state AFL-CIO officers. State COPEs coordinate their efforts with the national COPE, although they are not required to follow national COPE policies. Furthermore, state COPEs endorse gubernatorial candidates, candidates for state offices, and candidates for U.S. Congress, if two-thirds of the delegates approve. Endorsements for U.S. presidential candidates are traditionally made by the federation's General Board and are, in turn, supported by the national and state COPE bodies.

COPE is not aligned with a political party. At the merger convention of the AFL-CIO in 1955, it was resolved: "We affirm labor's traditional policy of avoiding entangling alliances with any other group and of supporting worthy candidates regardless of party affiliation. We will seek neither to capture any organization nor will we submit our identity to any group in any manner." However, the "worthy" candidates are usually Democrats rather than Republicans, probably because the legislative emphases of the former have been on labor reform and civil rights. In late August of 1988, the federation announced formal support of the Democratic ticket of Massachusetts Governor Michael S. Dukakis and Texas Senator Lloyd Bentsen.[18] An endorsement of a political candidate, of course, does not guarantee

---

[17] Sol C. Chaikin (interview), "Look for the Union Label," in Philip L. Quaglieri, *America's Labor Leaders* (Lexington, Massachusetts: Lexington Books, 1989), p. 59. Reprinted with permission.
[18] The Bureau of National Affairs, Inc., "AFL-CIO Dukakis Approval," *Collective Bargaining Negotiations & Contracts* (Washington, D.C.: The Bureau of National Affairs, Inc., September 8, 1988), p. 1.

that union workers will vote for the candidate favored by organized labor. The philosophy that led to the establishment of COPE was later summed up by the AFL-CIO's president, the late George Meany: "We don't tell people how to vote; we just want as many people as possible to go to the polls. Whatever the decision may be, we want it to be a real majority decision—a majority of all the people."[19]

Community Services

Activities of the AFL-CIO go beyond the workplace as evidenced by the federation's public service role. These activities range from aiding Red Cross disaster relief teams and establishing community blood banks to United Way campaigns and consumer protection programs. Educational programs on subjects such as installment buying, health insurance, retirement planning, and scores of other topics are provided through local community service organizations. Member unions provide assistance to their communities on a voluntary basis. For example, unions from the building trades have assisted disaster-torn communities with volunteer labor.

Presently, there are 300 full-time AFL-CIO Community Services representatives in 195 cities. The United Labor Agencies for Community Service provide a mechanism to deliver services and counseling to union members. These agencies have been established in a number of metropolitan areas and in regions where there are large concentrations of union members. The AFL-CIO Department of Community Services coordinates public service activities with international and local unions as well as with community organizations and national service organizations.

The Office of Housing and Monetary Policy of the AFL-CIO is concerned with the issues of substandard housing, housing shortages, and urban blight. Because many workers live in urban areas or desire to own homes, the quality of neighborhoods and the individual's ability to secure a home mortgage are of interest to the federation. The federation coordinates its efforts in this area with the Department of Housing and Urban Development and other governmental agencies, as well as with banks and financial institutions. Specifically, the federation has attempted to reduce housing shortages in some areas by encouraging the investment of excess union funds and pension reserves in government-insured mortgages.

International Affairs

The AFL-CIO seeks to promote a better understanding of the American labor movement and its foreign and domestic policies through the federation's Department of International Affairs. In order to help labor promote world-wide peace and freedom, the AFL-CIO maintains contacts with the State Department, the Labor Department, the Agency for International Development, and the U.S. Information Agency. The Department of International Affairs furthers its policies through conferences and orientation for foreign visitors, as well as through the *Free Trade Union News,* which

---

[19] *This Is the AFL-CIO,* (Washington, D.C.: The AFL-CIO, 1984), p. 10. However, there is some reason to believe that AFL-CIO leaders might hope that union members with Republican leanings would stay away from the polls on election day. Also see, John Thomas Delaney, Marick F. Masters, and Susan Schwochau, "Union Membership and Voting for COPE-Endorsed Candidates," *Industrial and Labor Relations Review* (July 1990), pp. 621–635.

is published 11 times a year in English, Spanish, and Portuguese. The Department also coordinates AFL-CIO participation in the Trade Union Advisory Committee of the Organization for Economic Cooperation & Development (OECD), the International Confederation of Free Trade Unions, and the International Labor Organization.

To help the advancement of representative trade unions in the developing nations, the AFL-CIO maintains institutes for three continents: the American Institute for Free Labor Development (for Latin America), The African-American Labor Center, and the Asian-American Free Labor Institute. These institutes are involved in worker and trade union education, cooperatives, vocational training, credit unions, and social and community projects such as housing. Each institute has offices in the major countries of the continent on which it operates. Another body, the Free Trade Union Institute, handles international labor exchanges and is an instrument through which the American labor movement assists trade union development in Third World countries and in certain areas of Western Europe.

Civil Rights

A primary mission of the AFL-CIO is to ensure the equitable treatment of all workers without regard to race, creed, color, sex, or national origin. The federation was a strong advocate of civil rights legislation in the 1960s and, before that, pushed to merge separate black and white local unions in the South. Emphasis was placed on eliminating discriminatory hiring practices and consolidating segregated seniority lists and lines of job progression that placed racial minorities and women at a disadvantage in the workplace.

The AFL-CIO has established a Civil Rights Committee and a compliance procedure whereby a worker can file a complaint against a local or international union. Member international unions have established policies against discrimination in employment referral and apprenticeship programs. The federation's Building and Construction Trades Department has instituted a program to foster the recruitment of women, blacks, and other racial minorities into apprenticeship training programs and gives minorities the necessary training to enable them to meet entrance qualifications into these programs. The Department of Civil Rights works closely with the AFL-CIO's Human Resources Development Institute (HRDI) in furthering employment and training programs for workers who have traditionally been victims of employment discrimination.

Civil rights activities by the AFL-CIO go beyond the workplace and union membership into such areas as voting rights, fair housing, school integration, and discrimination against the aged and handicapped. In addition to political lobbying, the federation's civil rights platform is conveyed through its educational programs and liaisons with civil rights groups. The AFL-CIO carries on programs of mutual assistance with the Equal Employment Opportunity Commission, the Labor Department's Office of Federal Contract Compliance Programs, the Civil Rights Commission, the Community Relations Services and other federal agencies. Continuing relationships are also maintained with organizations such as the Leadership Conference on Civil Rights, the A. Philip Randolph Institute, the National Urban League, the National Association for the Advancement of Colored People, the Coalition of Labor Union Women, the Labor Council for Latin American Advancement, and the Jewish Labor Committee.

Employment Training and Education

The federation's Human Resources Development Institute (HRDI) is responsible for developing employment opportunities and providing training programs for the disadvantaged and unemployed. The national staff of HRDI is in Washington, D.C., and field offices are located throughout the country. The HRDI works with state and local labor organizations to promote labor's full employment and equal opportunity goals and makes use of a range of technical services to help unions participate in employment and training programs. For union members who have lost their jobs due to plant closings or obsolete skills, HRDI works directly with unions in conducting worker assistance workshops and other employment services. The institute also operates handicapped placement and training programs to enhance employment opportunities for disabled workers.

One of the AFL-CIO's legislative concerns deals with public education. The federation has endorsed federal aid for the elementary and secondary schools and has pressed for the expansion of educational programs for adults. In addition, it has advocated state and federal legislative measures to assure that academically qualified students are not denied a college education because of financial reasons. The AFL-CIO supports vocational education, especially for displaced workers who are victims of unemployment, industrial dislocation, and skills obsolescence caused by technological changes.

The AFL-CIO is extensively involved in labor education through its Department of Education. Developing educational programs and materials, distributing pamphlets, coordinating a speaker's bureau, and maintaining an extensive film library are examples of functions performed by the federation's educational arm. The department offers assistance to AFL-CIO member unions in preparing and conducting courses ranging from shop-steward training to the study of international affairs. Courses vary from one-day seminars to week-long institutes and are held in union halls, in residential training centers, and on college campuses. The AFL-CIO's George Meany Center for Labor Studies was established in 1969 and is located on a 47-acre campus in Silver Spring, Maryland. The George Meany Center offers a number of tuition-free institutes for union officers and members, and, through Antioch College, offers a baccalaureate degree program in labor studies. The center houses the American Institute for Free Labor Development, which provides leadership training for Latin American and Caribbean trade unionists.

Worker Well-Being and Social Security

The AFL-CIO has supported measures that provide a "network of personal security" for both unionized and nonunionized employees. To enhance the security and well-being of workers, the federation encourages collective bargaining agreement provisions covering employee benefits such as pensions and health insurance. In addition, the AFL-CIO supports social security, workers' compensation, health and safety, and other legislation.

Organized labor supported the original social security law passed in 1935. William Green, then president of the AFL, was a member of the 23-member advisory council that helped design the law. As the law was amended to include survivorship coverage (1939), disability insurance (1954), and health insurance for the elderly (passed in 1965 and better known as Medicare), the AFL and CIO leaders served on various advisory committees and provided input as the amendments were drafted. For example, the federation believes that the concept of Medicare should be expanded into "a medically advanced and economically sound program of national health insurance" covering all Americans and available without the requirement of a pauper's oath. The AFL-CIO also supports federal standards that require states to improve and standardize laws governing workers' compensation and unemployment insurance.

A prominent concern of organized labor is worker health and safety. The AFL-CIO maintains a Department of Occupational Safety, Health, and Social Security that monitors government agencies that administer safety, health, and environmental laws. It works with affiliated unions in developing safety and health programs. In addition, the department provides technical support to unions on general occupational safety and health concerns, and it works through colleges and universities to educate the public on workplace safety issues. Representatives of the department serve on a number of advisory panels associated with government agencies, such as the Occupational Safety and Health Administration and the Toxic Substances Control Administration. The department also works with environmental groups, as well as with the Environmental Protection Agency, on problems of air and water pollution, noise, pesticides, solid wastes, and the impact of environmental programs on growth and employment.

Research and Public Relations

The AFL-CIO is interested in research and in disseminating information on trends in the economy, labor force, and other areas that have an impact on unions and workers. The federation uses its Department of Economic Research to analyze and report on economic, tax, trade, collective bargaining, and related issues that are of interest to AFL-CIO affiliates. The department provides advice and technical assistance in specialized areas such as industrial engineering, consumer activities, and natural resource development. It also prepares publications and testimony for Congressional hearings and maintains liaisons with various government agencies, such as the U.S. Department of Labor (Bureau of Labor Statistics), the Joint Council on Economic Education, and the Clergy Economic Foundation. Economists and staff members of the department serve on various government and private advisory groups and committees that are concerned with employment statistics, wages and productivity, technological change, inflation, and foreign labor conditions. The AFL-CIO maintains a labor library that provides materials on industrial relations and collective bargaining and contains a valuable collection of books, periodicals, and archival materials.

The Department of Information is responsible for conveying news on the policies and programs of the AFL-CIO to affiliate unions as well as to the general public. This department communicates with the news media, prepares news releases, and arranges press conferences. The AFL-CIO created the Labor Institute of Public Affairs (LIPA) to help the federation and its affiliate unions use electronic communications media more effectively. Teleconferences between the federation and its affiliates are one application. LIPA has developed a wide range of programming for commercial and public television to enhance the public's awareness of critical labor issues.

A two-year, $13 million advertising campaign to improve the public's image of organized labor and to stem declines in union membership was launched by the AFL-CIO in 1988. The drive is designed to "get people to appreciate what unions can do for them and to increase the threshold of respect for what unions do in society." The drive is directed largely at younger workers who do not necessarily appreciate the advantages of a union membership. Approximately 90 percent of the $13 million budget was used for radio and television advertising time.[20]

The AFL-CIO publishes a weekly newspaper, which is distributed to its affiliates, and a vast array of pamphlets, leaflets, and books on labor matters. In addition, the federation has joined forces with the Canadian Labour Congress to participate in the International Labor Communications Association, which sets standards for labor publications and advertising.

The AFL-CIO: A Summary

Through its large and complex structure, the AFL-CIO deals with a vast number of social, economic, and legal issues that have traditionally concerned the U.S. labor movement. James Wallihan has delineated four basic political concerns of unions and workers:[21]

1. *Institutional issues* involve labor law issues that are of concern to unions. For example, section 14(b) of the Taft-Hartley Act, which allows the individual states to outlaw union security clauses in collective bargaining agreements, has been a persistent thorn in the side of organized labor. The Labor Law Reform Bill, which fell before a Senate filibuster, is another example. Any legal threat or opportunity that affects the survival and status of labor unions falls within the category of institutional issues.
2. *Jobs and employment issues* involve preserving and expanding employment opportunities for unionized employees. For example, building trades unions could be expected to support federal funding for highways and the construction of municipal buildings and federal housing because of the impact that such projects have on the employment opportunities for construction workers.
3. *Class issues* deal with legislative and political efforts affecting income, employment standards, and working conditions. Some examples that fall into this category are safety and health, equal employment opportunity, unemployment compensation, and employee benefit concerns.

---

[20] From The Bureau of National Affairs, Inc., "AFL-CIO Media Campaign," *Collective Bargaining Negotiations & Contracts* (Washington, D.C.: The Bureau of National Affairs, Inc., January 14, 1988), p. 3.
[21] James Wallihan, *Union Government and Organization* (Washington, D.C.: The Bureau of National Affairs, Inc., 1985), pp. 182–185.

4. *Societal issues* represent the broadest classification of labor movement concerns. Issues such as educational opportunities, urban decay and crime, consumer protection, and environmental quality fall into the societal category of labor issues.

In essence, the AFL-CIO forms a broad umbrella that not only looks after the common interests of its 90 affiliate unions, but also those of all unionized and nonunionized workers throughout the United States as well as in many foreign countries.

▲ The International Unions

The international union is the kingpin structure in the U.S. labor movement. As mentioned previously, the AFL-CIO occupies the top rung in the hierarchy of the labor movement, but the international unions possess the resources and power that most directly affect the wages, hours, and working conditions of their members. There are approximately 200 international unions in the United States and they vary considerably in terms of size, organizational structure, financial resources, organizing tactics, jurisdictional boundaries, internal governance, and collective bargaining strategies. Because of the diversity that exists among international unions, it is difficult to generalize about their structure and operations. Therefore, an attempt is made not only to portray the broad features common to most international unions, but also to illustrate the differences that characterize these organizations.

The Size of the International Unions

Unions are usually ranked by number of members rather than on measures commonly used to rank corporate size, such as financial resources, assets, or geographic dispersion. The International Brotherhood of Teamsters (IBT) was, for a number of years, the largest labor union in the United States, with a membership that had approached the 2-million mark. Teamsters' membership has dwindled somewhat and is now approximately 1.6 million members. However, unions that have experienced the most impressive membership growth over the past 25 years are those that have centered their organizing efforts on public-sector employees. Unions such as the National Educational Association (NEA), with over 1.7 million members, and the American Federation of State, County, and Municipal Employees (AFSCME), with 1.1 million members, are prime examples of high-growth public-sector unions.[22]

Approximately 40 unions in the United States (about 20 percent) have memberships of more than 100,000. Furthermore, membership in labor organizations is heavily concentrated in the largest national unions. In the mid-1980s, the 10 largest labor unions accounted for over one half of all unionized employees in the United

---

[22] Courtney D. Gifford, *Directory of U.S. Labor Organizations*, 1988–89 edition (Washington, D.C.: The Bureau of National Affairs, Inc., 1988).

States and Canada. Nearly 6.9 million (or almost 35 percent) of all unionized employees were members of the five largest international unions.[23] A number of the smaller international unions have lost members because of layoffs and job displacement arising from technological and economic changes. Some of these unions have merged with larger unions; this trend increases membership concentration.

At the other end of the spectrum, some international unions, such as the Composers and Lyricists Guild of America, the National Hockey League Players Association, the International Union of Journeymen Horseshoers of the United States and Canada, the National Basketball Players Association, and the American Watch Workers Union have less than 1,000 members. The International Association of Sideographers and the Trademark Society, Inc. have fewer than 100 members. In fact, about 10 percent of the international unions in the United States have less than 1,000 members and about 2 percent have no more than 100.[24]

International Union Functions

International unions perform a multitude of functions. These functions vary from one international to another, but most internationals are responsible for organizing nonunionized workers, negotiating collective bargaining agreements, educating union officers and agents on labor matters, communicating with members on recent developments, and assisting political lobbying efforts at the state and federal level. The extent to which an international performs these functions depends on the union's constitution, the types of workers it represents, the industries it targets for organizing, the degree of decentralization in the union's organizational structure, and whether the union is affiliated with the AFL-CIO.

The international provides the major impetus in union organizing campaigns. Most union organizers are employed by and use international union headquarters as their operations base. In many cases, union officials at the international level select the target group of nonunion employees and plot the strategy for the organizing campaign. Representatives from the international are usually responsible for recruiting and training local employees and union members who will assist in the organizational campaign. Planning mass meetings and distributing and collecting authorization cards are also frequently coordinated through international union officials. Because of their legal expertise, employees of the international are usually responsible for initiating and pursuing unfair labor practice charges against employers that arise during an organizing campaign. In short, the international often determines which employees it will attempt to organize and then coordinates the entire organization campaign to its conclusion.

Negotiation of the collective bargaining agreement is another important function of most international unions. The increasing complexity of collective bargaining agreements requires expertise at the bargaining table. Thus negotiating contracts has become a primary responsibility of the international, which often employs a

---

[23] Courtney D. Gifford, *Directory of U.S. Labor Organizations*, 1988–89 edition (Washington, D.C.: The Bureau of National Affairs, Inc., 1988).
[24] Courtney D. Gifford, *Directory of U.S. Labor Organizations*, 1988–89 edition (Washington, D.C.: The Bureau of National Affairs, Inc., 1988).

cadre of professional negotiators, economists, compensation specialists, health and safety professionals, and labor lawyers. A large number of contracts are negotiated on a multi-plant or industry-wide basis, and the international becomes the focal point for contract talks with the employer. In many instances, the international negotiates a master agreement with the company and the local unions supplement the master agreement with contracts that deal with concerns in a plant or locale. International unions also collect vast amounts of data that are germane to the collective bargaining process and organize it so that it is readily available for use by union officials and negotiators.

Because the international often negotiates collective bargaining agreements that cover employees working at multiple locations or with more than one employer, it frequently administers employee benefit programs such as group life and health insurance, retirement, and disability income insurance plans. In addition, international unions establish and regulate monies used for strike funds that provide union members with an income during work stoppages.

The education of local union officers and shop stewards is an important function for many international unions. Courses in collective bargaining agreement provisions, processing member grievances, contract negotiations at the local level, and the latest developments in labor law are representative of the educational programs sponsored by international unions. Educational programs such as these may be conducted by international staff members or by private consultants or university faculty members.

In addition to their educational efforts, most internationals try to maintain an open channel of communication with their members. The primary communications vehicle for most large internationals is a union newspaper, magazine, or journal. Examples of these publications include *International Teamster*, *Airline Pilot*, *Public Employee*, (AFSCME), and *Sheet Metal Worker*. International union publications contain news on legislative developments, executive board minutes, editorials by union officers, financial reports, and summaries of local union events. At contract negotiation time, information is provided on talks with management. Most unions also publish general information on union history, general bargaining goals, descriptions of the union's organizational structure, and biographical sketches of prominent union officers.

International unions also engage in political lobbying as a means of influencing state and federal legislators to pass laws of benefit to their members. In some cases, lobbying efforts supplement those of the AFL-CIO, whereas in other instances, an international union may take the sole initiative in pushing for legislative action.

The Governance of International Unions

International unions are governed primarily by elected officials whose authority is established by the union's constitution and by-laws. The supreme governing body for most internationals is the annual or biennial convention, which makes general policy decisions, amends the union's constitution, elects union officers and establishes their salaries, adjusts initiation fees and dues, and approves specific policies formulated by the international union staffs. Most international unions are headquartered in metropolitan areas. Washington, D.C. is one of the major hubs of international union activity because international officers and lobbyists have access to members of Congress and other important government officials. The Teamsters, the National Education Association, and several of the building trades unions have headquarters in the Washington, D.C. area. Interestingly, the nonmanagerial, nonsupervisory employees of the National Labor Relations Board have their own union, which is headquartered in Seattle and has 33 locals throughout the United States. Other international unions locate their offices near the employees and industries that they serve. The United Auto Workers are based in Detroit, the Associated Actors and Artistes of America are headquartered primarily in New York City, and the United Steelworkers are located in Pittsburgh.

Two types of employees work at international headquarters: the elected union officials and the nonelected staff members and managers. International presidents, vice-presidents, and secretary-treasurers usually work out of the international union headquarters. They are assisted by staff members who specialize in economics, labor law, compensation and employee benefits, management information systems, union organizing strategies, and other areas of expertise that are important to the union. The Landrum-Griffin Act mandates that union officials at the international level face re-election at least every five years.

International union presidents generally wield considerable power in making decisions on bargaining strategy, organizing campaigns and jurisdictional issues, interpretation of the union's constitution and by-laws, and other operational matters. However, many international union presidents must either answer to an executive board or bring major policy issues before the board. Executive boards of international unions are often comprised of selected local union presidents who represent geographic areas or industry segments. International officers are usually brought up through the union ranks. Most presidents, although elected by the members, previously held a lower office at either the international or local level. In some cases, union presidents served as prominent staff members or were groomed for the presidency by their predecessors.

Once in office, most international union presidents manage successfully to thwart political opposition and may remain at their posts for long periods of time by repeatedly winning the Landrum-Griffin Act-mandated elections every five years. Although an incumbent president is occasionally ousted from office, most leave through voluntary resignations, retirement, or death rather than through defeat in a union election. The vast majority of high-level union officers retain their positions because they adequately respond to membership needs. In addition, they occupy a central role in the union power structure and usually have sizeable budgets and staffs at their disposal. These factors make it difficult for an upstart candidate to unseat a current union officer. However, one of the most dramatic struggles for control of a union took place in 1969 when Joseph A. Yablonski opposed incumbent president Tony Boyle for the presidency of the United Mine Workers.

> Yablonski saw much to criticize in Boyle. He claimed he was a "corrupt dictator" who used union funds as if they were his own, kept relatives on the payroll at fat salaries, and maintained an unhealthy alliance with operators of the coal mines where the members worked. He said that despite inflation, retired miners had

not had their pensions improved in years, yet the union's top officers secretly had voted themselves pensions at full salary, which in Boyle's case was $50,000 a year. He said that the union, in collusion with mine owners, was doing nothing to improve safety and health in the mines even though men were being killed and injured and others were being disabled by "black lung" disease.

Boyle denied none of this. Instead he campaigned vigorously for re-election, visiting union hall after union hall, vowing to make the union "a democratic servant of the members." Under Yablonski's goading, he joined the effort to improve safety and health in the mines. He also saw to it that pensions were increased. Yablonski, meanwhile, filed complaint after complaint with the Federal government, charging that Boyle was using union funds and union staff members in his campaign. At one point he sued the union to force its weekly newspaper . . . to report that he was running against Boyle. . . . Only when he won his suit did the paper acknowledge that he was a candidate. Violence also played a role. Toward the end of the campaign an unknown assailant knocked Yablonski unconscious with a karate blow to the neck.[25]

Yablonski lost the election by a sizeable margin and then demanded a government investigation. As a UMW vice-president, he vowed to continue to fight for union reform, but was assassinated three weeks later (along with his wife and daughter in their Clarksville, Pennsylvania home). Twenty thousand miners walked off their jobs in protest. Union officials denied knowledge of the crime and posted a $50,000 reward for the conviction of those responsible. Boyle was convicted of ordering the slayings and the Yablonski case led to an investigation of the union by the U.S. Department of Labor.

The large salaries paid to top officials of some international unions are frequently controversial. An examination of the salaries of international union presidents and secretary-treasurers reveals that most presidents of the large unions make over $100,000 annually while the salaries of those who are second-in-command are in the $80,000 to $90,000 range. There is a great deal of variation in the salaries of these officials, however. Before his resignation and death in 1988, Teamsters president Jackie Presser's annual salary exceeded $500,000 whereas Farm Workers president Cesar Chevez made less than $10,000. Between these two extremes are the following 1987 salaries: Henry Duffy (Air Line Pilots), $243,382 (including an allowance for personal expenses); William H. Wynn (Food and Commercial Workers), $200,000; William W. Winpisinger (Machinists) $109,126; and Lynn R. Williams (Steelworkers), $76,195. These salaries include expense allowances or other benefits such as access to union-owned aircraft, private club memberships, and use of union recreational facilities. AFL-CIO president Lane Kirkland received a total salary of $150,000 in 1987 and the federation's secretary-treasurer, Thomas R. Donahue, was paid $125,000. With the possible exception of the Teamsters, the salaries paid to international union presidents are well below those paid to chief executive officers of most large corporations. For example, Chrysler chairman Lee Iacocca received a 1987 salary and bonus of $1,740,000, as compared to the United Auto Workers' president, Owen F. Bieber, whose income totaled $85,651.[26] Even

---

[25] Alvin Schwartz, *The Unions* (New York: The Viking Press, 1972), pp. 82–83. Reprinted with permission of Curtis-Brown, Ltd., Copyright 1972 by Alvin Schwartz.
[26] "Executive Pay," *Business Week* (May 2, 1988), p. 56.

the lucrative Teamsters president's salary appears more reasonable when viewed from the fact that it represents approximately 30¢ per Teamsters member. One union president justified his salary by comparing his compensation with that of corporate executives:

> You know, it even troubled me that union officers' salaries were disproportionate to the ability of their own members to earn.... You say to yourself that you deal at a higher level, you negotiate contracts with employers, you match wits with them, and the chances are you work longer hours than your management counterparts because they don't go around the country talking to stockholders every Monday and Wednesday as union leaders must with their constituents. So you say the guy who's across the table from you earns $720,000 a year, aren't you entitled to $110,000?[27]

Unlike corporate chief executives whose performance can be partially assessed on financial measures such as profits, rates of return, and changes in stockholders' equity, union presidents have no such objective measures on which to base their salaries. Tangible measures such as wage and benefit increases won at the bargaining table or number of new members organized might be used to assess some union leaders, but probably not for those serving employees in declining industries such as steel and mining.[28]

International Union Organizational Structures

Organizational structures of international unions vary widely and are largely designed to enable the union to respond most effectively to members' needs. Some unions such as the United Auto Workers are highly departmentalized; at one time, it had 27 bargaining departments, 17 technical and administrative departments, and 7 departments designed for special blocs of members.[29] One of the more interesting union organizational structures is that of the Associated Actors and Artistes of America (AFL-CIO), which is divided into the following eight subunions: (1) Actors' Equity Association (has nearly 40,000 members and represents actors involved in Broadway plays, primarily in the New York City area); (2) American Federation of Television and Radio Artists (38 local unions and approximately 63,000 members); (3) American Guild of Musical Artists (5,700 members who are involved in opera and ballet); (4) American Guild of Variety Artists (5,000 members in five local unions who perform in circus, hotel, and ice shows); (5) Hebrew Actors Union, Inc. (approximately 250 members); (6) Italian Actors Union (less than 100 members); (7) Screen Actors Guild (approximately 70,000 members in the Hollywood motion picture industry); and (8) Screen Extras Guild (5,000 members and 5 local

---

[27] Sol C. Chaikin (interview), "Look for the Union Label," in Philip L. Quaglieri, *America's Labor Leaders* (Lexington, Massachusetts: Lexington Books, 1989), p. 63. Reprinted with permission.
[28] "Why Union Bosses Are Also-Rans in the Big Bucks Derby," *Business Week* (May 6, 1985), pp. 102–103.
[29] James Wallihan, *Union Government and Organization* (Washington, D.C.: The Bureau of National Affairs, Inc., 1985), p. 118.

unions). The first six divisions of the Associated Actors and Artistes of America are headquartered in New York and the remaining two are located in Hollywood.[30]

The departmental structures of international unions reflect the array of services offered to constituent local unions and their members. Wallihan categorizes international union departments into three types: bargaining departments, representation and service departments, and internal administration departments.[31] Bargaining departments are chiefly concerned with collective negotiations with employers. The United Auto Workers has three bargaining departments: one each for General Motors, Ford, and Chrysler. Representation and service departments serve a multitude of functions ranging from organizing campaigns to public relations, publications, research, safety and health, and retirement programs. Internal administration departments take care of matters pertaining to accounting, record keeping, administration of group insurance programs, and union personnel. Some departments provide services to all of the international union's local affiliates, whereas others serve the needs of specific industrial or occupational groups. Many of the larger international unions have intermediate bodies that lie between the international headquarters and the local unions. Intermediate bodies generally coordinate the organizing, bargaining, and administrative activities of locals in a certain geographic region or employment group.

International Union Finances

Unions depend on initiation fees and member dues to generate income. When a worker joins a union, he or she is often required to pay an initiation fee. In some instances, the initiation fee is waived for workers who join during an organizing campaign. Once recruited into the union, a member pays dues to remain in good standing. Union dues are frequently deducted from an employee's pay by the employer who then turns the money over to the local union. A payroll deduction arrangement of this nature is known as the dues *checkoff* and it eliminates the need for the union to collect individually from each member, a task that can be time-consuming and sometimes disruptive to the work routine. Union dues approximate 1 percent of the annual income for most workers; craft union members pay a somewhat higher amount.[32]

Local unions forward about 40 percent of the dues collected to the international and, as noted earlier, internationals affiliated with the AFL-CIO pay the federation a monthly per capita member fee.[33] Thus, the money in the labor movement flows primarily upward from the locals through the international to the federation.

---

[30] Information supplied by the Associated Actors and Artistes Guild of America, New York and supplemented with information from Courtney D. Gifford, *Directory of U.S. Labor Organizations*, 1988–89 edition (Washington, D.C.: The Bureau of National Affairs, Inc., 1988), pp. 38, 45, 46, 49, 55, and 57.
[31] James Wallihan, *Union Government and Organization* (Washington, D.C.: The Bureau of National Affairs, Inc., 1985), p. 119. The description within the text differs somewhat from Wallihan's outline of these departmental functions.
[32] Martin Estey, *The Unions: Structure, Development, and Management*, 3rd ed. (New York: Harcourt, Brace, and Jovanovich, 1981), p. 80.
[33] Charles W. Hickman, "Labor Organizations Fee and Dues," *Monthly Labor Review*, (May 1977), pp. 21–22.

Dues are the financial lifeblood of the labor movement. Union officer and staff salaries, and administrative and educational expenses, are paid with dues revenues. Unlike their corporate counterparts, however, most labor unions depend heavily on the volunteer work of local union members to accomplish their tasks. Local union officers and shop stewards often work for little or no pay and many unions would find it financially difficult to operate without the uncompensated services of their members.

Labor unions also put money aside for strike funds and investments. Although unions accumulate considerable wealth, their assets do not compare with those of Fortune 500 corporations. Large strike funds are subject to rapid depletion in the event of a work stoppage. Perhaps as a result, unions tend to invest in assets that can be readily converted to cash. Most unions are also reluctant to invest in high-risk endeavors that offer a more lucrative return on investment. Despite reports of financial corruption in a few unions, most follow conservative financial management policies that are designed to protect member interests and ensure solvency.

The Central Role of International Unions

International unions are the most powerful component of the U.S. labor movement. The AFL-CIO occupies the top rung in the labor movement, but its power chiefly depends on informally persuading member unions to comply with its ideologies and policies. Nonconforming member unions may be expelled by the AFL-CIO, although such action is extremely rare. Even if expelled, an international union may continue to operate as it pleases as long as it complies with federal and state laws. In fact, an international union may have an economic incentive to disassociate from the AFL-CIO because the international will no longer be obligated to pay a per capita tax to the federation.

International unions are powerful because they have a direct impact on the wages, hours, and working conditions of their members and they exercise considerable control over the administration of the collective bargaining agreement, changes in membership fees and dues, and disciplinary matters involving union members. In cases of mismanagement or malfeasance by local union officers, the constitution and by-laws of most internationals allow them to seize control of a member local. Furthermore, in heavily unionized industries such as the construction trades, transportation, and automobile manufacturing, the international unions have a pervasive impact on the labor costs and price competitiveness of individual firms.

The rising prominence of the international unions appears to be directly related to the increasing centralization of collective bargaining in the United States. From an economic standpoint, many product markets have become regional or national in scope rather than local; market expansion transfers power from local unions to the internationals. For example, since the end of World War II the beer industry has changed from one consisting primarily of local breweries and beer distributors to one dominated by large nationally known brewers.[34] Labor organizations in this

---

[34] See Douglas J. Workman, Neil H. Snyder, Rich Bonaventura, John Cary, Scott McMasters, and Karen Cook, "Anheuser-Busch Companies, Inc.," in William F. Glueck and Lawrence R. Jauch, *Business Policy and Strategic Management*, 4th ed. (New York: McGraw-Hill Book Company, 1984), pp. 622–639.

industry undoubtedly had to shift to a more centralized bargaining posture to accommodate this change. National product markets often mean broader labor markets, such as might be found when large construction firms are involved with highway building projects over large geographic expanses. The mobile nature of employees in the airline, trucking, and railroad industries also precludes bargaining on a local level and places more responsibility on international unions. Large manufacturing firms, such as those in the steel and automobile industries, have plants spread throughout the country. Because of the similar jobs and working conditions that are found among these plants, it is more feasible to negotiate multi-plant labor agreements. Unions are generally eager to "take the wages out of competition" and standardize collective bargaining agreement provisions among firms and plants within the same industry. Therefore, the bargaining process must be the responsibility of the international union if this goal is to be achieved.

The increasing complexity of collective bargaining agreements noted earlier is another reason why the international union has become more involved in contract talks. Local unions cannot afford to maintain the staff of experts that is needed to negotiate complex compensation, employee benefit, and other provisions in the labor agreement. Preparations for future contract talks may require the full-time efforts of a large and sophisticated staff over several months or longer to ensure that union negotiators are fully prepared when they reach the bargaining table. Because it assumes the major burden of negotiating the labor agreement, the international union accumulates power and influence in the labor movement.

The proliferation of federal laws that regulate both union-management relations and other personnel practices has also helped to centralize collective bargaining at the international level. Collective bargaining agreements must be drafted to ensure compliance with legislation pertaining to equal employment opportunity, health and safety, retirement programs, wage and salary structures, and affirmative action programs. Again, the expertise required to deal with these complex issues and the accompanying personnel legislation is most likely found at the international level.

Many labor unions must negotiate collective bargaining agreements with corporations that employ large, centralized personnel/human resource management staffs. To counteract the centralized personnel function, international unions have centralized contract negotiations. In other instances, international unions have held the bargaining reins and management has responded by centralizing bargaining at the corporate level. Multi-plant bargaining units create a centralized bargaining posture by management and influence the union to consolidate collective bargaining efforts at the international level. Union leaders may prefer to centralize bargaining efforts in order to shift power away from local unions, reduce the number of collective bargaining agreements that must be negotiated and administered, and standardize many of the compensation and employment provisions among union members as a means of reducing inequities and dissension among rank-and-file members.

Finally, the administration of union-wide employee benefit programs is often the responsibility of the international union. Group health insurance programs, such as major medical and disability income insurance, are usually created under the master collective bargaining agreement and are administered by the international.

Retirement programs are also a prime responsibility of administrators and fiduciaries, who are either part of the international staff or who report directly to international headquarters. The administration of employee benefit programs not only enhances the centralization of power at the international level, but also places the international in the position of collecting, safeguarding, and investing large sums of money. Furthermore, international union officials influence the cost of group life and health insurance programs through their selection of insurance companies that provide benefits to union members.

▲ The Local Unions

The local serves as the most accessible point of contact for union members. Most local unions are chartered by internationals and are ultimately governed by the constitution, by-laws, and policies that are promulgated at the international level. Other locals are independent entities that are affiliated with neither an international nor the AFL-CIO. Still others are directly affiliated with the AFL-CIO, but have no international. Most locals serve union members who work in a factory or a relatively small geographic area. However, local unions differ considerably with regard to their governance, geographical scope, occupational variety, employers covered, and types of employees served.

Local unions can be categorized into *factory* and *nonfactory* locals. As the name implies, factory locals serve union members who work in single or multi-plant units. Nonfactory locals serve union members who switch worksites or employers. That is, members of factory locals work in a permanent location, whereas nonfactory local union members are mobile. For example, United Auto Workers Local 600 serves workers who are employed at the Ford Rouge plant in Dearborn, Michigan. Local 320 of the United Brotherhood of Carpenters and Joiners of America is the local affiliate for carpenters working in the Augusta and Waterville, Maine area. Carpenters working in this locality may be either permanently or temporarily employed by a general contractor; they move from one job or employer to another, but they remain members of Local 320 unless they relocate to another part of Maine or to another state.

The membership in *industrial* local unions is made up of workers with different occupational skills and employment situations. Other local unions, such as *craft* unions, are comprised of members whose jobs and skills are much more homogeneous. Industrial locals may cover both single employers and plants as well as multiple employers. Steelworkers Local 1010 consists of 18,000 members working for one employer, Inland Steel, in East Chicago, Indiana, whereas Transport Workers Local 225 in Hackensack, New Jersey includes members employed by five different bus lines. In the building trades, local craft unions serve members who work for different construction firms in a metropolitan area or region of a state. The International Brotherhood of Electrical Workers, Local 3 in New York City is an example of a local with hundreds of employers under contract.[35]

---

[35] James Wallihan, *Union Government and Organization* (Washington, D.C.: The Bureau of National Affairs, Inc., 1985), pp. 91 and 93.

Local Union Functions

Local unions are actively involved in the initial stages of the contract administration process. The responsibility of collecting initiation fees, membership dues, and payments for union-sponsored employee benefit programs usually falls on the local unions. Local unions keep members abreast of developments at the international. Nonfactory locals are heavily involved in organizing activities within their geographic jurisdictions. Nearly all local unions hold monthly meetings and conduct social functions for their members. Finally, many local unions operate union hiring halls that provide employment referrals.

Of these local union functions, contract administration is typically the most important. Although the international unions have become increasingly responsible for the negotiation of the collective bargaining agreement, the local union is given the task of administering the contract on the shop floor. In factory locals, the *shop steward* is the initial contact for an employee who desires to file a grievance or obtain clarification on a provision in the collective bargaining agreement. Many grievances are quickly resolved by a brief conversation between the shop steward and the employee's first-line supervisor. For more complex problems, the local is often responsible for preparing a written statement of the grievance and dispatching it in a timely manner to higher stages of the grievance procedure. In short, the local union serves as the first line of defense in the contract administration process and acts as a watchdog to ensure that management adheres to the provisions of the collective bargaining agreement. Contract administration can be a delicate function. Union members who believe that they have been wronged by the employer may vehemently demand a grievance hearing. Local union stewards and officers may find themselves in a politically awkward situation if an employee's grievance has little merit. Sometimes the local union must walk a thin line between processing meritorious grievances and tactfully rejecting those that are ill-founded or do not represent violations of the collective bargaining agreement.

Although the international union assumes responsibility for negotiating the collective bargaining agreement, local unions are often required to negotiate supplemental labor agreements. Supplemental agreements extend or modify the master labor contract to accommodate local conditions. Local unions can create serious labor problems and work stoppages when their members refuse to ratify a supplemental contract.

As mentioned previously, the local union is chiefly responsible for collecting fees and dues payments from its members and remitting a pro-rata share of these collections to the international. When a dues checkoff is in effect, the employer deducts the members' dues from their pay checks and forwards them to the union. However, if there is no provision for a dues checkoff, the shop stewards and local union officials must collect from each member. Union officials may view this arrangement as burdensome and time-consuming; some employers avoid a dues checkoff agreement in order to hinder the union. The union may prefer the personal approach to collecting dues because it provides officials with regular opportunities to visit members and solicit their opinions on matters related to the job. Employers are aware that dues collections made on company property or during work hours may be disruptive; thus, most agree to a checkoff arrangement.

Local unions conduct regular meetings to make policy decisions and address membership concerns. Most local union meetings are not well attended unless there are important issues to be decided, such as a strike vote or an election of union officers. Local union meetings are often held after working hours and, in some cases, are dominated by local officers who fail to listen to member concerns. In other instances, a local union is so heavily dominated by the international that the local meetings serve primarily to relay news of international developments to members. Some local meetings are social events that are designed to increase solidarity among members and their families. Although attendance at routine local union meetings may be as low as 10 percent of the membership, many members participate in union affairs through what has been labeled a "shop society."[36] That is, local union members often have considerable input into job concerns through informal consultation with shop stewards, business agents, and union officers, as well as through committees, newsletters, grievance efforts, social events, and educational programs.

Despite the apathy that surrounds many local union meetings, union leaders exert pressure on members to maintain an unswerving loyalty to the labor organization. To ensure such loyalty, local unions have an informal code of behavior for members. Renegade members who become too friendly with management, attempt to undermine the efforts of local union officers, or start a rival union are likely to be viewed as traitors. Local leaders must occasionally deal with member misuse of union funds, working on a job at less than the union wage, or crossing a picket line during a strike. The constitution and by-laws of most unions provide for disciplinary action when members commit offenses against the union. If the officers decide that an infraction has occurred, they arrange for an internal hearing that is conducted in accordance with union by-laws. A member who is found guilty may be subjected to a reprimand, fine, or dismissal from the union. Although most fines are small, there was one instance in which a number of television news personnel were fined up to $14,000 for working during a strike.[37]

Craft local unions often attempt to control the availability of labor. One means of controlling the supply of skilled workers is through apprenticeship training programs, which are frequently found in the building trades unions. Local unions use the apprenticeship training program primarily to ensure the proper training of skilled craft workers. In practice, however, the restrictive admissions policies of such programs mean that the union can limit the number of trained workers who will be available to work in a locale. Local unions can control the supply of labor through hiring halls and job referrals. Available jobs are posted in the hiring halls and any qualified worker may apply. Although hiring halls are operated by unions, they are legally required to refer both union and nonunion members on an equal basis. Furthermore, the employer, not the union, is supposed to have the final hiring authority. If all employees were referred equally and the employer had total control over hiring, then the local union could not control the labor supply. However, when one or both of these conditions are violated, the local becomes increasingly able to manipulate the availability and price of labor.

---

[36] Joseph Kovner and Herbert Lahne, "Shop Society and the Union," *Industrial and Labor Relations Review*, (October 1953), pp. 3–14, and James Wallihan, *Union Government and Organization* (Washington, D.C.: The Bureau of National Affairs, Inc., 1985), pp. 100–101.

[37] Alvin Schwartz, *The Unions* (New York: The Viking Press, 1972), p. 101.

Local Union Governance and Politics

Large local unions generally employ full-time elected officers and staff members to conduct union business. Most factory locals are governed by an elected president, secretary-treasurer, and executive board. The salaried, full-time *business agent* elected or appointed by the international is a central figure in the operation of nonfactory locals. Business agents handle member grievances, enforce contracts, and perform other daily tasks for the union. Smaller locals often depend on the uncompensated services of union members to carry out their functions. Because of their proximity to rank-and-file union members, an important aspect of the local union officers' job is to keep a close watch on member problems and concerns. The partisan nature of some local unions can place local union officers in a precarious position as they attempt to maintain internal peace and soothe harsh feelings among factions within the local. When local union members face layoffs, reduced work hours, or other cutbacks precipitated by economic declines, the job of the local union officer becomes more difficult. An added element of uncertainty is that local officers must face re-election every three years according to the Landrum-Griffin Act. Local union officers have high visibility among the rank-and-file and their offices are often less secure than their international counterparts. Perhaps this uncertainty has best been summarized by Schwartz:

> Like all governments, those that run the local unions consist of an executive (the officers), a legislature (the members), and a judiciary (the officers or the members). The typical local is administered by part-time volunteers who serve in a dozen different positions....
>
> But even for an officer who does not receive pay, there are compensations, particularly if his regular job is a monotonous dead end. Thus, he may spend as much as half the week away from his regular job, for which his union or employer pays him. Usually he also has an expense account and is exempt from paying union dues. Moreover, he is a man of consequence in his union and in his community. He deals with his employer as an equal. His support may be sought by civic leaders and political figures. His ideas may be reported in the local newspaper. He also may attend leadership schools and conventions his international union sponsors and, if he is a good officer, eventually he may be offered a job as an international representative. If he is defeated in a bid for re-election, therefore, it may be a decided wrench to return to the more ordinary life he led earlier.[38]

Some union leaders are well entrenched and manage repeatedly to win re-election every three years. However, most officers in factory locals do not have a long-term orientation to their jobs as have their international counterparts who make a career out of being a union officer or working in an international staff position.

One of the most important groups in many local unions are the shop stewards. Most shop stewards are full-time employees for the company and work for the union on a voluntary basis; they are either elected by their fellow employees or are appointed by local union officers. The responsibilities of the shop steward vary

---

[38] Alvin Schwartz, *The Unions* (New York: The Viking Press, 1972), pp. 97–98. Reprinted with permission of Curtis-Brown, Ltd., Copyright 1972 by Alvin Schwartz.

depending on the union and the industry in which the union operates. Shop stewards serve as the initial contact for employees who file grievances against management. Some stewards are also involved with union political activities, community services, counseling, educational work, dues collection, and union organizing. The number of employees to which a shop steward is responsible varies. A steward may serve all bargaining unit employees or employees who work in a department, shift, or production area. The power of a shop steward appears to be stronger in industrial locals than in craft or white-collar locals. However, the power of many shop stewards has eroded due to the complexity of collective bargaining agreements, the diminishing influence of the first-line supervisor with whom shop stewards consult when resolving grievances, and the increasing centralization of the collective bargaining process at the international level. Some shop steward positions are highly coveted because of the protection afforded from layoffs (through superseniority) and the status and work freedom associated with the job. However, the shop steward often sacrifices personal off-duty time to attend training programs and conduct union business. Shop stewards can get caught up in the crossfire of union politics and they run the risk of becoming management targets for retaliation. Nevertheless, shop stewards form the backbone of local union activities; in some cases, these individuals are "the union" in the eyes of rank-and-file employees.[39]

Craft union locals are run by business agents who engage in bargaining and contract administration activities for union members working in a metropolitan area or region. Business agents are often responsible for organizing nonunion craft workers in their jurisdictions. In addition, they may administer employee benefit programs, coordinate local activities with the international, and engage in political lobbying. A leading reason for the importance of the business agent to the nonfactory or craft local stems from the transient nature of the local union members' jobs. Business agents add continuity and stability to a mobile job market. For example, in the construction industry, where a skilled craft worker is employed by one contractor after another, the business agent plays a prominent role in the quick resolution of worker grievances. Unlike their counterparts in industrial unions, business agents are more likely to have to deal with multi-employer contracts or multiple contracts with several firms.

▲ Merger Activities and Organized Labor

Union Mergers

Like their corporate counterparts, labor unions may elect to acquire or merge with other unions. Union mergers occur in two ways: *amalgamations*, in which two unions merge and assume a new identity, and *absorptions*, in which one union merges with another and loses its original identity. Amalgamations usually occur between two unions that are approximately the same size, whereas absorptions

---

[39] Al Nash, *The Union Steward: Duties, Rights, and Status* (Ithaca, New York: ILR Press, Cornell University, 1977).

often involve a larger union merging with a smaller union.[40] When the AFL and the CIO merged in 1955, it was expected that the federation's original 135 international and national unions would gradually merge with one another until approximately 50 unions remained. Today, the federation contains 90 unions, so it is doubtful that the goal of 50 strong unions will be realized. However, merger talks and activities among unions are commonplace and occasionally generate considerable controversy. In 1984, the International Typographical Union (ITU) considered a merger with the Teamsters, a move that caused concern among factions within the union as well as with the AFL-CIO. The proposed merger was further clouded because of campaign irregularities in the election of ITU officers. AFL-CIO President Lane Kirkland notified the ITU that a merger with the unaffiliated Teamsters would result in its expulsion from the federation.[41]

The motivations underlying the merger of unions are similar to those behind corporate mergers. First, a small union may merge with a larger union in order to gain access to greater resources and expertise. By merging, a union may have more personnel and money for organizing and may be able to offer its members a wider range of services. In addition, a small union that merges with a larger union may enhance its effectiveness during contract negotiations because of added expertise and power at the bargaining table.

In some cases, union mergers do not involve similar occupational groups.[42] For example, the 2,500-member Brewery Workers Local 9 in Milwaukee merged with the United Auto Workers. Similarly, the 34,000-member Upholsterers International Union merged with the 1 million-member United Steel Workers Union.[43] Second, unions that have traditionally competed with each other for members may merge in order to eliminate interorganizational conflicts; resources that had been used to compete with a rival union could be used for more constructive purposes once the rivals have merged. Third, unions whose members' skills have been outmoded by technological and economic changes may merge with a stronger union in order to maintain job security and institutional survival.[44] Occupational obsolescence may, in part, explain the merger of the United Cement, Lime, Gypsum, and Allied Workers International Union with the Brotherhood of Boilermakers. By combining the 29,000 members of the Cement Workers with the Boilermakers' 105,000 members, the new union (known as the Boilermakers) became the 20th largest in the United States.[45]

---

[40] Gary N. Chaison, "A Note on Union Merger Trends, 1900–1978," *Industrial and Labor Relations Review*, (October 1980), p. 116.
[41] The Bureau of National Affairs, Inc., *Collective Bargaining Negotiations & Contracts* (Washington, D.C.: The Bureau of National Affairs, Inc., May 10, 1984), p. 3.
[42] See John L. Conant and David L. Kaserman, "Union Merger Incentives and Pecuniary Externalities," *Journal of Labor Research* (Summer 1989), pp. 243–253.
[43] The Bureau of National Affairs, Inc., *Collective Bargaining Negotiations & Contracts* (Washington, D.C.: The Bureau of National Affairs, Inc., November 7, 1985), p. 3.
[44] See Larry T. Adams, "Labor Organization Mergers 1979–84: Adapting to Change," *Monthly Labor Review* (September 1984), p. 21.
[45] The Bureau of National Affairs, Inc., *Collective Bargaining Negotiations & Contracts* (Washington, D.C.: The Bureau of National Affairs, Inc., May 10, 1984), p. 3. Also see Thomas A. Kochan and Harry C. Katz, *Collective Bargaining and Industrial Relations*, 2nd ed. (Homewood, Illinois: Richard D. Irwin, Inc., 1988), pp. 179–180, for a discussion of union mergers.

Most union mergers benefit their respective memberships. However, some mergers appear to be poorly conceived because they involve unions whose jurisdictions, occupational and industry groupings served, and mode of operations are radically different. Union officials who desire to increase their membership numbers, financial base, and personal power in the labor movement may be tempted to merge with unions with which they have little in common.[46] Although a number of unions discuss the possibility of merging with other labor organizations, the annual number of actual mergers in the United States is small. Between 1900 and 1978, there was an average of 1.8 union mergers per year, and between 1970 and 1978, there were approximately 3.0 mergers per year.[47] Nevertheless, union mergers can have an important impact on the labor movement and contract talks, especially when large unions are involved.[48] At the time of this writing, the United Mine Workers were looking at the possibility of merging with another labor organization whose identity has not been publicized. Since most coal operations are now controlled by multinational corporations, the UMW has realized that management has the capacity to "act quickly and decisively to consolidate and amass even greater economic security." In the face of these threats to the security of UMW members, union officials said that they "must be equally armed and capable of garnering support beyond our ranks."[49]

The Impact of Unions on Corporate Mergers and Buyouts

The 1980s witnessed numerous corporate leveraged buy-outs and takeovers. Perceiving that their interests are at stake when a company contemplates a merger or acquisition, organized labor may attempt to buy out a company that is in financial distress. According to New York investment banker Eugene J. Keilin, "unions have organized to try to take an active role, and have increasingly been successful. . . . Indeed they have become part of the corporate picture."[50]

For example, the leveraged buy-out of Safeway Stores' Kansas City Division by a group of former division managers and the New York investment firm of Morgan, Lewis, Githens & Ahn was contingent upon cooperation by the United Food and Commercial Workers (UFCW) union. Three-year concessionary agreements were successfully negotiated between the parties involved in the buyout and three UFCW

---

[46] The previously mentioned example of the Brewery Workers local in Milwaukee, which merged with the Auto Workers, might be such an example. Earlier, this local had split from the Brewery Workers when that union affiliated with the Teamsters. Whether UAW leaders seized the opportunity to increase their sphere of influence is subject to speculation.
[47] Gary N. Chaison, "A Note on Union Merger Trends, 1900–1978," *Industrial and Labor Relations Review* (October 1980), p. 117.
[48] See Zachary Schiller, "Merger Phobia Has Unions Wheeling and Dealing," *Business Week* (March 23, 1987), p. 118.
[49] The Bureau of National Affairs, Inc., *Collective Bargaining Negotiations & Contracts* (Washington, D.C.: The Bureau of National Affairs, Inc., September 25, 1986), p. 1.
[50] The Bureau of National Affairs, Inc., "Union Mergers and Acquisitions," *Collective Bargaining Negotiations & Contracts* (Washington, D.C.: The Bureau of National Affairs, Inc., June 16, 1988), p. 4.

locals. The new contracts cover 3,500 workers in 66 stores under the name of Food Barn Stores, Inc.[51]

Unions typically become involved in corporate merger activities in order to preserve jobs for their members. The job-preservation goals of unions may run counter to the financial orientation of other parties involved in corporate takeovers or mergers. Labor attorney Bruce H. Simon says that "unions are often thinking in a different currency than others at the table, who can usually translate their goals into a bottom-line figure." Union and management, however, tend to be in the same predicament when a hostile takeover threatens a company. The involvement of unions in protecting a company from the advances of a corporate raider requires that labor and management take a cooperative rather than an adversarial stance. In addition, exorbitant legal fees may be required to thwart a takeover bid. According to Keilin, unions must first decide whether to make a "significant investment in developing outside counsel with the capacity to deal intelligently with the issues." He adds that unions need outside investment and financial advice and, by and large, they are "not comfortable with the five-zero and six-zero [legal] fees."[52]

▲ Unions as Democratic Institutions

Labor unions have occasionally been criticized for not being egalitarian and democratic. To bolster their charges that unions are not responding adequately to the needs of their members, critics of organized labor have cited member apathy over union governance and the internal corruption of some unions. The issue of union democracy has created a number of questions. What do we mean by the term "union democracy"? Is the lack of democracy a widespread problem in the labor movement or is it confined to only a few unions? Are locals more democratic than their internationals? Although the Landrum-Griffin Act (1959) was passed to eliminate corruption within the ranks of organized labor and to ensure a more democratic environment for union members, the concern over union democracy persists.

Democracy Defined

Most observers of the labor movement in the United States believe that democracy in labor unions is important.[53] The following statement by Seidman provides a concise explanation of why democracy is important to members of organized labor:

> The labor union, it should be noted, bases its reason for existence on peculiarly democratic grounds. It exists to force management to consider the rights of its

---

[51] The Bureau of National Affairs, Inc., "Concessionary, Buy-Out Agreements," *Collective Bargaining Negotiations & Contracts* (Washington, D.C.: The Bureau of National Affairs, Inc., February 25, 1988), pp. 1–2.
[52] Based on "Union Mergers and Acquisitions," *Collective Bargaining Negotiations & Contracts* (Washington, D.C.: The Bureau of National Affairs, Inc., June 16, 1988), p. 4.
[53] See Kenneth O. Alexander, "The Worker, the Union, and the Democratic Workplace," *The American Journal of Economics and Sociology* (October 1987), p. 385.

employees along with considerations of efficiency and profitability. It provides a counterpower to the power of management, which would otherwise have complete authority to hire and fire, determine wages and working conditions, and otherwise affect the livelihood and welfare of its employees, subject to the laws of the land and the state of the labor market. For this reason, the union that ceases to be democratic in its internal structure weakens its moral cause for existence.[54]

Although the ideals of democracy are widely accepted among proponents of organized labor in the United States, the definition of what constitutes a democratic union is subject to debate. If democracy is defined as member participation in the policy-making activities of unions, then most unions are not very democratic. However, if democracy is measured by the extent to which union members influence the actions of their leadership (who formulate policies), then most unions in the United States are democratic institutions.[55] That is, union officers heavily consider desires of the rank-and-file even though the members do not directly participate in contract negotiations or major policy decisions. Ignoring the needs of union members will eventually lead to internal dissatisfaction and possibly to leadership demise, a point that is obvious to all but the most autocratic union leaders.

Barriers to Union Democracy

Several forces are responsible for the lack of democracy in a few labor unions. First, the constitutions of some unions give their leadership very broad powers to conduct business and unilaterally make important decisions. For example, the constitutions of the Teamsters, United Mine Workers, and the American Federation of Musicians have contained (or still contain) clauses that not only bestow a great deal of power on union officials, but these constitutional provisions also make it difficult for members to challenge the legitimacy of decisions made by union leaders.

Second, we have seen that unions have a right to discipline their members for misconduct that is detrimental to union interests. Problems arise when disciplinary actions are used to suppress free speech or punish political opponents. Under the guise of using the disciplinary process to punish members for violating such vague constitutional prohibitions as "improper conduct," "disturbing the harmony of meetings," or "insubordination," union officials can control members who question the wisdom of leadership actions and union policies. Union disciplinary procedures are rarely nonpartisan, nor are they usually designed to ensure a fair and impartial hearing. In effect, the union serves as prosecutor, judge, and jury when exercising internal disciplinary measures against its members. The United Auto Workers (UAW) has used an independent public review board to overcome this problem. Under this arrangement, UAW members who feel that the union has treated them unfairly can appeal to the public review board, which is comprised of influential citizens who examine evidence and render a verdict that is binding on the union.

---

[54] Joel Seidman, *Democracy in the Labor Movement* (Ithaca, New York: New York State School of Industrial and Labor Relations, Cornell University, 1969), p. 4.
[55] Alvin Schwartz, *The Unions* (New York: The Viking Press, 1972), p. 101.

The UAW public review board is an exception rather than a rule among labor unions, who generally exercise sole disciplinary authority over their members.[56]

Membership apathy is probably the most often-cited reason for a lack of democracy in labor unions. Most union members demonstrate little interest in attending local union meetings unless there are issues of pressing concern such as contract negotiations, a strike vote, a major grievance, or the election of union officers. Topics covered at routine union meetings hold little interest to the average union member, who is content to let union officers take care of the more mundane business affairs. As long as the union member believes that the officers are doing a competent job, there is usually little concern over attending meetings that are often laden with parliamentary procedure and dominated by the long-winded and boring rhetoric of a few outspoken members. The incentive for attending meetings may diminish further when most important decisions are made at the international rather than the local level. As noted earlier in this chapter, a union member still has daily access to union officials and shop stewards at work. Rank-and-file members who do not attend union meetings still have ample opportunities to air their views to union officials.

Union democracy may be hindered by the fact that most international union officials are well entrenched in office and normally face little opposition when they run for re-election. Most union members regard union leaders as masters rather than servants and are reluctant to challenge leader authority unless there is a crisis or serious malfeasance. Union members who sue leaders for malfeasance may find that relief by way of a civil suit is expensive, time-consuming, and uncertain. Despite organized labor's stand against totalitarianism and communism, many unions are quite autocratic in their operations. At the 1947 convention of the International Longshoremen's and Warehousemen's Union, Harry Bridges drew the following parallel between totalitarianism in the Soviet Union and the one-party system in his union:

> What is totalitarianism? A country that has a totalitarian government operates like our union operates. There are no political parties. People are elected to govern the country based upon their records.... That is totalitarianism. If we started to divide up and run a Republican set of officers, a Democratic set, a Communist set and something else we would have one hell of a time.[57]

When the United Mine Workers powerful president, John L. Lewis, was challenged by Ray Edmundson in 1944, Lewis wasted no time in expressing his views about his challenger as well as the security of his job as UMW president:

> I have been reading in the public press ... that it was all up with old John L. when he came to this convention, that Browder, Hillman, and Roosevelt had hired themselves a man to come here and dethrone the old man right on his

---

[56] Joel Seidman, *Democracy in the Labor Movement* (Ithaca, New York: New York State School of Industrial and Labor Relations, Cornell University, 1969), p. 31.

[57] Joel Seidman, *Democracy in the Labor Movement* (Ithaca, New York: New York State School of Industrial and Labor Relations, Cornell University, 1969), p. 31. See *Proceedings of the Thirty-Eighth Constitutional Convention of the United Mine Workers of America* (1944), p. 16.

own ground.... Why, gentlemen, there isn't any mincing, lackadaisical, lace-pantied gigolo going to dethrone John L. in his own organization and in his own convention.[58]

By excluding Edmundson from the convention because he was allegedly not a member in good standing and by using violence against his supporters, Lewis successfully subverted Edmundson's attempt to challenge him for office.

Restrictive or discriminatory admissions policies to unions and apprenticeship training programs can have an adverse impact on union democracy. As late as 1964, blacks were excluded from membership in some unions or were forced to join racially segregated locals. Another practice by craft unions was the "permit" system that allowed nonunion members to work when there was an oversupply of jobs, but would not allow these workers to belong to the union. When the number of available jobs dwindled, those with "permits" were discharged and only full-fledged union members continued to work. In some instances, a worker seeking a permit had to pay a bribe to a local union official. High initiation fees and unequal union dues are other means by which a union can discriminate. As noted in Chapter 3, these practices are now illegal. Finally, favoritism on the part of craft unions in admitting trainees into apprenticeship training programs can be detrimental to democracy. Unions have been known to admit the relatives of current members (usually a son or daughter) to the exclusion of "outsiders" who are better qualified. Of course, there is likely to be little or no opposition to such nepotism by union members, who would be expected to favor preferential admissions policies for family members.

Some Suggestions for Making Unions More Democratic

There are a number of measures that can be taken to ensure greater democracy in U.S. labor unions. Seidman suggests the following nine points to help achieve union democracy:[59]

1. The officers must exercise restricted authority, subject to instructions from and periodic reports to the membership.
2. The members must have the supreme power—the right to decide important matters whenever they choose to do so.
3. Freedom of speech, including freedom to criticize, must be safeguarded.
4. Disciplinary procedures within the union must be administered fairly.
5. The members must enjoy job security.
6. There must be frequent, regular, and free elections.
7. Freedom to organize groups within the union must be safeguarded, to ensure choice among rival candidates.
8. Rival groups must have approximately equal access to membership.
9. The salaries of officers should not be too far above their earnings in the trade.

---

[58] Joel Seidman, *Democracy in the Labor Movement* (Ithaca, New York: New York State School of Industrial and Labor Relations, Cornell University, 1969), p. 52.
[59] Joel Seidman, *Democracy in the Labor Movement* (Ithaca, New York: New York State School of Industrial and Labor Relations, Cornell University, 1969), p. 36.

Seidman claims that democracy might be somewhat better at the local level than at the international level. Because local union members have daily contact with local officers and are more aware of their views and actions, such a claim sounds reasonable. Unions of professional workers may also enjoy a higher degree of democracy than other unions, according to Seidman. He cites the following reasons: professional workers enjoy high occupational prestige, union officers' salaries are at approximately the same level as members' salaries, and many professional unions do not have union security clauses that force bargaining-unit members to join or remain in the union. Thus, dissatisfied union members have the option of leaving the union without jeopardizing their job security.[60]

▲ Labor Unions and Organized Crime

The problem of labor racketeering has existed for decades in some international and local unions. Although the passage of the Landrum-Griffin Act was directed at reducing internal corruption in unions, labor racketeering still persists and has received considerable attention from the President's Commission on Organized Crime.[61] Labor racketeering has been defined as "the infiltration, domination, and use of a union for personal benefit by illegal, violent, and fraudulent means."[62] Most labor racketeering in the United States is conducted by organized crime families and syndicates who raid workers' benefit funds, enter into various sweetheart deals with employers, and exact "insurance" payments from companies whose business could be irreparably damaged by an untimely strike. Labor unions controlled by organized crime can create monopolies in certain industries; as a result, businesses owned or run by criminals and crime syndicates gain an economic advantage over their competition. By controlling the cost of labor, organized crime can raise its competitors' costs, force legitimate businesses to deal with illicit companies, and engage in price fixing, bid rigging, and other practices that destroy fair competition in an industry. Some companies regard dealing with organized crime as simply another cost of doing business. As a result, firms may do little to rid themselves of the economic burdens associated with labor racketeering.[63]

How Big Is the Problem of Labor Racketeering and Who Is Involved?

Labor racketeering has been characterized as a "cancer that almost destroyed the labor movement," as "a serious national problem," and as a threat comparable to "organized crime in international drug traffic."[64] Despite these sweeping statements,

---

[60] Joel Seidman, *Democracy in the Labor Movement* (Ithaca, New York: New York State School of Industrial and Labor Relations, Cornell University, 1969), p. 36.
[61] President's Commission on Organized Crime, *The Edge: Organized Crime, Business, and Labor Unions* (Washington, D.C.: U.S. Government Printing Office, March 1986).
[62] President's Commission on Organized Crime, *The Edge: Organized Crime, Business, and Labor Unions* (Washington, D.C.: U.S. Government Printing Office, March 1986), p. 9.
[63] President's Commission on Organized Crime, *The Edge: Organized Crime, Business, and Labor Unions* (Washington, D.C.: U.S. Government Printing Office, March 1986), p. 1.
[64] President's Commission on Organized Crime, *The Edge: Organized Crime, Business, and Labor Unions* (Washington, D.C.: U.S. Government Printing Office, March 1986), p. xv.

the influence of organized crime in the labor movement is confined to only a few international and local unions.[65] The *Quality of Employment Survey* published by the Institute of Social Research at the University of Michigan indicates that only three percent of the blue-collar employees surveyed reported problems of corruption in their unions.[66] Former Attorney General Benjamin Civiletti estimated during a Senate subcommittee hearing on organized crime that approximately 300 local unions were "severely influenced by racketeers."[67] When one considers that there are over 65,000 locals in the United States, then the number controlled by organized crime is miniscule. When the approximately 60,000 locals covered by the ethical procedures of the AFL-CIO are factored out, however, the percentage of racketeer-controlled local unions becomes more significant. Despite the small number of unions involved, the impact of labor racketeering goes beyond union members and causes problems for society as well.

The report issued by the President's Commission on Organized Crime focuses on the "big four" unions: the International Longshoremen's Association, the International Brotherhood of Teamsters,[68] the Laborers International Union of North America, and the Hotel Employees and Restaurant Employees International Union. According to the Commission, each of these unions has been found to be substantially influenced or controlled by organized crime. The Commission also investigated two New York City industries: meat distribution and construction.

The committee uncovered a number of racketeering practices that make unions an attractive target for organized crime. One objective of labor racketeers is to plunder the financial resources of a labor union. In some cases, union funds are simply embezzled by organized crime figures. In other instances, more sophisticated devices are used to bleed the financial resources of a local or international union. These include paying excessive salaries or administrative fees to union officials or "consultants" who have connections with organized crime. Family members of known organized crime figures have been placed on jobs at lucrative salaries, yet they performed little or no work and, in some cases, had no idea of the responsibilities and duties associated with their union jobs. Union treasuries were also tapped to purchase automobiles and houses for organized crime figures.[69] The President's Commission points to the following illustrative example:

> For instance, former union leader Daniel Cunningham was found guilty of embezzling union funds while serving as trustee of the Allied International Union Health and Welfare Fund. He gave "no show" jobs to friends and family members, disbursed approximately $38,000 in union and welfare fund checks to his wife,

---

[65] "Trade Unions: The Usual Suspects," *The Economist* (May 4, 1985), p. 29.
[66] Institute for Social Research, University of Michigan, *Quality of Employment Survey (QES)* (original 1969 title: *Survey of Working Conditions*). Cited in Richard B. Freeman and James L. Medoff, *What Do Unions Do?* (New York: Basic Books, Inc., 1984), pp. 210 and 214.
[67] Richard B. Freeman and James L. Medoff, *What Do Unions Do?* (New York: Basic Books, Inc., 1984), p. 214.
[68] See Laurence Zuckerman "Breaking a Devil's Pact: This Time A Crusade Against Teamsters Corruption Might Win," *Time* (July 11, 1988), p. 17; "A Credible Response to Union Mobsters," *The New York Times* (July 21, 1988), p. A24; Philip Shenon, "For Teamster Brotherhood, Some Tenacious Family Ties," *New York Times* (July 21, 1988), p. E5, and "Operation Decapitation," *The Economist* (June 20, 1987), p. 32.
[69] See James Cook, "The Invisible Enterprise," *Forbes* (September 29, 1980), p. 60.

ex-wife, and girlfriend, used union funds for personal travel expenses and merchandise, and during the 6 years that he was looting the union, purchased $147,000 of municipal bonds and amassed a cash kitty of more than $190,000.[70]

Because unions collect and safeguard large sums of money for retirement, health, and other benefit programs, these funds become the prey of corrupt trustees and executors with connections to organized crime. According to the President's Commission, Allen Glick served as a front man for several organized crime figures and obtained a $62.7 million loan from the Teamsters Central States Pension Fund without even submitting a personal financial statement. The money was used to finance Las Vegas casino operations.[71] Legitimate businesses are sometimes used as fronts in these financial schemes in order to protect organized crime figures who work behind the scenes. In some cases, professional asset managers, doctors, lawyers, and accountants have fronted for organized crime in health insurance schemes designed to pay kickbacks and inflated administrative fees. Such fronts make it difficult to prosecute those who are ultimately responsible for illegal activities.

Members of organized crime occasionally provide financial support to candidates for public office in return for favors and protection from prosecution. Although most politicians find such alliances unsavory, there are a few who are willing to become involved. Through business fronts, contributions can be made to campaigns without disclosing the identities of the donors. Union members may also provide assistance to favored candidates under the direction of organized crime figures who work behind the scenes.

Sweetheart contracts are collusive devices that are used by employers and corrupt union officials to violate or ignore collective bargaining agreement provisions. Because they force employers to make illicit payments to union officials, sweetheart agreements are of interest to organized crime figures. In most sweetheart arrangements, an employer pays a bribe to the union, which, in return, allows the employer to pay workers less, use fewer workers on a project, or employ nonunion labor for bargaining unit jobs. During contract negotiations, sweetheart arrangements allow an employer to select members of the union bargaining team. Sweetheart contracts are most likely to be found in industries such as construction and trucking, where labor costs are important and substantial differences between union and nonunion wages provide incentives for an employer to collude illegally with the union.

Strike "insurance" schemes allow members of organized crime to extort payments from management in return for promises of labor peace. Firms that are most susceptible to extortion through strike-insurance arrangements are those whose businesses can be damaged severely or irreparably by a work stoppage. For example, the construction industry is especially vulnerable to strikes because most building projects proceed in stages whereby one set of workers completes a job and then another group begins work at a site. If a group of workers or suppliers is plagued

---

[70] President's Commission on Organized Crime, *The Edge: Organized Crime, Business, and Labor Unions* (Washington, D.C.: U.S. Government Printing Office, March 1986), pp. 12–13.

[71] President's Commission on Organized Crime, *The Edge: Organized Crime, Business, and Labor Unions* (Washington, D.C.: U.S. Government Printing Office, March 1986), p. 14.

by labor difficulties, then an entire project can be delayed well beyond the anticipated completion date.[72] A classic example of how organized crime has established a firm grip on the New York City construction industry is exemplified by the following excerpt from the report issued by the President's Commission on Organized Crime:

> New York construction businesses cooperating with organized crime have formed a cartel, and the union is the enforcing agent. General contractors are told what suppliers to use and who the subcontractors will be. If a contractor does not comply, either he will never get the job (having been purposefully underbid by the cooperating companies) or he will never be able to complete it. Construction contractors have told Commission representatives that they simply cannot go into the New York market because they are underbid or cannot get work done when they get a bid.[73]

Other industries such as the garment, trucking, and retail meat industries have also been plagued by strike insurance and other forms of extortion by organized crime. Payments to unions under such schemes are often made through ghost employees who are racketeers posing as legitimate employees of the business under pressure. In addition, payoffs are made through employer advertisements paid to union newspapers, exorbitant charges paid by employers who participate in union social events, and fees paid to "consulting firms" run by organized crime figures.

The Effects of Organized Crime on Unions, Business, and Society

Labor racketeering has an immediate impact on union members as well as on the employers for which they work. Union members may be forced to work for wages that are less than the amounts prescribed by the collective bargaining agreement. In other instances, union members may be forced to work under conditions that are contrary to the labor contract. Members of organized crime may also engage in loansharking and gambling activities at worksites. In the longshoring industry, theft of cargo has been a problem at some ports, along with drug trafficking, insurance scams, and the exportation of stolen property.[74] Among the more publicized effects of organized crime's infiltration into the labor movement are the abuses of employee benefit plans in which premiums for group life and health insurance are overpriced and then skimmed by criminals.[75] The Teamsters Central States Pension Fund scandal remains as a landmark example of how pension funds were embezzled by union officials. As a result, some Teamsters members completely lost pension

---

[72] Also see Casey Ichniowski and Anne Preston, "The Persistence of Organized Crime in New York City Construction: An Economic Perspective," *Industrial and Labor Relations Review* (July 1989), pp. 549–565.
[73] President's Commission on Organized Crime, *The Edge: Organized Crime, Business, and Labor Unions* (Washington, D.C.: U.S. Government Printing Office, March 1986), p. 21.
[74] Also see Peter B. Levy, "The Waterfront Commission of the Port of New York: A History and Appraisal," *Industrial and Labor Relations Review* (July 1989), pp. 508–523.
[75] "How Mafia Raids Union Trust Funds," *U.S. News & World Report* (November 16, 1981), p. 13.

benefits or were forced to accept lower benefits than they had expected upon retirement.[76]

Labor racketeering practices in unions also have an adverse impact on society. When organized crime activities pervade an entire market, the consumer unknowingly pays what amounts to a surcharge on a wide range of goods and services. As noted earlier, organized crime has inflated building costs in the New York City construction industry. When cargo thefts occur in shipping ports, insurance premiums for carriers and shippers increase. Kickbacks, payoffs, and bribes inflate labor and product costs; higher costs are passed on to the consumer through higher prices. Because of pension plan abuses and other acts of corruption within unions, taxpayers bear the brunt of supporting federal enforcement efforts by the Internal Revenue Service and the Department of Labor. For employers who refuse to cooperate in strike insurance schemes, work stoppages and violence not only threaten a business and its employees, but also impose inconveniences on customers who depend on uninterrupted sources of supplies, merchandise, and services. Finally, the presence of organized crime in a few unions places legitimate labor organizations in a bad light. The majority of U.S. labor leaders are ethical individuals who give top priority to the interests of constituent members and attempt to run democratic labor organizations. Unfortunately, the news media and crime commissions focus on the unsavory elements of the labor movement; this emphasis on the seamy side of organized labor conveys the mistaken impression that union corruption is widespread.

Government Action against Labor Racketeering

The President's Commission on Organized Crime illustrates the problems associated with eliminating labor racketeering in unions in the following statement:

> Despite many prosecutorial successes, the government's efforts to remove organized crime's influence over unions and legitimate businesses have been largely ineffective. This situation does not stem simply from too few laws or unavailable remedies. It arises from a lack of political will, a lack of fixed responsibility, and a lack of a national plan of attack.[77]

The commission continues by noting that labor racketeering is not confined to a few major unions or labor leaders. Rather, organized crime has brought broad-based economic corruption to a number of industries and it operates through various instruments: unions, trade associations, and both legitimate and illegitimate businesses. The commission also recognizes that enforcing federal criminal laws will not suffice to eliminate labor racketeering because organized crime has estab-

---

[76] See, for example, "Casino Loans All Repaid, Teamsters Fund," *New York Times* (February 5, 1986), pp. 9 and 17; Joann S. Lublin, "White House Pushes Bill Widening Power of U.S. to Act on Pension-Fund Misdeeds," *The Wall Street Journal* (July 26, 1982), p. 6; and George Ruben, "Legal Action Against Teamsters Pension Fund Ends," *Monthly Labor Review* (July 1983), p. 43.

[77] President's Commission on Organized Crime, *The Edge: Organized Crime, Business, and Labor Unions* (Washington, D.C.: U.S. Government Printing Office, March 1986), p. 307.

lished economic cartels that eliminate free competition by maneuvering businesses and labor officials through a type of ownership that is not recognized by the law.

As a result of their investigations, the President's Commission on Organized Crime has made a number of recommendations for eliminating or diminishing the influence of labor racketeering. They suggest that the President of the United States adopt a national strategy against organized crime in the marketplace. This strategy would include the establishment of task forces for each industry plagued by organized crime. Both the Department of Justice and the Department of Labor were encouraged to take a more aggressive and consolidated role in eliminating organized crime's influence in businesses and unions. The Department of Justice's historic racketeering suit against the Teamsters is a prime example of the increased aggressiveness that the federal government has taken toward organized crime in labor unions. Just hours before the trial was supposed to start, the suit was settled when Teamsters leaders agreed to a permanent overseer by outsiders and court-appointed administrators. The settlement marked the departure of several Teamsters officials with alleged connections with organized crime and it heralded similar action against other unions that have been controlled by racketeers.[78]

The commission recommended that the National Labor Relations Act be amended to help deal with organized crime. It said, specifically, that it should be an unfair labor practice for either a union to be dominated by organized crime or an employer to assist members of crime syndicates in the domination of a union. The commission also suggested enacting a labor-bribery statute and augmenting other laws, such as the Landrum-Griffin Act, the Hobbs Act (federal anti-extortion statute), the pension laws, and antitrust laws to help fight organized crime. Furthermore, the commission believes that the private sector should do more to eliminate the influence of racketeering activities by taking a stronger stance against doing business with known members of organized crime.

▲ Union Goals in Collective Bargaining

Our discussion thus far illustrates that the labor movement in the United States pursues a combination of economic, social, and political goals. At the federation level, the AFL-CIO is interested in broad reforms that affect all workers, whereas international and local unions focus primarily on their members' economic concerns and place a lower priority on social and political issues. The exact collective bargaining goals of a union depend on a number of factors, such as economic, social, organizational, and political pressures, as well as union leadership preferences, employer responses, and rank-and-file expectations.[79] Figure 6–3 summarizes both the determinants of union bargaining goals and the nature of these goals.

---

[78] Aaron Bernstein, "Overhauling the Teamsters," *Business Week* (March 27, 1989), pp. 34–35.
[79] Thomas A. Kochan and Harry C. Katz, *Collective Bargaining and Industrial Relations*, 2nd ed., (Homewood, Illinois: Richard D. Irwin, Inc., 1988), pp. 168–170.

FACTORS AFFECTING UNION BARGAINING GOALS

ECONOMIC CONDITIONS
- Unemployment levels
- Consumer price index changes

INDUSTRY AND FIRM CONDITIONS
- Financial status
- Market conditions
- Technological levels
- Status of suppliers, creditors, and stockholders
- Merger and divestiture activities

POLITICAL AND LEGAL CLIMATE
- Public policies
- NLRB and court decisions

CONDITIONS WITHIN THE LABOR MOVEMENT
- Current contract settlements within the industry
- Contract settlements in other industries
- AFL-CIO concerns

→ Union leadership preferences ↕ Union member preferences →

NATURE OF UNION BARGAINING GOALS

- Wages and salaries
- Employee benefits
- Working conditions
- Union–management working relationship
- Employee job security and advancement

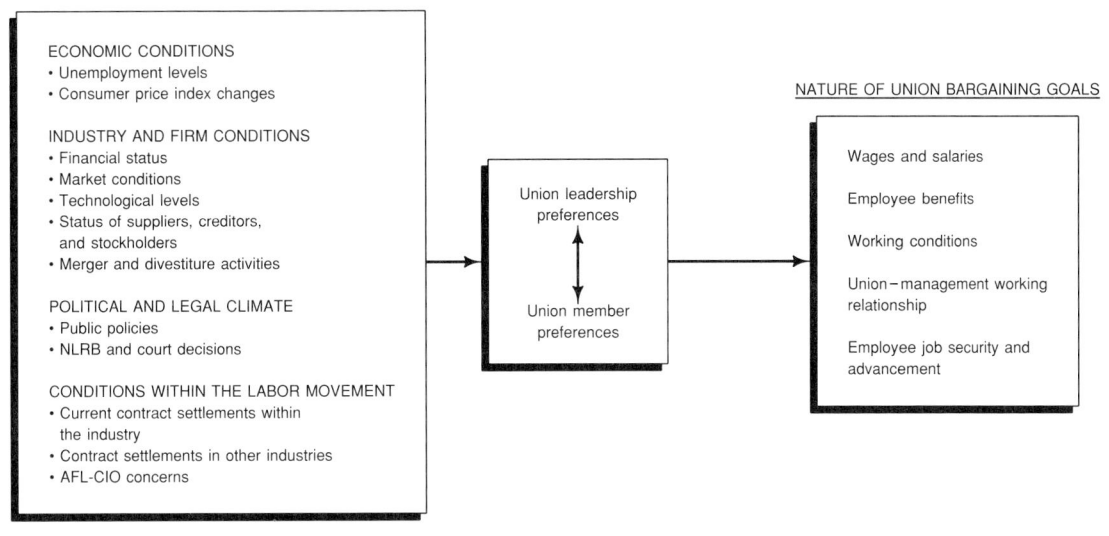

FIGURE 6–3 Union Goals in Collective Bargaining

Determinants of Union Goals

Unions are responsive to economic pressures and structure their bargaining agenda to changes in the consumer price index and the financial condition of firms having contracts with the union. For example, much publicity was given to the United Auto Workers' negotiations with the Chrysler Corporation in the late 1970s and early 1980s after Lee Iacocca took the reins as president. Chrysler was precariously close to bankruptcy and could not grant wage and other concessions to the UAW. As a result, union leaders had to structure their negotiations around cutbacks at a time when inflation rates were relatively high and the purchasing power of auto workers was declining. Later, under the leadership of Iacocca, who convinced Congress to grant Chrysler $1.5 billion in federally guaranteed loans, the auto manufacturer rebounded and the union's bargaining goals changed dramatically. Concession bargaining was also used in other economically depressed industries such as the steel, railroad, meatpacking, and airline industries.[80] In fact, 1982 was labeled "The Year of the Concession" because many unions were caught between accepting wage reductions and cutbacks in benefits or suffering job losses and plant closings.[81]

Labor unions respond to social and organizational pressures when formulating bargaining strategies.[82] In mid-February 1986, the AFL-CIO set up an office to mount anticorporate campaigns against firms who are the most notorious labor law vio-

---

[80] See, for example, James B. Dworkin, Sidney P. Feldman, James M. Brown, and Charles J. Hobson, "Workers' Preferences in Concession Bargaining," *Industrial Relations* (Winter 1988), pp. 7–20.
[81] "Labor Concessions: More Fable Than Fact?," *Industry Week* (February 8, 1982), pp. 19–21 and "Bad Bargain for Labor," *Newsweek* (November 23, 1981), pp. 85–86.
[82] See Charles R. Perry, *Union Corporate Campaigns* (Philadelphia: Industrial Research Unit, Wharton School, University of Pennsylvania, 1987), and Paul Jarley and Cheryl Maranto, "Union Corporate Campaigns: An Assessment." *Industrial and Labor Relations Review* (July 1990), pp. 505–524.

lators. Earlier, the Amalgamated Clothing and Textile Workers Union (ACTWU) had employed a corporate campaign strategy to pressure J.P. Stevens & Company into negotiating a collective bargaining agreement for employees working at the company's Roanoke Rapids, North Carolina plant.

Some of organized labor's newer tactics include pressuring a company's banks and creditors, challenging corporate applications for industrial revenue bonds and zoning variances, opposing management in proxy battles, suing corporate officers for breach of fiduciary duty or fraud, and engaging in consumer boycotts. The United Food & Commercial Workers launched a public attack on Albertson's Inc. in an attempt to obtain back pay for union members at six stores in Albuquerque, New Mexico. By using an embarrassing parody of an Albertson's television ad, the union forced the company to "coincidentally" grant a total of $47,000 in back pay less than a week after the ads were aired. Unions are also plotting strategies that attempt to save members' jobs that might otherwise be eliminated because of corporate takeovers. Consulting firms are now helping unions fight mergers and takeovers that threaten job security or jeopardize the bargaining relationship. In 1985, the Air Line Pilots Association (ALPA) prevented the nonunion Texas Air Corporation from buying Trans World Airlines and Frontier Airlines, both of which are unionized carriers. The ALPA was willing to grant bargaining concessions to other prospective buyers in order to prevent a takeover by Texas Air.[83]

Political pressures have shaped union bargaining and administrative policies. The most noteworthy pressure occurred during the Cold War period of the 1950s, when communists and socialists were banned or expelled from unions. As mentioned earlier, the AFL-CIO does not allow unions controlled by Communists, fascists, or other totalitarians to remain in the federation. And even before the passage of civil rights laws, there was political pressure to eliminate racial segregation in many unions.

Public policies have both expanded and limited the bargaining topics of unions. Unions must adapt not only to changes brought about by the passage and amendment of labor legislation, but also to important court decisions affecting collective bargaining. For example, many unions began to include nondiscrimination clauses in collective bargaining agreements after the equal employment opportunity laws were passed. The inclusion of section 14 (b) in the Taft-Hartley Act prevented unions from requiring mandatory membership for bargaining unit employees in states enacting right-to-work legislation. Furthermore, the legal distinction between mandatory and voluntary (or permissive) bargaining subjects has prevented unions from engaging in strikes in order to force employers to bargain over voluntary items that do not directly affect wages, hours, and working conditions.

The preferences of union leaders are especially important in determining a union's bargaining goals. As we have seen, international union officials heavily influence the union's objectives and strategies. Union leaders must decide on wage and benefit demands, union security issues, and the circumstances under which they will engage in economic strikes. Union leaders also make important decisions on contract administration and grievance processing that can have far-reaching

---

[83] "The Unions Are Learning to Hit Where It Hurts," *Business Week* (March 17, 1986), pp. 112–114.

implications for their members. Most union leaders creditably respond to their members' needs and preferences. The actual bargaining demands established by union leaders are normally determined by input from local union officers, the rank-and-file, and other influential union members. The membership has the final say in ratifying a collective bargaining agreement. From a political standpoint, failure to ratify may be construed as a vote of "no confidence" for the union leadership. Finally, union leaders must consider the long-term survival of their institutions when establishing bargaining priorities. For this reason, they may place a greater emphasis on union security provisions than their members would prefer.[84] Union leaders may also be willing to make economic concessions to ensure the survival of the firm. Firms in financial straits provide little job security for union members; recognizing this, union leaders may be willing to hold off on desired bargaining items in exchange for assurances on job security. The highly publicized 1989 machinists' strike at Eastern Airlines is a prime example of how union members were forced to grant concessions in order for the airline to survive. Finally, the machinists decided that they were unwilling to continue bearing the brunt of what they perceived to be poor and unenlightened management by Eastern chairman Frank Lorenzo. Six days into the strike, the ailing airline filed for bankruptcy under Chapter 11. In April of 1990, a federal judge stripped Lorenzo of his authority to run Eastern Airlines and placed the company under the control of a trustee. Officials of unions affiliated with Eastern were especially pleased with this development.

A Look at Some Typical Union Bargaining Goals

Labor unions can be viewed as institutions that *sell* the services of their members to an employer. Naturally, the union would like to sell its members' services at the highest possible price, whereas the employer is interested in obtaining quality labor at a reasonable cost. Most union bargaining concerns look beyond the immediate economic interests of their members and cover employee benefits, working conditions, and job security. The seller-buyer relationship between the union and employer is not a one-time affair; rather, the relationship spans years and even decades. A union is paid for its services through revenues that are generated from dues and initiation fees; it also receives gratification from satisfying its members' needs and watching the organizations grow and acquire power.

Collective bargaining provisions can be subdivided into several categories:

1. *Wages and Salaries*: Base hourly wages and salaries, call-out pay, shift differentials, job evaluation methods and rate setting processes, overtime pay, holiday pay and weekend premiums, temporary pay changes, and wage progressions.
2. *Employee Benefits*: Group life and health insurance, pensions, funeral pay, employee equipment allowances (clothing, gloves, hats, and shoes), jury pay, severance allowances, paid vacations, and leaves of absence.
3. *Employee Working Conditions*: Attendance policies, discipline procedures, accommodations for handicapped employees, occupational safety and health pro-

---

[84] Thomas A. Kochan and Harry C. Katz, *Collective Bargaining and Industrial Relations*, 2nd ed., (Homewood, Illinois: Richard D. Irwin, Inc., 1988), p. 170.

visions, hours of work, interchange of work, job classifications, promotion criteria, lunch and rest breaks, overtime and holiday work requirements, transfers, transportation between jobs, relationship with supervisors, and clean-up time.

4. *The Union-Management Working Relationship*: Grievance procedure, union bulletin boards on company premises, duration of collective bargaining agreement, union dues checkoff, union security, management rights, shop steward duty pay, leave of absence to conduct union business, and strike provisions.
5. *Employee Job Security and Advancement*: Individual skills and abilities needed for promotions and transfers, access to the grievance procedure, discipline and discharge criteria, service credit rules, disability and sick leave, layoff and recall criteria, probationary period, seniority provisions, and job progression.[85]

The emphasis that a union places on a set of bargaining goals will vary, depending on the economic, social, political, and legal factors discussed earlier. Union bargaining goals also change from one round of contract talks to another. When a contract is negotiated for the first time with an employer, the union may place great emphasis on union security provisions. Later, more effort may be directed toward wages and employee benefits.[86] During poor business conditions, a union may place a high priority on employee job security issues. The dynamics of contract negotiations are explored more fully in Chapters 8 and 9. Many of the collective bargaining provisions noted here are discussed in more detail in later chapters.

▲ Summary and Conclusions

This chapter describes the structure and goals of labor unions in the United States. Unions are economic institutions that deal with management and seek to raise wages and gain other advantages through collective bargaining. Unions are political institutions with officers, members, and machinery for internal governance. On occasion, unions become fighting institutions; they call strikes and engage in industrial warfare. Unions are also social institutions that give their workers a sense of belonging and a vehicle for social relations.[87]

In summary, there are several points that should be made about unions as they approach the 21st century. First, unions exert some political influence in the United States through the lobbying efforts of the AFL-CIO and international unions, but this influence is far from overwhelming. There is no labor party in the United States, and union members do not vote in a united front in political elections. Second, it is difficult to stereotype unions, union officials, or union members. There are a

---

[85] For a survey of collective bargaining provisions, see The Bureau of National Affairs, Inc., *Basic Patterns in Union Contracts*, 11th ed., (Washington, D.C.: The Bureau of National Affairs, Inc., 1986).

[86] Nearly two-thirds of the strikes involving the initial collective bargaining agreement are the result of union organization and security issues, whereas strikes involving renegotiation of a contract center on wages, hours, and other contractual matters. See P. K. Edwards, *Strikes in the United States, 1881–1974* (New York: St. Martin's Press), p. 183.

[87] Joel Seidman, *Democracy in the Labor Movement* (Ithaca, New York: New York State School of Industrial and Labor Relations, Cornell University, 1969), p. 10.

variety of industrial, craft, and mixed unions in the United States serving a number of occupational groups. Each union has its own organizing strategies, structure, mode of operations, and bargaining goals. Third, most unions are democratic institutions whose leaders make a good-faith effort to respond to members' needs. Only a very few unions are influenced by organized crime or other corrupt elements. Finally, unions have both a direct impact on the wages, hours, and working conditions of unionized workers and an indirect impact on those of nonunionized workers.

The public is often less aware of how unions operate than they are of developments in the managerial realm. Most of the media exposure given to unions focuses on major strikes, violence, and instances of corruption in the labor movement. Recently, unions have received additional exposure because of concession bargaining in depressed industries. One topic pertaining to unions that is more fully developed in Chapter 18 is the decline in membership that many unions are experiencing.

▲ Discussion Questions and Exercises

1. Why is the AFL-CIO's political, economic, and social agenda so broad? Do you believe that AFL-CIO affiliate unions might be better served if the federation focused exclusively on the needs of organized labor and ignored the concerns of nonunion workers?
2. The outcome of the election of international union officers is rarely in doubt. In most cases, the incumbent administration's slate wins and lower-echelon leaders must wait for the current union officers to retire or die before having a legitimate shot at office. It is therefore very difficult for an upstart candidate to unseat an incumbent officer. Discuss whether this situation is good for the U.S. labor movement.
3. Why are the international unions the most powerful level in the U.S. labor movement?
4. Explain why there has never been a viable labor party in the United States. Why has the Labour Party in Great Britain endured for so many years?
5. Do you believe that U.S. labor unions are democratic institutions? Is democracy always good for organized labor? Discuss.
6. Since organized crime is confined to a relatively small number of unions, why has the President's Commission on Organized Crime given so much attention to this problem?
7. Consult a recent book on strategic management. What factors do corporations evaluate when contemplating a merger or acquisition? Should unions considering a merger evaluate similar factors? Discuss.
8. How might organized labor either help or hinder corporate mergers or takeovers involving their members?

7
Management Structure, Goals, and Policies for Collective Bargaining

- **Introduction**
- **Management Goals and Strategies**
- **The Personnel/Human Resource Management Function**
- **Major Differences between Unionized and Nonunionized Firms**
  Recruitment and Selection of Employees
  Training and Development of Employees
  Employee Performance Appraisal
  Compensation and Employee Benefits
  Work Rules and Job Security Measures
  Employee Discipline and Control
  Bargaining with the Union
- **Management Bargaining Goals**
  Factors Affecting Management Bargaining Goals
     Compensation Objectives
     Employee Benefit Objectives
     Nonwage Bargaining Objectives
  Recent Trends in Management Bargaining Objectives
- **Balancing Management and Union Power Structures**
- **Multi-employer Bargaining**
- **Union-Management Cooperative Efforts**
  Opportunities Created by Cooperative Efforts
  Potential Fears and Drawbacks of Cooperative Programs
- **Summary and Conclusions**
- **Discussion Questions and Exercises**

▲ Introduction

Now that the collective bargaining process has been viewed through the eyes of organized labor, this chapter attempts to balance the material from Chapter 6 by examining the personnel management-industrial relations function in large and medium-sized organizations. Corporate objectives and strategies, along with the issue of organized labor's impact on management, are addressed. Finally, management's response to unions and the changes they create in organizational structures and personnel policies are examined.

Chapter 5 explains the legal and illegal tactics used by management to prevent unions from organizing their employees. It should be noted, however, that few companies have a reputation for being militantly antiunion.[1] Most unionized firms attempt to make the best of the situation by bargaining in good faith with the union and by adhering to the terms and conditions of the collective bargaining agreement. Firms not yet unionized may take available legal measures to prevent unions from engaging in successful organizing drives, but only a small percentage will openly and illegally attempt to subvert a union and violate employee rights under the National Labor Relations Act.

▲ Management Goals and Strategies

All organizations are guided by goals set by top management. Goals may be expressed in terms of: financial performance (such as profit or earnings per share goals); market share percentages for products or services; production and efficiency objectives; and social responsibility aims. In larger corporations, goals or objectives may be very explicit, based on extensive analysis and planning. Other organizations may have less well-defined goals. Managers, however, in all public and private entities have criteria by which they measure organizational performance. Private firms advance the interests of their stockholders by monitoring financial and market performance. Administrators in nonprofit and public organizations must stay within prescribed budgetary limits; they must also take into account nonfinancial criteria such as clients served, political influence, and growth potential of the organization.

Organizations face a number of environmental threats and opportunities. Technological changes, political and legal forces, changing economic conditions, international market forces, and pressures from outside interest groups affect an organization's ability to achieve its goals. Labor unions are generally regarded by management as an external threat whose presence may make it difficult or even impossible for the organization to fulfill its goals. Unions force management to relinquish some of its authority to make personnel decisions. Labor unions have been known to resist technological changes in the workplace and they occasionally insist on restrictive work rules that make it difficult for management to adapt to changing business needs. Many employers believe that the presence of a union

---

[1] Fred K. Foulkes, *Personnel Policies in Large Nonunion Companies* (Englewood Cliffs, New Jersey: Prentice-Hall, Inc., 1980), p. 8.

causes inflation.[2] In highly competitive industries, a unionized firm may lose important labor cost advantages. Finally, the presence of a union introduces the threat of inopportune strikes.

Once an organization has established its goals and identified environmental threats and opportunities that affect its ability to operate, its next step is to formulate organizational strategies. Goals represent a proposed *destination* or end result for an organization, whereas strategies are the *route* that it will follow to reach a destination or goal. An organization chooses among different strategic options, each offering certain advantages and disadvantages. Organizations make strategic decisions about customer targets, product and service mixes, product prices and quality, geographical market boundaries, production methods and technology, capital structure, and other factors. The strategic route selected by an organization may be altered if it must bargain with a union. A nonunion firm may undercut a unionized competitor on the basis of lower labor costs and lower product prices. Nonunion firms may meet with less resistance than unionized firms when shifting to more efficient capital-intensive methods of production.[3] Organizations that operate in rapidly changing markets may encounter obstacles when labor unions restrict their ability to move employees quickly to new assignments or locations. Some firms may be reluctant to become involved with seasonal product lines because of problems arising from laying off and rehiring unionized employees. Decisions about plant size and location are also affected by organized labor. The textile industry relocated plants from New England to the southeastern United States in order to take advantage of a nonunion labor force that was willing to work for relatively low wages.

In short, management must account for the threat or presence of labor unions when formulating corporate strategy. Some organizations deal with labor unions through avoidance tactics. Others may bargain in good faith with a union, but attempt to minimize the disruptive effect that a union has on the firm's strategic choices and goals. Still other managers view the presence of unions as simply another cost of doing business.

▲ The Personnel/Human Resource Management Function

The personnel/human resource management (PHRM) department is the focal point for hiring, training, evaluating, compensating, and disciplining employees in most organizations.[4] Furthermore, PHRM administrators are usually responsible for their employees' health and safety as well as for the administration of employee benefit

---

[2] See Steven G. Allen, "Can Union Labor Ever Cost Less?," *Quarterly Journal of Economics* (May 1987), p. 235; Assar Lindbeck, Dennis J. Snower, Michael L. Wachter, George L. Perry, and Daniel J. B. Mitchell, "Changes in Wage Norms," (4 articles), *American Economic Review* (May 1986), p. 235; Richard Edwards and Paul Swaim, "Union-Nonunion Earnings Differentials and the Decline of Private-Sector Unionism," *American Economic Review* (May 1986), p. 97; Anil Verma, "Union and Nonunion Wages at the Firm Level: A Combined Institutional and Econometric Analysis," *Journal of Labor Research* (Winter 1987), p. 67; and Janet C. Hunt, B. F. Kiker, and C. Glyn Williams, "The Effect of Type of Union on Member-Nonmember Wage Differentials," *Journal of Labor Research* (Winter 1987), p. 59.
[3] See S. G. Allen, "Productivity Levels and Productivity Change Under Unionism," *Industrial Relations* (Winter 1988), pp. 94–113.
[4] For a comprehensive treatment of personnel/human resource management, see Terry L. Leap and Michael D. Crino, *Personnel/Human Resource Management* (New York: Macmillan Publishing Company, 1989).

plans such as group health insurance and pension programs. In unionized firms, either the personnel department or a separate industrial relations department that is under the control of the corporate PHRM director deals with contract negotiations and administration. Figure 7–1 illustrates the organizational structure for the personnel function in a large organization.

Personnel functions such as job analysis, recruitment and selection, performance appraisal, compensation management, and labor-management relations are often required to meet rigorous standards. The field of personnel/human resource management is rapidly changing and has become increasingly complex; personnel managers today enjoy greater professionalism than their counterparts did 30 years ago.[5] Corporations now depend heavily upon the PHRM function to help

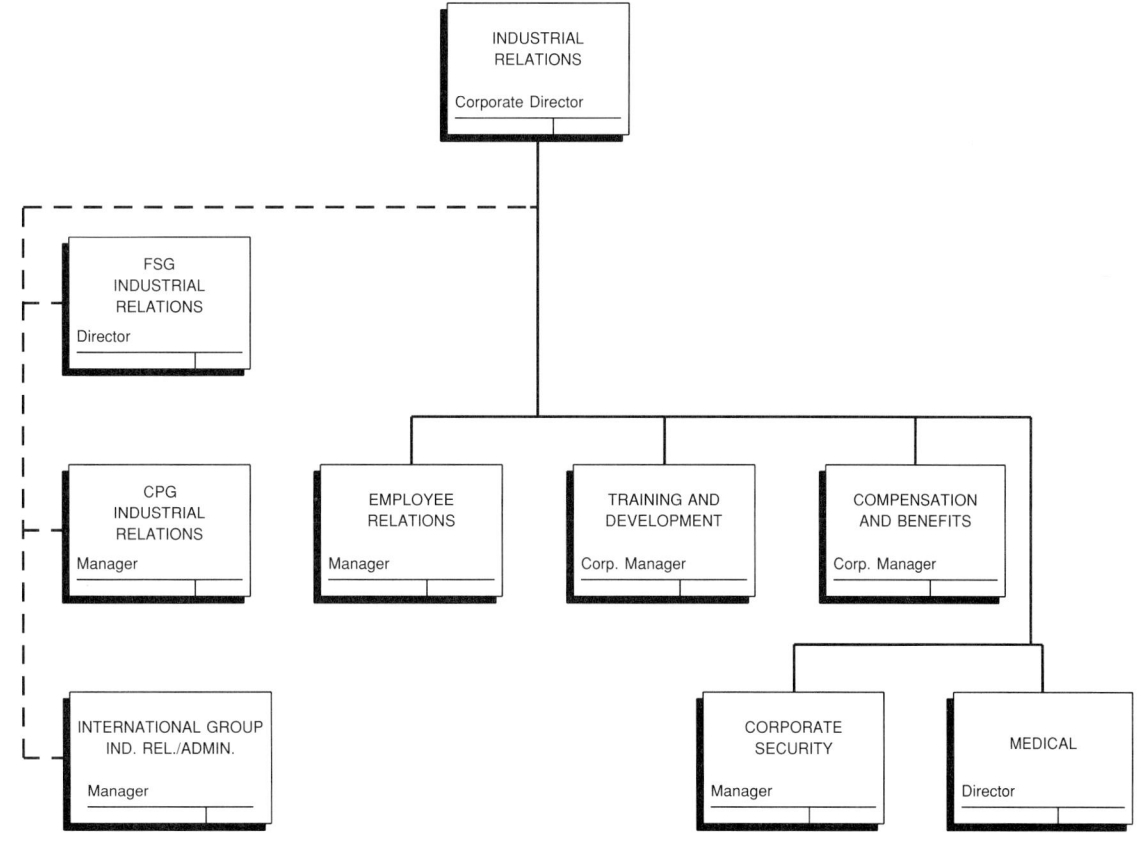

FIGURE 7–1 Organization Chart: Large Northeastern Electronics Firm
Reprinted by permission of The Bureau of National Affairs, Inc., 1986.

---

[5] The primary professional organization for personnel/human resource managers is the Society for Human Resource Management (Alexandria, Virginia). Other organizations include the American Compensation Association (Scottsdale, Arizona), American Society for Industrial Security (Arlington, Virginia), the American Society for Training and Development (Alexandria, Virginia), the Association of Training and Employment Professionals (South Windsor, Connecticut), International Association of Personnel Women (Los Angeles, California), and the Personnel Accreditation Institute (Alexandria, Virginia).

manage human resources in a manner that ensures organizational goal attainment, well-being for employees, and compliance with federal and state personnel legislation. To be effective, personnel/human resource managers must possess a knowledge of sociology, psychology, law, statistics, and economics.[6] Since it is impossible for one person to possess expertise in all areas of personnel management, many corporations employ PHRM staff specialists.

PHRM is generally regarded as a staff function. From a traditional management point of view, this means that the primary task of the personnel department is to advise and facilitate the work done by the organization's chief decision makers.[7] The PHRM department provides two major types of staff functions: support staff functions and advisory staff functions. Supportive staff functions involve the performance of administrative duties such as employment testing, retirement plan administration, and record-keeping. These are tasks that line managers would have to perform in the absence of the PHRM department. Advisory staff functions entail advising supervisors and managers on technical and legal matters such as equal employment opportunity law, disciplinary matters, and labor relations. Figure 7–2 provides an overview of the supportive and advisory staff functions.

The extent to which a PHRM department performs the staff functions shown in Figure 7–2 depends on the size, structure, and strategy of the organization. The PHRM function performs a different role in large organizations than it does in smaller ones. Small organizations may not have a separate personnel function or, when they do, it may be staffed with fewer than five persons. A survey jointly conducted by the American Society for Personnel Administration and The Bureau of National Affairs reveals that only one-third of the organizations with less than 250 employees have a personnel department, whereas over 80 percent of firms with more than 1,000 employees have separate PHRM departments.[8] A typical firm employs approximately four persons in the personnel function per 100 employees and allocates 1 percent of the firm's total budget or five percent of the total payroll to personnel managers and their staffs.[9]

---

[6] The educational background and qualifications of personnel managers are discussed in "Entry Level Requirements for HR Professionals," *Personnel Journal* (June 1987), p. 124; Thomas J. Bergman and M. John Close, "Preparing for an Entry Level Position in Personnel," *S. A. M. Advanced Management Journal* (Summer 1980), p. 62; Michael B. Arthur, Lotte Bailyn, Daniel J. Levinson, and Herbert A. Shepard, *Working With Careers* (New York: Columbia University Career Development Publication, 1985); William J. Traynor, *Opportunities in Personnel Management*, 2nd ed. (Lincolnwood, Illinois: VGM Career Horizons, 1983); Tom Jackson and Alan Vitberg, "Career Development Part I: Careers and Entrepreneurship," *Personnel* (February 1987), pp. 12–17; John Belt and James Richardson, "Academic Preparation for Personnel Management," *Personnel Journal* (May 1973), pp. 373–380; John Sussman, "Profile of the Successful Personnel Executive," *The Personnel Administrator* (February 1980), p. 81.
[7] See Dale S. Beach, *Personnel: The Management of People at Work* (New York: Macmillan Publishing Company, 1985), pp. 43–46.
[8] "ASPA-BNA Survey No. 40: Personnel Activities, Budgets, and Staffs 1979–1980," *Bulletin to Management* (Washington D.C.: The Bureau of National Affairs, Inc., 1980), p. 6.
[9] In 1986, an estimated $593 per employee was spent on the personnel/human resource function. This amounts to 2.4 percent of the company payroll or an average of $520,000 annually per organization. As might be expected, these figures vary substantially from one organization to another. In the manufacturing sector, there was one personnel staff member for every 100 employees whereas the nonmanufacturing sector employed 1.3 personnel staff members per 100 employees. Both the cost and the staffing ratios tend to decline as the organization becomes larger. See American Society for Personnel Administration and The Bureau of National Affairs, Inc., *Personnel Policies Forum*, "Personnel Activities, Budgets, and Staffs: 1985–1986" (ASPA-BNA Survey No. 49, June 5, 1986).

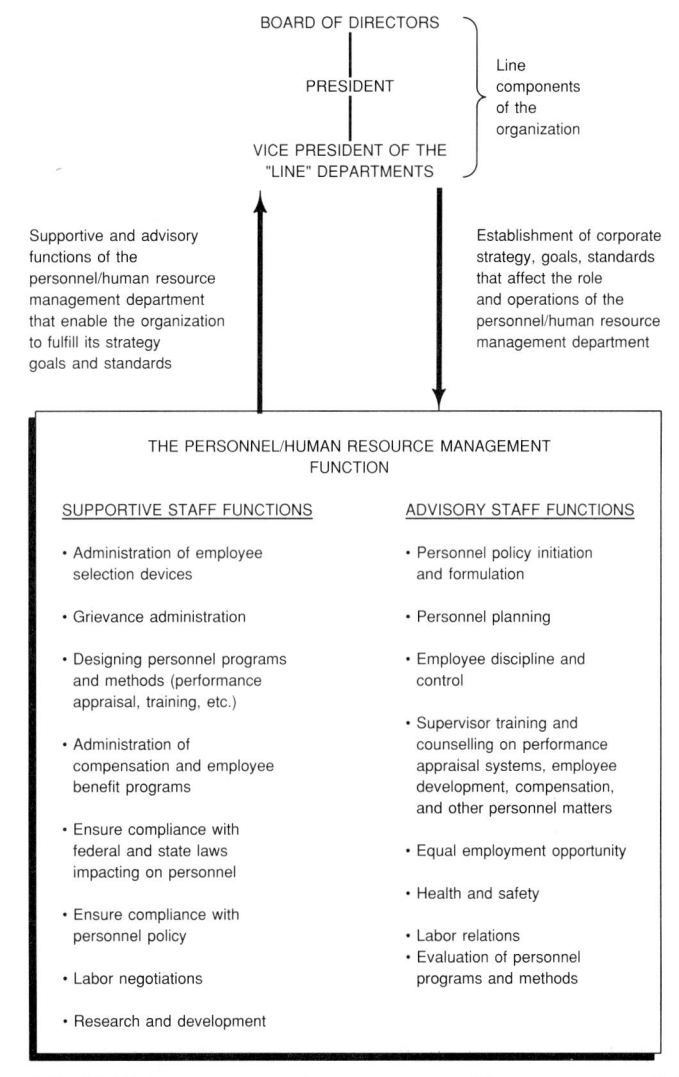

```
                        BOARD OF DIRECTORS  ⎫
                                |           ⎪  Line
                            PRESIDENT        ⎬  components
                                |           ⎪  of the
                                |           ⎪  organization
                      VICE PRESIDENT OF THE ⎭
                         "LINE" DEPARTMENTS
                              ↑    ↓
Supportive and advisory                    Establishment of corporate
functions of the                           strategy, goals, standards
personnel/human resource                   that affect the role
management department                      and operations of the
that enable the organization               personnel/human resource
to fulfill its strategy                    management department
goals and standards
```

┌───┐
│   THE PERSONNEL/HUMAN RESOURCE MANAGEMENT   │
│   FUNCTION   │
│   │
│   SUPPORTIVE STAFF FUNCTIONS   ADVISORY STAFF FUNCTIONS │
│   │
│   • Administration of employee   • Personnel policy initiation │
│   selection devices   and formulation   │
│   │
│   • Grievance administration   • Personnel planning   │
│   │
│   • Designing personnel programs   • Employee discipline and │
│   and methods (performance   control   │
│   appraisal, training, etc.)   │
│   • Supervisor training and │
│   • Administration of   counselling on performance │
│   compensation and employee   appraisal systems, employee │
│   benefit programs   development, compensation, │
│   and other personnel matters │
│   • Ensure compliance with   │
│   federal and state laws   • Equal employment opportunity │
│   impacting on personnel   │
│   • Health and safety   │
│   • Ensure compliance with   │
│   personnel policy   • Labor relations   │
│   • Evaluation of personnel │
│   • Labor negotiations   programs and methods   │
│   │
│   • Research and development   │
└───┘

FIGURE 7-2 Personnel/Human Resource Management as a Staff Function

Differences in an organization's size, jobs, and type of employee affect the structure and mission of the personnel department. In firms where employees are exposed to hazardous duties, toxic substances, or stress, a separate health and medical services department may be established outside the PHRM department. Large organizations employ PHRM *specialists* who often hold graduate or professional degrees. A firm may employ an attorney who is an expert on equal employment opportunity law or a person holding a master's degree in industrial or environmental engineering who is a safety and health specialist. Specialists such as these are usually found at corporate headquarters or in large plants. Smaller firms and plants usually employ PHRM *generalists* who perform a combination of personnel functions such as recruitment and selection of new employees, training and development, and compensation program management. Many PHRM generalists started their careers in areas outside of personnel management and have acquired knowledge of the field through on-the-job experience, professional journals, and management development programs.

▲ Major Differences between Unionized and Nonunionized Firms

Personnel-industrial relations policies and practices in unionized firms differ somewhat from those found in nonunionized organizations.[10] Unions tend to favor certain personnel policies and avoid others. Seniority, for example, plays an important role in employee promotion and retention decisions in unionized companies. Incentive or merit pay plans, on the other hand, are not favored by most unions. PHRM practices that rarely exist in nonunion organizations become commonplace once a firm is unionized. For instance, few nonunion companies have grievance procedures that include binding arbitration, yet over 95 percent of all collective bargaining agreements in unionized companies contain such provisions.[11] A union may require joint administration of some PHRM practices that are common to both unionized and nonunionized firms. Unions often insist on monitoring a firm's health and safety program to ensure compliance with the Occupational Safety and Health Act. Table 7–1 summarizes the differences and similarities between unionized and nonunionized firms. Detailed explanations are provided in this section.

Recruitment and Selection of Employees

Employee *recruitment* refers to the organization's establishing a pool of applicants, whereas *selection* refers to the process of determining which applicants are the most suitable for hiring.[12] An organization may establish a pool of 100 job applicants by using public and private employment agencies, newspaper ads, and word-of-mouth recruiting by incumbent employees. If 20 job vacancies exist, the firm will attempt to select the 20 best-qualified applicants (out of the 100) to fill these jobs. Devices such as application forms, interviews, reference checks, and tests are commonly used to help the organization predict the likelihood of an applicant's job success if hired.

Nonunion firms face few restrictions when hiring employees. As long as EEO and affirmative action guidelines are met, nonunion firms are free to use whatever applicant sources and selection devices that they deem appropriate. Federal and

---

[10] Martin M. Perline and David J. Poynter, "Union Versus Managerial Prerogative," *Personnel Journal* (September 1988), p. 126; and Fred K. Foulkes, "How Top Nonunion Companies Manage Employees," *Harvard Business Review* (September-October 1981), p. 90.

[11] For an excellent discussion and analysis of how grievances are resolved in the nonunion workplace, see David W. Ewing, *Justice on the Job: Resolving Grievances in the Nonunion Workplace* (Boston: Harvard Business School Press, 1989).

[12] See Terry L. Leap and Michael D. Crino, *Personnel/Human Resource Management* (New York: Macmillan Publishing Company, 1989), pp. 183–266; Richard D. Arvey and Robert H. Faley, *Fairness in Selecting Employees*, 2nd ed. (Reading, Massachusetts: Addison-Wesley Publishing Company, 1988); and Robert D. Gatewood and Hubert S. Feild, *Human Resource Selection* (Chicago: The Dryden Press, 1989).

Table 7-1 ▲ Personnel Policies in a Large Organization

Functions That Differ Little Between Unionized and Nonunionized Firms	▲ Employee Recruitment and Selection ▲ Training and Development ▲ Absenteeism Control
Personnel Policies Specifically Favored By Unions	▲ Promotions, Transfers, Layoffs, Compensation, and Job Rights Based on Seniority ▲ Apprenticeship Training ▲ Grievance Procedures and Arbitration ▲ Checkoff of Union Dues ▲ Subcontracting Restrictions ▲ Protective Work Rules (e.g., prohibiting supervisors from performing bargaining unit work)
Personnel Policies Specifically Disfavored By Unions	▲ Merit Pay Plans ▲ Individual and Group Incentives ▲ Behavioral or Output-Based Performance Appraisal Systems
Personnel Policies In Which The Union Wants Joint Control With Management	▲ Safety and Health Programs ▲ Plant Closing Decisions ▲ Quality of Worklife Programs ▲ Employee Benefits ▲ Wage and Salary Administration ▲ Employee Discipline and Control

state equal employment opportunity (EEO) laws prohibit unfair discriminatory hiring practices against protected groups of applicants. Affirmative action programs require that an effort be made to hire qualified females, blacks, persons over 40, and the physically and mentally handicapped.[13]

Federal labor law has attempted to give employers the freedom to hire whomever they desire without undue interference from labor unions. When a firm hires from several recruitment sources (for example, public and private employment agencies, technical and vocational schools, unsolicited walk-in applicants, and so forth), qualified applicants are less likely to be overlooked and the employer is not forced to hire substandard employees that might be favored by the union. As mentioned in Chapter 3, it is illegal for a union to force an employer to hire only union members (closed shop) or to hire nonunionized members only after the available supply of unionized workers has been exhausted (preferential shop).[14] Section 8(f) of the Landrum-Griffin Act legalizes prehire agreements in the construction industry that, in effect, permit the closed shop in the building trades.[15] Unions operating in

---

[13] Affirmative action programs apply to organizations that do business with the federal government or receive federal financial assistance.
[14] See Edward Brankey and and Mel E. Schnake, "Exceptions to Compulsory Union Membership," *Personnel Journal* (June 1988), p. 114.
[15] Benjamin J. Taylor and Fred Witney, *Labor Relations Law*, 5th ed. (Englewood Cliffs, N.J.: Prentice-Hall, Inc., 1987), p. 376.

other industries may partially circumvent the closed shop restriction by negotiating a provision in the collective bargaining agreement that gives hiring preference to employees who have work experience in the same industry. A union may also attempt to persuade an employer to give hiring preference to individuals residing in a defined geographic area.

A major source of labor for some firms is the union hiring hall. Union hiring halls are commonly used in the skilled trades and they enable employers to hire workers without the need for extensive advertising and recruitment. Hiring halls are especially useful for firms in the building trades that hire workers on a temporary basis. However, when a hiring hall is used in employee recruitment, closed shop conditions may occur if the union restricts employment referral to union members only. Union hiring halls are obliged to refer both union and nonunion members and they are supposed to post all known job vacancies so that qualified workers have an equal opportunity to apply. However, unions are able to restrict the size and quality of a firm's labor supply if an employer agrees to hire only persons referred by the union (or if they hire only apprentices from union-sponsored training programs). Unions may also influence the *internal* recruitment and selection of incumbent employees through collective bargaining agreements that control employee promotions, transfers, and job assignments.

Training and Development of Employees

Newly hired employees frequently spend the first several weeks learning about organizational policies and rules and acquiring the skills necessary to perform their jobs competently. Workers who have been employed by the firm for a period of time also receive training in order to avoid deterioration of current job performance and to upgrade their knowledge, skills, and abilities.[16]

Because many organizations view their employees as human capital and wish to get the best return possible on their investment, they are willing to spend large sums of money on training and development. The personnel management function is responsible for employee training and development in most corporations. Some companies employ full-time training directors and specialists who coordinate on-the-job and classroom programs on an in-house basis. In such instances, a corporation may have elaborate training facilities. Other firms train employees through programs offered by consultants, vocational-technical schools, and colleges.

Nonunionized firms have a great deal of freedom to identify training needs, select trainees, determine training methods, and evaluate the effectiveness of training and development programs. However, unions may regulate both the admission standards into training programs as well as what such programs offer. Employers may have to coordinate with the union the content of their training programs and the selection of employees who will participate in these programs. Furthermore,

---

[16] See Terry L. Leap and Michael D. Crino, *Personnel/Human Resource Management* (New York: Macmillan Publishing Company, 1989), pp. 272–314; Bernard M. Bass and James A. Vaughan, *Training in Industry: The Management of Learning* (Belmont, California: Wadsworth Publishing Company, 1969); and Kenneth N. Wexley and Gary P. Latham, *Developing and Training Human Resources in Organizations* (Glenview, Illinois: Scott, Foresman, 1981).

collective bargaining agreements may contain restrictive work rules that allow only properly trained bargaining-unit employees to perform certain tasks or jobs. For example, a railroad employee who performs routine maintenance on tracks and roadbeds may be prohibited from doing maintenance work on other equipment such as locomotives; any attempt to train a roadbed maintenance employee to perform work on other equipment may be restricted by the collective bargaining agreement.

Unions may control admission to apprenticeship training programs that provide avenues for employees who want to expand their job skills and promotion opportunities. Apprenticeship training programs are used in the skilled trades and may replace training that would otherwise be done solely by the employer. Apprenticeship training may be jointly administered by the union and the employer or done in conjunction with a vocational-technical school. Most apprenticeship programs combine work experience with technical instruction.[17] The length of an apprenticeship program varies with the particular skilled trade. Barbers serve an apprenticeship of two years, meatcutters three years, electrical workers four to five years, and printers five to six years.[18] Successful completion of the training program allows admission into the journeyman ranks. Although few unions and employers extensively use apprenticeship training programs, the collective bargaining agreements for those that do attempt to regulate both the training programs and the wages for the apprentices. The number of apprentices may be controlled through limiting the number per shop or worksite, fixing the ratio of apprentices to skilled workers, requiring unduly long periods of apprenticeship, and forcing firms to pay excessive wages to apprentices.[19] Such restrictive practices are designed to limit the size of the skilled workforce in a locale by establishing barriers to entry in a skilled trade.[20]

Unions are not the only groups that attempt to control the supply of labor. Hairdressers and taxi drivers, for example, employ restrictive labor market tactics through licensing requirements. Some licensing requirements are based on the need for public safety. Certainly, there is little doubt about requiring an air transport rating, extensive experience in the aircraft to be flown, and recurrent training and certification requirements for airline pilots. Similarly, the rigorous admission standards of U.S. medical schools reflects the public concern for quality medical care.

Employee Performance Appraisal

Organizations are interested in monitoring and evaluating the performance of employees. Performance appraisal systems are based on the assumption that the work outputs and behaviors of individual employees differ in terms of quality and quan-

---

[17] Robert E. Doherty, *Industrial and Labor Relations Terms: A Glossary*, ILR Bulletin Number 44, (Ithaca, New York: ILR Press, Cornell University, 1979), p. 3.
[18] U.S. Department of Labor Manpower Administration, *The National Apprenticeship Program*, (Washington, D.C.: U.S. Government Printing Office, 1965), pp. 9–27.
[19] Richard Scheuch, *Labor in the American Economy*, (New York: Harper and Row Publishers, 1981), pp. 511–512.
[20] See John M. Barron, Scott M. Fuess, Jr., and Mark Loewenstein, "Further Analysis of the Effect of Unions on Training," *Journal of Political Economy* (June 1987), p. 632.

tity. Performance appraisal systems analyze and document these differences so that management can make informed decisions on employee pay, promotions, transfers, training, and disciplinary matters. In recent years, many organizations have become increasingly aware of the value of performance appraisal systems as a means of validating hiring procedures and protecting the firm in the event of an equal employment opportunity or wrongful discharge suit. There has been a proliferation of performance appraisal methods designed to reflect and document actual employee behaviors and output.[21] Personnel managers have attempted to design performance appraisal systems that reflect all (or nearly all) facets of job performance and that are free from unnecessary biases stemming from a supervisor's dislike of an employee's race, sex, religion, lifestyle, or beliefs.

Performance appraisal systems allow employers to make pay adjustments and promotion assignments based on an employee's *merit*, rather than his or her seniority. The concept of merit assumes that some employees are superior to others in terms of job knowledge, skills, abilities, and performance. Organizational rewards such as pay raises, promotion, and assignment to desirable jobs are awarded to the most deserving employees. Because most labor unions have an egalitarian focus and tend to view each member as an equal insofar as job capabilities are concerned, organized labor generally opposes merit systems. Unions prefer that personnel decisions be based on an employee's seniority, and therefore look askance on formal performance appraisal systems.

Seniority is an employee's length of service with an organization. There are several ways in which seniority can be calculated. Seniority may be company-wide, plant-wide, or department-wide. *Competitive seniority* determines which employees obtain promotions, desirable shift assignments, and protection from layoffs. *Benefit seniority* is used to measure employee entitlement to benefits such as paid vacation time.[22] Seniority systems also vary in terms of their applications. For example, a pure seniority system would totally exclude merit from consideration in a promotion decision; the employee with the greatest seniority would be promoted regardless of qualifications or ability.

Organized labor's aversion to merit systems creates a certain amount of inflexibility for personnel administrators; however, most collective bargaining agreements allow for some consideration of merit in employment decisions. Finally, it should be noted that the use of seniority systems is often touted by employers, even in nonunion settings. Seniority represents an objective yardstick and employment decisions geared to seniority are less likely to offend employees or create controversy than are merit-based decisions that depend on accurate and timely performance appraisals. Seniority systems are discussed in further detail in Chapter 15.

---

[21] See Terry L. Leap and Michael D. Crino, *Personnel/Human Resource Management* (New York: Macmillan Publishing Company, 1989), pp. 315–349; Howard P. Smith and Paul J. Brouwer, *Performance Appraisal and Human Development: A Practical Guide to Effective Managing* (Reading, Massachusetts: Addison-Wesley Publishing Company, 1977); and Gary P. Latham and Kenneth N. Wexley, *Increasing Productivity Through Performance Appraisal* (Reading, Massachusetts: Addison-Wesley Publishing Company, 1980).

[22] Robert E. Doherty, *Industrial and Labor Relations Terms: A Glossary*, ILR Bulletin Number 44 (Ithaca, New York: ILR Press, 1979), p. 27.

Compensation and Employee Benefits

An important responsibility of the personnel department is to design and administer a company's compensation program.[23] Compensation may take a number of forms. It may be immediate pay in the form of a weekly or monthly salary, or it may take the form of deferred pay, as with annual profit or productivity bonuses. Some types of compensation are payable contingent upon an event or occurrence such as sickness, disability, or retirement. Still other forms of pay such as sick leave, paid holidays, and vacations are provided for time not worked. Benefits such as Social Security, unemployment, and workers' compensation are mandated by federal and state law. Collective bargaining agreements normally specify the exact compensation package for bargaining-unit employees. Nonunionized firms may do likewise in employee handbooks, but they generally have more flexibility in designing and administering compensation programs. They also are more likely to integrate merit and incentive components into their programs than are their unionized counterparts.

Personnel managers must address several important issues in establishing a compensation program. One issue is the concept of *external equity,* which deals with how much an organization is willing to pay its employees as compared to what other firms in the same locale or industry are paying. *Internal equity* pertains to how employees within the same firm are paid relative to each other for performing different jobs. A process known as job evaluation is used to assign values to various jobs for calculating wage and salary scales. Personnel managers must also decide whether to use incentive programs to increase productivity. Individual incentives such as commissions or piece rates are common for sales and certain manufacturing jobs. A variety of group incentives that reward employees in a department or plant for profitability, cost savings, or productivity also exist. Finally, the organization must decide what types of employee benefits that it wishes to offer. On the average, nearly 40 percent of the total compensation package for U.S. firms is comprised of employee benefits such as group life and health insurance, retirement programs, sick leave, and paid vacations.

An extensively debated topic is whether unions force employers to pay more than they would otherwise want to pay workers. As is the case with most controversial issues, there is no simple answer. However, unions are more likely to increase the compensation for workers who are at an economic and social disadvantage. The union wage effect is larger for young, short-tenure, and nonwhite workers.[24] Unions also do a better job of raising the pay of blue-collar workers and workers in the South.[25] There are also likely to be greater wage differentials between small union-

---

[23] See Terry L. Leap and Michael D. Crino, *Personnel/Human Resource Management* (New York: Macmillan Publishing Company, 1989), pp. 350–473; George T. Milkovich and Jerry M. Newman, *Compensation,* 2nd ed. (Plano, Texas: Business Publications, Inc., 1987).
[24] Richard B. Freeman and James L. Medoff, *What Do Unions Do?* (New York: Basic Books, Inc., 1984), p. 50 and Martin Estey, *The Unions: Structure, Development, and Management,* 3rd ed. (New York: Harcourt, Brace, Jovanovich, 1981), p. 134.
[25] Richard B. Freeman and James L. Medoff, *What Do Unions Do?* (New York: Basic Books, Inc., 1984) p. 50.

ized and nonunionized firms. As the size of firms increase, the unionized-nonunionized pay differential is eliminated because larger firms more often pay union scale and offer employee benefits that are competitive with unionized firms. Unions generally have more success at raising pay levels in industries that are heavily unionized, have inelastic product demand that allows labor cost increases to be passed on to consumers, and where pay increases are not likely to result in layoffs or financial hardship for the firm. Because of their desire to remain nonunionized, an unorganized firm may not only match the pay and benefits of unionized firms in the same industry or locale, but they may even exceed the union pay and benefit scale in what has been termed "a clear purchase of nonunionism."[26] The following statement best summarizes this point:

> It is no secret that some of the best employers in the country—firms offering the highest wages and benefits, job security and desirable work conditions—are large nonunion or primarily nonunion firms. IBM is the example most often cited. While not all large employers seek to match labor contracts ... enough large nonunion companies appear to offer desirable employment packages for the purpose of deterring unionism....[27]

Merit pay systems that regulate pay increases on individual performance are most likely to be used in nonunion firms. As noted previously, unions are generally opposed to reward systems that are geared to individual differences in job performance. According to one expert, "most unionized employees have not accepted the validity of supervisory judgments, and rarely does a union agree to a merit pay plan."[28] Even in nonunionized firms, a number of personnel managers have abandoned merit pay systems because of difficulties in accurately evaluating employee job performance. Some employees do not want first-line supervisors to set pay increases because of fears of favoritism, personnel vendettas, and subjectivity. Finally, some jobs do not lend themselves to measuring performance differences among employees. Assembly line jobs, jobs in which the performance of one employee is dependent on the work of others, and jobs in which tangible behaviors or outputs are difficult to observe are examples.

Despite the reluctance of some firms to use individual incentives, a number of companies have instituted group-incentive programs for their employees. Profit sharing plans, cash bonus plans, employee stock ownership plans, and investment plans are examples of such programs. Plans such as these allow employees to identify more closely with the company's goals and have an economic stake in its future. The "we-they" barrier between management and employees is lowered and workers are better able to identify with the production, cost, and profit concerns of the firm. The degree to which these objectives are met depends on the exact nature of the group-incentive plan, its administration, the extent of employee involvement in the plan, and the control that employees feel they have over the economic destiny of

---

[26] Fred K. Foulkes, *Personnel Policies in Large Nonunion Companies* (Englewood Cliffs, New Jersey: Prentice-Hall, Inc., 1980), p. 159.
[27] Richard B. Freeman and James L. Medoff, *What Do Unions Do?* (New York: Basic Books, Inc., 1984), p. 151.
[28] Herbert H. Meyer, "The Pay for Performance Dilemma," *Organizational Dynamics*, (Winter 1975), p. 170.

the firm. Unions, in most cases, would not favorably view any economic incentive plan that would encourage employees to identify with management. Although little research is available on organized labor's view on group incentives, any employment arrangement—financial or nonfinancial—that would encourage cohesion between management and bargaining unit employees is likely to be regarded as a threat by unions.

Employee benefits, such as group insurance, retirement programs, and paid vacations are a major component of many corporate compensation programs. Companies offer benefits to their employees for numerous reasons. Some benefits such as Social Security are required by law; other benefits such as retirement programs (above and beyond Social Security) and group life and health insurance coverage are provided by companies that wish to offer compensation packages comparable to those of their competitors. A liberal employee benefit program will attract and retain better-qualified employees. Firms also offer generous employee benefits because of social responsibility motives and concern for employee welfare. Finally, nonunionized firms use employee benefits to discourage overtures by union organizers.

Unions tend to support deferred forms of compensation favoring senior workers.[29] Specifically, unions negotiate hardest for retirement programs, group life and health insurance, and paid vacations whose length is geared to seniority. Unionized firms often have more generous benefits than their nonunion counterparts and the company frequently pays a greater share of the total premium for retirement, health, and other benefit plans. Chapters 13 and 14 provide a more comprehensive examination of compensation and employee benefits.

Work Rules and Job Security Measures

Nonunion employers have few restrictions on directing their workforces, scheduling workshifts, determining employee duties, and making decisions on layoffs and plant closings. Unionized firms often have to make managerial decisions that comply with the collective bargaining agreement. However, they do not automatically relinquish managerial authority to unions unless specifically required by the collective bargaining agreement. Management retains the right to direct its workforce and may reassign employees to different jobs, work shifts, or locations in order to meet production, service, and customer needs. In fact, over three-fourths of all collective bargaining agreements contain management-rights clauses that give the employer the right to direct the workforce unilaterally and manage the firm's business.[30] However, an employer may bargain away some of these rights. Some collective bargaining agreements prohibit an employer from subcontracting work to other firms. Supervisors are frequently prohibited from performing tasks normally assigned to bargaining unit members. Technological changes are restricted in approximately

---

[29] Richard B. Freeman and James L. Medoff, *What Do Unions Do?* (New York: Basic Books, Inc., 1984), p. 77.
[30] The Bureau of National Affairs, Inc., *Basic Patterns in Union Contracts*, 11th ed. (Washington, D.C.: The Bureau of National Affairs, Inc., 1986), p. 80.

one-fourth of all collective bargaining agreements and some agreements place limitations or conditions on plant shutdowns and relocations.

The primary objective of collectively bargained restrictions placed on managerial autonomy is to protect the job security of bargaining unit members. If management could freely subcontract work, allow supervisors to perform nonsupervisory tasks, add labor-saving machinery, or shut down a plant without notice, then the jobs of union members and, ultimately, the security of the union could be jeopardized.

Employee Discipline and Control

One of the most significant differences between unionized and nonunionized firms is the discretion that management has in disciplining employees.[31] Problems such as incompetence, absenteeism and tardiness, insubordination, theft, drug use, or rule violations may force an organization to take disciplinary action. Disciplinary measures range from an oral reprimand to suspension without pay and, at the most serious extreme, discharge. Unless there are violations of equal employment opportunity or civil service laws, nonunionized firms are free to discipline or discharge workers with little concern for due process. There is no legal requirement to warn employees or provide a hearing prior to taking disciplinary action; in fact, approximately 60 percent of the U.S. labor force is employed at-will and can be discharged for good cause, bad cause, or no cause at all. Although the courts in a number of states have permitted some protection for at-will employees, many nonunionized employees are not safeguarded from wrongful discharges.

Nearly all collective bargaining agreements have grievance procedures through which employees can contest disciplinary actions. Although bargaining-unit employees can be disciplined or fired for just cause, they are usually entitled to union representation when they have a meritorious grievance. Most grievance procedures provide binding arbitration as the final step, so the disposition of a disciplinary case may rest on the the arbitrator who is empowered to reinstate a worker or sustain the employer's initial disciplinary action. The employer's hands are not tied with respect to disciplinary procedures, but it is difficult to reprimand, suspend, or dismiss a unionized worker without allowing the union representative to challenge the employer's action. A grievance procedure is not likely to protect an employee who is clearly in violation of a work rule or guilty of other misconduct. The greatest difference between a nonunion and a unionized firm is that the former is more likely to discipline or discharge an employee erroneously whereas the latter must adhere to procedural safeguards outlined in the grievance procedure.

Bargaining with the Union

Employers dealing with a certified bargaining representative are legally obligated to bargain in good faith with the union. Extensive research and preparation on wages, hours, and working conditions are necessary before management can face

---

[31] See Terry L. Leap and Michael D. Crino, *Personnel/Human Resource Management* (New York: Macmillan Publishing Company, 1989), pp. 480–511; and James R. Redeker, *Discipline Policies and Procedures* (Washington, D.C.: The Bureau of National Affairs, Inc., 1983).

union negotiators at the bargaining table. The corporate labor relations staff is usually responsible for developing contract proposals, making cost estimates on specific wage and benefit proposals, drafting contract language, establishing upper and lower limits for certain wages and benefits, and formulating strike plans in the event that negotiations are not successful.

Members of the management negotiating team are often selected from the corporate labor relations staff and they influence the final terms of the collective bargaining agreement. Management negotiators must avoid wage and benefit settlements that impose a financial burden on the firm or force it to raise prices. Negotiators must also avoid restrictive work rules that limit management's ability to make strategic decisions. Thus, preparations for collective bargaining as well as the selection of management's negotiating team have vital strategic implications for the entire firm. According to two leading labor researchers, companies that are involved heavily with organized labor not only have large and sophisticated labor relations staffs, but they also tend to centralize most of the decisions pertaining to unions and collective bargaining at the corporate level. Although the labor relations staff controls the collective bargaining process, in many corporations top management reserves the right to approve major decisions such as the final provisions of the collective bargaining agreement and strike preparation.[32]

Responsibility for contract administration is normally decentralized and placed in the hands of supervisors and managers at the plant or local level. This task requires managers to become familiar with the provisions of the collective bargaining agreement. Beyond knowing the content of the provisions, management must understand how they are applied in the work setting on a daily basis. Effective contract administration can spell the difference between a work environment marked by cordial supervisor-employee relations and efficient production and one that is plagued with an endless stream of complaints, grievances, and work disruptions. Most collective bargaining agreements require management to address a formal grievance in a timely manner. Personnel managers at the local level generally attempt to resolve most grievances quickly. Occasionally a controversial grievance may arise that has long-term and expensive implications for the corporation. In such instances, industrial relations specialists at the corporate level may become involved to avoid setting a precedent that could pose a financial or administrative burden on the company.

▲ Management Bargaining Goals

Management formulates bargaining goals based on several general factors that have been discussed in preceding sections of this chapter. To summarize, management attempts to attain the following broad objectives:

1. In profit-oriented firms, management tries to maximize revenues and control labor and production costs. The presence of labor unions represents a threat

---

[32] Thomas A. Kochan and Harry C. Katz, *Collective Bargaining and Industrial Relations* (Homewood, Illinois: Richard D. Irwin, Inc., 1988), pp. 201–205.

to the control of labor costs. Likewise, nonprofit organizations with limited budgets are threatened by labor cost increases imposed by collective bargaining agreements.
2. Profit-oriented and nonprofit firms formulate strategies in order to attain the goals established by organizational leaders and decision makers. All organizations must deal with environmental threats that make it either difficult or impossible to adhere to a selected corporate strategy. Labor unions pose a major environmental threat to strategy formulation for many organizations.
3. Unions pose a greater threat to some firms than to others. Firms that are in highly competitive industries or markets, require significant labor inputs for production, have financial difficulties, or cannot pass labor costs on to consumers in the form of higher prices are generally more threatened by unions than firms that do not have these characteristics.
4. When given a choice, the vast majority of managers prefer to operate in a union-free environment. If a union is present, however, managers tend to do whatever is legally permissible to minimize the impact of unions. In some instances, illegal tactics may be employed.

Factors Affecting Management Bargaining Goals

The bargaining goals of management can be subdivided into three categories: direct compensation, employee benefits, and nonwage goals. Goals vary from one round of contract negotiations to the next, depending on economic, social, and industrial conditions. Because of the extensive preparation that precedes the actual contract negotiations, most management bargaining teams have a well-defined set of bargaining goals in mind; however, these goals are not rigid and may be altered after negotiations have started. General factors that affect bargaining goals are listed in Figure 7–3.

Compensation Objectives

Unionized firms are concerned about the magnitude and timing of wage and merit pay increases. Firms in which labor costs comprise a substantial portion of the total budget are more drastically affected by negotiated wage increases than firms whose labor cost percentages are relatively small. Furthermore, a firm may be more willing to grant a deferred wage increase rather than one that must be paid immediately; a 6 percent wage increase phased in over 18 months may be preferred to a 4.5 percent wage increase that is effective immediately.

One of the major determinants of a firm's compensation bargaining goals is the compensation level of its competition. Unions often force firms to look at what similar firms are paying their employees. The concept of pattern bargaining is based on the notion that a contract settlement in one firm will establish a precedent for other firms within the same industry. As noted earlier, unions attempt to alleviate competitive pressures in an industry by taking wages out of competition, a strategy that forces firms to compete in terms of quality, market penetration, product differentiation, advertising, and manufacturing strategies rather than on differences in

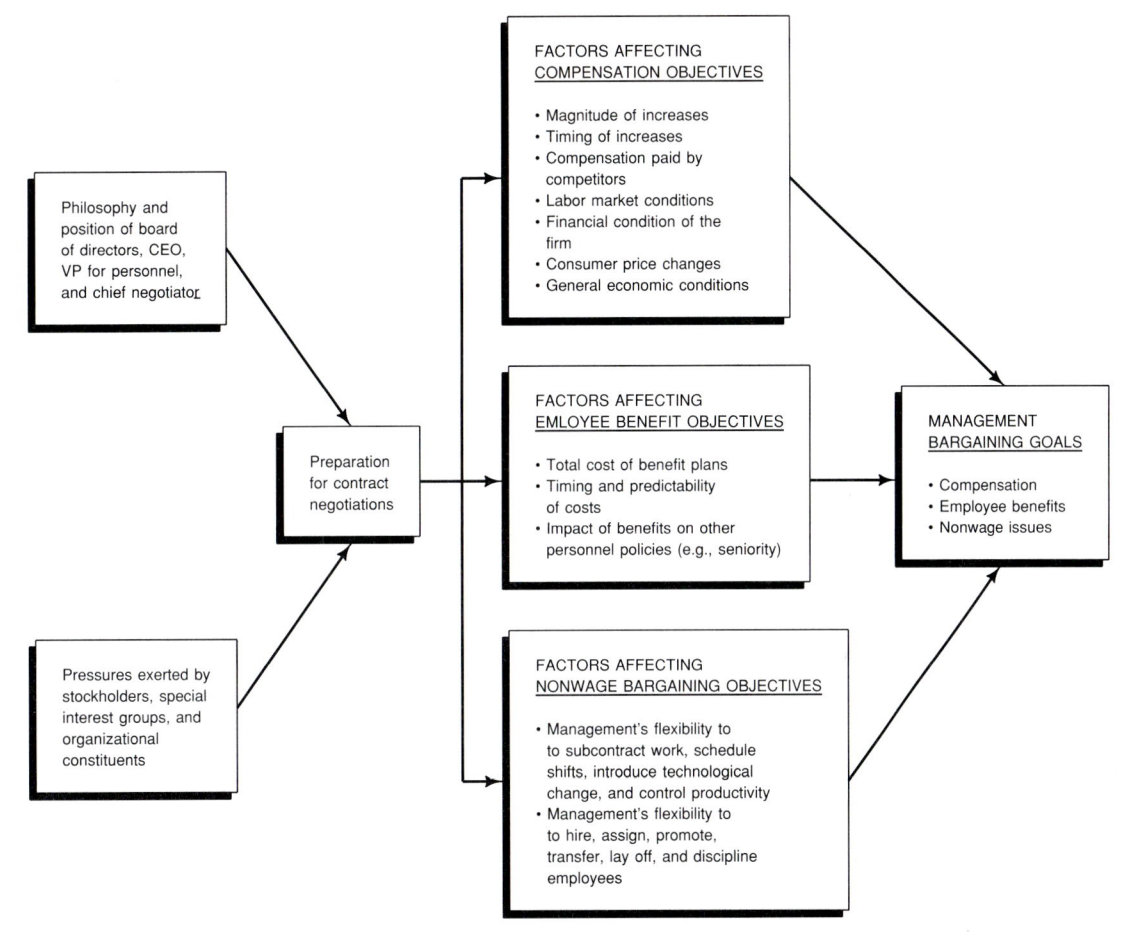

FIGURE 7-3 Management Bargaining Goals

```
Philosophy and
position of board
of directors, CEO,
VP for personnel,
and chief negotiator

Pressures exerted by
stockholders, special
interest groups, and
organizational
constituents

          → Preparation
            for contract
            negotiations

FACTORS AFFECTING
COMPENSATION OBJECTIVES
• Magnitude of increases
• Timing of increases
• Compensation paid by competitors
• Labor market conditions
• Financial condition of the firm
• Consumer price changes
• General economic conditions

FACTORS AFFECTING
EMLOYEE BENEFIT OBJECTIVES
• Total cost of benefit plans
• Timing and predictability of costs
• Impact of benefits on other personnel policies (e.g., seniority)

FACTORS AFFECTING
NONWAGE BARGAINING OBJECTIVES
• Management's flexibility to to subcontract work, schedule shifts, introduce technological change, and control productivity
• Management's flexibility to to hire, assign, promote, transfer, lay off, and discipline employees

MANAGEMENT
BARGAINING GOALS
• Compensation
• Employee benefits
• Nonwage issues
```

labor cost.[33] When Bethlehem Steel agreed to a settlement with the United Steelworkers in May of 1989, Bethlehem's major competitor USX (formerly U.S. Steel) gained a temporary advantage. USX was working under a four-year contract with a January 1991 expiration date. Between May of 1989 and January 1991, USX gained a significant labor-cost advantage over Bethlehem Steel. USX Chairman David Roderick estimated that his firm would have an $8 a ton cost advantage during the first year of the contract and a $12 per ton advantage during the second year (1990–1991). At the time of the settlement, domestic steel prices averaged $530 a ton.[34]

---

[33] See George Ruben, "Auto Industry Update," *Monthly Labor Review* (February 1988), p. 70; Daniel J. B. Mitchell, "Alternative Explanations of Union Wage Concessions," *California Management Review* (Fall 1986), p. 95.

[34] Industry analysts also point out that USX had to "earn" its advantage by enduring a five-month strike in 1987 before coming to terms with the United Steel Workers. See Clare Ansberry, "Bethlehem Steel Tentative Labor Accord Hands the Cost Edge to Industry Leader USX," *The Wall Street Journal* (May 15, 1989).

Management must also consider local labor market conditions. A firm that pays above the community market rate may attract a more stable and productive workforce. By paying more than other firms in the local area, a company may actually save on labor costs in the long run because of reduced turnover, absenteeism, and productivity problems. Unions may encourage an employer to consider pay levels in the local labor market if the firm pays its employees less than other firms in the community.

The financial condition of a firm is a major consideration when management formulates bargaining goals for wages and salaries. Profitability is a double-edged sword: profitable firms will be pressed by unions to share the wealth with bargaining unit members, whereas firms operating marginally or at a loss will be hard pressed to grant wage and benefit increases. Concessions may be necessary for firms experiencing financial difficulties; they must be willing to make other tradeoffs in lieu of pay increases.[35] A firm that is either unable to grant pay increases or must make wage cuts in order to remain in business may promise additional job security for older employees.[36] Financially strapped firms may also resort to two-tier wage systems and agree to provide improved pay and benefits once profits are restored.[37]

Other factors that affect management's compensation include productivity and labor cost trends in the company, the costs of allowing a strike to occur, consumer price index changes, unemployment levels and economic growth, and major contract settlements in other industries. Large firms may base their bargaining objectives on national or international conditions, whereas smaller firms may focus on local economic, social, and industrial conditions. Management must also consider the bargaining power and expertise of union bargaining team members in establishing bargaining goals for their firms.

Employee Benefit Objectives

As noted earlier, employee benefits comprise approximately 40 percent of the total compensation package and are a major bargaining item for unionized firms. Both unions and employers recognize the aforementioned advantages of employee benefits. Employers must decide on the type and amount of benefits to offer. As discussed in more detail in Chapter 14, there are a multitude of employee benefits including group life insurance, retirement programs, and guaranteed annual income programs. Some employee benefit programs, such as coverage for biannual ophthalmology examinations and coverage for eyeglasses, may be relatively inexpensive, whereas employer contributions to a retirement program can involve substantial cash outlays.

At the bargaining table, employers are concerned not only about the total cost of an employee benefit, but also about the timing and predictability of such costs. Management negotiators are often reluctant to commit the firm to large initial expenditures that could impose a financial burden. Management will likely resist a

---

[35] See Suhail Abboushi, "Union Willingness to Negotiate Concessions," *Journal of Labor Research* (Winter 1987), p. 47.
[36] "Deere Contract Protects Employees Against Layoffs," *Monthly Labor Review* (September 1986), p. 36.
[37] Terry L. Leap and Michael D. Crino, *Personnel/Human Resource Management* (New York: Macmillan Publishing Company, 1989), p. 413.

retirement program proposal that gives generous previous service credit to senior employees because of the large expenditures that the firm would have to make to bring employees with lengthy service records up to date in the retirement system. Company negotiators may also be unwilling to agree to benefits that have unpredictable costs. Suppose that a union proposes a short-term disability income plan that pays a disabled employee weekly or monthly benefits in the event of accident or sickness. Disability income benefits are usually provided by insurance companies on an experience-rating basis; the premiums are based on the firm's disability rates and benefits provided to employees. Because of the uncertainties surrounding future employee disabilities and the unpredictability of insurance premiums, the employer may resist providing such coverage.

When bargaining over employee benefits, management must be aware of the impact that a benefit may have on other personnel policies. The group disability income policy mentioned above may encourage absenteeism and malingering by disabled employees. Retirement programs often require that senior employees remain with the organization to avoid losing substantial sums in employer contributions. Retirement programs create a stable and experienced work force for the employer, but they can also force dissatisfied employees to remain with the firm.

The plethora of employee benefits available today complicates the bargaining process and requires that management understand the provisions of the major types of benefits as well as the social, economic, and legal consequences of each benefit program. The range of benefits is so wide and the provisions so complex that negotiators need the advice of the experts when establishing bargaining objectives for employee benefits. Employee benefits also allow negotiators greater leeway regarding bargaining tradeoffs. Firms desiring to defer compensation because of adverse economic conditions may be more receptive to some form of employee benefit rather than to an outright wage increase. However, deferred compensation arrangements often assume that a firm's financial position will improve in the future; when this is not the case, serious problems can arise if management is unable to meet its obligations under the collective bargaining agreement.

Nonwage Bargaining Objectives

The final category of management bargaining goals involves nonwage issues such as management rights, subcontracting, assignment of employees, technological changes, layoff and recall of employees, and other matters that affect management's ability to establish organizational goals and strategies as well as direct the work force. Although the term "nonwage bargaining goals" has a nonmonetary connotation, it has a direct impact on a firm's financial and profitability picture. Nonwage issues also affect management's flexibility to decide how the organization will be run and how its profits will be divided among stockholders, workers, and the firm. Management must be concerned about nonwage issues because of the effect that they have on productivity, costs, and management's ability to make decisions that are in the best interest of the company.

An important nonwage issue is the duration of the collective bargaining agreement. Most labor contracts remain in effect for three years. Management will not negotiate a new contract until the three-year time period has nearly expired, but they may agree to alter specific contract provisions during the life of the agreement. Some contracts allow negotiations to be reopened over wages, employee benefits, or cost-of-living adjustments. Others remain in effect beyond the expiration date unless either the union or management specifically requests modification or termination of the agreement.[38] In establishing its bargaining goals, management must be aware that it will have to abide by the terms and conditions of the contract for the entire duration unless there are provisions that allow for renegotiation. Finally, the timing of the contract expiration date can strongly affect the bargaining power of labor or management. If, for example, the contract expires during a peak business period for the employer (such as during the summer months for a construction firm), the employer's bargaining position may be weakened because of the threat of an economic strike.

Another major nonwage issue involves the employer's ability to assign, lay off, and recall employees. Most collective bargaining agreements contain provisions for the standard five-day, 40-hour work week and about 40 percent require the employer to notify or obtain approval from the union if it becomes necessary to deviate from the standard work week. Nearly all contracts require premium pay for overtime and approximately two-thirds stipulate the manner in which employees will be given the opportunity to work overtime. A majority of labor contracts currently provide that advanced notice will be given when layoffs are planned. Seniority usually determines which employees are laid off and recalled. Some contracts provide for worksharing as an alternative to layoffs.[39]

Because of uneven customer demands, fluctuating economic conditions, and unexpected equipment breakdowns, some firms must occasionally resort to subcontracting work to other companies. Subcontracting allows the employer latitude in scheduling employees and expediting production. In some instances, the employer may find subcontracting less expensive than having the firm's employees perform the work. Unions often attempt to limit subcontracting because it poses a threat to the jobs of bargaining unit members. Very few contracts strictly prohibit subcontracting; however, a number of contracts require the employer to notify and discuss subcontracting plans with the union. About one-third of the major collective bargaining agreements allow subcontracting only if the employer does not have the proper personnel or equipment to perform the work in-house. Roughly one-fourth of the contracts prohibit subcontracting if there are employees already on layoff or if subcontracting would result in layoffs.[40]

Firms may desire to make technological changes such as using new equipment to speed production, improve product quality, and reduce manufacturing costs. When technological advances threaten the job security of employees, the union will try to prevent these changes. On the other hand, unions may encourage advances that enhance safety and allow employees to switch from jobs that are monotonous to those that are more enjoyable.

---

[38] The Bureau of National Affairs, Inc., *Basic Patterns in Union Contracts*, 11th ed. (Washington, D.C.: The Bureau of National Affairs, Inc., 1986), pp. 1–6.
[39] The Bureau of National Affairs, Inc., *Basic Patterns in Union Contracts*, 11th ed. (Washington, D.C.: The Bureau of National Affairs, Inc., 1986), pp. 49–52 and pp. 68–71.
[40] The Bureau of National Affairs, Inc., *Basic Patterns in Union Contracts*, 11th ed. (Washington, D.C.: The Bureau of National Affairs, Inc., 1986), p. 81.

The above examples illustrate some of the nonwage bargaining issues that management must be prepared to negotiate at the bargaining table. Such issues restrict management and affect production schedules and costs. To protect its ability to run the company and minimize union interference, management typically inserts a management rights clause in the contract. The issue of management rights is both controversial and important and is treated in detail in Chapter 15. Management may go to great lengths to negotiate management rights clauses as well as provisions dealing with employee work schedules, layoffs, subcontracting, and other nonwage issues, in order to prevent the union from usurping managerial prerogatives. Many unions are content to allow management to run the firm and do not interfere with its decisions unless those decisions conflict with the collective bargaining agreement. When management perceives that unions are encroaching on their "right" to run the firm, however, hostilities may develop.

Recent Trends in Management Bargaining Objectives

According to Bureau of National Affairs, Inc. (BNA) survey data, many firms have adopted a get-tough negotiating attitude with unions.[41] Unless economic, social, or legal conditions change, the rigid stance that employers are taking when bargaining with labor unions is likely to continue through the turn of the century. The BNA report states that union wage increases have been pushed to record lows and cost-of-living protections are being eliminated from many collective bargaining agreements.[42] Two-tier wage structures, a form of union concession to financially strapped firms, pay newly hired employees significantly lower pay rates than senior employees in order to control total labor costs. Although two-tier pay systems were popular among employers during the early 1980s, they have been losing popularity as some firms regain financial strength.[43] Lump-sum (one-time) bonus payments are also being used in lieu of general pay increases because they do not permanently obligate an employer to adhere to a more costly pay scale.[44] Lump-sum payments (in lieu of permanent wage increases) were largely responsible for a strike between Ameritech and the Communications Workers of America (CWA) in the summer of 1989. A CWA spokesperson said that Ameritech offered too much of the pay increase in a lump-sum payment, rather than adding to the amount of the wage base.[45]

Employers are becoming more reluctant to guarantee job security for workers.

---

[41] The Bureau of National Affairs, Inc., *1987 Employer Bargaining Objectives* (Washington, D.C.: The Bureau of National Affairs, Inc., 1986); and The Bureau of National Affairs, Inc., "Employer 1989 Bargaining Goals," *Collective Bargaining Negotiations & Contracts* (Washington, D.C.: The Bureau of National Affairs, Inc., October 6, 1988), p. 4.

[42] Between 1977 and 1988, the percent of workers covered by cost-of-living clauses in major collective bargaining agreements fell from 61.2 percent to 38.4 percent. See Craig T. Norback, *The Human Resources Yearbook*, 1988 Edition (Englewood Cliffs, New Jersey: Prentice-Hall, Inc., 1988), p. 8.12.

[43] *The Wall Street Journal*, Labor Letter (June 16, 1987), p. 1.

[44] A pay increase of 6 percent, for example, means that the employees' *base pay* will increase by 6 percent. Subsequent pay raises will be a percentage of the new base pay. A lump-sum bonus, on the other hand, is not a permanent pay raise. Subsequent pay raises are expressed as a percentage of the base pay (*not counting* the lump-sum bonus).

[45] Mary Lu Carnevale, " Ameritech, Union Are Set to Resume Contract Talks," *The Wall Street Journal* (August 23, 1989), p. A10.

Many of the companies polled in the survey indicated that their contracts had job security provisions ranging from advanced notice of plant closings and layoffs to worksharing arrangements.[46] However, few employers had plans for liberalizing job security provisions. Over three-fourths of the employers indicated a willingness to replace striking workers in order to maintain operations during a work stoppage, while 84 percent said they would attempt to remove or relax restrictive work rules. A number of firms also indicated a desire to tighten employee absenteeism policies.

There is strong indication that employers are less likely to grant significant increases in employee benefits and are more likely to install cost controls on the more expensive benefit plans.[47] Health care cost containment provisions such as higher deductibles (that require the employee to pay a larger amount of a hospital bill before the insurance coverage takes effect) and increased employee health insurance premiums are being used more frequently. About one-fifth of the employers polled said that they would increase employee benefits such as group life insurance, accident and disability coverage, and disability income insurance. Approximately one-fifth claimed to be contemplating cutbacks in life and health insurance coverage. Despite recent attention on issues such as drug testing, formal policies for dealing with employees who are AIDS victims, and child care facilities, the firms surveyed expressed only mild interest in these bargaining topics.

Although The Bureau of National Affairs study indicates that firms are adopting a tougher bargaining stance, this survey covers only 261 employers and their views may not be entirely representative. Furthermore, stating a bargaining objective is not a guarantee of achieving it. Bargaining objectives are often shrouded in secrecy because neither the employer nor the union wants to risk revealing its position prior to negotiations, so it is difficult to determine an employer's actual bargaining objectives before negotiations. When asked whether they met their bargaining objectives after negotiations have been concluded, employers will probably answer affirmatively; to answer negatively makes it appear that management negotiators were ineffective at the bargaining table.

▲ Balancing Management and Union Power Structures

The relationship between organized labor and management has been depicted as a power struggle, with union and management being adversaries. As a result, the organizational structures of both unions and management have evolved to provide a system of checks and balances to ensure that one side does not secure a significant power advantage over the other. Figure 7–4 illustrates the interorganizational power points that exist in most union-management relationships.

At the lowest level in both union and management organizational structures is the relationship between first-line supervisors and shop stewards, sometimes

---

[46] Effective February 4, 1989, the federal plant closing bill became law. See chapter 15 for details on this legislation.

[47] For an excellent discussion of health care cost containment, see The Bureau of National Affairs, Inc., *Compensation: Personnel Policy and Practice Series* (Washington, D.C.: The Bureau of National Affairs, Inc., 1986), Section 339.

7 MANAGEMENT STRUCTURE, GOALS, AND POLICIES FOR COLLECTIVE BARGAINING ▲ 243

MANAGEMENT		UNION
U.S. Chamber of Commerce; National Association of Manufacturers	↔	AFL-CIO
Corporate CEO or vice president of industrial relations/personnel	↔	International union president or top leadership
Plant manager, superintendent, or personnel director	↔	Local union president or business agent
Departmental supervisor	↔	Business agent or chief steward
First-line supervisor	↔	Local union steward

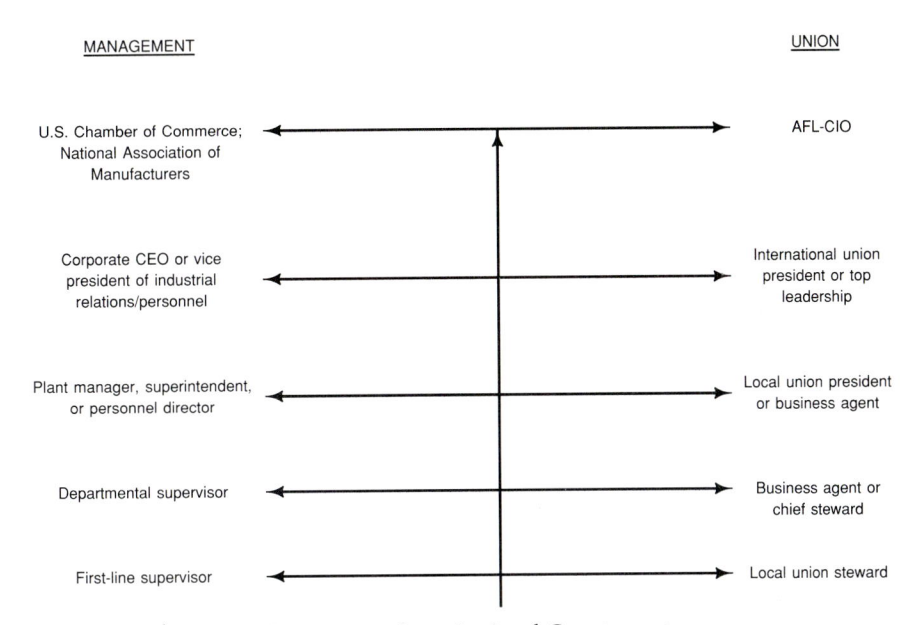

FIGURE 7–4 Union-Management Organizational Counterparts

referred to as the shop-floor level. The primary concern at this level is enforcement and administration of the collective bargaining agreement. As discussed in Chapter 6, the shop steward is charged with ensuring that management adheres to the spirit and terms of the labor contract. When complaints or formal grievances arise, first-line supervisors and shop stewards are often the initial points of contact. Despite being the lowest bargaining level, it has an important impact on the overall union-management relationship. When first-line supervisors and stewards handle complaints and grievances in a competent and timely fashion, they perform a valuable service to their respective organizations. Conflict can be minimized before it escalates and leads to chronic productivity and morale problems. Because of their intimate knowledge of working conditions and employee concerns, supervisors and stewards are also able to provide useful information during preparations for contract negotiations.

In large organizations, a departmental supervisor is the counterpart of the business agent or chief steward. When contract negotiations are conducted at the local level, these people may be part of their respective bargaining teams. Departmental supervisors, chief stewards, and business agents are usually involved with formal employee grievances. Typically, minor complaints or grievances arising under the collective bargaining agreement are resolved by first-line supervisors and shop stewards. If the grievance cannot be settled at this stage, then it is usually put in writing and jointly submitted to the departmental supervisor and chief steward for resolution. Resolving complex grievances requires extensive knowledge of the contract, past practices, and other considerations.

Plant managers or superintendents usually deal primarily with the local union president and leadership. When bargaining is done at the local level, plant managers and local union leaders may be the chief negotiators for their respective sides. If collective bargaining is done at the company-wide level, these individuals may have significant input into bargaining preparations and they may be responsible for negotiating a supplemental collective bargaining agreement that covers local conditions. Furthermore, plant managers and local union leaders must convince employees to approve a company-wide contract once a settlement has been reached between the union and management bargaining teams. The most serious grievances also receive attention by plant managers and local union leaders. Often such grievances are precipitated by confusing contract terms and have important long-term implications for both the union and the employer. Finally, plant and local union leaders occasionally meet away from the bargaining table to resolve matters of mutual concern. Examples include health and safety problems, local economic conditions, and unexpected problems arising in the workplace.

Establishing broad industrial relations policies that regulate personnel functions is a primary concern of the CEO and the corporate vice president for personnel/human resource management. Because of the high degree of centralization in the collective bargaining process, many contract negotiations take place between international union leaders and their counterparts at corporate headquarters. Union bargaining team members may consist of the international president who is the chief negotiator, along with various other international leaders and staff experts. The vice president for personnel or the industrial relations director may serve as management's chief negotiator with the assistance of personnel experts in compensation, employee benefits, and other functional areas. Corporate and international union leaders do not generally become involved with grievances unless the grievance is both exceptional and has important managerial or financial ramifications. As noted earlier, these parties may meet to discuss matters of mutual concern. Difficult issues, such as the bargaining rights of employees who are transferred to a newly opened plant, can be resolved in a leisurely fashion without later disrupting contract negotiations.

At the pinnacle of Figure 7–4 are the organizations that represent the common interests of organized labor and business. Labor's major advocate, the AFL-CIO, is discussed in Chapter 6 and will not be further examined here. The vast interests of business are represented by a variety of groups. Perhaps the best known are the U.S. Chamber of Commerce and the National Association of Manufacturers (NAM). Both organizations lobby on behalf of business interest groups to achieve a number of goals. Among NAM's recent concerns are the federal deficit and tax reform measures.[48] Occasionally, business and labor leaders will clash openly over important issues such as plant closings.[49] In most instances, however, the two groups independently pursue their objectives. Both the NAM and the Chamber of Commerce have antiunion reputations. The South Carolina Chamber of Commerce, for example, periodically makes statements about the negative effects of organized labor on businesses in that state.

---

[48] "NAM Will Have No Narrow 'Wish List' Under Pace," *Industry Week* (January 7, 1985).

[49] Mark Sfiligoj, "Union Chiefs, NAM At Odds On Plant Closing Notice Bill," *American Metal Market* (May 20, 1985), p. 32.

▲ Multi-employer Bargaining

Multi-employer bargaining through employer associations represents a viable arrangement for a group of small firms that must bargain with a large powerful union. Because the advantages and disadvantages of multi-employer bargaining are discussed in Chapter 4, these issues will not be treated here. Firms considering multi-employer bargaining arrangements should be aware that once they have become contractually committed to the association, it is often legally difficult to withdraw until the collective bargaining agreement has expired.

Multi-employer bargaining may be on the decline both in the United States and in Canada. In the United States, employer associations in coal and trucking have been weakened in recent years by employers who desire to bargain on their own rather than in concert with other firms in the same industry.[50] Trucking Management, Inc. (TMI), a major bargaining group in the trucking industry, experienced employer attrition during the 1980s. A number of small trucking firms that were organized under another association, the Motor Carrier Labor Advisory Council, sought to split from TMI and seek a labor contract that was more responsive to the needs of small trucking firms.[51] Employers in the steel industry disbanded their coordinated bargaining committee in 1985, bringing an end to 30 years of industry-wide national bargaining in the U.S. steel industry.[52] The construction industry has also witnessed an erosion of multi-employer bargaining arrangements. The above examples notwithstanding, there are still a number of successful multi-employer bargaining structures in the United States.

▲ Union-Management Cooperative Efforts

Labor-management relations in the United States have been largely built on a foundation of mutual distrust. Collective bargaining and contract administration have been viewed as a situation whereby the gains of one party result in losses to the other party. In recent years, however, it has become more apparent that both the employer and the union may benefit from cooperative rather than adversarial relations. Labor and management both have areas of mutual concern such as quality of worklife and productivity bargaining, the threat of increasing government regulation, foreign competition, employee health and safety, and bargaining in declining industries. Many instances of labor-management cooperation have been precipitated by economic downturns that have threatened the survival of unionized firms. The aforementioned concessionary bargaining of the early 1980s is one example. According to the United Steelworkers' Paul Rusen and to Joseph Scalise, vice president

---

[50] Joseph B. Rose, "Legislative Support For Multi-Employer Bargaining: The Canadian Experience," *Industrial and Labor Relations Review* (October 1986), p. 3.
[51] The Bureau of National Affairs, Inc., *Labor Relations Yearbook, 1984* (Washington, D.C.: The Bureau of National Affairs, Inc., 1985), p. 12.
[52] Joseph B. Rose, "Legislative Support for Multi-Employer Bargaining: The Canadian Experience," *Industrial and Labor Relations Review* (October 1986), p. 3.

of the Wheeling-Pittsburgh Steel Corp., one great motivator for labor cooperation is survival. A former counsel for the United Auto Workers has noted:

> Keys to successful programs ... are empathy, information-sharing and openness, egalitarian principles, and a willingness to take risks. But by far the most important factor ... is whether the parties demonstrate that they are unwilling to take advantage of the other during bad times.[53]

Not all labor-management cooperative efforts are undertaken when the survival of a company is at stake. Quality of worklife and productivity programs are also used to enhance the work environment of employees and to boost productivity efficiency. These factors can improve profits for employers and raise pay levels for employees. Joint health and safety programs help employers avoid legal entanglements under federal and state law, reduce workers' compensation costs, and enhance the work environment. Health care cost containment measures that are jointly controlled by labor and management reduce medical insurance premiums and allow employees to get the best possible medical coverage for the premium dollar.[54]

Opportunities Created by Cooperative Efforts

Although cooperative union-management programs are not a new idea, such programs have arisen mainly during the late 1970s and throughout the 1980s. The content and scope of these cooperative endeavors vary substantially from one union and employer to another. Some of the more ambitious programs have attempted to give unions and workers broad input into management decisions, whereas others have a narrow focus. An examination of a number of programs reveals three areas of benefit: (1) benefits to the employer, (2) benefits to employees and the union, and (3) benefits to the union-management relationship.[55]

Management enters into cooperative arrangements with the union because of potential advantages in product quality,[56] productivity improvements, labor cost reductions, and reduced turnover, absenteeism, and tardiness.[57] Some programs specify both the topics that are subject to discussion through joint union-management committees and those that are forbidden. Xerox Corporation entered into an agreement with the Amalgamated Clothing and Textile Workers Union (ACTWU)

---

[53] Michael Schuster, "Problems and Opportunities in Implementing Cooperative Union-Management Programs," in *Proceedings of the Thirty-fifth Annual Meeting, Industrial Relations Research Association*, Barbara D. Dennis, ed. (Madison, Wisconsin: Industrial Relations Research Association, 1983), pp. 189–197. Also see, William N. Cooke, "Factors Influencing the Effect of Joint Union-Management Programs on Employee-Supervisor Relations," *Industrial and Labor Relations Review* (July 1990), pp. 587–603.

[54] The National Association of Manufacturers (NAM) has made a strong endorsement for certain types of union-management cooperative programs. See John Hoerr, "The Strange Bedfellows Backing Workplace Reform," *Business Week* (April 30, 1990), p. 57.

[55] See Jerome M. Rosow, ed., *Teamwork: Joint Labor-Management Programs in America* (New York: Pergamon Press/Work in America Institute Series, 1986).

[56] Arthur A. Whatlay and Wilma Hoffman, "Quality Circles Earn Union Respect," *Personnel Journal* (December 1987), p. 89.

[57] The Bureau of National Affairs, Inc., *Labor Relations Yearbook, 1984*, p. 204.

to form problem-solving teams. These teams were allowed to deal with issues that did not "tamper with the collective bargaining agreement."[58] Permissible subjects of investigation included product quality, safety and health, inventory cost savings, and the location of equipment and materials. Nonpermissible subjects included salaries, grievances, company policy, working hours, breaks, discipline problems, and production standards.

Both unionized and nonunionized employees may benefit from joint union-management cooperative efforts.[59] Advantages include increased job satisfaction, job influence and involvement, greater loyalty and commitment to the employer, improved working conditions and supervision, reduced job frustration, improved earnings, job enrichment, and job security.[60] Some of these benefits are difficult to document. Union-management cooperative programs may list all or some of the above goals at the outset of the program only to discover later that they were never realized.[61] Furthermore, there may be debate among union, management, and the employees regarding the extent of such benefits. Employers and the union may believe that a joint quality of worklife program has increased job satisfaction and improved working conditions, whereas the employees may remain unconvinced of this.

Finally, cooperative programs may create changes in the union-management relationship. A more cooperative stance by labor and management may increase mutual trust between labor and management and soften the adversarial relationship. Unions that have been commonly regarded as critics by management may be regarded as partners with respect to certain issues. The proverbial "putting yourself in someone else's shoes" may be relevant to joint union-management efforts because, for the first time, both sides are working toward resolving common problems. Cooperative programs may reduce the number of grievances filed by bargaining unit employees, reduce the potential for future strikes, and improve communications between union and management. As a result, new ideas can be generated through on-going problem solving. The natural tensions between labor and management may be reduced.

Potential Fears and Drawbacks of Cooperative Programs

Most innovations and changes are accompanied by a certain degree of skepticism. Union-management cooperative programs are no exception. Unions are apprehensive that such programs will ultimately weaken labor unions and divert attention

---

[58] Charlotte Gold, *Labor-Management Committees: Confrontation, Cooptation, or Cooperation?* (Ithaca, NY: ILR Press, Cornell University, 1986), p. 10.

[59] See William N. Cooke, "Improving Productivity and Quality Through Collaboration," *Industrial Relations* (Spring 1989), pp. 299–319; and Paula B. Voos, "The Influence of Cooperative Programs on Union-Management Relations, Flexibility, and Other Labor Relations Outcomes," *Journal of Labor Research* (Winter 1989), pp. 103–117.

[60] Charlotte Gold, *Labor-Management Committees: Confrontation, Cooptation, or Cooperation?* (Ithaca, New York: ILR Press, Cornell University, 1986), p. 11.

[61] See Gordon DiGiacomo, "Trade Unions and the Reform of the Quality of Work Life: Ergonomic and Other QWL Reforms Have Limited Goals and Are No Substitute for Labor Involvement," *The American Journal of Economics and Sociology* (October 1987), p. 399.

away from the time-honored practices of collective bargaining and contract administration. As one labor leader noted, there is the possibility that management will reap the fruits of cooperation while "mugging the union at the plant gate."[62] Unions are concerned that management will improve productivity and profits with little or no benefit accruing to workers. Union leaders are also concerned that joint participation with management may later undermine unions at the bargaining table. Employees may also worry that the union will become alienated from their own needs and become too closely aligned with management.[63]

Management has misgivings about losing its decision-making authority if a formal cooperative program is established with the union. It has been argued that workers will not be able to make contributions to management decision making "because they are not acquainted with the intricate and complicated factors involved in running an enterprise."[64] There is also concern that cooperative programs will impair managerial decisions because of the added bureaucratic layer that is created. Many middle managers may fear that they will lose the ability to control employees, whereas upper level management may believe that the use of "innovations" is simply another gimmick and a mask for poor management. Managers may be more receptive to union-management cooperative programs during times of crises, but once the crisis ends so may the cooperative efforts. It is possible that cooperative programs will be "too little, too late" for firms beset by serious economic and market problems.[65]

Pressures exerted by foreign competition, deregulation of key industries, and other factors have forced some companies to adopt a more flexible and cost-effective way of conducting business. Kochan, Katz, and McKersie, in *The Transformation of American Industrial Relations*, discuss a number of workplace innovations that have involved collaborative efforts between union and management, as well as union involvement in managerial decisions. These programs include quality circles, enhanced worker-supervisor communications, work restructuring, gain sharing, and union representation on managerial planning committees. A number of these programs have been implemented in the auto, steel, and communications industries. Kochan, Katz, and McKersie reached the following conclusions:

1. The success of cooperative work reform efforts depends on the ability of union and management to sustain high levels of trust. Trust must be fostered through support from higher levels of the industrial relations system (e.g., through international union officials and corporate top management).
2. The ability to introduce and sustain cooperative work reform efforts will vary

---

[62] Charlotte Gold, *Labor-Management Committees: Confrontation, Cooptation, or Cooperation?* (Ithaca, New York: ILR Press, Cornell University, 1986), p. 23. This comment is attributed to William W. Winpisinger, former president of the International Association of Machinists and Aerospace Workers.
[63] Charlotte Gold, *Labor-Management Committees: Confrontation, Cooptation, or Cooperation?* (Ithaca, New York: ILR Press, Cornell University, 1986), p. 25.
[64] Charlotte Gold, *Labor-Management Committees: Confrontation, Cooptation, or Cooperation?* (Ithaca, New York: ILR Press, Cornell University, 1986), p. 27.
[65] Charlotte Gold, *Labor-Management Committees: Confrontation, Cooptation, or Cooperation?* (Ithaca, New York: ILR Press, Cornell University, 1986), p. 29.

across organizational settings, depending on a range of factors such as a firm's technological and market constraints.
3. It is difficult and politically risky for both union and management officials to introduce cooperative work reform efforts. Such programs often require modification of the terms of the collective bargaining agreement.
4. Unions generally become involved in helping management make strategic decisions (e.g., those regarding production schedules and job design) when:
   a. the parties are faced with severe environmental pressures (e.g. a foreign competitor) and there are few alternatives for dealing with the threat other than through union-management cooperation.
   b. labor is able to overcome resistance to change by management.
   c. unions already have considerable bargaining power.
   d. both parties can overcome internal dissension and criticism among those who are skeptical of the cooperative efforts.
5. The use of extensive cooperative work reforms is relatively limited. Even if such reforms were widespread, it may not be sufficient to alter the decline in unionism in the United States.[66]

Chapter 18 further discusses the use of union-management cooperative programs as well as environmental threats and opportunities affecting U.S. labor relations.

▲ Summary and Conclusions

This chapter has described the management structure used to deal with organized labor and the preceding chapter described the structure and operation of labor organizations. Together these two chapters portray both the individual characteristics of union and management organizations as well as the ways in which the two organizations interact.

Private- and public-sector organizations exist to achieve various goals and objectives. As discussed in this chapter, these goals and objectives may be geared to financial performance, market share, productivity, social responsibility, public service, or other criteria. Ultimately, the management of profit-oriented firms must answer to a corporate board of directors and to the stockholders. Managers in public sector and nonprofit organizations are accountable to the taxpayers, elected officials, and special interest groups. Furthermore, management is expected to achieve success for their organizations and, when they fail, they are likely to receive little sympathy from those who put them in office and to whom they must answer. Boards of directors, stockholders, taxpayers, and constituent groups are interested in good performance, not excuses for poor performance.

---

[66] Thomas A. Kochan, Harry C. Katz, and Robert McKersie, *The Transformation of American Industrial Relations* (New York: Basic Books, Inc., 1986), pp. 175–177 and pp. 201–205. Also see, Adrienne E. Eaton, "The Extent and Determinants of Local Union Control of Participative Programs," *Industrial and Labor Relations Review* (July 1990), pp. 604–620.

Labor organizations represent a threat to an organization's ability to attain its goals and achieve success. Unions may force a firm to alter its corporate strategy and modify its personnel policies. A primary responsibility of management is dealing with external threats to the firm; unions represent one such threat. However, unions represent only one among the many market, social, economic, and legal threats with which management must cope. Most organizations handle numerous employee matters through personnel or human resource management departments. When organized labor becomes a threat, the personnel department may establish an industrial or labor relations function that is staffed with experts in union organizing, collective bargaining, and contract administration. The industrial relations function is expected to deal with organized labor and minimize any negative impact that it might have on the organization.

This chapter examines the various personnel functions with special emphasis on how these functions differ between unionized and nonunionized organizations. A discussion of management bargaining goals provides insight into some of the concerns of managers in unionized settings. An analysis of how the union and management structures are designed to balance the bargaining power relationship is also important in understanding the concept of collective bargaining power. Finally, the union management relationship is not always adversarial. Examples of union-management cooperative efforts are noted here (along with their advantages and disadvantages); these innovations are also discussed in subsequent chapters.

The stage is now set to examine the most prominent and notorious facet of labor relations—the collective bargaining process. In order to fully appreciate the process, some understanding is needed of topics such as labor history, labor legislation, union organizing efforts, bargaining units, the nature of organized labor, and the personnel function. Chapters 1 through 7 have covered these topics and provide the background for subsequent chapters.

▲ Discussion Questions and Exercises

1. Briefly summarize the major differences between unionized and nonunionized firms with respect to the following PHRM functions:
   a. recruitment and selection of employees
   b. training and development of employees
   c. employee performance appraisal
   d. compensation and employee benefits
   e. work rules and job security measures
   f. employee discipline and control
2. Select a unionized firm in your area. Analyze the firm and its recent bargaining history with the union. What factors appear to affect the company's bargaining goals? Discuss.

3. Do you believe that union-management cooperative efforts will increase during the 1990s? Why or why not?
4. Under what circumstances are union-management cooperative programs most likely to be successful? Discuss.
5. Are union-management relations going to become more adversarial or less adversarial during the 1990s?

Part IV

Collective Bargaining Agreement Negotiations

▲ ▲

Part IV examines bargaining theory, the process of collective bargaining, and the resolution of labor disputes. Chapter 8 presents a general discussion of bargaining theory. Several prominent bargaining theories are described, and their similarities and differences are discussed. This chapter outlines the basic concepts of the bargaining process and establishes a foundation for an in-depth treatment of the actual contract negotiations in Chapter 9.

Chapter 9 examines the bargaining preparations of both union and management as well as face-to-face negotiations at the bargaining table. The extensive preparation needed for successful collective bargaining is analyzed, along with negotiation tactics. Among other topics, Chapter 9 discusses the process of developing proposals, bargaining protocol, and the financial costs of wage and employee-benefit proposals.

Chapter 10 focuses on what happens when union and management cannot reach an agreement and become involved in a labor dispute. The role of industrial conflict is discussed, along with sources of conflict. A discussion of the dynamics and legal issues associated with strikes and lockouts is also presented. Finally, Chapter 10 discusses the role of labor mediation in resolving private-sector labor disputes. The facts surrounding several work stoppages are presented at the end of Chapter 10. These examples provide practical insights into the anatomy of labor disputes and their resolution.

8 The Collective Bargaining Process: A Theoretical Overview

- **Introduction**
- **The Role and Spectrum of Bargaining Theories**
  Mathematical/Economic Bargaining Models
  Behavioral Bargaining Models
  Descriptive Approaches to Bargaining
- **Some Selected Bargaining Theories**
  Pigou's Original Bargaining Model
  A Behavioral Theory of Labor Negotiations
  The Hicks Bargaining Model
- **Similarities among Bargaining Theories**
  Settlement Points and Ranges
  Costs of Agreeing and Disagreeing
  The Rationality Assumption
  The Element of Timing
  Communications Issues and Policies
  Bargaining Tactics and Concessions
- **A Model of Collective Bargaining Power**
  Sources of Bargaining Power
  Factors that Dilute Bargaining Power
  Relative, Absolute, and Total Bargaining Power
  Problems with the Bargaining Power Concept
- **Collective Bargaining Tactics and Outcomes**
  Reaching a Settlement
  Work Stoppages: Strikes and Lockouts
  Dissolution of the Bargaining Relationship
  Assessing the Outcome of Collective Bargaining
- **Summary and Conclusions**
- **Discussion Questions and Exercises**

▲ Introduction

The terms *bargaining* and *negotiations* cover a variety of situations that range from haggling over the price of a sports car with an automobile salesperson, to plea bargaining in a criminal trial, to economic summits between the United States and major world powers. Most discussions use the terms interchangeably. Both terms encompass several key elements. First, bargaining takes place between at least two individuals or groups. Common examples of individual bargains include negotiating the price of a piece of merchandise or resolving interpersonal differences in a domestic dispute. Collective bargaining between union and management teams or high-level conferences between national leaders are examples of group bargaining. Second, bargaining represents an attempt to divide resources or resolve a problem of mutual concern. That is, the negotiators must have something in common before bargaining can take place. In labor-management relations, the group of bargaining-unit employees whose wages, hours, and working conditions must be established is the mutual concern. Third, both sides must be able to grant concessions and impose penalties on the opposite side. Concessions and penalties not only compel an opponent to bargain, but also they ensure that proposals and counterproposals made during the course of negotiations will be taken seriously. If an automobile dealer fails to give in to the price demands of a prospective buyer, then the penalty imposed by the buyer is to look elsewhere for a better deal. Likewise, both union and management can impose sanctions if negotiations are not successful. The best-known penalty is the economic strike. Strikes are a major sanction imposed by the union against the employer.

This chapter establishes a framework for analysis of collective bargaining between labor unions and management. The first part of the chapter examines the role of bargaining theories and provides examples of several of the better-known theories. Because of its central importance, the concept of bargaining power is analyzed as it pertains to labor-management negotiations. Finally, bargaining tactics and outcomes are discussed.

▲ The Role and Spectrum of Bargaining Theories

Theories or models of the collective bargaining process range from descriptive accounts of what occurs at the bargaining table to complex theories that make extensive use of mathematical models and economic utility functions. Bargaining theories illustrate the dynamics of negotiating behavior and they often predict a point or range in which the parties will reach a settlement. Bargaining theories help to *explain* the behavior of negotiators and, in many cases, *predict* the outcome of bargaining. Most collective bargaining theories focus on economic issues such as wage settlements. A number of behavioral bargaining theories emphasize social and psychological variables. Behavioral theories examine the presence of mediators, the location of bargaining sites, the imposition of strike deadlines, and differences in the personality characteristics of negotiators to determine the effects of these factors on the bargaining process. Descriptive approaches present a realistic view of events at the bargaining table and do not attempt to isolate and analyze specific variables pertaining to bargaining behavior and outcomes. In fact, descriptive approaches are not true bargaining theories. Rather, they often represent an anecdotal account of collective or individual negotiations.

Mathematical/Economical Bargaining Models

Some of the most complex bargaining models are of a mathematical/economic nature.[1] Most mathematical/economic models focus on bargaining outcomes that maximize the joint utility of the respective negotiators (or negotiating teams). The term *utility* pertains to the value that a party attaches to a bargaining settlement or outcome. Most of us have a positive utility for money in that we value $500 more than $100. In the same vein, union negotiators would attach a higher utility to a 7 percent wage increase than they would to a 6 percent increase. Management would attach a higher utility to the lower wage increase because it allows the firm to pay less to its employees and save the money for other purposes.

The concept of utility becomes less precise when it is used to place a value on nonmonetary items such as union security clauses, grievance procedures, and seniority provisions. Although most of us would agree that $200 has twice the utility of $100, how do we compare the utility of a union shop clause with that of a company-wide seniority arrangement? For this reason, mathematical/economic models lose some of their usefulness or realism when the entire spectrum of economic and noneconomic collective bargaining provisions is considered.

Management would maximize its utility if it could pay whatever wage it desired without considering demands by the union. On the other hand, the union would maximize its utility if it could obtain its highest wage demand without being limited by management's financial and profitability position. In the real world of bargaining, it is probable that neither the union nor management will receive exactly what it wants. Collective bargaining is a practice in compromise and reason. Many labor-management settlements split the difference between the two extreme positions and most mathematical/economic models recognize the typical proposal-concession-counterproposal sequence of collective bargaining. Some mathematical/economic models of bargaining recognize that there is a cost or disutility for *not* reaching an agreement. A work stoppage stemming from an economic strike or lockout is a major cost of this kind.

Finally, mathematical/economic portrayals of the bargaining process define a settlement point or settlement range. The settlement point may be defined as the point in which the two parties maximize their respective *joint* utilities. In other words, a party may be willing to settle once the cost of disagreeing exceeds the cost of agreeing with the other side. Of course, models that define settlement points in this manner assume that the union and management are fully aware of their respective utilities for specific combinations of wages, hours, and working condi-

---

[1] Examples of mathematical/economic bargaining models can be found in Alan Coddington, *Theories of the Bargaining Process* (Chicago: Aldine Publishing Co., 1968). Also see John H. Pencavel and Thomas E. MaCurdy, "Testing Between Competing Models of Wage and Employment Determination in Unionized Markets," *Journal of Political Economy* (June 1986).

tions or can fully comprehend the costs of agreeing or disagreeing with their opponent. To the extent that these assumptions are not true, then the value of these models may be diminished.

Behavioral Bargaining Models

A number of bargaining models have their roots in social psychology.[2] Behavioral bargaining models focus on human variables such as the size and composition of bargaining teams, the impact of time limits and deadlines on bargaining, the number of bargaining issues at stake, attitude changes during negotiations, and communications styles of negotiators. Although the emphasis in mathematical/economic bargaining models is primarily on the point or range at which the parties will reach a settlement, behavioral models focus on the dynamics of collective bargaining. Some behavioral models account for bargaining outcomes. However, sociologists and psychologists are primarily interested in analyzing variables or factors that affect negotiating behavior rather than predicting the terms of the settlement.

Behavioral theories address issues such as the impact of the physical setting on negotiations. For example, most negotiators would prefer contract talks behind closed doors than before a public audience. The presence of an audience may encourage negotiators to place too much emphasis on conveying a positive image. As a result, negotiators may be reluctant to compromise with an opponent because they want to appear to be bargaining from a position of strength. Behavioral theories may attempt to account for the effects of mediators who are available to help unions and management resolve conflicts that arise during negotiations. It has been suggested that mediators discourage good-faith bargaining because both sides know the mediator will be available to resolve conflicts and soften unreasonable demands. Behavioral theories also examine the size of the bargaining team and the psychological characteristics of negotiators. These examples do not encompass the entire spectrum of sociological-psychological research, but are an illustration of the kinds of issues addressed by behavioral theories.

Descriptive Approaches to Bargaining

Nearly all of the research on bargaining behavior and outcomes is conducted in laboratory or simulated bargaining settings in order to scientifically control and measure the variables being analyzed. Research on actual collective bargaining sessions is almost nonexistent because union and management negotiators are reluctant to allow observers into the room where negotiations are taking place. Observers may distract negotiators from the critical business at hand, and there is the fear that they may reveal confidential information to outsiders. For these reasons, descriptions of what takes place during contract talks are usually sanitized before being released to the news media, bargaining-unit employees, and other interested parties.

---

[2] See Jeffrey Z. Rubin and Bert R. Brown, *The Social Psychology of Bargaining and Negotiation* (New York: Academic Press, Inc., 1975); Richard E. Walton and Robert B. McKersie, *A Behavioral Theory of Labor Negotiations* (New York: McGraw-Hill Book Company, 1965); Max H. Bazerman and Roy J. Lewicki, eds., *Negotiating in Organizations* (Beverly Hills, California: Sage Publications, 1983).

A number of published accounts of realistic collective negotiations are available.[3] Many of these are based on the experiences of union and management negotiators as well as labor mediators. Although they make no attempt to formulate a comprehensive theory of the collective bargaining process, descriptive accounts of bargaining preparation and tactics provide insights obtained through the personal experiences of negotiators. These accounts can be a valuable resource for people who plan careers as professional negotiators or mediators. (See Chapter 9 for a practical discussion of union-management contract talks).

▲ Some Selected Bargaining Theories

Three collective bargaining models are examined here to illustrate the differences in the structure, complexity, and assumptions underlying the various kinds of theories. The first, Pigou's original bargaining range theory, is probably the best-known depiction of wage bargaining. The second theory, that of Walton and McKersie, is among the most prominent of the behavioral theories. Finally, a slightly more complex economic bargaining theory, the Hicks model, is discussed.

Pigou's Original Bargaining Model

The late Professor A. C. Pigou formulated a model of short-run wage determination during the 1920s.[4] Pigou's bargaining range theory explains the process by which labor and management establish upper and lower wage limits within which a final settlement is made. Pigou observed that when wage rates are set by collective bargaining rather than through the free market forces of supply and demand, the wage rate can no longer be set at a single point (that is, the wage at which labor supply equals the employer's demand for labor). Instead, a "range of indeterminateness" is established during collective bargaining. The union's initial wage demand defines the upper limit of the range, whereas the employer's initial wage offer to the union defines the lower limit. Typically, the union demands a wage that is above the competitive rate and management initially offers a wage that is below the competitive rate.

Figure 8–1 illustrates Pigou's range theory under conditions that should result in a wage settlement between labor and management. The union's upper limit (point A) represents the union's ideal wage. Management will initially offer a wage well below that acceptable to the union (point D). From these two extremes, the union and management negotiating teams will normally proceed through a series of proposals, concessions, and counterproposals. The union will gradually reduce its wage

---

[3] See Thomas R. Colosi and Arthur Eliot Berkeley, *Collective Bargaining: How It Works and Why* (New York: American Arbitration Association, 1986). Colosi and Berkeley do an excellent job of describing what happens at the bargaining table; their book also elucidates why behaviors occur and provides some unique insights into the process. Gene Daniels and Kenneth Gagala, *Labor Guide to Negotiating Wages and Benefits* (Reston, Virginia: Reston Publishing Company, Inc., 1985); and Charles S. Loughran, *Negotiating A Labor Contract: A Management Handbook* (Washington, D.C.: The Bureau of National Affairs, Inc., 1984).

[4] A.C. Pigou, *The Economics of Welfare*, 4th ed. (London: Macmillan and Co., Ltd., 1933), pp. 450–461.

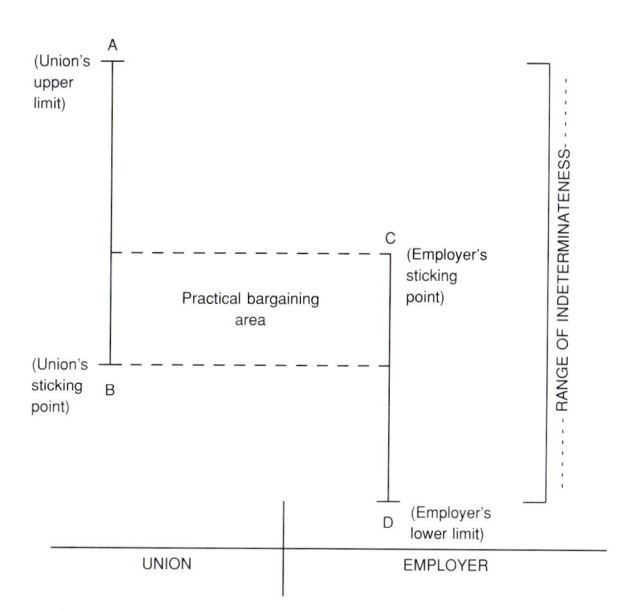

FIGURE 8–1 Pigou's Bargaining Range Theory

demands and the employer will also concede by raising its wage offer. Both sides, however, have established limits as to how far they are willing to concede. The union establishes a sticking point (point B) at which it is willing to endure the lost wages and hardships of a strike or lockout rather than accept a wage rate lower than point B. Management is also willing to accept the costs of a work stoppage before it grants a wage concession greater than point C.

Both union and management regard their sticking points as confidential and may go to great lengths to avoid revealing this information to the opposing side. In some instances, one side may attempt to mislead the other as to where the actual sticking point lies. Because the employer and union sticking points overlap in Figure 8–1, a settlement (without a strike) is likely. That is, the union is willing to accept a wage rate that is less than what management is ultimately willing to offer. The overlap between the two sticking points creates a practical bargaining area. Suppose that the union's sticking point is a three percent wage increase, whereas management is willing to provide a maximum increase of seven percent. A wage settlement somewhere between three and seven percent is in the offing. According to Pigou, the exact settlement point will depend on the respective bargaining skills and strengths of the union and management negotiators. If management possesses superior bargaining power and skill, then a settlement at or near three percent may be reached. Should the union hold the upper hand, then the settlement may be closer to seven percent. If the two sides are equally matched in terms of bargaining skills and strength, then the final outcome may be a split-the-difference settlement in the vicinity of five percent.

Numerous factors play a role in the determination of sticking points. In essence, sticking points represent each side's perception of its bargaining power. For example, during prosperous economic times when labor supplies are tight (that is, relatively few workers are available), the union may have superior bargaining strength. As a result, the union may raise its sticking point. An employer may be unwilling to endure a strike during prosperous times because of the potential loss of customers and profits and may therefore raise its sticking point. Sluggish economic conditions leading to higher unemployment rates increase the employer's bargaining power and decrease the union's power. Under these circumstances, the sticking points for both sides will be lower.

As noted earlier, neither the union nor management wants to reveal its sticking point to the other side. According to Morgan:

> One of the major problems which arise in the whole procedure of collective negotiation, of course, is that neither side can be certain of the exact location of the other party's sticking point. Hence, a great deal of uncertainty exists until, by virtue of the verbal probing that goes on through tortuous hours of negotiation, either a range of practical bargaining is discovered and a wage agreement is signed, or no such range is found and a work stoppage ensues. By the same token, if an arbitrator... is called into the dispute, a like amount of uncertainty confronts the neutral party... since neither side confides....the location of its sticking point. It then becomes the principal task of the third party to try to "hit" the range of practical bargaining if such a range actually exists.[5]

If the union's sticking point is greater than the employer's, then there is no overlap and no area of practical bargaining. When negotiators realize there is no overlap, a strike or lockout is likely unless at least one side alters its sticking point. Sticking points may be altered during a work stoppage, especially if one side becomes convinced that its original bargaining position was unrealistic. The union, with the help of a labor mediator, may decide that its original wage demands were unreasonably high because they failed to consider fully the deteriorating financial condition of the employer. Likewise, management may underestimate the willingness of rank-and-file union members to endure a long strike to achieve concessions at the bargaining table. The party with less bargaining power is more likely to alter its sticking points than its more powerful opponent. If the employer can replace a substantial number of striking workers, then the union may be at a power disadvantage and may lower its sticking point. Once sticking points are altered and a practical bargaining area is established, a settlement is usually imminent.

Professor Pigou's bargaining model focuses exclusively on wages and ignores other types of bargaining issues, such as employee benefits and nonwage items; however, to the extent that monetary values can be placed on bargaining issues, Pigou's theory may be useful. Pigou's theory illustrates some of the important dynamics of collective bargaining, and its consideration of sticking points is especially relevant. However, Pigou's theory does not define a precise point of settlement. Nor does it make any judgments as to what constitutes a fair and equitable settlement. Nevertheless, it is one of the better-known theories and it forms the foundation for understanding more complex economic bargaining theories.

---

[5] Chester A. Morgan, *Labor Economics*, 3rd ed. (Austin, Texas: Business Publications, Inc., 1970), p. 87.

A Behavioral Theory of Labor Negotiations

Richard E. Walton and Robert B. McKersie in their book, *A Behavioral Theory of Labor Negotiations*, established a comprehensive behavioral view of the bargaining process. Specifically, Walton and McKersie view collective bargaining as four subprocesses: distributive bargaining, integrative bargaining, attitudinal structuring, and intraorganizational bargaining. Although these subprocesses each have their own function and logic, their interplay ultimately determines the goals and tactics of union and management negotiators as well as bargaining outcomes.[6]

Walton and McKersie acknowledge that labor negotiations contain a mixture of "conflictful and collaborative items." They state that "the need to defend one's self-interest and at the same time engage in joint problem solving vastly complicates the selection of bargaining strategies and tactics." The authors also note that collective bargaining relationships "involve complex social units in which the constituent members are very interested in what goes on at the bargaining table and have some influence over the negotiators."[7]

Distributive bargaining applies to situations in which the two parties' goals are in conflict. Some bargaining subjects present conflicts in which one person's gains will result in an equal loss to the opponent (known as a zero-sum situation among game theorists). Distributive bargaining normally occurs over items such as wages and premium pay (e.g., overtime rates or hazardous duty pay). When union negotiators extract a wage increase from management negotiators, the company is left with less money than it would otherwise have in the absence of the increase. That is, the company's losses will equal the union's wage gains. Distributive bargaining is central to contract negotiations and is usually regarded as the dominant activity in the union-management relationship.[8] It is not surprising, therefore, that distributive bargaining issues become the most heated and controversial at the bargaining table. Distributive bargaining issues are a factor in most labor disputes and work stoppages.

Not all labor relations issues involve distributive bargaining or zero-sum situations. There are a number of subjects, such as quality of worklife and employee safety and health, that are of mutual concern to both labor and management. *Integrative bargaining* refers to bargaining issues that are not necessarily in conflict with those of the other party. According to Walton and McKersie, "Integrative potential exists when the nature of a problem permits solutions that benefit both parties, or at least when the gains of one party do not represent equal sacrifices by the other."[9] Walton and McKersie note that although the distributive and integrative bargaining subprocesses are dissimilar, they both represent rational responses to

---

[6] Richard E. Walton and Robert B. McKersie, *A Behavioral Theory of Labor Negotiations* (New York: McGraw-Hill Book Company, 1965), pp. 1–10.
[7] Richard E. Walton and Robert B. McKersie, *A Behavioral Theory of Labor Negotiations* (New York: McGraw-Hill Book Company, 1965), p. 3.
[8] Richard E. Walton and Robert B. McKersie, *A Behavioral Theory of Labor Negotiations* (New York: McGraw-Hill Book Company, 1965), p. 4.
[9] Richard E. Walton and Robert B. McKersie, *A Behavioral Theory of Labor Negotiations* (New York: McGraw-Hill Book Company, 1965), p. 5.

different situations. Thus, bargaining situations involving economic issues are characterized by distributive bargaining, whereas situations conducive to cooperation and mutual problem solving are characterized by integrative bargaining.

The issues, rights, and obligations pertaining to distributive and integrative bargaining are often written into the collective bargaining agreement. Walton and McKersie recognize that an additional function of collective bargaining is the manner in which each side influences and builds a relationship with the other. *Attitudinal structuring* is the subprocess by which the bargaining parties cultivate friendliness, trust, respect, and cooperation. Unlike some bargaining relationships, labor-management relationships often continue for years and even decades. Thus, the personal attitudes and reputations of negotiators and key union and management figures are crucial to the long-term bargaining relationship and should be incorporated into a behavioral theory of negotiations.[10]

The final subprocess in Walton and McKersie's theory is *intraorganizational bargaining*. Most observers of the collective bargaining process focus their attention on interaction *between* union and management. However, before the union and management negotiating teams meet at the bargaining table, each side must determine its own bargaining goals and priorities. Intraorganizational bargaining refers to the subprocess of bringing the expectations of the negotiators and principals for each side into alignment with their chief negotiator. According to Walton and McKersie:

> The chief negotiators often play important but limited roles in formulating bargaining objectives. On the union side, the local membership exerts considerable influence in determining the nature and strength of aspirations, and the international may dictate the inclusion of certain goals in the bargaining agenda. On the company side, top management and various staff groups exert their influence on bargaining objectives. In a sense the chief negotiator is the recipient of two sets of demands—one from across the table and one from his own organization.[11]

Intraorganizational bargaining is important for three reasons. First, a bargaining team cannot effectively negotiate a contract unless it has formulated its goals and prepared a strategy to attain them. Second, each side needs to decide the point and cost at which it is willing to endure a work stoppage if negotiations are not successful. Third, it is imperative for each respective negotiating team to present a united front at the bargaining table. If, for example, the management negotiating team perceives that there is internal dissension among the union negotiators, they may employ a conquer-and-divide strategy on the union bargaining team to obtain bargaining concessions.

The discussion presented here of Walton and McKersie's behavioral theory of negotiations is quite brief. Their complete discussion of these four subprocesses and the relationships among each is extensive and encompasses both behavioral and economic variables. However, the behavioral theory provides a multitude of insights into the dynamics of collective bargaining.

---

[10] See William H. Ross, Jr., "Situational Factors and Alternative Dispute Resolution," *Journal of Applied Behavioral Science* (August 1988), p. 251.

[11] Richard E. Walton and Robert B. McKersie, *A Behavioral Theory of Labor Negotiations* (New York: McGraw-Hill Book Company, 1965), pp. 5–6.

The Hicks Bargaining Model

The well-known bargaining model proposed by Professor Hicks focuses on the length and costs of work stoppages.[12] Hicks proposed that union and management negotiators use a cost-benefit approach to collective bargaining and anticipating work stoppages. That is, the cost-benefit approach will determine the demands and concessions of employers and unions at the bargaining table. Each side makes concessions to avoid a strike, resulting in an agreement between union and management negotiators. Because of miscalculations, unrealistic expectations, or political reasons, strikes occasionally occur. Once a strike has occurred, further concessions are determined by union and management's estimation of the strike length and costs associated with the strike.

Hicks's model is diagrammed in Figure 8–2. In the absence of the union, the employer would prefer to pay the wage indicated by the point W1. On the other hand, the union would prefer wage W2, if it could be obtained without calling a strike. As the negotiations progress, both the union and the employer modify their

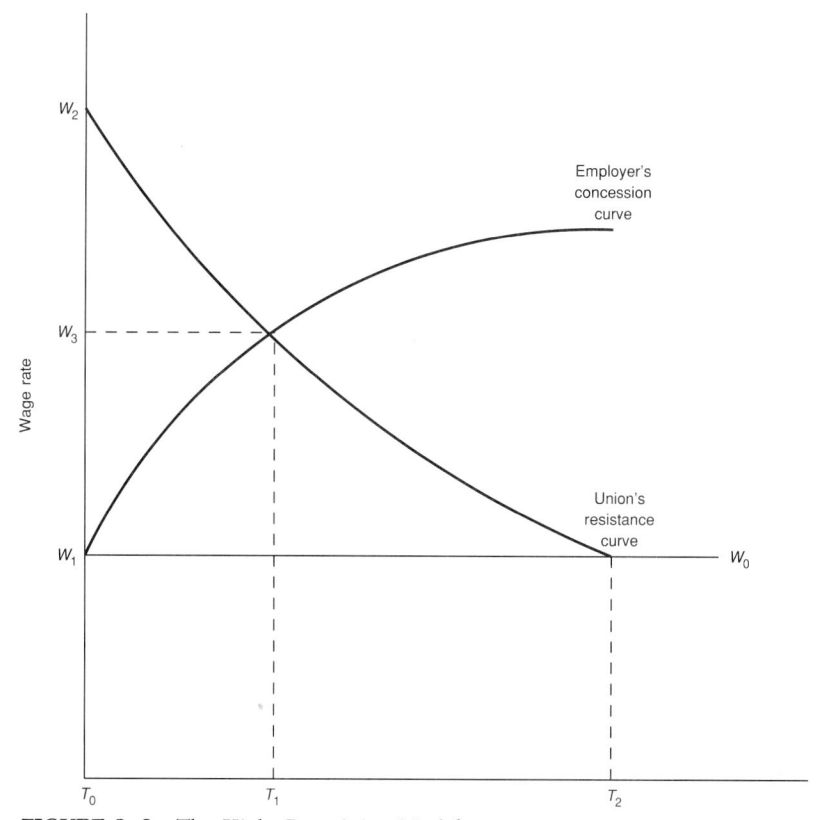

FIGURE 8–2 The Hicks Bargaining Model

[12] John R. Hicks, *The Theory of Wages* (New York: St. Martin's Press, 1966), pp. 136–157.

demands along respective concession curves in order to avoid a work stoppage. The union gradually makes concessions and lowers its wage demands, whereas management makes higher wage concessions until their positions intersect at wage W3. A primary difference between the Hicks model and the previously discussed bargaining range theory is that Hicks pinpoints a precise wage settlement, whereas Pigou's bargaining range theory does not. The Hicks bargaining model has served as a basis for the development of more sophisticated and complex bargaining theories.[13] The Hicks model, like its bargaining range counterpart, has several fundamental weaknesses. First, the model unrealistically assumes that the parties are aware of their opponent's willingness to make concessions. Second, it assumes that concession curves are fixed and are not subject to the vicissitudes and dynamics of the collective bargaining process. Hicks's model does not recognize the possibility that negotiators may increase their willingness to make concessions as contract talks progress. Third, the model may overestimate the precision with which union and management negotiators calculate strike costs. In many instances, strike costs are considered only when a negotiations deadlock (impasse) is reached and a strike vote is taken by bargaining unit employees. Since most contract negotiations are settled without resorting to a strike or lockout, it is doubtful that work stoppage costs are considered until necessary; in fact, strike costs cannot be determined until the barriers to an agreement are known. Union and management negotiators remain aware of a potential work stoppage during negotiations, but the length and costs of the work stoppage cannot be estimated until a strike or lockout becomes imminent.

▲ Similarities among Bargaining Theories

Because the large number of economic, behavioral, and descriptive models cannot be discussed in detail here, this section will provide a summary of some common threads in the various theories and descriptions of the collective bargaining process. Through a description of these common elements, a more realistic picture of collective bargaining will emerge.

Settlement Points and Ranges

A number of the mathematical/economic bargaining theories establish a point or range within which the parties will reach a settlement. Theories that define an exact settlement point make two assumptions: (1) the respective parties will behave in an economically rational manner, and (2) both sides fully understand not only their own bargaining preferences (utilities), but also their opponent's preferences. In

---

[13] See Harold W. Davey, Mario Bognanno, and David L. Estenson, *Contemporary Collective Bargaining*, 4th ed. (Englewood Cliffs, New Jersey.: Prentice-Hall, Inc., 1982), pp. 315–317; and Robert L. Bishop, "A Zeuthen-Hicks Theory of Bargaining," in Oran R. Young, ed., *Bargaining* (Urbana, Illinois: University of Illinois Press, 1975), pp.145–163, 183–190, and 253–266.

actual collective bargaining situations, neither of these assumptions is reasonable. Predicting a precise point of settlement is nearly impossible because one side rarely has a complete understanding of its opponent's bargaining objectives; this difficulty is intensified by the complexity of most collective bargaining agreements.

A more realistic approach is predicting bargaining outcomes within a range. Predictions within a specified range can be made on a number of social phenomena such as political elections or sporting events. Oddsmakers can predict that a political candidate will win by two to three percent of all votes cast. Likewise, Las Vegas bookmakers may predict that one college basketball team will defeat another by no more than seven points. The same type of predictability holds true in collective bargaining. We may be able to predict that the United Auto Workers and General Motors will reach a settlement that falls between a four and six percent wage increase, but predicting the exact settlement is not possible. However, the more information that we have on past negotiations, economic and industry conditions, and collective bargaining settlements at the other major automobile manufacturers, the more accurate our predictions will be on future UAW-GM negotiations.

Costs of Agreeing and Disagreeing

Models that emphasize the concept of collective bargaining power often note that a party is willing to reach an agreement once the costs of disagreeing with an opponent exceed the costs of agreeing.[14] To continue negotiating beyond this point would be counterproductive and more expensive than immediately reaching a settlement. A major problem with this approach is accurately assessing the cost of disagreeing. For example, the union may indicate that it will settle for a six percent wage increase, whereas the employer has most recently offered four percent. Management must decide whether the inconveniences of a strike and the potential loss of business are worth the labor-cost savings of standing firm on the four percent offer. The union must decide whether the lost wages of its membership warrants a strike even if management later concedes to the full six percent demand.

As noted earlier, neither side can fully measure the economic costs of risking a work stoppage. Even the most skilled PHRM and industrial relations directors, union leaders, and negotiators find it difficult to predict the duration and costs associated with a strike or lockout. The cost-of-disagreeing issue is compounded by the fact that not all costs are strictly pecuniary. Most work stoppages have noneconomic consequences such as tarnished working relationships, lingering animosity between labor and management officials, and the loss of public goodwill. It is difficult to convert such costs into dollars and cents, but they have an important impact on management, the employees, and the union.

Given the inaccuracies of estimating one's *own* costs, it is even more difficult to estimate an opponent's costs of disagreeing. Management may have little idea as to how long the union and its members are willing to endure a strike because they do not have complete information about the importance of bargaining items to

---

[14] See Neil W. Chamberlain and James W. Kuhn, *Collective Bargaining*, 2nd ed. (New York: McGraw-Hill Book Company, 1965), p. 182.

union negotiators. Nor do they always fully comprehend the determination of union members to achieve their objectives. Likewise, the union cannot be certain of management's ability to endure a strike. Some firms have stockpiled inventory and can hire replacements for striking employees in order to continue operations. Other firms may actually welcome a work stoppage and use it as an opportunity to perform maintenance, repair, and remodeling work in a plant.

The Rationality Assumption

Nearly all economic models of the collective bargaining process assume that the negotiators are behaving in a rational manner in attempting to maximize utility for their respective sides. Occasionally an observer will make the accusation that union and management negotiators do not behave rationally. Such arguments are bolstered by pointing to the economic damages caused by a work stoppage. In many cases, these damages far exceed the costs that would have been incurred had the parties settled earlier. Unfortunately, negotiators must make decisions with incomplete information. Critics who evaluate the process once the work stoppage is over have the advantage of perfect hindsight. The rationality of negotiator behavior must be assessed in the context of when the decision is made—not later, when the entire script of the bargaining process is known.

Negotiators with any semblance of sophistication come to the bargaining table well prepared. They and their staffs have prepared a list of proposals and counterproposals and have organized the necessary information and data to defend and substantiate their proposals. If their opponents prepare with the same degree of thoroughness, there will be few major surprises regarding proposals and counterproposals. Usually, the union's goal is to get the best settlement for its bargaining unit members without placing an onerous and unrealistic financial or managerial burden on the company. Management is usually willing to bargain in good faith and make reasonable proposals and concessions to the union. Of course, there are exceptions, but over 90 percent of all negotiations are concluded without a work stoppage, testifying to the fact that most negotiators perform in a rational manner.

At times management or union negotiators do not appear to behave in an economically rational manner, particularly when a power struggle between union and management arises in the early stages of a bargaining relationship. A company may be willing to endure a strike to demonstrate to the union that it will not be intimidated at the bargaining table. Although the company may lose business in the short run, it will set a precedent that may make the union reconsider strike threats at future negotiations. Thus, actions that may appear irrational from a short-term economic standpoint may be rational from a longer social or organizational standpoint. A prime example of this occurred in the summer of 1981, when President Reagan fired air traffic controllers who struck in violation of federal law. From an economic standpoint, these mass firings were probably not rational; air travel disruptions and concern for air safety led to criticism of the Reagan administration. Regardless of the mixed feelings that the actions of the president and the strikers may have evoked, the mass firings undoubtedly sent a message to all federal employees about the dangers of engaging in future illegal work stoppages.

The Element of Timing

Nearly all theories of the collective bargaining process recognize that union and management negotiators require time in order to reach a settlement. Behavioral theories and descriptive approaches also take into account the large amount of time that must be consumed in preparing for contract talks. It must also be recognized that collective bargaining is more than a series of talks that end once a contract settlement is reached. Unlike some bargaining situations, collective bargaining is an ongoing relationship that continues after the parties have reached an agreement. For this reason, negotiators are usually reluctant to maximize short-term economic gain by taking unfair advantage of an opponent. Although collective bargaining sometimes appears cutthroat, both union and management understand the dangers of pushing too hard and forcing an opponent to the brink of disaster. Such behavior may be detrimental to the union-management relationship in the long run and most astute bargainers are fearful of the proverbial "winning the battle and losing the war."[15]

Another important element that sets collective bargaining apart from some other types of negotiations is that most contract talks take place under time pressures. Deadlines imposed by contract expiration dates force union and management negotiating teams to reach an agreement within a stipulated period of time. Failure to settle before the deadline may lead to a work stoppage, so collective bargaining sessions often reach a frenzied pace prior to the deadline.

Communications Issues and Policies

Many economic bargaining models assume unbiased communications and perfect knowledge of the opponent's utilities and preferences, and most do not account for negotiating teams' attempts to bluff and deceive the other side. Neither bargaining team has a complete understanding of its opponent's preferences and sticking points. Because of the rapid exchange of information and abundance of talking in a bargaining session, the probability of misunderstandings among the negotiators is high.

During collective bargaining sessions, negotiators try to camouflage sticking points and gain tactical advantages through bluffing and deceptive behavior. Most negotiators, however, will stop short of outright dishonesty. A chief negotiator for management may claim that the firm's profits are low, but he or she is unlikely to provide erroneous financial data from an income statement. Lying or providing erroneous data may be construed as bad-faith bargaining, an unfair labor practice. The degree of familiarity and trust between union and management has an effect on bluffing. Parties who have been successfully negotiating agreements for years may employ few bluffs or threats; neither side is likely to succeed by glossing over

---

[15] The "winning the battle and losing the war" phenomenon was noted by Virgil B. Day, vice president, General Electric Company, in a speech at the January 1967 National Seminar of the Federal Mediation and Conciliation Service, in which Mr. Day noted succinctly: "It is of benefit to nobody to perform a hysterectomy on the goose that lays the golden eggs." Cited in William E. Simkin and Nicholas A. Fidandis, *Mediation and the Dynamics of Collective Bargaining*, 2nd ed., (Washington, D.C.: The Bureau of National Affairs, Inc., 1986), pp. 15–16.

the truth, and a trusting relationship obviates the need for such maneuvers. Hostile relations, on the other hand, may foster a tendency to issue strike threats or ultimatums.

Bargaining Tactics and Concessions

Nearly all models of the collective bargaining process depict negotiations between union and management as a series of proposals, concessions, and counterproposals. The parties often initiate contract talks by making offers or demands that they know the other side is unlikely to accept. For example, the union's chief negotiator may request a 20 percent wage increase—a demand that management probably views as ludicrous. Management may counter by offering no wage increase for employees under the new collective bargaining agreement. Both sides realize that they will have to compromise to reach a settlement. The rate at which the parties are willing to concede is a key concern in bargaining behavior. Giving in to the opponent's demands too soon may indicate weakness. Conceding too slowly, however, may lead to a failure to settle before the contract expiration deadline.

Another aspect of bargaining behavior is the use of threats. The ultimate threat is the economic strike or lockout. Other threats include expressing unwillingness to concede on a bargaining issue that is important to an opponent, adopting an unyielding attitude on certain bargaining topics, and threatening to create an impasse by withdrawing from negotiations. There are two keys to an effective threat. First, the threat must be believable. If bargaining opponents do not believe that an ultimatum has substance, they will not take it seriously. An idle threat may be worse than no threat because it erodes the credibility of the party who issues it. Second, the opponent being threatened must realize that the cost of disagreeing and ignoring the threat is greater than the cost of agreeing. Negotiating parties who are risk-averse may be more susceptible to threats than those who are risk-prone. Risk-averse negotiators want to reach a contract settlement while simultaneously minimizing danger to themselves and their respective constituencies. Management normally prefers to negotiate and reach a settlement without becoming subjected to burdensome labor costs and restrictive work rules. The union normally prefers to settle without a long work stoppage that results in lost wages, depletion of union strike funds, and lost job security for its members.

▲ A Model of Collective Bargaining Power

The concept of power is an important element in the collective bargaining process because it ultimately affects the contract settlement, the administration of the collective bargaining agreement, and the overall relationship between the union and management. A number of definitions of collective bargaining power have been set forth. Bacharach and Lawler discuss bargaining power in terms of one party's dependence on the other. If the union becomes more dependent on management, then management's bargaining power is increased.[16] Chamberlain and Kuhn define bargaining power as "the ability to secure agreement on one's own terms."[17] An early definition by John R. Commons describes bargaining power as "the proprietary ability to withhold products or production pending the negotiations for transfer of ownership of wealth."[18] A more basic definition, "the cost to A of imposing a loss upon B," was proposed by Slichter.[19] Although these definitions are intuitively appealing, they say little about what creates collective bargaining power, how power fluctuates over time, and how power is used. Figure 8–3 presents a model of collective bargaining power formulated by Leap and Grigsby.[20] The basic components of this model are discussed in order to provide an idea of how bargaining power is generated and used.

Sources of Bargaining Power

A major concern when discussing the collective bargaining power of a union or a company is the source of its power. Each party involved in collective negotiations can tap a number of power sources, as illustrated in Figure 8–3. Some sources of bargaining power are controllable during actual negotiations (that is, in the short term), others are only controllable during the long term, and some power sources are not controllable at all. It might be possible for management to increase its bargaining power in the short run by hiring an experienced and influential chief negotiator to lead contract talks. In the longer run, management may gain a power advantage by introducing technological changes that make the firm less dependent on unionized labor. The union also has various sources of power that it can tap in short- and long-run situations. Bargaining power is increased by both the number of power sources available to union and management and the amount of power that can be generated from each source. In addition, the more control a party has over a power source, the more power it will have available for use in collective bargaining. Suppose a company recently received a favorable ruling in an Internal Revenue Service (IRS) tax hearing and, as a result, has substantially bolstered its cash reserves. If the union does not learn about the company's fortunate turn of events, it may have lost an important source of bargaining power. Had the union known about the company's excess cash, it might have used this as a reason to ask for a higher wage demand. Of course, it could also be argued that the cash windfall

---

[16] Samuel B. Bacharach and Edward J. Lawler, *Bargaining Power, Tactics, and Outcomes* (San Francisco: Jossey-Bass, 1981), pp. 59–79.
[17] Neil W. Chamberlain and James W. Kuhn, *Collective Bargaining*, 2nd ed. (New York: McGraw-Hill Book Company, 1965), pp. 162–190.
[18] John R. Commons, *Institutional Economics: Its Place in Political Economy* (New York: Macmillan, 1934), p. 331.
[19] Sumner Slichter, "Impact of Social Security Legislation Upon Mobility and Enterprise," *American Economic Review*, Vol. 30, Supplement (1940), pp. 44–77.
[20] Terry L. Leap and David W. Grigsby, "A Conceptualization of Collective Bargaining Power," *Industrial and Labor Relations Review* (January 1986), pp. 202–213. Also see Paul S. Kirkbride and James W. Durcan, "Power and the Bargaining Process: A Comment on Leap and Grigsby," *Industrial and Labor Relations Review* (July 1988), pp. 618–621; and Terry L. Leap and David W. Grigsby, "Reply," *Industrial and Labor Relations Review* (July 1988), pp. 622–626.

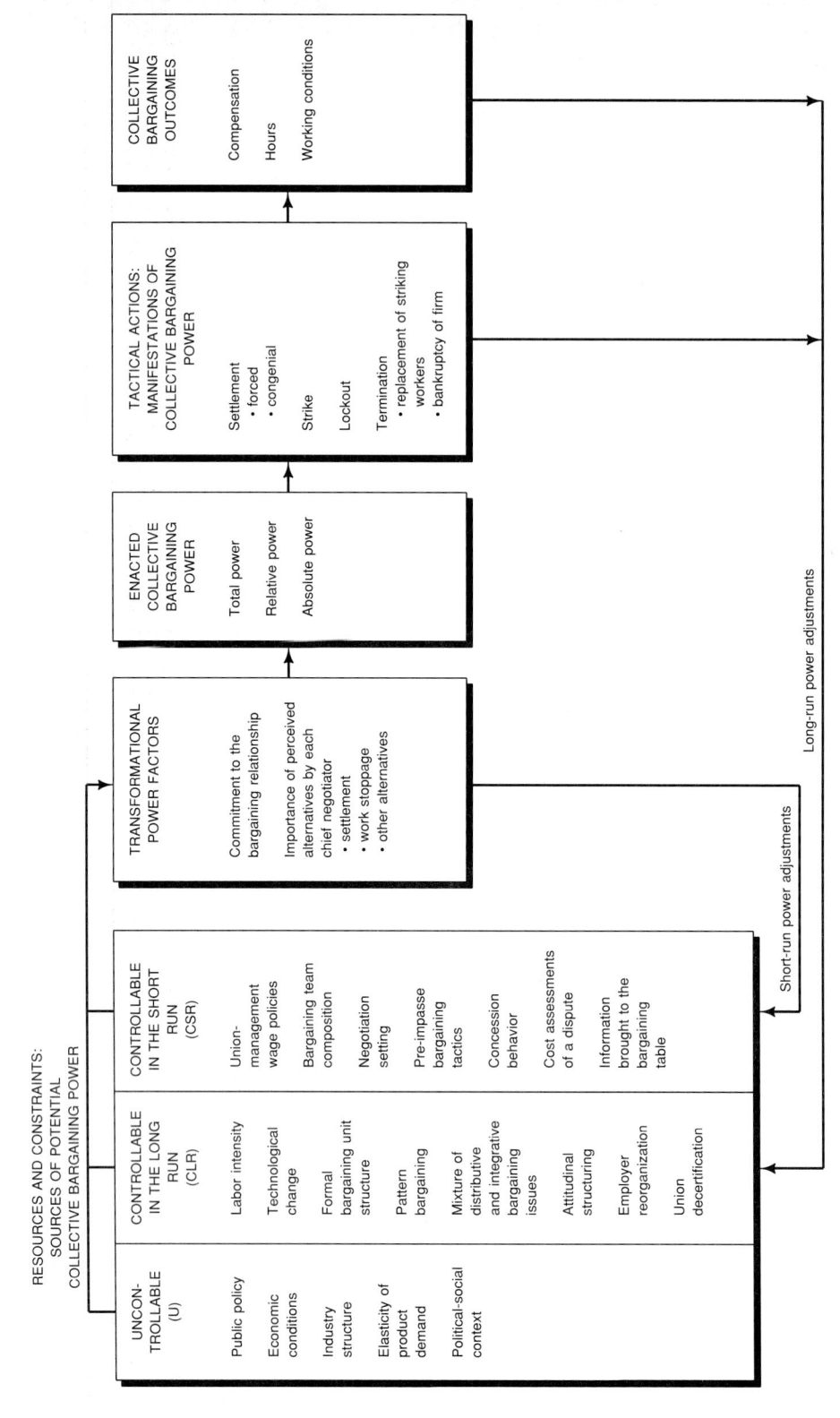

FIGURE 8–3 A Model of Collective Bargaining Power

increased the company's bargaining power because it could conceivably allow the firm to endure a lengthy strike by bargaining unit employees.

Although both unions and management possess potential bargaining power, there is no guarantee that they will take full advantage of it during contract negotiations. The bargaining power model outlined in Figure 8–3 makes the distinction between power that is available and power that is actually brought to bear on contract talks. *Enacted power* is the power that either union or management elects to use. It is regulated by two factors: (1) a party's commitment to the bargaining relationship, and (2) the number of settlement alternatives available to a party during negotiations. In summary, management's bargaining power is enhanced when it is represented by an experienced and skilled bargaining team, when the union has a stronger dependence on the bargaining relationship than management, and when the company is in a better position to endure a work stoppage than the union. If the union is superior in these respects, then labor may have the power advantage. The key to the bargaining power model is not how much power one side or the other possesses, but rather the amount of power that is used.

Factors that Dilute Bargaining Power

A number of factors diminish the bargaining power of labor and management. Some of the constraints on bargaining power are the result of intelligent actions by an opponent. In the aforementioned example of the company's favorable IRS ruling and financial windfall, union representatives who were preparing to bargain could have discovered the presence of the excess cash through careful probing at the bargaining table. This discovery would have diluted management's bargaining power while simultaneously enhancing the power of the union. Management may gradually attempt to reduce the union's bargaining power by opening new plants and facilities in rural areas of the South rather than in the more unionized Northeast and upper Midwest. In essence, many of the tactical actions taken by unions or management are efforts to decrease the bargaining power of the opponent while increasing their own power.

Not all constraints on collective bargaining power are the result of an opponent's actions. Constraints are also posed by market, economic, and legal forces. If section 8(a)(5) of the National Labor Relations Act did not require employers to bargain in good faith with labor organizations, then management would have an almost insurmountable power advantage over unions. When unemployment is low, the union has more bargaining power than when unemployment levels are high. The lack of suitable employment opportunities undoubtedly prompted a number of striking Eastern Airlines pilots to abandon their five-month-old strike in August of 1989 and return to work. During a ten-day span, 164 pilots returned to Eastern, bringing a total of 535 pilots back to work (out of a total of 3,500).[21] To the extent that pilots continued to defect (allowing Eastern to meet its projected flight schedules), the bargaining power of Eastern's management increased. These factors and

---

[21] Bridget O'Brian, "More Eastern Pilots Returning to Work As Strike Continues," *The Wall Street Journal* (August 9, 1989), p. A4.

others listed in Figure 8–3 have an effect on collective bargaining power that cannot be controlled by either side.

Relative, Absolute, and Total Bargaining Power

Figure 8–3 lists three types of enacted collective bargaining power: relative, absolute, and total power. Most discussions of bargaining power focus on *relative* power. Relative power is one party's dependence on the bargaining relationship as compared to that of the other party. Thus, relative bargaining power is inversely related to a party's dependence on achieving a satisfactory contract settlement. If management is less dependent on a satisfactory contract settlement than the union, then management has greater relative bargaining power. The party using the most relative power could be expected to secure the most favorable settlement at the bargaining table. Multi-employer bargaining structures are a prime example of how companies with little individual bargaining power attempt to equalize relative power between labor and management.

Absolute bargaining power is defined as the power of an individual party irrespective of the other party's power. Many corporations possess significant amounts of absolute power because of their large product markets and assets in the billion dollar range. Companies with large amounts of absolute power may pose a serious threat to the national well-being if they become involved in a major work stoppage. This problem was recognized by Congress when the National Emergencies section of the Taft-Hartley Act was passed. If the president of the United States believes that a strike will affect a substantial part of an industry that is vital to the well-being of the nation, then an 80-day injunction can be used to delay the work stoppage. The 80-day injunction allows a presidential-appointed board of inquiry to investigate the labor dispute and make recommendations for its resolution.

Total bargaining power is the sum of the parties' dependence on each other. Union and management bargaining teams with high levels of total bargaining power may be reluctant to engage in a work stoppage because of the potential damage that each side may inflict on the other. Parties with low total bargaining power may be more likely to engage in a work stoppage because neither side is in a position to damage the opponent severely. In essence, total bargaining power is diametrically opposed to relative bargaining power.

Problems with the Bargaining Power Concept

Power is clearly important to collective bargaining outcomes. However, collective bargaining power is an elusive concept. Bargaining power must originate from a source, yet it is often difficult to pinpoint where collective bargaining power comes from, as well as the amount that is available at a particular time. Enacted collective bargaining power is the amount of power that is actually used by a bargaining team and it is less than potential power. Yet, little is known about how negotiators interpret and use power sources. Although more research is needed to understand collective bargaining power better, it is safe to conclude that much of what union and management negotiators do before and during negotiations is an attempt to manipulate relative power.

▲ Collective Bargaining Tactics and Outcomes

Negotiators use bargaining tactics to gain concessions from their opponents. They employ tactics such as threatening, bluffing, and misleading the other party about bargaining priorities during negotiations. Talks at the bargaining table may result in agreeing to a contract settlement, engaging in a strike or lockout, or terminating the bargaining relationship. All of these tactics ultimately effect the compensation, hours, and working conditions contained in the collective bargaining agreement.

Reaching a Settlement

Most, but not all, collective negotiations end in a settlement. Three important questions arise with regard to settlements. First, will a settlement occur? As noted earlier in this text, about two-thirds of all legally certified bargaining relationships are consummated with a collective bargaining agreement between the company and the union. Accordingly, one-third of the certification elections won by unions do not result in a written agreement.[22] In some instances, bad faith bargaining charges may be brought against either the employer or the union. However, there are numerous other cases in which neither side is guilty of an unfair labor practice, yet an agreement is not reached.

Second, when will a settlement occur? An agreement may be reached in a reasonable amount of time, or one may be reached only after a prolonged work stoppage, extensive legal action, or violence. Bethlehem and National Steel settled early during their 1989 negotiations with the United Steelworkers in order to avoid losing customers in the highly competitive steel industry.[23] At the other extreme, J.P. Stevens subdued the textile workers union (now known as the Amalgamated Clothing and Textile Workers International Union) for nearly a quarter of a century before signing a collective bargaining agreement in 1980.[24] In order to maintain the health of his firm, Pittston Company CEO, Paul W. Douglas, vowed to strike indefinitely with the United Mine Workers (UMW) over reduced health benefits, changes in work rules, and an end to Pittston's contributions to a multi-employer

---

[22] Thomas Reed, "Union Attainment of First Contracts: Do 'Progressive' Unions Possess a Competitive Advantage?," *Proceedings*, Southwest Division, Academy of Management (Denton, Texas: Southwest Division, Academy of Management, 1989), pp. 324–328.
[23] Clare Ansberry, "Inland Steel Stands Fast in Union Talks, Demanding Concessions From Workers," *The Wall Street Journal* (June 15, 1989), p. C17.
[24] George Ruben, "J. P. Stevens Settlement Provides for Job Security," *Monthly Labor Review* (August 1985), p. 50.

pension fund. Pittston and the UMW reached a settlement in January of 1990.[25] Greyhound Lines' chief labor negotiator, P. Anthony Lannie, refused to resume negotiations with the Amalgamated Transit Union until violence directed at Greyhound buses and facilities ceased. Mr. Lannie issued the ultimatum after two Greyhound buses had been hit by sniper fire and a bomb threat was phoned into the company's Chicago terminal.[26]

Admittedly, these cases are unique. However, there have been a number of instances in which union and management battled through strikes, negotiation delays, and National Labor Relations Board hearings before reaching a settlement. During this time, employees were forced to seek work elsewhere and, in some cases, employers have closed plants or relocated their operations.

Third, what conditions will exist once a settlement is reached? A settlement may represent a satisfactory contract that was negotiated through a process of mutual understanding and give-and-take at the bargaining table. If this is the case, both union and management may believe that the settlement is "fair" and they may have harmonious labor relations throughout the life of the collective bargaining agreement. However, if one party possesses superior relative bargaining power and is able to impose its will on the other, then a settlement may be "forced." The stronger party can force the weaker party to accept a contract that differs significantly from what the weaker believes is equitable. Suppose that management is able to use strong-arm bargaining tactics on a union because high local unemployment rates make it easy to replace striking workers. The union may be forced to accept little or no wage and benefit increases. Forced settlements may pose future labor relations problems once a relative bargaining power advantage is lost, since union negotiators may harbor a desire for revenge because of earlier incidents of harsh or unfair treatment.

Work Stoppages: Strikes and Lockouts

Although strikes and lockouts are discussed in Chapter 10, the brief discussion here focuses on their use as a bargaining tactic. Strikes and lockouts are used to exert pressure on an opponent to modify bargaining demands or make bargaining concessions. Perhaps the most effective use of a strike or lockout is as a *threat* rather than as an actual work stoppage. Labor and management negotiators are cognizant of the need to complete contract talks prior to the contract deadline; to do otherwise is to encourage a strike or lockout.

---

[25] See The Bureau of National Affairs, Inc., "UMW Strike at Pittston," *Collective Bargaining Negotiations & Contracts* (Washington, D.C.: The Bureau of National Affairs, Inc., April 20, 1989), p. 1; The Bureau of National Affairs, Inc., "Continuing Turmoil at Pittston Co.," *Collective Bargaining Negotiations & Contracts* (Washington, D.C.: The Bureau of National Affairs, Inc., June 15, 1989), p. 1; The Bureau of National Affairs, Inc., "Resumed UMW-Pittston Talks," *Collective Bargaining Negotiations & Contracts* (Washington, D.C.: The Bureau of National Affairs, Inc., July 27, 1989), p. 1; The Bureau of National Affairs, Inc., "Pittston-UMW Negotiations Resumption," *Collective Bargaining Negotiations & Contracts* (Washington, D.C.: The Bureau of National Affairs, Inc., November 16, 1989), p. 1; The Bureau of National Affairs, Inc., "Pittston-UMW Settlement," *Collective Bargaining Negotiations & Contracts* (Washington, D.C.: The Bureau of National Affairs, Inc., January 11, 1990), p. 1.

[26] "Greyhound Lines Refuses To Bargain After Violence," *The Wall Street Journal* (March 2, 1990), p. A8.

The entire complexion of the collective bargaining process would change if the threat of a work stoppage were eliminated. If unions were deprived of the right to engage in economic strikes, incentives to engage in good-faith bargaining by management would be curtailed and the relative bargaining power of labor would be drastically diminished. The lack of a work stoppage threat has posed some interesting problems for federal and state government employees who either have no right to strike or have a very limited right to engage in work stoppages. However, alternative impasse resolution procedures are available to public-sector labor and management negotiators. These procedures restore some of the incentive to engage in good-faith bargaining. Public-sector impasse resolution procedures are discussed in Chapter 17.

Dissolution of the Bargaining Relationship

From the union's standpoint, the worst scenario is a dissolution of the bargaining relationship. A dissolution is most often the result of a prolonged work stoppage. An employer may continue operations during an economic strike by subcontracting work to other firms, substituting machines for workers on some jobs, and replacing striking workers with nonunion employees. Management may be able to sustain operations indefinitely by employing these tactics. Under such circumstances, the employer is under no obligation to re-employ striking workers as long as company negotiators have engaged in good-faith bargaining and have not committed other unfair labor practices. A 1983 U.S. Supreme Court decision has provided additional protection for workers employed as strike replacements. The high court ruled that an employer is not privileged to discharge strike replacements if it has promised them permanent employment.[27] Traditionally, employees serving as strike replacements lose their jobs once the strike is ended, but this decision gives them some employment rights. Eventually the replacement employees may petition for a decertification election in order to eliminate the union's influence.

Bankruptcy of the employer or elimination of a unionized plant or department may also dissolve the bargaining relationship.[28] A collective bargaining contract may be invalidated by a bankruptcy judge under the amended U.S. Bankruptcy Code.[29] Controversy has also arisen regarding an employer's right to close or relocate a unionized operation. It now appears that an employer has some right to relocate an operation without obtaining approval from the union.[30] If the National Labor Relations Board and courts allow employers to move or eliminate unionized

---

[27] See *Belknap Inc. v. Hale*, 463 U.S. 591 (1983).
[28] In *NLRB v. Bildisco and Bildisco*, 465 U.S. 513 (1984), the U.S. Supreme Court held that an employer could abrogate a labor agreement immediately upon filing for bankruptcy under Chapter 11. See Benjamin J. Taylor and Fred Witney, *Labor Relations Law*, 5th ed. (Englewood Cliffs, New Jersey: Prentice-Hall, Inc., 1987), p. 270; William A. Wines, "An Overview of the 1984 Bankruptcy Amendments: Some Modest Protections for Labor Agreements," *Labor Law Journal* (December 1985), pp. 911–918; and Mark S. Pulliam, "The Collision of Labor and Bankruptcy Law: *Bildisco* and the Legislative Response," *Labor Law Journal* (July 1985), pp. 390–401.
[29] BNA Editorial Staff, *Labor Relations Yearbook—1984* (Washington D.C.: The Bureau of National Affairs, Inc., 1985), pp. 100–106.
[30] Antone Aboud, ed., *Plant Closing Legislation* (Ithaca, New York.: ILR Press, Cornell University, 1984).

operations that have higher labor costs and restrictive work rules, then the employer's relative bargaining power is increased.

Assessing the Outcome of Collective Bargaining

Because of the high stakes associated with the collective bargaining process, assessing the outcomes of the bargaining process becomes important. However, examining bargaining outcomes after the fact is a subjective process. Furthermore, most bargaining theories do not have a mechanism for assessing the outcomes of negotiations. A number of bargaining outcomes from the point of view of management have been analyzed. These include management's ability to achieve bargaining goals, adjust to technological changes, maintain worker productivity, endure a strike, and avoid legalistic maneuvering.[31] The union would presumably desire to achieve bargaining outcomes that would increase its relative bargaining power, enhance the image of its leadership, and satisfy union members.

Satisfaction (or a lack of satisfaction) with negotiation outcomes is likely to vary between rounds of negotiations as well as over the duration of the collective bargaining agreement. Upon reaching a settlement, both the union and management may be satisfied with the outcome (or one side may be satisfied and the other side dissatisfied). At issue is whether the dissatisfied party will voice concern over the bargaining outcomes or remain silent. To express disappointment over the terms and conditions of the collective bargaining agreement may be tantamount to admitting that the opponent secured an advantage at the bargaining table. The union or management is more likely to be initially satisfied with the newly negotiated agreement and later express disenchantment after it has had the opportunity to deal with the agreement on a daily basis. Thus, the dissatisfied party can use its discontent with the current collective bargaining agreement to prepare for the next round of contract talks.

▲ Summary and Conclusions

This chapter presents a theoretical overview of the bargaining process. It serves as a foundation for Chapters 9 and 10. A number of bargaining theories exist, some are very simple and straightforward, and others are complex and attempt to examine a large number of variables that affect the bargaining process. However, most conceptualizations of the collective bargaining process have several elements in common. These include settlement points or ranges, assessments of costs associated with agreeing or disagreeing with an opponent, rationality assumptions, timing elements, communications assumptions, and the use of bargaining tactics and concessions.

The concept of power is central to the bargaining process. In this chapter, a model of collective bargaining power is presented and discussed. Sources of bar-

---

[31] See Thomas A. Kochan and Harry C. Katz, *Collective Bargaining and Industrial Relations* (Homewood, Illinois: Richard D. Irwin, Inc., 1988), pp. 215–230.

gaining power are outlined along with factors that can increase or dilute bargaining power. Distinctions between absolute, relative, and total bargaining power are also noted. Power by itself is an abstract concept unless it is used to gain advantages during negotiations. Thus, tactics that are commonly employed as part of collective bargaining are briefly examined. Tactics such as settlements, work stoppages, and dissolution of the bargaining relationship are considered here and are discussed more fully in subsequent chapters.

Now that a theoretical base has been established, Chapters 9 and 10 focus on how union and management deal with collective bargaining and labor disputes. Chapter 9 illustrates how both sides make extensive preparations to negotiate. In addition, the legal requirements associated with collective bargaining are discussed, along with the tactics that are used at the bargaining table. Chapter 10 deals with negotiation impasses and labor disputes. The causes and consequences of labor-management conflict are discussed, along with strikes and the use of labor mediation. Several major labor disputes are also discussed and analyzed.

▲ Discussion Questions and Exercises

1. How would Walton and McKersie's behavioral theory of negotiations explain the 1989 labor turmoil at Eastern Airlines? Discuss.
2. Examine a collective bargaining agreement. Select two provisions that represent distributive bargaining topics and two that represent integrative topics.
3. Are collective bargaining negotiations as rational as most bargaining theories would lead us to believe? Discuss.
4. Obtain information on the Pittston Coal-United Mine Workers strike. Based on the model set forth in Figure 8–3, what bargaining power factors are especially important to the company? What factors are critical to the UMW?
5. Research a recent contract settlement using a local newspaper, *The Wall Street Journal*, *Business Week*, or other publication. What criteria would you use to evaluate the outcome of the contract negotiations? Discuss.

9 The Collective Bargaining Process: Preparation, Tactics, and Issues

- **Introduction**
- **Stages of the Bargaining Process**
- **Preparation for Collective Bargaining**
  Beginning Preparations
  Selecting a Bargaining Team and Chief Negotiator
  Reviewing Previous Negotiations
  Examining the Current Contract with an Eye Toward Change
  Gathering Data on the Firm and the Industry
  Economic Data Relevant to Collective Bargaining
  Input From Employees and Supervisors
  Formulating Proposals, Priorities, and Bottom-Line Positions
  Selecting the Bargaining Site
  Organizing the Plethora of Bargaining Information
- **The Legal Requirements for Collective Bargaining**
  Notification of Intent to Bargain
  The Concept of Good-Faith Bargaining
    Totality of Conduct by the Parties
    The Employer's Duty to Furnish Information
    Surface Bargaining and Dilatory Tactics
    Concessions, Proposals, and Demands in Bad-Faith Bargaining
    Mandatory, Permissive, and Illegal Bargaining Subjects
    Reaching an Impasse
- **Strategies and Tactics at the Bargaining Table**
  The Initial Proposal Stage
  The Primary Bargaining Stage
    Conduct at the Bargaining Table
    Making Proposals and Counterproposals

The Use of Caucuses
Making Cost Estimates on Proposals
Drafting Contract Language
The Eleventh-Hour Bargaining Stage
Moving Toward a Settlement
Identifying the Need for a Mediator
Implementing a Strike Plan
Post-Settlement Issues
▲ **Summary and Conclusions**
▲ **Discussion Questions and Exercises**

▲ Introduction

Negotiations between labor and management are the most prominent and publicized aspects of collective bargaining. Representatives from both sides meet at the bargaining table to negotiate the terms and provisions of a labor contract that can affect the worklife and economic well-being of hundreds and even thousands of workers. The atmosphere at the bargaining table is usually serious and sometimes tense, especially when large numbers of employees are affected by negotiations or a work stoppage is threatened. Most negotiators are professionals who maintain decorum during contract talks, but occasionally negotiations become heated. Management negotiators know that a mistake at the bargaining table may cost their company millions of dollars in operating and labor costs. Union negotiators realize that the contract settlement not only affects the worklives of bargaining unit employees, but it can also set an important precedent with regard to the union's effectiveness in future negotiations. Negotiators on both sides of the bargaining table understand that the final contract settlement is a reflection of their bargaining skills. The professional reputations of negotiators, corporate industrial relations directors, and union officers can be immeasurably enhanced or irreparably damaged, based on their performance during contract talks. Both union and management negotiators risk large sums of money and power when they sit down at the bargaining table; therefore, it is not surprising that contract talks involve extensive preparations, ingenious tactics, and occasional emotional outbursts.

This chapter provides a practical view of contract negotiations. Special emphasis is placed on preparations for negotiations as well as on the strategies and tactics employed at the bargaining table. An examination of the stages of bargaining provides a point of departure. Because of its crucial importance to the success of collective bargaining, a detailed discussion of bargaining preparations comprises the chapter's first major section. Following this, an analysis of the legal requirements of good-faith bargaining is presented. The third major section of the chapter discusses the strategies and tactics commonly used by unions and management in each stage of negotiations.

▲ Stages of the Bargaining Process

The process of contract negotiations between labor and management can be divided into four stages: (1) preparations for negotiation, (2) the initial proposals, (3) primary bargaining, and (4) "eleventh-hour" bargaining. The preparation stage occurs before the parties meet for formal negotiations. It is often the most time-consuming and important part of collective bargaining; however, bargaining preparations usually are not conducted under pressure because the contract deadlines and potential work stoppages are not yet of major concern to the negotiators. When the collective bargaining agreement is voluminous, complex, and covers a large number of employees, preparation may take a year or more to complete. Likewise, when difficult contract talks are anticipated, bargaining preparations may be quite extensive. Less complex and controversial bargaining situations may require only a few weeks of preparation.

Once the parties meet at the bargaining table to formally open contract talks, the pressure and excitement begin to build. Union and management negotiators exchange initial demands and proposals on the terms and the provisions of the prospective collective bargaining agreement. It is difficult to describe a typical sequence of events once the parties meet. In some instances, the union and management bargaining teams start slowly and cautiously in an attempt to probe the position of the other side. In other situations, the union presents its demands, management then remarks on the ridiculous nature of the union's requests, and negotiations start with "both barrels blazing." Depending on the complexity of the collective bargaining agreement, negotiations normally span a period of several months. The parties do not necessarily meet every day during this period, nor do the meetings always turn into marathon sessions. As the contract deadline nears, however, the negotiating sessions are likely to increase both in frequency and duration. As the target date approaches, negotiations may turn into all-night, pressure-packed sessions as both sides attempt to reach a settlement and avoid a strike or lockout.

Figure 9–1 summarizes the various bargaining stages. As noted earlier, collective bargaining starts with the preparation stage and proceeds through the initial demands, primary bargaining, and eleventh-hour bargaining stages. If the parties reach an impasse, a mediator may be called in to help union and management negotiators regain their bargaining momentum and avoid a work stoppage. Most union and management bargaining teams reach an agreement before the contract deadline. If the parties are unable to reach an agreement, then the union may call a strike or the employer may engage in a lockout. The parties also may decide to forsake a work stoppage and continue negotiations, especially when a settlement is near and a work stoppage would serve no useful purpose. Once the collective bargaining agreement is negotiated and approved by union members, the terms of the new contract are often retroactive to the expiration date of the original contract.

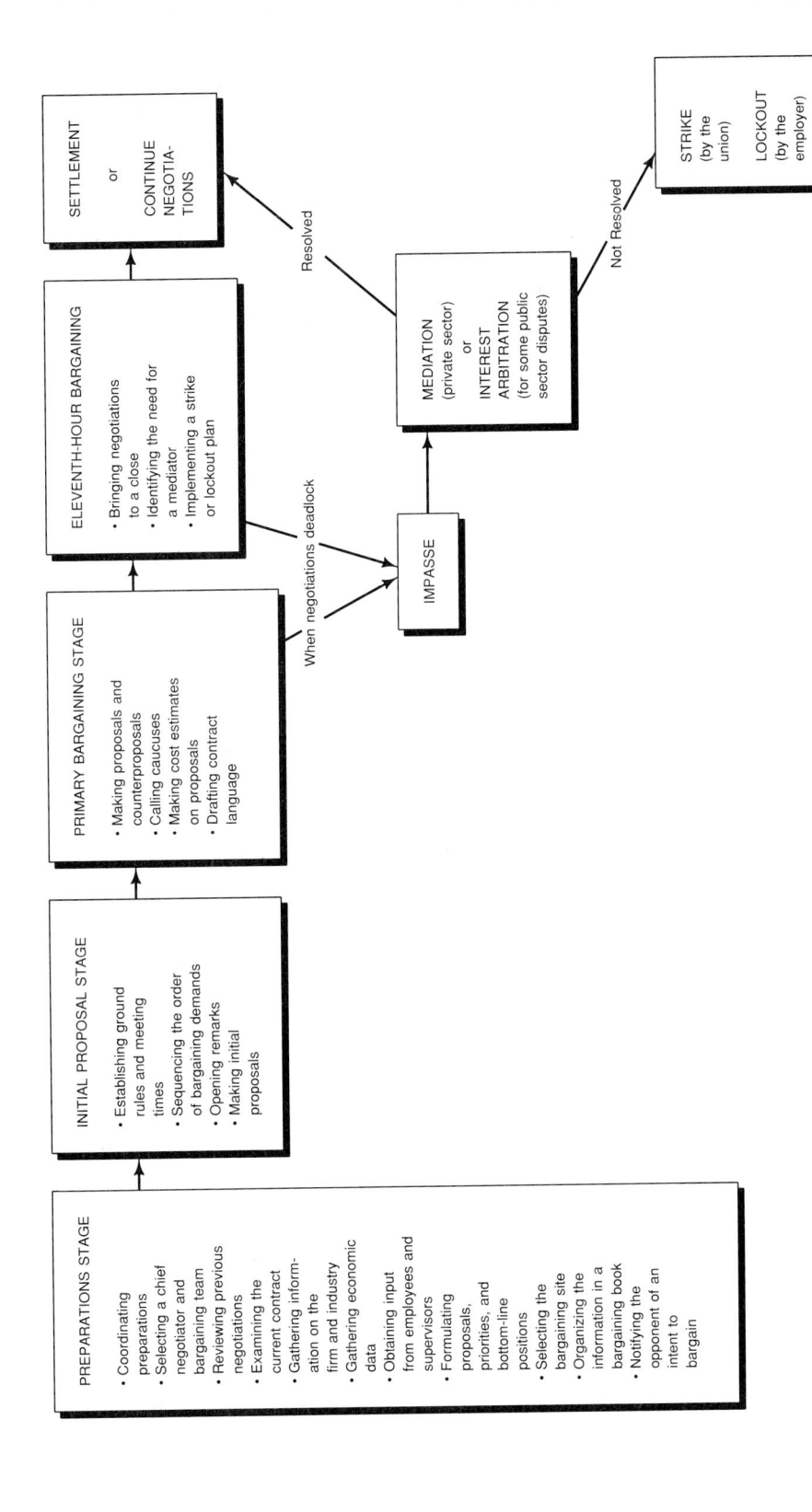

FIGURE 9–1 Stages of the Collective Bargaining Process

▲ Preparation for Collective Bargaining

Perhaps the most critical stage of the collective bargaining process is the groundwork that is established prior to the actual negotiations. As veteran negotiator Fritz Ihrig has stated:

> My own view is that 90 percent of what is accomplished in the negotiations process occurs behind the scenes. A good part of this is simply preparation—doing your homework.[1]

Experience at the bargaining table can be an important asset for a negotiator, but there is no substitute for careful and thorough preparation. There are three fundamental reasons for bargaining preparation:

1. Preparation enables each bargaining team to *determine its bargaining objectives* and the limits to which it is willing to concede before enduring a strike or lockout. Bargaining demands can be carefully formulated and ranked in order of importance to the union and management.
2. Preparation enables a negotiating team to *substantiate and defend its proposals*. By collecting and organizing information germane to collective bargaining, negotiators can quickly refer to economic, industrial, and financial information that has an important bearing on the contract provision under discussion.
3. Preparation enables a negotiating team to *anticipate the demands of an opponent*. In a fashion similar to a football coach scouting an upcoming foe in order to detect its strengths, weaknesses, and tendencies, extensive preparation by a negotiating team will minimize surprises at the bargaining table.

In a sense, pre-negotiation preparations represent an attempt by unions and management to increase their relative bargaining power. When both sides extensively prepare for upcoming negotiations, it is possible that they will adopt a more realistic outlook on contract negotiations and reduce the possibility of a strike or lockout. If one side is well-prepared and the other is not, then a mismatch with unsavory repercussions may occur.

Beginning Preparations

Pre-negotiations preparation can be a time-consuming process that requires coordinating large amounts of information. Often the job of collecting data and information associated with the collective bargaining process is the responsibility of a number of people. Therefore, two important points should be considered. First, bargaining preparations must be coordinated. Management is most likely to give this responsibility to the personnel or industrial relations director at the plant, division, or corporate level. The union coordinates preparations through its local, regional, or international leadership. Often the chief negotiator for each side coordinates bargaining preparations. One important coordinating activity is to estab-

---

[1] Fritz Ihrig (Interview), "Labor Contract Negotiations: Behind the Scenes," *Personnel Administrator* (April 1986), p. 55.

lish committees to draft proposals for various parts of the collective bargaining agreement. For example, there may be a committee responsible for the wage and salary structure, a committee for employee benefits, a committee for work rules and security provisions, and a committee for safety and health. Preparing time tables containing schedules of committee meetings and deadlines for completing assigned tasks is another important aspect of coordination. The person responsible for coordinating pre-negotiation preparations must also ensure that duplication of effort among the various committees is minimized and, perhaps most importantly, that an important bargaining subject is not allowed to fall between the cracks. For instance, the wage and salary committee may assume that the benefits committee is in charge of researching the provisions of a new overtime pay schedule. Meanwhile, the benefits committee mistakenly believes that the wage and salary committee is performing this task. A blunder of this type may force negotiators to make last-minute and hurried preparations that could hurt the effectiveness of their bargaining.

A second important aspect of preparations is deciding when to start. Some negotiators claim that pre-negotiations preparations begin anew as soon as a collective bargaining agreement has been negotiated. Thus, if a collective bargaining agreement spanning three years is negotiated and goes into effect on May 15, 1991, negotiators adhering to this school of thought would begin pre-negotiation preparations for the 1994 negotiations sometime in late May of 1991. Although it is probably better to err on the side of starting too early, much of the economic and industrial information needed for the 1994 negotiations is not yet available. It is imperative to allow as much time as possible for the preparation stage. A year or more may be needed for complex or troublesome negotiations, whereas a few months may suffice for simple contracts covering local conditions.

Selecting a Bargaining Team and Chief Negotiator

A critical concern in collective bargaining is the size and composition of the negotiating team. The bargaining team is ultimately responsible for making proposals and counterproposals to the opposing bargaining team; it has the power to approve a tentative contract settlement. Members of the negotiating team must be able to draft proposals, analyze the short- and long-term implications of counterproposals made by the opponent, present cogent arguments during contract talks, and obtain a settlement without unduly compromising the interests of their constituents. Individual qualifications for bargaining team membership include a knowledge of labor-management relations, an intimate familiarity with the contract, and an understanding of economic and industry conditions affecting the negotiations. Personal requisites for a negotiator would include intelligence, an ability to speak clearly and concisely, an even temperament, patience, and physical stamina. Each negotiator must be carefully selected in order to form a team that functions as a unit rather than in a disjointed, individualized fashion. Bargaining team members should know what each is thinking and trying to accomplish; members should understand their respective roles, when they should speak, and when they should listen and remain silent. Normally, the chief negotiator is responsible for molding the individual negotiators into an effective bargaining team.

The optimal number of members needed to negotiate a contract successfully is a prime consideration in assembling a bargaining team. Simply stated, negotiating teams should be neither too large nor too small. In the simplest bargaining situation, one union representative and one management representative negotiate an entire collective bargaining agreement. An arrangement such as this may be acceptable when the contract is not complex and covers a small number of employees in a single location. Many collective bargaining agreements, however, are lengthy, complex documents covering a large number of employees at multiple sites, so most bargaining teams have several negotiators. If a bargaining team has too many negotiators, then pre-negotiations conferences and contract talks may become long-winded and cumbersome. Some bargaining teams become too large because union and management officials consider it a status symbol to be included in the negotiations. Large bargaining teams also create an opportunity for leakages of confidential and sensitive information from contract talks or from meetings that precede contract talks. Bargaining teams that have too few negotiators may place an unreasonable burden on each negotiator and small bargaining teams may lack the expertise to deal intelligently with the multitude of provisions found in complex labor contracts. An experienced management negotiator suggests using the following types of bargaining team members:[2]

1. An *operating specialist* who understands the production methods, equipment, and working conditions in a plant or facility is an important bargaining team member. Management may use a plant superintendent or departmental supervisor who has extensive work experience in a plant, whereas the union may select a senior shop steward to perform this role.
2. Most chief negotiators need to have a *cost specialist* on hand to assist in the preparation and evaluation of wage and employee benefit proposals. The team member may be a cost accountant, industrial engineer, or other expert with access to economic and financial information. In addition to making cost projections, this person must be able to illustrate the effect that cost increases will have on the firm's financial picture. Cost specialists play an especially prominent role on management negotiating teams.
3. At least one member of the bargaining team should be designated as a *note taker*. It is important that accurate records be kept on proposals, counterproposals, and what was agreed upon during negotiations. Union and management negotiators may need to refer to the details of a conversation that took place earlier in the bargaining session. By writing down or outlining agreements on contract provisions, union and management negotiators are less likely to have misunderstandings later. Finally, a written account of contract talks may be

---

[2] Charles S. Loughran, *Negotiating a Labor Contract: A Management Handbook* (Washington, D.C.: The Bureau of National Affairs, Inc., 1984), pp. 55–58. This book provides an excellent, extensive, and practical discussion of bargaining preparations, tactics, and issues. Although written for management negotiators, its superb insights and suggestions make it an ideal sourcebook for all negotiators.

useful later if a grievance or arbitration case arises. Arbitrators often consider the intent of negotiators in deciding how to rule on a grievance.[3]

4. A bargaining team should either include a *language draftsperson* or have one readily available for consultation. Contract language may be drafted before presenting a demand at the bargaining table. Once a tentative agreement has been reached on a contract provision, then union and management negotiators must carefully draft its wording in order to capture the intent of the negotiators and avoid ambiguities that could later cause problems. The draftsperson is often a labor lawyer, but this qualification is not as important as obtaining someone who is experienced in drafting contract language. Before the provision is put in its final form, it should be reviewed by other members of the union and management negotiating teams and by the supervisors and union stewards who will interpret the contract on a daily basis.

Regardless of the size of the negotiating team, all members should understand their respective roles at the bargaining table. Some bargaining team members do little talking and are primarily responsible for making cost estimates and supplying necessary information as needed to the chief negotiator. Other members may lead contract talks that involve provisions in their areas of expertise. Some bargaining team members may be used for tactical purposes. For example, a hard-nosed, disagreeable negotiator may be allowed to take center stage during part of the negotiations. After dealing with this difficult individual for several hours, the other side may be relieved when a more cordial and reasonable negotiator takes over. This ploy is known as the "good guy-bad guy" tactic. The demands of the "good guy" appear reasonable and are accepted by the other side; the party using this tactic often achieves exactly what it had originally wanted.

The personalities of negotiators also warrant close attention as the bargaining team is being selected. Some potential negotiators have the intelligence, knowledge, and experience to be effective bargaining team members, but they may lack the patience, temperament, and attitude to be effective. Two labor relations professionals with considerable mediation and arbitration experience believe that negotiator personalities fall into three categories: (1) stabilizers, (2) destabilizers, and (3) quasi-mediators.[4] *Stabilizers* are individuals who strongly desire to reach an agreement, sometimes at any cost. A sales manager who is part of a negotiating team may be a stabilizer because of fears that sales opportunities will be lost if a strike occurs. *Destabilizers*, on the other hand, often have little patience for collective bargaining; they may view the other side with contempt and regard a work stoppage as a means of destroying an opponent. A corporate controller who believes that labor's demands are exorbitant may want to engage in a long strike in order

---

[3] Charles S. Loughran, *Negotiating a Labor Contract: A Management Handbook* (Washington, D.C.: The Bureau of National Affairs, Inc., 1984), pp. 56–57. It may be prudent to avoid using stenographers or tape recorders during negotiations because of the inhibiting effect that they have on negotiations. The NLRB has held that a party does not have to bargain if the other party is using a stenographer or tape recorder. See *Morton-Norwich Products*, 94 LRRM 1696 (1977).

[4] Thomas R. Colosi and Arthur Eliot Berkeley, *Collective Bargaining: How It Works and Why* (New York: American Arbitration Association, 1986), pp. 57–59.

to bring the union to its knees. The middle ground is occupied by *quasi-mediators,* who want a settlement that is reasonable and workable, yet they will neither sell out to nor try to ruin the opposition. Thus a negotiating team that is influenced by stabilizers may prematurely settle on an unacceptable contract. Stabilizers on a management bargaining team may accept a contract that is a financial and managerial disaster, whereas stabilizers on a union negotiating team may agree to a contract that is subsequently rejected by the rank-and-file. On the other hand, bargaining teams influenced by destabilizers are likely to drive negotiations into an unnecessary impasse, strike, or lockout.

Arguments have been made against having the highest-ranking union or management official present at the bargaining table. Corporate chief executive officers and union presidents may be very effective in bargaining sessions; however, the principal of "unseen authority" can be used to the advantage of both union and management negotiators.[5] This strategy allows a chief negotiator to consult with a higher authority before agreeing to a contract provision. By so doing, a chief negotiator can buy additional time to contemplate a proposal or counterproposal. It also allows the chief negotiator to save face and avoid excessive debate over an unwanted contract term by simply stating that the corporate chief executive officer (or the union members, in the case of labor's chief negotiator) "won't buy" the proposal. The unseen-authority ploy can result in a bad-faith bargaining charge, however, because continued insistence on having every proposal and counterproposal approved by an official who is not present at negotiations may be regarded as an unreasonable delaying tactic by the National Labor Relations Board.

Although labor and management negotiators may differ in terms of their personality and tactics, the one ingredient that is vital to all negotiators is integrity. Because of the long-term nature of the union-management relationship, integrity before, during, and after negotiations is of paramount concern. According to one experienced negotiator:

> You can make a quick deal with a lie, a breach of confidence or a broken promise, but over the long haul, both you and the organization you represent will lose credibility, and probably much more. You don't have to like the person on the other side and they don't have to like you, but everyone has to recognize that when you make a deal you stand behind it—and when you agree to something *away* from the table, you agree to it when you *sit down* at the table. To be successful, whether it's in negotiations or in anything else dealing with people, you have to live by your words. You have to have integrity. (Emphasis in the original)[6]

Many of the general criteria used in selecting bargaining team members also apply to the selection of a chief negotiator. Chief negotiators are chosen because of their expertise in labor relations and their experience at the bargaining table. Union chief negotiators are often employed by the international union and are

---

[5] Charles S. Loughran, *Negotiating a Labor Contract: A Management Handbook* (Washington, D.C.: The Bureau of National Affairs., Inc., 1984), pp. 53–54.
[6] Fritz Ihrig (Interview), "Labor Contract Negotiations: Behind the Scenes," *Personnel Administrator* (April 1986), p. 57.

veterans of numerous contract talks. In fact, they may negotiate a contract at one location and then move elsewhere to another round of contract talks with a different employer. Management chief negotiators come from the ranks of the personnel and industrial relations staff or they may be temporarily hired from outside the company to serve as the spokesperson for management.

Whether management uses an in-house staff member or hires a chief negotiator from the outside depends primarily on the level of expertise that management needs at the bargaining table. Union negotiators often bargain more frequently than management chief negotiators. If management hires an experienced negotiator from the outside, then the union negotiator is less likely to have an edge. Chief negotiators hired from the outside may be more familiar with broad bargaining concerns such as economic and industrial conditions, recent compensation trends, and other contract settlements within an industry or region. However, an outsider is not as familiar with the day-to-day operations of the company as would be a chief negotiator who comes from inside the firm. Obtaining the services of an outside chief negotiator can also be expensive, but this expense pales in comparison to the costs associated with reaching an unacceptable settlement. Thus management may want to consider employing an outside chief negotiator when: (1) there is no suitable experienced person available from within the organization, (2) the collective bargaining agreement is complex and covers a large number of employees, (3) the negotiations are likely to be complicated and difficult, and (4) the parties are negotiating a contract for the first time.

Reviewing Previous Negotiations

Preparation for collective bargaining entails gathering a plethora of information related to wages, hours, and working conditions. A good starting point for the information-gathering process is to review previous negotiations between the union and the company. When there are no previous negotiations, management may find it instructive to look at the bargaining experiences of other firms in the same industry who have dealt with the union. The union may also find it useful to examine the company's negotiating history with other labor organizations.[7]

The review might start with an examination of the opponent's proposals and "must-win" items at the previous negotiations. If detailed minutes were kept of the previous contract talks, it would be wise to look at the contract provisions on which the opponent was willing to concede versus those on which a hard bargain was driven. Suppose that the union settled for a modest wage increase during negotiations two years ago, but was adamant about securing a union shop clause that required new bargaining unit employees to join the union within 30 working days. Management might infer that two events are likely to occur at the next round of contract talks. First, the union will not consider any modification of the union shop clause because it is the strongest form of legal union security arrangement

---

[7] Much of the following discussion is based on the detailed outline set forth in Charles S. Loughran, *Negotiating a Labor Contract: A Management Handbook* (Washington, D.C.: The Bureau of National Affairs., Inc., 1984), Appendix 4, "Negotiations Preparation Checklist", pp. 425–435.

available and the union will be extremely reluctant to give it up. Second, the union is likely to argue for a substantial pay increase, citing the fact that the increase from the previous contract talks was modest. The union must also look at the bargaining subjects on which management was willing to concede versus those on which it held firm in order to anticipate management's bargaining behavior during upcoming negotiations.

Both sides must study the successes and failures of the previous negotiations. If management failed to persuade the union to lift restrictive work rules that make it difficult to assign bargaining unit employees to work outside the unit temporarily, then the union must anticipate that management might again attack this subject. Unless the union is willing to concede on this issue, they must be prepared to offer counterproposals and arguments on the restrictive work rules. It is not only important to determine what bargaining objectives were attained or not attained at the previous negotiations, but each side must also study its opponent's tactics and willingness to concede on different bargaining subjects. Management may have rapidly conceded on increasing the employees' group life insurance benefits, but may have slowly and begrudgingly conceded on increased retirement benefits. The union must decide whether a similar concession pattern is likely to occur at the next round of contract talks.

An analysis of previous negotiations should not overlook the composition of the opposing bargaining team. Who were the dominant personalities on the previous negotiations? Will they be involved in the next negotiations and, if so, how can they be effectively handled? By anticipating a domineering or troublesome negotiator, it may be possible to formulate tactics that will minimize his or her influence. If, for example, a pair of union negotiators attempted the previously mentioned "good guy-bad guy" ploy at the bargaining table, then management should anticipate a possible reenactment of this tactic. By ignoring the theatrics of the "bad guy" and focusing attention on the validity of the "good guy's" arguments, management will not be lulled into a premature settlement by the good guy's supposedly reasonable demands.

Examining the Current Contract with an Eye Toward Change

When preparing to bargain over the terms and conditions of a new collective bargaining agreement, negotiators must determine what changes should be made in the current contract. Some provisions may have outlived their usefulness and need to be eliminated. Others may have created administrative problems during the life of the collective bargaining agreement and require modification. Provisions involving pay scales and employee benefits may require updating because of changes in economic conditions, tax laws, or health care costs, whereas other provisions may necessitate little or no alteration.

Each provision in the collective bargaining agreement must be scrutinized with an eye toward change. First, employee problems encountered on the shop floor often become union demands at the bargaining table. Normally the union takes the initiative in seeking employee opinions, but management should also consider using attitude surveys for this purpose. As bargaining preparations proceed, management usually obtains input from first-line supervisors. Supervisors have daily contact with bargaining unit employees and are aware of their subordinates' complaints and concerns. Similarly, employee concerns are relayed to shop stewards who pass them along to union negotiators.

An analysis of formal grievances and arbitration cases is another useful source of information that will help to identify weaknesses in the collective bargaining agreement. If a disproportionate number of grievances were centered on the seniority provision of the labor agreement, then strong consideration should be given to renegotiating or modifying the seniority clause to prevent future problems. Arbitration awards stemming from formal grievances should also be analyzed. Both union and management need to examine unfavorable arbitration decisions that could have been the result of ambiguous contract language. Suppose management discharged an employee who refused to submit to a "for reasonable cause" drug test after the employee exhibited erratic behavior at work. An arbitrator later ordered reinstatement for the employee because the collective bargaining agreement did not clarify what constitutes "reasonable cause" nor did the agreement stipulate that an employee's refusal to submit to a drug test would result in discharge. Because of increasing concerns about drug abuse in the workplace, management may be anxious to add specific "reasonable cause" standards to the contract to avoid another adverse arbitration ruling.

Poorly drafted contract language may lead to personnel problems during the life of the agreement. A sick-leave policy that is not well designed may precipitate absenteeism problems. Seniority clauses that protect long-term employees and provide them with a disproportionate share of employee and job benefits may create high turnover rates among young workers. The collective bargaining agreement may be silent on recently emerging personnel issues such as drug abuse on the job, employees who are AIDS victims, and changes in affirmative action guidelines. Contract provisions covering these issues may be drafted for inclusion in the upcoming round of contract talks. Incidents that have arisen over the life of the contract should also be analyzed for their effect on the contract terms. Have employees expressed displeasure over personnel policies and working conditions by walking off the job, demanding a meeting with the plant manager or personnel director, or posting anonymous complaints on company bulletin boards? If employees are dissatisfied to the extent that they are willing to publicize their complaints, they are also likely to push the union to address these issues at the bargaining table.

Gathering Data on the Firm and the Industry

As pre-negotiation preparations proceed, information on the internal operations and personnel policies of the firm must be gathered. A chronology of wage and employee benefit changes that have occurred over the past 10 years should be compiled, along with information on changes that have taken place with labor cost ratios (e.g., labor costs to total costs and labor costs per unit of output). A wage and salary summary of employees by pay grade, job classification, or pay interval (e.g., the number of employees who make between $9.50 and $9.75 per hour) can be useful when assessing the impact of pay increases. Information should also be assembled on the number of overtime hours worked by bargaining-unit employees, along with premium hours worked during holidays and weekends. Because employee benefit costs have continued to increase as a proportion of total compensation costs in most firms, it is important to prepare detailed cost breakdowns on group life, medical, and disability insurance plans as well as on retirement programs. Cost estimates such as these serve two important purposes. First, they will be readily available when needed at the bargaining table. Second, by analyzing labor cost data, negotiators can detect trends and problems that may have previously gone unnoticed. Management may have failed to realize, for example, that the shipping department in an Ohio plant has paid an inordinate amount of premium pay to its employees over the past two years. Information such as this may have useful implications for contract negotiations, cost control, and contract administration.

Noneconomic information germane to the collective bargaining agreement should be compiled and analyzed. Information such as who worked or refused to work overtime may be useful. A breakdown of bargaining unit employees by age, sex, job, and seniority may have important bargaining implications, especially when contract talks center on employee benefits. A summary of work schedules by shift and department, along with an analysis of peak and slack productivity periods, may help negotiators when discussing overtime and premium pay. Information on job posting and bidding activities, employee promotions and transfers, along with data on layoffs, retirements, employee resignations, and discharges, should be gathered.

Industry-wide bargaining information should be collected as part of prenegotiation preparations. Information on wage rates paid by other employers for comparable job classifications in comparable facilities is an important item for most contract talks. A summary of employee benefits for both unionized and nonunionized companies within an industry is generally useful. It should be noted that benefit costs can vary considerably from one firm to another even when group life, health, and retirement benefits are similar. Therefore, employee benefit cost comparisons among firms within the same industry can be misleading.[8]

Recent contract settlements involving comparable firms provide especially useful information for union and management negotiators and should be obtained, if possible. Management negotiators should contact personnel/human resource managers at other companies who have negotiated with the union in order to obtain insights on possible proposals, innovative issues, personalities of the negotiators, concessions, and potential sticking points. Agreeing to reciprocate when other firms need similar information is the key to obtaining their cooperation.

Economic Data Relevant to Collective Bargaining

General data on local, regional, national, and even international economic conditions should be collected and analyzed before negotiations. Information on inflationary trends, unemployment rates, consumer spending, investment trends, and government spending are all relevant to the bargaining process. Specific information on the company's product and labor markets is especially important. When gath-

---

[8] Frederick S. Hills, *Compensation Decision Making* (Chicago: The Dryden Press, 1987), p. 250.

ering economic data, union and management negotiators must know how trends in consumer price changes, unemployment, government economic policies, and international economic forces will affect upcoming negotiations. It is important to remember that a firm's demand for labor depends on the demand for its products and services. As a firm produces and sells more, it is usually willing to hire additional employees and pay them better wages. Firms in declining product markets may be forced into layoffs and less attractive levels of compensation for its employees. Wage increases are affected by economic conditions. Most notably, changes in the consumer price index (CPI) play a prominent role in the compensation demands made by union negotiators.

Economic data may be obtained from a number of sources. The federal government publishes an array of information through the U.S. Department of Labor's Bureau of Labor Statistics (BLS). BLS data is available on CPI trends, employment and earnings, family budgets, union wage scales, area and industry wage surveys, and other factors.[9] State governments also supply economic information that is useful for regional and local negotiations. Private organizations such as the U.S. Chamber of Commerce and The Bureau of National Affairs, Inc., publish economic, industry, and bargaining information that is relevant to contract negotiations.

Because of its general nature, published economic information should be used to supplement the more specific firm and industry information. Negotiators should be careful not to use economic information that is either out of date or not relevant to the bargaining situation at hand. Data that is gathered from samples of large firms in urban areas may not be useful for negotiating contracts involving bargaining-unit employees working in small firms or in rural areas. Private consulting companies such as Hay Associates, or professional associations such as the Battelle Institute, provide specialized compensation data that can be used by negotiators.[10] Union and management can also conduct their own wage and salary surveys. When wage and salary information is collected for a specific client, however, the question of sampling biases may arise. Information garnered from wage and salary surveys collected by one side should not be blindly accepted by the other side. If one side presents such information at the bargaining table, the other side has a right to know the type of organizations from which the data was obtained and the similarities between the jobs used in the survey and jobs in the bargaining unit.

Input from Employees and Supervisors

As noted earlier, union and management negotiators need to obtain input from employees and supervisors prior to negotiations. Shop stewards and local union officials may poll bargaining unit members in an attempt to determine their needs. This process typically yields a list of reasonable demands along with an inventory of pet peeves, complaints, and unrealistic requests; the list is then reduced to the most sensible and realistic demands. The opinions of bargaining-unit members are

---

[9] Economic information is available from the Superintendent of Documents, U.S. Government Printing Office, Washington, D.C. 20402 and the Bureau of Labor Statistics, U.S. Department of Labor, Washington, D.C. 20210. Most large libraries also have this information available.
[10] Frederick S. Hills, *Compensation Decision Making* (Chicago: The Dryden Press, 1987), pp. 240–242.

vital for several reasons. First, not all negotiators are intimately acquainted with the working conditions of bargaining-unit employees. Second, the contract is likely to be more reflective of the needs and concerns of bargaining-unit employees. Third, there is a greater likelihood that the contract will be ratified by bargaining-unit members once it is negotiated. Fourth, a contract that satisfies the employees will likely result in harmonious labor-management relations.

There are several ways in which information can be obtained from bargaining-unit members. The demands of the union membership have traditionally been solicited during local union meetings. Unfortunately, the demands of the more vocal members may take precedence over those who are less assertive. To ensure that all bargaining-unit members have an opportunity to air their views, other methods such as suggestion boxes, questionnaires, and telephone surveys can be used.[11] Some bargaining-unit members may find it difficult to articulate their ideas before a large group of union members. Suggestion boxes and questionnaires allow employees to state their ideas in writing and present them privately without fear of ridicule or political retaliation. Formal questionnaires also allow union and management bargaining team members to compile systematically and analyze data on proposals submitted by bargaining-unit members.

Formulating Proposals, Priorities, and Bottom-Line Positions

Before negotiating team members are ready to meet the opposing team at the bargaining table, they must first formulate bargaining objectives that are understood and accepted by the entire team. Pre-negotiation preparations provide union and management with the information necessary to formulate bargaining objectives and strategies. By establishing a bargaining agenda, negotiators will have a better understanding of their goals, they are less likely to argue among themselves during contract talks, and they are more likely to agree on what concessions and tradeoffs they are willing to make.

Some union and management negotiating teams establish only a rough set of bargaining objectives, whereas others formulate a detailed set of proposals, priorities, and bottom-line positions. A chief negotiator who is told, "Get the best deal that you can," is given a great deal of flexibility, but he or she may also be uncertain about what constitutes an acceptable settlement. At the other extreme, a bargaining agenda containing detailed and rigid criteria for each provision of the collective bargaining agreement may make it difficult for negotiators to be flexible, make tradeoffs, and adjust to the bargaining proposals and tactics of the opponent. Table 9–1 illustrates the degrees of detail (Models A through D) that can be used when formulating a bargaining agenda. Model A represents the most general set of objectives, whereas Model B and Model C represent increasingly more specific objectives. Model D presents both bargaining targets and walls; *targets* represent what the bargaining team would like to have and *walls* represent the limits to which a party is willing to concede before enduring a work stoppage.

---

[11] Gene Daniels and Kenneth Gagala, *Labor Guide to Negotiating Wages and Benefits* (Reston, Virginia: Reston Publishing Company, 1985), p. 4.

Table 9-1 ▲ Models of Bargaining Parameters and Objectives

Least Detailed Objectives

Model A

1. Contract term to be longer than 1 year.
2. Cost increases no greater than 7.5 percent in any one year.

Somewhat More Detailed Objectives

Model B

1. Three-year contract term.
2. Limit overall cost increases to a maximum of 7.5 percent in any one year, and a cumulative cost package of no more than 20 percent for a three-year contract or 14 percent for a two-year contract.
3. Wage increases in any one year to be no greater than 7.5 percent nor average more than 7 percent in each year of a multiple-year contract.
4. Limit medical insurance cost obligations to a rate of increase no greater than the percentage wage increase in any year.
5. Grant no additional paid time-off benefits.
6. Eliminate restrictive seniority practices in the following areas:
    a. Selection for promotion to skilled trade jobs.
    b. Assignment of overtime requiring additional penalty/premium payments.
    c. Retention of critical skills during layoff periods.
7. Alter grievance/arbitration provisions in order to:
    a. Eliminate current backlog of grievances pending arbitration.
    b. Prevent recurrence of unreasonable backlogs.
    c. Prevent grievants and union from circumventing first step of grievance procedure (oral discussion with supervisor).

The Most Detailed Set of Objectives

Model C

1. Lay a foundation through specific actions for a long-term improvement in our labor-management relationship with this union.
2. Term of contract, two or three years.
3. Total package cost (wage and employee benefits):
    a. Two years—maximum increase of 7.5 percent in any one year and 14.5 percent cumulative increase over term of contract.
    b. Three years—maximum increase of 8 percent in any one year and 22.5 percent cumulatively.
    c. "Dividend" of additional package cost increase of up to 1 percent per year if concessions can be attained in items 7 and 8 below, which will result in savings over the term of the contract equal to twice the amount of the dividend, based upon conservative cost estimates.
4. Wage increases are to be as follows:
    a. No less than 5 percent nor more than 7.75 percent in any one year.
    b. Increases in all but one year of the contract must be in percentage terms or otherwise comparably graduated to recognize skill differences.
5. Any increases resulting from COLAs (cost-of-living adjustments) must be taken from amounts available under items 3 and 4 above, based upon an assumed increase of 5 percent per year in the national CPI.
6. Any increases in employee benefits are limited by the following:
    a. No additional holidays.

Table 9-1 ▲ Models of Bargaining Parameters and Objectives (Continued)

The Most Detailed Set of Objectives

Model C

    b. May grant one additional week of vacation except for employees with less than five years of service, and no employee may receive more than a maximum of five weeks of vacation, regardless of service.
    c. No increases in medical insurance benefits except where recommended by benefits consultants, with a maximum of improvements equal to 0.5 percent in total labor cost.
    d. Pension improvements may not result in a monthly benefit rate of more than $15 per year of service.
    e. Fringe benefit improvements in excess of the stated amounts may be increased to the extent they are taken out of the wage package, except that no improvements may exceed the maximums provided by other comparable employers in our industry in the same geographical area.

7. Change scheduling and overtime provisions to:
    a. Eliminate premium pay for work on Saturday "as such."
    b. Permit scheduling of extra shifts with less than 48 hours notice.
    c. Permit scheduling of split shifts in departments X, Y, and Z when business conditions so require.

8. Change seniority provisions to:
    a. Allow use of part-time employees to avoid scheduled overtime.
    b. Eliminate all "grandfather" agreements (permit buy-outs up to twice annual loss of pay).
    c. Prohibit interdepartmental bidding except in base rate jobs.

9. Stengthen no-strike clause to:
    a. Completely preclude self-help in grievance situations.
    b. Prohibit honoring of stranger picket lines.

Objectives with Targets (Like to Have) and
Walls (Willing to Agree to Avoid a Strike)

Model D

TARGET

1. Three-year contract term.
2. Maximum average overall cost increase of 6 percent per year with a maximum of 7 percent in any one year.
3. First year general wage increase not to exceed 5.5 percent per year; average annual wage increase over term of contract not to exceed 6.5 percent and a maximum of 7.5 percent in any one year.
4. No medical insurance benefit increases; company contribution to be "capped" each year at a level 6 percent above contribution rate for the preceding year.
5. No pension improvements.
6. No additional holidays.
7. No additional vacation benefits except for employees who have more than 25 years of service.
8. Eliminate COLA clause: can buy out over term of contract with a lump sum payback equal to a two-year payment assuming an average annual CPI increase of 6 percent.
9. Reduce sick-pay benefits by 50 percent—no specific buy-out money available.

Table 9-1 ▲ Models of Bargaining Parameters and Objectives (Continued)

Objectives with Targets (Like to Have) and
Walls (Willing to Agree to Avoid a Strike)

Model D

WALL

1. Two-year contract term or longer.
2. Total annual average labor cost increase of 8.5 percent per year; maximum of 7 percent in first year.
3. First year general wage increase not to exceed 7 percent average annual wage increase not to exceed 8.5 percent.
4. Increase medical insurance benefits by no more than $10 per month (composite cost) for each year of contract.
5. No increase in past service benefits under pension plan and limit future service benefits to a rate of increase in percentage terms no greater than the wage increase for that year.
6. Maximum of two additional paid holidays per year for three-year contract; one additional for a two-year contract.
7. Vacation improvement only for employees with more than 10 years service.
8. No increase in COLA formula.

Reprinted with permission from Charles S. Loughran, *Negotiating A Labor Contract: A Management Handbook* (Washington, D.C.: The Bureau of National Affairs, Inc., 1984), pp. 92–97.

When formulating a bargaining agenda, negotiators may decide to rank or classify their preferences. For example, the union decides that it must have at least a six percent pay increase, even if this means granting major concessions on other bargaining demands or engaging in a lengthy economic strike. Although the union would like an increase in the group major medical insurance coverage, this objective is secondary to the six percent pay increase. In addition, the union might like to have the Friday after Thanksgiving as an additional paid holiday, but they are not willing to press management to obtain this concession. Thus, bargaining items can be classified as "must" items (the six percent pay increase), "important, but not vital" items (the additional major medical coverage), and "nice to have if we can get them" items (the extra paid holiday). By ranking or categorizing bargaining topics, negotiators are less likely to lose sight of their priorities during the heat of contract talks. Collective bargaining is a process of give-and-take; chief negotiators may not be willing to make concessions on the "must" items, but they may make wholesale trades on the "nice-to-have" items. Negotiators usually maintain secrecy regarding their bargaining priorities because this information would give the opposing team an edge at the bargaining table.

The bargaining plan should also include provisions for a possible work stoppage. Management may decide to formulate plans to maintain total or partial operations if the union calls an economic strike. The union must decide the conditions under which it wants to strike and make provisions for picket lines, strike funds, and dealing with problems that accompany a strike. In addition, both sides must make a rough estimate of the costs associated with engaging in a work stoppage (these topics are discussed in Chapter 10).

Selecting the Bargaining Site

Selection of a suitable bargaining site is important for two reasons. First, the union and management negotiating teams spend a great deal of time at or near the bargaining table; comfortable surroundings ease the arduous task of contract negotiations. Second, negotiators need time to think and privately discuss matters without unnecessary disruptions from bargaining-unit employees, the news media, and other interested parties. The bargaining site selected should be satisfactory to both bargaining teams.

Union and management negotiators can select from a number of potential bargaining sites. The company may make conference rooms available for negotiators; however, this arrangement can give management a "home-court" advantage because of their ability to schedule meeting times and control seating arrangements, breaks, and access to telephones. Sites arranged by the union, such as local or international headquarters, pose similar problems for the management negotiating team. Both bargaining teams should avoid sites where union members and the news media can influence and distract negotiators with frequent inquiries about the progress of contract talks. A hotel conference room is often a suitable setting because negotiators can be shielded from outside distractions, food and refreshments can be provided by hotel personnel, and negotiators can retreat to a room or suite for private conferences. The major drawback to using a hotel conference room for negotiations is that facilities must be reserved in advance and, depending on the progress of negotiations, the parties may have to pay for rooms they do not use.

Organizing the Plethora of Bargaining Information

As noted earlier, bargaining teams collect large volumes of information as they prepare to negotiate a complex and lengthy collective bargaining agreement. This information must be organized so that it can be quickly accessed at the bargaining table. A bargaining book is commonly used to organize economic, industry, and company information. Each section of the book usually corresponds to each section of the collective bargaining agreement. For example, if the parties were discussing the seniority clause, a section of the bargaining book would contain a copy of the existing seniority clause, industry-wide information on seniority, summaries of arbitration cases involving the clause, an outline of problems that the union and management have encountered with seniority issues, and a draft of proposed changes in the clause.

A well-prepared and detailed bargaining book can save considerable time and effort at the bargaining table. Information that is kept in binders can be removed, copied, shared with the other side, and updated as necessary. As negotiations proceed, both bargaining teams can add copies of proposals, counterproposals, and notes taken during negotiations to the appropriate section of the book. One key to successful negotiations is to be well-armed with relevant information. A second key is to manage the information with a minimum of confusion and paper shuffling; the bargaining book is an important negotiating tool for achieving this second objective.

▲ The Legal Requirements for Collective Bargaining

Two legal requirements that union and management negotiators must fulfill are (1) formal notification of intent to bargain, and (2) good-faith bargaining. Both of these requirements are part of the good-faith bargaining provisions of the National Labor Relations Act (NLRA), as amended, and they are respectively designed to allow the parties time to prepare for negotiations and ensure that a reasonable attempt is made to reach a settlement once negotiations begin.

Notification of Intent To Bargain

Bargaining relationships covered by the NLRA (private sector firms meeting the standards set forth in the Act except for the airlines and railways) must provide written notice to the other party 60 days prior to the time they wish to terminate or modify an existing collective bargaining agreement. Because of concerns for patient care in the event of a strike, health care institutions must make this notification no later than 90 days before modification or termination of a labor contract.[12] The party initiating changes in the collective bargaining agreement must also offer to meet and confer with the other party to negotiate a new contract or revise the existing one. Usually the union notifies management of the proposed changes; however, management is usually aware of the forthcoming changes and has started preparations well in advance of the 60-day (or 90-day) limit.[13]

The National Labor Relations Act also requires that the parties notify the Federal Mediation and Conciliation Service (FMCS) and any state or territorial mediation agency 30 days after the notice to modify or terminate has been given, unless an agreement has already been reached. The Act implies that a dispute exists if the parties have not reached an agreement within 30 days.[14] The 30-day notice allows the FMCS to monitor the negotiations and offer the services of federal mediators if it appears that an impasse or work stoppage is pending. Neither the union nor management is legally obliged to accept the services of a federal mediator, except health care institutions, which must make efforts to avoid work stoppages by participating "fully and promptly" in meetings called by the FMCS.

Once the 60-day or 90-day notice has been given, all terms and conditions of the existing collective bargaining agreement must continue.[15] The union cannot strike within 60 days of the notification to modify or terminate the labor contract. Employees who are discharged for engaging in a strike during the 60-day period may not have recourse through the National Labor Relations Act. In most cases, the existing collective bargaining agreement is still in effect during the 60-day warning period and the union will not call a strike until the contract has expired.

---

[12] For an interesting discussion of labor disputes in health care institutions, see Woodruff Imberman, "Rx: Strike Prevention in Hospitals," *Hospital & Health Services Administration* (Summer 1989), pp. 195–211.
[13] National Labor Relations Act (NLRA), Sec. 8(d)(1) and (2).
[14] National Labor Relations Act, Sec. 8(d)(3).
[15] National Labor Relations Act, Sec. 8(d)(4).

The Concept of Good-Faith Bargaining

One of the most complex legal issues in labor-management relations is good-faith bargaining. Section 8(a)(5) of the NLRA imposes the duty of good-faith bargaining on the employer, and section 8(b)(3) imposes a similar duty on unions. Section 8(d) of the Act provides a general description of the good-faith bargaining requirement:

> For the purposes of this section, to bargain collectively is the performance of the mutual obligation of the employer and the representative of the employees to meet at reasonable times and confer in good faith with respect to wages, hours, and other terms and conditions of employment, or the negotiation of the agreement, or any question arising thereunder, and the execution of a written contract incorporating any agreement reached if requested by either party, but such obligation does not compel either party to agree to a proposal or require the making of a concession.[16]

From this general statement, the NLRB and courts have fashioned and refined the nebulous concept of good-faith bargaining. Both management and labor must bargain in good faith over mandatory bargaining items until an impasse is reached. The NLRB and courts are often forced to answer three questions: (1) How is good-faith bargaining defined? (2) What are mandatory bargaining subjects? and (3) How do the negotiators, the NLRB, and the courts know exactly when an impasse has been reached? Once negotiations reach an impasse and the current labor contract expires, the employer may unilaterally change wages, hours, and working conditions.

Totality of Conduct by the Parties

An overriding consideration when deciding whether one party or the other has engaged in bad-faith bargaining is to look at their total conduct, both at the bargaining table and in other aspects of the labor-management relationship. Suppose that a company has used stalling or evasive tactics during negotiations over a shift pay differential. If the company has committed unfair labor practice violations during negotiations or has a history of unfair labor practice violations involving such actions as firing union supporters and disrupting organizing campaigns, the NLRB may be more likely to regard this particular evasive maneuver as a violation of section 8(a)(5) of the NLRA. The NLRB may not regard this tactic as bad-faith bargaining if the company has maintained harmonious relations with the union and has no record of unfair labor practice violations.

Many bad-faith bargaining cases hinge on circumstantial evidence. Although the NLRA does not require that the parties reach a settlement, they must maintain an open mind and a sincere desire to reach an agreement. According to the U.S. Supreme Court:

> The object of this Act was ... to ensure that employers and their employees could work together to establish mutually satisfactory conditions. The basic

---

[16] National Labor Relations Act, Sec. 8(d).

theme of the Act was that through collective bargaining the passions, agreements, and struggles of prior years would be channeled into constructive, open discussions leading, hopefully, to mutual agreement.[17]

Determining whether talks at the bargaining table are constructive and open often hinges on evaluating the total conduct of the parties, rather than focusing on specific incidents that may be misinterpreted when viewed in isolation.

The Employer's Duty to Furnish Information

Because the union generally does not have access to the employer's production, financial, and personnel information, the NLRB and courts have held that management must furnish information requested by union negotiators if such information is relevant to contract talks. This duty is based on the belief that the union would be unable to bargain on behalf of its members without information on wages, hours, and other terms of employment. Management must also furnish information promptly and in a reasonably usable form, but they do not have to provide information that is unduly burdensome to collect, nor do they have to reveal business or trade secrets to union negotiators.

When the union requests information, the employer may question its relevance to collective bargaining. Management may decide that the union does not have a legitimate "need to know" and may refuse to honor the request. The NLRB has taken a liberal view as to what constitutes relevant information. Information requested by the union is more likely to be regarded as relevant if it is needed to settle an issue currently under discussion at the bargaining table. If a change in the seniority system is being negotiated, then the union's request for an itemized listing of the ages and employment dates for all bargaining unit employees is relevant and reasonable. Generally, management must furnish any information that directly pertains to bargaining-unit employees; information not directly relevant may also be requested and must be provided if it is germane to the bargaining issues at hand. For example, if an employer is gradually transferring additional work from its unionized to its nonunionized facilities, then wage, production, and other information on the nonunionized facilities may be deemed relevant by the NLRB. The U.S. Supreme Court has ruled that employers must furnish financial information if they claim an inability to grant concessions to the union because of the company's financial condition. An employer's *inability* to pay should be contrasted to its *unwillingness* to pay. Once an employer claims financial inability to meet the demands of the union negotiators, it must provide relevant financial statements to substantiate the claim.[18] For this reason, most employers will stop short of pleading inability to pay and will instead claim they are unwilling to agree to the union's demands because of labor costs or competitive conditions.

---

[17] *H.K. Porter, Inc.*, 397 U.S. 99 (1970). Cited in Charles J. Morris, ed., *The Developing Labor Law* (Washington, D.C.: The Bureau of National Affairs, Inc., 1971), p. 278.
[18] *NLRB v. Truitt Manufacturing Co.*, 351 U.S. 149 (1956). Also see James T. O'Reilly, *Unions' Right to Company Information* (Philadelphia: Industrial Research Unit, The Wharton School, University of Pennsylvania, 1980).

Surface Bargaining and Dilatory Tactics

Surface bargaining occurs when one party or the other goes through the motions of negotiating without making a sincere effort to reach an agreement. The employer, rather than the union, usually engages in surface bargaining because of its desire to maintain the status quo and impede a settlement that could create a financial and managerial burden. Thus, a party's *intent* to reach an agreement is an important consideration with surface bargaining. Examples of surface bargaining include reneging on previously agreed upon proposals, waiting until late in the contract negotiations to inform the union that all proposals must be approved by the company board of directors, failing to offer counterproposals, maintaining an inflexible attitude at the bargaining table, and using filibustering tactics to turn negotiations into marathon sessions.

Dilatory tactics are used to delay meeting the opponent at the bargaining table. The duty of good-faith bargaining requires that the parties meet and confer at a reasonable time and place. If an employer refuses to meet with the union, it has violated its duty to bargain in good faith; however, management is not obligated to meet at a time and place dictated solely by the union. Employers not making outright refusals to engage in contract talks occasionally try to delay the meeting as long as possible in order to disrupt the union's bargaining momentum. Neither the union nor management may refuse to bargain because they regard a member of the opposing team as obnoxious, unreasonable, or otherwise unacceptable. Additional dilatory tactics include failure to supply relevant information in a reasonable amount of time, slowing negotiations by seeking the company president's approval on all proposals and concessions, sending a chief negotiator to the bargaining table without granting him or her the authority to make concessions and approve proposals, and scheduling unreasonably long periods of time between bargaining sessions.

Concessions, Proposals, and Demands in Bad-Faith Bargaining

Willingness to compromise during negotiations is one primary indication of good-faith bargaining. Making a preposterous demand, however, does not necessarily constitute bad-faith bargaining. In the early stages of negotiations such demands are not unusual, and in some union-management relationships they are traditional. Negotiators should maintain a flexible attitude and remain willing to listen to proposals submitted by the other side and make counteroffers on those proposals.

The NLRB and courts have examined a number of factors regarding proposals, demands, and concessions. A party who adopts a take-it-or-leave-it posture is probably bargaining in bad faith unless the record indicates it had made significant and frequent concessions earlier in the contract talks. The classic example of making proposals in bad faith is the *General Electric* case.[19] In 1960, General Electric, under the guidance of its vice president, Lemuel R. Boulware, formulated a final offer to the union after 6 weeks of meetings spanning 18 bargaining sessions. General Electric's final offer was based on extensive research by the company, and management negotiators regarded it as both fair and firm, although General Electric subsequently

---

[19] *NLRB v. General Electric Company*, 418 F. (2d) 736 (1969).

made four changes in the offer. The NLRB ruled that the company had engaged in bad-faith bargaining.[20] The Board based their decision on the company's failure to furnish information requested by the union, its attempt to bypass negotiating with the international union by bargaining directly with the locals, its presentation of an insurance proposal on a "take-it-or-leave-it" basis, and its overall attitude toward negotiations (the aforementioned totality of conduct criterion).[21] The term "Boulwarism" in commemoration of Lemuel Boulware is often associated with a "take-it-or-leave-it" posture at the bargaining table. The term is somewhat broader than this, however, and generally describes a strategy whereby management gives the employees its "best" deal and then disregards inputs from the union.[22]

Other bad-faith bargaining tactics associated with proposals, demands, and concessions include making a large number of new demands just before the contract deadline and imposing unreasonable conditions on the opponent (e.g., insisting that the union waive all grievances pending under the old contract before management will sign the new one). Bypassing union negotiators and appealing directly to the rank-and-file is also regarded as bargaining in bad faith. Finally, unilateral changes in wages, hours, and working conditions by management during negotiations, as well as during the life of the contract, usually constitutes bad-faith bargaining.

Mandatory, Permissive, and Illegal Bargaining Subjects

Labor and management are required to bargain in good faith over mandatory bargaining subjects such as wage changes and employee drug testing. That is, if one side wants to discuss a mandatory subject at the bargaining table, the other side is legally obliged to negotiate until a settlement or an impasse is reached. However, neither party is legally required to negotiate over permissive bargaining subjects (also known as voluntary subjects). Suppose the union wants to discuss the working conditions of supervisors, a permissive subject, and management flatly refuses to negotiate the issue. In this case, management is not guilty of bad-faith bargaining and the union commits an unfair labor practice if it calls a strike as a result of management's refusal to negotiate a permissive subject. A third type of bargaining subject, illegal subjects, are banned from negotiations. Closed-shop provisions in which only union members can be hired, and racially or sexually discriminatory provisions are examples of illegal subjects.

The mandatory-permissive-illegal categorization of bargaining subjects was created by the NLRB in the *Borg-Warner* case, a ruling that was eventually upheld by the U.S. Supreme Court.[23] Mandatory bargaining subjects are those directly related

---

[20] *General Electric Co.*, 150 NLRB 192 (1964). In a split decision, a U.S. Court of Appeals affirmed the Board's 1964 decision that General Electric had failed to bargain in good faith. See *NLRB v. General Electric Company*, 418 F 2d 736 (1969).

[21] Charles J. Morris, *The Developing Labor Law* (Washington, D.C.: The Bureau of National Affairs, Inc., 1971), p. 280.

[22] See Herbert R. Northrup, *Boulwarism* (Ann Arbor, Michigan: Graduate School of Business, University of Michigan, 1964).

[23] *NLRB v. Borg-Warner, Wooster Div.*, 356 U.S. 342 (1958). In Borg-Warner, the employer insisted on including a "recognition" clause and a "ballot" clause in the collective bargaining agreement. Both of these clauses were regarded by the NLRB and courts as *permissive* bargaining subjects. By insisting that these clauses be included in the collective bargaining agreement, the employer committed an unfair labor practice when negotiations over these permissive issues reached an impasse.

to wages, hours, and other terms of employment. Subjects falling into the broad mandatory category include wages, salaries, incentive pay, shift differentials, vacations, pension benefits, rest and lunch periods, job duties and work assignments, and seniority provisions, to name a few. Some other mandatory items are subcontracting arrangements, rental of company housing, successorship clauses that protect bargaining-unit employees if the company is sold or merged with another firm, provisions for polygraph testing, and the presence of vending machines on company property. Recently, the NLRB issued an opinion that compulsory drug testing of employees is a mandatory bargaining topic. Thus, if an employer desires to institute a random drug-testing program, it must negotiate the terms and conditions of the program with the union.[24] Permissive subjects include employer-provided performance bonds for employees, use of the union label on company products, strike insurance plans, and changes in pension benefits for employees who have already retired.

Most debates over the categorization of a contract provision center on whether it should be placed in the mandatory or the permissive category. In the course of hearing bad-faith bargaining cases, the NLRB and courts have categorized bargaining topics cases and therefore have had a direct influence on the substance of collective bargaining. A dilemma is created when union and management negotiators are uncertain of the status of a bargaining issue. A mandatory subject must be negotiated; a permissive item, however, is negotiated only if both sides choose to discuss it.[25] Rather than refusing to negotiate an issue because it falls into the permissive category, the safest strategy might be to bargain over the issue with the written understanding that any settlement on a permissive item is subject to revocation. This strategy is indicative of a desire to bargain in good faith and will minimize the likelihood of unfair labor practice charges.

Reaching An Impasse

The duty to bargain in good faith requires that the parties engage in contract talks with the intent to reach an agreement. Although "good faith" is difficult to define, it generally describes a bargaining posture in which the parties continuously display a desire to settle. Evidence of this desire can be found in a party's receptivity to proposals and counterproposals, its willingness to make concessions and furnish information, and an absence of surface bargaining and dilatory tactics. When irreconcilable differences arise between the positions of the parties after exhaustive good-faith negotiations, the law recognizes that an impasse exists.[26] Once an impasse occurs, the obligation to bargain in good faith is suspended and management may unilaterally make changes in wages, hours, and working conditions that are not inconsistent with proposals made by the union during negotiations. That is, if

---

[24] The Bureau of National Affairs, Inc., "Drug Testing Policy Review," *Collective Bargaining Negotiations & Contracts* (Washington, D.C.: The Bureau of National Affairs, Inc., May 19, 1988), p. 4.
[25] For an analysis of how the mandatory-permissive categorizations affect bargaining outcomes, see John Thomas Delaney and Donna Sockell, "The Mandatory-Permissive Distinction and Bargaining Outcomes," *Industrial and Labor Relations Review* (July 1989), pp. 566–583.
[26] Charles J. Morris, *The Developing Labor Law* (Washington, D.C.: The Bureau of National Affairs, Inc., 1971), p. 330.

the union requested a seven percent wage increase during negotiations and management later provided employees with a 10 percent raise during the impasse, then management's actions are inconsistent with the union's earlier demands.[27]

Because the law only requires that parties bargain to an impasse, defining an impasse becomes important. If the parties have reached a deadlock in which further negotiations appear futile, then an impasse exists. There is also less controversy surrounding the existence of an impasse if the parties can demonstrate that they have engaged extensively in good-faith bargaining prior to the stalemate. Some impasses degenerate into strikes or lockouts, whereas other impasses end when the bargaining or economic position of one of the parties changes. An impasse is usually temporary and the employer cannot immediately capitalize on one as a means of avoiding all bargaining obligations and undermining the strength of the union.

▲ Strategies and Tactics at the Bargaining Table

The Initial Proposal Stage

At the outset of contract talks, the parties usually agree to establish ground rules that will reduce confusion and allow negotiations to proceed smoothly. A schedule of proposed meeting times should be established by the union and management chief negotiators; scheduling will enable each side to have adequate time to present and discuss their demands before the contract expires. Adequate time between meetings should be allowed for both sides to prepare responses to its opponent's proposals. Chief negotiators should also schedule the meetings far enough in advance to avoid the need for lengthy and tiring marathon sessions during the latter stages of contract talks.

Union and management chief negotiators should decide how they wish to sequence the bargaining topics. They may elect to negotiate all noneconomic items (e.g., seniority, union security, safety and health, and discipline and discharge issues) before discussing economic items. Alternatively, the negotiators may first bargain over the easy-to-resolve items (e.g., employee parking spaces and the location of union bulletin boards) before embarking on the more difficult issues such as wages. This approach gives the negotiators an opportunity to build momentum and goodwill early in the bargaining process, which may make it easier to resolve the difficult economic issues. Along with establishing the order of bargaining topics, the negotiators may make provisions for a tentative settlement on each issue. As each contract provision is negotiated to a conclusion, the chief negotiators may want to sign a statement indicating tentative approval, subject to final agreement on all outstanding issues. The latter approach minimizes potential misunderstandings between union and management chief negotiators over which items have been settled and which remain open, an important point because both chief negotiators must agree on the terms and conditions of the final settlement. The union usually submits the completed contract to the rank-and-file for ratification, whereas management obtains approval from the company president or board of directors.

[27] An employer might use such a strategy to subvert a union.

Once the preliminary ground rules are established, both chief negotiators usually make a brief opening statement. The opening statement performs a ceremonial function and sets the tone for the negotiations. Management may discuss general economic conditions, developments in the industry, the current and future condition of the company, and its relationship with the union. The union's chief negotiator voices the general economic and job-security concerns of its members, along with his or her perception of the current relationship with management. Both sides usually emphasize the seriousness of the negotiations along with their intent to bargain in good faith and reach a mutually satisfactory settlement. Opening statements are usually general in nature and do not touch on specific proposals or items in the collective bargaining agreement.

After the opening ceremony is concluded, the union normally presents its list of demands to management. Union demands may be presented in writing before negotiations begin, in order to speed up the bargaining process. Regardless of when the union presents its initial demands, management needs time to evaluate them and offer proposals and counterproposals of their own. The management chief negotiator either asks questions about the union's demands as they are presented or waits until all demands have been made before obtaining clarification from the union's chief negotiator. To avoid surprise proposals at a later date that could smack of bad-faith bargaining, both chief negotiators may decide not to allow further proposals on new bargaining topics once each side has made its initial demands.

The Primary Bargaining Stage

Most of the progress made at the bargaining table occurs during the primary bargaining stage. During this stage, union and management make proposals and concessions, debate points of contention, make cost estimates on proposals, call caucuses to discuss bargaining matters privately, consider the ramifications of possible work stoppages, and gain insights as to what the opponent is thinking and willing to accept as a final offer.

Conduct at the Bargaining Table

Union and management negotiators approach collective bargaining with a pragmatic and professional attitude. Typically, the union negotiators sit on one side of the table and management negotiators on the other. Chief negotiators sit in the middle and are flanked by an equal number of bargaining team members on each side. This traditional seating arrangement conveys two points. First, the union-management relationship is adversarial because the negotiating teams sit on opposite sides. Second, the chief negotiators occupy center stage for their respective sides and are seated in the middle. The seats are arranged so that direct eye contact is possible, but the table is wide enough to prevent opposing negotiators from seeing the contents of confidential files and papers. Chief negotiators usually will not allow the opposing side to secure a physical or psychological advantage through more comfortable seating arrangements or higher chairs.

Negotiators generally avoid using loud, abusive, or profane language. Behavior of this nature is no substitute for thorough preparation prior to negotiations and it is unlikely to persuade an experienced opponent to grant concessions. If a negotiator feels compelled to use loud and abusive language at the bargaining table, it should be used sparingly and only when necessary to emphasize a critical issue that could mean the difference between a settlement and a strike. Ultimatums, extreme statements, and statements attacking someone's personal integrity should likewise be avoided unless their use is absolutely imperative. Suppose management tells the union that it will not agree to a company-wide seniority system under any circumstances. An extreme statement of this nature forces management to spend one of its "bargaining chips" because it will not be able to use a company-wide seniority proposal later for leverage to obtain an important concession or a tradeoff on wages. Should management negotiators later back down from such an extreme statement, they may lose credibility in the eyes of the union negotiators. However, if a bargaining team is forced to retract an extreme statement, a wise opposing chief negotiator will allow them to do so with as much dignity as possible; rubbing salt into the wounds of an opponent may provide short-term gratification at the expense of serious long-term damage to the relationship.

Negotiations often appear to be long-winded and tedious. It is important that negotiators remain patient (or at least appear patient) and avoid pressing for a premature settlement. Negotiators must possess the tenacity to grind through a series of long and tiring negotiation sessions and pay attention to detail without getting bogged down in trivia. As contract talks progress, bargaining team members must distinguish between important issues that emerge and those that are less vital to reaching a settlement. Focusing on and resolving issues that could cause an impasse or work stoppage will, in turn, permit the negotiators to reach an agreement on more mundane issues.

Because negotiators are human, their talking skills are often vastly superior to their listening skills. Effective negotiators, however, are usually effective listeners. The chief negotiator must listen carefully and take notes on what the opposition says. Asking questions is acceptable, but the chief negotiator must insist that the other side be allowed to fully explain their position without undue interruption. According to Professor Joseph F. Byrnes, an expert on negotiations:

> Some people are poor negotiators because they talk too much. As a rule of thumb, if you are talking more than 50 percent of the time, you are talking too much. Try to relax and let the other side do more talking. As one professional negotiator has said, "You never give anything away if you keep your mouth shut."
> Silence is a simple but powerful negotiating tool.[28]

It is advisable not to feign knowledge about an unfamiliar topic; negotiators should confess ignorance and either seek clarification from the other side or obtain the necessary information at the earliest opportunity. As Professor Byrnes notes:

> It is not a sign of weakness to ask for more time to prepare adequately.... Common beliefs to the contrary, negotiation is usually a contest of preparation, not a macho battle where contestants are willing to lose rather than admit they are not ready to fight.[29]

---

[28] Joseph F. Byrnes, "Ten Guidelines for Effective Negotiating," *Business Horizons* (May-June 1987), p. 10. Reprinted with permission.

[29] Joseph F. Byrnes, "Ten Guidelines for Effective Negotiating," *Business Horizons* (May-June 1987), p. 8. Reprinted with permission.

Making Proposals and Counterproposals

Collective bargaining in the United States traditionally starts with the union making unrealistically high demands and management countering with an equally unrealistic low offer. After the initial demands are made, the parties begin to make more reasonable proposals. Proposals made early in negotiations can convey a message about a party's credibility and willingness to reach an agreement. If the union initially demands a 15 percent general wage increase and then later counters at 14.5 percent, management may get the impression that the union's slow rate of concession is an early warning of a possible strike over wages. On the other hand, if the union starts at 15 percent and quickly moves to 10 percent, management will assume the second offer indicates that the union wants to move toward a settlement without a strike.

There are three general rules regarding concessions at the bargaining table. First, counterproposals should not be offered without carefully considering the implications of the opponent's proposal. Some proposals made by an opponent may, at first glance, seem harmless and of little consequence. If management has recently opened a new plant and hires a new group of employees, it may accept a union proposal that provides five weeks of paid vacation to employees having at least ten years of seniority. Since there will be no employees with ten years of seniority for quite some time, management probably feels safe in accommodating the union on this demand. However, if the workforce at the new plant remains stable, this provision will become a financial and operational nightmare in the years ahead as large numbers of employees suddenly become eligible for liberal paid vacation benefits.

Second, concessions should not be made too quickly. Once a proposal or concession is offered by a chief negotiator, it often becomes "chiseled in stone." If management proposes a five percent wage increase, it cannot later offer a four-and-one-half percent increase without risking a bad-faith bargaining charge or a strike. By making concessions in small increments, the chief negotiator does not overcommit his or her position and, perhaps more importantly, does not send a message to the other side of being anxious to settle. From the union negotiators' standpoint, an early settlement could be viewed with suspicion by the rank-and-file, who believe that the union bargaining team has sold out to management. A corporate board of directors or company president may likewise believe that the management team did not drive a hard enough bargain if they settled well in advance of the contract expiration date. Conceding too slowly, however, may cause an unnecessary work stoppage if an agreement is not reached before the deadline.

Third, when agreeing to a proposal, negotiators should try to obtain a concession from the other side. With economic issues such as wages, the union gradually lowers its demands and management gradually raises its offer. Noneconomic items present a thornier issue in terms of acceptable tradeoffs. Suppose management wants more flexibility to subcontract excess work in order to avoid expensive overtime payments to bargaining-unit employees. The union, on the other hand, may press to obtain a job-bidding system that places more emphasis on seniority and gives management less discretion in promotion and transfer decisions. How do negotiators evaluate a tradeoff between a subcontracting arrangement and a job-bidding system? Management would be unlikely to give the union the job-bidding system without getting something in return. Some tradeoffs involve swapping one contract provision for another:

> The essence of excellent bargaining is to trade what is cheap for you, but valuable to another, for what is valuable to you but cheap to another. In this way, both parties are able to more fully satisfy their needs at no enormous cost to the other side. Of course, this is not possible on all issues. However, with a little imagination, such trade-offs are often attainable.[30]

For example, management negotiators may be reluctant to provide an additional paid personal day off for bargaining-unit personnel. However, by stipulating that only employees with no more than two absences within the past six months were entitled to the extra personal day off, the company calculated that the reduced cost savings generated by lower absenteeism rates would offset the expense of the extra personal holiday.[31]

Another potential tradeoff is for management to grant the union's demand if the union agrees to drop a proposal to which management is totally opposed. Occasionally, one party will use a "blocking" tactic whereby they refuse to give favorable consideration to any of the opponent's proposals until the opponent agrees to drop an unacceptable demand. Management, for example, may be against considering *any* union demands until labor negotiators drop their request for a union shop provision. Finally, a dilemma is created when one party makes a proposal and the other party neither accepts the offer nor makes a counteroffer. Suppose management agrees to provide a pay increase of six percent and the union negotiators do not counter with a proposal of their own. What course of action is open to management? The company's chief negotiator can either remain silent and risk a premature impasse over wages or make a second offer at a higher pay rate; the latter strategy may weaken the company's bargaining position in the eyes of the union. If an opponent refuses to make a counteroffer, the original offer should be either withdrawn or left unchanged until the other side eventually makes a counteroffer.

Negotiators must carefully examine the opponent's proposal before responding with a counteroffer. If the union proposes a job-bidding system that places a premium on seniority, management must consider several questions. Why does the union want a job-bidding system? Are there problems with the current method of assigning jobs? Will the union's proposal eliminate these problems? How important is this issue to the union's chief negotiator and the rank-and-file? The answers to these questions will determine whether management accepts the union's proposal as written, suggests a modified version of the union's job-bidding proposal in its counteroffer, or totally rejects any form of job bidding.

The acceptability of a counteroffer can be enhanced or diminished by the

---

[30] Joseph F. Byrnes, "Ten Guidelines for Effective Negotiating," *Business Horizons* (May-June 1987), p. 11. Reprinted with permission.
[31] Joseph F. Byrnes, "Ten Guidelines for Effective Negotiating," *Business Horizons* (May-June 1987), p. 11.

manner in which it is presented to the opposing side. Counteroffers should be made in writing to reduce the possibility for misunderstandings. An offer or counteroffer should be carefully explained and the chief negotiator should invite questions regarding its terms. A proposal should be presented in a positive tone that encourages the other side to see its merits and accept it. If the opponent's previous demand is rejected, the manner in which the answer of "no" is expressed is significant. A "soft" no might be expressed as follows: "We must reject the union's proposal as it now exists because they are placing too much weight on seniority in their job-bidding proposal." The "soft" no leaves room for additional counteroffers and keeps the job-bidding issue alive. A "hard" no may sound like this: "The use of seniority in job bidding is completely contrary to our managerial philosophy and under no circumstances will we consider this proposal." This statement will make it difficult if not impossible to reach an agreement on the use of seniority and job bidding.

The Use of Caucuses

A caucus is an adjournment for a private conference by either the union or management bargaining team. Caucuses are often called to discuss a proposal made by the other side. They are also used to plan bargaining strategy and tactics, draft contract proposals, obtain additional data and information, make cost estimates, and obtain approval from a higher authority on a pending contract proposal. Caucuses are working sessions, not rest breaks, and each member of the bargaining team should have assigned tasks during this time. The intelligent use of caucuses can have an important impact on the effectiveness of negotiators at the bargaining table.

The number and length of caucuses taken by a bargaining team over the course of contract negotiations sends important signals to the opponent. A chief negotiator who calls too many caucuses can appear poorly prepared or lacking control of the bargaining team. Too many caucuses can also slow negotiations down to the point where the parties will be unable to reach a settlement before the contract expiration date. Refraining from calling caucuses also pose difficulties: If a negotiator stays at the bargaining table to discuss a complex issue without giving it adequate thought and preparation, the results can be disastrous.

The timing and length of a caucus is also important. If the union rejects a management proposal and then immediately calls a caucus, management negotiators may get the impression that the issue is not dead and that the union has caucused in order to discuss the proposal in more detail, and perhaps to buy additional time before making a concession. The longer a caucus lasts over a bargaining issue, the more important the issue is likely to be to negotiators. Suppose that the union proposes Martin Luther King's birthday as an additional paid holiday and in return is willing to drop its proposal for double time premium pay (instead of time and a half) for employees working on Sundays during peak business periods. If management calls a brief caucus of 20 minutes before rejecting the proposal, then the union chief negotiator may perceive that management's "no" is, in fact, final. On the other hand, if management spends two hours discussing the proposal, then the union may believe that the rejection is a "soft" no and a settlement on this issue is still possible.

Making Cost Estimates on Proposals

Management negotiators, perhaps more than union negotiators, must be able quickly and accurately to make cost estimates on contract proposals.[32] Chief negotiators often use accountants to make cost calculations; however, persons who prepare the cost estimates should have an understanding of the collective bargaining process as well as a familiarity with the financial condition of the firm. In addition, the chief negotiator must understand the basis on which cost estimates are made. An accountant who mechanically computes costs without appreciating the impact that such costs have on the firm, coupled with a chief negotiator who does not understand the basis of the cost estimates, can lay the foundation for some expensive mistakes. The availability of personal computers and software now makes it possible to make cost calculations quickly and easily. Estimates that once required tedious calculations by hand or with an electronic calculator can now be done in a matter of seconds with a personal computer. Printouts and graphs can also be made using modern software to illustrate quickly the cost implications for alternative proposals. If computers are used, negotiators should be cautioned against leaving printouts and software disks in rooms that are accessible to the opposing bargaining team. This warning is not to imply that espionage is common during contract talks, but carelessly discarded printouts or a misplaced computer disk may provide valuable information to the opposing bargaining team.

Cost estimates are largely a matter of knowing how much money will be spent and when the expenditure will be made. Many negotiators incorporate the present value or time value of money into their calculations. Simply stated, a dollar today is worth more than a dollar at some future date. From management's standpoint, it is better to defer wage and benefit increases as long as possible. The union, of course, wants to receive these increases for its members at the earliest possible date. Management's chief negotiator may have to decide whether it would be less expensive to provide a four percent wage increase for each year of a three-year contract or provide three percent the first year, another four percent the second year, and an additional six percent during the third year. If the employer's present value for money is high, it may opt for the second plan because a smaller wage increase will be required during the first year of the contract. However, the employer should realize that wages will increase by more than 13 percent at the end of the three-year period under the second plan as opposed to 12 percent under the first. Thus the second plan provides a higher starting point for wages when the contract is renegotiated in three years. A one percent wage difference may not seem large, but if the firm employs 1000 full-time employees, each working 2000 hours per year, at an average wage of $8.00 per hour, then a one percent difference in pay will amount to approximately $160,000 per year in labor costs (excluding employee benefits).

---

[32] See Michael H. Granoff, *How To Cost Your Labor Agreement* (Washington, D.C.: The Bureau of National Affairs, Inc., 1973); Charles S. Loughran, *Negotiating a Labor Contract: A Management Handbook* (Washington, D.C.: The Bureau of National Affairs, Inc., 1984), pp. 229–259; and Gene Daniels and Kenneth Gagala, *Labor Guide to Negotiating Wages and Benefits* (Reston, Virginia: Reston Publishing Company, 1985), Chapters 3 and 4.

Negotiators often make the distinction between "old money" and "new money" when discussing cost estimates. Old money represents costs that are perpetuated from the previous collective bargaining agreement, whereas new money represents additional costs imposed by the new contract. If the firm's average wage under the previous contract was $8.00 per hour and the wage under the new contract is $8.48, then the 48 cent differential is new money. Likewise, any increase in employee benefits will be regarded as new money if there is a cost impact on the employer during the life of the new contract. However, not all benefit increases result in new money. Suppose the new collective bargaining agreement provides employees having 20 or more years of seniority with an additional week of paid vacation per year. If the firm currently has no workers with this much seniority, then there are no new money liabilities for the employer.[33]

An important element to consider when making cost estimates are "rollup" or "loading" costs. Rollup costs occur because wage increases lead directly to cost increases for some employee benefits. If a collective bargaining agreement calls for a 6 percent increase, then not only will the employer's total wage costs increase, but costs for overtime, holiday and vacation pay, and sick leave will also rise. Other payments such as social security, unemployment compensation, and pension contributions may be affected as well. The rollup factor is usually between 20 and 40 percent of total wages, depending on the firm's employee benefit program. If a company's rollup factor is 30 percent, then a six percent wage increase will add an additional 1.8 percent (6.0 percent × 30 percent) to total labor costs. Rollup costs can be a significant expense and should be considered whenever cost estimates are made.

Rollup costs are not the only costs that can surprise the inexperienced negotiator. Noneconomic provisions such as seniority also have a cost impact. Suppose that a new contract provision is negotiated which provides the most senior employees first refusal rights on overtime assignments. As a general rule, senior employees will have higher hourly wage rates than less senior employees. Under this provision, overtime costs can be considerably higher if a large number of senior employees exercise their option to work at one and a half or two times their normal wage. Hidden indirect costs are also incurred when paid vacation benefits are increased. As more employees are granted time off with pay, the employer may be forced to either hire new employees or use additional overtime hours. These indirect costs need to be considered when cost calculations are made at the bargaining table. A detailed examination of cost calculations is presented at the end of Chapter 14.

Drafting Contract Language

The written word of the collective bargaining agreement determines the rights and responsibilities of bargaining-unit employees and management; therefore, it is important that the contract language is drafted carefully so that it accurately reflects

---

[33] Charles S. Loughran, *Negotiating a Labor Contract: A Management Handbook* (Washington, D.C.: The Bureau of National Affairs, Inc., 1984), pp. 232–234.

what was agreed upon at the bargaining table. Drafting contract language as the terms are settled during negotiations will minimize the possibility for misunderstandings. Once a provision is tentatively drafted, then a labor attorney or expert in contract language can review the provision to determine if there are any loopholes or legal problems that could cause trouble in the future. Occasionally one side will propose the insertion of a contract provision that has been used in another collective bargaining agreement. Unless the provision perfectly fits the intent of the parties, standard contract provisions should be avoided. A contract clause that worked in another collective bargaining agreement will not necessarily fit the current labor-management situation.[34]

Contract language must be clearly written. Provisions must be understandable to the supervisors, shop stewards, and employees who must interpret the contract. However, the provisions must also be written knowing that an arbitrator, the National Labor Relations Board, or a judge may have to read and interpret the collective bargaining agreement. The contract draftsperson should constantly anticipate how the provisions *might* be misconstrued or used to the advantage of the other side. A contract should not necessarily be written by a lawyer who employs all of the latest legal terms—to do so makes the contract difficult to understand for supervisors, shop stewards, and employees. To avoid misconstruing contract provisions, both sides should play the devil's advocate by constantly surmising how the contract can be interpreted in different situations.

The following contract term was incorporated into a collective bargaining agreement:

> Being absent from work for four (4) working days without reporting to the Company shall be reason for discharge. However, in such cases where an employee is unable to call in or report due to a condition beyond his control, this section does not apply.[35]

This clause presents several problems for management. First, the phrase "reporting to the Company" does not specify exactly to whom the employee must report. Is it a supervisor or a department head? Is it permissible for the employee to notify the company through a co-worker or spouse? The phrase that is especially troublesome is: "However, in such cases where an employee is unable to call in or report due to a condition beyond his control, this section shall not apply." Suppose that an employee does not come to work because of a common cold and does not call his supervisor. The employee claims that he did not call the company because the telephone company had disconnected his service for nonpayment. Is this "a condition beyond his control?" The employer could argue that the employee has no legitimate excuse for failing to call in, whereas the union could insist that no

---

[34] The U.S. Department of Labor maintains a Union Contract File. The Bureau of National Affairs, Inc., publishes *Collective Bargaining Negotiations & Contracts*, a loose-leaf service that contains, among other things, sample contract provisions. Union and management negotiators may find these sample clauses helpful.

[35] This clause was taken from a collective bargaining agreement in the food service industry.

disciplinary action is warranted. Problems such as these could be eliminated by drafting the contract language as follows:

> Being absent from work for four (4) working days without personally contacting his immediate supervisor, department head, or the plant personnel manager, shall be reason for discharge. However, in such cases where an employee is unable to call in or report because of confinement to a hospital or because adverse weather or power outages preclude the use of telephones, this section shall not apply.

A clause such as this is clear and contains few ambiguities that could create contract administration problems; it allows the employer and union to excuse employees with legitimate reasons for not calling in, yet makes it difficult for employees to abuse the system.

Contract provisions should be kept simple and consistent with other sections of the collective bargaining agreement. It is advisable not to use multiple terms for the same object. For example, a contract making reference to "employees" in one section should not refer to them as "persons" or "individuals" in another section because of the potential for confusion. Legal terms make the contract difficult to read and do not guarantee that it will stand up any better before an arbitrator or in court than a contract written in simpler language; words like "hereunto" or "provided however" are no more exacting than "to this" or "except." When inserting new contract provisions, be sure that they do not conflict with or change the meaning of other contract provisions. If the seniority system is changed from a department-wide to a plant-wide system during contract talks, it would be short-sighted to ignore how this change might affect job assignment, overtime, retirement eligibility, and vacation provisions. Finally, the contract should be free of overly general and vague terms such as "etc.," and "so forth,"; it should have frequent headings and subheadings to enhance readability, and it should specify the dates that provisions are to take effect if they differ from the date that the contract goes into effect.[36]

The Eleventh-Hour Bargaining Stage

Union and management negotiators enter the eleventh-hour or crisis stage of bargaining when they realize that the contract expiration date is near and a substantial number of issues remain unresolved. Negotiations evolve into marathon sessions that often are accompanied by heated discussions, strike threats, final offers, and last-minute maneuvering to reach a settlement and avoid a work stoppage. Eleventh-hour bargaining situations are filled with pressure and the long sessions at the bargaining table can be fatiguing. Negotiators must guard against succumbing to the fatigue of marathon bargaining sessions by conceding too quickly or making proposals that are ill-advised.

Several important questions must be addressed by union and management negotiators during the eleventh-hour stage. How hard should a chief negotiator

---

[36] Charles S. Loughran, *Negotiating a Labor Contract: A Management Handbook* (Washington, D.C.: The Bureau of National Affairs, Inc., 1984), pp. 260–281.

push to reach a settlement and what tactics can be used to bring negotiations to a successful conclusion? When should mediators be called in to help avoid a possible work stoppage? When should the contingency plan for a work stoppage be implemented? What post-negotiation matters need to be resolved?

Moving Toward a Settlement

The process of contract negotiations can appear endless. Once the crisis stage is reached and the pressure to settle begins to build, negotiators from both sides can employ a number of tactics to bring contract talks to a close. An experienced negotiator can often detect when the other side is attempting to conclude contract talks. When the opposing chief negotiator makes concessions at a faster rate than before, drops less important demands, proposes final package offers, or agrees to concessions without obtaining a concession of equal value in return, then it is likely that he or she is becoming anxious to reach a settlement. When a final offer is made, it should be done in earnest. The term *final* means that no further concessions are likely on a contract provision; making a final offer and then later agreeing to additional concessions can damage a negotiator's credibility.

If union and management negotiators are close to agreement on all major contract terms, a skilled chief negotiator can use a little creativity to bring contract talks to a close. Suppose that management has offered a seven-percent wage increase for a three-year collective bargaining agreement, but the union has issued a "final" demand of 7.5 percent. The union chief negotiator has perhaps unwisely spread the word to the rank-and-file that he will stand firm on the 7.5 percent wage demand; if the chief negotiator later reduces this demand, he or she will lose credibility with union members and management negotiators. An astute management negotiator who wants to reach a settlement and avoid a work stoppage might concede to the 7.5 percent wage demand by making the pay raise effective at the beginning of the next calendar year rather than at the beginning of the contract date. Thus if the new contract is effective June 1st, the 7.5 percent wage increase can be deferred for seven months. In the meantime, the company saves labor costs with a lower wage rate and the union chief negotiator is able to save face and maintain credibility.

Negotiators often become committed to principles that are no longer valid because of social, legal, or economic changes. Labor negotiators often try to preserve the union shop clause because of past problems with free riders who did not join the union or pay dues, but who received all of the benefits of union membership. Labor leaders maintain that many employees will not join the union unless membership is mandated by the union shop clause. As a result, the union loses dues revenues and the camaraderie among bargaining-unit members may be destroyed if some employees are union members and others refuse to join. This objection could pose a serious roadblock to a settlement unless the union reconsiders the provision. Will the absence of a union shop clause still create free riders among the company's current employees? If so, how much dues revenue will be lost? If the union has built a good reputation among employees so that nearly all are willing to join, the union chief negotiator should seriously consider removing the union shop clause as a settlement roadblock. A willingness to engage in creative bargaining and to re-examine antiquated principles is sometimes necessary in the eleventh-hour stages of negotiations. Bargaining behavior that emphasizes creativity and willingness to reach a mutually acceptable settlement not only avoids unnecessary work stoppages, but also improves the quality of union-management relations.

Identifying the Need for a Mediator

At some point in the contract talks, the parties may realize that a settlement is unlikely without the help of an outside third party known as a mediator. Mediators are commonly provided free-of-charge by the Federal Mediation and Conciliation Service (FMCS). The primary responsibility of a mediator is to help the parties help themselves; a mediator normally does not attempt to impose a settlement, but rather conciliates, persuades, and assists parties in order to avoid a work stoppage. As noted earlier, neither the union nor the management bargaining team is obligated to accept the services of an FMCS mediator.

The best time to make arrangements for mediation is once the chief negotiators recognize that the possibility of an impasse exists. If the chief negotiators wait until the contract expiration date is at hand, then the mediator may not have enough time to help the parties resolve the deadlock in contract talks. Likewise, if conflict associated with contract talks escalates to hostility, then the mediator may be unable to resolve the differences and avoid a work stoppage. The dynamics of mediation are discussed in Chapter 10.

Implementing a Strike Plan

As a part of bargaining preparations, many bargaining teams formulate a strike plan. Management's strike or lockout plan usually addresses issues such as whether to maintain full or partial operations during a work stoppage, arrangements to serve customers, supplier arrangements, plant security, availability of jobs to bargaining-unit employees who do not wish to participate in the strike, and strike replacements for workers who do. The union's strike plan includes staffing picket lines, making strike fund payments to eligible union members, and keeping international officials abreast on pertinent events associated with the dispute. Both sides may also want to arrange further contract talks during the work stoppage.[37]

When contract negotiations near the deadline, negotiators must decide when to begin putting strike or lockout plans into effect. If management begins to recruit employees to serve as strike replacements, several questions arise. Is management actually intending to endure a strike or are they making a last ditch effort to bluff the union? Could management be guilty of bad-faith bargaining if they shift their attention from the bargaining table in order to procure strike replacements? How will the company's customers and suppliers react? The union may send a signal to management that it expects a strike or is willing to endure a strike when it polls bargaining-unit members regarding their desire to withstand a work stoppage. Strike threats during eleventh-hour negotiations bring up two important points for the

---

[37] See Charles R. Perry, Andrew M. Kramer, and Thomas J. Schneider, *Operating During Strikes* (Philadelphia: Industrial Research Unit, The Wharton School, University of Pennsylvania, 1982).

negotiators' consideration. First, initial strike preparations just before an impasse or contract expiration date can provide the catalyst for a settlement. Of course, such preparations can backfire and push the opposing side into a work stoppage. Second, negotiators must remember that innocent bystanders can be injured by a work stoppage. The welfare of customers, suppliers, nonunion employees working outside the bargaining unit, and others affected by the work stoppage must be considered. If a work stoppage appears likely, management should inform supply and sales personnel so that those doing business with the company are not caught off guard. Likewise, the personnel department should notify nonunion employees who are likely to suffer a layoff or reduction in work hours if negotiations end in a strike. Chapter 10 provides a detailed discussion on the costs and legal ramifications of work stoppages.

Post-Settlement Issues

In most negotiations, a mutually satisfactory settlement will be reached without a work stoppage. If management negotiators have the authority to settle without further approval or ratification by the corporate president or board of directors, a written memorandum of agreement is drafted, subject to final ratification by the union members. Most collective bargaining agreements are ratified by the rank-and-file when the union leadership wholeheartedly endorses its terms and conditions. When union leaders do not enthusiastically endorse the contract or when they discourage ratification in hopes of a more favorable settlement, a contract rejection is likely.[38] For this reason, management may request that the union negotiators sign a contract provision to fully support ratification by the rank-and-file. This tactic imposes a moral obligation on union negotiators to encourage ratification.[39] Until the contract is ratified, it is wise not to publicize widely the terms of the agreement. Management should use caution when discussing the terms of the tentative settlement with employees because of the potential for bad-faith bargaining charges. Union negotiators should ensure that the terms and conditions of the contract are thoroughly explained to the rank-and-file. If the contract is rejected, management must be careful about granting additional economic concessions that will encourage future rejections. A negative ratification vote can often be reversed by repackaging contract items, isolating dissident membership elements and selling the offer to them, re-explaining troublesome provisions to the rank-and-file, and warning union members about the consequences of a work stoppage.

Occasionally a negotiator will attempt to add minor provisions to the contract after negotiations have been closed. These provisions are usually minor and a work stoppage is not likely to occur even if they are rejected. In most instances, last-minute add-on provisions represent unethical chiseling by a negotiator who is out to squeeze whatever concessions he or she can from the other party. Since a work stoppage is unlikely, proposals made after the close of negotiations should be flatly

---

[38] Union negotiators may desire a negative ratification vote so that they can tell the employer that they were right (i.e., "We told you so.") about the position of their member constituents.

[39] Charles S. Loughran, *Negotiating a Labor Contract: A Management Handbook* (Washington, D.C.: The Bureau of National Affairs, Inc., 1984), p. 372.

rejected. Negotiators should avoid the temptation to accept these minor add-on provisions in order to maintain goodwill between the union and management.[40]

Once the contract language has been drafted in final form and the ratification vote has been completed, then the collective bargaining agreement usually goes into effect and the new wage scale, benefits, and other changes become a part of the union-management relationship. Management should conduct training programs to ensure that supervisors understand the new contract provisions. Union and management negotiating teams can also arrange to have minutes of the negotiations drafted. Both the supervisory training programs and the minutes of the negotiations can later become valuable aids if arbitration hearings are needed to resolve grievances under the new contract. Each side should analyze and critique their performance at the bargaining table. Did the parties achieve their goals? Were prenegotiations preparations sufficient? What unexpected tactics did the opposing side use? Was the original bargaining strategy followed and, if not, what turn of events precluded successful pursuit of the strategy? What mistakes were made that could be avoided in future negotiations? Answers to these questions provide a foundation for the next round of negotiations.

▲ Summary and Conclusions

This chapter presents a practical view of bargaining preparations and strategy. Contract negotiations can be extremely complex, and no two union-management negotiating situations are alike. The key to successful negotiations is to prepare extensively, use care in making proposals and counterproposals, and bargain in good faith. Most union and management negotiators are prudent individuals who understand the process of bargaining. Although negotiators are hired and paid to drive a hard bargain, they are usually not attempting to take unfair advantage and destroy the other side. Unlike bargains struck over temporary business deals, collective bargaining relationships endure for years and even decades. Therefore, both sides must learn when to apply pressure and when to accommodate the needs of the other side.

Chapter 10 discusses the problems that arise when negotiations lead to impasses and work stoppages. Conflict occasionally arises in collective bargaining and skillful conflict resolution is an important facet of industrial and labor relations. Tools such as labor mediation and interest arbitration have been successfully used when contract talks disintegrate. Although many conflicts can be avoided by following some of the suggestions made in this chapter, other conflicts are rooted deeply in the fabric of the union and management relationship.

---

[40] Charles S. Loughran, *Negotiating a Labor Contract: A Management Handbook* (Washington, D.C.: The Bureau of National Affairs, Inc., 1984), p. 372.

▲ Discussion Questions and Exercises

1. Examine the stages of the bargaining process outlined in this chapter. Assume you are going to purchase a new automobile. How might your recognition of these stages and the procedures within each stage prove useful in negotiating over the terms and price of your purchase?
2. You are a member of the local school board. Recently, the teachers became unionized and now want to negotiate over wages, hours, and working conditions. What criteria will you use to select negotiators to represent the school board when they meet the teachers' union bargaining team?
3. Two years ago, a bicycle manufacturer negotiated a contract with the International Pedal Assemblers' union. The bicycle company "took a beating" at the bargaining table, primarily because their inexperienced negotiators were poorly prepared. The firm's president has hired you to help the negotiating team avoid the same mistake during the next round of negotiations. How will you proceed?
4. In his article, "Ten Guidelines for Effective Negotiating," published in *Business Horizons* (May-June 1987), Professor Joseph Byrnes lists the following suggestions that are useful to a wide variety negotiations:
   a. Preparing for negotiations;
   b. Recognizing different perceptions;
   c. Avoiding corners;
   d. Using creativity and imagination;
   e. Appreciating the power of silence;
   f. Making tradeoffs;
   g. Helping the other side to agree;
   h. Taking notes;
   i. Valuing deadlines; and
   j. Anticipating no agreement.

Read this article and discuss the specific application of these 10 guidelines to union-management contract talks.

Part V

Resolving Interest and Rights Disputes Over the Collective Bargaining Agreement

▲ ▲

The labor relations system in the United States places a strong emphasis on the resolution of disputes. Part V discusses two types of disputes: **interest disputes**, *which arise when contract negotiations do not result in a settlement, and* **rights disputes**, *which arise over the interpretation of an existing collective bargaining agreement.*

Chapter 10 focuses on interest disputes and examines the role and causes of labor-management conflict. The role of labor mediation in resolving interest disputes is discussed. Although most contract negotiations do not lead to a strike and lockout, such tactics make front-page news when they occur. Chapter 10 discusses the various types of strikes, union and management preparation for work stoppages, and the rights of striking employees.

Chapters 11 and 12 deal with rights disputes. Chapter 11 focuses on the role of contract administration in industrial relations. Since the contractual grievance procedure serves as the centerpiece for contract administration, a great deal of attention is given to how grievance mechanisms are designed and administered. In addition, Chapter 11 discusses the union's duty of fair representation and criteria for evaluating the effectiveness of a grievance procedure.

Chapter 12 deals with the final stage of most grievance procedures: binding arbitration. Labor arbitration has assumed an important role in resolving rights disputes in the United States. Chapter 12 discusses labor arbitrator qualifications, arbitration arrangements, and the legal status of arbitration. Factors used by arbitrators in rendering their decisions are also discussed.

10 Negotiation Impasses and Labor Disputes

- **Introduction**
- **Conflict in Labor-Management Relations**
  The Role of Conflict
  Sources of Conflict in Labor-Management Relations
    Bargaining Structure Problems
    Inadequate Decision-Making Power of Negotiators
    Intraorganizational Conflicts
    Antagonistic Policies and Actions
    Procedural Sources of Conflict
    Economic and Labor Market Conditions
    Foreign and Domestic Competition
    The Public Interest
- **The Role of Mediation in Preventing Labor Disputes**
  Federal and State Mediation Agencies
  The Functions of Labor Mediators
    Procedural Mediation Functions
    Communications Functions during Mediation
    Substantive Mediation Functions
  Mediation Effectiveness
- **Strikes and Lockouts**
  The Economic Strike
    Economic Strike Costs to the Employer
    Economic Strike Costs to the Union and Striking Employees
    Maintaining Operations during an Economic Strike
    Union Preparations for an Economic Strike
    The Employment Rights of Economic Strikers
    Dealing With Violence, Harassment, and Sabotage

The Unfair Labor Practice Strike
Sympathy Strikes
Wildcat Strikes and Slowdowns
Lockouts
▲ **National Emergency Disputes**
▲ **Summary and Conclusions**
▲ **Discussion Questions and Exercises**
▲ **Selected Labor Disputes**
The San Francisco Nurses Strike
The Screen Actors and Screen Extras Strike
The New York University Clerical Workers Strike

▲ Introduction

This chapter examines impasses and disputes in union-management relations. Most union-management contract negotiations avoid major disputes and end in a settlement. Some labor disputes are resolved with the help of a mediator after a temporary impasse. Less than 10 percent of negotiations end in a strike or lockout. The majority of work stoppages last two to three weeks. However, a few work stoppages continue for several months and occasionally involve hostilities, picket line skirmishes, and violence. Along with organized crime's influence on some unions, strikes and lockouts receive more media attention than any other aspect of labor relations.

The discussion of negotiation impasses and labor disputes in this chapter begins with a brief discussion of conflict in labor relations. The institution of labor mediation as a means of resolving union-management conflicts is then examined. Finally, the various types of work stoppages are discussed. The legal rights of strikers and employers are described along with the dynamics of work stoppages.

▲ Conflict in Labor-Management Relations

The Role of Conflict

The union-management relationship has traditionally been viewed as one of competition and conflict. Perhaps the relationship can be summarized as follows:

> The easiest thing for unions to do is to continue to stress a strongly adversarial approach to management. Because management is often insensitive to the needs of employees, the unions are able to cite a long list of management actions and inactions that seem to justify retaining an emphasis on challenging management action. To a large degree the unions have become captives of their origins. Born in adversity and conflict, they continued to act as opponents of management when their strength had become much greater. In some instances unions have created a web of rules which immobilize management, just as spiders build webs to ensnare prey. When the webs of rules have crippled productivity, the unions

have discovered that not only managers but also unions have been caught in the trap. Plants have declined in competitiveness and jobs have been lost. The unions have discovered too late that a snare is no less a snare because you have set it yourself.[1]

Tradition carries a great deal of weight in labor-management relations. As the labor movement gained tremendous momentum after the Wagner Act was passed in the 1930s, it was probably necessary for unions to challenge management's every move. However, as the 20th century draws to a close, the role of labor-management conflict may be diminishing. It is possible that a certain degree of conflict is both inevitable and beneficial; it keeps both sides alert and on the defensive and neither side is likely to become complacent and let its guard down. On the other hand, conflicts lead to mutual distrust, difficulties at the bargaining table, and damaging strikes and lockouts. Whether labor and management's interests are irreconcilable is subject to debate. Some experts argue that labor-management cooperation is a necessity if American industry is to remain competitive.[2] Because the relationship between unions and management is adversarial and will likely remain so in the foreseeable future, persons involved with labor relations will have to deal with impasses and work stoppages.

Sources of Conflict in Labor-Management Relations

The following hypothetical scenario provides some interesting insights into union-management conflict:

Once there was a president of a small unorganized company who believed firmly in labor unions. He was therefore gratified when his employees notified him that they were joining a union and wished to bargain collectively with him. The negotiating committee submitted its demands in advance and the president studied them carefully. As he compared those demands with contracts in other companies in his industry, he could find nothing that seemed unreasonable. The employees were simply asking for conditions that would put them in line with those exisiting in plants which had been organized for several years. So when the negotiating committee came in to bargain he simply told them that he was prepared to accept their terms in full and sign a contract at once. Such a magnanimous attitude, he thought, would establish a firm basis for harmonious relations.

In legal and economic terms, the union had won without effort the gains that had been achieved with great difficulty by other organizations. You would think, therefore, that the union people would have been very happy. This was not so. The employer's troubles began as soon as he had signed the contract. Productivity fell off, there were wildcat strikes in one department after another,

---

[1] Daniel Quinn Mills and Janice McCormick, *Industrial Relations in Transition: Cases and Text* (New York: John Wiley & Sons, Inc., 1985), Chapter 13. Reprinted in Harvard Business School, *Course Development & Research Profile*, 1987 (Boston: Harvard Business School, 1987), p. 95.

[2] See The Bureau of National Affairs, Inc., "Labor-Management Cooperation Key to Improving Productivity," *Labor Relations Reporter*, Vol. 127 (Washington, D.C.: The Bureau of National Affairs, Inc., April 18, 1988), pp. 481–482.

and it was many months before relations settled down into the harmonious pattern that the employer's friendly attitude should have made possible.[3]

An explanation as to why the union and employees were not happy even though the employer granted each and every one of their demands sheds some light on the origins of union-management conflict. First, it could be argued that workers are never satisfied; no matter what one has in terms of wages, hours, and working conditions, there is always room for improvement. Second, the ease with which the settlement occurred probably made the workers believe that an even better contract was possible if the negotiators would have exerted more pressure on management. Third, the workers may have felt that the contract was "negotiated" with little or no input from them. Since the contract terms were based on what other unions had obtained from firms in the same industry rather than on what the employees felt was a "just" settlement, they probably felt like outsiders in the collective bargaining process. In a nutshell, the union and workers did not have to fight for an acceptable contract. The company simply gave the employees what they wanted without any of the usual haggling, bluffing, and threats that accompany contract talks. As a result, the workers missed the excitement of challenging management in a heated series of contract talks. This scenario suggests that some union-management conflict is probably inevitable in the Western culture. Conflict can stem from a number of sources, some of which are discussed below.

Bargaining Structure Problems

As discussed in Chapter 4, the structure of the bargaining unit forms an important foundation for union-management relations and can either heighten or diminish labor-management conflict. Narrow bargaining units that serve a group of employees who share similar pay, working conditions, and skill levels may have less difficulty reaching an agreement than a large, diversified bargaining unit.

There are likely to be differences among companies or unions regarding bargaining demands and strategies when employer associations (more than one company bargaining with a single union over a single contract) or coordinated bargaining (more than one union bargaining with a single employer) are used. Employer associations (also known as multi-employer bargaining units) comprised of competing firms may have a particularly difficult time during the preparation stages of negotiations and during contract talks. Strong companies within the employer association may be willing to make concessions that a weak company might find financially ruinous.[4] On the other hand, if an employer association caters to the bargaining demands of its weakest firm, it may have a difficult time reaching a settlement with union negotiators.

Inadequate Decision-Making Power of Negotiators

Negotiators who do not have the authority to reach an agreement without consulting a higher authority in the organization are likely to cause bargaining delays,

---

[3] Donald E. Cullen, *Negotiating Labor-Management Contracts* (Ithaca, New York: New York State School of Industrial and Labor Relations, Cornell University, 1965), pp. 8–9.

[4] A firm cannot disassociate from an employer association during contract negotiations.

frustrations, and conflict. The "unseen authority" tactic (discussed in Chapter 9) is used when a negotiator discusses a proposal with a higher-ranking union or management official before reaching an agreement or making a counterproposal. An excessive use of the "unseen authority" tactic can slow negotiations and cause the opposing side to lose patience. When the parties must tolerate constant interruptions, the contract deadline may be reached with a number of unsettled issues still on the agenda.

The problem of inadequate decision-making power is most prevalent in public-sector bargaining, where negotiators must obtain approval from budgetary authorities such as a state legislature before final approval can be given for pay and benefit increases. In the private sector, the good-faith bargaining requirement of the National Labor Relations Act makes the "unseen authority" tactic a legal risk. Agencies that regulate public-sector labor relations recognize that negotiators who must wait for legislatively approved budgets are not guilty of bad-faith bargaining. Nevertheless, frustrations and feelings of helplessness among public-sector unions and employees may precipitate an illegal strike in order to gain the attention of government officials and the general public.

Intraorganizational Conflicts

Union and management negotiators are frequently faced with a multitude of demands. The union bargaining team must appease diverse interests from bargaining-unit members whose age, sex, skill levels, seniority, commitment to the job, marital status, and family obligations may vary considerably. In addition, union members are often aware of wage levels and employee benefits negotiated by other unions in the same geographic region or industry. All of these factors affect the expectations of bargaining-unit members as the union prepares to negotiate a collective bargaining agreement. When bargaining-unit member interests are diverse or another nearby union has been successful at the bargaining table, it may be difficult for union negotiators to reach an agreement with management that satisfies members' needs and expectations. Once the collective bargaining agreement is negotiated, the members must vote to accept its terms (known as a contract ratification). For example, flight attendants at United Airlines soundly rejected a tentative agreement because of their dislike for the two-tier pay system.[5] Teamsters members voted to reject a contract covering some 20,000 truckers employed by 15 companies because of their dissatisfaction with wage proposals contained in the contract.[6] The United Rubber Workers rejected a tentative three-year agreement with Goodyear Tire and Rubber Co., because the contract would have frozen wages for 15,000 employees at 11 Goodyear locations nationwide.[7] In these examples, it appears that union negotiators misjudged the desires of bargaining-unit members.

---

[5] The Bureau of National Affairs, Inc., "UAL Contract Rejection," *Collective Bargaining Negotiations & Contracts* (Washington, D.C.: The Bureau of National Affairs, Inc., January 14, 1988), pp. 1–2.
[6] The Bureau of National Affairs, Inc., "Rejected Teamsters Agreement," *Collective Bargaining Contracts & Negotiations* (Washington, D.C.: The Bureau of National Affairs, Inc., August 11, 1988), p. 1.
[7] The Bureau of National Affairs, Inc., "Goodyear Settlement Disapproval," *Collective Bargaining Negotiations & Contracts* (Washington, D.C.: The Bureau of National Affairs, Inc., May 5, 1988), p. 1.

In large bargaining units, informal employee factions may attempt to push their special interests. For example, employees with a great deal of seniority may have a strong desire to link job assignments, working conditions, and employee benefits to seniority. Younger employees might prefer to use a strict definition of individual qualifications and ability to perform a job in making job assignments; they might also prefer that employee benefits be based on wage rates or number of dependents rather than on seniority. As factions develop among union members with different interests, the likelihood of intraorganizational conflicts arises. These conflicts may lead to contract rejections and strikes.

Management negotiators also face conflicting demands that must be resolved prior to negotiations. Corporate boards are often responsible for setting broad labor relations policies. Boards, chief executive officers, and vice presidents for industrial relations must balance the sometimes competing needs of stockholders and employees along with their own personal stake in the organization. When board members either disagree among themselves or are unrealistic about the demands that should be pursued by management negotiators, the seeds for conflict may have been planted.

Antagonistic Policies and Actions

The old saying that "familiarity breeds contempt" may form the basis for some labor disputes. Union or management negotiators who develop an antagonistic approach toward collective bargaining may set the stage for labor turmoil. Negotiators may actually go to the bargaining table planning to withstand a strike or lockout before a contract settlement is reached. Because of the long-term nature of the union-management relationship, future contract negotiations may be hindered by hostile or unethical actions by supervisors, labor relations and personnel directors, and union officials.

As is the case with most long-term relationships, each party must learn to cooperate and develop a "give-and-take" attitude with the other side. Union officials who rigidly enforce the contract, file grievances against supervisors over trifling matters, and zealously challenge management's every decision will likely create a working relationship filled with distrust and animosity. Suppose a union files a grievance against a supervisor who picked up a piece of material that had fallen off a conveyer belt and placed it back on the belt. The union contested the action and claimed that the supervisor was performing work normally done by bargaining-unit employees. Grievances such as these waste time and money, and create hard feelings that can smolder and later erupt into a labor dispute. Management policies and actions can also antagonize the union. Suppose management unilaterally makes changes in working conditions without consulting the union. In doing so, management is not only engaging in bad-faith bargaining, but is also damaging its relationship with union officials and employees.

Labor disputes do not necessarily end when a new contract is approved by negotiators and ratified by bargaining-unit members. Hard feelings may persist long after negotiations come to a close, and such feelings may carry over into a new round of negotiations several years later. As one veteran National Football League player remarked after the 1987 National Football League Players Association (NFLPA) strike:

> Management wanted it [the settlement] and they got it. They squeezed the players to a certain point, and I really don't think the NFL will be the same until you get a whole new crop of players in who haven't gone through the situation. I think there's a lot of bitterness still going on between players. Players are back doing their jobs, but I don't think things will be the same again in the NFL for a while.[8]

Clashes between personnel directors, supervisors, and union officials may also be remembered when contract negotiations occur. Gloating over previous successes at the bargaining table, failing to cooperate when administering the agreement, and using loopholes in the contract to take advantage of the other side all serve to breed contempt. In addition, vendettas spawned by personality differences or disagreements between union and management officials may increase the potential for labor disputes.

Procedural Sources of Conflict

Some labor disputes arise because of procedures and arrangements associated with the collective bargaining process. If the union makes its initial demands orally rather than in writing, the likelihood of misunderstandings and conflicts may be increased. As noted earlier, negotiators who must obtain approval from a higher authority may slow the proceedings down to the point where the opposition becomes impatient or there is inadequate time to complete negotiations prior to a strike deadline. Chief negotiators who fail to plan carefully regarding the negotiating ground rules, the scheduling of meetings, or obtaining the services of a mediator may also find themselves embroiled in a labor dispute that could have otherwise been avoided.

Informal bargaining relationships that become disrupted can also enhance conflict. Some negotiators prefer to present all written demands to the other side well ahead of the actual contract talks; others are skillful at extracting concessions from an opponent away from the bargaining table during coffee breaks or caucuses. There may be instances in which a group of union and management negotiators have become comfortable with a particular bargaining site, meeting schedule, or mode of bargaining. For example, negotiators may have traditionally held their contract negotiations at a particular hotel; they may also have followed a specific bargaining protocol such as presenting their initial demands in writing, exchanging relevant information freely, and allowing each side ample time to consider new proposals. If negotiators are forced to abandon their methods of bargaining because of changes in union or management policy or because new negotiators resist the "old way" of doing business, then a conflict may arise.

---

[8] See Martha I. Finney, "Owners Play Hardball, Win Football Strike," *Resource* (Arlington, Virginia: American Society for Personnel Administration, November 1987), p. 18; and Terry L. Leap and Michael D. Crino, *Personnel/Human Resource Management* (New York: Macmillan Publishing Company, 1989), p. 681.

Economic and Labor Market Conditions

The outcome of contract talks and the likelihood of a labor dispute may be affected by economic and labor market conditions. During periods of high inflation, unions attempt to press for higher wages by citing increases in the consumer price index and the need to maintain the union members' *real* income.[9] Inflationary periods may also prompt employers to cite the upward-spiraling costs associated with doing business as a reason for *not* granting generous wage or salary increases. Employers are often reluctant to commit to wage and salary increases for two reasons. First, once pay concessions are granted, they cannot be easily revoked. It is much easier to deny employees a wage or salary increase than to make pay cuts later should financial difficulties occur. During the 1980s two-tier wage plans gained acceptance by organized labor as a means of avoiding across-the-board pay cuts by financially-strapped companies.[10] Second, pay increases also increase employee benefit costs because of the roll-up costs discussed in Chapter 9. Thus, when the union uses inflationary trends as a reason for raising pay and the employer balks at making pay concessions, the probabilty of a labor dispute increases.

Labor markets have been characterized as either "tight" or "loose." A tight labor market is one having a shortage of qualified personnel, whereas a loose labor market is one in which there is an abundant supply of qualified labor.[11] The ability of either the union or management to withstand a labor dispute may depend on the tightness or looseness of a labor market. A tight labor market may be advantageous to the union because it will be difficult for the employer to hire strike replacements. When management cannot easily obtain an adequate amount of labor to continue operations during a strike, they may be forced to concede to union demands. Tight labor markets also make it more likely that union negotiators will press company negotiators to make generous concessions; if union negotiators press too hard, however, management may elect to endure a strike or call a lockout.

Foreign and Domestic Competition

Private-sector firms operate in competitive environments. Companies compete with each other on dimensions such as price, product innovations, quality, production methods, service, and market segment. In unionized industries, a firm's labor costs and product price are often its most crucial competitive factors. Foreign competitors in the steel and textile industries have been especially successful at competing with U.S. steel and textile companies because of labor cost advantages.[12] In indus-

---

[9] *Real income* represents the purchasing power of a person's wage or salary. Thus, if an employee received a five percent raise, yet inflation increased prices by eight percent, the employee's real income would have decreased, although his or her *monetary income* increased.

[10] Two-tier wage plans appear to be declining. "Labor Letter," *The Wall Street Journal* (June 16, 1987), p. 1. Such pay plans may also create problems among members of the same bargaining unit since less senior employees paid in the lower tier may feel like second-class citizens.

[11] The following jingle has been used to make the distinction between loose and tight labor markets: "When the labor market's tight, tell your employer to fly a kite. When the labor market's loose, saying that can cook your goose!"

[12] Cost competitiveness is a major reason why U.S. textile firms have traditionally been strong opponents of organized labor.

tries such as apparel manufacturing, retail grocery, the airlines, and food services, labor costs must be held in check if a firm is to price its product or service competitively. As noted in earlier chapters, unions have attempted to "take wages out of competition" in an industry in order to force firms to compete on some basis other than labor costs.

When management is asked by union negotiators to raise pay levels, it must first consider how the pay raise will affect product or service prices and sales. In industries where there are large differences in unit labor costs from one firm to another, management may strongly resist granting economic concessions to the union if such concessions would place the firm at a competitive disadvantage. When a firm perceives that it will be less competitive because of a union's economic demands, management negotiators may be willing to resist and endure a work stoppage.

The Public Interest

Contract talks affecting a large number of employees in an industry on which the public heavily depends, may receive considerable attention by the news media. The general public may become interested and follow the progress of negotiations, especially if a strike is imminent. One of the costs of a labor dispute, for both the union and the company, is the adverse publicity associated with a work stoppage. Strikes that lead to public inconveniences, such as a major transportation, sanitation workers', or teachers' strike, can lead to public outcries about the irresponsibility of those who caused the work stoppage. The news media may inflame public opinion or "take negotiations away from the bargaining table" by publicizing information leaks or rumors surrounding eleventh-hour negotiations.

Once negotiators believe they have achieved widespread attention from the news media, they may appeal to the general public to sympathize with their position. Negotiators may adopt a hard-nosed approach at the bargaining table and risk a work stoppage in order to demonstrate determination and solidarity to their constituents, the opponent, and the general public. Union negotiators may focus on the plight of the underpaid worker and attempt to portray management as having a cavalier or uncaring attitude toward employees. Management may counter by publicly denouncing the union as unrealistic and irresponsible because labor negotiators are asking for economic concessions that will place the company at a competitive disadvantage. If union or management negotiators publicly announce that they are willing to endure a work stoppage unless certain concessions are granted, they may have painted themselves into the proverbial corner; it will now be difficult to make concessions without losing face in the eyes of the public. As a result, the chances of a work stoppage are enhanced.

▲ The Role of Mediation in Preventing Labor Disputes

As contract negotiations proceed through the primary bargaining stage and into the eleventh hour, union and management negotiators may encounter difficulties. One difficulty is the realization by both sides that a number of important issues remain unresolved as the strike deadline draws closer. Furthermore, the parties may reach an impasse whereby further negotiations appear to be fruitless. Impasses at the bargaining table may occur because of pressures exerted by constituents, unrealistic bargaining demands, and personality conflicts among negotiators. Union and management negotiators may be able to avoid a work stoppage only with the aid of a labor mediator. Because of their training in dispute resolution techniques and their general acceptability to negotiators, mediators have been successful in maintaining industrial peace in the United States. Most mediators working private-sector collective bargaining disputes play a conciliatory role: they "help the parties to help themselves." However, mediators have no legal authority to compel the parties either to accept their services or to reach a settlement.

Federal and State Mediation Agencies

The Federal Mediation and Conciliation Service (FMCS) was created by the Taft-Hartley Act and is both the largest mediation agency in the United States and the largest single source of labor mediators. Although private-sector unions and employees have the right to engage in economic strikes and other forms of work stoppages, the FMCS was established to promote collective bargaining, provide mediation assistance to union and management negotiators, and promote "sound and stable industrial peace."[13] To meet this basic objective, the FMCS employs a staff of approximately 300 mediators nationwide. Many FMCS mediators previously worked as union or management negotiators and receive extensive training by the agency in mediation duties and techniques. The FMCS, headquartered in Washington, D.C., is directed by a presidential appointee. FMCS regional offices, located throughout the United States, engage in "crisis bargaining" mediation for private-sector organizations, provide technical and educational assistance to parties interested in collective bargaining, and assist parties in obtaining labor arbitrators to hear grievances arising out of existing collective bargaining agreements.[14]

The National Mediation Board (NMB) was originally created in 1926 (and reorganized in 1934 into its present form). The primary function of the NMB is to mediate disputes in the railway and airline industries. In addition to the mediation function, the NMB deals with union representation matters within these two industries (a function performed by the National Labor Relations Board in other private-sector industries). Disputes arising out of grievances or the interpretation of an existing collective bargaining agreement in the railway industry are referred to the National Railroad Adjustment Board. The NMB is headquartered in Washington, D.C., but has no regional offices.[15]

A number of states also provide mediation services. In most instances, state mediation agencies are created to handle labor disputes and avoid work stoppages among state or municipal workers (teachers, police officers, firefighters, health care

---

[13] 61 Stat. 136, Title II, Section 201(a) (June 23, 1947).
[14] William E. Simkin and Nicholas A. Fidandis, *Mediation and the Dynamics of Collective Bargaining*, 2nd ed. (Washington, D.C.: The Bureau of National Affairs, Inc., 1986), p. 38.
[15] "National Mediation Board," *The Human Resources Yearbook: 1988 Edition* (Englewood Cliffs, New Jersey: Prentice-Hall, Inc.), pp. 6.39–6.40.

workers, and so forth). Since strikes by public-sector employees are illegal in most states, mediation is used to help the parties minimize disagreements before more forceful measures such as interest arbitration are taken under public-sector bargaining law. Some states also provide mediators for the resolution of private-sector impasses.

The Functions of Labor Mediators

The key objective of private-sector mediation is to encourage union and management negotiators to reach an agreement with as little assistance as possible from the mediator. A basic premise of labor mediation is that the "best" settlement is the one reached by the negotiators without undue influence by outsiders such as mediators. Negotiators who find themselves at an impasse may need only a small "push" from the mediator in order to regain bargaining momentum and reach an agreement before the strike deadline. In other instances, a mediator may have to play a more prominent and decisive role if a work stoppage is to be avoided. Nevertheless, a skilled mediator does no more than what is absolutely necessary to bring about a settlement. By limiting mediator involvement, the parties are allowed to reach their own settlement, rather than having one imposed by a third party.

One important skill associated with labor mediation is to determine when the mediator should enter a dispute. Private-sector negotiators must notify the FMCS at least 30 days before a contract is terminated or modified.[16] This legal requirement allows the FMCS regional office to monitor the progress of negotiations and remain on an informal "standby" status in the event that the parties request mediation services. To monitor the progress of negotiations, a representative from the FMCS may periodically contact the union and management negotiators by telephone and inquire whether the parties anticipate the need for mediation. When a mediator makes an appearance at the bargaining table, the parties may try to sell their proposals to the mediator rather than continue bargaining on their own. If the mediator becomes involved in the bargaining process too early, there is a risk that his or her presence may impede progress at the bargaining table. At the other extreme, the mediator who waits until the dispute has deteriorated to the point where hostilities are intense and bargaining has come to a standstill may find it impossible to avoid a work stoppage.

Once a labor mediator enters a dispute, he or she may employ a number of tactics to help union and management negotiators break an impasse and bargain to a final settlement.[17] Two experienced mediators with the FMCS, William E. Simkin and Nicholas A. Fidandis, have delineated three major categories of mediator functions: (1) functions that are essentially procedural, (2) functions intended to facil-

---

[16] There is no notification requirement for negotiating an *initial* contract. Sec. 8(d)(A) of the Taft-Hartley Act requires that health care institutions give 60 days notice to modify or terminate an existing contract and 30 days notice when negotiating an initial contract. A union representing health care employees must give 10 days notice of its intent to strike.

[17] According to FMCS reports, mediators are called into approximately one-fifth of all contract talks. Thus, the vast majority of union and management negotiators are able to reach an agreement without the assistance of a mediator.

Table 10-1 ▲ Mediation Functions

Procedural Functions

a. Schedule Bargaining Meetings
b. Recess Meetings
c. Arrange Joint and Separate Bargaining Meetings
d. Influence the Duration of Bargaining Meetings
e. Change Location of Meetings
f. Chair Meetings and Maintain Order during Contract Talks
g. Propose a Discussion Sequence or Grouping of Bargaining Issues
h. Suggest Subcommittees during Negotiations
i. Arrange for Orderly Record-Keeping during Negotiations
j. Propose and Develop Procedures for Contract Extensions or Strike Postponements
k. Propose and Develop Procedures for Settlement of Limited Issues
l. Fend Off Outside Intervention
m. Continue Negotiations after the Strike Begins
n. Create Alternative Deadlines after the Strike Begins

Communication Functions

a. Keep Communication Channels Open
b. Try Bargaining Proposals on for Size during Private Meetings with the Mediator
c. Help Assess the Rigidities of the Negotiators' Positions
d. Help Assess the Negotiators' Ability to Sell the Agreement to Constituents
e. Arrange for Top-Level Direct Communications

Substantive Functions

a. Smoke Out the Negotiators' Priorities
b. Deflate Extreme and Unreasonable Positions
c. Offer Creative Suggestions on Specific Issues
d. Assess the Costs of a Work Stoppage
e. Recommend a Package Settlement

Adapted from William E. Simkin and Nicholas A. Fidandis, *Mediation and the Dynamics of Collective Bargaining* (Washington, D.C.: The Bureau of National Affairs, Inc., 1986), pp. 59–88. Reprinted with permission.

itate communications between union and management negotiators, and (3) functions that focus on substantive issues surrounding the dispute. Table 10–1 summarizes the three mediator functions.

Procedural Mediation Functions

Procedural mediation functions involve tasks such as scheduling meetings, record keeping, dealing with the news media, and proposing extensions for contract talks. When parties have reached a stalemate, neither side may want to appear weak by requesting another bargaining session. The mediator allows both sides to save face by scheduling the meeting and requesting that both sides attend. If contract talks become hostile or the parties are simply repeating previous arguments to no avail, the mediator may suggest that the negotiators recess for several days. A mediator may also suggest that negotiators call a recess when fatigue has taken its toll and the negotiators no longer appear capable of making careful judgments about critical bargaining issues. Mediators often hold separate meetings with union and management negotiators in order to obtain better insights into each side's bargaining demands than would be possible during joint union-management sessions. In addition, mediators may suggest a change in the location of contract talks if the conference room or hotel facilities are not suitable or if the news media and other interested parties create distractions.

When negotiation sessions appear to lack order or continuity, the mediator may chair the meetings and arrange for orderly record keeping on contract proposals, concessions, and agreements. In order to help the parties gain momentum, the mediator may suggest that easy-to-resolve items (e.g. the number of vending machines in a plant or the location of bulletin boards) be addressed before tackling the "hard" bargaining items, such as wages and major employee benefits. Once the "easy" items are negotiated, a spirit of cooperation and trust between the union and management negotiators may make it easier to resolve the more difficult topics. The mediator may also appoint a union-management bargaining team subcommittee to work out the details of the contract clauses that have been tentatively approved by the chief negotiators. The use of subcommittees to iron out the final details allows the chief negotiator to proceed to other important bargaining topics without becoming bogged down. Subcommittees make full use of bargaining team expertise and give team members a greater sense of personal involvement.[18]

As the strike deadline approaches and important issues remain unresolved, a mediator must decide whether to suggest an extension of the deadline. An extension is most likely to be accepted by the parties if a number of issues have been resolved and only one or two remain. For example, Ford Motor Company and the United Auto Workers agreed to a day-to-day extension of their current contract 45 minutes before their strike deadline in September of 1987. Sources close to the bargaining said that the parties needed additional time to discuss the critical issue of job security.[19] However, a mediator involved in negotiations in which the parties are far apart on important items may decide that an extension would only delay the inevitable strike. When one or two important items remain unresolved, but the parties have negotiated in good faith and have reached a satisfactory settlement on all other items, the mediator may suggest postponing the strike and resolving the remaining issues through a special subcommittee, arbitration, or other method that is acceptable to both chief negotiators. If a strike or lockout is not avoided, the mediator may take responsibility for scheduling further contract talks during the work stoppage.

Communications Functions during Mediation

Successful negotiations require a two-way exchange of information. One of the major functions of labor mediation is to keep the channels of communication open between union and management negotiators. In private meetings, a union or man-

---

[18] Subcommittees are also useful for isolating a particularly disagreeable negotiator who is hampering progress at the bargaining table.
[19] The Bureau of National Affairs, Inc., "UAW/Ford Contract Extension," *Labor Relations Reporter*, Vol. 126 (Washington, D.C.: The Bureau of National Affairs, Inc., September 21, 1987), pp. 34–36.

agement negotiator may discuss alternative contract proposals with a trusted mediator without making commitments or revealing sticking points to the opposing side. Mediators must be especially careful not to disclose details of private talks to the opponent. Such a breach of confidentiality is a cardinal sin in labor mediation. However, when a labor mediator is aware of overlaps in the bottom-line positions of each side, it may be possible to steer them toward a settlement without breaching confidences.

When a mediator is reasonably certain that a party has reached its bottom-line position and is not likely to make further concessions, he or she may try subtly to convey this information to the opposite side. Suppose, for example, that the union negotiating team wrongly believes that management will eventually capitulate on the issue of subcontracting certain types of bargaining-unit work. Such a mistaken belief may create an impasse or strike. If the mediator has explored the subcontracting issue with company officials and truly believes that the company has made its final offer, the mediator may tell the union negotiators that further concessions by management on subcontracting are not likely. Finally, mediators may attempt to help the sides determine whether the union members are likely to ratify the contract.

Substantive Mediation Functions

Substantive mediation functions deal with contract proposals made by union and management negotiators. One substantive function is to smoke out the bargaining priorities of each side by the mediator. As noted in Chapter 9, union and management negotiators often rank order bargaining items; some items are so important that they are worth enduring a work stoppage to obtain, whereas others would be "nice to have," but not at the cost of a major dispute. According to Simkin and Fidandis:

> A mediator's usefulness will be limited if he or she is unable to distinguish between the substantial and the relatively trivial issues. Moreover, it may be necessary or advisable to seek to assist the parties in the sorting-out process.[20]

By helping the parties determine their bargaining priorities, the mediator may be able to reduce conflict within a bargaining team, prevent negotiations from getting off on a tangent, and indirectly assist management in matching their "must" items with the union's "must" items (or vice versa).

When a bargaining team insists on obtaining a concession that is unreasonable, the mediator may attempt to deflate the team's extreme position. Extreme positions are those that the opposing team is either totally unable or unwilling to grant. Such positions may be unreasonable because they are radically different from other collective bargaining agreements or practices in the industry. A demand may also be extreme if management simply does not have the financial ability to grant it. If the mediator encourages a party to deflate an extreme demand, he or she should be careful to avoid any showing of favoritism toward either union or management. To

---

[20] William E. Simkin and Nicholas A. Fidandis, *Mediation and the Dynamics of Collective Bargaining* (Washington, D.C.: The Bureau fof National Affairs, Inc., 1986), p. 81.

do otherwise could destroy the mediator's credibility. Although mediators usually stop short of making specific contract proposals, mediator Doug Hammond successfully used this strategy in reaching a tentative settlement between striking workers represented by the Machinists union and striking Boeing Company employees. Mr. Hammond claimed that his strategy was "unusual and, for me, a rare step." Both union and management representatives praised the mediator for proposing the settlement.[21]

As the strike deadline approaches, the mediator may help union and management negotiators assess the costs of a work stoppage. Costs associated with strikes and lockouts are both economic and noneconomic (as discussed later in this chapter). The cost of a work stoppage must be assessed in relation to the importance of the issues that have yet to be resolved. A strike may be worth the effort if important wage or job security issues remain unresolved, but a work stoppage over minor differences in a holiday pay schedule may not be prudent. Experienced negotiators are usually well aware of strike costs, but their less experienced counterparts may not fully understand the far-reaching effects of a strike.

Another substantive mediation function designed to help parties move toward a settlement is for the mediator to suggest a package settlement to the parties. Package settlements may allow the parties to save face and quietly back down on earlier "final" demands or threats. In addition, package settlements allow the parties to view the final offer in its entirety, rather than as a disjointed series of individual proposals. Once the negotiators see the entire proposal, they may be willing to accept it. However, there may be situations where the mediator realizes that a strike is inevitable. As one mediator stated:

> I just start wrapping up my papers and sticking them in my briefcase. And somebody'll say, "What are you doing?" and I'll say, "Hell, you guys are going to strike anyway so why waste my time?"

According to this particular mediator, some parties would ask him to stay, whereas others would not.[22]

Mediation Effectiveness

Mediators use a variety of styles and tactics in their work. The effectiveness of a mediation effort depends heavily on the degree to which the parties accept and trust the individual mediator. Factors such as the timing of the mediation effort, the differences between union and management bargaining demands, the level of hostility between the bargaining teams, and the pressures exerted on the parties to reach a settlement and avoid a strike all affect the success of mediation.[23] If the union and management negotiators do not totally accept the presence of the mediator, then they will not confide in him or her for help. Mediators may make the mistake of entering negotiations after bargaining positions have become solidified

---

[21] Associated Press, "Mediator Prompts Agreement Between Boeing, Machinists," *The Greenville News* (November 20, 1989), p. 1C.
[22] Alvin Schwartz, *The Unions* (New York: The Viking Press, Inc., 1972), p. 188. Reprinted with permission, Curtis-Brown, Ltd., Copyright 1972 by Alvin Schwartz.
[23] William H. Ross, Jr., "Situational Factors and Alternative Dispute Resolution," *Journal of Applied Behavioral Science* (August 1988), p. 25.

or after hostilities have escalated to the point where a work stoppage becomes a virtual certainty. Mediation is more likely to be effective if the bargaining positions of the parties overlap and a positive bargaining range exists. Thus, if union negotiators are willing to accept a five percent hourly wage increase and management's sticking point is six percent, then mediation is more likely to yield a settlement than in a situation where the union's sticking point is 6.5 percent and management's sticking point is 5.5 percent (see Chapter 8 for a discussion of bargaining range theory and sticking points).

The question regarding how well mediation works is difficult to answer. Mediators undoubtedly help parties reduce hostility toward each other. They also help negotiators clarify their bargaining demands and the demands of their opponents. In addition, mediators perform administrative duties that allow negotiations to proceed smoothly and they often help negotiators assess risks and save face when the bargaining climate becomes inhospitable.[24] The exent to which mediators help parties avoid work stoppages is difficult to assess because of uncertainties in predicting the course of negotiations in the absence of mediation.[25]

▲ Strikes and Lockouts

- ▲ A 45-day strike over job security occurred in the spring of 1987 between the Writers Guild of America and CBS. Once the dispute was settled, 315 employees received a series of three percent pay increases. CBS agreed to drop a proposal to deny dismissed employees access to arbitration and to restrict temporary jobs to 60 days. The Guild, in turn, agreed to contribute to spouse and dependent health insurance premiums and to permit managers and on-air reporters to write stories.[26]
- ▲ A seven-week walkout by approximately 6,700 workers at General Electric Co.'s Aircraft Engine plant in Cincinnati ended with agreement on a modified job consolidation program and a subcontracting provision. The striking employees were represented by the United Auto Workers Local 647 and International Association of Machinists Local 912. The strike was called in protest over the company's impending implementation of a program that would have eliminated about 10 percent of all hourly jobs.[27]
- ▲ United Rubber Workers members employed at Armstrong Tire Co.'s Des Moines, Iowa plant walked off their jobs in August of 1988, after rejecting a tentative contract covering 1,700 employees at four company facilities.[28]
- ▲ About a dozen striking meatpackers were arrested for throwing rocks at workers hired by John Morrell & Co. to replace 2,500 production workers who refused

---

[24] See Ahmad Karim and Richard Pegnetter, "Mediator Strategies and Qualities and Mediator Effectiveness," *Industrial Relations* (Winter 1983), pp. 352–359.
[25] For a discussion of alternative dispute resolution techniques, see William L. Ury, Jeanne M. Brett, and Stephen B. Goldberg, *Getting Disputes Resolved* (San Francisco: Jossey-Bass, Inc., 1988).
[26] The Bureau of National Affairs, Inc., "CBS-Writers Guild Settlement," *Collective Bargaining Negotiations & Contracts* (Washington, D.C.: The Bureau of National Affairs, Inc., April 23, 1987), p. 2.
[27] The Bureau of National Affairs, Inc., "GE Strike Settlements," *Collective Bargaining Negotiations & Contracts* (Washington, D.C.: The Bureau of National Affairs, Inc., April 21, 1988), p. 1.
[28] The Bureau of National Affairs, Inc., "Rubber Workers Strike," *Collective Bargaining Negotiations & Contracts* (Washington, D.C.: The Bureau of National Affairs, Inc., August 11, 1988), p. 1.

to cross a picket line set up by striking Morrell workers from Sioux City, Iowa. The demonstrators were charged with disorderly conduct and criminal property damage.[29]

▲ After contract talks broke down between Harter Equipment, Inc., of Englishtown, New Jersey, and Operating Engineers Local 825, the company locked out employees and hired temporary replacements.[30]

These examples typify strike and lockout activities in the United States. *Strikes* are called by the union in order to exert economic pressure on employers (economic strikes) or to protest alleged unfair labor practices (unfair labor practice strikes). Although rare compared to strikes, *lockouts* are used by employers to place pressure on unions to achieve bargaining concessions, avoid inopportune work stoppages, or protect the integrity of a multi-employer bargaining arrangement.

Peaceful and uneventful contract settlements do not make front-page news. However, work stoppages are another matter. Newspaper, radio, and television accounts often give the public a distorted view of the severity and impact of strikes and lockouts, especially when work stoppages accompanied by violence receive extensive media publicity. However, an examination of statistics associated with work stoppages in the United States reveals that strikes and lockouts have caused little disruption to industrial society:[31]

1. The largest number of strikes involving more than 1,000 employees since 1947 occurred in 1952, when 470 work stoppages were recorded.[32] In 1984, only 62 strikes involving more than 1,000 workers occurred.[33] By 1986, the six-year decreasing trend in work stoppages began to turn slightly.[34]
2. A more significant statistic is the number of employees involved in strikes.[35] In 1952, a record 2.7 million workers were idled by work stoppages, whereas in 1963 only 512,000 workers participated in strikes.
3. The largest number of working days lost, 60,850,000, came in 1959 in 245 strikes, whereas in 1982 a low of 96 strikes resulted in only 9,061,000 lost working days.

---

[29] The Bureau of National Affairs, Inc., "Arrests in Morrell Sympathy Strike," *Labor Relations Reporter*, Vol. 124 (Washington, D.C.: The Bureau of National Affairs, Inc., May 18, 1987), pp. 43–44.
[30] *Operating Engineers, Local 825 v. NLRB*, CA 3, No. 86–3641 (September 25, 1987).
[31] The Bureau of National Affairs, Inc., *Labor Relations Yearbook, 1984* (Washington, D.C.: The Bureau of National Affairs, Inc., 1985), p. 522.
[32] The U.S. Department of Labor, Bureau of Labor Statistics began maintaining statistics on work stoppages in 1947. However, 1946 is generally regarded as the most strike-prone year. In that year, 4,985 strikes occurred resulting in 116 million worker-days of lost production. See Benjamin J. Taylor and Fred Witney, *Labor Relations Law*, 5th ed. (Englewood Cliffs, New Jersey: Prentice-Hall, Inc., 1987), p. 211.
[33] Work stoppages continued to decline in the late 1980s. See "Number of Strikes Declined in 1987 to 40-Year Low," *The Wall Street Journal* (February 25, 1988), p. 24.
[34] The Bureau of National Affairs, Inc., "Rise in Major Strike and Lockout Activity," *Labor Relations Reporter*, Vol. 124 (Washington, D.C.: The Bureau of National Affairs, Inc., March 16, 1987), pp. 172–173.
[35] According to Jack W. Skeels, Paul McGrath, and Gangadha Arshanapalli, "The Importance of Strike Size in Strike Research," *Industrial and Labor Relations Review* (July 1988), p. 582. " 'Small' strikes are found to differ significantly from 'large' strikes, whatever the size criterion, in terms of industry, strike issue, region of the country, and contract status."

4. Perhaps the most telling statistic is the percentage of working time lost. In 1959, approximately four tenths of one percent (.0043) of total work time was lost to work stoppages. A low of four one-hundredths of one percent (.0004) was lost in 1982. Thus, work stoppages have not had a crippling effect on the flow of commerce.
5. According to Federal Mediation and Conciliation Service reports, strikes occur in only two to three percent of all negotiations in which the required 30-day notice is filed (see Chapter 9).[36] However, the incidence of strikes in large bargaining units (more than 1,000 employees) appears to exceed 10 percent.[37]
6. The majority of strikes are precipitated by economic issues such as wage and salary demands.[38]

The Economic Strike

The economic strike usually occurs when contract talks are unsuccessful and the union is attempting to put pressure on the employer to meet its bargaining demands.[39] Several issues are of importance when the union calls an economic strike. First, both the union and the employer must carefully consider the monetary and nonmonetary costs associated with economic strikes. Second, the 1980s has witnessed increased efforts by employers to maintain business operations during a strike. When employers attempt to soften the impact of an economic strike, careful planning is required. Third, the employment rights of workers who engage in economic strikes continues to be a controversial issue. The conditions under which striking employees may be reinstated have been the subject of considerable litigation.[40]

---

[36] Thomas A. Kochan and Harry C. Katz, *Collective Bargaining and Industrial Relations*, 2nd ed. (Homewood, Illinois: Richard D. Irwin, Inc., 1988), pp. 242–243.
[37] In a study of manufacturing firms with bargaining units of more than 1,000 employees, it was revealed that 13.8 percent of the negotiations involved a strike. See Cynthia L. Gramm, "The Determinants of Strike Incidence and Severity: A Micro-Level Study," *Industrial and Labor Relations Review* (April 1986), pp. 361–376.
[38] Also see Stanley J. Modic, "Striking Statistics: Work Stoppages Fewer, But Cost Is High," *Industry Week* (March 23, 1987), p. 18; David A. Dilts, "Strike Activity in the United States: An Analysis of Stocks and Flows, *Journal of Labor Research* (Spring 1986), p. 187; and David Card, "Longitudinal Analysis of Strike Activity," *Journal of Labor Economics* (April 1988), p. 147.
[39] See John M. Abowd and Joseph S. Tracy, "Market Structure, Strike Activity, and Union Wage Settlements," *Industrial Relations* (Spring 1989), pp. 227–250, Cynthia L. Gramm, Wallace E. Hendricks, and Lawrence Kahn, "Inflation Uncertainty and Strike Activity," *Industrial Relations* (Winter 1988), pp. 114–129; Kern O. Kymn and Catherine Palomba, "The Strike Experience Model: Adaptive Expectations Applied to Strikes," *Journal of Behavioral Economics* (Spring-Summer 1986), p. 135; W. Stanley Seibert, Philip V. Bertrand, and John I. Addison, "The Political Model of Strikes: A New Twist," *Southern Economics Journal* (July 1985), p. 23; and Joseph S. Tracy, "An Investigation into Determinants of U.S. Strike Activity," *American Economic Review* (June 1986), p. 423.
[40] See James E. Martin, "Predictors of Individual Propensity to Strike," *Industrial and Labor Relations Review* (January 1986), pp. 214–227; Michele I. Naples, "An Analysis of Defensive Strikes," *Industrial Relations* (Winter 1987), pp. 96–105; Sean Flaherty, "Strike Activity, Worker Militancy, and Productivity Change in Manufacturing," *Industrial and Labor Relations Review* (July 1987), pp. 406–417, Joseph S. Tracy, "An Investigation into the Determinants of U.S. Strike Activity," *American Economic Review* (June 1986), p. 423.

Economic Strike Costs to the Employer

The union's decision to call a strike or the employer's willingness to endure a strike involves potentially severe, long-term costs for both sides. Perhaps the major cost of an economic strike from the employer's standpoint is lost business and permanent damage to customer goodwill. The union's bargaining power is significantly reduced when the employer is able to continue manufacturing and selling its products or serving customers. It is primarily for this reason that an increasing number of firms are maintaining total or partial operations during economic strikes.

One cost of continuing operations is the hiring of workers to replace those who have gone on strike. Hiring strike replacements often means additional advertising, interviewing, training, and administrative expenses. A company may not be able to hire an adequate number of replacements to maintain normal business operations. Under such conditions management may elect to use partial or "skeleton" crews, an arrangement that may pose scheduling problems and require the use of overtime payments. It may also be necessary to provide additional security measures to ensure that replacement employees (or employees who refuse to participate in the strike) are not subjected to physical harm or verbal harassment by striking personnel. Even when operations are maintained, management may discover that customers, suppliers, and others may be unwilling to enter the struck facility.

When operations are totally or partially suspended during an economic strike, there are costs associated with shutting down facilities, protecting company property, and later restarting operations after a settlement is reached. Maintenance costs often continue during shutdowns. Additional security in and around a plant or facility may be necessary to reduce the likelihood of vandalism and sabotage by striking workers or strike sympathizers. According to a former security manager of a large food processing firm, employees anticipating a strike have damaged locks, made duplicate keys to company facilities and vehicles, and sabotaged water and electrical sources. Saboteurs have also been known to plant radio-controlled explosive devices inside company facilities that can be activated from outside a facility.[41]

Economic Strike Costs to the Union and Striking Employees

Employees who engage in economic strikes not only lose their pay check, but in many states are also not eligible for unemployment compensation benefits.[42] In such instances, economic strikers may soon find themselves financially strapped as savings or other resources dwindle and personal obligations mount.[43] Unions often

---

[41] The former security manager has requested anonymity.
[42] An employer, however, may not be able unilaterally to revoke employee medical and hospitalization benefits during a strike. See D. Diane Hatch, Wayne E. Barlow, and Betty Southard Murphy, "Termination of Health Benefits During Strikes Can Violate CBAs," *Personnel Journal* (March 1985), p. 28.
[43] A 1988 U.S. Supreme Court ruling (*Lyng v. Automobile Workers*, U.S. Supreme Court, March 3, 1988) upheld the disqualification of strikers and their families from participation in the federally funded Food Stamp Program. The Court ruled that the Food Stamp Act was passed by Congress to reduce hunger, cut malnutrition, and boost the agricultural economy, but not to subsidize those who reject their companies' contract offers and participate in an economic strike. See Jay S. Siegel, "Strikers Denied Food Stamp Assistance," *New England Business* (May 2, 1988), p. 65; and The Bureau of National Affairs, Inc., "Constitutionality of Food Stamp Act's Ban on Striker Households," *Labor Relations Reporter*, Vol. 127 (Washington, D.C.: The Bureau of National Affairs, Inc., March 28, 1988), pp. 385–386.

help striking members through the use of strike funds, which typically provide a small amount of money to help with food, clothing, and other necessities. If the strike is prolonged, however, the union strike fund may become depleted. The union's financial dilemma is also exacerbated because union members do not customarily pay dues while participating in a work stoppage.

Because employers have the right to replace economic strikers permanently, an employee who participates in a work stoppage runs the risk of losing his or her job. Even in instances where a striking employee is not permanently replaced, he or she may suffer interruptions in accumulated vacation, sick leave, seniority, and retirement benefits.[44] The permanent replacement of strikers also poses a critical risk to the union: the loss of majority employee support in the bargaining unit and the danger of decertification. (The reinstatement rights of economic strikers and their right to vote in certification or decertification elections are discussed in a later section of this chapter.)

Even after a settlement is reached, relationships among union officials, employees, and the company may be irreparably damaged. Some strikes have even divided close friends and families, as illustrated by a sawmill strike in the small town of Darrington, Washington, involving the Summit Timber Co., and mill workers represented by Industrial Workers Union, Local 2860:

> A bitter, five-month-old strike at a sawmill has traumatized a logging town's 1,200 residents, splitting apart families, friends and union members who find themselves on opposite sides of a picket line.
>
> Divisions within the town 55 miles northeast of Seattle have run deep since 177 Summit Timber Co. mill workers went on strike August 1 [1988] after a three-year contract expired and the town's largest employer hired replacement workers.
>
> Twenty-three union members also returned to work, while 90 who once were paid as much as $13 an hour remain on the picket line at $60 a week. Others have left to find other jobs.
>
> Friendships in the small town are now measured against which side of the picket line people are on.
>
> "Oh no. Oh no. He's one of them!" said Gary Ensley, a striking worker, as he watched a pickup truck drive into the Summit plant. "He's one of those who went back. His bills caught up with him, and he started losing things, so he went back... I don't like him anymore."
>
> Nancy Stull, 43, a 13-year Summit employee, and her husband, a 22-year mill veteran, walked out together with her two brothers.
>
> One brother found another job and, with his first paycheck, bought her $250 worth of groceries, she said. The other, now referred to as her "ex-brother", crossed the picket line about six weeks into the walkout.
>
> When she and her family drive to her parents' home for a traditional Christmas dinner, she said, "if my ex-brother is there, we won't stay. We will just turn around and go home and have our own dinner."[45]

Strikes also precipitate domestic problems among families who are involved in

---

[44] Employees may still be entitled to receive workers' compensation or sick leave benefits during a strike, according to the NLRB. See *Gulf & Western Manufacturing Co.*, 127 LRRM 1018 (1987).
[45] The Associated Press, "Bitter Strike Divides A Town," *Anderson Independent Mail* (December 26, 1988), p. 2. Reprinted with permission.

work stoppages. During the 1985 strike by employees of Hormel & Company in Austin, Minnesota, incidents of domestic violence and child abuse increased drastically, according to a local police official.[46]

Maintaining Operations during an Economic Strike

In recent years, an increasing number of companies have decided to maintain operations during an economic strike. Perhaps the most vivid illustration of continuing operations was the dramatic handling of the flight controllers' strike in August of 1981, by President Reagan and Secretary of Transportation, Drew Lewis. Federal government officials had decided that the Professional Air Traffic Controllers' Organization (PATCO) would undoubtedly call a strike unless its demands were met. Rather than give in to what federal officials believed to be expensive proposals by PATCO, a detailed strike plan was drawn up. Although commercial air carriers were subjected to flight cancellations and delays, overtime compensation, and other hardships, the federal government managed to staff critical air traffic control functions and kept air traffic moving without jeopardizing air safety.[47]

In 1988, Eastern Airlines President Frank Lorenzo planned to maintain operations during a machinists union strike by leasing aircraft from Orion Air and having Orion's nonunion pilots fly the aircraft during the strike. Eastern had a history of labor relations turmoil during the 1980s that was intensified by airline industry deregulation and Eastern's unsuccessful attempt to thwart hostile takeovers by Lorenzo's Texas Air. Lorenzo's plan to use Orion's aircraft and crews, however, was prevented by a U.S. District court ruling.[48]

When union workers struck Nynex Corp., Bell Atlantic Corp., and Pacific Telesis Group in 1989, managers filled in for striking telephone operators, installers, and repair workers. Although there were gaps in services offered by these companies, computer-driven telecommunications networks blunted the effect of the strikes. As a result, customers encountered few problems in placing or receiving calls.[49]

Before the April 6, 1990, expiration date of its labor contracts with 10 unions, the *New York Daily News* began to advertise "competitive pay and generous benefits" for candidates to replace employees who had earlier voted to strike. The ads solicited applications from prospective drivers and press operators to apply in person at the *News'* production plants in Brooklyn, Long Island, and northern New Jersey.[50]

The decision to operate facilities during a strike requires careful planning and

---

[46] Marj Charlier, "'Togetherness Town' Is Getting a Divorce on Grounds of a Strike," *The Wall Street Journal* (February 26, 1986), p. 1. Family problems also surfaced in the strike between Pittston Co. and the United Mine Workers. See Alecia Swasy, "Coal-Mine Strike Divides a Family and a Community," *The Wall Street Journal* (June 22, 1989), p. A1.

[47] Much of the discussion on operating during strikes is taken from Charles R. Perry, Andrew Kramer, and Thomas J. Schneider, *Operating During Strikes* (Philadelphia: Industrial Research Unit, The Wharton School, University of Pennsylvania, 1982).

[48] The Bureau of National Affairs, Inc., "Continuing EAL Labor Strife," *Collective Bargaining Negotiations & Contracts* (Washington, D.C.: The Bureau of National Affairs, Inc., April 7, 1988), p. 4.

[49] Mary Lu Carnevale, "Union Workers Begin Strike at Nynex, Bell Atlantic and Pacific Telesis Group," *The Wall Street Journal* (August 7, 1989), p. A3.

[50] "Newspaper Advertises Jobs as Pact with Unions Expires," *Greenville News* (April 2, 1990), p. 3C. Copyrighted by *Newsday*.

preparation. A company must first decide what it hopes to gain by maintaining production or customer service during a work stoppage. Some firms continue operations because management regards a production facility, distribution center, or store as critical to the long-term competitive position of the company. Other firms may use the threat of operating during a strike to show the union that they can get along without the services of striking employees. Such a tactic may be a bargaining ploy designed to make the union reconsider calling a strike. Still other firms may continue business as usual as a means of destroying employee support for the union. Regardless of the company's objective, careful planning is important. According to one labor expert:

> Employers who do not plan for possible strikes when they are embroiled in bargaining disputes may end up making expensive concessions at the negotiating table.
>
> While many employers do no strike planning at all, others make the equally critical error of drawing up a strike plan without relating it to what is occurring in negotiations.[51]

Table 10–2 outlines the specific preparations that should be considered prior to a work stoppage.

Union Preparations for an Economic Strike

Union leaders must also carefully anticipate how they will prepare for and endure a work stoppage. A primary concern for the union is staffing picket lines. Picket lines are used to publicize the economic strike and they are regarded as a form of constitutionally-protected free speech. Union officials must not only ensure that picket lines are adequately staffed, but they must also inform striking workers about the appropriate and inappropriate types of conduct on a picket line. Employers may obtain court injunctions against union officials to prevent picket-line members from blocking plant entrances, intimidating customers and suppliers who want to enter the company's premises, or engaging in violence. Union officials may elect to monitor plant entrances to determine if members are crossing picket lines and returning to work. When striking members return to work before the labor dispute has ended, the union may decide to levy fines or impose other disciplinary sanctions.

The union may set up a strike fund to help employees purchase basic necessities such as food and clothing. Strike funds may pay the same amount to all striking employees or they may pay varying amounts to employees, depending on factors such as individual seniority and the employee's wage rate. Unions may also arrange to purchase food, clothing, and other items and offer them to striking workers free of charge or at a substantial discount.

Union leaders also must establish channels of communication with striking workers. If negotiations with management continue during the strike, members must be kept abreast of developments at the bargaining table. Informal polls may be used to determine union members' reactions to management's latest proposals. In addition, local union leaders must keep international union officials informed on the progress of local negotiations.

---

[51] Comments of labor attorney Harry R. Stang. The Bureau of National Affairs, Inc., *Collective Bargaining Negotiations & Contracts* (Washington, D.C.: The Bureau of National Affairs, Inc., May 21, 1987), p. 4.

Table 10–2 ▲ Strike Preparation Plan and Checklist

1. *Production Planning*: Decide which units will remain open and which will be closed; decide on staffing requirements and work schedules for operations that will remain open; arrange to subcontract work to other firms if current personnel and equipment are unable to perform the work "in-house."
2. *Supply Preparations*: Determine raw material requirements and inventories needed to maintain production levels; arrange for shipments of raw materials to the locations where they will be needed (anticipate the possibility that transportation firms may be unable or unwilling to cross picket lines once the strike is underway); purchase work equipment and arrange for food, clothing, medical, and sleeping accommodations for employees who will work during the strike.
3. *Maintenance Preparations*: Review maintenance needs; complete all outside contracting work prior to the anticipated date of the work stoppage; make staffing plans to ensure that qualified maintenance personnel are available; contact firms that might be needed to make repairs in the event of major equipment breakdowns.
4. *Personnel Preparations*: Compile an updated list of employee names, addresses, and telephone numbers; determine whether striking workers will be allowed to return to work before the dispute is resolved; arrange to use managerial workers to perform bargaining unit work; decide whether to hire strike replacements, the means by which such replacements will be hired, and whether the replacements will be temporary or permanent; determine what licensing requirements and training will be needed to ensure that employees will perform their assigned tasks legally and competently; make provisions regarding the means by which employees will report to work in order to minimize problems in crossing picket lines; establish policies on pay periods, record-keeping of work hours, and overtime pay.
5. *Security Preparations*: Check fences, property lines, and work area perimeters for possible areas of vulnerability; arrange for controlled entrance and exit to company property; establish additional security lighting, if necessary; arrange for alternate modes of communication (such as CB radios) in the event that telephone service is disrupted; arrange for in-plant fire fighting equipment and personnel trained in fighting fires; monitor picket line activities and be prepared to videotape acts of misconduct and violence.
6. *Communications Preparations*: Establish a means of communicating the latest strike developments to interested parties (suppliers, customers, top management); assign a trained individual to handle press releases and communications with the news media.
7. *Legal Preparations*: Retain a labor attorney to assist in securing injunctions to stop violence and other illegal activities by striking workers and to provide counsel on the use of strike replacements and other legal matters.

Adapted from Charles R. Perry, Andrew M. Kramer, and Thomas J. Schneider, *Operating During Strikes* (Philadelphia: Industrial Research Unit, The Wharton School, University of Pennsylvania, 1982), pp. 45–48. Reprinted with permission.

The union should employ legal counsel to help them deal with unfair labor practice charges that might arise during the strike. Unfair labor practice charges may be initiated by employers against the union or the union may file unfair labor practice charges against the employer. In the former case, the employer may charge that the union is engaging in intimidation tactics against employees, customers, and others who desire to enter company property. An employer may also seek an injunction against a union for illegal picketing at sites away from the primary labor dispute. Likewise, unions may elect to bring charges against employers for bad faith bargaining, harassment of union members walking the picket line, or illegal surveillance of union activities.

Finally, union officials must make arrangements to recall workers once the strike has ended. Some workers use a strike as an opportunity to take a vacation, so it is important that union officials be able to contact striking employees once the dispute is resolved. Other striking workers may obtain temporary employment elsewhere and they too must be contacted to determine whether they want to return to work or risk forfeiting their jobs.

The Employment Rights of Economic Strikers

Employers normally have the right to replace economic strikers permanently. Federal labor law has provided unions and employees with the right to engage in economic strikes, but public policy also grants employers the right to maintain operations during a strike. Some employees may elect to remain on the job during the strike or return to work before the strike has ended. As long as the employer is willing to allow members of the striking bargaining unit to work, the union cannot prevent members from working (or returning to work). However, the union can fine or discipline members who work during an economic strike.[52] Employees facing financial pressures may cross the picket line and continue working while their fellow union members strike.

> Without an income no one can strike for very long. To help their members make ends meet, some international unions pay a strike benefit... A local union may try to supplement this by soliciting money and food from other local unions and by getting its members temporary jobs. But when a strike fund runs out or when there is none to begin with, a union is vulnerable.
>
> Time is another factor. A strike may isolate a worker who earlier had led a busy, productive life. Manning a picket line and attending strike meetings may take but a few of his hours each week. Moreover, the bargaining sessions so crucial to his future are secret and the bulletins both sides issue often say nothing. If he does not find another job, and most strikers do not, inevitably the strike becomes a waiting game, a bleak period of empty days marked by a growing need. At such times a worker's loyalty to his union may be severely tested.[53]

Another option available to employers is to hire employees—either permanently or temporarily—to replace those who are on strike.[54] When striking em-

---

[52] For a discussion of the advantages or disadvantages of union disciplinary actions against members who refuse to join a strike, see Derek C. Bok and John T. Dunlop, *Labor and the American Community* (New York: Simon and Schuster, 1970), pp. 105–107.
[53] Alvin Schwartz, *The Unions* (New York: The Viking Press, 1972), p. 205. Reprinted with permission of Curtis-Brown, Ltd., Copyright 1972 by Alvin Schwartz.
[54] At the AFL-CIO's biennial convention on October 27, 1987, Wayne Glenn, president of the Paperworkers union, said that during the 1930s and 1940s, there was a stigma associated with hiring replacements during a strike and few employers were willing to do it. The Reagan Administration may have ushered in a new feeling about strike replacements when they fired the air traffic controllers for striking in 1981. Since then, there has been a "wave" of hiring strike replacements. Gene Upshaw, president of the National Football League Players Association, described strike replacements this way: "I like to call the son of a bitches scabs because that's what they are." The Bureau of National Affairs, Inc., "AFL-CIO on Strike Replacements," *Labor Relations Reporter*, Vol. 126 (Washington, D.C.: The Bureau of National Affairs, Inc., November 2, 1987), pp. 138–139.

ployees are replaced, the replacements are often hired on a temporary basis; once the labor dispute is resolved, the employer and union agree to reinstate economic strikers and terminate the temporary strike replacements. However, the employer may elect to make the replacements permanent. When this situation occurs, economic strikers may lose the right to reclaim their jobs. The issue of replacement workers became a major point of contention during the highly publicized Eastern Airlines machinists' strike of 1989. Three weeks into the strike, management decided to run newspaper ads to find replacements for the 3,400 Eastern pilots who supported the machinists and refused to cross picket lines.

> Eastern Airlines went shopping Sunday for the new pilots it needs to survive a crippling strike now in its third week ... The ads promise an "outstanding opportunity for the very best," and try to put the best light on the strike, telling pilots to "also understand that this is an unprecedented opportunity for growth and success."
>
> Pilot union spokesman J. B. Stokes said, "They [Eastern management] want to test the marketplace, and they also want to frighten our pilots into thinking that they're being replaced. They should have learned by now that intimidation isn't going to work."
>
> "They're going to be disappointed," Stokes predicted. "There isn't a pool of pilots out there." Stokes said that other major carriers are hiring pilots and offer better working conditions and long-term stability.
>
> [Robin] Matell [Eastern spokesman] said that Stokes was engaging in "ALPA [airline pilot's union] propaganda." He said that Eastern had received more than 100 unsolicited resumes from qualified pilots before the ads began running."[55]

Strike replacements are not always easy to find. For example, Greyhound Lines, Inc., found it difficult to replace the striking 9,000 Amalgamated Transportation Union members (6,300 of whom are drivers). Only 363 Greyhound drivers remained on the job. The company was able to hire an additional 744 permanent replacements, a woefully inadequate number. As a result, Greyhound was able to serve only 1,800 of its 9,500 locations.[56] The problem of finding replacements for striking workers was undoubtedly compounded by shooting incidents and threats of violence against Greyhound buses.

As a general rule, there are three ways that an economic striker may lose the right to return to his or her former job. First, as noted, a striker may be permanently replaced. Assuming that an employee possesses the proper job qualifications, however, economic strikers must be rehired in a nondiscriminatory fashion as job openings become available.[57] An employer who refuses to hire a former economic striker

---

[55] Dan Sewell, "Eastern Hunts for New Pilots," *Anderson Independent Mail* (The Associated Press, March 20, 1989), p. 6B. Reprinted with permission of the Associated Press.
[56] Robert Tomsho, "Greyhound Lines Struggles to Restart 'Full' Operations," *The Wall Street Journal* (March 13, 1990), p. A18.
[57] A 1989 Supreme Court case allowed replacements for striking TWA flight attendants to retain seniority rights over striking flight attendants who later returned to work. See "Employers Can Favor Strikebreakers, Supreme Court Rules," Copyright 1989 by the *Washington Post,* reprinted in *The Greenville News* (March 1, 1989), p. 9A.

as a retaliatory measure may violate the employee's rights under the National Labor Relations Act.[58] Furthermore, economic strikers that have been permanently replaced may vote in a certification or decertification election for up to 12 months after the commencement of the strike. This provision makes it difficult for the employer to lure a union into an economic strike, permanently replace all economic strikers, and then allow the replacements to decertify the union.

Second, an economic striker may forfeit his or her job by accepting employment elsewhere and failing to return to work after being notified that the economic strike is over. Economic strikers may also forfeit their right to vote in a certification or decertification election if they accept a job with another firm that is substantially equivalent to the struck job. However, when an employee holding a substantially equivalent job continues to picket or informs the employer of a continuing interest in the former job, then the economic striker may retain the right to vote in an NLRB-conducted election.

Third, an economic striker may be dismissed for engaging in violence or other serious acts that would make the employee unfit for further employment.[59] According to the NLRB:

> The applicable test in determining whether strikers accused of misconduct should be returned to work "is whether the misconduct is so violent or of such serious character as to render the employees unfit for further service, or whether it merely constitutes a trivial rough incident occurring in a moment of animal exuberance." This distinction has been drawn on the theory that some types of "impulsive behavior" being "normal outgrowths of the intense feelings developed on the picket lines." "must have been within the contemplation of Congress when it provided" for the right to strike.[60]

Thus "anticipated animal exuberance" such as cursing, hostile stares or gestures at persons crossing a picket line, or other rowdy behavior that does not cause property damage or bodily injury is not grounds for refusing to reinstate an economic striker. Vandalism resulting in extensive property damage, physical assaults on supervisors or strike replacements, or preventing persons from crossing a picket line through threats of bodily harm may be legitimate grounds for refusing reinstatement. However, if management provokes strikers into violence, the NLRB or, courts may decide that employees cannot be discharged.[61]

---

[58] An employer cannot discriminate against strikers or hold out inducements such as superseniority or favorable jobs for strike replacements after the strike has been resolved. *NLRB v. Erie Resistor Corp.*, 373 U.S. 221 (1963).

[59] For an excellent treatise on union violence, see Armand J. Thiebolt and Thomas R. Haggard, *Union Violence: The Record and the Response by Courts, Legislatures, and the NLRB* (Philadelphia: Industrial Research Unit, The Wharton School, University of Pennsylvania, 1983).

[60] See *W.C. McQuaide, Inc.*, 220 NLRB 165 (1975), *modified*, 552 F.2d 519 (3rd Circuit, 1977). Cited in Charles R. Perry, Andrew M. Kramer, and Thomas J. Schneider, *Operating During Strikes* (Philadelphia: Industrial Research Unit, The Wharton School, The University of Pennsylvania, 1982), p. 88.

[61] Bruce Feldacker, *Labor Guide to Labor Law*, 2nd ed. (Reston, Virginia: Reston Publishing Company, Inc., 1983), p. 225.

Dealing With Violence, Harassment, and Sabotage[62]

Most strikes are not accompanied by serious or widespread incidents of violence, harassment, or sabotage. However, there are cases in which picket line conduct may precipitate violence. Strike replacements, suppliers, and even customers attempting to enter a struck facility may encounter hostile strikers walking the picket line. The few physical assaults that mar strikes, however, usually occur against the wishes of union officials.

When violence occurs, the results can be devastating from both a personal and economic standpoint. The A.T. Massey Coal Company of Richmond, West Virginia, and the United Mine Workers ended a four-year labor dispute over the firing of 92 workers for alleged violence during a 1984 strike. After the company decided to maintain operations during the strike, miners lined roadways from the mines to the processing facilities; there were numerous reports of vandalism to cars and trucks. Anticipating picket line violence, the company hired a security firm to film the strikers' actions and identify those committing violent activities. Several shootings also took place and a truck driver transporting coal was killed. After the strike was terminated in late 1985, the company announced that it would not rehire workers who had engaged in violence. The union insisted on rehiring all strikers and subsequently filed an unfair labor practice charge with the NLRB. Massey agreed in 1988 to reinstate the workers and pay them $2.4 million in back pay or severance.[63]

Employers may take steps to prevent picket line and other forms of violence near the perimeter of the struck facility. First, strike replacements may be brought in by bus, perhaps with a police escort. Buffer zones can be established inside the plant and employees should be instructed to remain inside these zones and away from picket lines, gates, fences, or windows, where they might become targets for strikers armed with rocks, slingshots, or air rifles. Second, fences should be repaired or fortified and other points of access to the struck facility should be sealed to prevent unauthorized personnel from entering. Some firms board windows that face streets. Third, employers may resort to legal action. Court injunctions may be obtained to prevent violence; once injunctions are obtained, law enforcement officials will generally cooperate in preventing further trouble. Management may attempt to hold individuals or the union liable for acts of property damage to employee automobiles or company property.

Harassment associated with a strike often takes place away from the struck facility. Harassment may range from making annoying telephone calls to throwing eggs or paint to firebombing the homes of supervisors or strike replacements. Suppliers and trucking firms doing business with a struck firm are also vulnerable to vandalism and harassment by strikers. Compared to picket line violence, which is confined to a well-defined area, harassment or other acts of intimidation are often sporadic and, therefore, difficult to prevent. Persons committing such acts are difficult to apprehend; they are usually aggressive individuals acting on their own and the strike is simply an outlet for their aggression.

---

[62] This discussion is based primarily on Charles R. Perry, Andrew M. Kramer, and Thomas J. Schneider, *Operating During Strikes* (Philadelphia: Industrial Research Unit, The Wharton School, The University of Pennsylvania, 1982), pp. 87–99.

[63] The Bureau of National Affairs, Inc. "Dispute Settled Over Strike Violence," *Labor Relations Reporter*, Vol. 129 (Washington, D.C.: The Bureau of National Affairs, Inc., November 21, 1988), pp. 372–373.

Strike-related sabotage is of two types: (1) prestrike sabotage committed by employees prior to the strike deadline, and (2) sabotage that occurs during the course of a strike.[64] Both types of sabotage are designed to make it more difficult for the employer to operate during a work stoppage. Sabotage may be directed at machinery, water and power sources, merchandise, and sources of raw materials. Bomb and arson threats are frequently used to disrupt the operation of a struck facility. However, not all sabotage attempts are successful, as is related by former Teamsters organizer Joseph Franco.

> We hit a big electrical company with a strike. They had about forty or fifty trucks, closed panel trucks, and we had them on strike for about four weeks and it started to drag. After the fourth week, I decided something had to be done to get this thing off dead center. I started getting into their trucks and started putting sugar and molasses in their gas tanks, and I did it to better than 50 percent of their trucks. The funny thing about the whole [expletive] thing is that the first day I didn't expect anything to happen, but I felt that by the second day, these trucks would start spitting and sputtering and then would jam up because the sugar and molasses crystallize and freeze up the piston and destroy the motors, and they would have to buy all new gas lines, carburetors, fuel pumps, motors, the whole works. It would have been a very costly thing to replace that many parts in the twenty, twenty-five trucks I fixed up. But the thing is that the next two, three days, those trucks would start up and start roaring like you'd think I put some power in there. They never backfired, they never smoked, they never did a [expletive] thing, they never ran better. It was like whatever those trucks needed it wasn't gasoline, it was sugar and molasses. They just ran beautifully. I couldn't believe it.[65]

In recent years, the presence of computers has opened up new avenues for potential saboteurs who may plant logic bombs or viruses that destroy data and wreck havoc with equipment and production processes. Most acts of sabotage are criminal acts and, in addition to the aforementioned remedies, those caught engaging in them may face prosecution, jail sentences, and fines. According to a U.S. Court of Appeals ruling, a union and its business agents may be liable for triple damages under the Racketeer Influenced and Corrupt Organizations Act (RICO) for destruction of property and threatened violence directed at a bus company during an organizing drive.[66] It seems likely that a similar line of reasoning applies to violence associated with strikes.

The Unfair Labor Practice Strike

Unfair labor practice strikes occur when employees or the union call a strike in response to an alleged unfair labor practice by the employer. Strikes precipitated by disputes over union recognition, discrimination against union members, and a

---

[64] For a recent discussion of vandalism associated with strikes by Nynex and Bell Atlantic, see "Telephone Strikes Continue As Officials Assess Support," *The Wall Street Journal* (August 15, 1989).
[65] Joseph Franco with Richard Hammer, *Hoffa's Man: The Rise and Fall of Jimmy Hoffa as Witnessed by His Strongest Arm* (New York: Dell Publishing, 1987), p. 72.
[66] *Yellow Bus Lines, Inc. v. Teamsters*, 127 LRRM 2607 (1988).

refusal to bargain in good faith are examples of unfair labor practice strikes. An economic strike may convert to an unfair labor practice strike because of actions taken by the employer, such as unlawfully discharging economic strikers or inciting violence on the picket line. The key difference between an economic strike and an unfair labor practice strike lies in the reinstatement rights of employees. Although economic strikers can be permanently replaced, unfair labor practice strikers may only be temporarily replaced.[67] Thus, once an unfair labor practice strike ends, the strikers are unconditionally entitled to reinstatement to their former jobs (or a substantially equivalent job) with full seniority and benefits.

Sympathy Strikes

Sympathy strikes occur when employees not directly involved in a work stoppage decide to honor the picket line of striking employees. The following situations typify the issues faced by those who contemplate engaging in a sympathy strike.

> You work in an office where there is a union, but you are not a member. The union goes on strike. Do you cross its picket line to get to your job or do you stay home until the strike ends?
>
> You work on an assembly line in a factory. Your union negotiates a new contract. But another union in the plant fails to do so and strikes. Your leaders urge that you join their members in a sympathy strike. Do you follow their advice or do you continue to work?
>
> The clerks in the supermarket where you regularly shop strike for a higher wage. But the store remains open for business. Do you cross the picket line or do you shop elsewhere?[68]

Many companies and plants are organized into several different bargaining units or have groups of nonunion employees working in the same location as unionized employees. Some of a firm's employees may be on strike, whereas other employees are not striking. For example, unionized employees in a bargaining unit of clerical employees may engage in a sympathy strike by voluntarily refusing to cross a picket line set up by striking employees in a manufacturing bargaining unit. Nonunion workers may likewise refuse to cross a picket line out of respect or sympathy for their unionized counterparts. Truck drivers or others who normally enter the facilities of a struck firm may express their sympathy by refusing to cross a picket line (sometimes called a "stranger" picket line). For example, Communications Workers of America members refused to cross picket lines of the International Brotherhood of Electrical Workers during work stoppages at Bell of Pennsylvania and New Jersey Bell.[69]

Strikes may also elicit sympathy from customers who refuse to do business with a struck firm. Unions generally have the right to set up picket lines or distribute

---

[67] An employer that hires permanent replacements and later lays off permanent replacements in order to reinstate economic strikers may be sued in a state court for breach of contract. See *Belknap v. Hale*, 463 U.S. 591 (1983).

[68] Alvin Schwartz, *The Unions* (New York: Viking Press, 1972), p. 204. Reprinted with permission from Curtis-Brown Ltd., Copyright 1972 by Alvin Schwartz.

[69] Mary Lu Carnevale, "Pacific Telesis, CWA Sign Agreement On New Contract Ending 15-day Strike," *The Wall Street Journal* (August 21, 1989), p. A10.

leaflets outside retail stores informing the public about a strike as long as they do not intimidate customers who want to enter the store. In assessing whether a picket line or the distribution of leaflets is permissible near retail establishments, the NLRB and courts have attempted to balance the employees' freedom of speech and the employers' right to protect their property and maintain business operations.

Employers must treat sympathy strikers in the same manner as those engaged in the primary strike. Thus, sympathy strikers responding to an economic strike may be permanently replaced and those responding to an unfair labor practice strike may only be temporarily replaced. Sympathy strikers such as delivery truck drivers who refuse to cross a picket line at a struck facility can be replaced (and have their pay docked) only for the time that it takes a replacement to complete the delivery; these sympathy strikers cannot be discharged if they are willing to make deliveries at other nonstriking facilities along their routes. Sympathy strikers must *voluntarily* decide to honor a picket line; if they refuse to cross a picket line because of legitimate fears of bodily harm, the employer may not have the right to replace them.[70] However, sympathy strikers who support the efforts of an illegal secondary boycott or who violate a specific no-strike clause may be discharged.[71]

Employees may also engage in a limited sympathy strike by refusing to handle work or goods produced by a struck facility. Two or more firms have a right to maintain their normal business relationship during a strike. If employees for a tool manufacturer customarily work on products supplied by a metal casting firm, they cannot refuse to handle these goods if employees at the metal casting firm call a strike. There are occasions, however, when a firm will attempt to maintain operations by subcontracting struck work to other firms. In this case, an employer cannot discipline workers who refuse to handle the work or goods of a firm that is subcontracting only because its employees are on strike.

Wildcat Strikes and Slowdowns

Occasionally a group of employees will protest working conditions, a disciplinary action, or an unpopular managerial decision by calling a "wildcat" strike that is not authorized by the union.[72] In 1989, wildcat strikes among United Mine Workers members closed nearly every UMW-organized mine east of the Mississippi River. According to *The Wall Street Journal:*

> The union insists it didn't instigate the wildcat strikes, which have involved as many as 50,000 of the union's 65,000 active members. "This is a grassroots movement that rolled across the country," says Tony Kujawa, a UMW executive board member from Springfield, Ill.

---

[70] Section 502 of the Taft-Hartley Act permits an employee to refuse work when "abnormally dangerous" conditions exist.
[71] See *OCAW Local 1–547 v. NLRB*, 127 LRRM 3164 (1988) and *Indianapolis Power & Light Co.*, 130 LRRM 1001 (1988).
[72] See Dennis M. Byrne and Randall H. King, "Wildcat Strikes in U.S. Manufacturing, 1960–1977," *Journal of Labor Research* (Fall 1986), p. 387; and C. Frederick Eisele, "Work Stoppages during the Term of a Collective Bargaining Agreement: Protected or Unprotected Activity," *Labor Law Journal* (December 1985), pp. 902–909.

But rank-and-file members say otherwise. At a union rally in Ebensburg, Pa., last month, for example, UMW leaders didn't openly tell non-Pittston workers to strike because that would have violated the existing contract with the BCOA [Bituminous Coal Operators Association, the industry group that has a contract with the UMW]. But one international officer poured a lunch pail of water on the ground, the unspoken strike signal, miners say.

That signal alone was enough to prompt a show of force in support of 1,700 Pittston strikers.[73]

Many collective bargaining agreements contain no-strike clauses that allow the employer to discharge employees engaging in unauthorized work stoppages. A union may be liable to the employer for damages caused by a wildcat strike that violates a no-strike clause, regardless of whether a union or its officers sanctioned the strike. To reduce the possibility of a lawsuit for unauthorized strikes, unions have negotiated *nonsuability clauses* in which the company agrees not to sue a union because of wildcat strikes. Nonsuability clauses often stipulate that a union cannot, in any manner, condone an unauthorized strike and must take steps to end the work stoppage. The union may be required to disavow the strike, order workers back to their jobs, and refrain from providing any financial or other relief to striking workers.[74] The U.S. Supreme Court has held that local and international unions are not liable for wildcat strikes that they did not provoke or encourage.[75] Individual union members are also not liable for damages caused by an unauthorized strike. However, wildcat strikers may be discharged and may forfeit reinstatement rights to their jobs.

Instead of engaging in a wildcat strike, employees may use a work slowdown to express their dissatisfaction with management or show their support for other striking workers. Unless the employer can demonstrate that a work rule has been broken, it may be difficult to discipline employees for slowdowns. In fact, many slowdowns are the result of slavish adherence to work rules by employees who want to slow the work routine and create bottlenecks. Table 10–3 illustrates how sympathetic airline pilots engaged in slowdown activities during the Eastern Airlines strike of 1989. A letter from the president of the Air Line Pilots Association (ALPA) asked its 41,000 members for "100% vigilance" to Federal Aviation Administration air traffic regulations. Officially, the union claims that the idea of the vigilance is to ensure safety in a time of turmoil caused by the strike at Eastern Airlines. In order to expedite the flow of air traffic, pilots are normally given discretion by air traffic controllers to bypass certain departure and arrival procedures, especially when weather conditions are good and no safety hazards are posed. However, the ALPA's insistence on completely following all procedures has the potential not only to delay individual flights, but to create log jams for subsequent flights.[76]

---

[73] Alecia Swasy, "Proliferating Strikes Threaten Mines—And Mine Union Too," *The Wall Street Journal* (July 17, 1989), p. A1. Reprinted by permission of *The Wall Street Journal,* Dow Jones & Company, Inc., 1989. All rights reserved worldwide.
[74] Benjamin J. Taylor and Fred Witney, *Labor Relations Law,* 5th ed. (Englewood Cliffs, New Jersey: Prentice-Hall, Inc., 1987), pp. 435–437.
[75] *Carbon Fuel v. United Mine Workers of America,* 444 U.S. 212 (1979).
[76] Robert L. Rose, "How Pilots Hope to Slow Air Travel," *The Wall Street Journal* (March 7, 1989), p. B1.

Table 10–3 ▲ How Pilots Create Air Travel Delays

1. *Request a full reading of flight plans before takeoff*: Because they have already filed their flight plans with air traffic controllers, pilots can accept a "cleared as filed" clearance from departure controllers. Many flight plans involve lengthy and complicated routings. The ALPA, however, is asking pilots to require that controllers read the entire clearance to the pilot; the pilot then repeats ("reads back") the clearance to the controller for confirmation. Such lengthy exchanges between the pilot and controller often take much longer than the standard "cleared as filed" clearances.
2. *Insisting on instrument approaches when landing*: If visibility is poor due to fog, haze, or heavy rain, pilots must execute instrument landing approaches. When instrument approaches are necessary, controllers must sequence incoming flights and require lengthy final landing approaches, and inbound aircraft must be spaced at least five miles apart. These precautions are necessary because aircraft crews cannot see other air traffic when the visibility is poor and there is a need to keep aircraft from flying in close proximity. When the weather is clear, pilots are often given "visual approaches" in order to expedite arrivals. Under a "visual approach," the pilots are responsible for seeing and avoiding other aircraft. However, by insisting on an instrument approach during clear weather, airline pilots can potentially delay air traffic and increase the workload of air traffic controllers.
3. *Refusing "parallel" approaches*: Many high-volume traffic airports, such as Chicago's O'Hare field, Atlanta's Hartsfield airport, and New York's John F. Kennedy International have parallel runways in which traffic simultaneously arrives and departs. Under federal regulations, pilots have the right to refuse simultaneous approaches on parallel runways, a request that can cause traffic snarls at large airports.

Adapted from Robert L. Rose, "How Pilots Hope to Slow Air Travel," *The Wall Street Journal* (March 7, 1989), p. B1; and Federal Aviation Administration, *Federal Aviation Regulations*, Part 91 (Washington, D.C.: U.S. Government Printing Office, 1990).

Lockouts

The lockout is used by employers to place pressure on unions by barring bargaining-unit members from the workplace. Lockouts are of two types: defensive and offensive. *Defensive lockouts* are used by firms to "head unions off at the pass" and prevent work stoppages from occuring at inopportune times. Firms such as retail stores, resort hotels, and construction firms experience peak and slow times during a typical year. If a union calls a strike during a slow time, it may cause only minimal inconvenience, whereas a strike during a peak business period could be devastating to a firm. Companies that produce perishable raw materials are also susceptible to damaging work stoppages. Suppose a union bargains in good faith during a slow period, but appears to be stalling negotiations so that it can strike during a busy time when the firm is vulnerable. The employer may counter this tactic by calling a defensive lockout rather than risking a severe strike later. By so doing, management puts pressure on the union to settle before the firm reaches its busy season.

Defensive lockouts are also used to protect the integrity of a multi-employer bargaining arrangement (employer association). Unions have used a tactic known as *whipsawing*. Whipsawing occurs when a union calls an economic strike against a firm that is a member of an employer association. A firm that is struck by way of the whipsawing tactic is in a difficult position because other members of the association are competitiors who stand to acquire some of the struck firm's customers and business. Thus, the struck employer is often under a great deal of pressure to settle and may be forced to grant high wage increases and accept unfavorable contract terms. Once the first strike is settled, the union targets another firm in the association and again employs the whipsawing strategy. The union uses the wages and the contract terms from the first settlement as a bargaining target for the second struck firm. The whipsawing continues until all firms in the employer association either have been struck or have agreed to contract terms that approximate those negotiated with the first firm. Although a firm may initially obtain a competitive advantage when a strike is called against a competitor, it is only a matter of time before it will fall victim to whipsawing. For this reason, firms belonging to an employer association may lockout their employees in order to discourage whipsawing by the union.[77] The U.S. Supreme Court has long defended a firm's right to a lockout under these circumstances.[78]

Offensive lockouts are the direct counterpart to the union's economic strike weapon because they are used to force a union to accept an employer's bargaining demands.[79] An offensive lockout is generally permissible once the collective bargaining agreement has expired and a bargaining impasse is reached. Offensive lockouts, however, are not legal if they are designed to discourage union membership. In recent years, the NLRB and lower federal courts have granted employers the right to hire temporary replacements during lockouts. Two separate U.S. Court of Appeals decisions have held that employers may hire temporary workers to strengthen their bargaining positions and remain in business after lawfully locking out employees. The Gold Bond Building Products Division of National Gypsum Company resorted to such action after reaching an impasse in bargaining with the Boilermakers' union in Portsmouth, New Hampshire. After the parties reached a settlement, the temporary employees were dismissed and the regular employees returned to work. When the union filed an unfair labor practice charge against the firm and sought to recover the workers' lost wages during the lockout, the U.S. Court of Appeals held that the employer had no antiunion motivation and the company's action was not "inherently destructive" of employee rights. The court claimed that the lockout had a "comparatively slight" adverse impact on employee rights and the company had a legitimate and justifiable business reason for calling the lockout during the bargaining impasse.[80] A similar decision was also reached

---

[77] Management may also engage in whipsawing. The practice by large corporations of forcing workers at one of its plants to grant concessions or lose work to employees at another plant is a form of managerial whipsawing. The United Auto Workers was concerned about the prospect of whipsawing when it drew up its 1987 collective bargaining program. See The Bureau of National Affairs, Inc., "Approval of Bargaining Strategy by Auto Workers," *Labor Relations Reporter*, Vol. 124 (Washington, D.C.: The Bureau of National Affairs, Inc., April 27, 1987), pp. 265–266.

[78] *NLRB v. Truck Drivers Local Union No. 449 et al. (Buffalo Linen Supply Company)*, 353 U.S. 85 (1956).

[79] *American Ship Building Company v. NLRB*, 380 U.S. 300 (1965).

[80] *Boilermakers v. NLRB*; CA DC, No. 8–1189 (September 30, 1988). Discussed in The Bureau of National Affairs, Inc., "Hiring of Temporary Workers during a Lockout," *Collective Bargaining Negotiations & Contracts* (Washington, D.C.: The Bureau of National Affairs, Inc., October 20, 1988), pp. 1–2.

when Harter Equipment, Inc. of Englishtown, New Jersey, locked out members of the Operating Engineers, Local 825.[81]

▲ National Emergency Disputes

As noted earlier in this chapter, strikes have not posed major problems in the United States. When the Taft-Hartley Act was passed, however, Congress recognized the possibility that some strikes could create serious societal and economic threats. As a result, the Act included a "National Emergencies" section (sections 206–212) designed to deal with strikes or lockouts affecting an entire industry (or a substantial part of an industry) that would imperil the national health or safety.[82] If a labor dispute is regarded as a major threat, the president of the United States is empowered to appoint a board of inquiry composed of neutral, disinterested individuals to inquire into the issues involved in the dispute and to return a written report to the president. The report normally includes a statement of the facts surrounding the dispute, along with each party's final offer. However, the board of inquiry is not supposed to make recommendations regarding how the dispute should be settled.[83] Once the board of inquiry completes its investigation, the president decides whether a true emergency exists. The president may then petition a federal district court for an 80-day injunction to end the work stoppage.[84] The court must determine whether the work stoppage: (1) affects an entire industry (or a substantial part of an industry), and (2) would imperil the national health and safety if permitted to continue. Once the 80-day injunction expires, the parties are free to strike. However, they must make an effort to settle their differences during this time and use the services of the Federal Mediation and Conciliation Service. The board of inquiry makes a report to the president on the current status of the work stoppage 60 days after the injunction has been issued. Within 15 days after this report is made, the NLRB holds a secret-ballot election to determine whether the employees are willing to accept management's final offer of settlement. The NLRB certifies the election results and makes the report available to Congress. In the 1980s, however, these procedures were used sparingly.[85]

The Taft-Hartley provisions dealing with national emergency disputes have been a subject of controversy.[86] First, there is no strict set of guidelines that helps the president determine whether a genuine national emergency exists. A strike

---

[81] *Operating Engineers, Local 825 v. NLRB (Harter Equipment, Inc.)*, CA 3, No. 86–3641 (September 25, 1987). Discussed in The Bureau of National Affairs, Inc., "Replacements During Lockout Ruling," *Collective Bargaining Negotiations & Contracts* (Washington, D.C.: The Bureau of National Affairs, Inc., November 5, 1987), p. 3.
[82] 61 Stat. 136, section 206, (June 23, 1947).
[83] 61 Stat. 136, Title II, section 206, (June 23, 1947).
[84] 61 Stat. 136, Title II, section 208, (June 23, 1947).
[85] See Charles M. Rehmus, "Emergency Strikes Revisited," *Industrial and Labor Relations Review* (January 1990), pp. 175–190.
[86] For an excellent discussion of national emergency disputes, see Benjamin J. Taylor and Fred Witney, *Labor Relations Law*, 5th ed. (Englewood Cliffs, New Jersey: Prentice-Hall, Inc., 1987), pp. 556–583.

affecting a large segment of the steel industry might constitute a national emergency if steel inventories are low. A key issue is determining what constitutes an adequate inventory. Second, it must be decided whether a "public inconvenience" constitutes a national emergency. A strike encompassing most of the trucking industry might pose an inconvenience for customers who depend on deliveries, but the line between "public inconvenience" and "public suffering" is difficult to determine. If taken literally, the definition of an "emergency" dispute is quite narrow; only a very few number of labor disputes in the United States would fall into this category.[87] Third, the board of inquiry must confine its efforts to reporting the facts of the dispute and it is not allowed by law to mediate or arbitrate a national emergency dispute. The Taft-Hartley provisions merely extend the strike or lockout deadline without placing a great deal of formal pressure on the parties to resolve their differences. Furthermore, last-offer votes by employees are almost universally rejected. Without pressure to resolve their differences at the bargaining table, the parties may be tempted to engage in perfunctory bargaining during the 80-day cooling-off period.[88] Once the 80-day injunction period has expired, Congress may take the drastic measure of enacting legislation to end the work stoppage; a threat to do so may be all that is necessary to bring the dispute to an end.

▲ Summary and Conclusions

Labor disputes have long been intertwined with the collective bargaining process, not only in the United States but also in other nations. In the United States, strikes and lockouts have had a relatively small impact on the flow of commerce, whereas in European countries, general strikes can affect large segments of the economy. Perhaps a certain degree of tension between union and management is not only to be expected, but might even be regarded as healthy. However, collective bargaining relationships that are fraught with conflict usually work to the disadvantage of both sides. Organizations such as the Federal Mediation and Conciliation Service and the American Arbitration Association will continue to play a prominent role in labor-management conflict resolution.

Several trends in labor disputes have emerged in the 1980s and early 1990s. First, labor disputes have become legally complex insofar as the rights and conduct of unions, employees, and management are concerned. Second, there have been fewer strikes and lockouts over the past decade, but those that have arisen are often bitter. Third, companies have become increasingly willing to operate during work stoppages. Management may be driven by the need to ensure the survival of the firm and, in some cases, to destroy the power of the union.

The frequency and magnitude of labor disputes in the future will undoubtedly be affected by the state of the economy, foreign competition, labor law develop-

---

[87] Derek C. Bok and John T. Dunlop, *Labor and the American Community* (New York: Simon and Schuster, 1970), p. 251.

[88] "In spite of these flaws, the procedures have worked out better than might have been expected. The ingenuity of public officials in designing mediation and special fact-finding procedures has often compensated for the formal deficiencies of the law." Derek C. Bok and John T. Dunlop, *Labor and the American Community* (New York: Simon and Shuster, 1970), p. 251.

ments, union and management labor relations strategies, and changes in the way in which employees view their jobs. Perhaps the most certain prediction that can be made is that labor disputes and their resolution will remain as a major topic of concern among labor practitioners and researchers.

▲ Discussion Questions and Exercises

1. Much has been said in recent years about the need for organized labor and management to assume a less adversarial role than has occurred in years past. Is such an idea feasible? Do you believe that a certain degree of conflict might be worthwhile in the union-management relationship?
2. Interview a labor mediator. What is the mediator's professional background? What techniques does he or she employ in resolving impasses?
3. Why, in your opinion, are some companies and unions more prone to strike than others? Discuss.
4. Why is labor violence not as common in recent years as it has been in the past?
5. Research either the Eastern Airlines-International Association of Machinists or the Pittston Co.-United Mine Workers labor disputes of 1989. Why did these disputes receive so much media attention?
6. Explain how strike preparations (or lack thereof) by union and management can either increase or decrease bargaining power.
7. What legal problems do sympathy strikes and wildcat strikes pose? Discuss.
8. Why, in your opinion, do strikes in the U.S. result in such a small percentage of lost work days?

▲ ▲ ▲ ▲ ▲ SELECTED LABOR DISPUTES

The San Francisco Nurses Strike[89]

In the early-morning hours of August 18, 1988, negotiators for the Affiliated Hospitals of San Francisco and the California Nurses Association (CNA) reached a tentative agreement on a new 36-month contract that was to end a strike by 2,000 registered nurses at six San Francisco hospitals. The agreement was the result of four days of intensive negotiations, which were assisted by San Francisco mayor Art Agnos and FMCS mediator Dorothy Christiansen. However, the nurses rejected the agreement by a 2-to-1 margin and the 16-day strike continued.

CNA spokeswoman Maureen Anderson said that the nurses rejected the proposed contract primarily because the wage package was "virtually the same as it was before the strike." The rejected contract would have raised wages

---

[89] Condensed from The Bureau of National Affairs, Inc., "San Francisco Nurses Remain on Strike," *Labor Relations Reporter*, Vol. 128 (Washington, D.C.: The Bureau of National Affairs, Inc., August 29, 1988), pp. 568–569.

by 7.5 percent in the first year, 6.5 percent in the second year, and 6 percent in the third. However, the nurses wanted increases of 11 percent in the first year and 10 percent in the second. Under the old contract, nurses earned between $31,152 and $35,892. In addition, Anderson said the nurses were seeking a two-year contract rather than a three-year pact. The nurses also wanted a larger weekend shift differential than was offered by management.

The hospitals' chief negotiator, Karen Henry, said that the rejected agreement would have provided the "average full-time nurse with more than $18,000 in increased compensation over the life of the contract," placing them among the highest paid nurses in the United States. CNA's Anderson said that salaries at Affiliated Hospitals were currently about 8 percent behind those of other area hospitals. She added that nurses' salaries have not kept up with the cost of living in San Francisco and that the nurses were "no longer willing to work for substandard wages." Anderson noted that the average salary in San Francisco hospitals rose 39 percent during a nursing shortage in the 1970s. She said that the current shortage was "more severe" than in the 1970s and that salaries would have to go up at least that much over the next several years.

John G. Williams, president of Affiliated Hospitals, said: "We really stretched to offer our nurses a package which exceeds all others in the area. We did this even though our hospitals are facing tremendous financial pressures, and even though the increases far exceed what we have given other employees." He added that the hospitals had "no choice but to continue to operate our hospitals without our CNA nurses."

When the nurses struck, they joined the picket lines of members from the Service Employees International Union, Local 250, who had walked out one week earlier at seven hospitals represented by Affiliated Hospitals. Local 250 members ratified a new two-year contract, but refused to return to work until the nurses had ratified their contract.

Discussion Questions

1. Given the difference between the nurses' demands and the contract offered by Affiliated Hospitals, what is the likelihood that a settlement would be imminent?
2. San Francisco mayor Agnos insisted that both sides confront not only the issues, but also the mutual obligations of union and management to the community. Evaluate this argument in light of the positions of the parties.
3. What tactics could the federal mediator follow to help the California Nurses Association and Affiliated Hospitals reach a settlement?
4. Why did the Service Employees International Union members who had already ratified their contract wait until the nurses settled before going back to work? What were the possible motives behind the SEIU members' return-to-work strategy?

The Screen Actors and Screen Extras Strike[90]

Three unions, the Screen Actors Guild (SAG), the American Federation of Television and Radio Artists (AFTRA), and the Screen Extras Guild ended a 15-day strike and returned to work on April 5, 1988, after reaching a tentative agreement with both the American Association of Advertising Agencies and the Association of National Advertising. The three unions represented 100,000 artists nationwide, and their strike centered on pay to performers for commercials viewed on cable television. Prior to the agreement, if an actor's commercial ran on cable television, he or she received no payment. The actors were looking for payments that were tied to the size of each cable network's subscription base.

The settlement calls for a residual payment of $366 for a 13-week cycle on cable television. Thus, if a commercial airs anytime within a 13-week period, an actor gets a check. If the commercial appears on cable television any time after that, the actor receives another payment for that 13-week cycle. AFTRA/Los Angeles public relations director Pam Thayer referred to this pay schedule as a "336 percent pay increase." In addition, the cable payment will increase by five percent in the 18th month of the three-year contract. The contract also provides a 10 percent increase in the session fee ($333 under the previous contract) paid to actors, a 10 percent increase for "wildspot" or nonnetwork commercials, and a 13.5 percent increase for radio commercial sessions.

In reflecting on the strike, it is difficult to assess its impact. The unions claimed that commercial production had come to a halt. SAG spokesman Mark Locher noted that many advertising campaigns are written around a particular actor and production would have necessarily been stopped in the absence of the familiar character. But John McGuinn, chief negotiator for mangement, claimed that non-union performers were able to fill many spots and business continued during the work stoppage.

Discussion Questions

1. This strike is a textbook example of the entertainment strikes of recent years, which cast unions in the role of catching up with the technological leaps in video and television viewing. Research other strikes involving actors and writers. What labor problems do you foresee in the future in the entertainment industry?
2. Once a strike ends, union negotiators typically talk about the great gains achieved and management makes the point that the employees gained very little for their sacrifices as the result of the work stoppage. Why do you believe statements such as these are made?

[90] Condensed from The Bureau of National Affairs, Inc., "Actors Unions End Strike," *Labor Relations Reporter*, Vol. 127 (Washington, D.C.: The Bureau of National Affairs, Inc., April 25, 1988), pp. 535–536.

3. Discuss whether it would be easy for management to replace actors in television commercials.

The New York University Clerical Workers Strike[91]

In a contract dispute centering on wages, clerical and technical employees struck New York University on August 29, 1988, an hour before in-person student registration for the fall term was set to begin. Striking employees were members of Local 3882 of the American Federation of Teachers (AFT), which represents some 1,600 New York University clerical and technical employees (900 of these employees are union members). Union members voted 600–10 in favor of the strike after negotiators for the union and the university failed to reach an agreement in a bargaining session held the previous day. Between 500 and 600 union members participated in picketing at several locations on the university's Washington Square campus in the Greenwich Village area of New York City; few members crossed the picket lines.

The central issue of the work stoppage was pay equity. Union statistics show that the median salary in the bargaining unit was $17,000 a year. This figure represented at least $2,000 per year less than what was earned by other unionized support staff, such as guards and elevator operators. The AFT unit was largely female, whereas the other support units were largely male. The AFT sought an 8 percent increase each year as well as improvements in the pension plan (which paid $64 a week for a person retiring after 20 years). The university's final offer was a 5.5 percent wage increase and it also planned on a further 5.5 percent increase during the life of the contract.

On September 20, 1988, the clerical workers voted overwhelmingly to end the three-week strike. The vote to end the walkout followed an announcement of a tentative contract settlement that would give the clerical workers a 17 to 20 percent pay raise over a three-year term. Acceptance of the tentative settlement was made, according to union spokeswoman Eleanor Lee, "because they did not feel they could move NYU any further." The university administration adamantly refused to include an agency shop agreement in the settlement. An agency shop clause requires bargaining unit employees who elect not to join the union to pay union dues. Asked if the university viewed the absence of the agency shop clause as a victory, university spokesman Howard Levine commented, "This is not like the Olympics or a ballgame—we're not looking for victories and defeats. The agency shop was something we did not want to offer, and we did not have to."

---

[91] Condensed from The Bureau of National Affairs, Inc., "New York University Strike," *Labor Relations Reporter*, Vol. 129 (Washington, D.C.: The Bureau of National Affairs, Inc., September 5, 1988), p. 20; and The Bureau of National Affairs, Inc., "End of Clerical Workers Strike at NYU," *Labor Relations Reporter*, Vol. 129 (Washington, D.C.: The Bureau of National Affairs, Inc., September 26, 1988), pp. 120–121.

Other terms of the settlement include additional merit pool money to boost salaries to a minimum of $385 a week, lowering the overtime threshold from 37.5 to 35 hours per week, increasing the pension formula multiplier, providing pay raises retroactive to September 1st, and permitting the accumulation of vacation and other benefits during the strike.

Discussion Questions

1. Why did the employees call a strike just before fall registration?
2. Explain why the AFT represents 1,600 employees, yet only 900 actually belong to the union. Why, in your opinion, did only 610 actually cast a strike vote? What does this signify to union and management negotiators?
3. Given NYU's annual wage increases of 5.5 percent, do you believe that the 17 to 20 percent pay increases over a three-year period represented a significant victory for the AFT and the clerical employees?
4. Evaluate the poststrike statements of Eleanor Lee and Howard Levine.
5. During the strike, an FMCS mediator called two bargaining sessions, neither of which was successful. However, a third session, called on September 18 eventually yielded a settlement. Students and faculty demonstrations supporting the strikers were also held. What might have happened had the mediator, students, and faculty not intervened?

11 Contract Administration: The Grievance Procedure

- **Introduction**
- **The Role of Contract Administration in Labor Relations**
- **Sources of Grievances in Union-Management Relations**
  Disciplinary Problems
  Disputes over Compensation Practices
  Problems Associated with Working Conditions
  Inconsistent Enforcement of Personnel Policies by Supervisors
  Economic Conditions Leading to Layoffs and Reduced Working Hours
  Ambiguous Contract Language
  Conflicts Regarding Past Practices
  The Effect of Individual Employee Characteristics and Grievance Filing
- **Components of Grievance Procedures**
  Parties to a Grievance
  Defining the Grievance
  Time Limits between Stages of the Grievance Procedure
  Persons Involved in Processing and Evaluating Grievances
  Resolving Grievances
- **Processing Grievances**
  The Initial Stage
  Processing Grievances to Higher Stages
    A Written Definition of the Grievance
    Presenting the Grievance
    Preparing the Case for Arbitration
- **Abuse and Misuse of Grievance Procedures**
- **The Union's Duty of Fair Representation in Grievance Administration**
- **Criteria for Evaluating Grievance Procedures**
- **Summary and Conclusions**

▲ Discussion Questions and Exercises
▲ Appendix: Boeing-International Association of Machinists and Aerospace Workers Grievance Procedure

▲ Introduction

Rights disputes arise over the interpretation and application of the collective bargaining agreement. The effective resolution of rights disputes can spell the difference between a labor-management relationship that is stable and harmonious and one that is acrimonious and hostile. Grievance procedures that have been incorporated into collective bargaining agreements are the primary means for administering the contract and resolving rights disputes. The parties are provided with a mechanism for resolving alleged contract violations economically, expeditiously, and without a work stoppage. Grievance procedures allow the grievant and representatives from the union and management to explain their respective positions fully and, when necessary, to submit the dispute to final and binding arbitration. In short, the grievance resolution process plays an integral role in maintaining industrial peace and has been referred to by one arbitrator as "the lifeblood of a collective bargaining relationship."[1]

This chapter discusses the role of contract administration in labor relations. Topics include the major sources of grievances, the primary components of grievance procedures, strategies used in processing grievances, and criteria for evaluating the effectiveness of a grievance procedure.

▲ The Role of Contract Administration in Labor Relations

If the collective bargaining agreement is the "law of the shop," then contract administration is the system of industrial jurisprudence designed to give life and meaning to that law. As noted in earlier chapters, the process of negotiating a collective bargaining agreement generally takes only a few months; yet the union, employer, and workers usually live with the terms and conditions of the agreement from one to five years.[2] During the life of the contract, a number of unanticipated problems and issues may arise. For example, a male nursing home attendant who contemplated transsexual surgery received permission from his employer to wear

---

[1] Quoting Arbitrator Michael I. Komaroff in *North American Aviation*, 16 LA 747 (1951), in Frank Elkouri and Edna Asper Elkouri, *How Arbitration Works*, 4th ed. (Washington, D.C.: The Bureau of National Affairs, Inc., 1985), p. 154.

[2] According to The Bureau of National Affairs, Inc. survey data, over 80 percent of the collective bargaining agreements are 3 years in length; only 5 percent of the agreements span 4 years or more. See The Bureau of National Affairs, Inc., *Basic Patterns in Union Contracts*, 11th ed. (Washington, D.C.: The Bureau of National Affairs, Inc., 1986), pp. 1–3.

the female nursing attendant uniform. After wearing the female uniform for three years without undergoing surgery, he was terminated.[3] Contract provisions allowing management to discipline or fire employees for "just cause" are written in general language and must be applied to specific problems such as the bizarre grievance just described.

Even when contract provisions appear to be specific, the parties are likely to have differing opinions as to the exact meaning and application of these terms. Seniority provisions, for example, are troublesome in this respect, especially when job promotions are based on a combination of seniority and the employee's qualifications and ability to perform the job competently. Rights disputes also arise over a host of other topics such as vacation scheduling, employee grooming and dress codes, sick-leave policies, and safety issues.

For anyone who has had to endure the expense, long delays, extensive motions and briefs, legal technicalities, and appeals associated with civil court proceedings, the process of contract administration offers a refreshing change in speed, economy, and simplicity. Many rights disputes are settled quickly through a conference between a union shop steward and a first-line supervisor. Even when a dispute reaches the arbitration stage, it is resolved much faster and at considerably less cost than disputes processed through a state or federal court.[4] Arbitrators and others involved in resolving rights disputes generally possess a familiarity with the job, working environment, and past union and management practices, whereas judges in a civil court rarely possess the industrial expertise of arbitrators. Union and management have little control over the selection of a judge in a civil proceeding, yet the parties using a contractual grievance procedure have a great deal of control in selecting both their grievance representatives and the arbitrator. Thus, the parties develop a sense of ownership in the grievance and arbitration process, a fact that normally makes it easier to accept the settlement of a rights dispute.

Finally, the parties understand that the resolution of a rights dispute is almost always final. Arbitration decisions are rarely appealed to a state or federal court and, as discussed in Chapter 12, the U.S. Supreme Court has stated that the courts should not tamper with or alter an arbitration decision, except under unusual circumstances. As a result, the parties can present their grievances, resolve them either through mutual agreement or through binding arbitration, and then put the problem behind them without resorting to a work stoppage. If the outcome of a grievance is particularly dissatisfying to a party, they have the option of negotiating new contract language during the next round of contract talks.

---

[3] *Greater Harlem Nursing Home*, 76 LA 680 (1981).

[4] For example, a woman who was fired from her job as a bartender on December 16, 1983 because she used "unladylike" language after her supervisor made sexually-suggestive remarks to her filed a sex discrimination charge under Title VII of the 1964 Civil Rights Act. After her case was heard by the Equal Employment Opportunity Commission and U.S. federal district court, she finally received a judgment in her favor on June 29, 1987, three and one-half years after she was discharged. *EEOC v. FLC & Brothers Rebel, Inc.*, 44 FEP Cases 362 (1987). The time needed to resolve civil cases such as this may be five to six years if the case is appealed to a higher court. The same case could probably have been settled through labor arbitration in less than eight months.

▲ Sources of Grievances in Union-Management Relations

Grievances are precipitated for a number of reasons. An examination of published arbitration awards reveals a variety of grievances arising over factors such as disciplinary problems, inconsistent enforcement of personnel policies by supervisors, managerial actions that threaten job security, and disagreements regarding the administration of pay and benefit plans. Grievances also arise because of personal conflicts between union officials and members and management.[5]

Disciplinary Problems

The most common type of grievance arises over disciplinary actions taken against employees by management. In fact, some collective bargaining agreements use two grievance procedures, one exclusively for disciplinary matters and one for all other grievances. Disciplinary problems arise because of excessive employee absenteeism, damage to company property, negligence, safety violations, dishonesty and theft, alcohol and drug abuse, assault and fights with other employees, insubordination, and incompetency.

Under most collective bargaining agreements, management clearly has the right to discharge employees for "just cause." A prime objective of the grievance procedure insofar as disciplinary issues are concerned is due process and equal protection for the employee. Grievance procedures help to ensure that management has fully investigated the facts surrounding a disciplinary incident. The presence of a grievance procedure also prevents the company from making a hasty decision to suspend or terminate an employee. The grievance procedure is used to determine whether the employee was properly disciplined in accordance with the company rules and the applicable provisions of the collective bargaining agreement. Factors such as the nature of the individual offense, extenuating circumstances, and the employee's previous work and disciplinary record are commonly considered in the course of disciplinary proceedings. Chapter 16 deals with employee rights, job security, and discipline. Among the many examples of grievances arising over disciplinary issues are the following:

▲ An employee was fired from his job in a paper mill because the absences stemming from accidents and illnesses comprised almost one quarter of his 18 years' employment.[6]
▲ A city fire department driver was discharged after he pleaded *nolo contendre* to a felony charge of second-degree manslaughter arising from horseplay while operating his boat that resulted in the drowning of a passenger who was riding in another boat.[7]

---

[5] For an excellent analysis of a variety of grievances, see BNA Editorial Staff, *Grievance Guide*, 7th ed. (Washington, D.C.: The Bureau of National Affairs, Inc., 1987).
[6] *Mead Paper*, 91 LA 52 (1988).
[7] *City of Shawnee, Oklahoma*, 91 LA 93 (1988).

▲ An auto mechanic filed a grievance after he was discharged for punching a co-worker several times because of a dispute over the playing of the co-worker's radio.[8]

Disputes over Compensation Practices

The application and coverage of pay and employee benefit policies may also foster grievances. For example, an employee (or the union) may file a grievance to protest the job evaluation and pay classification of a job. The assignment of overtime work that is paid at a higher rate than the initial eight hours of work might be contested if assignments are not made in accordance with the collective bargaining agreement. Unions may contest the employer's choice of a health insurance carrier that provides group hospitalization coverage to bargaining-unit employees, especially if the insurance company has not been paying claims promptly. Compensation issues are addressed in Chapters 13 and 14. Examples of compensation grievances include the following:

▲ Teachers who were allegedly not informed of a newly negotiated tax-sheltered annuity benefit filed a grievance to obtain retroactive benefits.[9]
▲ Employees filed a grievance after management refused to grant a 25-cent wage increase. The collective bargaining agreement required that the employer "talk about" a wage increase "if the economy and profitability of the company allows."[10]
▲ Employees who worked overtime on the eve of a July 4th holiday filed a grievance to obtain premium holiday pay. The employees contended that a side agreement between the union and management provided premium pay for work on the eve of a holiday.[11]

Problems Associated With Working Conditions

Working conditions or "other terms and conditions of work" cover a wide array of contract provisions pertaining to work rules, schedules of work hours, seniority, layoff, and health and safety conditions. A variety of potential grievances may arise that affect working conditions. For example, the union-management tug-of-war over management's right to control operations, change production standards, hire employees, introduce technological improvements, and subcontract work to employees outside of the bargaining unit all represent potential grievances. Grievances pertaining to working conditions also occur when employees refuse to perform unsafe work or when the employer disciplines a worker for safety-rule violations. The following are some relevant examples:

▲ A grievance was filed by maintenance employees as to whether the employer could subcontract concrete-block work. The maintenance workers cited a con-

---

[8] *Marin Honda*, 91 LA 185 (1988).
[9] *Alameda Unified School District*, 91 LA 60 (1988).
[10] *Technocast, Inc.*, 91 LA 164 (1988).
[11] *St. Louis Post Dispatch*, 92 LA 23 (1988).

tract provision that prohibited contracting out "work normally performed" by maintenance employees.[12]
- ▲ The Electrical Workers union filed a grievance after a telephone company transferred the duty of assigning telephone numbers to non-bargaining-unit commercial department employees. The shift in job duties was in response to a technological change.[13]
- ▲ An accident-prone mining employee filed a grievance against his employer after he was ordered to attend an accident-repeater training course.[14]

Inconsistent Enforcement of Personnel Policies by Supervisors

Collective bargaining agreements are designed to ensure that all employees are treated consistently and fairly with regard to personnel matters. Immediate or first-line supervisors occupy an integral position in contract administration. A supervisor who fails to abide by the terms, conditions, and spirit of the collective bargaining agreement can create numerous grievances. Supervisors can precipitate grievances when they demonstrate favoritism among employees, fail to supervise and direct subordinates in their work properly, and overreact in taking disciplinary action. Grievance procedures also provide a means of checking up on the decisions and practices of first-line supervisors. Immediate or first-line supervisors who are in daily contact with employees are often in the best position to either create or halt a grievance. The following examples are illustrative:

- ▲ Shipyard supervisors discharged an employee for sleeping on the job and gave only a three-week suspension for two co-workers who were allegedly loafing on the job. The company later equalized the penalties by reducing the discharged employee's punishment to a three-week suspension.[15]
- ▲ An employee was observed shopping by a supervisor after the employee had called in sick on two successive mornings. The employee was subsequently fired even though the company failed to prove that the employee was no longer ill, and the company had no "24-hour stay-at-home rule."[16]
- ▲ Supervisors at an air conditioning and heating equipment manufacturer discharged an employee without investigating the circumstances surrounding the case after the employee entered a guilty plea on gross sexual imposition, a third degree felony in Ohio.[17]

Economic Conditions Leading to Layoffs and Reduced Working Hours

Unions are deeply concerned about the job security of their members. When poor economic conditions and declining business conditions necessitate cutbacks in a firm's operations, layoffs and reduced working hours are often inevitable. Grievances

---

[12] *Champion International Corp.*, 91 LA 245 (1988).
[13] *United Telephone Company of Ohio*, 91 LA 317 (1988).
[14] *Eastern Coal Corp.*, 89 LA 759 (1987).
[15] *Todd Pacific Shipyards*, 91 LA 30 (1988)
[16] *Central Illinois Public Service Company*, 91 LA 127 (1988).
[17] *Bard Manufacturing Co.*, 91 LA 193 (1988).

arise when union leaders or employees perceive that layoffs are not being made in accordance with seniority and layoff provisions in the collective bargaining agreement. Issues such as the ability of senior employees to "bump" less senior employees from their jobs in order to avoid layoffs may create grievances, especially if the senior employees are not as capable of performing the jobs as their junior counterparts. Controversies also arise when it is believed that management may be making extensive cutbacks in its unionized facilities while maintaining normal operations in its nonunion plants. Plant closings often create heated disputes between union and management. An issue that has arisen is whether employees at the closed facility have the right to transfer to other company facilities. If so, what are their seniority rights at the new location?

Layoffs and plant closings also raise the issue of employee rights to severance pay and employee benefits. Employees who permanently lose their jobs are entitled to unemployment compensation, but they may also be entitled to other payments, such as supplemental unemployment benefits under the collective bargaining agreement. Disputes may arise regarding the eligibility of some employees to receive such benefits, especially if they are on sick leave or have had breaks in employment with the company.

Finally, problems occur when a financially declining company (the *acquired* company) is purchased by another company (the *acquiring* company). The extensive amount of merger activity among U.S. corporations during the 1980s and early 1990s has created new labor relations issues. Whether the collective bargaining agreement negotiated by the acquired company will apply to the acquiring company depends on factors such as the language of the collective bargaining agreement, the purchase agreement between the two companies, and the degree to which the acquired firm's original business is changed because of the merger. Grievances can therefore arise over issues such as seniority and job security rights of employees from both the acquired and acquiring firms. Chapter 15 further discusses problems associated with seniority, layoffs, and plant closings. Examples of grievances arising over these issues include the following:

▲ A marine construction company laid off employees when it ceased operating part of its business. A grievance was filed when the company entered into a new joint business venture with a firm whose employees performed tasks that were similar to the previous business.[18]
▲ Employees of a Volkswagen dealership that was sold filed a grievance requesting severance pay. Although the employees were permanently terminated by the former employer, they were subsequently rehired by the firm's buyer.[19]
▲ A dispute arose over the entitlement to vacation days by employees who had worked for a grocery store that had ceased operations during the life of the collective bargaining agreement.[20]

---

[18] *Crowley Constructors*, 91 LA 32 (1988).
[19] *Ala Moana Volkswagen*, 91 LA 1331 (1988).
[20] *Mahoning Sparkle Markets*, 91 LA 1366 (1988).

Ambiguous Contract Language

The collective bargaining agreement is the source of rights and responsibilities for employers, unions, and employees. At the same time, the agreement also contains the seeds of future disputes, due, in part, to the climate in which negotiations take place. Compromises made between union and management negotiators, the haste that surrounds the last-ditch, all-night bargaining sessions, the lack of foresight by negotiators who fail to anticipate the consequences of what appears to be an innocuous contract provision, and poorly drafted language all create potential problems when the contract must be interpreted and administered.

Phrases such as "just cause," "and so forth," "all normal prerogatives of management," "due consideration," and "appropriate regard for," are examples of ambiguous terms that are commonly found in collective bargaining agreements. All collective bargaining agreements contain clauses of a *general* nature that must be interpreted when *specific* grievances arise. Some collective bargaining agreements contain legal prose that makes sense to attorneys, but is totally incomprehensible to first-line supervisors, shop stewards, and others who must interpret the contract. Furthermore, enlightened self-interest often helps to shape a party's perception of the meaning of a contract provision.

Even the most airtight collective bargaining agreements fail to anticipate all of the possible legal, social, economic, and ethical questions that can arise. Given the multitude of union and management interests and the variety of contract clauses, grievances are sometimes difficult to avoid because the drafting of contract language is not an exact science. When contract language is *ambiguous*, the outcome of a grievance may hinge on past practices, local customs, and industry policies. If the contract language relevant to a particular grievance is *nonexistent*, then the employer may have unilateral control over the issue. Chapter 12 further discusses the arbitrator's role in interpreting ambiguous contract language. However, the following exemplify such grievances:

▲ A grievance was filed over hiring "preferred employees" for "job or projects" of less than $2,500,000. Ambiguities arose regarding the definition (and hence, the value) of a "job or project."[21]
▲ A social worker filed a grievance after being denied "call back" pay (at time-and-one-half the regular pay rate) for arranging emergency care for a minor child. The social worker handled the request by telephone while on standby duty. The collective bargaining agreement did not specify whether telephone contacts fall within the one-quarter pay provision for standby duty or the premium-pay provision "for time worked as a result of a callback to duty."[22]
▲ An equipment operator filed a grievance to obtain an out-of-class wage adjustment after he acted for one day as foreman of his excavation team. The company claimed that an equipment operator "directs employees of small work crews and acts for [the] foreman."[23]

[21] *California Drilling and Blasting Company*, 91 LA 66 (1988).
[22] *County of Ventura*, 91 LA 107 (1988).
[23] *City of Duluth*, 91 LA 238 (1988).

Conflicts Regarding Past Practices

Not all grievances arise over the interpretation and meaning of contract language. Workplace customs and practices that have been established by management and accepted by the union and employees can form an integral part of the labor-management relationship. For example, when management supplies employees with coffee during rest breaks or allows them to leave their work stations 10 minutes prior to the end of a shift in order to shower and change their clothing, the company may have instituted a clear and consistent practice. Grievances typically arise when a company attempts to abolish a practice that has been in effect for a period of time and the union claims that management must continue the practice, at least until the collective bargaining agreement expires. Grievances arising over past practices are among the most difficult to resolve; they are discussed in more detail in Chapter 12. Examples of such grievances include the following:

- A grievance was filed after an employer implemented a flexible benefits plan that required payroll deductions for benefit costs that exceeded an employee's "benefit dollars" allowance. The grievants claimed that the deductions were contrary to the past practice of no employee payroll contributions.[24]
- Editorial employees filed a grievance over a newspaper's unilateral, company-wide smoking policy because the company had allowed editorial employees to smoke in the past.[25]
- An employer allegedly violated a past practice by training a lift-truck operator for a backup leadperson position, where past practice was to train a senior employee for the backup leadperson job.[26]

The Effect of Individual Employee Characteristics on Grievance Filing

Interpersonal conflicts between management, union officials, and employees may create conflicts. Union officials may adopt the posture of "keeping management honest" by challenging nearly all personnel decisions, even those not addressed in the collective bargaining agreement. Some union stewards precipitate grievances by allowing favoritism to cloud their judgments when dealing with bargaining-unit employees. Unions that fail to acquaint shop stewards thoroughly with the collective bargaining agreement may create unnecessary conflicts when the stewards make ill-informed attempts to administer the contract. Militant employees may also desire to file grievances at the slightest provocation. Union officials may be faced with a dilemma when chronically agitated and embattled employees insist in filing grievances over trivial matters.

Overzealous managers with an antiunion bent who insist on making unilateral personnel decisions that conflict with the terms of the collective bargaining agreement also cause problems. Not only do such managers create unnecessary grievances, but their actions may also result in bad-faith bargaining or other unfair labor

---

[24] *Hertz Corporation*, 91 LA 261 (1988).
[25] *Dayton Newspapers*, 91 LA 201 (1988).
[26] *Atlas Powder Co.*, 92 LA 17 (1988).

practice charges against the company. Another antiunion tactic is for the company to adopt a strategy of denying all union grievances, regardless of merit. This tactic forces the union to decide which grievances they can afford to process through arbitration.

Although research on grievance activity is relatively sparse, studies indicate that factors such as a person's age, gender, and work experience have an impact on individual grievance-filing behavior.[27] Furthermore, good union-management relationships are associated with lower levels of grievance activity.[28] Organizations with technologies requiring high levels of worker responsibility and close supervision also engender higher grievance rates, as do organizations with a centralized management structure.[29] Likewise, workers who are poor performers on the job, union activists, highly educated workers, workers with high rates of absenteeism, and workers in lower job classifications have a greater tendency to file grievances than other employees.[30]

▲ Components of Grievance Procedures

Grievance procedures represent the centerpiece of the contract administration process and, as such, they play an integral role in enforcing the "law of the shop," ensuring democracy in the workplace, and maintaining industrial peace. The stages of a grievance procedure are usually outlined in the collective bargaining agreement. Figure 11-1 presents the major elements of a typical grievance procedure, and the Appendix illustrates a grievance procedure from the aerospace industry. As noted earlier, grievance procedures almost always culminate in binding arbitration. The major components of grievance procedures are discussed below.

Parties to a Grievance

The majority of grievances are filed by employees (or by the union on behalf of an employee). Unions also file grievances on behalf of a group of employees because of an alleged violation of their rights under the collective bargaining agreement. For example, a union may file a grievance on behalf of a group of production employees who lost the opportunity to receive overtime pay because management subcontracted bargaining unit work to an outside firm. Occasionally, a former employee or the estate of a deceased employee will file a grievance (with the help of

---

[27] See Ignace Ng and Ali Dastmalchian, "Determinants of Grievance Outcomes: A Case Study," *Industrial and Labor Relations Review* (April 1989), pp. 393–394; and Philip Ash, "The Parties to the Grievance," *Personnel Psychology*, Vol. 23, No. 1 (1970), pp. 13–37.
[28] Jeffrey Gandz and J. David Whitehead, "The Relationship Between Industrial Relations Climate and Grievance Initiation and Resolution," *Proceedings of the Thirty-Fourth Annual Meeting, Industrial Relations Research Association* (Madison, Wisconsin: Industrial Relations Research Association, 1982), pp. 320–328.
[29] David Peach and E. Robert Livernash, *Grievance Initiation and Resolution: A Study in Basic Steel* (Boston: Graduate School of Business Administration, Harvard University, 1974).
[30] Howard Q. Sulkin and Robert Pranis, "Comparison of Grievants and Non-Grievants in a Heavy Machinery Company," *Personnel Psychology* (Summer 1967), pp. 111–119.

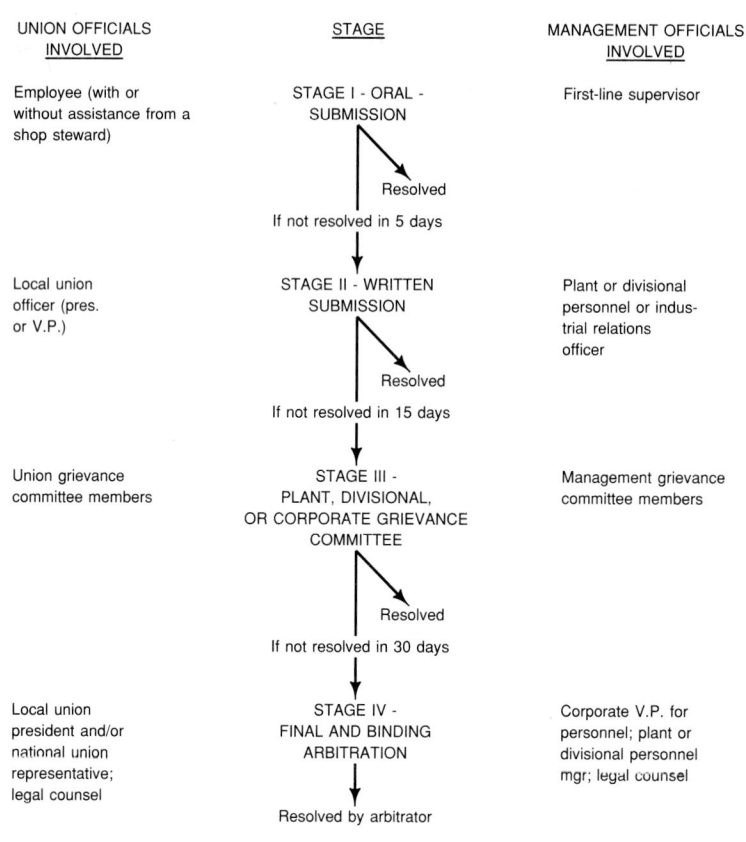

UNION OFFICIALS INVOLVED	STAGE	MANAGEMENT OFFICIALS INVOLVED
Employee (with or without assistance from a shop steward)	STAGE I - ORAL - SUBMISSION → Resolved *If not resolved in 5 days*	First-line supervisor
Local union officer (pres. or V.P.)	STAGE II - WRITTEN SUBMISSION → Resolved *If not resolved in 15 days*	Plant or divisional personnel or industrial relations officer
Union grievance committee members	STAGE III - PLANT, DIVISIONAL, OR CORPORATE GRIEVANCE COMMITTEE → Resolved *If not resolved in 30 days*	Management grievance committee members
Local union president and/or national union representative; legal counsel	STAGE IV - FINAL AND BINDING ARBITRATION ↓ Resolved by arbitrator	Corporate V.P. for personnel; plant or divisional personnel mgr; legal counsel

FIGURE 11-1 A Grievance Procedure with Final and Binding Arbitration

the union) in order to collect insurance or accrued vacation benefits. Although employees and the union file the vast majority of grievances, the company may file a grievance, especially to enforce a no-strike clause under the collective bargaining agreement.[31]

Defining the Grievance

Most collective bargaining agreements place restrictions on the problems and issues that can be submitted as grievances. Parties to a collective bargaining agreement may encounter a number of problems within the web of relationships that exists between management, employees, and union officials. However, there is generally a distinction between a *grievance* and a *complaint*; a meritorious grievance must generally be based on a violation of the collective bargaining agreement. For ex-

---

[31] Employers also have the right to sue the union for breach of contract under section 301 of the Taft-Hartley Act. If a union violates a no-strike clause in the contract, the company may find it more expedient to obtain an injunction to enforce the clause.

ample, employees may harbor a dislike for a supervisor because of his aloof and arrogant demeanor. Unless the employees can show that the supervisor has somehow violated their rights under the collective bargaining agreement, they probably do not have a meritorious grievance. The only recourse that employees have against such a supervisor is to complain to management. However, management probably will not violate the terms and conditions of the collective bargaining agreement if it ignores the employees' complaint regarding the supervisor.

Management generally prefers a narrow interpretation of what constitutes a grievance, whereas union officials prefer a broader definition. The narrowest definition of a grievance is one that violates the express terms of the collective bargaining agreement. At the other end of the spectrum is a broad grievance definition that allows *any* dispute to be processed through the grievance procedure.[32] Some grievance procedures contain liberal definitions of the topics that can be submitted to a grievance procedure (an open definition of a grievance). Other grievance procedures restrict the topics that are grievable; if a topic is excluded, it cannot be processed through the grievance procedure (a closed definition of a grievance). Some grievance procedures have an open definition of grievances up to the arbitration stage, but limit the types of grievances that may be heard by an arbitrator. The U.S. Supreme Court has held that doubts over whether a grievance is subject to arbitration should be resolved in favor of submitting the grievance to an arbitrator. Unless a grievance over a contract provision is specifically excluded from arbitration, it is subject to arbitration.[33]

The key to determining whether a valid grievance exists is twofold. First, does the alleged grievance violate the terms, conditions, or spirit of the collective bargaining agreement? Second, is this type of grievance expressly excluded from the grievance procedure? If the answer to the first question is affirmative and the answer to the second question is negative, then a legitimate grievance probably exists.

During the first step of the grievance procedure, the employee (with or without the help of a shop steward) may present a grievance to his or her supervisor without putting the charges in writing. In many cases, the grievance arises over a simple misunderstanding and is quickly resolved at the first stage. For example, a supervisor may have inadvertently scheduled a less senior employee to work overtime in violation of the contract. Once the matter is brought to the supervisor's attention, he or she may simply change the work schedule and avoid further problems.

Beyond the first stage of the grievance procedure, nearly all grievances are put into writing. The grievance should be clearly written and provide specifics on dates, the contract provisions in question, and other relevant information. Putting the grievance in writing establishes a record of the grievance. In addition, by forcing the grievant to define and formulate the grievance carefully, he or she may be amazed to discover that there is no legitimate grievance after all. Reducing an issue to writing forces the grievant to think carefully about the grievance and may serve to eliminate those that are frivolous or lack merit.

---

[32] Donald S. McPherson with Conrad John Gates and Kevin N. Rogers, *Resolving Grievances: A Practical Approach* (Reston, Virginia: Reston Publishing Company, 1983), p. 15.
[33] *United Steelworkers v. Warrior & Gulf Navigation Company*, 363 U.S. 574 (1960).

Time Limits between Stages of the Grievance Procedure

The hallmark of a good grievance procedure is one that permits a quick resolution of the problem at the earliest possible stage. An examination of Figure 11–1 reveals that time limits between each stage of the grievance procedure have been established. Time limits prevent the grievance from "dying on the vine" and they force the parties to resolve the grievance in an expeditious fashion. The prompt resolution of grievances prevents issues from smouldering and creating unrest in the workplace. Without time limits, the party who is the "defendant" in the grievance (usually management) might attempt to stall in hopes that the "moving" party (usually the union or the employee) will eventually lose interest and drop the grievance. Grievance procedures that have no time limits may also allow a grievant to dredge up a grievance from years past. For example, a grievance was filed because of a typographical error that allegedly first appeared 12 years earlier. Despite the inordinate amount of time that had passed, the arbitrator held that the grievance was filed in a timely fashion because the grievance procedure had no time limits.[34]

There is no set formula for deciding how much time should be allowed between stages of the grievance procedure. Time limits should be long enough to allow the parties ample opportunity to prepare their case, yet short enough to resolve the dispute without drawn-out proceedings and frustrating delays. When union and management negotiators draft the provisions of the grievance procedure during contract talks, they generally allow for longer periods of time between the higher stages than the lower stages. Thus, in Figure 11–1, only five days are allowed between stages one and two, whereas 30 days are allowed between the third and fourth stages.[35] The reason for the longer time periods between higher stages is because grievances reaching higher stages are usually more complex and there is often a need to include prominent union and management officials at the higher stages. Some grievance procedures contain a process known as "advance-step" filing, which typically allows the parties to bypass the first or second stage. Grievances involving employee disciplinary actions or other complex issues having important, long-term implications to the union-management relationship are often filed at an advanced stage (e.g., the third stage) of the grievance procedure. The reason behind advance-step filing is that first-line supervisors and shop stewards do not have the authority or expertise to resolve critical issues.

Under most grievance procedures, if a moving party fails to adhere to a time limit, he or she may lose the right to continue the grievance unless extenuating circumstances have caused the delay. When management grievance committee members fail to move to the next step of a grievance procedure, the company may automatically forfeit its position. For example, such "company-default" provisions could result in the automatic reinstatement of a terminated employee if the company fails to move the grievance to the next stage within the prescribed time limits. However, when the existence of a grievance is not known until some time after

---

[34] See *Food Employers Council, Inc.*, 87 LA 514 (1986).
[35] Some grievance procedures use an *overall* time limit (e.g., 30 days to resolve the entire grievance excluding the arbitration stage), rather than specific limits between each stage.

the event occurred, a grievance may still be valid even though the time limit has expired. A pregnant laboratory worker who was denied a transfer to a less physically demanding job did not realize that she had a grievance until two years later, when she discovered that a male employee was granted a transfer because of recent gall bladder surgery. The arbitrator ruled that the grievance was timely because "an employee cannot be expected to file a grievance until he or she is made aware of the action upon which the grievance is based."[36] The same logic also applies to continuous and repetitive violations, such as pay discrimination cases or workplace safety hazards.[37]

Arbitrators have ignored strict time limits when both sides have been lax about following the limits established in the grievance procedure. Time limits may also be waived if the mail has delayed the receipt of a grievance letter or if there is doubt as to when the contract violation that created a grievance actually occurred. In cases where there is controversy over whether a grievance has been processed in a timely fashion, the parties may allow the arbitrator to resolve the timeliness issue prior to hearing the case.

Persons Involved in Processing and Evaluating Grievances

Shop stewards usually serve as the initial repository for grievances filed by employees. The employer is generally required to deal with whomever the union and employee designate as their grievance representative; to do otherwise constitutes bad-faith bargaining by management.[38] To ensure that shop stewards will be able to process grievances during periods of layoffs, most collective bargaining agreements grant them superseniority and place them at the top of the seniority list. Superseniority for shop stewards is limited to layoffs and recall and does not entitle them to additional paid vacations, overtime work, or retirement benefits.[39] Shop stewards must often perform the initial investigation and gather facts surrounding the grievance. To properly investigate grievances, shop stewards are generally allowed access to company facilities outside of their own work areas. It is also a common practice for management to compensate union representatives and other employees for time spent processing grievances during normal working hours.[40] Although management cannot discipline militant grievance representatives who zealously attempt to enforce the collective bargaining agreement, shop stewards who use abusive language toward supervisors during the course of a grievance investigation may be subject to disciplinary action.[41]

---

[36] *Cities Services Co.*, 87 LA 1209 (1986).
[37] *West Penn Power Co.*, 31 LA 297 (1958).
[38] See *Frankline, Inc.*, 127 LRRM 1132 (1988).
[39] *Dairylea Coop., Inc.*, 219 NLRB 656 (1975).
[40] Many collective bargaining agreements stipulate that shop stewards will continue to receive their hourly pay rate while they are serving as grievance representatives. However, some agreements control the amount of time that stewards spend on grievances by requiring time limits on grievance processing (beyond which stewards are not paid) and by requiring that stewards fill out a form on their grievance activity or report to their supervisor before leaving the work area.
[41] Frank Elkouri and Edna Asper Elkouri, *How Arbitration Works*, 4th ed. (Washington, D.C.: The Bureau of National Affairs, Inc., 1985), pp. 183–184.

Union and management officials are somewhat divided as to the merits of having union representatives accompany a grievant to meet with the supervisor during the first stage of the grievance procedure.[42] Unions favor having a representative present from the outset because: (1) all facts surrounding the grievance will be known by the union from the start; (2) the steward is in a better position to counsel the employee to ensure that his or her contractual rights are not compromised; (3) union representatives want to ensure that an employee will not say something that could later make it difficult to win the grievance; (4) first-line supervisors may display favoritism among employees; and (5) by having a grievance representative present at the first stage, the union is in a better position to screen grievances that lack merit.

Management, on the other hand, often feels that an employee and his or her supervisor should have the opportunity to quietly resolve the grievance without interference from the union. Some managers also believe that the seriousness of the grievance may be overstated when the union representative is present.[43] The right to have a union representative present during the initial stages of the grievance procedure is especially critical when there is a likelihood that the employer may take disciplinary action against the employee. Under the U.S. Supreme Court's *Weingarten* ruling, individual employees who reasonably believe that they may be subject to disciplinary action have the right to refuse to submit to an investigatory interview unless a union representative is present.[44] Although management is not obliged to discuss the matter with the union representative who is present, the employer cannot deny the representative the right to speak during the course of the investigatory interview.[45] Interestingly, the courts have upheld the right of employers to deny union representation where the imposition of discipline has already been determined.[46]

Employees may try to settle a problem without using the grievance procedure. Workers may also refuse to perform a task assigned by a supervisor because they believe that it would violate the collective bargaining agreement. Such practices by grievants are known as "self-help." Although employees may refuse to perform tasks that pose an imminent safety hazard or result in criminal or immoral acts, other forms of self-help may jeopardize an employee's right to pursue the matter later under the grievance procedure. In short, the union should not encourage employees to disobey reasonable orders by management (sometimes called "obey now, grieve later"), even when an order appears to clearly violate the contract. Rather, the

---

[42] Neal Orkin and Louise Schmoyer, "*Weingarten* Rights, Remedies, and the Arbitration Process," *Labor Law Journal* (September 1989), pp. 594–602.
[43] Frank Elkouri and Edna Asper Elkouri, *How Arbitration Works*, 4th ed. (Washington, D.C.: The Bureau of National Affairs, Inc., 1985), p. 171.
[44] *NLRB v. J. Weingarten, Inc.*, 88 LRRM 2689 (1975).
[45] *Taracorp Industries*, 117 LRRM 1497 (1984).
[46] *Baton Rouge Water Works*, 103 LRRM 1056 (1979); *San Antonio Portland Cement Company*, 121 LRRM 1234 (1985); *Eagle Discount*, 120 LRRM 1047 (1985). See Marlin M. Volz and Edward P. Goggin, *How Arbitration Works*, 4th ed. (Washington, D.C.: The Bureau of National Affairs, Inc., 1988), p. 45. 1985-87 Supplement to Frank Elkouri and Edna Asper Elkouri, *How Arbitration Works*, 4th ed. (Washington, D.C.: The Bureau of National Affairs, Inc., 1985).

grievance procedure should be used to determine the legitimacy of management's orders.[47]

As the grievance progresses to more advanced stages, higher-level union and management officials become involved. If the grievance mechanism is functioning properly, only the more important, complex, and precedent-setting issues will rise to the upper levels of the procedure. Such grievances require the scrutiny of higher union and management officials for four reasons. First, these grievances have no easy solution because of their complex nature. Second, the settlement of grievances may have important managerial and financial consequences to the firm. Third, the outcome of a grievance may change the relative bargaining power of either union or management. For example, an arbitration decision that supports management's right to shut down production facilities temporarily when inventories are high gives the company more bargaining power and flexibility in layoff decisions. Fourth, certain grievances may expose weak or troublesome provisions in the collective bargaining agreement that will require change during the next round of contract talks.

Resolving Grievances

Grievances are normally regarded as resolved when the parties mutually agree on a settlement. Suppose that for safety reasons, management prohibits employees from wearing radio headsets while working on a production line. The union then files a grievance claiming that there is no legitimate safety reason for banning headsets. However, after hearing the testimony of several safety experts, the plant grievance committee, composed of union and management representatives, realizes that headsets do, in fact, pose a safety problem and the union withdraws its grievance. By so doing, the union usually cannot later refile the grievance and insist on an arbitration hearing.

Mutual settlements may be overturned if conditions surrounding the dispute later change. For example, an employee who is terminated by the company for excessive absenteeism, but is later reinstated during the third stage of the grievance procedure, may be terminated if he continues to miss work for no legitimate reason. Some collective bargaining agreements also stipulate that mutual settlements automatically occur against a party that fails to adhere to the time limits imposed by the grievance procedure.

The union may not have the right to settle a grievance affecting an individual employee's contract rights without the employee's consent.[48] However, many ar-

---

[47] Management cannot generally bypass the grievance procedure and offer to resolve the problem for the grievant. Unless prohibited by the collective bargaining agreement, however, an employee has the right, under section 9 (a) of the Taft-Hartley Act, to present a grievance to management without following the grievance procedure. If an employee elects to do so, the U.S. Supreme Court has held that he or she may be banned from instituting a court suit to later enforce his or her rights under the collective bargaining agreement. *Republic Steel Corp. v. Maddox*, 58 LRRM 2193 (1965).

[48] *Kister Lumber Co.*, 37 LA 356 (1961).

bitrators have recognized that an individual grievant's interest does not take precedence over the majority interests of bargaining unit members.[49] In addition, arbitrators have held that the employer does not always have the right to settle a grievance with the individual employee without the knowledge or approval of the union.[50]

A criticism that arises in grievance administration is the issue of trading or compromising among several grievances. For example, the union might agree to drop a relatively insignificant grievance in turn for a favorable settlement on what union officials regard as an important grievance. Although the parties have a right to drop grievances that lack merit, they violate the collective bargaining agreement and run the risk of legal suits by individual employees if they fail to process meritorious grievances. Dropping grievances that have merit in favor of a quick and favorable settlement on another grievance could violate the union's duty of fair representation. Thus, both union and management grievance representatives must process grievances on their individual merits and avoid the temptation of making tradeoffs. Union and management grievance representatives may agree upon a compromise settlement as long as a grievant's contractual rights are not violated. For example, an employee terminated for suspected drug use may be reinstated to a lower-paying job where he cannot create a safety hazard for himself or other employees. Or, management may agree not to subcontract maintenance work on grinding machines in the future if the union agrees not to demand reimbursement of back wages to workers who lost work in the past because of subcontracting. Because contract language is often general or ambiguous, compromise settlements may be possible without violating the duty of fair representation. The key to such settlements is to adhere to the terms and spirit of the collective bargaining agreement and avoid jeopardizing the rights of individual bargaining-unit members for the sake of political expediency.

Unless the grievance is settled at an earlier stage, the proverbial buck stops at binding arbitration. As noted in earlier chapters, an arbitrator is a neutral, disinterested party who is jointly selected by union and management to hear, decide, and finally resolve a grievance. Both union and management have agreed in the collective bargaining agreement to accept the arbitrator's decision as *final* (it will not normally be appealed in a court of law) and *binding* (the parties agree to abide by the decision regardless of whether they agree with it). When union and management officials agree to submit a grievance to arbitration, they relinquish their power to reach a mutually satisfactory settlement on their own and, perhaps, forfeit an opportunity to win the respect of the other side. As one labor expert said:

> Arbitration can be a form of Russian roulette, with the party who presents a case rarely knowing how it will come out.

---

[49] See The Bureau of National Affairs, Inc., "Grievances," *Labor Relations Expediter* (Washington, D.C.: The Bureau of National Affairs, Inc., 1988), Section 540.
[50] See *Bendix Corp.*, 38 LA 909 (1962).

Preferable is a negotiated settlement of grievances, with both parties protecting their vital interests, through a process of compromise and accommodation.[51]

Chapter 12 discusses the role of labor arbitration in resolving rights disputes.

▲ Processing Grievances

The Initial Stage

The manner in which a grievance is processed at the initial stages may have a significant bearing on the overall union-management relationship. As noted earlier, the initial stage of most grievance procedures is an informal meeting between the employee, the first-line supervisor, and the shop steward. There are, however, four basic considerations in processing a grievance at the first step: (1) presenting the grievance to the supervisor; (2) gathering the relevant facts surrounding the grievance; (3) determining whether the grievance has merit; and (4) either resolving the grievance at that point or laying the groundwork for processing the grievance to higher stages of the procedure.

As noted earlier, there is a difference between a grievance and a complaint. Supervisors and shop stewards should understand the importance of listening to the grievant during the first stage of the grievance, regardless of whether they believe there is merit to the grievant's problem. Employees who are denied the chance to air their gripes, no matter how trivial they may seem to the supervisor or steward, may continue to be a source of discontent. Some employees who believe they have a legitimate grievance simply want to vent their frustrations and anger by talking to someone in authority. Supervisors and shop stewards must sometimes "read between the lines" to determine what a grievant is really trying to say. For example, an employee may be upset because of the hot and dirty conditions associated with the job. A supervisor handled such a situation as follows:

> A very angry employee complained vehemently to his foreman that he had been unjustly assigned to do a job which he considered to be especially undesirable. The job called for heavy physical effort and it was a hot and dirty one. The foreman listened patiently and sympathetically to the employee's tirade until he stopped, but said nothing, just waited attentively. The employee repeated the grievance, but in a much calmer manner. When he stopped talking this time, the foreman asked, "If you were in my place, how would you settle this grievance?" The employee hesitated briefly, then replied, "I guess I don't really have a grievance after all. Other guys have had to do this same job before me. I feel better now that I've shot off my mouth."[52]

---

[51] Quoting Duane Beeler, *Roles of a Labor Leader*, in Donald S. McPherson with Conrad John Gates and Kevin N. Rogers, *Resolving Grievances: A Practical Approach* (Reston, Virginia: Reston Publishing Company, 1983), p. 37.

[52] Maurice S. Trotta, *Handling Grievances: A Guide for Management and Labor* (Washington, D.C.: The Bureau of National Affairs, Inc., 1976), p. 80.

In situations where a grievance does exist, the supervisor and shop steward must use the preliminary discussion as a starting point for gathering facts. The shop steward and supervisor must determine what incidents precipitated the grievance. If there are witnesses to the incident, written or tape-recorded accounts should be made as soon as possible after the incident to ensure that the recollections of witnesses are fresh and vivid. Conflicting accounts among witnesses must also be evaluated because they may have important implications later. Times, places, and dates of important incidents must be also be noted. Absenteeism, work schedules, and employee performance appraisals should be checked if they are likely to have a bearing on the grievance.[53] The shop steward should contact other union officials at the local level to determine what collective bargaining agreement provisions or past practices may have been violated as well as whether similar grievances have ever arisen. Supervisors should do likewise with the plant personnel or industrial relations manager. The best time to gather facts is immediately after the grievance has been initiated. Fact-finding during the early stages avoids potential surprises during the latter stages of the grievance procedure or in arbitration. By having all, or nearly all, of the facts at the outset of the grievance, the parties are in a better position to resolve their differences at an early stage and avoid needlessly expensive and time-consuming grievance committee and arbitration proceedings.

Once the initial investigation has been completed, a determination must be made regarding the merits of the grievance. Unions are in a particularly sensitive position when screening grievances because they run the risk of alienating union members who have paid their dues and, in return, expect union officials to process their grievances. There is also the risk of an unfair labor practice charge if a grievant believes that the union has not processed a meritorious grievance properly. As a result, some unions process even frivolous grievances, a strategy that is both expensive and wasteful. The issue of merit is discussed more extensively later in this chapter. However, the union must make a decision on merit based on contract language, previous grievances, and past practices and customs, among other factors. If there is doubt as to whether a grievance has merit, the union should probably err on the side of processing the grievance, rather than dropping it or allowing the time limits to expire.

If the grievance is meritorious, each side must establish a "theory of the case;" that is, each side must demonstrate why the grievance should be resolved in its favor. The theory of a grievance must be built on facts, evidence, and logical arguments. Often, the theory is only developed in rough form at the initial stages of the grievance and may not be fully and clearly developed until the latter stages. Nevertheless, the parties must begin to develop a theory of their case at the earliest possible stage and refine and polish it as new evidence and arguments are presented.

A shop steward or first-line supervisor may decide that a grievance cannot be settled at the initial stage, either because he or she lacks the authority to settle it or because he or she disagrees as to how it should be settled. Even the most

---

[53] As noted in Chapter 9, the employer has an obligation to furnish information relevant to the collective bargaining process. Information associated with processing grievances is regarded as germane to collective bargaining and employers are obligated to furnish such information to union officials. See *EPE Inc.*, 125 LRRM 1166 (1987) and *Hall Industries Ltd.*, 126 LRRM 1162 (1987).

mundane individual grievances may have ramifications as to how other employees in a plant or department will be treated in the future. Management may feel comfortable only allowing a first-line supervisor to settle the most basic types of grievances; all other grievance settlements may require the approval of a department head, plant manager, or corporate personnel staff.

Processing Grievances to Higher Stages

A Written Definition of the Grievance

Once the grievance progresses beyond the initial stage, a formal written definition of the issue is usually made. A standard grievance form may be used to frame the basic issues. Figure 11–2 presents an example of a grievance form. It is especially

```
                  SEIU GRIEVANCE FORM
                        (Sample)
      Make original and three copies to be distributed to:
        (1) management, (2) steward, (3) business agent,
                    (4) aggrieved worker

    Employee                         I.D. Number

    Job Title              Dept.          Shift

    Date of Hire           Supervisor

    Name of Employer
    Nature of Grievance



    (use additional sheets of paper if necessary)
    Adjustment Desired



    Management Reply



    Steps Taken

    Disposition
    Date

    Signature of Employee     Signature of Steward
```

FIGURE 11–2   Grievance Form

In Figure 11–2 is included: 1) employee's name, address and home and work phone numbers, 2) name of employer, 3) clock number, 4) department, 5) shift, 6) classification, 7) length of employment, 8) name of supervisor, and 9) rate of pay.

WHEN: Refers to the time element. Often information regarding more than one date is needed to properly complete the form: 1) the date on which the grievance is officially written, 2) the time and date on which the grievance actually happened, 3) the date on which the grievance was filed in the first step with the supervisor, and 4) the date on which the supervisor gave a decision. It is particularly important in matters involving back pay that all dates be clearly stated. All dates should include month, day, and year.

WHERE: Refers to the exact place where the grievance took place—the department, ward, machine, building, floor, etc.

WHY: Refers to the reasons why the complaint is considered a grievance. This is the heart of the grievance and should be written under the section headed "Nature of Grievance." It is important to remember that it's possible to have a legitimate grievance without being able to point to a violation of a specific clause of the contract. (Reread "What is a Grievance?")

WHAT: Refers to what should be done about the grievance—the settlement desired. Many grievance forms do not have a separate section headed "Settlement Desired." In those cases, the steward should list the settlement request at the end of the section "Nature of Grievance." It is extremely important that this be done since an arbitrator will often base the award solely on the original request. *Therefore, the steward should be sure to ask for the maximum possible remedy.*

Source: The Bureau of National Affairs, Inc., "SEIU Steward's Manual, Collective Bargaining Negotiations and Contracts (Washington, D.C.: The Bureau of National Affairs, Inc., May 15, 1982), Section 17.

important that the grievance be properly defined so that all of the important facts and relevant contract provisions are included. In addition, a poorly defined grievance may be a signal to the opposing side that the party presenting the grievance has not thoroughly prepared its case or is bluffing in an attempt to secure a settlement.

Some grievance statements are brief:

Mr. Joseph R. Roberts was discharged without reasonable cause by the company in violation of Section XIV, part A of the agreement. The union requests that Mr. Roberts be reinstated with full back pay and benefits.

On the other hand, a grievance statement may be lengthy:

On April 3, 1990 at 8:05 A.M., James Morrison, a supervisor in the casting department of the East Mill, ordered millwright Joseph R. Roberts to report to the plant physician's office for a urinalysis test to detect the use of drugs. Morrison allegedly observed Roberts fall to the ground as he was walking across a set of railroad tracks near the East Mill. Roberts, who was carrying his lunch pail in one arm and a tool box in the other arm, failed to break his fall and sustained minor abrasions on his arms and face. Because he failed to stop himself from falling, Morrison suspected that Roberts was under the influence of alcohol or a controlled substance. Roberts claimed that he was unable to break his fall because he was attempting to hold on to his lunch pail and tool box. When Roberts refused to submit to the drug test, Morrison immediately terminated him for insubordination.

Joseph R. Roberts was improperly charged with insubordination and terminated in violation of Section XIV, part A of the agreement. The supervisor, James Morrison, did not have reasonable cause for the discipline. The union requests that Mr. Roberts be reinstated with full back pay and benefits.

Several points should be made regarding written grievance statements. First, the statement should stipulate the time, date, relevant contract provisions, and individuals involved. The grievance examples given pertain only to the discharge of Joseph Roberts. In other grievances, all employees in a particular job classification, department, or work area may be involved and the grievance statement must clearly define this point. Some grievance procedures do not allow new contract provisions, grievants, or issues to be added once the grievance is put into writing. Second, there is no need to mention arguments or evidence in the grievance statement, since these items will be presented during the grievance hearing. Thus, mentioning why Roberts did not break his fall is probably unnecessary at this point. In fact, the use of arguments and evidence in the grievance statement may give the opposing party a better chance to prepare a defense. Finally, the grievance statement should stipulate the remedy being sought. In the above example, the union representing Mr. Roberts is seeking reinstatement with full back pay and benefits.[54]

Presenting the Grievance

The parties generally schedule a grievance meeting in accordance with the time limits and procedures specified in the grievance procedure. Since the union is usually the moving or "prosecuting" party, the union grievance representative must be prepared to set forth a statement of the grievance, the reasons underlying it, and arguments as to why it should be settled in favor of the grievant. If the grievant is to be present at the hearing, the union must ensure that he or she has been properly briefed on how the case will proceed, what questions might be asked of him or her, and the grievant's code of conduct during the hearing.[55] The grievance should be presented in a concise, logical, easy-to-understand fashion. Emphasis should be placed on stipulating facts, presenting evidence to back up the allegations and opinions, and illustrating how the provisions of the collective bargaining agreement have been violated. Arguments that cannot be substantiated with hard facts and evidence should be avoided. Union representatives must also avoid the temptation of arguing with management over past grievances or complaints that are not relevant to the present case. Table 11–1 provides some definitions that should be kept in mind when presenting a grievance.[56]

As the "defending" party, management representatives usually listen to the union's grievance presentation and then counter with a presentation of their own. Management representatives should show respect for the union grievance representatives or, at a minimum, avoid outward displays of hostility. By adopting a cooperative posture and a willingness to listen, management can defuse a conflict

---

[54] See Donald S. McPherson with Conrad John Gates and Kevin N. Rogers, *Resolving Grievances: A Practical Approach* (Reston, Virginia: Reston Publishing Company, 1983), pp. 54–57.

[55] Grievants must be cautioned not to argue with management representatives or engage in actions that could jeopardize their case. A grievant may insist on presenting his or her case; a move such as this is unwise since most grievants do not have the expertise or understanding of contract interpretation to represent themselves competently. See Donald S. McPherson with Conrad John Gates and Kevin N. Rogers, *Resolving Grievances: A Practical Approach* (Reston, Virginia: Reston Publishing Company, 1983), p. 58.

[56] Based on Maurice S. Trotta, *Handling Grievances: A Guide for Management and Labor* (Washington, D.C.: The Bureau of National Affairs, Inc., 1976), pp. 120–126.

Table 11–1 ▲ Factors Used in Making Decisions Regarding Grievances

Facts:

A fact is something that is not in dispute. To establish a fact, it is necessary to keep accurate records that can be produced at a grievance hearing. It is often a good practice for union and management representatives to stipulate to the facts before arguing the grievance. Examples of facts include the following:
- ▲ An employee's age, employment date, position on a seniority list.
- ▲ Employee A struck Employee B in the face at a specified time and place (if both the union and management agree to stipulate this as a fact).
- ▲ An accident involving a forklift caused $14,268 in property damage.

Allegations:

An allegation is a claim made against someone. It must be distinguished from a fact and proven during the course of the grievance hearing. Examples of allegations include the following:
- ▲ An employee states that her supervisor has not given her a fair share of the overtime work.
- ▲ A supervisor claims that an employee engaged in insubordination when he refused to perform an assigned task within a prescribed period of time.
- ▲ A personnel manager claims that an employee reported to work intoxicated.

Assumptions:

An assumption is a concept one assumes to be true without proof. A large number of disagreements that result in grievances are based upon faulty assumptions. Assumptions are often based on culture and values. Examples of assumptions include the following:
- ▲ A supervisor refuses to allow a woman to bid on a job because the job requires lifting sections of pipe that weigh 50 pounds and he believes that women are incapable of lifting heavy weights.
- ▲ A manager refuses to promote an employee who was observed sitting, and reading a newspaper at his work station. The manager cites this one incident to claim that the employee is lazy.
- ▲ A supervisor assigns a higher percentage of black employees to work on jobs requiring exposure to 90 degree and above temperatures because he believes that blacks can tolerate heat better than whites.

Opinions:

Opinions are conclusions arrived at by persons who have a special technical or professional expertise to evaluate a situation. In order for an opinion to be valid, the person expressing it must have expertise in the subject matter evaluated *and* sufficient evidence on which to base his or her conclusion. Examples of opinions include the following:
- ▲ An industrial hygienist claims that radiation levels in a work area are not hazardous to employees who work in that area less than 20 hours a week.
- ▲ A cardiologist states that a blast furnace operator cannot perform his job without undue risk to his health.
- ▲ An industrial engineer, who is a recognized expert in ergonomics, claims that the equipment used to monitor pressure readings and levels in chemical tanks is difficult for only one person to operate without causing excessive levels of fatigue that could pose a safety hazard.

Table 11-1 ▲ Factors Used in Making Decisions Regarding Grievances (Cont.)

Weighting:

Weighting refers to the importance that the decision maker gives to a fact, allegation, or opinion. Grievances may arise if a supervisor applies an unreasonably heavy weight to an employee's action. For example, one supervisor may view an employee's refusal to accept an overtime assignment as insubordination, whereas another supervisor may not be upset by such a refusal. Facts and opinions are generally given more weight than accusations and assumptions.

Quantum of Proof:

The amount of proof needed varies directly with the seriousness of the case. Thus, the quantum of proof would be highest for a grievance involving an employee who has been discharged; the quantum of proof would be somewhat less for an employee filing a grievance because he was denied overtime.

Adapted, in part, from Maurice S. Trotta, *Handling Grievances: A Guide for Management and Labor* (Washington, D.C.: The Bureau of National Affairs, Inc., 1976), pp. 120–125.

or prevent one from escalating. If the union's definition of the grievance is unclear or unacceptable, management should attempt to redefine or clarify the grievance statement, especially if it is likely that the grievance will proceed to arbitration. Questions to the union grievance representatives should be designed to elicit clear responses; they should be posed in a clear, deliberate, and nonjudgmental manner.[57]

Once management is satisfied that they have heard all of the facts, allegations, assumptions, and opinions from the union, they will either propose a settlement or reject the grievance. Should management representatives decide that the grievance has no merit or that it involves an important policy issue that can only be settled at a higher level of the grievance procedure, then they may firmly reject the grievance without further explanation. If management decides to reject the grievance or a union's offer to settle, they should put the rejection in writing and minimize the use of arguments (except to set the record straight on allegations made by union representatives). Another option is for management to accept a compromise settlement, if one was discussed during the grievance hearing. When accepting a settlement, management must ensure that it is not undercutting the authority and integrity of its supervisory personnel. If a supervisor precipitated a grievance because of a failure to follow the contract or because of an incorrect interpretation of the contract language, management should privately counsel the supervisor to avoid future problems. Likewise, management should also correct any unprofessional supervisory behavior that created a grievance. However, supervisory counseling should be done in private, not during the course of a grievance hearing.

Preparing the Case for Arbitration

If the parties are unable to resolve the grievance, they must consider the prospect of submitting the dispute to an arbitrator or a panel of arbitrators. By this point, both the union and management grievance representatives should have a well-

---

[57] Donald S. McPherson with Conrad John Gates and Kevin N. Rogers, *Resolving Grievances: A Practical Approach* (Reston, Virginia: Reston Publishing Company, 1983), p. 60.

developed theory of their case, complete with adequate evidence, statements from witnesses, and other supporting documentation. The parties should consider the risks of going to arbitration. Presumably, both sides have fully considered any feasible compromise settlements and have reserved the use of arbitration to resolve only those disputes that are important but irreconcilable. According to three labor relations experts, Donald S. McPherson, Conrad John Gates, and Kevin N. Rogers, in their book, *Resolving Grievances*, union and management should ask themselves the following questions before preceding to arbitration:

1. Are we convinced that our interpretation of the agreement is correct?
2. Is the issue important enough to risk arbitration?
3. What would be the effect of winning?
4. What would be the effect of losing?
5. Can we afford the cost and delay in final resolution?
6. Based on known arbitration principles and what we know about the case of the other party and our own, can we win?[58]

Collective bargaining agreements usually stipulate a requirement and time limit for giving notice that a party wishes to arbitrate a grievance.[59] As noted earlier, the parties are generally expected to adhere to the contractual time limits unless extenuating circumstances, such as the illness or unavailability of a key party in the grievance, prevent a case from proceeding within the allotted time period. Other issues related to the selection of an arbitrator and the arbitration hearing are discussed in Chapter 12.

▲ Abuse and Misuse of Grievance Procedures

A sound grievance procedure is one that resolves meritorious grievances in a timely and mutually satisfactory fashion. Grievance procedures that are successful are usually so characterized, not because of the way they are designed and written in the collective bargaining agreement, but because of the manner in which union and management representatives handle and administer the grievance machinery. Well-trained union and management personnel who know how to evaluate and process grievances may be the single most important element in effective contract administration.

There are several hallmarks of a good grievance procedure. First, a grievance procedure should settle grievances at the lowest possible stage. By nipping a problem or complaint in the bud, the issue has less chance to proliferate into a more serious, time-consuming, and expensive grievance. Second, an effective grievance procedure sifts out unmeritorious claims and retains meritorious grievances. A well-

---

[58] Donald S. McPherson with Conrad John Gates and Kevin N. Rogers, *Resolving Grievances: A Practical Approach* (Reston, Virginia: Reston Publishing Company, 1983), p. 63

[59] An oral notice to arbitrate is generally not sufficient when the contract calls for a written notice. See Frank Elkouri and Edna Asper Elkouri, *How Arbitration Works*, 4th ed. (Washington, D.C.: The Bureau of National Affairs, Inc., 1985), p. 209.

designed and properly administered grievance procedure should be capable of screening a variety of grievances that can conceivably arise under the collective bargaining agreement. Grievance procedures that are hopelessly bogged down with an abundance of claims may exacerbate hostilities among shop stewards and managers. Third, a grievance procedure should provide an opportunity for the parties to fully investigate and discuss their grievances. Due process is a critical element of any grievance procedure and the parties should be able to fully present their case, submit evidence to substantiate their contentions, view the evidence submitted by the other side, and explore various remedies at the grievance hearing. Fourth, an efficient grievance procedure should give priority handling to serious grievances (e.g., discharge cases). Fifth, the grievance machinery should be viewed as a problem-resolution technique. Grievance procedures provide insights and solutions to important workplace problems, give meaning to ambiguous contract terms, and form the foundation for negotiating new and improved contract language at future bargaining sessions. Finally, the parties to a grievance procedure should emphasize settling rather than winning grievances. The grievance procedure is not a sporting event where won-loss records are of paramount concern. Both parties win when a grievance is resolved in a mutually satisfactory manner.

A distressed grievance procedure is one that fails to meet some or all of the above criteria and, as a result, either becomes inundated with grievances or fails to settle them in a timely and satisfactory fashion. Management can create distressful conditions if first-line supervisors take a hard-line stance on all grievances, regardless of their merit. In other instances, top management undermines the authority of first-line supervisors or personnel managers by failing to support them when they attempt to resolve grievances. Union grievance representatives create a distressed grievance procedure by failing to screen and eliminate unmeritorious grievances. Shop stewards may also favor one grievant over another, especially when there is factional strife within the union. Some union officials may fail to investigate grievances thoroughly prior to submitting them to the grievance procedure. Other union officials may indiscriminately file grievances in order to create work for themselves and justify their existence as union leaders.

▲ The Union's Duty of Fair Representation in Grievance Administration

One of the most controversial and unsettled aspects of labor law is the duty of fair representation.[60] The duty of fair representation first received attention because of segregated local unions and racial discrimination.[61] Because a union is the exclusive bargaining representative for bargaining-unit employees, it is obligated to process meritorious grievances in good faith without discrimination.[62] Furthermore, a union

---

[60] See Jean T. McKelvey, ed., *The Changing Law of Fair Representation* (Ithaca, New York: ILR Press, Cornell University, 1985).
[61] *Steele v. Louisville and Nashville Railroad*, 15 LRRM 708 (1944); *Wallace Corp., v. NLRB*, 323 U. S. 248 (1944); and *Syres v. Oil Workers Union*, 350 U.S. 892 (1955).
[62] *Ford Motor Co. v. Huffman*, 31 LRRM 2548 (1948).

must avoid processing grievances in an arbitrary, perfunctory, or negligent manner.[63]

The duty of fair representation has been described as a "no-win" situation for unions. Although there is a growing body of legal opinion on the fair representation issue, there are no precise standards for determining what constitutes a "meritorious" grievance, "arbitrary conduct" by union representatives, or "perfunctory or negligent processing of a grievance." Because of the uncertainty as to when the duty of fair representation has been breached, unions may be tempted to expend time and money on grievances that have little or no merit and, perhaps, divert valuable resources from more deserving grievants with legitimate claims. According to one prominent labor attorney, Seymour M. Waldman:

> If the union does not arbitrate a grievance because it regards the claim as lacking merit, then it may be liable to the prospective grievant for "arbitrary" representation.[64] If it processes the grievance to the final stage but loses the arbitration, it may be liable to the grievant for "perfunctory" representation.[65] If it hires lawyers to handle some but not all arbitrations, on the reasonable premise that some disputes involve larger, more important issues with significant precedential effect, it may be liable to a grievant to whom it has not assigned counsel.[66] If it does not engage an expert witness to testify at an arbitration because it does not deem such expertise necessary for proper presentation of the case, it may be liable if a judge—or a jury—subsequently disagrees with its strategic decision.[67]

Unions have violated the duty of fair representation by refusing to process grievances filed by union members who have evoked the displeasure of union officials. For example, a union cannot deny a bargaining-unit employee's grievance in retaliation for speaking out against union leadership.[68] In right-to-work states, bargaining unit employees may decide not to join or lend financial support to the union certified as the employees' exclusive bargaining representative.[69] Yet the union must bear the cost of processing grievances of union members and nonmembers alike as long as they hold a job in the bargaining unit and are covered by the

---

[63] Section 8(b)(1)(A) of the NLRA prohibits labor organizations, when acting in a statutory representative capacity, from taking action against any employee upon considerations or classifications, which are irrelevant, invidious, or unfair. Thus, employees who believe that a union has violated the duty of fair representation can file an unfair labor practice charge under the Taft-Hartley Act. In addition, breach of contract suits can also be filed by employees under section 301 of the Act.

[64] See *Bowen v. United States Postal Service*, S. Ct., 112 LRRM 2281 (1983) and *Vaca v. Sipes*, 64 LRRM 2369 (1967). The legal definition of "arbitrary" includes "done capriciously, ... without adequate determining principle ... not done or acting according to reason or judgment ... without fair, solid or substantial cause ..." Henry Campbell Black, *Black's Law Dictionary* (St. Paul, Minnesota: West Publishing Co., 1968).

[65] See *Hines v. Anchor Motor Freight, Inc.*, 91 LRRM 2481 (1976); *Holodnak v. Avco Corp.*, 90 LRRM 2614 (1975).

[66] See *Del Casal v. Eastern Airlines, Inc.*, 106 LRRM 2276 (1981).

[67] Seymour M. Waldman, "A Union Advocate's View," in Jean T. McKelvey, ed., *The Changing Law of Fair Representation* (Ithaca, New York: ILR Press, Cornell University, 1985), pp. 109–110.

[68] *Sargent Electric Co.*, 209 NLRB 630 (1974) and *General Motors Corp., Delco Moraine Division* 237 NLRB 167 (1978).

[69] Benjamin J. Taylor and Fred Witney, *Labor Relations Law*, 5th ed. (Englewood Cliffs, New Jersey: Prentice-Hall, Inc., 1987), p. 429.

collective bargaining agreement. Union officials must process meritorious grievances with competence and care, regardless of whether the bargaining-unit employee supports the union or enjoys a cordial working relationship with other union members.

Union officials are faced with the difficult task of deciding whether a grievance has merit. In *Vaca v. Sipes,* an employee by the name of Owens had been discharged because of poor health, despite his contention that he was able to continue working. He filed a grievance and the union processed the grievance up to, but not including, arbitration. The union paid for a medical examination by a physician, who indicated that Owens was unfit to work. Although the union urged Owens's employer to give him a less physically demanding job, the company refused and the union subsequently dropped the grievance. Owens then sued the union in a state court, claiming that it had arbitrarily and capriciously dropped his grievance. A jury awarded Owens $10,000 in damages. The case was appealed and eventually reached the U.S. Supreme Court, where it was reversed. The Supreme Court said that a union breaches its duty of fair representation if it represents an employee arbitrarily, discriminatorily, or in bad faith. According to the Court:

> Though we accept the proposition that a union may not arbitrarily ignore a meritorious grievance or process it in a perfunctory fashion, we do not agree that the individual employee has an absolute right to have his grievance taken to arbitration regardless of the provisions of the applicable collective bargaining agreement. In providing for a grievance and arbitration procedure which gives the union discretion to supervise the grievance machinery and to invoke arbitration, the employer and the union contemplate that each will endeavor in good faith to settle grievances short of arbitration. Through this settlement process, frivolous grievances are ended prior to the most costly and time-consuming step in the grievance procedure. Moreover, both sides are assured that similar complaints will be treated consistently, and major problem areas in the interpretation of the collective bargaining contract can be isolated and perhaps resolved.
>
> If a union's decision that a particular grievance lacks sufficient merit to justify arbitration would constitute a breach of the duty of fair representation because a judge or jury later found the grievance meritorious, the union's incentive to settle such grievances short of arbitration would be seriously reduced....[70]

A key to determining the extent to which a grievance has merit often lies in the language of the collective bargaining agreement. A bargaining-unit member files a grievance with the expectation that his or her rights, which are clearly stated under the collective bargaining agreement, cannot be ignored or traded away because of personal vendettas or internal union politics. The issue of whether a grievance has merit becomes more of a judgment call by the union when the contract language is ambiguous or incomplete. However, the grievant has a right to expect that the union grievance representatives will make a diligent effort to evaluate the ambiguous contract language and resolve the grievance, perhaps by allowing an arbitrator to interpret the unclear language. The assessment of merit also depends

---

[70] *Vaca v. Sipes,* 64 LRRM 2369 (1967).

heavily on conducting a thorough investigation of the grievance at an early stage. Union representatives are obliged, first, to investigate and discover the relevant facts surrounding a grievance and, second, to weigh the available facts in deciding whether to process the grievance.

Another difficult issue to resolve is the degree of competency with which a union must process a grievance. Unions must not process legitimate grievances in a perfunctory manner. "Perfunctory" means to act in a superficial manner without care or interest.[71] In *Hines v. Anchor Motor Freight*, the U.S. Supreme Court addressed the issue of processing a grievance in a perfunctory fashion.[72] Several truck drivers had turned in travel expense vouchers for motel room rentals. The company subsequently accused the drivers of padding their travel expenses when it was discovered that they had submitted vouchers for an amount higher than the actual rental rate of the motel room. Although maintaining their innocence, the drivers were discharged. The union processed the grievance through arbitration and the arbitration board sustained the discharge. The drivers then sued the union for breach of fair representation (and the employer for breach of contract). Upon further investigation, the motel clerk later admitted that he had overcharged the drivers and pocketed the difference. Although the drivers were exonerated, the employer argued that the arbitration board's decision was final and binding.

The U.S. Supreme Court held that an arbitration board's decision is not binding if the union violates its duty of fair representation in processing the grievance. The Court held that the union violated the duty of fair representation because it handled the grievance in a perfunctory manner. Had the union agent acted fairly or diligently, the drivers' innocence could have been established before the arbitration panel heard the case. (Note: the arbitration board made the decision in good faith, based upon the available evidence, and the employer was also innocent of wrongdoing). According to the Court, the duty of fair representation is not necessarily violated because the union used bad judgment or failed to conduct an error-free investigation of the grievance. However, a union cannot process a grievance in a cavalier fashion, without regard for the truth or the grievant's welfare. Several other court decisions indicate that inadvertently missing a grievance deadline is not regarded as perfunctory processing unless there are other factors that point to the likelihood that the union was careless or unconcerned in processing the grievance.[73]

In processing grievances, the following points made by University of Pennsylvania labor law professor Clyde Summers should be kept in mind:

1. The union must determine the merits of the grievance on the basis of the collective bargaining agreement and the available facts.
2. If the collective bargaining agreement and the facts are clear and show a breach of the individual's contract right, the union cannot ignore and thereby destroy that contract right.

---

[71] Bruce Feldacker, *Labor Guide to Labor Law*, 2nd ed. (Reston, Virginia: Reston Publishing Company, 1983), pp. 381–382.
[72] *Hines v. Anchor Motor Freight*, 91 LRRM 2481 (1976).
[73] See *Hughes v. Teamsters Local 683*, 95 LRRM 2652 (1977); *Russom v. Sears Roebuck and Company*, 95 LRRM 2914 (1977); *Riley v. Letter Carriers Local 380*, 109 LRRM 2772 (1981); *Hoffman v. Lozna, Inc.*, 108 LRRM 2772 (1981).

3. If the collective agreement is unclear and unsettled, the union has a wide range of reasonableness in resolving ambiguity or filling gaps, so long as the agreement is applied consistently to all employees.
4. If the union's action requires exercise of judgment, such as weighing conflicting evidence, determining the likelihood of winning in arbitration, or determining the facts and arguments to be used in arbitration, the measure of the union's exercise of judgment is only that it must have a rational basis and be even-handedly applied.
5. If the union's action involves a policy decision, such as the resources to be expended in investigation or carrying cases to arbitration, then the decision must again only have a rational basis and be consistently applied.
6. In performing the mechanical functions of processing grievances, the union owes the standard of at least ordinary care, taking account of the nature of the process and the expectations of those represented.
7. When the union, in representing one employee's individual contract rights, directly opposes another employee's contract rights, as in seniority and promotion cases, the union cannot claim the exclusive right to represent the one whose interest it opposes, but must allow him to represent his own interests.[74]

Both the union and the employer may be liable for damages in unfair representation suits. Damages against a union are limited to an employee's lost wages and other actual damages.[75] Thus, punitive damages are not permissible in unfair representation cases. Damages may be apportioned between the union and company. In *Bowen v. United States Postal Service*, an international union refused to arbitrate an employee's discharge case even though the employee's grievance was supported by lower levels of the union hierarchy.[76] The U.S. Supreme Court held that the union had failed to fulfill its statutory obligation of fair representation when it refused to submit the case to arbitration. The Court ordered the union to pay $30,000 of the total $53,000 in back pay (with the employer paying the remaining $23,000).

▲ Criteria for Evaluating Grievance Procedures

Several studies have analyzed the outcomes of grievances. An analysis of 1,160 grievances among Canadian federal employees noted that the highest percentages of decisions favorable to grievants (1) occurred in the early stages of the grievance procedure; (2) involved higher-paid employees; and (3) dealt with grievances over working conditions rather than over the assignment of work duties.[77] Studies have

---

[74] See Clyde W. Summers, "Measuring the Union's Duty to the Individual: An Analytical Framework," in Jean T. McKelvey, ed., *The Changing Law of Fair Representation* (Ithaca, New York: ILR Press, Cornell University, 1985).
[75] *Electrical Workers v. Foust*, 101 LRRM 2365 (1979).
[76] *Bowen v. United States Postal Service*, 112 LRRM 2281 (1983).
[77] Ignace Ng and Ali Dastmalchian, "Determinants of Grievance Outcomes: A Case Study," *Industrial and Labor Relations Review* (April 1989), pp. 393–403.

also examined the aftermath of grievance and arbitration cases.[78] These studies indicate that less than half of discharged grievants who are reinstated through a grievance procedure enjoy a satisfactory working relationship with their employer.[79] There is also some indication that workers are reluctant to submit their most important problems to the grievance procedure.[80]

These studies point to the need for additional research before drawing firm conclusions about the effectiveness of grievance procedures. Most observers would judge that union-management grievance procedures are quite efficient compared to the time and expense of taking a grievance to a state or federal civil court. An AFL-CIO staff member reported that the average time to process a case through arbitration in 1975 was over seven months (233 days).[81] Yet little is known about how satisfied employees, managers, and union officials are with their grievance procedures.

Grievance procedures such as those described here are used almost exclusively by unionized organizations and are much less frequently used in nonunion firms.[82] This state of affairs suggests that management sees little value in grievance procedures and will use them only when forced by the union in a collective bargaining relationship. Research also indicates that employees may be reluctant to pursue certain grievances, perhaps because they fear retaliation by management or union officers. In addition, it appears that grievance procedures do not help the majority of reinstated employees "turn over a new leaf" once they regain their former jobs. Although there is a paucity of research on the aftermath of grievance procedures, there is some indication that the parties do not always learn from their experiences and may repeat the same mistake.[83]

Grievance mediation and *expedited arbitration* have been used to make grievance procedures more effective. *Grievance mediation* appears to have gained in-

---

[78] See David Meyer and William Cooke, "Economic and Political Factors in Formal Grievance Resolution," *Industrial Relations* (Fall 1988), pp. 318–335.

[79] Arthur M. Ross, "The Arbitration of Discharge Cases: What Happens After Reinstatement?" Critical Issues in Arbitration: *Proceedings of the Tenth Annual Meeting of the National Academy of Arbitrators* (Washington, D.C.: The Bureau of National Affairs, Inc., 1956), pp. 21–56; Thomas J. McDermott and Thomas H. Newhams, "Discharge-Reinstatement: What Happens Thereafter?" *Industrial and Labor Relations Review* (July 1971), pp. 526–540; and Charlotte Gold, Rodney E. Dennis, and Joseph Graham III, "Reinstatement After Termination: Public School Teachers," *Industrial and Labor Relations Review* (April 1978), pp. 310–321. All cited in Thomas A. Kochan and Harry C. Katz, *Collective Bargaining and Industrial Relations*, 2nd ed. (Homewood, Illinois: Richard D. Irwin, Inc., 1988), p. 326. Also see William E. Simkin, "Some Results of Reinstatement by Arbitration," *The Arbitration Journal* (September 1986), pp. 53–58.

[80] Janice A. Radle, "A Cry for Justice: An Examination of Formal and Informal Grievance Settlement," M. A. Thesis (Ithaca, New York: Cornell University, 1978). Cited in Thomas A. Kochan and Harry C. Katz, *Collective Bargaining and Industrial Relations*, 2nd ed. (Homewood, Illinois: Richard D. Irwin, Inc., 1988), p. 326.

[81] John Zalusky, "Updating A Vital Process," *American Federationist* (November 1976), p. 1. Cited in Thomas A. Kochan and Harry C. Katz, *Collective Bargaining and Industrial Relations*, 2nd ed. (Homewood, Illinois: Richard D. Irwin, Inc., 1988), p. 307.

[82] "One clear distinction exists between the unionized and the nonunion employer. Although the unionized company generally has a formal grievance procedure with a final step for binding arbitration of disputes, the nonunion company generally does not have this." Fred K. Foulkes, *Personnel Policies in Large Nonunion Companies* (Englewood Cliffs, New Jersey: Prentice-Hall, Inc., 1980), p. 299.

[83] See Thomas R. Knight, "Feedback and Grievance Resolution," *Industrial and Labor Relations Review* (July 1986), pp. 585–598.

creasing acceptance in recent years. By employing mediation functions similar to those described in Chapter 10, the grievance mediator meets with the parties and attempts to help them resolve their differences. "Using creative suggestion, thoughtful questioning, and gentle persuasion, the mediator attempts to guide the two sides towards a mutually acceptable settlement."[84] Unlike most arbitrators, the grievance mediator has no authority to compel the parties to reach an agreement. However, grievance mediation allows them to settle a rights dispute without the risks, time, and expense of arbitration.[85] Perhaps most important is the fact that disputes resolved through grievance mediation do not have a "winner" and a "loser"; rather, both sides come away from the process with the feeling that they have achieved a mutually satisfactory settlement.

Expedited arbitration is used to resolve relatively straightforward and simple cases quickly and economically. Arbitrators may hear several expedited cases within a single day and will issue arbitration decisions soon thereafter (usually within two to five days). Expedited procedures often dispense with using transcripts and briefs, a move that reduces arbitration costs and saves time. Since relatively inexperienced arbitrators often hear expedited cases, the costs may be less than when better-known arbitrators are used. Finally, some expedited arbitration arrangements do not allow the use of lawyers, perhaps to reduce the temptation of becoming involved in long-winded and overly legalistic proceedings.[86]

It appears that the improvements made in grievance processing have focused on two important concerns: time and expense. However, research suggests that there may be other concerns. First, are certain types of grievants less likely to have their cases carefully processed by unions? Second, are employees reluctant to submit certain problems to the grievance procedure? If so, what are the causes for their reluctance? Third, are union and management grievance representatives well-equipped to handle all categories of grievances or do they lack the expertise to handle specific types of complex problems competently? Fourth, how satisfied are employees, union officials, and management with the current grievance machinery?

▲ Summary and Conclusions

This chapter provides a discussion of the structure, process, and legal issues associated with the grievance procedures found in the vast majority of collective bargaining agreements. As the centerpiece for contract administration, the grievance

---

[84] Martin M. Volz and Edward P. Goggin, *How Arbitration Works,* 4th ed. (Washington, D.C.: The Bureau of National Affairs, Inc., 1988), p. 43. 1985-87 Supplement to Frank Elkouri and Edna Asper Elkouri, *How Arbitration Works,* 4th ed. (Washington, D.C.: The Bureau of National Affairs, Inc., 1985).

[85] Grievance mediation has been used in the coal mining industry. "The cost and time savings of mediation was substantial. The average cost per mediation case was $295 (mediator's fee and expenses), less than one-third of the average cost of arbitration. (The average cost of arbitration—arbitrator's fee and expenses—in the experimental districts was $1,034 per case). The average time between the request for mediation and the mediation conference (at which nearly all grievances were resolved) was 15 days; the average time between the request for arbitration and the issuance of the arbitrator's decision was 109 days." See William L. Ury, Jeanne M. Brett, and Stephen B. Goldberg, *Getting Disputes Resolved: Designing Systems to Cut the Costs of Conflict* (San Francisco: Jossey-Bass Publishers, 1988), p. 158.

[86] See John Zalusky, "Arbitration: Updating A Vital Process," *American Federationist* (November 1976), p. 4.

procedure often sets the tone for the collective bargaining climate. A grievance procedure that functions efficiently allows the parties to resolve disputes over the interpretation of the collective bargaining agreement with a minimum of disruption. Contract administration can also set the stage for the next round of contract talks; problems with the language and application of the collective bargaining agreement are frequently highlighted by the grievance procedure and help the parties to prepare for upcoming negotiations.

Chapter 12 focuses on the important final step of the grievance procedure—final and binding arbitration. An adequate grievance procedure should prevent all but the most complex grievances from going to the final step of arbitration. The presence of binding arbitration may encourage the parties to settle the dispute among themselves rather than place their fate in the hands of a third-party neutral.

▲ Discussion Questions and Exercises

1. Using the *Labor Arbitration Reports*, published by The Bureau of National Affairs, Inc., select a case from one of the categories discussed earlier in this chapter under Sources of Grievances in Union-Management Relations. Discuss the central issue(s) of the grievance. What factors do you believe created the grievance? Why were the parties unable to resolve the grievance prior to arbitration?
2. How can grievances be prevented? Outline the conditions necessary to minimize the incidence of grievances under a collective bargaining agreement.
3. Draft a short paper describing how grievances should be handled by shop stewards and first-line supervisors.
4. Examine a collective bargaining agreement that contains a grievance procedure. What are the strengths and weaknesses of the procedure? How could the structure of the grievance procedure be improved? Is the structure of the grievance procedure or the manner in which the procedure is administered the most important aspect of contract administration?
5. Why is the union's duty of fair representation such an important concept in U.S. industrial relations?

Appendix: Boeing-International Association of Machinists and Aerospace Workers Grievance Procedure*

ARTICLE 19. GRIEVANCE PROCEDURE AND ARBITRATION.

Section 19.1 Establishment of Grievance and Arbitration Procedure.

Grievances or complaints arising between the Company and its employees subject to this Agreement, or the Company and the Union, with respect to the interpretation or application of any of the terms of this Agreement, shall be settled according to the following procedure. Subject to the terms of this Article 19 relating to cases of dismissal or suspension for cause or of involuntary resignation, only matters dealing with the interpretation or application of terms of this Agreement shall be subject to this grievance machinery.

Section 19.2 Employee Grievances.

In the case of grievances on behalf of employees and subject to the further provisions of Section 19.3 below, relating to cases of layoff or dismissal or suspension for cause or involuntary resignation:

Step 1. Oral Discussion. The employee first shall notify his supervisor of his grievance and then, if he so desires, shall discuss his grievance with the steward or the Union business representative, and if the steward or the business representative considers the grievance to be valid, then the employee and the steward or business representative will contact the employee's supervisor and will attempt to effect a settlement of the complaint. This procedure, however, will not prevent an employee from contacting his supervisor if he so chooses. If the purpose of the employee's contacting his supervisor is to adjust the grievance, the steward or the business representative shall be given an opportunity to be present and such adjustment shall be in conformity with this Agreement.

Step 2. Grievance Reduced to Writing—Handling at Supervisory Level. If no settlement is reached in Step 1, the business representative, if he considers the grievance to be valid, may at any time reduce to writing a statement of the grievance or complaint which shall contain the following:

(a) The facts upon which the grievance is based.

(b) Reference to the section or sections of the Agreement alleged to have been violated (this will not be applicable in cases of dismissal or suspension for cause or of involuntary resignation).

(c) The remedy sought.

The business representative shall submit the written statement of grievance to the supervisor for reconsideration, with a copy to the designated representative of the Company. After such submission the supervisor and the business representative may, within the next five workdays (unless mutually extended), settle the written grievance and, over their signatures, indicate the disposition made thereof. Otherwise, promptly after the expiration of such five-day period (or agreed extensions thereof) the supervisor and the business representative shall sign the grievance and their signatures will indicate that the grievance has been discussed and reconsidered by them and that no settlement has been reached.

Step 3. Written Grievance: Handling at Business Representative-Company Representative Level. If no settlement is reached in Step 2, within the specified or agreed time limits, the busines representative may at any time thereafter submit the grievance to the designated representative of the Company. After such submission the designated representative of the Company and the business representative may, within the next ten workdays (unless mutually extended), settle the grievance and, over their signatures, indicate the disposition made thereof. Otherwise, promptly after the expiration of such ten-day period (or agreed extension thereof) the designated representative of the Company and the business representative shall sign the grievance and their signatures will indicate that the grievance has been discussed and reconsidered by them and that no settlement has been reached.

Step 4. Arbitration. If no settlement is reached in Step 3 within the specified or agreed time limits, then either party may in writing, within ten workdays thereafter, request that the matter be submitted to an arbiter for a prompt hearing as hereinafter provided in Sections 19.6 to 19.9, inclusive.

Section 19.3 Dismissals, Suspensions, Layoffs, Etc.

In cases of layoff, or of dismissal or suspension for cause, or of involuntary resignation, the employee shall be given a copy of the layoff, suspension or termination of service slip, as the case may be, if he is available to be presented with such copy. If he is not available, copies of the slip will be sent to the employee and to the Union office. The employee shall have the right to appeal the action shown on the slip providing the business representative files a written grievance with the designated representative of the Company within seven workdays after the date of layoff, dismissal, suspension for cause or involuntary resignation, or within seven workdays after the date of the mailing of the copy of the slip, provided, however, that any dismissal or suspension of an employee who has committed a sex crime victimizing a child or children shall be deemed to be for cause and shall not be subject to the grievance and arbitration procedure of this Article 19. The written grievance then may be processed through subsequent steps.

Section 19.4 Union Versus Company and Company Versus Union Grievances.

In the case of any grievance which the Union may have against the Company or the Company may have against the Union, the processing of such grievance shall begin with Step 3 and shall be limited to matters dealing with the interpretation or application of terms of this Agreement. Such grievance shall be submitted in writing to the designated representative of the Company or the designated representative of the Union, and shall contain the following:

19.4(a) Statement of the grievance setting forth the facts upon which the grievance is based.

19.4(b) Reference to the section or sections of the Agreement alleged to have been violated.

19.4(c) The correction sought.

The grievance shall be signed by the designated representative of the Union or the designated representative of the Company. If no settlement is reached within ten workdays (unless mutually extended) from the submission of the grievance to the designated representative of the Company or the designated representative of the Union, as the case may be, both shall sign the grievance and indicate that it has been discussed and reconsidered by them and that no settlement has been reached. Within ten workdays thereafter either party may in writing request that the matter be submitted to an arbiter for a prompt hearing as hereinafter provided in Sections 19.6 to 19.9, inclusive.

Section 19.5 Retroactive Compensation.

Grievance claims involving retroactive compensation shall be limited to thirty calendar days prior to the written submission of the grievance to Company representatives, provided, however, that this thirty-day limitation may be waived by mutual consent of the parties.

Section 19.6 Selection of Arbiter— By Agreement.

In regard to each case reaching Step 4, the parties will attempt to agree on an arbiter to hear and decide the particular case. If the parties are unable to agree to an arbiter within ten workdays after submission of the written request for arbitration, the provisions of Section 19.7 (Selection of Arbiter— From Arbitration Panel) shall apply to the selection of an arbiter.

Section 19.7 Selection of Arbiter— From Arbitration Panel.

Immediately following execution of this Agreement the parties will proceed to compile a list and agree upon two separate panels of arbiters. One such panel shall be referred to as the Seattle-Renton-Portland Panel, and the other shall be referred to as the Wichita Panel. The Seattle-Renton-Portland Panel shall be comprised of five arbiters, and the Wichita Panel shall be comprised of two arbiters. Insofar as practicable the arbiters on each panel shall be located in the general vicinity of the location identified with the title of their panel.

If a case reaches Step 4, and the parties are unable to agree to an arbiter within the time limit specified in Section 19.6, the case shall be heard and settled by an arbiter on the panel geographically identified with the grievance, if available. An available arbiter is one who is available to conduct a hearing within sixty days (unless mutually extended) after expiration of the time limit specified in Section 19.6. Selection of an arbiter from the Seattle-Renton-Portland Panel to hear a particular case shall be accomplished by the parties taking turns in striking a name from the panel until one name remains. The arbiter whose name remains shall be the arbiter for that case. The right to strike first shall be determined by lot. Assignment of cases to arbiters on the Wichita Panel shall be rotated in the alphabetical order of the last names of those available on the panel.

Section 19.8 Procedure Where Corporate Panel Arbiter Not Available.

In the event, as to any case, that there is no available arbiter on the applicable Corporate Panel, the parties shall jointly request the American Arbitration Association to submit a panel of seven arbiters. Such request shall state the general nature of the case and ask that the nominees be qualified to handle the type of cases involved. When notification of the names of the panel of seven arbiters is received, the parties in turn shall have the right to strike a name from the panel until only one name remains. The remaining person shall be the arbiter. The right to strike the first name from the panel shall be determined by lot.

Section 19.9 Arbitration—Rules of Procedure.

Arbitration pursuant to Step 4 shall be conducted in accordance with the following:

19.9(a) The arbiter shall hear and accept pertinent evidence submitted by both parties and shall be empowered to request such data as he deems pertinent to the grievance and shall render a decision in writing to both parties within fifteen days (unless mutually extended) of the completion of the hearing.

19.9(b) The arbiter shall be authorized to rule and issue a decision in writing on the issue presented for arbitration, which decision shall be final and binding on both parties.

19.9(c) The arbiter shall rule only on the basis of information presented in the hearing before him and shall refuse to receive any information after the hearing except when there is mutual agreement, in the presence of both parties.

19.9(d) Each party to the proceedings may call such witnesses as may be necessary in the order in which their testimony is to be heard. Such testimony shall be limited to the matters set forth in the written statement of grievance. The arguments of the parties may be supported by oral comment and rebuttal. Either or both parties may submit written briefs within a time period mutually agreed upon. Such arguments of the parties, whether oral or written, shall be confined to and directed at the matters set forth in the grievance.

19.9(e) Each party shall pay any compensation and expenses relating to its own witnesses or representatives.

19.9(f) The Company and the Union shall, by mutual consent, fix the amount of compensation to be paid for the services of the arbiter. The Union or the Company, whichever is ruled against by the arbiter, shall pay the compensation of the arbiter including his necessary expenses.

19.9(g) The total cost of the stenographic record (if requested) will be paid by the party requesting it. If the other party also requests a copy, that party will pay one-half of the stenographic costs.

Section 19.10 Extension of Time Limits by Agreement.

Time limits designated in this Article 19 for processing grievances and for bringing a matter to arbitration may only be extended by mutual written consent.

Section 9.11 Agreement Not to Be Altered.

In arriving at any settlement or decision under the provisions of this Article 19, neither the parties nor the arbiter shall have the authority to alter this Agreement in whole or in part.

Section 9.12 Conferences During Working Hours.

All conferences resulting from the application of provisions contained in this Article 19 shall be held during working hours.

Section 19.13 Business Representative, When Not Avalable, May Authorize Designee.

For any period that the business representative is unavailable to serve in that capacity under this Article 19, he may designate an accredited steward or another accredited business representative to act for him, as his designee. As to each such period of unavailability, authorization of the designee will be accomplished by the business representative informing the appropriate Company representative of the expected period of the business representative's unavailability and naming the designee. When the business representative again is available to perform his duties under this Article 19, he shall promptly notify the Company representative of the fact and such notice will terminate the period during which the designee is authorized to act.

Section 19.14 Signing Grievance Does Not Concede Arbitrable Issue.

The signing of any grievance by any employee or representative either of the Company or of the Union shall not be construed by either party as a concession or agreement that the grievance constitutes an arbitrable issue or is properly subject to the grievance machinery under the terms of this Article 19.

Section 19.15 Union Jurisdictional Claims.

Union jurisdictional claims arising under the provisions of Section 1.3 of this Agreement, except those identified in Section 1.3(f), shall be handled pursuant to the provisions of Section 19.4 and 19.6 through 19.14, inclusive, except that the following requirements shall apply:

19.15(a) The written statement of grievance shall identify the job involved, state the Union's contention or contentions in detail, and shall contain a detailed statement of the reasons for the position taken by the Union.

19.15(b) If the Company and the Union are unable to agree upon the contents and scope of the record to be presented to the arbiter, either party may present to the arbiter whatever evidence, testimony and written argument it deems relevant to the question to be submitted to the arbiter. A written summary of such evidence, testimony and written argument will be submitted to the other side at least ten days in advance of the hearing.

19.15(c) If the parties are unable to agree upon the question that it is to be submitted to the arbiter for decision, the question to be submitted to, and answered by, the arbiter shall be:

"On the basis of the evidence, information, and arguments submitted by the parties in reference to the Union's contention in this case, is the Company violating Article I, Section 1.1, paragraph 1.1(a), 1.1(b), 1.1(c), or 1.1(d)?"

19.15(d) The arbiter shall answer the question submitted to him under 19.15(c) or the agreed statement of the issue presented by both parties. The arbiter's answer shall either be in the affirmative or the negative. The arbiter shall confine the proceedings before him to the questions presented to him in accordance with this Section 19.15 and he shall not have authority to specify any change in a job or any change in the work assignments under a job or the creation of a new job or any other remedy or type of award.

19.15(e) If the arbiter's answer sustains the Union's contention, the Company shall, within thirty days (or any longer period to which the parties may mutually agree) after receiving the arbiter's decision, take whatever corrective action is necessary to eliminate the basis for the Union's jurisdictional claim in the particular case.

19.15(f) Any resolution of any claim of controversy under Section 1.3, whether by mutual agreement or by arbitration, that requires corrective action on the part of the Company shall be prospective in effect from the date of the corrective action taken by the Company.

---

* Source: The Bureau of National Affairs, Inc., "Contracts in Text," *Collective Bargaining Negotiations & Contracts* (Washington, D.C.: The Bureau of National Affairs, Inc., March 12, 1987), Section 20. Reprinted with permission.

12 Labor Arbitration

- **Introduction**
- **Arbitrator Selection**
  Arbitrator Qualifications
  The Arbitration Tribunal
    Ad Hoc Arbitrators
    Permanent Arbitrators
    Tripartite Arbitration Boards
- **The Legal Status of Arbitration**
  The Enforceability of Arbitration Clauses: The Lincoln Mills *Decision*
  The Arbitration Tribunal and the Courts: The Trilogy Cases
  Grievances and Unfair Labor Practices: NLRB Deferral Policies
  Civil Rights Grievances: Alexander v. Gardner-Denver
  Arbitration and the Law: A Summary
- **The Issue of Arbitrability**
- **Preparing a Case for Arbitration**
- **Conducting the Arbitration Hearing**
  The Setting
  Stating the Issue to Be Heard by the Arbitrator
  Procedural Rules and Practices
    Grievance Representatives
    Presenting the Case
    Selecting and Examining Witnesses
    Using Exhibits and Evidence
    Briefs and Transcripts
    The Arbitrator's Award and Decision
- **Common Errors in Arbitration**

> ▲ **Factors Affecting Arbitration Decisions and Awards**
>   *Interpreting the Collective Bargaining Agreement*
>   *Sifting through the Evidence*
>   *Evaluating the Testimony of Witnesses*
>   *Considering the Role of Custom and Past Practice*
>   *Incorporating External Law into Arbitration Decisions*
>   *Assessing the Precedent Value of Arbitration Awards*
> ▲ **Professional and Ethical Standards for Arbitrators**
> ▲ **Summary and Conclusions**
> ▲ **Discussion Questions and Exercises**
> ▲ **Appendix: Code of Professional Responsibility for Arbitrators**

▲ Introduction

When union and management representatives are unable to settle a grievance on their own, the final stage of the grievance procedure almost always stipulates binding arbitration as the last resort for resolving a dispute. The institution of labor arbitration has played a prominent role in resolving labor-management disputes. Although this chapter focuses on the final and binding arbitration of rights disputes, arbitration is also used to resolve bargaining impasses (interest disputes) and various commercial disputes. The institution of labor arbitration has generally been held in high esteem by union officials and managers.[1] Over the years, labor arbitrators have developed professional and ethical standards of conduct that are probably unparalleled by any other profession.[2] The status of labor arbitrators has been enhanced by the fact that the U.S. Supreme Court has granted labor arbitrators a great deal of power in making decisions affecting rights disputes.

This chapter discusses the qualifications and selection of labor arbitrators, the legal status of arbitration, and the issue of arbitrability. The focus then shifts to the manner in which the parties conduct an arbitration hearing along with factors affecting the arbitrator's award.

Arbitrator Selection

Arbitrator Qualifications

Unlike most professions, labor arbitrators are not required to meet any formal educational or licensing requirements. The key to working as an arbitrator is *acceptability* by the union and management officials who hire a neutral party to hear a case and render a decision.

---

[1] According to the Bureau of National Affairs, Inc., *Basic Patterns in Union Contracts*, 11th ed. (Washington, D.C.: The Bureau of National Affairs, Inc., 1986), 98 percent of grievance procedures use final and binding arbitration to resolve rights disputes.
[2] Arbitrators are also referred to as "neutrals" or "third-party neutrals."

> [There] has not been a single instance in which an arbitrator has been accused and proved of having committed misconduct....And one of the reasons is that we serve in a "fish bowl." Everything that is done is seen. And we serve on acceptability. We are not appointed by the government, and we don't have lifetime tenure like a judge.... And we police our own profession. The parties do too; when someone does a poor job, he or she is not acceptable anymore.[3]

The majority of active arbitrators have law degrees and are well-versed on conducting hearings, weighing evidence, hearing testimony, and writing opinions once a decision has been reached in a case.[4] However, a number of highly successful arbitrators come from other backgrounds. Some possess extensive industry or union experience, whereas others are college professors who arbitrate on a part-time basis.

Most arbitrators are selected from lists provided by the American Arbitration Association (AAA), the Federal Mediation and Conciliation Service (FMCS), or a state agency. Inclusion on one of these lists means that an arbitrator meets the standards set forth by the above agencies, but it does not necessarily mean that the individual is acceptable to union and management officials who appoint arbitrators to hear their grievances. In fact, a large number of individuals on the AAA, FMCS, and state agency lists arbitrate few, if any, cases. An unfortunate aspect of arbitrator selection is that union and management officials only want veteran arbitrators and few parties are willing to risk selecting arbitrators who are untried and not well known.[5] A relatively small percentage of arbitrators are in extremely high demand; some parties are willing to wait long periods of time to have their case heard by a high-profile arbitrator. To help alleviate the uneven demand for arbitrators, the AAA, the FMCS, and the National Academy of Arbitrators have instituted programs to give training, experience, and acceptability to new arbitrators.[6]

Perhaps the key to an individual's acceptability as an arbitrator is impartiality and integrity. Arbitrators are usually expected to refuse an assignment or disqualify themselves from a case if there is any likelihood that their personal relationship or business endeavors create a conflict of interest. An arbitrator is normally expected to avoid cases involving companies in which they have a financial interest or with parties who are close friends or relatives. Furthermore, it is important that arbitrators do not behave in such a way so as to indicate either a labor or management bias.[7] If there is a question regarding a possible conflict of interest between the

---

[3] Comments of Eric J. Schmertz, Dean of Hofstra University School of Law, in Friedman, "Arbitrators in Oral History Interview: Looking Back and Ahead," *Employee Relations Law Journal*, Vol. 12 (1986), pp. 444–445. Cited in Marlin M. Volz and Edward P. Goggin, *How Arbitration Works*, 4th ed. (Washington, D.C.: The Bureau of National Affairs, Inc., 1988), p. 35. 1985–87 Supplement to Frank Elkouri and Edna Asper Elkouri, *How Arbitration Works*, 4th ed. (Washington, D.C.: The Bureau of National Affairs, Inc., 1985).
[4] See Sprehe and Small, "Members and Nonmembers of the National Academy of Arbitrators: Do They Differ?" *Arbitration Journal*, Vol. 39 (1984), pp. 25 and 28.
[5] See Nels E. Nelson, "The Selection of Arbitrators," *Labor Law Journal*, Vol. 37 (1986), pp. 703–709.
[6] Frank Elkouri and Edna Asper Elkouri, *How Arbitration Works*, 4th ed. (Washington, D.C.: The Bureau of National Affairs, Inc., 1985), p. 139.
[7] In selecting an arbitrator, some parties review an individual's previous arbitration awards and count the number that favored the union and management. If the awards are not evenly distributed, there is the implication that the arbitrator is biased. However, such an assumption may be erroneous. It is possible that an arbitrator simply heard a sample of grievances in which management had the stronger case. To conclude from this that the arbitrator is biased would be patently unfair. Thus, arbitrators must avoid the temptation of "splitting awards" for the sake of maintaining an even "win rate" for union and management; to do so implies a lack of integrity.

arbitrator and the parties, the arbitrator is generally obliged to fully reveal such conflicts to all concerned.[8] Should the parties believe that the arbitrator will render a fair decision, they may decide to allow the arbitrator to proceed with the case. However, it is crucial that arbitrators avoid even the *appearance* of partiality.[9]

Arbitrators are often selected because of their expertise in an industry or with a particular type of grievance. The parties may prefer that an arbitrator possess specific qualifications, such as a law degree, when hearing certain types of cases. For example, an arbitrator might become familiar with workplace practices and terminology that could make him or her especially competent to hear airline industry cases. Other arbitrators, because of their knowledge of occupational health issues, may become experts in health and safety cases.[10] However, arbitrators do not necessarily have to be experts in a particular topic in order to render well-reasoned decisions.[11] According to Elkouri and Elkouri, an arbitrator's ability should be viewed in the following light:

> Naturally, extensive arbitration experience is one indication of ability. But at the outset a labor-management arbitrator should have a broad background of social and economic study or experience. He should have an analytical mind and should be able to orient himself quickly when dealing with new subject matter. Maturity of judgment is indispensable. Diplomacy helps too.[12]

The Arbitration Tribunal

The manner in which an arbitrator or panel of arbitrators is selected is usually specified by the collective bargaining agreement. Most agreements provide for the selection of an ad hoc arbitrator who is selected on an "as needed," case-by-case basis.[13] Other parties use permanent arbitrators who are retained and used when-

---

[8] Arbitrators are also professionally obligated to decline a case if they cannot schedule a hearing within a reasonable amount of time. See *Code of Professional Responsibility for Arbitrators of Labor-Management Disputes of the National Academy of Arbitrators, the American Arbitration Association, and the Federal Mediation and Conciliation Service* (amended May 25, 1985), section J (a). The *Code* is contained in an appendix to this chapter.

[9] The AFL-CIO's Department of Economic Research has launched a major project to compile data on the performance of individual arbitrators in an effort to "help improve the quality of justice in the workplace." The database will ultimately be available for use by unions to help them select arbitrators. See Craig T. Norback, ed., *The Human Resources Yearbook, 1988 Edition* (Englewood Cliffs, New Jersey: Prentice-Hall, Inc., 1988), p. 17.47.

[10] For example, in a contract between Phelps Dodge Magnet Wire Company and the Electronic Workers union, rate and work standards disputes must be heard by an arbitrator qualified in industrial engineering techniques. See The Bureau of National Affairs, Inc., "Selection of Arbitrators," *Collective Bargaining Negotiations & Contracts* (Washington, D.C.: The Bureau of National Affairs, Inc., April 24, 1986), Section 51.

[11] Also see David E. Bloom and Christopher L. Cavanaugh, "An Analysis of the Selection of Arbitrators," *American Economic Review* (June 1986), p. 408.

[12] Frank Elkouri and Edna Asper Elkouri, *How Arbitration Works,* 4th ed. (Washington, D.C.: The Bureau of National Affairs, Inc., 1985), p. 141.

[13] The FMCS requests that the union and management representatives alternately strike unacceptable arbitrators from the list until one remains. The AAA, on the other hand, asks the parties to eliminate all unacceptable arbitrators on the list and rank order the remaining candidates. The AAA then matches the ranks and the arbitrator with the lowest combined ranking is selected.

ever unresolved grievances arise. Still other parties use either an ad hoc or permanent panel of arbitrators.[14]

Ad Hoc Arbitrators

Ad hoc arbitrators are selected to hear and decide a case as the need arises. Once an ad hoc arbitrator hears a case and renders a decision, the relationship between the parties has ended. If the union and management grievance representatives are pleased with the manner in which the case was handled, they may select the arbitrator to hear subsequent cases. However, if the parties were not satisfied with the arbitrator's decision, they are under no obligation to employ him or her in the future.

Temporary or ad hoc arbitration allows the parties to select arbitrators who they believe are best qualified to hear a particular case. Union and management grievance representatives who must only arbitrate a few cases during the life of their collective bargaining agreement will probably find the use of ad hoc arbitration to be less expensive than retaining a permanent arbitrator. Another potential advantage of ad hoc arbitration is that the arbitrator is usually not well acquainted with either the union or management and, as a result, is less likely to harbor biases toward either side.

There are certain disadvantages to using ad hoc arbitrators. First, the parties must select an arbitrator every time a case reaches the arbitration stage. As noted earlier, arbitrators are normally selected from a list provided by the AAA or FMCS. The process of eliminating names from the list until one acceptable candidate remains can be time-consuming.[15] Second, the use of ad hoc arbitration eliminates the advantage of continuity, so that arbitrators knowing little about the union-management relationship or the collective bargaining agreement must spend additional time learning about company and union practices, customs, and workplace issues. Finally, an ad hoc arrangement may encourage the losing party not to call upon an arbitrator in the future, even when the arbitrator's decision is sound.

Permanent Arbitrators

Permanent arbitrators are retained during the life of the collective bargaining agreement and are paid a retainer for being available to hear cases as they arise.[16] Permanent arbitrators offer the advantage of a stable and consistent relationship with union and management officials. There is no need to take a great deal of time in

---

[14] According to a Bureau of National Affairs, Inc., survey, approximately three-fourths of the collective bargaining agreements calling for arbitration use a single arbitrator and the remaining agreements call for multiple arbitrators. The vast majority of single arbitrators are selected on an ad hoc basis. See The Bureau of National Affairs, Inc., *Basic Patterns in Union Contracts*, 11th ed. (Washington, D.C.: The Bureau of National Affairs, Inc., 1986).

[15] Some parties schedule an arbitrator for nearly every grievance that arises in order to impress the other side with the seriousness of the case. For this reason, arbitrators often charge cancellation fees to parties who schedule a hearing and later cancel.

[16] Permanent arbitrators may be appointed for the life of the collective bargaining agreement or used as long as they remain acceptable to the parties. Some permanent arbitrators are paid on a case-by-case basis rather than on a retainer. In addition, permanent arbitration panels may be used in which the arbitrators on the panel rotate case assignments.

appointing an arbitrator, a fact that allows the parties to resolve grievances without waiting several months before an acceptable ad hoc arbitrator can be scheduled. Permanent arbitrators are likely to be much more familiar with the collective bargaining agreement, firm and industry past practices and customs, and workplace issues than their ad hoc counterparts. Furthermore, the parties can use the decision of the permanent arbitrator as a guide for resolving future grievances.

Because the parties have a sunk cost in paying a retainer to the permanent arbitrator, they may be tempted to take grievances to arbitration simply to get their money's worth. This strategy is inconsistent with resolving grievances at the lowest possible level of the grievance procedure. A permanent arbitrator may develop a bias for a party, especially if one side or the other develops an open animosity toward the arbitrator or insists on pursuing trivial grievances to arbitration. Another criticism of permanent arbitrators is that they may be tempted to split awards in order to balance the won-loss record of union and management. As noted earlier, compromise awards defeat the purpose of meaningful contract administration and may taint the reputation of a labor arbitrator.

Tripartite Arbitration Boards

Rather than using a single arbitrator, some collective bargaining agreements stipulate the use of a tripartite arbitration board. A tripartite board generally consists of an arbitrator selected by the union and one selected by management. A third nonpartisan arbitrator is then jointly selected by the union and management arbitrators. The tripartite panel hears a grievance and decides the outcome either through a majority vote (two out of three deciding) or by discussing the issue with the nonpartisan arbitrator who renders a decision.

Tripartite panels offer the potential advantages of additional knowledge and insight (compared to a single arbitrator) when complex issues must be evaluated. The nonpartisan arbitrator, who usually controls the final outcome of the grievance, has the advantage of obtaining the opinions of knowledgeable union and management advocates. When the decision among the three arbitrators is unanimous, the parties are more likely to view the decision as fairer than one rendered by a single arbitrator. On the negative side, permanent tripartite panels may be expensive and temporary tripartite panels may take a great deal of time to select and schedule. Because two members of the panel are partisan, the decision often rests on the shoulders of the lone nonpartisan arbitrator. Thus, it could be argued that the parties should have used one arbitrator and avoided the time and expense of an arbitration panel.

▲ The Legal Status of Arbitration

Over the years, the U.S. Supreme Court has adjudicated a number of cases that have strengthened the institution of labor arbitration by providing arbitrators with a great deal of power and latitude in resolving rights disputes. There are four major issues that have evolved regarding the legal status of labor arbitration. First, are collective bargaining provisions calling for arbitration enforceable in a state or federal court? Second, what is the relationship between the arbitrator's authority (under the collective bargaining agreement) and the authority of the courts (under federal labor law)? Third, how does the National Labor Relations Board (NLRB) view arbitration cases that also involve unfair labor practices? Fourth, under what circumstances can a court relitigate and reverse an arbitrator's award?

Today it is clear that agreements to arbitrate are clearly enforceable in state and federal courts. The Supreme Court has generally taken the position that labor arbitrators have performed their duties in a competent, judicious, and honorable fashion. As a result, the courts rarely tamper with or reverse arbitration rulings; rather, they allow the parties to resolve industrial disputes without judicial intervention. Furthermore, the NLRB defers to an arbitrator's decision to rule on grievances that involve unfair labor practices if certain conditions are met. These issues are now discussed in further detail.

The Enforceability of Arbitration Clauses: The *Lincoln Mills* Decision

The decision that heralded the rising influence of labor arbitrators was *Textile Workers of America v. Lincoln Mills of Alabama*.[17] The key question in *Lincoln Mills* was whether Section 301(a) of the Taft-Hartley Act allowed the courts to apply federal substantive law to require adherence to a labor contract provision calling for the arbitration of disputes.[18] The Court held that Congress authorized specific performance of promises to arbitrate grievances and "that the substantive law to apply in suits under Section 301(a) is federal law, which the courts must fashion from the policy of our national laws." *Lincoln Mills* requires that when a collective bargaining agreement contains an arbitration clause and the employer refuses to proceed to arbitration, the union may compel arbitration by obtaining an injunction in a federal court.[19]

In upholding the enforceability of arbitration clauses in *Lincoln Mills*, the U.S. Supreme Court recognized that arbitration was socially desirable. The Court noted that:

> it will promote a higher degree of responsibility upon the parties to such agreements [to arbitrate], and will thereby promote industrial peace.... Yet, to repeat, the entire tenor of the [legislative] history indicates that the agreement to arbitrate grievance disputes was considered as *quid pro quo* of a no-strike agreement.[20]

The *quid pro quo* relationship to which the Court refers, means that both parties give up something of value in a contractual relationship. Management relinquishes

---

[17] 353 U.S. 448 (1957).
[18] Section 301(a) states: "Suits for violation of contracts between an employer and a labor organization... may be brought in any district court of the United States having jurisdiction of the parties..."
[19] The Supreme Court also held that the Norris-LaGuardia Act's anti-injunction provision (Section 4) does not bar injunctive relief.
[20] Clyde Summers, Harry H. Wellington, and Alan Hyde, *Labor Law: Cases and Materials* (Mineola, New York: The Foundation Press, Inc., 1982), p. 766.

some of its decision-making authority to the arbitrator whose decision will be binding on the company. The union, in turn, agrees to give up its right to strike if the arbitrator's decision is not acceptable to the grievant or union officials.

The Arbitration Tribunal and the Courts: The Trilogy Cases

The *Lincoln Mills* decision stated that Section 301 constituted an authorization to the federal district courts to put together a substantive body of federal law for the interpretation and enforcement of collective bargaining agreements. Justice Douglas stated that the federal "common law" of labor contracts could be based on state law, federal law, and national labor policy.[21] The three Supreme Court cases granting the greatest amount of authority to arbitrators are known collectively as the Steelworkers Trilogy of 1960.[22]

The first two Trilogy cases dealt with the rules of arbitrability and the enforcement of an agreement to arbitrate. The term *arbitrability* refers to whether the issue in dispute falls within the arbitrator's jurisdiction.[23] In *Warrior & Gulf Navigation*, the union sought a court order forcing the employer to proceed to arbitration.[24] The union contended that the company violated the collective bargaining agreement by subcontracting bargaining unit work and reducing the firm's maintenance workforce by nearly one half. Management claimed that the decision to subcontract work was solely within its prerogative and not subject to arbitration. The Supreme Court, however, held that unless the arbitration clause *expressly excludes* a subject from arbitration, the parties are obligated to submit unresolved grievances to an arbitrator. The Court viewed arbitration as a system of industrial self-government, with the labor arbitrator being selected because of his or her knowledge of "the common law of the shop." Arbitration was viewed by the Court as a substitute for labor strife rather than a substitute for litigation in a federal court.

The Supreme Court has ruled that the arbitrator, rather than the courts, will decide whether a grievance has merit. In the Trilogy's *American Manufacturing Company* case, the employer felt that the grievance of an employee with a permanent partial disability who wanted to return to work was "a frivolous patently baseless one, not subject to arbitration under the collective bargaining agreement."[25] However, the Supreme Court disagreed with the employer's position. Although a court may direct arbitration (because a grievance is arbitrable), the arbitrator must decide whether a grievance has merit. The Court said that national labor policy favors labor arbitration and because "the processing of even frivolous

---

[21] Theodore J. St. Antoine, "Arbitration and the Law," in Arnold M. Zack, ed., *Arbitration in Practice* (Ithaca, New York: ILR Press, Cornell University, 1984), p. 14.

[22] The Trilogy cases were all decided on June 20, 1960. *United Steelworkers of America v. American Manufacturing Company*, 363 U.S. 564 (1960); *United Steelworkers of America v. Warrior & Gulf Navigation Company*, 363 U.S. 574 (1960); *United Steelworkers of America v. Enterprise Wheel & Car Corporation*, 363 U.S. 593 (1960).

[23] Robert E. Doherty, *Industrial and Labor Relations Terms: A Glossary*, 4th ed., ILR Bulletin Number 44 (Ithaca, New York: ILR Publications Division, New York State School of Industrial and Labor Relations, Cornell University, 1979), p. 3.

[24] 363 U. S. 574 (1960).

[25] 363 U. S. 593 (1960).

claims may have therapeutic values [to the grievant, union, or management] of which those who are not part of the plant environment may be quite unaware."

Whereas the first two Trilogy cases deal with the issue of whether a case should be heard by an arbitrator, the third case, *Enterprise Wheel & Car Corporation*,[26] deals with the enforcement of an arbitrator's award *after* the arbitrator has completed the case. Pursuant to a grievance, an arbitrator ordered the reinstatement (with back pay) of several employees. The back pay included a time period beyond the termination date of the collective bargaining agreement. As a result, the company refused to comply with the award. The Supreme Court held that an arbitrator's award is enforceable in court as long as it was within the arbitrator's jurisdiction (arbitrable) and "draw[s] its essence" from the collective bargaining agreement. Thus, the integrity of arbitration awards are upheld, even in situations where a federal judge believes that an arbitrator's decision was unfair, unwise, or inconsistent with the collective bargaining agreement.[27] Arbitration awards, however, may be overturned for the following reasons:

1. The arbitrator lacks jurisdiction to decide a case based on explicit contractual language (the issue of arbitrability).
2. The arbitrator disregards the essence of the collective bargaining agreement in rendering an award.
3. The arbitration award is illegal or contrary to strong public policy. For example, an arbitrator who upholds a racially discriminatory contract clause may have his or her award reversed by a court.
4. The arbitrator exhibits a biased or partial attitude toward a party directly involved in the grievance. Financial or personal relationships that create a conflict of interest could lead to a court reversal of an arbitration award.
5. The arbitrator prejudicially excludes important evidence or commits a gross error of fact in rendering an award.
6. The arbitrator violates his or her remedy power. For example, an arbitrator who decides to discharge an employee who is not a party to the grievance may have the award overturned.[28]

In 1987, the U.S. Supreme Court unanimously ruled that courts are not free to overturn an arbitrator's award in the absence of proof of fraud or dishonesty. This decision stemmed from the case of a machine operator who was fired after being apprehended on company property in the back seat of a car in which a marijuana cigarette was found burning in the front seat ashtray. Finding insufficient evidence that the employee either possessed or smoked marijuana, the arbitrator subsequently ordered reinstatement. However, a federal court overturned the arbitrator's award and stated that reinstatement of the employee would violate public policy "against the operation of dangerous machinery by persons under the influence of drugs." The U.S. Supreme Court overturned the lower court's decision and noted

---

[26] 363 U. S. 593 (1960).
[27] Benjamin J. Taylor and Fred Witney, *Labor Relations Law*, 5th ed. (Englewood Cliffs, New Jersey: Prentice-Hall, Inc., 1987), pp. 444–445.
[28] See Frank Elkouri and Edna Asper Elkouri, *How Arbitration Works*, 4th ed. (Washington, D.C.: The Bureau of National Affairs, Inc., 1985), p. 30.

that the courts have limited power to reverse labor arbitration awards and may not do so simply because they disagree with an arbitrator's findings, contract interpretations, or choice of remedies. The Supreme Court also said that an arbitrator's decision can be overturned only if it violates some explicit public policy that is grounded in "laws and legal precedents." However, courts may not reverse arbitration decisions that involve "general considerations of supposed public interests."[29]

The Steelworkers Trilogy and subsequent decisions have given labor arbitrators considerable power to evaluate the merits of a grievance and render a final and binding award that the courts cannot reverse except under unusual circumstances. As a result, the success of the institution of labor arbitration depends heavily on arbitrators who perform their work with professional competence and integrity. The final and binding nature of the award is perhaps the major reason why union and management officials generally want experienced arbitrators who have proven performance records.

Grievances and Unfair Labor Practices: NLRB Deferral Policies

A grievance may involve both a contractual violation and an alleged unfair labor practice by the employer. For example, a shop steward fired for incompetency may claim that his termination was actually based on the employer's union animus, rather than on his poor job performance. Although an employer may legitimately discharge a worker for poor performance, a firing that is the result of antiunion sentiments by a supervisor violates the National Labor Relations Act (NLRA). When grievances involving potential unfair labor practices arise, does the arbitrator or the NLRB ultimately have the final word in resolving the dispute? The discharged employee has the right to a grievance and arbitration hearing under the disciplinary provision of the collective bargaining agreement; the employee also has a right (under sections 8(a)(1) and (3) of the NLRA) to be protected from discrimination resulting from an employer's animosity toward unions.

Federal law (the NLRA) normally takes precedence over the terms and conditions of a contract (the collective bargaining agreement). Using this logic, an unfair labor practice hearing before the NLRB should take precedence over an arbitration hearing. However, the NLRB has agreed to defer unfair labor practice cases to arbitrators when such cases also involve potential violations of the collective bargaining agreement.

In 1955, the NLRB decided to honor arbitration awards that were made *prior* to the union's filing of an unfair labor practice charge. According to the *Speilberg Manufacturing Company* case, the NLRB will give full weight to arbitration awards that also involve unfair labor practices when: (1) the arbitration proceedings were "fair and regular," (2) all parties agreed to be bound by the arbitrator's decision, and (3) the arbitrator's award was not "clearly repugnant to the purposes of the Act [NLRA]."[30] The Board later required that it was also necessary that the arbitrator

---

[29] *United Paperworkers v. Misco, Inc.*, 126 LRRM 3113 (1987).
[30] 112 NLRB 1080 (1955).

explicitly consider the unfair labor practice issue.[31] However, the explicit standard was somewhat relaxed during the years of the Reagan-appointed NLRB in the *Olin Corporation* case.[32] *Olin* held that the NLRB would defer to an arbitrator's award if the contractual issue was factually parallel to the unfair labor practice issue and if the arbitrator was presented with the general facts relevant to resolving the unfair labor practice.[33] Later, a federal court of appeals held that *Olin* improperly presumed that an arbitration award resolves all relevant unfair labor practice issues.[34] Thus, the standard of determining whether an arbitration award is "repugnant" to the NLRA remains somewhat unclear. However, the arbitration award need not be totally consistent with the NLRA.[35] Thus, an arbitrator may resolve an unfair labor practice issue in a manner different from the NLRB (had the NLRB heard the case instead of the arbitrator) as long as the award does not subvert the intent of the NLRA.[36]

The NLRB later began deferring unfair labor practice charges (that also involved contract disputes) even when the parties had not originally pursued the dispute through arbitration.[37] In the controversial *Collyer Insulated Wire* case, the Board dismissed a refusal-to-bargain case against an employer that had unilaterally raised the wages of skilled employees and made job reassignments.[38] The Board deferred to the arbitrator to determine the merits of the unfair labor practice charge filed by the union as well as whether the employer had violated its bargaining obligations under the NLRA. However, the Board retained jurisdiction over the case and was willing to hear the unfair labor practice charge if the dispute was not settled with reasonable promptness or if the grievance and arbitration procedures were not fair or reached a result repugnant to the NLRA.[39] Since the *Collyer* case, the NLRB has deferred many other types of disputes to arbitration. However, the NLRB will not defer cases under the *Collyer* doctrine if:

1. the collective bargaining agreement does not contain a provision for final and binding arbitration or if the employer refuses to agree to final and binding arbitration;[40]

---

[31] *Raytheon Company*, 140 NLRB 883 (1963).
[32] 268 NLRB No. 86 (1984).
[33] 268 NLRB No. 86 (1984). Benjamin J. Taylor and Fred Witney, *Labor Relations Law*, 5th ed. (Englewood Cliffs, New Jersey: Prentice-Hall,Inc., 1987), p. 413.
[34] *Taylor v. NLRB*, 122 LRRM 2084 (1986).
[35] There is concern that *Olin* may permit the NLRB to defer too many cases to arbitrators and, perhaps, compromise the statutory rights of charging parties. See Patricia A. Greenfield, "The NLRB's Deferral to Arbitration Before and After *Olin*: An Empirical Analysis," *Industrial and Labor Relations Review* (October 1988), pp. 34–49.
[36] Also see Leanne M. Swenson, "Labor Law—the Rejection of the *Olin* Standard for Deferral to an Arbitrator's Award," *Journal of Corporation Law* (Summer 1987), pp. 801–814.
[37] See Benjamin W. Wolkinson, "The Impact of the *Collyer* Policy of Deferral: An Empirical Study," *Industrial and Labor Relations Review* (April 1985), pp. 377–391; and Mark A. Shank, "Deferral to Arbitration: Accommodation of Competing Statutory Polices," *Hofstra Labor Law Journal*, Vol. 2 (1985), pp. 211–263.
[38] 192 NLRB 837 (1971).
[39] The Bureau of National Affairs, Inc., "Arbitration," *Labor Relations Expediter* (October 1988), section 410.
[40] *Tulsa-Whisenhunt Funeral Homes*, 195 NLRB 106 (1972).

2. the bargaining history between the union and employer has been marred by friction and hostility;[41]
3. the employer has engaged in serious unfair labor practices;[42]
4. the union was decertified prior to the expiration of the collective bargaining agreement.[43]

Civil Rights Grievances: *Alexander v. Gardner-Denver*

Grievants who obtain a fair hearing before an arbitrator are not usually entitled to have their case heard a second time before an administrative agency or in a state or federal court. *Alexander v. Gardner-Denver* involved the arbitration of an employee's race discrimination claim in which the arbitrator upheld the discharge of a black employee. The Supreme Court held that race discrimination claims heard by arbitrators could be relitigated in an Equal Employment Opportunity Commission (EEOC) or court hearing under Title VII of the 1964 Civil Rights Act.[44] Furthermore, *Gardner-Denver* allows the EEOC or courts to decide the extent to which they want to weigh the previous arbitration opinion when hearing a discrimination case. The EEOC and courts may hear the case *de novo* and give no weight to the arbitrator's previous ruling, or they may attach a great deal of significance to the arbitration decision, depending on the arbitrator's expertise and the extent to which the arbitrator considered the employee's Title VII rights.[45]

The question arising in the aftermath of the *Gardner-Denver* case was why are arbitration cases involving civil rights issues allowed to be relitigated, whereas the arbitrator's opinion is final when other issues are in dispute?[46] Professor Theodore J. St. Antoine provides a concise answer:

> The employee was not bound by the adverse arbitral award under the contract because he had a separate and independent statutory right. Title VII rights may be considered peculiarly personal—they belong to the individual— as well as exceptionally sensitive, in contrast to NLRA rights, which are more organizational and institutional.[47]

An issue discussed later in this chapter is the extent to which arbitrators should consider external laws in fashioning their decisions and awards.[48]

---

[41] *Borden, Inc., Dairy & Services Division*, 196 NLRB 1170 (1973) and *Kansas Meat Packers*, 198 NLRB 543 (1972).
[42] *Mountain State Construction Company*, 203 NLRB 1085 (1973).
[43] *Seng Company*, 205 NLRB 200 (1973).
[44] 415 U. S. 36 (1974).
[45] The impact of an arbitration award in a race-discrimination case under Title VII is discussed in footnote 21 of *Gardner-Denver*.
[46] Also see William A. Carmell and Patrick Westercamp, "Arbitration of EEO Claims a Decade After *Gardner-Denver*," *Employee Relations Law Journal* (Summer 1986), pp. 80–97.
[47] Theodore J. St. Antoine, "Arbitration and the Law," in Arnold M. Zack, ed., *Arbitration in Practice* (Ithaca, New York: ILR Press, Cornell University, 1984), p. 20.
[48] Also see Deborah R. Willig, "Arbitration of Discrimination Grievances: Arbitral and Judicial Competence Compared," in Walter J. Gershenfeld, ed., *Arbitration 1986: Current and Expanding Roles, Proceedings of the Thirty-Ninth Annual Meeting National Academy of Arbitrators* (Washington, D.C.: The Bureau of National Affairs, Inc., 1987), pp. 101–120.

Arbitration and the Law: A Summary

Table 12–1 presents a capsule summary of some of the more significant court decisions affecting the institution of labor arbitration.[49]

Table 12–1 ▲ Significant Court Rulings Affecting Labor Arbitration

Enforcing an Agreement to Arbitrate

Textile Workers v. Lincoln Mills, 353 U.S. 448 (1957): Section 301 (of the National Labor Relations Act) allows the federal courts to fashion a body of federal "law" to enforce arbitration provisions in a collective bargaining agreement.

Application of State and Federal Law to Arbitration

Dowd Box v. Courtney, 368 U.S. 502 (1962): State and federal courts have concurrent jurisdiction over Section 301 cases.

Teamsters, Local 174 v. Lucas Flour, 49 LRRM 2619 (1962): State courts must apply federal substantive law to Section 301 cases.

The Arbitrability and Finality of Arbitration Awards

Steelworkers Trilogy
- *American Manufacturing Company*, 363 U.S. 564 (1960): The courts determine the arbitrability, whereas arbitrators evaluate the merits of a grievance. Doubts regarding arbitrability should be resolved in favor of arbitrating the grievance. Also see *AT&T Technologies v. Communication Workers*, Docket No. 84–1913, April 7, 1986.
- *Warrior Gulf & Navigation Company*, 363 U.S. 574 (1960): A grievance is arbitrable unless expressly excluded by the collective bargaining agreement.
- *Enterprise Wheel & Car Corp.*, 363 U.S. 593 (1960): The courts will not review an arbitrator's decision as long as it "draws its essence" from the collective bargaining agreement.

Alexander v. Gardner-Denver, 415 U.S. 36 (1974): A grievant claiming race discrimination who is not satisfied with the arbitrator's decision may re-litigate his or her case through the EEOC or courts under Title VII of the 1964 Civil Rights Act.

Nolde Bros., Inc., v. Bakery and Confectionery Workers, Local 358, 430 U.S. 243 (1977): An employer may be obligated to arbitrate a dispute arising during the life of the agreement even though the collective bargaining agreement has expired.

United Paperworkers v. Misco, Inc., 126 LRRM 3113 (1987): The courts have a limited power to reverse arbitration awards and cannot do so just because they disagree with the arbitrator's finding, contract interpretations, and choice of remedies.

Procedural Issues in Arbitration

Packinghouse Workers, Local 721 v. Needham Packing Company, 55 LRRM 2580 (1963): Arbitration must still be used to determine whether strikers discharged because they violated a no-strike clause were discharged for just cause.

John Wiley and Sons v. Livingston, 55 LRRM 2769 (1964): Once it is determined that a grievance is arbitrable, procedural questions arising from the dispute (e.g., determining whether the parties have filed a timely grievance) are resolved by the arbitrator. Answering procedural questions may require that the arbitrator examine the merits of a dispute.

---

[49] The case summaries are designed to show basic trends in the legal status of labor arbitration. For a detailed explanation of the facts and judgment of the NLRB and courts, the reader is advised to examine the published cases.

Table 12–1 ▲ Significant Court Rulings Affecting Labor Arbitration (Cont.)

Procedural Issues in Arbitration

Boys Markets, Inc. v. Retail Clerks, Local 770, 398 U.S. 235 (1970): Injunctions may be used to stop strikes that violate a no-strike clause if: (1) the grievance is arbitrable under the contract, (2) arbitration has been used unsuccessfully to prevent the strike, and (3) if principles of equity needed to obtain an injunction (e.g., the employer will be irreparably damaged) have been met.

The Relationship between the NLRB and Arbitration

Spielberg Manufacturing Company, 112 NLRB 1080 (1955): The NLRB will give great weight to an arbitration award involving an unfair labor practice if the arbitration proceedings are fair, the parties agree to abide by the arbitrator's award, and the arbitrator's award was not repugnant to the NLRA.

Smith v. Evening News Association, 51 LRRM 2646 (1962): The NLRB has the authority to hear Section 301 suits, which also involve unfair labor practices. The courts, however, retain the right to hear Section 301 suits. Individual employees can sue under Section 301 to enforce their rights under the collective bargaining agreement when there is no arbitration clause.

Carey v. Westinghouse, 55 LRRM 2042 (1964): Arbitration can be used to resolve jurisdictional disputes (disputes over which group of employees performs a certain job or task), but the NLRB has superior jurisdiction.

Collyer Insulated Wire, 192 NLRB 837 (1971): The NLRB will defer to a private arbitrator a grievance involving an unfair labor practice when such a dispute involves a contract violation as well as a violation of the NLRA.

Olin Corporation, 268 NLRB No. 86 (1984): The NLRB will defer to an arbitrator's award provided that the contractual issue was factually parallel to the unfair labor practice issue, and if the arbitrator was presented with generally the same facts relevant to resolving the unfair labor practice.

United Technologies, 268 NLRB No. 83 (1984): The NLRB will defer discharge cases to arbitrators even when the discharge potentially violates an employee's rights under the NLRA.

Arbitration and the Union's Duty of Fair Representation

Vaca v. Sipes, 386 U.S. 171 (1967): Employees may sue a union for not processing a meritorious grievance.

Hines v. Anchor Motor Freight, 96 S. Ct. 1048 (1976): An arbitration award can be relitigated only when the process has malfunctioned by reason of bad-faith performance by the union.

Bowen v. U.S. Postal Service, 459 U.S. 212 (1983): A union may be liable for damages if the union violates its duty of fair representation to an employee.

▲ The Issue of Arbitrability

As noted earlier, the issue of arbitrability deals with the arbitrator's jurisdiction or authority to hear an arbitration case and render an award. Arbitrability is of two types. *Procedural arbitrability* involves deciding whether the parties adhered to the requirements of the grievance procedure. An arbitrator, for example, may refuse to hear a grievance because the moving party has failed to adhere to prescribed time limits. *Substantive arbitrability* issues arise when there is a debate over whether a grievance is within the scope of the collective bargaining agreement. If a grievance arises over management's refusal to allow employees to transfer to a recently-opened facility in a nearby town, the arbitrator may refuse to hear the case on the grounds that such a grievance falls outside the scope of the current contract. According to the Steelworkers Trilogy (*American Manufacturing Company*), the courts must decide substantive arbitrability.[50] Arbitrators, however, generally determine whether a grievance is procedurally arbitrable.

Arbitrability is generally not a problem if both union and management grievance representatives agree to submit the dispute to arbitration. The issue of arbitrability may be raised by the party seeking an arbitration hearing. A party may also seek a determination on arbitrability *after* the other party refuses to arbitrate. In the latter case, the party who does not believe that the dispute is subject to arbitration may seek a "stay" of arbitration until a court has made an arbitrability ruling.

Arbitrators routinely determine arbitrability in order to avoid the time, expense, and controversy of hearing a dispute over which the arbitrator has no power. When the issues of arbitrability and merit are intertwined, the arbitrator may hear the entire case before rendering a decision on the arbitrability of a grievance.

▲ Preparing a Case for Arbitration

By the time a case has proceeded through several stages of the grievance procedure, a great deal of preparation for the arbitration hearing has already been completed. The parties must bear in mind that arbitrators base their decisions on the collective bargaining agreement as well as on what they see and hear during the course of the hearing. If the parties fail to present important evidence or testimony, the arbitrator will not have all of the relevant facts needed to make an informed decision. Preparation also allows the parties to build a sound theory of their case. When both sides thoroughly prepare their cases, they may discover that they can settle without the need for arbitration. Careful preparation may also eliminate irrelevant issues and reduce the length and expense of the arbitration hearing.[51]

Table 12–2 illustrates some important steps that should be taken in preparing a case for arbitration:

Table 12–2 ▲ Preparing a Case for Arbitration

1. Carefully examine the written grievance, all supporting documentation, and notes from each stage of the procedure.
2. Analyze the current collective bargaining agreement to determine which clauses have a bearing on the grievance.

---

[50] Arbitrators may determine substantive arbitrability if the collective bargaining agreement so specifies. When the contract allows the arbitrator to assess arbitrability, the courts will not usually overturn the arbitrator's arbitrability determination. Even when the contract is silent on the matter, the parties often allow the arbitrator to decide on the arbitrability issue; a party would still have the right to challenge the arbitrability in court.

[51] Raymond L. Britton, *The Arbitration Guide* (Englewood Cliffs, New Jersey: Prentice-Hall, Inc., 1982), pp. 82–83.

Table 12–2 ▲ Preparing a Case for Arbitration (Cont.)

3. Obtain information on previous collective bargaining agreements and the negotiating history of the contact provisions that are relevant to the current grievance.
4. Examine past practices and customs that have a bearing on the grievance (both in the company and in the industry).
5. Interview the grievant, all prospective witnesses in the case, and other persons who have knowledge of the grievance. Be prepared to account for any contradictions in their version of the facts surrounding the grievance. Use the information garnered from the interviews to identify the need for other types of evidence (e.g., exhibits, records, plant visits by the arbitrator). Once witnesses are selected, prepare them for the arbitration hearing. Witnesses should be briefed on how to answer questions as well as on their demeanor during the hearing.
6. If the grievance involves a workplace issue, accident, or safety issue, a visit to the work site may shed some important light on how to use diagrams, photographs, and other types of evidence.
7. If the grievance involves a dispute over wage rates, incentive systems, or employee benefits, research and analyze economic and statistical data that might be relevant. Government reports, industry wage and benefit data, and the results of scientific research may be used to help the parties establish a theory of their case.
8. If the grievance involves a disciplinary issue, obtain as much information as possible about the grievant's work history, performance evaluations, and disciplinary record.
9. Research previous arbitration awards under the contract that involve issues similar to the current grievance. Previous arbitration awards under the same contract may serve as a precedent for the current grievance, especially when the facts of the current grievance and the previous grievance are similar.
10. Once steps 1–9 are complete, develop a theory of the case. That is, determine what facts and arguments are necessary to convince the arbitrator to rule in your favor. Outline the plan of attack that will be taken during the arbitration hearing. The outline should include the order in which evidence and witnesses will be presented, the major points of contention to be proven, and how arguments from the other party will be refuted.
11. Select and prepare exhibits (e.g., diagrams, photographs, statistics, and employment records) that will be presented during the arbitration hearing.
12. Meet with the other party and the arbitrator to establish procedural ground rules (e.g., the hearing will be held in a plant conference room and the union will present its case first), fact stipulations (e.g., both union and management agree that a grievant was absent for 28 work days during 1990), and a definition of the grievance.

Adapted, in part, from Raymond L. Britton, *The Arbitration Guide* (Englewood Cliffs, New Jersey: Prentice-Hall, Inc., 1982), pp. 83–86.

▲ Conducting the Arbitration Hearing

The Setting

Arbitration hearings are usually conducted in a quasi-judicial setting; arbitration proceedings are formal in that evidence is admitted and witnesses are examined and cross-examined. However, the strict procedural rules that are used in the state and federal courts are relaxed in arbitration hearings. Both the union and management grievance representatives are allowed ample opportunity to present whatever evidence and arguments are necessary to explain their case fully. Procedural rules associated with defining the grievance, submitting evidence, cross-examining witnesses, and the use of pre- and post-hearing briefs are established by the parties and the arbitrator.

The parties often meet in a company, union, or hotel conference room. Arbitration hearings are also conducted in meeting rooms provided by the American Arbitration Association (AAA) or Federal Mediation and Conciliation Service (FMCS). Union and management representatives along with the grievant are usually seated at a conference table with the arbitrator at the head of the table. Witnesses and other interested parties are often seated in the room, unless the arbitrator believes that the presence of these individuals will bias testimony or disrupt the hearing. The parties may also use a reporter to compile a transcript of the hearing.

Stating the Issue to be Heard by the Arbitrator

Arbitration cases are initiated either through a demand for arbitration (based on an arbitration clause in the collective bargaining agreement) or through a submission agreement. A submission agreement defines an arbitrator's authority to hear a grievance. For example, a submission agreement often poses a question that the arbitrator must answer: "Was Mary Smith discharged for just cause in accordance with Section 12, part d of the contract, and, if not, what shall the appropriate remedy be?" or "Did management at the Ajax Manufacturing, Pleasantburg plant have the right to subcontract maintenance work on 24 air hammers to the Ace Machine and Maintenance Shop? If not, to what remedies are Ajax maintenance employees entitled?" Submission agreements also outline procedural details associated with the arbitration hearing.[52]

Union and management grievance representatives may jointly define the issue to be decided and then submit it to the arbitrator. The grievance has usually been well-defined by the time it reaches the arbitration stage. However, the grievance may be narrowed immediately prior to the arbitration hearing or during the initial stages of arbitration. For example, in a discharge case, management may decide to reinstate the employee as a result of grievance procedure hearings, but the decision of whether the employee is entitled to back pay and benefits may be left to the arbitrator. When the parties cannot agree upon a formal definition of the grievance, the arbitrator may help the parties define the issue and draft a submission agreement. In some instances, the arbitrator will proceed with the case and, once the facts are fully known, properly define the issue.

---

[52] Sam Kagel, *Anatomy of a Labor Arbitration* (Washington, D.C.: The Bureau of National Affairs, Inc., 1961), p. 55.

Procedural Rules and Practices

Grievance Representatives

Each side selects grievance representatives to help present its case. A grievance representative should have a thorough understanding of the case, the collective bargaining agreement, and the arbitration tribunal. Grievance representatives should have the ability to present their case in a clear and concise fashion. Some parties prefer to use attorneys as grievance representatives. Attorneys understand how to secure evidence and use it to maximum effect. In addition, they are skilled at preparing witnesses to testify and they are adept at examining and cross-examining witnesses. Attorneys are also trained to build a theory of a case and present it in an effective manner. However, attorneys add to the expense of a hearing and they may not understand certain workplace issues as well as experienced union stewards, first-line supervisors, and other union and management representatives. Since the strict rules of evidence and other procedural requirements are relaxed, the use of an attorney is much less critical in arbitration than in a court of law.

Arbitration hearings are not public meetings and either the parties or the arbitrator may restrict the admission of spectators. Some grievances have important consequences for employees who are not named as grievants in the case. For this reason, co-workers may want to attend the hearing to satisfy their own curiosity or to lend moral support to the grievant. Too many spectators, however, may distract the parties and hinder the presentation of a case. In addition, the employer may find it inconvenient to excuse employees from their jobs unless they are needed as witnesses. Arbitrators insist on maintaining decorum during the hearing and generally will not tolerate unsolicited comments, talking among spectators, or other actions that detract from the hearing. In order to prevent the testimony of one witness from influencing the testimony of another, some witnesses may be sequestered for all or part of the hearing.

Presenting the Case

In a court of law, the plaintiff usually makes the opening presentation. Since the union is normally the moving party, it often presents its case first. However, in employee discipline and discharge cases, management proceeds first and attempts to justify the disciplinary action. Once the moving party has presented its case, the other side presents and rebuts the contentions of the moving party.

Normally the party filing the grievance (the moving party) has the burden of proof in an arbitration case. However, the burden of proof issue is relaxed in arbitration tribunals because the arbitrator has a chance to fully explore evidence and testimony without being constrained by rules of evidence and procedure commonly found in a court of law. For example, in a discharge case, the employer may carry the burden of proof to show that a discharge was for just cause (even though the union is the moving party). Regardless of which side has the burden of proof, arbitration cases are built on showing how a grievance violates the contract language as well as presenting convincing facts, evidence, and testimony to the arbitrator.[53]

Once it has been decided that party A will present its case first, the usual procedure is for party A to make an opening statement, followed by party B's opening statement. Then party A presents evidence and witnesses. Party B follows by cross-examining A's witnesses as well as presenting its own witnesses and evidence. Party A then cross-examines B's witnesses and rebuts testimony and evidence presented by party B. Parties A and B continue presenting evidence, cross-examining witnesses, and making rebuttals until both sides are satisfied that they have fully presented their respective cases. In making closing arguments, party B may proceed first, on the theory that the party who opens the hearing (party A) should have the last word.[54]

Selecting and Examining Witnesses

Witnesses often hold the key to helping the union or company prove its case. It is therefore crucial that witnesses be carefully selected and briefed prior to testifying at the arbitration hearing. Table 12–3 summarizes the roles that a witness may serve during an arbitration hearing.[55]

Witness selection must be made on three criteria. First, does the witness possess the information necessary to help prove the case? Second, will the witness's appearance add to the information already presented? Third, once on the stand, is the witness capable of imparting information to the arbitrator in an effective and persuasive manner?[56] Some witnesses may be reluctant to testify because they fear retaliation by the employer (or co-workers) or embarrassment if certain aspects of their personal lives are exposed. Other witnesses may be unacceptable to the union or company because of their general appearance, demeanor, propensity to lie, or the fact that they harbor racial or sexist biases. Witnesses who are easily flustered, prone to engage in argumentative or comical behavior, or quick to lose their tempers may damage their party's case.

Once selected, a prospective witness must be briefed on his or her role in the arbitration hearing. When appearing before an arbitrator, the witness's testimony will be evaluated on two elements: (1) the extent to which the witness has a grasp of the relevant facts, and (2) the credibility displayed by the witness. Grievance representatives must make certain that a witness has a complete understanding of the documents and evidence associated with his or her testimony. Witnesses must also be well briefed on the questions that will likely be asked by both sides during

---

[53] To borrow from a legal anecdote: "When you are strong on the facts, pound on the facts. When you are strong on the contract language, pound on the contract language. When you are strong on neither the facts nor the contract language, pound on the table."

[54] Martin F. Scheinman, *Evidence and Proof in Arbitration* (Ithaca, New York: New York State School of Industrial and Labor Relations, Cornell University, 1977), pp. 2–3.

[55] Adapted, in part, from Edward Levin and Donald Grody, *Witnesses in Arbitration* (Washington, D.C.: The Bureau of National Affairs, Inc., 1987), pp. 40–47.

[56] Edward Levin and Donald Grody, *Witnesses in Arbitration* (Washington, D.C.: The Bureau of National Affairs, Inc., 1987), p. 39.

Table 12–3 ▲ Roles of Witnesses in Arbitration Hearings

Foundation Witnesses:

Witnesses who verify the authenticity of a document or piece of evidence. A personnel director may serve as a foundation witness to verify that an employee's absenteeism record is authentic.

Explanatory Witnesses:

Witnesses who can explain or amplify the meaning of a document. For example, a departmental supervisor may be called upon to explain how absenteeism records are maintained. Or, a member of the union negotiating team may testify regarding the intent of the parties when they negotiated a contract clause.

Participating Witnesses:

Witnesses who participated in events or conversations that represent disputed elements in the case. In an insubordination case, both the supervisor and the grievant who allegedly engaged in the insubordination would be called as participating witnesses, since both were directly involved in the incident.

Eyewitnesses and Observers:

Persons who observed events, but did not actually participate. Another supervisor or co-worker may have witnessed the insubordination described above, although neither was directly involved in the dispute.

Character and Credibility Witnesses:

Witnesses who are in a position either to bolster or damage the credibility and testimony of other witnesses. Character witnesses are also used to substantiate personal traits of other witnesses or the grievant. A character witness might be called to defend an employee who has been disciplined for assaulting another employee. The character witness might testify as to the employee's calm, easygoing personality and aversion to violence.

Expert Witnesses:

Witnesses who provide an opinion (as opposed to supplying facts) that is within their realm of expertise. A physician might testify as to the employability of a grievant who has been discharged because of supervisory fears that the grievant's epilepsy poses a safety hazard.

---

the hearing.[57] Grievance representatives should coach witnesses to listen carefully to questions, ask for clarification if a question is not understood, and direct their answers to the arbitrator in a forthright, honest manner. Some witnesses also need to be advised on their dress and demeanor during testimony.

Witnesses are commonly sworn in prior to giving their testimony. The *direct examination* pertains to questions asked of witnesses by the representative who called the witness to the stand. On direct examination, the representative is attempting to establish the factual background of the case by asking the witness about

---

[57] Reputable grievance representatives should not coach a grievant to lie when providing answers to questions. Lying not only undermines the integrity of the grievance procedure and arbitration hearing, but it can also represent a fatal blow to a case if a witness is caught in a lie or gross contradiction of the facts. Perhaps more importantly, encouraging a witness to lie can irreparably damage the credibility of the grievance representatives involved.

his or her knowledge of the grievance.[58] The grievance representative may ask the witness to "tell us the story in your own words" in a narrative fashion, or the representative may ask the witness specific questions to which there must be specific answers. The strategy chosen by the grievance representative usually depends on whether the witness is articulate as well as the witness's ability to remember specific incidents surrounding the grievance. Some grievance representatives may ask leading questions such as, "You saw the grievant walk into the spray paint booth with a lighted cigarette in his hand, didn't you?" Leading questions on direct examination may be objectionable when they contain an assumption that may be untrue or when they "put words in a witness's mouth." The question: "What did the grievant say after he struck his supervisor?" is an example of a leading question that may be unacceptable to the arbitrator if it has not yet been established that the grievant struck the supervisor.[59] The parties have the right to make timely objections to misleading or irrelevant questions. Since the arbitrator serves as both judge and jury, the arbitrator may allow the question and then disregard the answer if it is baseless or not relevant to the case.

The grievant usually testifies during the arbitration hearing. A failure of the grievant to testify may be looked upon with disfavor by an arbitrator. Grievants are expected to testify fully and truthfully. However, the testimony of a grievant may present problems when the grievant's testimony results in self-incrimination. For example, the company may call upon a discharged grievant to testify as an *adverse witness*.[60] Some arbitrators will allow a grievant to refuse testifying as an adverse witness, whereas other arbitrators believe that a grievant should not refuse to take the stand.[61]

Some arbitration cases hinge on the testimony of expert witnesses. As noted in Chapter 11, expert witnesses differ from ordinary witnesses in that the former provide opinions based on their expertise, whereas the latter confine their testimony to statements of fact. Testimony as an expert witness is confined to the witness's realm of expertise. A grievance representative may first wish to question the expert witness to determine whether the witness has the proper knowledge, expertise, or credentials to proceed with the expert testimony.[62]

Once the direct examination has been concluded, the opposing party has the right to *cross-examine* the witness about matters brought up during the direct examination. When cross-examining a witness, the opposing grievance representatives should ensure that the witness completely answers the question without providing extraneous information. Questions should be short and to the point. Finally, cross-examinations are designed to clarify earlier testimony; their purpose is not to harass or degrade an opposing witness unduly. Most arbitrators will not tolerate personal insults by grievance representatives when cross-examining a witness. Ef-

---

[58] Raymond L. Britton, *The Arbitration Guide* (Englewood Cliffs, New Jersey: Prentice-Hall, Inc., 1982), p. 126.
[59] Boaz Siegel, *Proving Your Arbitration Case* (Washington, D.C.: The Bureau of National Affairs, Inc., 1961), pp. 16–18.
[60] An adverse witness is one who is called by one side, but who is identified with the opposing side.
[61] Raymond L. Britton, *The Arbitration Guide* (Englewood Cliffs, New Jersey: Prentice-Hall, Inc., 1982), p. 125.
[62] Testing the expertise of an expert witness is known as *voir dire*.

forts to discredit a witness can be made by demonstrating that the witness (1) did not have the opportunity to observe the matter in question, (2) has a faulty memory, (3) did not understand the questions from the direct examination, (4) is biased or prejudiced, (5) has demonstrated questionable character, prior bad acts, or a tendency to lie or exaggerate, or (6) has made prior statements that are inconsistent with current testimony.[63] The process of examination and cross-examination continues until both sides are satisfied that they have received a full account from the witness. It should be borne in mind that a party must build a theory of their case using their *own* witnesses, not the opponent's witnesses. Arbitrators may also question witnesses during direct and cross-examination. The arbitrator may explore points made during the testimony or ask the witness to elaborate on an earlier comment in order to develop a complete picture of the case.[64]

Using Exhibits and Evidence

Exhibits such as photographs, written depositions, charts, graphs, records, and other physical evidence are frequently used to substantiate a claim or contention. An exhibit may be submitted either by one party or jointly by both union and management.[65] All exhibits may be introduced at the beginning of the hearing or the parties may present them as they are discussed during the proceedings. An exhibit may also be introduced at the same time a witness is called upon to provide related testimony. Exhibits become part of the record of the case and are generally available for examination by either party. If the opposing side does not object, an exhibit is admitted as evidence. Should an objection arise, the arbitrator will hear arguments as to why the evidence should either be admitted or excluded. Evidence that is either irrelevant to the case or of questionable reliability is often excluded by the arbitrator. Even when evidence is admitted, it does not necessarily mean that the arbitrator considers it factual or will give it significant weight when rendering an award.

There are four primary reasons for the liberal attitude toward admissibility of evidence in arbitration. First, the arbitrator serves as both judge and jury and has the expertise to distinguish between relevant and irrelevant evidence. Second, most arbitrators would rather examine too much irrelevant evidence than not enough relevant evidence. It is sometimes difficult for an arbitrator to know what evidence is important until it has been presented and compared with other evidence. Third, presenting evidence and testimony may have a therapeutic value to the parties because it allows them to air bothersome issues. Fourth, there is always the possibility that an arbitrator's award could be reversed by a court if he or she fails to review material evidence or hear relevant testimony.[66]

---

[63] Raymond L. Britton, *The Arbitration Guide* (Englewood Cliffs, New Jersey: Prentice-Hall, Inc., 1982), pp. 128–130.

[64] For an excellent treatment of the role of witnesses in arbitration, see Edward Levin and Donald Grody, *Witness in Arbitration* (Washington, D.C.: The Bureau of National Affairs, Inc., 1987).

[65] Exhibits are commonly labeled sequentially in the order presented, i.e., "union exhibit 1," "management exhibit 1," or "joint exhibit 1."

[66] Martin F. Scheinman, *Evidence and Proof in Arbitration* (Ithaca, New York: New York State School of Industrial and Labor Relations, Cornell University, 1977), pp. 6–7.

Table 12–4 summarizes some important types and rules of evidence in labor arbitration.

Table 12–4 ▲ Major Types and Rules of Evidence in Arbitration

Direct Evidence:

Direct evidence is evidence that directly proves a point made by a party. An employee may have observed a co-worker driving a forklift into the side of a warehouse. The eyewitness account is a form of direct evidence.[67]

Circumstantial Evidence:

Circumstantial evidence is evidence that raises an inference with respect to an issue in a grievance. An employee might be disciplined for violating a no-smoking rule after he was discovered alone in a smoke-filled room. Although the employee was not observed smoking, he was (a) alone in the room, that (b) was filled with smoke, and (c) there were no other employees in the immediate area. Conditions (a), (b), and (c) create a web of circumstances that resulted in disciplinary action against the employee.[68]

Confessions:

Arbitrators weigh confessions according to the circumstances surrounding the confession. Little weight is given to signed confessions obtained through threats or deception.

Hearsay Evidence:

Hearsay is an oral or written statement made by a person who is not a direct witness to an event. For example, a witness testifies that she heard employee A claim that he saw employee B leave his work station without authorization. Courts tend to exclude hearsay evidence because: (1) there is no opportunity to cross-examine the person making the original statement; (2) there is a great risk of inaccuracy in the repetition of the story; (3) such evidence is often unreliable; and (4) it does not permit a person to face his or her accusers. Arbitrators may admit hearsay evidence, but limit the weight accorded to such evidence unless "it is corroborated by stronger or direct evidence."[69]

New Evidence:

New evidence is evidence not discussed before the arbitration hearing (nor even mentioned in the grievance procedure). There are two types of new evidence: (1) evidence that one side had in its possession during earlier stages of the grievance, but elected to suppress for tactical or "surprise" reasons; and (2) evidence that was not uncovered until after a grievance had been processed.[70] Arbitrators generally do not admit the first type of new evidence if the collective bargaining agreement requires full disclosure of all evidence prior to the arbitration hearing. However, arbitrators are divided on whether to admit the first type of evidence in the absence of a contract clause requiring full disclosure. Arbitrators generally admit the second type of new evidence if it is relevant to the case.

---

[67] Marvin Hill, Jr., and Anthony V. Sinicropi, *Evidence in Arbitration* (Washington, D.C.: The Bureau of National Affairs, Inc., 1980), p. 4.

[68] Fred Elkouri and Edna Asper Elkouri, *How Arbitration Works*, 4th ed. (Washington, D.C.: The Bureau of National Affairs, Inc., 1985), p. 327.

[69] Martin F. Scheinman, *Evidence and Proof in Arbitration* (Ithaca, New York: New York State School of Industrial and Labor Relations, Cornell University, 1977), p. 16.

[70] Martin F. Scheinman, *Evidence and Proof in Arbitration* (Ithaca, New York: New York State School of Industrial and Labor Relations, Cornell University, 1977), pp. 24–25.

Table 12-4 ▲ Major Types and Rules of Evidence in Arbitration (Cont.)

Best Evidence Rule:

The best evidence of the contents of a document is the document itself, rather than a copy of the original document or oral testimony regarding the contents of an original document. In a disciplinary case involving a tardy employee, an original time card indicating exactly when an employee clocked in at work is normally "better" evidence than a supervisor's recollection of when the employee reported for work.

Competency, Relevancy, and Materiality:

Competency refers to the ability of a witness to testify fully, accurately, and truthfully. Relevancy and materiality refer to whether evidence is both truthful and has a connection to the issues in the case. If employee A observes employee B writing racially offensive graffiti on a restroom wall, such an observation may be relevant if employee B is being disciplined for the racial harassment of a co-worker. However, the fact that employee B has had his driver's license revoked for reckless driving is not material (has no connection) with the issue of whether he is guilty of racially harassing a co-worker.

Parole Evidence Rule:

The parole evidence rule holds that when the parties agree that the written collective bargaining agreement is the entire final agreement between the parties, the arbitrator will not admit prior written or oral agreements as evidence if such agreements alter or contradict the final agreement. The rule permits the arbitrator to consider and interpret only the collective bargaining agreement that was in effect at the time of the grievance and ignores previous written or oral agreements.[71]

De minimus Rule:

Trifling or immaterial matters will not be taken into account when the action precipitating the grievance is of such slight departure from what is required by the agreement that there was no injury to the party filing the grievance. Suppose a union files a grievance because a supervisor performed bargaining unit work by picking up a part that had fallen from a conveyer belt. The arbitrator may apply the de minimus rule because the supervisor's action did not damage bargaining-unit employees' job security or their chances for earning overtime pay.

Offers of Settlement or Compromise:

Offers of settlement or compromise at an earlier stage of the grievance procedure are usually given little weight by the arbitrator.

Privileged Communication:

Arbitrators may allow witnesses to refuse testimony when there is a danger of revealing confidential information. Relationships such as attorney-client, physician-patient, husband-wife, and labor mediator-client are often subject to the protections associated with privileged communications.

Briefs and Transcripts

Union and management grievance representatives may desire to file pre- and post-hearing briefs and maintain a record of the arbitration proceedings. Pre-hearing briefs outline each party's theory of the case. Post-hearing briefs summarize contentions made during the arbitration hearing, pertinent contract clauses, critical

---

[71] Raymond L. Britton, *The Arbitration Guide* (Englewood Cliffs, New Jersey: Prentice-Hall, Inc., 1982), pp. 158–159.

facts and evidence, and previous arbitration awards and legal precedents that support the party's position. Pre- and post-hearing briefs help the parties focus their thoughts and prepare their respective cases; they also help the arbitrator obtain a summary of the case. Arbitrators generally disregard new evidence that is presented in the post-hearing brief, but was not mentioned during the arbitration hearing.[72]

Transcripts of the arbitration hearing may prove beneficial, especially when the grievance involves complex issues. Arbitrators can review transcripts after the hearing to refresh their memory on testimony, evidence, and other critical points. When transcripts are used, the parties jointly share the cost of using a court recorder in most instances. Tape recordings of the arbitration hearing may be used as a substitute for a written transcript.

The Arbitrator's Award and Decision

Once all testimony, evidence, and closing briefs have been presented, the arbitration hearing is closed. Most arbitrator's agree to submit a written award and opinion within a stipulated period of time (usually 30 days).[73] An *award* or *remedy* describes what the arbitrator is granting to a party or is requiring a party to perform.[74] For example, an arbitrator may order the reinstatement of a discharged employee with full back pay and benefits. The arbitrator may either stipulate the amount of back pay or leave it to the parties to determine the amount.[75] In the latter case, the arbitrator may retain jurisdiction of the case in the event that the parties cannot agree upon the amount owed to the grievant.

Arbitration remedies include awarding overtime pay to employees who were denied the opportunity to work after hours, ordering an employer to cease and desist from subcontracting repair work to an outside firm, expunging a written reprimand from an employee's personnel file, or requiring a reinstated employee to attend a drug rehabilitation program. Remedies must not be contrary to the language of the collective bargaining agreement. Most arbitration remedies are "make-whole," rather than punitive. That is, a reinstated employee may receive full back pay and benefits as restitution for the economic loss that occurred while the employee was suspended without pay pending arbitration. However, arbitrators avoid remedies designed to punish an errant employer or compensate the employee for more than his or her net economic loss.

The written *opinion* discusses the major points of contention made by the parties and explains the arbitrator's reasoning and logic for rendering the award. Written opinions not only shed light on the arbitrator's reasoning, but they also help to educate the parties and may eliminate similar grievances in the future.

---

[72] Most arbitrators will not accept post-hearing briefs from only one side unless both parties have been given the opportunity to file briefs and only one does so.
[73] The AAA requires an award within 30 days and the FMCS, within 60 days of the close of the record.
[74] Also see Marvin F. Hill, Jr. and Anthony V. Sinicropi, *Remedies in Arbitration* (Washington, D.C.: The Bureau of National Affairs, Inc., 1981).
[75] Arbitrators frequently reduce the amount of back pay to which an employee is entitled when (1) the employee worked during the time he or she was suspended, or (2) the employee failed to act promptly in obtaining other employment that was reasonably available between the time the employee was discharged and later reinstated, or (3) the arbitrator decides that the employee was partially at fault and is entitled to reinstatement, but not full back pay.

Written opinions, however, also open up potential avenues for additional grievances by a party who is not satisfied with the arbitration award.

▲ Common Errors in Arbitration

The American Arbitration Association has developed a list of potential problems and abuses of labor arbitration that are detrimental to harmonious labor relations. Grievance representatives involved in processing arbitration cases can reduce the time and expense associated with arbitration hearings by avoiding the pitfalls listed in Table 12-5.[76]

Table 12–5 ▲ Common Errors in Arbitration

1. Using arbitration and arbitration costs as harassing techniques.
2. Overemphasis of the grievance by the union or exaggeration of an employee's fault by management.
3. Reliance on a minimum of facts and a maximum of arguments.
4. Concealing essential facts; distorting the truth.
5. Holding back books, records, and other supporting documents.
6. Tying up proceedings with legal technicalities.
7. Introducing witnesses who have not been properly instructed on demeanor and on the place of their testimony in the entire case.
8. Withholding full cooperation from the arbitrator.
9. Disregarding the ordinary rules of courtesy and decorum.
10. Becoming involved in arguments with the other side. The time to try to convince the other party is before arbitration, during grievance processing. At the arbitration hearing, all efforts should be concentrated on convincing the arbitrator.

▲ Factors Affecting Arbitration Decisions and Awards

The arbitrator's decision and award hinges on several important factors. First and foremost, arbitrators must look to the language and spirit of the collective bargaining agreement. As creatures of the contract, arbitrators simultaneously derive their power from and are constrained by the collective bargaining agreement. In fashioning their decisions, arbitrators also examine and weigh evidence and testimony, customs and past practices within the firm and industry, and previous arbitration awards.[77] Each of these factors is discussed below.[78]

---

[76] American Arbitration Association, *Labor Arbitration Procedures and Techniques* (New York: American Arbitration Association, 1961), pp. 20–21. Cited in Frank Elkouri and Edna Asper Elkouri, *How Arbitration Works*, 4th ed. (Washington, D.C.: The Bureau of National Affairs, Inc., 1985), p. 293.

[77] Of course, arbitrators also rely on a good dose of common sense to sort through the evidence and testimony. Arbitrators must decide which version of the events makes the most sense or appears the most logical.

[78] In a study of the consistency and predictability of grievance arbitration awards, 177 arbitrators rendered awards on a series of hypothetical cases. There was considerable inconsistency on the part of arbitrators in making their awards. Furthermore, these inconsistencies did not appear to be related to the arbitrator's age, gender, educational degree, or experience. See Robert J. Thornton and Perry Zirkel, "The Consistency and Predictability of Grievance Arbitration Awards," *Industrial and Labor Relations Review* (January 1990), pp. 294–307.

Interpreting the Collective Bargaining Agreement

Arbitrators examine both the letter and spirit of the collective bargaining agreement in fashioning their decision on a grievance.[79] When the contract contains explicit language that permits resolution of a grievance, the arbitrator's decision is clear-cut.[80] In fact, grievances that are resolvable because of clear contract language should not reach arbitration unless the grievance machinery is malfunctioning.

Arbitration cases often involve ambiguous contract language. Some ambiguities are caused by unclear language that permits conflicting interpretations by union and management grievance representatives. Ambiguities of this nature may be the result of contract language that was hurriedly and poorly drafted during the latter stages of negotiations, misunderstandings about the meaning of a contract clause, or enlightened self-interest by those who read and interpret the contract to suit their own needs. Contract language can also be unclear and ambiguous when different clauses within the collective bargaining agreement conflict or contradict each other.

When evaluating ambiguous contract language, an arbitrator may inquire into the intent of the parties when the contract was negotiated. If records of the contract negotiations are available, the arbitrator may examine these for insight into the meaning of unclear language. Negotiation bulletins that are used to keep union members updated during contract talks may also help clarify the meaning of contract language. Arbitrators often consider factors such as company manuals and handbooks, custom and past practices established by union and management officials, prior grievance settlements, and any other clues that are available to ascertain the intent of the parties when they drafted the contract language.

In resolving a grievance, arbitrators must give meaning to unclear contract language without, in effect, "rewriting" the contract provision in question. Arbitrators generally try to avoid reading contract clauses in isolation; rather, they attempt to read individual clauses in the context of the entire agreement. Specific contract language generally supersedes general contract language. If a contract clause contains misspelled or misused words, the arbitrator will not provide a literal interpretation that could lead to harsh, absurd, or nonsensical results.[81] Furthermore, arbitrators give words their ordinary and popularly-accepted meanings. Words such as *union shop* or *work day* can have different meanings to different parties. For example, the term *union shop* might refer to a union shop security clause, which requires newly hired bargaining unit employees to join the union within 30 days,

---

[79] See Frank Elkouri and Edna Asper Elkouri, *How Arbitration Works*, 4th ed. (Washington, D.C.: The Bureau of National Affairs, Inc., 1985), pp. 342–365.

[80] A contract clause is clear when the arbitrator can read and understand it without clarification by another person or without reference to other documents.

[81] Suppose a contract clause requires a medical doctor's (M.D.) statement documenting the illness of an employee who takes three or more days of sick leave. An arbitrator would not likely uphold the discharge of an employee who was absent because he had wisdom teeth removed and took four days sick leave on the advice of an oral surgeon (dentist) who provided a written statement to the employer. The arbitrator would probably rule that a written statement from a dentist carried the same weight as a statement from a medical doctor. To do otherwise would appear nonsensical. See *Consolidated Coal Co.*, 83 LA 1158 (1984), cited in Marlin M. Volz and Edward P. Goggin, eds., *How Arbitration Works* (Washington, D.C.: The Bureau of National Affairs, Inc., 1988), p. 71. 1985–87 Supplement to Frank Elkouri and Edna Asper Elkouri, *How Arbitration Works*, 4th ed. (Washington, D.C.: The Bureau of National Affairs, Inc., 1985).

or the term may simply refer to a part of the plant that is unionized. Likewise, the term *work day* may mean an eight-hour, one-shift day in some plants, and a 24-hour, three-shift day in other plants.[82]

Sifting through the Evidence

Arbitrators have a great deal of discretion in evaluating and weighing evidence.[83] The major types of evidence, evidentiary rules, and factors used in weighing evidence are presented in Table 12–3. In fashioning a decision, arbitrators must distinguish between evidence that is relevant and material from that which should be discounted or ignored. Arbitrators may allow seemingly unimportant evidence to be admitted during the hearing for two reasons. First, some "irrelevant" testimony may give the arbitrator a better understanding of the case and, second, the relevance of evidence is not always immediately discernible until other aspects of the case become known.

The various pieces of evidence have to be examined collectively, especially when circumstantial evidence is being used to establish a theory of the case. Arbitrators base their decisions on a "preponderance of the evidence." As noted in Chapter 11, the quantum of proof is greater for serious grievances, such as discharge cases, than for minor grievances. In rendering an award, arbitrators must be careful about drawing inferences based on inadequate evidence. Although arbitrators may engage in a certain amount of speculation in deciding on a course of action in a grievance, their award must be grounded primarily in case facts. In a case study of the late, preeminent arbitrator Saul Wallen, it was noted:

> There is, however, an inherent difficulty in attempting to quantify and compare such subjective judgments or standards. While some arbitrators might equate proof by a preponderance of the evidence with probability, others would declare that this standard means "more than quantitative probability, and requires at least sufficient evidence to remove the matter from the realm of conjecture." Wallen himself defined this standard. . . to be "sufficient to persuade one to moral certainty," and further stated that "this is something beyond mere suspicion—even strong suspicion. It must rest on a modicum of tangible evidence." He declared. . . that "the possibility of other courses must be so remote as to strain the credulity of a reasonable man."[84]

Arbitrators may draw adverse inferences from a party's failure or refusal to produce important evidence. For example, an arbitrator may rule in favor of a grievant fired for absenteeism and tardiness if the company refuses to submit employee attendance records as evidence during the hearing. According to arbitrator Wallen:

> An arbitrator has no right to compel the production of documents by either side. He may, however, give such weight as he deems appropriate to the failure

---

[82] Also see Sheri L. Bocher, "Contract Interpretation in Arbitration," *Employment Relations Today* (Summer 1987), p. 181; and Clyde Scott and Trevor Bain, "How Arbitrators Interpret Ambiguous Contract Language," *Personnel* (August 1987), p. 10.
[83] See Frank Elkouri and Edna Asper Elkouri, *How Arbitration Works*, 4th ed. (Washington, D.C.: The Bureau of National Affairs, Inc., 1985), pp. 296–341.
[84] Brook I. Landis, *Value Judgments in Arbitration: A Case Study of Saul Wallen* (Ithaca, New York: New York State School of Industrial and Labor Relations, Cornell University, 1977), p. 70.

of a party to produce documents on demand. The degree of weight to be attached to such failure will depend upon the relevancy of the documents requested to the issues at hand. If the information withheld appears to be strongly pertinent, the withholding of it may be vital in the making of a decision. If it is of doubtful relevancy, and merely represents an attempt by one party to rove through the files of another on the mere chance that its position may be generally strengthened thereby, then the failure to produce such records should be disregarded.[85]

A number of arbitration cases involve determining an employee's fitness either to continue working or to return to work after a medical disability. Arbitrators who have little or no medical expertise may have difficulty evaluating medical evidence. Companies that refuse to allow employees with health problems to work are often fearful that the employee will pose a safety hazard, become reinjured on the job, or be unable to perform in an efficient manner. Employees with heart conditions, back problems, diabetes, epilepsy, visual and hearing impairments, and mental problems often pose dilemmas for arbitrators who must sift through complex and sometimes conflicting medical evidence.

An analysis of arbitration decisions involving handicapped and medically impaired employees reveals several points. First, in the absence of contract language to the contrary, most arbitrators will abide by the employer's recommendation as to whether an employee should be allowed to work. Arbitrators generally believe that the employer has the most complete understanding of an employee's medical impairment and working conditions and is therefore best qualified to determine a grievant's fitness to work. For this reason, arbitrators often give the company physician's opinion greater weight than the employee's personal physician. Second, the results of recent physical examinations carry greater weight than an examination that is somewhat dated. Third, the results of an extensive medical examination carry greater weight in the eyes of most arbitrators than a superficial, cursory examination. Fourth, the medical opinion of a specialist (e.g., a cardiologist or psychiatrist) is given greater consideration by the arbitrator than that of a general practitioner. Finally, arbitrators will more likely give deference to medical evaluations that are geared to an employee's job and work environment.[86]

Evaluating the Testimony of Witnesses

Arbitrators must evaluate the credibility of witnesses and the accuracy of their testimony. Determining whether a witness is telling the truth is a subjective and often difficult process. Some arbitrators examine the witness's demeanor (gestures, voice, and attitude) and the "ring of truth" associated with the testimony. Arbitrators often pay special attention to the witness's ability to recall facts; a "selective" ability to recall certain events may be construed as dishonesty on the part of the witness. Consideration is given to the witness's ability to speak with clarity. Arbitrators must also be aware of potential biases that may be harbored by a witness. A supervisor testifying as an eyewitness in a disciplinary case may give biased testimony that damages a grievant's case in order to protect a fellow supervisor. The perceived

---

[85] *Curtis-Wright Corporation* (1955). Cited in Brook I. Landis, *Value Judgments in Arbitration: A Case Study of Saul Wallen* (Ithaca, New York: New York State School of Industrial and Labor Relations, 1977), p. 71.
[86] See Terry L. Leap, *Health and Job Retention* (Ithaca, New York: ILR Press, Cornell University, 1984).

accuracy of the person's testimony and whether the witness has made contradictory statements also have an important bearing on how the arbitrator weighs the testimony.[87] However, according to attorney and arbitrator Edgar A. Jones, Jr., even the most experienced arbitrators may find it difficult to determine whether a witness is telling the truth:

> The core problem of credibility is that, no matter how insistent may be the conventional wisdom about a trier observing demeanor, it is simply impossible to tell by observation if someone is lying under oath. You cannot tell by looking at and listening to the person. A trial judge in Chicago once compiled a list of tests to see if a witness is telling the truth: does he perspire; lick his lips; fidget in his seat; is he shifty-eyed? From my experience as an arbitrator I can tell you that shifty-eyed people often tell the truth, while the most honest-looking people will lead you by the nose down the primrose path. It is going to happen to *you*, too. The only way you can hope to cope with this is by careful attention to circumstantial evidence: the old saw that direct evidence is the best evidence is not necessarily true. The best evidence is that which snares the truth in a web of circumstance.
>
> In one particular case early in my career, a very earnest, calm young man got on the stand and said that he had been sick in bed, unable to phone in, so he should not be viewed as a voluntary quit. Then the company called a rebuttal witness, a retired policeman who had investigated and discovered that the witness was working for another employer at the time. He was collecting sick pay while working at another job. Of course, all the time the ex-officer is testifying, I am watching the grievant like a hawk. If I had to pick out a credible witness, I'm thinking, it would have to be *this* character! Then by golly he went back on the witness chair and convinced me again! He had an explanation, an improbable one, true, but what delivery! I really believed him! Such a demeanor! But that good old arbitral nerve twitched a bit even so (I actually felt embarrassed at my instinctive instant of cynicism!). So I said to the union representative, "Well, it's about 4:30 now. I suggest we recess for today and you go check out the story." I really wanted this guy to win! I had acquired a vested interest in him. I believed him and then believed him again. A few days later, the union called to tell me they were withdrawing the grievance. The grievant had been lying. He had conned me twice! So be careful. Don't think you can always tell who is telling the truth.[88]

Considering the Role of Custom and Past Practice

As part of the decision-making process, arbitrators may be required to examine the role of custom and past practice.[89] Custom and past practice affects every type of human activity, including labor-management relations. The typical workplace is

---

[87] See John J. Flagler, "Modern Shamanism and Other Folderol—The Search for Certainty," in Walter J. Gershenfeld, ed., *Arbitration 1986: Current and Expanding Roles, Proceedings of the Thirty-Ninth Annual Meeting National Academy of Arbitrators* (Washington, D.C.: The Bureau of National Affairs, Inc., 1987), pp. 194–204.
[88] Edgar A. Jones, Jr., "Selected Problems of Procedure and Evidence," in Arnold M. Zack, ed., *Arbitration in Practice* (Ithaca, New York: ILR Press, Cornell University, 1984), pp. 62–63. Reprinted with permission.
[89] See Frank Elkouri and Edna Asper Elkouri, *How Arbitration Works*, 4th ed. (Washington, D.C.: The Bureau of National Affairs, Inc., 1985), pp. 437–456.

replete with customs and understandings between employees and management. For example, the company may allow employees to listen to personal radios in work areas. Supervisors may allow office and clerical employees to take an extra break to celebrate the birthday of a co-worker. Management may decide to pay the expenses of rehabilitating an employee with drug problems, even when not required to do so under the collective bargaining agreement. According to U.S. Supreme Court Justice Douglas, "the labor arbitrator's source of law is not confined to express provisions of the contract, as the industrial common law—past practices of the industry and shop—is equally a part of the collective bargaining agreement although not expressed in it."[90]

In resolving a dispute involving a custom or past practice, the arbitrator must first determine whether a past practice actually exists. A past practice must generally meet the following criteria: (1) clarity and consistency—is the practice well-defined and understandable? (2) longevity and repetition—has the practice occurred repeatedly over a period of time?, and (3) acceptability—have the parties expressly or through implication condoned the practice?[91] For example, an employer who has provided a ham or turkey to plant employees at Christmas for the past ten years has established a past practice under the above criteria. The practice is well-defined, has been done every Christmas for the past decade, and is in all likelihood accepted and appreciated by the employees. Suppose, however, that management at a Racine, Wisconsin plant allowed employees to bring televisions to work when the Milwaukee Brewers were playing in the 1982 World Series. (To date, the Brewers have played in the Series only once, losing to the St. Louis Cardinals in seven games.) Now suppose the Milwaukee Bucks played in the National Basketball Association championship play-off series and management refused to allow the employees to view the games during work hours. Could the union demonstrate that the television privilege was an established past practice? It is doubtful that a past practice could be established based on a management policy that was implemented only once.

Arbitrators generally define custom and past practice as narrowly as possible. For example, a practice that has been established on a night shift does not necessarily apply to employees working the day shift. In a multi-plant bargaining unit, a custom or practice in a Pennsylvania plant may not be applicable to a plant in Missouri, even though both plants are covered under the same collective bargaining agreement.

When hearing grievances that have been precipitated by a dispute over a custom or past practice, arbitrators must distinguish between the right of management to make unilateral decisions and the right of employees to benefit from established practices. Some arbitrators will not challenge minor changes in customs or practices unless management is prohibited by the collective bargaining agreement from making such changes. For example, if management paints the walls in a work area green (when they were previously blue) and employees file a grievance, an arbitrator will

---

[90] *United Steelworkers of America v. Warrior & Gulf Navigation Co.*, 363 U.S. 574 (1960). Cited in Richard Mittenthal, "Past Practice and the Administration of Collective Bargaining Agreements," in Arnold M. Zack, ed., *Arbitration in Practice* (Ithaca, New York: ILR Press, Cornell University, 1984), pp. 181–182.
[91] Richard Mittenthal, "Past Practice and the Administration of Collective Bargaining Agreements," in Arnold M. Zack, ed., *Arbitration in Practice* (Ithaca, New York: ILR Press, Cornell University, 1984), pp. 183–184.

likely regard such a change as minor and uphold the company's right to alter the paint scheme.

Another approach to analyzing the legitimacy of changing customs and past practices is to distinguish between practices that are of benefit to employees versus those that are purely the prerogative of management. A ham or turkey at Christmas is of obvious benefit to employees, whereas the color of the walls does not economically benefit employees. Similarly, some arbitrators also rule that customs and past practices affecting working conditions are enforceable, but those that are simply gratuities (such as the Christmas ham or turkey) are subject to unilateral change by management (in the absence of contract language to the contrary). Finally, arbitrators may rule that a past practice mutually agreed upon by employees and management is enforceable, whereas those instituted unilaterally by management are also subject to unilateral revocation by the company. The problem with the latter approach is determining whether a mutual agreement must be explicit or implicit.

Customs and past practices serve several functions in contract administration.[92] First, customs and past practices may clarify ambiguous contract language. Past practice may define the term *dinner* to mean the evening meal. Thus, a contract provision that provides the evening meal at company expense for employees working overtime may not apply to paying for breakfast when employees perform early overtime work by reporting at 5 A.M. Second, customs and past practices may implement general contract language. If a company has previously terminated several employees for sleeping on the job (even when safety and productivity were not compromised), a past practice has been established that will help the arbitrator define the contract phrase "discharge for just cause" in subsequent grievances. Third, customs and past practices may modify or amend apparently unambiguous language. Consider the following contract clause:

> Where skill and physical capacity are substantially equal, seniority shall govern in the following situations only: promotions, downgrading, layoffs, and transfers.[93]

Did the parties intend to exclude overtime assignments from the above clause? If not, should the past practice of awarding overtime based primarily on seniority modify a clear contract provision such as the one above? Finally, customs and past practices may exist as a separate, enforceable condition of employment. Some collective bargaining agreements allow unwritten practices to remain in effect for the life of the contract. A company may have allowed employees to take a day of paid leave to attend the funeral of a family member or close friend (although the contract is silent on the matter of paid funeral leave). If the company tries to revoke this practice during the life of the collective bargaining agreement, an arbitrator may rule that the practice must remain in effect until the contract expires. Arbitrators

---

[92] Based on Richard Mittenthal, "Past Practice and the Administration of Collective Bargaining Agreements," in Arnold M. Zack, ed., *Arbitration in Practice* (Ithaca, New York: ILR Press, Cornell University, 1984), pp. 187–196.

[93] Richard Mittenthal, "Past Practice and the Administration of Collective Bargaining Agreements," in Arnold M. Zack, ed., *Arbitration in Practice* (Ithaca, New York: ILR Press, Cornell University, 1984), p. 191.

have also held that established practices that were in existence when the agreement was negotiated (and that were not discussed during negotiations) must be continued for the life of the agreement.

Customs and past practices may be altered or eliminated when the collective bargaining agreement is renegotiated or amended. A custom or past practice may be revoked when new conditions arise that render the old practice meaningless or obsolete. For example, the past practice of allowing truck drivers operating vehicles without air conditioning to stop and take a break every two hours during the summer months may no longer be legitimate if new, air conditioned trucks are purchased. Likewise, the practice of using a five-person crew may no longer be necessary to operate a set of machines if new equipment is installed and can be operated by only two workers.[94]

Incorporating External Law into Arbitration Decisions

A controversial issue among arbitrators is the extent to which they should incorporate relevant law into their decisions.[95] Union and management negotiators should be expected to draft collective bargaining agreements whose provisions do not conflict with state and federal laws. However, arbitrators must hear grievances that not only violate the terms of the collective bargaining agreement, but also run afoul of the law. Table 12-6 summarizes some of the federal laws that are likely to be violated.

Many states have enacted laws that are often more comprehensive than the federal laws listed in Table 12-6. Arbitrators may hear off-duty misconduct cases in which a grievant has allegedly violated state or municipal criminal codes. Some arbitration cases also involve issues of contract law.

Arbitrators differ regarding their willingness to incorporate external law into their decisions. There are three schools of thought on the application of external law to arbitration decisions:[96]

1. The *isolationist approach*: the arbitrator makes his or her decision strictly on contract provisions, even when such provisions contradict the law. Suppose the arbitrator discovers that the employer followed the collective bargaining agreement and violated the Fair Labor Standard Act's (FLSA) prohibition of allowing persons under the age of 18 to work at a hazardous job. Under the isolationist approach, the arbitrator would ignore the law and follow the contract.
2. The *totality approach*: the arbitrator will ignore contract provisions that contradict state or federal law and apply substantive terms of the law in making a decision. In the above example, the arbitrator would rule that an employee

---

[94] There are instances in which the union insists on maintaining the same crew size or work methods, even in the face of technological change. See the discussion of featherbedding in Chapter 3.
[95] See Frank Elkouri and Edna Asper Elkouri, *How Arbitration Works*, 4th ed. (Washington, D.C.: The Bureau of National Affairs, Inc., 1985), pp. 366–413.
[96] Raymond L. Britton, *The Arbitration Guide* (Englewood Cliffs, New Jersey: Prentice-Hall, Inc., 1982), pp. 46–47.

Table 12–6 ▲ Major Federal Laws Affecting Arbitration Decisions

Equal Employment Opportunity Laws (see Chapter 16)

Title VII of the 1964 Civil Rights Act
Age Discrimination in Employment Act of 1967
Immigration Reform and Control Act of 1986
Rehabilitation Act of 1973
Vietnam Era Veterans Readjustment Act
Equal Pay Act
Federal Executive Orders Mandating Affirmative Action

Compensation and Employee Benefit Laws (see Chapter 13)

Fair Labor Standards Act
Workers Compensation Laws
Federal Laws Regulating Government Contractors
Social Security Act (1935)
Unemployment Compensation Laws
Consumer Credit Protection Act
Federal/State Child Support Enforcement Program (1975), Child Support Amendments of 1984
Employee Retirement Income Security Act (1974)
Health Maintenance Act (1973)
Tax Reform Act (1986)
Consolidated Omnibus Budget Reconciliation Act of 1985 (COBRA)

Health and Safety Laws

Occupational Safety and Health Act (1970)

Labor-Management Relations Laws (see Chapter 3)

Norris-LaGuardia Act (1932)
Wagner Act (1935)
Taft-Hartley Act (1947)
Landrum-Griffin Act (1959)

---

under the age of 18 must be removed from the hazardous job because the practice violates federal law (FLSA).

3. The *middle-of-the-road approach*: the arbitrator will apply relevant external law only when the contract provisions are sufficiently general or unclear so as to allow the application of external law in making a decision. Thus, the external law becomes another factor to be considered in interpreting ambiguous contract language.

Under the isolationist approach, the arbitrator may give the appearance of supporting parties who break the law. Arbitrators adhering to the isolationist approach also run the risk of having their decisions overturned in court. Union and management grievance representatives may stipulate, either in the collective bargaining agreement or prior to arbitration in the submission agreement, that the arbitrator may incorporate external law into the decision. Under the totality and middle-of-the road approaches, however, the arbitrator may be accused of usurping the power of state and federal courts and administrative agencies (e.g., the Equal

Employment Opportunity Commission or the Occupational Safety and Health Administration).[97] There is also the question regarding the wisdom of allowing arbitrators who are not attorneys to interpret external law.[98] If the arbitrator applies external law, it is important that the decision not exceed the scope and authority of the contract.

Assessing the Precedent Value of Arbitration Awards

Judges in the state and federal judicial system often follow precedents established in earlier cases having similar facts and circumstances. Arbitrators may also examine arbitration awards made by others, but these awards are not given as much weight as the courts are likely to give prior judicial decisions. Because of variations in contract language, an arbitrator hearing two factually similar grievances may make two totally different decisions *if the grievances are arbitrated under two different contracts.*

Prior arbitration awards serve several functions. First, the parties to the collective bargaining agreement can use previous awards as guidelines that may help them resolve a similar grievance in the future without going to arbitration. Second, arbitration awards fashion the "industrial law of the shop" that is cited in federal court decisions. Third, prior awards provide arbitrators with an indication of what other arbitrators have done under similar circumstances. Even when arbitrators do not use prior awards as precedents, they provide insight and wisdom for arbitrators faced with difficult decisions. Fourth, published arbitration awards are used to help the parties select ad hoc arbitrators. Arbitrator selection, in many cases, is based upon the arbitrator's industrial expertise, reputation for fairness, and decision-making tendencies. Published arbitration awards also make arbitrators more accountable for their decisions and, it is hoped, more responsible in executing their duties. Finally, arbitrators frequently cite other arbitration decisions in written case awards to support the reasoning and logic behind their decisions. By including relevant case citations in an award, the parties are more likely to be convinced that the arbitrator's decision is well-reasoned and sound.[99]

There are two types of case precedent in arbitration: authoritative and persuasive.[100] *Authoritative precedents* carry the greatest weight because the parties may agree in the collective bargaining agreement to allow previous cases to control similar cases in the future. Permanent arbitrators may also hold that their earlier decisions (involving similar facts over the same contract language) are authoritative precedents. Ad hoc arbitrators may also give authoritative weight to decisions made by other arbitrators in cases involving similar circumstances and under the same collective bargaining agreement.

---

[97] As noted earlier in this chapter, grievances involving civil rights issues that have been heard by an arbitrator may be relitigated by the EEOC or courts.
[98] As noted earlier in this chapter, the NLRB will defer grievances involving unfair labor practice charges to arbitrators.
[99] See Frank Elkouri and Edna Asper Elkouri, *How Arbitration Works*, 4th ed. (Washington, D.C.: The Bureau of National Affairs, Inc., 1985), pp. 414–436.
[100] Frank Elkouri and Edna Asper Elkouri, *How Arbitration Works*, 4th ed. (Washington, D.C.: The Bureau of National Affairs, Inc., 1985), pp. 421–433.

Persuasive precedents are used primarily by arbitrators to garner wisdom from previous awards. The actual influence of a prior award may range from very significant to completely insignificant, depending on the applicability of the award to the present case, its logic and reasoning, and the professional reputation of the arbitrator rendering the previous award.[101]

▲ Professional and Ethical Standards for Arbitrators

As noted earlier in this chapter, arbitrators enjoy an excellent reputation for professional and ethical behavior. Arbitrators must meet specific professional requirements to be included on the lists of the American Arbitration Association (AAA) and the Federal Mediation and Conciliation Service (FMCS). In addition, arbitrators admitted to the National Academy of Arbitrators are among the most active and highly regarded in the country.[102] The AAA, FMCS, and National Academy of Arbitrators have established a *Code of Professional Responsibility* that covers arbitrator qualifications, responsibilities, and conduct associated with arbitration hearings. Appendix A contains the full text of the *Code of Professional Responsibility*.

▲ Summary and Conclusions

This chapter illustrates the manner in which labor arbitration is used to resolve rights disputes. If collective bargaining agreements were written in clear, unambiguous language and grievance procedures allowed the resolution of contractual disputes at the earliest possible stage, then there would be little need for labor arbitrators. Many grievances arise between parties who are competent and conscientious; the grievants simply have honest differences of opinion as to how the collective bargaining agreement should be interpreted regarding a compensation, workplace, or disciplinary issue. However, grievances may also involve complex issues that require an expert analysis of contract language, evidence, testimony, external law, and previous arbitration awards.

The profession of labor arbitration has risen in prominence since World War II because arbitrators have been able to meet the challenges posed by ever-changing workplace issues. The legal decisions discussed in this chapter have provided arbitrators with a great deal of power to resolve disputes, free from intervention by the state and federal courts. Nearly all grievance procedures use binding arbitration as the final step, an indication that arbitrators have earned the respect of union and

---

[101] Published arbitration awards are the primary means of examining the awards of other arbitrators. The Bureau of National Affairs, Inc., *Labor Arbitration Reports*, provides a compilation of published arbitration decisions that are thoroughly indexed by the type of dispute and the issues raised in the arbitration case.

[102] For an interesting commentary on the quality and significance of labor arbitration, see National Academy of Arbitrators, Special Committee on Professionalism, "Arbitration Promise and Performance" (New Orleans: National Academy of Arbitrators, 40th Annual Meeting, May 1987). Reprinted in The Bureau of National Affairs, Inc., *Collective Bargaining Negotiations & Contracts* (Washington, D.C.: The Bureau of National Affairs, Inc., July 16, 1987), section 17.

management representatives through the professional and ethical ways in which they have conducted hearings and rendered awards.

This chapter, along with Chapter 11, provides a foundation for illustrating how contracts are administered and grievances resolved. Chapters 13 through 16 cover various terms and conditions of collective bargaining agreements. Sample cases are presented at the end of these chapters to illustrate further some of the issues that are resolved through grievance procedures and arbitration.

▲ Discussion Questions and Exercises

1. What advantages does labor arbitration enjoy over the state and federal courts insofar as resolving rights disputes is concerned?
2. Unlike most professions, the field of labor arbitration does not have rigorous educational requirements and formal licensing standards. Explain why the profession of labor arbitration has nonetheless enjoyed such wide respect among labor and management practitioners and the federal courts.
3. Summarize the criteria used to select arbitrators. Most arbitrators are legally trained. In your opinion, does this background aid or handicap the arbitration process?
4. A dispute over an arbitration case between a local truck drivers' union and Synergy Gas Corporation of Farmingdale, New York, has dragged on for over eight years. The employer refused to abide by the arbitrator's award and reinstate a terminated driver (with back pay). When the union pressed the AAA to have the arbitrator's award enforced, a second arbitrator heard the case and also ruled in favor of the union and employee. Synergy appealed and claimed that the second arbitrator had exceeded his authority under the contract. Both a federal district court and a U.S. Court of Appeals held for the union and employee. As a result, Synergy has appealed to the U.S. Supreme Court. What had originally amounted to an arbitration award of "a few thousand dollars" ballooned into a claim of over $100,000. The grievant was never reinstated to his job and ultimately retired on Social Security.[103]
    a. What potential impact could the U.S. Supreme Court's ruling have on the institution of labor arbitration? Discuss.
    b. If the grievant and union ultimately win this case, to what damages are they entitled?
    c. What might have motivated Synergy's management to allow a relatively small grievance to become such a major issue?
5. An arbitrator is a "creature of the contract" in that he or she must fashion an arbitration award in accordance with the terms of the collective bargaining agreement. What advantages and disadvantages does the "creature of the contract" posture have on labor arbitration and the "law of the shop"?
6. Assume that the union business agent is inexperienced or unprepared when

[103] Selwyn Feinstein, "Eight-Year Arbitration Dispute Shows How Process Can Be Messy," *The Wall Street Journal* (November 21, 1988), p. B9.

appearing at an arbitration hearing on behalf of a grievant who was fired after an off-duty fight with a supervisor at a local bar. The labor arbitrator evaluates the evidence and testimony given and rules in favor of the employer. Later it is discovered that the supervisor provoked the fight with scurrilous remarks about the virtue of the grievant's wife. It is also discovered that the local union president was aware of the supervisor's remarks to the grievant *before* the case came to arbitration. Can the arbitrator's decision be reversed? Why or why not?

Appendix: Code of Professional Responsibility for Arbitrators of Labor–Management Disputes of the National Academy of Arbitrators, the American Arbitration Association, and the Federal Mediation and Conciliation Service

PREAMBLE

Background

Voluntary arbitration rests upon the mutual desire of management and labor in each collective bargaining relationship to develop procedures for dispute settlement which meet their own particular needs and obligations. No two voluntary systems, therefore, are likely to be identical in practice. Words used to describe arbitrators (Arbitrator, Umpire, Impartial Chairman, Chairman of Arbitration Board, etc.) may suggest typical approaches but actual differences within any general type of arrangement may be as great as distinctions often made among the several types.

Some arbitration and related procedures, however, are not the product of voluntary agreement. These procedures, primarily but not exclusively applicable in the public sector, sometimes utilize other third party titles (Fact Finder, Impasse Panel, Board of Inquiry, etc.). These procedures range all the way from arbitration prescribed by statute to arrangements substantially indistinguishable from voluntary procedures.

The standards of professional responsibility set forth in this Code are designed to guide the impartial third party serving in these diverse labor–management relationships.

Scope of Code

This code is a privately developed set of standards of professional behavior. It applies to voluntary arbitration of labor-management grievance disputes and of disputes concerning new or revised contract terms. Both "ad hoc" and "permanent" varieties of voluntary arbitration, private and public sector, are included. To the extent relevant in any specific case, it also applies to advisory arbitration, impasse resolution panels, arbitration prescribed by statutes, fact-finding, and other special procedures.

The word "arbitrator," as used hereinafter in the Code, is intended to apply to any impartial person, irrespective of specific title, who serves in a labor-management dispute procedure in which there is conferred authority to decide issues or to make formal recommendations.

The Code is not designed to apply to mediation or conciliation, as distinguished from arbitration, nor to other procedures in which the third party is not authorized in advance to make decisions or recommendations. It does not apply to partisan representatives on tripartite boards. It does not apply to commercial arbitration or to other uses of arbitration outside the labor-management dispute area.

Format of Code

Bold Face type, sometimes including explanatory material, is used to set forth general principles. *Italics* are used for amplification of general principles. Ordinary type is used primarily for illustrative or explanatory comment.

Application of Code

Faithful adherence by an arbitrator to this Code is basic to professional responsibility.

The National Academy of Arbitrators will expect its members to be governed in their professional conduct by this Code and stands ready, through its Committee on Ethics and Grievances, to advise its members as to the Code's interpretation. The American Arbitration Association and the Federal Mediation and Conciliation Service will apply the Code to the arbitrators on their rosters in cases handled under their respective appointment or referral procedures. Other arbitrators and administrative agencies may, of course, voluntarily adopt the Code and be governed by it.

In interpreting the Code and applying it to charges of professional misconduct, under existing or revised procedures of the National Academy of Arbitrators and of the administrative agencies, it should be recognized that while some of its standards express ethical principles basic to the arbitration profession, others rest less on ethics than on considerations of good practice. Experience has shown the difficulty of drawing rigid lines of distinction between ethics and good practice and this Code does not attempt to do so. Rather, it leaves the gravity of alleged misconduct and the extent to which ethical standards have been violated to be assessed in the light of the facts and circumstances of each particular case.

1. ARBITRATOR'S QUALIFICATIONS AND RESPONSIBILITIES TO THE PROFESSION

A. General Qualifications

1. Essential personal qualifications of an arbitrator include honesty, integrity, impartiality and general competence in labor relations matters.

An arbitrator must demonstrate ability to exercise these personal qualities faithfully and with good judgment, both in procedural matters and in substantive decisions.

a. Selection by mutual agreement of the parties or direct designation by an administrative agency are the effective methods of appraisal of this combination of an individual's potential and performance, rather than the fact of placement on a roster of an administrative agency or membership in a professional association of arbitrators.

2. An arbitrator must be as ready to rule for one party as for the other on each issue, either in a single case or in a group of cases. Compromise by an arbitrator for the sake of attempting to achieve personal acceptability is unprofessional.

B. Qualifications for Special Cases

1. An arbitrator must decline appointment, withdraw, or request technical assistance when he or she decides that a case is beyond his or her competence.

a. An arbitrator may be qualified generally but not for specialized assignments. Some types of incentive, work standard, job evaluation, welfare program, pension, or insurance cases may require specialized knowledge, experience or competence. Arbitration of contract terms also may require distinctive background and experience.

b. Effective appraisal by an administrative agency or by an arbitrator of the need for special qualifications requires that both parties make known the special nature of the case prior to appointment of the arbitrator.

C. Responsibilities to the Profession

1. An arbitrator must uphold the dignity and integrity of the office and endeavor to provide effective service to the parties.

a. To this end, an arbitrator should keep current with principles, practices and developments that are relevant to his or her own field of arbitration practice.

2. An experienced arbitrator should cooperate in the training of new arbitrators.

3. An arbitrator must not advertise or solicit arbitration assignments.

a. It is a matter of personal preference whether an arbitrator includes "Labor Arbitrator" or similar notation on letterheads, cards, or announcements. *It* is inappropriate, however, to include memberships or offices held in professional societies or listings on rosters of administrative agencies.

b. *Information provided for published biographical sketches, as well as that supplied to administrative agencies, must be accurate.* Such information may include membership in professional organizations (including reference to significant offices held), and listings on rosters of administrative agencies.

2. RESPONSIBILITIES TO THE PARTIES

A. Recognition of Diversity in Arbitration Arrangements

1. An arbitrator should conscientiously endeavor to understand and observe, to the extent consistent with professional responsibility, the significant principles governing each arbitration system in which he or she serves.

a. Recognition of special features of a particular arbitration arrangement can be essential with respect to procedural matters and may influence other aspects of the arbitration process.

2. Such understanding does not relieve an arbitrator from a corollary responsibility to seek to discern and refuse to lend approval or consent to any collusive attempt by the parties to use arbitration for an improper purpose.

B. Required Disclosures

1. Before accepting an appointment, an arbitrator must disclose directly or through the administrative agency involved, any current or past managerial, representational, or consultative relationship with any company or union involved in a proceeding in which he or she is being considered for appointment or has been tentatively designated to serve. Disclosure must also be made of any pertinent pecuniary interest.

a. The duty to disclose includes membership on a Board of Directors, full-time or part-time service as a representative or advocate, consultation work for a fee, current stock or bond ownership (other than mutual fund shares or appropriate trust arrangements) or any other pertinent form of managerial, financial or immediate family interest in the company or union involved.

2. When an arbitrator is serving concurrently as an advocate for or representative of other companies or unions in labor relations matters, or had done so in recent years, he or she must disclose such activities before accepting appointment as an arbitrator.

An arbitrator must disclose such activities to an administrative agency if he or she is on that agency's active roster or seeks placement on a roster. Such disclosure then satisfies this requirement for cases handled under that agency's referral.

a. It is not necessary to disclose names of clients or other specific details. It is necessary to indicate the general nature of the labor relations advocacy or representational work involved, whether for companies or unions or both, and a reasonable approximation of the extent of such activity.

b. *An arbitrator on an administrative agency's roster has a continuing obligation to notify the agency of any significant changes pertinent to this requirement.*

c. When an administrative agency is not involved, an arbitrator must make such disclosure directly unless he or she is certain that both parties to the case are fully aware of such activities.

3. An arbitrator must not permit personal relationships to affect decision-making.

Prior to acceptance of an appointment, an arbitrator must disclose to the parties or to the administrative agency involved any close personal relationship or other circumstance, in addition to those specifically mentioned earlier in this section, which might reasonably raise a question as to the arbitrator's impartiality.

a. Arbitrators establish personal relationships with many company and union representatives, with fellow arbitrators, and with fellow members of various professional associations. There should be no attempt to be secretive about such friendships or acquaintances but disclosure is not necessary unless some feature of a particular relationship might reasonably appear to impair impartiality.

4. If the circumstances requiring disclosure are not known to the arbitrator prior to acceptance of appointment, disclosure must be made when such circumstances become known to the arbitrator.

5. The burden of disclosure rests on the arbitrator. After appropriate disclosure, the arbitrator may serve if both parties so desire. If the arbitrator believes or perceives that there is a clear conflict of interest, he or she should withdraw, irrespective of the expressed desires of the parties.

C. Privacy of Arbitration

1. All significant aspects of an arbitration proceeding must be treated by the arbitrator as confidential unless this requirement is waived by both parties or disclosure is required or permitted by law.

   a. Attendance at hearings by persons not representing the parties or invited by either or both of them should be permitted only when the parties agree or when an applicable law requires or permits. Occasionally, special circumstances may require that an arbitrator rule on such matters as attendance and degree of participation of counsel selected by a grievant.

   b. *Discussion of a case at any time by an arbitrator with persons not involved directly should be limited to situations where advance approval or consent of both parties is obtained or where the indentity of the parties and details of the case are sufficiently obscured to eliminate any realistic probability of identification.*

   A commonly recognized exception is discussion of a problem in a case with a fellow arbitrator. *Any such discussion does not relieve the arbitrator who is acting in the case from sole responsibility for the decision and the discussion must be considered as confidential.*

   Discussion of aspects of a case in a classroom without prior specific approval of the parties is not a violation provided the arbitrator is satisfied that there is no breach of essential confidentiality.

   c. *It is a violation of professional responsibility for an arbitrator to make public an award without the consent of the parties.*

   An arbitrator may request but not press the parties for consent to publish an opinion. Such a request should normally not be made until after the award has been issued to the parties.

   d. It is not improper for an arbitrator to donate arbitration files to a library of a college, university or similar institution without prior consent of all the parties involved. When the circumstances permit, there should be deleted from such donations any cases concerning which one or both of the parties have expressed a desire for privacy. As an additional safeguard, an arbitrator may also decide to withhold recent cases or indicate to the donee a time interval before such cases can be made generally available.

   e. *Applicable laws, regulations, or practices of the parties may permit or even require exceptions to the above noted principles of privacy.*

D. Personal Relationships with the Parties

1. An arbitrator must make every reasonable effort to conform to arrangements required by an administrative agency or mutually desired by the parties regarding communications and personal relationships with the parties.

   a. *Only an "arm's-length" relationship may be acceptable to the parties in some arbitration arrangements or may be required by the rules of an administrative agency. The arbitrator should then have no contact of consequence with representatives of either party while handling a case without the other party's presence or consent.*

b. *In other situations, both parties may want communications and personal relationships to be less formal. It is then appropriate for the arbitrator to respond accordingly.*

E. Jurisdiction

1. An arbitrator must observe faithfully both the limitations and inclusions of the jurisdiction conferred by an agreement or other submission under which he or she serves.

2. A direct settlement by the parties of some or all issues in a case, at any stage of the proceedings, must be accepted by the arbitrator as relieving him or her of further jurisdiction over such issues.

F. Mediation by an Arbitrator

1. When the parties wish at the outset to give an arbitrator authority both to mediate and to decide or submit recommendations regarding residual issues, if any, they should advise the arbitrator prior to appointment. If the appointment is accepted, the arbitrator must perform a mediation role consistent with the circumstances of the case.

a. Direct appointments, also, may require a dual role as mediator and arbitrator of residual issues. This is most likely to occur in some public sector cases.

2. When a request to mediate is first made after appointment, the arbitrator may either accept or decline a mediation role.

a. Once arbitration has been invoked, either party normally has a right to insist that the process be continued to decision.

b. If one party requests that the arbitrator mediate and the other party objects, the arbitrator should decline the request.

c. An arbitrator is not precluded from making a suggestion that he or she mediate. To avoid the possibility of improper pressure, the arbitrator should not so suggest unless it can be discerned that both parties are likely to be receptive. In any event, the arbitrator's suggestion should not be pursued unless both parties readily agree.

G. Reliance by an Arbitrator on Other Arbitration Awards or on Independent Research

1. An arbitrator must assume full personal responsibility for the decision in each case decided.

a. The extent, if any, to which an arbitrator properly may rely on precedent, on guidance of other awards, or on independent research is dependent primarily on the policies of the parties on these matters, as expressed in the contract, or other agreement, or at the hearing.

b. When the mutual desires of the parties are not known or when the parties express differing opinions or policies, the arbitrator may exercise discretion as to these matters, consistent with acceptance of full personal responsibility for the award.

H. Use of Assistants

1. An arbitrator must not delegate any decision-making function to another person without consent of the parties.

a. Without prior consent of the parties, an arbitrator may use the services of an assistant for research, clerical duties, or preliminary drafting under the direction of the arbitrator, which does not involve the delegation of any decision-making function.

b. If an arbitrator is unable, because of time limitations or other reasons, to handle all decision-making aspects of a case, it is not a violation of professional responsibility to suggest to the parties an allocation of responsibility between the arbitrator and an assistant or associate. The arbitrator must not exert pressure on the parties to accept such a suggestion.

I. Consent Awards

1. Prior to issuance of an award, the parties may jointly request the arbitrator to include in the award certain agreements between them, concerning some or all of the issues. If the arbitrator believes that a suggested award is proper, fair, sound, and law-

ful, it is consistent with professional responsibility to adopt it.

    a. Before complying with such a request, an arbitrator must be certain that he or she understands the suggested settlement adequately in order to be able to appraise its terms. If it appears that pertinent facts or circumstances may not have been disclosed, the arbitrator should take the initiative to assure that all significant aspects of the case are fully understood. To this end, the arbitrator may request additional specific information and may question witnesses at a hearing.

J. Avoidance of Delay

1. It is a basic professional responsibility of an arbitrator to plan his or her work schedule so that present and future commitments will be fulfilled in a timely manner.

    a. When planning is upset for reasons beyond the control of the arbitrator, he or she, nevertheless, should exert every reasonable effort to fulfill all commitments. If this is not possible, prompt notice at the arbitrator's initiative should be given to all parties affected. Such notices should include reasonably accurate estimates of any additional time required. To the extent possible, priority should be given to cases in process so that other parties may make alternative arbitration arrangements.

2. An arbitrator must cooperate with the parties and with any administrative agency involved in avoiding delays.

    a. An arbitrator on the active roster of an administrative agency must take the initiative in advising the agency of any scheduling difficulties that he or she can forsee.

    b. Requests for services, whether received directly or through an administrative agency, should be declined if the arbitrator is unable to schedule a hearing as soon as the parties wish. If the parties, nevertheless, jointly desire to obtain the services of the arbitrator and the arbitrator agrees, arrangements should be made by agreement that the arbitrator confidently expects to fulfill.

    c. An arbitrator may properly seek to persuade the parties to alter or eliminate arbitration procedures or tactics that cause unnecessary delay.

3. Once the case record has been closed, an arbitrator must adhere to the time limits for an award, as stipulated in the labor agreement or as provided by regulation of an administrative agency or as otherwise agreed.

    a. If an appropriate award cannot be rendered within the required time, it is incumbent on the arbitrator to seek an extension of time from the parties.

    b. If the parties have agreed upon abnormally short time limits for an award after a case is closed, the arbitrator should be so advised by the parties or by the administrative agency involved, prior to acceptance of appointment.

K. Fees and Expenses

1. An arbitrator occupies a position of trust in respect to the parties and the administrative agencies. In charging for services and expenses, the arbitrator must be governed by the same high standards of honor and integrity that apply to all other phases of his or her work.

An arbitrator must endeavor to keep total charges for services and expenses reasonable and consistent with the nature of the case or cases decided.

Prior to appointment, the parties should be aware of or be able readily to determine all significant aspects of an arbitrator's bases for charges for fees and expenses.

    a. Services Not Primarily Chargeable on a Per Diem Basis

By agreement with the parties, the financial aspects of many "permanent" arbitration assignments, of some interest disputes, and of some "ad hoc" grievance assignments do not include a per diem fee for services as a primary part of the total understanding. *In such situations, the arbitrator must adhere faithfully to all* agreed-upon arrangements governing fees and expenses.

b. Per Diem Basis for Charges for Services

(1) When an arbitrator's charges for services are determined primarily by a stipulated per diem fee, the arbitrator should establish in advance his or her bases for application of such per diem fee and for determination of reimbursable expenses.

Practices established by an arbitrator should include the basis for charges, if any, for:

(a) hearing time, including the application of the stipulated basic per diem hearing fee to hearing days of varying lengths;

(b) study time;

(c) necessary travel time when not included in charges for hearing time;

(d) postponement or cancellation of hearings by the parties and the circumstances in which such charges will normally be assessed or waived;

(e) office overhead expenses (secretarial, telephone, postage, etc.);

(f) the work of paid assistants or associates.

(2) Each arbitrator should be guided by the following general principles:

(a) Per diem charges for a hearing should not be in excess of actual time spent or allocated for the hearing.

(b) Per diem charges for study time should not be in excess of actual time spent.

(c) Any fixed ratio of study days to hearing days, not agreed to specifically by the parties, is inconsistent with the per diem method of charges for services.

(d) Charges for expenses must not be in excess of actual expenses normally reimbursable and incurred in connection with the case or cases involved.

(e) When time or expense are involved for two or more sets of parties on the same day or trip, such time or expense charges should be appropriately prorated.

(f) An arbitrator may stipulate in advance a minimum charge for a hearing without violation of (a) or (e) above.

(3) An arbitrator on the active roster of an administrative agency must file with the agency his or her individual bases for determination of fees and expenses of the agency so requires. Thereafter, it is the responsibility of each such arbitrator to advise the agency promptly of any change in any basis for charges.

Such filing may be in the form of answers to a questionnaire devised by an agency or by any other method adopted by or approved by an agency.

Having supplied an administrative agency with the information noted above, an arbitrator's professional responsibility of disclosure under this Code with respect to fees and expenses has been satisfied for cases referred by that agency.

(4) If an administrative agency promulgates specific standards with respect to any of these matters which are in addition to or more restrictive than an individual arbitrator's standards, an arbitrator on its active roster must observe the agency standards for cases handled under the auspices of that agency, or decline to serve.

(5) When an arbitrator is contacted directly by the parties for a case or cases, the arbitrator has a professional responsibility to respond to questions by submitting his or her bases for charges for fees and expenses.

(6) When it is known to the arbitrator that one or both of the parties cannot afford normal charges, it is consistent with professional responsibility to charge lesser amounts to both parties or to one of the parties if the other party is made aware of the difference and agrees.

(7) If an arbitrator concludes that the total of charges derived from his or her normal basis of calculation is not compatible with the case decided, it is consistent with professional responsibility to charge lesser amounts to both parties.

2. An arbitrator must maintain adequate records to support charges for services and expenses and must make an accounting to the parties or to an involved administrative agency on request.

3. RESPONSIBILITIES TO ADMINISTRATIVE AGENCIES

A. General Responsibilities

1. An arbitrator must be candid, accurate, and fully responsive to an administrative agency concerning his or her qualifications, availability, and all other pertinent matters.

2. An arbitrator must observe policies and rules of an administrative agency in cases referred by that agency.

3. An arbitrator must not seek to influence an administrative agency by any improper means, including gifts, or other inducements to agency personnel.

    a. It is not improper for a person seeking placement on a roster to request references from individuals having knowledge of the applicant's experience and qualifications.

    b. Arbitrators should recognize that the primary responsibility of an administrative agency is to serve the parties.

4. PREHEARING CONDUCT

1. All prehearing matters must be handled in a manner that fosters complete impartiality by the arbitrator.

    a. The primary purpose of prehearing discussions involving the arbitrator is to obtain agreement on procedural matters so that the hearing can proceed without unnecessary obstacles. If differences of opinion should arise during such discussions and, particularly, if such differences appear to impinge on substantive matters, the circumstances will suggest whether the matter can be resolved informally or may require a prehearing conference or, more rarely, a formal preliminary hearing. When an administrative agency handles some or all aspects of the arrangements prior to a hearing, the arbitrator will become involved only if differences of some substance arise.

    b. Copies of any prehearing correspondence between the arbitrator and either party must be made available to both parties.

5. HEARING CONDUCT

A. General Principles

1. An arbitrator must provide a fair and adequate hearing which assures that both parties have sufficient opportunity to present their respective evidence and argument.

    a. Within the limits of this responsibility, an arbitrator should conform to the various types of hearing procedures desired by the parties.

    b. An arbitrator may: encourage stipulations of fact; restate the substance of issues or arguments to promote or verify understanding; question the parties' representatives or witnesses, when necessary or advisable, to obtain additional pertinent information; and request that the parties submit additional evidence, either at the hearing or by subsequent filing.

    c. An arbitrator should not intrude into a party's presentation so as to prevent that party from putting forward its case fairly and adequately.

B. Transcripts or Recordings

1. Mutual agreement of the parties to use or non-use of a transcript must be respected by the arbitrator.

    a. A transcript is the official record of a hearing only when both parties agree to a transcript or an applicable law or regulation so provides.

    b. An arbitrator may seek to persuade the parties to avoid use of a transcript, or to use a transcript if the nature of the case appears to require one. However, if an arbitrator intends to make his or her appointment to a case contingent on mutual agreement to a transcript, that requirement must be made known to both parties prior to appointment.

    c. If the parties do not agree to a transcript, an arbitrator may permit one party to take a transcript at its own cost. The arbitrator may also make appropriate arrangements under which the other party may have access to a copy, if a copy is provided to the arbitrator.

    d. Without prior approval, an arbitrator may seek to use his or her own tape recorder to supplement note taking. The arbitrator should not insist on such a tape recording if either or both parties object.

C. Ex Parte Hearings

1. In determining whether to conduct an ex parte hearing, an arbitrator must consider relevant legal, contractual, and other pertinent circumstances.

2. An arbitrator must be certain, before proceeding ex parte, that the party refusing or failing to attend the hearing has been given adequate notice of the time, place, and purposes of the hearing.

D. Plant Visits

1. An arbitrator should comply with a request of any party that he or she visit a work area pertinent to the dispute prior to, during, or after a hearing. An arbitrator may also initiate such a request.

    a. Procedures for such visits should be agreed to by the parties in consultation with the arbitrator.

E. Bench Decisions or Expedited Awards

1. When an arbitrator understands, prior to acceptance of appointment, that a bench decision is expected at the conclusion of the hearing, the arbitrator must comply with the understanding unless both parties agree otherwise.

    a. If notice of the parties' desire for a bench decision is not given prior to the arbitrator's acceptance of the case, issuance of such a bench decision is discretionary.

    b. When only one party makes the request and the other objects, the arbitrator should not render a bench decision except under most unusual circumstances.

2. When an arbitrator understands, prior to acceptance of appointment, that a concise written award is expected within a stated time period after the hearing, the arbitrator must comply with the understanding unless both parties agree otherwise.

6. POST HEARING CONDUCT

A. Post Hearing Briefs and Submissions

1. An arbitrator must comply with mutual agreements in respect to the filing or non-filing of post hearing briefs or submissions.

    a. An arbitrator, in his or her discretion, may either suggest the filing of post hearing briefs or other submissions or suggest that none be filed.

    b. When the parties disagree as to the need for briefs, an arbitrator may permit filing but may determine a reasonable time limitation.

2. An arbitrator must not consider a post hearing brief or submission that has not been provided to the other party.

B. Disclosure of Terms of Award

1. An arbitrator must not disclose a prospective award to either party prior to its simultaneous issuance to both parties or explore possible alternative awards unilaterally with one party, unless both parties so agree.

    a. Partisan members of tripartite boards may know prospective terms of an award in advance of its issuance. Similar situations may exist in other less formal arrangements mutually agreed to by the parties. In any such situation, the arbitrator should determine and observe the mutually desired degree of confidentiality.

C. Awards and Opinions

1. The award should be definite, certain, and as concise as possible.

    a. When an opinion is required, factors to be considered by an arbitrator include: desirability of brevity, consistent with the nature of the case and any expressed desires of the parties; need to use a style and form that is understandable to responsible representatives of the parties, to the grievant and supervisors, and to others in the collective bargaining relationship; necessity of meeting the significant issues; forthrightness to an extent not harmful to the relationship of the parties; and avoidance of gratuitous advice or discourse not essential to disposition of the issues.

D. Clarification or Interpretation of Awards

1. No clarification or interpretation of an award is permissible without the consent of both parties.

2. Under agreements which permit or require clarification or interpretation of an award, an arbitrator must afford both parties an opportunity to be heard.

E. Enforcement of Award

1. The arbitrator's responsibility does not extend to the enforcement of an award.

2. In view of the professional and confidential nature of the arbitration relationship, an arbitrator should not voluntarily participate in legal enforcement proceedings.

Reprinted with permission of the American Arbitration Association and National Academy of Arbitrators.

Part VI

Substantive Provisions of the Collective Bargaining Agreement

▲ ▲ ▲ ▲ ▲ ▲ ▲ ▲ ▲ ▲ ▲ ▲ ▲ ▲ ▲ ▲ ▲ ▲ ▲ ▲

Collective bargaining agreements set the stage for the labor–management relationship; they are often lengthy, complex documents that are the products of extensive preparations and negotiations. The compensation and benefits received by employees are described in detail in the collective bargaining agreement, along with management rights clauses, seniority provisions, subcontracting rules, disciplinary policies, grievance mechanisms, and other provisions.

Chapter 13, Economic and Compensation Issues, analyzes wage provisions that are commonly addressed in collective bargaining agreements. Factors affecting compensation provisions are discussed, as well as the techniques that are used to ensure that pay systems are both reflective of labor market conditions and equitable in the eyes of bargaining-unit employees. The use of seniority and merit in making pay adjustments and incentive programs are among the topics discussed in Chapter 13.

Chapter 14, Employee Benefit Programs, outlines both the government's role in employee benefits and the collectively bargained benefits typically found in labor contracts. Because of their significant growth during the 1970s and 1980s, approximately 40 percent of the total compensation package in U.S. firms is composed of various employee benefits. Major employee benefits include group life and health insurance, retirement programs, paid vacations and holidays, income maintenance benefits, and childcare and eldercare. Chapter 14 discusses both the prevalence and complexities of the major types of employee benefit programs.

Chapter 15, Institutional Issues: Balancing Management Rights against Union and Employee Security, portrays the delicate balancing act that occurs between union and management. Management wants to maintain its right to make business decisions, whereas the union wants to ensure institutional security for itself and job security for its members. Issues discussed in Chapter 15 include management rights provisions, seniority systems, the impact of technological change on labor relations, employee health and safety concerns, and union security.

Chapter 16, Employee Rights, Job Security, and Discipline, deals with a problem that accounts for the highest percentage of grievances: employee discipline problems. Management's right to discharge and discipline employees is analyzed, along with the causes and categories of employee discipline problems. The manner in which discipline procedures are designed and implemented is discussed. Also explored are the arbitral criteria used in dealing with disciplinary matters.

Part VI is intended to reveal the complexities and seemingly endless array of problems and questions that can arise when dealing with collective bargaining provisions. This section of the book also illustrates the importance of carefully designing and drafting collective bargaining clauses that deal with these issues.

13 | Economic and Compensation Issues

- **Introduction**
- **Factors Influencing Compensation in Collective Bargaining**
  Economic Influences and External Labor Markets
  Organizational Influences and Internal Labor Markets
  Financial Condition of the Organization and Industry
  Inflation and Cost-of-Living Considerations
  Pay Equity
  Laws Regulating Compensation and Employee Benefits
  The Impact of Unions on Pay Levels
- **The Pay Level Decision**
  The Concept of External Equity
  Sources of Wage and Salary Data
    Pay Information Gathered by Third Parties
    Wage and Salary Surveys Tailored to a Specific Organization
  Using the Wage and Salary Data
- **The Pay Structure Decision**
  The Concept of Internal Equity
  Job Evaluation: The Major Steps
  Job Evaluation: Some Important Considerations
  Computerized Job Evaluation and Skill-Based Pay
- **Merging the Pay Level and Pay Structure**
  Establishing the Pay Policy Line
  Determining the Number of Pay Grades or Job Classifications
  Determining the Range of Pay Grades
  Determining Overlap between Pay Grades
  The Use of Seniority and Merit in Pay Increases
    Seniority as the Sole Factor

The Use of Merit in Compensation Decisions
   Combining Seniority and Merit
Supplementary Pay
Wage Adjustments during the Life of the Collective Bargaining Agreement
Two-Tier Compensation Systems
Wage Rates for Promotions, Demotions, and Transfers
▲ **Individual and Group Incentive Programs**
   Individual Incentive Programs
   Examples of Individual Incentive Programs
   Group and Organizational Incentives
   Examples of Group Incentive Programs
▲ **Sex Discrimination in Compensation Programs**
   Equal Pay for Equal Work
   Comparable Worth: The Unsettled Issue
▲ **Summary and Conclusions**
▲ **Discussion Questions and Exercises**
▲ **Cases in Compensation**
   The Misclassified Studio Artists
   Double Time Dilemma
▲ **Appendix: Major Methods of Job Evaluation**
   The Ranking Method
   The Classification Method
   The Factor Comparison Method
   The Point Method

▲ Introduction

Among the most important parts of the collective bargaining agreement are the provisions dealing with employee compensation. As noted in Chapter 10, most economic strikes are precipitated by disputes over wages. In the absence of a collective bargaining agreement, the employer may unilaterally establish and administer wage rates. Collective bargaining agreements contain detailed provisions regulating pay schedules, incentive systems, and the relationship between pay, seniority, and performance. Employee compensation may be *immediate* (payable within a short period of time) or *deferred* (payable at a later date). An employee's hourly, weekly, or monthly pay is an example of an immediate payment, whereas a pension, profit-sharing, or bonus plan typifies a deferred payment. Compensation may either be paid in-kind or in nonmonetary forms where the employee has little discretion as to how the compensation will be spent (e.g., on work clothing, use of a company automobile, and group life and health insurance). Some forms of compensation are *contingent* upon performing certain types of work (e.g., working in a hazardous environment or meeting work quotas) or working during specified hours (e.g., overtime). The types of compensation found in collective bargaining agreements can be categorized as follows:

1. *Wages and salaries*: "Wages" typically pertain to hourly rates of pay (the more hours worked, the greater the pay) and the term "salary" generally applies to a fixed weekly, monthly, or annual rate of pay (regardless of the number of hours worked). The amount of an employee's wage or salary depends on the type of job held by an employee, as well as individual seniority and job performance (merit).
2. *Incentive programs*: Some collective bargaining agreements provide additional compensation above and beyond the employee's wage or salary through incentive programs. Incentive programs provide additional pay based on productivity, sales, profits, or cost-reduction efforts. The major objective of most incentive compensation programs is to motivate and reward employee productivity and cost effectiveness. Incentive programs are of two types:
   a. *Individual incentive programs* provide compensation based on the sales, productivity, or cost savings attributable to a *specific* employee.
   b. *Group incentive programs* allocate compensation to a group of employees (by department, division, or work group) for meeting or exceeding profit, production, or cost-savings standards.
3. *Supplementary pay*: Includes pay for working under unusual, inconvenient, or hazardous conditions. Shift differentials, reporting pay, call-back pay, pay for temporary transfer, or hazardous work premiums are examples of supplementary pay.
4. *Employee benefit programs*: Group life and health insurance, paid vacations and holidays, pension programs, and other benefits associated with an employment relationship or membership in a union are examples of employee benefit programs. Employee benefits now comprise approximately 40 percent of total compensation costs in the United States.
5. *Perquisites*: Employees may receive amenities such as discounts on the purchase of company merchandise or services or the use of company vehicles or club facilities.[1]

Nearly all forms of compensation fall into one of the five categories listed above. Table 13–1 presents a summary of basic compensation provisions (excluding employee benefits, which are discussed in Chapter 14) found in The Bureau of National Affairs, Inc., survey of major collective bargaining provisions.[2] Because of their complexity, these provisions often require extensive negotiation by union and management officials.

---

[1] See A.W. Smith, Jr., "Will Perquisites Survive?" *Compensation and Benefits Review* (November-December, 1985), pp. 44–52.
[2] The Bureau of National Affairs, Inc., *Basic Patterns in Union Contracts*, 11th ed. (Washington, D.C.: The Bureau of National Affairs, Inc., 1986).

Table 13-1 ▲ Major Pay Provisions in Collective Bargaining Agreements

1. Base Wage or Salary
a. Two-tier wage systems (17%)
b. Variable rate ranges (45%)
c. Single wage rates (55%)

2. Provision for General Wage Increases
a. Deferred wage increases (80%)
b. Cost-of-living adjustments (42%)
c. Wage reopeners allowing renegotiation of wages during the life of the contract (10%)

3. Supplementary Pay
a. Second and third shift differentials (86%)
b. Reporting pay (when no work is available) (74%)
c. Call-back pay (Premium pay to cover call-in of employee outside of regular working hours) (68%)
d. Pay for temporary transfer (62%)
e. Hazardous work premium (11%)
f. Travel expenses (31%)
g. Work clothes (33%)

4. Overtime (96%)
a. Premium pay for weekend work (70%)
b. Double pay for Sunday work (76%)
c. Meals during overtime (34%)

Source: The Bureau of National Affairs, Inc., *Basic Patterns in Union Contracts*, 11th ed. (Washington, D.C.: The Bureau of National Affairs, Inc., 1986), based on a sample of 400 contracts from industries throughout the United States. The percentages in parentheses indicate the prevalence with which a provision appears in the sample of collective bargaining agreements. Since a collective bargaining agreement may contain more than one type of pay provision, the totals for each of the categories above exceed 100 percent. Reprinted with permission.

▲ Factors Influencing Compensation in Collective Bargaining

A number of factors influence the amount of pay that workers receive. When union and management negotiate collective bargaining agreement provisions covering pay, several factors are usually taken into account. Among these are external and internal labor markets, inflationary trends, the firm's demand for labor, financial and strategic factors within the organization, union and management views on pay equity, and legislation affecting compensation programs.

Economic Influences and External Labor Markets

A firm's demand for labor is *derived* from the demand for the firm's products and services. The demand for labor (employment level) within a firm rises and falls respectively as the demand for its products increases or decreases. When the general aviation industry began to experience plummeting light aircraft sales, companies such as Cessna and Beechcraft were forced to curtail production and lay off workers. The skyrocketing cost of fuel and higher interest rates in the mid-1970s and early 1980s made the use of large, gas-guzzling recreational vehicles less attractive, and manufacturers such as Winnebago closed production facilities and laid off employees as sales declined. Zenith Electronics Corporation froze the salaries of 6,000 employees in the fall of 1989 after suffering lower-than-expected sales that resulted in third-quarter losses.[3] Thus, the supply and demand for a firm's product has a direct impact on both employment levels and wages.

The supply of labor available to a firm is obtained, in part, from *external labor markets*, a geographical area or occupational group from which an organization recruits employees into the organization. A firm's external labor market may be restricted to a community or metropolitan area or it may be nationwide. As a general rule, the external labor market for unskilled employees is confined to a small geographical area, whereas the external labor market for skilled and professional employees covers a large area.

External labor markets are composed of buyers and sellers of labor; organizations *demand* (buy) units of labor (employees) and employees are willing to *supply* (sell) their labor to an employer for a certain price (wage or salary rate). Thus employers must set wage rates at a level that will enable them to hire an adequate number of qualified workers. This concept is known as the *exchange value*. When labor markets are "tight," employees are scarce and wage levels tend to increase; labor markets that are "loose" have an abundance of qualified workers and encourage employers to pay lower wages and salaries.[4] Another explanation for establishing pay rates is the *marginal revenue productivity theory*, which states that an employer will hire workers up to the point where the cost of hiring an additional worker (the worker's pay) equals the productivity or revenue added by hiring another worker. If the cost of labor becomes too high, the employer may substitute machinery for workers or take advantage of technological advances in order to lower production costs. The fallacy of the exchange value and marginal revenue productivity theories is that both assume that employers have a precise understanding of market forces and labor and product costs. In reality, most employers have only a general idea regarding labor supply, demand, and costs. Standard economic explanations may appear to be precise, but they depend on data that are either imprecise or incomplete. Economic wage theories, however, provide insights into the dynamics of establishing pay levels and structures. When negotiators set wage and salary rates to coincide with the pay levels within an industry or external labor market, they are approximating the exchange value concept. Wages that are tied to production costs and profits are following the marginal revenue productivity theory. In practice, union and management negotiators usually follow some combination of these two approaches.

---

[3] Robert L. Rose, "Zenith Electronics To Post a Loss, Freeze Salaries," *The Wall Street Journal* (September 15, 1989).
[4] See footnote 11, Chapter 10, for a jingle on "tight" and "loose" labor markets.

Organizational Influences and Internal Labor Markets

Even within the same labor market, there are likely to be significant differences in what organizations are willing to pay an employee for the same job. A secretary working for a state governmental agency may receive 15 percent less than one doing comparable work for a large life insurance company located in the same city. Some organizations attempt to keep labor costs in check by paying less than competing firms in the same labor market. The labor economics literature often portrays the employer as wanting to pay the lowest possible wage needed to secure an adequate amount of labor. Some managers, however, have discovered that a low wage strategy can be costly in the long run. By paying lower than average wages, firms are often able to hire only the less desirable employees. Lower wage firms may experience higher than normal rates of turnover, lower productivity, and other problems associated with a marginally competent and poorly motivated workforce. By paying employees above the market rate, a firm may save money in the long run because of its ability to attract more productive and stable employees.

Internal labor markets are a series of related jobs within the organization.[5] Internal labor markets tend to develop pay rates that are unique to a specific organization and somewhat isolated from supply and demand forces in the external labor market. The longer a person stays in an organization, the less influence external labor markets have on his or her pay. Part of this phenomenon is due to the lack of mobility that employees possess as they become "tied" to an organization because of pension and seniority benefits. As one progresses upward in an organization, jobs become more specialized and less standardized relative to the external labor market. In addition, employees who remain with an organization for long periods of time become culturally attuned to their organization, more entrenched in their communities, and less willing to leave.[6] Compensation schedules that link seniority to pay in collective bargaining agreements tend to strengthen the internal labor markets and make them more visible than might be the case in nonunionized firms.[7]

Financial Condition of the Organization and Industry

An important factor in union-management contract talks is the organization's *ability to pay* high salaries and wages. Firms that are highly profitable and are predicting a strong future demand for their products and services are in a better position than financially strapped firms to pay higher wages and salaries and attract the best workers in the labor market. The ability of an organization to pay a certain wage level depends on factors such as the firm's product demand and labor intensity.

---

[5] Beverly Kaye and Kathryn McKee, "New Compensation Strategies for New Career Patterns," *Personnel Administrator* (March 1986), p. 61; Paul Osterman, "Choice of Employment Systems in Internal Labor Markets," *Industrial Relations* (Winter 1987), pp. 46–67.

[6] See David B. Bills, "Costs, Commitment, and Rewards: Factors Influencing the Design and Implementation of Internal Labor Markets," *Administrative Science Quarterly* (June 1987), pp. 202–221.

[7] Collective bargaining agreements containing job-posting-and-bidding systems as a means of filling vacancies from within (as opposed to hiring workers from outside the organization to fill these jobs) also strengthen internal labor markets.

Companies who sell products or provide services that have an inelastic demand (where product price increases resulting from increases in labor costs can be passed on to the consumer without a significant loss of sales) are in a better position to pay higher salaries than firms with elastic product demands. A distillery manufacturing a fine (and expensive) brand of scotch probably has an inelastic product demand. The firm can grant a modest wage increase to its workers and pass all or part of the increase on to its customers by raising the price of a bottle of scotch without significantly decreasing total revenues. That is, a seven percent price increase in the price of a bottle of scotch would result in *less* than a seven percent decline in total sales. A firm whose product has an elastic demand, such as dairy manufacturer producing milk, would find that a price increase of seven percent would decrease sales by *more* than seven percent.[8] Thus, it could be expected that unions will win larger wage gains for their members when they bargain with firms having an inelastic product demand.[9]

An organization's ability to pay is affected by its *labor intensity*. Service organizations such as hospitals and educational institutions are labor intensive because a high percentage of their total budgets are allocated to personnel costs. If a community hospital spends 60 percent of its total budget on salaries, employee benefits, and other personnel costs, a ten percent pay increase will result in a six percent increase in the hospital's budget (10% × 60% = 6%). Thus, wage increases for employees working in educational institutions and health care facilities would likely cause tuition and patient fees to increase. A capital-intensive chemical manufacturer whose personnel expenditures are only 15 percent of the firm's total budget will experience only a 1.5 percent budget increase if a ten percent raise is given.

In recent years, increasing attention has been given to the relationship between organizational strategy and pay policies. An organization's strategy defines its business in terms of product line, quality emphasis, market segment, geographical market limits, diversity, and size. Some firms are expanding and diversifying, whereas others are remaining stable both in size and in terms of product lines. Firms in declining product markets often elect to retrench by eliminating unprofitable products and reducing their workforce. In an extreme case, a firm may divest large segments of its operations or go out of business completely. Firms that are growing and expanding frequently de-emphasize low base salaries and benefits and emphasize incentive programs. Firms in a stable or mature market have a tendency to use competitive base pay and high employee benefits, whereas firms in declining markets may abandon incentive programs altogether.[10]

---

[8] Milk is a fungible product with little consumer brand loyalty.
[9] Robert J. Flanagan, Lawrence M. Kahn, Robert S. Smith, and Ronald G. Ehrenberg, *Economics of the Employment Relationship* (Glenview, Illinois: Scott, Foresman and Company, 1989), pp. 82–84. The greater the elasticity of demand for the firm's product, the greater will be the firm's elasticity of demand for labor.
[10] George T. Milkovich and Jerry M. Newman, *Compensation*, 2nd ed. (Plano, Texas: Business Publications, Inc., 1987), p. 16. Also see Richard I. Henderson and Howard W. Risher, "Influencing Organizational Strategy through Compensation Leadership," Stephen J. Carroll, "Business Strategies and Compensation Systems," and Joseph E. McCann, "Rewarding and Supporting Strategic Planning," all contained in David B. Balkin and Luis R. Gomez-Mejia (Eds.), *New Perspectives on Compensation* (Englewood Cliffs, New Jersey: Prentice-Hall, Inc,, 1987), pp. 328–363.

During austere times, organizations may be hard pressed to grant pay increases. Under the 39-month National Steel contract negotiated in 1986, steel industry workers took a 42-cent-an-hour pay cut and had their cost-of-living adjustment (COLA) suspended.[11] Perhaps the most dramatic example of concession bargaining occurred in 1980 and 1981 when the United Auto Workers agreed with Chrysler Corporation on wage and benefit concessions amounting to $865 million.[12]

Organizations experiencing profits or budgetary surpluses are often pressured or feel obligated to raise pay levels. In the aerospace industry, high government and commercial production orders foretold high profits for companies such as Boeing and Lockheed. Productivity payments were scheduled in 1986, 1987, and 1988. The first productivity payment at Boeing, made in December of 1986, was 12 percent of all hours worked between October 4, 1985, and October 3, 1986. The COLA clause was also liberalized for Boeing employees.[13]

In making pay level increases, management negotiators need to look beyond the immediate profit picture and forecast the financial condition of the company in the future. It is generally easier to avoid large pay increases than it is to cut pay levels later because of financial hardship. Organizations that provide generous pay raises during prosperous times may be planting the seeds of disaster if the firm's business declines. Thus pay level decisions should be made carefully to avoid overcommitting the organization's resources. Labor unions are also quick to point out the need to share profits during prosperous times with the employees who "helped make it all possible." However, a dilemma exists for capital stock firms that have obligations to shareholders who also expect to share in the firm's profitability.[14]

Inflation and Cost of Living Considerations

Increases in the cost of living also have a substantial impact on pay levels. The most relevant measure of economic well-being is *real* income, which measures purchasing power, whereas *monetary* income is expressed in absolute dollars. An employee who receives a pay increase of three percent will experience a three percent change in monetary income. If the consumer price index increases by five percent, however, the employee's real income has actually decreased by approximately two percent. Because of the importance of real income, multi-plant collective bargaining agreements covering workers in areas with a high cost of living, such as the San Francisco Bay area, Hawaii, Alaska, or New York City, must not underestimate the effects of the costs required to enjoy a decent standard of living in these locations. A $30,000 a year job in Fayetteville, Arkansas, will provide a substantially higher

---

[11] George Ruben, "Labor-Management Scene in 1986 Reflects Continuing Economic Difficulties," in *The Human Resources Yearbook*, 1987 edition (Englewood Cliffs, New Jersey: Prentice-Hall, Inc., 1987), p. 8.13.

[12] See The Bureau of National Affairs, Inc., "Wage Patterns and Wage Data," *Collective Bargaining Negotiations & Contracts* (Washington, D.C.: The Bureau of National Affairs, Inc., 1987), section 18.

[13] George Ruben, "Labor-Management Scene in 1986 Reflects Continuing Economic Difficulties," in Craig T. Norback, ed., *The Human Resources Yearbook*, 1987 edition (Englewood Cliffs, New Jersey: Prentice-Hall, Inc., 1987), pp. 8.16–8.17.

[14] See Aaron Bernstein, Michael Schroeder, and Susan B. Garland, "Labor is Slowly Raising Its Fist," *Business Week* (February 27, 1989), p. 36.

real income than a $40,000 position in Boston. Variations in the cost of living from one location to another may partially explain why there has been a shift toward decentralized bargaining in the United States; unions want to get the best wage bargain for their members at the local level.

Periodic increases in wages and salaries are often tied directly to changes in the consumer price index (CPI). During inflationary times, union negotiators have pushed for cost-of-living adjustment formulas (COLAs) in collective bargaining agreements that provide an automatic across-the-board pay raise as the CPI increases.[15] A discussion of COLA provisions is presented later in this chapter.

Pay Equity

Bargaining-unit employees often compare their pay to the pay received by other employees.[16] When employees perceive pay inequities, they may pressure the union into making exorbitant wage demands, a move that could lead to an economic strike. Pay equity appears to be especially important to unions, which are egalitarian organizations. Research indicates that unions tend to reduce pay inequalities within firms and between firms within an industry.[17] Union and management negotiators also examine the pay policies and practices of other firms when bargaining over pay provisions. Although collective bargaining agreements tend to emphasize standardized pay scales and strong seniority provisions, there are three types of equity associated with wage negotiations and compensation:

1. *External equity* compares the pay of *similar* jobs in *comparable* organizations. An employee working for General Motors might compare his or her pay with a Ford Motor Company employee. External equity deals with the concept of *pay levels. Wage and salary surveys* are the primary means of collecting information on pay levels.
2. *Internal equity* compares the pay of *dissimilar* jobs within the *same* organization. A checkout clerk in a grocery store might compare his or her wage rate

---

[15] During periods of low inflation employers usually try to abolish COLA provisions.
[16] Under equity theory an employee provides *inputs* to his or her job; these include factors such as education, knowledge, skills, abilities, and effort. In return, an employee receives pay, employee benefits, and other inducements such as job satisfaction, challenge, and the prestige of working for a well-known company. In the above example, an employee (the focal person) evaluates job outputs and inputs with another person (referent others) to determine whether he or she is equitably treated. The other person is usually an individual who is in a position similar to that of the focal person. Collective bargaining agreements tend to standardize outputs within an organization and, in many cases, within an industry affected by pattern bargaining. For a study of how employees select referent others, see Richard W. Scholl, Elizabeth A. Cooper, and Jack F. McKenna, "Referent Selection in Determining Equity Perception: Differential Effects on Behavioral Attitude Outcomes," *Personnel Psychology* (Spring 1987), pp. 113–124. A second motivational theory, instrumentality-expectancy theory, focuses on two links: (1) an employee's effort on the job and and the likelihood that such effort will lead to improved performance, and (2) the rewards received as the result of improved job performance. Under collective bargaining agreements with standard pay scales and emphasis on seniority for making pay raises and promotions, the second link of the instrumentality-expectancy theory is broken. See Victor H. Vroom, *Work and Motivation* (New York: John Wiley & Sons, 1964); and J.R. Hackman and L.W. Porter, "Expectancy Theory Prediction of Work Effectiveness," *Organizational Behavior and Human Performance*, Vol 12, (1968), pp. 417–426.
[17] See Richard B. Freeman and James L. Medoff, *What Do Unions Do?* (New York: Basic Books, Inc., 1984), pp. 78–93.

with a produce clerk or a meatcutter working in the same store. Internal equity deals with *pay structures. Job evaluation* is the method used to place a value on a job within the pay structure.

3. *Procedural equity* determines the fairness with which pay rates are set and pay changes such as annual raises are made. Pay increases may be made on an across-the-board basis, with all employees receiving the same dollar or percentage increase, or pay raises may be geared to seniority or job performance.[18]

Laws Regulating Compensation and Employee Benefits

A number of federal and state laws regulate compensation and employee benefits, and it is important that union and management officials understand the content of these laws as well as the manner in which they are interpreted by the regulatory bodies and courts. The major laws affecting compensation management are summarized in Table 13-2.

Table 13–2 ▲ Laws Affecting Compensation Provisions in Collective Bargaining Agreements

- *Fair Labor Standards Act* (1938): The FLSA regulates minimum wage and hour provisions that apply to most private-sector organizations, federal and state agencies, and labor unions. The FLSA distinguishes between *exempt* and *nonexempt* employees. Executives, administrators, professionals, and outside salespersons are in the exempt category and are not subject to the Act's overtime provisions. Nonexempt employees working more than 40 hours per week must be paid one and a half times their normal rate for each hour worked beyond 40 hours. The FLSA regulates the working hours of children under age 16 and also specifies that persons under age 18 cannot work in hazardous jobs. The Act requires that employers keep detailed records on employee compensation, and its enforcement lies with the Wage and Hour Division of the U.S. Department of Labor.
- *Workers' Compensation Laws*: Each state has enacted and administers workers' compensation legislation that provides benefits for employees who suffer job-related injuries. Workers' compensation laws provide disability income payments while the employee is out of work, payments for catastrophic losses (limbs, eyesight, permanent injuries, and so on), burial expenses, and payment of medical bills.
- *Federal Laws Regulating Government Contractors*: Several laws regulate the minimum wages that are to be paid by firms holding federal government contracts. The *Davis-Bacon Act* (1931) requires that construction contractors pay the prevailing wage in the area in which the contract is held and the *Walsh-Healy Act* (1936) extends the Davis-Bacon Act to most nonconstruction contractors and requires overtime pay (one and a half time) for work beyond eight hours per day and 40 hours per week. In 1965, the *McNamara-O'Hara Act* extended the above obligations to service contractors.
- *Social Security Act* (1935): The current Social Security program is comprised of four major programs: the retirement program (1935), which provides an income to eligible retirees; the survivorship program (1939), which provides income to the family of a deceased worker (a form of life insurance); the disability program (1956), which pays

---

[18] See Jerald Greenberg, "Reactions to Procedural Injustice in Payment Distributions: Do the Means Justify the Ends?" *Journal of Applied Psychology* (February 1987), pp. 55–61.

Table 13–2 ▲ Laws Affecting Compensation Provisions in Collective Bargaining Agreements (Continued)

disability benefits to eligible workers who are totally and permanently disabled; and the health insurance program (enacted in 1965 and better known as Medicare) for eligible persons above age 65. These programs are administered by the federal Social Security Administration and are funded through payroll taxes on employees and employers.

▲ *Unemployment Compensation Laws*: State-administered programs generally provide payments to workers during periods of joblessness that occur for reasons beyond the employee's control. In most states, unemployment compensation insurance is available to an unemployed person for up to 26 weeks. Unemployment insurance is financed by employers in all but three states.

▲ *Consumer Credit Protection Act* (1968): This law regulates wage garnishments in which an employee has pay withheld by someone to whom he or she owes money. Under this law, wage garnishments can be obtained only by a court order and limits are placed on the amount subject to garnishment. The Consumer Credit Protection Act also makes it illegal for an employer to terminate an employee for garnishments over a single debt. The Wage and Hour Division of the U.S. Department of Labor enforces the Act.

▲ *Federal/State Child Support Enforcement Program* (1975) *Child Support Enforcement Amendments of 1984*: This law allows automatic mandatory wage withholding for child support payments. This amendment provides a means of obtaining delinquent child support payments and mandatory payroll deductions to ensure that payments are made on time. State child support enforcement agencies can order employers to withhold pay without the need of a court review. Employers cannot discipline, discharge, or refuse to hire employees who have wages withheld under this law.

▲ *Employee Retirement Income Security Act* (1974): Retirement programs are regulated under this federal law. The major purpose of ERISA is to safeguard pension funds so that they will be available to employees when they retire. The Act sets forth standards on funding, fiduciary responsibilities, vesting, and eligibility to join a retirement program, and it created the Pension Benefit Guaranty Corporation to insure pension funds in the event of mismanagement or bankruptcy of the employer.

▲ *Health Maintenance Act* (1973): This act requires firms with 25 or more employees to provide the option of a health maintenance organization (HMO) as part of their health insurance plan if an HMO exists in the local area. HMOs provide comprehensive medical care through a group of health care providers. HMOs have traditionally emphasized preventive medical care. The Act is an amendment to the FLSA.

▲ *Tax Reform Act* (1986): This act makes significant changes in corporate and individual tax structures and imposes a number of changes on the regulation and taxation of employee benefits. The Act is indicative of the federal government's desire to become more involved in the regulation of employee benefit programs.[19]

▲ *Consolidated Omnibus Reconciliation Act* (passed in 1985 and known as COBRA): This law allows continued health insurance protection for the family of an employee who dies. COBRA also allows continued health insurance coverage for employees who are involuntarily or voluntarily terminated (except for gross misconduct), as well as for other "qualified" events that could otherwise terminate health insurance coverage. COBRA provides employees or their families the option of purchasing continuing

---

[19] Jack H. Schecter, "The Tax Reform Act of 1986: Its Impact on Compensation and Benefits," *Compensation and Benefits Review* (November-December 1986), pp. 11–24.

Table 13-2 ▲ Laws Affecting Compensation Provisions in Collective Bargaining Agreements (Continued)

health insurance coverage (at the expense of the employee or family) regardless of their insurability.[20]

▲ *Equal Pay Act* (1963): This act protects against sex discrimination in pay by mandating equal pay for equal work. Jobs do not have to be identical to be "equal" and the factors of responsibility, effort, working conditions, and skills are used to evaluate the equality of two or more jobs to determine pay equity. Unequal pay is permissible for differences in employee seniority, merit, and productivity. The EPA is administered by the Equal Employment Opportunity Commission (EEOC). Pay discrimination can also violate *Title VII of the Civil Rights Act* (1964), the *Age Discrimination in Employment Act* (1967), and other federal and state equal employment opportunity laws.

These laws are designed primarily to protect employees from unfair pay discrimination and the loss of employee benefits. They also provide protection from economic hazards such as injury, sickness, and unemployment. Some of these laws require that personnel departments or unions administering benefit programs maintain certain records on pay and employee benefits.

The Impact of Unions on Pay Levels

Labor unions are often thought to have a strong influence on pay levels.[21] Because of the profound impact that wage settlements have on the financial condition of the firm and its employees, labor and management negotiators make extensive preparations prior to contract talks. The wage settlements reached as the result of collective bargaining are based on the employer's ability to pay, changes in the consumer price index, wage and benefit trends for other firms, as well as the bargaining strength and skills of the respective negotiators.

Labor unions often attempt to standardize wages among unionized firms in a particular industry.[22] The phenomenon of pattern bargaining explains why assembly line workers at General Motors, Ford, and Chrysler have traditionally received similar wages and benefits. Within a heavily unionized industry such as automobiles, the wage level settlement between the United Auto Workers and Ford heavily influences the wage settlement for General Motors and Chrysler.[23] By standardizing

---

[20] See Paul M. Hamburger, "Compliance Overview of COBRA Health Care Continuation Coverage," in *The Human Resources Yearbook*, 1987 edition, (Englewood Cliffs, New Jersey: Prentice-Hall, Inc., 1987), pp. 2.103–2.124; and Muriel N. Feldman, "COBRA Compliance: Guidelines for Employers," *Employment Relations Today* (Spring 1988), pp. 1–8.
[21] See Thomas A. Kochan and Harry C. Katz, *Collective Bargaining and Industrial Relations*, 2nd ed. (Homewood, Illinois: Richard D. Irwin, Inc., 1988), pp. 328–337; and Daniel J. B. Mitchell, *Unions, Wages, and Inflation* (Washington, D.C.: Brookings Institute, 1980).
[22] Barry T. Hirsch and John I. Neufald, "Nominal and Real Union Wage Differentials and the Effects of Industry and SMSA Density," *Journal of Human Resources* (Winter 1987), p. 138; and Anil Verma, "Union and Nonunion Wages at a Firm Level: A Combined Institutional and Econometric Analysis," *Journal of Labor Research* (Winter 1987), p. 67.
[23] See Kathryn J. Ready, "Is Pattern Bargaining Dead?" *Industrial and Labor Relations Review* (January 1990), pp. 272–279.

or "taking wages out of competition" within an industry, a low-wage employer cannot undercut a rival company and gain a competitive edge through lower prices obtained through labor cost savings. Companies are thus forced to compete on product quality, production efficiencies, and customer brand loyalty, rather than labor costs. As Sol C. Chaikin, president of the International Ladies' Garment Workers' Union (ILGWU) stated:

> We've told our employers, compete on style; compete on merchandising; compete on deliveries; compete on who is able to raise capital for less; compete on manufacturing efficiency, your own talent, your effort, your knowledge, drive—but no way do we want you to compete on the backs of the workers.[24]

Nonunionized firms often attempt to maintain pay levels that are equal to or, perhaps, greater than their unionized counterparts. This phenomenon is known as the "threat effect" of unions. Although there are other antiunion strategies that can be followed (some of which are illegal), the equalization-of-pay strategy is legal (except for giving employees pay raises during union organizing campaigns) and it enables nonunion firms to obtain quality labor.

Unions probably raise pay levels the most when union bargaining power is high relative to the bargaining power of the employer. Bargaining power is determined by factors such as the degree of unionization within an industry, the economic condition of the employer, the employer's vulnerability to a strike, the availability of replacements for striking workers, general economic conditions, and the bargaining savvy of negotiators. Unions also affect pay levels through their support of cost-of-living adjustment formulas (COLAs) that were incorporated into many collective bargaining agreements during the inflationary periods of the 1970s and early 1980s. However, a blanket statement that unions increase pay levels by some specified percentage is tenuous because of the uncertainty surrounding the collective bargaining process. In recent years, a number of studies have attempted to assess the impact of unions on wage levels. H. Gregg Lewis analyzed over 200 studies of organized labor's impact on wages. Several points emerge from Lewis's work:[25]

1. The union relative-wage advantage (over nonunion employees in the same occupational group) averaged 15 percent between the mid-1950s and late 1970s.[26]
2. Union wage effects are neither constant across time nor constant across groups. During the 1960s, when unemployment was low, unionized workers earned about 12 percent more than their nonunion counterparts. By the mid-1970s,

---

[24] Sol C. Chaikin (interview), "Look for the Union Label," in Philip Quaglieri, *America's Labor Leaders* (Lexington, Massachusetts: Lexington Books, 1989), p. 55. Reprinted with permission.
[25] H. Gregg Lewis, *Union Relative Wage Effects: A Survey* (Chicago: University of Chicago Press, 1986). Cited in Robert J. Flanagan, Lawrence M. Kahn, Robert S. Smith, and Ronald G. Ehrenberg, *Economics of the Employment Relationship* (Glen View, Illinois: Scott, Foresman and Company, 1989), pp. 551–555. Also see Thomas A. Kochan and Harry C. Katz, *Collective Bargaining and Industrial Relations*, 2nd ed. (Homewood, Illinois: Richard D. Irwin, Inc., 1988), pp. 333–337.
[26] Union-nonunion wage differentials may be larger than indicated by early research. See Sanford M. Jacoby and Daniel J. B. Mitchell, "Measurement of Compensation: Union and Nonunion," *Industrial Relations* (Spring 1988), pp. 215–231.

when unemployment was higher, the union-nonunion differential increased to 20 percent.[27]

3. Unions appear to help increase the wages of blacks more than whites, but make little difference in wages between males and females. According to Freeman and Medoff, there is a diverse pattern of union effects on male and female wages. Union-nonunion wage differentials are also highest for younger, lower-paid workers as well as for workers with relatively little seniority.[28]

4. Because unions negotiate absolute increases in wages rather than across-the-board percentage increases, the relative impact of unions on wages tends to favor lower-paid, blue-collar workers. That is, there is a larger difference in pay between union and nonunion blue-collar workers than between union and nonunion white-collar and professional employees.

5. Union wages differ across industries. Union wage effects, for example, are much larger for construction (43 percent) and much smaller in durable goods manufacturing (9 percent).[29] The ability of a union to maintain a large difference between union and nonunion wages in an industry may depend on the barriers to entry faced by new firms desiring to enter an industry and set up nonunion operations. In addition, the ability of a firm to move to areas such as the South where less expensive, nonunion labor is available also tends to reduce union-nonunion wage differentials.[30] Freeman and Medoff have noted that the union-nonunion wage differential is greater in the southern United States and smaller in the Northeast and central part of the country.[31]

Unions also have an important impact on pay structures through their emphasis on seniority in pay decisions and their egalitarian nature. Most union leaders attempt to de-emphasize merit and job performance in determining individual pay increases and promotions and, instead, want seniority to control these decisions. Labor unions have also been a major driving force behind the expansion of employee benefit programs. Thus it is a certainty that labor unions *do* make a difference in pay levels, pay structures, and employee benefits. The extent to which unions affect employee compensation varies by time period, occupation, industry, and other factors.

---

[27] Also see Richard B. Freeman and James L. Medoff, *What Do Unions Do?* (New York: Basic Books, Inc., 1984), pp. 52–54.

[28] Richard B. Freeman and James L. Medoff, *What Do Unions Do?* (New York: Basic Books, Inc., 1984), pp. 49–50.

[29] Orley Ashenfelter, "Union Relative Wage Effects: New Evidence and a Survey of Their Implications for Wage Inflation," in Richard Stone and William Peterson, eds., *Econometric Contributions to Public Policy* (New York: St. Martin's Press, 1978), pp. 31–60. Cited in Thomas A. Kochan and Harry C. Katz, *Collective Bargaining and Industrial Relations*, 2nd ed. (Homewood, Illinois: Richard D. Irwin, Inc., 1988), p. 364.

[30] This phenomenon is known as the union's ability to maintain its jurisdictional control over an industry. See Robert J. Flanagan, Lawrence M. Kahn, Robert S. Smith, and Ronald G. Ehrenberg, *Economics of the Employment Relationship* (Glenview, Illinois: Scott, Foresman and Company, 1989), p. 554.

[31] Richard B. Freeman and James L. Medoff, *What Do Unions Do?* (New York: Basic Books, Inc., 1984), p. 50.

▲ The Pay Level Decision

The Concept of External Equity

In negotiating pay provisions, both union and management negotiators are interested in what other organizations pay employees within the same industry, occupational group, or labor market. This comparison deals with the concept of *external equity*. External equity (also called the pay level decision) is assessed by comparing the pay of similar jobs *between* comparable organizations. In making such comparisons, two conditions must be satisfied: (1) the jobs being compared must be the same or nearly the same, and (2) the organizations surveyed must be similar in size, function, mission, and sector. The wage rate of production workers in a medium-size manufacturing firm would be compared to the wages of production workers employed by a firm that is similar in size, product market, and geographic region. To compare the wages of production workers of a medium-size tool manufacturer in the Southeast United States with production workers in a high-tech firm in the California Silicon Valley would be inappropriate and misleading; there are vast differences in the job descriptions and qualifications of the two groups of production workers as well as the type of product and location of the firms.

Sources of Wage and Salary Data

Bargaining demands and offers made by union and management negotiators are based heavily on wage and salary surveys of comparable firms. Once the survey is completed and the wage and salary data is analyzed, negotiators can establish pay-level targets for individual jobs or groups of jobs where the pay is "out of line" with the labor market.[32] Wage and salary information is generally gathered from two sources: (1) surveys conducted by third parties, such as state and federal departments of labor, consulting firms, labor groups, or industry associations, and (2) surveys tailored to a specific organization that are conducted by personnel specialists, consultants, or unions. International unions may conduct wage and salary surveys and make this information available to member locals.

Pay Information Gathered by Third Parties

Federal and state governments gather large amounts of wage and salary information that are useful to those engaged in collective bargaining. The U.S. Department of Labor, Bureau of Labor Statistics (BLS), for example, conducts area, industrial, and other surveys covering a variety of jobs and occupations.[33] Private organizations, such as The Bureau of National Affairs, Inc., the Society for Human Resource Administration, the Hay Group, and various professional, trade, and industrial associations all perform wage and salary surveys.

---

[32] Sara L. Rynes and George L. Milkovich, "Wage Surveys: Dispelling Some Myths About the 'Market Wage,'" *Personnel Psychology* (Spring 1986), p. 71.
[33] John D. Morton, "BLS Prepares to Broaden the Scope of Its White Collar Pay Survey," *Monthly Labor Review* (March 1987), p. 3.

A major advantage of ready-made or "canned" surveys is their low cost. Federal government wage and salary survey data is available at most large public or university libraries. Most surveys range in cost from $300 to $3,000 per year, depending on the source and the amount of information purchased. These surveys include a broad variety of jobs surveyed across wide geographical areas. Ready-made surveys also pose several problems. First, there may be an imperfect match between the jobs surveyed and the jobs on which the survey information will be applied. Comparing the surveyed salary of an administrative assistant for a chemical manufacturer may be an "apples and oranges" comparison if the firm buying the information employs administrative assistants whose tasks and duties differ from the one contained in the survey. There may be a mismatch between the relevant labor market of the employer and the labor market covered by the survey. Many surveys focus on large firms in urban areas and exclude small organizations and rural communities. Surveys that are industry specific and cover banks, insurance companies, or government organizations may have little relevance to firms outside those industries. Other surveys are geared to specific professions such as accounting, engineering, or health care. Therefore, negotiators must carefully examine the sample from which a survey is made before using the data to formulate bargaining proposals.[34] Finally, by the time a wage and salary survey has been collected, organized, and published, six months to one year may have elapsed. Thus it is important to know when the data were collected before they are used to make pay level decisions. During periods of high inflation, it is necessary to compensate for lags between the time when survey data are collected and published as well as the lag between when the data are published and when pay level changes will actually go into effect.[35]

Wage and Salary Surveys Tailored to a Specific Organization

Many of the problems associated with ready-made wage and salary surveys can be eliminated by designing a wage and salary survey that specifically meets the needs of a particular organization. In essence, a tradeoff is made between cost and accuracy when selecting between third-party and tailor-made surveys.[36] Once the decision has been made to perform a wage and salary survey, those in charge of preparing for contract talks can decide whether to use in-house compensation specialists or obtain the services of a compensation consultant. Regardless of the avenue chosen, several important points must be kept in mind:

1. The organizations selected to participate as respondents in the survey must be carefully selected. Ideally, the firms surveyed should be approximately the same size, offer the same products and services, and be located in the same geographical region.

---

[34] See Theodore E. Weinberger, "A Way to Audit Job Matches of Salary Survey Participants," *Compensation Review* (Third Quarter 1984), pp. 47–58.
[35] Steven D. Beggs, "The 'Lead-Lag' Problem: Adjustments Needed for Salary Comparisons," *Compensation and Benefits Review* (November-December 1986), pp. 44–54.
[36] Herbert Z. Halbrecht, "Compensation Surveys: Misleading Guideposts," *Personnel Journal*, (March 1987), p. 122; and D.W. Belcher, N. Bruce Ferris, and John O'Neill, "How Wage Surveys Are Being Used," *Compensation and Benefits Review* (September-October 1985), p. 34.

2. The jobs for which the survey information is being gathered must be carefully chosen. A survey may focus on either *job-based* or *skill-based* systems. To keep the length of the survey reasonable, only those jobs that are essential to the successful completion of the survey should be included. In some industries such as the airlines there are a number of standard or "benchmark" jobs that have essentially the same tasks, duties, responsibilities, and working conditions from one firm to another. By surveying benchmark jobs, the company can obtain an estimate of how its pay levels compare with those of other firms. An alternative approach is to focus the survey on the skills that employees bring to the job rather than on the job itself. Thus, a survey may ask how much an electrician with an associate degree from a technical school is paid (regardless of the job this person holds). The skill-based approach assumes that employers will make every effort to place employees in jobs that are commensurate with their knowledge, skills, and abilities. If employee benefits are to be surveyed, it might be wise to gather information only on the more expensive benefits, such as paid vacations, retirement plans, and group health insurance.
3. Wage and salary questionnaires must be carefully constructed and pretested if accurate and timely information is to be obtained. The foundation for designing a survey is a comprehensive and current job analysis system that describes job duties, tasks, and responsibilities and specifies the employee education, experience, and skills necessary to perform the job. Survey data may be collected by personal interview, mail questionnaires, or telephone interviews. Regardless of the method used, survey questions must be clear and concise so that the respondent will understand the type of information being requested.
4. Respondents are more likely to provide wage and salary information on their firms if a *summary* of the survey results will be shared with them. In order to ensure confidentiality, most surveys *do not* reveal salary and benefits data for a specific firm.
5. Wage and salary survey results should be summarized and analyzed in a form that is understandable and useful to those needing the information. Charts, graphs, tables, and illustrations usually enhance and clarify the information being presented.

Table 13–3 provides a summary of the types of information that should be included when designing a wage and salary survey.

Using The Wage and Salary Data

Data collected in a wage and salary survey are usually summarized by calculating the average pay levels for the jobs surveyed and examining the ranges and distribution of pay for each surveyed job. If the average pay for a job within an organization is considerably different from the average pay for the surveyed firms, then further investigation is required. Suppose that the survey reveals that the market rate salary for a diesel mechanic is $2,500 per month, but the surveying firm is paying $2,800 monthly to diesel mechanics. It is possible that the diesel mechanic job in the organization conducting the survey has more responsibility or must

Table 13-3 ▲ Information Included in a Wage and Salary Survey

I. Data on the Organizations Surveyed
a. Number of employees in the bargaining unit
b. Major products and services
c. Financial data: total assets, annual sales, profits
d. Location of jobs surveyed
e. Organizational charts
f. Union representing the bargaining-unit employees

II. Job Analysis and Pay Information
a. Job description (tasks, duties, responsibilities, hazardous conditions)
b. Job specification (knowledge, skills, and abilities required to perform the job)
c. Pay scale of job surveyed
   1. Pay quartiles
   2. Rate ranges
d. Means by which job incumbents receive pay increases
   1. Merit increases (and frequency with which merit increases are given)
   2. Seniority increases (and frequency with which seniority increases are given)
e. Pay incentives
   1. Individual pay incentives (amount and basis for rewarding incentive pay)
   2. Group incentives (amount and basis for rewarding incentive pay)
f. Supplementary pay
   1. Shift differentials (amount for each shift)
   2. Reporting pay
   3. Call-back pay
   4. Hazardous work
   5. Other
g. Overtime and premium pay
   1. Basis for computing overtime pay
   2. Amount of overtime pay
h. Perquisites and special allowances

III. Employee Benefits
a. Group life insurance
   1. Total amount of coverage for employees or formulas for calculating life insurance coverage
   2. Average cost per employee
b. Group health insurance
   1. Dollar limits of coverage
   2. Scope of coverage (e.g., hospitalization, surgical, ancillary services)
   3. Deductibles and co-insurance
   4. Major exclusions and restrictions
c. Group disability insurance
   1. Definition of disability (in order to receive benefits)
   2. Waiting period
   3. Percentage of gross income paid during disability
d. Retirement programs
   1. Funding mechanisms
   2. Vesting schedules
   3. Benefit plans

Table 13–3 ▲ Information Included in a Wage and Salary Survey (Continued)

III. Employee Benefits

e. Compensation for time not worked
    1. Paid vacations (amount of pay and number of days)
    2. Leaves of absence
f. Child care programs
    1. Arrangements
    2. Funding
g. Other benefits

endure more hazardous working conditions than diesel mechanics in other firms within the industry.

Prior to beginning contract talks, summary statistics can be compiled for inclusion in the bargaining book (see Chapter 9):

▲ *Mean wages and salaries*: The average salary for each job surveyed.
▲ *Median wage*: The wage level for a particular job at which half of the wage rates are less and half of the wage rates are greater.
▲ *Modal wage rates*: The wage most frequently paid for a particular job.
▲ *Pay percentiles*: Wages are calculated for the 25th, 50th, and 75th percentiles. A job paid at the 25th percentile means that 25 percent of the organizations pay less than the surveying organization for this job and 75 percent pay more. The median wage equals the 50th percentile.
▲ *Pay distributions*: Considerations such as the range in pay and the shape of the pay distribution can be important.

By calculating summary statistics, union and management negotiators can compare the pay in their organization to that of other organizations. Employee benefit statistics can be analyzed in a similar fashion. By plotting pay and employee benefit data on graphs and charts, it is possible to obtain an overview of distributions and trends that are not apparent when raw data and numbers are examined.

Once information is available on the internal structure of jobs, the final pay level and structure can be determined.

▲ The Pay Structure Decision

The Concept of Internal Equity

Internal equity deals with the variation in pay among different jobs within an organization. The question posed by internal equity is how much more (or less) should Job A be paid than Job B? Internal equity can have an important impact on employee morale, satisfaction, productivity, and turnover because internal inequities may be more visible, in many instances, than external inequities. Many employees have only a vague idea of what other organizations are paying, but they are usually aware of what their fellow employees are being paid. A lack of internal equity may create dissension among bargaining-unit employees and lead to grievances over pay classifications and job assignments.

Job Evaluation: The Major Steps

Job evaluation places a *value* on a job. This "value" may be expressed directly in dollars or indirectly through a ranking, classification, or point scheme.[37] In some organizations, management has exclusive control over job evaluation techniques, whereas other collective bargaining agreements stipulate that jobs may not be evaluated (or re-evaluated) without input by the union.[38] The appendix at the end of this chapter briefly describes several common job evaluation techniques. Although numerous job evaluation techniques are available, the following steps are common to most methods:[39]

1. *Sampling benchmark jobs.* Job evaluation systems are often developed and validated on the basis of a select sample of jobs known as *benchmark or key jobs.* Large organizations contain a variety of jobs that can be categorized on the basis of similarities in locations, duties, skills required, and other characteristics. A general hospital that is conducting a job evaluation for all of its jobs may use six broad job classifications: (1) physicians, (2) administrators, (3) registered nurses and licensed practical nurses, (4) laboratory, x-ray, and other technical employees, (5) secretarial and clerical employees, and (6) all others (such as physical plant employees and food service workers).

    Benchmark jobs are then selected from each job classification or cluster, based on two important characteristics. First, benchmark jobs are highly visible and well-known throughout the organization. Second, the wage and salary rate of a benchmark job is generally considered to be "in line" and stable relative to both external labor market conditions and with other jobs in the organization. That is, benchmark jobs are neither overpaid nor underpaid.

2. *Establishing compensable factors.* Factors that determine the relative worth of a job (responsibility, mental and physical effort, skill required to perform the job, etc.) are known as *compensable factors.* Compensable factors should meet the following criteria. First, a compensable factor must be found in all (or nearly all) of the jobs being evaluated. Second, the amount of a compensable factor should vary from one job to another. If all jobs within a classification require the same amount of physical effort, then physical effort will not be a good *distinguishing* factor for the jobs being evaluated. Physical effort will make a

---

[37] Job evaluation is normally based on a *job analysis* system, which gathers data on the tasks, duties, and responsibilities associated with a job (known as the *job description*) and the knowledge, skills, and abilities required of the employee to perform the job properly (known as the *job specification*).

[38] See The Bureau of National Affairs, Inc., "Evaluating and Setting Rates for Jobs," *Collective Bargaining Negotiations & Contracts* (Washington, D.C.: The Bureau of National Affairs, Inc., 1985), section 93. Unions may become more interested in influencing the design of pay systems in the 1990s. See David B. Balkin, "Union Influences on Pay Policy: A Survey," *Journal of Labor Research* (Summer 1989), pp. 299–307.

[39] Thomas A. Mahoney, "Compensating for Work" in Kendrith M. Rowland and Gerald R. Ferris (Eds.) *Personnel Management* (Boston: Allyn and Bacon, Inc., 1982), pp. 242–248.

good compensable factor if some jobs require little physical effort while others are physically demanding. Third, a compensable factor should be measurable. For example, physical effort may be measured by the amount of lifting, bending, walking, and climbing ordinarily done on a job during a typical workday. A compensable factor that is difficult to measure can make the job evaluation process subjective and uncertain. Fourth, the compensable factor should be accepted and well understood by those performing the job evaluation. The collective bargaining agreement may stipulate the manner in which the union and company select the compensable factors.

3. *Development of a job evaluation system.* Four major types of job evaluation systems are the ranking, classification, factor comparison, and point methods. The selection of a particular job evaluation method will depend on factors such as the number and complexity of the jobs being evaluated, the degree of accuracy desired, and the time and money available to perform the evaluation.

4. *Implementation.* Once an evaluation method has been selected, benchmark jobs identified, and the final instrument designed, the job evaluation process begins. Most job evaluations are conducted by a committee familiar with the organization's jobs or by consultants specializing in compensation management.

Job Evaluation: Some Important Considerations

Several important points regarding job evaluation should be emphasized. First, as the name implies, job evaluation is an attempt to assess and evaluate a specific job or category of jobs, *not* the person holding the job. The latter issue is the function of performance appraisal and individual seniority. Thus, a janitor who holds a master's degree in electrical engineering is paid on the same basis as a janitor with an eighth-grade education.

Second, job evaluation is a subjective process. Even when the job evaluation contains a number of detailed and well-designed compensable factors, an element of subjectivity is involved. If poorly constructed, a job evaluation may create a false sense of precision that, in the end, may contribute little to improving the pay structure. It is therefore vital that job evaluations be conducted under the auspices of union and management representatives who are familiar with the organization and its jobs.

Third, job evaluation creates a *job hierarchy* that provides a foundation for setting pay rates as long as job descriptions and specifications do not change. If additional tasks or responsibilities are added to a job, then the job should be re-evaluated. Arbitration cases frequently arise over wage adjustment disputes related to technological and operational changes that alter the content of a job.[40] A job may be overpaid (a red-circle job) or underpaid (a blue-circle job) relative to what the job evaluation dictates is an equitable pay rate. Employees in red-circle jobs who are overpaid will resent having their pay cut to conform with the job evalu-

---

[40] For an excellent discussion of arbitrating job classification and job evaluation disputes, see Jack Stieber, "Job Classification, Overtime, and Holiday Pay," in Arnold M. Zack, ed., *Arbitration in Practice* (Ithaca, New York: ILR Press, Cornell University, 1984), pp. 103–113.

ation.[41] For red-circle jobs, it might be wise to wait until the employee is promoted, transferred, or quits his or her job before hiring a successor at the new and lower rate. Of course, employees who are in blue-circle jobs are usually pleased to have their pay increased. Before making a decision to alter the pay rate for a job, wage and salary survey information should also be considered.

Computerized Job Evaluation and Skill-Based Pay

Much of the time-consuming effort spent on maintaining a job evaluation program can be reduced by combining personal computers with job evaluation software. Computer-aided systems simplify the administration of job evaluation programs and provide a more expedient means of processing job evaluation information. Job data can be collected from supervisors by using a structured, machine-scoreable questionnaire.[42] Computer software can be used to analyze the questionnaire responses and to perform the job evaluation. With the advent of skill-based pay, which focuses on an employee's education, experience, and skills developed in training programs, a computer program can update employee knowledge and skills as they are acquired. Pay adjustments are then made to reflect the employee's increased knowledge and skills.[43] Collective bargaining agreements covering elementary and secondary public school teachers, for example, provide pay increases for college credits earned beyond the bachelor's degree.

▲ Merging the Pay Level and Pay Structure

At some point during contract talks, union and management negotiators must combine the information from the wage and salary survey and job evaluations to determine (1) the organization's pay policy line, (2) the number of pay grades, (3) the range or monetary spread for each pay grade, and (4) the degree of overlap between pay grades.

Establishing the Pay Policy Line

The pay policy line represents the organization's pay level relative to what competitors pay for similar jobs.[44] Figure 13–1 illustrates the relationship between wage

---

[41] Paul Reed and Mark J. Kroll, "Red Circle Employees: A Wage Scale Dilemma," *Personnel Journal* (February 1987), p. 92.
[42] Jill Kanin-Lovers, "Salary Practices," in the *Human Resources Yearbook*, 1987 edition (Englewood Cliffs, New Jersey: Prentice-Hall, Inc., 1987), p. 2.133
[43] See Gerald E. Ledford, Jr., *The Design of Skill-Based Pay Systems*, CEO Publication No. G89–15(158) (Los Angeles: Center for Effective Organizations, Graduate School of Business, University of Southern California, October 1989) and Edward E. Lawler, III, and Gerald E. Ledford, "Skill Based Pay: A Concept That Is Catching On," *Management Review* (February 1987), p. 46
[44] George T. Milkovich and Jerry M. Newman, *Compensation* , 2nd ed. (Plano, Texas: Business Publications, Inc., 1987), pp. 249–256 and 626.

EXTERNAL EQUITY (PAY LEVEL)

Major Issue: How does an organization's pay compare to the pay received by employees in similar firms?

Pay levels are affected by:
- Minimum wage legislation
- Compensation paid by similar firms
- Labor unions
- Labor market and economic conditions
- Financial condition of the firm

Pay levels are analyzed through wage and salary surveys

Merging the pay level and the pay structure
- Pay policy lines
- Pay grades

Base wage or salary

INTERNAL EQUITY (PAY STRUCTURE)

Major Issue: How does an organization place a relative value on their jobs?

Pay structures are affected by:
- Job descriptions
- Job specifications
- Benchmark jobs
- Compensable factors
- Judgments by those responsible for job evaluation

Pay structures are established through job evaluation
- Ranking method
- Classification method
- Factor comparison
- Point method
- other methods

Total individual compensation (excluding employee benefits)

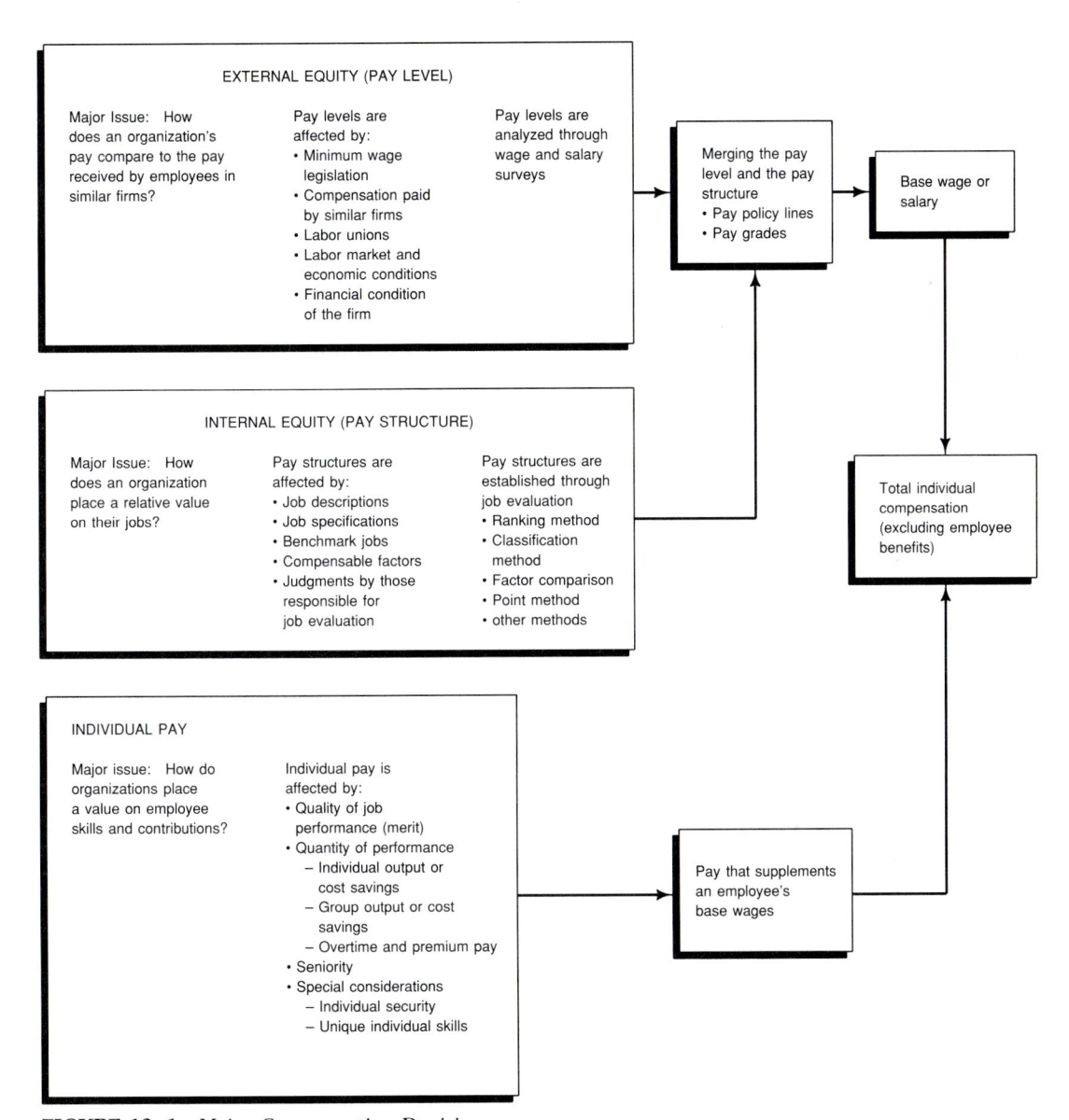

INDIVIDUAL PAY

Major issue: How do organizations place a value on employee skills and contributions?

Individual pay is affected by:
- Quality of job performance (merit)
- Quantity of performance
  - Individual output or cost savings
  - Group output or cost savings
  - Overtime and premium pay
- Seniority
- Special considerations
  - Individual security
  - Unique individual skills

Pay that supplements an employee's base wages

FIGURE 13–1 Major Compensation Decisions
Source: Terry L. Leap and Michael D. Crino, *Personnel/Human Resource Management* (New York: Macmillan Publishing Company, 1989), p. 382. Reprinted with permission.

and salary survey data and the pay policy options.[45] When negotiating the pay provisions within a collective bargaining agreement, the employer has three options for competing in the labor market. One option is for a firm to be a pay *leader* and offer wages and salaries that are higher than most industry or labor market competitors.[46] Firms may adopt the pay-leader strategy as a means of discouraging union organizing campaigns. A second option is to *meet* the competition and pay approximately the same rates as labor market competitors for comparable jobs. Finally, the employer may elect or be forced (because of tight operating budgets) to be a *follower* in the labor market and pay less than most competitors. A company that is a follower would likely receive pressure from the union to raise pay levels to the point of at least meeting the labor market competition. However, there is usually more to a pay increase than meets the eye, especially for firms with comprehensive employee benefits. As noted in Chapter 9, roll-up costs must be considered whenever a pay increase is planned. Pay raises not only increase salaries and wages, but they also increase the cost of employee benefits such as retirement plans, paid vacations, holiday pay, sick leave, overtime, and other benefits. Roll-up costs may comprise an additional 30 percent of a total pay increase. Thus an employer granting a ten percent pay increase would actually raise total labor costs by 13 percent (10% + [10% × 30%] = 13%). A complete discussion of calculating settlement costs is contained in the Appendix to Chapter 14.

Determining the Number of Pay Grades or Job Classifications

A number of collective bargaining agreements provide for a single wage rate for employees performing a job. Under a single-wage rate system, an employee is usually paid the initial rate specified in the contract and is given pay increases based on seniority and cost-of-living adjustments. Some single rate systems have no upper

---

[45] The formula for a straight line is $y = a + bX$, where y is the wage or salary rate, a is the point at which the line crosses or intercepts the y axis, X is the number of job evaluation points for each job, and b is the slope of the wage line. The straight line formula for a set of job evaluation points and pay rates can be derived through a process known as the *least squares method*, which is a component of regression analysis. Any elementary statistics book will provide the formula for the least squares method. An alternative to using least squares is to plot the wage line by drawing a straight line through the center of the scatter graph and then deriving the linear equation by sampling several points along the line to determine the slope (that is, the change in y divided by the change in x). Suppose that a set of annual salary data generate the following pay line for a manufacturing plant.
$$y = \$3.60 + 0.09X$$
If the job of an assembly-line employee working in a plant is worth 300 points (out of 500 maximum), then the *average* hourly wage paid to this position would be:
$$y = \$3.60 + 0.09(300)$$
$$= \$6.30$$
Some assembly-line workers would receive an hourly wage above $6.30 and some would receive a salary that is less than this amount. The $6.30 represents the approximate *midpoint* salary for all assembly-line workers employed at the manufacturing plant.

[46] Firms that adopt a pay-leader strategy may offset some of their higher wage costs through improved productivity and lower hiring and turnover costs. According to research by labor economist Harry J. Holzer, cost savings may be greater for firms that have *chosen* high wage levels than for firms in which unions have imposed high wage levels. See Harry J. Holzer, "Wages, Employer Costs, and Employee Performance in the Firm," *Industrial and Labor Relations Review* (February 1990, Special Issue), p. 147-S.

limit.[47] However, approximately half of the contracts surveyed by The Bureau of National Affairs, Inc., use pay grades (also known as pay ranges).[48] Pay grades stipulate minimum and maximum pay rates for each job. In essence, each pay grade becomes a form of job classification. When a variety of jobs are found in an organization, job evaluation is used to place each job into a pay grade. Jobs within a pay grade usually receive the same salary or wage, subject to individual differences in employee job performance (merit), seniority, or productivity. Figure 13–2 illustrates the determination of pay grades using the point method of job evaluation (see appendix). Under the point method, jobs with higher point values are generally paid at a higher rate. Point values and a corresponding salary have been previously established for the category of 45 jobs (one dot per job) evaluated under the point method.

Six pay grades were established for the 45 jobs illustrated in Figure 13–2. For example, jobs evaluated as having between 550 and 700 points would fall into pay grade IV and would all have the same base salary or wage rate even though there can be a 150-point difference among jobs in this pay grade. Too few pay grades can create employee morale problems because jobs with significantly different tasks, responsibilities, and working conditions would be paid the same base salary or wage rate. On the other hand, too many pay grades can create pay differentials among jobs that are essentially the same.

The pay grades depicted in Figure 13–2 are equally spaced at 150-point intervals. However, unequal point intervals may be appropriate if the point values of the jobs are not evenly distributed between low and high point values. Gaps in point values or clusters in point values may also require the use of unequal point intervals.

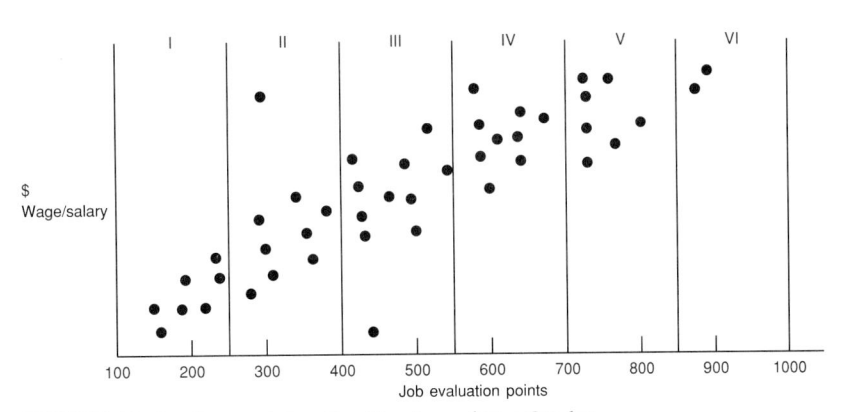

FIGURE 13–2 Determining the Number of Pay Grades
Source: Terry L. Leap and Michael D. Crino, *Personnel/Human Resource Management* (New York: Macmillan Publishing Company, 1989), p. 382. Reprinted with permission.

---

[47] The Bureau of National Affairs, Inc., "Wages," *Collective Bargaining Negotiations & Contracts* (Washington, D.C.: The Bureau of National Affairs, Inc., 1987), section 93.
[48] The Bureau of National Affairs, Inc., "Wages," *Collective Bargaining Negotiations & Contracts* (Washington, D.C.: The Bureau of National Affairs, Inc., 1989), section 93.

Determining the Range of the Pay Grades

Because jobs within a pay grade receive the same base wage or salary rate (with individual differences in pay being geared to seniority, merit, productivity, and shift differentials), it is necessary to determine the minimum and maximum pay that can be earned for each pay grade. Jobs at the lower end of the point value spectrum have narrower pay grade ranges than those at the upper end of the point scale. Figure 13–3 illustrates the application of this idea. Notice that the height of the pay grade "boxes" increases when one moves from the lower to the higher pay grades. The primary reason for having "taller" pay grades at the upper end of the structure is that it is possible to have greater variations in employee performance for the higher-value jobs. However, unions often prefer to negotiate absolute pay increases (employees receive an hourly wage increase of 98 cents) as opposed to an across-the-board percentage increase. Absolute pay increases have the effect of compressing pay rates so that the *percentage* wage differential between lower-paid workers and higher-paid workers is diminished or compressed.[49]

Determining Overlap between Pay Grades

An examination of Figure 13–3 illustrates that overlap exists between adjacent pay grades. A set of pay grades may have little or no overlap or a high degree of overlap, depending on a number of factors. First, if there are considerable differences between jobs from one grade to another (based on point values), then there will be

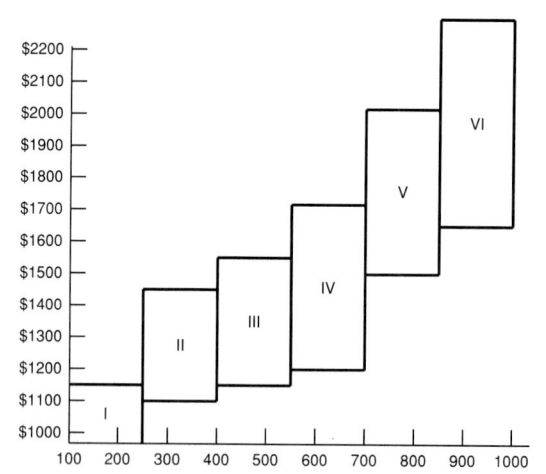

FIGURE 13–3 Determining Pay Grade Ranges
Source: Terry L. Leap and Michael D. Crino, *Personnel/Human Resource Management* (New York: Macmillan Publishing Company, 1989), p. 409. Reprinted with permission.

---

[49] A $1.00 wage increase represents a ten percent raise for an employee earning $10.00 an hour, but only a five percent increase for an employee earning $20.00 per hour.

little overlap between pay grades. Conversely, small differences denote a greater degree of overlap. If the amount of overlap extends beyond adjacent pay grades (for example, the maximum pay rate of grade III is greater than the minimum pay rate for grade V), then there may be too many pay grades. Second, if seniority is used as a primary means of providing pay increases, a greater degree of overlap may be necessary. The height of the pay grades may be increased to avoid the "dead-end street" phenomenon encountered by long-term, senior employees who are trapped at the top of the pay grade. Third, a higher degree of overlap may reduce the total compensation cost to the organization. On the other hand, less overlap increases the steepness and may also increase the cost of the pay structure (see Figure 13–3).[50]

The Use of Seniority and Merit in Pay Increases

Two or more employees doing identical work do not always receive the same level of pay. A compensation system that uses pay grades must have a procedure that allows employees to progress upward through a pay range from the minimum to the maximum pay rate. An employee may advance upward in a pay grade because of seniority, superior performance ratings, or a combination of these.

Seniority as the Sole Factor

Unless there are significant differences in job performance between two employees performing the same job, the one with the greater seniority will probably receive more pay. According to The Bureau of National Affairs, Inc., survey data, 57 percent of contracts containing pay grades and progression scales use length of service *alone* to determine pay increases.[51] These are two reasons for using seniority in compensation decisions. First, for jobs in the lower pay grades, differences in the caliber of job performance among employees may be minimal. For example, the difference in quality of performance between an "average" and a "good" assembly-line worker may be slight because the job is controlled by the pace of the conveyer line. When it is not possible for employees to engage in distinctive job performance, seniority often plays a central role in determining pay increases.

Second, some organizations have no satisfactory performance appraisal system. The use of seniority in compensation decisions has the advantage of being totally objective and therefore is legally defensible; it also takes pressure off supervisors who must otherwise justify individual performance ratings and compensation decisions. Seniority is a more objective and less controversial yardstick for making pay adjustments than merit systems, which are often based on subjective performance appraisals. Unions favor promoting equality among employees and pay increases linked to seniority provide for objective distinctions among employees

---

[50] The overall cost of the pay structure is also affected by the number of employees in each pay grade. If a large number of employees hold jobs in higher pay grades, then the pay structure will be "high cost" even though it is relatively flat.

[51] The Bureau of National Affairs, Inc., *Basic Patterns in Union Contracts*, 11th ed. (Washington, D.C.: The Bureau of National Affairs, Inc., 1986).

that cannot be altered because of internal politics, favoritism, and individual ambition. Table 13-4 provides an excerpt from a contract clause that uses seniority to regulate pay increases.

The Use of Merit in Compensation Decisions

A well-designed and well-administered performance appraisal system can provide a foundation for determining and justifying merit pay increases.[52] The Bureau of National Affairs, Inc., survey data indicate that 29 percent of the contract clauses base wage progression on length of service only if performance merits progression. Seven percent of the contracts base initial progression (usually to the midpoint of the pay grade) on seniority, with further advancement depending on merit. An additional seven percent of the contracts base wage progression *solely* on merit.[53]

Care must be taken to tailor the performance appraisal system to job-relevant behaviors and results. Merit pay increases are based on noteworthy job performance and should be distinguished from pay adjustments geared to seniority or changes in the cost of living.

Table 13-5 provides an example of how pay adjustments are made by combining merit and cost-of-living increases. An employee's pay within a pay grade falls into a percentile or quartile. Suppose monthly salaries in a pay grade range from $1,500 to $2,300. Assuming that employee pay is evenly distributed throughout the pay grade, then the first quartile (0 to 25th percentile) is approximately $1,500 to $1,700, the second quartile (26th to 50th percentile) $1,700 to $1,900, the third quartile (51st to 75th percentile) $1,900 to $2,100, and the fourth quartile (76th to 99th percentile) $2,100 to $2,300. According to Table 13-5, if an organization decides to give employees a five percent cost-of-living adjustment, then an employee in the *60th percentile* with a *superior* rating would receive a 12 percent increase (7 percent + 5 percent). On the other hand, a marginal employee in the same pay grade and percentile would receive only a 2 1/4 percent raise (1 percent + 5 percent/4 percent).

Several factors pertaining to Table 13-5 should be noted. First, employees in the higher quartiles receive a slightly smaller *percentage* increase than those in the

Table 13-4 ▲ Pay Increases Based on Seniority

All new hires . . . shall be paid on the following basis:	
First year of employment:	85% of Union Wage Scale
Second year of employment:	90% of Union Wage Scale
Third year of employment:	95% of Union Wage Scale
Fourth year of employment:	To be brought to Union Wage Scale

Source: Collective bargaining agreement between Six Hundred Superior Corporation and Hotel Employees and Restaurant Employees International Union (expired October 1988) in The Bureau of National Affairs, Inc., "Wages," *Collective Bargaining Negotiations & Contracts* (Washington, D.C.: The Bureau of National Affairs, Inc., 1986), section 93. Reprinted with permission.

---

[52] Robert H. Rock, "Pay for Performance: Measures and Standards," *Compensation Review* (Third Quarter 1984), pp. 15–25.
[53] The Bureau of National Affairs, Inc., *Basic Patterns in Union Contracts*, 11th ed. (Washington, D.C.: The Bureau of National Affairs, Inc., 1986).

Table 13–5 ▲ Pay Adjustments Based on Merit and Cost of Living

Maximum		Location in Pay Grade	Superior	Good	Marginal	Unacceptable
	100th Percentile					
		4th Quartile	6% + X	3% + X	0	0
	75th Percentile					
		3rd Quartile	7% + X	1% + X	$1\% + \frac{X}{4}$	0
	50th Percentile					
		2nd Quartile	8% + X	5% + X	$1\% + \frac{X}{3}$	0
	25th Percentile					
Minimum		1st Quartile	9% + X	6% + X	$2\% + \frac{X}{3}$	0
	0th Percentile					

X = percentage cost-of-living adjustment.
Source: Terry L. Leap and Michael D. Crino, *Personnel/Human Resource Management* (New York: Macmillan Publishing Company, 1989), p. 412. Reprinted with permission.

lower quartiles because of the higher wage and salary rates in the upper end of a pay grade. Second, the percentage increase in cost-of-living (denoted by X) is calculated separately from merit increases. Third, employees whose performance is marginal will receive little or no merit increase and will run the risk of having their *real* income (income adjusted for changes in the cost of living) reduced. A merit plan such as this is easy for employees to understand and should encourage superior job performance. Employees receiving marginal or unacceptable ratings should be evaluated more frequently to detect job performance changes that can be used for pay adjustments or other personnel actions.

Combining Seniority and Merit

When seniority and merit are combined, management must decide how much weight should be given to each. Even in situations where merit has a strong influence on pay, small seniority-based increases can be used to reward loyalty and to account for the fact that superior job performance associated with seniority is often difficult to measure. For example, an employee who has a long association with a firm understands the internal politics and informal organizational structure; this situation may be an aid to better working relationships and job performance. Employees with lengthy service records often have "learned the ropes" and have developed an ability to cut through red tape and the bureaucratic maze in order to get things done in an expedient fashion. Pay increases that are, in part, based on seniority recognize this phenomenon.[54]

---

[54] See John E. Buckley, "Wage Differences Among Workers in the Same Job and Establishment," *Monthly Labor Review* (March 1985), p. 11.

An employee moves through a pay grade in an elevator-like fashion based on merit, seniority, or some combination of the two. In general, movement from the bottom to the midpoint (50th percentile) of a specific pay grade is more rapid than movement from the midpoint to the top. When seniority and merit are combined, employees with average job performance may move from the bottom to the middle of the pay grade primarily on seniority. However, to receive pay beyond the midpoint might require superior job performance. Another alternative is to make seniority a *necessary, but not sufficient condition* for pay raises into each quartile or percentile of a pay grade. For example, an organization may decide that two years of seniority is *necessary* for an employee to move into the second quartile of a pay grade. However, an employee will not be given a pay raise unless his or her performance is also above average.

Employees who reach the top of a pay grade have limited opportunity to receive additional pay raises. Unless the employee is promoted or his or her job is reclassified to a higher pay grade (because the job is enlarged and given additional tasks, duties, and responsibilities), pay increases may be limited to annual cost-of-living adjustments. As a result, the incentive for superior performance may be diminished for employees who are hemmed in at the top of a pay grade. To combat this problem, pay systems may provide limited merit increases or bonuses for employees who demonstrate superior performance or loyalty. Gold-circle rates are applied to superior employees who are at the top of their pay grade and receive a merit wage or salary increase, whereas silver-circle rates are used for senior employees.[55] An alternative to gold- and silver-circle rates are 10-year, 15-year, or 20-year cash bonuses for high-seniority employees who are at the top of a pay grade and display meritorious job performance. Bonuses allow the company to reward employees and satisfy the union without raising base pay rates and becoming "locked in" to a more expensive pay structure.

Supplementary Pay

Collective bargaining agreements often require that employees who work at inconvenient hours or perform hazardous duties receive supplementary pay. One common type of supplementary pay is the *shift differential*. Shift differentials are designed to compensate an employee for working undesirable hours and are commonplace for firms having more than one work shift. Organizations using three eight-hour shifts generally pay employees who work in the evenings (e.g., 4 P.M. until midnight) a higher rate than those working during the day. Employees working the night shift (e.g., midnight until 8 A.M.) receive the highest shift differential since these work hours are usually regarded as the least desirable. A shift differential may consist of a flat cents-per-hour bonus or a percentage of hourly earnings. Some agreements stipulate that an employee working only part of an evening or night shift will receive a full eight-hours' pay. If an employee's eight-hour work schedule overlaps between evening and night shifts, some contracts apply the shift differential of the higher-paying shift for the entire eight-hour period.

---

[55] Richard I. Henderson, *Compensation Management: Rewarding Performance*, 2nd ed. (Reston, Virginia: Reston Publishing Co., Inc., 1979), p. 293.

Many collective bargaining agreements provide guarantees for employees who report for regularly scheduled work without having been told that no work is available. A provision such as this is known as a *reporting pay guarantee* and it usually pays the employee for several hours of work even when the employee performs little or no work. For example, a construction industry contract may compensate workers who report to a building site and are told by the contractor that no work is available. Reporting pay provisions may provide a minimum guarantee of three or four hours of pay.

Another form of supplementary pay is *call-back* pay. Employees who are called in outside of their regularly scheduled hours frequently are offered a minimum pay guarantee or some payment over and above their usual rate as compensation for the inconvenience of working at an irregular hour. Such guarantees may be paid straight time, time-and-one-half, or at a double-time rate. Contracts calling for a guaranteed call-back pay of at least three hours, for example, may allow the employee to quit work once the purpose of the call back is accomplished (e.g., a repair job that lasts only two hours) or the contract may require that the employee remain and perform other duties in order to fill the three-hour period.

Collective bargaining agreements usually contain contracts for special wage differentials when employees must perform supervisory or work leader duties. In addition, contracts frequently provide for supplementary pay when employees are required to work outside of their normal job or perform hazardous or "dirty" work.[56] Airlines sometimes pay higher rates for crew members who must fly at night or on transcontinental routes.

Overtime and premium pay schedules are used for two major reasons. First, the Fair Labor Standards Act (FLSA) requires that nonexempt employees receive one and one half times their normal pay for time worked in excess of 40 hours per week.[57] The penalties for failing to comply with the Act can be expensive. El Paso Natural Gas Company was ordered by the U.S. Department of Labor to pay $7.6 million to workers who were entitled to overtime wages. These individuals were employed as operators and repair personnel at the company's remote cites in Texas and New Mexico.[58] Second, employers are often willing to pay higher hourly rates or salaries to employees who work during weekends or holidays. Organizations also provide meal allowances for employees who must work outside the traditional daytime hours.

The purpose of premium and overtime pay is to motivate employees to accept additional and less desirable working hours or, at least, make the acceptance of such work more palatable. Collective bargaining agreements dealing with overtime typically address two issues: (1) *who* is entitled to overtime work, and (2) the *amount* of pay that an employee receives for working overtime. Overtime assignments are often offered based on an employee's skill and ability to perform the work, as well as on individual seniority. Some collective bargaining agreements call

---

[56] The Bureau of National Affairs, Inc., "Wages," *Collective Bargaining Negotiations & Contracts* (Washington, D.C.: The Bureau of National Affairs, Inc., 1987), section 93.
[57] Gina Ameci, "Overtime Pay: Avoiding FLSA Violations," *Personnel Administrator* (February 1987), p. 117.
[58] *The Wall Street Journal*, Labor Letter (October 14, 1986), p. 1.

for one-and-a-half times the regular pay rate to employees working more than eight, but less than 12 hours per day and double time for any work beyond 12 hours. Employees who must remain on call during off-duty hours are often paid a guaranteed minimum number of hours to compensate for the social disruption and uncertainty associated with being on call.[59] About one fourth of the collective bargaining agreements surveyed by The Bureau of National Affairs, Inc., contain sixth- and seventh-day premiums for employees who work six or seven days consecutively.[60]

The vast majority of collective bargaining agreements contain provisions that prohibit the "pyramiding" of overtime pay. Pyramiding occurs when an employee is receiving premium pay, such as pay for working on a holiday, and then collecting overtime on top of the premium pay for working more than eight hours (e.g., time-and-a-half *of the holiday rate*). Nonexempt employees who must work overtime are sometimes given compensatory time off or additional pay even though this is not required by the FLSA.

Wage Adjustments during the Life of the Collective Bargaining Agreement

Since collective bargaining agreements often have a duration of three or more years, union negotiators often press for provisions that will allow wages and salaries either to be renegotiated or automatically adjusted during the life of the contract. One type of wage adjustment during the life of the contract is a *deferred wage increase*. Most contracts of more than one year's duration contain deferred increases of some stipulated amount. For example, Table 13–6 presents a contract provision that provides semiannual wage increases.

Deferred increases may also be based on productivity or efficiency improvements. Occasionally, the amount of a deferred increase in a firm is based on amounts provided to workers in other firms within an industry.[61]

Table 13–6 ▲ Deferred Wage Increase Provision

General increases in the base rates negotiated by the parties for all work done at the Grand Haven, Michigan plant will be effective as follows:

March 4, 1985	$10.54	per hour (Journeyman)
September 2, 1985	$10.75	per hour (Journeyman)
March 3, 1986	$10.97	per hour (Journeyman)
September 1, 1986	$11.19	per hour (Journeyman)
March 2, 1987	$11.41	per hour (Journeyman)
August 31, 1987	$11.64	per hour (Journeyman)

Source: Bastian Blessing and Sheet Metal Workers contract (expired March 1988). In The Bureau of National Affairs, Inc., "Wages," *Collective Bargaining Negotiations and Contracts* (Washington, D.C.: The Bureau of National Affairs, Inc., 1987). Reprinted with permission.

[59] Gary S. Marx, "Is On-Call Time Compensable?" *Journal of Property Management* (November-December 1986), p. 70.
[60] The Bureau of National Affairs, Inc., "Wages," *Collective Bargaining Negotiations & Contracts* (Washington, D.C.: The Bureau of National Affairs, Inc., 1989), section 93.
[61] The Bureau of National Affairs, Inc., "Wages," *Collective Bargaining Negotiations & Contracts* (Washington, D.C.: The Bureau of National Affairs, Inc., 1987), section 93.

Many contracts provide wage adjustments that are directly linked to the cost of living. *Cost-of-living adjustments* (COLAs) usually tie increases to changes in the Bureau of Labor Statistics Consumer Price Index. Most COLA provisions contain the following components:

1. *Adjustment intervals*: Most escalators adjust wages at a specified interval such as quarterly (most common), semiannually, or annually and reflect price changes from the preceding period.
2. *Adjustment formulas*: Most clauses include a specific formula for making wage increases. A common formula is a 1-cent increase for every 0.3 point change in the consumer price index. COLAs may also have corridors, which require that the index rise by a given percentage before pay adjustments are made. As a general rule, COLA formulas do not grant wage increases for the full amount of the CPI change. Thus if the CPI increases by five percent, a COLA formula may provide for a three percent adjustment.
3. *CPI*: Most escalators use the national All-Cities CPI (1967 = 100) as a base.[62]
4. *Minimum and maximum adjustments*: Some COLAs have provisions for minimum raises and impose ceilings that would limit COLA increases during periods of high inflation.
5. *Fold-ins or roll ins*: COLAs stipulate the extent to which adjustments will be "folded" into the base rate as well as the extent to which increases will be reflected in benefits such as paid vacation and personal leave. In addition, some COLAs provide that a certain amount of the adjustment will be diverted to employee benefit costs. These provisions can have a significant effect on overtime premiums, incentive earnings, paid vacations, and other benefits that are tied to *base* wage and salary rates.[63]

Another method of changing wage and salary rates during the life of the contract is through *wage reopeners*. Wage-reopening provisions allow renegotiation of pay scales at specified intervals. Approximately 10 percent of the contracts surveyed by The Bureau of National Affairs, Inc., contained wage reopener provisions.[64] Wage-reopening clauses generally stipulate which contract clauses are subject to renegotiation (e.g., wage rates, but not overtime, shift differentials, or supplementary pay). Such clauses also stipulate when wages can be renegotiated (e.g., 30 days prior to the beginning of the second anniversary of the agreement).

Two-Tier Compensation Systems

In order to contain total labor costs without cutting the pay of long-term, senior employees, some organizations such as the U.S. Postal Service and the airlines have adopted two-tier compensation systems.[65] Under a two-tier system, employees

---

[62] In addition, most escalators use the index for Urban Wage Earners and Clerical Workers—Revised (CPI-W) rather than the All Urban Consumers (CPI-U).
[63] The Bureau of National Affairs, Inc., "Wages," *Collective Bargaining Negotiations & Contracts* (Washington, D.C.: The Bureau of National Affairs, Inc., 1987), section 93.
[64] The Bureau of National Affairs, Inc., "Wages," *Collective Bargaining Negotiations & Contracts* (Washington, D.C.: The Bureau of National Affairs, Inc., 1989), section 93.
[65] David Wessel, "Two-Tier Pay Spreads, But the Pioneer Firms Encounter Problems," *The Wall Street Journal* (October 14, 1985), pp. 1 and 9; and Jane Seaberry, "Two-Tiered Wages: More Jobs v. More Worker Alienation," *Washington Post* (April 7, 1985), pp. G1-G3.

hired after a specific "cutoff" date receive less pay than employees hired before the cutoff date. New employees often receive fewer employee benefits than senior employees. Two-tier pay systems in collective bargaining agreements represent a union concession to an employer who is financially pressed by high labor costs. Senior employees are able to maintain their accustomed pay levels and standard of living while job applicants know that, if hired, they will be paid less than current employees. Whether new employees suffer morale problems because of these pay differentials is uncertain. However, a study of airline employees found that lower-wage ('B' tier) workers felt significantly more satisfied with their pay, work, supervision, and job security than higher-paid ('A' tier) workers.[66] Some organizations gradually phase employees into the higher tier as they accumulate seniority. There is some evidence that two-tier systems had begun to decline in the late 1980s.[67]

Wage Rates for Promotions, Demotions, and Transfers

Employees who are moved to new jobs normally receive the contractual pay rate for the new job. Some contracts, however, provide for gradual pay adjustments. For example, an employee who is promoted to a higher-paying job may not receive the higher rate until the employee completes a probationary period or demonstrates that he or she is fully capable of performing the new job. Employees who are demoted may have their pay cut gradually to avoid the shock of a large pay decrease. Some contracts allow older or disabled employees to transfer to less-demanding, lower-paying jobs and retain the pay rate from their previous position. Other contracts permit individuals who are temporarily transferred to a different job to receive either the pay rate for the new job or their previous pay rate, whichever is higher.

▲ Individual and Group Incentive Programs

Incentive programs are usually geared to measurable performance results such as units of production, sales volume, cost savings, or profitability.[68] Performance-based compensation systems that are properly designed and administered can be instrumental in increasing productivity and lowering costs.[69] On the other hand, a mismanaged incentive program may have side effects that are counterproductive both to the plan's objectives and to harmonious union-management relations. According

---

[66] Peter Cappelli and Peter Sherer, "Assessing Worker Attitudes Under a Two-Tier Wage Plan," *Industrial and Labor Relations Review* (January 1990), pp. 225–244.
[67] *The Wall Street Journal*, Labor Letter (June 16, 1987), p. 1. Also see Marvin J. Levine, "The Evolution of Two-Tier Wage Agreements: Bane or Panacea in Labor Relations?" *Labor Law Journal* (January 1989), pp. 12–20.
[68] Incentive plans differ from merit plans. Incentive pay is directly linked to the amount of work or cost savings, but does not affect an employee's permanent wage or salary. Merit pay is linked to quality of work and generally affects the employee's permanent wage or salary.
[69] Hoyt Doyel and Thomas Riley, "Considerations in Developing Incentive Plans," *Management Review*, (March 1987), p. 34; and Jerry McAdams, "Rewarding Sales and Marketing Performance," *Management Review* (April 1987), p. 33.

to The Bureau of National Affairs, Inc., survey data, incentive or piecework pay is addressed in 32 percent of the collective bargaining agreements sampled, most of which are in the manufacturing sector. Of these agreements, seven percent either prohibit the establishment of an incentive plan or require union consent to adopt a plan. Most agreements that mention incentive programs do not elaborate on the details of the system. Provisions dealing with incentive pay systems often outline the means by which rates are set and the conditions under which the union may file a grievance over rates that are regarded as unfair. Seventy-two percent of the contracts with incentive pay provisions in The Bureau of National Affairs, Inc., sample allow the company to establish new rates without union participation, 21 percent require consultation with the union, and seven percent require union consent before setting incentive rates.[70]

Individual Incentive Programs

A variety of individual incentive plans have been used to promote productivity, increase efficiency, and improve employee job satisfaction. Frederick W. Taylor and his colleagues in the scientific management school paved the way for individual incentive programs by carefully establishing performance standards and linking pay to work output.[71]

Several conditions are important to the successful operation of individual incentive programs. First, individual jobs must not be too interdependent. Production delays that are not controllable by the employee make it difficult to link effort, performance, and pay. Employee frustration, lower morale, and grievances may arise if mechanical problems or supply shortages create "down time" and destroy the opportunity to earn incentive pay.[72]

Second, individual incentive programs require that output be objectively and accurately measured. Employees must understand the basis for their incentive pay and must trust management to keep accurate records of employee output.

Third, production standards upon which the individual incentive plan is based must be carefully established and maintained. Productivity and incentive standards must be neither too "loose" nor too "tight." A "loose" standard means that an employee can produce at levels that will enable him or her to attain high amounts of pay. Although employees will undoubtedly appreciate a "loose" rate, the organization's labor costs may become prohibitively high. "Loose" rates may cut into profitability or, worse, cause financial problems for the organization. If the employer attempts to tighten a "loose" rate, employee morale will suffer. "Tight" rates, on the other hand, make it difficult to earn adequate incentive pay and discourage individual effort. Establishing standards that are neither too "loose" nor too "tight" requires careful time-and-motion study and adjustments for employee deception

---

[70] The Bureau of National Affairs, Inc., "Wages," *Collective Bargaining Negotiations & Contracts* (Washington, D.C.: The Bureau of National Affairs, Inc., 1989), section 93.
[71] Daniel A. Wren, *The Evolution of Management Thought* (New York: Ronald Press, 1972), pp. 111–146.
[72] See Charles Brown, "Firms' Choice of Method of Pay," *Industrial and Labor Relations Review* (February 1990, Special Issue), p. 165-S.

(usually slowdowns in the presence of time-and-motion analysts), fatigue, and other potential interruptions to the work flow.[73]

Once the production standards are established, they must be linked to pay rates. Incentive rate scales may be fixed, increasing, or decreasing. *Fixed* scales pay the same amount for each additional unit of output or sales. For example, an employee who receives 25 cents for each unit produced is on a fixed scale. An *increasing* incentive rate might provide 25 cents for the first 50 units produced in a work day and then 30 cents per unit for production above the daily standard of 50 units. A *decreasing* scale might provide a 25-cent unit incentive for the first 50 units and a 20-cent rate for all production over 50 units per day. Because overhead costs per unit typically decrease as production or sales volume increases, an increasing incentive rate allows the employee to share in these cost savings. Decreasing incentive rates also reduce unit costs, but it is the organization rather than the employee who benefits from such cost savings.

A fourth consideration in deciding whether to implement an individual incentive system is the tradeoff between quantity and quality of output. A potential problem with persons who are on an incentive plan is that they may focus on work speed at the expense of product quality. Quality may be safeguarded by linking monetary rewards to error rates, customer complaints, or product rejections.

Finally, the amount that an employee can potentially earn under an individual incentive system must be high enough to motivate increased effort and productivity. A basic premise of any incentive plan is that employees value money and are willing to work for additional amounts. The problem with incentive systems is determining how much additional monetary incentive is necessary to motivate employees to produce more. Most employees will not notice a difference in take home pay when two percent is added to base compensation, but nearly all employees will notice a 20 percent addition to base pay. The next question is whether employees are willing to exert the additional effort needed to earn the incentive pay. Research indicates that the amount of additional pay needed to increase productivity varies considerably among individuals.[74] Factors such as inflation rates, the employee's total compensation level, and personal perceptions of what constitutes a noticeable pay increment are all relevant to the value that an employee attaches to different amounts of incentive pay.[75]

Collective bargaining agreements may place the following restrictions on the use of incentive programs:[76]

1. Most incentive provisions give management the right to establish new rates or revise existing rates. However, the union may challenge rate adjustments through the grievance procedure.
2. Some collective bargaining agreements specify conditions under which rates

---

[73] Frederick S. Hills, *Compensation Decision Making* (Chicago: The Dryden Press, 1987), pp. 352–353.
[74] P. Varadarajan and C. Futrell, "Factors Affecting Perceptions of Smallest Meaningful Pay Increases," *Industrial Relations*, Vol. 23 (1984), pp. 278–286.
[75] Edward E. Lawler, III, *Pay and Organization Development* (Reading, Massachusetts: Addison-Wesley Publishing Company, 1981), p. 88.
[76] See The Bureau of National Affairs, Inc., "Wages," *Collective Bargaining Negotiations & Contracts* (Washington, D.C.: The Bureau of National Affairs, Inc., 1987), section 93.

may be changed. Rate adjustments may be allowed only if there is a change in machinery, methods, or processes. In other instances, rates may be changed if they do not yield the expected earnings or if the original rate was not calculated correctly.

3. When rates are changed, some contracts stipulate that management cannot use the new rate to pay employees less than they made while working under the previous rate.
4. When time and motion studies are used to recalibrate the incentive system, the contract may contain provisions that the union be notified. Collective bargaining agreements may also regulate the qualifications of those performing the study, the employees to be analyzed, union access to records and data gathered from time-and-motions studies, and the union's right to appeal changes in work design or incentive rates.
5. Contracts occasionally deal with how employees will be paid for spoiled or damaged work as well as the conditions and pay rates associated with redoing or repairing such work.

Examples of Individual Incentive Programs

A common type of incentive program is the *piecework plan* in which an employee is paid a base wage or salary plus an incentive for each unit produced. The more an employee produces, the more pay he or she receives. Many plans provide a base pay, which assumes that the average employee will produce at least a standard number of units per hour. Once the employee exceeds the hourly standard output, additional pay is given for each unit over standard. These plans are called *standard hour plans* and they have been designed in a variety of ways.[77]

Employee stock ownership plans (ESOPs) involve employer contributions to an employee trust that are then invested in company stock. ESOPs provide tax and cash flow advantages to the employer; ESOPs also give an incentive to employees because they own stock in the corporation. Payments by the employer into the ESOP trust are tax deductible and serve as a major form of investment capital. Stock-owning employees are provided with an incentive to remain with the firm and help keep it profitable.[78]

Group and Organizational Incentives

Many organizations link pay to the efforts of an employee group. Compensation programs such as the Scanlon plan, a group cost savings plan that is designed to lower labor costs without lowering productivity, and the Lincoln Electric plan, a combined profit-sharing, year-end bonus, and piecework incentive plan, are two noteworthy examples. Profit-sharing programs represent another major form of

---

[77] See Frederick S. Hills, *Compensation Decision Making* (Chicago: The Dryden Press, 1987) for a discussion of the Halsey, Rowan, and Gantt Plans, all of which are standard hour plans.
[78] See Katherine J. Klein, "Employee Stock Ownership and Employee Attitudes: A Test of Three Models," *Journal of Applied Psychology* (May 1987), p. 319.

group and organizational incentive plans designed to allocate a fixed share of profits among employees based on a predetermined formula.

Group incentive systems may promote productivity and efficiency under circumstances in which individual incentive systems are not practical. For example, labor unions generally have not favored the use of individual incentive programs, but as a compromise during contract negotiations, may agree to a group or organization-wide plan. In addition, several other factors may preclude individual incentive plans and yet favor group incentives. Organizations that are technologically complex and characterized by a large number of interdependent jobs, such as a computer manufacturer, may be better served by group rather than individual incentive plans. However, the success of a group incentive plan is also dependent on a high degree of employee trust within the organization, good communications channels, and explicit organizational goals and performance measures.[79] Some union leaders also fear that group incentive programs may create an alliance between management and employees that could undermine the power and influence of the union.

The frequency with which incentive pay is given must be determined; frequent payments (more than once per year) can lead to an overemphasis on short-term results, such as minimizing costs, to the detriment of long-term concerns, such as safety or the proper maintenance of equipment. Longer time spans between incentive payments (less than once per year) can cause the plan to lose its motivational value because most employees do not want to defer monetary rewards for long periods of time. However, if an employee waits for a longer period to receive an incentive bonus, the employer has a better chance of paying a larger and more meaningful amount.

Examples of Group Incentive Programs

Among the more prominent group-incentive or gainsharing systems are the Scanlon Plan, the Lincoln Electric Plan, the Rucker Plan, and Improshare.[80] The Scanlon Plan was developed in 1935 by labor leader Joseph Scanlon; it provides a monthly cash bonus for the improved productivity of a plant or employee group. Emphasis is placed on encouraging employees to cut labor costs. A suggestion system and departmental and plantwide production committees are used to explain the plan to employees, to encourage them to submit cost-saving suggestions, and to evaluate these suggestions. Bonus systems are established on a formula basis that measures productivity gains and sets a procedure for sharing these gains equitably among workers. Under the Scanlon Plan, bonus payments are based on the ratio of total labor costs to total production costs. For example, if the ratio of the total labor cost to the total production cost is 40 percent, then employees receive a bonus whenever their cost savings efforts reduce this ratio below 40 percent. The monthly

---

[79] Edward E. Lawler, *Pay and Organization Development* (Reading, Massachusetts: Addison-Wesley Publishing Company, 1981), p. 83.

[80] The descriptions for these plans are based on a discussion in The Bureau of National Affairs, Inc., *Compensation: BNA Policy and Practice Series* (Washington, D.C.: The Bureau of National Affairs, Inc., 1981), section 321.

bonus is split three ways: the employer's share, the employees' share, and a percentage placed into the reserve fund. Employers typically receive about 25 percent of the savings and employees 60 percent. The remaining amount is placed in a reserve fund for months when the labor cost ratio is above 40 percent.

The Lincoln Electric plan combines generous year-end cash bonuses, guaranteed employment (30 hours per week for 49 weeks a year), and an individual incentive system. Tight controls are used to ensure quality control, and employees must correct errors on their own time. In financially strong years, Lincoln Electric employees have received bonuses equal to 100 percent of their base pay. Lincoln Electric employees are among the highest paid production employees in the United States, and the company has experienced very low employee turnover and cordial labor-management relations.

The Rucker Plan focuses on labor cost productivity. Labor cost productivity is the payroll divided by a concept known as "value added." Value added is the difference between net sales and costs required to produce the product. If a firm has sales of $4,000,000 and total costs of $2,500,000, then value added is $1,500,000. By examining labor cost data over a period of several years, the firm arrives at an appropriate ratio between labor costs and value added. Suppose the ratio is 50 percent. Using the above figures, assume that labor costs were $525,000, or 35 percent of value added. Employees would reap the benefits of a $225,000 cost savings ($1,500,000 × 50% minus $525,000). As in the Scanlon Plan, the employer receives a share, employees receive the largest share, and some of the savings are set aside in a reserve fund.

An Improshare Plan uses a standard labor hours *per unit* measure to assess employee efficiency and productivity. In essence, Improshare compares a standard productivity per unit measure with the actual labor cost per unit achieved by employees.

▲ Sex Discrimination in Compensation Programs

Compensation programs have been the subject of extensive litigation because females have been paid less than males for performing essentially the same work. When union and management negotiators set wage rates and formulate employee benefit plans, they must be cognizant of potential discriminatory effects of compensation programs. There are two types of sex discrimination cases involving compensation management: (1) cases involving *equal pay for equal work*, and (2) cases involving the concept of *comparable worth*. Both of these legal issues deal with aspects of internal equity because they are concerned with paying employees (without regard to sex) for the effort they expend and the contributions they make to the organization. However, there are several important distinctions between the equal pay and comparable worth concepts. First, the equal pay for equal work concept is based *explicitly* on the Equal Pay Act of 1963, whereas the comparable worth concept has been *inferred* from Title VII of the 1964 Civil Rights Act. Second, the equal pay concept is well-defined relative to the comparable worth concept, which is still legally uncertain. Third, the equal pay concept involves comparing rates of pay for jobs that have similar tasks, duties, responsibilities, and working conditions and that require approximately the same amount of effort and skill to perform. Comparable worth involves comparing jobs with substantially different characteristics that allegedly have the same value to the organization and society.

Figure 13–4 illustrates the comparisons between the equal pay and comparable worth concepts. The equal pay concept involves comparing the pay of male and female licensed practical nurses (LPNs); the comparable worth concept involves comparing the pay of a predominantly female group of LPNs and a predominantly male group of groundskeepers and landscapers, all of whom work for a large state hospital. Thus, equal pay issues involve "apples-and-apples" comparisons, whereas comparable worth deals with "apples-and-oranges" comparisons.

Equal Pay for Equal Work

The well-established concept of equal pay for equal work has its roots in the fact that males have traditionally earned more than females.[81] As of 1990, females continued to work for the "69-cent dollar." That is, pay levels for females continued to lag approximately 31 percent behind those of their male counterparts, despite the fact that the Equal Pay Act was passed in 1963 to ensure that men and women performing the same job are paid at the same rate.

A man and woman working at the same job do not have to perform identical sets of tasks for the work to meet the "sameness" test. Rather, the jobs must be similar with respect to *responsibility*, physical and mental *effort, working conditions,* and *skills* required to perform the job satisfactorily. If two jobs are essentially the same insofar as these four compensable factors are concerned, then there should be no significant pay differentials between males and females.

The U.S. Supreme Court held that the Equal Pay Act was violated when a glass company paid male "selector-packers" 21½ cents an hour more than female packers. The company contended that the differential was justified because the men were occasionally required to perform heavier work.[82]

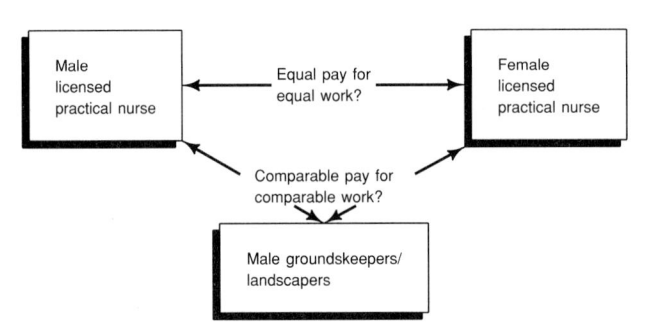

FIGURE 13–4 The Equal Pay and Comparable Worth Concepts

---

[81] Robert Drazin and Ellen R. Auster, "Wage Differences Between Men and Women: Performance Appraisal Ratings vs. Salary Allocation as the Locus of Bias," *Human Resource Management* (Summer 1987), p. 157.
[82] *Schultz v. Wheaton Glass*, 9 FEP Cases 502 (1970).

Not all male-female pay differentials violate the Act. A group of male physician assistants employed by the State of Georgia who were paid more than a group of predominantly female nurse practitioners did not violate the Equal Pay Act because of different responsibilities associated with the two jobs. Although many similarities between the physician assistants and nurse practitioners were noted, the former group had greater latitude in making decisions as to how to treat patients. Nurse practitioners, on the other hand, "must not diagnose or treat the condition without direct physician involvement."[83] In another case, the U.S. Court of Appeals in Chicago ruled that a university that raised female professors' salaries did not violate the Act because the university was trying to restore the salary of women to levels that they would have enjoyed in the absence of such discrimination.[84]

The best protection against equal pay violations is to use a carefully designed job evaluation system and a periodic equal pay audit.[85] However, there are certain exceptions to the Equal Pay Act that permit paying an employee of one sex more than another for *individual* differences that are geared to seniority, merit, productivity, or factors other than sex. Thus, an employee who has longer service, superior job performance, or higher levels of production or sales is entitled to receive greater pay, regardless of sex. Changes in job titles assigned to employees mean very little when the Equal Employment Opportunity Commission (EEOC) examines male and female jobs to determine whether pay discrepancies are justified. However, males and females who work for the same employer but in different departments or plants may receive different pay rates under most conditions. Organizations that violate the Equal Pay Act are liable for back pay.

Comparable Worth: The Unsettled Issue

The concept of comparable worth deals with assessing the economic and organizational values of dissimilar jobs. That is, should the licensed practical nurses working for a large hospital be paid the same as the institution's groundskeepers and landscapers (Figure 13–4)? Should physical plant employees working for a university receive greater pay than the school's clerical workers? Should state library employees be paid an amount equal to prison guards employed by the state's corrections department? Each of these comparisons involves evaluating the pay of male-dominated occupations (landscapers, physical plant employees, and prison guards) with female-dominated occupations (nurses, university clerical employees, state library employees).

The comparable worth debate stems from a phenomenon known as the *dual labor market*. Some occupations such as engineering, accounting, and truck driving, have been traditionally dominated by males. Other jobs are almost exclusively occupied by females. For example, 99.1 percent of all secretaries are female, as are 86.2 percent of cashiers, 96.8 percent of registered nurses, 80.1 percent of those

---

[83] *Beall v. Curtis*, 37 FEP Cases 644 (1985).
[84] *Ende v. Board of Regents of Regency Universities*, 37 FEP Cases 575 (1985).
[85] Frederick S. Hills and Thomas J. Bergmann, "Conducting an 'Equal Pay for Equal Work' Audit," in David B. Balkin and Luis R. Gomez-Mejia, (Eds.) *New Perspectives On Compensation* (Englewood Cliffs, New Jersey: Prentice-Hall, Inc., 1987), pp. 80-89.

who wait on tables in restaurants, and 83.6 percent of elementary school teachers.[86] Traditionally male-dominated occupations are paid, on the average, more than those traditionally dominated by females.[87] Advocates of the comparable worth concept claim that the dual labor market consists of a *primary* segment of desirable, higher-paying jobs and a *secondary* segment of less desirable, lower-paying, "dead-end" jobs. Females and minorities, the advocates claim, are more likely to be relegated to jobs in the secondary segment of the dual labor market. Even for jobs involving comparable skills and characteristics, proponents of the comparable worth concept believe that females are shortchanged.[88]

Although labor economists and civil rights leaders have cogently argued that the dual labor market phenomenon has increased pay differences between the sexes, the proper solution to the comparable worth problem is a controversial and thorny issue. Traditional job evaluation techniques may not provide a complete answer because the vast differences between jobs may make it impractical to use a common set of compensable factors. A set of compensable factors useful for evaluating nursing jobs would not be useful for evaluating some of the male-dominated jobs mentioned above. In fact, both wage and salary surveys and job evaluation methods have been viewed as culprits that perpetuate and exacerbate comparable worth problems rather than eliminate them.[89]

Several court cases have provided partial answers, but they have also raised a number of questions regarding the solution and fate of the comparable worth issue.[90] The legal question presented by comparable worth is whether Title VII claims of sex discrimination can be pursued beyond the equal-pay-for-equal work doctrine of the Equal Pay Act. In *County of Washington v. Gunther*, the U.S. Supreme Court decided that *intentional* sex-based pay discrimination that goes beyond the equal pay concept can be challenged under Title VII.[91] The Court said that female employees who claim that their jobs are undervalued because of intentional sex discrimination may file suit under Title VII even when they do not perform the same work as their male co-workers. Unfortunately, the *Gunther* case focused on the pay of male and female prison guards rather than on radically different jobs and therefore did not provide a stern test of the comparable worth theory. A U.S. Court of Appeals (San Francisco) dealt a setback to comparable worth when it reversed a lower court's decision that the State of Washington had engaged in unlawful sex discrim-

---

[86] Lawrence Z. Lorber, J. Robert Kirk, Stephen L. Samuels, and David J. Spellman, III, *Sex and Salary: A Legal and Personnel Analysis of Comparable Worth* (Alexandria, Virginia: The ASPA Foundation, 1985), p. 7 and Robert S. Smith, "Comparable Worth: Limited Coverage and the Exacerbation of Inequality," *Industrial and Labor Relations Review* (January 1988), pp. 227–239.

[87] According to one study, women in female-dominated jobs earned 6 to 15 percent less than women with the same characteristics in other occupations. See Elaine Sorrensen, "Measuring the Pay Disparity between Typically Female Occupations and Other Jobs: A Bivariate Selectivity Approach," *Industrial and Labor Relations Review* (July 1989), pp. 624–639.

[88] Carl C. Hoffman and Kathleen P. Hoffman, "Does Comparable Worth Obscure the Real Issues?" *Personnel Journal*, (January 1987), p. 82.

[89] See Michael Evan Gold, *A Dialogue on Comparable Worth*, (Ithaca, New York: ILR Press, Cornell University, 1983), pp. 38–54.

[90] See Doug Grider and Mike Shurden, "The Gathering Storm of Comparable Worth," *Business Horizons*, (July-August 1987), pp. 81–86.

[91] U.S. Supreme Court, 25 FEP Cases 1521 (1981).

ination in its pay practices. The state performed a job evaluation study of 121 job classifications in its personnel system and found that women were paid 20 percent less ($175 per month on the average) than men for performing jobs that received the same number of job evaluation points. A public-sector union, the American Federation of State, County, and Municipal Employees (AFSCME) filed suit against the state under Title VII in order to secure remedial pay adjustments and back pay. In ruling against the union, the U.S. Court of Appeals noted that the state's job evaluation "may be useful as a diagnostic tool" but that the state "should also be able to take into account market conditions, [union] bargaining demands, and the possibility that another study will yield different results." Stressing that "[the] economic reality is that the value of a particular job to an employer is but one factor influencing the rate of compensation for that job," the court held that reliance on the free market system to set pay rates in dissimilar female-dominated jobs is not in and of itself a violation of EEO laws.[92] The same Court of Appeals in San Francisco also rejected the comparable worth theory when it found that faculty members in the University of Washington College of Nursing could not press a discrimination claim merely by citing statistics indicating that they were paid less than faculty members in other colleges within the University. The fact that the pay rates are different does not necessarily imply intentional sex discrimination, according to the Court. The U.S. Supreme Court decided not to hear an appeal on this case.[93]

The comparable worth debate poses some tough questions that are not likely to be answered in the near future. Even if personnel/human resource managers, union leaders, civil rights advocates, feminist groups, legislators, and the courts all agreed that comparable worth is a noble goal that should be attained, the means of resolving the issue is difficult to determine.[94] Those involved in contract negotiations, however, can do several things to minimize comparable worth problems in their organizations:

1. Use carefully conceived job evaluation systems containing a variety of well-defined compensable factors. Do not use overly broad or narrow job categories. An overly broad category will result in "apples-and-oranges" comparisons that could lead to comparable worth suits. Narrow job categories may create artificial and unimportant distinctions among jobs; this too could lead to equal pay or comparable worth suits. A job evaluation system should be labeled as "experimental" until experience has shown that it is workable and valid.
2. Identify job classes that are dominated by males or females. The employer or union may, for example, define a "dominated" class as one that has at least 70 percent males or females. When a job category is predominantly one sex or the other, decide what can be done in terms of recruitment and selection or training and development programs to achieve a more balanced distribution of male and female employees.

---

[92] *American Federation of State, County, and Municipal Employees, AFL-CIO, v. State of Washington,* 38 FEP Cases 1353 (1985).
[93] *Spaulding v. University of Washington,* 35 FEP Cases 217 (1984), U.S. Supreme Court, cert. denied, U.S. SupCt, 36 FEP Cases 464 (1985).
[94] Thomas A. Mahoney, Benson Rosen, and Sara Rynes, "Where Do Compensation Specialists Stand on Comparable Worth?" *Compensation Review* (Fourth Quarter 1984), pp. 27–40.

3. Stay abreast of federal and state court decisions and legislation that may have an impact on comparable worth.

▲ Summary and Conclusions

Negotiating a compensation program that is equitable and cost-effective, provides incentives to employees, and meets the standards of the federal and state compensation laws is a challenging task.[95] This chapter has illustrated that compensation management is actually a series of separate yet interrelated functions: ensuring external equity through wage and salary surveys, establishing internal equity using job analysis and job evaluation, making individual pay adjustments, and properly using individual and group incentive programs. Persons responsible for negotiating compensation provisions in collective bargaining agreements should understand equal pay and comparable worth issues. However, equal pay problems will be minimal *if* the job evaluation and wage and salary surveys have been carefully conducted.

A well-designed and well-administered compensation program can improve union-management relations, control labor costs, and enhance employee morale. However, there is no "ideal" structure for a compensation program. A program that works well in a young and growing private-sector corporation may be poorly suited for a stable corporation whose products are in a declining market cycle. The Bureau of National Affairs, Inc., survey data discussed in this chapter also illustrates the diversity in compensation provisions in collective bargaining agreements, especially between the manufacturing and other sectors. The temptation to borrow or copy the successful compensation program of another organization in a wholesale fashion should be avoided. In preparing for contract talks, the parties should examine the compensation programs of other organizations and incorporate provisions that appear relevant to their respective organizations and bargaining climate. Even the best designed and administered compensation programs require frequent fine tuning. Job changes, organizational restructuring, changes in the organization's workforce, and legal developments occasionally require changes in the compensation program. Unless the collective bargaining agreement gives management the right to change compensation provisions unilaterally, changes must be negotiated with the union.

▲ Discussion Questions and Exercises

1. Why is pay equity so important for unions and employers? What problems arise when a pay system contains external and internal inequities?
2. Why, in your opinion, have the federal and state governments passed so many laws that affect pay and employee benefits? Discuss.
3. Discuss the use of seniority and merit in pay raises. Why do unions typically want to de-emphasize merit and use seniority as a primary means of making pay adjustments? Why do employers often agree with the union on this matter?

---

[95] See James L. Whitney, "Pay Concepts for the 1990s, Part 1," *Compensation and Benefits Review* (March-April 1988), pp. 33–44.

4. Under what circumstances are (1) individual incentive programs, and (2) group incentive programs most likely to be successful? What factors should union and management negotiators consider when bargaining over such programs?
5. What effect will wage and salary surveys and job evaluation have on sex discrimination in pay systems? Will wage and salary surveys and job evaluation perpetuate or eliminate sex discrimination? Discuss.
6. You have been selected to moderate a local television debate on whether labor unions have a significant impact on wages and inflation. The debate will be between officials from several local unions and several plant managers and personnel/human resource managers. What issues will each side likely present? How will they defend their respective positions?

▲ ▲ ▲ ▲ **CASES IN COMPENSATION**

The Misclassified Studio Artists

Gill Studios, Inc., is engaged in the business of producing decals, bumper stickers, signs, posters, and other silk screen products. The company distributes its products through jobbers and is attempting to increase its volume of production. Because of its increasing emphasis on high-volume production and profits, the company makes an effort to avoid projects that require custom-made, individual designs. As a result of their changing business strategy, the company is standardizing much of the work performed by its employees.

The grievants who are classified as "production layout artists" contend that the company is violating the current collective bargaining agreement by not classifying them as higher-paid "creative artists." The two job classifications were proposed by the company during contract negotiations and accepted by the union. The grievants who are classified as "production layout artists" perform the following duties:

Grievant Anita Edmonds: Receives her work orders from Bert Petrie, supervisor in the art department. Edmonds then takes the order and does what is necessary to complete the design, has it photographed, and submits it for inspection and transmission to the customer. If the design for a decal or other product ordered by the customer is not complete, the artist completes it. This process may involve searching for additional pictures or lettering in the necessary wording, color separation, and performing freehand drawing and shading. Edmonds testified that she is now instructed in greater detail as to how her work should be performed than was formerly the case. In many cases, Edmond's work consists of refining color arrangement of designs transmitted to the company by the customer in a nearly complete state. Only in about one percent of the cases does a production layout artist design a product based only on a general written description provided by the customer.

Grievant Ethel Strunk: Testified that she had been working on bumper stickers for nearly nine years. Most of her work consisted of lettering and refining the likeness of the finished product when the figure sent by the customer was not sharp enough. The lettering used by Strunk is cut primarily from photographed letters.

Grievant Coy Shay: Shay's work is similar to that performed by Strunk. Shay's primary job is lettering. Most of his letters are reproduced from book copies, rather than designed by him.

Gill Studio's only classified "creative artist," Emmett Ryburg, spends 90 percent of his time doing art work for Gill Studio's catalog and other advertising material. In performing such work, Ryburg selects a design that he feels will best illustrate the object to be sold. He rarely duplicates an object sent to him; rather, he refines catalog items so that they will look attractive to customers. The other 10 percent of Ryburg's time is spent in producing special orders where the design is his own, made on general directions from the customer.

The union contends that the grievants are not correctly classified as "production and layout artists" and they should be reclassified as "creative artists." Management attempted to reach a compromise settlement on the grievance by offering production and layout artists a small hourly wage increase. There was some confusion as to whether the union's representative had agreed to accept the wage increase on behalf of the grievants. No evidence was produced that indicated that either party had agreed to the proposed wage increase.

Discussion Questions

1. Based on the brief descriptions of the grievants' jobs and Mr. Ryburg's job, do you believe that the "production layout artist" and "creative artist" job duties were similar enough to warrant a reclassification?
2. What factors should the arbitrator consider in reaching a decision in this case?
3. What steps would you suggest that union and management representatives take if they desire to make changes during the life of a collective bargaining agreement?
4. What collective bargaining and wage structure problems might be encountered by firms that constantly change their business strategy and production-service emphasis?

Double Time Dilemma

The Trent Engineering Company is a subsidiary of the Parker Pen Company. Employees are represented by the United Rubber Workers union, Local 891. Shortly after the company activated a third shift in its operations, a dispute arose with respect to the proper rate of pay for regularly scheduled hours worked by third-shift employees who began their shift at 11 P.M. on Saturday and continued until 7:00 A.M. on Sunday. The union's grievance is as follows:

Members of Local #891 request that third shift employees be paid double time for all hours worked on Sunday.

One month later, the company made the following reply:

> Grievance denied for the reasons contained in Article, Section 6.1.
>
> The Wage and Hour Act indicates that twenty-four hour (24) hours constitutes a work day. Our work week begins at 7:00 A.M. Monday, which is the first work day of the week. This work day is completed at 7:00 A.M. on Tuesday. Likewise, the sixth work day begins Saturday at 7:00 A.M. and is completed at 7:00 A.M. Sunday. This is considered the sixth work day, or Saturday work.

Section 6 of the collective bargaining agreement defines the normal work day as being eight hours and work beginning after midnight constitutes the third shift. Section 6.2 of the contract stipulates as follows:

> Time and one-half the regular rate shall be paid for all hours worked in excess of eight (8) hours in a work day and forty (40) in a work week. Double time will be paid for all hours worked on a Sunday.

The union insists that the last sentence of Section 6.2 is clear and unambiguous; the company is clearly obligated to pay employees at double time rates for all hours worked on a calendar day, which begins at midnight on Saturday night. The union also claims that there was full and complete agreement on the meaning of Section 6.2 by both sides during contract negotiations. Furthermore, there was no second or third shift in operation during the period in which negotiations were underway and there was no thought that additional shifts would be activated at Trent Engineering during the life of the contract. The union argues that the company is attempting to nullify or modify a clearly and concisely stated contract provision, which an arbitrator has no power to modify.

The company argues that the Saturday night-Sunday morning third shift should be paid in accordance with Saturday wages, rather than at the double-time Sunday rate. Thus, the company argues that the Sunday work day does not begin until until 7:00 A.M. on Sunday. The company, like the union, argues that the provisions of the agreement with respect to premium pay for Sunday hours worked, are clear and unambiguous. In addition, the company claims that at no time during the negotiations did it agree with the union to pay double time for hours worked by employees on Sundays prior to 7:00 A.M.

Discussion Questions

1. Is the language in Section 6.2 of the agreement clear and unambiguous? What other factors should be examined by the arbitrator in assessing the language of this section?
2. In this case, the company argues that the work week "shall begin at 7:00 A.M. on Monday", and it does not end until 7:00 A.M. on the following Monday. Thus, the company argues that for purposes of calculating overtime pay, the rate for the *starting time* of a shift should be used. They point out that this method of calculation is common in other collective bargaining agreements. Evaluate this argument.

> 3. The company's post-hearing brief contains numerous citations and references to other arbitration decisions (between other companies and unions). What effect might these cases have on the arbitrator's decisions in the current case?

Appendix: Major Methods of Job Evaluation

THE RANKING METHOD

The simplest approach to job evaluation is the ranking method. As the name implies, each job within an organization, corporate division, or department is ranked relative to other jobs in the same group. The ranking is usually based on an analysis of all tasks, duties, responsibilities, and requisite skills needed to perform a job. In some cases, specific compensable factors may be used to determine rank. However, the final ranking is an *overall* rating, with one job being ranked first in value, one job ranked second in value, and so forth.

The ranking method has the advantage of simplicity and expediency, especially when there are significant differences in the value of the jobs and the number of jobs being evaluated is small. Problems arise with the ranking method when large numbers of complex jobs must be evaluated. The assignment of rankings is a subjective process and disagreements may arise if several persons evaluate and rank each job. Perhaps the major disadvantage of the ranking method is its failure to determine absolute differences among the values of each job. A job that is ranked third is obviously more valuable than one ranked fourth, but there is little indication as to how much of a pay difference should exist between the two jobs.

THE CLASSIFICATION METHOD

Job classifications are established by using a set of general compensable factors. Each job is evaluated and placed in a classification according to the amount of compensable factors present in the job. Classifications are then ranked and compensated according to their relative worth. Persons holding jobs within the same job classification are paid at the same rate (or within the same rate range). Some classification methods also incorporate the qualifications of individual employees when determining a pay rate. According to The Bureau of National Affairs, Inc., job classification procedures for changing or establishing new categories of jobs during the contract term are contained in over half of the collective bargaining agreements sampled.[96]

The federal government uses a classification system of job evaluation for white-collar and professional employees. If a person was hired by the U.S. Park Service as an administrator in a job at Yellowstone National Park, that individual would be assigned a General Schedule (GS) rating, depending on the nature and complexity of the job.[97]

The classification method provides a practical means of evaluating a large number of jobs, some of which vary considerably in

---

[96] See The Bureau of National Affairs, Inc., "Wages," *Collective Bargaining Negotiations & Contracts* (Washington, D.C.: The Bureau of National Affairs, Inc., 1989), section 93.
[97] General Schedule (GS) ratings are established by the federal government's Office of Personnel Management. The GS ratings are based primarily on the differences in level of difficulty among jobs and are based on nine factors: Knowledge required by the position, supervisory controls, guidelines, complexity, scope and effect, personal contacts, purpose of contacts, physical demands, and work environment.

terms of tasks, duties, working conditions, and skill requirements. Distinctions between job classifications rather than individual jobs are emphasized. Two jobs that are placed in the same classification and paid at the same rate may be completely different (e.g., a secretary working in a plant distribution center and a truck driver assigned to make local pickups and deliveries). When the content, responsibility, or qualifications for a job are changed, then it can be reclassified to either a higher or a lower classification.

THE FACTOR COMPARISON METHOD

The factor comparison approach to job evaluation places dollar amounts on compensable factors within a group of similar jobs. Although there are several variations of the factor comparison method, the following steps are common:

1. *Select benchmark jobs from each cluster or classification.* (Note the definition of benchmark jobs earlier in this chapter). The base wage or salary rates for benchmark jobs are assumed to be *fixed*, and other wage and salary rates are subject to adjustment based on the pay allocated to benchmark jobs.

2. *Select and define compensable factors that are common to jobs within a cluster or classification.* These factors may include responsibility, mental and physical effort, working conditions, as well as education, skill, and experience requirements. Each compensable factor contributes a certain monetary value to the job.

3. *Allocate the base wage or salary rate for benchmark jobs across each compensable factor.* The sum of the monetary values for each compensable factor will be exactly equal to the rate *currently* paid for the benchmark job. (Remember that the pay rates for benchmark jobs have already been determined to be acceptable and are *fixed*.)

4. *Compare nonbenchmark jobs on a factor-by-factor basis with the fixed rates for benchmark jobs.* Once the basic structure is determined using benchmark jobs, the basis for determining the internal equity and pay rates for *nonbenchmark* jobs is established.

5. *Sum the monetary values for each nonbenchmark job.* This produces the *new* and, hopefully, internally equitable wage or salary rate for each job.

THE POINT METHOD

The point method, when properly designed and administered, is probably the most detailed approach to job evaluation. Unlike the factor comparison method, the point method does not directly place a dollar value on a job. Rather, each job receives a total point value and the points are then converted into pay rates.[98]

The preliminary stages of the point method are similar to the factor comparison method. First, the compensable factors or dimensions for a job category must be specified. Second, each factor must be defined, measured, and weighted. Third, each job is evaluated on a factor-by-factor basis by comparing job analysis information with the compensable factor scales. The extent to which a factor is present in a job determines the points awarded to that job. The point method of job evaluation does not directly compare one job with another, as is done in the factor comparison method. Instead, the compensable factor scales are used to assign points; the points are then summed for each job. Point totals for each job are used along with wage and salary survey data to determine the final pay rate.[99]

---

[98] Edward E. Lawler, III, "What's Wrong With Point-Factor Job Evaluation," *Compensation and Benefit Review* (March-April 1986), pp. 29–40.

[99] For a detailed description of the various methods of job evaluation, see Terry L. Leap and Michael D. Crino, *Personnel/Human Resource Management* (New York: Macmillan Publishing Company, 1989), pp. 392–406.

14 Employee Benefit Programs

- **Introduction**
- **The Role of Employee Benefit Programs in Collective Bargaining Agreements**
- **The Government's Role in Employee Benefit Plans**
  Mandatory and Government-Provided Employee Benefits
    Workers' Compensation
    Unemployment Compensation
    Social Security
    Some Important Issues Surrounding Social Insurance
  Government Regulation of Employee Benefits
- **Collectively-Bargained Benefits**
- **Group Life Insurance**
- **Accidental Death and Dismemberment Insurance**
- **Group Health Insurance**
  Medical Expense Insurance
  Health Maintenance Organizations
  Disability Income Insurance
  Other Important Health Care Contract Provisions
  Health Care Cost Containment Measures
- **Retirement Programs**
  The Concept of a Pension
  The Employee Retirement Income Security Act of 1974
  Retirement Plan Terminology and Provisions
- **Income Maintenance Benefits**
- **Paid Vacations, Holidays, and Sick Leave**
- **Childcare and Eldercare Benefits**
- **Employee Assistance Programs**

▲ Other Employee Benefit Programs
▲ Communicating Employee Benefits
▲ Summary and Conclusions
▲ Discussion Questions and Exercises
▲ Cases in Employee Benefits
  The Misunderstanding over Health Insurance Benefits
  Double-Dipping Under Medicare
▲ Appendix: Calculating the Cost of Compensation and Benefit Provisions

▲ Introduction

Employee benefit programs have become an integral part of most collective bargaining agreements. Group life and health insurance programs, retirement programs, paid vacations and holidays, leaves of absence, and dental and optical insurance coverage are among the types of employee benefits commonly found in private- and public-sector organizations. Table 14–1 summarizes The Bureau of National Affairs, Inc., survey data on employee benefits commonly found in collective bargaining agreements.[1]

Table 14–1 ▲ Employee Benefits Found in Collective Bargaining Agreements

1. Life and Health Insurance
a. Life Insurance (96%)
b. Accidental death and dismemberment insurance (74%)
c. Sickness and accident insurance (86%)
d. Supplemental occupational accident insurance (26%)
e. Long-term disability insurance (21%)
f. Hospitalization insurance (79%)
g. Surgical insurance (77%)
h. Major medical insurance (74%)
i. Miscellaneous medical expense benefits (61%)
j. Maternity benefits (54%)
k. Health care cost containment measures (55%)
l. Dental care (79%)
m. Prescription drugs (35%)
n. Optical care (40%)
o. Alcohol and drug abuse benefits (32%)

---

[1] Compiled from The Bureau of National Affairs, Inc., *Basic Patterns in Union Contracts*, 11th ed. (Washington, D.C: The Bureau of National Affairs, Inc., 1986), based on a sample of 400 contracts throughout the United States. The percentages in parentheses indicate the frequency with which a provision appears in the sample of collective bargaining agreements. Reprinted with permission.

Table 14–1 ▲ Employee Benefits Found in Collective Bargaining Agreements (Continued)

2.	*Retirement Programs (almost all contracts)*
3.	*Income Maintenance Programs*
a.	Guarantees of work or pay (13%)
b.	Severance (separation) pay (41%)
c.	Supplemental unemployment benefits (16%)
4.	*Holidays (99%)*
a.	Holiday pay (88%)
b.	Pay for holidays worked (97%)
5.	*Leave of Absence*

a.	Personal leave (72%)		e.	Civic duty leave (82%)
b.	Union leave (77%)		f.	Paid sick leave (28%)
c.	Maternity leave (36%)		g.	Unpaid sick leave (52%)
d.	Funeral leave (84%)		h.	Military leave (72%)

6.	*Vacations*
a.	Vacations based on length of service (90%)
b.	Pay for employees who work during vacation (55%)

▲ The Role of Employee Benefit Programs in Collective Bargaining Agreements

The trend in employee benefits has been toward increasing the amount and variety of programs available to employees.[2] Labor unions have provided a major impetus behind the rise of employee benefit programs over the past 40 years.[3] One role of employee benefits such as pension programs is to defer an employee's income until retirement while simultaneously allowing both employers and employees to take advantage of current tax laws.[4] Furthermore, a comprehensive array of employee benefits may help the organization attract high-quality employees and increase the morale and job satisfaction of current employees. As employees accumulate seniority in an organization, collectively bargained employee benefits may reduce turnover because of health care coverage and pension vesting arrangements that "tie" workers to a firm. Benefits such as group life and health insurance are often less expensive for employees than those purchased individually from local insurance agents, partially because the employer often subsidizes administrative costs and premium payments.

Employee benefits help employees manage personal risks. During their income-earning years, employees face several risks that have unfavorable financial conse-

---

[2] Robert E. Perkins, "The Employer's Role in Benefits Evolution," *Personnel* (February 1987), p. 66.
[3] The NLRB has ruled that pension and employee welfare plans are mandatory bargaining items. The U.S. Supreme Court refused to hear the case, thereby upholding the circuit court's ruling. See *Inland Steel Company*, 77 NLRB 1, enforced 170 F. (2d) 247 (1948), cert. denied 336 U.S. 960 (1949).
[4] Philip C. Hunt, "Tax Reform: Its Impact on Compensation and Benefits," *Employee Relations Today* (Spring 1987), pp. 39–52.

quences. These risks are especially critical for family members or others who are economically dependent on the employee's ability to continue working. The following risks pose a threat to the economic security of workers and their dependents:

1. *Premature death*: A person may die during the years in which he or she is earning an income. Although most persons regard any form of death as premature, the financial loss suffered by the dependents of deceased income earners is especially devastating. Life insurance is the primary means of dealing with the risk of premature death.
2. *Superannuation*: A person may outlive his or her ability to generate an income. Most of us do not worry about the "risk" of living to a ripe old age, but *financially* those who live well beyond retirement must make provisions for their post-retirement years. Public and private pension programs are a primary means of dealing with superannuation.
3. *Interruption or loss of income*: Events such as disability, accidents, illness, or layoff result in either a temporary or permanent loss of employment and earnings. Disability income insurance, workers' compensation, and unemployment compensation are commonly used to deal with this risk.
4. *Extraordinary medical expenses*: Large medical bills can impose severe financial burdens or lead to financial ruin. Because most employees do not have adequate resources to cover large and fortuitous expenses (e.g., surgery that results in a $30,000 hospital bill), employee benefits such as hospitalization and surgical insurance are used to protect against this risk.

These four categories of risk have two characteristics. First, they impose financially severe obligations that cannot be met through the personal resources of most middle-income employees. Second, these risks are contingent or fortuitous in nature. They occur in a somewhat random and unpredictable fashion. Most employees will not die prematurely, but a small percentage will. Thus, some employee benefits are paid in the event of premature death, disability, or hospitalization. The real satisfaction of such benefits is the employee's security of knowing that they are available if needed.[5]

[5] In addition to analyzing the *types* of risks faced by workers, union and management negotiators should consider the *severity and probabilities* associated with these risks. Although events such as premature death, total and permanent disability, and extraordinary medical expenses pose catastrophic financial burdens, they affect relatively few employees. Other occurrences, such as routine dental care, jury duty, the need for eyeglasses, and maternity care, affect a large percentage of employees. Fortunately, the more common events present the least trouble financially. From the standpoint of risk management, the dollars used to purchase employee benefits are better spent by insuring against those events that have a *small probability of occurrence* but impose *severe financial losses*. Thus, group life, hospitalization, and disability income insurance will afford more protection per premium dollar than items such as dental, eyeglass, or maternity insurance policies. Employee benefits that provide protection against relatively certain, yet financially insignificant "losses" are usually not good bargains in terms of cost because the premiums (cost of the insurance) are nearly equal to the benefits received. That is, the company, the union, or the employee is merely "trading dollars" with the insurance company. Unfortunately, some employees hold frivolous benefits (that require a high insurance premium relative to the amount of coverage received) in high regard. It is probably better for the employer or the worker to pay for the small, high-probability risks out-of-pocket rather than insuring them. A dilemma is created when employee benefit dollars are used for minor benefits to the neglect of benefits such as major medical insurance or long-term disability income insurance. Responsible union and management officials should attempt to convey to employees the importance of securing protection against the potentially severe losses such as major medical expenses and long-term disability.

▲ The Government's Role in Employee Benefit Plans

Employee benefits found in collective bargaining agreements often supplement benefits that are provided under state and federal programs. The federal and state governments play two important roles with regard to employee benefit programs. First, they either mandate or provide certain types of benefits such as Social Security retirement benefits, workers' compensation, and unemployment compensation. These and other government programs are often referred to as "social insurance." Second, many nonmandatory benefits are regulated through federal legislation or state insurance codes. There is a definite trend toward increased governmental regulation of employee benefits. Perhaps the two most significant federal interventions into employee benefits over the past 20 years are the Employee Retirement Income Security Act of 1974, which regulates pension programs, and the Tax Reform Act of 1986.

Mandatory and Government-Provided Employee Benefits

Workers' Compensation

Workers' compensation programs are regulated by the individual states and provide protection against job-related injuries and illnesses. The goals of workers' compensation laws are to help rehabilitate injured workers and provide them with cash benefits and medical care for disabilities incurred during the course of employment. According to The Bureau of National Affairs, Inc., most state workers' compensation laws have the following objectives:[6]

- ▲ Replacement of lost earnings and payment of medical care expenses for those injured on the job.
- ▲ Elimination of an employee's need to file a civil suit against his or her employer for damages arising from on-the-job injuries.
- ▲ Encouragement of employer interest in worker safety and the reduction of preventable injuries.

Nearly all states require employer participation in workers' compensation programs. Employers are responsible for financing their workers' compensation programs (employees do not contribute money to the program) through premiums paid on an "experience-rating" basis. Experience rating penalizes firms with high rates of worker injuries.[7] The logging industry, for example, has historically had one of the highest workers' compensation insurance rates, whereas policies covering office and clerical personnel usually have low premiums because of the few safety

---

[6] The Bureau of National Affairs, Inc., *Compensation: Personnel Policy and Practice Series* (Washington, D.C.: The Bureau of National Affairs, Inc., 1987), Section 365.
[7] "Wal-Mart Stores Must Pay $16.8 Million For Premiums," *The Wall Street Journal* (July 10, 1987), p. 4; Stephen Tarnoff, "Monsanto Has Coverage for $108 Million Verdict, *Business Insurance*, Vol. 20 (December 22, 1986), p. 1; James R. Chelius and Robert S. Smith, "Firm Size and Regulatory Compliance Costs: The Case of Workers' Compensation Insurance," *Journal of Policy Analysis and Management* (Winter 1987), p. 193; and Michael L. Murray, "Reducing the Impact of Workers' Compensation," *Risk Management* (February 1986), p. 48.

hazards associated with white-collar jobs. Organizations typically purchase workers' compensation insurance through private insurance companies or through a state-operated program. Nearly all states allow employers to self-insure their workers' compensation programs if certain standards are met. The amount that a worker receives under workers' compensation depends on the extent of his or her injuries and earnings at the time of injury. Because each state has different workers' compensation laws, benefits vary. However, most states have no maximum on rehabilitative and hospitalization benefits. Occupational diseases are covered by all state laws, and some jurisdictions now provide workers' compensation benefits for stress-induced occupational illnesses.[8] A major advantage of workers' compensation is that the injured employee avoids the trauma and uncertainty of time-consuming legal proceedings. Workers' compensation benefits are paid to the employee as prescribed by law; determining who is at fault or liable for an employee's on-the-job injury is not at issue. A few states also provide *state disability insurance* for employees who become disabled for reasons other than job-related injuries.

Unemployment Compensation

In addition to the perils of death, disability, and extraordinary medical expenses stemming from on-the-job injuries and illnesses, workers face the risk of losing their income through unemployment. Because private insurance companies are not willing to sell insurance coverage for unemployment, the government has established a joint federal-state system of unemployment compensation. The basic objective of unemployment compensation is to promote financial security for workers by encouraging employers to stabilize their workforce and avoid repeated layoffs and rehires. Unemployment compensation promotes individual financial security by providing emergency income to workers during periods of high unemployment.[9] The Federal Unemployment Tax Act (FUTA) requires that employers (not employees) pay unemployment taxes. Individual states must impose a payroll tax on employers under an experience-rating plan that penalizes firms with high rates of involuntary unemployment rates and rewards firms whose unemployment history is low. Most states require that the worker have earned a minimum income during the year preceding unemployment and maintain an attachment to the labor force by reporting to a local public employment office. States also differ with respect to the amount of unemployment compensation benefits offered. Weekly benefit amounts range from a minimum of several dollars to a maximum of several hundred dollars, depending on the state in which the employee works and the income of the employee prior to layoff. The majority of states provide up to 26 weeks of unemployment benefit payments.[10]

Unemployment compensation laws are designed to protect the employee who,

---

[8] John M. Ivancevich, Michael T. Matteson, and Edward P. Richards III, "Who's Liable For Stress on the Job?" *Harvard Business Review* (March 1985), p. 60; and Meg Fletcher, "Employers Facing More Mental Stress Claims," *Business Insurance* (April 13, 1987), p. 34.

[9] The Bureau of National Affairs, Inc., *Compensation: Personnel Policy and Practice Series* (Washington, D.C.: The Bureau of National Affairs, Inc. 1986), Section 356.

[10] E. Cohn and M. Capen, "A Note on the Adequacy of UI Benefits," *Industrial Relations* (Winter 1987), pp. 106–111.

through circumstances beyond his or her control, suffers a layoff. States often disqualify employees from receiving unemployment compensation (or limit the amount received) under the following conditions: voluntary resignation without good cause; discharge for misconduct; failure to accept suitable employment through a public employment agency; participation in a strike; receipt of Social Security, workers' compensation, or pension benefits; quitting work to attend school; plant shutdowns for vacation periods; voluntary resignations precipitated by marriage or family obligations; and various types of fraud.[11] Supplements to unemployment compensation can be addressed by unions and employers through the collective bargaining agreement. Supplemental unemployment compensation (SUB) provisions are discussed later in this chapter.

Social Security

The federal government provides the well-known Social Security program (whose proper title is the Old Age, Survivors, Disability, and Health Insurance [OASDHI] program). The Social Security program provides retirement, life insurance, disability income, and Medicare (health insurance) benefits to eligible recipients. Unlike workers' compensation and unemployment compensation programs, Social Security is financed through mandatory payroll taxes on *both* the employer and the employee.[12] Employers match the taxes paid by employees.[13] The more Social Security taxes paid by an employee, the higher the benefit levels for which he or she is eligible. Thus, an employee who pays at or near the maximum tax each year would be entitled to a larger monthly retirement benefit at age 65 than would an employee who pays less Social Security taxes. A qualified employee is currently entitled to receive full retirement benefits at age 65 (or reduced benefits at age 62). However, the normal retirement age will rise to age 66 by the year 2009 and age 67 by the year 2027. Survivors' benefits (a form of life insurance coverage) are payable to the family of a deceased worker.[14] Disability benefits are provided to workers under Social Security for workers who are unable to engage in any meaningful employment for at least 12 months. Medicare provides health insurance coverage primarily for persons age 65 and over, as well as for persons who are permanently disabled or suffering from a life-threatening illness.[15]

---

[11] See G. Solon, "The Effects of Unemployment Insurance Eligibility Rules on Job Quitting Behavior," *The Journal of Human Resources* (Winter 1984), pp. 118–126.
[12] In 1988, employees paid a payroll tax of 7.51 percent on the first $45,000 of taxable wages and salary. The tax rate remained at 7.51 percent for the first $48,000 of taxable compensation in 1989 and was increased to 7.65 percent for the first $51,300 of taxable income in 1990. Employers match payroll taxes paid by employees.
[13] "A Bite Too Big to Swallow," *American Demographics* (March 1987), p. 20.
[14] Eligible survivors include a widowed spouse age 65 (age 60 for reduced benefits or age 50 if disabled), surviving divorced spouse, age 60 or older, dependent parents age 62 or older, unmarried surviving spouse caring for a child under age 16, and unmarried surviving children under age 18 (under age 19 if a full-time high school student or under age 22 if disabled).
[15] See Warren Boroson, "What Social Security Owes You and How to Get It All," *Medical Economics*, (August 25, 1986).

Some Important Issues Surrounding Social Insurance

The rationale behind the benefits described in the workers' compensation, state temporary disability programs, unemployment compensation, and Social Security appear to be twofold. First, the federal and state governments have attempted to ensure that workers and their families enjoy at least a minimal level of economic security from the risks of premature death, old age, disability, and unemployment. This line of thought stems from former President Franklin D. Roosevelt and the New Deal era, which emphasized antipoverty programs as a means of stimulating economic recovery and growth. Some critics argue that programs such as Social Security only allow benefit recipients to eke out a meager existence. However, the programs would probably impose a severe and politically unsavory tax burden on employers and workers if benefits were substantially increased. Critics also feel that the government should not require employers and employees to participate in programs such as Social Security. Rather, they argue that each worker should be responsible for his or her own welfare. Opponents of the Social Security program claim that it is unfair to persons in higher-income brackets because the retirement benefits redistribute income toward workers in the lower-income brackets. Some employees feel that if they were allowed to invest the amount that is regularly deducted from their paychecks for Social Security, they could obtain better investment results. This argument overlooks the fact that employers match employee contributions to the program; those who make their own investments in retirement in lieu of Social Security also run the risk of losing their nest egg through mismanagement or fraud. The decreasing number of workers paying payroll taxes into the program, coupled with the increasing number of retirees and others who are drawing benefits, have created financial pressures and uncertainty regarding the future of the Social Security program.[16]

Federal and state governments provide insurance protection if private insurance companies are either unable or unwilling to do so. Some workers may not be able to obtain life and health coverage from insurance companies because of poor health history or exposure to occupational hazards. Other workers, if left on their own, would neglect to provide for their retirement or seek life, health, and disability insurance protection; they are therefore "forced" to obtain protection through the mandatory payroll deductions of Social Security. It should be noted that workers' compensation, unemployment compensation, and Social Security benefits are only available under conditions prescribed by law. Thus, a person requiring large amounts of life insurance to protect the needs of a growing family with young children or a person who suffers a three-month partial disability because of an off-the-job injury would need protection above and beyond that provided by the government programs described here.

---

[16] See George E. Rejda, *Social Insurance and Economic Security* (Englewood Cliffs, New Jersey: Prentice-Hall, Inc., 1976), pp. 108–172; William C. Birdsall and John L. Hankins, "The Future of Social Security," *Annals of the American Academy of Political and Social Science* (May 1985), p. 82; and "Slip Sliding Away," *American Demographics* (April 1987), p. 13.

Government Regulation of Employee Benefits

Employee benefit programs are regulated by both federal and state laws. Federal laws regulating employee benefits (as briefly described in Chapter 13) include the Employee Retirement Income Security Act of 1974 (ERISA), the Consolidated Omnibus Budget Reconciliation Act of 1985 (COBRA), the Tax Reform Act of 1986, and the various equal employment opportunity laws, such as Title VII of the 1964 Civil Rights Act, the Pregnancy Discrimination Act, and the Age Discrimination in Employment Act of 1967. State insurance codes regulate collectively bargained group life and health insurance programs by setting the minimum employee group size, insurance rates, employee participation standards, coverage limits, and other aspects of group insurance.

Employee benefits are regulated by the federal and state governments for four reasons. First, employee benefits that accumulate over a number of years (such as pension assets) may be mismanaged by incompetent or unscrupulous administrators. Second, employers may knowingly or inadvertently engage in unfair sex discrimination (usually to the detriment of female employees) because of unequal pension and health insurance benefits. Third, state insurance codes focus heavily on the problem of adverse selection—a situation in which high-risk (i.e. older or unhealthy) employees participate heavily in group life and health insurance plans whereas the lower-risk (i.e. younger or healthy) employees choose not to participate. Adverse selection increases the cost of group insurance. By requiring minimum participation standards (e.g., 70 percent of all employees must join the health insurance group), state insurance codes negate some of the problems associated with adverse selection. Finally, all 50 states require employers who offer group health insurance to provide certain benefits.[17] State insurance codes also regulate the management practices and solvency of insurance companies that provide employee benefits. Because the insurance industry is highly competitive, the states regulate group insurance rates to prevent insurers from charging unrealistically low rates that could lead to insolvency and an inability to pay claims.

▲ Collectively-Bargained Benefits

Unions and employers recognize that government-provided benefits furnish only a minimal amount of protection from the risks of premature death, superannuation, extraordinary expenses, and loss of income. For example, most employees faced with retirement and depending *only* on Social Security for an income would be forced into a frugal lifestyle. Many employees also lack the personal resources, such as large savings accounts, to meet these risks. Thus, employee benefit provisions in collective bargaining agreements *supplement* existing government-sponsored programs such as workers' compensation, unemployment compensation, and Social

---

[17] For example, Minnesota law requires that health plans pay for wigs for men and women suffering from alopecia areata, a rare disease that causes hair loss. Kentucky law requires newborn nursery care; California, prenatal care; New Mexico, care by midwives; New York, breast reconstruction. See David Stipp, "Laws on Health Benefits Raise Firms' Ire," *The Wall Street Journal* (December 28, 1988), p. B1.

Security. Collective bargaining agreements often supplement workers' compensation with disability income insurance; unemployment compensation might be bolstered by supplemental unemployment benefits or guaranteed pay provisions; Social Security benefits might be enhanced by collectively bargained pensions as well as group life, health, and disability insurance.

▲ Group Life Insurance

Nearly all collective bargaining agreements provide some form of group life insurance for bargaining-unit members. Group life insurance protects the family of an employee against economic losses that would occur if a worker died during his or her years of gainful employment. Most group life policies contain term insurance. Term insurance is the least expensive form of life insurance because it does not contain the "savings" (cash value) element that is found in whole life and similar policies. Thus, term insurance provides pure life insurance protection; once the term policy expires, the insured employee has no vested financial interest (cash value) in the policy. A collective bargaining agreement may provide for a master contract with an insurance company that covers employees on a bargaining-unit or multi-plant basis. Each employee receives a certificate or handbook that explains the type and amount of life insurance protection. Group life insurance as an employee benefit offers several advantages:[18]

1. Premiums usually cost less under a group policy than they would under a comparable individual policy purchased by the employee directly through an insurance company.
2. Group policies usually do not require a physical examination or proof of insurability. Employees who would otherwise have difficulty obtaining life insurance because of poor health or occupational hazards are automatically eligible for group life insurance benefits when they are hired.
3. Employers may receive a business expense tax deduction on the premiums paid for group life insurance.
4. If an employee resigns or is terminated, he or she has the right to convert to an individual life insurance policy (usually within 30 days) without further evidence of insurability.

Group life insurance is an especially important benefit for employees with children or other economic dependents. Many employees who need life insurance the most are often the ones who have the fewest resources to pay high insurance premiums. For example, a 25-year-old worker with an unemployed spouse and two dependent children, ages 2 and 4, may need $200,000 of life insurance in order to protect the family adequately in the event that the worker suffers premature death. A whole-life insurance policy containing a cash value or savings program with a $200,000 face value might cost this 25-year-old worker approximately $3,000 per

---

[18] The Bureau of National Affairs, Inc., *Compensation: Personnel Policy and Practice Series* (Washington, D.C.: The Bureau of National Affairs, Inc., 1987), section 339.

year, an amount that is prohibitive for many employees. A less expensive term insurance policy providing $200,000 in coverage might cost $500 a year. However, a term policy may expire and not be renewable if the employee's health deteriorates. Group life insurance is often provided without cost to the employee under a *noncontributory* plan whereby the employer pays the entire premium. Even when the employee pays part of the premium, the cost is usually low. Group insurance policies are sold directly to the employer, thereby eliminating sales calls to each employee. Similarly, there is usually no requirement for a medical examination or an extensive insurance application detailing the employee's medical history. Premiums paid by the employer on behalf of the employee are not taxable as ordinary income to the employee for the first $50,000 in life insurance coverage. If the employee had to purchase a life insurance policy on his or her own, the premium would be paid in after-tax dollars—a definite disadvantage.

The primary problem with group life insurance is that an employee may be lulled into a false sense of security regarding his or her personal life insurance program. Most group programs do not provide an adequate amount of insurance protection to meet all of an employee's life insurance needs, especially for employees with dependent children. The Bureau of National Affairs, Inc., survey data indicates that 19 percent of the contracts have a maximum coverage of $10,000—a woefully inadequate amount. A number of group life insurance contract provisions also allow employees to purchase additional coverage at their own expense. It is often necessary for the employee to supplement group life insurance coverage by purchasing additional protection under an individual policy. In addition, group life insurance coverage terminates when an employee leaves the company. Employees should therefore determine how much life insurance coverage is necessary to provide their dependents with a comfortable standard of living in the event that they suffer premature death (rather than depend only on the life insurance provided by the employer). Table 14-2 summarizes The Bureau of National Affairs, Inc., data on life insurance provisions found in U.S. collective bargaining agreements.[19]

Table 14–2 ▲ Group Life Insurance Contract Provisions

1. *Amount of insurance*
   a. Maximum coverage of $10,000 or more (81%)
   b. Flat amount of insurance for all employees (69%)
   c. Based on employee's earnings (26%)
   d. Based on employee's length of service (5%)
   e. Option for employees to purchase additional coverage (36% in manufacturing and 30% in nonmanufacturing)
2. *Post-retirement group life insurance (56%)*
3. *Company-paid coverage during layoffs (55%)*
4. *Transition and bridge benefits for family members of deceased employees (12%)*

---

[19] The Bureau of National Affairs, Inc., *Collective Bargaining Negotiations & Contracts* (Washington, D.C.: The Bureau of National Affairs, Inc., 1989), section 44. Reprinted with permission.

▲ Accidental Death and Dismemberment Insurance

Coverage for accidental death and dismemberment is provided in 74 percent of the contracts surveyed by The Bureau of National Affairs, Inc. Such provisions often pay an amount equal to the employee's group life insurance coverage (double indemnity) for death from accidental causes. Thus, if an employee has $40,000 in group life insurance coverage, his or her beneficiaries may be entitled to an *additional* $40,000 under the accidental death and dismemberment policy. Dismemberment benefits generally pay as much as one half the life insurance benefit for the loss of either a limb or an eye and up to the full life insurance coverage for the loss of more than one limb (or both eyes).[20]

▲ Group Health Insurance

Group health insurance can be divided into three categories: (1) medical expense insurance, (2) health maintenance organizations, and (3) disability income insurance.

Medical Expense Insurance

Between 75 and 80 percent of the contracts surveyed by The Bureau of National Affairs, Inc., provide various forms of medical expense insurance. Medical expense insurance covers charges for surgical, hospitalization, and ancillary services such as x-ray and laboratory services, prosthetic devices, drugs, and other medical items. Plans such as hospital indemnity contracts, Blue Cross and Blue Shield, surgical service plans, major medical insurance, Medicare supplement policies, and various limited health insurance policies covering specific diseases such as cancer all fall under the rubric of medical expense insurance.

Hospital indemnity contracts (also called cash-benefit plans) pay a stipulated amount (e.g., $150 per day for up to one year for a semi-private hospital room) when the insured employee or eligible dependents are hospitalized. The employee is reimbursed up to the policy limits of coverage and is responsible for any charges in excess of these limits. Most collective bargaining agreements provide for one to two years of hospitalization coverage. Blue Cross plans (known as *service plans*) maintain contracts with *member hospitals* that have agreed to accept a specific fee schedule as full payment for persons carrying this type of hospitalization coverage. The Bureau of National Affairs, Inc., survey data indicates that 22 percent of the contracts provide service benefits.[21] Both hospital indemnity contracts and Blue Cross plans also provide ancillary services. Indemnity (cash benefit) plans are gen-

---

[20] The Bureau of National Affairs, Inc., "Basic Patterns: Insurance," *Collective Bargaining Negotiations & Contracts* (Washington, D.C.: The Bureau of National Affairs, Inc., 1989), section 44.
[21] The Bureau of National Affairs, Inc., "Basic Patterns: Insurance" *Collective Bargaining Negotiations & Contracts* (Washington, D.C.: The Bureau of National Affairs, Inc., 1989), section 44.

erally less expensive than service plans (Blue Cross), but the latter often provides more comprehensive coverage.[22]

Surgical insurance covers the physician's bill for health care services (not just for surgery, as the name implies). Surgical coverage is offered on both an indemnity contract and a service contract (Blue Shield) basis. Indemnity plans reimburse the worker according to a *schedule of benefits* that lists the amounts that the policy will pay for a variety of surgical procedures (e.g., $800 for an appendectomy, $700 for a gallbladder removal, $950 for a hysterectomy, and so on). Surgical service plans generally pay "usual, customary, and reasonable fees" for a physician's services. Most group health insurance policies cover hospital care and surgical services under a single package. Approximately three-fourths of the contracts sampled by The Bureau of National Affairs, Inc., stipulate that the employer will pay the entire premium for hospital and surgical insurance (known as a noncontributory plan).[23]

Major medical insurance covers catastrophic hospitalization, surgical, and other medical expenses. There are two types of major medical plans: one that supplements basic hospital/surgical medical expense programs and one that provides basic coverage that includes regular hospital and surgical insurance along with major medical insurance. The maximum limits on a major medical policy commonly range upward from $10,000 for any single illness or injury. Some collective bargaining agreements place a *lifetime* limit on coverage in the range of $300,000, whereas other contracts have *annual* limits ranging from less than $30,000 to more than $100,000.[24] Major medical insurance covers a wide variety of health care costs such as hospital care, physician's fees, surgery, anesthesia, oxygen, drugs, services of a private duty nurse, artificial limbs, ambulance services, and services by radiologists and physical therapists. From a risk management standpoint, major medical insurance is an excellent buy because it protects against severe financial losses that most persons would find devastating. Although major medical insurance affords a great deal of protection from financially ruinous medical bills, it is not prohibitively expensive. The relatively low cost of major medical insurance is a result of its substantial deductible ($50 to $100) plus a co-insurance (or co-payment) provision for amounts above the deductible. The vast majority of contracts contain an 80–20 co-insurance provision; the health insurance pays 80 percent of covered expenses and the employee pays the remaining 20 percent.[25] Co-insurance payments are designed to discourage malingering by covered employees and reduce the cost of group health insurance.

Suppose that a major medical policy has a $30,000 annual limit, a $100 deductible, and a 20 percent co-insurance clause for medical expenses above the deductible. The insured employee with covered medical bills totaling $23,000 would pay $4,680 ($100 for the deductible plus 20 percent of the remaining

---

[22] The Bureau of National Affairs, Inc., *Compensation: Personnel Policy and Practice Series* (Washington, D.C.: The Bureau of National Affairs, Inc., 1984), Section 339.
[23] The Bureau of National Affairs, Inc., "Basic Patterns: Insurance," *Collective Bargaining Negotiations & Contracts* (Washington, D.C.: The Bureau of National Affairs, Inc., 1989), section 44.
[24] The Bureau of National Affairs, Inc., "Basic Patterns: Insurance," *Collective Bargaining Negotiations & Contracts* (Washington, D.C.: The Bureau of National Affairs, Inc., 1989), section 44.
[25] The Bureau of National Affairs, Inc., "Basic Patterns: Insurance," *Collective Bargaining Negotiations & Contracts* (Washington, D.C.: The Bureau of National Affairs, Inc., 1989), section 44.

$22,900 under the co-insurance provision); the insurance company would pay the remaining $18,320. Although many employees would find the $4,680 payment to be financially inconvenient, this amount pales in comparison to $18,320—a sum that may force an employee to deplete savings, sell property, borrow heavily, or file for bankruptcy. In addition, a number of major medical policies waive co-insurance payments when medical bills exceed certain amounts (e.g., the health insurance pays 100 percent of medical expenses above $10,000).

The quality of a group medical expense policy such as major medical insurance depends on several factors. It is obvious that the higher the dollar limits of coverage, the better the policy. However, several additional considerations are important. First, union and management officials who are responsible for negotiating a group medical insurance plan should carefully consider the *exclusions* and the application of the *deductible clause*. Typical exclusions are war-related injuries, self-inflicted injuries, expenses payable under workers' compensation, and elective cosmetic surgery. Hospitalization coverage often excludes outpatient care (where the employee is treated at home or in a physician's office rather than being admitted to a hospital). Pre-existing conditions are often excluded. A pre-existing condition is one that had been diagnosed prior to the employee's eligibility under the group health insurance plan. For example, an employee who is diagnosed with a stomach ulcer on April 3, 1990, and accepts employment with a company on June 18, 1990, may not have health insurance coverage for treatments on the ulcer because the condition existed *prior* to the employee's eligibility under the group insurance plan. All other conditions diagnosed after June 18, 1990 would be covered. Medical expense insurance often excludes coverage for mental illness and drug and alcohol addiction. Dental care and prescription eyeglasses are also excluded and can be insured under separate group health policies.

Most health insurance plans use a deductible that ranges from $50 to $1,000 dollars. Deductibles eliminate frequent small claims and reduce the cost of group health insurance. Most health insurance plans use an annual deductible rather than a per-illness deductible. For example, a company may use a maximum $500 annual family deductible, with a $100 deductible for each family member until the $500 maximum is reached. In other group policies, the deductible is more restrictive and is applied on a *per-illness* basis. Thus, an employee who is treated for a leg injury in February and then is treated for an eye disorder in July may have to satisfy two $100 deductibles, one for the leg injury and one for the eye disorder.

Federal law requires employers to offer the same health insurance coverage to workers who are age 65 or older (and not yet retired). Employees age 65 or older have the option of selecting Medicare rather than the employer's group health insurance plan. However, the law stipulates that benefits provided by Medicare cannot be supplemented by the employer's health insurance plan.[26] A number of collective bargaining agreements also provide health insurance to retirees.[27] How-

---

[26] The Bureau of National Affairs, Inc., "Basic Patterns: Insurance," *Collective Bargaining Negotiations & Contracts* (Washington, D.C.: The Bureau of National Affairs, Inc., 1989), section 44.

[27] Daniel L. Klein and Jeffrey P. Petertil, "Health Coverage for Retirees: A Timebomb," *Personnel* (August 1986), p. 54; and Meg Delaney, "Who Will Pay Retirees Health Care?," *Personnel Journal* (March 1987), p. 82.

ever, the cost of such coverage can be quite expensive. One consulting firm estimated that a corporation with 200 retired workers will pay $153,000 a year for the retirees' health insurance.[28] Some health insurance provisions covering retirees and their dependents coordinate benefits with those of Medicare and cover the deductibles and co-insurance not paid by the Medicare program.[29] There is also concern in Congress that legislation is needed to protect the health insurance benefits of retirees in the event that the employer faces bankruptcy. Congressional concern was precipitated by the adverse publicity associated with the termination of retiree health insurance coverage by LTV Steel.[30]

Maternity benefits typically cover hospitalization and related expenses associated with childbirth. Forty-five percent of the contracts surveyed by The Bureau of National Affairs, Inc. include maternity coverage.[31] Most group hospitalization plans provide maternity coverage for 10–14 days for workers who have been employed with the organization for at least nine months.[32] Persons responsible for negotiating maternity provisions must comply with the Pregnancy Discrimination Act of 1978, which requires that pregnancy and related conditions be treated in the same manner as other disabilities and medical conditions.[33] The Act does not permit employers to discriminate between men and women with regard to medical and disability benefits. For example, the Pregnancy Discrimination Act would be violated if a collective bargaining agreement provided a health or disability policy that does not cover pregnancy or imposed a high cost to employees for such coverage.

Health Maintenance Organizations

Some collective bargaining agreements permit employees to choose between different types of health insurance coverage. For companies and employees who elect not to purchase medical expense insurance, Health Maintenance Organizations (HMOs) are an attractive alternative. HMOs provide a comprehensive array of health care services such as medical examinations, x-ray and laboratory services, maternity

---

[28] *The Wall Street Journal*, Labor Letter (March 10, 1987), p. 1.
[29] The Medicare Catastrophic Protection Act (1989) has reduced the Medicare deductible and co-insurance amounts paid by the elderly. For example, the Act provides 365 days of hospital coverage per year after the patient pays a one-day deductible. Previously, Medicare patients received only 60 days coverage after a $540 deductible. Outpatient medical expenses are paid in full once a $1,400 deductible is satisfied (as opposed to an 80% co-insurance provision before the Act was passed). See "Medicare Catastrophic Protection Act," in Craig T. Norback, ed., *The Human Resources Yearbook, 1989 Edition* (Englewood Cliffs, New Jersey: Prentice-Hall, Inc., 1989), pp. 2.36–2.37.
[30] Richard J. Donahue, "78,500 LTV Retirees Lose Health Coverage: Pensions Safe," *National Underwriter—Life and Health Insurance Edition* (July 26, 1986), p. 3.
[31] The Bureau of National Affairs, Inc., "Basic Patterns: Insurance," *Collective Bargaining Negotiations & Contracts* (Washington, D.C.: The Bureau of National Affairs, Inc., 1989), section 44.
[32] The Bureau of National Affairs, Inc., *Compensation: Personnel Policy and Practice Series* (Washington, D.C.: The Bureau of National Affairs, Inc., 1987), section 339. Under the Pregnancy Discrimination Act, disabilities arising from pregnancies must be treated in the same manner as other disabilities under a firm's group health insurance plan. There can be no special conditions placed on the number of days or dollar amounts for maternity coverage *unless* these limitations apply to other disabilities under an employer's group insurance plan.
[33] Public Law 95–555 (1978) adds a new section, Section 701 (k) to Title VII of the 1964 Civil Rights Act. The Pregnancy Discrimination Act does not require the employer to establish health and disability where none previously existed. There is also no requirement for employers to pay for health insurance benefits covering abortions except where the life of the mother would be endangered if the fetus were carried for the full term of pregnancy or where medical complications have arisen from an abortion.

care, hospitalization, and surgical services for persons residing in a defined geographic area. The original HMO concept offered comprehensive health care for members within a single organization and encouraged a preventive approach to medical care (rather than the curative approach of waiting for illnesses or diseases to occur) as a means of reducing illnesses and controlling health care costs. Most HMOs follow the *group practice model* in which a contract is established with a physician group and area hospitals who provide health care to HMO members. Under this arrangement, physicians are employed by the HMO and members can select a personal physician from within the group and enjoy more personalized medical care. HMOs are funded through premium payments much in the same manner as group health insurance plans; members pay little or no additional fees whenever they consult a physician or are admitted to an HMO-member hospital. HMOs are operated as a private business and there is an incentive for HMOs to reduce costs in order to earn a profit or, at least, to break even. Supporters of HMOs claim that they offer a more economic and efficient means of health care delivery because of their emphasis on diagnostic services, preventive medical care, and outpatient treatment of illnesses. The traditional modes of health care, on the other hand, focus on the treatment of acute illnesses and inpatient hospital care rather than on the prevention of health problems.[34]

The Health Maintenance Organization Act of 1973 was passed to encourage the formation and use of HMOs and to provide grant and loan monies to HMOs that meet federal standards. A federally-qualified HMO must provide a wide array of health care services, such as physician services, inpatient and outpatient hospital services, emergency medical care, outpatient and evaluative mental health services, treatment and referral services for drug and alcohol addiction, preventive care and immunizations, well-child care from birth, periodic health evaluations for adults, voluntary family planning services, and children's eye and ear examinations.

Employers with 25 or more employees must offer an option of participating in a qualified HMO. This requirement assumes that the employer offers alternative forms of health insurance and has received a written request from a qualified HMO that operates in the local area.[35] Once the employer has accepted the HMO request, it must allow the HMO periodic access to its employees, provide employees with the option of joining the HMO and arrange for payroll deductions to the plan, along with several other requirements.

Disability Income Insurance

Disability income insurance provides protection against a loss of income during periods when an employee is unable to work because of illness or injury. Provisions for nonoccupational sickness and accident benefits are found in over 80 percent of the contracts surveyed by The Bureau of National Affairs, Inc.[36] Some employee benefit experts argue that protecting against a loss of income is more important

---

[34] The Bureau of National Affairs, Inc., *Compensation: Personnel Policy and Practice Series* (Washington, D.C.: The Bureau of National Affairs, Inc., 1983), section 339.
[35] See "Employer Perceptions of HMOs: Survey Shows Mixed Feelings on Effectiveness as Cost Savings Vehicles," *Medical Benefits: The Medical-Economic Digest* (April 30, 1987), p. 1.
[36] The Bureau of National Affairs, Inc., "Basic Patterns: Insurance," *Collective Bargaining Negotiations & Contracts* (Washington, D.C.: The Bureau of National Affairs, Inc., 1989), section 44.

than life insurance protection because disability, in an economic sense, is a form of "living death." Disabled workers do not generate an income, but they incur expenses that are equal to or even greater than those of people who are employed. Furthermore, the odds of becoming disabled are higher than the odds of premature death. According to the American College of Life Underwriters,

> At age 35, the chance of experiencing total disability of three months or more before age 65 is about 33%. The average length of disability will exceed five years. Moreover, nearly 30% of all disability cases will be permanent.[37]

From a risk management point of view, disability income insurance should be at or near the top of the employee's priority list of benefits. For employees injured on the job, workers' compensation will provide periodic monthly payments up to the maximum specified by law. Some employees will also qualify for disability benefits under Social Security. However, for workers who are not injured on the job or who are ineligible for Social Security benefits, group disability insurance fills a critical need. Short-term disability income group insurance policies normally provide protection up to one year and long-term policies may provide protection for five years, ten years, or until the disabled employee reaches age 65. Some long-term policies provide lifetime income protection. Approximately one-fifth of the contracts in The Bureau of National Affairs, Inc., survey provide long-term disability insurance.[38]

A primary consideration when the union and management negotiate a disability income insurance group policy is the plan's *definition of "disability."* The disability definition is of the utmost importance because it determines the conditions under which the weekly or monthly benefits are paid. Several examples of disability definitions are the following:

▲ The inability of the insured employee to engage in *his or her* occupation.
▲ The inability of the insured to engage in any *reasonable* occupation (commensurate with the employee's education and work experience) for which he or she might become qualified through training within a two-year period.
▲ The inability of the insured to engage in *any* occupation.

The first definition of disability is the most liberal because the worker is only required to be physically or mentally incapable of performing his or her occupation. For example, a machinist sustaining a broken hand would probably not be able to continue working at his or her chosen occupation, although there are many other jobs that such an individual could fill. Under a definition similar to the first two, a machinist with a broken hand could collect disability income benefits. However, the third definition is quite restrictive and would not allow payment of benefits unless the worker were severely disabled and incapable of performing any job. Some disability income policies contain a provision of "presumptive disability." Under such a provision, a worker who suffers the loss of a limb or eyesight is automatically eligible for income benefits even though he or she is still employable.

Another important feature of a group disability income insurance plan is the

---

[37] Emmett J. Vaughan, *Fundamentals of Risk and Insurance*, 3rd ed. (New York: John Wiley and Sons, 1982), p. 256.
[38] The Bureau of National Affairs, Inc., "Basic Patterns: Insurance," *Collective Bargaining Contracts & Negotiations* (Washington, D.C.: The Bureau of National Affairs, Inc., 1989), section 44.

waiting period (also called the elimination period) between the time an employee becomes disabled and the date on which benefit payments actually begin. Short-term disability policies usually require a waiting period of at least one week, whereas a long-term policy may require a one year waiting period. The waiting period serves as a form of deductible and reduces the cost of the disability income policy by eliminating small claims for very short periods of disability. Most group disability income insurance policies do not pay more than 60 percent of an employee's gross income because Social Security disability benefits partially cover the difference between payments made under the disability income policy and the employee's gross income. By paying only two-thirds of an employee's gross pay, disability income policies discourage malingering by disabled workers.[39] Under the Tax Reform Act of 1986, disability income benefits are subject to withholding for federal income tax purposes.

Many group disability income insurance plans require that an employee undergo rehabilitative treatment to reduce disabilities and regain employability. As is the case with most forms of health insurance, disability income insurance is subject to exclusions under which benefits will not be paid. Benefits may be reduced because of payments made by workers' compensation or Social Security. Pre-existing conditions, mental and nervous disorders, and time lost from work for drug and alcohol rehabilitation are frequently excluded. Benefits are also denied for disabilities arising from acts of war, self-inflicted injuries, and injuries suffered while committing a crime.

Other Important Health Care Contract Provisions

A number of other important health care benefits are also found in many collective bargaining agreements. Eighty-three percent of the contracts surveyed by The Bureau of National Affairs, Inc., contain dental care coverage and nearly all of these include dental care for dependents. Nealy half of the surveyed contracts cover the cost of prescription drugs, optical care, and alcohol and drug abuse benefits. When contracts provide dental and optical care for employees, they typically provide the same care for dependents. Collective bargaining agreements may also provide for the continuation of health care benefits during layoffs (but not strikes).

Health Care Cost Containment Measures

Health care is one of the most expensive employee benefits and business executives and labor leaders have devoted much attention to keeping employee health care expenditures in check.[40] One survey indicates that a typical employer annually paid $2,226 per employee for health care benefits.[41] Most group health insurance policies

---

[39] Carol Cain, "Employer Meddling Can Hasten Mending," *Business Insurance* (January 13, 1986), p. 19.
[40] "Group Health Insurance Survey," (Touche Ross, December 1986). Summarized in Regina E. Herzlinger and Jeffrey Schwartz, "How Companies Tackle Health Care Costs," *Harvard Business Review* (July-August 1985), p. 58.
[41] Albert G. Holzinger, "The Real Costs of Benefits," *Nation's Business* (February 1988), p. 31. This total includes state sickness benefits insurance ($211), medical insurance for current employees ($1,604) and retired employees ($157), dental insurance ($148), and other medical payments ($86).

are only vaguely understood by employees who often care little about health care costs as long as "the insurance company takes care of it." Prior to 1984, health care costs were increasing by at least 10 percent annually.[42] For example, between September 1988 and September 1989, the wages and salaries of private-sector workers rose 4.4 percent, the consumer price index jumped 4.3 percent, and health insurance costs increased by 13.7 percent.[43] Part of this increase is the result of inflationary forces that have affected the price of almost every consumer good and service. Some of the rising health care costs can be attributed to the improved quality of health care created by advances in medical diagnoses and treatment, technological innovations, and improved pharmaceuticals.[44]

Health care costs have also gone unchecked because of a lack of market forces affecting prices charged for physicians' services, hospital stays, and ancillary medical care. Consumers do not necessarily seek out the least expensive sources of health care and may, in fact, avoid health care providers who offer their services at low rates for fear that they are inferior to their more expensive counterparts. The market mystique of health care prices is compounded by the fact that doctors and other health care providers do not usually advertise their services or prices; persons in need of health care do not shop around for the best buy as they would for most other goods and services.[45] The dilemma posed by rising health care costs has been expressed by one labor advocate as follows:

> Health premium increases [have]....dwarfed negotiated wage increases and pension improvements. This disparity will mean even greater pressure from employers in the future to shift the rising costs of care onto the backs of workers and get it off corporate or public employers' budgets. As federal and state health plans cut back on public programs and tighten payments to hospitals and physicians, the crisis situation for privately negotiated plans will worsen. Hospitals and physicians have demonstrated in the past that they are more than willing to stop a potential reduction in their income from one source by simply shifting costs onto other payers—namely privately-insured patients. For unions, this means the costs of negotiating retiree supplementary and unemployed worker coverage will rise dramatically due to less public program coverage, and costs of current worker coverage will soar beyond even the double digit (15–20%) health care inflation rate. In other words, protecting health benefits will continue to remain a central and difficult negotiating issue *unless* something is done to contain costs.[46]

---

[42] The Bureau of National Affairs, Inc., *Compensation: Personnel Policy and Practice Series* (Washington, D.C.: The Bureau of National Affairs, Inc., 1986), section 339.
[43] David Wessel, "Labor Costs Rose 1.2% in Third Quarter as Health Care Costs Continued to Soar," *The Wall Street Journal* (November 1, 1989).
[44] By April of 1990, health care costs were increasing at an annual rate of eight percent, well above the Federal Reserve Board's estimated overall inflation rate of between four and 4.5 percent. See Kathleen Madigan and Mike McNamee, "Inflation's Split Personality," *Business Week* (April 30, 1990), p. 24.
[45] Bruce A. Lepore, "Consumerism and Health Care Costs: It Pays to Shop Around," *National Safety and Health News* (June 1985), p. 63; and James M. Burcke, "Cost No Object: Big Health Care Users Don't Shop Around: Study," *Business Insurance* (November 3, 1986), p. 3.
[46] Cathy Schoen, "Maintaining and Improving Health Benefits by Containing Costs," originally written for an AFL-CIO health benefits conference held in Washington D.C. in December, 1983. Reprinted in The Bureau of National Affairs, Inc., "Union Guide to Bargaining Over Health Care Cost Containment," *Collective Bargaining Negotiations & Contracts* (Washington, D.C.: The Bureau of National Affairs, Inc., 1984), section 14.

Group health insurance policies have traditionally used deductibles, co-insurance, and exclusions to contain health care costs and insurance premiums.[47] As employers have become increasingly cost conscious, additional measures have been taken. Employers and unions have begun to analyze health care expenditures closely. Monthly, quarterly, and annual health services data are collected on the length of hospital stays by employees, physician fees, outpatient costs, expenditures on certain ailments, and other items. A number of firms, in cooperation with health insurance companies, have formed coalitions to examine health care costs and establish alternative health care provider systems to contain costs.[48] Some companies audit health insurance claims for accuracy and may save as much as 10 percent in health care costs. Carson Pirie Scott and Co. in Chicago started a program urging its employees to examine their medical bills carefully for errors; the employee receives 20 percent of any savings from a billing error. Other employers and health insurance companies are focusing their cost containment efforts on health care providers.[49]

Employers have begun monitoring the hospitalizations of their employees to eliminate unnecessary hospital stays and medical services. Health insurance companies are often willing to pay for second medical opinions to determine whether surgical or other expensive medical treatments are necessary. Preadmission certification programs can help reduce hospitalizations by ensuring that less costly alternatives are used whenever possible. For example, some minor surgery can be performed in a physician's office rather than in a hospital. *Preferred provider organizations* (PPOs) work through hospitals and doctors to cut medical fees.[50] *Professional standards review organizations* (PSROs) are used to help eliminate inadequate or inappropriate treatments by physicians and other health care professionals.[51]

Health care costs may also be contained through employee involvement and education. Some firms have attempted to educate employees regarding group health insurance provisions and cost concerns. Other companies have stressed the use of wellness and fitness programs as a means of preventing heart disease and other health problems.[52] A four-year study of 15,000 Control Data Corporation employees showed that workers with the worst lifestyle habits had the highest medical bills. Employers may attempt to control health care costs by either penalizing workers who smoke or are overweight, requiring them to pay larger premiums for health

---

[47] "Deductibles, Co-insurance Up in Health Care," *Employee Benefit Plan Review* (December 1986), p. 82.
[48] Rick Lee, "Business-Health Coalitions," *Compensation and Benefits Review* (January-February 1986), pp. 18–25; and "Employer Health Care Coalitions Work with Insurers and Providers to Manage Costs, Quality," *Employee Benefit Plan Review* (December 1986), p. 114.
[49] "Guidelines on Diagnostic Testing Will Lead to Cost Savings, Better Patient Care," Blue Cross and Blue Shield Association (March 30, 1987).
[50] *The Wall Street Journal*, Labor Letter (February 17, 1987), p. 1; and Eileen McCabe, "Preferred Provider Organizations: PPO's May Offer A New Way to Manage Health Care Costs," *Personnel Administrator* (December 1984), p. 53.
[51] See Michael M. Biehl and Linda M. Laarman, "Legal Problems of Health Care Cost Containment," *Employment Relations Today* (Spring 1988), pp. 1-8.
[52] For an excellent discussion on health care cost containment, see The Bureau of National Affairs, Inc., *Compensation: Personnel Policy and Practice Series* (Washington, D.C.: The Bureau of National Affairs, Inc., 1986), section 339.

insurance or reducing their benefits. Employees with health-conscious lifestyles, on the other hand, might have their premiums reduced or benefits expanded. According to one state insurance commissioner, "It just isn't fair for the person who leads a clean lifestyle to subsidize the debauchery of those who don't."[53]

According to The Bureau of National Affairs, Inc., survey data, provisions designed to lower the cost of health care rose dramatically during the 1980s. Most of these provisions were directed at reducing hospitalization costs. The following health care cost containment measures are commonly used in collective bargaining agreements:[54]

1. Increasing emphasis on paying for minor surgical procedures at a physician's office or outpatient clinic, rather than admitting a patient to the hospital.
2. Requiring second (and even third) medical opinions prior to many surgical procedures.
3. Increased coverage for home health care or care in a skilled nursing facility in lieu of keeping a patient in the hospital.
4. Increasing deductibles and requiring employees to pay part of the health insurance premiums.
5. Using comprehensive insurance plans that integrate medical, dental, and other types of health insurance into a single group policy in order to reduce administrative costs and minimize duplication of coverage.

There is some evidence that labor and corporate leaders are attempting to cooperate in reducing health care costs. Both the AFL-CIO and the National Association of Manufacturers are calling for measures to control health care costs.[55] However, as private-sector companies place a greater burden on employees to help pay health insurance premiums, assume responsibility for higher deductibles and co-insurance percentages, or accept reduced benefits, problems will arise. Rising health care costs have been at the heart of several recent labor-management disputes. The strike between the United Mine Workers and the Pittston Company centered on the company's refusal to pay royalties to trusts that fund the miners' health care and pensions. Similarly, the strike by the communications and electrical workers unions against Nynex (a telecommunications firm serving the Northeast) was sparked by a controversy over health care premium payments.[56] United Auto Workers, Local 278, went on strike against Borg-Warner Corporation over a continuing battle over the cost of health care benefits.[57] In the summer of 1988, members of the Hospital and Health Care Workers Union (an affiliate of the Service

---

[53] Frank E. James, "Study Lays Groundwork For Tying Health Costs to Workers' Behavior," *The Wall Street Journal* (April 14, 1987).
[54] The Bureau of National Affairs, Inc., "Basic Patterns: Insurance," *Collective Bargaining Negotiations & Contracts* (Washington, D.C.: The Bureau of National Affairs, Inc., 1989), section 44.
[55] Kenneth H. Bacon, "Business and Labor Reach a Consensus on Need to Reduce Health-Care Costs," *The Wall Street Journal* (November 1, 1989), p. A16.
[56] Christopher Elias, "Nasty Battle over Health Care Has Labor Relations in a Knot," *Insight* (December 4, 1989), pp. 40–41.
[57] Gregory A. Patterson, "UAW Local Strikes Borg-Warner Over Benefits Costs," *The Wall Street Journal* (September 8, 1989), p. C15.

Employees International Union) walked off the job to protest a management demand for higher co-insurance payments and reduced health benefits.[58]

▲ Retirement Programs

Retirement (pension) programs represent the primary source of retirement income for many employees, with Social Security and individual retirement plans providing supplementary income. Nearly all collective bargaining agreements provide for some form of retirement program. Collectively-bargained retirement programs may cover either a single employer or multiple employers. There is also considerable variation among retirement programs in terms of funding mechanisms, vesting provisions, and benefit schedules. Furthermore, the Employee Retirement Income Security Act of 1974 (ERISA) as well as Title VII of the 1964 Civil Rights Act and the Age Discrimination in Employment Act have affected the structure of pension plans. This discussion outlines the basic characteristics of retirement programs and the laws affecting these programs.[59]

The Concept of a Pension

In its simplest form, a pension is an *accumulation* of funds during an employee's working years followed by a *liquidation* of these funds once the employee retires (the funds may also be partially liquidated if an employee becomes permanently disabled, resigns or is terminated, or dies prematurely). Figure 14-1 provides an illustration of this concept.

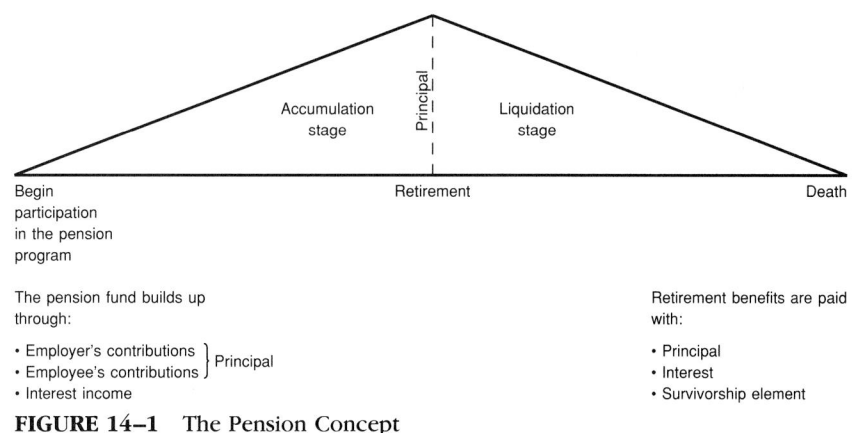

FIGURE 14–1 The Pension Concept
Source: Terry L. Leap and Michael D. Crino, *Personnel/Human Resource Management* (New York: Macmillan Publishing Company, 1989), p. 458. Reprinted with permission.

The pension fund builds up through:
- Employer's contributions ⎫ Principal
- Employee's contributions ⎭
- Interest income

Retirement benefits are paid with:
- Principal
- Interest
- Survivorship element

---

[58] Joan O'C. Hamilton, "Health Care Costs Take a Turn for the Worse," *Business Week* (October 31, 1988).

[59] Harry E. Allen, "Recent Developments in Private Pensions," *Management Review* (January 1987), pp. 54–56; Allen Stiteler, "Finally Pension Plans Defined," *Personnel Journal* (February 1987), pp. 44–53; and Judy Olian, Stephen J. Carroll, Jr., and Craig Eric Schneier, *Pension Plans: The Human Resource Management Perspective* (Ithaca, New York: ILR Press, Cornell University, 1986).

The employer and/or the worker contribute periodic payments (usually every pay period) to a pension program or individual employee pension account. The person or organization responsible for the safekeeping and investment of these funds is known as a *fiduciary*. Over a period of time, the invested funds accumulate interest income. Upon his or her retirement, the amount paid to the employee in a monthly or biweekly retirement check is based on three components: (1) the principal (sums of the employer's and employee's contributions over the years), (2) interest income earned on the principal, and (3) a survivorship element. Although the reader is probably familiar with the principal and interest components, the survivorship component requires further elaboration. The survivorship component is a recognition of the fact that some retirees will live for a number of years after retirement—perhaps well into their 90s—whereas others will survive for only a few years. A retiree who lives to age 97, for example, will probably use up the entire principal and interest income allocated to his or her retirement. On the other hand, a person who dies two years after retirement will not use up his or her entire principal plus interest. The survivorship component allows pension plan administrators and actuaries to establish benefit levels so that those dying soon after retirement will partially subsidize those who live longer.

A retiree's income also depends on the age at which he or she retires; the longer a person waits to retire, the larger the pension benefit. Many retirement programs provide some form of *guaranteed benefit option* that allows payments to continue to survivors of deceased retirees. For example, a retiree may elect a 10-year certain benefit that guarantees a retirement income for as long as the retiree lives *or* for 10 years, whichever is longer. If an employee dies six years after retirement, then benefits are payable to a designated beneficiary for an additional four years. One popular form of guaranteed benefit option is a *joint and survivor annuity,* which provides a retirement income for the retiree and his or her spouse. Should the retiree die, the surviving spouse will continue to receive a lifetime income that is the same or slightly less than the amount received before the retiree's death. When a retiree elects a guaranteed benefit option, the biweekly or monthly retirement income is usually less than what would have been received under a straight life annuity with no guaranteed minimum.

The Employee Retirement Income Security Act of 1974

The Employee Retirement Income Security Act of 1974 (ERISA) regulates nearly all pension benefit plans sponsored by employers and unions (except for government plans, Railroad Retirement, church plans, and a few others). ERISA establishes standards that protect the retirement benefits of employees from misuse or mismanagement by persons charged with the safekeeping of pension funds so that these funds will be available upon his or her retirement.[60] The impetus behind the passage of ERISA was several pension plan scandals, the most notable being the Central States Fund incident involving the Teamsters union. Employees have been denied their retirement benefits because of bankruptcies, loans from the pension funds that

---

[60] Alfred Klein, "Why You Can't Afford to Ignore ERISA," *Personnel Journal* (June 1986), p. 72.

were never repaid, embezzlement, and investment of pension funds in risky endeavors. ERISA now provides a myriad of rules and requirements pertaining to employee eligibility to participate in a retirement program, minimum vesting standards, reporting requirements for pension fund administrators, disclosure rules, contribution and benefit limits, distribution of plan proceeds, and benefit guarantees.

Companies without private pension plans are *not* required to establish a pension in order to comply with ERISA. In fact, some critics initially argued that the presence of ERISA might discourage the growth of pension plans and possibly lead to the termination of existing plans. However, this problem has not materialized.[61] What ERISA has done is to improve the quality of existing retirement programs by providing greater income security to the worker.[62]

Retirement Plan Terminology and Provisions

Retirement or pension plans differ from one organization to another. However, they all contain common provisions that are defined and discussed here. These provisions are discussed in light of ERISA and changes mandated by the Tax Reform Act of 1986.

1. *Participation or eligibility standards.* An employer may exclude employees from participating or making contributions to the company's pension plan until they have accumulated two years of service. Employers are also required to have a minimum percentage of employees participating in the pension plan.
2. *Contributory and noncontributory plans.* A *contributory plan* is one in which *both* the employer and employee make payments into the pension plan. Under a *noncontributory plan*, only the employer makes contributions. The majority of pension plans in collective bargaining agreements surveyed by The Bureau of National Affairs, Inc., are noncontributory.[63]
3. *Defined-contribution and defined-benefit plans.* A *defined contribution plan* fixes the amount of the employer's contribution by formula, but the level of the benefits paid to the worker upon retirement is not guaranteed. Under a *defined benefit plan*, the income that an employee will receive is either (a) fixed at a specific dollar amount or (b) determined by a fixed formula (e.g., 50 percent of an employee's average annual income 3 years immediately prior to retirement). Approximately half of The Bureau of National Affairs, Inc.-surveyed contracts have defined-benefit pensions that guarantee a flat dollar amount per month for each year of service. For example, a monthly benefit formula of $20 for every year of service would pay a retiree with 25 years of service $500 per month ($20 x 25 years).

---

[61] Johannes Ledoltes and Mark L. Power, "A Study of ERISA's Impact on Private Retirement Plan Growth," *The Journal of Risk and Insurance*, Vol. LI, No. 2, pp. 225–243. Also see Jozetta H. Srb, "Pension Policy for the Eighties," *Industrial and Labor Relations Report* (Ithaca, New York: New York State School of Industrial and Labor Relations, Cornell University, Fall 1981), pp. 7–9.
[62] See Benson Rosen and Thomas H. Jerdee, "Retirement Policies for the 21st Century," *Human Resource Management* (Fall 1986), p. 405.
[63] The Bureau of National Affairs, Inc., "Basic Patterns: Pensions," *Collective Bargaining Negotiations & Contracts* (Washington, D.C.: The Bureau of National Affairs, Inc., 1986), section 48.

Thus, a defined contribution plan holds contributions constant and allows benefits to vary, whereas a defined benefit plan guarantees benefits, but requires that contributions be periodically changed. Contributions to the pension fund accumulate over long periods of time (over 40 years in some cases) and investment income tied to economic growth and interest rates cannot be accurately predicted years in advance. Thus, it becomes necessary to change pension contributions *or* benefits as economic conditions dictate.

4. *Funding*. Somewhat related to the previous definitions of defined contribution and defined benefit plans is the concept of funding. ERISA requires that funding be based on a "pay-as-you-work" basis, with contributions made during the employee's working years. Employers and unions cannot fund pension benefits to retirees from current operating revenues, nor can they design a pension program that purchases a lump sum retirement benefit for an employee who is about to retire. Under either of these latter two arrangements, there are no guarantees that the funds will be available to employees upon retirement if the company goes out of business or is acquired by another firm. The most common method of funding collectively-bargained retirement benefits is through the establishment of a trust fund. A bank or insurance company is usually designated as a trustee for the pension assets.[64]

5. *Vesting*. Vesting refers to the employee's ability to claim all or part of the *employer's* contribution to a pension program that was made on behalf of the employee. The money that an employee contributes on his or her behalf is nonforfeitable (that is, it cannot be taken away from the employee). The issue of vesting becomes important, however, when an employee resigns or is terminated and wants to obtain all or part of the employer's contribution. Thus, an employee who is "50-percent vested" would be entitled to 50 percent of the employer's contributions (plus *all* of the *employee's* contributions). If a person resigns or is terminated before becoming fully vested, he or she loses the unvested portion of the employer's contribution (known as a *forfeiture*). Persons who have been employed for several years by a firm may be entitled to a substantial sum of money if they leave the organization, depending on the vesting provisions of a particular pension plan. However, the employer has the option of either paying the worker a lump sum or retaining the vested amount and paying it to the employee upon retirement. Some companies use *portable pensions*, which allow workers to move funds from one plan to another (e.g., when changing jobs) without incurring a tax liability.

Under the Tax Reform Act of 1986, employees are now required to be 100 percent vested after five years of service. An employee with four years of service would have no vested pension rights, but would go from zero to full (100%) vesting after five years of service (five-year, 100 percent rule). Vesting may also be phased in between an employee's third and seventh year of service, with 20 percent vesting after three years and 20 percent increases per year such that 100 percent vesting is achieved after seven years. The latter option provides

---

[64] The Bureau of National Affairs, Inc., "Basic Patterns: Pensions," *Collective Bargaining Negotiations & Contracts* (Washington, D.C.: The Bureau of National Affairs, Inc., 1987), section 48.

earlier vesting rights than the five-year, 100 percent rule, but delays full vesting until the seventh year of service. Plans that condition participation on more than one year of service must provide full and immediate vesting rights. Multi-employer plans may protract full vesting for ten years. Pension administrators are, of course, free to use vesting standards that allow more rapid vesting than is required under federal law.

6. *Qualified and nonqualified pension plans.* A qualified pension plan must meet certain Internal Revenue Service requirements that entitle both the employee and employer to substantial tax breaks. Employers receive a tax deduction for contributions made to a pension plan, and investment income on pension funds are not subject to taxation. Employees do not incur a tax liability on the employer's contributions until pension benefits are paid (usually at retirement). Employee contributions to a qualified pension can be made in before-tax dollars, which provides greater disposable income (take home pay). Nonqualified plans do not offer the aforementioned tax advantages.

7. *Integrated pension plans.* Pension plans that coordinate benefits with Social Security retirement benefits on a formula basis are known as integrated plans. There are a number of methods by which retirement benefits may be coordinated with Social Security. For example, employees making more than the Social Security base ($51,300 in 1990) may have their contributions increased to offset the "loss" of Social Security retirement benefits. According to The Bureau of National Affairs, Inc., survey data, only a small percentage of collectively bargained retirement programs are integrated.[65]

8. *Fiduciary standards and the protection of pension assets.* Fiduciaries who safeguard, control, and invest pension funds are required to meet "prudent person" standards as well as numerous record and reporting requirements. In the event that pension monies are lost through fraud, embezzlement, or mismanagement, the Pension Benefit Guaranty Corporation (created by ERISA) protects employees through a mandatory plan termination insurance program.[66]

9. *Conditions for retirement*: The 1987 amendments to the Age Discrimination in Employment Act now make the involuntary retirement of most employees illegal, regardless of age. A number of agreements, however, allow voluntary early retirement. For example, the United Auto Workers collective bargaining agreements contain three early-retirement options: (1) retirement at age 60 after 10 years of service; (2) retirement between ages 55 and 60 when age plus service equals 85; or, (3) retirement after 30 years of service regardless of age.[67] Most pension plans allow disabled employees to retire early and receive

---

[65] The Bureau of National Affairs, Inc., "Basic Patterns: Pensions," *Collective Bargaining Negotiations & Contracts* (Washington, D.C.: The Bureau of National Affairs, Inc., 1986), section 48.

[66] In 1988, firms had to pay the Pension Benefit Guaranty Corporation an annual premium of $16.00 per employee. Firms with underfunded pension plans had to pay as much as $50.00. See *The Wall Street Journal*, Labor Letter (January 5, 1988), p. 1. The Pension Protection Act amendments now require that pension administrators pay a variable-rate premium that is based to the level of funding in a pension program. See Kathleen P. Utgoff, "Defined Benefit Plans: Still A Good Deal," *Labor Law Journal* (July 1988), p. 444.

[67] The Bureau of National Affairs, Inc., "Basic Patterns: Pensions," *Collective Bargaining Contracts & Negotiations* (Washington, D.C.: The Bureau of National Affairs, Inc., 1986), section 48.

some form of disability benefit. In addition, some plans allow early retirement for plant shutdowns or permanent layoffs.

The legal and economic factors affecting retirement plans are complex and often beyond the expertise of union and management negotiators. Assistance from tax experts and pension specialists may be needed during bargaining preparations and contract talks to ensure that eligibility requirements, contributions, vesting standards, benefits, and other facets of a retirement plan meet the standards of ERISA and the latest changes in the tax laws.

▲ Income Maintenance Benefits

Organizations whose production or service levels fluctuate may be forced to lay off and, possibly, recall employees as business demands dictate. Income maintenance benefits that supplement state unemployment compensation payments are useful in attracting and retaining workers for employment in cyclical business operations. Over half of the contracts surveyed by The Bureau of National Affairs, Inc., contain income maintenance benefits. Three income maintenance programs are discussed here: guaranteed minimum amounts of work or pay, supplemental unemployment benefits, and severance pay (for employees who are subject to permanent layoffs).[68]

Guaranteed work and pay programs ensure that employees can count on receiving a minimum number of work hours or base pay per month or year, regardless of layoff status. Many of the guaranteed work and pay programs only apply to employees who have worked with an organization for a specified number of years. Other arrangements void the minimum guarantee if employees refuse assigned work as well as for work stoppages caused by economic strikes or matters beyond the employer's immediate control such as floods, power outages, or inclement weather.[69]

Supplemental unemployment benefit (SUB) plans provide additional income for laid-off employees above and beyond the amount paid by state unemployment compensation. First negotiated by the United Auto Workers in 1955, SUB plan benefits are usually based on the level of unemployment compensation benefits in a particular state. In some cases, the state unemployment compensation plus the SUB will restore income to 95 percent of the level received when the employee was working, minus a small deduction for incidental work-related expenses. Some SUB plans also have a ceiling on weekly payments.

SUB plans fall into two categories—the pooled-fund system and the individual account plan. Employers having SUB plans generally contribute a percentage of their payroll to the plan. The pooled-fund system provides benefits only in the event that no work is available. Individual account plans, on the other hand, allow the worker to withdraw his or her full amount at termination. In some cases, individual SUB plans also permit employees to withdraw money from the account for reasons other than layoff or termination.

---

[68] The Bureau of National Affairs, Inc., *Compensation: Personnel Policy and Practice Series* (Washington, D.C.: The Bureau of National Affairs, Inc., 1982), Section 331.
[69] The Bureau of National Affairs, Inc., "Basic Patterns: Income Maintenance," *Collective Bargaining Negotiations & Contracts* (Washington, D.C.: The Bureau of National Affairs, Inc., 1987), section 53.

According to The Bureau of National Affairs, Inc., survey of collective bargaining agreements, some SUB plans use a system of credit units. An employee generally accrues a specified number of credit units per work week or pay period, subject to a maximum limit. When the employee begins to collect benefits, credit units are cancelled. The rate at which credit units are cancelled may depend upon the amount of money in the SUB trust fund and the employee's seniority. When the trust fund is at its highest level, one credit unit per benefit is cancelled, regardless of the employee's seniority. As the fund level drops, more than one credit unit is cancelled per unit of benefit. When the fund drops below a certain level, SUB benefits may cease entirely. In order to receive SUB benefits, an employee must be willing to accept a company's offer to work, accept suitable work by a state unemployment service, or receive (or be eligible to receive) unemployment compensation.[70]

Severance pay (or separation pay) may be paid to employees who are permanently terminated because of plant or departmental shutdowns or layoffs due to a lack of work or technological change. Several reasons may prompt an employer to provide severance pay. First, severance pay gives an employee time to search for a new job without becoming economically desperate. Second, severance pay may be used to decrease an employee's desire to sue the employer for wrongful discharge. Third, severance pay may be a means of enhancing a firm's social responsibility and improving its corporate image. Employees covered by collective bargaining agreements commonly receive severance pay based on a length of service and seniority formula. Under this arrangement, the greater the length of service and earnings, the greater the severance pay. Severance pay arrangements often contain payment restrictions. Benefits may not be payable to employees who quit voluntarily, are eligible for retirement benefits, or refuse other work offered by the employer. Some contracts state that the company will not pay a severance allowance for layoffs or shutdowns caused by conditions beyond the employer's control, such as fires, floods, and strikes.[71]

▲ Paid Vacations, Holidays, and Sick Leave

Paid vacations and holidays represent a common employee benefit and the trend over the years has been to increase compensation for time not worked because of union pressures and employer concerns for attracting and retaining employees.[72] Entitlement to *paid vacations* is often determined by an employee's seniority. As a worker accumulates seniority, the amount of paid vacation time increases. It is common for employees with only one year of service to receive one week of paid

---

[70] The Bureau of National Affairs, Inc., "Basic Patterns: Income Maintenance," *Collective Bargaining Negotiations & Contracts* (Washington, D.C.: The Bureau of National Affairs, Inc., 1985), section 53.

[71] Severance pay arrangements may be both innovative and attractive. The Norfolk Southern Corp. offered a voluntary severance program for certain train-service employees at its Central of Georgia Railroad Co. subsidiary. The program offered a $100,000 separation allowance and medical care coverage. The separation allowance includes a one-time $50,000 payment in exchange for elimination of the annual productivity-fund payments provided under a collective bargaining agreement. See "Central of Georgia Workers Are Offered Severance Program," *The Wall Street Journal* (September 6, 1989).

[72] The Bureau of National Affairs, Inc., *Compensation: Personnel Policy and Practice Series* (Washington, D.C.: The Bureau of National Affairs, Inc., 1987), section 335.

vacation, whereas employees with eight or more years of service are commonly provided with three to six weeks of paid vacation. Some industries, such as the steel industry, have provided extended vacation periods of up to 13 weeks at five-year intervals. In addition, two-tier vacation clauses specify different eligibility requirements for newly hired employees, much in the same manner as two-tier pay plans. Collective bargaining agreements may also specify the minimum amount of time that must be worked during a calendar year in order to qualify for vacation benefits.

Some contracts allow vacation time to continue accruing if an employee has a break in service caused by a disability or layoff. Collective bargaining agreements often contain provisions for employees who desire to work during all or part of their vacation time for personal or financial reasons. Some contracts prohibit employees from working during vacation time, whereas others allow work only in emergency situations. More than three-fourths of the work-during-vacation clauses in contracts surveyed by The Bureau of National Affairs, Inc., allow employees to collect *both* their vacation pay and work pay.[73]

Most contract clauses governing paid vacations also have a system for determining *when* an employee will take the paid vacation. A number of contracts allow senior employees to have first choice regarding vacation dates. Vacation policies should also stipulate whether employees must take their vacation time all at once or whether they will be allowed to take several shorter vacations. If the latter practiced is used, the contract should stipulate the smallest permissible increment of vacation time. Vacation splitting may be necessary for employees who have more than two weeks of vacation entitlement. For firms having cyclical product or service demands, the contract should address whether employees will be allowed to take vacations during peak business months or only during periods when business is slow. A paid-vacation policy must also have a method for resolving conflicts that arise when two or more employees want to take their vacations on the same date (when it is necessary that at least one worker remain on the job). A contract may have a cumulation clause that either allows or prohibits carrying unused vacation time from one year to the next.

Collective bargaining agreements usually specify the basis upon which vacation pay is calculated. For example, many agreements stipulate that an employee's shift differential will be used in computing vacation pay if the employee customarily works the evening shift.

The Bureau of National Affairs, Inc., survey data reveal that collective bargaining agreements contain a median number of 11 *paid holidays* per year. Over 90 percent of the contracts include the "traditional six" holidays of Thanksgiving, Labor Day, Christmas, Independence Day, New Year's Day, and Memorial Day.[74] Paid holidays pose fewer administrative problems than vacations because their dates coincide with or fall near the observed holiday date. Some contracts require that an employee work both the day before and the day after the holiday in order to receive holiday

---

[73] The Bureau of National Affairs, Inc., "Basic Patterns: Vacations," *Collective Bargaining Negotiations & Contracts* (Washington, D.C.: The Bureau of National Affairs, Inc., 1989), section 91.
[74] The Bureau of National Affairs, Inc., "Basic Patterns: Holidays," *Collective Bargaining Negotiations & Contracts* (Washington, D.C.: The Bureau of National Affairs, Inc., 1989), section 58.

pay. In addition, employees may also have to meet minimal seniority requirements before being eligible for holiday pay. If a holiday falls on a scheduled day off, such as during the weekend or when an employee is on vacation, the contract may provide an alternative holiday such as Easter Monday or may compensate employees with a holiday bonus. Most contracts also pay an employee for a holiday taken while on vacation. Employees who work on a holiday listed in the collective bargaining agreement usually receive their regular pay plus the holiday pay.

Employees who are ill are assured continued pay through *sick-leave* provisions. Organizations typically grant between five and 12 sick-leave days per year; some provide all employees with the same number of paid sick leave days whereas others base paid sick-leave entitlement on seniority. About half of the firms surveyed by The Bureau of National Affairs, Inc., allow employees to accumulate sick-leave days from one year to the next subject to a maximum limit that fluctuates between 30 and 90 days.[75] Some companies allow an employee to elect reduced paid sick-leave benefits in exchange for payments over a longer period. In order to discourage short periods of absenteeism, an employee may have to wait several days before drawing sick-leave benefits. Some contracts pay sick leave only if an employee obtains a physician's statement certifying illness, and some also impose penalties for misuse of sick-leave policies. As noted earlier, the Pregnancy Discrimination Act requires that female employees who use sick leave for maternity-related disabilities must be treated in the same manner as other employees. Other forms of compensated time off found in collective bargaining agreements include jury duty leave, bereavement or funeral leave, military leave, and childcare leave.

▲ Childcare and Eldercare Benefits

As more women and single parents have entered the labor force and dual-career couples have become more commonplace, providing care for the children of working parents has become an important issue. The growing concern and publicity about the plight of "latchkey" children who must spend time at home without adult supervision while their parents are at work has also prompted corporate action.[76] Parents who must deal with the guilt and worry of leaving children unattended at home may suffer from low morale and reduced productivity.[77] Employers have incentives for providing childcare benefits because they help to attract and retain employees and provide a tax deduction (as an ordinary and necessary business expense). On-site or near-site daycare programs can reduce the amount of commuting required by working parents and reduce absenteeism and tardiness. Childcare arrangements also provide favorable publicity to the sponsoring company.

[75] The Bureau of National Affairs, Inc., *Compensation: Personnel Policy and Practice Series* (Washington, D.C.: The Bureau of National Affairs, Inc., 1983), section 335.
[76] Mary F. Cook, "Child Care Programs and Options," In Craig T. Norback, ed., *The Human Resources Yearbook*, 1987 edition (Englewood Cliffs, New Jersey: Prentice-Hall, Inc., 1987), pp. 2.68–2.71.
[77] Fern Schumer Chapman, "Executive Guilt: Who's Taking Care of the Children? And How Will Kids Raised By Nannies and in Day Care Centers Turn Out?" *Fortune* (February 16, 1987), p. 30; "Child Care Woes," *The Wall Street Journal* (May 14, 1987), p. 29.

In addressing problems at the other end of the age spectrum, an increasing number of companies are offering to help employees with aging parents. Some experts believe that eldercare will replace childcare as the top workplace issue in the 1990s. According to the Older Women's League (OWL), a Washington, D.C.-based group, 89 percent of all women will be caregivers of children and elders during their lifetime. Women who work full time are four times as likely to be primary caregivers to the elderly as working men. The average caregiver to the elderly is 45 years old; 65 percent are under age 65. Ninety-five percent of the elderly and 90 percent of the disabled elderly live at home under the care of family members, most of whom receive little or no financial assistance from sources outside the family. Furthermore, the cost of caring for the elderly is much greater than the cost of childcare; the average annual cost of childcare is $3,000 as compared to $25,000 for a year's stay in a nursing home.[78] These trends suggest that provisions for eldercare will appear with increasing regularity in collective bargaining agreements in the 1990s. Corporations such as IBM have already introduced the Eldercare Referral Service. This service provides IBM employees with consultation and assistance in determining the proper care available for elderly relatives.[79]

A three-year labor contract between American Telephone & Telegraph (AT&T) and the Communications Workers of America includes a comprehensive package of benefits for single parents and dual-career couples. Provisions include $5 million for the creation of childcare facilities around the country, doubling the length of unpaid childcare leaves up to one year, payment of certain adoption expenses, and setting aside tax-free funds for payment of dependent care, unpaid time off to take care of seriously ill dependents, and flexible time off to attend to family emergencies. Other unions such as the American Federation of State, County, and Municipal Employees (AFSCME) have negotiated provisions for on-site childcare and dependent-care financial assistance.[80]

▲ Employee Assistance Programs

An employee benefit that increased in popularity in the 1980s and is continuing to grow in the early 1990s, is the employee assistance program (EAP). Employee assistance programs are designed to "prevent problems that interfere with an employee's ability to perform his or her job and to rehabilitate those employees who are experiencing problems that affect the employee's performance on the job."[81] Employee assistance programs offer a wide variety of services. According to one survey, the most common EAP service is alcohol and drug counseling, followed by

---

[78] The American Occupational Therapy Association, "Elder Care Projected to Replace Child Care as Top Workplace Issue of the Next Decade," *O. T. Week*, Vol. 3, No. 20 (1989).
[79] *Employee Benefit Plan Review* (January 1988), pp. 15–16. Also see John L. Utz, "Employers and Long-Term Health Care Insurance: What to Buy, Where to Get It, and How to Fund It," *Employee Benefits Journal* (March 1988), p. 13.
[80] Amanda Bennett and Cathy Trost, "Benefit Package Set by AT&T, Unions Show Power of Families in Workplace," *The Wall Street Journal* (May 31, 1989), p. A6.
[81] D.W. Myers, *Employee Assistance Programs* (Chicago: Commerce Clearing House, Inc., 1986), p. 4.

preretirement counseling and emotional stress counseling. Career, marital, and financial counseling are also offered by many EAPs.[82]

The trend is clearly toward incorporating treatment of drug and alcohol abuse programs into collective bargaining agreements. According to The Bureau of National Affairs, Inc., 1989 survey data, provisions for drug and alcohol abuse appeared in 49 percent of the sample contracts, compared to 32 percent in 1986.[83] Some collective bargaining agreements contain general statements about alcohol and drug abuse and leave it up to the employer to establish programs to combat these problems. In other cases, the union and employer may jointly design an EAP. Attention should be given to the design, administration, and effectiveness of an EAP as well as to avoiding potential liabilities. The following guidelines should be kept in mind by union and management negotiators when bargaining over provisions relating to EAPs:

1. Determine what EAP services will be offered "in-house" versus those that will be offered on a referral basis. For example, services such as career and preretirement counseling may be offered by the employer, whereas alcohol and drug problems might be referred to medical professionals who are retained by the company to provide these services.
2. Carefully review potential legal liabilities associated with an EAP. EAPs that provide medical and psychological services may subject the employer to malpractice liabilities if improper treatments are given. Information on an employee's medical condition should be held in strict confidence.
3. Ensure that supervisors and shop stewards fully understand the EAP functions and programs, as well as the nature of employee problems such as alcohol and drug abuse.
4. Develop methods for monitoring the effectiveness of the EAP. One insurance company estimated that an EAP may return as much as $5 for every $1 invested in the program.[84] McDonnell Douglas Corporation estimated that it may save as much as $5 million by providing employees with quality psychiatric care and alcohol and drug treatment at the earliest possible time.[85] EAP effectiveness may be measured in terms of reduced employee absenteeism, turnover, and lost-time accidents as well as improved employee performance and lower health care costs.

▲ Other Employee Benefit Programs

The types of employee benefit programs are varied and seem to be limited only by the imagination and negotiating skills of union and management representatives. In recent years, new and innovative benefit plans have been designed; some are gaining

[82] 1986 AMS New Benefits Survey, *Medical Benefits* (April 15, 1986), p. 8.
[83] The Bureau of National Affairs, Inc., "Health Care Cost-Cutting Measures," *Collective Bargaining Negotiations & Contracts* (April 20, 1989), p. 1.
[84] See Mary F. Davis, "Worksite Health Promotion," *Personnel Administrator* (December 1984), pp. 45–50.
[85] Ron Winslow, "Spending to Cut Mental-Health Costs," *The Wall Street Journal* (December 13, 1989), p. B1.

acceptance among corporations. *Prepaid legal plans* are designed to offer affordable legal services to employees. Under a prepaid legal plan, employees are able to obtain counseling on matters such as income and property taxes, civil actions, criminal matters, bankruptcy, consumer complaints, real estate matters, adoptions, the preparation of wills, and traffic offenses.[86]

Management's interest in developing a better-educated workforce has led to the use of *tuition-aid plans* for employees. Some companies provide tuition assistance for all courses taken at an approved institution, whereas others grant tuition aid only for "job-related" course work. Companies may grant total or partial cash advances (or reimbursements), provide educational leaves of absence, or loan employees money for educational purposes.[87]

Some employee benefits are more directly tied to the workplace. For example, travel allowances, moving expenses, uniform and tool expenses, and meal allowances permit employees to perform more efficiently and enhance morale. Suggestion systems provide financial incentives to employees for submitting cost-saving ideas to management. Retail and service firms may provide discounts to employees who purchase their products and services, a tactic that creates brand loyalty and knowledge of the company's products.

▲ Communicating Employee Benefits

Employee benefit programs are complex because they deal with legal, financial, and tax-related issues. Most employees find that the actuarial assumptions, tax regulations, and behavioral implications associated with certain employee benefits such as pension programs can be complicated. The problem is compounded when one realizes that benefits are often discussed at orientation programs for new employees at a time when the employee is already under stress and is being inundated with more pressing information about job responsibilities. Most companies provide employees with a booklet or brochure that outlines the benefits program. Such information is frequently ignored because it is difficult to understand and not very exciting to read. As a result, employees often do not learn the facts about their benefits until they need to make a claim. They may then learn, either to their delight or to their chagrin, that employee benefits cover certain contingencies but not others.[88]

If employees are given choices in selecting benefits (such as under a cafeteria or flexible benefits plan), it is important that they understand the options available to them. Employees should understand their benefits and how certain choices can affect their personal financial situation.[89] Two key points to remember in commu-

[86] The Bureau of National Affairs, Inc., *Compensation: Personnel Policy and Practice Series* (Washington, D.C.: The Bureau of National Affairs, Inc., 1987), section 339.
[87] Marvin S. Katzman, "Tuition Benefits: Are They Not Being Used Wisely Because of a Lack of Planning and Counseling?" *Employee Benefits Journal* (September 1985).
[88] "Never Enough: Communications Aids in the Acceptance of Employee Benefit Changes," *Employee Benefit Plan Review* (October 1985), p. 12.
[89] Richard J. Anthony, "A Communication Program Model For Flexible Benefits: Keeping Employees Informed Takes Time, Effort, and Planning," *Personnel Administrator* (June 1986), p. 65; and Peter R. Schleger, "Effective Benefits Communication: Delivery Counts Too!" *Employee Benefits Journal* (March 1988), pp. 24–26.

nicating employee benefits are (1) employees must understand the basic coverage and restrictions that apply to their benefit programs, and (2) employees should be personally counseled about their benefits on a periodic basis. Internal company and union memos, newsletters, and brochures can provide up-to-date information on changes in employee benefits. However, such information must be carefully written to avoid an overly detailed and technical presentation that most employees will find difficult to comprehend. Individual benefits counseling should probably be done on an annual basis or whenever requested by the employee. Benefits counseling allows the employee to make changes in his or her benefit program based on changes in the family structure (e.g., births, deaths, or divorces), income levels, tax laws, age, health status, and other factors.

▲ Summary and Conclusions

The employee benefit programs discussed in this chapter represent those currently found in collective bargaining agreements as well as those that will likely appear with increasing regularity in the future. However, the amount and extent of benefit coverage varies considerably from one contract to another. Employees face certain risks such as premature death, outliving one's ability to earn a living, loss of income caused by disabilities and unemployment, and extraordinary medical expenses. Public programs such as Social Security, workers' compensation, and unemployment compensation provide some protection from these risks, but employer- and union-sponsored programs such as life, medical, and disability insurance, and retirement plans enhance the benefits established by public programs and improve economic security for many workers. Other benefits such as paid vacations, holidays, and perquisites enhance the quality of work life and the public image of the union and the employer.

Although there is evidence that the growth of employee benefits has reached a plateau, their presence is likely to have a lasting effect on a company's ability to attract, retain, and motivate employees. The extent to which union officials are able to negotiate employee benefits that meet the diverse needs of their members may play an important role in the future viability of labor organizations. Furthermore, both employers and unions must maintain concern over how limited benefit dollars will best serve employees. Employees, in turn, must view employee benefits as a tool for protecting their income and managing personal risks.

The types of employee benefits found in future collective bargaining agreements will likely reflect those found in organizations at large. A survey by Hewitt Associates indicates that employees will continue to covet medical benefits as a primary employee benefit followed (in descending order) by pensions, paid vacations and holidays, disability and sick leave, dental care, profit sharing plans, long-term disability, and life insurance. Future employee benefits cited by the Hewitt Associates survey include flexible medical plans that allow employees to tailor their coverage to personal needs, long-term care coverage and eldercare benefits, and flexible work schedules.[90]

[90] Jolie Solomon, "The Future Look of Employee Benefits," *The Wall Street Journal* (September 7, 1988), p. 29.

▲ Discussion Questions and Exercises

1. Do you believe that the federal and state governments should increase or decrease their legislative involvement in employee benefit plans? Discuss.
2. Should collective bargaining agreements allow bargaining-unit employees to select the array of employee benefits that best suits their personal needs and tastes? If so, how should a flexible or cafeteria benefit plan be established and administered?
3. Some experts believe that health care costs are increasing rapidly, and current measures (e.g., co-insurance, deductibles, cost sharing with employees, etc.) to contain health care costs are inadequate. Research the problem of escalating health care costs and discuss how you believe they should be curtailed.
4. What problems do you believe will accompany the increasing use of childcare and eldercare programs? How will union and management negotiators overcome these problems?

▲ ▲ ▲ ▲ CASES IN EMPLOYEE BENEFITS

The Misunderstanding Over Health Insurance Benefits

CWC Textron had entered into a collective bargaining agreement with the International Molders' and Allied Workers' Union of North America. The contract included provisions for major medical and surgical health insurance benefits. Approximately a year prior to renegotiating the contract with the union, the company changed to a new health insurance carrier, Aetna Life and Casualty Company. Shortly thereafter, Aetna issued a new booklet that explained the employees' health insurance coverage. Surgical benefits under the Aetna plan were listed on a schedule that stipulated what would be paid for a specific procedure (e.g., $220 for an appendectomy). These benefits were comparable to those paid by the previous insurance carrier. A section of the book entitled "Medical Expense Benefits Exclusions" stated that charges for services would not be paid if they "are unreasonable." Whether a physician's fee was "reasonable" was based on what constituted "customary and reasonable" charges within the community where the medical services were rendered.

Once the union and management began to negotiate a new contract, a number of disagreements arose and a four-week strike ensued. Part of the dispute seems to have been over the union's proposal that the company pay whatever the doctor charged for performing a surgical procedure; the company, however, wanted to retain a surgical fee schedule that listed a dollar amount for each procedure. Nevertheless, the company was willing to bargain over increased amounts of coverage for surgical fees. Both sides eventually agreed to adopt a new schedule of fees that would provide one and a half times the benefit coverage of the previous fee schedule. Thus, the maximum insurance coverage for an appendectomy under the old schedule was $220;

under the new schedule this amount was increased to $330. However, some problems and misunderstandings remained.

The fact that a misunderstanding had occurred surfaced several months later when Aetna refused to pay some surgical claims that did not exceed the limits of the new schedule. The company explained that "these claims were denied on the basis that, while less than the schedule limit, the claims exceeded the usual and customary amount charged for the procedure in the locality [where the surgical procedures were performed]." Although the company agreed to omit the "customary and reasonable" limitation with regard to surgical coverage, there was confusion as to whether the limitation still applied to major medical coverage. Thus, employees who were not fully reimbursed under the surgical coverage might receive additional payments under the major medical coverage.

Two employees filed a grievance over the payment of surgical benefits. One employee, Robert East, was charged $475 by a physician for a surgical fee (breast surgery for his wife). The insurance company paid $300 under surgical benefits and allowed an additional $50 under major medical coverage because $350 was deemed to be the customary local fee in this case. The second employee, Clyde Whitehead, was charged $375 for surgical services (an appendectomy) and the insurance company paid $330 (all under the surgical coverage), but refused to pay any additional coverage because they claimed that $325 was customary for this particular surgical procedure. (Why Aetna paid $5 more than the customary fee was not revealed). The union wanted the company to reimburse the grievants for the unpaid amounts ($125 to East and $45 to Whitehead).

Discussion Questions

1. Neither the union nor management did an adequate job of communicating the health insurance benefit changes to the rank-and-file employees. Will this mistake likely have an impact on the arbitrator's decision?
2. At one point in the hearing, the company's counsel asked whether the employer would always be required to pay a fee, regardless of its reasonableness. In addition, company counsel inquired as to how a determination of a fee's "reasonableness" could be made. How should the arbitrator address these issues?
3. Since the case involved a series of misunderstandings between union and management representatives, the arbitrator decided to check with several insurance companies, insurance consultants, members of the medical profession, and executives of a county medical society. Can the information obtained from these inquiries play a prominent role in the arbitrator's award?
4. From a strategic standpoint, should management have agreed to pay East $125 and Whitehead $45 in order to avoid the time and expense of processing a grievance through arbitration. Why or why not?

Double-Dipping Under Medicare

Indiana General Corporation, a manufacturer of precision electric motors, has for many years engaged in collective bargaining with the United Motor Workers, Federal Labor Union. In fulfillment of its obligations under Article XVII of the collective bargaining agreement, which went into effect in 1965, the company purchased a group health insurance policy from Liberty Mutual Insurance Company. The policy provided hospitalization coverage for employees and their dependents. The benefit schedule listed the maximum daily amount that the policy would pay for hospitalization coverage.

On July 1, 1966, Medicare, an amendment to the Social Security program, went into effect. Medicare provides medical insurance coverage primarily for persons over age 65. Liberty Mutual subsequently issued a rider to Indiana General's group health policy that "took credit" for any payment made to employees or their dependents under Medicare. That is, the insurance company refused to pay any amounts that it would normally be paid under its group policy if Medicare already covered the medical expense. Neither the union nor the employees were aware of this provision, nor did Liberty Mutual reduce the policy premiums as a result of their potential savings (through lower claims) from the Medicare program.

Between September 1966 and March 1967, five dependents of Indiana General Corporation employees, who were also eligible for Medicare, incurred medical expenses and submitted claims through the company's group health insurance plan. The claims were paid in accordance with the benefits scale *less* the amounts paid by Medicare. At a labor-management meeting held shortly thereafter, the union objected to the deduction of Medicare benefits. The company asserted that the claims had been handled in accordance with "customary and standard procedures involving Medicare." Approximately one month later, the company and union entered into a new collective bargaining agreement. The new contract provided for increased group health insurance benefits, but like the previous contract, it made no mention of Medicare deductions against health insurance claims.

The union filed a grievance on behalf of the five employees and argued that the contract did not permit the company to take credit for benefits paid under Medicare. Moreover, the union asserted that insured individuals whose sickness or hospitalization started during the life of the 1965 agreement, but extended into the life of the 1967 agreement were entitled to the higher benefits of the latter agreement.

The company denied that it violated the contract. Management claimed that the union was aware of the Medicare program and knew how insurance carriers generally handled claims under health insurance group policies after Medicare became effective. Furthermore, the company pointed out that to pay employees the full amount under the group health policy would have resulted in employees or their dependents "making money" by "double dipping" from both the company policy and Medicare. The general objective of insurance is to restore the insured (employees or their dependents) to his or her original economic position and not allow them to make a profit from health insurance benefits. In addition, the company claimed that the initial date of a disability or sickness governed the insurance coverage to which an employee (or dependents) was entitled. The company also said that an employee had to be on the active payroll and at work when the 1967 agreement went into effect in order to receive the higher insurance benefits of the 1967 contract.

Discussion Questions

1. What impact does an insurance rider issued by Liberty Mutual Insurance Company (amending the health insurance benefits) have on the arbitrator's interpretation of the collective bargaining agreement?
2. Evaluate the company's argument that "the union should have known how insurance carriers generally handled claims ... after Medicare became effective."
3. Does the arbitrator generally have the power to modify a collective bargaining agreement to comply with the provisions of a newly enacted federal law? Discuss.
4. If an employee became ill before October 1967 (when the 1967 contract went into effect) and remained on medical leave, should he or she have the right to collect the higher benefits under the 1967 contract even though he or she was not on the payroll when the new contract went into effect?

Appendix: Calculating the Cost of Compensation and Benefit Provisions

A Simple Example

The ability to calculate the cost of wage, salary, and employee benefit increases is not only a valuable tool for bargaining preparation, but it also helps management and union negotiators to assess the long-term cost of a compensation package. In some instances, employers enter negotiations prepared to pay a fixed amount of money for wages and employee benefits. When this is the case, the employer may be indifferent as to the final composition of the wage and benefit package—any settlement that does not exceed the total amount allocated by management is satisfactory. However, there are several considerations that must be kept in mind when calculating pay and benefit costs. The simplified example below of a small grocery store assumes the following:

Job Classification	Number of Employees	Hourly Wage
Checker	16	$5.00
Stock and Produce Clerks	10	$4.50
Meatcutters	6	$8.00

Half of all employees work the day shift and receive these hourly wages. Those working the evening shift receive an hourly 50-cent shift differential. Thus, a checker working the evening shift receives $5.50 an hour, a stock clerk $5.00 an hour, and so forth. Overtime work is required for approximately 200 hours per year per employee and employees are paid at time-and-one-half of the day rate. All employees receive one week of paid vacation, paid at a rate of 40 hours times an employee's day-shift rate. Employees are not allowed to work during vacation periods. Each employee also receives 10 paid holidays, paid at the employee's day-shift rate. Thus, employees are paid approximately 1,880 straight-time hours per year (including vacations and holidays) and 200 overtime hours. The employer pays $50.00 per month for each employee's group health insurance coverage and 6 percent of gross wages to a multi-employer pension fund.

STEP 1: DETERMINE BASE COMPENSATION COSTS.

    Checkers: 8 x $5.00 (day rate) x 1880 hours = $75,200
    Checkers: 8 x $5.50 (night rate) x 1,880 hours = $82,720
    Checkers 16 x 200 overtime hours x $7.50 overtime rate = $24,000
    Total annual base compensation for checkers = $181,920

    Stock and Produce Clerks: 5 x $4.50 (day rate) x 1,880 hours = $42,300
    Stock and Produce Clerks: 5 x $5.00 (night rate) x 1,880 hours = $47,000
    Stock and Produce Clerks: 10 x 200 overtime hours x $6.75 overtime rate = $13,500
    Total annual base compensation for stock and produce clerks = $102,800

    Meatcutters: 3 x $8.00 (day rate) x 1,880 hours = $45,120
    Meatcutters: 3 x $8.50 (night rate) x 1,880 hours = $47,940
    Meatcutters: 6 x 200 overtime hours x $12.00 overtime rate = $14,400
    Total annual base compensation for meatcutters = $107,460

    Total annual base wage costs for the bargaining unit = $392,180

STEP 2: DETERMINE EMPLOYEE BENEFIT COSTS

1-Week Paid Vacation:
    Checkers: 16 x $5.00 x 40 hours = $3,200
    Stock and Produce Clerks: 10 x $4.50 x 40 hours = $1,800
    Meatcutters: 10 x $8.00 x 40 hours = $3,200
Total Cost of Paid Vacation = $8,200

10 Paid Holidays:
    Checkers: 16 x $5.00 x 10 days x 8 hours = $6,400
    Stock and Produce Clerks: 10 x $4.50 x 10 days x 8 hours = $3,600
    Meatcutters: 10 x $8.00 x 10 days x 8 hours = $6,400
Total Cost of Paid Holidays = $16,400

Group Health Insurance:
    36 employees x $50.00 per month x 12 months = $21,600

Pension Program:
    .06 x ($392,180 [total base wages] + $8,200 [for paid vacations] + $16,400 [for paid holidays]) = $25,006.80
    The Cost of the Total Wage and Benefit Package for the 36 Bargaining Unit Employees = $463,386.80

STEP 3: DETERMINE THE TOTAL COST OF A BARGAINING DEMAND

Assume the following bargaining demand by the union:
    1. 10 percent wage increase.
    2. Adding Martin Luther King, Jr.'s Birthday as a paid holiday.
    3. Increasing the employer's pension contribution from 6 percent to 7 percent.

A 10-percent wage increase would increase total base wage and overtime costs from $392,180 to $431,398 ($392,180 x 1.10). Paid vacation costs would rise from $8,200 to $9,020 ($8,200 x 1.10). The cost of the current 10 paid holidays would rise from $16,400 to $18,040 (16,400 x 1.10). The cost of adding Martin Luther King, Jr.'s

Birthday as the 11th paid holiday would be calculated as follows:

Checkers: 16 x $5.50 (new wage rate) x 8 hours x 1 additional paid holiday = $704

Stock and Produce Clerks: 10 x $4.95 (new wage rate) x 8 hours x 1 additional paid holiday = $396

Meatcutters: 10 x $8.80 (new wage rate) x 8 hours x 1 additional paid holiday = $704

Total Cost of Adding the 11th Paid Holiday = $1,804

Increasing the employer's contribution to the pension program from 6 percent to 7 percent would result in a new pension cost of

.07 x ($431,398 + $9,020 + [$18,040 + $1,804]) = $32,218.34

Thus the above set of demands, if accepted by management, can be summarized as follows:

	Previous Contract	New Contract
Base Compensation	$392,180	$431,398
Paid Vacations	8,200	9,020
Paid Holidays	16,400	19,844
Group Health Insurance	21,600	21,600
Pension	25,006.80	32,218.84
Total Cost	$463,386.80	$495,080.84

The above exercise is a simplified example of how wage and benefit settlement costs may be calculated. Nearly all cost calculations ignore the fact that a firm may adapt to a new labor contract by reducing the size of its labor force, shifting work to nonunion plants, or reducing the need for overtime work. In addition, some collective bargaining agreements are "frontloaded," whereas others are "backloaded." A frontloaded contract is one in which pay and benefit increases go into effect immediately. A backloaded contract is one in which pay and benefit increases are phased in over the life of the contract; that is, a firm may grant a pay increase that does not go into effect until the second or third year of a contract. Recognizing the cash flow concerns and time value of money, employers prefer backloaded contracts, whereas unions prefer frontloaded contracts.[91]

A More Complex Example

For readers who want a somewhat more complex and realistic illustration of settlement cost calculations, a U.S. Department of Labor publication example is presented below.[92]

"[C]ompensation" consists of both salaries and/or wages and fringe benefits. It encompasses all forms of wage payments (including, for example, bonuses, commissions, and incentive payments) as well as the cost to the employer of all types of fringes.[93] Obviously, the higher-paid, senior employees in the bargaining unit tend to enjoy higher compensation, while the compensation of those at the opposite end of the salary and seniority spectrums tends to be lower.

For bargaining purposes, the most relevant statistic is the unit's average compensation or, more specifically, its *weighted* average compensation. The weighted average compensation (hereafter "average compensation" or, simply, "compensation") is merely an expression of how much it costs the employer, on the average, for each per-

---

[91] See Michael H. Granof, *How to Cost Your Labor Contract* (Washington, D.C.: The Bureau of National Affairs, Inc., 1973).
[92] From a U.S. Department of Labor, Labor-Management Services Administration publication entitled, *The Use of Economic Data in Collective Bargaining* (Washington, D.C.: U.S. Government Printing Office, 1978).
[93] Technically, employee compensation may also include the cost of legally-required employer payments for programs such as social security, unemployment compensation, and worker's compensation. These items are disregarded in this analysis.

son on the payroll. It is this figure which presumably will be increased through negotiations.[94]

Although precision in computing these compensation costs depends very much on detailed data usually available only in the employer's payroll records, it is possible to develop some reasonably accurate approximations even without such detailed information.

Indeed, the ability to do so may be quite important in making judgments as to whether a settlement proposal is or is not satisfactory. Moreover, an awareness of the concepts and techniques that are involved in these computations can prove invaluable in carrying on the bargaining dialogue or in dealing with a third-party neutral.

These computations, it must be remembered, are not performed simply to engage in a mathematical exercise. The reason for seeking out this type of information is its usefulness at the bargaining table.

The value of salaries and fringe benefits must be known so that the value of any bargaining offer or settlement can be judged. Logically, therefore, the base compensation costs as of the point in time of negotiations—or, more accurately, immediately prior to the receipt of an increase—must be known.

The information that is needed in most cases in order to compute compensation costs is (a) the salary scales and benefit programs, (b) the distribution of the employees in the unit according to pay steps, shifts, and length of service, and (c) for purposes of some medical care programs, the employees' coverage status. If this information is in hand, just about all but one item of compensation can be readily computed.

The sole exception is the cost of the overtime premium. Overtime is apt to vary widely from week-to-week or month-to-month. Consequently, the data for any one pay period are an inadequate gauge where overtime is concerned. Simply by chance, it may cost the employer more one week than the next. It is common practice, therefore, to cost-out the overtime premium by averaging the cost of that benefit over the prior 12 months.

So far as the other elements of compensation are concerned, however, it is not necessary to study a full year's experience. With salaries, vacations, holidays, etc., the costs can be based on a snapshot taken at a fixed point in time on the basis of the provisions in the current collective bargaining agreement and the current distribution of the employees in the bargaining unit. That snapshot of compensation costs should be made as of the time the parties are at the bargaining table.

The purpose of this section is to provide guidance on how to perform those computations, as well as the computations to determine the cost—the value—of an *increase* in compensation. The development of such compensation information gives the parties a basis for weighing the value of any particular wage and fringe benefit package.

Before the value or cost impact of any increase in compensation—whether in salaries, fringes, or both—can be gauged, the first step is to develop the base, or existing, compensation figure. A pay increase of $500 per employee, for example, means something different for a bargaining unit whose existing salary and fringe benefit cost per employee amount to $20,000 per year than for a unit whose compensation is $10,000. In the latter case, it represents an increase of 5 percent, but on a base of $20,000 it amounts to only 2½ percent. Thus, the base compensation figure is essential in determining the percentage value of any increase in compensation.

In order to demonstrate the computation methods for arriving at the base compensation figure, a Sampling Bargaining Unit has been constructed and certain levels of employment, salaries, fringe benefits and hours of work have been assumed:

---

[94] It is also referred to as the "base" compensation—that is, the compensation figure against which the cost of any settlement will be measured in order to determine the value of the settlement.

Sample Bargaining Unit

(a) Employment and Salaries

Classification	Number of Firefighters	Salary
Probationary		
Step 1	5	$10,100
Step 2	10	11,100
Private	65	12,100
Lieutenant	15	13,500
Captain	5	14,500
	100	

(b) Longevity Payments

Longevity Step	Number of Firefighters	Longevity Pay
Step 1	20 Privates	$ 500
Step 2	10 Privates	1,000
Step 3	15 Lieutenants	1,000
Step 4	5 Captains	1,000

(c) Hours of Work

The scheduled hours consist of one 24-hour shift every three days (one on; two off), or an average of 56 hours per week and a total of 2,912 hours per year.

(d) Overtime Premium

All overtime hours are paid at the rate of time-and-one-half. The sample bargaining unit is assumed to have worked a total of 5,000 overtime hours during the preceding year.

(e) Shift Differential

The shift differential is 10 percent for all hours between 4 p.m. and 8 a.m. However, 10 members of the unit work exclusively on the day shift, from 8 a.m. to 4 p.m.

(f) Vacations

15 employees—(probationers) 5 shifts
35 employees—(privates) 10 shifts
50 employees—(all others) 15 shifts

(g) Holidays

Each firefighter is entitled to 10 paid holidays, and receives 8 hours pay for each holiday.

(h) Clothing Allowance

$150 per employee per year.

(i) Hospitalization

Type of Coverage	Number of Firefighters	Employer's Monthly Payment
Single Coverage	15	$20.00
Family Coverage	85	47.00

(i) Pensions

The employer contributes an amount equal to six percent of the payroll (including basic salaries, longevity, overtime and shift differentials).

1. Computing Base Compensation

On the basis of the foregoing information on employment, salaries, and benefits, we are now in a position to compute, for the Sample Bargain Unit, its average base compensation—in essence the cost of compensation for the average employee.

(a) *Average Straight-time Salary*

(1) Classification	(2) Number of Firefighters	(3) Salary	(4) Weighted Salaries (2) × (3)
Probationary Step 1	5	$10,100	$ 50,500
Step 2	10	11,100	111,000
Private	65	12,100	786,500
Lieutenant	15	13,500	202,500
Captain	5	14,500	72,500
	100		$1,223,000

Average Annual Basic Salary =
$1,223,000 ÷ 100;
or $12,230 per year

(b) *Longevity Pay*

(1) Longevity Step	(2) Number of Firefighters	(3) Longevity Pay	(4) Total Longevity Pay (2) × (3)
Step 1	20	$ 500	$10,000
Step 2	30	1,000	30,000
			$40,000

Average Annual Longevity Pay =
$40,000 ÷ 100; or $400 per year

*Since the unit is trying to determine its average base compensation—that is, all the salary and fringe benefit items its members receive collectively—the total cost of longevity pay must be averaged over the entire unit of 100.

The combined average salary cost and average longevity cost amount to $12,630 per year. On an hourly basis, this comes to $4.337 ($12,630 + 2,912 hours). This hourly rate is needed to compute the cost of some fringe benefits.

(c) *Average Cost of Overtime*

Overtime work for the Sample Bargaining Unit is assumed to be paid for at the rate of time-and-one-half. This means that part of the total overtime costs is an amount paid for at straight-time rates and part is a premium payment.

	(1) Annual Cost	(2) Number of Firefighters	(3) Average Annual Cost (1) ÷ (2)
Straight-time cost ($4.337 × 5,000 overtime hours)	$21,685.00	100	$216.85
Half-time premium cost (½ × $21,685.00)	10,842.50	100	108.43
Total Overtime Cost	$32,527.50		$325.28

It can be seen from these overtime-cost calculations that the half-time premium is worth $108.43 per year on the average, while the straight-time portion is worth $216.85. This means, of course, that total pay at straight-time rates amounts to $12,846.85 ($12,630 plus $216.85) per firefighter.

(d) Average Cost of Shift Differential

The Sample Bargaining Unit receives a shift differential of 10 percent for all hours worked between 4 p.m. and 8 a.m. But 10 members of the unit who work in headquarters are assumed to work hours that are not subject to the differential. This leaves 90 employees who receive the differential.

Since the differential is paid for hours worked between 4 p.m. and 8 a.m., it is applicable to only two-thirds of the normal 24-hour shift. It, therefore, only costs the employer two-thirds of 10 percent for each 24 hours. That is the reason for column (5) in the following calculation. Each employee receives the differential for only two-thirds of his 24-hour tour.

(1) Classification	(2) No. on Shift Pay	(3) Salary	(4) 10% of Col. (3)	(5) .667 of Col. (4)	(6) Total Cost (2) × (5)
Probationary					
Step 1	5	$10,100	$1,010	$ 674	$ 3,370
Step 2	10	11,100	1,110	740	7,400
Private					
Longevity-0	35	12,100	1,210	807	28,245
Longevity-1	17	12,600*	1,260	840	14,230
Longevity-2	7	13,100*	1,320	880	6,160
Lieutenant	12	14,500*	1,450	967	11,604
Captain	4	15,500*	1,550	1,034	4,136
	90				$75,195

Average Annual Cost of Shift Differential = $75,195 ÷ 100;** or $751.95 per year

*   Basic salary plus longevity pay.
** Since the unit is trying to determine its average base compensation—that is, all the salary and fringe benefit items its members receive collectively—the total cost of the shift differential must be averaged over the entire unit of 100.

(e) Average Cost of Vacations

Vacation costs for the unit are influenced by (a) the amount of vacations received by the employees with differing lengths of service, and (b) the pay scales of those employees.

(1) Classification	(2) Number of Firefighters	(3) Hourly Rate*	(4) Hours of Vacation**	(5) Total Vacation Hours (2) × (4)	(6) Total Vacation Costs (3) × (5)
Probationary					
Step 1	5	$3,468	120	600	$ 2,080.80
Step 2	10	3,312	120	1,200	4,574.40

(1) Classification	(2) Number of Firefighters	(3) Hourly Rate*	(4) Hours of Vacation**	(5) Total Vacation Hours (2) × (4)	(6) Total Vacation Costs (3) × (5)
Private					
Longevity-0	35	4,155	240	8,400	34,902.00
Longevity-1	20	4,327	360	7,200	31,154.40
Longevity-2	10	4,499	360	3,600	16,196.40
Lieutenant	15	4,979	360	5,400	26,888.60
Captain	5	5,323	360	1,800	9,581.40
	100				$125,376.00

Average Annual Vacation Cost = $125,376 ÷ 100; or $1,253.76 per year

* Derived from annual salaries (including longevity pay), divided by 2.912 hours (56 hours × 52 weeks). The 10 firefighters who do not receive shift differential would be on a regular 40-hour week and would, therefore, have a different hourly rate and vacation entitlement. The impact on cost, however, would be minimal. It has, therefore, been disregarded in this computation.

** Since each firefighter works a 24 hour shift, the hours of vacation are arrived at by multiplying the number of work shifts of vacation entitlement by 24 hours. For example, the figure of 120 hours is obtained by multiplying 5 shifts of vacation × 24 hours (one work shift).

(f) *Average Cost of Paid Holidays*

Unlike vacations, the number of holidays received by an employee is not typically tied to length of service. Where the level of benefits is uniform, as it is with paid holidays, the calculation to determine its average cost is less complex.

In the Sample Bargaining Unit, it is assumed that each firefighter receives 8 hours of pay for each of his 10 paid holidays, or a total of 80 hours of holiday pay:

(1) Average Annual Cost of Paid Holidays = $346.96 (80 hours × $4.337 average straight-time hourly rate), or

(2) Total Annual Cost of Paid Holiday hours per year = 8,000 (80 hours × 100 employees)

Total annual cost of paid holidays = $34,696.00 (the unit's average straight-time hourly rate of $4.337 × 8,000 hours)

Average annual cost of paid holidays = $346.96 (34,696.00 + 100 employees)

(g) *Average Cost of Hospitalization*

(1) Type of Coverage	(2) Number of Fire-fighters	(3) Yearly Premium Cost to Employer	(4) Total Cost to Employer (2) × (3)
Single	15	$240	$ 3,600
Family	85	564	47,940
	100		$51,540

Average Annual Cost of Hospitalization = $51,540 ÷ 100; or $515.40 per year

(h) *Other Fringe Benefits*

(1) Pensions cost the employer six percent of payroll. The payroll amounts to $1,370,723 (salary cost—$1,223,000; longevity cost—$40,000; overtime cost—$32,528; and shift differential cost—$75,195). Six percent of this total is $82,243 which, when divided by 100, yields $822.43 as the average cost of pensions per firefighter, per year.

(2) The yearly cost of the clothing allowance is $150 per firefighter.

As the recapitulation below indicates, total compensation—salary plus fringes—for each firefighter averages $16,795.78 per year.

Once having determined the base compensation costs, it is now possible to compute the value—or cost—of any increase in the items of compensation. The methods used to make these computations are essentially the same as those used to compute the base compensation data.

Before proceeding to that exercise, however, a general observation about the computation of base compensation should be made. Since the purpose is to produce an average *total* cost per employee—whether by the hour or by the year—it follows that the objective must be to capture and include in the computation, for each item of compensation, the full amount of the employer's expense. This is why accurately maintained payroll records are desirable. Among other things, such records can help to resolve what might otherwise be protracted debates over approaches to the costing-out process on certain complicated benefit programs.

One such item that comes to mind is paid sick leave. Many paid sick leave programs permit the employee to accumulate unused sick leave. Suppose, for example, the employees are allowed five paid sick leave days each year, with the opportunity to "bank" the unused days and, upon separation or retirement, to receive pay for one-half of the days in the "bank."

With such a program, it is likely that not all of the employees in the unit would use all five days each year. It would be incorrect, however, to cost out sick leave on the basis of the days actually taken each year since, at some subsequent point, there would be partial reimbursement for the unused days. Further complicating matters is the fact that the employee's rate of pay at the time the reimbursement takes place will very likely be higher than it is when the unused days are put in the "bank." Obviously, there is no way of knowing what that future rate of pay will be, so there is no way to determine now how much those "banked" days will be worth at the time of reimbursement.

One way to cost out the unit's paid sick leave in any year may be simply to charge everyone with five days. Needless to say, this may mistake the true cost and may generate controversy and debate.

Such disputes may be avoided if the actual total dollar cost of the sick leave program for the year can be derived. To do this, however, it would be necessary to have the dollar costs for each piece—that is, in our example, the cost of the days used in the year plus the cost of the reimbursements made in the year—in order to produce a total annual cost. That total, divided by the number of employees in the unit or by the number of hours worked by the unit during the year, would then yield the cost per employee or per hour for this particular benefit.

In a case such as the sick leave program cited above, the availability of dollar amounts reflecting total annual costs would, as mentioned earlier, help to forestall controversy over the procedure to be used for costing out the benefit. And this approach would be consistent with the basic concept that is involved in costing out the other elements of employee compensation. That approach, as was also mentioned earlier, seeks to capture and include in the computation the full amount of the employer's expense for each item of compensation.

Average Annual Base Compensation for the Sample Bargaining Unit

(a) *Straight-time earnings* $12,846.85

Basic salary	$12,230.00
Longevity pay	400.00
Overtime	216.85*

(b) *Fringe benefits* $ 3,948.93

Overtime premium	$ 108.43
Shift differential	751.95
Vacations	1,253.76
Holidays	346.96
Hospitalization	515.40
Clothing allowance	150.00
Pension	822.43

(c) *Total* $16,795.78

* This is only the straight-time portion of overtime pay. The premium portion appears with the fringe benefits.

2. Computing the Cost of Increases in Items of Compensation

In order to demonstrate how to cost-out any increases in compensation, it will be assumed that the Sample Bargaining Unit negotiates a settlement consisting of the following package:

—An increase of 5 percent in basic salaries;
—Two additional shifts of vacation for all those at the second step of longevity;
—An improvement in the benefits provided by the hospitalization program, which will cost the employer an additional $4.00 per month for family coverage and $2.50 for single coverage.

The cost of this settlement—that is, the amount of the increase in compensation that it represents—would be computed in the manner presented below, starting first with the cost-impact of the salary increase. As will be noted, the objective of the computation is to find the *average* cost of the increase—that is, the cost per firefighter, per year.

(a) Increase in Cost of Salaries. The increase in average annual basic salary (0.05 × $12,230) is $611.50. The cost of longevity pay does not increase. This is because longevity increments for the unit are fixed dollar amounts. If these payments were based on a percentage of salary—that is, if they were linked to the pay scales—then the cost of the longevity payments would also have risen by 5 percent. However, as a fixed dollar amount, these payments remain unaffected by the increase in basic salaries.

As a result, the increase in the unit's total average salary ($12,230 in basic salary plus $400 in longevity) is, in reality, not 5 percent, but only 4.8 percent ($611.50 + $12,630).

This difference is important because of the way in which pay increases impact on the cost of fringe benefits. This is commonly referred to as the "roll up".... As salaries increase, so does the cost to the employer of such fringes as vacations, holidays, overtime premiums, etc. This increase in cost comes about even though the benefits are not improved.

Some fringes, however, are not subject to

the roll up. This is the case with respect to those fringe benefits that are not linked to pay rates. Examples of this type of fringe benefit include shift differentials that are stated in cents-per-hour (in contrast to a percentage of salary), a flat dollar amount for clothing allowance, and most group insurance programs.

(b) Cost Impact of the "Roll up". The increase in average straight-time pay (basic salary plus longevity pay) of the Sample Bargaining Unit was shown to be 4.8 percent. This means that the average cost of every benefit linked to salary will likewise increase by 4.8 percent. In our example, therefore, the average cost of compensation will go up by $611.50 per year in salaries, *plus,* however much this adds to the costs of the fringe benefits as a result of the roll up.

But there is more. For our example, it is also to be assumed that the Sample Bargaining Unit will gain a vacation improvement—two additional shifts at the second step of longevity—and an improved hospitalization program.

The employer's contribution for the hospitalization program of the Sample Bargaining Unit is a fixed dollar amount and is, therefore, not subject to any roll up. Thus, we need in this instance be concerned only with the costing-out of the improvement in that benefit.

This is not the case with the vacations. Here the cost-increase is double-barreled—the cost of the improvement *and* the cost of the roll up.

None of the other fringe benefits of the Sample Bargaining Unit will be improved. Consequently, so far as they are concerned, we need only compute the increases in cost due to the roll up. The fringes which fit this category are overtime premiums, holidays, sick leave, shift differentials, and pensions.

(1) Fringe Benefit	(2) Base Average Annual Cost	(3) Roll up Factor	(4) Increased Cost (2) × (3)
Overtime Straight-time	$216.85	0.048	$ 10.41
Premium	108.43	0.048	5.20
Shift differential	751.95	0.048	36.09
Holidays	346.96	0.048	16.65
Pensions	822.43	0.048	39.48
			$107.83

As is indicated in the table [above], column (3)—the added cost due to the roll up—is obtained by multiplying the base (pre-settlement) cost by 0.048. Obviously, if shift differentials and/or pensions were based on a set dollar (or cents) amount (instead of a percentage of salary), there would be no roll up cost associated with them. The only increase in cost that would result in such a situation would be associated with an improvement in the benefit item.

Having performed this computation, we can now begin to see the impact of the roll up factor. As a result of the increase in pay, the four fringe benefit items will together cost the employer an additional $107.83 per firefighter, per year.

(c) Increase in Cost of Vacations. As noted earlier, the vacation improvement of two shifts—48 hours (2 shifts × 24 hours)—is to be limited to those whose length of service is equal to the time required to achieve the second step of longevity in the salary structure. Thus, it will be received by 30 members of the unit—10 privates, 15 lieutenants, and 5 captains.[95]

---

[95] In costing out an improvement in vacations, the computation should cover the cost impact in the first year *only*. There is no need to be concerned with the impact in subsequent years when, supposedly, more and more employees become eligible for the improved benefit. For computational purposes, it must be assumed that the average length of service in the unit remains constant. This constancy is caused by normal personnel flows. As the more senior staff leave because of retirement or death, the staff is replenished by new hires without any accumulated seniority. Thus, for this type of computation, it must be presumed that the proportion of the workforce which benefits from the improved vacation will be constant year after year.

It should be noted that an improvement in vacations (or any other form of paid leave) that is offset by corresponding reductions in on-duty manning does not represent any increase in cost to the employer.

The first step in the computation is to determine the cost of the *new* benefit under the *existing* (old) salaries—that is, before the 4.8 percent pay increase:

(1) Number of Firefighters	(2) Hours of Increased Vacation	(3) Total Hours (1) × (2)	(4) Existing Hourly Rates	(5) Cost of Improvement (3) × (4)
10 Privates	48	480	$4.499	$2,159.52
15 Lieutenants	48	720	4.979	3,584.88
5 Captains	48	240	5.323	1,277.52
				$7,021.92

The calculation thus far reflects only the additional cost of the vacation improvement based on the salaries existing *prior* to the 4.8 percent pay raise. In other words, if there had been no pay increase, the vacation improvement would result in an added cost of $7,021.92. But there was a pay increase. As a result, the base year vacation costs—including now the added cost of the improvement—must be rolled up by the 4.8 percent factor. Every hour of vacation—the old and the new—will cost 4.8 percent more as a result of the pay increase:

(1) Classification	(2) Existing Vacation Costs*	(3) Increase in Cost**	(4) Adjusted Base Costs (2) + (3)	(5) Roll up Factor	(6) Increased Cost from Roll up (4) × (5)
Probationary					
Step 1	$ 2,080.80	—	$ 2,080.80	0.048	$ 99.38
Step 2	4,574.40	—	2,574.40	0.048	219.57
Private					
Longevity-0	34,902.00	—	34,902.00	0.048	1,675.30
Longevity-1	31,154.40	—	31,154.40	0.048	1,495.41
Longevity-2	16,196.40	$2,159.52	18,355.92	0.048	881.08
Lieutenant	26,886.60	3,584.88	30,471.48	0.048	1,462.63
Captain	9,581.40	1,277.52	10,858.92	0.048	521.23
	$125,376.00	$7,021.92	$132,397.92	0.048	$6,355,10

By adding the two "new" pieces of cost—$7,021.92, which is the cost of the improvement, and $6,355.10, which is the cost due to the impact of the wage increase—we obtain the total increase in the cost of vacations. It amounts to $13,377.02. In order to figure the *average* cost, this total must be divided by the number of firefighters in the Sample Bargaining Unit. The increase in the average cost of vacations, therefore; is

$13,377 ÷ 100, or $133.77

Had the vacation improvement been granted across-the-board, to everyone in the unit, the calculation would have been different—and considerably easier. If the entire unit were to receive an additional 48 hours of vacation, the total additional hours would then be 4,800 (48 hours × 100 employees). These hours would then be multiplied by the unit's old average straight-time rate ($4.337), in order to arrive at the cost of the additional vacation improvement which, in this case, would have come to $20,817.60 (4,800 hours × $4.337). And, in that case, the total cost of vacations—that is the across-the-board improvement, plus the impact of the 4.8 percent salary increase—would have been computed as follows:

(a) Roll up of old vacation costs
= $ 6,018.05
($125,376 × 0.048)
(b) Cost of vacation improvement
= $20,817.60
(c) Roll up cost of improvement
= $ 999.24
($20,817.60 × 0.048)

These pieces total to $27,834.89. When spread over the entire Sample Bargaining Unit, the increase in the average cost of vacations would have been $278.35 per year ($27,834.89 ÷ 100 employees).

This latter method of calculation does not apply only to vacations. It applies to any situation where a salary-related fringe benefit is to be improved equally for every member of the unit. An additional paid holiday would be another good example.

(d) Increase in Cost of Hospitalization. In this example, it has been assumed that the Sample Bargaining Unit has negotiated as part of its new package an improvement in its hospitalization plan. As with most hospitalization programs, the one covering this unit is not linked to salaries.

This improvement, it is assumed, will cost the employer an additional $4.00 per month ($48 per year) for family coverage, and $2.50 per month ($30 per year) for single coverage. Thus, based on this and previous information about the breakdown of employees receiving each type of coverage . . . , the calculation of the increase in hospitalization cost is as follows:

(1) Type of Coverage	(2) Number Covered	(3) Annual Cost of Improvement	(4) Total New Cost (2) × (3)
Single	15	$30	$ 450
Family	85	48	4,080
			$4,530

The unit's average hospitalization cost will be increased by $45.30 per year ($4,530 ÷ 100 employees).

3. The Total Increase in the Average Cost of Compensation

At this point, the increase in the costs of all the items of compensation which will change because of the Sample Bargaining Unit's newly-negotiated package have been calculated. All that is left is to combine these individual places in order to arrive at the total increase in the unit's average cost of compensation. This is done in the tabulation which appears below.

As the recapitulation shows, the average increase in salary costs amounts to $621.91 per year, while the average increase in the cost of the fringe benefits (including *new* benefit costs, as well as *roll up* costs) comes to $276.49, for a total increase in average annual compensation of $898.40 per firefighter, per *year*. That is the total annual cost of the settlement per firefighter.

Increase in Average Annual Cost of Compensation for Sample Bargaining Unit

(a) *Straight-time earnings* $621.91
   Basic salary $611.50
   Longevity pay   —
   Overtime (straight-
      time portion)   10.41

(b) *Fringe benefits*	$276.49
Overtime premium	$ 5.20
Shift differential	36.09
Vacations	133.77
Holidays	16.65
Hospitalization	45.30
Clothing allowance	—
Pensions	39.48
(c) *Total Increase in Average Annual Cost of Annual Compensation*	$898.40

There remains one final computation that is really the most significant—the *percent* increase that all of these figures represent. The unit's average base compensation per year was $16,796. The total dollar increase amounts to $898. The percent increase, therefore, is 5.3 percent ($898 + $16,796), and that is the amount by which the unit's package increased the employer's average yearly cost per firefighter.

4. Computing the Hourly Cost of Compensation

The increase in the cost of compensation per *hour* will be the same. The approach to the computation, however, is different than that which was used in connection with the cost per year. In the case of the hourly computation, the goal is to obtain the cost per hour of *work*. This requires that a distinction be drawn between hours worked and hours paid for. The difference between the two is leave time.

In the Sample Bargaining Unit, for example, the employee receives an annual salary which covers 2,912 regularly scheduled hours (56 hours per week, times 52). In addition, he works an average of 50 hours of overtime per year. The sum of these two—regularly scheduled hours and overtime hours, or 2,962—are the total hours paid for.

But they do not represent hours worked, because some of those hours are paid leave time. The Sample Bargaining Unit, for example, receives paid leave time in the form of vacations and holidays. The number of hours actually worked by each employee is 2,600 (2,962 hours paid for, minus 362 hours[96] of paid leave).

The paid leave hours are, in a sense, bonuses—hours paid for, above and beyond hours worked. Thus, in order to obtain the hourly cost represented by these "bonuses"—that is, the hours of paid leave—the annual dollar cost of these benefits is divided by the annual hours *worked*.

It is the same as if we were trying to compute the per-hour cost of a year-end bonus. The dollar amount of that bonus would simply be divided by the total number of hours worked during the year.

So it is with *all* fringe benefits, not only paid leave. In exchange for those benefits the employer receives hours of work (the straight-time hours and the overtime hours). Consequently, the hourly cost of any fringe benefit will be obtained by dividing the annual cost of the benefit by the annual number of hours *worked*. In some instances that cost is converted into money that ends up in the employee's pocket, as it does in the case of fringe benefits like shift differentials, overtime premiums and clothing allowances. In other instances—such as hospital-

---

[96] Each firefighter receives 80 hours in paid holidays per year. The average number of hours of vacation per year was derived as follows:

15 firefighters × 120 hours (five 24-hour shifts)	= 1,800 hours
35 firefighters × 240 hours (ten 24-hour shifts)	= 8,400 hours
50 firefighters × 360 hours (fifteen 24-hour shifts)	= 18,000 hours
	28,200 hours

This averages out to 282 hours of vacation per firefighter (28,200 + 100) which, together with 80 holiday hours, totals 362 paid leave hours).

ization and pensions—the employee is provided with benefits in the form of insurance programs. And in the case of paid leave time—holidays,[97] vacations, sick leave, etc.—the return to the employee is in terms of fewer hours of work.

The average annual costs of the fringe benefits of the Sample Bargaining Unit were developed earlier in this chapter in connection with the computations of the unit's average annual base compensation. They appear in column (2) below.

In order to convert the costs of those fringe benefits into an average hourly amount, they are divided by 2,600—the average hours worked during the year by each employee in the unit. As can be seen, the hourly cost of all fringe benefits amounts to $1.518.

(1) Fringe Benefit	(2) Average Annual Cost	(3) Average Hours Worked	(4) Average Hourly Cost (2) ÷ (3)
Overtime Premium*	$ 108.43	2,600	$0.042
Shift Differential	751.95	2,600	0.289
Vacations	1,253.78	2,600	0.482
Holidays	346.96	2,600	0.133
Hospitalization	515.40	2,600	0.198
Clothing Allowance	150.00	2,600	0.058
Pensions	822.43	2,600	0.316
	$3,948.93		$1.518

* Includes only the premium portion of the pay for overtime work.

In addition to the fringe benefit costs, compensation includes the basic pay. For our Sample Bargaining Unit this is $12,630 per year (average salary plus average cost of longevity payments). On a straight-time hourly basis, this comes to $4.337 ($12,630 ÷ 2,912 hours). Even with the straight-time portion for the year's overtime included ($216.85), the average straight-time hourly rate of pay will, of course, still remain at $4.337 ($12,846.45 ÷ 2,962 hours).

A recapitulation of these salary and fringe benefit cost data produces both the average *annual* base compensation figure for the Sample Bargaining Unit and the average *hourly* figure.

As indicated, on an annual basis, the average compensation cost comes to $16,795.78, a figure that was also presented earlier in this chapter. And on an hourly basis, the average compensation of the unit amounts of $5.856.

Essentially the same process is followed if the *increase* in compensation is to be measured on an hourly (instead of an annual) basis.

The five percent pay increase received by the Sample Bargaining Unit would be worth 21 cents ($12,230 × 0.05 = $611.50; $611.50 ÷ 2,912 = $0.21). The annual increase in the unit's fringe benefit costs per firefighter—$276.49 for all items com-

---

[97] Typically, of course, firefighters do not receive time off, but are paid an extra day's pay for working a holiday. Excerpted from *The Use of Economic Data in Collective Bargaining* published in 1978 by the Labor-Management Services Administration, details the methods use to calculate the cost of increases in wages and fringe benefits.

bined—works out to 10.6 cents per hour (276.49 ÷ 2600 hours).

Together, these represent a gain in average compensation of 31.6 cents per hour, or 5.4 percent ($0.316 ÷ $5.856). This is one-tenth of a percentage point off from the amount of increase (5.3 percent) reflected by the annual data—a difference due simply to the rounding of decimals during the computation process.

	Hourly	Yearly
Earnings at Straight-time	$12,846.85 ÷ 2,962 = $4.337	
Fringe Benefits	3,348.03 ÷ 2,600 = $1.519	
Total Compensation	$16,795.78	$5.856

15 Institutional Issues: Balancing Management Rights Against Union and Employee Security

- **Introduction**
- **Management Rights**
  The Residualist and Implied Obligation Views of Management Rights
  Management Rights Clauses
  Legal Factors Affecting Management Rights
  Management Rights and Arbitration
- **Seniority Arrangements**
  The Application of Seniority Provisions
  Calculating Seniority
  The Effect of Mergers, Acquisitions, and Plant Closings on Seniority
  Seniority Systems and Discrimination
- **Technological Change and Worker Displacement**
  Work Rules
  Robotics Technology
  Plant Closings and Layoffs
- **Subcontracting**
- **Health and Safety in the Workplace**
  Health and Safety Provisions in the Collective Bargaining Agreement
  The Occupational Safety and Health Act of 1970
  Health and Safety Grievances: Arbitrators, OSHA, and the Courts
    Refusing to Perform Unsafe Work
    Physical or Mental Conditions as a Safety Hazard
    Violation of Plant Safety Rules
  Emerging Health and Safety Rules
    Substance Abuse and Dependency
    Acquired Immune Deficiency Syndrome (AIDS)
    Smoking in the Workplace

▲ **Union Security Issues**
  Types of Union Security Arrangements
  Checkoff Provisions
  Arguments for and against Union Security
  Right-to-Work Laws
▲ **Summary and Conclusions**
▲ **Discussion Questions and Exercises**
▲ **Cases on Institutional Issues**
  The Disputed Seniority Date
  The Terminated AIDS Victim

▲ Introduction

In a collective bargaining relationship, union and management are constantly balancing managerial rights against employee rights and union security. Management wants to maintain as much control as possible on decisions regarding product and service lines, business strategies, personnel policies, and the firm's daily business operations. The union and employees, on the other hand, want to have a voice in matters that affect members' work lives, job security, and safety in the workplace. Critical institutional issues include management rights clauses, seniority systems, management's right to subcontract bargaining unit work, automation and technological changes, layoffs and plant closings, employee health and safety, and union security. This chapter discusses the issues, contract provisions, legislation, and arbitration decisions affecting the major institutional issues of collective bargaining.

▲ Management Rights

Among the most important provisions in a collective bargaining agreement are those dealing with management rights. The management rights issue centers on drawing a line between management's obligations under the collective bargaining agreement and their right to operate the business and direct the workforce as they see fit. Management generally believes that it should have the right to hire employees and assign them to specific jobs. Management almost always wants to have sole discretion in formulating business strategies, developing product lines, deciding on the best means to produce a product or service, and making technological changes. Although labor leaders have traditionally taken a "hands-off" approach in allowing management full discretion in establishing product lines and setting prices for their goods and services, conflicts have arisen when managerial decisions affect wages, hours, and working conditions.

A major problem with management rights is that employers would have a difficult time managing the firm if they had to negotiate every proposed managerial action with the union. On the other hand, the union must enforce bargaining-unit members' rights under the collective bargaining agreement. For this reason, the issue of management rights is controversial, especially for parties who are in the developing stages of a collective bargaining relationship. Parties who have been negotiating with each other for years seem to have fewer problems with management rights than do less experienced parties.[1]

The Residualist and Implied Obligation Views of Management Rights

There are two schools of thought on management rights. The school of thought most favored by management is the concept of *residual or reserved rights*. Under this approach, management retains all rights except those expressly relinquished in the collective bargaining agreement. For example, suppose the contract is silent on the issue of whether management has the right to redesign bargaining-unit jobs. Redesigning a job may include introducing new machinery to a work shop, changing the size of a work crew, or requiring employees, rather than custodial workers, to clean up debris around their work areas. Under the residual rights approach, management has the right to make such changes without consulting union representatives. The residualist position is justified by the fact that management had full control of all personnel policies and practices *before* the union became the employees' exclusive bargaining representative. Unless management has agreed to give up a certain degree of control to the union when making personnel decisions, the residualist position holds that management has a right to limit the power of the union.

A second view of management rights, favored primarily by labor leaders, is known as the *implied obligations* concept of managerial authority.[2] This approach emphasizes that union and management should not defend their absolute rights and prerogatives; rather, each side should do whatever is necessary to maximize the long-term benefits for both employees and management. Proponents of the implied obligations approach believe that management must be willing to concede that there are no bargaining subjects over which they have exclusive control. The union-management cooperative programs discussed in Chapters 7 and 18 illustrate the implied obligations approach. Employee involvement (EI) programs represent another recognition of implied obligations between labor and management. EI programs may consist of problem-solving teams that meet one or two hours a week to discuss ways of improving product quality, production efficiency, or the work environment. Special purpose teams may allow unionized workers and management to design and introduce work reforms and new technology jointly. EI programs may also use self-managing work teams of five to 15 employees to produce an entire product. Self-managing work teams take over managerial duties, including ordering materials and work and vacation scheduling. Unions such as the United Auto Workers and companies such as Boeing, Caterpillar, and Champion International are using various forms of EI programs. Although a great deal of skepticism still surrounds EI programs they are recognized as a means of enhancing the productivity, flexibility, and competitiveness of many firms.[3]

---

[1] Charles C. Killingsworth, "Management Rights and Union-Concerted Action," in Arnold M. Zack, ed., *Arbitration in Practice* (Ithaca, New York: ILR Press, Cornell University, 1984), pp. 81–82.
[2] The implied obligations position is also called the *trusteeship theory* of management rights.
[3] See John Hoerr, "The Payoff from Teamwork," *Business Week* (July 10, 1989), pp. 56–62.

Management Rights Clauses

According to The Bureau of National Affairs, Inc., survey data, nearly 80 percent of the collective bargaining agreements have some form of management rights clause. Management rights clauses typically preserve management's ability to direct the workforce, manage the business, control production, establish work rules, determine employee duties, close or relocate production facilities, and make technological changes. Over half of the management rights clauses surveyed have a *savings clause*, which stipulates that management retains all rights not specifically modified or restricted by the contract (the residualist approach). A number of management rights clauses also contain restrictions on management that (1) limit management's ability to subcontract bargaining unit work to other firms, independent contractors, or employees outside the bargaining unit; (2) prohibit supervisors from performing work normally done by nonsupervisory bargaining unit employees; (3) control management's right to introduce technological changes or shut down or relocate production facilities without consulting the union.[4]

Management rights clauses may be either brief or lengthy. The short contract clause below represents a residualist approach to management rights.

> It is expressly understood and agreed that all rights heretofore exercised by the Company or inherent in the Company as the owner of the business or as an incident to the management not expressly contracted away by specific provision of this Agreement are retained solely by the Company.[5]

Other management rights clauses may be quite lengthy in an attempt to spell out every conceivable managerial function over which the company wishes to retain full authority:

> Section 1. It is expressly agreed that all rights which ordinarily vest in and are exercised by employers such as COMPANY, except such as are clearly relinquished herein by COMPANY, are reserved to and shall continue to vest in COMPANY. This shall include, this enumeration being merely by way of illustration and not by way of limitation, the right to:
> (a) Manage the plant and direct the working forces, including the right to hire and to suspend, discipline or discharge employees for proper cause.
> (b) Transfer employees from one department and/or classification to another.
> (c) Lay off or relieve employees from duty because of lack of work or for other legitimate reasons.
> (d) Promote and/or transfer employees to positions and classifications not covered by this agreement, it being understood employees in the bargaining unit cannot be forced to take a position outside the bargaining unit.
> (e) Make such operating changes as are deemed necessary by it for the efficient and economical operation of the plant, including the right to change normal work-week, the length of the normal workday, the hours of work, the

---

[4] The Bureau of National Affairs, Inc., "Basic Patterns: Management and Union Rights," *Collective Bargaining Negotiations & Contracts* (Washington, D.C.: The Bureau of National Affairs, Inc., 1989), section 65.

[5] Contract between Amana Refrigeration, Inc., and Machinists Union (expired December, 1990). Reprinted in The Bureau of National Affairs, Inc., "Basic Patterns: Management and Union Rights," *Collective Bargaining Negotiations & Contracts* (Washington, D.C.: The Bureau of National Affairs, Inc., 1989), section 65. Reprinted with permission.

beginning and ending time of each shift or assignment, and the number of shifts to be operated.
   (f) Transfer persons from positions and classifications not covered by this agreement to positions and/or classifications covered hereby.
   (g) Maintain discipline and efficiency.
   (h) Hire, promote, demote, transfer, discharge, or discipline all levels of supervision or other persons not covered by this agreement.
   (i) Determine the type of products to be manufactured, the location of work within the plant, the schedules of production, the schedules of work within work periods, and the methods, processes, and means of manufacture and the conduct of other plant operations.[6]

The above management rights clause vests all unrelinquished rights with the company. The phrase "this enumeration being merely by way of illustration" is an attempt to avoid limiting management to the prerogatives listed in parts (a) through (i). Management rights clauses that present a laundry list of managerial functions that are within the exclusive domain of the company may risk omitting a function that they would like to control. For this reason, general management rights clauses may be preferred to lengthy, detailed clauses.

Legal Factors Affecting Management Rights

The erosion of managerial prerogatives goes beyond the terms of the management rights and other clauses in the collective bargaining agreement. Over the past quarter of a century, the passage of equal employment opportunity, health and safety, and compensation legislation has also restricted management's ability to fashion personnel policies. As noted in earlier chapters, Section 8 (d) of the National Labor Relations Act (NLRA) also requires that the employer bargain in good faith over wages, hours, and working conditions.[7] Following the U.S. Supreme Court's *First National Maintenance* decision,[8] the NLRB held in *Otis Elevator*[9] that "decisions which affect the scope, direction, or nature of the business" are excluded from section 8(d) of the NLRA.[10] However, when wages, hours, or working conditions are affected, the issue falls within the broadly defined mandatory bargaining category and must be negotiated in good faith. Even when the contract is silent on a specific issue, management may still be obligated to discuss it with the union prior to taking action.[11] Suppose that the contract does not have any form of incentive pay clause and management decides to institute a piecework plan on an experimental basis. If the company fails to discuss the plan with the union, management may be guilty of bad-faith bargaining. As a means of avoiding this problem, employers have negotiated *zipper clauses* into collective bargaining agreements.

[6] Frank Elkouri and Edna Asper Elkouri, *How Arbitration Works*, 4th ed.(Washington, D.C.: The Bureau of National Affairs, Inc., 1985), pp. 478–479. Reprinted with permission.
[7] As noted in earlier chapters, the duty to bargain in good faith does not imply that a settlement must be reached on a particular mandatory bargaining issue.
[8] 101 S. Ct. 2573 (1981).
[9] 116 LRRM 1075 (1984).
[10] Marlin M. Volz and Edward P. Goggin, eds., *How Arbitration Works*, 4th ed. (Washington, D.C.: The Bureau of National Affairs, Inc., 1988), p. 103. 1985–87 Supplement to Frank Elkouri and Edna Asper Elkouri, *How Arbitration Works*, 4th ed. (Washington, D.C.: The Bureau of National Affairs, Inc., 1985).
[11] *Jacobs Manufacturing Co.*, 28 LRRM 1162 (1951), affirmed, 196 F. 2d. 680 (CA 2, 1952).

Zipper clauses stipulate that certain issues will not be subject to negotiation during the life of the contract. However, zipper clauses have been narrowly interpreted by the NLRB and must be very specific as to the bargaining subjects that cannot be negotiated.[12]

Management Rights and Arbitration

When management takes action without informing the union on an issue that affects wages, hours, or working conditions, the union may file a grievance. To determine whether expressed or implied restrictions have been placed on management's ability to make a decision, arbitrators first look to relevant contract provisions for guidance. Although the management rights clause is often a key provision affecting an arbitrator's decision, other contract provisions dealing with the hiring of employees, technological change, production standards, job classification and job evaluation methods, subcontracting, and work scheduling must also be carefully examined by the arbitrator.

Arbitrators have held that management cannot make personnel decisions that are arbitrary, capricious, or in bad faith. For example, a management rights clause may give the employer sole discretion in hiring matters. However, if an employer's hiring practices intentionally screen out union members in violation of the NLRA, the arbitrator may rule that such an action was done in bad faith.

When the contract language surrounding a management rights case is unclear or nonexistent, arbitrators may look at customs and past practices for guidance (see Chapter 12). However, arbitrators generally give management a wide range of discretion in taking actions that are not expressly prohibited by the collective bargaining agreement.

▲ Seniority Arrangements

Seniority clauses are an integral part of most collective bargaining agreements. *Competitive-status seniority* governs an employee's eligibility for overtime assignments, promotions, and transfers. Perhaps most importantly, competitive-status seniority determines the order in which an employee is subject to temporary or permanent layoff. *Benefit seniority* regulates an employee's entitlement to income maintenance protection, paid vacations, and pension benefits.[13] According to The Bureau of National Affairs, Inc., over 90 percent of the collective bargaining agreements contain some form of seniority provision.[14] As noted in previous chapters, unions favor seniority because it represents an objective measure that is uncontaminated by supervisory favoritism and workplace politics. Seniority also protects older workers who, if laid off, might be unable to find another job because their skills and abilities have been eroded by technological changes or health impairments.

---

[12] Frank Elkouri and Edna Asper Elkouri, *How Arbitration Works*, 4th ed. (Washington, D.C.: The Bureau of National Affairs, Inc., 1985), pp. 467–468.
[13] Richard B. Freeman and James L. Medoff, *What Do Unions Do?* (New York: Basic Books, Inc., 1984), p. 122.
[14] The Bureau of National Affairs, Inc., "Basic Patterns: Seniority," *Collective Bargaining Negotiations & Contracts* (Washington, D.C.: The Bureau of National Affairs, Inc., 1989), section 75.

Older workers also have a greater stake in employee benefit programs (such as pensions) that are regulated by seniority provisions. Thus, seniority systems may shift income from younger workers to older workers.

Opponents of seniority systems argue that young or ambitious employees have their promotion opportunities blocked when seniority is the primary criterion in personnel decisions. In addition, critics claim that seniority provisions protect technologically obsolete and unproductive employees. Arbitrators also consider an employee's seniority in discipline and discharge grievances. Employees who have created disciplinary problems or those whose productivity is marginal may be able to use seniority as a mitigating factor in an arbitration hearing to reduce a disciplinary penalty or avoid termination.[15]

A retired airline captain made the following observations about how seniority systems affected his career:

> You watch them board a [Boeing] 727—pilot, copilot and flight engineer or, in airline parlance, captain, first officer and second officer. . .
> Did the captain have more college credits or the most logged [flight] time? Did he score the highest in ground school? Did he know someone in management?. . . .
> The answer is none of the above. He's number one in the crew because he was hired before the copilot who, in turn, was hired before the engineer. . . and they are locked in their relative positions for as long as they work for their [airline]. . . .
> And if you think 80 numbers [on a seniority list] are not worth worrying about on a 3,000-pilot roster, listen to someone who has been there.
> Early on, 25 numbers would have put me on extended furlough. My long-awaited checkout as captain took place six months after the fellow five numbers my senior got his [captain's] stripes. One number put an interesting international schedule beyond my reach. Three numbers avoided an undesirable base assignment. A single number can cost a pilot many thousands of dollars in income over the years. . . .
> Seniority is everything. Number one has it all. Number two must settle for second best and number 100 gets what 99 seniors leave. . . .[16]

The Application of Seniority Provisions

The narrowest and most restrictive form of seniority is departmental seniority. Under a departmental seniority arrangement, an employee accumulates seniority as long as he or she remains in the same department. Employees who transfer to another department must start at the bottom of seniority list. Plant-wide seniority systems allow employees to move from one department to another within the same plant without losing seniority. The broadest forms of seniority are multi-plant and organization-wide systems that permit employees to transfer from one location to another within the company while retaining their seniority. Some collective bargaining agreements use occupational seniority based on job classifications or occupational groupings.

---

[15] Also see Carl Gersuny, "Erosion of Seniority Rights in the U.S. Labor Force," *Labor Studies Journal* (Spring 1987), p. 62.
[16] Len Morgan, "The Numbers Game," *Flying* (June 1989), pp. 118–119.

The extent to which competitive-status seniority controls personnel decisions such as promotions, filling vacancies, and designating employees for layoffs is extremely important.[17] Table 15–1 summarizes several ways in which seniority affects employee promotion and transfer decisions.[18]

When promotion and transfer decisions are based on a combination of seniority and ability, management generally reserves the right to determine an employee's ability to safely perform and competently perform. According to the veteran airline captain quoted earlier:[19]

> The seniority system does guarantee a chance at promotion, but not promotion itself. The new-hire who automatically imagines his stint as a flight engineer automatically leads to a copilot's slot will learn differently. First, there's ground school, and then simulator training. He advances only if he cuts the mustard. . .

Under many collective bargaining agreements, however, managerial assessments of an employee's ability may be challenged by the union or employee.[20]

Table 15–1 ▲ The Use of Seniority in Promotion and Transfer Decisions

Seniority is the sole factor:

Seniority is the *only* factor considered in promotion and transfer decisions. Other factors such as an employee's knowledge, skills, and abilities are not considered. Under a seniority system of this nature, management would probably have to show a clear safety hazard or gross incompetency on the part of the senior employee before giving preference to an employee with less seniority.

Seniority is the determining factor (the most common approach):

Seniority controls a promotion or transfer decision if an employee has *sufficient ability* to perform the job. Suppose Employee A and Employee B are competing for the same promotion. Assume that Employee A has greater seniority than Employee B, but of the two candidates, Employee B has superior job-relevant knowledge, skills, and abilities. If Employee A has sufficient ability to perform the job, then under the "seniority-is-the-determining-factor" approach, Employee A would receive the promotion.

Seniority is a secondary factor (the second most common approach):

Seniority controls a promotion and transfer decision if two employees have the same degree of job-relevant knowledge, skills, and abilities. This approach uses *relative ability* as the primary factor in promotion and transfer decisions. Assume that Employee A has greater seniority than Employee B, but Employee B has superior job-relevant abilities. Under the relative ability approach, Employee B would receive the promotion.

Seniority is given equal consideration:

Seniority is only one factor among several that governs promotion and transfer decisions. That is, seniority is not used as a primary or secondary (tie-breaking) factor.

---

[17] Also see Dan A. Black and Darrell F. Parker, "Unions, Seniority, and Public Choice," *Journal of Labor Research* (Fall 1986), p. 337; Jeff Frank, "Trade Union Efficiency and Overemployment with Seniority Wage Scales," *Southern Economic Journal* (December 1985), p. 1020; Lawrence M. Kahn, "Unions, Seniority, and Turnover," *Industrial Relations* (Fall 1983), pp. 362–373.
[18] Also see D. Quinn Mills, "Seniority vs. Ability in Promotion Decisions," *Industrial and Labor Relations Review* (April 1985), pp. 421–425.
[19] Len Morgan, "The Numbers Game," *Flying* (June 1989), pp. 118–119.
[20] See Richard R. Cerbone and Joseph Walsh, "Management Judgment vs. Seniority—Grist for the Arbitration Mill," *Employee Relations Law Journal* (Winter 1988), pp. 429–437.

Table 15–2 summarizes factors that management, union officials, and arbitrators may use to measure an employee's job-relevant knowledge, skills, and abilities under a promotion and transfer system that considers both seniority and ability.[21]

Table 15–2 ▲ Factors Used to Assess Employee Abilities for Promotion and Transfer

Tests of job knowledge, skill, aptitude, or personality:

Tests must be: (1) administered and evaluated competently and fairly and (2) job-relevant measures that are predictive of future job performance.

Job experience:

Experience is measured by the extent to which an employee has engaged in a particular job, type of work, training, or occupation. Experience must be assessed in terms of its length and relevance to the job for which the employee is being considered. A trial or break-in period may be used as a substitute for experience, especially when a senior employee is competing for a job and there is a reasonable doubt about the employee's ability to perform. The trial period should be long enough to allow the company to evaluate adequately the employee's potential for safe and competent job performance. However, the company is not normally obliged to continue the trial period once it becomes clear that the employee is not qualified. The length of a trial period may be stipulated in the collective bargaining agreement. Furthermore, employers are not normally required to spend lengthy periods of time or large sums of money training an employee if other well-qualified employees are already available to perform the work.

Opinions of supervisors:

The opinions of supervisors are often given heavy weight by arbitrators if the supervisors are familiar with the knowledge, skills, abilities, and work record of the job candidate.

Performance evaluations:

Evaluations that objectively and fairly measure an employee's job performance may be used to measure ability.

Educational background:

Education or other formal training that is relevant to the knowledge, skills, and abilities needed to safely and competently perform the job (as well as jobs for which the employee may seek through normal career progression) are used as measures of ability. However, it may be wise not to automatically eliminate an employee from promotion or transfer consideration who lacks a specific educational requirement (e.g., a high school diploma).

Production, attendance, and disciplinary records:

Production, attendance, and disciplinary records may be useful insofar as they provide insight into job-relevant qualifications and are predictive of future performance.

Employee's physical and psychological fitness:

Physical and psychological fitness and abilities as measured by physical and other examinations may be useful for evaluating safety concerns and the employee's ability to perform physically demanding or stressful job functions.

Adapted from Frank Elkouri and Edna Asper Elkouri, *How Arbitration Works*, 4th ed. (Washington, D.C.: The Bureau of National Affairs, Inc., 1985), pp. 617–649. Reprinted with permission.

---

[21] See Daniel G. Gallagher and Peter A. Veglahn, "Arbitral Standards in Cases Involving Testing Issues," *Labor Law Journal* (October 1986), pp. 719–730.

Calculating Seniority

Seniority is generally defined as continuous service. Collective bargaining agreements typically date seniority from the first day of employment, but often withhold accumulated seniority rights until employees have served a probationary period. Probationary periods usually last 60 to 90 days. Seniority lists are commonly posted on a company bulletin board and employees who believe that the list is in error are required to lodge a protest within a limited period of time. Problems arise when one or more employees are hired and report to work on the same date. A collective bargaining agreement or past practice may hold that the employee who reports in or clocks in first will be placed higher on the seniority list than an employee who clocks in at a later time on the same date. Thus, it is possible for an employee to have a permanent advantage over another based on several minutes difference in seniority. A more practical way of breaking ties in competitive-status seniority for employees hired on the same date is to use individual ability or merit as a factor in making job placement or promotion decisions.

Controversies arise when employees have a break in service or accept a temporary assignment outside of the seniority unit. Virtually all contracts specify that employees who quit, retire, or are discharged for just cause lose all seniority rights. Some contracts allow credit for prior service if the employee is rehired within a specified period, whereas other contracts cancel seniority if an employee is laid off and not recalled within a certain period of time. Collective bargaining agreements generally do not penalize employees who have breaks in service for maternity leave, union leave, civic leave, or sick leave. In fact, seniority may continue to accumulate under such circumstances. Employees who take military leave are entitled to continue accumulating seniority under federal law.[22]

Part-time employees who transfer to full-time positions within a company may receive seniority credit on a pro-rata basis under some collective bargaining agreements. For example, an employee who worked on a half-time basis for two years may receive one-year's credit toward seniority upon assuming a full-time position. In addition, contract provisions covering employees who are temporarily transferred to a job outside of the seniority unit may permit seniority to accumulate in the permanent unit while the employee is temporarily transferred. Other contracts allow employees to retain seniority, but do not allow them to accumulate seniority while on temporary assignment. Still other contracts require that seniority be forfeited as a result of transfers requested by the employee.

The Effect of Mergers, Acquisitions, and Plant Closings on Seniority

The number of mergers, acquisitions, and plant closings during the 1980s and early 1990s has brought increasing attention to the seniority and job security rights of displaced employees. Some union and management officials have anticipated the dangers associated with the merger of plants or companies and have negotiated provisions designed to protect employees against a total loss of seniority. According

---

[22] The Bureau of National Affairs, Inc., "Basic Patterns: Seniority," *Collective Bargaining Negotiations & Contracts* (Washington, D.C.: The Bureau of National Affairs, Inc., 1985), section 75.

to The Bureau of National Affairs, Inc., survey data, merger provisions are most often found in transportation industry collective bargaining agreements, where there is frequent consolidation and pooling of operations.[23] The previously-cited airline captain's discussion of seniority explains the dilemma of Braniff airline pilots after the company merged with Mid Continent Airlines, and later when Braniff collapsed:

> A pilot regards any fiddling with his seniority number as he would a pass at his wife. Whatever the result, it is certain to be greeted with howls of dismay by many. When Braniff acquired Mid Continent, a smaller line, the merged list worked out, but only after heated debate that produced bitterness in both camps. The grudge was cemented in some cases. "And it will last until we're all retired," I said to a friend.
>
> "No, it will last until we're all dead," he said.
>
> In some cases the job security known prior to deregulation evaporated. In 1982 Braniff's collapse idled 1,200 pilots with little warning. . .Today Braniff veterans fly with a score of airlines. But seniority is nontransferable, so it was back to the bottom at the new job.
>
> Individual seniority can be affected in strange ways. After 17 years with Braniff, one captain was number 325 out of 1,200. After seven years with Piedmont he was 715 out of 2,525, and the merger with US Air puts him at 2,300 out of 5,630. He's gone from the top 27 percent to 41 percent. A younger pilot who ranked 54 percent with Braniff now ranks 40 percent after the merger of Piedmont and US Air. Both pilots are ahead of Braniff friends hired later, some of whom were once their seniors.[24]

Suppose Company A purchases Company B. Company A is known as the *acquiring* (or successor) company and Company B is the *acquired* (or predecessor) company. In other instances two companies may merge. For example, Company A and Company B may merge and form a new company, Company C. If a collective bargaining agreement does not provide for companywide seniority or the integration of seniority lists, employees from the acquired company may be regarded as "new hires" and lose all seniority rights. However, a successor company is obligated to bargain with the union that represented the predecessor's employees if the operations and workforce of the predecessor firm remain essentially the same. This point was made by the U.S. Supreme Court in the *Fall River Dyeing & Finishing Corp.* case.[25] Citing the "continuity of the bargaining relationship," the Court upheld an NLRB order requiring a successor employer to bargain with the union that had represented the predecessor's employees. The Court noted that "during this unsettling transition, the union needs the presumptions of a majority status to which it is entitled to safeguard its members' rights and to develop a relationship with the successor."[26]

---

[23] The Bureau of National Affairs, Inc., "Basic Patterns: Seniority," *Collective Bargaining Negotiations & Contracts* (Washington, D.C.: The Bureau of National Affairs, Inc., 1989), section 75.
[24] Len Morgan, "The Numbers Game," *Flying* (June 1989), p. 119.
[25] *Fall River Dyeing & Finishing Corp. v. NLRB*, 107A S. Ct. 2225 (1987).
[26] See Marlin M. Volz and Edward P. Goggin, eds., *How Arbitration Works*, 4th ed. (Washington, D.C.: The Bureau of National Affairs, Inc., 1988), p. 125. 1985–87 Supplement to Frank Elkouri and Edna Asper Elkouri, *How Arbitration Works*, 4th ed. (Washington, D.C.: The Bureau of National Affairs, Inc., 1985).

There are several ways of merging seniority lists after corporate mergers, acquisitions, or plant closings. Table 15–3 summarizes five methods for merging seniority lists.

Table 15–3 ▲ Merging Seniority Lists

The surviving-group principle:

If Company A purchases or acquires Company B, the employees of Company A receive seniority preference over the employees of Company B. The seniority lists are merged by adding the names of Company B employees to the *bottom* of Company A's seniority list.

The length-of-service principle:

If Company A purchases or acquires Company B, then the seniority lists from the two companies are combined based on each employee's length of service. Thus, a new seniority list is created in which an employee with 10 years service in Company B would have greater seniority (under the new seniority list) than a Company A employee with 9 years of service.

The follow-the-work principle:

When companies merge or when departments are consolidated within a single firm, the employees are given the opportunity to "follow their work" (if such work has not been eliminated), usually under a departmental or occupational seniority list.

The absolute-rank principle:

If Company A purchases or acquires Company B, then employees are placed on a seniority list on the basis of the rank that they held on their respective seniority lists. Thus, the most senior employee from Company A and the most senior employee from Company B are given the top two spots on the new seniority list; the second most senior employees from Companies A and B respectively are given the third and fourth places on the seniority list. Unlike the length-of-service principle, which focuses on how long an employee has worked, the absolute-rank principle focuses on the employee's relative position on the seniority lists that were in effect before the merger or acquisition.

The ratio-rank principle:

Assume Company A (with 400 employees on its seniority list) purchases or acquires Company B (with 200 employees on its seniority list). Therefore, the Company A to Company B seniority list ratio is 2 to 1 (400 employees to 200 employees). Of the top three places on the new seniority list, two will go to the most senior employees from Company A and the third spot will go to the most senior employee from Company B. Places four and five on the new seniority list will go to the third and fourth most senior employees from Company A, and the sixth position on the new list will go to the second most senior employee from Company B. The seventh and eighth positions on the list will go the employees who were ranked fifth and sixth on Company A's original seniority list and the ninth position on the new list will go to Company B's third most senior employee. This process will continue until all 600 employees are placed on the new list.

Adapted from Frank Elkouri and Edna Asper Elkouri, *How Arbitration Works*, 4th ed. (Washington, D.C.: The Bureau of National Affairs, Inc., 1985), pp. 608–609. Reprinted with permission.

Seniority Systems and Discrimination

Seniority systems have presented problems when they have either caused or perpetuated illegal race or sex discrimination.[27] Title VII of the 1964 Civil Rights Act outlaws certain types of discrimination in employment that are based on race, sex, religion, color, or national origin. Section 703(h) of the Act permits the "routine application of a bona fide seniority system"[28] Section 703(h) provides:

> Notwithstanding any other provision of this subchapter, it shall not be an unlawful employment practice for an employer to apply different standards of compensation, or different terms, conditions, or privileges of employment pursuant to a bona fide seniority or merit system ... provided that such differences are not the result of an intention to discriminate because of race, color, religion, sex, or national origin ...

To qualify as a bona fide seniority system under Title VII, the system must be established without discriminatory intent. For example, collective bargaining agreements that have separate seniority systems for men and women would be illegal under Title VII. However, employers are no longer liable for acts of discrimination that took place before Title VII went into effect, even though a seniority system perpetuates the effect of such discrimination beyond the Act's effective date.[29] In the following situations, the courts have held that seniority systems were bona fide under Title VII:

1. A seniority system that gave preference to current employees over outside applicants was bona fide even though there was a disparity between the number of blacks employed by the company and the number of blacks in the firm's local labor market.[30]
2. A seniority system was bona fide despite its discriminatory impact on black employees who were rejected in their bids for promotions.[31]
3. A seniority system that perpetuated disparities and disadvantages associated with race (that existed prior to the passage of Title VII) is not illegal since neither the union nor the company had been motivated by racial considerations.[32]
4. Police officer candidates who achieved a score of 70 percent on a battery of job-related tests were eligible to receive points for seniority. The court held that the seniority point system was neutral, legitimate, and equally applicable to all races.[33]

However, a seniority system that is intentionally discriminatory would not be regarded as bona fide under section 703(h). Remedies for intentional discrimination

---

[27] See, for example, William L. Kandel and Peter Janovsky, "Reducing Potential for ADEA Liability in Reductions in Force," *Employee Relations Law Journal* (Summer 1988), pp. 107–115.
[28] *Trans World Airlines v. Hardison*, 97 S. Ct. at 2275 (1977).
[29] *International Brotherhood of Teamsters v. United States*, 97 S. Ct. 1843 (1977).
[30] *Allen v. Prince George's County*, 38 FEP Cases 1220 (1984).
[31] *Calloway v. Westinghouse Electric Corp.*, 41 FEP Cases 1715 (1986).
[32] *Goodman v. Lukens Steel Co.*, 39 FEP Cases 617 (1984).
[33] *Black Law Enforcement Officers v. City of Akron*, 40 FEP Cases 322 (1986).

include reinstatement and race-conscious affirmative action. Problems arise when a Title VII consent decree ordering an employer or union to cease discrimination conflicts with the provisions of a collective bargaining agreement. However, it appears that the courts are reluctant to override a bona fide seniority agreement in the absence of intentional discrimination.[34]

▲ Technological Change and Worker Displacement

Since the 1960s, there has been increasing concern among business, government, and union officials regarding the meager productivity gains among U.S. companies and the growing threat of competition from the Japanese and Western European countries.[35] The issues of productivity and global competition go well beyond the unionized sector and include issues such as the education level of the labor force and the ability of U.S. firms to introduce technological innovations. In order to improve productivity, efficiency, and safety, management may desire to introduce technological innovations into the workplace.

Firms may become involved in productivity bargaining with unions over the automation of certain jobs and the abolishment of outmoded work practices. Unions typically welcome technological changes that improve safety or lead to higher wages and improved benefits. However, technological innovations that threaten union members' job security are often strongly resisted. Technological changes have severely damaged the employment opportunities for some union members. Until 1960, approximately 90 percent of all steel in the United States was produced by open hearth furnaces. However, in the past 30 years a shift to the basic oxygen process sharply reduced the time required to produce steel and requires only one-fifth the labor of the open-hearth process.[36] The advent of jet aircraft and improved communications and navigation equipment have largely eliminated the need for the flight engineer on most airliners.[37] In Atlantic City and Las Vegas, musicians are being laid off at most big casino hotels and live orchestra music is being replaced with pre-recorded tapes.[38] The transition from 35 millimeter films to videoproduction methods in the movie-making industry has required that union members undergo job retraining and has created jurisdictional disputes among craft unions.[39] The introduction of robotics and computer-integrated manufacturing systems in the

---

[34] See *W. R. Grace & Co. v. Rubber Workers Local 759*, 113 LRRM 2641 (1983); *Firefighters Local 1784 v. Stotts*, 34 FEP Cases 1702 (1984); and *Wygant v. Jackson Board of Education*, 40 FEP Cases 1321 (1986).

[35] See Bruce R. Scott and George C. Lodge, "U.S. Competitiveness in the World Economy," *Course Development & Research Profile, 1987* (Boston: Harvard Business School, 1987), p. 107 and pp. 249–273.

[36] Jack Stieber, "Steel," in Gerald G. Somers, ed., *Collective Bargaining: Contemporary American Experience* (Madison, Wisconsin: Industrial Relations Research Association, 1980), pp. 152–153.

[37] Mark L. Kahn, "Airlines," in Gerald G. Somers, ed., *Collective Bargaining: Contemporary American Experience* (Madison, Wisconsin: Industrial Relations Research Association, 1980), pp. 333–334.

[38] "Musicians Lose Hotels on Boardwalk," *The Wall Street Journal* (March 23, 1989), p. A12.

[39] Susan Christopherson and Michael Storper, "The Effects of Flexible Specialization on Industrial Politics and the Labor Market: The Motion Picture Industry," *Industrial and Labor Relations Review* (April 1989), p. 344.

workplace will undoubtedly lead to the future displacement of unskilled and semi-skilled employees.

Although technological innovations jeopardize job security and often force workers to change occupations, they also improve productivity, enhance a firm's competitiveness, stimulate economic demand, and create long-term benefits that may outweigh their short-term effects on unemployment. As noted, the introduction of automation or other technological innovations that lead to higher levels of unemployment for members of organized labor may be strongly opposed by union leaders. More often than not, however, employers eventually overcome union opposition and are able to abolish restrictive work rules and institute technological advances. Labor leaders such as John L. Lewis of the United Mine Workers realized that technological change was both desirable and necessary to protect job security and mine safety.[40] In reality, employers are generally more concerned about technological changes than organized labor because maintaining high levels of productivity, controlling costs, and remaining competitive are the lifeblood of a business. It should also be noted that work rules and restrictions on technological changes cannot be maintained indefinitely if they unduly impair management's ability to operate profitably. For these reasons, unions are not likely to mount strong and enduring opposition to technological advances; rather, they often allow management to institute changes and then negotiate contract provisions to protect the job security of their members.[41]

Work Rules

Work rules are often designed to protect employee job security against technological innovation. After the introduction of diesel locomotives eliminated the need for locomotive firemen, the railroad brotherhoods forced the railroads to continue employing firemen in the cabs of diesel locomotives.[42] Musicians unions have insisted that orchestras employ more musicians than are necessary to play the music properly. Electricians union contracts have enforced protective work rules that permit only electricians to change light bulbs in work areas.[43] Unions have been blamed for perpetuating inefficient and wasteful work practices. However, it must be remembered that restrictive work rules are jointly negotiated by union and management. In some cases, unions obtained such work rules in exchange for making concessions that management regarded as important.

The following example illustrates the effect of an overly restrictive work rule:

> A crew of four railroad maintenance employees was assigned the task of sandblasting and repainting a trestle. Since the trestle could not be reached by truck,

---

[40] See William H. Miernyk, "Coal," in Gerald G. Somers, ed., *Collective Bargaining: Contemporary American Experience* (Madison, Wisconsin: Industrial Relations Research Association, 1980), pp. 26–27.

[41] For an insightful discussion of these issues, see Neil W. Chamberlain, Donald E. Cullen, and David Lewin, *The Labor Sector*, 3rd ed. (New York: McGraw-Hill Book Company, 1980), pp. 245–248; and Leonard M. Apcar, "Unions React to Automation by Stressing Job Security and Retraining," *The Wall Street Journal* (May 3, 1983), p. 1.

[42] Diesel locomotives were introduced on most railroads in the early 1950s. In 1970, the railroads and the unions agreed to allow a gradual phasing out of locomotive firemen through a policy of attrition.

[43] See Richard B. Freeman and James L. Medoff, *What Do Unions Do?* (New York: Basic Books, Inc., 1984), p. 162.

the maintenance workers traveled to the work site on a motorized car designed to run on railroad tracks. A battery connection on the motorized car became disconnected several miles from the work site and, as a result, the vehicle's engine failed. All that was needed to repair the vehicle was to reconnect the cable, a task that could be performed by an unskilled worker within a few minutes. However, the work crew leader (who was allegedly knowledgeable of the collective bargaining agreement) would not allow any members of the crew to repair the disconnected cable and, instead, called a mechanic from the company's shop. It took over four hours for the mechanic to reach the disabled vehicle and another sixty seconds to make the repair. As a result, the work crew did not have sufficient time to continue their journey to the trestle and set up their equipment. They returned to the shop where they spent the remainder of their shift loitering. Each member of the crew was paid for eight hours of work.[44]

Many work rules are designed to protect the job security of bargaining unit employees. Restrictive work rules arise through featherbedding practices discussed in earlier chapters.[45] Some work rules help promote employee discipline (see Chapter 16), health and safety, and efficiency. Work rules such as the one described above may create inefficiencies, higher productivity costs, poor product and service quality, and tensions in the workplace. Since some work rules seem almost absurd, it is sometimes difficult to comprehend how they were formulated in the first place. Bok and Dunlop provide a portrayal of how work rules often evolve.

> In the normal case the employer imposes a rule or agrees with the union on a rule which seems to make perfect sense under the conditions then prevailing. In the course of time, however, minor changes in working conditions or technology gradually diminish the appropriateness of the rule. The job may be simplified or made safer or more automatic, or the men working on the job may discover short cuts, so management comes to disregard the rule. In the early stages, however, management may not feel that it is worth a serious conflict to press for a change in the rule. As time passes, the gap between current conditions and those envisaged at the outset of the rule grow steadily wider. The more out-of-date the rule becomes, the larger the number of men who would be displaced if the rule were abandoned. Hence, there is growing opposition on the part of the members and the union to making a change. At the same time, as the inefficiency grows more apparent, management regards perpetuation of the rule as a mounting threat to its competitive position. In short, the prospects rise for a major confrontation between the parties.[46]

Work rules are often based on the idea that workers have a property right to their jobs.[47] When management desires to eliminate restrictive work rules or introduces improved technology, they are often required to make tradeoffs or conces-

---

[44] This example is based on the author's experience while working on a summer job in 1969.
[45] Also see Cynthia B. Costello, "Technological Change and Unionization in the Service Sector," *Monthly Labor Review* (August 1987), p. 45; Janet Stern Solomon, "Union Responses to Technological Change: Protecting the Past or Looking to the Future?" *Labor Studies Journal* (Fall 1987), p. 51.
[46] Derek C. Bok and John T. Dunlop, *Labor in the American Community* (New York: Simon and Schuster, 1970), p. 271.
[47] See William Gomberg, "The Work Rule Problem and Property Rights in the Job," *Monthly Labor Review* (June 1961), pp. 595–596.

sions to labor. In 1959, the International Longshoremen's and Warehousemen's Union (ILWU) and the Pacific Maritime Association signed a Modernization Agreement in which the union agreed to give up restrictive work practices in return for job security guarantees.[48] In order to modernize one of its plants, Armco Steel and the United Steelworkers agreed to more than $22 million in wage and benefit concessions during the three-year period of modernization; but once the new plant becomes operational, all of the plant's hourly employees will recover their lost wages and benefits (plus 7 percent interest).[49] The 1987 contract negotiated between the United Auto Workers (UAW) and the Ford Motor Company established committees to ensure that labor and management officials at the local level reviewed individual operations and formulated plans to increase efficiency, productivity, and quality. The concessions on productivity efficiency were likely a tradeoff to the UAW by Ford on wage and layoff provisions.[50] The Santa Fe Railway Company and the United Transportation Union reached an accord on reduced train size in return for $75,000 in benefits for each of the 1,300 workers involved.[51] Pittston Company's labor pact with the United Mine Workers in January of 1990 also proposed more flexible work rules that would allegedly improve productivity in Pittston mines.[52]

Robotics Technology

Robotics technology is becoming an integral part of the manufacturing process in many U.S. and multinational firms. A robot is a mechanical device having a reasonably high level of intelligence, the ability to make elementary decisions, and the dexterity and flexibility to perform an intricate sequence of different motions without human intervention.[53] Robots are different from automatic machines in that they can be reprogrammed to carry out a number of functions and in the fact that their adaptability competes closely with that of humans. Robots increase productivity because of their ability to work at a faster and more continuous pace than human workers. Quality of production is enhanced by robotics technology due to the elimination of human error caused by fatigue, boredom, and inattention on the job. Safety hazards may be reduced or eliminated by placing robots in jobs that are dangerous or monotonous. Finally, robots may reduce labor costs in the long run; they do not require overtime pay or expensive employee benefits; nor do they file unemployment and workers' compensation claims.

The introduction of robotics technology into a firm's production process raises a number of issues with regard to union-management relations. First, the union's

---

[48] See Robert J. Flanagan, Lawrence M. Kahn, Robert S. Smith, and Ronald G. Ehrenberg, *Economics of the Employment Relationship* (Glenview, Illinois: Scott, Foresman and Company, 1989), pp. 519–520.
[49] Laurence J. Cohen, "New Bargaining Approaches to New Economic Conditions: Pursuing a Mutuality of Interests," *The Labor Lawyer* (Spring 1989), p. 268.
[50] The Bureau of National Affairs, Inc.,"Wage Patterns: Automobiles," *Collective Bargaining Negotiations & Contracts* (Washington, D.C.: The Bureau of National Affairs, Inc., 1989), section 18.
[51] "Santa Fe Pacific Unit, Union Reach Accord On Train Crew Size," *The Wall Street Journal* (August 8, 1989), p. C13.
[52] Alecia Swasy, "Pittston Accord, if Ratified, May Bring Work-Rule Changes, Productivity Gains," *The Wall Street Journal* (January 5, 1990), p. A2.
[53] Parvez Salim, "The Robots Are Coming," *Professional Safety* (March 1983), pp. 18–19.

reaction to robotics will likely depend on the extent to which bargaining-unit jobs are threatened. Unions will probably support robotics if few jobs are lost and safety and job enrichment are enhanced. Union and management must decide whether robots should replace human workers when there is little difference in their productivity levels. Union organizing strategies and bargaining unit structures may also change as robotics make inroads into U.S. organizations. Robotics may make blue-collar jobs virtually obsolete, further eroding what has traditionally been the most heavily unionized category of employee.

In bargaining units where robots assume the task normally performed by unskilled and semiskilled workers, an increasing number of professional and technical workers will be needed to program and maintain robots. Professional and technical employees require different organizing tactics than less skilled employees. Furthermore, the coverage of supervisors under the National Labor Relations Act may require alteration. For example, persons who program robots to perform a certain task or job might be regarded by the NLRB or courts as supervisors or managers who "formulate and effectuate management policies by expressing and making operative the decisions of the employer."[54] Persons who program robots to perform a security function could conceivably be required to form a separate bargaining unit similar to those of plant guards and other security personnel (see Chapter 4).

The types of grievances filed by bargaining unit employees may change as a firm shifts to robotics technology. Robotics technology may eliminate tedious, monotonous, and dangerous jobs. As a result, grievances involving discharges for excessive absenteeism, tardiness, and insubordination may decrease, whereas disputes regarding professional prerogatives, job displacement, layoffs, seniority rights, and compensation may become more prevalent.[55]

Plant Closings and Layoffs

Plant closings have become a controversial issue in labor-management relations. Outmoded factories are being replaced by high-tech facilities that require smaller workforces. Intense international competition has also had a strong influence on industrial restructuring.[56] During the 1980s, managers, union officials, and politicians debated over the rights and protection of displaced workers. Although a majority of companies have notified their employees well in advance of impending plant closings, an estimated 30 percent of firms failed to give their employees notice of plant closings.[57] Employers are concerned that advance notice of mass layoffs and plant closings will result in impaired production, sabotage, or a mass exodus of employees before the facility closes. However, those who advocate advance notice of closings claim that relatively few employees leave before the actual clos-

---

[54] *Bell Aerospace Co.*, 219 NLRB 384 (1985).
[55] Terry L. Leap and Allayne Barrilleaux Pizzolatto, "Robotics Technology: The Implications for Collective Bargaining and Labor Law," *Labor Law Journal* (November 1983), pp. 697–698.
[56] Paul D. Staudohar, "New Plant Closing Law Aids Workers in Transition," *Personnel Journal* (January 1989), pp. 87–90.
[57] U.S. Congress, General Accounting Office, "GAO's Preliminary Analysis of U.S. Business Closures and Layoffs During 1983 and 1984," cited in U.S. Congress Office of Technology Assessment, *Plant Closing: Advance Notice and Rapid Response* (Washington, D.C.: U.S. Government Printing Office. 1986), p. 8.

ing.[58] When employees have little or no notice of plant closings, they are often unable to make financial and psychological adjustments to losing their jobs and they are less able to find new jobs before depleting their personal savings.[59] Advance-notice requirements for firms closing facilities or laying off employees en masse may also save approximately $400 million in unemployment insurance costs and may increase the earnings of displaced workers by more than $1 billion.[60]

As a result of the plight facing displaced workers as well as the benefits that could accrue from giving advance notice to employees of plant closings, Congress passed the Worker Adjustment and Retraining Notification Act (WARN). WARN requires that companies with more than 100 full-time employees give a 60-day notice of certain plant closings and mass layoffs.[61] Notice is required if a total or partial plant closing will result in the displacement of 50 or more employees at one location. WARN also requires notice for mass layoffs for 6 months or more involving at least 50 employees who constitute more than 33 percent of the plant's workforce, or if the layoff involves more than 500 employees.[62] In addition to the requirements of WARN, advance notice of layoff is called for in many union contracts. The notification period varies from a few hours to 30 days or more. Notice may be required for the employees involved, the union, or both. By notifying the union or employees about an impending layoff, the parties may be able to negotiate alternative measures, such as work sharing, that will either eliminate the proposed layoff or reduce its severity.[63] Some contracts also provide for pay in lieu of layoff notice.[64]

Layoff provisions are included in 91 percent of the collective bargaining agreements surveyed by The Bureau of National Affairs, Inc. Because of the central role that seniority plays in regulating an employee's job status and entitlement to benefits, it is not surprising that seniority is also a major determinant in layoff decisions. Seniority is the sole factor in 46 percent of the surveyed contracts. Thus, junior employees with superior work records and skills are subject to layoff before their more senior, but less competent counterparts. Other contracts allow employers to use seniority as either a determining or as a secondary factor in layoffs. When

---

[58] See Paul O. Flaim and Ellen Sehgal, "Displaced Workers of 1979–83: How Well Have They Fared?" *Monthly Labor Review* (June 1985), p. 3.
[59] For a discussion on the impact of plant closings on workers, see Carolyn C. Perrucci, Robert Perrucci, Dena B. Tang, and Harry R. Tang, *Plant Closings: International Context and Social Costs* (New York: Aldine De Gruyter, 1988).
[60] Comments of Conte Silvio, *Congressional Record*, No. 105 (July 13, 1988), p. H5507. Cited in Paul D. Staudohar, "New Plant Closing Law Aids Workers in Transition," *Personnel Journal* (January 1989), p. 88.
[61] 29 U.S.C., Sec. 2101 (1988). WARN is an exceedingly complex statute. The U.S. Department of Labor recommends to employers that they give advance notice even where it is not strictly required because such notice is preferable to "the possibility of expensive and time-consuming litigation to resolve disputes where notice has not been given." See John T. Canoni, ed., "The Final Plant Closing Law Regulations Provide Guidance and Advice to Employers," *Personnel Practices Newsletter* (New York: Townly & Updike, April 27, 1989).
[62] Part-time employees working less than 20 hours per week or working less than six of the preceding 12 months before the notice is required are exempt from the Act.
[63] See Steven Briggs, "Allocating Available Work in a Union Environment: Layoffs vs. Work Sharing," *Labor Law Journal* (October 1987), pp. 650–657.
[64] A year after WARN went into effect, employers and unions reported few legal problems. According to one union leader: "Until we can keep manufacturing jobs in the U.S., advance notice doesn't help much." See "Labor Letter," *The Wall Street Journal* (January 9, 1990), p. A1.

seniority is a determining factor and two employees both have *sufficient* ability to perform a job, the less senior employee will be laid off. Collective bargaining agreements that use seniority as a secondary factor allow the employer greater latitude in considering the *relative* abilities of employees. Two employees may both be sufficiently skilled to perform a job. When seniority is a secondary factor, management may elect to retain the more competent, but less senior employee. Seniority rules may be waived during temporary (less than two weeks) or emergency layoffs.[65] In addition, union stewards (because of superseniority) and employees with specialized skills, whose employment is necessary for continuous and efficient company operations, may be exempt from layoff provisions.[66]

Many contracts allow employees who are scheduled for layoff to "bump" less senior employees in other jobs.[67] The majority of contracts require that employees be qualified to perform the job that they desire to bump into and they may be required to demonstrate their ability through a test or trial period. A few contracts require that an employee meet a minimum service requirement (e.g., five years) before being allowed to bump another employee from a job. An employee may be restricted from bumping outside his or her department or job classification. Recall of employees after layoff is most commonly done in reverse order of layoff. That is, the first person laid off is the last recalled. When employees are recalled to a job different from the one held prior to layoff, they may have to demonstrate their ability to perform the new job.

The impact of layoffs may be softened by allowing employees covered by multi-plant agreements to transfer to another plant. Some interplant transfer provisions permit transfers only for employees affected by permanent shutdowns, whereas others allow transfer during temporary layoffs. Interplant transfers provisions may also provide moving and other relocation expenses to displaced employees.[68]

▲ Subcontracting

Management's right to subcontract bargaining unit work (also called "contracting out") has been the subject of heated contract talks as well as the source of a number of grievances and arbitration cases. To run a business effectively and produce a good or service at a reasonable cost, management may decide to subcontract work to outside firms, independent contractors, or employees who work outside of the bargaining unit. For example, management may hire another firm to perform maintenance or janitorial work in a plant. A production manager may decide that it

---

[65] This discussion in no way implies that older or more senior employees are generally less competent or reliable than younger, less senior workers.

[66] The Bureau of National Affairs, Inc., "Basic Patterns: Layoff, Rehiring, and Work Sharing," *Collective Bargaining Negotiations & Contracts* (Washington, D.C.: The Bureau of National Affairs, Inc., 1989), section 60.

[67] The *least* senior employee holding a particular job is usually the first employee bumped. Some contracts allow *any* less senior employee to be bumped, thereby giving management more discretion in deciding who shall be removed from a job or laid off.

[68] Also see Antone Aboud, ed., *Plant Closing Legislation*, (Ithaca, New York: ILR Press, Cornell University, 1984).

would be less expensive to have a part manufactured by a tool-and-die firm rather than manufacturing the part "in-house."[69] Some firms subcontract their customer billing to firms that have specialized computer equipment to handle such work. Work is often subcontracted because management believes that another firm or group of workers can produce better-quality work, reduce production costs, or complete the job faster or more efficiently than bargaining unit employees. However, the union may view subcontracting as a threat to the job security of its members. As a result, the union may try to negotiate contract language that will limit management's ability to subcontract work.

According to The Bureau of National Affairs, Inc., over half of the collective bargaining agreements contain provisions dealing with management's right to subcontract work. Most contracts with subcontracting provisions require that management notify or discuss proposed subcontracting work with the union. About one-fourth of the contracts prohibit subcontracting if there are employees on layoff status or if contracting out work would create layoffs. One-third of the contracts surveyed allow subcontracting only if bargaining-unit employees do not possess the necessary skills or the proper equipment to perform the work.[70] In addition, management rights, seniority, union recognition, and other contract clauses may also affect management's ability to subcontract bargaining unit work.

Subcontracting has been held to be a mandatory bargaining topic by the U.S. Supreme Court. In the *Fibreboard* case, the employer subcontracted certain maintenance work during the life of the collective bargaining agreement without first consulting the union. Consequently, a number of employees lost their jobs. The Supreme Court held that management had violated the National Labor Relations Act by refusing to bargain over a mandatory issue. The employer was ordered to resume the maintenance operation that had been subcontracted and to reinstate the employees who had suffered layoffs as a result of the subcontracting.[71] The current NLRB approach for determining whether an employer's decision is a mandatory subject of bargaining is reflected in the *Otis Elevator Company* case.[72] In *Otis Elevator*, the Board held that a duty to bargain arises when a managerial decision is based on labor costs. However, management is not necessarily obligated to discuss with the union changes in the direction or nature of the business.[73]

In the absence of a specific contract clause regulating management's ability to subcontract work, a typical management rights clause generally allows the firm to subcontract work as long as the decision is made in good faith. That is, subcontracting that represents a reasonable business decision, does not subvert the col-

---

[69] A U.S. Court of Appeals has ruled that an employer is required to bargain with a union prior to subcontracting bargaining unit work if the decision to contract out is based primarily on labor costs. See *NLRB v. Plymouth Stamping Division*, CA 6, No. 88-5469 (March 27, 1989).

[70] The Bureau of National Affairs, Inc., "Basic Patterns: Management and Union Rights," *Collective Bargaining Negotiations & Contracts* (Washington, D.C.: The Bureau of National Affairs, Inc., 1989), section 65.

[71] *Fibreboard Paper Products Corporation v. NLRB*, 379 U. S. 203 (1964). It should be noted that an employer may make changes in working conditions such as subcontracting *after* it has negotiated with the union and has reached an impasse.

[72] *Otis Elevator Company*, 269 NLRB No. 62 (1984).

[73] Also see *First National Maintenance Corp.*, 107 LRRM 2705 (1981); and *Steelworkers Local 2179 v. NLRB*, 125 LRRM 3313 (1987).

lective bargaining agreement, and does not seriously weaken the bargaining unit would likely be viewed by the NLRB, courts, and arbitrators as being "in good faith."[74] Table 15-4 summarizes standards that arbitrators use to evaluate the legitimacy of subcontracting by management.

Management may also elect to assign bargaining-unit work to company employees who do not work in the bargaining unit. Unions officials may become especially upset when bargaining-unit work is reassigned to supervisory or professional employees. As in the case of subcontracting, management's ability to assign bargaining-unit work to nonunit employees may be specifically regulated by the collective bargaining agreement. When the contract does not explicitly address the issue of work assignments, arbitrators may consider factors such as the quantity of work assigned to "outside" employees, whether the work contains supervisory duties, the duration of the work (temporary versus permanent), custom and past practices, whether automation or technological changes have been recently made, or whether an emergency or other special situation has arisen.[75]

Table 15-4 ▲ Factors Used by Arbitrators in Evaluating Subcontracting Disputes

1. Past practice.

Has the company subcontracted similar work in the past?

2. Justification.

Was the subcontracting done for reasons such as economy, maintenance of secondary production and personnel sources, augmenting the regular workforce, plant security, or other sound business reasons?

3. Effect on the union or bargaining unit.

Was the subcontracting being used as a method of discriminating against the union? Did it substantially jeopardize the status and strength of the bargaining unit?

4. Effect on bargaining unit employees.

To what extent were members of the bargaining unit discriminated against, displaced, deprived of regular or overtime work, or laid off? It should be noted that other important business factors may still justify subcontracting even when layoffs are created. Arbitrators may also evaluate the legitimacy of a subcontracting decision by the results *expected* by management *prior* to the decision, rather than by what actually occurred after the subcontracting took place. That is, management may have anticipated 20 layoffs because of the subcontracting. However, the fact that management eventually laid off 30 employees does not necessarily mean that the decision to subcontract work was made in bad faith.

5. Type of work involved.

Is the subcontracted work normally performed by bargaining unit employees or is the work in question frequently subject to subcontracting in the firm or industry?

---

[74] Citing Arbitrator McDermott in *Shenango Valley Water Co.*, 53 LA 741 (1969), see Frank Elkouri and Edna Asper Elkouri, *How Arbitration Works*, 4th ed. (Washington, D. C.: The Bureau of National Affairs, Inc., 1985), p. 540.

[75] Adapted from Frank Elkouri and Edna Asper Elkouri, *How Arbitration Works*, 4th ed. (Washington, D.C.: The Bureau of National Affairs, Inc., 1985), p. 548–549.

Table 15-4 ▲ Factors Used by Arbitrators in Evaluating Subcontracting Disputes (Continued)

6. *Availability of properly qualified employees.*	
Are bargaining-unit employees properly qualified to perform the subcontracted work? If not, can such employees be readily trained?	
7. *Availability of equipment and facilities.*	
Are the necessary equipment and facilities presently available or can they be economically purchased?	
8. *Regularity of subcontracting.*	
Is the work in question frequently or only intermittently subcontracted?	
9. *Duration of the subcontracted work.*	
Is the work subcontracted for a temporary or limited period or is it subcontracted for a permanent or indefinite period?	
10. *Unusual circumstances.*	
Was the subcontracting necessitated by an emergency or urgent need to complete the work?	
11. *History of negotiations on the right to subcontract.*	
Has management's right to subcontract been the subject of contract negotiations? If so, how successful was the union at obtaining concessions from management on the subcontracting issue?	

Adapted from Frank Elkouri and Edna Asper Elkouri, *How Arbitration Works*, 4th ed. (Washington, D.C.: The Bureau of National Affairs, Inc., 1985), pp. 540–543. Reprinted with permission.

▲ Health and Safety in the Workplace

Occupational safety and the health of employees have traditionally focused on hazards that were part of the work environment. Unsafe working conditions; inadequate ventilation; dangerous machinery; and exposure to toxic chemicals, airborne particles, and extreme temperatures have been traditional safety concerns. In recent years, safety and health issues such as job-related stress, drug abuse and dependency, smoking in the workplace, and employee exposure to acquired immune deficiency syndrome (AIDS) have received increasing attention. Unions and management must deal with several health and safety concerns. First, what contract language is needed to deal with health and safety issues? Second, what impact does the Occupational Safety and Health Act of 1970 have on the collective bargaining relationship? Third, how are health and safety grievances handled? Finally, what role will union and management take with regard to emerging health and safety issues such as employee stress and emotional health, chemical dependency, AIDS, the special occupational health risks faced by women, and smoking in the workplace?

Health and Safety Provisions in the Collective Bargaining Agreement

Safety and health provisions appear in 86 percent of the sample contracts surveyed by The Bureau of National Affairs, Inc. Some contracts contain a general statement of responsibility for the safety and health of employees, whereas others go into detail and address issues such as safety equipment, first aid, physical examinations, investigation of accidents, employee obligations, hazardous work, safety committees, and substance abuse. Table 15–5 lists safety provisions commonly found in collective bargaining agreements.

The Occupational Safety and Health Act of 1970

The Occupational Safety and Health Act of 1970 (commonly known as OSHA or the OSHAct) was enacted to hold employers responsible for protecting worker safety and health. The Act establishes two categories of employer responsibility: (1) a broad duty to provide a working environment "free from recognized hazards that... are likely to cause death or serious physical harm," and (2) a specific duty to follow standards created by OSHA administrators. OSHA also evaluates the health and safety implications of technological changes, promotes research on workplace safety, and encourages industry cooperation with state health and safety officials. Employers are not responsible for the prevention or elimination of unknown hazards nor are they responsible for hazards that cannot be reasonably eliminated. Also, employers are not usually held responsible when employees disregard safety rules that are consistently enforced.

Table 15–5 ▲ Safety and Health Provisions Found in Collective Bargaining Agreements

Provisions
Safety equipment (hard hats, goggles, safety shoes, etc.) to be worn by employees (43%)
First-aid facilities and supplies (22%)
Registered nurse on duty (19%)
First-aid training for employees or supervisors (19%)
Physical examinations
For new hires (25%)
When employees are rehired or returned from layoff (34%)
Periodically or at management's request (63%)
Employee appeal of an unfavorable physical examination (39%)
Investigation of on-the-job accidents (18%)
Employee obligations to maintain safety (40%)
Obedience of all safety rules (65%)
Use of safety equipment (38%)
Report job-related injuries (18%)
Disciplinary action for violation of safety rules (39%)
Restrictions on employee performance of hazardous work (26%)
Guarantee employees the right to refuse hazardous work (29%)
Employees not required to perform work that they *believe* to be unsafe (58%)
Employees may file a grievance if faced with hazardous work (34%)
Employees' "right-to-know" about hazardous substances (2%)
Joint union-management safety and health committees (48%)
Union officers accompany government officials on safety inspections (12%)

Source: The Bureau of National Affairs, Inc., "Basic Patterns: Working Conditions—Safety and Health; Discrimination," *Collective Bargaining Negotiations & Contracts* (Washington, D.C.: The Bureau of National Affairs, Inc., 1989), section 95. Reprinted with permission.

Employees or unions can file a complaint with the U.S. Department of Labor, Occupational Safety and Health Administration, which is empowered to investigate complaints, inspect work areas, and establish safety standards. Should investigation reveal an immediate danger to employees and others, a court order can be obtained to shut down the work facility or remove the dangerous condition.[76] Fines can also be levied against companies found violating safety and health regulations. For example, the United Food and Commercial Workers (UFCW) mounted a sophisticated campaign to spotlight unsafe work practices against IBP, Inc., that led to $5.6 million in fines against the nation's largest meatpacker.[77] In 1986, Union Carbide was fined $1.3 million for 221 health and safety violations, 127 of which were described as a "willful disregard of the law," at its Institute, West Virginia chemical plant. Union Carbide eventually agreed to pay $405,500 for the violations. In 1987, Chrysler Corporation was fined and paid a record $1.5 million for 811 safety violations at its Newark, Delaware, automobile assembly plant.[78] The U.S. Labor Department proposed fines of $754,000 against a Cargill, Incorporated turkey-processing plant in California, Missouri, after the firm failed to protect workers from cumulative trauma disorders caused by fast and repetitive meatcutting tasks.[79] UFCW officials claim that packing companies increased workers' risk of repetitive-motion injuries in the early 1980s by speeding up their production lines in order to increase profits.[80] Most fines are much smaller than those cited here. However, the fines and associated bad publicity are an incentive for most employers to maintain safe working conditions.

An issue that is not completely resolved is the proper relationship between OSHA and collective bargaining agreements. Over one-third of the contracts contain statements that the company will comply with federal, state, and local laws.[81] In the event of a conflict, federal law takes precedence over the terms of a labor agreement negotiated between union and management. Many of the collective bargaining provisions cited in Table 15–5, in effect, encourage employers to conform to the provisions of OSHA. An important question regarding employee health and safety is whether employers can legitimately refuse to bargain with unions over safety and health measures falling directly within the province of OSHA regulation. The National Labor Relations Act requires employers to bargain in good faith over working conditions, and it would seem that safety and health are mandatory subjects for bargaining. However, collective bargaining demands that conflict with OSHA could be regarded as potentially illegal bargaining subjects.

---

[76] The Secretary of Labor, however, is not authorized to order permanent closure of a plant or facility.
[77] Aaron Bernstein and Sandra D. Atchison, "How OSHA Helped Organize the Meatpackers," *Business Week* (August 29, 1988), p. 82.
[78] See Terry L. Leap and Michael D. Crino, *Personnel/Human Resource Management* (New York: Macmillan Publishing Company, 1989), p. 521.
[79] See Marj Charlier, "Cargill Faces Fines Over OSHA Charges At Plant in Missouri," *The Wall Street Journal* (November 15, 1989).
[80] The Bureau of National Affairs, Inc., "Ongoing Meatpacking Safety Strife," *Collective Bargaining Negotiations & Contracts* (Washington, D.C.: The Bureau of National Affairs, Inc., January 26, 1989), p. 4.
[81] The Bureau of National Affairs, Inc., "Basic Patterns: Working Conditions—Safety and Health; Discrimination," *Collective Bargaining Negotiations & Contracts* (Washington, D.C.: The Bureau of National Affairs, Inc., 1989), section 95.

Health and Safety Grievances: Arbitrators, OSHA, and the Courts

Employers have long been obligated to provide a safe place for employees to work; safe machinery, tools, and equipment; safe and competent fellow employees; adequate instruction and warnings regarding dangers in the workplace; and rules of conduct designed to promote workplace safety. Compliance with OSHA is generally a strong indication that an employer has fulfilled these conditions. Nevertheless, grievances over health and safety issues typically revolve around three issues: (1) Does an employee or group of employees have the right to refuse to work when conditions are perceived as being unsafe? (2) Is an employee with a medical problem or handicap fit to perform his or her job safely? (3) Was an employee who violated a plant safety rule disciplined for just cause?

Refusing to Perform Unsafe Work

The U.S. Supreme Court has recognized that employees have the right to refuse an unsafe work assignment under certain circumstances. Likewise, arbitrators continue to recognize the safety exception to the "obey now—grieve later" doctrine. As noted in Chapter 11, employees must generally obey orders and carry out their job assignments, even if they believe that the collective bargaining agreement is violated. An employee may then file a grievance to contest management's job assignment. However, it is of little consolation for an employee to know that he or she can later file a grievance while continuing to perform dangerous work.

In *Whirlpool Corp. v. Marshall*, the U.S. Supreme Court upheld a regulation issued under OSHA, which provided that it "is the right of an employee to choose not to perform his assigned task because of a reasonable apprehension of death or serious injury coupled with a reasonable belief that no less drastic alternative is available."[82] Suppose that an employee fears for his or her safety and refuses to perform a task only to discover later that the refusal was unwarranted. Some arbitrators might decide that an employee's subjective opinion of safety hazard is "reasonable," whereas other arbitrators may decide that the employee must be quite certain that the danger is serious or life-threatening. Most arbitrators adhere to a "reasonable person" approach in determining whether an employee's refusal to perform unsafe work was legitimate. This standard holds that a refusal to perform an unsafe task is warranted if other reasonable persons would have reached a similar conclusion about the safety hazard in question. Arbitrators, however, have generally held that an employee owes management an explanation as to why he or she refused to perform the work.

Examples of cases in which arbitrators have supported employees who refused to perform unsafe work include the following:[83]

▲ A control room operator was given a three-day suspension when he did not finish removing ash from inside a hopper after a slab of ash fell on him. The

---

[82] *Whirlpool Corp. v. Marshall*, 100 S. Ct. 883 (1980).
[83] Taken from Marlin M. Volz and Edward P. Goggin, eds., *How Arbitration Works*, 4th ed. (Washington, D.C.: The Bureau of National Affairs, Inc., 1988), pp. 149–150. Supplement to Frank Elkouri and Edna Asper Elkouri, *How Arbitration Works*, 4th ed. (Washington, D.C.: The Bureau of National Affairs, Inc., 1985).

arbitrator ruled that the grievant "reacted as a reasonable person would under the circumstances in failing to return inside the hopper to complete ash removal work."[84]
- ▲ An arbitrator reduced the disciplinary penalty of a crew chief when he refused to continue the gravity defueling of a helicopter because the operation would have been unsafe.[85]
- ▲ An arbitrator held that an employee on light duty less than 24 hours after a work-related accident was justified in refusing to check operating equipment in a low-visibility basement.[86]
- ▲ An employee who demanded to see a safety committee member after he activated a breaker by touching a high-voltage plug to his leg acted reasonably and "in good faith" and should not have been suspended, according to an arbitrator.[87]

However, the following examples illustrate situations where an employee's refusal to perform work was not warranted:

- ▲ Several refinery workers were discharged when they refused to perform a routine asbestos-removal job. In upholding management's decision to dismiss the employees, the arbitrator noted that "the safety exception is not applicable—obedience did not involve an unusual or abnormal safety hazard once the right equipment was supplied. Under the facts and circumstances, a reasonable person would not have feared for his life."[88]
- ▲ A grievant with a history of insubordination refused to wear an organic vapor mask, claiming that it made her feel dizzy. Although the arbitrator reduced her disciplinary penalty from discharge to reinstatement without backpay, he observed that wearing the mask "did not pose any major hazard to her health, so she could not invoke that exception to the fundamental work now, grieve later principle."[89]
- ▲ An arbitrator upheld the five-day suspension of an employee who refused to temporarily transfer to another machine, but failed to explain to management that her refusal was based upon her high blood pressure and the fact that the machine was not in an air-conditioned area.[90]

Employees frequently complain about room temperatures, fumes and dust, cigarette smoke, excessive noise, and other annoyances that are found in many work areas. Arbitrators must distinguish between serious and immediate safety hazards versus those that make an employee's job uncomfortable, but do not pose a risk of serious injury or death. The items in the above list of "hazards" do not generally pose an immediate danger to employee health, although they may be harmful when an employee is exposed over a long period of time. Thus, employees who walk off the job because they do not like the room temperature or because

---

[84] *Indianapolis Power & Light Co.*, 87 LA 559 (1986)
[85] *U.S. Army Armor Center & Fort Knox*, 82 LA 464 (1984).
[86] *Minnesota Mining & Manufacturing Co.*, 85 LA 1179 (1985).
[87] *Beth Energy Mines*, 87 LA 577 (1986).
[88] *Amoco Oil Co.*, 87 LA 889 (1986).
[89] *Roemer Industries*, 86 LA 232 (1986).
[90] *Morton Thiokol, Inc.*, 88 LA 254 (1987).

they object to cigarette smoke are not usually protected from disciplinary action by management.

A potential conflict may arise between collective bargaining agreement provisions and the right of employees to walk off an unsafe job. Since most collective bargaining agreements contain a no-strike clause, mass refusals to work may be regarded by employers as a strike that violates the collective bargaining agreement. However, Section 502 of the National Labor Relations Act stipulates that "the quitting of labor by an employee or employees in good faith [shall not] be deemed a strike under this Act." In *Gateway Coal v. United Mine Workers*, the U.S. Supreme Court held that Section 502 "provides a limited exception to an express or implied no-strike obligation," but that "a union seeking to justify a contractually prohibited work stoppage under Section 502 must present 'ascertainable, objective evidence supporting its conclusion that an abnormally dangerous condition for work exists.' "[91] In addition, employees who complain about working conditions that allegedly pose an immediate danger are engaging in concerted activity that is protected under Section 7 of the National Labor Relations Act.[92]

Physical or Mental Conditions as a Safety Hazard

An employee's physical or mental condition may create a safety hazard to himself, fellow employees, customers, and others. Most handicapped or health-impaired employees are removed from their jobs for safety reasons, even though they have not been involved in a mishap. That is, employers typically remove such employees from their jobs because of perceived rather than actual safety problems.[93] Persons with diabetes, heart problems, and epilepsy are often banned from the workplace by employers because of the fear that a worker will experience sudden incapacitation from insulin shock, heart attacks, or seizures. Employers fear that workers with back or other orthopedic problems will either re-injure themselves or further aggravate their injuries.

Handicapped and health-impaired employees who suffer discrimination may seek relief under the Rehabilitation Act of 1973 or the Americans with Disabilities Act of 1990.[94] The definition of a "handicapped individual" under the two federal laws is broad and includes "any person who (1) has a physical or mental impairment which substantially limits one or more of such person's major life activities, (2) has a record of such an impairment, or (3) is regarded as having such an impairment."[95] Although discrimination against handicapped or health-impaired individuals is forbidden, there is no obligation by the employer to hire persons who are either unable to perform the job competently or safely or who are less qualified than other nonimpaired employees. The law only protects "qualified handicapped

---

[91] *Gateway Coal Co. v. United Mine Workers*, 85 LRRM 2049 (1974).
[92] See *NLRB v. City Disposal Systems, Inc.*, 115 LRRM 3193 (1984).
[93] See Terry L. Leap, Jozetta H. Srb, and Paul F. Petersen, "Health and Job Safety: An Analysis of Arbitration Decisions," *The Arbitration Journal* (September 1986), p. 43.
[94] Public Law No. 95–602 (1973), and H.R. 2273 and S. 933 (1990).
[95] For example, a definition such as this protects not only persons with obvious types of handicaps such as amputated limbs, impaired vision or hearing, and partial paralysis, but cancer victims, diabetics, and those with a history of heart disease as well.

individuals" who are capable of performing a particular job with "reasonable accommodation" to his or her handicap. Reasonable accommodation to an employee's handicap might included modifying job tasks and duties so that they can be more easily performed by the employee, installing ramps for persons confined to wheelchairs, or providing additional rest or medication breaks.

Arbitrators are also frequently required to determine whether management has dismissed for just cause a handicapped or health-impaired employee. Arbitrators must examine a grievant's medical condition, job duties and requirements, and other personal factors to assess the likelihood and severity of a safety hazard.[96] However, as one arbitrator stated, employees cannot be expected to work in a risk-free environment:

> No doubt there is a certain risk in employing [the] Grievant. But since he has been employed for almost seven years with no epileptic-related injuries, the risk seems very small.
> The grievance is sustained. In balancing the risk, the social benefits to be derived by [the] Grievant's continued employment, the questions of safety and job performance, I must conclude [the] Grievant's discharge is without just cause.[97]

When there is a clear and present danger that the employee may injure him- or herself or others, most arbitrators will uphold a discharge or indefinite suspension by management. The prevailing view of arbitrators is that management not only has the right, but also the responsibility to take corrective action when an employee has a physical or mental disability that creates a safety hazard.

Most collective bargaining agreements do not provide "reasonable accommodation" for handicapped employees, and arbitrators generally have held that management has no obligation to transfer a handicapped employee to a less-demanding job. In fact, giving handicapped employees preference for light-duty jobs may violate seniority or other provisions of a collective bargaining agreement.[98]

Violation of Plant Safety Rules

Management has a right to formulate and administer reasonable plant safety rules. Organizations consisting of professional and white-collar employees may have few safety rules, whereas manufacturing facilities and transportation firms may have numerous safety rules. Many organizations spend large sums of money and devote considerable personnel hours to safety training programs. Because of the heavy emphasis that some firms place on employee health and safety, employees who violate safety rules are subject to discipline or termination. Safety violations may include failure to wear protective safety equipment, carelessness or negligent ac-

---

[96] In *Mantolete v. Bolger*, 38 FEP Cases 1081 (1985), a U.S. Court of Appeals held that safety determinations cannot be based only on medical reports or subjective evaluations by employers. The court stated that an "elevated risk" must be demonstrated by assessing "all relevant information" on individual medical and work histories on a case-by-case basis.
[97] *Samuel Bingham Co.*, 67 LA 706 (1976).
[98] It is not likely that the courts will view the violation of a collective bargaining agreement as reasonable accommodation, as required by the Rehabilitation Act or the Americans with Disabilities Act of 1990.

tions, and horseplay. Because the violation of safety rules is a disciplinary matter, the topic is discussed in greater detail in Chapter 16.

Emerging Health and Safety Issues

The scope of employee health and safety issues has expanded considerably in recent years. Issues discussed here that have received major attention are substance abuse and dependency, exposure to the AIDS virus, and smoking in the workplace. In addition, health hazards facing women, employee stress, and genetic testing are also important.

Substance Abuse and Dependency

The abuse of chemical substances is a major social problem.[99] It has been estimated that 60 percent of the world's illegal drugs are consumed by Americans.[100] According to the U.S. Chamber of Commerce, drug and alcohol abuse costs employers $60 billion per year in lost productivity, turnover costs, increased health insurance claims, accidents, absenteeism, and criminal behavior at work.[101] Nearly all companies surveyed by the American Management Association reported that they had dealt with drug abuse problems within the year preceding the survey.[102] Approximately 75 percent of the persons calling a cocaine hotline admitted that using cocaine on the job had impaired their performance. Nearly half of the cocaine users claimed that they sold the drug to fellow employees and almost one-fifth said they had stolen from co-workers to support their habit.[103] Because of the high incidence of drug and alcohol abuse among employees, many firms have resorted to some form of drug testing. The most common form is urinalysis testing. Drug testing has generated controversy among employers, unions, workers, and other interested groups. Supporters of drug testing claim that an employer has the right to maintain a drug-free workplace, not only because of safety reasons, but also because drug abuse impairs productivity and increases crime on the job. Opponents believe that the procedures associated with drug testing are degrading to employees. They argue further that drug tests are unreliable and may falsely indicate that innocent employees have taken drugs. Even when traces of an illegal substance are detected in an employee's urine, it does not necessarily mean that the employee is physically or mentally impaired. Unless the employer can demonstrate that an employee is actually under the influence of drugs, the employee's off-duty conduct should not be regulated by the company. In short, management often wants to test employees for drugs to ensure workplace safety and efficiency. Union leaders, on the other hand, are less likely to approve of widespread drug testing and would rather see such tests only for employees whose jobs involve safety and security concerns.

---

[99] For a more complete discussion of workplace drug abuse and drug testing, see Terry L. Leap and Michael D. Crino, *Personnel/Human Resource Management* (New York: Macmillan Publishing Company, 1989), pp. 536–542.
[100] "America on Drugs," *U.S. News and World Report* (July 28, 1986), pp. 48–54.
[101] See William Hoffer, "Business' War On Drugs," *Nation's Business* (October 1986), p. 19.
[102] Dale Masi, "Company Responses to Drug Abuse From AMA's Nationwide Survey," *Personnel* (March 1987), p. 41.
[103] Ed Lopez, "Companies Urged to Fight Drug Abuse," *Rochester Democrat and Chronicle* (June 26, 1986); and William Hoffer, "Business' War On Drugs," *Nation's Business* (October 1986), p. 19.

The NLRB has held that testing employees for drugs is a mandatory subject for bargaining because it constitutes a material condition in the terms and conditions of employment.[104] Ruling on a charge filed by the International Association of Machinists, the NLRB found that the Johnson-Bateman Co., violated the NLRA by unilaterally implementing a work rule requiring employees who receive medical treatment for injuries on the job to also submit to drug and alcohol screening.[105] In a companion case decided on the same day, however, the Board ruled that an employer need not bargain over a drug and alcohol testing requirement for job applicants.[106] According to the Board, job applicants are not employees represented by the union for bargaining purposes. In addition, the Board noted that an employer's use of testing as part of its hiring criteria does not so "vitally affect" the interests of current employees as to bring it within the scope of bargaining under the Act.[107]

The extent to which *public* employers and unions may negotiate drug-testing provisions is still uncertain because the Fourth Amendment's constitutional prohibition of searches and seizures applies only to public employees or firms with federal government contracts. A wide range of employers, including private and public transportation firms and federal contractors, are subject to drug-testing rules of the U.S. Department of Transportation, the Department of Defense, and the Drug-Free Workplace Act of 1988.[108] Private employers, however, have fewer legal obstacles to surmount before they can lawfully impose drug testing programs on their employees. Court cases in several states have granted private employers the right to engage in drug testing, even when such testing encroaches on an employee's privacy.[109] When establishing drug testing provisions, management and union negotiators should keep the following points from Table 15-6 in mind:

Table 15-6 ▲ Standards for Drug Testing Programs

1. Rules regarding the possession, use, or sale of drugs should be clearly communicated to all employees and consistently enforced. Employees should understand the nature of the drug testing program and the consequences of refusing to participate in drug testing.
2. Random or routine drug testing of all employees must be based on a real concern for public and workplace safety.

---

[104] *Johnson-Bateman Co.*, 295 NLRB No. 26 (June 15, 1989).

[105] In a Railway Labor Act (RLA) case stemming from Conrail's implementation of a testing program over the objection of its numerous unions, the U.S. Supreme Court ruled that in light of management's claim of an existing contractual right to included drug testing as part of employee physical exams, the dispute is a "minor" one within the meaning of the RLA. Therefore, the unions have the option of taking their challenge of the drug testing program to compulsory and binding arbitration under the RLA. *Consolidated Rail Corp., v. Railway Labor Executives Association*, U.S. Sup Ct., No. 88-1 (June 19, 1989).

[106] *Minneapolis Star Tribune*, 295 NLRB No. 63 (June 15, 1989).

[107] See The Bureau of National Affairs, Inc., "Drug Testing Rulings," *Collective Bargaining Negotiations & Contracts* (Washington, D.C.: The Bureau of National Affairs, Inc., June 29, 1989), p. 4.

[108] See The Bureau of National Affairs, Inc., "Workplace Drug Regulations," *Collective Bargaining Negotiations & Contracts* (Washington, D.C.: The Bureau of National Affairs, Inc., March 23, 1989), p. 4.

[109] See *Greco v. Halliburton*, 674 F. Supp 1447 (1987); *Texas Employment Commission v. Hughes*, 3 IER Cases 451 (1988); *Di Tomaso v. Electronic Data Systems*, 3 IER Cases 1700 (1988), and *Luedtke v. Nabors Alaska Drilling* (1989), cited in Townley & Updike, "Private Employer May Require Its Employees to Submit to Drug Tests," *Personnel Practices Newsletter* (New York: Townley & Updike, July 1989), pp. 2-4.

Table 15-6 ▲ Standards for Drug Testing Programs (Continued)

3. Selective testing (as opposed to random testing) that isolates a single employee or group of employees should be based upon reasonable suspicion of drug involvement.
4. Tests should be conducted so as to preserve the dignity and privacy of employees.
5. Employees should be assured of accurate test results, regardless of the expense. This includes a secure chain of custody for the urine or blood samples, and multiple tests when samples "test positive."
6. Employees who test positive for drug use (and the positive results are confirmed by subsequent tests) should be afforded the opportunity to participate in a rehabilitation program. If possible, the employee should be reinstated to his or her job (or an equivalent job) upon successful completion of the rehabilitation program. Employees who refuse treatment or who do not successfully complete the rehabilitation program may be subject to termination. Terminated employees should be assured of confidentiality with reference to the cause of their dismissal.

Adapted from Terry L. Leap and Michael D. Crino, *Personnel/Human Resource Management* (New York: Macmillan Publishing Company, 1989), pp. 540–541. Reprinted with permission.

Acquired Immune Deficiency Syndrome (AIDS)

Acquired Immune Deficiency Syndrome (AIDS) has become a serious general health concern that has only begun to make its presence known in the workplace. AIDS is caused by a retrovirus that attacks the body's immune system, eliminating its ability to combat infection, and leaving the individual open to fatal infections and opportunistic diseases. It is estimated that over 2 million persons in the United States have been infected with the AIDS virus (such persons are regarded as *seropositive*), but show no outward symptoms of the disease. Of these individuals, 45 percent will eventually develop AIDS-related complex (ARC). Once AIDS has been contracted, it is usually fatal within 18 months.

AIDS is transmitted primarily through intimate sexual contact. AIDS can also be contracted through sharing a drug needle with an infected person or by receiving a transfusion of blood that contains the AIDS virus. There is no evidence to date that AIDS can be contracted through the typical casual social encounters of the workplace. Nevertheless, employers and co-workers often fear that a person carrying the AIDS virus can spread the disease by sharing restroom facilities and eating utensils as well as through airborne contamination. As a result of these fears, AIDS victims may be unjustly terminated, even though it is safe for them to remain on the job.

Although workplace exposure to AIDS is unlikely for most employees, there are a few professions in which persons may be exposed to blood or other body fluids as part of the job. These professions include dentists, dental assistants, nurses, emergency medical personnel, firefighters, police officers, laboratory technicians, prison guards, and physicians. In professions where employees may come into contact with the AIDS virus, management (perhaps in conjunction with union officials) should ensure that the proper precautions are taken to eliminate the risk of infection.[110] Citing the general duty clause in OSHA, the U.S. Department of Labor has

---

[110] These steps include the use of puncture-resistant containers the size of small waste baskets for the disposal of used needles, syringes, and scalpel blades and provisions for gloves, masks, and goggles for health care workers who may come into contact with body fluids contaminated with the AIDS virus.

begun to levy fines against hospitals not taking specific steps to ensure protection of health care workers.[111]

AIDS victims and others with contagious diseases appear to enjoy protection under the Rehabilitation Act as well as under various state equal employment opportunity laws. A number of state courts and civil rights agencies have categorized the AIDS infection as a handicap under state laws prohibiting discrimination against the handicapped. The U.S. Department of Justice has reached a similar conclusion in interpreting the Rehabilitation Act. Since these laws prohibit discrimination and require reasonable accommodation, AIDS victims may not be terminated solely because they are infected with the AIDS virus.[112]

AIDS in the workplace may generate three types of grievances that union representatives, management, and arbitrators must consider. First, AIDS victims may believe that they have been unjustly suspended from work or terminated. Although AIDS victims whose conditions have advanced to the latter stages of the disease may be too sick to work, persons who have been diagnosed as seropositive may be fully capable of performing their jobs. Resolving a grievance of this nature requires a careful examination of the relevant medical evidence and job demands of the grievant. Second, co-workers who harbor irrational fears about working around AIDS victims may create disturbances in the workplace that can result in disciplinary action.[113] An example of such misinformed hysteria occurred among Immigration and Naturalization Service employees who demanded to wear gloves when they processed the applications of Haitians.[114] Finally, if employees act in concert to protest working with an AIDS-infected co-worker, their actions might represent a form of protected concerted activity under the NLRA.[115] However, these employees would not likely be able to invoke the safety exception to the "obey now—grieve later" doctrine under Section 502 of the NLRA.

Smoking in the Workplace

Smoking in the workplace has become a sensitive issue, primarily because of concerns voiced by nonsmokers who do not wish to be exposed to sidestream smoke (smoke from the tobacco products used by smokers). Nonsmokers cite research literature that indicates that sidestream smoke is hazardous to their health. Sidestream smoke may aggravate allergies and increase the probability of respiratory problems, eye irritation, throat discomfort, and other problems. Although smokers argue that nonsmokers exaggerate the hazards of sidestream smoke, there is evi-

---

[111] Joint Advisory Notice (U.S. Department of Labor and U.S. Department of Health and Human Services) 52 *Federal Register* 41,818 (1987), Associated Press, "AIDS Cases Prompt Government to Enforce Guidelines on Hospitals," *The Greenville News* (July 24, 1987). In August of 1987, the Centers for Disease Control warned that all patients should be treated as potentially infected, and emphasized that the risk faced by health care workers is increasing.

[112] Thomas H. Barnard and Martin S. List, "Defense Perspective on Individual Employment Rights," *Nebraska Law Review*, Vol. 67, Nos. 1 and 2 (1988), pp. 205–207.

[113] Under a contract covering prison guards, the employer was required to notify personnel if any prisoners had a contagious disease. An arbitrator found that prison administrators had breached the contract when they failed to reveal the names of inmates who tested positive for the AIDS virus. See *Delaware Department of Corrections*, 86 LA 849 (1986).

[114] "Confronting AIDS With a Sense of Realism," *New York Times* (February 17, 1988), p. A1.

[115] Thomas H. Barnard and Martin S. List, "Defense Perspective on Individual Employment Rights," *Nebraska Law Review*, Vol. 67, Nos. 1 and 2 (1988).

dence that smokers also have higher absenteeism rates and health insurance costs than nonsmokers. In addition, smoking causes damage to furniture and sensitive electronic equipment and increases cleaning and maintenance costs.

Union and management may elect to negotiate provisions to control smoking in the workplace. Contract provisions covering workplace smoking should accommodate both smokers and nonsmokers. Designated smoking and nonsmoking areas may alleviate tensions between smokers and nonsmokers. In addition, a means of resolving disputes over smoking issues should be included in the smoking provision.[116]

▲ Union Security Issues

Unions exist only as long as they have members who are employed and support the organization through the payment of fees and dues. For this reason, a union tries to protect the job security of its members by limiting management's ability to transfer, lay off, or discharge employees. The use of seniority systems, work rules, and restrictions on management's ability to make technological changes and to subcontract work are some of the ways in which unions protect employment opportunities for their members.

Unions are also vitally concerned about their ability to maintain a strong nucleus of members. Ideally, unions would prefer that employers hire only loyal, dues-paying union members. Public policy, however, does not permit unions to insist that employers hire only those applicants who belong to the union. Furthermore, some employees may not wish to join the union, for either personal or financial reasons. Unions must therefore protect their membership levels through union security arrangements.

Types of Union Security Arrangements

There are several types of union security arrangements. The *union shop* is by far the most prevalent form of security. Under a typical union shop provision, an employee is not required to be a union member when hired, but once hired, he or she must join the union within 30 working days.[117] However, section 8(f) of the Landrum-Griffin Act permits *prehire agreements* in the construction industry. A prehire agreement permits compulsory union membership seven days after employment. Under a union shop or prehire agreement, an employee who fails to join the union is discharged. *Modified union shop* provisions typically do not require union membership of temporary employees or employees working before the con-

---

[116] See Terry L. Leap and Michael D. Crino, *Personnel/Human Resource Management* (New York: Macmillan Publishing Company, 1989), pp. 551–555.

[117] In 1980, Congress amended the NLRA and exempted employees who were religious objectors from compulsory union membership or financial support of a union. The amendment allows unions and employers to negotiate contract provisions that require religious objectors to make a contribution that is equivalent to the union dues. In addition, unions may make reasonable charges to nonmembers for processing their grievances.

tract went into effect. *Agency shop* provisions require payment of union service fees (usually an amount equal to union dues) by employees who do not wish to join the union.[118] Although union negotiators prefer the union shop provision, an agency shop arrangement ensures the financial, but not necessarily the moral support of employees. *Maintenance-of-membership* provisions require present union members to remain in the union during the life of the contract, but impose no such obligation on other bargaining unit employees who are nonmembers.[119] Some maintenance-of-membership clauses allow union members to escape membership once the contract expires.[120]

Two types of illegal union security arrangements are the *closed shop* and the *preferential shop*. The closed shop requires that employees be union members *before* they are hired, whereas as the aforementioned union shop requires membership *after* hiring. The preferential shop is similar to the closed shop in that union members are given first hiring preference and nonunion members are hired only if the supply of union labor is exhausted. The crucial difference between the closed and preferential shops versus other legal forms of union security is that the former restrict the employer's applicant pool and force the firm to discriminate against nonunion employees in violation of Sections 8(a)(1) and 8(a)(3) of the NLRA.

Even after the closed and preferential shop provisions were declared illegal, some unions and employers continued to use them. Closed shops were also maintained under the guise of union hiring halls; if an employer hires almost exclusively from a union hiring hall and the union provides job referrals only to its members, then closed or preferential shop conditions exist. When discriminatory hiring practices occur, the NLRB must look at the administrative operation of the hiring hall and formulate remedies to prevent further problems.

Checkoff Provisions

All organizations depend on revenues to survive and unions are no exception. The ability to collect member dues is therefore vital to union security. A primary means of conveniently collecting dues from union members is through an arrangement known as the *checkoff*. According to The Bureau of National Affairs, Inc., over 90 percent of surveyed contracts contain this provision.[121] A checkoff allows the union to have dues deducted directly from the member's paycheck and it eliminates the need for union representatives to either bill members or personally collect money

---

[118] Nonunion employees who are assessed agency shop fees may request that the union apply those fees only to collective bargaining activities. Agency shop fees used to support the union's ideological positions are subject to refund if nonmembers object to the subsidization of such activities. See *Chicago Teachers Union, Local No. 1, v. Hudson*, U.S. Sup Ct., No. 84–1503, March 10, 1986).
[119] Union shop provisions are found in 62 percent of the contracts surveyed by The Bureau of National Affairs, Inc. In addition, modified union shop provisions are found in 13 percent of the contracts, agency shop provisions are in 11 percent, and maintenance of membership, 4 percent. The Bureau of National Affairs, Inc., "Basic Patterns: Union Security," *Collective Bargaining Negotiations & Contracts* (Washington, D.C.: The Bureau of National Affairs, Inc., 1989), section 87.
[120] If a contract is renegotiated with a "new" maintenance-of-membership clause, current union members may be given an "escape period" such as 15 days.
[121] The Bureau of National Affairs, Inc., "Basic Patterns: Union Security," *Collective Bargaining Negotiations & Contracts* (Washington, D.C.: The Bureau of National Affairs, Inc., 1989), section 87.

from them each month.[122] Checkoff arrangements also offer two advantages for employers. First, by having union fees and dues deducted from employee paychecks, the workplace disruptions associated with having union representatives collecting dues is eliminated. Second, some employees will inevitably be lax about paying their dues unless it is deducted directly from their pay. Under a contract containing a union shop but no checkoff provision, the employer may be forced to initiate discharge proceedings against union members whose fees are in arrears; in most instances, the union member makes payment once it becomes obvious that termination is imminent.[123] This situation is both costly and time-consuming for the employer.[124]

Arguments for and against Union Security

Supporters of organized labor believe that union security arrangements are vital. However, there are also those who argue against union security. Table 15-7 summarizes these issues.

Table 15-7 ▲ Arguments for and against Union Security Arrangements

Arguments Favoring Union Security

1. Bargaining-unit workers who do not join the union will receive the benefits of collective bargaining without bearing the financial burden of union membership.
2. Union leaders must devote more effort to encouraging bargaining-unit employees to join the union. Increased organizing efforts detract from other union obligations such as grievance administration and bargaining preparations.
3. When union membership is compulsory, unions can better control and discipline their members. As a result, violations of the collective bargaining agreement are less likely to occur.
4. Unions need an adequate and cohesive membership base in order to achieve sufficient bargaining power and mount a serious strike threat.

Arguments Against Union Security

1. Compulsory union membership violates an employee's freedom of association.
2. Some union leaders may feel less compelled to satisfy a captive membership and, as a result, workers do not receive their money's worth from the union.
3. Compulsory union membership may deprive a person of his or her freedom to work.
4. Unions may obtain too much power if membership is compulsory.

Adapted, in part, from Benjamin J. Taylor and Fred Witney, *Labor Relations Law*, 5th ed. (Englewood Cliffs, New Jersey: Prentice-Hall, Inc., 1987), pp. 366-368.

---

[122] Union members must authorize, in writing, the checkoff of union dues and fees. Such an authorization is valid for no more than one year or until the current collective bargaining agreement expires, whichever occurs first. Some agreements allow the employee to revoke the checkoff at any time and other contracts automatically renew the checkoff unless an employee revokes the authorization.

[123] A union may expel a member for violating its rules or bylaws. However, a union cannot force an employer to fire an expelled member who no longer pays fees and dues, even when a valid union shop provision is in effect. Unions can only compel an employee's discharge for nonpayment of dues. In addition, unions may fine members for infraction of union rules, but they cannot compel the employer to fire a member for nonpayment of the fine. Unions can collect delinquent fines from members through civil action.

[124] See Benjamin J. Taylor and Fred Witney, *Labor Relations Law*, 5th ed. (Englewood Cliffs, New Jersey: Prentice-Hall, Inc., 1987), pp. 395-396.

Most of what has been said about the pros and cons of union security provisions are based on speculation rather than on an organized, scientific study of the issues. Nevertheless, union security remains a controversial issue, especially in right-to-work states where various types of union security may be outlawed by a state statute or constitutional amendment.

Right-to-Work Laws

Compulsory union membership or financial support is illegal in some states. Currently, 20 states have enacted right-to-work laws or constitutional amendments. Section 14 (b) of the NLRA (as amended in 1947 under the Taft-Hartley Act) invited states to pass laws outlawing union security provisions.

> Nothing in this Act shall be construed as authorizing the execution or application of agreements requiring membership in a labor organization as a condition of employment in any State or Territory in which such execution or application is prohibited by State or Territorial law.

The states that have passed right-to-work laws are located primarily in the south and southwestern sections of the United States. State legislators have enacted right-to-work legislation in order to give their constituents the freedom to either join or reject union membership.[125] Lawmakers have also wanted to use right-to-work legislation as a means of attracting industry to their states. Section 14(b) may have created unequal competition between right-to-work and non-right-to-work states.[126] Unfortunately, there are no conclusive studies on the effects that right-to-work laws have on the labor climate in states.[127]

Union leaders strongly oppose right-to-work legislation because they fear that it undermines union strength and solidarity. "Free riders" are bargaining unit employees who do not join the union, but who benefit from the terms and conditions of the collective bargaining agreement. Unions have the duty to fairly represent all bargaining unit members, regardless of union membership. Although unions have tried to assess non-members for a portion of collective bargaining costs and have also fought to repeal Section 14 (b) of the NLRA, they have been unsuccessful to date.[128]

---

[125] Based on the author's experience in two right-to-work states, Louisiana and South Carolina, most employees do not understand the right-to-work concept and believe that they are compelled to join a union. Some employees claim that the union told them that they "had to join." To the extent that this is true, the effect of right-to-work laws may be primarily symbolic.
[126] Benjamin J. Taylor and Fred Witney, *Labor Relations Law*, 5th ed., (Englewood Cliffs, New Jersey, Prentice-Hall, Inc., 1987), p. 386.
[127] Railroad and airline employees working in states that have enacted right-to-work laws are still compelled to abide by union security provisions in their collective bargaining agreements.
[128] See Benjamin J. Taylor and Fred Witney, *Labor Relations Law*, 5th ed. (Englewood Cliffs, New Jersey: Prentice-Hall, Inc., 1987), pp. 383–386.

▲ Summary and Conclusions

Balancing the institutional rights of management and organized labor is an on-going process that requires careful contract negotiations and administration. This chapter has attempted to illustrate some of the major institutional issues that arise in collective bargaining relationships. Management rights, seniority, subcontracting, employee health and safety, and union security are complex topics that affect bargaining power and the quality of the union-management relationship. In most instances, union and management representatives are able to satisfactorily negotiate contract provisions on these issues and maintain a balance between the rights and obligations between labor and management. When disputes arise regarding managerial prerogatives or union security, the parties often resolve the problem on their own without third-party intervention. Occasionally, however, complex disputes over management rights, technological changes, subcontracting, seniority, employee health and safety, and union security must be resolved through arbitration, the NLRB, or in court.

We now shift from the collective rights of management, employees, and unions to the issue of individual rights. Chapter 16 deals with the individual rights in labor-management relations and the issues that arise when employees face disciplinary action.

▲ Discussion Questions and Exercises

1. Why must negotiators pay close attention to the wording and structure of management rights clauses? Discuss.
2. In light of the increase in flexible working schedules, temporary workers, and part-time employees, do you believe that seniority systems will increase or decrease in importance during the 1990s? Defend your position.
3. What types of technological changes will occur during the 1990s? How will companies and unions likely adapt to these technological changes? How will these changes be reflected in collective bargaining agreement provisions?
4. Draft collective bargaining provisions to reflect the following health and safety concerns in the workplace:
   a. The issue of workers who are known carriers of the AIDS retrovirus.
   b. The rights of smokers and nonsmokers.
   c. Employee drug testing.
5. How important are right-to-work laws? In your opinion, what would occur in the U.S. labor movement if
   a. all right-to-work laws were abolished.
   b. all 50 states enacted a right-to-work statute.

▲ ▲ ▲ ▲ ▲ CASES ON INSTITUTIONAL ISSUES

The Disputed Seniority Date

Charles B. Reichert was hired as a part-time driver by Columbus Retail Merchants Delivery on July 28, 1971. He was in the continuous employ of the

Company from that date and on May 1, 1974, he was granted a transfer from part-time to full-time employee status. Between the two above dates, Reichert averaged over 25 hours of work per week. Article I of the contract defines a part-time employee as one "whose work week does not average in excess of twenty-five (25) hours per week." Except for having access to the grievance procedure, part-time employees are not entitled to participate in any benefits that have been established under the agreement.

The Company contends that Reichert's seniority date should be May 1, 1974. In addition, both union and management representatives disagreed as to whether a part-time anniversary date should be the date that the employee was hired on a part-time basis or the date the employee was transferred to full-time status. Both issues were submitted to an arbitrator for resolution.

The union asserts that Reichert was employed on July 28, 1971 and over the span of his employment as a part-time driver, he averaged 29.48 hours per week. As a result, the union contends that he should be classified as a full-time employee. During his first two years with the firm, Reichert did not work the required 1,400 hours per year to receive paid vacation benefits (Article VIII of the contract). However, during his third year of employment, he exceeded the 1,400 hours and, at that time, he allegedly became eligible for a two-week vacation, based on three years of continuous service under the contract.

The company contends that during his first two years on the job, Reichert averaged less than 25 hours of work per week. Starting in July of 1973, his average weekly employment exceeded 25 hours. Furthermore, Reichert's written request for full-time status was not made until May 1, 1974. The company cited Article I of the agreement and noted that part-time employees are excluded from employee benefits. In addition, the company claims that part-time employees are not working on a "continuous service basis" and are therefore not entitled to vacation benefits. The company claims that permitting part-time employees (whose working hours might be minimal and sporadic) to use their original date of hire for seniority purposes would be "manifestly unfair" to employees who worked for the firm on a regular 40-hour-a-week basis.

Excerpts From Relevant Contract Provisions

Article I—Recognition

Section 1.2 Part-time employees are defined as employees who are not hired to work on a regularly scheduled basis, and whose work week does not average in excess of twenty-five (25) hours per week.

Section 1.3 No part-time employee shall be entitled to participate in any of the terms and conditions of this Agreement, except that relating to the grievance procedure.

Article VIII—Vacations

Section 8.1 An employee subject to this Agreement shall receive vacation with pay in accordance with the following schedule, provided that such employee has worked a minimum of 1,400 hours during the preceding calendar year.

Excerpts From Relevant Contract Provisions (Continued)

Article VIII—Vacations (Continued)

    If employed 1 year at April 1, 1 week vacation with pay;
    If employed 2 years at April 1, 2 weeks vacation with pay;
    If employed 8 years at April 1, 3 weeks vacation with pay.

Article X—Seniority

Section 10.1 An employee's seniority shall, in all cases, be determined from the employee's date of hire, except as otherwise provided in this contract. It being understood, however, that an employee shall not be placed on any seniority list until he has completed his probationary period.

Discussion Questions

1. Although the agreement stipulates that a part-time employee is one who works less than 25 hours a week, the agreement is silent as to how the average is to be determined. What implications does this "silence" have on the arbitrator's decision?
2. How crucial is Article I, section 1.3 in the outcome of this case? Discuss.
3. How much paid vacation time should Reichert receive? Explain your reasoning.
4. When the collective bargaining agreement is renegotiated, what modifications might the union and management negotiators propose to Articles I, VIII, and X?

The Terminated AIDS Victim

An anonymous grievant employed by a nursing home had been hospitalized in July of 1986 and again in January of 1987. The grievant was treated for pneumocystis carinii pneumonia, a disease related to his AIDS condition. A grievance was filed by the union when the grievant was fired by nursing home management. Two separate arbitration hearings were held. At the first hearing, the arbitrator ruled in favor of the grievant on the issues of arbitrability and timely filing of the grievance. The second hearing was held to deal with the questions surrounding AIDS as a disease and the proper employment status of the grievant. This case deals with the second grievance only. The parties agreed to let the arbitrator decide the following issues:

1. Is AIDS a communicable disease as defined by state law?
2. Are Centers for Disease Control (CDC) Guidelines appropriate and adequate in a nursing home setting?
3. If not, what is the appropriate employment status of the grievant?
4. What are appropriate remedies for the improper discharge?

    AIDS has been described by the U.S. Public Health Service as a bloodborne virus that is transmitted primarily by sexual contact. It is also remotely possible that a "needle stick" or open sore might also transmit the disease. An individual with AIDS is assumed to be a carrier for the rest of his or her life. In this case, applicable state law requires that institutions must have

> Written policies for [the] control of communicable disease in effect to ensure that employees with symptoms or signs of communicable disease or infected skin lesions are not permitted to work.

Nursing home management established a written policy that an employee with a communicable disease "is suspended until a negative report is received."

In addressing the second question set forth by the parties, substantial testimony was given concerning the adequacy and appropriateness of CDC guidelines when applied to health care workers. Counsel for the employer argues that because state law covering nursing home employees deals with communicable diseases, CDC guidelines are irrelevant to this case. The union counters by noting that the guidelines reduce the chances of spreading the virus to a minimal level.

Discussion Questions

1. Based on the issues briefly presented above, how should the arbitrator rule on questions 3 and 4 of the submission agreement?
2. To what extent should arbitrators become involved in interpreting state law and federal guidelines such as those discussed above?
3. Because the incidence of AIDS is expected to continue to increase in the future, what types of provisions are collective bargaining agreements likely to incorporate as a means of dealing with problems similar to the one described here?
4. If the AIDS victim is discharged, he will lose his health insurance coverage after 30 days. This loss will compound the employee's problems because of the likelihood that he will continue to incur high medical expenses. What is the arbitrator's responsibility in dealing with this issue?

16 Employee Rights, Job Security, and Discipline

- **Introduction**
- **Management's Right to Discharge and Discipline Employees**
  Contractual Rights to Employment
  Tenured Employees
  At-Will Employees
  The Quasi-Contractual Rights of Employees under a Collective Bargaining Agreement
- **Causes of Employee Discipline Problems**
- **Categories of Employee Discipline Problems**
  The Attendance Problem: Absenteeism and Tardiness
  Rule Violations
  Drug and Alcohol Problems
  Dishonesty
    Falsification of Employment Applications and Work Records
    Employee Theft
    Gambling
  Off-Duty Misconduct
  Insubordination and Abusive Behavior
  Incompetency
  Carelessness, Negligent Actions, and Horseplay
- **Some Issues Affecting Disciplinary Measures**
  Use of Reasonable Rules and Standards
  Burden of Proof, Due Process, and Equal Protection
  The Concept of Just Cause
  Discharge: The Ultimate Penalty

- ▲ **Corrective Disciplinary Policy and Procedures**
  Categories of Violations
  The Penalty Structure
  Corrective Discipline: The Bottom Line
- ▲ **Arbitral Review and Modification of Disciplinary Sanctions**
- ▲ **Arbitral Remedies in Discharge and Discipline Cases**
- ▲ **Summary and Conclusions**
- ▲ **Discussion Questions and Exercises**
- ▲ **Cases on Employee Discipline**
  An Argument with Fatal Results
  Caught by an Undercover Agent
- ▲ **Appendix: Excerpt from USX Corporation Collective Bargaining Agreement**

▲ Introduction

The largest single source of grievances among unionized employees are those that arise in conjunction with management's attempt to discipline or discharge employees. Organizations employ workers with the expectation that they will perform their jobs in a safe, reliable, and competent manner. Likewise, the employee who accepts and abides by the employer's work rules generally expects entitlement to job security, respect for individual dignity, and reasonable compensation, free from unfair or capricious action by management. In the majority of cases, the employee and employer satisfactorily fulfill their mutual obligations. Unfortunately, there are instances in which employees either do not conform to organizational policies and rules or create difficulty at work. Examples of such behavior include poor attendance, alcohol or drug abuse, carelessness and negligence, theft, insubordination and abusive language, misconduct, rule violations, and poor performance. Some individuals mistakenly believe that the union will automatically protect them from discharge, even when the employee is guilty of a serious infraction. Similarly, organizations may violate employees' expectations of fair treatment. Examples include ordering employees to break the law, terminating employees for off-duty behaviors that have no bearing on job performance, and firing employees in order to avoid the payment of incentive pay.

Although it is easy to view the employee as the villain when organizational policies and rules are violated or when performance is poor, organizations sometimes contribute to the problem. Poor recruitment and selection, inadequate orientation and training programs, sporadic supervision, and lack of communication often contribute to employee disciplinary problems. Furthermore, management may fail to follow the fundamental precepts of due process and fairness in administering disciplinary measures. As a result, employee trust in management is diminished and union-management hostilities may be exacerbated. Some employees may feel that their only alternative is to seek legal recourse through the Equal Employment Opportunity Commission (EEOC) or civil proceedings. However, employees represented by a union will, in all likelihood, file a grievance in accordance with the collective bargaining agreement. Regardless of the outcome, disciplinary problems create disruptions, cost money, and waste time for both management and union representatives. This chapter discusses employee rights, the causes of and appropriate responses to disciplinary problems, and the role of grievance procedures and arbitration in resolving grievances.

The resolution of discipline and discharge cases is rarely a simple task. Professor and arbitrator Jean T. McKelvey gives the following advice to arbitrators embarking on disciplinary cases:

> Discipline and discharge cases are among the most difficult to decide. The facts are often complicated; credibility is difficult to evaluate; emotions may run high at the hearing; and the misconduct itself may be sordid and shocking even to one who professes sophistication. Do not be misled by parties who assure you at the outset of a hearing that "this is a simple case." There is no such thing as a simple case.[1]

▲ Management's Right to Discharge and Discipline Employees

Discharge cases raise a number of questions. Under what conditions, for example, does an employee have the right to contest the employer's decision to discharge? Federal and state equal employment opportunity (EEO) laws protect persons against unfair job treatment that is rooted in race, sex, religion, color, national origin, age, handicap, or other protected categories. However, many individuals who are discharged cannot show that they have suffered discrimination as part of a protected class. Furthermore, a number of these persons are discharged for flimsy reasons or for no reason at all. In recent years, the courts in some states have begun to take a closer look at questionable discharge cases.

Essentially an employee falls into one of four categories with respect to employment rights (or lack thereof). First, some employees have *contractual* rights to employment. Second, others are *tenured* employees. Third, a large group of employees are employed *at-will* and have no specific job security rights. Finally, *employees represented by a union and covered by a collective bargaining agreement* usually have certain contractual rights (or quasi-contractual rights) that protect them from unfair discipline or discharge. As a backdrop to the discussion on the discipline and discharge of unionized employees, a brief comparison will be made between the rights of union and nonunion workers.

Contractual Rights to Employment

Some managerial, professional, and other types of employees may sign an employment contract that affords protection against unjust dismissal during the life of the contract. College and professional football coaches, for example, typically sign con-

---

[1] Jean T. McKelvey, "Discipline and Discharge," in Arnold M. Zack, ed., *Arbitration in Practice* (Ithaca, New York: ILR Press, Cornell University, 1984), p. 101.

tracts for a specified number of years. An employment contract stipulates the terms and conditions of the employment relationship between the worker and the employer. For instance, the employee is expected to perform his her job in a competent and reliable manner. The employment contract may explicitly define the tasks, duties, and performance standards, or the contract may simply outline the employee's obligations in general terms. Some employment contracts may spell out, in detail, the conditions under which an employee may be dismissed during the life of the contract (e.g., after failure to perform, dishonesty, or financial insolvency of the employer).

Contracts are not one-way streets. The employer is also generally obligated to provide compensation according to the terms of the contract and must fulfill any other agreements that may have been made. Should the employer fail to allow an employee to work in accordance with the contract terms, the employee may sue for lost wages and benefits.

Tenured Employees

Probably the strongest form of job security and protection against unjust dismissal is afforded to tenured employees. Tenure is most commonly used in academic institutions; a prime example is college professors, who normally receive tenure after four to seven years of service if their teaching, research, and total work record is meritorious. Tenure for university professors is awarded as a protection of academic freedom. Some state and local government employees and public school teachers also enjoy job security that is equivalent to tenure. Once tenure is received, an employee can generally be discharged only for gross incompetence, neglect of duty, or moral turpitude. Many institutions, however, reserve the right to dismiss tenured employees in the event of a financial crisis or emergency.

At-Will Employees

Individuals not covered by contractual or tenure arrangements are regarded as "at-will" employees.[2] An "at-will" employee can be terminated by the employer for good cause, bad cause, or no cause at all. Traditionally, little legal protection for those employed at will has been available. The National Labor Relations Act (NLRA), equal employment opportunity (EEO) laws, and health and safety laws have prevented employers from engaging in various forms of discrimination and retaliatory actions against workers. However, many people are discharged without cause yet "fall through the cracks" and have no legal recourse under the laws mentioned above. In its purest form, the employment-at-will doctrine means that no protection

---

[2] Stephen P. Pepe and Michael A. Curley, "Fire at Will? Not Necessarily," *ABA Banking Journal* (July 1984), pp. 24–33; D.A. Cathcart and M.S. Dichter, (Eds.), *Employment-At-Will: A State by State Survey*, American Bar Committee on Employment and Labor Relations Law, 1983; W.J. Issacson and G.B. Axlerod, "Employment at Will: An Idea Whose Time Is Done?" *Legal Times of New York* (June 20, 1983), p. 14; I.M. Shepard and N.L. Moran, *Employment At Will: A Personnel Director's Guide* (Washington, D.C.: College and University Personnel Association, 1983); William H. Holley and Roger S. Wolters, "Employment at Will: An Emerging Issue," *Journal of Small Business* (October 1987), pp. 1–6.

is available for an employee who is terminated because he or she refuses to engage in illegal or unethical behavior.

Although the common law interpretation of employment-at-will still favors the employer, recent court decisions and denouncements by employee advocates have created the speculation that the at-will doctrine may be eroding.[3] Unfortunately, some companies have drawn attention to themselves by discharging employees for reasons that appear highly unreasonable by nearly anyone's standards. Not only were the tenets of due process, equal protection, and progressive discipline not followed, but some discharges have been contrary to the public interest or have been based on malice and bad faith.[4]

Proponents of the traditional employment-at-will position claim that employers should have the right to terminate employees as they see fit; after all, the employee *also* has the right to terminate an at-will employment relationship if he or she is dissatisfied or if a better employment opportunity arises. To a certain extent, this proposition assumes that an employee has the same degree of power as the employer and that employment on a new job is readily available. Some employees, however, may find it difficult or impossible to obtain a new job without a great deal of hardship. Factors such as age, poor economic conditions, and poor health may preclude employees from finding a new job. Although an employer is within proper bounds to discharge employees who are incompetent, unreliable, disloyal, or troublesome, there are instances in which the courts have stepped in and overturned an employer's decision to discharge at-will employees. Employees are appealing discharge decisions in record numbers. In the late 1970s, there were 200 wrongful discharge suits pending in state courts. In 1988, there were an estimated 25,000 suits pending.[5] Table 16–1 outlines reasons under which state courts have reinstated at-will employees who were unfairly discharged by employers:[6]

Table 16–1 ▲ Cases in Which Terminated At-Will Employees Have Been Reinstated

Discharges Contrary to the Public Interest

By far the most common exception to the employment-at-will doctrine occurs when an employee is discharged for reasons that contravene the public interest. The "public interest" may include specific statutes, accepted principles of law, high moral standards, or established interests of society. The following are examples of discharge that might violate public policy:
- An employee is discharged for filing a legitimate workers' compensation claim.
- An employee refuses to knowingly file false reports to the Environmental Protection Agency (EPA) and is fired as a result.

---

[3] Terry L. Leap and Michael D. Crino, "Protecting a Bank from Punitive Damage Suits for Discharging Employees," *Banking Law Review* (May–June 1988), pp. 40–46; David L. Bacon and Angel Gomez, III, "How to Prevent Wrongful Termination Lawsuits," *Personnel* (February 1988), pp. 70–72.
[4] See "See You in Court," *Nation's Business* (July 1989), pp.17–26.
[5] John Hoerr, "It's Getting Harder to Pass Out Pink Slips," *Business Week* (March 28, 1988), p. 68.
[6] See Sami M. Abbasi, Kenneth W. Hollman, and Joe H. Murray, "Employment At Will: An Eroding Concept in Employment Relationships," *Labor Law Journal* (January 1987), pp. 21–33; and Kenneth L. Sovereign, *Personnel Law* (Reston, Virginia: Reston Publishing Co., 1984), pp. 299–310.

Table 16–1 ▲ **Cases in Which Terminated At-Will Employees Have Been Reinstated (Continued)**

Discharges Contrary to the Public Interest (Continued)

- An employee is summoned for jury duty and the employer discharges him or her for missing work for 10 days.
- An employee faces dismissal for reporting details of a company's price-fixing arrangement to the Department of Justice.
- An employee refuses to dump hazardous waste material into a river and is discharged for insubordination.

Most discharges affecting the public interest rest on the issue of employee disloyalty or lack of respect toward management. Steeped in tradition, management has long been accustomed to giving orders and expecting compliant behavior from employees. Persons who question management's authority, speak out against management policies and actions, or contact the authorities with details of a company's illegal actions have, in the past, placed themselves in a precarious position. However, the public interest increasingly appears to be taking precedence over management's right to rule the workplace and its employees with an iron hand.

Although an employee has the right to disobey orders that violate the law and speak up when violations occur, there are limits.[7] First, no employee has a right to divulge confidential information about legal and ethical organizational practices. Second, damaging accusations or slurs against management in general or against specific members of management need not be tolerated if they are unfounded. Third, management still has the exclusive prerogative to plan, organize, direct, and control its operations without acts of insubordination or undue interference from employees. The crux of the issue here is an employee's right to stand up to management when the public interest is threatened.

Malice and Bad Faith

Employee dismissals are occasionally so out of line and repugnant to a normal person's sense of decency that the courts will step in and overturn the discharge. Examples of discharges made in malice and bad faith might include the following:

- Mass firings of employees because of the misconduct of one employee.
- Discharging an employee to avoid further payment of sales commissions that had already been earned.
- Discharging employees shortly before they achieve full vesting rights under a pension plan.
- Firing an employee who had a legitimate physical need to use the restroom even when the employer had a "no restroom" policy during working hours.
- Discharging an employee suspected of theft who refused to submit to a "strip search."

Organizations with any semblance of reasonable and enlightened personnel practices are not likely to find themselves being accused of malice and bad faith. However, the courts appear willing not only to examine such cases, but to reverse the employer's decision to discharge. What remains to be seen is how the courts will, in the future, interpret malice, bad faith, and actions violative of the public interest. The courts may continue to reverse more and more at-will discharges or they may retreat to their original "hands-off" position. The latter seems unlikely, especially in light of legislative proposals at the state level that may give at-will employees statutory protection.

---

[7] David W. Ewing, *Freedom Inside the Organization: Bring Civil Liberties to the Workplace* (New York: McGraw-Hill Book Company), p. 109.

Table 16-1 ▲ Cases in Which Terminated At-Will Employees Have Been Reinstated (Continued)

The Implied Contract

Under certain conditions, an at-will employee may be inadvertently transformed into an employee who possesses certain contractual rights. The employer, because of statements made or actions taken, may have unknowingly given an employee more job security than originally intended. Examples of situations that may create implied contract rights include the following:

- ▲ Promising an employee that he or she can expect to work for the company until reaching retirement age.
- ▲ Convincing an employee to leave a secure job by promising a better job and then failing to keep the promises after the employee is hired.
- ▲ Quoting salaries on an annual basis and thereby creating an implied employment contract for one year.
- ▲ Clauses in employee handbooks which state that employees who are not on probationary status may expect an indefinite term of employment.

A contractual relationship need not be secured in writing. If an employee is led to believe that he or she can expect permanent employment if satisfactory standards of job performance are maintained, then an implied contract may exist.

Adapted from Terry L. Leap and Michael D. Crino, *Personnel/Human Resource Management* (New York: Macmillan Publishing Company, 1989), pp. 505–507. Reprinted with permission.

The Quasi-Contractual Rights of Employees under a Collective Bargaining Agreement

The employment rights of a bargaining-unit employee who is disciplined or discharged by management are protected under the grievance procedure. The grievance machinery forces management to justify its disciplinary actions, and it ensures that employees are allowed to have an opportunity to present their case fully and explain any mitigating circumstances. For this reason, grievance procedures enable the parties to hear the entire story before deciding the employee's fate. The following bizarre case illustrates how there is often more to a disciplinary incident than meets the eye.

> The employer had dismissed two employees for horseplay. The employer's witnesses testified at length as to the large amount of time the women spent together, and their unusually close friendship—"almost like they were married." One day they got into a shoving match—they said friendly jostling. One fell down, and both were fired. The employer made it clear that one of the reasons for such a severe penalty was its belief, from their constant companionship, that they were lesbians and that was causing disruption in the plant. During the hearing, one of the women was cross-examined about inconsistencies on her application form. When she disclaimed any knowledge of it, she was given the form and told to read it aloud. She refused to do so and when pressed said, to the surprise of both the union and the employer, "I can't read." It then emerged that she relied upon the other woman for all reading, and they were always together because she needed the other one to read all instructions and directions on the job and manage affairs off the job. Out of this dependency had grown a

friendship based not on lesbianism but on illiteracy. Without the grievants present, the crucial facts would never have been known, and the decision would have been misdirected.[8]

Most disciplinary grievances do not involve surprises such as the one encountered in the case above. However, some of the employer abuses listed in Table 16–1 would be difficult for management to defend in a grievance or arbitration hearing. Even when disciplinary action might otherwise be justified, arbitrators have ruled against management when they fail to adhere to the prescribed disciplinary procedure or other terms of the contract.

▲ Causes of Employee Discipline Problems

Table 16–2 examines two major sources of employee disciplinary problems: organizational sources and individual (employee) sources. In many cases, the organization's inadequate personnel practices contribute to discipline problems. For example, persons with a history of unacceptable or troubled work performance may be hired if references are not carefully checked and verified. Careless placement of employees into jobs for which they are not suited often creates difficulties. Similarly, haphazard and inadequate training programs may lead to employee inefficiencies, feelings of inadequacy and frustration, and safety hazards, all of which can lead to disciplinary incidents. Supervisors may contribute to the problem through unequal application of rules, favoritism, an unduly harsh posture toward employees, and failure to communicate performance standards and expectations adequately. Although most employees are willing to abide by policies and work rules that they perceive to be reasonable and equitable, they may question and test those that appear to be unreasonable or antiquated.

Table 16–2 ▲ Sources and Types of Employee Discipline Problems

Organizational Causes	Individual Causes	Types of Disciplinary Problems
Poor recruitment and selection	Alcohol and drug use	Absenteeism and tardiness
Inadequate training	Personal financial difficulties	Rule violations
Lack of communication	Domestic problems	Drug and alcohol abuse
Poor supervision	Physical/mental illness	Dishonesty and theft
Unreasonable rules and policies	Personality	Off-duty misconduct
		Insubordination and abusive behavior
		Incompetency
		Carelessness and horseplay

Adapted from Terry L. Leap and Michael D. Crino, *Personnel/Human Resource Management* (New York: Macmillan Publishing Company, 1989), p. 483. Reprinted with permission.

---

[8] Clyde W. Summers, "Individual Rights in Arbitration," in Arnold M. Zack, ed., *Arbitration In Practice* (Ithaca, New York: ILR Press, Cornell University, 1984), pp. 149–150.

Other discipline problems are rooted in an employee's personal life. Alcohol and drug abuse (or addiction), financial worries, and domestic problems all take their toll and may adversely affect an employee's work performance. Physical and mental disorders can also play an integral part in employee problems at work. Personal characteristics such as an employee's high level of aggression toward others, intolerance for monotony and routine work, carelessness, and poor individual initiative and reliability, are common factors that underlie disciplinary problems.

▲ Categories of Employee Discipline Problems

The most commonly encountered types of employee disciplinary problems will now be examined.[9] No attempt is made to provide a psychological profile of the typical "problem employee." Rather, the objective is to describe the problems that management and union representatives must periodically face.

The Attendance Problem: Absenteeism and Tardiness

For many organizations, absenteeism and tardiness are a pressing concern. Although the overall absenteeism rate for organizations in the United States is approximately two to three percent of scheduled work time, some organizations experience much higher rates.[10] Absenteeism may be the result of illness, inclement weather, imprisonment, overstaying a period of paid leave or vacation, or personal problems that the employee does not wish to reveal. Furthermore, employees are often voluntarily absent on either Friday or Monday (or both) in order to lengthen their weekend.[11] Periods of high absenteeism may disrupt work schedules and create expensive production and service delays for some companies. Transportation firms, for example, operate on tight schedules and find absenteeism and tardiness to be especially troublesome.

Although nearly all employees are occasionally forced to be late or absent from work, the chronic absentee or tardy employee presents a difficult problem. Some absenteeism is involuntary; however, other incidents of absenteeism and tardiness are clearly voluntary. Some employees make every effort to attend work, in spite of illness, family conflicts, or transportation problems. Others seize the opportunity to stay away from work whenever a plausible (or semiplausible) excuse presents itself. For example, inclement weather that is likely to slow or delay travel to work may mean leaving the house 45 minutes early for one employee. The chronically late or absent employee will use the same inclement weather as a reason either to arrive late or skip work entirely. Some employees are willing to come to work with a common cold, whereas others will remain away for several days.

From the perspective of employee supervision and discipline, absenteeism and tardiness present a thorny dilemma. First, the supervisor must determine whether

---

[9] See James R. Redeker, *Discipline: Policies and Procedures* (Washington, D.C.: The Bureau of National Affairs, Inc., 1983), pp. vii and viii.
[10] "Job Absence and Turnover," *Bulletin to Management* (Washington, D.C.: The Bureau of National Affairs, Inc., 1985).
[11] Frank E. Kuzmits, "What to Do About Long-Term Absenteeism," *Personnel Administrator* (October 1986), p. 93.

the absence or lateness is legitimate. The supervisor is forced into the poorly suited role of detective. Second, management should establish a reasonable absenteeism policy. A policy may be included in the collective bargaining agreement or left solely to the discretion of management. Third, the policy should be communicated and enforced in a consistent fashion.

Arbitrators generally hold that chronic or excessive absenteeism is reasonable grounds for discharge. Of course, what constitutes "excessive" absenteeism is subject to debate. In the absence of specific contract language, arbitrators typically examine the particular facts and circumstances of each individual case. For example, illness is probably the most common excuse given by employees who are absent from work. Although it is reasonable for employees to be excused for occasional absences due to illness, management does have the right to discipline for excess absences and false claims of sickness. Arbitrators often consider whether an employee's attendance record has fallen below an acceptable range for an unreasonable period of time. The employee's previous work and attendance record, length of service, individual efforts to improve attendance, the extent to which the employee's absences exceed those of other employees, and the impact of the employee's absences on efficiency and morale are among the factors evaluated by arbitrators in absenteeism cases.[12] Most employers also require both a notice that the employee will be absent as well as the reason for the absence. Failure to provide either of these usually results in disciplinary action. As with the case of absenteeism, excessive and consistent tardiness is also grounds for discipline or discharge.

To develop a clear-cut means of dealing with absenteeism, some companies have instituted *no-fault absenteeism programs*. Under a no-fault plan, the employee accumulates absences (or points for absences or tardiness) and is dismissed if a certain number of absences or points are accumulated during a specified time period.[13] The rationale of a no-fault system is to relieve supervisors of the burden of determining whether an absent or tardy employee has a legitimate excuse. However, no-fault plans may unfairly penalize employees who must experience lengthy absences for a serious illness. In addition, certain employees may view the no-fault arrangement as a "permissive limit" and will be absent or late up to the maximum amount allowed by the system. Arbitrators generally do not challenge the legitimacy of a no-fault absenteeism plan; however, they may reinstate an employee when the accuracy of attendance records is in doubt or when enforcement of the plan is inconsistent.

Rule Violations

Employees occasionally violate work rules.[14] In some instances, a rule is violated unknowingly. In other cases, it is broken by an employee who is fully aware of the transgression. Inadequate training programs and poor communications between

---

[12] The BNA Editorial Staff, *Grievance Guide*, 7th ed. (Washington, D.C.: The Bureau of National Affairs, Inc., 1987), p. 21.
[13] See Darrell Olson and Ruth Bangs, "No-fault Attendance Control: A Real World Application," *Personnel Administrator* (June 1984), pp. 53–63 and Frank E. Kuzmits, "Is Your Organization Ready For No-Fault Absenteeism?" *Personnel Administrator* (December 1984), pp. 119–127.
[14] Frans Mulder, "Characteristics of Violation of Formal Company Rules," *Journal of Applied Psychology*, Vol. 55 (1971), pp. 500–502.

supervisors and employees may lead to accidental rule violations. Employees who purposely violate work rules often do so to test what they feel is an unreasonable or outmoded policy. Others intentionally violate rules or fail to follow prescribed work procedures simply for the thrill involved or to show off in front of fellow employees.

Arbitrators usually agree that management has the inherent right to make and to post reasonable rules of conduct that are not inconsistent with the collective bargaining agreement. However, rules may be challenged through the grievance procedure if they are believed to violate the contract or are regarded as arbitrary, unfair, or discriminatory. A rule, however, is generally regarded as reasonable if it is related to a legitimate objective of management. For example, a rule that requires employees to wear seat belts when operating company vehicles would likely be regarded as legitimate. The seat-belt rule is directly related to management's objective of workplace safety and the need to comply with conditions in the firm's liability insurance policies. Rules must generally be reasonable not only in their content, but also in their application. For example, an employer had a safety rule that prohibited employees from wearing loose clothing or jewelry when working around moving machinery. Such a rule is entirely reasonable. However, the employer went too far when it would not allow employees to walk to and from the plant gate wearing casual beach attire. The arbitrator held that such a prohibition constituted unreasonable interference with the personal freedom of employees in going to and from their workplaces.[15]

Rules must also be clear and enforced in a consistent fashion. An arbitrator is likely to reduce the disciplinary penalty of an employee who has violated a rule that has not previously been enforced by management. Arbitrators may also set aside disciplinary actions when management has enforced a rule for nonsupervisory employees, but has ignored similar violations by supervisors. However, management may mete out different penalties to two employees who commit the same infraction. Factors such as an employee's work and disciplinary record may warrant a harsher penalty for one employee than for another, even though the same rule was violated by both.[16]

Management can most effectively deal with rule violators by communicating applicable rules to employees and stressing the reasons underlying specific rules. Most employees are willing to abide by purposeful rules. When reasonable policies and rules are violated, employees should be warned or disciplined in a consistent and fair manner.

Drug and Alcohol Problems

Alcohol and drug use among employees has the potential to create numerous performance problems, some of which have tragic consequences.

What are we to do when private vices become public tragedies?

---

[15] *Babcock & Wilcox*, 73 LA 443 (1979).
[16] See The BNA Staff, *Grievance Guide*, 7th ed. (Washington, D.C.: The Bureau of National Affairs, Inc., 1987), pp. 6–7.

Joseph Hazelwood had a drinking problem. Upon his completion of a treatment program, Exxon restored him to his position as captain of an oil tanker. Then, with Capt. Hazelwood in his cabin, possibly under the influence of alcohol, a junior officer ran the Exxon Valdez aground. The resultant oil spill has befouled the Alaskan coast and destroyed the livelihood of many. Whatever personal penalty Capt. Hazelwood eventually may pay for the spill, virtually all of the cost will be imposed on others. Already taxpayers, Exxon and Exxon's customers are bearing the expense of the cleanup.[17]

An Alaska jury later acquitted Captain Hazelwood of the major charges against him. Nevertheless, employers and unions must deal with those who are either under the influence of alcohol or drugs, or have traces of illicit substances in their systems. Poor performance, unreliability, absenteeism, interpersonal conflicts, job-related safety hazards, and violations of federal or state laws are common problems among employees who abuse alcohol and drugs. In hearing cases involving drug and alcohol abuse, managers, union representatives, and arbitrators will likely have to deal with increasing amounts of medical evidence and testimony. Employees may abuse alcohol or drugs without being addicted. Regardless of an employee's level of dependence on potentially addictive substances, however, the problem lies with the impact that alcohol and drug use has on worklife.

A great deal of research has been done on employee alcohol and drug use. Some studies focus on the causes of abuse and addiction. Factors such as an individual's genetic predisposition to substance abuse, as well as social and organizational forces that contribute to alcohol and drug usage, have been examined. Job-based risks, such as low job visibility, absence of clear goals, freedom to set work hours, occupational obsolescence, stress, required on-the-job drinking, and other factors appear to contribute to alcohol and drug problems. Other research studies have focused on the consequences of illicit alcohol and drug consumption. Alcohol and drug use appears to impair job performance in many, but not all, cases. Some employees have the ability to cover up even severe alcohol or drug problems, sometimes with the help of close co-workers and supervisors.[18]

Alcoholism or drug abuse can serve two purposes in disciplinary proceedings. First, and most obvious, is that disciplinary action may be brought against an employee who is caught using alcohol or drugs on the job, regardless of whether the individual's usage impaired job performance or created a safety hazard. Employees may also be disciplined if they have on-the-job problems stemming from alcohol or drug use. Second, and less obvious, is that alcoholism or drug dependency may serve as a defense to explain inappropriate conduct at work, thereby avoiding or reducing disciplinary penalties. That is, alcohol or drug problems can create mitigating or extenuating circumstances in some cases.[19] Nevertheless, discharge may

---

[17] Daniel Quinn Mills, "Society, Employers Owe Hazelwoods Only So Much," *The Wall Street Journal* (May 16, 1989). In his editorial, Professor Mills argues that corporations may have gone too far in employing (and re-employing) people with chronic drug and alcohol problems. Reprinted by permission of *The Wall Street Journal*, Dow Jones & Company, Inc., 1989. All rights reserved worldwide.

[18] For an excellent treatment of drug and alcohol use at work, see Harrison M. Trice and Paul M. Roman, *Spirits and Demons at Work: Alcohol and Drugs on the Job*, 2nd ed. (Ithaca, N.Y.: Cornell University, New York State School of Industrial and Labor Relations, 1978).

[19] James R. Redeker, *Discipline: Policies and Procedures* (Washington, D.C.: The Bureau of National Affairs, Inc., 1983), p. 81.

still be warranted when alcohol or drug abuse results in frequent absenteeism, leads to other misconduct or improper behavior having serious consequences (e.g., physical attack on a supervisor or co-worker), renders the employee unable to perform the job safely and competently, results in a definite destructive effect on the employer's business, or significantly impairs the morale of other employees.

Organizations and society are often more tolerant of alcohol abuse than drug use. Employers are more likely to show leniency for alcohol abusers, whereas individuals caught with illegal drugs are automatically discharged. Specific policies that address the use of alcohol before work, at work, during lunch breaks, or after hours should be established to provide guidance for supervisors, union representatives, and arbitrators. For example, if an employee comes to work heavily intoxicated, the employer may use this incident as grounds for immediate dismissal or severe disciplinary action. When an employee is disciplined for alleged intoxication, a dispute often arises as to whether there is sufficient evidence to evaluate his or her sobriety. Radical changes in an employee's behavior (as noticed by one or more supervisors) and the odor of alcohol may be sufficient grounds in the eyes of some arbitrators to establish that an employee was intoxicated. When there are no outward signs of intoxication (other than the odor of alcohol or the presence of open containers of an alcoholic beverage), the employer may elect to have the company physician, safety officer, or other qualified person administer a breathalyzer or blood alcohol content (BAC) test. When plant rules clearly forbid the possession of alcoholic beverages on company property, management may use the discovery of an open container as grounds for disciplining an employee. However, an innocent employee may conceivably stumble upon an open container at the wrong moment and suffer unwarranted disciplinary action. Although such a sequence of events seems unlikely, an arbitrator held that there was inadequate evidence to discipline an employee found squatting behind a car in a company parking lot after a security guard found a styrofoam cup hidden behind the rear wheel of the car, which allegedly contained some type of alcoholic beverage.[20]

Employers may wish to consider the merits of having a policy against drinking alcoholic beverages during off-premises lunch breaks if this will result in improvements in work performance or reductions in safety hazards. The precise nature of such drinking policies will depend on the tasks and responsibilities of the employees' jobs, safety considerations, applicable drinking laws, and the employer's posture on alcohol use.[21] Interestingly, some arbitrators take a more liberal view of employees who are caught drinking alcoholic beverages on the job during the holiday season.[22] However, even off-duty drinking may be grounds for discipline or discharge for employees who are supposed to be undergoing alcohol rehabilitation.[23]

---

[20] *Kast Metals Corp.*, 65 LA 783 (1975).
[21] See August Ralston, "Employee Alcoholism: Response of the Largest Industrials," *Personnel Administrator* (August 1977), p. 50; and Carol Durtis, *Drug Abuse as a Business Problem—The Problem Defined with Guidelines for Policy* (New York: U.S. Chamber of Commerce, 1970).
[22] As one arbitrator noted in reinstating an employee who was disciplined for drinking alcoholic beverages at a warehouse party: "If we were all angels at all times, we would sprout wings and fly up to Heaven." See *Ashland Oil, Inc.*, 59 LA 292 (1972).
[23] The BNA Staff, *Grievance Guide*, 7th ed. (Washington, D.C.: The Bureau of National Affairs, Inc., 1987), p. 123.

A number of organizations are now attempting to help employees with drug and alcohol problems through the use of employee assistance programs (EAPs).[24] EAPs provide counseling and other assistance for employees who are addicted to or who abuse chemical substances.[25] Employees may voluntarily seek assistance from an EAP as part of a disciplinary process. The burden usually falls on the worker to demonstrate that he or she has made a sincere and substantial effort to deal with an alcohol or drug problem.[26] Since there is increasing recognition that substance abuse and dependency is an illness that often requires extensive professional treatment, management is generally justified in firing employees who fail to make a good-faith effort to undergo rehabilitation.[27]

Dishonesty

Acts of employee dishonesty may range from falsifying job applications, to stealing merchandise or money, to sabotage that results in hundreds of thousands of dollars in damage to the firm. Some of the major problems associated with employee dishonesty and sabotage are discussed here. Management wants to minimize acts of dishonesty in the workplace, whereas union representatives want to ensure that employees accused of dishonesty are afforded a thorough investigation of their case and fair treatment through the grievance mechanism.[28]

Falsification of Employment Applications and Work Records

Employees who falsify employment applications may do so to cover up a poor medical history, criminal record, or firing by a previous employer. In addition, applicants may falsify their employment history by overstating their qualifications or by falsely claiming to have held certain jobs in order to increase their chances of being hired. Arbitrators often support a discharge when it is discovered that an employee has deliberately and substantially misrepresented a fact that is material to the employment relationship. Material facts might include information about an applicant's previous employment, criminal record, or medical condition. Whether a fact is "material" might depend on its relevance to the job. Suppose an employee answers "no" to the question, "Have you ever had a back injury for which you received medical or rehabilitative treatment?" If the job for which the employee has applied involves lifting heavy objects and bending, then the misrepresentation

---

[24] See "On the Job Against Drugs," *Nation's Business* (July 1989), pp. 29–31.
[25] See Martin Shain and Judith Groenveld, *Employee Assistance Programs: Philosophy, Theory, and Practice* (Lexington, Massachusetts: Lexington Books, 1980); N.R. Berg and J.P. Moe, "Assistance for Troubled Employees" in D. Yoder and H.G. Heneman, Jr., eds., *ASPA Handbook of Personnel and Industrial Relations, PAIR Policy and Program Management* (Berea, Ohio: American Society for Personnel Administration, 1979) Vol. VII, pp. 1-59–1-77.
[26] A number of companies make the distinction between an employee who comes forward and accepts an offer for drug or alcohol rehabilitation as compared to seeking rehabilitation *after* an offense has occurred. Leniency may be more likely in the former case.
[27] The BNA Editorial Staff, *Grievance Guide*, 7th ed. (Washington, D.C.: The Bureau of National Affairs, Inc., 1987), pp. 122–123.
[28] This statement in no way implies that union representatives condone employee dishonesty or want to protect those who are guilty of dishonest acts.

is deliberate, substantial, and material to the job. However, erroneous statements that are made because of an oversight or lapse of memory are not usually grounds for disciplinary action. In addition, arbitrators may be reluctant to uphold the discharge of an employee because of false statements that are discovered after a long period of time. When the employee's work record is otherwise satisfactory and the employer had an opportunity to discover the falsification earlier, arbitrators are reluctant to support a disciplinary action.

Falsifying work records such as time cards, expense accounts, or production records under an individual incentive program is regarded as a serious offense. Some employers regard such falsification as a form of theft and, unless there are strong mitigating factors, management may terminate for a first offense. Mitigating factors that may save an employee from termination are a long and otherwise unblemished work record, an "honest mistake" in filling out the form, or proof that the error was the result of actions taken by others.[29]

Employee Theft

Most organizations will move swiftly to dismiss an employee who is caught or found guilty of stealing merchandise, supplies, or money from the employer.[30] However, several important issues can arise when employees are involved in theft or illegal acts. First, companies may prefer not to press criminal charges if an employee admits to the theft or illegal act and accepts an uncontested discharge. Second, when an employee does not admit to such an act, the employer must decide whether to use internal channels to investigate and discipline the wrongdoer or resort to filing criminal charges. If criminal charges are filed, the organization and the employee should be prepared to weather adverse publicity and time-consuming investigatory and criminal proceedings. Third, arbitrators must determine the credibility of the testimony given by an employee who is accused of theft.[31]

When the employer suspects employee theft, an internal investigation may be held. As part of it, an employee or group of employees may be required to submit to a polygraph test. Polygraph or lie detector tests have been used for many years,

---

[29] The reader may recall the discussion of *Hines v. Anchor Motor Freight* in Chapter 11 in which several truck drivers were discharged for padding their travel expenses. It was later learned that a motel clerk, not the truck drivers, was the culprit.

[30] See William L. Taylor and Joseph P. Cangemi, "Employee Theft and Organizational Climate," *Personnel Journal* (October 1979); August Bequai, *White Collar Crime: A Twentieth Century Crisis* (Lexington, Massachusetts: D.C. Heath, 1978); and R.J. Healy and T.J. Walsh, "Security Policies, Programs, and Problems," in D. Yoder and H.G. Heneman, eds., *ASPA Handbook of Personnel and Industrial Relations, PAIR Policy and Program Management* (Berea, Ohio: American Society for Personnel Administration, 1979), pp. 1-79–1-93.

[31] Because of the stigma associated with a discharge for theft or dishonesty, arbitrators may be reluctant to support the termination of an employee who offers any plausible excuse. According to one experienced arbitrator: "When an employee is caught with the goods, in his or her locker, in a handbag or briefcase, in a car or even at home, the employee's defenses (and I have heard all of them) are usually among the following: 'The material was scrap'; 'I was framed by someone who put it in my locker, car, or home.'; 'I borrowed the tools overnight'; 'The tools were mine'; 'I carried the stuff off by mistake.'; 'I intended to return it later in the day.' Although these defenses are frequently incredible, they are often sufficient to create the doubts in the arbitrator's mind as to the employee's guilt or intentions that lead to a reversal of the penalty." Jean T. McKelvey, "Discipline and Discharge," in Arnold M. Zack, *Arbitration in Practice* (Ithaca, New York: ILR Press, Cornell University, 1984), p. 94.

but the reliability of such tests is so questionable that the results are usually given little weight in an arbitration hearing. In recent years, more cases of innocent employees having been dismissed for theft because of polygraph test results have appeared in the courts. Increasingly, the employees involved are suing for damages, and are collecting substantial settlements.[32] The American Psychological Association, the American Civil Liberties Union, the AFL-CIO, and the American Medical Association Council on Scientific Affairs have denounced polygraph testing as an inaccurate means of assessing honesty.[33] Kevin McGuiness, counsel for the Senate Committee on Labor and Human Resources, believes that in addition to the reliability problems associated with lie detector tests, "there is overwhelming evidence that employers are using polygraphs to justify activities that otherwise would be prohibited. Some employers use the test to screen out minority applicants and union sympathizers, or to get rid of employees who aren't liked."[34] Many states have, for years, banned the use of polygraph tests in the workplace.[35] The misuse of polygraph tests in employment decisions led to the passage of the Polygraph Protection Act of 1988, which outlaws the use of polygraphs for most pre-employment testing as well as for the random testing of employees. Employers may continue to use polygraph examinations on employees who are suspected of thefts or other criminal acts on the job.

Polygraph tests are not without their advocates. Days Inn of America has stated that between 1975 and 1985 the use of polygraphs reduced annual employee theft from $1 million to $115,000. Further, the company claims that the tests have resulted in $1 million in employee restitutions.[36] In spite of the success of Days Inn of America, polygraph testing in the workplace has been severely curtailed by state and federal legislation.

Some organizations have had considerable success in reducing employee theft by instituting an aggressive antitheft program that includes the following:[37]

1. Conscientious pre-employment screening. Reference checks may uncover employees who have stolen from previous employers.
2. A strong antitheft policy (perhaps incorporated into the collective bargaining agreement) should be established and communicated to all employees. Some employees wrongly believe that it is acceptable to take small or inexpensive items, scrap materials, or "discarded" supplies and equipment. An antitheft pol-

---

[32] One example, of two employees fired for theft at a securities firm, is described in Benjamin Kleinmuntz, "Lie Detectors Fail the Truth Test," *Harvard Business Review* (July–August 1985), p. 36.
[33] "Trends," *Bulletin to Management* (Washington, D.C.: The Bureau of National Affairs, Inc., September 25, 1986), p. 323. See also Lisa J. McCue, "Employee Screening: Who's Behind The Mask?" *Bottomline* (April 1986), pp. 19, 37–38.
[34] The Bureau of National Affairs, Inc., "No Future For Polygraphs," *Bulletin to Management* (Washington, D.C.: The Bureau of National Affairs, Inc., November 20, 1986), p. 381.
[35] As of early 1987, 22 states had outlawed lie detector use. Ed Bean, "More Firms Use 'Attitude Tests' to Keep Thieves Off the Payroll," *The Wall Street Journal* (February 27, 1987), p. 41.
[36] Washington Roundup, "It's A Lie," *Nation's Business* (December 1985), pp. 12–13.
[37] Ron Zemke, "Employee Theft: How To Cut Your Losses," *Training* (May 1986), p. 77. An alternative view is presented by Robert R. Taylor, "A Positive Guide to Theft Deterrence," *Personnel Journal* (August 1986), pp. 36–40. This article describes aggressive antitheft programs as oppressive and suggests a more positive program emphasizing employee dignity, respect, and support.

icy could, for example, make it clear that taking any of the employer's property, regardless of its apparent value, is grounds for discharge.
3. Orientation programs for new employees should include a discussion of the firm's antitheft policy and the impact of theft on all employees. Training programs can be used to teach employees how to spot and report employee theft.
4. Security controls, including computerized inventory control, frequent physical inventories, and routine package checking often help to reduce employee theft.
5. Once antitheft programs are in place, management and union representatives must continue to show concern about employee theft and a determination to end it.

Gambling

Because of its illegality in most states, gambling on company property may also be regarded as a form of dishonesty. Gambling may involve informal betting on sporting events among a few employees or it may involve organized "numbers" rackets run by outsiders who contact employees at work. Gambling can be disruptive to workplace morale and productivity and, in some cases, may encourage theft or fighting and assaults among employees. Arbitrators uphold disciplinary actions involving gambling when the employer has a well-publicized rule prohibiting such conduct. However, management must be able to offer specific proof that a worker was involved in illicit gambling activities.[38]

Arbitrators frequently reinstate employees who have been discharged for dishonesty. Unlike offenses such as absenteeism or rule violations, an employee discharged for dishonesty is forced to carry a stigma that can threaten his or her career. According to one arbitrator, when an employee is accused of criminal behavior, such as theft of property, the worker is likely to suffer a "diminution" of reputation of the "severest sort" in the employment community.[39] Because of a reluctance to label an employee as a thief, management may seize on an employee's violation of other company rules to justify termination.[40]

Off-Duty Misconduct

Employees may be charged with criminal misconduct not associated with their employment.[41] Arbitrators have generally held that employers may not discipline a worker for off-duty activities, since "to do so would constitute an invasion of the

---

[38] The BNA Staff, *Grievance Guide*, 7th ed. (Washington, D.C.: The Bureau of National Affairs, Inc., 1987), pp. 69–71.
[39] *General Electric Co.*, 70 LA 1097 (1978). Cited in BNA Editorial Staff, *Grievance Guide*, 7th ed. (Washington, D.C.: The Bureau of National Affairs, Inc., 1987), p. 54.
[40] The BNA Editorial Staff, *Grievance Guide*, 7th ed. (Washington, D.C.: The Bureau of National Affairs, Inc., 1987), p. 54.
[41] See Terry L. Leap, "When Can You Fire for Off-Duty Conduct?" *Harvard Business Review* (January–February 1988), pp. 28–30, 34, and 36; and Marvin F. Hill, Jr., and Mark L. Kahn, "Discipline and Discharge for Off-Duty Misconduct," in Walter J. Gershenfeld, ed., *Arbitration 1986: Current and Expanding Roles, Proceedings of the Thirty-Ninth Annual Meeting, National Academy of Arbitrators* (Washington, D.C.: The Bureau of National Affairs, Inc., 1987), pp. 121–154.

employee's personal life by the employer and would place the employer in the position of sitting in judgment on neighborhood morals, a matter which should be left to civil officers."[42] Most organizations do not attempt to influence the conduct of an employee's private life directly. However, a dilemma is created when off-duty conduct irreparably damages the employee's integrity, makes it exceedingly difficult for the employee to continue working with customers or co-workers, or significantly tarnishes the organization's image.[43] As one arbitrator noted, "there [must be] a direct and demonstrable relationship between the illicit conduct and the performance of the employee's job." The arbitrator further noted that it "cannot be merely assumed that particular conduct—even conduct so gross as to result in a criminal conviction—is related to job performance."[44] Cases in which arbitrators established that an employee's off-duty conduct had a negative impact on job performance or the organization's image have included the following:

▲ The Elyria, Ohio Board of Education dismissed a high school counselor after her conviction on a misdemeanor for permitting her husband to use their house for drug trafficking. The arbitrator said the board's action was reasonable because the counselor's conduct related directly to her work of advising students and parents on drug abuse.[45]

▲ Two truck drivers employed by a retail grocery chain went on a drinking spree during a layover and assaulted two other drivers employed by the same firm. Their intoxication, coupled with the injuries they inflicted on the other pair, disrupted the company's delivery schedule. According to the arbitrator, such misconduct was adequate grounds for discharge.[46]

▲ A woman was involved in a shooting incident during an argument at a friend's home. She was fired from her job in the laundry at the Maimonides Institute, a New York City institution for emotionally disturbed young people. The arbitrator upheld the institution's action because her presence at work made the residents apprehensive.[47]

▲ Northwest Airlines dismissed a flight attendant after he had admitted photographing an 18-year-old man in the nude during off-duty hours. He had recently returned to duty after being suspended for a similar offense. The arbitrator upheld the dismissal on the basis that "some people might be given pause" about traveling on an airline that is "under the control of persons so inept at managing their own affairs."[48]

There are also a number of cases in which the arbitrator ruled that an employee's off-duty conduct had little or no bearing on job performance or the organization's image.

---

[42] *Menzie Dairy Co.*, 45 LA 283 (1965).
[43] See Jolie Solomon, "Strategies for Handling the Arrest of an Employee," *The Wall Street Journal* (March 29, 1990), p. B1.
[44] *Internal Revenue Service*, 77 LA 19 (1981).
[45] *Elyria Board of Education*, 86 LA 921 (1985).
[46] *Lucky Stores, Inc.*, 83 LA 760 (1984).
[47] *Maimonides Institute*, 69 LA 876 (1977).
[48] *Northwest Airlines, Inc.*, 53 LA 203 (1969).

- The Potomac Electric Power Company fired a credit collector for making obscene telephone calls, while off duty, to the teenage daughter of a customer of the utility. The collector had met her during a business call at the customer's home. An arbitrator reinstated the man without back pay because the firm had no policy regulating employee off-duty conduct, coupled with the offender's satisfactory work record, which spanned more than two decades.[49]
- Air California discharged a service employee who, after leaving his work shift, took a $20 dare from several fellow employees and "streaked" in front of the airport terminal building, wearing only a ski mask, t-shirt, and cowboy boots. The arbitrator reinstated the man and stated that his conduct was not lewd, caused no moral problems among other employees, and resulted in only minimal negative publicity.[50]
- Management fired a female employee after discovering that she was involved in an extramarital affair with a co-worker (who had earlier been pressured into resigning). The arbitrator dismissed the contention that the employee had been fired in order to protect the firm's reputation. It was noted that the two were "consenting adults" whose behavior had no adverse impact on the workplace.[51]
- An asphalt refining company discharged an employee for selling a small amount of marijuana to a friend from his high school days. The friend was working as an undercover agent. An arbitrator reinstated the worker on the ground that the publicity surrounding his arrest and his three-year suspended sentence did not unreasonably harm the company's reputation or product, nor did it render him incapable of safely performing his duties.[52]

Employees who are arrested and incarcerated for various crimes present a difficult problem for employers, union representatives, and arbitrators. Individuals arrested and charged with serious crimes may spend lengthy periods of time in jail before authorities can arrange for a trial. Some companies adopt the stance of "standing by" their employees and assuming their innocence until they are proven guilty, whereas others may suspend or even dismiss employees who are accused of felonies or other serious misconduct. Arbitrators generally uphold discharges when an employee is convicted of a serious crime, even when the sentence is suspended and the employee is released. A liquor store clerk fatally injured an elderly woman who intervened in a dispute between the man and his wife on a downtown Pittsburgh street. The clerk was discharged, convicted of manslaughter, and later released through a prison work program. The arbitrator sustained the discharge on the ground that the store's customers would be reluctant to enter the premises if the perpetrator of such a violent deed were working in the store.[53]

Even when employees are acquitted as the result of criminal proceedings, they are not necessarily entitled to reinstatement. Persons may be acquitted because evidence is discovered that strongly indicates innocence, because a lack of evidence

---

[49] *Potomac Electric Power Co.*, 83 LA 449 (1984).
[50] *Air California*, 63 LA 350 (1974).
[51] *Operating Engineers*, 68 LA 254 (1977).
[52] *Vulcan Asphalt Refining Company*, 78 LA 1311 (1982).
[53] *Commonwealth of Pennsylvania*, 65 LA 280 (1975).

makes it unlikely that guilt can be established beyond a reasonable doubt, or because they "beat the system" on a legal technicality. Although a collective bargaining agreement or past practice may require that the company reinstate an employee who is acquitted, arbitrators are not bound by the outcome of criminal proceedings. As one arbitrator noted: "It matters not that rigorous protection in the criminal law saved the individual from criminal penalties because such fact does not constitute a bar to the employer's right to protect itself and other employees."[54]

In summary, illegal acts committed outside the realm of employment present a difficult issue to resolve. The nature of the job and the offense generally determine the employer's action. For example, a teacher accused of immoral conduct off the job might be more likely to face suspension than would a machinist because of the potential risk to students. A bank employee accused of armed robbery would probably be removed from the job pending the outcome of a trial because of the nature of the crime, whereas a laborer may not be suspended. An airline pilot found guilty of driving under the influence of alcohol would probably face more severe employment consequences than would a clerk. The accused employee's rights to retain his or her job must be balanced against the employer's right to protect property, employees, and customers. Unfortunately, such dilemmas are difficult to resolve; clear-cut solutions are rarely apparent. Keeping this in mind, Table 16–3 offers some general guidelines for union and management representatives who must evaluate employee off-duty misconduct.

Table 16–3 ▲ Disciplinary Guidelines For Off-Duty Misconduct

Establish written prohibitions for specific types of off-duty conduct that management regards as unacceptable.

Some organizations have rules that result in automatic discharge for a guilty plea or conviction of a felony. Others list specific behaviors such as drug possession, theft, or assault that are grounds for immediate disciplinary action.

Use caution in initiating disciplinary actions that are heavily influenced by the moral or political views of one decision maker.

Occasionally an otherwise prudent manager who has no tolerance for extramarital affairs, homosexuality, or unorthodox lifestyles will overreact in suspending or discharging an employee.

Formulate procedures for employees who are charged with a crime and awaiting trial.

An employer is not obligated to retain a worker who faces a long period of incarceration before being tried, but employees released on bail may want to return to work. If the nature of the crime makes it inadvisable to allow the employee to work, the company may opt for temporary suspension. Final disciplinary action can then be taken once the case is resolved. As a gesture of good faith, the company may offer to reimburse the employee for lost income if the case is later dropped or there is an acquittal.

---

[54] *New York City Health and Hospital Corp.*, 76 LA 387 (1981).

Table 16–3 ▲ Disciplinary Guidelines For Off-Duty Misconduct (Continued)

Stipulate how the organization will deal with employees who receive suspended sentences.	Individuals who either plead guilty or who are convicted often receive suspended sentences that, once again, make them available for work. In some instances, the suspended sentence is contingent upon the employee having a full-time job. Arbitrators tend to show leniency when the courts do likewise. In the absence of an arbitration award or state statute protecting the employment rights of convicted felons, however, the employer must decide whether reinstatement is advisable by considering factors such as the employee's trustworthiness, propensity for violence or drug abuse, and the reaction of customers and co-workers.
Anticipate the possibility that an employee who is guilty of a serious crime may "beat the system."	Employees who avoid criminal prosecution because of legal technicalities in the face of overwhelming evidence of guilt may still be disciplined by management. Unless the employer has agreed to base disciplinary action on the outcome of a criminal proceeding, then the use of double jeopardy is legally permissible.
Consider the impact that an employee's off-duty acts will have on co-workers and formulate plans for dealing with their concerns.	It may be possible to calm co-worker fears by thoroughly explaining why the employee is being reinstated. Co-workers should understand that the reinstatement is based on an extensive investigation of the off-duty incident and its impact on the employee's job. Care should be taken to set the record straight on exaggerated or distorted stories surrounding the employee's conduct while protecting sensitive information surrounding the case. Management should also consider transferring the employee to a different location if irreconcilable differences and tensions persist.
Decide how much negative public opinion can be tolerated before sacrificing an employee.	When customers object to an employee's reinstatement, consider the following points. First, how many customers have complained? One or two complaints out of several thousand potential customers may not be a reasonable basis for disciplinary action. Negative public reaction can be strong, however, when employees holding jobs requiring high moral values engage in off-duty misconduct (especially where contact with children is involved). Second, can a competitor exploit the bad publicity of an unsavory off-duty incident and harm the employer's business? In the latter case, the employer may have little choice other than discharge unless effective public relations tactics can be used to offset the competitor's claims.

Reprinted by permission of the *Harvard Business Review*, "When Can You Fire For Off-duty Conduct?," by Terry L. Leap (January–February 1988). Copyright 1988 by the President and Fellows of Harvard College; All rights reserved.

Employee Insubordination and Abusive Behavior

Insubordination is one of the more common disciplinary problems. Employees are generally expected to comply with reasonable management orders because such compliance is considered essential to the employer's business operations. The "obey–now–grieve later" requirement discussed in previous chapters is based on management's right to direct work activities without unnecessary interruptions by employees who refuse to obey supervisory orders. When an employee willfully disobeys or disregards a supervisor's directive, the organization usually has the right to discipline the employee for insubordination. In addition, the use of profane language or threats by employees toward supervisory personnel is a form of insubordination because it diminishes the employer's authority to direct the workforce.[55] Work slowdowns or mass refusals to work may also be regarded as a form of insubordination. Lamson & Sessions Co. fired 95 hourly workers at its Midland Steel Products truck-frame plant when they disregarded written warnings and failed to report for weekend overtime work. The discharged employees had been working without a collective bargaining agreement after the contract between the company and the United Auto Workers had expired two months earlier.[56]

In order to establish a case of insubordination, management must show that (1) the supervisor issued a direct order (either orally or in writing), (2) the employee received and understood the order, and (3) the employee refused to obey the directive through an explicit statement of refusal or through nonperformance. For example, employees have been disciplined for acts such as refusing to move an automobile to a proper parking space on company property,[57] displaying an "air of insubordination" toward management,[58] refusing to sign company forms making an employee responsible for work tools,[59] and failing to report to a supervisor as required before and after a shift,[60] to name a few. In addition, employees who fail to follow standard operating procedures may be guilty of insubordination. A teacher was given a one-day suspension after ignoring a bomb threat and requiring students to remain in the classroom to complete an exam. Although the teacher claimed that false alarms were common, the fact that he "deliberately and willfully" disobeyed "clear and reasonable policy" was adequate grounds for suspension.[61]

Another type of insubordination involves physical assaults and the use of abusive language toward supervisors and others. Physical aggression toward supervisors by employees is almost always grounds for immediate discharge, even when such assaults occur off-duty and away from company property.[62] Physical attacks are regarded by arbitrators as uncivilized behavior that carries a criminal liability and undermines management's authority in the workplace.[63]

---

[55] The BNA Editorial Staff, *Grievance Guide*, 7th ed. (Washington, D.C.: The Bureau of National Affairs, Inc., 1987), p. 29.
[56] "Lamson & Sessions Dismisses 95 Workers In Overtime Dispute," *The Wall Street Journal* (May 11, 1989).
[57] The BNA Staff, *Grievance Guide*, 7th ed. (Washington, D.C.: The Bureau of National Affairs, Inc., 1987), p. 30.
[58] *Federal Correctional Institution*, 75 LA 295 (1980).
[59] *Washington Hospital Center*, 75 LA 32 (1980).
[60] *Budd Company*, 75 LA 281 (1980).
[61] *Whitehall-Copley School District*, 76 LA 325 (1981).
[62] Arbitrators have held that off-duty encounters between supervisory and nonsupervisory personnel may not be grounds for discharge if the encounter is purely personal. It is hard to imagine, however, that such altercations would not have some negative impact on workplace relations.
[63] Some arbitrators believe that a distinction should be made between persons who attack supervisors and those who attack nonsupervisory personnel. However, the author believes that any form of unprovoked aggression is serious and warrants severe disciplinary action or discharge.

Abusive and threatening language is also a form of insubordination. In determining whether an employee was properly disciplined for abusive or threatening language, managers, union representatives, and arbitrators should consider the following factors: (1) whether the abusive language was provoked by the supervisor, (2) whether it was done in the presence of other employees or customers, and (3) whether abusive or profane language is part of the "shop talk" in the particular workplace.[64] Employees who use racist, sexist, or religious epithets in the workplace may create a legal liability for the employer under Title VII of the 1964 Civil Rights Act. A more difficult-to-resolve issue involves instances of employee grumbling and disparaging remarks that stop short of defiance and disrespect. Such remarks might be regarded as a healthy venting of frustrations and not as grounds for disciplinary action. However, there are occasions when the work environment becomes polluted with derogatory remarks that are malicious and that undermine management's authority. Before management takes disciplinary action, employees who make such remarks should be given a clear warning that such behavior will not be tolerated.

Arbitrators are occasionally called upon to hear cases in which an employee was disciplined because of abusive behavior toward the firm's customers or other members of the public. Although abusive behavior of this nature is often grounds for severe disciplinary action, arbitrators must distinguish between hearsay evidence and conclusive evidence that an employee was disrespectful or abusive. As noted in Chapters 11 and 12, arbitrators admit hearsay evidence only when other corroborating evidence is available to help determine the truth. A bus driver accused of trying to kiss a 17-year-old female passenger was not properly discharged, according to an arbitrator, since the woman could not provide dates or descriptions of other passengers who might have witnessed the event.[65] Employees of public service organizations, such as hospital workers or public transportation workers, are often held to a higher standard of conduct toward patrons than employees of other organizations. However, arbitrators carefully examine accusations of discourtesy by hospital patients who are likely to misinterpret the actions of health care personnel. For example, a hospital orderly who physically restrains a violent mental patient is not guilty of abusive behavior unless unnecessary force was used. Furthermore, arbitrators may view, as a mitigating circumstance, the fact that a customer or member of the public provoked an employee into abusive behavior.

Employee Incompetency

Employee incompetency poses a somewhat different dilemma than the previously discussed disciplinary cases, because the employee may not be directly at fault. Incompetency refers to an *inability* rather than an unwillingness to perform in an acceptable manner. Employees may have been carelessly hired, lack proper training, or possess physical or mental impairments that prevent satisfactory job performance. A good performance appraisal system can be used to document incompetency, and it may also provide a basis for suggesting appropriate remedies. Incompetency, for example, may be eliminated through remedial training or through

---

[64] James R. Redeker, *Discipline: Policies and Procedures* (Washington, D.C.: The Bureau of National Affairs, Inc., 1983), pp. 170–181.
[65] *Capital District Transportation Authority*, 72 LA 1313 (1979).

transfer to a less demanding job. Dismissal should be used only as a last resort, especially for older or handicapped employees.[66] Improved hiring practices should be considered as a means of preventing incompetent applicants from becoming incompetent employees. Management may have the right under some collective bargaining agreements to discharge probationary employees for incompetency without challenge from the union.

Carelessness, Negligent Actions, and Horseplay

Carelessness and negligent actions may range from gross negligence to inattention to job responsibilities. Gross negligence is a willful disregard for safety procedures that places employees or customers in an unsafe or life-threatening predicament or causes extensive damage to buildings, equipment, and materials. At the other extreme, unintentional carelessness might result in minor property damage, but no threat of bodily injury. However, arbitrators have upheld the discharge of employees who are habitually careless, even when no single incident results in severe damage.[67] Furthermore, arbitrators are usually less lenient with employees who are disciplined because of safety violations while driving company motor vehicles.

The disciplinary sanctions taken against an employee who commits a careless or unsafe act often depends on the employee's skill level or training. An act may be deemed "inappropriate" if it is done by an employee who, by virtue of his or her experience, training, and capabilities, should not have committed such an act. For example, an employee trained in the proper use of a forklift truck who carries an oversized or unbalanced load that overturns is probably guilty of carelessness and negligence. An untrained operator who is requested by a supervisor to drive a forklift with an unbalanced load may, on the other hand, not be guilty of wrongdoing. Personnel policies or collective bargaining agreements might also distinguish between careless acts that do not result in injury or damage and acts that carry some negative consequence. Should an organization only discipline employees for unsafe acts that result in damage, or should all acts of carelessness or negligence be punished regardless of the outcome? The potential severity of the damage is a prime consideration. An employee who places the lives of co-workers in jeopardy (even if no lives were lost or injuries sustained), is probably a prime candidate for immediate discharge. Another consideration is the presence of mitigating factors. For example, an employee who is occasionally required to work a double shift (16 hours) may commit a careless act because of fatigue. In addition, an employee without a history of negligent behavior is generally granted more leniency than one whose record contains acts of aberrant behavior.

Unlike gross negligence, horseplay does not involve a malicious or willful attempt to cause bodily injury or property damage.[68] Nevertheless, the consequences of horseplay can be serious. Arbitrators will generally support the discharge of

---

[66] Incompetency is probably the only valid reason for using *demotion* as an employee discipline and control measure.
[67] The BNA Editorial Staff, *Grievance Guide*, 7th ed. (Washington, D.C.: The Bureau of National Affairs, Inc., 1987), p. 147.
[68] Horseplay has been referred to as the "'first cousin' to willful intent to damage." See *Ozark Lead Co.*, 69 LA 1227 (1978).

an employee whose horseplay poses a serious danger; otherwise, lesser forms of punishment are usually warranted.

▲ Some Issues Affecting Disciplinary Measures

Use of Reasonable Rules and Standards

Employees are more likely to accept and abide by policies, standards, and rules that are perceived as being reasonable. Of course, the definition of what is "reasonable" will vary from one employee to another. Generally speaking, employees and arbitrators will regard a policy, standard, or rule as being reasonable *if* he or she understands its underlying rationale. That is, why does this policy exist? What benefits accrue from having such a policy? What negative consequences might occur if this policy or rule were violated? For example, as a means of reducing employee theft, female employees in retail establishments may not be allowed to carry purses or pocketbooks with them while they are in customer areas. Most employees are willing to accept such a rule if (1) it is applied uniformly, (2) it is clearly communicated to each employee, and (3) the reasoning behind the policy is understood and accepted.

Policies that were reasonable in the past may become antiquated due to changes in the workplace. Technological advances in security systems, for example, may make the "no-purse" policy obsolete. Therefore, management must periodically assess policies, standards, and rules to ensure that they remain relevant. A prime test for reasonableness is to carefully examine rules that represent employee disciplinary troublespots. Rules that are repeatedly violated may need elimination, restructuring, or re-emphasis to employees regarding their importance.

Burden of Proof, Due Process, and Equal Protection

As a general rule, the burden of proof in demonstrating wrongdoing by an employee falls on management. In nearly all grievances involving disciplinary action, the employer assumes the role of plaintiff and the worker that of the defendant. The employer has the responsibility of initiating disciplinary action, collecting evidence, and presenting a case against the employee. The quantum of proof required of the employer is higher in discharge cases than in disciplinary proceedings, where the penalty imposed on the grievant is less severe. Discharge has perhaps been over harshly characterized as the "capital punishment" of industrial relations. Nevertheless, arbitrators require a high degree of proof before sustaining management's decision to discharge an employee, especially when an offense involves criminal intent or moral turpitude.

Although the concept of due process is somewhat elusive and subject to varying degrees of interpretation, four elements appear essential. First, the employee must be made aware that he or she has committed a violation of the rules. Second, the employer must supply credible evidence that supports whatever accusation is being made against the employee. Third, the employee must be made aware of the nature of such evidence. Fourth, the employee must have the opportunity to question and refute the evidence against him or her.

Another hallmark of a sound disciplinary procedure is equal protection or treatment. The term "equal" does not necessarily mean that each employee committing the same offense will receive *exactly* the same treatment or punishment. Differences in employees in terms of seniority, work record, and past disciplinary incidents will ultimately mean that some employees are treated differently than others. In addition, extenuating or mitigating circumstances can play a paramount role. The key to equal protection lies in the employees' perception of whether fair treatment was accorded in a specific case. As long as there are not radical differences in punishments for similar offenses and there is the belief that management tailored the disciplinary action to the offense, there should be little controversy over equal protection. The key is not to ignore offenses by some employees while punishing others. Furthermore, the employer should keep records on employee offenses, circumstances surrounding each offense, and the penalties handed out. By reviewing previous cases, union and management representatives are better able to handle new cases involving similar facts and circumstances equitably.

The Concept of Just Cause

Discipline procedures frequently call for discipline or discharge for "cause" or "just cause."[69] The concept of "just cause" is rarely defined in any precise fashion. As in all grievances, arbitrators look first to the terms, provisions, and spirit of the collective bargaining agreement for guidance. In addition, custom and past practice play a prominent role in defining "just cause" in many disciplinary grievance hearings. Arbitrator Lawrence Stessin defines "just cause" as "what a reasonable person mindful of the habits and customs of industrial life and standards of justice and fair dealing, would decide."[70] Arbitrators rely heavily on common sense to determine what constitutes "just cause." Much of what constitutes "just cause" comes from the "common law of the shop." In writing their opinions, arbitrators frequently read published arbitration awards (see Chapter 12). The wisdom garnered from published opinions often ensures that arbitration decisions and awards will reflect the principles of "just cause."

Discharge: The Ultimate Penalty

Discharge is the common penalty for serious infractions as well as the final penalty for employees who have committed multiple offenses of a less serious nature. When discharging an employee, management runs the risk of creating a wrongful discharge

---

[69] According to The Bureau of National Affairs, Inc., 86 percent of the agreements surveyed contain the "cause" or "just cause" provisions. The remaining provisions specify individual offenses for which an employee can be discharged. See The Bureau of National Affairs, Inc., "Basic Patterns: Discharge, Discipline, and Resignation," *Collective Bargaining Negotiations & Contracts* (Washington, D.C.: The Bureau of National Affairs, Inc., 1989), section 40.
[70] Lawrence Stessin, *Employee Discipline* (Washington, D.C.: The Bureau of National Affairs, Inc., 1973), cited in Jean T. McKelvey, "Discipline and Discharge," in Arnold M. Zack, ed., *Arbitration in Practice* (Ithaca, New York: ILR Press, Cornell University, 1984), p. 90.

liability. Wrongful discharges have been characterized as "the tort of the 1980s"; such suits will likely continue into the 1990s. Terminated employees are suing their former employers at increasing rates and, in many cases, are winning large judgments. Unions also run the risk of becoming embroiled in unfair representation suits if they fail to process the grievance of discharged employees in a competent and timely manner. Table 16–4 summarizes the procedures that should be used to protect employers and unions from wrongful discharge and unfair representation suits.

Table 16–4 ▲ Factors to Consider in Discharging Employees

1. *Make sure that you have supporting evidence and documentation.*

These should include letters regarding previous disciplinary incidents; testimony from witnesses; photographs and other evidence of property damage or bodily injury at the hands of the discharged employee; performance evaluations; records from earlier grievance proceedings; documentation pertaining to criminal or civil proceedings; notes from the employee's file on previous disciplinary counseling sessions.

2. *Adhere to the established grievance or corrective disciplinary procedures.*

Follow the grievance procedure as outlined in the collective bargaining agreement. Comply with the spirit and language of the collective bargaining agreement. Adhere to time limits in the grievance procedure.

3. *Put the conditions and terms of the discharge in writing.*

Explain why the employee is being discharged in specific terms. Glittering generalities such as "you didn't work out" are not acceptable and may create a legal liability.

4. *If the employee is given severance pay or other benefits in exchange for signing an agreement to hold the employer harmless from legal liability, do not allow the employee to sign the agreement immediately.*

Make the employee wait several days and encourage him or her to consult a trusted friend, relative, or legal counsel before signing the agreement. By establishing a short waiting period, terminated employees cannot claim that they were coerced into signing and later use this as a reason to file a civil suit.

5. *Respect the dignity of the employee.*

Avoid anger or personal confrontations during termination proceedings. Terminations should be made in private. Information surrounding the termination should be kept confidential.

6. *Be careful about writing letters of recommendation or releasing information to other companies who may want to hire the employee.*

Generally speaking, the good-faith release of truthful information about a terminated employee will not create a legal liability. However, information should be released only to those who have a "need to know." Be extremely careful about writing positive letters of recommendation that are not indicative of an employee's job performance. Companies may sue former employers for providing inaccurate information that led to the hiring of an incompetent or dangerous employee.

7. *Employees who "voluntarily" resign may cause legal problems.*

Employees who resign under pressure may be regarded by the courts as "constructively discharged." The courts often view this form of discharge in the same vein as an outright firing.

▲ Corrective Disciplinary Policy and Procedures

To ensure due process and equal protection, management may adopt what is known as a corrective (or progressive) disciplinary system. Such systems usually contain the following elements:

1. A categorization of violations that either specifies "minor, moderate, and serious" offenses or provides a set of criteria for categorizing such offenses.
2. A system of penalties to match the respective violations. The severity of the penalties increases with each subsequent violation.
3. An appeal mechanism that is either part of the regular grievance procedure contained in the collective bargaining agreement or a separate procedure for discipline and discharge cases.

Categories of Violations

As an initial step, union and management officials should categorize violations as minor, moderate, and serious. Categories of violations may be written into the collective bargaining agreement or the employee handbook. For example, serious violations are those that could result in the discharge of an employee on the first offense. Theft, physical attack on a supervisor or co-worker, and acts that endanger the lives of others would likely fall into this category. Moderate violations are those that normally warrant definite disciplinary action, but not discharge for a first offense. Neglect of duty, absence without permission, insubordination, and sleeping on the job are typically regarded as "moderate" violations. Minor infractions are those that generally result in discharge only after repeated violations and warnings. Examples of minor violations might include occasional loafing on the job, tardiness, minor safety violations, and the like.

When categorizing violations, management must consider the skill level and professionalism of its employees, the nature of their jobs, and the impact of the infraction upon safety, workflow, other employees, customer image, and other factors affecting the organizational culture. Violations that might be regarded as "minor" in one organization could be regarded as "serious" in another. For example, a librarian who arrives at work after a night of heavy drinking may not experience a subpar level of job performance that would warrant disciplinary action (in fact, the severe headache and nausea is probably sufficient punishment). A bus driver reporting to work in the same condition, however, could pose a very serious threat to passenger safety. Under these circumstances, the violation would probably be regarded as serious and could result in an immediate discharge.

Ultimately, each firm must determine how it wishes to categorize various violations. It is not possible to think of and classify every conceivable violation. Therefore, management may wish to establish a set of criteria that will aid in determining whether a violation should be regarded as serious, moderate, or minor. Table 16–5 provides a possible set or criteria.

The criteria listed in Table 16–5 are intended to categorize offenses only—not to determine the final disposition of a disciplinary incident. Previously mentioned factors, such as extenuating circumstances, the employee's disciplinary and work record, and so forth, are normally used in determining the ultimate outcome of a specific disciplinary case.[71] The criteria of Table 16–5 should serve to guide managers as they categorize a multitude of potential employee offenses. However, the final categorization will depend on the nature of the employees, their jobs, and the organizational culture.

Table 16–5 ▲ Violation Categories

Minor	Moderate	Serious
1. Little or no disruption to workflow.	1. Moderate disruption to workflow.	1. Severe and expensive disruption to workflow.
2. No damage to products or equipment.	2. Some damage to products or equipment.	2. Severe and expensive damage to products and equipment.
3. Inconsequential safety hazard posed to employee or others.	3. Employee and possibly others were exposed to a definite safety hazard.	3. Employee and others were placed in a life-threatening situation.
4. Conduct was unacceptable for this type of worker (skill and professional level), but not grossly "out of line."	4. Conduct was definitely unacceptable for this type of worker. Employee fully understood that actions were wrong.	4. Conduct was outside the scope of that normally expected of a prudent, rational person.
5. Employee's behavior can be corrected by simply discussing it with him or her.	5. Employee's behavior may be corrected by further training and counseling.	5. Employee's behavior was either not correctable or was correctable only through extensive training or psychiatric counseling.
6. No state or federal law was violated.	6. The act committed was a misdemeanor (on the job).	6. The act committed was a felony (on the job).
7. Morale and welfare of employees was not significantly disrupted.	7. Morale and welfare of other employees was disrupted.	7. Morale and welfare of other employees was significantly disrupted and possibly irreparably impaired.

---

[71] See Patrick L. McConnell, "Is Your Discipline Process the Victim of Red Tape?" *Personnel Journal* (March 1986), pp. 64–71; and Roger B. Madsen and Barbara Knudson-Fields, "Productive Progressive Discipline Procedures," *Management Solutions* (May 1987), pp. 17–25.

The Penalty Structure

An equitable penalty system has two characteristics: it tailors the penalty to the offense, and it ensures that employees who commit similar transgressions are treated in similar fashion. Table 16–6 provides an example of a penalty structure associated with a corrective disciplinary system. Penalties generally range from a written warning to discharge.

Table 16–6 portrays a system of increasingly severe penalties, with the ultimate sanction being discharge. Serious violations *can* result in discharge on the first offense and *will* result in discharge on the second. Minor violations, on the other hand, do not result in discharge before the third offense; the employee may be offered as many as four chances. The use of minimum and maximum penalties for each offense allows management a degree of flexibility to consider both the precise nature of the offense and any extenuating circumstances.

There are two additional noteworthy considerations regarding the penalty structure depicted in Table 16–6. First, the system should impose time limits between offenses. That is, a statute of limitations is necessary. For example, should an employee who committed a minor violation five years ago be credited with a second offense if another minor violation occurs? An employee's disciplinary record may be expunged if no further violations occur within one or two years. This rule offers a fresh start to employees who improve their behavior. Second, what happens if an employee commits a combination of violations? For example, if an employee is caught loafing on the job (a minor violation) and six months later has an unexcused absence (another minor violation), then the absence is generally considered to be a second minor offense that carries more stringent penalties. If an employee commits a minor violation and then follows with a moderate violation (first offense),

Table 16–6 ▲ Corrective Discipline System

Serious Violations

1st Offense		2nd Offense
minimum Suspension (1 month)	*maximum* Discharge	Discharge

Moderate Violations

1st Offense		2nd Offense		3rd Offense
minimum Suspension (1 week)	*maximum* Suspension (1 month)	*minimum* Suspension (1 month)	*maximum* Discharge	Discharge

Minor Violations

1st Offense		2nd Offense		3rd Offense		4th Offense	
min. oral warning	*max.* written reprimand	*min.* written reprimand	*max.* suspension (1 week)	*min.* suspension (1 week)	*max.* discharge	*min.* discharge	*max.*

Adapted from Terry L. Leap and Michael D. Crino, *Personnel/Human Resource Management* (New York: Macmillan Publishing Company, 1989), p. 500. Reprinted with permission.

then the employer will probably credit the worker with a first moderate offense, but may elect to impose the maximum penalty (a one-month suspension). Regardless of how multiple violations are handled, the key is to be as consistent as possible. Otherwise, employees will begin to view the entire process as capricious and arbitrary.

Corrective Discipline: The Bottom Line

Union and management officials who carefully design and administer a corrective discipline system are likely to reap the benefits of improved employee performance and morale as well as protection if grievance proceedings or lawsuits arise. The underlying rationale of a corrective discipline system is that employees are expected to perform in a safe, competent, and reliable manner; otherwise, they can expect that sanctions will be imposed. In return, the employee has a right to expect fair and consistent treatment from the employer. The essence of corrective discipline consists of the following features:[72]

1. An adequate *warning system* is established. Incidents of employee misconduct are well documented, and the employee is counseled and fully aware that further incidents will lead to more severe penalties.
2. *Enforcement is consistent* among employees. The employee is assured of equal protection, free from discriminatory application of discipline policies.
3. *The penalties are matched with the offense.* A penalty structure such as the one outlined in Table 16–6 prevents management from overreacting to a specific offense.
4. *Due process* is ensured. Each employee receives a full hearing, cognizant of the evidence brought against him or her. Furthermore, the system allows the employee to rebut evidence presented by management.
5. Management has *adequate flexibility* to tailor the penalty to a specific violation by considering an employee's work record and extenuating circumstances. Corrective discipline systems with minimum and maximum penalties provide consistent enforcement and yet allow a certain degree of flexibility when circumstances warrant it.

▲ Arbitral Review and Modification of Disciplinary Sanctions

A corrective disciplinary system should allow grievances involving employee infractions to be resolved in a fair and expeditious manner. Disciplinary cases that reach the arbitration stage, however, often involve important contractual or man-

---

[72] Jill Hauser List, "In Defense of Traditional Discipline," *Personnel Administrator* (June 1986), p. 42; and Rodney P. Beary, "Discipline Policy–A Neglected Personnel Tool," *Administrative Management* (November 1985), pp. 21–24, for a discussion of some of the listed points. On occasion, employees engage in very peculiar or bizarre behaviors both on and off the job. These behaviors create difficult disciplinary problems, and standard approaches to discipline may not provide guidance. For a discussion of bizarre employee behavior, see Terry L. Leap and Michael D. Crino, "How to Deal with Bizarre Employee Behavior," *Harvard Business Review* (May–June 1986), pp. 18–22.

agerial principles. Arbitrators must examine the facts surrounding a discipline case along with relevant contract provisions to determine whether the penalty imposed on the grievant by management is "for just cause." Most collective bargaining agreements either implicitly or explicitly allow arbitrators to modify disciplinary penalties. Arbitrators are reluctant to overturn disciplinary penalties imposed by management when the proceedings were fair, the decision was not made in haste, and there was no evidence of capricious or arbitrary treatment of the grievant. The mere fact that management has imposed a somewhat different or more severe penalty than the arbitrator would have imposed is not, by itself, justification for reversing management's decision. However, arbitrators are not reluctant to modify disciplinary action by management if the disciplinary proceedings were not fair, extenuating circumstances were ignored,[73] or the evidence suggests that management's actions were unfairly discriminatory. Table 16–7 summarizes criteria that arbitrators use in evaluating disciplinary penalties.

Table 16–7 ▲ Arbitral Evaluation of Disciplinary Penalties

Nature of the Offense:

Arbitrators must judge whether the offense was sufficiently severe to warrant immediate discharge rather than giving the grievant a second chance. A related issue is whether corrective discipline could be used (if permitted by the contract or because of past practice) to avoid further offenses by the grievant.

Due Process and Procedural Requirements:

The arbitrator is interested in whether management fully investigated the facts surrounding the offense before initiating disciplinary action. It must be determined whether the grievant was informed of the reasons for the disciplinary action when the penalty was imposed. Grievant and union representatives should be allowed to question management officials about the offense and examine evidence obtained by management. Management should not conceal or withhold pertinent evidence. Disciplinary penalties have been modified when the arbitrator discovered that the procedural requirements and the spirit of the disciplinary procedure were not followed. Arbitrators may overturn a disciplinary penalty if management attempted to place the grievant in "double jeopardy" by imposing a disciplinary penalty and then later increasing its severity.

Grievant's Employment Record:

An offense may be mitigated by a good employment record or aggravated by a poor one. A series of disciplinary incidents may serve to establish a "course of conduct" by an employee that warrants careful consideration by the arbitrator. Arbitrators often do not consider past rule infractions by the grievant if management failed to provide a warning or reprimand for the earlier offense. Some collective bargaining agreements place a time limit on the extent to which management may consider prior disciplinary incidents.

---

[73] Modification of an overly severe disciplinary penalty by an arbitrator should not be confused with the exercise of leniency (clemency). An arbitrator may sustain the penalty imposed by management, yet *recommend* leniency. Management may then decide whether to follow the arbitrator's suggestion and reduce the penalty. See Frank Elkouri and Edna Asper Elkouri, *How Arbitration Works*, 4th ed. (Washington, D.C.: The Bureau of National Affairs, Inc., 1985), pp. 669–670.

Table 16–7 ▲ Arbitral Evaluation of Disciplinary Penalties (Continued)

Length of Service with the Organization:

Employees with lengthy service records that are relatively free of disciplinary problems are often given the benefit of the doubt by arbitrators, especially when the loss of seniority and employee benefits (e.g., retirement benefits) would create a severe hardship on the employee.

Knowledge of Company Rules:

A rule must be reasonable, consistently applied, and widely disseminated. To the extent that these conditions are not met, an arbitrator may decide to modify a disciplinary penalty that was given because of a rule violation. Social norms that dictate normally accepted conduct might also be regarded as "reasonable and widely disseminated rules" by arbitrators. For example, prohibitions against theft, bringing firearms to the workplace, or physical assault are well understood by civilized people and need not be put in writing or communicated to employees.

Lax Enforcement of Rules by Management:

Arbitrators are likely to overturn disciplinary penalties when management has known about, but ignored, similar violations in the past. When management decides to crack down and begin stricter enforcement of such rules, they should provide adequate warning to employees. However, management's lax enforcement of minor violations of a rule (e.g., employees "stealing" small quantities of scrap materials) does not imply that more serious violations of the same rule will be condoned (e.g., stealing large quantities of scrap materials).

Management Contributes to a Disciplinary Offense:

Arbitrators may overturn a penalty if management contributed to the violation. A supervisor might provoke an act of employee insubordination, or employees might observe management violating certain rules and conclude that it is acceptable for them to do likewise.

Unequal or Discriminatory Treatment:

It is generally accepted that enforcement of rules and assessment of discipline must be exercised in a consistent manner. Arbitrators usually hold that employees who engage in the same type of misconduct should be disciplined similarly unless there are differing degrees of fault or different mitigating or aggravating circumstances. Arbitrators may be especially suspicious of disciplinary actions taken against union officers and supporters.

Adapted from Frank Elkouri and Edna Asper Elkouri, *How Arbitration Works*, 4th ed. (Washington, D.C.: The Bureau of National Affairs, Inc., 1985), pp. 670–688. Reprinted with permission.

▲ Arbitral Remedies in Discharge and Discipline Cases

When examining a disciplinary grievance and penalty, the arbitrator will either uphold management's action, modify the penalty, or decide that the grievant was not disciplined or discharged for just cause. Employees who have been fired as the result of a disciplinary incident may be reinstated with full back pay, seniority, and employee benefits; discharged employees may also be reinstated with total or partial *loss* of back pay, seniority, and benefits. In addition, reinstated employees may be required to abide by certain conditions such as remaining drug-free, resigning from an outside job, losing weight, or faithfully attending sessions at an alcohol rehabilitation center.

The extent to which an arbitrator is allowed to modify a penalty may be controlled by the contract. Some agreements provide that the arbitrator is limited to the finding of guilt or innocence only. If the grievant is guilty of the infraction, the penalty stands; otherwise, the grievant is entitled to reinstatement with full back pay and benefits. Other contracts limit the recovery to a specified period of time or give the arbitrator free rein in fashioning a remedy. However, arbitrators who have a great deal of latitude may find it difficult to determine an appropriate remedy. Suppose an arbitrator reinstates an employee, but decides that a suspension is warranted. The arbitrator must now wrestle with the question of how long the employee should be suspended. A number of arbitrators will reinstate an employee without back pay; in effect, the period during which the employee was out of work serves as the period of suspension. However, there is no way of knowing whether this period of time is appropriate unless the arbitrator examines other cases in which employees were suspended. In addition, arbitrators often decide to deduct (from the back pay award) wages earned or unemployment compensation received by the employee during the suspension. Arbitrators must also decide whether a reinstated employee is entitled to full seniority and other employee benefits. Such decisions may have to be made with little guidance from the contract or reference to previous disciplinary cases.[74]

▲ Summary and Conclusions

This chapter discusses the sources and types of disciplinary problems, the mechanisms for dealing with disciplinary incidents, and the arbitral considerations surrounding discharge cases. Many organizations have adopted a "firefighting" approach to dealing with employee problems as they arise. Management and union officials are best served by carefully selecting, training, and rewarding employees rather than punishing poor performance or unacceptable behavior. The ideal situation would be to establish a well-designed corrective discipline system that is *never* used.

The discipline and control function in modern-day organizations has gone well beyond the dictatorial, "fire now, ask questions later" posture of the 1920s and early 1930s. Today, employers seem to be exhibiting greater social responsibility toward employees and their problems than in the past. This trend has been most markedly demonstrated by employee assistance programs, which provide counseling for personal, domestic, financial, and alcohol and drug problems. Perhaps also, spillover effects from the Japanese management concept of lifetime employment

---

[74] See Jean T. McKelvey, "Discipline and Discharge," in Arnold M. Zack, ed., *Arbitration in Practice* (Ithaca, New York: ILR Press, Cornell University, 1984), pp. 100–101.

624 ▲ PART VI SUBSTANTIVE PROVISIONS OF THE COLLECTIVE BARGAINING AGREEMENT

are gradually making inroads in the United States, with companies now willing to help with employee problems.[75]

Nevertheless, both employers *and* employees occasionally exhibit gross insensitivities toward their responsibilities to each other. Employers, in some instances, still treat workers with a lack of dignity, failing to respect even the most fundamental notions of due process and fairness, and showing little concern for employee welfare. Likewise, some employees fail to fulfill their job responsibilities, create trouble with supervisors and co-workers, and disrupt harmony and productivity in the workplace. Under these circumstances, disciplinary concepts and systems are important.

▲ Discussion Questions and Exercises

1. Explain the relationship between the job security enjoyed by bargaining-unit members (who are covered by a comprehensive collective bargaining agreement) and the job security of contractual, tenured, and at-will employees.
2. In your opinion, to what extent do employers and unions have a legal and moral obligation to help employees overcome personal problems such as alcohol and drug addiction? Justify your position.
3. What are the advantages and disadvantages of having numerous rules to guide the conduct of employees in the workplace?
4. Select a discipline case from a recent volume of the *Labor Arbitration Reports,* published by The Bureau of National Affairs, Inc. Using the criteria in Table 16–5, determine the seriousness of the offense. How did the arbitrator evaluate the offense and establish a remedy?

▲ ▲ ▲ ▲ CASES ON EMPLOYEE DISCIPLINE

An Argument With Fatal Results

Quality Electric Steel Castings, Inc., operates a foundry in Houston, Texas, and manufactures various types of steel castings for use primarily in the oil industry. The company has had a collective bargaining relationship with the United Steel Workers of America for the past 25 years. The unnamed grievant (referred to by the arbitrator as W) had worked for the company for approximately eight years. At the time of the grievance, W worked on the evening (second) shift as a "burn man." His job involved burning slag and excess metal

---

[75] Two books on employee responsibilities and rights that go beyond the treatment commonly found in labor relations textbooks are: David W. Ewing, *Justice on the Job: Resolving Grievances in the Nonunion Workplace* (Boston: Harvard Business School Press, 1989); and Chimezie A.B. Osigweh, ed., *Communicating Employee Responsibilities and Rights* (Westport, Connecticut: Greenwood Press, 1987).

off rough steel castings. In addition, he assisted in the movement of the steel castings from his area to the heat treat area.

Although W had told his supervisor, Tollie Kiel, that he did not want to work that day, he nevertheless reported for duty 45 minutes late on October 8, 1979. After arriving at his work area, W claimed that he had no work to do. Approximately 2 hours and 15 minutes later, W's supervisor approached him and instructed him to help another employee, J. W. Wofford, load a car with material for the heat treat operation. Instead of assisting Wofford, W continued to talk with another employee and then went to the restroom. Kiel and Wofford then loaded the car by themselves. Approximately 45 minutes later, Kiel and the shift foreman, Oscar Greenleaf, went to the restroom where they found W. The two men warned W to stop loafing and report to his work area.

After the employees on the evening shift had finished their "lunch break" (between 7 and 7:30 P.M.), W and Wofford were standing at W's work area when Kiel approached and began talking with Wofford. The two men talked about a broken windshield in Kiel's truck and Wofford offered to give Kiel a windshield from a junk truck that he owned. Wofford told Kiel that he would bring the windshield with him to work the next day and the two men apparently discussed the price of the windshield. Kiel then remarked that "Whoever broke out my windshield, I hope they had good luck." W thought Kiel was accusing him of vandalizing the truck and immediately launched into a violent argument with the supervisor.

W, who was holding a 12-inch steel rod, began waiving it at Kiel and poked it at his head and chest. Another employee, Mr. Jackson, witnessed the event from approximately 100 feet away and walked over to try to break up the argument. Jackson later testified that the noise in the plant prevented him from hearing what W and Kiel were saying, but he could tell by the expression on W's face that the argument was heated. As Jackson approached, he saw W put the rod up to Kiel's face such that it was touching the supervisor's nose. Kiel told W to get the rod out of his face. Jackson tried unsuccessfully to pull W away from the supervisor and told him to "leave Kiel alone." At this point W said, "I wouldn't go anywhere for killing a black man" (both W and Kiel are black). Jackson then pulled W away from Kiel and W said, "I'll leave Kiel alone."

As Jackson turned to leave, Kiel moaned and fell over backwards. Jackson turned around and heard Wofford yell, "Lord have mercy. He done hit that man." Although medical assistance was called immediately, Kiel was dead. W was arrested and taken to the police station. Shortly thereafter, a coroner determined that Kiel had died of a heart attack. There was no evidence that W had struck Kiel and he was released from jail. On Tuesday, October 9, 1979, W reported for work and was told by the personnel director that he was suspended pending an investigation of the incident. The personnel director discussed the findings of the investigation with other company officials and it was decided that W should be discharged. A grievance was subsequently filed on W's behalf.

The union argued that Kiel's unfortunate death was not caused by W's actions since he did not physically attack the supervisor; nor did he verbally attack him in an insubordinate or abusive manner. The union also stated that W had no previous disciplinary actions that would indicate a "disrespectful attitude" on his part. The company claimed that the argument, together with W's threats and use of the steel rod, put a great deal of stress on Kiel. Management grievance representatives presented witnesses who testified that W made unprovoked verbal threats to Kiel and escalated the conflict by poking a steel rod at him. The company also claimed that such verbal threats and physical actions showed a disrespectful attitude toward company supervisors.

Discussion Questions

1. Evaluate the merits of the union and company arguments.
2. How should the arbitrator view the eyewitness accounts of Wofford and Jackson in this case? What arguments might the union make to discredit the testimony of Wofford and Jackson?
3. The company grievance representatives did not raise the issue of W's insubordination when he ignored Kiel's order to help load the truck (and, instead, went to the restroom for an extended period of time). Should the arbitrator nevertheless take W's insubordination into account in deciding this case?

Caught By an Undercover Agent

During the latter part of 1981, management at Pacific Bell's Junction Avenue facility in San Jose, California, received reports that marijuana had been found in company trucks and on company premises. Management contacted the California Bureau of Narcotics Enforcement (BNE) and arranged for an undercover agent to be hired as an employee at the Junction Avenue facility. The BNE referred an undercover agent by the code name of "Paris" to Pacific Bell. Several years earlier, Paris had been arrested for selling cocaine and intimidating a witness. The charges against Paris were dismissed after he agreed to work with the BNE as an informant.

Based on observations allegedly made during his employment at the company, Paris reported to his supervisors at the BNE that he had observed various co-workers using marijuana, cocaine, and heroin. Most of the drug activity allegedly occurred in the company parking lot in vehicles used by the grievants. As a result of Paris's undercover activities, six employees were discharged for the use or possession of illegal drugs on company property. The Communications Workers' union subsequently filed a grievance on behalf of the terminated employees.

There were a number of problems surrounding Paris' undercover activities. First, Paris admitted to having used marijuana, cocaine, and marijuana laced with PCP while working undercover on certain cases, but he denied doing so when working as an informant for Pacific Bell. However, both the discharged grievants and another co-worker claimed that Paris came to work on several occasions under the influence of marijuana and PCP. Second, Paris testified at the grievance hearing that he had kept a notebook recording his observations of employee drug activities, but that the book had been eaten by his dog. Paris also had some notes that he brought to a company meeting, but he said that the notes were "too vague" to refresh his memory. As a result, he discarded them. Most of Paris's allegations were were not specific as to the dates and times that the grievants were involved in illicit drug activities. Third, Paris did not retain any samples of the drugs allegedly used by the grievants, nor were there any laboratory tests, photographs, or tape recordings to corroborate his allegations. Thus, he was the only "witness" claiming to have observed the possession or use of drugs by Pacific Bell employees while at work.

The union contended that since the grievants were charged with criminal wrongdoing, the truth of the allegations against them had to be proven "beyond a reasonable doubt." Under this standard, a dismissal could not be upheld based on the uncorroborated testimony of an undercover informant. The union emphasized that the company could have obtained corroboration by photographs, tape recordings, chemical analysis, or observations by other individuals. However, the company failed to do so. It also pointed out that the informant's notes were either discarded or destroyed under questionable circumstances. The union furthermore attacked Paris's credibility on the basis of his own alleged drug use, past criminal activities, and inability to provide specific times and dates of illicit drug activities.

The company contended that the standard of proof should be beyond a preponderance of the evidence rather than proof beyond a reasonable doubt. It suggested that under the former standard, no corroboration of the informant's allegations were necessary. Furthermore, the company contended that some corroboration was supplied by the involvement of the BNE; the company also pointed to the successful apprehension of individuals in other drug busts based on information supplied by Paris. As to the informant's credibility, the company emphasized that persons involved in drug undercover work can hardly be expected to have clean prior records and that any inconsistencies in the informant's testimony were not significant.

Discussion Questions

1. Discuss which standard of proof—"beyond a preponderance of the evidence" or "beyond a reasonable doubt"—is most appropriate in this case.

2. How should the arbitrator evaluate the questionable character and testimony of undercover informant Paris?
3. The use of undercover agents to detect drug possession and usage in the workplace is becoming more commonplace. Does management have an obligation to inform the union that it uses such agents?
4. Since grievants discharged for drug use will likely institute grievance proceedings, what precautions should be taken by management when using undercover agents in the workplace? That is, how can management ensure that the rights of both the company and the employees are protected?

Appendix: Excerpt from the Collective Bargaining Agreement between USX Corporation and the United Steelworkers (Expires February 1, 1991)

SECTION 8—SUSPENSION AND DISCHARGE CASES

A. Purpose

The purpose of this Section is to provide for the disposition of complaints involving suspension or discharge and to establish a special procedure for the prompt review of cases involving discharge or suspension of more than 4 calendar days. Complaints concerning suspensions of 4 calendar days or less shall be handled in accordance with Section 6 — Adjustment of Complaints and Grievances, Section 7 — Arbitration and Appendix J — Grievance and Arbitration. Complaints concerning suspensions of 5 calendar days or more and discharges shall be handled in accordance with the procedure set forth below, including Section 6 — Adjustment of Complaints and Grievances, Section 7 — Arbitration, and Appendix J — Grievance and Arbitration.

B. Procedure

An employee shall not be peremptorily discharged. In all cases in which Management may conclude that an employee's conduct may justify suspension or discharge, he shall be suspended initially for not more than 5 calendar days, and given written notice of such action. In all cases of discharge, or of suspension for any period of time, a copy of the discharge or suspension notice shall be promptly furnished to such employee's grievance committeeman.

If such initial suspension is for not more than 4 calendar days and the employee affected believes that he has been unjustly dealt with, he may initiate a complaint and have it processed in accordance with Section 6 — Adjustment of Complaints and Grievances, Section 7 — Arbitration, and Appendix J — Grievance and Arbitration.

If such initial suspension is for 5 calendar days and if the employee affected believes he has been unjustly dealt with, he may request and shall be granted, during this period, a hearing and a statement of the offense before a representative (status of department head or higher) designated by the **general manager** of the plant with or without an assistant grievance committeeman or grievance committeeman present as the employee may choose. At such hearing the facts concerning the case shall be made available to both parties. After such hearing, or if no such hearing be requested, Management may conclude whether the suspension shall be affirmed, modified, extended, revoked, or converted into a discharge. In the event the suspension is affirmed, modified, extended, or converted into a discharge, the employee may, within 5 calendar days after notice of such action, file a grievance in the Second Step of the complaint and grievance procedure. Final decision shall be made by the Company in this Step within 5 calendar days from the date of the filing thereof. Such grievance shall thereupon be handled in accordance with the procedures of Section 6 — Adjustment of Complaints and Grievances, Section 7 — Arbitration, and Appendix J — Grievance and Arbitration. Grievances involving discharge which are appealed to the Board shall be docketed, heard, and decided within sixty (60) days of appeal, unless the Board determines that circumstances require otherwise. Such grievances shall be identified by the Union as discharge grievances in the appeal to the Board.

An initial suspension for not more than calendar days to be extended or converted into a discharge must be so extended or converted within the 4-day period, in which case the procedures outlined in the immediately preceding paragraph shall be followed and the 5-calendar-day period for requesting a hearing shall begin when the employee receives notice of such extension or discharge.

The Company in arbitration proceedings will not make use of any personnel records of previous disciplinary action against the employee involved where the disciplinary action occurred five or more years prior to the date of the event which is the subject of such arbitration.

An employee who is summoned to meet in an office with a supervisor other than his own immediate supervisor for the purpose of discussing possible disciplinary action shall be entitled to be accompanied by his grievance committeeman or assistant grievance committeeman if he requests such representation, provided such representative is then available, and provide further that, if such representative is not then available, the employee's required attendance at such meeting shall be deferred only for such time during that shift as is necessary to provide opportunity for him to secure the attendance of such representative.

C. Revocation of Suspensions or Discharges

Should any initial suspension, or affirmation, modification, or extension thereof, or discharge be revoked by the Company, the Company shall reinstate and compensate the employee affected on the basis of an equitable lump sum payment mutually agreed to by the parties or, in the absence of agreement, make him whole in the manner set forth in Section 8-D below.

D. Jurisdiction of the Board

Should it be determined by the Board that an employee has been suspended or discharged without proper cause therefor, the Company shall reinstate the employee and make him whole for the period of his suspension or discharge, which shall include providing him such earnings and other benefits as he would have received except for such suspension or discharge, and offsetting such earnings or other amounts as he would not have received except for such suspension or discharge. In suspension and discharge cases only, the Board may, where circumstances warrant, modify or eliminate the offset of such earnings or other amounts as would not have been received except for such suspension or discharge.

Should it be determined by the Board that an employee has been suspended or discharged for proper cause therefor, the Board shall not have jurisdiction to modify the degree of discipline imposed by the Company; provided, however, that in a discharge case arising out of a strike or work stoppage the Board shall have discretion, if it finds that the Company has proper cause for discipline but does not have proper cause for discharge, to modify the penalty; provided, further, that in case the Board modifies the discipline the Board shall have discretion to reduce or not require the Company to pay the compensation provided above if, in its judgment, the facts warrant such an award.

The provisions of this Subsection apply to all suspensions regardless of the number of days involved.

E. Suspension of Hearing

When a strike, work stoppage, or interruption or impeding of work is in progress at any plant or subdivision thereof, Management shall not be required to hold any hearings or notify employees under this Section if the employees are participating in such violation of this Agreement or if it is impracticable for Management to do so because of such violation. In such cases, the time limits for holding hearings or notifying employees shall start to run upon the termination of the strike, work stoppage, or interruption or impeding of work.

Reprinted with permission of USX Corporation and the United Steelworkers.

Part VII

Public-Sector Labor Relations

▲ ▲

To this point the major focus of this book has been on private-sector labor relations. However, there are significant differences between the manner in which collective bargaining is conducted between the private and public sectors. Federal, state, and local government employees are unique in that they typically enjoy high levels of job security. In addition, they are subject to standardized wage and salary scales and uniform personnel/human resource management policies. Public employees such as police officers and firefighters provide unique services for which there is no readily available substitute from private-sector sources. Other public employees, such as school teachers, health care workers, and sanitation workers provide services for which there is a substitute, but are nonetheless essential.

Chapter 17, Public-Sector Labor Relations, provides an overview of public-sector unions as well as the unique legal structure surrounding public-sector labor relations. Major differences between public- and private-sector labor relations are discussed along with collective bargaining among federal, state, and local government workers. Special attention is given to the restrictions placed on public-sector employees to engage in work stoppages and impasse resolution techniques used to resolve public-sector interest disputes.

17 Public-Sector Labor Relations

- **Introduction**
- **The Growth of Public-Sector Unionism**
  The Early Days
  The 1960s and Beyond
- **Types of Unions Representing Public Employees**
- **Major Differences Between Public- and Private-Sector Collective Bargaining**
  The Right of Public Employees to Bargain Collectively
  The Right of Public Employees to Engage in Work Stoppages
  Multilateral Bargaining
  Budgeting Issues and the Nonprofit Status of Governmental Agencies
  Unique Organizational Issues
- **Collective Bargaining among Federal Government Employees**
- **Collective Bargaining among State and Local Employees**
  Sources of Bargaining Rights for State and Local Employees
  Organizing and Bargaining in the Absence of Statutory Protections
  Components of State and Local Collective Bargaining Laws
    Employee Groups Covered and Bargaining-Unit Determination
    Union Recognition, Certification, and Decertification
    Scope of Bargaining
    Unfair Labor Practices
    Strikes and the Treatment of Striking Employees
    Impasse Resolution Provisions
    The Administration of Public-Sector Collective Bargaining Agreements
    State and Municipal Collective Bargaining Agencies
- **Summary and Conclusions**

▲ **Discussion Questions and Exercises**
▲ **Public-Sector Strike Case**
  The Los Angeles Teachers' Strike

▲ Introduction

Compared to private-sector labor relations, collective bargaining in the public sector is a relatively new development in the United States. Prior to the 1960s, unionization and collective bargaining among federal, state, and local government employees were scattered and undeveloped. From the 1960s through the mid-1970s, public employees were increasingly attracted to organized labor. Teachers, health care personnel, municipal workers, and other government workers joined unions, partially offsetting the decline in unionization among private-sector employees. Since the mid-1970s, collective bargaining among government employees has not grown as rapidly. However, the extent of organization among federal, state, and local government employees now greatly exceeds that of private-sector workers.

Public-sector collective bargaining contains a number of unique characteristics that set it apart from the more established private sector. Table 17–1 summarizes these differences. This chapter discusses the dynamics of public sector collective bargaining and places special emphasis on the unique problems that are encountered when public employees bargain with federal, state, and local governmental agencies over wages, hours, and working conditions. Although a number of similarities exist between public- and private-sector labor relations, there are also some significant differences. For example, many of the laws regulating public-sector bar-

Table 17–1 ▲ **Differences Between Public- and Private-Sector Collective Bargaining**

	Private Sector	*Public Sector*
Statutory Framework	Uniform federal statutes (National Labor Relations Act, Railway Labor Act).	A federal statute for federal government employees plus numerous state and local statutes.
Unionization Trends	Gradually declining number of organized workers. Currently 16 percent unionization.	Growth during the 1960s to mid-1970s, followed by stabilization. Currently over 40 percent unionization.
Bargaining Power of the Employees	In the event of a strike by one firm, other firms can continue providing services. Less potential bargaining power for private-sector employees.	Public services may be unavailable or in limited supply during a strike. Greater potential bargaining power for government employees.

Table 17–1 ▲ Differences Between Public- and Private-Sector Collective Bargaining (Continued)

	Private Sector	*Public Sector*
Negotiations Climate	Negotiators usually have full authority to agree to settlements without consulting higher authorities. Identity of the employer having final authority is well-defined.	Negotiators may be restricted in their ability to make bargaining concessions. Concessions may be dependent on legislative approval. The identity of the employer having final authority is not well-defined.
Third-Party Interests	Because alternative goods and services are available, consumers and other constituents are less concerned about the prospects of a work stoppage. Little pressure is placed on negotiators by "outside" parties.	Constituents are generally interested in the outcome of a strike because alternative services are not readily available. As a result, more pressure may be exerted by taxpayers and special-interest groups to quickly and, perhaps, prematurely resolve an impasse. Diverse political interests often affect bargaining.
Bargaining Structure	Ranging from highly centralized (employer associations) to highly decentralized (local negotiations).	Generally highly decentralized. Almost all bargaining is done on a single-employer basis.
Scope of Bargaining	Broad scope of mandatory bargaining topics.	A narrow scope of bargaining topics in many instances.
Right to Strike	Broad right to engage in economic strikes and other types of work stoppages.	Limited or no right to engage in work stoppages.
Impasse Resolution Procedures	Primarily mediation.	Mediation, fact-finding, interest arbitration (in which the arbitrator determines the final provisions of the collective bargaining agreement if the parties are unable to reach an agreement).
Contract Provisions	Relatively few legal restrictions on contract provisions. Contracts are of several years duration.	Contracts are often pre-empted by civil service statutes and regulations. Contracts are of shorter duration.
Contract Administration	Influenced primarily by the terms of the collective bargaining agreement.	Influenced by the collective bargaining agreement as well as civil service regulations.

gaining were patterned after National Labor Relations Act provisions. However, public employees generally do not have the right to strike, whereas their private-sector counterparts have a broad right to engage in economic and other types of strikes. Contract negotiations in the public sector follow many of the traditions of the private sector, yet are often strongly influenced by diverse political interests and taxpayer groups. The differences between private and public-sector collective bargaining are important because employer and union bargaining power is altered, different impasse resolution techniques are used, and contract terms and provisions are often narrower in scope.

As Table 17–1 suggests, the differences between public-sector and private-sector collective bargaining are significant, especially with regard to the statutory framework and the right of employees to engage in economic strikes. The issues summarized in Table 17–1 are discussed in greater detail throughout this chapter.

▲ The Growth of Public-Sector Unionism

The Early Days

During the first half of the 20th century, there was little semblance of collective bargaining among state and municipal employees. Public-sector employment was characterized by the *public service patrician model,* in which the government employer unilaterally set compensation and personnel policies. Early employee associations used political lobbying rather than direct collective bargaining with government employers to achieve improved wages, hours, and working conditions. In 1902, President Theodore Roosevelt issued an executive order to prohibit federal employees from lobbying on their own behalf. President William Howard Taft, in 1909, affirmed Roosevelt's executive order. However, in 1914 Congress passed the Lloyd-LaFollette Act allowing employees to organize unions and petition Congress. Nonetheless, Presidents Herbert Hoover and Franklin D. Roosevelt continued to take a dim view of collective bargaining among federal employees. Later, the *patronage model* evolved and based public employment on a worker's political party affiliation. Chicago mayor Daley and Philadelphia mayor Rizzo were known for their use of the patronage system in recent years.[1] In many locations, the patronage system was replaced by the *civil service model*, which emphasized merit, political neutrality, and bureaucratic personnel rules and regulations. In addition to the civil service model, police officers, firefighters, and prison guards work in paramilitary organizations; their employment relationship is based on the *military/public safety model*, which is characterized by a well-defined chain of command and an authoritative leadership style.

These models allowed little input from employees. By the late 1950s and early 1960s, however, government employees were no longer content to allow elected public officials and political appointees to dictate compensation and personnel pol-

---

[1] Limits on permissible political activities of public employees are regulated by the federal Hatch Act and similar state statutes. These laws are intended to prevent government employees from being pressured into supporting a particular party.

icies. Unions and government employee associations began to serve as a voice for federal, state, and municipal employees with regard to compensation and personnel policies. Thus the *collective bargaining model* was born.[2] The early successes of unionized groups, such as the New York school teachers, demonstrated to other public servants that unionization and collective bargaining could be both practical and beneficial.

Prior to the 1960s, public-sector employees enjoyed reasonable, although not spectacular, levels of compensation and benefits. Persons working for federal, state, or municipal governments typically enjoyed strong job security and were nearly immune from layoffs caused by poor business conditions or the reorganization of government agencies.[3] The low unemployment rates for government workers often compensated for any undesirable conditions associated with their work. State laws and civil service statutes prohibited the use of economic strikes. The inability to engage legally in strikes diluted potential union bargaining power and created an inhospitable organizing climate for labor unions in the public sector.[4]

The 1960s and Beyond

The early 1960s marked the beginning of public-sector collective bargaining on a large scale. Most of the early public-sector bargaining activity focused on municipal employees such as elementary and secondary school teachers, sanitation workers, police officers, and firefighters. In the years following the unionization of local government workers, state and federal employees began to organize in large numbers. Although it is difficult to separate cause from effect, a number of reasons have been set forth to explain the rise of public-sector collective bargaining in the United States.

Government employees who performed diverse jobs began to realize that they had a community of interest because they worked for the same employer and were covered by a uniform set of civil service personnel policies.[5] Subgroups of government employees such as police officers and firefighters realized that they had common concerns because of their similar skills, training, and job duties. Police officers, firefighters, and health care personnel, for example, are highly trained specialists who perform duties that are often hazardous yet essential to the public safety and welfare. As government workers developed an interest in collective bargaining, employee associations that had originally engaged in political lobbying and had

---

[2] For a more extensive discussion of these models, see Michael T. Leibig and Wendy L. Kahn, *Public Employee Organizing and the Law* (Washington, D.C.: The Bureau of National Affairs, Inc., 1987), pp. 14–28.

[3] See Steven G. Allen, "Unions and Job Security in the Public Sector," in Richard B. Freeman and Casey Ichniowski, eds., *When Public Sector Workers Unionize* (Chicago: University of Chicago Press, 1988), pp. 271–296.

[4] See John F. Burton, Jr., and Terry Thomason, "The Extent of Collective Bargaining in the Public Sector," in Benjamin Aaron, Joyce M. Najita, and James L. Stern, eds., *Public Sector Bargaining*, 2nd ed. (Washington, D.C.: The Bureau of National Affairs, Inc., 1988), pp. 14–27.

[5] E. Wright Bakke, "Reflections on the Future of Bargaining in the Public Sector," *Monthly Labor Review* (July 1970), pp. 21–25.

provided professional development programs, insurance, and other benefits to public servants evolved into bargaining organizations.[6]

The growth of public-sector unionism may have been fueled by the expansion of public services and the increasing number of governmental employees.[7] During the 1960s, federal and state governments expanded their missions because private-sector organizations were either unable or unwilling to provide programs such as interstate highways, health care, and social services. Today, government employees perform a wide range of professional and nonprofessional jobs ranging from elementary, secondary, and college teachers; to police officers, firefighters, and prison guards; to accountants and health care personnel; to sanitation workers and zookeepers. By the late 1980s, employees of the federal, state, and local governments comprised 15 percent (17 million employees) of the U.S. workforce.[8]

The wages and salary of many government workers did not keep up with the inflationary period of the early 1970s, thereby making unions more attractive to public employees. Many low-paid government employees saw unions as a means of raising both their pay and job status. The job security traditionally enjoyed by government workers was not enough to offset the fact that their wages and benefits were beginning to lag behind those of comparable private-sector workers.

The 1960s also heralded a more militant attitude by citizens toward the government. Perhaps because of the Viet Nam conflict, the public began to question the government's wisdom about certain aspects of public policy. A questioning of the established order led to student activism on college campuses and a greater tolerance for protest and civil disobedience.[9] The spirit of unrest fostered by the civil rights movement of the 1960s undoubtedly added fuel to the public-sector labor movement.

Finally, President John F. Kennedy signed Executive Order 10988 in 1962, allowing federal government employees the right to engage in limited collective bargaining. President Kennedy's order served as a catalyst for state and local legislation permitting the recognition of public-sector unions and bargaining for government workers. On one hand, public officials felt threatened by the prospect of collective bargaining among governmental employees; on the other hand, the same officials found it difficult to deny public workers the right to unionize and bargain collectively in light of the fact that private-sector workers had enjoyed such privileges since the 1930s. As Supreme Court Justice Potter Stewart noted in *Abood v. Detroit Board of Education*, "Public employees are not basically different from private employees: on the whole they have the same sort of skills, the same needs, and seek the same advantages."[10]

---

[6] John F. Burton, Jr., and Terry Thomason, "The Extent of Collective Bargaining in the Public Sector," in Benjamin Aaron, Joyce M. Najita, and James L. Stern, *Public-Sector Bargaining*, 2nd ed. (Washington, D.C.: The Bureau of National Affairs, Inc., 1988), p. 15.

[7] See Marick F. Masters and John D. Robertson, "The Impact of Organized Labor On Public Employment: A Comparative Analysis," *Journal of Labor Research* (Fall 1988), p. 347.

[8] *Monthly Labor Review*, Vol. 109, No. 9 (1986), p. 60.

[9] Derek C. Bok and John T. Dunlop, *Labor and the American Community* (New York: Simon and Schuster, 1970), p. 314.

[10] *Abood v. Detroit Board of Education*, 95 LRRM 2411 (1977).

▲ Types of Unions Representing Public Employees

There are a variety of unions that represent public-sector employees, ranging from all-public unions whose membership is comprised almost exclusively of federal, state, or municipal employees; to brotherhoods of police and firefighters; to mixed unions that organize both private- and public-sector workers. Furthermore, decentralized bargaining requires that unions and their officials fill different roles, depending on the state or municipality where the bargaining takes place.

> Just the fact that labor relations legislation may be unique to one group of employees provides sufficient grounds for differences in the way the union conducts itself in a particular locality. Clearly, in jurisdictions where unions have not secured legal bargaining rights, their priorities will differ somewhat from union activities emphasized in localities where this goal has been achieved. And the union structure, and even its finances, and the role of the union leader will be affected.[11]

Despite the large number of unions that represent public employees, membership is concentrated in a half dozen or so large unions.[12] Unions that evolved from professional associations often have concerns that go beyond the pay and employment conditions of their members.[13] Teachers and postal workers unions have not been especially influential within the U.S. labor movement. However, teachers and postal workers have traditionally been strong lobbyists at the state and federal levels respectively long before they turned to organized labor.[14] The two major teachers' unions, the National Education Association (NEA) and the American Federation of Teachers (AFT), have pursued a number of professional concerns.[15] Former NEA president Mary Hatwood Futrell, for example, is credited with shifting the NEA's focus from self-protection to a more professional concern for better education. Recent NEA concerns include curriculum innovations, grants for dropout and illiteracy prevention programs, and higher certification standards for teachers.[16] AFT president Albert Shanker has gone on record as favoring the de-emphasis of standardized testing programs.[17] Interestingly, a large percentage of the major

---

[11] James L. Stern, "Unionism in the Public Sector," in Benjamin Aaron, Joyce M. Najita, and James L. Stern, eds., *Public-Sector Bargaining*, 2nd ed. (Washington, D.C.: The Bureau of National Affairs, Inc., 1988), p. 52.

[12] The federal government as well as a number of state governments have outlawed various forms of union security, thereby creating "open shop" conditions that allow bargaining-unit workers to avoid joining a union. As a result, it is not unusual to see large differences between bargaining-unit membership and union membership in public-sector organizations. That is, the number of "free riders" is often considerably higher in public-sector bargaining units than in private-sector units.

[13] For a related discussion of the evolution of government employee associations toward the more traditional bargaining-unit membership, see Casey Ichniowski and Jeffrey S. Zax, "Today's Associations, Tomorrow's Unions," *Industrial and Labor Relations Review* (January 1990), pp. 191–208.

[14] Walter J. Gershenfeld, "Public Employee Unionization—An Overview," in Muriel K. Gibbons, Robert D. Helsby, Jerome Lefkowitz, and Barbara Z. Tener, eds., *Portrait of a Process—Collective Negotiations in Public Employment* (Fort Washington, Pennsylvania: Labor Relations Press, 1979), pp. 10–11.

[15] The NEA started as a professional association, shifted to a collective-bargaining orientation, and has now reverted back at least partially to an increasing emphasis on professional concerns.

[16] Associated Press, "NEA Must Fill Shoes of Leader," *Greenville News* (June 25, 1989), p. A20.

[17] Associated Press, "Teachers Union Chief Wants Ending to Standardized Tests," *Greenville News* (October 29, 1989).

teachers' unions members do not engage in collective bargaining, but use the union to focus primarily on professional concerns.[18]

Table 17–2 lists the major public-sector employee unions along with pertinent information on their size and operations.

Table 17–2 ▲ The Major Public-Sector Unions

Teachers

National Education Association (NEA):

Originally founded in Philadelphia in 1875, the NEA has promoted the cause of public education and the improvement of teaching. The NEA has approximately 1.4 million members and is an active political lobbying group for educators in public schools, colleges, and universities. In states where there is extensive collective bargaining, the NEA uses UniServ districts to administer bargaining activities. UniServ districts provide experienced negotiators and staff for school districts that do not need a full-time representative for each bargaining unit. The NEA has maintained that affiliation with the AFL-CIO is not desirable.

American Federation of Teachers (AFT):

Formed in 1916, the AFT currently has approximately 500,000 members and is affiliated with the AFL-CIO. The AFT is the primary union for teachers in major cities such as New York, Chicago, Philadelphia, Detroit, Boston, Pittsburgh, Cleveland, Minneapolis, and Baltimore. Unlike the NEA, the AFT gives educational support personnel (e.g., school secretaries) membership rights and has also organized health care and state civil service employees.

The American Association of University Professors (AAUP):

Serves to promote higher education and protect academic freedom and tenure for college professors. Originally the AAUP opposed exclusive bargaining representation for faculty members in colleges and universities, but has since modified its position and now pursues collective bargaining as a goal. The AAUP has found it difficult to compete with the NEA and AFT in representing faculty members and has experienced financial pressures because of declines in its membership base.

State and Local Government Employees

American Federation of State, County, and Municipal Employees (AFSCME):

The dominant union of state, county, and municipal employees (excluding teachers), AFSCME has nearly 1 million members. Under the leadership of the late Jerry Wurf, AFSCME membership increased from 200,000 to 1 million between 1964 and 1981 and it is the largest AFL-CIO-affiliated union. Forty percent of its members work in health care, 20 percent are clerical workers, 10 percent are in law enforcement, and 11 percent are technical and professional employees. AFSCME bargains on a decentralized basis and has approximately 3,500 contracts in 47 states.

---

[18] James L. Stern, "Unionism in the Public Sector," in Benjamin Aaron, Joyce M. Najita, and James L. Stern, eds., *Public-Sector Bargaining* (Washington, D.C.: The Bureau of National Affairs, Inc., 1988), p. 73.

Table 17–2 ▲ The Major Public-Sector Unions (Continued)

State and Local Government Employees (Continued)

Service Employees International Union (SEIU):

Founded in 1917, the SEIU is an AFL-CIO affiliate with 850,00 members in 350 locals. The SEIU represents employees in educational and health care institutions as well as a variety of other occupations such as police officers.

Assembly of Governmental Employees (AGE):

Performs the unique function of an umbrella agency for independent state civil-service employee associations. Some affiliates have left the AGE and have re-affiliated with AFSCME and other unions. Despite these and other loses, the AGE serves as a clearinghouse for independent associations.

Other large unions representing state and municipal employees include the **Teamsters**, the **American Nurses Association**, and the **Laborers' International**.

Uniformed Protective Services

International Association of Fire Fighters (AFL-CIO):

Founded in 1918 in Washington, D.C. The IAFF is the dominant fire fighters union, with approximately 142,000 members in nearly 2,000 locals.

Fraternal Order of the Police (FOP):

Founded in 1915 in Pittsburgh, Pennsylvania. The FOP contains approximately one half of all unionized police officers in the United States. 187,000 members are spread across 1,680 locals.

Federal Government Employees

American Federation of Government Employees (AFGE):

Founded in 1932 in Washington, D.C., the AFGE is an AFL-CIO affiliate with 200,000 members in 1,300 locals. The AFGE has been plagued with severe declines in membership and excessive numbers of "free riders" who do not pay union dues and fees. Because of federal government prohibitions against union security provisions that mandate union membership or financial support by federal employees, it is estimated that the AFGE represents approximately 400,000 nonmembers.

Other unions representing federal employees include the **National Treasury Employees Union** and the **National Federation of Federal Employees**, both of which are independent of the AFL-CIO.

Postal Service Employees

American Postal Workers Union (APWU):

Founded in 1971 through the merger of several postal unions, the APWU is an AFL-CIO affiliate with 350,000 employees in 2,500 locals. The APWU is a multi-craft union with 50 percent of its membership being female.

National Association of Letter Carriers (NALC):

Founded in 1899 in Milwaukee, Wisconsin, NALC is an AFL-CIO affiliate with over 300,000 members spanning nearly 3,800 locals. The NALC is a single craft union that has a more homogeneous membership than the APWU.

Adapted from James L. Stern, "Unionism in the Public Sector," in Benjamin Aaron, Joyce M. Najita, and James L. Stern, eds., *Public-Sector Bargaining,* 2nd ed. (Washington, D.C.: The Bureau of National Affairs, Inc., 1988), pp. 52–89; and Courtney D. Gifford, *Directory of U.S. Labor Organizations, 1988–89 Edition* (Washington, D.C: The Bureau of National Affairs, Inc., 1988). Reprinted with permission.

▲ Major Differences Between Public- and Private-Sector Collective Bargaining

The Right of Public Employees to Bargain Collectively

Considerable debate has centered on the right of federal, state, and municipal government employees to unionize and bargain with their employers. The debate centers on two issues. First, do public employees have the right to join a union or form an association whose primary mission is to address employment concerns? If the first question is answered affirmatively, then a second question must be addressed: Do public employees have the right to bargain collectively with governmental agencies over wages, hours, and working conditions?

Prior to the turn of the century, the courts viewed public employment as a "privilege" and held that federal and state governments could force public employees to give up their constitutional rights as a condition of continued employment.[19] However, this view has been reversed. Public employees have constitutional rights that generally allow them to join or form a union.[20] The First Amendment of the U.S. Constitution protects public employees and other citizens from unwarranted interference with their freedom of speech, expression, and association. Constitutional rights are particularly important in states without public-sector collective bargaining statutes. For example, under most state public-sector bargaining statutes, it is an unfair labor practice to fire an employee for joining a union or urging others to join. If there is no public-sector bargaining law, public employees must look to a state constitution or the U.S. Constitution for protection.[21] Although the courts generally have upheld the rights of public employees to join or form a union (or association), there are a few restrictions.[22] Police officers have been allowed to join a union that also admits persons whose jobs do not involve law enforcement. However, the union was not allowed certification as the exclusive bargaining representative for police officers; such a proviso avoids potential conflicts of interest that arise in the course of law enforcement. In other cases, police officers and firefighters have been excluded from joining unions that also represent other public-sector workers.[23] Likewise, public-sector supervisors have been legally excluded from unions with nonsupervisory employees because of concerns associated with divided loyalties.[24]

The second question deals with whether public employees have the right to bargain collectively with their governmental-agency employers. The sovereignty issue is the well-worn and somewhat specious argument used to justify prohibiting collective bargaining by government employees. Although the right of public em-

---

[19] See, for example, *McAuliffe v. Mayor of New Bedford*, 155 Mass. 216, 29 N. E. 517 (1892).
[20] See *Adler v. Board of Education*, 342 U.S. 485 (1952); *Keyishian v. Board of Regents*, 385 U.S. 589 (1967); and *Shelton v. Tucker*, 364 U. S. 479 (1960).
[21] For an excellent discussion of the constitutional and statutory rights of public employees, see Michael T. Leibig and Wendy L. Kahn, *Public Employee Organizing and the Law* (Washington, D.C.: The Bureau of National Affairs, Inc., 1987), pp. 46–66.
[22] See *Brennan v. Koch*, 564 F. Supp. 322 (S.D.N.Y., 1983).
[23] See, for example, *Key v. Rutherford*, 107 LRRM 2321 (1981); *Elk Grove Firefighters Local 2340 v. Willis*, 90 LRRM 2447 (1975), aff'd 93 LRRM 2019 (1976); and *Police Associations Local 189 v. Barrett*, 111 LRRM 2728.
[24] *Key v. Rutherford*, 107 LRRM 2321 (1981).

ployees to associate might be constitutionally protected, such a right does not prevent the government employer from protecting the "public interest." The sovereignty argument usually proceeds along the following lines: Elected officials have been given the authority to make decisions affecting the public interest; they cannot abdicate these responsibilities to other individuals or groups such as union and management negotiators or interest arbitrators. Negotiating with labor organizations allegedly limits governmental discretion on matters such as personnel policies, compensation, and employee benefits. Collective bargaining agreements and work stoppages designed to pressure government officials into acceding to employee demands are regarded as invasions of the sovereign's absolute authority to act in the public interest.[25] The principle of governmental sovereignty has been summarized as follows:

> In Hobbesian terms, government is identified as the sole possessor of final power, since it is responsive to the interests of all its constituents. To concede to any special interest group a right to bargain for terms which the sovereignty believes contravenes the public interest is to deny the government's single responsibility. The government must remain in possession of the sole power to determine, on behalf of all, what shall be public policy. And public policy includes the determination of what proportion of tax revenues shall be allocated for the conduct of any service, whether it be police protection or sanitation or teaching. No union can be allowed to bargain up the rates for its members through threat or pressure, thereby curtailing what the city can afford to do in other areas.[26]

Although federal and state government officials make decisions on legislative, administrative, and judicial issues, they routinely delegate administrative decisions to civil servants who are appointed rather than elected. Furthermore, state and local governments have granted public employees and unions bargaining rights through the passage of statutes and ordinances. Thus, using the sovereignty issue as an argument against allowing public-sector employees to bargain collectively is both outmoded and unconvincing.

The Right of Public Employees to Engage in Work Stoppages

> "Come back from your vacations young men; there is sport and diversion for you right here in Boston," read a letter in the *Boston Herald* of August 27, 1919. Edwin H. Hall, Rumford professor of physics at Harvard was urging his students to return to Cambridge early and volunteer to patrol Boston if the city's policemen went on strike as they were threatening to do. Several weeks later a young Harvard lecturer made headlines by siding with the workers, proclaiming that "the demands of the striking policemen were justified" and that "labor will never surrender." Harold J. Laski, an Englishman whose fields were history and government, was addressing a solidarity meeting held by the wives of the policemen—who in fact had struck on September 9 . . .

[25] B. V. H. Schneider, "Public Sector Labor Legislation—An Evolutionary Analysis," in Benjamin Aaron, Joyce M. Najita, and James L. Stern, *Public-Sector Bargaining*, 2nd ed. (Washington, D.C.: The Bureau of National Affairs, Inc., 1988), pp. 192–193.
[26] Neil W. Chamberlain, "Public vs. Private Sector Bargaining," in J. Joseph Loewenberg and Michael H. Moskow, *Collective Bargaining in Government: Readings and Cases* (Englewood Cliffs, New Jersey: Prentice-Hall, Inc., 1972), p. 13.

Led by Professor Hall, more than four hundred Harvard "volunteers," mainly students, rallied to the call. President A. Lawrence Lowell urged that returning students "in a time of crisis... prepare themselves for such service," which would "maintain order and support the laws of the Commonwealth." An emergency headquarters for volunteer activity was set up on the first floor of University Hall and was open night and day. Posters displayed in the windows of Leavitt and Peirce [halls] emphasized President Lowell's assurance that students who missed registration or even classes would suffer in no way "from their devotion to public service"...

The Guard would patrol the city for 102 days, the last soldier leaving on December 21. The striking police would never be allowed to return to work, even though most of them had disowned the strike by the middle of September ... By December more than 1,500 new police had been hired. This hard-line response to the strikers was reinforced by the emergence of Calvin Coolidge, the Republican Governor, as a key player in the drama ... Coolidge, the shrewd Yankee, saw political capital to be earned in the strike ... [he] took personal control of the Guard after the first week of the crisis. His simple, blunt pronouncement as he did so would make its way into many an anthology: "There is no right to strike against the public safety by anybody, anywhere, any time."[27]

Seven decades later, the words of Calvin Coolidge still ring true in the minds of many elected public officials. In most states, as well as in the federal sector, public employees have no legal right to engage in economic strikes or other work stoppages. Nine states have granted the right to strike to employee groups whose jobs typically do not affect the public safety or welfare. The right to strike by government employees is the single most controversial issue in public-sector collective bargaining.[28] As discussed in previous chapters, the economic strike weapon is the union's primary means of pressuring employers into reaching an acceptable settlement on contract terms. Because of strike prohibitions, the incidence of strikes among public employees is considerably lower than among private-sector workers. Most public-sector strikes occur at the local level, primarily involving public elementary and secondary teachers.[29] Without the strike threat, bargaining power during contract negotiations often favors the employer. However, illegal strikes do occur, especially when the cost to public employees of striking is low. When public employees strike, labor leaders are often subject to fines and imprisonment. Unions may be decertified and striking employees are frequently subject to discharge. As a condition of settlement, however, the government may grant amnesty to union leaders and strikers.

The debate as to whether government employees should be allowed to strike has generated a great deal of controversy on both sides of the issue. Table 17–3 summarizes these arguments.

[27] Isaac Kramnick, "The Professor and the Police," *Harvard Magazine* (September-October 1989), pp. 42–43. Reprinted by permission of *Harvard Magazine*. Copyright 1989 by the President and Fellows of Harvard College; All rights reserved.
[28] For an excellent discussion of the issues surrounding public-sector employee strikes, see Grace Sterrett and Antone Aboud, *The Right to Strike in Public Employment*, Key Issues Series, No. 15 (Ithaca, New York: ILR Press, Cornell University, 1982).
[29] See, for example, George Ruben, "New Orleans Teachers, Related Workers Settle," *Monthly Labor Review* (March 1988), p. 48; and George Ruben "Schools Reopen In Akron," *Monthly Labor Review* (May 1989), p. 59.

Table 17–3 ▲ Major Arguments Supporting and Opposing Public Sector Strikes in the United States

Arguments Against Strikes by Public Employees

1. There are no alternative sources for many of the services provided by federal, state, and local governments. The public would therefore be left without important services such as police and fire protection, health care, and the services of teachers and sanitation workers if strikes by government employees were legal.
2. Strikes and the public pressures to settle strikes may force wages and employee benefits to exceed budgetary levels imposed by legislative bodies. As a result, taxes must be increased to support these "artificially high" wages and benefits.
3. Public employees accepted their job with a federal, state, or local agency with the understanding that strikes were illegal. The employee is obligated to live up to this condition of employment and not engage in strikes.
4. Most public-sector collective bargaining statutes have created procedures for the resolution of interest disputes. Unions, employees, and governmental agencies should be able to resolve contract disputes effectively through mediation, fact-finding, and interest arbitration rather than through work stoppages.
5. Public-sector strikes deprive citizens of services for which they have already paid through federal, state, and local taxes. Taxpayers have a right to receive these services as promised.
6. Strikes by public servants distort political power and place too much influence in the hands of public-sector union leaders.

Arguments Favoring Strikes by Public Employees

1. The right to strike is a fundamental part of the American collective bargaining process and should be extended to public employees. Strikes are a means of achieving industrial democracy and balancing the bargaining power of employers and employees.
2. Except for police and fire protection, most public services are either not essential or can be acquired through private-sector sources. Public employers can substitute capital for labor; they can also subcontract governmental services such as sanitation services, street repair work, and the maintenance of public facilities to private firms. Thus, public-sector employers can endure a strike as well as their private-sector counterparts.
3. Public employers have the right either to permanently or temporarily replace striking employees rather than grant exorbitant wage and benefit demands.
4. Dispute resolution techniques such as mediation, fact finding, and interest arbitration do not encourage meaningful negotiations at the bargaining table; since negotiators know that a third party (e.g., an interest arbitrator) will impose a settlement if negotiations reach an impasse, union and management negotiators may avoid serious bargaining. If strikes were legal, negotiators would be more likely to bargain in good faith.
5. When public-sector strikes occur, the governmental agency saves money because they do not pay wages or provide employee benefits during the work stoppage (although tax dollars continue to flow into public coffers).
6. The voters have a right to elect officials who are willing to adopt a "hard-line" stance on unions and employees who strike. Contrary to popular belief, public-sector unions are not able to gather a disproportionate amount of political and economic power. Unions and employees who use the strike threat are simply one among a number of political pressure groups confronting public officials.

It is not unusual for contract talks involving state and local employees to extend well beyond the expiration date of the preceding contract. In part, this trend reflects the time-consuming nature of the bargaining process as well as the need for the parties to wait until funds are appropriated by state or local legislative bodies or special agencies. When public employees engage in strikes, they are often doing so either as a last resort or as a means of gaining public attention. Most public-sector collective bargaining disputes are settled through the negotiators' own volition or through some form of statutory impasse resolution technique. Statutory strike and antistrike provisions, along with public-sector impasse procedures, are discussed in subsequent sections of this chapter.

Multilateral Bargaining

Private-sector labor disputes generally do not attract a great deal of attention from persons or interest groups outside of the corporation and union directly involved in the contract talks. Public-sector bargaining and disputes, on the other hand, may attract the attention of special interest groups who pressure negotiators, public officials, and workers into changing their bargaining demands during an impasse or work stoppage.[30] The issue of multilateral collective bargaining in the public sector arises as follows:

> Because general government services must be paid for by the public through the tax system, public management has a relationship to its public that is very different from that of private management to its firm's customers. In the latter case, typically, a concerned customer can exercise the choice of buying or not buying, but lacks the power to influence the private management's collective bargaining policies or procedures. In the former case, a concerned public may seek to replace the responsible managers or force a change in bargaining policies.[31]

Multilateral pressures are probably strongest in collective bargaining involving public school teachers. For example, when teachers in a school district strike or threaten to strike, parents may apply pressure to school board officials to resolve the labor dispute. Similarly, there may be widespread public attention if police officers, firefighters, or health care workers threaten a work stoppage.[32]

The presence of multilateral bargaining issues creates several problems. First, it forces the contract talks to "go public." Public-sector negotiators do not necessarily bargain in the isolation of a conference room. Some states and municipalities have "sunshine" laws. The majority of these laws require that records from negotiations be made available to the public, but do not allow interested citizens to attend bargaining sessions. Four states—Alaska, Florida, Minnesota, and Texas—

---

[30] See Thomas A. Kochan and Hoyt N. Wheeler, "A Theory of Multilateral Collective Bargaining in City Governments," *Industrial and Labor Relations Review* (July, 1974), pp. 525–542.
[31] Milton Derber, "Management Organization for Collective Bargaining in the Public Sector," in Benjamin Aaron, Joyce M. Najita, and James L. Stern, eds., *Public-Sector Bargaining*, 2nd ed. (Washington, D.C.: The Bureau of National Affairs, Inc., 1988), p. 91.
[32] See Kenneth McLennan and Michael H. Moskow, "Multilateral Bargaining in the Public Sector," in J. Joseph Loewenberg and Michael H. Moskow, eds. *Collective Bargaining in Government: Readings and Cases* (Englewood Cliffs, New Jersey: Prentice-Hall, Inc., 1972), p. 230.

require open negotiations.[33] When negotiators must perform in the public eye, they may find it difficult to make concessions; there is a temptation to "perform" before an audience composed of special-interest group members. As noted in Chapter 9, a lack of privacy may make it difficult for negotiators to analyze and formulate proposals and make concessions, all of which are important ingredients in good-faith collective bargaining. Second, union negotiators may use the "end-run" tactic: rather than negotiate with management, union negotiators appeal directly to a legislative body, city council, school board, or special interest group for support. Third, the news media may inflame public opinion by reporting on difficulties at the bargaining table, printing the rhetoric of militant union leaders and employees, or predicting dire consequences if a work stoppage occurs.[34] Finally, when a contract settlement is reached, political pressures by constituent groups may cause employees to vote against ratification.[35]

McLennan and Moskow propose three necessary conditions for demonstrating the existence of multilateral bargaining:

1. *Some of the goals of the interest group relate to topics included in the scope of negotiations.* For example, in negotiating a collective bargaining agreement between a teachers' union and a school board, the issue of a teacher transfer clause is commonly addressed. Community groups interested in quality education might believe that the best teachers would leave the school district if a transfer clause allowed the superintendent to assign teachers to any location within the district. Civil rights groups, on the other hand, might oppose a voluntary transfer clause for fear that it would result in faculty segregation as the better teachers moved away from schools located in lower-income areas.
2. *Interest groups pursue their goals by trying to influence the parties involved in negotiations either directly or through an intermediary.* Persons or groups concerned with the teacher transfer clause may approach members of the negotiating team directly, write editorials in local newspapers, or attempt to influence public figures who are not directly involved in negotiations.
3. *At least one of the participants in the actual negotiations believes that the group represents segments of the public and responds to the pressure from interest group leaders.* If, for example, negotiators believe that civil rights groups possess sufficient power to sway public opinion, they may agree to a transfer clause that gives the school district superintendent considerable discretion in assigning and transferring teachers.

Budgeting Issues and the Nonprofit Status of Governmental Agencies

Public-sector organizations have several unique fiscal characteristics that set them apart from private-sector firms. Federal, state, and municipal organizations are often labor intensive. Public hospitals, schools, prisons, and police departments spend a

---

[33] B. V. H. Schneider, "Public-Sector Labor Legislation—An Evolutionary Analysis," in Benjamin Aaron, Joyce M. Najita, and James L. Stern, eds. *Public-Sector Collective Bargaining*, 2nd ed. (Washington, D.C.: The Bureau of National Affairs, Inc., 1988), p. 218.

[34] See Thomas A. Kochan, "A Theory of Multilateral Collective Bargaining in City Governments," *Industrial and Labor Relations Review* (July 1974), pp. 525–542.

[35] Also see Thomas R. Colosi and Arthur Eliot Berkeley, *Collective Bargaining: How It Works and Why* (New York: American Arbitration Association, 1986), pp. 72–79.

large portion of their operating budgets on wages, salaries, and other personnel expenditures. Thus, even a modest wage settlement such as a four percent pay increase can have a profound effect on the overall budget of a governmental agency or school district.

Federal, state, and municipal agencies derive revenues either directly or indirectly through the collection of taxes. Few public agencies have the authority to raise the money they need; instead, budgets for governmental agencies are generally established by elected officials and their political appointees. State and municipal agencies obtain funds not only from taxes paid by their constituents, but also from federal grants and assistance. Budgeting and collective bargaining are therefore closely intertwined in the public sector. Budgets are typically established on an annual basis and depend on the fiscal allocations made by governors, mayors, and other high-ranking officials. When budgets for federal, state, or municipal agencies have been established prior to bargaining, it would appear that the amounts allocated for personnel matters would determine the bargaining targets for union negotiators. Union negotiators, however, do not necessarily view the size of a governmental agency's budget as a finite, rigid amount that cannot be exceeded. Rather, they may ignore the budget and establish bargaining goals on other factors such as cost-of-living index changes and the wages that other governmental jurisdictions are paying their workers.

Problems arise when negotiators and budget makers in public-sector organizations do not communicate with each other and coordinate their efforts in some manner. Moreover, private-sector firms usually have more flexible budgeting systems than federal, state, or local government agencies. Even when union and management negotiators agree on a settlement, they may be forced to wait for legislative approval on the funds needed to meet the newly negotiated compensation package and other contract provisions. There is always the risk that legislative bodies will deny these budgetary requests, resulting in a protracted labor dispute. From the standpoint of collective bargaining strategy, the budgetary process in governmental agencies may dilute the final authority of management negotiators to reach a settlement. However, public administrators frequently have the authority to move funds from one budgetary category to another. Funds originally allocated for equipment expenditures may be reallocated to wages and salaries in some cases. Appeals may also be made to legislative bodies for additional monies to fund wage, salary, and benefit demands. For these reasons, the rigid and bureaucratic budgeting process that is commonly characteristic of governmental entities does not necessarily impose a constraint on the collective bargaining process.[36]

Public-sector organizations operate on a nonprofit basis, a fact that makes their bargaining strategies somewhat different from private-sector firms that operate for a profit. The nonprofit-profit distinction may be overemphasized, however. Organizations that operate on a for-profit basis typically reinvest profits into the firm through increased retained earnings or additional capital expenditures. Privately

---

[36] Also see Casey Ichniowski and Jeffrey Zax, "The Effects of Public Sector Unionism on Pay, Employment, Department Budgets, and Municipal Expenditures," in Richard B. Freeman and Casey Ichniowski, eds., *When Public Sector Workers Unionize* (Chicago: University of Chicago Press, 1988), pp. 323–361. Also see Daniel G. Gallagher, "Teacher Bargaining and School District Expectations," *Industrial Relations* (May 1978), pp. 231–237.

held firms earning profits also pay dividends to stockholders. Nonprofit organizations generate surpluses when revenues exceed expenses. Financial surpluses in government agencies may be used either to finance capital expenditures or may be saved for subsequent fiscal years. Some governmental agencies are required to return surpluses to a central budgetary authority or legislative body; for this reason, a public agency may frantically spend surplus funds at the end of a fiscal year in order to avoid returning them. Union negotiators may cite budgetary surpluses to justify wage and benefit demands. There is also evidence that municipal unions are able to increase the demand for public services and increase municipal expenditures through the use of political power and multilateral bargaining.[37]

> Among the characteristics that may be unique in public-sector unionism in the United States, perhaps the most important is the ability of public employees to alter labor demand through the use of political influence over the budgetary process. This influence is likely to be significant at the municipal level, where public employee unions can exercise a combination of lobbying and multilateral bargaining power ...
>
> By affecting wage and employment outcomes, municipal unions are likely to increase municipal department expenditures. If these effects are large and not completely offset by reduction in expenditures in other departments, total municipal expenditures will also increase.[38]

In recent times, public officials in large cities have been faced with severe financial crises. The most noteworthy of these crises was the near-bankruptcy of New York City in the mid-1970s.[39] Even when the threat of bankruptcy is not imminent, state and city elected officials and administrators have faced tax-payer revolts and pressures to cut costs and improve the productivity. Proposition 13 in California in 1978 and proposition two and-one-half in Massachusetts in 1980 are prominent examples of revolts against high taxes. As a result, public officials have been forced to operate on a more economical and efficient basis; negotiators representing state and municipal governments have begun to take a more hard-line, take-it-or-leave-it stance toward the bargaining demands of public-sector unions.[40] According to John A. Gannon, president of the International Association of Fire Fighters (IAFF):

> The cities started playing hardball with us right after President Reagan broke PATCO. It's just been take-away time since then. For example, there've been locals that had full family hospitalization, and the cities are moving them to single coverage. And a lot of our affiliates have gone through no-pay-raise years, or just gotten an insult of a 1 percent raise. And these are in cities where taxes are

---

[37] Robert G. Valetta, "The Impact of Unionism on Municipal Expenditures and Revenues," *Industrial and Labor Relations Review* (April 1989), pp. 430–442.
[38] Richard B. Freeman, "Unionism Comes to the Public Sector," *Journal of Economic Literature*, Vol. 24, No. 1, pp. 41–86. Cited in Robert G. Valetta, "The Impact of Unionism on Municipal Expenditures and Revenues," *Industrial and Labor Relations Review* (April 1989), p. 430.
[39] See Raymond D. Horton, "Fiscal Stress and Labor Power," *Proceedings of the Thirty-Eighth Annual Meeting* (Madison, Wisconsin: Industrial Relations Research Association, 1986), pp. 304–315.
[40] See Milton Derber, "Management Organization for Collective Bargaining in the Public Sector," in Benjamin Aaron, Joyce M. Najita, and James L. Stern, eds., *Public-Sector Bargaining*, 2nd ed. (Washington, D.C.: The Bureau of National Affairs, Inc., 1988), pp. 115–116.

good. So we've gotten to the point now where we send economists into cities to examine their budgets before we begin negotiating. And oftentimes we're able to find out they're hiding money, or just not properly managing it.

For example, we found one city that kept most of their general fund in a checking account at a local bank. We figured that the amount of interest they lost by keeping it there would've doubled the salary demands that this particular board wanted. So when we got that information I called the mayor, told him what we found, and that we wanted to meet with him.

Later on the city's finance director told us that the mayor would agree to our 10 percent wage demand if we agreed not to take any of what we found public . . .[41]

Unique Organizational Issues

In private-sector labor relations, there is little question as to who has the final authority to make decisions on behalf of management. Whomever the company designates to negotiate and administer the contract typically has final authority to act on behalf of the employer. The identity of the persons having final authority with regard to contract negotiations and administration is much less clear, however. Public-sector administration is often fragmented; the responsibility for enforcing public personnel policies and dealing with labor-management relations may be spread across various legislative, executive, and judicial branches. The final authority in some states may be the governor, whereas in other jurisdictions it may be a labor relations officer, school superintendent, or middle-level government official. Some states have attempted to identify the public employer responsible for negotiating and administering collective bargaining agreements.[42] Even when the labor relations authority of public officials is well-defined, an especially strong or unusually weak public official may cause the power structure to shift. For example, a strong mayor may heavily influence the contract negotiations involving sanitation workers, even though the "final" authority for such negotiations has been legislated to the city's chief of public works.

Still another problem that plagues public-sector collective bargaining is drawing the line between supervisory and nonsupervisory personnel. As discussed in Chapter 4, the National Labor Relations Act (NLRA) has defined what constitutes supervisory work for private-sector firms; yet, the distinction between supervisory and nonsupervisory employees in the public sector is often blurred. Contrary to labor relations in the private sector, first-line supervisors and middle-level managers in governmental agencies have often assumed a leadership role in union organizing campaigns and collective bargaining. Although many states have adopted a definition

---

[41] "Protecting Fire Fighters" (Interview with John A. Gannon) in Philip L. Quaglieri, *America's Labor Leaders* (Lexington, Massachusetts: Lexington Books, 1989), p. 107. Reprinted with permission.
[42] For example, New York's Taylor Law defines the various political units (state, county, municipal district, etc.) that fall within the meaning of the term "government." The Connecticut Municipal Employee Relations Act specifies that "the chief executive officer, whether elected or appointed, or his designated representative or representatives shall represent the municipal employer in bargaining . . ." Discussed in Milton Derber, "Management Organization for Collective Bargaining in the Public Sector," in Benjamin Aaron, Joyce M. Najita, and James L. Stern, eds., *Public Sector Bargaining*, 2nd ed. (Washington, D.C.: The Bureau of National Affairs, Inc., 1988), p. 95.

of "supervisor" similar to that found in the NRLA, the collective bargaining rights of public-sector supervisors are far from settled.[43]

The distribution of managerial authority is also related to the bargaining-unit structure of a public-employee group. According to Derber, the wider and more comprehensive a public-sector bargaining unit, the greater the likelihood that management responsibility for bargaining will be centralized. Smaller, narrower, and more fragmented bargaining units, on the other hand, are characterized by a more decentralized administration (including contract negotiations). In the latter case, responsibility for contract negotiations and administration is often vested with a variety of agencies, departments, and institutions.[44] Centralization of the collective bargaining process in many instances is based on the recognition that contract negotiations and administration are time-consuming and require professional skills, specialized knowledge, and access to a large data bank of bargaining information (see Chapter 9).[45] Small government units (municipalities, school boards, etc.) often hire a lawyer or negotiator on an ad hoc basis to represent management at the bargaining table. Both small and newly-organized public-sector entities may encounter problems of inexperience at the bargaining table unless they secure the services of an experienced labor-relations specialist.

Larger governmental units may employ a full-time labor relations specialist. The specialist may be the full-time personnel/human resource manager who deals with a variety of issues such as hiring, personnel planning, and employee health and safety or the specialist may deal with labor relations matters only. Full-time labor specialists must coordinate contract negotiations with higher public officials as well as with line managers working in the governmental agencies that are involved with labor relations. When the central labor relations specialist fails to communicate with other public officials and managers who are affected by the contract negotiations and administration, morale and efficiency problems may arise.

> Professional management negotiators, whether at the central or agency level, are usually sensitive to the internal communication problem. However, they have not always been successful in coping with it, either because of limitations of staff and time or because bargaining strategy impels them to hesitate to reveal their plans to others for fear of leaks. Moreover, in large and complex organizations (a major city, a large school district, or a state), size creates serious communications barriers. In addition, organizational politics, competition for power, interpersonal relations, differences in age, and experience in office, geographical spread of offices, and a host of other internal factors may encourage close involvement with some officials and total neglect of others.[46]

---

[43] See Stephen L. Hayford and Anthony V. Sinicropi, "Bargaining Rights Status of Public Sector Supervisors," *Industrial Relations* (February 1976), pp. 44–61.

[44] Milton Derber, "Management Organization for Collective Bargaining in the Public Sector," in Benjamin Aaron, Joyce M. Najita, and James L. Stern, eds., *Public-Sector Bargaining*, 2nd ed. (Washington, D.C.: The Bureau of National Affairs, Inc., 1988), pp. 99–100.

[45] Milton Derber, "Management Organization for Collective Bargaining in the Public Sector," in Benjamin Aaron, Joyce M. Najita, and James L. Stern, eds., *Public-Sector Bargaining*, 2nd ed. (Washington, D.C.: The Bureau of National Affairs, Inc., 1988), p. 102.

[46] Milton Derber, "Management Organization for Collective Bargaining in the Public Sector, " in Benjamin Aaron, Joyce M. Najita, and James L. Stern, eds., *Public-Sector Bargaining*, 2nd ed. (Washington, D.C.: The Bureau of National Affairs, Inc., 1988), p. 107.

The authority of the centralized labor-relations specialist becomes more uncertain and subject to conflict when there is an overlap between the provisions of the collective bargaining agreement and various civil service rules. However, the above problems are not unique to public-sector labor relations; large private-sector firms with geographically-dispersed operations may also encounter difficulties similar to those described above.

▲ Collective Bargaining among Federal Government Employees

Although some agencies within the federal government have bargained collectively for a number of years, the bargaining rights of federal employees were recognized on a much broader basis when President Kennedy formulated Executive Order 10988 in 1962.[47] The current framework for collective bargaining among federal government employees is based on the Civil Service Reform Act of 1978, Title VII (CSRA).[48] The CSRA states that it is within the public interest for federal employees to join labor organizations and bargain collectively in reaching "amicable settlements" over employment conditions with federal government agencies. According to the CSRA, the federal government demands the highest standards of employee performance and the Act must be interpreted in a manner consistent with "effective and efficient" government.[49] Table 17–4 summarizes the major provisions of the CSRA.

Table 17–4 ▲ Collective Bargaining Rights among Federal Government Employees

Administration:

There are four key agencies charged with personnel matters affecting federal employees. The Office of Personnel Management (OPM) is the major personnel rule-making agency, the Merit System Protection Board (MSPB) reviews personnel regulations to ensure that they are not prohibited under the CSRA (Title I), and the Federal Labor Relations Authority (FLRA) establishes regulations and procedures for collective bargaining among federal employees. The FLRA functions in a fashion similar to the National Labor Relations Board. The Federal Service Impasse Panel (FSIP) helps to resolve labor disputes and impasses.[50]

---

[47] President Nixon subsequently revised Kennedy's executive order with Executive Order 11491 (1970); the Ford administration revised Nixon's order in 1975 with Executive Order 11838.
[48] P. L. 95–454, effective January, 1979. Unlike the aforementioned executive orders, which can be abolished at any time, a law such as the Civil Service Reform Act can be abolished only by an act of Congress or through a court decision that nullifies the constitutionality of the law.
[49] CCH Editorial Staff, *Labor Law Course*, 26th ed. (Chicago: Commerce Clearing House, Inc., 1987), p. 5922.
[50] There has been some controversy surrounding the duplication of effort in dealing with labor-management disputes arising in the federal sector. See David L. Feder, " 'Pick A Forum—Any Forum': A Proposal for A Federal Dispute Resolution Board," *Labor Law Journal* (May 1989), pp. 268–280.

Table 17-4 ▲ Collective Bargaining Rights among Federal Government Employees (Continued)

Recognition of Labor Organizations:

Exclusive recognition may be granted only after a secret-ballot certification election (similar to those conducted by the National Labor Relations Board for private-sector employees). "National consultation" rights may be granted to unions representing a substantial number (but not necessarily a majority) of a federal agency's employees if the employees have no exclusive bargaining representative. National consultation rights require the federal agency to inform the union "of any substantive change in conditions of employment" so that a union has the opportunity to present its "views and recommendations" on proposed changes. Unions must be free of corrupt influences in order to represent federal government employees. Employees have the right to refrain from union membership without fear of reprisal.

Bargaining-Unit Determination:

The FLRA determines the appropriate bargaining unit. Managerial employees are not eligible for bargaining-unit membership except when represented by unions that have historically represented managerial workers. Other employees who are either excluded from a bargaining unit or placed in a separate unit include confidential employees, employees who administer provisions of a labor relations law, and employees who are engaged in internal or national security (except guards). Military personnel (except for civilian employees working in military installations) are forbidden from union membership under the Thurmond Act of 1979.

Scope of Bargaining:

No bargaining outcome is permitted to change federal law or interfere with the federal merit system. Compensation adjustments are ultimately determined by the President of the United States, not through collective bargaining. The CSRA does not permit bargaining over an agency's mission, budget, number of employees, or procedures for internal security. Management has the full authority to decide whether agency work will be subcontracted. Permissible bargaining items include the methods, means, and technology of conducting agency operations. Illegal bargaining items include retirement programs, life and health insurance, and suspending or terminating an employee for national security reasons. Collective bargaining agreements are binding between an exclusive bargaining agent and management after approval by the federal agency head or after 30 days (if the agreement has been neither approved nor disapproved).

Unfair Labor Practices:

The unfair labor practices applicable to federal employees are similar to those under the National Labor Relations Act. In addition, unions cannot interfere with a member's performance as an employee nor can they discriminate with regard to race, color, creed, national origin, sex, age, handicap, marital status, civil service status, or political affiliation. Strikes, slowdowns, or picketing that interferes with an agency's operations are also unfair labor practices.

Grievance Arbitration Procedures:

Collective bargaining agreements must provide a means for the resolution of grievances. Employees may present a grievance and have it adjusted without assistance from the union, but the union has the right to be present at the grievance hearing. Binding arbitration is required in the final step of a grievance procedure. However, arbitration may be initiated only by the exclusive bargaining representative or by management.

Table 17-4 ▲ Collective Bargaining Rights among
Federal Government Employees (Continued)

Impasses and Strikes:

The Federal Mediation and Conciliation Service is the first agency to become involved in a bargaining impasse. Either the union or federal agency may then request the services of the Federal Service Impasse Panel (FSIP). The FSIP may choose from an "arsenal of weapons" in resolving the dispute, including fact-finding, recommendations for a settlement, and directed settlements. It is an unfair labor practice for a union to call, participate in, or condone a strike, work stoppage, or slowdown of a federal agency involved in a labor dispute. The Federal Labor Relations Authority may revoke the exclusive representation status or impose other appropriate sanctions against a union that engages in strike-related activities.

Collective bargaining for employees working for the U.S. Postal Service are covered under the Postal Reorganization Act of 1970 (PRA). The National Labor Relations Board regulates bargaining unit determination, certification elections, and unfair labor practices under the PRA. Postal employees are not allowed to strike under current federal regulation. Federal Reserve employees also have their collective bargaining activities regulated separately from the Civil Service Reform Act.[51]

▲ Collective Bargaining Among State and Local Employees

Unlike federal employees who enjoy uniform regulation under the Civil Service Reform Act of 1978, collective bargaining for state, county, and municipal employees is regulated by a patchwork quilt of state and local laws. This section will discuss the major components of state and municipal collective bargaining legislation.

Sources of Bargaining Rights for State and Local Employees

As noted earlier, public employees have a right to join or form a union, but they do not necessarily have the right to bargain collectively with public employers. State and municipal employees have achieved collective bargaining rights from several sources. First, bargaining rights may be based on a *state or local statute*. Until the 1960s, few state and local jurisdictions provided statutory recognition of public-sector collective bargaining. Wisconsin, a state with a rich history of innovations in collective bargaining, passed a bargaining law in 1959 for municipal employees. The Wisconsin law created an administrative agency similar in function to the National Labor Relations Board (NLRB) and provided a means of resolving bargaining impasses through mediation and fact-finding.[52] By the late 1980s, public

---

[51] For a more detailed discussion of the regulation collective bargaining for postal and federal reserve employees, see Benjamin J. Taylor and Fred Witney, *Labor Relations Law*, 5th ed. (Englewood Cliffs, New Jersey: Prentice-Hall, Inc., 1987), pp. 630–632.

[52] B. V. H. Schneider, "Public-Sector Labor Legislation—An Evolutionary Analysis," in Benjamin Aaron, Joyce M. Najita, and James L. Stern, eds., *Public-Sector Bargaining*, 2nd ed. (Washington, D.C.: The Bureau of National Affairs, Inc., 1988), p. 196.

employees in 34 states had statutory bargaining rights. State and municipal bargaining laws may cover nearly all public employees or may be limited to specific employee groups such as police officers, firefighters, and teachers. State and municipal bargaining statutes are often similar in content to the National Labor Relations Act (NLRA), although most statutes restrict the right of public employees to strike and contain limitations on other issues such as the scope of bargaining, union certification, and bargaining-unit structure.[53]

Bargaining rights for state and municipal employees may also be based on executive orders, court decisions, attorney general opinions, and past practices. Unlike the statutory right to bargain, the right to bargain through means other than a statute is subject to revocation. An executive order or attorney general's opinion allowing public employees to bargain collectively may be issued by a governor, mayor, or attorney general. However, once these public officials leave office, their successors may nullify an executive order or attorney general's opinion and rescind the collective bargaining rights of public employees. Likewise, court decisions may be negated by a statute or reversed by a higher court. State courts may also nullify local bargaining statutes or executive orders.

Organizing and Bargaining in the Absence of Statutory Protections

The lack of a state or municipal collective bargaining statute does not necessarily imply that government employees are unable to organize or bargain. Since few jurisdictions actually make it illegal for a governmental agency to enter into a bargaining relationship with its employees, most public employers have the right to enter into an enforceable collective bargaining agreement. However, the public employer is in a stronger position to resist the concerted efforts of employees if it so decides. According to Leibig and Kahn:

> The difference between jurisdictions with a collective bargaining law and those without a law is that in the latter, no matter how much the employees support a union and let the employer know of this support, the employer does not have to deal with any union, except if the employer chooses to do so. And the employer can pretty well establish the ground rules on which it will deal with unions. For example, the employer can decide whether it will voluntarily recognize a union or will require an election. The employer can decide whether it will deal with the union as a representative of its members only or as an exclusive representative of all people in a "bargaining unit." Also the employer can unilaterally define the appropriate bargaining unit if there is no statute.[54]

Components of State and Local Collective Bargaining Laws

State and municipal bargaining laws have borrowed heavily from NLRA language and provisions in many cases. Nevertheless, a great deal of variety exists among these laws from one state and municipality to another. This section summarizes the

---

[53] Also see Jeffrey S. Zax and Casey Ichniowski, "Bargaining Laws and the Unionization in the Local Public Sector," *Industrial and Labor Relations Review* (April 1990), pp. 447–462.

[54] Michael T. Leibig and Wendy L. Kahn, *Public Employee Organizing and the Law* (Washington, D.C.: The Bureau of National Affairs, Inc., 1987), p. 81.

common elements and differences that characterize state and municipal public-sector bargaining laws.

Employee Groups Covered and Bargaining-Unit Determination

Some state and municipal collective bargaining laws cover nearly all employees under one statute, whereas other jurisdictions use multiple statutes for different occupational groups. For example, the comprehensive bargaining statute for Minnesota covers state employees, including employees of the University of Minnesota, state, and junior colleges.[55] Similarly, Iowa has a single, comprehensive statute that covers nearly all public employees, including state, county, municipal, school, and special-purpose district personnel.[56] Other jurisdictions that rely primarily on one statute to cover collective bargaining for governmental employees include the District of Columbia, Florida, Hawaii, New Hampshire, New York, Ohio, Oregon, and South Dakota.[57]

The majority of states have more than one set of public-sector bargaining laws. California, for example, has five public employee bargaining statutes. State civil service employees and teachers employed by the state Department of Education or the Superintendent of Public Instruction are covered by one law. State noncivil service workers, local government employees, public school workers, and employees of higher education are covered by the other four California statutes.[58] Washington has seven public employee bargaining statutes; four separate laws cover municipal employees, teachers, academic employees in community college districts, and classified personnel in institutions of higher education. Three additional Washington statutes cover port district employees, marine employees of the state ferries system, and utility district workers.[59]

State and municipal bargaining laws typically exclude certain groups of employees from protection. An analysis of the various state laws reveals that there is a wide variety of excluded employees. Excluded employees include managerial and confidential employees, elected and appointed public officials, school superintendents, professional employees engaged in budget preparations, board or commission members, part-time employees, inmates, judges, legislative employees, members of the militia, employees working for small municipalities (e.g., Georgia firefighters working in municipalities with less than 20,000 in population), employees working directly for a governor, students in state institutions, security personnel, persons employed less than six months, seasonal employees, interns, and employees engaged in collective bargaining for management.

Bargaining units of state and local government employees are determined using criteria similar to those found in the National Labor Relations Act (for private-sector

---

[55] Minnesota Statutes Annotated, Chapter 179A.01 et seq. (1984).
[56] Code of Iowa, Chapter 20, Sec. 20.1 et seq. (1974).
[57] The AFL-CIO, Public Employee Department, *AFL-CIO Public Sector Bargaining Law Report* (Washington, D.C.: The AFL-CIO, February 1987).
[58] Government Code Annotated, Title 1, Division 4, Sections 3500 et seq. (1977), 3525 et seq. (1971), 3500 et seq. (1961), 3540 et seq. (1975), and 3560 et seq. (1978).
[59] Revised Code of Washington, Sections 41.56.010 et seq. (1967), 41.59.010 et seq. (1975), 28B.52.010 et seq. (1971), 28B.16.100 et seq. (1971), 53.18.010 et seq. (1967), 47.64.010 et seq. (1961), and 54.04 (1963).

workers). The agency designated to enforce the bargaining law (commonly called a public employment relations board) may have considerable discretion in drawing bargaining-unit lines. In such cases, the desires of union and management officials may carry considerable weight in bargaining-unit determination. Other jurisdictions use specific criteria in determining the composition of bargaining units. Hawaii, for example, has designated the following state-wide bargaining units:

> Nonsupervisory blue-collar employees; supervisory blue-collar employees; white-collar employees; supervisory white-collar employees; teachers; educational officers; University of Hawaii and community college faculty; non-faculty personnel of the University of Hawaii and community colleges; registered nurses; nonprofessional hospital and institutional employees; fire fighters; police officers; professional and scientific employees. The last 5 groups may vote to be included in the general white- or blue-collar units. Supervisors may vote to be included in nonsupervisory units.[60]

The public-sector bargaining law in Kansas, on the other hand, provides a more general set of criteria for bargaining unit determination. Kansas law employs criteria such as efficient administration of government, community of interest, history and extent of organization, geographical location, recommendations of the parties, and separate units for uniformed police, security guards, and fire fighters.[61]

Union Recognition, Certification, and Decertification

States and municipalities that have collective bargaining laws usually allow exclusive union representation. Unions may be certified either by voluntary recognition or by a formal certification election. Voluntary recognition is typically allowed if the union can demonstrate majority interest by bargaining-unit employees through authorization card signatures, formal petition, or other means.

Certification elections are commonly conducted by a state or local public employment relations board. When a certification election is conducted, most jurisdictions require a "show of interest" by bargaining unit employees. Under most statutes, the existence of a collective bargaining agreement prevents a rival union from seeking recognition (known as a "contract bar"). Contract bars may remain in effect for as long as three years in some states, although petitions for a new certification election involving a rival union may be held during designated periods (known as a "window"). Window periods typically go into effect 90 to 120 days prior to the expiration of the current collective bargaining agreement and may last for up to 30 days. If a union loses a certification election, most states provide for 12-month election bars before another union can seek certification. State and local public-sector bargaining statutes also provide for decertification proceedings, conditions under which the employer may withdraw union recognition, and the elimination of inactive unions that no longer desire to represent bargaining-unit employees.[62]

---

[60] Hawaii Revised Statutes, Chapter 89, Section 89–1 et seq. (1970).
[61] Kansas Statutes Annotated, Chapter 264, Section 75–4321 et seq. (1971).
[62] See Michael T. Leibig and Wendy L. Kahn, *Public Employee Organizing and the Law* (Washington, D.C.: The Bureau of National Affairs, Inc., 1987), pp. 93–98.

Scope of Bargaining

A critical issue in public-sector bargaining is the scope or breadth of issues that are subject to negotiation and inclusion in the collective bargaining agreement.[63] In the private sector, the range of mandatory bargaining subjects is very broad. However, the range of bargaining topics in public-sector negotiations is often more limited. The majority of state laws define the scope of bargaining to include "wages, hours, and working conditions." However, these same statutes often provide a list of excluded topics that remain under the control of the public employer and are not subject to negotiation. A few states such as California have "meet and confer" statutes that do not require the employer to engage in good-faith bargaining. Meet-and-confer statutes allow employers more discretion in dealing with labor organizations and determining contract provisions. Table 17–5 lists *excluded* bargaining subjects for selected states.

Table 17–5 ▲ Bargaining Subjects Excluded from Negotiations in Selected States

State	Bargaining Law	Exclusions
Alaska	Public Employees (General)	General policies describing the function and purposes of the employer.
California	State Civil Service Employees	Merits, necessity, or organization of any service provided by law or executive order. Rental rates for state-owned housing rented to employees.
	Local Government Employees	Merits, necessity, or organization of any service provided by law or executive order.
Hawaii	All Public Employees	Classifications and reclassifications; benefits to the public employee's health fund, retirement, salary ranges provided by law; matters inconsistent with merit principles and the equal pay for equal work principle; managerial discipline and control.
Kansas	Public Employees in General	Subjects preempted by federal, state, or municipal law; employer and employee rights; and state merit system.
Kentucky	Police Officers	Managerial policy.

[63] Scope-of-bargaining concerns are often difficult to resolve. In *Pennsylvania Labor Relations Board v. State College Area School District*, 337A .2d 285, Sup. Ct. of Pennsylvania (1975), the court tried to sort out what subjects were mandatory items of negotiation and what subjects the school district could refuse to negotiate without committing an unfair labor practice.

Table 17–5 ▲ Bargaining Subjects Excluded from Negotiations in Selected States (Continued)

State	Bargaining Law	Exclusions
Maine	State Employees	Matters proscribed by law; regulations governing application for state service; merit system principles and personnel laws.
Massachusetts	Police and Fire Fighters	Appointments, promotions, assignments, and transfers.
Minnesota	All Public Employees	Retirement contributions or benefits; employer's personnel policies; educational policies of a school district.
Ohio	Public Employees in General	Civil service examinations.
Vermont	Municipal Employees	Managerial prerogatives.
Wisconsin	State Employees	Employer rights; mission and goals of agency; merit system; and matters related to employee occupancy of houses or other lodging provided by the state.

Alaska Statutes Titles 14 and 23, as amended; California Government Code Annotated Title 1, (1977), as amended; Hawaii Revised Statutes, Chapter 89, (1970), as amended; Kansas Statutes Annotated, Chapter 264, Section 72 and 75 (1971), as amended; Kentucky Revised Statutes, Chapters 78 and 345 (1972), as amended; Maine Revised Statutes, Title 26 (1973), as amended; Minnesota Statutes Annotated, Chapter 179A (1984) as amended; Ohio Revised Code, Chapter 4117 (1984); Vermont Statutes Annotated Titles 6, 16, and 21 (1969), as amended; and Wisconsin Statutes Annotated, Chapter 111 (1966), as amended.

Rather than use the general "wages, hours, and working conditions" categorization, some state public-sector bargaining statutes provide a lengthy list of bargaining topics that are subject to negotiation. For example, the scope of bargaining provision for local government employees, teachers, and nurses in Nevada includes the following:

> Salary, wage rates, or other forms of direct monetary compensation; sick leave, vacation leave, holidays, and other nonpaid leaves of absence; insurance benefits; total hours of work required of an employee on each work day or work week; total number of days of work required in a work year; discharge and disciplinary procedures; recognition clause; method used to classify employees in the bargaining unit; deduction of dues for the recognized union; protection of employees in the bargaining unit from discrimination because of participation in recognized unions; no strike provisions; grievance and arbitration procedures for resolution of disputes relating to interpretation or application of collective bargaining agreements; general savings clauses; duration of collective bargaining agreement[s]; safety; teacher preparation time; procedures for reduction in [the] workforce.[64]

---

[64] Nevada Revised Statutes, Section 288.010 et seq. (1969).

Specific scope of bargaining clauses such as the one above may be used to limit the union's ability to include a wide range of topics in contract talks. However, specific definitions can create controversies as to whether a certain topic can be legally discussed at the bargaining table. For example, does the "safety" topic in the Nevada law allow teachers to bargain over the issue of using physical force against students who pose a threat to other students and school personnel? When such controversies arise, it may take more time to determine whether an issue is negotiable than to negotiate it.

Certain occupational groups such as teachers have their own unique scope of bargaining provisions. For example, the bargaining law affecting Indiana teachers allows negotiators to discuss curriculum developments and revisions, textbook selection, teaching methods, student discipline and expulsion, pupil-teacher ratios, class sizes, and budget appropriations.[65] Interestingly, the scope of bargaining provisions for police and firefighters is generally confined to the generic "wages, hours, and working conditions." However, police and firefighters have unique bargaining concerns. An analysis of interest arbitration cases involving police officers, for example, include issues such as court appearance pay, false arrest insurance, type of sidearm carried, and special assignment pay.[66]

Unfair Labor Practices

Nearly all public-sector collective bargaining statutes have unfair labor practice provisions for both employers and unions. These unfair labor practice charges are often similar to those found in the NLRA. For example, bad-faith bargaining is a common unfair labor practice in both private- and public-sector labor relations. In addition, there are unfair labor practices that are unique to state and municipal collective bargaining. Table 17–6 summarizes employer and union unfair labor practices in selected states.

Table 17–6 ▲ Selected Public-Sector Employer and Union Unfair Labor Practices

State	Bargaining Law	Unfair Labor Practices
Alaska	Public Employees in General	Employer: Interfere with, restrain, or coerce employees; dominate labor organizations; discriminate on account of labor organization membership or testimony.
		Union: Restrain or coerce employees or the employer's representative; refusal to bargain in good faith.

---

[65] Indiana Code Title 20, Article 7.5, Section 20–7.5–1 et seq. (1973).
[66] John Delaney and Peter Feuille, "Police Interest Arbitration: Awards and Issues," in David Lewin, Peter Feuille, Thomas A. Kochan, and John Thomas Delaney, eds., *Public Sector Labor Relations: Analysis and Readings*, 3rd ed. (Lexington, Massachusetts: Lexington Books, 1988), p. 393.

Table 17-6 ▲ Selected Public-Sector Employer and Union Unfair Labor Practices (Continued)

State	Bargaining Law	Unfair Labor Practices
California	State Civil Service Employees	Employer: Interfere with, intimidate, restrain, coerce, or discriminate against employees; deny union rights guaranteed under the statute; refusal to meet and confer in good faith; dominate unions; refusal to participate in the mediation procedure. Union: Cause or attempt to cause an employer to commit an unfair labor practice; interfere with, restrain, coerce, or discriminate against employees; refusal to meet and confer in good faith; refusal to participate in the mediation procedure.
	Higher Education Employees	Employer: Threaten, discriminate, interfere with, restrain, or coerce employees; deny union's rights guaranteed under statute; refusal to meet and confer; dominate unions; refusal to participate in the impasse procedure; consult with groups other than the exclusive representative. Union: Interfere with, restrain, or coerce employees; cause or attempt to cause an employer to commit an unfair labor practice; refusal to meet and confer; refusal to participate in the impasse procedure; failure to represent all employees fairly; charge excessive service fees; cause or attempt to cause an employer to pay for services not rendered.
Connecticut	State Employees	Employer: Interfere with, lockout, or discriminate on account of union membership or testimony; refusal to bargain in good faith; violation of SBLR rules regarding the conduct of representation elections. Union: Refusal to reduce an agreement to writing and sign it.
	Municipal Employees	Employer: Refusal to discuss grievances; refusal to comply with an arbitration award.
	Teachers	Employer: Refusal to participate in mediation or arbitration in good faith. Union: Solicit or advocate support of students.

Table 17–6 ▲ Selected Public-Sector Employer and Union Unfair Labor Practices (Continued)

State	Bargaining Law	Unfair Labor Practices
Delaware:	Teachers	Employer: Refusal to disclose public records. Union: Soliciting employees during working hours; hindering or preventing the pursuit of work; solicit or advocate support of students on school property.
	Police and Fire Fighters	Union: Distribute union literature or solicit employees during work hours; hinder or prevent the pursuit of work.
District of Columbia	All Public Employees	Union: Participate in a work stoppage, recognitional strike, or secondary boycott.
Illinois	Public Employees in General	Employer: Violation of the board's rules and regulations. Union: Picketing to force an employer to bargain.
Kansas	Public Employees in General	Union: Endorse or make contributions to political candidates.
Maine	Municipal, County, School, and Turnpike Employees	Employer: Blacklist employees. Union: Engage in work stoppages, slowdowns, strikes, or blacklisting.
Minnesota	All Public Employees	Employer: Refusal to provide budget information to a union. Union: Call for a jurisdictional strike; damage property or endanger safety of persons while on strike; force or require an employer to assign work to certain employees in a particular union; cause or attempt to cause an employer to pay for services not performed; engage in an unlawful strike; picketing that has an unlawful purpose; picketing that unreasonably interferes with access to an employer's facilities; seize, occupy, or destroy employer's property.
Montana	Public Employees in General	Union: Use of agency shop fees for political purposes.
Nevada	Local Government Employees, Teachers, and Nurses	Employer and Union: Discriminate on account of race, color, religion, sex, age, physical or visual handicap, national origin, political or personal reasons or affiliations.
New Hampshire	All Public Employees	Employer: Adopt any law or regulation that would invalidate any part of the agreement; breach of a collective bargaining agreement.

Table 17–6 ▲ Selected Public-Sector Employer and Union Unfair Labor Practices (Continued)

State	Bargaining Law	Unfair Labor Practices
New Mexico	State Employees in Classified Service	Union: Coerce or discipline an employee in an effort to hinder job performance.
New York	Public Employees in General	Employer: Refusal to continue the terms of an expired contract until a new contract is negotiated.
Oregon	Public Employees in General	Employers and Unions: Communicate with outside parties other than bargaining representatives during negotiations regarding employment conditions.
Pennsylvania	Public Employees in General	Employer and Unions: Violate PLRB rules and regulations regarding conduct of representation elections.

In selecting representative employer and union unfair labor practices from state statutes, only those practices that were somewhat unique were chosen in order to avoid repetition. The reader should refer to the actual text of a particular state law for a full listing of employer and union unfair labor practices. Alaska Statutes Title 23, Chapters 20 and 40, as amended; California Government Code Annotated, Title 1, Division 4, (1977), as amended; Connecticut General Statutes, Titles 5, 7, and 10 (1975), as amended; Delaware Code Titles 2, 14, and 19 (1965), as amended; District of Columbia Law 2–139 (1978), as amended; Illinois Public Act 1012 (1984), as amended; Kansas Statutes Annotated, Chapter 264 (1971), as amended; Maine Revised Statutes, Title 26 (1969), as amended; Minnesota Statutes Annotated, Chapter 179A (1984), as amended; Montana Compiled Laws, Chapters 31 and 32 (1973), as amended; Nevada Revised Statutes, Section 288 (1969), as amended; New Hampshire Revised Statutes Annotated, Chapter 273-A (1975), as amended; New Mexico State Personnel Board (rules and regulations for labor-management relations for state classified employees), (1983); New York Civil Service Law, Section 200 (1967), as amended; Oregon Revised Statutes, Section 243 (1963), as amended; Pennsylvania Acts 288 (1967), 111 (1968), and 195 (1970), as amended.

Strikes and the Treatment of Striking Employees

As discussed earlier, the majority of state and municipal collective bargaining statutes prohibit strikes by public employees.[67] States and municipalities that follow this practice often establish penalties for union officials who condone work stoppages. In Iowa, for example, strikes may be enjoined by a state court; individuals who engage in strikes may be fined up to $500 a day and unions up to $10,000 a day. Iowa law also provides for up to six months imprisonment, loss of employment rights for one year, and union decertification for one year.[68] Nevada law prohibits strikes and may fine a union up to $50,000 a day; union leaders may be fined $1,000 a day or jailed.[69] Other states that prohibit strikes either have less severe penalties than those described above or they do not list any penalties associated with work stoppages. In addition, some statutes establish penalties for striking employees that

---

[67] Strikes are generally prohibited in Alabama, Arizona, Arkansas, California (except municipal employees), Colorado, Connecticut, Delaware, District of Columbia, Florida, Georgia, Idaho, Indiana, Iowa, Kansas, Kentucky, Louisiana, Maine, Maryland, Massachusetts, Michigan, Mississippi, Missouri, Nebraska, Nevada, New Hampshire, New Jersey, New Mexico, New York, North Carolina, North Dakota, Rhode Island, Virginia, Washington, and Wisconsin. Oklahoma, South Carolina, South Dakota, Tennessee, Texas, Utah, West Virginia, and Wyoming either do not have public-sector bargaining statutes or have statutes that are silent on the issue of strikes by public employees.
[68] Code of Iowa, Chapter 20, Sec. 20.1 et seq. (1974).
[69] Nevada Revised Statutes, Section 288.010 et seq. (1969).

include loss of pay and benefits, termination, and cancellation of the collective bargaining agreement. New York law stipulates that employees engaging in illegal public-sector strikes will lose two day's pay; the striking employee is penalized one day's pay for each strike day and this amount is added to the day's pay that the employee loses for not working.[70] Strike penalties may be of questionable value in some cases:

> The question of appropriate sanctions for the illegal strike is receiving increased attention. Early laws were extremely punitive calling for heavy fines, prison terms and strong institutional penalties including loss of representation rights.... There has been some movement toward more limited penalties. Imprisonment of union leaders does not take place lightly. It has been learned that a prison term may make a martyr of a union leader and seriously impair the ability of the parties to work out a settlement. Excessive organizational fines have been set aside either as a price of settlement or when it became clear that there was no realistic way for the union to meet the fine. If there is a trend in sanctions, it is toward individual and organizational penalties which are severe enough to have some deterrent value without becoming unreasonably excessive. Attention has turned to such fines for individuals as loss of two days' pay for each day of illegal strike and forfeiture of check-off rights for the union.[71]

Nine states allow a limited right to strike by public employees. Such statutes recognize that not all public employee services are essential. Table 17–7 summarizes the statutory provisions of states who allow their employees the right to strike.

Table 17–7 ▲ Statutes That Allow Public Sector Employees the Right to Strike

State	Bargaining Law	Strike Provisions
Alaska	Public Employees in General	Strikes are prohibited for law enforcement and fire protection employees; jail, prison, and correctional institution employees. Strikes may be enjoined. Public utility, snow removal, sanitation, public school, and other educational institution employees may strike until there is a threat to public safety, health, or welfare. At that time the superior court may enjoin the strike, and the parties shall submit to arbitration. All other employees may strike after majority vote.
Hawaii	All Public Employees	Limited right to strike 60 days after fact-finding report. Parties must give 10-day notice prior to the strike. The Hawaii Labor Relations Board (HLRB) must certify that the striking employees'

---

[70] New York Civil Service Law, Section 200 et seq. (1967).
[71] Walter J. Gershenfeld, "Public Employee Unionization—An Overview," in Muriel K. Gibbons, Robert D. Helsby, Jerome Lefkowitz, and Barbara Z. Tener, eds., *Portrait of a Process—Collective Negotiations in Public Employment* (Fort Washington, Pennsylvania: Labor Relations Press, 1979), p. 20.

Table 17–7 ▲ Statutes That Allow Public Sector Employees the Right to Strike (Continued)

State	Bargaining Law	Strike Provisions
		services are nonessential. HLRB may set requirements to remove danger to public health and safety. Strikes are forbidden over contributions to the public employees' health fund.
Illinois	Public Employees in General	Security employees, peace officers, firefighters, and paramedics are not allowed to strike. Other employees may strike only if they are represented by a union, their contract has expired (and does not prohibit a strike), disputed issues are not submitted to binding arbitration, mediation has been unsuccessful, and a 5-day notice has been given prior to the strike. A strike may be enjoined if public health and safety are endangered.
	Educational Employees	Strikes are allowed only if the employees are represented by a union, mediation has been unsuccessful, the contract has expired, the dispute was not submitted to binding arbitration, and a 5-day notice is given. A strike may be enjoined if public health and safety are endangered.
Minnesota	All Public Employees	Confidential, essential, and managerial employees may not strike. Nonessential employees may strike if the contract has expired and the mandatory mediation period has passed (or an impasse has arisen and there is no previous contract). Teachers may strike if the above requirements have been met plus neither party requests arbitration (or arbitration has been rejected), or the employer refuses to comply with an arbitration award.
Montana	Public Employees in General	All employees except firefighters may strike.
	Nurses	Nurses are permitted to strike upon a 30-day notice provided there is no other strike at a health care facility within a 150-mile radius.
Ohio	Public Employees in General	Strikes are prohibited for police, fire fighters, and state highway patrol. Other employees may strike after a 10-day

Table 17-7 ▲ Statutes That Allow Public Sector Employees the Right to Strike (Continued)

State	Bargaining Law	Strike Provisions
		notice. A strike may be enjoined for health and safety reasons. If a strike is enjoined, the parties must bargain for 60 days with the assistance of a state mediator.
Oregon	Public Employees in General	Strikes are prohibited for emergency telephone workers, police, firefighters, and guards at prisons and hospitals. All other employees may strike after the use of mediation and fact-finding, provided that a 10-day notice has been given and 30 days have elapsed since the fact-finding report has been made public. The employer may seek an injunction to prevent strikes that threaten public health, safety, and welfare. A court may order a dispute submitted to arbitration. Strikes are also prohibited when a union is not recognized by the employer or state Public Employment Relations Board (PERB), where there is an interest arbitration provision, or in response to an unfair labor practice by the employer. Employees normally prohibited from striking who refuse to cross a picket line are regarded as engaging in an illegal strike.
Pennsylvania	Public Employees in General	Prohibited for prison and mental hospital guards and court employees. Other employees may strike after mediation and fact-finding. The employer may seek an injunction if the strike creates a clear and present danger to public health, safety, and welfare.
Vermont	Municipal Employees	Municipal employees may strike 30 days after a fact-finder's report if the parties have not agreed to arbitration and there is no danger to public health, safety, and welfare. (State employees are prohibited from striking).

Alaska Statutes Titles 14 and 23 (1970), as amended; Hawaii Revised Statutes, Chapter 89 (1970), as amended; Illinois Public Acts 1012 and 1014 (1984), as amended; Minnesota Statutes Annotated, Chapter 179A (1984), as amended; Montana Compiled Laws, Chapter 31 and 32 (1969 and 1973), as amended; Ohio Revised Code Chapter 4117 (1984); Oregon Revised Statutes, Section 243 (1963), as amended; Pennsylvania Acts 111, 195, and 288 (1967, 1968, and 1970), as amended; Vermont Statutes Annotated, Titles 6, 16, and 21 (1969 and 1973), as amended.

As Table 17–7 indicates, none of the state and municipal public-sector collective bargaining laws provide the broad right-to-strike privileges that are possessed by private-sector employees. Most state legislatures have decided that strikes by government employees are somehow different than those by their private-sector counterparts. States such as Illinois and Ohio have recognized that some public employees do not provide essential services and should therefore be allowed to strike. Montana has taken an even broader view and allows nearly all public employees to strike; only firefighters are totally restricted from striking and nurses may strike if 30-day notice is given and there are no other health care strikes within a 150-mile radius. However, a number of labor experts and scholars believe that public-sector bargaining laws unnecessarily restrict the use of strikes by government employees.[72] Taylor and Witney summarize their concerns:

> Most public bodies with authority to decide strike legality will hold generally false conceptions of the effect that public employee strikes will have, and will prohibit them far beyond any real need to do so. In this respect, the politics of the moment may prevail over rational economic judgment. It has been demonstrated that because of technology, excess capacity, and the ability to substitute and postpone demand for services often performed by the public sector, most public employee strikes will impose little or no economic cost, and only some inconvenience in substituting or in delay. State legislatures should spend more time developing strike safeguards instead of evading the problem by merely outlawing strikes.[73]

Olson has drawn several conclusions regarding public policy and strikes among government employees. First, interest arbitration (in which an arbitrator determines the contract provisions when union and management negotiators reach an impasse) has been successful in reducing strike activity in the public sector. Second, strike penalties such as fines, termination of striking workers, and union decertification can deter strikes. As noted earlier, some states that have strike penalties fail to enforce them and, instead, grant amnesty to workers who engage in prohibited work stoppages. On the other hand, states that allow public employees to strike on a limited basis do not necessarily open the flood gates to strike activity. Olson cites Pennsylvania as an example in which the legal right to strike provided to municipal employees (other than police and firefighters) had little effect on the incidence of strikes. Third, state and municipal policies other than collective bargaining policies can have an important effect on strike activity. School teachers, for example, are less likely to strike when the school days missed because of the work stoppage will not be rescheduled.[74] Presumably, striking teachers realize that they will permanently lose income when school days are not made up; when state or municipal law require make-up days the teachers know that they will eventually recoup in-

---

[72] See Gary R. Grimes, "Strike Out Public-Sector Strikes," *Personnel* (April 1988), p. 104.
[73] Benjamin J. Taylor and Fred Witney, *Labor Relations Law*, 5th ed. (Englewood Cliffs, New Jersey: Prentice-Hall, Inc., 1987), p. 644.
[74] Craig A. Olson, "Dispute Resolution in the Public Sector," in Benjamin Aaron, Joyce M. Najita, and James L. Stern, eds., *Public-Sector Bargaining*, 2nd ed. (Washington, D.C.: The Bureau of National Affairs, Inc., 1988), pp. 165–166. Also see Craig A. Olson, "The Role of Rescheduled School Days in Teacher Strikes," *Industrial and Labor Relations Review* (July 1982), pp. 515–528.

come lost during the strike. Finally, there is evidence that both the incidence and duration of public-sector strikes are reduced when union and management negotiators are more experienced in collective bargaining.[75]

Impasse Resolution Provisions

In the private sector, failure to reach an agreement often leads to a work stoppage. As discussed in the previous section, state and municipal employees do not have the right to strike, except on a very limited basis. A strike or, more appropriately, the threat of a strike has been regarded as labor's primary weapon to ensure that the employer engages in meaningful collective bargaining. When the union and its members are deprived of the strike weapon, their bargaining power is seriously impaired unless they are provided with an alternative. The alternative in public-sector bargaining is an *impasse procedure* that is built into the state or municipal collective bargaining statute. Statutory impasse procedures typically consist of mediation, fact-finding, interest arbitration, or some combination thereof. The design and administration of an impasse procedure can have a significant effect on the negotiators' willingness to bargain in good faith and resolve impasses.

Most state and municipal public-sector bargaining laws include some form of mediation in their impasse procedure. The use of mediation in public-sector interest disputes is similar to that found in private-sector impasses.[76] Mediation may be used primarily in the initial stage of impasse resolution or it may be employed in conjunction with fact-finding and interest arbitration.[77] Fact-finders hear the positions of both parties and usually make recommendations to the state agency in charge of public-sector labor relations. Although fact-finders may attempt to mediate a dispute, they play a more formal role than the mediator in resolving public-sector interest disputes. In its report to the governor of New York, the Taylor Committee, which drafted New York's public-sector law, stated as follows:

> Fact-finding requires the parties to gather objective information and to present arguments with references to these data. An unsubstantiated or extreme demand from either party tends to lose its force and status in this form. The fact-finding report and recommendations provide a basis to inform and crystallize thoughtful public opinion and news media comment. Such reports and recommendations have a special relevance when the public's business is involved. The public has a special right to be informed on the issues, contentions, and merits of disputes involving public employees.[78]

---

[75] Edward Montgomery and Mary Ellen Benedict, "The Impact of Bargainer Experience on Teacher Strikes," *Industrial and Labor Relations Review* (April 1989), pp. 380–392.
[76] See Kenneth Kressel, "Labor Mediation: An Exploratory Survey," in David A. Lewin, Peter Feuille, Thomas A. Kochan, and John Thomas Delaney, eds., *Public Sector Labor Relations: Analysis and Readings* (Lexington, Massachusetts: Lexington Books, 1988), pp. 351–373.
[77] For an excellent discussion of public-sector mediation (most of which is equally applicable to private-sector), see Arnold M. Zack, *Public-Sector Mediation* (Washington, D.C.: The Bureau of National Affairs, Inc., 1985).
[78] *Governor's Committee on Public Employee Relations Final Report* (Albany, New York: State of New York, March 31, 1966), p. 37. Cited in Harold R. Newman, "Mediation and Fact-Finding," in Muriel K. Gibbons, Robert D. Helsby, Jerome Lefkowitz, and Barbara Z. Tener, eds., *Portrait of a Process—Collective Negotiations in Public Employment* (Fort Washington, Pennsylvania: Labor Relations Press, 1979), p. 202.

Approximately half of the state public-sector bargaining statutes employ fact finders in their impasse procedures.

Interest arbitrators are used to determine the terms of the contract when union and management negotiators are unable or unwilling to reach a settlement. Many interest arbitration provisions were designed primarily for police and firefighters. Some state statutes provide for *conventional arbitration*, which allows the arbitrator to fashion the award that he or she deems appropriate for the disputed issues. Other states call for *final-offer arbitration* in which the arbitrator chooses either labor's or management's final offer with no compromising between the two offers. Final-offer arbitration may be either final offer *by package* (where the arbitrator selects either the union's or management's final offer on *all* disputed issues) or final offer *by issue* (where the arbitrator selects either side's final offer on an *issue-by-issue* basis).[79] Over half of the states have included interest arbitration as the final step in resolving bargaining impasses in public-sector disputes.

Iowa, for example, uses a combination of mediation,[80] fact finding, and interest arbitration if the parties do not elect to use their own impasse procedure.[81] First, a mediator is selected by the Iowa Public Employment Relations Board (PERB). If mediation is unsuccessful, a fact finder is called upon to analyze the unsettled bargaining issues, make recommendations as to what the final contract terms should be, and file a report on the recommendations within 15 days.[82] The fact finder's report is made public after 10 days if the parties have still not reached an agreement. Finally, an interest arbitrator or tripartite panel of arbitrators is selected. The interest arbitrator(s) must select from among the employer's final offer, the union's final offer, or the fact finder's recommendation. Interest arbitrators hearing public-sector interest disputes in Iowa must pick a final offer from one of the three above.[83] Suppose an impasse has been reached over wages and mediation has not been successful in breaking the stalemate. The union's final demand is a nine percent wage increase, whereas management's final offer is four percent. The fact-finder subsequently recommends a seven percent increase. The interest arbitrator or arbitration panel must then decide on a wage settlement of four, seven, or nine percent; the interest arbitrators cannot select a compromise settlement of six percent. This procedure is known as final-offer-selection arbitration. Iowa statute also forbids interest arbitrators from engaging in mediation activities.[84] Figure 17–1 summarizes the procedure used in Iowa public-sector impasses.

---

[79] "Dispute Resolution," in David Lewin, Peter Feuille, Thomas A. Kochan, and John Thomas Delaney, *Public Sector Labor Relations Analysis and Readings*, 3rd ed., (Lexington, Massachusetts: Lexington Books, 1988), p. 339.

[80] See Ronald Hoh, "The Effectiveness of Mediation in Public Sector Arbitration Systems: The Iowa Experience," *The Arbitration Journal* (June 1984), pp. 30–40.

[81] See Daniel G. Gallagher and M. D. Chaubey, "Impasse Behavior and Tri-Offer Arbitration in Iowa," *Industrial Relations* (Spring 1982), pp. 129–147.

[82] Fact finding with recommendations is also known as *advisory arbitration*.

[83] Interest arbitrators do not make their decisions in a vacuum; rather, the applicable public-sector bargaining law frequently stipulates standards that must be followed in selecting a final offer. In Iowa, the criteria that the interest arbitrator or tripartite arbitration panel must follow are past agreements; comparison with comparable public employees, considering factors peculiar to the area or job; interest and welfare of the public; ability to pay; effect of award on standard of services; employers' taxing or appropriating power.

[84] Code of Iowa, Chapter 20, Sec. 20.1 et seq. (1974).

17 PUBLIC-SECTOR LABOR RELATIONS ▲ 669

MEDIATION
- Begins 120 days prior to budget submission date.
- Mediator appointed by PERB at request of either employer or union.

FACT FINDING
- Appointed by parties 10 days after mediator's appointment.
- Recommendations due within 15 days.
- Report made public 10 days later (if no settlement is reached).

INTEREST ARBITRATION
- Either employer or union may request single or tripartite arbitration.
- Arbitrator(s) select (1) union's final offer, or (2) employer's final offer, or (3) fact finder's recommendations.
- The arbitrator's decision is incorporated into the collective bargaining agreement.

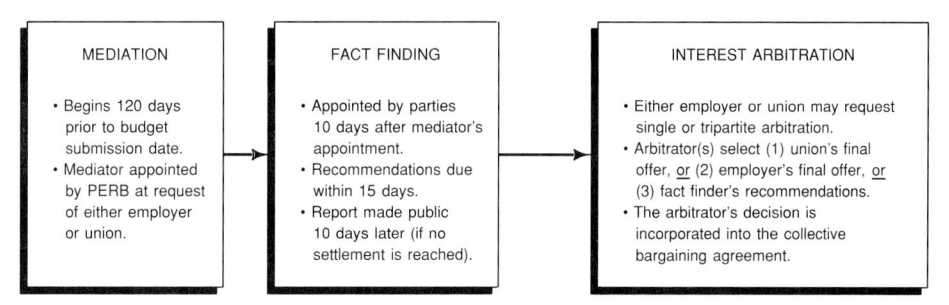

Figure 17–1 Iowa Public-Sector Impasse Resolution Procedure

In theory, final-offer-selection arbitration similar to that used in Iowa should force union and management negotiators to make a reasonable final offer. Similarly, a "package" form of final-offer arbitration is used in Massachusetts, Wisconsin, and Hawaii. Under the package form of final arbitration, each party must submit one final package incorporating all unsettled issues; the arbitrator or arbitration panel must select what is considered to be the most suitable package. Under package arbitration, interest arbitrators cannot pick and choose from among the best features of the union and management final offers.

The ideal form of interest arbitration discourages the parties from using it and, instead, places a high premium on reaching a settlement without third-party intervention. Final-offer-selection and package arbitration are supposed to encourage adequate preparation for contract talks and realistic proposals and concessions at the bargaining table. In reality, interest arbitration discourages resort to arbitration, but does not eliminate it. Research on interest arbitration indicates a usage range (as a percent of negotiated settlements) from 3.8 in Iowa to 29 percent for Pennsylvania police and firefighters.[85] The usage rate of interest arbitration probably depends on factors such as whether the public employees have a limited right to strike, whether final-offer-selection or package arbitration is used, and the union and management negotiators' willingness to control their own destiny rather than place their fate in the hands of an arbitrator or arbitration panel.[86]

Interest arbitration is not without its detractors.[87] One concern of the critics is that when union and management negotiators allow interest arbitration to resolve unsettled issues, arbitrators may be forced to choose not the best or most suitable package, but that which is the least inequitable.[88] Farber and Katz have formulated

---

[85] Richard A. Lester, *Labor Arbitration in State and Local Governments* (Princeton, New Jersey: Industrial Relations Section, Princeton University, 1984), cited in Craig A. Olson, "Dispute Resolution in the Public Sector," in Benjamin Aaron, Joyce M. Najita, and James L. Stern, eds., *Public-Sector Bargaining*, 2nd ed. (Washington, D.C.: The Bureau of National Affairs, Inc., 1988), pp. 167–168.

[86] See, for example, Arnold M. Zack, "The Arbitration of Interest Disputes: A Process in Peril," *Arbitration Journal* (June 1986), pp. 38–47; and Richard A. Lester, "Lessons from Experience with Interest Arbitration in Nine Jurisdictions," *Arbitration Journal* (June 1986), pp. 34–37.

[87] See, for example, John C. Anderson, "The Impact of Arbitration: A Methodological Assessment," *Industrial Relations* (Spring 1981), pp. 129–148; and David Bloom, "Is Arbitration *Really* Compatible with Bargaining?" *Industrial Relations* (Fall 1981), pp. 233–244.

[88] Charles M. Rehmus, "Interest Arbitration," in Muriel K. Gibbons, Robert D. Helsby, Jerome Lefkowitz, and Barbara Z. Tener, eds., *Portrait of a Process—Collective Negotiations in the Public Sector* (Fort Washington, Pennsylvania: Labor Relations Press, 1979), p. 218.

a theoretical model that demonstrates that parties with a low tolerance for risk (known as risk aversion) will concede to a wage that is beyond the expected arbitration award.[89] Compulsory arbitration has also been challenged on the grounds that illegal strikes still occur in jurisdictions mandating interest arbitration. However, this argument ignores the fact that the incidence of public-sector strikes is considerably less than private-sector strikes. Another criticism of interest arbitration is that it has a chilling effect on the bargaining process; rather than encouraging meaningful collective bargaining, interest arbitration is accused of fostering a conservative approach to bargaining and a reluctance to make concessions by negotiators at the bargaining table. Critics of interest arbitration claim that over time, negotiators develop a dependency on arbitrating rather than continue bargaining over unresolved issues (known as the *narcotic effect*).[90] Union and management negotiators may decide that it is easier to adopt a hard-line stance at the bargaining table and then "pass the buck" to the interest arbitrator in order to save face and avoid political pressures from constituents. To the extent that this point is valid, interest arbitration may stifle creativity in public-sector labor relations.[91] There are also concerns that interest arbitration may become systematically biased toward either management or labor, especially since statutes publish criteria for arbitrators to follow in making their awards.[92] There are those who believe that interest arbitration comes into conflict with the sovereignty doctrine discussed earlier. When interest arbitrators determine the final terms and provisions of a collective bargaining agreement, they are encroaching on the power of elected public officials. Opponents of interest arbitration believe that private citizens working as interest arbitrators may impose an unacceptable collective bargaining agreement on public officials and tax payers. Of course, this argument overlooks the fact that legislators enacted the interest arbitration provisions of the state or local bargaining statute in the first place.[93] In addition, public policy makers can amend interest arbitration statutes that prove unworkable.

> Charges that compulsory arbitration tends to have a "narcotic" effect on collective bargaining, whatever their merit, are likely to carry less weight with state legislatures than will the prospect of strike-free, definite, and certain disputes resolutions brought about by compulsory arbitration. A greater concern, perhaps, is the ever-present danger that arbitrators will grant wage awards that are unacceptably high or will decide noneconomic issues in ways that impermissibly intrude in areas intended to be the exclusive preserve of government management. Those fears can be assuaged, however, by the appropriate statutory re-

---

[89] Henry S. Farber and Harry C. Katz, "Interest Arbitration, Outcomes, and the Incentive to Bargain," *Industrial and Labor Relations Review* (October 1979), pp. 55–63.
[90] See Janet Currie, "Who Uses Interest Arbitration?: The Case of the British Columbia Teachers, 1947–1981," *Industrial and Labor Relations Review* (April 1989), pp. 363–379; and Richard J. Butler and Ronald G. Ehrenberg, "Estimating the Narcotic Effect of Public Sector Impasse Procedures," *Industrial and Labor Relations Review* (October 1981), pp. 3–20.
[91] See Thomas A. Kochan and Harry C. Katz, *Collective Bargaining and Industrial Relations*, 2nd ed. (Homewood, Illinois: Richard D. Irwin, Inc., 1988), p. 281.
[92] For a discussion of criteria used in interest arbitration, see Susan Schwochau and Peter Feuille, "Interest Arbitrators and Their Decision Behavior," *Industrial Relations* (Winter 1988), pp. 37–55.
[93] Also see Peter Feuille, "Selected Benefits and Costs of Compulsory Arbitration," *Industrial and Labor Relations Review* (October 1979), pp. 64–76.

striction of arbitral powers and by the exercise of judicial review in cases in which arbitrators have clearly exceeded the limits of their legal authority.[94]

The Administration of Public-Sector Collective Bargaining Agreements

Grievances arising over the terms and provisions of collective bargaining agreements in the public sector are usually handled in a fashion similar to private-sector contract grievances. Some state and municipal statutes require that collective bargaining agreements contain a grievance procedure. As in the private sector, most grievance procedures in public-sector contracts contain binding arbitration as the final step. The aforementioned sovereignty argument once again surfaces when the issue of arbitration is discussed in public-sector contract grievances. As a general rule, however, agreements to arbitrate have been upheld by state courts. Questions of arbitrability may arise if the grievance involves issues that deal with civil service regulations rather than collective bargaining provisions.

Although the courts in various states have made different rulings on the status of grievance procedures and arbitration in their respective jurisdictions, Grodin and Najita have noted the emergence of the following patterns:

1. The courts appear less inclined to defer to an arbitration award where a statute exists (such as an equal employment opportunity law or minimum wage law) that also deals with the subject matter of the grievance.
2. Courts in the public sector appear less tolerant than those in the private sector of awards that rely on past practice to establish obligations not expressed in the agreement.
3. Even when the arbitrator's award is based upon express contract language, courts in some cases have displayed a greater tendency to overturn the arbitrator's interpretation (than in the private sector).[95]

These points are generalizations. A state court may take a more liberal or more conservative view of grievance administration and arbitration in the public sector, depending on the state and the extent to which public-sector bargaining has developed in that state.[96]

State and Municipal Collective Bargaining Agencies

States that have public-sector bargaining laws usually have an agency that enforces the law, commonly known as a public employment relations board, commission, or agency.[97] Public employment relations boards function in a manner that is similar

---

[94] Benjamin Aaron, "The Future of Collective Bargaining in the Public Sector," in Benjamin Aaron, Joyce M. Najita, and James L. Stern, eds., *Public-Sector Bargaining*, 2nd ed. (Washington, D.C.: The Bureau of National Affairs, Inc., 1988), p. 319.

[95] Joseph R. Grodin and Joyce M. Najita, "Judicial Response to Public-Sector Arbitration," in Benjamin Aaron, Joyce M. Najita, and James L. Stern, eds., *Public-Sector Bargaining*, 2nd ed. (Washington, D.C.: The Bureau of National Affairs, Inc., 1988), pp. 229–252.

[96] See David L. Epp, "The Duty to Arbitrate Public Sector Employee Grievances After Expiration of the Collective Bargaining Agreement," *Labor Law Journal* (April 1989), pp. 195–207.

[97] There are few public employment relations boards at the county or city level. One such agency of note is the Office of Collective Bargaining in New York City. The District of Columbia has a PERB, as do a number of counties surrounding large urban areas. Some states delegate public-sector labor relations to agencies that previously administered laws covering private-sector labor relations not affecting interstate commerce (and therefore not under the purview of the National Labor Relations Act).

to that of the National Labor Relations Board (for private-sector labor relations). Most of these boards hear unfair labor practice cases, determine bargaining units, and conduct certification elections. In addition, state public employment relations boards provide mediators, fact finders, and arbitrators (both for grievances and bargaining impasses). These third-party neutrals may be employed by the state agency or they may work privately on an ad hoc basis.

Public employment relations boards are typically funded by the state. In fact, the level of funding to these agencies is a major indicator as to how seriously the state legislators view public-sector collective bargaining issues and the rights of state and municipal employees. The chairperson of the administrative agency is usually a political appointee, and staff members are civil servants employed on a full- or part-time basis.

▲ Summary and Conclusions

This chapter summarizes the major differences between public- and private-sector collective bargaining in the United States. Because of its relatively recent evolution, it is certain that public-sector bargaining will continue to change. What is less certain is the nature of these changes.

The federal, state, and local governments will undoubtedly continue to offer a wide array of services to the public. There is also some evidence that public-sector unions increase employment levels in governmental agencies.[98] Once public services are established, they may be permanently or temporarily transferred to private industry through a process known as privatization.[99] In addition, the decline of organized labor in the private sector will continue to make the organization of government employees an attractive target for union organizers.

It is doubtful that federal, state, and municipal employees will ever achieve the same right to strike as private-sector employees. However, state legislators and other public officials who make policy affecting government employees may gradually allow nonessential employees greater freedom insofar as bargaining and strikes are concerned. Of course, one debate that should continue is the definition of "essential." If essentiality is restricted to police, fire, health care, and security employees, then the vast majority of government employees may eventually have at least a limited right to strike.

Another area for potential change deals with the scope of issues negotiated during contract talks and included in public-sector collective bargaining agreements. Will bargaining gradually encroach on civil service policies or will such policies continue to dominate public personnel/human resource management?

---

[98] See Jeffrey Zax, "Employment and Local Public Unions," *Industrial Relations* (Winter 1989), pp. 21–31; and Jeffrey S. Zax, "Wages, Nonwage Compensation, and Municipal Unions," *Industrial Relations* (Fall 1988), pp. 301–317.
[99] See Werner Z. Hirsch, "The Economics of Contracting Out: The Labor Cost Fallacy," Industrial Relations Research Association 1989 Spring Meeting, reprinted in the *Labor Law Journal* (August 1989), pp. 536–542.

Public-sector collective bargaining will become much more influential if the scope of bargaining is gradually expanded.

The future of impasse procedures is another area of interest. Will union and management negotiators become sophisticated enough to reach contract settlements without resorting to mediation, fact finding, and arbitration? If not, will government officials attempt to maintain a great deal of control over impasse resolution techniques in order to avoid abdicating authority to third-party neutrals who are not elected officials?

▲ Discussion Questions and Exercises

1. Do you believe that public-sector union membership levels will remain the same through the 1990s? Discuss.
2. Much has been said about the differences between public- and private-sector collective bargaining. What *similarities* exist between the two sectors?
3. What types of multilateral bargaining issues might arise involving contract negotiations or work stoppages for the following categories of public employees?
    a. Elementary and secondary teachers
    b. Sanitation workers
    c. Police officers
    d. Air traffic controllers
4. What unique bargaining subjects might arise among the four groups of employees in question 3 above? Discuss.
5. Some observers believe that there are actually few differences between strikes by public- and private-sector employees. What factors or arguments might prompt such a statement?
6. Why is the scope of public-sector collective bargaining narrower than in the private sector? What subjects are excluded from bargaining under federal and state public-sector bargaining laws?
7. What unfair labor practices are unique to public-sector bargaining laws?
8. Table 17–7 summarizes the strike provisions in the nine states that allow public-sector work stoppages. Under what conditions are these employees allowed to strike? What strike limits are imposed in these states?
9. What does the future hold for public-sector collective bargaining? Do you believe that public-sector unions will eventually suffer declines similar to those in the private sector?

▲ ▲ ▲ ▲ ▲ PUBLIC-SECTOR STRIKE CASE

The Los Angeles Teachers' Strike

After teachers ended a nine-day strike at the Los Angeles Unified School District, union president Wayne Johnson claimed victory for its 22,000 members. However, the winners and losers in this strike are not clear cut.

The teachers won salary increases of 24 percent (eight percent for each of three years). Starting teachers for the 1990–91 school year earn $29,529; the maximum base salary is $53,938 plus bonuses for advanced degrees, bilingual instruction, and seniority. After the settlement, the average teacher's salary for 1989 was $39,500 (for 182 days of work). The benefit package includes fully paid medical, dental, vision, and surgical insurance for employees and their dependents.

The newly won economic concessions may have come at a high price. Although the teachers also won a sought-after school reform plan as part of the district's final offer, the school budget is so crippled by the teachers' raises that little money is left for real change. The raises required cutting between $120 million and $170 million from other programs between 1989 and 1991. Prior to the strike, the teachers had complained about poor security, outdated textbooks, a lack of air conditioning in many schools, and a lack of respect as professionals. Yet, without money to implement school reforms, the strike settlement may have done little more than give the teachers a short morale boost.

Teachers have felt that they have had little input into change and educational reform. One year after the contract goes into effect, school-based councils, half of whose members will be picked by the union, will be able to vote on issues such as staff development, school activities, discipline, and school expenditures. But according to one observer, the councils will not be able to eradicate the Los Angeles downtown bureaucracy's outrageous expenditures that have angered teachers. For example, the superintendent's chauffeur/bodyguard earned $91,000 in 1988. Parents have also been excluded from the councils. After the strike, the union and the school district appear to have equal power, but there is little cooperation between the two groups.

Addressing teachers after they had ratified the contract, union president Johnson said, "We ain't what we oughta be, we ain't what we're gonna be, but thank God, we ain't what we were." Unfortunately, Los Angeles teachers may be simply getting paid more to deal with all of their old problems.[100]

Discussion Questions

1. Why might the Los Angeles teachers' satisfaction with the contract be short-lived?

---

[100] From Debra J. Saunders, "L. A. Teachers 'Win,' but School Reform Doesn't," *The Wall Street Journal* (May 31, 1989).

2. How, in your opinion, did the teachers manage to get away with an illegal strike?
3. How might the concept of multilateral bargaining manifest itself in the case of the Los Angeles teachers?
4. What rights do students and parents have in disputes such as this?

Part VIII

Future Directions

▲▲▲▲▲▲▲▲▲▲▲▲▲▲▲▲▲▲▲▲▲▲▲

Collective bargaining and labor relations is a dynamic field that will undoubtedly change through the 1990s. Organized labor in the United States has been faced with a decline in membership over the past 30 years. A major reason for the shift away from the unionized sector is the decline in the industries that have traditionally been union strongholds. In addition, the deregulation of key industries, the legalistic encroachment on collective bargaining, the negative image of labor unions, and an antiunion political and managerial environment have all contributed to organized labor's decline.

Chapter 18, The Challenges Facing Collective Bargaining and Labor Relations, discusses union membership losses and assesses the future strategic choices of the U.S. labor movement. A number of innovations including union-management cooperative efforts, gainsharing, and employee ownership plans are also discussed.

18 The Challenges Facing Collective Bargaining and Labor Relations

- **Introduction**
- **Union Membership Losses**
  The Decline in Union Strongholds
  The Deregulation of Certain Unionized Industries
  The Legalistic Encroachment on Collective Bargaining
  The Negative Image of Labor Unions
  The Antiunion Managerial and Political Environment
- **Strategic Choices for the Future**
  The Continued Use of Adversarial Tactics or More Cooperation?
  Responding to Foreign Competition and the Specter of 1992 Europe
  Changing the Legal Structure
  Employee Ownership and Gainsharing
  Organized Labor's Use of Strategic Management Concepts
  Bargaining Innovations
- **Summary and Conclusions**
- **Discussion Questions and Exercises**

▲ Introduction

Collective bargaining in the United States is at a crossroads. Some observers believe that the U.S. labor movement will decline to the point where it is no longer an important political, economic, and social force. Other observers believe that if the labor movement is to survive, it must adapt to changing international economic conditions, advancing technology, and a flexible and innovative style of strategic management by companies that compete in a global economy. This chapter discusses some of the major changes that are currently taking place in labor-management relations and their implications for the future.

▲ Union Membership Losses

As noted in earlier chapters, labor union membership was at an all-time high in the late 1940s and early 1950s, when over 30 percent of the nonagricultural labor force was represented by a labor organization. The percentage of employees represented by unions in the early 1990s is approximately one half of the levels found four decades earlier. Union victory rates in certification elections hit a low of 41 percent in 1981. Although the certification election winning percentage of unions had increased to 49 percent by 1989, the number of defeats for unions in decertification elections continued to rise.[1] Much has been said and written about the factors causing the decline of labor unions in the United States. Before speculating on the future of the U.S. labor movement, the major factors surrounding the current state of organized labor are discussed.

The Decline of Union Strongholds

According to Donald Ratacjczak of Georgia State University, the primary reason for the drop in union membership is that union strength "is in the wrong part of the economy." Much of the unionized segment of the economy has traditionally been located in the declining steel, rubber, and other "smokestack" industries of the Northeast and upper Midwest states.[2] The decaying industrial sector has been faced with increasing foreign competition, and unions have been unable to assist heavy manufacturing firms in responding to threats from abroad.[3] In addition, the growth in high technology manufacturing, such as electronics, communications, and aerospace, has increased the number of skilled workers while reducing the number of traditionally unionized semiskilled workers.[4] Two union leaders summarize the

---

[1] One possible explanation for the increased success of unions is that union organizers may have become more selective about the employees targeted for representation campaigns.
[2] See The Bureau of National Affairs, Inc., *Unions Today: New Tactics to Tackle Tough Times* (Washington, D.C.: The Bureau of National Affairs, Inc., 1985), pp. 95-121.
[3] For an excellent discussion of the decline of the steel industry in the United States, see John P. Hoerr, *And the Wolf Came: The Decline of the American Steel Industry* (Pittsburgh: University of Pittsburgh Press, 1988).
[4] The Bureau of National Affairs, Inc., *Unions Today: New Tactics to Tackle Tough Times* (Washington, D.C.: The Bureau of National Affairs, Inc., 1985), p. 12.

woes that have plagued their unions. According to Charles W. Jones, president of the International Brotherhood of Boilermakers, Iron Ship Builders, Blacksmiths, Forgers, and Helpers (IBB), job losses in industries served by his union and other unions have led to declines in membership.

> Organized labor in the United States has shrunk to 13 million from about 19 million members, but so have the number of good jobs in this country shrunk. Our members didn't go because they were mad at us. They left because there were no more jobs in their plants, or in construction and shipbuilding. Their jobs have all gone overseas. Union after union lost—the Steelworkers, Auto Workers, Machinists, and the Boilermakers.
>
> Our members are having to work for some hamburger place or to pump gas. Like I saw a young fellow working at a gas station who had a Machinist emblem on his jacket, and I talked with him a bit to see whether he was moonlighting or what. Here's a guy who was a skilled aircraft mechanic but had lost out because of the merger mania, and now he's out pumping gas.[5]

A similar view was aired by Lynn Williams, president of the United Steelworkers of America (USWA):

> Now I don't deny that the labor movement has fallen on tough times. But it's not because people have all turned their backs on the movement and decided its irrelevant. It's because their jobs have gone overseas...
>
> We've lost jobs to overseas because of the changing world scene. It has to do with multinationals going out to see if they couldn't make any more money by exploiting cheap labor overseas. It has to do with the fact that for their economic development, Third World countries were encouraged by bankers and international investment companies to build a bunch of steel mills, and then invite the multinationals to come in and use their cheap labor. We have a global economy now, it's certainly not American unions and our collective bargaining efforts that have sent jobs overseas.[6]

The strength of organized labor through the 1990s will depend on several economic, social, and political factors. First, labor unions are more likely to flourish in a healthy economy. The concession bargaining of the early 1980s was brought about by the declining economic health in industries such as steel and auto manufacturing. These declines were, in turn, largely a response to changing international economic conditions as foreign firms continued to offer labor cost savings and product quality advantages over domestic firms. U.S. companies were often unable to overcome foreign competition, and as employers suffered, so did organized labor. Second, in order to compete with foreign firms, U.S. companies have begun to seek ways to control labor costs and regain a competitive advantage. Some companies have resorted to legal and illegal antiunion tactics. Such employer tactics have been at least partially responsible for the continued growth of the nonunion sector among U.S. firms. Other employers sought to regain a competitive edge through improved

---

[5] Interview with Charles W. Jones, "Back to the Basics," in Philip Quaglieri, *America's Labor Leaders* (Lexington, Massachusetts: Lexington Books, 1989), p. 142. Reprinted with permission.

[6] Interview with Lynn Williams, "Toughness and Idealism in Steel," in Philip Quaglieri, *America's Labor Leaders* (Lexington, Massachusetts: Lexington Books, 1989), pp. 236–237. Reprinted with permission.

production methods and technological advances. Still others made efforts to secure the cooperation of labor. Lacking success in any of these areas, a number of companies have been forced to divest or shut down plants and facilities. Third, the wage increases of unionized workers have lagged behind those of nonunion workers. This trend may be partially attributable to bargaining concessions in industries that have traditionally been union strongholds. Fourth, political and legal trends of the 1980s and early 1990s have not been conducive to the stability of organized labor.

Even when an industry is not declining, companies may decide to shift operations from a union plant to a nonunion plant. In some cases a firm's nonunion facilities are more modern or employ a workforce that is not supportive of organized labor. For example, Japanese automakers opening production facilities in the United States have built their plants in semirural areas of the Midwest. According to *Business Week*, "They [the Japanese automakers] hired mostly young workers with little industrial experience—and no love of unionism."[7] Companies are also relocating their operations to the Sunbelt states where labor costs are lower than in heavily unionized states and where the perceived likelihood of the union's winning a certification election is diminished.

There are also instances in which the employer resorts to foreign suppliers or subcontractors. When United Auto Worker members were threatened with the loss of bargaining-unit jobs due to changes in auto assembly technology and competition from cheaper overseas labor, the UAW instituted a six-day strike in 1984 at selected General Motors facilities. GM felt that any restrictions upon its right to close plants as well as to subcontract work or enter into production or import agreements with foreign firms would prevent it from competing effectively in international markets. Nevertheless, agreements were reached between GM and the UAW that protected eligible workers from the effects of doing business with foreign firms.[8]

Not all unions are suffering from membership declines. The Teamsters, United Food and Commercial Workers, as well as the various unions that focus on organizing health care workers have experienced recent membership increases. Some of these unions have prospered because of aggressive and innovative organizing campaign tactics, whereas others have been successful because they are directing their organizing efforts toward previously unorganized workers.

The Deregulation of Certain Unionized Industries

Another problem that has plagued organized labor in some industries is deregulation. Most private-sector firms operate in deregulated industries and are relatively free to establish their markets and set prices for their goods and services. Organizations in regulated industries are constrained with regard to the markets that they serve and the prices they set. Companies that have operated in regulated industries are protected from cutthroat competitive pressures. One benefit of being a regulated

---

[7] James B. Treece and John Hoerr, "Shaking Up Detroit: How Japanese Auto Makers Are Beating the Big Three on Their Own Turf," *Business Week* (August 14, 1989), p. 76.
[8] The Bureau of National Affairs, Inc., *Unions Today: New Tactics to Tackle Tough Times* (Washington, D.C.: The Bureau of National Affairs, Inc., 1985), p. 27.

company is that competition is either limited or controlled; "outside" firms are often restricted from entering an industry or market.

Starting in the 1970s, industries such as trucking (1976), airlines (1976), railroads (1980), and communications (1981) were deregulated. The major result of deregulation was to allow an increased number of firms to operate in these industries. Many of these new firms were nonunion and were able to compete on the basis of lower labor costs. New nonunion firms entering an industry may be able to undercut unionized firms on labor costs and reduce the number of union workers in an industry. Firms that have been accustomed to the stability and protection of a regulated industry are often forced to sell or shut down the less profitable segments of their businesses. For example, former Teamsters president Jackie Presser said that nearly 100,000 Teamsters members had lost their jobs in the trucking industry because of deregulation.[9] Charles Wheeler, international vice president of the Transportation Communications International Union (TCU) and general president of the Brotherhood Railway Carmen Division/TCU, voiced similar concerns:

> The Staggers Rail Act of 1980, which deregulated the railway industry, was the beginning of our downfall. And believe it or not, we even supported it. But once deregulation went through, the large lines began very quickly to set off miles of track, and they did it without having to hold public hearings as they had to previously. And as those lines were sold, thousands of our members were laid off by the major lines. As you might imagine, those layoffs came as quite a shock to a lot of our members who had worked twenty or thirty years with those companies. In fact, many of our members didn't even know what a reduction in force was when they first heard about it.[10]

Deregulation also attracts firms that provide few or no benefits to their employees. Addressing the Air Transport Labor Relations Conference, American Airlines CEO Robert L. Crandall said that airline deregulation had gone far beyond what "anyone had dreamed." Crandall said that low-cost carriers had taken advantage of deregulation to take labor relations "far beyond the bounds of cost control." He criticized government for allowing low-cost carriers to get away with abusing employees. The airline CEO asserted that "it's time for all of us— labor, management, and government to join forces and make it clear that our society will no longer tolerate an airline, or for that matter any company abusing its employees in order to beat the competition." Taking aim at Continental Airlines, Crandall noted that they did not provide medical benefits for retirees and require employees to bear most of the cost for medical coverage. He then noted that American Airlines spent $1,666 per employee for such coverage or $80 million annually for current employees, plus $16 million for retirees.[11] To the extent that deregulated firms attempt to take advantage of workers by slashing pay and benefits, unions might be

---

[9] The Bureau of National Affairs, Inc., *Unions Today: New Tactics to Tackle Tough Times* (Washington, D.C.: The Bureau of National Affairs, Inc., 1985), pp. 12-14.
[10] Interview with Charles E. Wheeler, "Commitment in a Declining Industry," in Philip L. Quaglieri, *America's Labor Leaders* (Lexington, Massachusetts: Lexington Books, Inc., 1989), p. 229. Reprinted with permission.
[11] The Bureau of National Affairs, Inc., *Collective Bargaining Negotiations & Contracts* (Washington, D.C.: The Bureau of National Affairs, Inc., July 2, 1987), p. 4.

able to use the abuses cited by Crandall as a means of organizing nonunion employees.

Regulated companies are often bureaucratic in their mode of operation, and rely heavily on extensive rules, regulations, and personnel policies. Deregulation within an industry forces a firm to adopt a more flexible competitive posture as well as more flexible personnel policies and practices. Collective bargaining agreements, on the other hand, are typically rigid in their approach to job assignments, promotions, and transfers. As deregulated firms offer lower pay and fewer benefits and implement more flexible personnel practices in an attempt to achieve a competitive edge, there is an increased probability that labor tensions will surface.

The Legalistic Encroachment on Collective Bargaining

The proliferation of labor legislation in the United States has both helped and hindered the labor movement. When organized labor began to make significant membership strides in the late 1930s, it did so because the Wagner Act protected employees who wanted to join, form, or assist a labor organization. Similarly, the passage of public-sector bargaining laws in the 1960s and 1970s helped federal, state, and local government employees engage in collective bargaining.

Labor legislation has also encroached on traditional union and collective bargaining activities. Prior to the 1960s, unions protected employees from racial discrimination, unfair treatment, unsafe working conditions; labor organizations also helped to obtain improved pay and employee benefits for their members. Since the 1960s, federal and state legislation has protected workers from many of the abuses that used to be policed by unions. Title VII of the 1964 Civil Rights Act and the Age Discrimination in Employment Act have formed the backbone of civil rights in employment over the past quarter of a century. The Occupational Safety and Health Act (OSHA) was passed in 1970 to reduce hazards in the workplace. Employees injured on the job receive medical and disability income benefits through workers' compensation. Employees now receive advance notice of plant closings because of recent federal legislation. As noted in Chapter 13, there are several compensation laws that protect employee wages, salaries, and benefits. Retirement programs are protected by the Employee Retirement Income Security Act (ERISA); interestingly, ERISA was passed in part because of abuses in the management of pension assets by the Teamsters union.

Nonunion employees now have a number of federal and state labor laws that afford protection; as a result, they have less need for organized labor than in the past. Ironically, the AFL-CIO and international union leaders lobbied for the passage of these laws. What nonunion employees may be overlooking, however, is that processing a case through an administrative agency such as the Equal Employment Opportunity Commission (EEOC) or the federal court system can take several years. A union grievance procedure can be much more expeditious than an administrative agency or court. In addition, there are adverse employment practices that are not protected by a law. For example, Chapter 16 provides illustrations of how "at-will" employees can be discharged for good cause, bad cause, or no cause at all. These terminations do not always violate a civil rights law; although such discharges are morally and ethically questionable, they are nonetheless legal.

A by-product of increased federal and state labor legislation is the improvement of personnel/human resource management programs and policies within many organizations. Examples include more equitable compensation programs, safer working conditions, better employee benefit programs, improved performance appraisal and promotion systems, and disciplinary programs that ensure equal protection and due process for employees. The more these improved personnel policies and practices are used in private- and public-sector organizations, the more difficult it will be for unions to organize nonunion employees.

The Negative Image of Labor Unions

The image of organized labor has been unfairly tainted by relatively rare (but well-publicized) work stoppages, scandals, and setbacks. As discussed in Chapter 6, a few unions have links with organized crime. Unfortunately, unions that are not affected by organized crime are often judged "guilty by association." Furthermore, strikes and violence associated with labor disputes are typically blamed on union leaders and members rather than management. Concession bargaining in the early 1980s also sent a signal to prospective union members that organized labor might be losing much of its political and economic clout.

In more recent times, the poor public image of unions has been exacerbated by the labor crisis at Eastern Airlines, the prolonged strike of Pittston Coal employees in Virginia, and the resounding defeat of the United Auto Workers in a certification election at the Nissan plant in Smyrna, Tennessee. Peaceful contract settlements and union victories in certification elections, on the other hand, usually receive little publicity in the news media.

Shortly after Nissan workers in Tennessee voted by a 2-to-1 margin against being represented by the United Auto Workers, Lane Kirkland, president of the AFL-CIO and Michael E. Avakian, general counsel of the Center on National Labor Policy were invited to participate as guest columnists and publish their views in *USA Today*. Mr. Kirkland discussed the role of organized labor in enhancing freedom and democracy in countries such as Poland, Chile, Hungary, and South Africa. Kirkland said that in the United States "unions are on the front lines of the battle against the ravages of corporate greed and for better health care, childcare, higher wages and safer jobs." He mentioned that the vast majority of contract negotiations are completed without serious dispute and that public approval for organized labor was at its highest level in more than a decade. Kirkland then cited that disputes in the airline, coal, and communications industries had "brought the fury of a unified labor movement."[12] Avakian countered by saying that "the 'decline' of organized labor is simply a self-created, homespun phenomenon." Avakian said that high-profile union defeats should not lull the public into complacency. "The union agenda is not to improve conditions of employment for more of the workforce but to seek crippling extractions from industries already under their influence and to brashly use political power to push everybody else around Capitol Hill." He cited the fact that the incomes of union members have increased despite the declining

---

[12] Lane Kirkland, "Union Labor is the Way of the Future," *USA Today* (September 1, 1989).

percentage of organized workers. Avakian noted that public opinion places union leaders below used-car salesmen.[13]; He concluded by saying that "the United Mine Workers strike [in Virginia] explains why: Violence and terrorism are part and parcel of union organizing and strike strategies, and Americans want no part of it."[14]

This debate illustrates how two intelligent and informed professionals, both with deeply seated views toward their respective camps, can have radically different viewpoints. Much of the public opinion on unions is based on fragmented and incomplete evidence that is distorted by personal values, self-interests, and preconceptions.

Perhaps a more damaging image of American labor unions is the belief on the part of unorganized workers that unions increase the risk of strikes and the likelihood of a company's going out of business.[15] The problem is compounded by the fact that plants in heavily unionized industries have been closed or relocated. Rather than attribute the shutdowns to declining economic conditions and foreign competition, antiunion commentators have tried to convince the public that organized labor is to blame. Although most of the American public has a poor image of unions in general, a large number of those surveyed still believe that organized labor serves a useful purpose.[16];

The Antiunion Managerial and Political Environment

Chapter 4 discusses the various proactive and reactive measures that employers have used to defeat unions in organizing campaigns. At one extreme are the proactive tactics in which employers attempt to discourage unionism while simultaneously complying with the law. One CEO, new to his company, wrote a letter to the firm's employees that stated in part:

> To the extent possible, we will operate all parts of our business without unions. Our interest in avoiding unions does not mean we are seeking cheap or compliant labor. Rather, since we are committed to providing a fair and attractive work environment for our employees, a valid reason for a third party (the union) simply does not exist. To make sure this environment prevails, we must always adhere to these four policies:
> 1. We will always pay above-average wages for good performance, and we will monitor the wage structure in each market so that we don't slip behind.
> 2. Our fringe benefits for nonunion employees will remain comparable with or better than those in union plants, and we will introduce new fringe pro-

---

[13] Mr. Avakian may be in error with regard to this point. In 1985, a random sample of Americans was asked to rate the moral and ethical practices of 25 occupational groups. Only car salesmen were rated more negatively than union leaders. See Seymour Martin Lipset, "Labor Unions in the Public Mind," in Seymour Martin Lipset, ed., *Unions in Transition* (San Francisco: Institute for Contemporary Studies Press, 1986), cited in Robert J. Flanagan, Lawrence M. Kahn, Robert S. Smith, and Ronald G. Ehrenberg, *Economics of the Employment Relationship* (Glenview, Illinois: Scott, Foresman and Company, 1989), p. 623.
[14] Michael E. Avakian, "Labor's in Decline—For Good Reason," *USA Today* (September 1, 1989).
[15] The AFL-CIO Committee on the Evolution of Work, *The Changing Situation of Workers and Their Unions* (Washington, D.C.: AFL-CIO, 1985), p. 13.
[16] Thomas A. Kochan, Harry C. Katz, and Robert B. McKersie, *The Transformation of American Industrial Relations* (New York: Basic Books, Inc., 1986), p. 216.

grams to our nonunion employees before the union secures them through negotiation.
3. We will agreeably try to accommodate individual preferences for work assignments and schedules. As long as employees perform well in their current positions, we will never penalize them for turning down new assignments. Nor will we penalize employees who decline to work overtime because of personal considerations.
4. We will encourage open communication with employees and try to respond to their criticisms and questions in a fair, sensitive, and intelligent way.

Employees must be encouraged to tell us when we are not following these policies. If for any reason they feel they can't, dissatisfaction and distrust will develop, and they will ultimately perceive the need for a union to protect their rights.[17]

At the other extreme are companies that openly defy union and employee organizing and bargaining rights by flagrantly violating federal labor laws. The middle ground is occupied by firms that hire consulting firms to prevent or defeat a labor union's organizing efforts. Regardless of the approach taken by management to curb organized labor, the results suggest that these tactics are effective and will pose a threat to the existence of unionism in the future.

Labor leaders are also concerned that the political climate of the 1980s has dealt a severe blow to the United States labor movement. President Reagan has been singled out by some labor leaders as a major culprit in the decline in unionism. Donald Dotson, chairman of the National Labor Relations Board during the Reagan administration, was also accused of being strongly pro-management. According to one union official quoted by The Bureau of National Affairs, Inc.: "The NLRB has been reduced to little more than a management tool, whose chief function is to delay, deny, and destroy the right of employees to freely and fairly organize and win union representation."[18]

Two union leaders expressed their opinions on the Reagan administration's impact on organized labor. John H. Serembus, president of the Upholstery and Allied Industries Division of the United Steelworkers, commented:

What's happened? Well, we now have a president [Reagan] in the White House who is antilabor, and with your right-to-work groups we're fast getting back to that era [the 1920s and 1930s when employers adopted a strong antiunion posture]. In fact, it's the first time in my lifetime that I've seen police dogs, security guards with clubs and guns and surveillance equipment out at picket lines, and I've been active as a member for forty-three years. When Ronald Reagan was elected in 1980, I thought that was the best thing that could happen to the labor movement. I said, "This can't be happening. He'll be out of there in

---

[17] Reprinted by permission of the *Harvard Business Review*, "Straight Talk from the New CEO," by B. Charles Ames (November-December 1989), p. 133. Copyright 1989 by the Presidents and Fellows of Harvard College; all rights reserved.
[18] Comment of United Food and Commercial Workers International Union's William H. Wynn. In The Bureau of Affairs, Inc., *Unions Today: New Tactics to Tackle Tough Times* (Washington, D.C.: The Bureau of National Affairs, Inc., 1985), p. 9.

four years, and he'll make people realize why they need unions." Well, he got a second term and just decimated our ranks.[19]

John J. Sweeny of the Service Employees International Union echoed similar sentiments:

> Labor's biggest disappointment has been our inability to defeat Ronald Reagan. With this administration, we have seen the worst gutting of social programs and worker related programs in the past fifty years, and its going to take years to reinstate many of them. And there's no question about it, Ronald Reagan set an example with the PATCO situation. Corporate America, along with the public sector employers, got the message that it was now time to take on the labor movement.[20]

To date, the Bush administration has not deviated significantly from the labor policies promulgated under Reagan. The NLRB and the Supreme Court are currently comprised of members with conservative leanings. Thus, organized labor will continue to battle both a hostile managerial and political environment into the foreseeable future.

▲ Strategic Choices for the Future

The Continued Use of Adversarial Tactics or More Cooperation?

A number of factions within U.S. corporations and organized labor appear willing to continue fighting with each other rather than adopting a conciliatory posture. Some corporate boards and executives will do whatever is necessary to rid themselves of labor unions. Unions have begun to counter with corporate campaigns against employers who do not provide reasonable wages, hours, and working conditions or who use illegal tactics to thwart organizing campaigns and certification elections (see Chapter 6). Tactics by unions include placing pressures on banks that do business with antiunion firms, conducting adverse publicity campaigns against selected firms, enlisting the support and sympathy of church groups, defeating attempts by private investors and antiunion firms to obtain industrial revenue bonds and federal grants, and holding consumer boycotts against firms that oppose organized labor.

A bizarre tactic of recent vintage was the intentional decertification of the National Football League Players Association by union president Gene Upshaw. By relinquishing its right to bargain with NFL team owners, the Players Association hoped to force the courts to rule in favor of the players' unrestricted right to sell their services to the highest-bidding team (full free agency). The intentional decertification was a reaction to a U.S. Court of Appeals decision that at least tem-

---

[19] Interview with John H. Serembus, "A People's Person," in Philip A. Quaglieri, *America's Labor Leaders* (Lexington, Massachusetts: Lexington Books, 1989), p. 199. Reprinted with permission.

[20] Interview with John J. Sweeney, "Attracting New Members to Labor," in Philip L. Quaglieri, *America's Labor Leaders* (Lexington, Massachusetts: Lexington Books, 1989), p. 219. Reprinted with permission.

porarily protected the team owners from antitrust laws while restricting a player's right to become a free agent. The strategy is risky for the union and it goes against the idea of power through collective action—the foundation upon which the American labor movement was built. NFL players will continue to pay dues to the union. However, Upshaw has calculated that if the union no longer bargains for the players, individual negotiations between the players and the team owners can be used successfully to attack the long-standing free agency issue.[21]

Although many of these tactics are innovative and are used to circumvent the ineffectiveness of U.S. labor laws (which are failing to protect the organizing rights of employees), such tactics may not be in the best interest of either the U.S. labor movement or the corporations. Resources used in union-management battles may be better spent fighting a more serious threat: increasing competition among firms operating within the international marketplace.

Organized labor will likely continue its decline through the turn of the century unless either economic, political, and legal factors change or labor leaders and employers agree to work together and develop workplace innovations that focus on union-management cooperation (rather than union-management adversity). If employers and union leaders decide to pursue cooperative efforts, such efforts will have to focus on making U.S. firms more productive and competitive relative to European and Japanese firms. There are several conditions that are necessary for union-management cooperative efforts to work:

1. Union leaders must realize that the adversarial nature of collective bargaining is no longer feasible; cooperating with management must not be viewed as a sign that union leaders are "selling out."
2. Management must realize that employees often hold the key to productivity gains.
3. Both union and management leaders must realize that they have a number of common (and permanent) problems including nonunionized competitors, an increasingly legalistic and litigious business environment, and foreign competition.

Peter Drucker envisions that U.S. labor organizations will follow one of three paths:

> The labor union can go in three directions. If it does nothing, it may disappear—or shrink to the point where it becomes irrelevant. This is clearly the direction in which the British, Italian, and French unions are moving, but also most of those in America.
>
> Secondly, it can try to maintain itself through dominating the political power structure and having government impose compulsory union membership. Such power positions could be "co-determination," which gives the union a veto power over company management. This may appear to be a rational course. Indeed, the unions in Germany, Holland, and Scandinavia have clearly chosen it. . .

---

[21] Aaron Bernstein, "The NFL's Union Could Win by Committing Suicide," *Business Week* (November 27, 1989), p. 84. The NFLPA has given up its status as a union and is now an association.

If the unions' power results in its country's industry becoming noncompetitive, those unions will lose control as membership shrinks and public opinion turns against them. The German unions are already impaled on the horns of this dilemma. . . .

There is a third possibility. The union can rethink its function. It might reinvent itself as the organ of society—and of the employing institution—concerned with building human potential and achievement, with optimizing the human resource altogether.

The union would still have a large role as the representative of employees against management stupidity and abuse of power, but the relationship would not be adversarial. Rather, it would resemble the Scandinavian "ombudsman." The union would work with management on productivity, quality, and whatever else keeps the enterprise competitive, thus maintaining the members' jobs and protecting their incomes and opportunities.[22]

Responding to Foreign Competition and 1992 Europe

We have already witnessed the competitive impact of Japanese auto manufacturing on the U.S. auto industry. Another major international threat now lurks on the horizon that should have an effect on the U.S. labor movement. In 1992, 12 Western European countries will merge as a single economy (known as EC'92). These 12 countries have a total population of 320 million. In combination with new technologies and improved transportation, reduced barriers to trade can improve production, simplify logistics, and cut costs. Companies with subsidiaries in Europe must learn to take advantage of the opportunities for improved productivity that lower regulatory barriers will bring. Even U.S. firms that have no business interests in Europe may have to compete with more productive and cost-efficient European firms who want to do business in the United States.[23]

Although the consequences of a unified European economy are difficult to predict, it would appear that EC'92 will place an even higher premium on labor-management cooperation. Unionized firms will be forced to maintain a sharper focus on productivity, quality, and labor costs. To do so, they will either have to enlist the support of organized labor or make an all-out effort to rid themselves of the inflexibilities and labor-cost constraints imposed by collective bargaining agreements.

There is also speculation that U.S. firms doing business in Europe will have to learn to deal with problems posed by foreign labor organizations. Because of codetermination, in which union officials sit on corporate boards, unions in nations such as West Germany expect to play a prominent consulting role in management decisions. The prospect of a unified Germany has also placed pressure on West German unions. In 1990, the average factory wage in West Germany was $21.00 per hour, compared to $5.40 for East German factory workers. Negotiators for West

---

[22] Peter F. Drucker, "Peter Drucker Asks: Will Unions Ever Be Useful Organs of Society?" *Industry Week* (March 20, 1989), p. 22.
[23] See John F. Magee, "1992: Moves Americans Must Make," *Harvard Business Review* (May-June 1989), pp. 78–89.

German unions such as I.G. Metall (2.6 million members) were forced to back down from their demands for a 8.5 percent wage hike and 35-hour week for fear that West German firms might accelerate their investments in East German firms.[24] Some firms are already plotting a "Sunbelt" strategy in Europe by locating in southern European countries such as Spain, where wages are low and unions are weaker.[25]

Workplace innovations by the Japanese will also dictate changes in the face of organized labor in the United States. The Big Three auto manufacturers are slowly reshaping management and production methods along Japanese lines. Japanese firms advocate greater delegation of authority to workers, extensive employee training and development programs, teamwork in the workplace, greater job security and no-layoff policies, and treating employees with dignity and trust (e.g., abolishing the use of time clocks and avoiding formal grievances). In short, the Japanese management philosophy focuses on eliminating the chasm between workers and management and enhancing product quality.[26] It is not known how popular Japanese workplace practices and philosophies will become in the United States. However, the traditional roles and objectives of unions in the U.S. conflict with the Japanese style of management. Labor and management, therefore, will be forced to make significant adjustments if Japanese management practices become widespread.

The Collective Bargaining Forum (CBF), a group of chief executive officers from major companies, international union presidents, and AFL-CIO officials, have attempted to resolve some of the issues associated with foreign competition. According to the CBF, "competitiveness" is defined as

> The ability of America in a world economy to produce domestically goods and services that will yield a competitive return on capital, provide jobs for the American work force, and promote a rising standard of living for the American people. For the individual firm, our view of competitiveness implies the achievement of a rate of return on capital adequate to attract sufficient resources and a commitment to creating and maintaining high quality employment opportunities for American workers.[27]

The CBF stresses the need for employee participation in the workplace to improve productivity, product and service quality, and employment security.[28] Specifically, the CBF advocates the adoption of business strategies that can support high productivity-high wage employment relationships. The CBF does not believe in competition based on being a low-wage producer. Instead, the CBF's focus is on

---

[24] Igor Reichlin and Gail E. Schares, "What's Haunting West German Unions: East Germans," *Business Week* (May 21, 1990), p. 60.
[25] *The Wall Street Journal*, Labor Letter (October 17, 1989), p. A1.
[26] James B. Treece and John Hoerr, "Shaking Up Detroit: How Japanese Carmakers Are Beating the Big Three on Their Own Turf," *Business Week* (August 14, 1989), pp. 74–80.
[27] U.S. Department of Labor, Bureau of Labor-Management Relations and Cooperative Programs, *New Directions for Labor and Management* (Washington, D.C.: U.S. Department of Labor, 1988), p. 3.
[28] Not all union members and leaders are convinced that labor-management cooperation is the answer to saving jobs. Dissidents in the United Auto Workers have charged that such measures are not saving jobs and force employees to work harder, pit UAW locals against each other, discourage the filing of grievances and brand those who do as "uncooperative," and create a bureaucracy of union appointees who are not directly accountable to the union membership. See Wendy Zellner, "The UAW Rebels Teaming Up Against Teamwork," *Business Week* (March 27, 1989), pp.110 and 114.

an ongoing process of adjustment to changing technology and new work design concepts. In addition, the CBF emphasizes the expansion of long-term labor-management activities such as training, quality improvement, work redesign, appropriate kinds of cost containment, and other activities that are tailored to meet the specific needs and competitive conditions of individual enterprises.[29]

Cooperative programs between labor and management require a change in both the organizational culture of the firm and a commitment by both sides to make the program work. At the A.O. Smith Corporation automotive works in Milwaukee, for example, employee problem-solving and work teams have improved quality and productivity.[30] However, worker-management teams at USX (formerly U. S. Steel Corporation), have been accused of perhaps being a management-driven strategy to build worker involvement outside the union contract.[31]

Changing the Legal Structure

An issue that must be addressed if labor and management are to embark on increasingly cooperative efforts is the need to change labor relations law. The U.S. Department of Labor has published a report dealing with U.S. labor law and the future of union-management cooperation.[32] The report represents a first step in a two-year project to review the nation's labor laws, bargaining traditions, and industrial practices that may inhibit improved labor-management relations. Table 18–1 illustrates potential conflicts between federal labor laws and union-management cooperative efforts.

Labor law reform will need to go beyond the potential legal restrictions associated with labor-management cooperation programs. If Congress and the president are interested in maintaining a viable labor movement, reforms will be needed to curb the abuses surrounding certification elections. The elimination of certification delays, harsher penalties for employers (and unions) who illegally threaten or coerce parties involved in a certification election, and a tightening of good-faith bargaining standards to help newly elected unions achieve an initial collective bargaining agreement are all necessary ingredients if public policy makers desire to slow the membership decline in private-sector unions.[33]

Employee Ownership and Gainsharing

Both employee ownership and gainsharing are receiving support within the labor community. Full or partial employee ownership theoretically eliminates the inherent conflict between union and management and should enhance product quality

---

[29] U.S. Department of Labor, Bureau of Labor-Management Relations and Cooperative Programs, *New Directions for Labor and Management* (Washington, D.C.: U.S. Department of Labor, 1988), pp. 9–10.
[30] John Hoerr, "The Cultural Revolution at A. O. Smith," *Business Week* (May 29, 1989), pp. 66–68.
[31] Gregory L. Miles, "Suddenly USX is Playing Mr. Nice Guy," *Business Week* (June 26, 1989), pp. 151–152.
[32] See U.S. Department of Labor, Bureau of Labor-Management Relations and Cooperative Programs, *U.S. Labor Law and the Future of Labor-Management Cooperation* (Washington, D.C: U.S. Department of Labor, 1987), p. 85.
[33] See Thomas A. Kochan, Harry C. Katz, and Robert B. McKersie, *The Transformation of American Industrial Relations* (New York: Basic Books, Inc., 1986), pp. 250–253.

Table 18–1 ▲ Conflicts Between Union-Management Cooperative Efforts and Labor Laws

National Labor Relations Act Problems

The Exclusion of Managerial Employees from Protection under the Act [Sections 2(3) and 9(b)]:

When employees take part in managerial decisions, do they lose their status as employees and become managerial employees? Will employees be hesitant to take part in cooperative efforts if such efforts will exclude them from bargaining units?

Definition of a Labor Organization [Section 2(5)]:

When does an employee committee become a labor organization? What kind of communication can exist between employees and management before a committee can be said to be "dealing with" an employer?

Illegal Domination or Interference with a Union by an Employer [Section 8(a)(2)]:

Where does employee-employer cooperation end and employer domination and support (company unions and sweetheart arrangements) begin?

Good-Faith Bargaining [Section 8(a)(5)]:

Does the distinction between mandatory and permissive subjects of bargaining impede cooperative programs and the sharing of information between union and management?

A Union's Duty of Fair Representation [Sections 8(b)(1)(a) and 9(a)]:

If a union delegates part of its authority to a joint employer-employee committee—and the committee makes decisions about scheduling, overtime, promotions, or disciplinary actions—has the union violated its duty of fair representation to its members? Or if a union official is involved in managerial decisions that affect bargaining unit employees, has he or she breached the union's duty to represent its members fairly?

Conflicts of Interest [Sections 8(a)(2), 8(b)(1)(a), and 8(b)(3)]:

Is there a conflict of interest when a union president is appointed to the board of directors of a corporation (whose employees the union represents), where the union also represents the employees of other competing corporations?

Taft-Hartley Act Problems

Restrictions on Payments to Employee Representatives [Sections 302(a), (b), and (c)]:

How may a corporation legally compensate union officials who sit on its board of directors, since the law prohibits an employer from paying money or other things of value to an employee's representative? Does the payment of director's fees to union officials come within the broad prohibition of the Act? Would it be a criminal violation of the law for a company to transport company and union officials in a corporate jet to view examples of innovative operations taking place in Japan or other countries?

Landrum-Griffin Act Problems

Fiduciary Responsibilities [Section 501(a)]:

May labor representatives on corporate boards serve two masters—the union and the shareholders— where the board of directors takes up issues involving labor relations policy or reviews confidential information that has not been disclosed to the union? Section 501(a) imposes a fiduciary responsibility on union officials and requires them to refrain from dealing with the union as an adverse party or from having any pecuniary or personal interest that conflicts with the interest of the union.

Table 18–1 ▲ Conflicts Between Union-Management Cooperative Efforts and Labor Laws (Continued)

Clayton Act Problems

Antitrust Provisions [Section 8]:

Does an international union's attempt to gain seats on the board of directors of more than one large corporation raise antitrust questions? Section 8 of the Clayton Act makes it illegal for a person to be a director of two or more corporations of a certain size if those corporations are competitors, which could eliminate competition by an agreement between them.

Adapted from U.S. Department of Labor, Bureau of Labor-Management Relations and Cooperative Programs, *U.S. Labor Law and the Future of Labor-Management Cooperation* (Washington, D.C.: U.S. Department of Labor, 1987), p. 85.

and customer service. Since the employee-owners have a direct interest in maintaining profit levels, close attention will likely be given to cost savings and production efficiencies. On the negative side, union officials are concerned that employee ownership will be used to undermine the union's status by persuading workers that they are owners who no longer need a union to represent them. There are also concerns that employees will lack the funding to buy healthy firms and, instead, will only be asked to buy companies that have become poor investments.[34]

Union members typically gain a share of ownership and decision making in a company in return for economic concessions. Employee stock option plans (ESOPs) are a primary means of transferring ownership to employees. However, the success of employee-ownership programs has been limited. Members of the United Food and Commercial Workers Local 46 in Waterloo, Iowa, were able to purchase a $3.6 million share (as part of a contract settlement of deferred wages and benefits) in the financially ailing Rath Packing Company. Unfortunately, the company did not make a financial turnaround.[35] Eastern Airlines negotiated an agreement with the International Association of Machinists that gave the union a seat on Eastern's board (along with union participation in various management decisions) in exchange for wage concessions. The success of this particular arrangement was short-lived after the union became disenchanted when Eastern continued wage cuts and the parties became embroiled in a lawsuit. Studies by the government's General Accounting Office and the private National Center for Employee Ownership indicate that employee ownership often does not improve productivity. In the case of Eastern Airlines, according to Rutgers University professor Joseph Blasi, "Both union leaders and senior managers kept letting their personal differences interfere."[36]

A more successful employee ownership venture involved members of the Independent Steelworkers Union and the Independent Guard Union. The members agreed to a buyout-concession plan with Weirton Steel (owned by the National

---

[34] The Bureau of National Affairs, Inc., *Unions Today: New Tactics to Tackle Tough Times* (Washington, D.C.: The Bureau of National Affairs, Inc., 1985), pp. 39–40.
[35] The Bureau of National Affairs, Inc., *Unions Today: New Tactics to Tackle Tough Times* (Washington, D.C.: The Bureau of National Affairs, Inc., 1985), pp. 44-45.
[36] Randall Smith and Judith Valente, "Can UAL Pilots Bury Their Old Animosities as Firm's Co-Owners?" *The Wall Street Journal* (September 18, 1989), p. A1. Also see Judith Valente, "UAL's Board Removes Wolf from Talks with Unions on New Buy-Out Proposal," *The Wall Street Journal* (January 12, 1990), p. A2.

Steel Corporation) that prevented massive layoffs. In the first three quarters of 1984, Weirton posted a $48 million after-tax profit and was the largest employee-owned firm in the United States.[37]

Obtaining ownership can be complicated and usually involves the cooperation of management, union officials, banks, and even government officials. Although the involvement of numerous parties may make it difficult to arrange an employee ownership plan, it may also ensure that the employees do not enter into a plan that is ill-fated from the outset. The complexities of employee-ownership plans are illustrated by the United Airline pilots' attempt to obtain at least partial ownership of their air carrier. The United pilots' $300 a share, $6.75 billion buyout bid was part of a bidding war with Los Angeles investor Marvin Davis. The pilots had the backing of British Airways and were attempting to finance the bid through wage and benefit concessions totalling $250 million annually. Other United Airline employee groups were being solicited to help in the bid by agreeing to an additional $120 million in concessions.[38] However, United's largest union, the machinist union, elected not to support the pilots in their bid to acquire 75 percent ownership in the airline.[39] Despite opposition by United Airline's chairman and CEO, Stephen M. Wolf, the pilots, machinists, and flight attendants unions had agreed to a new buy-out proposal of $185 a share or about $4 billion in March of 1990.[40]

Under gainsharing, employees share financially in productivity, profits, and other gains. Profit sharing is a primary method used in gainsharing. However, some union leaders are reluctant to give up guaranteed wage levels for the uncertainty of profit sharing.

During the 1980s, employee ownership efforts were limited primarily to "last-resort" efforts to save firms that have experienced severe financial problems and labor disputes. Directors and stockholders in financially solvent companies would, in all likelihood, resist employee ownership. Thus, the widespread use of employee ownership programs may not occur in the foreseeable future. However, inroads into labor-management cooperation may be feasible through the use of gainsharing plans. There is also evidence that more profitable firms may be targets for employee ownership.

Organized Labor's Use of Strategic Management Concepts

The leadership of American labor unions, like the leadership of other democratic institutions, has long been a subject of lively debate. Labor leaders have often been criticized by aspiring union leaders, "dissident" union groups, and man-

---

[37] The Bureau of National Affairs, Inc., *Unions Today: New Tactics to Tackle Tough Times* (Washington, D.C.: The Bureau of National Affairs, Inc.), pp. 40–44.
[38] The leader of the United Airlines pilots union, Frederick C. Dubinsky, told his 6,500 members that they would face pay cuts of up to ten percent, less overtime pay, and fewer vacation days in order to finance the takeover bid. See Judith Valente and Randall Smith, "United Air Pilots Face Cuts in Wages, Overtime Pay, Vacation to Finance Bid," *The Wall Street Journal* (September 11, 1989), p. A4.
[39] Judith Valente and Randall Smith, "UAL Machinists Decline to Join Offer and Urge Airline Directors to Reject It," *The Wall Street Journal* (September 15, 1989), p. A3.
[40] Judith Valente and Randall Smith, "UAL Chief Wolf, Bypassed in Latest Bid, Missed Opportunities, Alienated Unions," *The Wall Street Journal* (April 9, 1990), p. A4.

agement observers as being unresponsive, autocratic, or otherwise unsuited to the job. Now, with organized labor undergoing its most serious challenge in half a century, union leadership is under special scrutiny.

Most of today's labor leaders entered in the labor movement at a time when the movement's fortunes were better and when America's manufacturing sector—the foundation of the labor movement—was the centerpiece of the economy. Since then, American workers, as well as the American economy and legal environment have changed in several important respects. Today, potential union members are more highly educated. Many grew up unfamiliar with labor unions. There are many more working women. The growth areas of the economy are in the service industry, not manufacturing. Union job actions do not enjoy the same legal standing they once did, nor are they as effective as they once were.[41]

The labor-management cooperation programs discussed above (and in Chapter 8) imply that union officials and members will, in some way, play a role in helping management formulate organizational strategies. Organizational strategies typically involve decisions as to what products to produce, which customers and markets to serve, what sources of capital to use, and which production technologies to implement, among other considerations.

There is little evidence to suggest that labor organizations apply corporate strategic management concepts to their own operations. For example, union mergers are often undertaken haphazardly with little regard to the merits of the restructuring. Furthermore, there appear to be few labor leaders who make detailed long-range plans for organizing nonunion sectors, and little seems to be done to assess the internal strengths and weaknesses of their unions or the environmental threats and opportunities affecting their future. Once internal strengths and weaknesses are identified and environmental threats and opportunities are assessed, union leaders may be in a better position to make intelligent strategic choices. Strategic choices might include expansion of the union's membership (if organizing opportunities are available), merging with another labor organization, stabilizing membership levels and doing a better job of meeting the needs of current members, introducing new organizational arrangements such as non-union associations and associate memberships,[42] or perhaps divesting certain programs within the union that have become a financial drain. The point being made here is that union leaders must take a more systematic approach to running their labor organizations and making realistic strategic choices. To do otherwise may hasten the decline of organized labor in the United States.[43]

Bargaining Innovations

A critical question facing employers, unions, and workers is whether we will witness changes in the way collective bargaining is performed as well as changes in the

---

[41] The Bureau of National Affairs, Inc., *Unions Today: New Tactics to Tackle Tough Times* (Washington, D.C.: The Bureau of National Affairs, Inc., 1985), p. 118.
[42] See Paul Jarley and Jack Fiorito, "Associate Membership: Unionism or Consumerism?" *Industrial and Labor Relations Review* (January 1990), pp. 209–224.
[43] For a discussion of strategic planning in labor organizations, see John T. Dunlop, *The Management of Labor Unions* (Lexington, Massachusetts: Lexington Books, 1990), pp. 25-51.

terms and provisions of collective bargaining agreements. Although it is difficult to predict the course of collective bargaining over the next decade, several trends may be in the offing. First, the number and complexity of collective bargaining issues may force the parties either to allocate longer periods of time to complete contract talks (and avoid work stoppages) or to place more emphasis on informal joint consultation away from the bargaining table. Second, collective bargaining may become more emotional and intense because the outcome of contract talks may have important implications for the institutional survival of both the employer and the union.[44] Third, conflicts will continue to emerge from bargaining topics that are regulated by governmental agencies and are also of interest to groups outside the bargaining process. The government is involved in employee health and safety, civil rights, compensation management, individual employee rights, and other employment concerns. As the regulations, court decisions, and administrative rulings associated with federal and state labor laws proliferate, the potential for conflict may increase and the legality of collective bargaining provisions may be subject to greater scrutiny. When demands cannot be won at the bargaining table, labor leaders and workers may turn to political action. The plant closing bill discussed in Chapter 15 is a prime example of this phenomenon. Fourth, there have been predictions that the current model of unions will be replaced with a new form of labor organization that provides various services to members other than bargaining.[45]

Although change is inevitable, it is difficult to know what changes will occur and how fast they will take place. Perhaps Professor Daniel J. B. Mitchell of UCLA has made the most realistic prediction:

> A rapid change in union structure could happen only in response to some unforeseen political-economic cataclysm (inherently unpredictable) as occurred during the 1930s.
>
> It is more likely that in the 1990s there will develop "island unionism." Those unions that remain in relatively good bargaining positions will practice traditional wage bargaining tinged with a residue of the 1980s, i.e., labor-management cooperation systems. In that regard, I will stick with my early-1980s prediction of a return to normalcy. We will continue to see multi-year union agreements, COLA clauses, and other standard contractual features. A marked shift toward wages linked to real economic conditions does not seem likely, although in my view the economy would benefit from such a shift.
>
> The public sector will contain important islands of union activity, but there will be others, for example, in the automobile industry and certain still-regulated utilities. Within these islands there will be pattern bargaining. However, spheres of pattern imitation will be smaller than was the case in the 1970s; there will be fewer union workers to act as followers.

---

[44] See Joel Cutcher-Gershenfeld, Robert McKersie, and Richard Walton, "Dispute Resolution and the Transformation of U.S. Industrial Relations: A Negotiations Perspective," Industrial Relations Research Association, 1989 Spring Meeting, reprinted in *Labor Law Journal* (August 1989), pp. 480–481.
[45] Some AFL-CIO unions have established affiliate memberships. See Charles C. Heckscher, The *New Unionism: Employee Involvement* (New York: Basic Books, Inc., 1988) and Daniel J. B. Mitchell, "Will Collective Bargaining Outcomes in the 1990s Look Like Those of the 1980s?" Industrial Relations Research Association, 1989 Spring Meeting, reprinted in *Labor Law Journal* (August 1989), pp. 494-495.

Surrounding the bigger bargaining islands will be a largely nonunion sea and lesser union archipelagos. Key issues regarding human resources will be fought out in the political arena in the 1990s, especially as the workforce ages and job security becomes a more and more important concern. Employee concerns may well be voiced in the 1990s through litigation (wrongful discharge, complaints to the EEOC, etc.) and legislation, a pattern that was already emerging in the 1980s. Congress, the state legislatures, and the courts will become the employee representation plan of the next decade.[46]

▲ Summary and Conclusions

This final chapter has attempted to establish a foundation upon which predictions about the future of collective bargaining can be made. The U.S. labor movement is on the decline. Although union membership may continue to decrease, it will eventually level off, quite possibly at a point where less than 10 percent of all nonagricultural employees are represented by unions. (The number of companies with archaic, unenlightened management practices should ensure that traditional labor organizations will always be able to represent a small percentage of workers). In order for the U.S. labor movement to remain as a viable social, political, and economic force, four conditions are necessary: First, U.S. businesses must adapt to the threats of foreign competition. Second, labor must cooperate in helping U.S. firms remain competitive, even if it means moving away from traditional bargaining concerns and customs. Third, the government must modify existing labor laws to facilitate organizational campaigns and labor-management cooperative arrangements. Finally, union leaders must engage in strategic planning rather than run their organizations through short-term, incremental policies and decisions.

It is hoped that this book has illustrated the issues, complexities, and challenges associated with collective bargaining as they exist in the 1990s. An understanding of labor history should provide an appreciation of how collective bargaining has developed in the United States and, perhaps, provide insights into where it is going as we approach the 21st century. The chapter on labor law is designed to provide an understanding of the impact that public policy has on the U.S. labor movement. The chapters on bargaining units (Chapter 4), certification elections (Chapter 5), and union and management organizational structures (Chapters 6 and 7) illustrate the political, economic, and social characteristics of labor and management entities and the seemingly endless array of problems that can arise. Chapters 8 through 12 provide insights into the dynamics of bargaining and dispute resolution, areas that are often regarded as the core of collective bargaining and labor relations. The four chapters on collective bargaining agreement provisions (Chapters 13 through 16) covering compensation, employee benefits, institutional issues, and employee job rights and discipline are designed to illustrate the multitude of provisions and variations that can be found in labor contracts. These chapters also illustrate the im-

---

[46] Daniel J. B. Mitchell, "Will Collective Bargaining Outcomes in the 1990s Look Like Those of the 1980s?" Industrial Relations Research Association, 1989 Spring Meeting, reprinted in *Labor Law Journal* (August 1989), pp. 494–495.

portance of carefully negotiating and drafting contract language. The chapter on public-sector collective bargaining (Chapter 17) is designed to illustrate the different treatments afforded to governmental employees insofar as organizational rights, bargaining, and contract administration are concerned. The public sector may provide the brightest prospect for the U.S. labor movement in the 1990s.

The material covered in this book should be valuable to those who will be involved in the collective bargaining process, whether it be as a corporate personnel/human resource administrator, union or management negotiator, union officer, or an employee whose worklife will be affected by the bargaining process. In addition, the issues discussed here should provide insights for those who may never work in a unionized setting or be involved with collective bargaining. The union-nonunion distinction that is made between organizations may, at times, be overstated. All organizations have employees and all employees have concerns about wages, hours, and working conditions. The success of a book such as this one is probably best measured by the extent to which the reader has gained an appreciation for matters affecting the employment relationship.

▲ Discussion Questions and Exercises

1. Evaluate the three potential roads that Professor Peter Drucker believes American unions will follow. Which scenario appears most likely? Discuss.
2. Of the five causes of union membership losses discussed in this chapter, which has been most damaging to labor unions? Which factors are most likely to be corrected by public policy and economic restructuring? Which factors are least amenable to correction?
3. What methods would you recommend as being most practical and feasible for shifting U.S. labor relations from an adversarial to a more cooperative posture?
4. Consult a current strategic management textbook for a discussion on organizational strategy formulation, implementation, and evaluation. How can labor unions implement strategic management concepts to improve their operations and ensure their survival?
5. You have just been appointed as Secretary of Labor by the President of the United States. Outline your proposed agenda to help revitalize the American labor movement and improve the well-being of all American workers.

Glossary

AAA *See* American Arbitration Association.

Absenteeism A situation in which an employee fails to report to work as scheduled. Absenteeism is regarded as *voluntary* when the employee is physically able, yet elects not to report to work. *Involuntary* absenteeism occurs when an employee wants to work, but is prevented from doing so because of illness, inclement weather, or other circumstances beyond his or her control.

Ad hoc arbitration A system whereby the union and the employer jointly choose arbitrators on a case-by-case basis.

Administrative law judge An employee of the National Labor Relations Board who issues decisions in cases in which an unfair labor practice has been charged. Formerly called "trial examiner."

Affirmative action Providing special assistance and preference to certain minority groups in hiring, promotion, and other employment considerations. Affirmative action plans are designed primarily to overcome the effects of past discrimination. Organizations that have Federal contracts or receive Federal financial assistance usually have affirmative action obligations. Affirmative action is based primarily on Executive Order 11246, as amended, and Executive Order 12048.

AFL-CIO *See* American Federation of Labor-Congress of Industrial Organizations.

Age Discrimination in Employment Act (1967) Protects workers and job applicants age 40 and over from a wide range of discriminatory employment practices associated with hiring, promotions, working conditions, and employee benefits.

Agency shop A bargaining unit covered by a union security clause in the collective bargaining agreement stating that the nonunion employees in the unit must pay the union a sum equal to union fees and dues as a condition of continuing employment. The contract does not, however, require nonunion workers to join the union.

Alexander v. Gardner-Denver *See* Gardner-Denver.

Ally doctrine A neutral (secondary) employer becomes an ally of a primary employer when it accepts subcontracted work normally performed by striking workers of the primary employer. A neutral employer also becomes an ally when it has managerial ties with a primary employer. During the course of a labor dispute, ally employers may be subjected to picketing or other pressure by the union. Such pressure is not regarded as a secondary boycott.

Alter-ego employer A firm that goes out of business and then, under the same ownership, reopens the business under a new name. Alter-ego employers are obligated to continue bargaining with the certified bargaining representative and must honor a collective bargaining agreement that was in force before the business changed its name. *Compare with* Successor employer.

American Arbitration Association (AAA) A private nonprofit agency that encourages arbitration as a means of settling disputes. The AAA maintains panels of arbitrators in large American cities.

American Federation of Labor-Congress of Industrial Organizations (AFL-CIO) A federation of craft and industrial unions, as well as unions of a mixed structure, created in 1955 by the merger of two specialized federations.

Americans with Disabilities Act of 1990 Protects physically and mentally handicapped persons against employment discrimination. The Act covers employers affecting interstate commerce who employ 25 or more employees. Employers are required to make reasonable accommodation to "qualified individuals with a disability." Drug testing is permitted under the Act. *See* Rehabilitation Act of 1973.

Annual improvement factor A yearly adjustment rate used in granting wage increases in recognition of the workers' share in increased productivity.

Apprenticeship training An arrangement whereby an employee enters into an agreement with an employer and a union, and sometimes vocational school authorities, to learn a skilled trade by work experience and technical instruction. Successful completion of the training allows admission into journeyman ranks.

Arbitrability The potential of an issue in dispute to fall within an arbitrator's jurisdiction. Arbitrability is of two types: *procedural*, dealing with matters of timeliness and adherence to particular steps before arbitration, and *substantive*, related to the scope of an arbitration provision in a collective bargaining agreement.

Arbitration A method of settling a labor-management dispute by having an impartial third party, known as an arbitrator, render a decision that is binding on both the union and the employer. *See* Grievance; Rights dispute; Interest arbitration.

Areawide bargaining A type of multi-employer bargaining in which bargaining takes place between union and employer representatives on a local or city level. This form of bargaining is common in the construction, bakery, and laundry industries.

Attitudinal structuring An attempt by negotiators to alter the way in which a bargaining opponent views a set of bargaining issues or perceives the opposing negotiating team.

At-will employee *See* Employment at will.

Authorization card A statement solicited from individual employees by a union during an organizing drive. The statement either indicates the employee's desire for an election in which the question is whether there shall be a union, or it authorizes the union to represent the employees for purposes of collective bargaining.

Award The final decision of an arbitrator, binding on both parties to the dispute. Often a rationale or opinion accompanies the decision.

Back-loaded Providing a greater wage increase during the later part of a multi-year agreement. Used to describe a contract. *See* Deferred pay increases; Front-loaded.

Back pay Wages due an employee because of (1) employer violation of the overtime or minimum wage provisions of the Fair Labor Standards Act or an equal employment opportunity law; (2) suspension or discharge in violation of the collective bargaining agreement; or (3) adjustment of a piece rate following a grievance.

Back-to-work movement A return of strikers to their jobs before their union has declared an end to the strike.

Bargaining agent A union that is the exclusive representative to the employer of all workers, both union and nonunion, in a bargaining unit. *See* Exclusive bargaining representative.

Bargaining power The power that negotiators bring to play on a specific negotiating session. Bargaining power is often viewed in a relative sense (union's power versus management's power). Power is also defined as the cost of agreeing versus disagreeing with an opponent.

Bargaining unit A group of jobs in a firm, plant, or industry with sufficient commonality to constitute the unit represented in collective bargaining by a particular bargaining agent.

Benchmark job Jobs used as a point of reference during job evaluation and wage and salary administration. An organization's benchmark jobs have a stable set of tasks, duties, and responsibilities and are paid at a rate that is equitable with external labor market conditions. Also known as *key* jobs. *See* Factor comparison method.

Bill of Rights Provisions in the Landrum-Griffin Act that guarantee union members the right to meet with other members and express views on union business and to have a fair trial in matters of internal discipline.

BLS *See* Bureau of Labor Statistics.

Blacklist An antiunion tactic used extensively in the early part of this century and latter part of the 19th century. A list of union supporters was circulated among firms in a region or industry. Blacklisted employees were then barred from employment by these firms.

Blue-circle rate A job that is *underpaid* relative to what the job evaluation dictates is an equitable pay rate. Also called a green-circle rate. *See* Red-circle rate.

Blue flu A job action in which large numbers of uniformed workers of a law enforcement agency call in sick. The purpose of the blue flu is to win concessions from the employer without resorting to an illegal strike.

Bona fide occupational qualification (BFOQ) A provision in a civil rights law that permits an employer, employment agency, union, or other agency to legally discriminate against a protected group. Under Title VII of the 1964 Civil Rights Act, for example, BFOQs are permitted for sex, religious, or national origin, but not for race or color. BFOQs are typically granted very sparingly by the courts and usually involve safety concerns.

Boulwarism A bargaining strategy in which an employer attempts to persuade the employees that his or her initial offer is in their best interests, thus bypassing the union. The employer changes this offer only if it receives new information or persuasive arguments from the union.

Boycott An organized refusal by employees and their union to deal with an employer. Boycotts are used to win concessions. Primary boycotts usually take the form of putting pressure on consumers not to buy the goods of an employer who is directly involved in a dispute. Secondary boycotts are those in which pressure is exerted on employers who are not directly involved in a dispute.

Bumping A practice allowing a worker laid off from a job for lack of work to displace some other worker with less seniority in the same plant. Often provided for in collective bargaining agreements, bumping is designed to protect job rights of workers with the greatest seniority.

Burden of proof In an arbitration proceeding, the responsibility placed on one of the parties, depending on the issue, to prove (to the arbitrator's satisfaction) the correctness or truth of the allegations made. It can mean the burden of producing evidence, the burden of pleading, or the burden of ultimate persuasion.

Bureau of Labor Statistics (BLS) A unit of the U.S. Department of Labor that collects and publishes information on the cost of living, the volume of employment and unemployment, labor turnover, industrial disputes, and other matters relating to the world of work.

Business Agent A full-time officer of a local union who handles grievances, helps enforce contracts, and performs other tasks in the day-to-day operation of a union. To be distinguished from international representative and shop steward.

"C" cases A term used to denote unfair labor practice cases.

Call-back pay Compensation, often at higher rates, to workers called back on the job after completing their regular shift.

Call-in pay Compensation, usually from two to eight hours in wages, guaranteed to a worker who reports for work and finds there is insufficient work for him or her to do. *See* Reporting pay.

Captive audience A situation in which an employer requires workers to attend antiunion speeches prior to a certification election. Captive audience speeches are usually done during normal work hours. Such speeches are generally legal as long as they contain no threats of reprisal or promise of benefit, and are not conducted within 24 hours of the certification election.

Card check Checking authorization card signatures to determine whether a union represents the majority of bargaining-unit employees.

Casual employees Employees who do not work on a regular full- or part-time basis. Casual employees are usually excluded from bargaining units.

Cease and desist order A form of injunction that prohibits a party from performing a certain action. For example, a cease and desist order might be issued against management or a union to prevent them from engaging in an unfair labor or discriminatory practice.

Centralized bargaining An arrangement whereby contract negotiations are conducted primarily by top corporate and union officials. The resulting contract may cover an employer association, industry, or group of plants. *See* Decentralized bargaining.

Certification Determination by the National Labor Relations Board or an appropriate state agency that a particular union is the majority choice, and hence the exclusive bargaining agent, of all employees in a particular bargaining unit.

Checkoff The deduction of union dues, assessments, and initiation fees from the pay of all union members by the employer, who transmits these funds to the union.

Chief negotiator The person generally responsible for coordinating bargaining preparations, directing contract talks, and having the final authority to accept or reject a proposal or offer.

Civil service A central personnel bureau within a governmental unit. A civil service has a function similar to a corporate personnel unit in that it advises, formulates policy, and regulates employment procedures. The selection processes for many public sector jobs are based on the merit system and make use of tests standardized by civil service. Civil services were established in response to the problems stemming from the appointment of persons to government jobs for political reasons.

Civil Service Reform Act of 1978 A federal law enacted in 1978 to improve the federal civil service system. Among the important provisions of the law are (1) the reorganization of the Civil Service Commission into the Office of Personnel Management, which administers civil service policies, and the Merit System Protection Board, which is responsible for protecting civil service employees from prohibited employment practices; (2) the creation of a senior executive service, designed to attract and retain top-grade-level managers and supervisors by providing a more flexible means of linking salary increases to improved job performance; and (3) the regulation by statute of the federal labor-management relations program, which previously operated under Executive Orders 10988 and 11491.

Classification method A job evaluation technique whereby a group of similar jobs are placed in a common classification and assigned a single pay rate or variable-pay range.

Clayton Act A law passed in 1914 that remedied the inadequacies of the Sherman Antitrust Act (1890) in dealing with business mergers and monopolistic practices. The act exempted unions from the coverage of the Sherman Antitrust Act and stated that labor organizations were not illegal combinations or conspiracies.

Closed shop A bargaining unit covered by an agreement between an employer and a union that, as a condition of employment, all employees must belong to the union *before* being hired. This form of union security was declared illegal by the Taft-Hartley Act in 1947.

Coalition bargaining A form of collective bargaining in which several different unions representing different categories of employees of a single employer attempt to coordinate their bargaining. Some of the reasons for coordinating the bargaining include increasing the effectiveness of strikes, preventing divide-and-conquer tactics on the part of the employer, and countering the increasing numbers of nonunion members in corporations and conglomerates.

COBRA *See* Consolidated Omnibus Reconciliation Act of 1985.

Code of Ethical Practices A code of union ethics, drawn up in 1957 by the Ethical Practices Committee of the AFL-CIO and adopted by the convention of the AFL-CIO, that sets standards of trade union morality.

Co-determination An arrangement in which union officials have input into corporate policy. Co-determination is used in several European countries, most notably, West Germany.

Co-insurance The share of health care expenses that an insured employee must pay on a health insurance claim in addition to the deductible. Co-insurance clauses typically require that the employee pay 10 to 20 percent of health care expenses that are incurred above the deductible amount.

COLA *See* cost-of-living adjustment.

Collective bargaining A method of determining terms and conditions of employment by negotiation between representatives of the employer and union representatives of the employees. The results of the bargaining are set forth in a collective bargaining agreement.

Collective bargaining agreement A written contract resulting from negotiation between an employer (or a group of employers) and a union (or group of unions), which sets the terms and conditions of employment (such as wages, hours, and benefits) and the procedure to be used in settling disputes that may arise during the term of the contract. Contracts usually are in effect for a specified period (e.g., one, two, or three years).

Collusion A conspiracy engaged in by an employer and the certified representative of his or her employees to defraud the employees represented while providing the semblance of a genuine bargaining relationship. *See* Sweetheart contract.

Committee on Political Education (COPE) A division of the AFL-CIO. COPE's primary activity is to provide support for candidates for political office who have received the endorsement of organized labor. Its activities are supported by voluntary contributions.

Common law Legal doctrines that are fashioned through a series of court decisions rather than codified in statutory law. For example, the development of labor arbitration and the power of arbitrators in U.S. labor relations is primarily a product of common law.

Common law of the shop A set of precedents or an established way of doing things in a particular industrial setting. The interpretation of contract language, informal agreements, and custom and past practices often determine the common law of the shop. The common law of the shop varies from one firm or industry to another.

Common-situs picketing A form of picketing in which employees of a struck employer who work at a common site with employees of at least one neutral employer may picket only at their entrance to the work site. The employees of the neutral employers must enter the work site through other gates. Picketing is restricted to the entrance of the struck employer so as not to encourage a secondary boycott. *See* Reserve gate.

Company union An employee organization, usually of a single company, that is dominated or strongly influenced by management. Company unions were widespread in the 1920s and early 1930s. The National Labor Relations Act of 1935 declared that such employer domination is an unfair labor practice, and company unions have since been on the decline.

Comparable worth The notion that wages and benefits should be based on the worth of the job to the employer rather than on circumstances dictated by the vagaries of the labor market.

Concerted activity An action by two or more employees to improve wages, hours, and working conditions or to protect their mutual employment interests.

Concession bargaining Sometimes called employee or union givebacks, concession bargaining usually describes those instances when unions agree to modify terms in the existing contract in exchange for other benefits. During the 1980s, for example, many unions agreed to modify such issues as work rules and seniority provisions in exchange for greater job security.

Conciliation *See* Mediation.

Confidential employee An employee who, although he or she may have no supervisory responsibilities, has access to information about the organization's labor relations policy and is therefore ineligible for inclusion in a bargaining unit or coverage by a bargaining agreement.

Consent election A certification election that is held after the employer and union informally agree to the terms of the election.

Consolidated Omnibus Budget Reconciliation Act of 1985 (COBRA) Allows for continued health insurance protection for the dependents of an employee if the employee dies or terminates his or her employment. COBRA also provides the option of extended health insurance coverage for other "qualified" events.

Conspiracy doctrine The doctrine, developed in English common law, which holds that certain acts that are lawful when performed by an individual (e.g., a worker's demand for an increase in pay) are unlawful when performed by a group (e.g., several workers acting in concert to demand an increase in pay). In the early 19th century, American courts held that labor combinations (unions) formed to secure higher wages and other benefits were conspiracies. In 1842, in the case of *Commonwealth v. Hunt*, a Massachusetts court declared that labor combinations were not in themselves illegal. After that decision, prosecutions against unions were based on the illegality of methods used or ends sought rather than on the issue of conspiracy. *See* Clayton Act; Sherman Antitrust Act.

Constructive discharge A situation in which an employee resigns because of pressure or harassment by the employer. Equal employment opportunity commissions and the courts often view such discharges in the same light as an outright termination.

Consumer Price Index (CPI) *See* Cost-of-living index.

Contract *See* Collective bargaining agreement.

Contract bar The existence of a valid collective bargaining agreement that precludes a labor relations agency from honoring a request for an election by a rival union or a petition for a decertification election. The National Labor Relations Board will not deal with representation questions during the life of an agreement, unless a petition is filed at least 60 days before but not more than 90 days before the expiration of a current contract. Customarily, however, the NLRB will not permit a contract to bar an election for more than a three-year period.

Cooling-off period 1. A required period of delay (fixed by federal or state law) following legal notice of a pending labor dispute during which there can be neither a strike nor a lockout. 2. An 80-day period during which a strike or lockout is prohibited by injunction of the federal courts.

COPE *See* Committee on Political Education.

Corrective discipline A disciplinary system containing a categorization of offenses (e.g., minor, moderate, or serious) and a series of increasingly severe penalties for repeat offenders. Such a system typically enhances due process, equal protection, and fairness. Also known as *progressive* discipline.

Cost-of-living adjustment (COLA) A provision in a collective bargaining agreement that relates wage increases to the cost of living during the period of an agreement.

Cost-of-living index A measurement of changes in prices of goods and services purchased by urban wage earners and clerical workers.

Counterproposal A proposal by union or management negotiators that is made in response to an earlier proposal on contract terms.

Craft A manual occupation that requires extensive training and a high degree of skill, such as carpentry, plumbing, or operating a Linotype machine.

Craft union A union that limits its membership to those workers in a particular craft. Most craft unions today, however, have broadened their jurisdictions to include many occupations and skills that are not closely related to the originally designated craft.

Davis-Bacon Act A federal law that requires firms to pay a stipulated wage on federally funded construction projects.

Decentralized bargaining A situation in which bargaining is done primarily at the local level. For example, bargaining between a local union and a plant represents a decentralized bargaining arrangement. *See* Centralized bargaining.

Decertification election When bargaining-unit employees decide that they no longer wish to be represented by their union, they may call for a decertification election. Decertification procedures are similar to those used in certification elections. Employees may decertify a union if they believe that it no longer represents their interests or if they desire to be represented by another labor organization.

Deductible The amount that an insured employee must pay on a group health insurance claim before the insurance policy pays benefits. Disability income insurance policies use a waiting period in lieu of a deductible.

Deferred pay increase Pay increases that are to be granted at some later date. For example, an employer may agree to a seven percent wage increase, four percent of which is to be granted immediately and the remaining three percent deferred for one year. *See* Back-loaded.

De minimus rule In denying a grievance, an arbitrator may decide that trifling or immaterial matters will not be taken into account.

Deregulation A situation in which firms within a heavily regulated industry have the regulation abolished by the federal or state government. Deregulation typically allows a firm to establish its own pricing structure, formulate its own operating procedures, and select the markets it wishes to serve. Airlines, railroads, and communications are examples of industries that were once heavily regulated, but which have been deregulated.

Disability income insurance An insurance policy that pays an employee a weekly or monthly amount if that individual is disabled because of an accident or illness. A short-term disability income policy may pay only for several months, whereas a long-term policy may pay benefits until the employee reaches retirement age or dies.

Discharge A term used to describe the firing or involuntary termination of an employee. *See* Constructive discharge.

Distributive bargaining A bargaining issue in which one side gains and the other side loses. Known as a *zero-sum* bargaining situation. *See* Integrative bargaining.

Double breasting A practice, usually confined to the construction industry, wherein a single employer operates two subsidiaries, one unionized and the other nonunion. Employers believe that under this arrangement they can better compete with open shop firms.

Double jeopardy A situation in which an employee's off-duty misconduct results in criminal or civil charges as well as disciplinary action by the employer.

Dual-status employee An employee who works in a bargaining-unit job as well as in a nonbargaining unit job. Whether an employee is entitled to benefits under the collective bargaining agreement will depend on the percentage of work time that is spent in the bargaining unit job. *See* Part-time employee.

Due process A set of conditions that ensure the fair treatment of an employee who faces disciplinary action. The precepts of due process are normally fulfilled if the employee is informed of the charges, has an opportunity to examine and rebut adverse evidence, as well as present evidence and arguments on his or her behalf. When a grievance procedure is used, due process considerations dictate that the procedure be followed in a proper and timely fashion.

Duty of fair representation A union's obligation to represent fairly all individuals in the bargaining unit. The Supreme Court has held that the power of a majority representative to speak for all bargaining-unit employees gives rise to a duty to represent those employees fairly and in good faith. A bargaining representative has a duty both in collective bargaining negotiations and in the enforcement of the collective bargaining agreement to serve the interests of all members of the bargaining unit without hostility, discrimination, or arbitrary conduct—whether or not members of the bargaining unit are members of the union or voted for the union and whether or not they are members of some racial or ethnic minority group.

Economic strike A work stoppage resulting from a dispute over wages, hours, and other terms of employment. Economic strikers retain employee status but may be permanently replaced and are not entitled to bump their replacements upon termination of the strike.

EEO *See* Equal employment opportunity.

EEOC *See* Equal Employment Opportunity Commission.

Emergency dispute A labor-management dispute believed to endanger the public's health or safety. While there is little consensus on what conditions constitute an emergency dispute, federal law has attempted to provide mechanisms to resolve them.

Employee assistance programs An employer- or union-sponsored program that helps an employee deal with a variety of personal problems such as alcohol and drug abuse as well as domestic, legal, and financial problems.

Employee benefits Nonwage items and payments received by or credited to workers in addition to wages, often not in exchange for time worked: for instance, supplemental unemployment benefits, pensions, vacation and holiday pay, and health insurance.

Employee Retirement Income Security Act of 1974 (ERISA) Federal legislation that regulates private pensions. The law was enacted to ensure that all employees covered under pension plans would receive the benefits promised.

Employee stock ownership plans (ESOPs) Plans that give employees some sense of ownership in a company by purchasing stock or receiving stock bonuses.

Employment at will The doctrine that employment may be terminated by either the employee or the employer without cause. Under this concept all employees whose job security is not protected by a collective bargaining agreement, tenure, or civil service law are subject to employment at will discharge.

End run A tactic in which a bargaining agent bypasses one level of management or statutory authority and approaches a higher level with the intention of securing or negotiating a more favorable agreement.

Equal employment opportunity (EEO) In hiring and employment practices, the absence of discrimination on the basis of race, color, religion, sex, national origin, age, handicap status, or other protected classification under federal, state, or local law.

Equal Employment Opportunity Commission (EEOC) The Equal Employment Opportunity Commission was established by Title VII, Civil Rights Act of 1964, which prohibits employers and labor unions from discriminating against an individual because of race, color, religion, sex, or national origin.

Equal Pay Act (1963) A federal law that requires "equal pay for equal work" and prohibits pay differentials geared to an employee's sex. "Equal work" is defined as jobs having similar responsibilities, effort, working conditions, and skill requirements. A male and female employee performing the same job may receive different amounts of pay if such differentials are based on seniority, individual productivity, merit, or factors other than sex.

Equal protection Ensuring that an employee receives approximately the same type of disciplinary hearing and penalty as other employees received for similar transgressions.

ERISA *See* Employee Retirement Income Security Act of 1974.

Escalator clause *See* Cost-of-living adjustment.

Escape clause *See* Maintenance-of-membership clause.

Ethical Practices Committee A body within the AFL-CIO, established by the Executive Council in 1955, charged with the task of keeping the AFL-CIO "free from any taint of corruption or communism."

Exclusive bargaining representative The U.S. labor doctrine that allows only one bargaining representative for a group of bargaining-unit employees.

Executive Committee, AFL-CIO A policy-making and advisory body of the AFL-CIO composed of the president and secretary-treasurer of the AFL-CIO and six vice presidents selected by the Executive Council. The committee carries on the work of the AFL-CIO between meetings of the Executive Council.

Executive Council, AFL-CIO A body within the AFL-CIO consisting of the president, secretary-treasurer, and 27 vice presidents. The Executive Council, which meets three times a year, is the governing body of the organization. Many of its actions are subject to approval of the AFL-CIO convention, however.

Executive Order 11491 An order issued in 1969 by President Richard M. Nixon. It revised Executive Order 10988 issued by President John F. Kennedy in 1962, which established the first government labor relations program, by extending limited collective bargaining rights to federal employees.

Exempt employee An employee who is not subject to the provisions of the Fair Labor Standards Act. For the most part, employees whose compensation is based on an annual salary, rather than on an hourly rate, are considered exempt.

Factfinding Investigation of a labor-management dispute by a board or panel, or by an individual, usually appointed by a chief executive or a government or a state agency that administers a labor relations law. Factfinding boards and factfinders issue reports that describe the issues in the dispute and frequently make recommendations for their resolution.

Factor comparison method A form of job evaluation that uses a set of benchmark jobs and compensable factors to determine the pay rates for nonbenchmark jobs. *See* Benchmark job.

Fair employment practice (FEP) laws Federal, state, and municipal laws and ordinances designed to bar discrimination in hiring, promoting, discharging, and other conditions of employment on the basis of race, creed, color, national origin, and in some cases, age. *See* Affirmative action, Age Discrimination in Employment Act of 1967, Equal employment opportunity, Rehabilitation Act of 1973, and Title VII of the Civil Rights Act of 1964.

Fair Labor Standards Act (FLSA) A federal statute passed in 1938 that set minimum wages and maximum hours, requiring overtime rates for hours worked beyond the maximum, and restricting child labor in industries engaged in interstate commerce.

Featherbedding Labor practices, usually promoted by unions, that are inefficient or unprofitable for the employer. Featherbedding includes payment for work not performed, refusal to allow the adoption of labor-saving equipment, and the creation of nonessential jobs. Unions often argue that featherbedding practices are attempts to enhance safety and ensure quality work. The fear of workers that they might work themselves out of a job is another motivation for featherbedding.

Federal Mediation and Conciliation Service (FMCS) An independent federal agency created in 1947 to provide mediators for private sector labor-management disputes affecting interstate commerce.

Fiduciary An individual responsible for pension trust funds such as an attorney, a trustee, or an officer or director of a corporation.

Field examiner An employee of the National Labor Relations Board whose primary duties are to conduct certification elections and to carry out preliminary investigations of unfair labor practice charges. To be distinguished from an administrative law judge.

Final-offer arbitration A type of interest arbitration in which the arbitrator selects either the union's or the employer's final proposal. In some instances the arbitrator selects one side's entire *package* of issues; in other cases the arbitrator selects the final proposal of a party on an *issue-by-issue* basis. *See* Interest arbitration.

Flexible benefits Allowing employees to select from among a variety of employee benefits. Sometimes referred to as *cafeteria benefits.*

Flexitime A work scheduling system that allows workers to vary their arrival and departure times but does not change the number of hours they must work. Most flexitime schedules are based on a flexible workday rather than on a week or month. They require employees to be present for a specified period known as "core time," but allow them to complete the remainder of the required hours at their discretion.

FLSA *See* Fair Labor Standards Act.

FMCS *See* Federal Mediation and Conciliation Service.

Free rider A worker in a bargaining unit who is eligible for union membership but does not join the union. Union members maintain that free riders receive all the benefits of the union contract, yet do not pay the dues or fees that make these benefits possible.

Front-loaded Providing a greater wage increase in the early period of a multi-year collective bargaining agreement than in the later period. For instance, an eight-percent wage increase in the first year of a three-year agreement and a seven-percent increase in the two years following. *See* Back-loaded.

Gainsharing A system under which employees are paid a bonus because the company's profits or cost reductions.

Gardner-Denver (*Alexander v. Gardner-Denver*, 1974) The U.S. Supreme Court ruled that an employee alleging discrimination is not prevented from pursuing a remedy under Title VII of the Civil Rights Act, even though the employee has already pursued the claim through the grievance procedure and arbitration.

General strike A strike by all or most organized workers in a community or nation. Such strikes usually are politically motivated rather than an attempt to improve conditions of work. General strikes are rare in the United States.

Good-faith bargaining Negotiations in which two parties meet and confer at reasonable times and demonstrate a willingness to listen and be persuaded. Although the parties must negotiate with a view toward reaching an agreement on new contract terms, good-faith bargaining does not imply that either party is required to make concessions or reach an agreement on any proposal. Lack of good faith bargaining is an unfair labor practice.

Grievance An allegation by an individual, union, or management involving the misinterpretation or misapplication of a collective bargaining agreement. Grievances also arise over deviations from traditional work practices. *See* Rights dispute.

Grievance arbitration Usually the final step in adjudicating a grievance. The dispute is submitted to an arbitrator for a final and binding decision. The arbitrator's task is to determine whether the contract or long-standing work practice has been misinterpreted or misapplied. Sometimes referred to as "rights arbitration."

Group insurance A health or life insurance policy that covers a group of employees (e.g., a group of plant workers, all employees of a particular corporation, or members of a union). Group policies provide a master insurance contract to the employer or union; individual employees receive a handbook that summarizes their insurance benefits. Because the employer or union pays part of the administrative cost and premiums, group insurance is often less expensive for the employee than if he or she purchased a comparable individual policy.

Guaranteed annual wages *See* Income maintenance.

Hazardous work pay Pay that supplements an employee's base wage or salary because he or she is either required to perform hazardous duties or work in a hazardous environment.

Hospitalization insurance Medical insurance that covers the costs of a hospital stay as well as ancillary services such as nursing care. Hospitalization insurance often pays a specific daily amount (e.g., $200 per day) and requires that the insured employee be admitted to the hospital in order to collect benefits.

Hot cargo provisions Contract provisions that allow workers to refuse to work on or handle "hot cargo" or "unfair goods" that come from a plant where there is a labor dispute. The Landrum-Griffin Act of 1959 outlawed such provisions, except for those affecting suppliers or subcontractors in construction work and jobbers in the garment industry.

ILO *See* International Labor Organization.

Immigration Reform and Control Act (1986) Regulates the employment of aliens in the U.S. and requires that job applicants provide suitable documentation to verify their citizenship and eligibility to work.

Impact bargaining Labor-management negotiations over the effects of employer decisions. Even when an issue is not a mandatory subject of bargaining, the employer may be obliged to bargain over the effect of the unilateral decision on that issue. Thus, even though an employer may unilaterally reduce the number of workers employed, the order of layoffs (which workers go first) is a mandatory subject of bargaining.

Impasse A situation in which no further progress in reaching an agreement can be made by negotiators. Either party may determine the point at which an impasse has been reached. In the public sector, technical impasse occurs when an agreement has not been reached within a specified number of days before the deadline for budget submission, even though the parties are continuing to bargain in good faith.

Incentive wage plan A system of compensation in which workers' earnings are directly related to their output rather than being based on an hourly rate (e.g., 15 cents per unit). Incentive wage plans are widespread in textiles, clothing, and certain other manufacturing industries.

Income maintenance A program that guarantees an employee a minimum amount of income or work. Income maintenance programs typically guarantee a minimum level of annual income. Severance pay and supplemental unemployment benefits are also regarded as forms of income maintenance.

Increments A series of successive additions to salary, provided for in a salary schedule. Employees are granted a specific salary increase for each year of service, either in a dollar amount or as a percentage of the previous year's salary. Salary schedules containing increments are commonplace in the public sector. Teachers, for example, frequently have salary schedules containing 15 to 20 automatic increments.

Independent contractor A person hired to perform a job at a stipulated price. The independent contractor determines the means (materials, labor, processes) by which the job will be performed. The difference between the price paid for the job and the cost of performing the job represents the independent contractor's profits.

Independent union A union that is not affiliated with the AFL-CIO.

Industrial union A union representing all workers, both skilled and unskilled, in a plant or industry.

Industrywide bargaining A form of multi-employer bargaining that results in a master agreement negotiated for all employees in an industry by one or more unions. This form of bargaining is common in the coal and men's clothing industries.

Inflation A continuous rise in the general price level due to an increase in the supply of money or credit or a limited supply of goods and services.

Initiation fees Payment to a union required of a worker when he or she joins the union. The amount of the fee is usually set forth in the union's constitution.

Injunction A court order restraining individuals or groups from committing acts the court has determined will do irreparable harm. Injunctions are now issued in labor disputes that imperil the nation's health and welfare; they are also used to prevent certain unfair labor practices, stop violence associated with a strike, or abolish picket lines that prevent entrance to a plant or facility.

Integrative bargaining A bargaining issue in which the gains of one side may also result in gains by the bargaining opponent. Known as a *variable-sum* bargaining situation.

Interest arbitration Adjudication to resolve an impasse in contract negotiations. Interest arbitration has become widespread in the resolution of disputes in the public sector, particularly for police and fire fighters.

Interest dispute A dispute over the final terms and conditions of a collective bargaining agreement (as opposed to a dispute over the interpretation or application of such an agreement).

Internal disputes plan A method established by the constitution of the AFL-CIO for resolving disputes arising among affiliated unions.

International Labor Organization (ILO) An international body whose purpose is to better labor standards worldwide, founded during the peace conferences after World War I as part of the League of Nations. The ILO holds annual conferences of government, management, and labor representatives who discuss working conditions and set standards for improving them. The United States withdrew from the ILO in 1977.

International representative A staff officer of an international union who is appointed by the union's executive board, president, or regional vice president to serve as liaison between the international union and its locals. The international representative usually comes from the ranks of union members, and his or her duties include aiding in contract negotiations, assisting local unions in the handling of grievances and other matters, and organizing unorganized shops in the union's jurisdiction.

International union The national organization of a labor union, so called because many unions have affiliates in Canada. Financially supported by a per capita tax of all its members, its chief functions are extending union organization: chartering local unions; setting jurisdictional boundaries; conducting educational programs; doing research in areas related to trade union objectives; engaging in lobbying; aiding local unions in bargaining; and where multi-employer bargaining is used, negotiating directly with industry representatives.

Interstate commerce Trading goods or services across state lines. The federal government has the constitutional authority to regulate trade among the states. This authority has enabled the federal government to pass laws such as the National Labor Relations Act, ERISA, and others.

Intraorganizational bargaining Negotiations that occur among bargaining team members before they meet with the opponent at the bargaining table. Intraorganizational bargaining is used to establish a negotiating team's priorities and demands.

Job action A concerted activity by employees on the job designed to put pressure on an employer without resorting to a strike.

Job analysis Job analysis consists of a *job description* that outlines the tasks, duties, responsibilities, and working conditions associated with a job and a *job specification* that lists the knowledge, skills, and abilities required of the employee performing the job. Job analysis provides useful information for nearly all facets of personnel/human resource management such as hiring, training, performance appraisal, compensation, and collective bargaining.

Job evaluation The process of placing a value on a job for compensation purposes. *See* Classification method, Factor comparison method, and Point method.

Job posting The process of posting job openings on a company bulletin board so that current employees can apply for (or bid on) these jobs.

Job security Generally, the quest to retain one's job. Many union contracts contain provisions that protect jobs for bargaining-unit members and provide for fair dismissal or just cause procedures for individuals subjected to discharge.

Job sharing A system of allowing employees to share work on a part-time basis when jobs are scarce or the firm is forced to layoff employees. Instead of having some employees work full time while others are on layoff, job sharing allows more employees to remain on the job as part-time workers.

Journeyman A craft worker who has completed apprenticeship training and has been admitted to full membership in a craft, for instance, a journeyman plumber or journeyman carpenter.

Judicial review A court procedure to determine the legality of decisions issued by a labor relations board or an arbitrator. Judicial review is concerned solely with whether the decision is in violation of a statute and not with the merits or the substance of the decision.

Jurisdiction The area of jobs, skills, occupations, and industries within which a union organizes and engages in collective bargaining. International unions often assert exclusive claim to particular areas of employment.

Jurisdictional dispute A conflict between two or more unions over the right of their memberships to perform certain types of work. The term may also refer to a conflict between two or more unions over organizing or representing groups of workers.

Jurisdictional strike A strike resulting from a dispute between two rival unions over representation rights or the right to perform specific work. Jurisdictional strikes were declared unfair labor practices in 1947 by the Taft-Hartley Act.

Just cause When an arbitrator rules that there is sufficient reason to support an employer's disciplinary action. In making the determination, an arbitrator looks at the collective bargaining agreement, the customs and standards of the workplace and the community, standards of justice and equity, and the facts of the particular case.

Labor force All persons age 16 and over who are either employed, temporarily idle, between jobs, or looking for work. The total labor force includes all military personnel.

Labor-Management Reporting and Disclosure Act *See* Landrum-Griffin Act.

Labor market An area or employee pool from which a firm solicits job applicants. *External labor markets* are labor sources outside the firm; they may be limited to a local area or they may be regional or national in scope. *Internal labor markets* are the firm's current employees who are considered for job openings within the firm.

Landrum-Griffin Act (Labor-Management Reporting and Disclosure Act) A federal statute, passed in 1959, designed to rid unions of corruption and to ensure internal union democracy.

Layoff Temporary and indefinite separation from work, due usually to slack season, shortage of materials, temporary decline in the market, or other factors over which the worker has no control. Layoffs are distinguished from a discharge or firing, whereby the worker is permanently separated from his or her job for such reasons as insubordination, absenteeism, or poor job performance.

Leave of absence An employee who is absent from work with prior approval by the employer. A leave of absence may be for military, jury duty, maternity, or other personal reasons. Leaves of absence may be paid or unpaid. Many employers allow employees to maintain their benefits and seniority status while on a leave of absence.

Local union The organization of members of an international union in a particular plant, region, or locality. Craft union locals, such as those of plumbers and carpenters, are usually organized by regions or localities, whereas industrial union locals are often organized on plant-wide basis. Often a local union is referred to as simply a "local."

Lockout A suspension of work initiated by the employer as the result of a labor dispute. A lockout is the employer's counterpart of a strike, which is initiated by the workers. Used primarily to avert a threatened strike.

Maintenance-of-membership clause A provision in a collective bargaining agreement stating that a worker does not have to join the union as a condition of employment, but all workers who voluntarily join must maintain their membership for the duration of the contract in order to keep their jobs. Most maintenance-of-membership provisions include an escape clause, setting aside an interval, usually ten days or two weeks, during which members may withdraw from the union without penalty. *See* Agency shop, Preferential hiring, and Union shop.

Maintenance-of-standards clause A contract provision that precludes an employer from changing any condition of employment, even though it might not be specifically mentioned in the collective bargaining agreement, unless changes are negotiated with the union.

Major medical insurance Medical insurance that covers large or catastrophic medical bills. Group major medical policies also have few exclusions (e.g., no coverage for mental illness or alcohol and drug addiction). Most major medical policies have deductible and co-insurance clauses that require the sharing of medical expenses by the employee.

Make whole Compensation to a wrongfully-discharged employee. Typically such compensation includes back pay less any amounts received or earned by the worker during the period of suspension.

Management prerogatives Rights that management believes are exclusively its own, and hence not subject to collective bargaining. These rights are often expressly reserved to management in the collective bargaining agreement and usually include the rights to determine the products to be made, to schedule production, to determine the process of manufacture, and to hire employees.

Mandatory subject of bargaining *See* Scope of bargaining.

Master agreement A collective bargaining agreement covering a number of companies and one or more unions or covering several plants of a single employer. The master agreement is often supplemented by local agreements covering conditions that vary among the individual plants or companies within the overall bargaining unit.

Med arb An impasse resolution procedure whereby parties in a dispute agree to have the mediator empowered to render a final and binding decision (if initial mediation efforts fail to secure an agreement). Short for "mediation arbitration."

Mediation An attempt by a third party, usually a government official, to bring together the parties to an industrial dispute. Mediators typically try to help negotiators regain their bargaining momentum so that they will reach an accord on their own. The mediator has no power to force a settlement.

Meet-and-confer negotiations Public-sector negotiations in which the ultimate decision as to the terms and conditions of employment for government employees is made by the public employer.

Merit system An employment scheme in which the selection of an employee for an entry-level position, promotion, and pay raise are based purely on the employee's capabilities and experience. This practice is common in civil service.

Minimum wage Lowest wage rate allowed by either federal or state law. The Fair Labor Standards Act (1938) was the first national minimum wage law. Many states have minimum wage laws covering industries not engaged in interstate commerce. The majority of these states have minimums below the federal level.

Multi-employer bargaining Collective bargaining involving more than one company in an industry and resulting in a master agreement. Multi-employer bargaining takes various forms: areawide bargaining, industrywide bargaining, and regional bargaining.

Multilateral bargaining A situation primarily in public-sector labor negotiations in which certain public-interest groups try to pressure or influence negotiators. An example of multilateral bargaining would be parents putting pressure on a school board to avoid a city-wide teachers' strike.

Narcotic effect When a public-sector bargaining law has an impasse procedure with arbitration, the parties may avoid serious negotiation and instead rely on the arbitrator to create part of the collective bargaining agreement. Thus the narcotic effect is a dependency by negotiators on interest arbitration.

National emergency strike A strike not specifically forbidden by the Taft-Hartley Act, but which may be enjoined for up to 80 days if, in the opinion of the president of the United States and the appropriate court of competent jurisdiction, it threatens the nation's health or safety.

National Labor Relations Act (Wagner Act) A federal law passed in 1935 that had the effect of generally stengthening the position of organized labor. It is enforced by the National Labor Relations Board. The Act guaranteed workers the right to organize and join unions, to bargain collectively, and to act in concert in pursuit of their objectives. It provided for secret-ballot certification elections and gave the union the right to be the exclusive bargaining agent for all workers in a bargaining unit. The law declared five employer unfair labor practices.

National Labor Relations Board A body created by the National Labor Relations Act of 1935. The board's primary duties are to hold elections to determine representation and to interpret and apply the law concerning unfair labor practices. The courts may review the board's decisions on unfair labor practices, but the board's decisions on representation elections are final.

National Mediation Board An agency created by the Railway Labor Act to mediate interest disputes and conduct certification elections among railway and airline employees.

National Railroad Adjustment Board An agency created by the Railway Labor Act to resolve rights disputes involving railway employees.

National union *See* International union.

Negotiation The process by which representatives of labor and management bargain to set terms over wages, hours, benefits, working conditions, and the procedures for handling grievances. The fruits of these negotiations are usually reduced to writing and comprise the collective bargaining agreement.

Nepotism Favoring friends or relatives in hiring, promotion, or other personnel matters. Some unions may engage in nepotism when admitting members into apprenticeship training programs.

NLRB *See* National Labor Relations Board

No-raiding agreement A compact among individual international unions in which they promise not to persuade workers to leave one union and join another when the first union has established a bargaining relationship. AFL-CIO-affiliated unions in good standing are signators to a general no-raiding pact. In addition, several unions have signed bilateral agreements covering the organization of unorganized workers.

No-solicitation rule A company rule prohibiting any type of solicitation on company property.

Norris-LaGuardia Act (Anti-Injunction Act) A federal law passed in 1932 that restricted the rights of federal courts to issue injunctions aimed at restraining the activities of labor unions. The Taft-Hartley Act of 1947 restored some injunctive power to the courts. The Norris-LaGuardia Act also declared yellow-dog contracts unenforceable.

Occupational Safety and Health Act (OSHA) of 1970 A statute that gives the federal government the authority to develop and enforce nationwide safety and health standards for employees of businesses in the private sector. Under this law, employers must comply with OSHA standards, submit to inspections, maintain records, and report accidents and illnesses. The act also established the Occupational Safety and Health Administration and time-and-a-half pay.

Occupational Safety and Health Administration (OSHA) An agency within the United States Department of Labor established by the Occupational Safety and Health Act of 1970 to adopt and enforce workplace safety and health standards.

Open shop A shop, factory, or business establishment in which there is no union. Also sometimes applied to places of work in which there is a union, but where union membership is not a condition of employment or of continuing employment.

Organizational picketing Picketing that attempts to persuade employees to join a union.

OSHA *See* Occupational Safety and Health Act of 1970 and Occupational Safety and Health Administration.

Overtime When an employee works more than the normally scheduled number of work hours (usually eight hours per day or 40 hours per week). Overtime work is often compensated at time and a half pay and, in some cases at double or even triple time. *See* Fair Labor Standards Act and Time-and-a-half pay.

Paper locals A local union without members. The paper local is based on a charter that is used for illegitimate purposes. Charters are sometimes secured from national unions, but more frequently paper locals are self-chartered. The holder of the charter enters into a sweetheart contract with an employer or uses the charter as a vehicle for extortion, threatening to organize the plant unless he or she receives a payoff from the employer. Paper locals are denounced by the AFL-CIO in its Code of Ethical Practices. *See* Sweetheart contract.

Parity Equivalence established between the wage schedules of certain categories of employees. Used commonly in the public sector to describe the ratio maintained between the salaries of police and fire fighters.

Parole evidence A precept governing the admission of evidence to an arbitration proceeding. If two parties have made a written contract and have both assented that the contract is the complete agreement between the parties, then evidence of previous understandings and negotiations will not be admitted for the purpose of varying or contradicting the written contract.

Part-time employee An employee who normally works on a regular basis, but does not work the standard 40-hour work week. For example, an employee who regularly works three hours every evening or one who works only on the weekends is regarded as a part-time employee. *Compare with* Casual employee; Dual-status employee.

Past practice Workplace practices that are consistent and mutually recognized by the union and employer over an extended period of time. Past practices are typically not written into the collective bargaining agreement. Nevertheless, past practices may be regarded by arbitrators and the courts as part of the contract under certain conditions.

Pattern bargaining Negotiations in which key contract terms reached in a settlement in one company are closely followed by other companies. For example, pattern bargaining has historically played a prominent role in auto industry negotiations.

Pension *See* Retirement plan

Permanent umpire An arbitrator who is selected by both union and management to serve for a specified period of time, most often for the duration of the contract. The contract outlines the duties of the arbitrator.

Picketing Publicizing the existence of a labor dispute by patrolling near the location where the dispute is taking place, usually with placards that announce the nature of the dispute and the parties to it. Also an attempt to persuade workers to join a work stoppage or to discourage customers from patronizing a business establishment or both.

Point Method A form of job evaluation that places a point value on a job. The point value is then used to determine a specific wage, salary, or pay range for the job.

Portable pension plan A pension plan that allows an employee to transfer pension credits accrued with one employer to another.

Portal-to-portal pay Originally, payment for time spent in travel from the entrance of a mine to the actual place of work, both at the start and completion of a day's work. Subsequently adapted to other industries where travel time is a factor.

Preferential hiring A form of union security in which the employer agrees that in hiring new workers preference will be given to union members.

Pregnancy Discrimination Act of 1978 An amendment to Title VII of the 1964 Civil Rights Act. The Pregnancy Discrimination Act requires that employers treat female employees who are pregnant in the same fashion as they treat employees with disabilities. Thus, if an employer provides medical insurance coverage or leaves of absence for disabled employees, then it must do so for pregnant employees. The Act also eliminates sex discrimination with regard to group health and disability income insurance programs.

Premature extension An agreement to extend the duration of an existing collective bargaining contract. Such an agreement is made before the existing contract expires.

Premium pay An amount greater than the regular rate of pay paid because of a job's inconvenience or unpleasantness. Employees often receive premium pay for working overtime in late shifts, on holidays, or in hazardous working conditions.

Prevailing wage The wage paid for a particular job in a specific locale.

Production worker A worker connected directly with manufacturing or operational processes in industry, as contrasted with a supervisory or clerical worker (e.g., an assembly line worker in the automobile industry).

Productivity A measurement of the efficiency of production; a ratio of output to input.

Productivity bargaining A collective bargaining arrangement that provides for wage increases based upon the increased productivity of the operation. In many instances, wage increases are the quid pro quo for the union's agreement to abandon certain work practices that have tended to restrict productivity.

Professional employee An employee whose work is predominantly intellectual, who has undergone advanced specialized training, and whose work requires the exercise of independent judgement.

Profit sharing A form of compensation to employees based upon the profits of the company and paid in addition to wages. Usually, profit-sharing plans take one of two forms: (1) a cash plan, giving employees a share of profits on a cash basis quarterly, semiannually, or annually; or (2) a deferred plan, in which a trust fund is established and payments are made to workers at the time of their retirement, death, or disability. *See* Gainsharing.

Progressive discipline *See* Corrective discipline.

Public employment relations board or commission (PERB or PERC) An administrative agency empowered to carry out the provisions of public-sector labor relations law. In most instances, PERBs or PERCs resolve representation disputes, adjudicate unfair labor practice charges, and provide assistance to the parties in the resolution of interest disputes.

"R" cases NLRB representation cases. "RC" designates a union-filed petition, "RM" designates an employer-filed petition, and "RD" designates a decertification election.

Racketeer Influenced and Corrupt Organizations Act (RICO) A federal law that, among other things, allows for treble damages against union officials who engage in racketeering activities to the detriment of union members.

Racketeering The use of extortion, bribes, and theft to achieve certain means. A small number of labor unions have been used to promote the interests of organized crime through the mismanagement of union funds, illegal cartels, the theft of warehoused merchandise, and the use of strike threats.

Raiding A union's attempt to enroll members of another union, thereby encroaching on the other union's jurisdiction. Two reasons for raiding are (1) a union's belief that another union has workers that rightfully belong in its jurisdiction and (2) a union's desire to increase its size to protect its bargaining position.

Railway Labor Act, as amended A federal law passed in 1926 establishing administrative agencies and procedures for the prompt and orderly settlement of labor disputes between interstate rail and air carriers and their employees. The act also guarantees collective bargaining rights and self-organization to railroad and airline employees.

Rank and file Union members who do not hold union office.

Real wages The actual purchasing power of wages, as compared to a fixed time in the past. Often computed by dividing money wages by the cost-of-living index. For example, if money wages increase from $4.00 to $5.00 an hour but the cost-of-living index also increases from 1.00 to 1.25, real wages have remained constant. Changes in real wages indicate changes in living standards.

Recognition A formal acknowledgment by an employer that the majority of his or her employees in a given bargaining unit want a specific union to represent them in collective bargaining.

Recognition picketing Picketing that attempts to persuade the employer to recognize a union as the exclusive bargaining representative for a group of its employees.

Red-circle rate A job that is *overpaid* relative to what the job evaluation dictates is an equitable rate. *See* Blue-circle rate.

Regional bargaining A type of multi-employer bargaining whereby bargaining occurs between a union and representatives of several employers in an industry in a given region (e.g., the southwestern part of the United States). Over-the-road trucking, lumber, and maritime industries are usually involved in regional bargaining.

Rehabilitation Act of 1973 Prohibits employment discrimination against otherwise qualified employees who have physical or mental handicaps or who have a record of such handicaps. The Act also protects employees who are regarded as being handicapped even when such a handicap does not exist. *Also see* Americans with Disabilities Act of 1990.

Reinstatement Allowing a worker to return to work after he or she was discharged unlawfully or in violation of the collective bargaining agreement.

Remedial order An order by an administrative agency (e.g., the NLRB) that orders an employer, union, or individual to take remedial or corrective action for engaging in illegal conduct.

Reopening clause A provision in a collective bargaining agreement stating circumstances under which wages and other issues can be reconsidered while other terms of the agreement remain in force. Often called a "reopener."

Reporting pay Pay that an employee receives for reporting to work when it is subsequently discovered that no work is available. *See* Call-in pay.

Representation election A referendum held among employees in a bargaining unit to determine what bargaining agent, if any, will represent them for collective bargaining purposes.

Reserve gate A gate that is designed to separate striking from nonstriking employees at a work site in which several employers and unions are active. Reserve gates are commonly found at large construction sites when, for example, the carpenters are striking but members of other construction trades continue to work. *See* Common-situs picketing.

Residual rights The school of thought stipulating that management retains all rights not explicitly relinquished to the union in the collective bargaining agreement. *See* Management prerogatives.

Retirement plan A plan that allows for the accumulation of funds during an employee's working years and a systematic liquidation (payment) of funds to the employee after he or she retires. Also called a pension.

Retroactive pay 1. A delayed wage payment for work done previously at a lower rate. 2. Income due to workers when a new contract provides for a wage increase for work completed prior to the time the contract goes into effect, often dating back to the expiration of the previous contract.

Rights arbitration *See* Grievance arbitration.

Rights dispute A controversy over the interpretation or application of the terms of a collective bargaining agreement. Such a dispute is usually dealt with through the grievance procedure, sometimes ending up in grievance arbitration.

Right-to-work laws State laws prohibiting union shop, maintenance-of-membership clauses, preferential hiring, or any other contract provisions calling for compulsory union membership. State legislatures were authorized to pass such laws by the Taft-Hartley Act of

1947. Since that time, 20 states, mostly in the South and Midwest, have passed right-to-work laws.

Roll-up costs The increased cost of employee benefits that result from increases in a wage or salary rate. For example, if all employees receive a five percent pay increase, the cost of paid vacations, sick leave, overtime, and other employee benefits will also increase.

Roving pickets Pickets that follow a struck employer's trucks. When the truck stops (e.g., to make a delivery), the pickets display signs that the union is striking the employer.

Runaway shop A unionized business concern that moves to another state or area to escape the union.

Runoff election A second election directed by the NLRB to determine the union (if any) that has the majority support of the employees. Runoff elections occur when two or more unions are vying to represent a group of employees and the initial election does not result in a majority choice.

Saving clause A contract provision stating that if any part of the contract in held to be illegal, the rest of the contract will remain binding on the parties.

Scab A worker who refuses to go out on strike with his co-workers. Also a worker who is hired to replace a striking worker. Sometimes called *rats*.

Scope of bargaining The range of issues negotiated for a collective bargaining agreement. Most statutes require the parties to negotiate over subjects directly affecting wages, hours, and working conditions (*mandatory* subjects of bargaining). If an impasse is reached over a mandatory subject, a lawful economic strike may ensue. Failure to bargain over a mandatory subject of bargaining is an unfair labor practice under the National Labor Relations Act. *Permissive* subjects of bargaining (e.g., pension improvements for retirees) may be negotiated only if both sides agree to bargain over them. A strike over a permissive subject is not protected by the National Labor Relations Act.

Secondary boycott *See* Boycott.

Seniority An employee's standing as determined by length of continuous employment. There are two kinds of seniority: *competitive seniority*, which is used to determine which employees should secure advantages at the workplace (such as promotion, shift assignment, or layoff survival), and *benefit seniority*, which is used to measure employee entitlement to benefits.

Service worker A worker whose job is to provide personal assistance, protective service, or current maintenance for buildings and residences. Some examples of service workers are parking lot attendants, hospital orderlies, bartenders, and custodians.

Severance pay Compensation to a worker permanently separated from a company due to a permanent reduction of the work force, introduction of labor-saving machinery, plant shutdown, or any other cause for which the worker is not responsible.

Shadowing Keeping a person under surveillance, usually done to observe union organizing or strike-breaking activities.

Sherman Antitrust Act A federal law passed in 1890 that prohibits trusts and conspiracies that restrain interstate commerce and forbids parties to monopolize trade or commerce among the states. Many courts interpreted this law as forbidding unionization. The Clayton Act of 1914 later exempted labor organizations from the jurisdiction of the Sherman Antitrust Act.

Shift differential An hourly premium paid to employees who must work at inconvenient hours (usually during the evening or early morning hours).

Shop committee A body of employees elected by fellow workers or appointed by union officials to represent the bargaining unit in considering grievances and related matters.

Shop steward The local union representative who carries out union duties in the plant or shop. Stewards handle grievances, collect dues, and recruit new members. Elected by union members in the plant or appointed by higher union officials, the shop steward usually continues to work at his or her regular job and handles union duties only on a part-time basis. Often used interchangeably with "union steward." To be distinguished from a business agent.

Slowdown A deliberate reduction of output by workers in an attempt to win concessions from an employer. Not a work stoppage or strike. *See* Work-to-rule. Also known as *soldiering.*

Social Security Act of 1935, as amended The Act originally provided for old age (retirement) benefits and unemployment insurance. Today, old age, survivorship, disability, and Medicare benefits are provided. Benefits are financed through payroll taxes on employers and employees.

Speedup An increase in production by the employer without a compensating increase in wages to workers (e.g., an assembly line is speeded up, thus increasing production, but there is no increase in wages).

Steelworkers Trilogy A trio of 1960 Supreme Court decisions involving the United Steelworkers of America. The Supreme Court held that the arbitration of grievances is the quid pro quo for a no-strike agreement and is the preferred means of handling industrial disputes. The Court directed that a lower court should set aside an arbitration award only if the arbitrator exceeds his or her jurisdiction. The courts are not permitted to vacate an arbitrator's award solely on the merits of the decision.

Steward *See* Shop steward.

Stranger picketing Picketing by persons who are not employed by the firm to which the picketing is directed.

Stretch-out A situation in which workers are required to assume additional work duties, such as tending more machines, without additional compensation.

Strike *See* Economic strike, General strike, Sympathy strike, and Wildcat strike.

Strike benefits Union payments, usually a small proportion of regular income, to workers during a strike. Many unions do not supply monetary aid, but distribute groceries and other types of aid to needy striking families.

Strikebreaker An outsider brought in by an employer to fill a job temporarily vacated by a striker. Often an employer attempts to break a strike by hiring outsiders so as to lower the strikers' morale and to maintain production. Also known as a strike replacement. *See* Scab.

Strike fund Money held by an international union or local union for allocation during a strike to cover costs of strike benefits, legal fees, publicity, and the like. Some international unions assess each member a small amount each month to build the fund. Other unions use the international's general fund. The amount of the fund often determines the staying power of the workers and, consequently, the success or failure of the strike. Strike funds are often designated in union financial statements as "emergency," "reserve," or "special" funds.

Strike insurance Insurance used to offset the extraordinary expenses and loss of business that an employer experiences during a work stoppage.

Strike notice A notice filed with the Federal Mediation and Conciliation Service or appropriate state agency that the union has rejected the company's latest offer and a strike is impending. The National Labor Relations Act requires that, if a collective bargaining agreement exists between the union and the employer, the union may not call a strike until 60 days after it has notified the employer of its desire to modify or terminate the existing agreement. The union must also notify the Federal Mediation and Conciliation Service within 30 days of notifying the employer. If the union strikes without observing these rules, the strikers lose the rights granted to them by the act.

Struck work Work performed by a nonstriking company for a company whose employees are on strike.

Subcontracting An arrangement by a company to have its production, maintenance, or service work performed by another firm. When work is subcontracted out, the job security of a firm's workers may be threatened. Subcontracting may create union-management conflicts.

Submission agreement An agreement to submit a dispute to an arbitrator and a definition of the issue to be resolved by the arbitrator.

Successor employer A firm that purchases and assumes managerial control of another firm. Under certain conditions, successor employers may be obligated to bargain with a union that was certified by employees who worked for the previous employer. Successor employers may also be required to abide by the terms and conditions of a collective bargaining agreement negotiated by the previous owner. *Compare with* Alter-ego employer.

Sunshine bargaining Collective bargaining in which the public-at-large is permitted to attend the bargaining sessions. Sunshine bargaining is permitted in several states for public-sector negotiations. However, private-sector collective bargaining sessions are almost always closed to the public.

Superannuation When an employee outlives his or her economic usefulness. Thus retirees may be regarded as superannuated because they are still living, yet they generate no income from employment. Retirement programs are designed to deal with superannuation.

Superseniority The placement of an employee at the top of a seniority list. Shop stewards typically are granted superseniority for layoff purposes only.

Supplemental unemployment benefit (SUB) plans Private plans providing compensation for wage loss to laid-off workers, usually in addition to public unemployment insurance payments. The automobile, glass, and steel industries have the highest percentage of these plans. SUB plans are financed by employers.

Surgical insurance Health insurance that pays the cost of physicians' fees for office visits, treatments, and surgical procedures.

Suspension A disciplinary penalty in which an employee is not allowed to work and is not paid during his or her period of suspension. Suspension allows the employee to contemplate the gravity of his or her offense and is usually the second most severe disciplinary penalty imposed by an organization (discharge being the most severe).

Sweatshop A workplace where working conditions are substantially below accepted standards. Sweatshops are usually characterized by low wages, long hours, and an unsanitary work environment. Historically, sweatshops were often found in the garment industry.

Sweetheart contract A collective bargaining agreement, usually between a racketeer head of a paper local (but sometimes a legitimate union) and a corrupt employer. The employer's advantages in such an arrangement are that legitimate unions then have difficulty in organizing the shop, the employer pays less in wages and in other benefits, and he or she has to contend with few restrictions. The union racketeer benefits from the payoff received from the grateful employer or the dues collected from employees or both. Sweetheart contracts were denounced by the AFL-CIO in its Code of Ethical Practices.

Sympathy strike A strike by workers not directly involved in a labor dispute; an attempt to demonstrate labor solidarity and bring pressure on an employer in a labor dispute.

Taft-Hartley Act (Labor-Management Relations Act) A federal statute passed in 1947 amending the National Labor Relations Act of 1935. Among the important provisions of the law are (1) the proscription of the closed shop; (2) government authorization to seek an injunction preventing any work stoppage for 80 days in a strike that imperils the nation's health and welfare; (3) the authorization of the states to pass right-to-work laws; and (4) the establishment of union unfair labor practices.

Take-home pay The amount of pay the worker actually receives directly in his or her check: gross earnings minus federal and state income taxes, social security taxes, health insurance premiums, and other deductions.

Tax-sheltered annuity A plan whereby an employee (either individually or in conjunction with his or her employer) sets aside funds for retirement. Contributions to tax-sheltered annuities are made with income that is not subject to taxation. The proceeds from tax-sheltered annuities may be drawn without penalty (but subject to ordinary income taxation) at retirement or at an earlier age stipulated by tax laws.

Temporary restraining order *See* Injunction.

Tenure A form of job security, customarily confined to educational employees, although civil service employees also have a form of tenure protection. Tenure is achieved after a specified probationary period has been served (in academic institutions usually from three to six years). An individual with tenure has assurance of continuous employment and can be terminated only because he or she has reached the mandatory retirement age, because of unusual financial exigencies, or for just cause. In the latter instance a terminated employee often has the protection of a due process procedure.

Termination *See* Discharge.

Time-and-a-half pay Pay rate consisting of one and one-half times the employee's regular pay. The Fair Labor Standards Act of 1938 made time-and-a-half pay mandatory for all work performed beyond 40 hours a week by many workers engaged in interstate commerce. Enacted during the Depression, the law envisaged that the extra pay would serve as a penalty to employers and would force them to spread the work, thereby providing more jobs.

Title VII, Civil Rights Act of 1964 (as amended in 1972 and 1978) A federal law prohibiting employers, unions, employment agencies, and joint labor-management committees controlling apprenticeship training or other training programs from discriminating against any employee or applicant for employment on the basis of race, color, sex, religion, or national origin. Discrimination is illegal with regard to any employment practice, including compensation, hiring, firing, promotion, and admission to training programs.

Trial examiner *See* Administrative law judge.

Trilogy *See* Steelworkers Trilogy.

Trusteeship Assumption of control over a local union by an international union, which suspends the normal governmental process of a local union and takes over management of the local's assets and the administration of its internal affairs. The constitutions of many international unions authorize international officers to establish trusteeships over local unions in order to prevent corruption, mismanagement, and other abuses. The Landrum-Griffin Act of 1959 established controls over the establishment and administration of trusteeships.

Turnover The rate at which workers move into and out of employment, usually expressed as the number of accessions and separations per 100 employees during a given period. Monthly turnover rates, by industry and selected states and regions, are computed by the Bureau of Labor Statistics.

Two-tier wages An arrangement in which compensation for new hires is substantially below that of current employees doing the same work. Two-tier wage structures became widespread in the airline industry during the late 1970s and early 1980s in part because of the intense competition that resulted from the deregulation of that industry. Unions have objected strongly to this practice.

Unemployment insurance A joint federal-state program created by the Social Security Act of 1935 that provides benefit payments to persons experiencing involuntary unemployment. These benefits are paid out of funds derived from an employer-financed payroll tax that is mandated by the Federal Unemployment Tax Act (FUTA). Eligibility and the amount and duration of benefits vary from state to state.

Unfair labor practice Conduct on the part of either union or management that violates provisions of national or state labor relations acts. Failing to bargain in good faith and interference with the administration of a labor organization are examples of unfair labor practices on the part of management. Failing to bargain in good faith and engaging in a secondary boycott are examples of unfair labor practices on the part of unions. *See* National Labor Relations Act and Taft-Hartley Act.

Uniformed services Public employees, usually municipal employees, such as police, fire fighters, and sanitation workers.

Union hiring hall A form of employment agency run by a labor union. Job openings in a local labor market are posted in the hiring hall. Under federal law, both union members and nonmembers must be allowed access to the hiring hall.

Union label An imprint attached to a product (e.g., clothing or printed materials) indicating that work on the article was done by union workers. Unions often encourage their members and the public-at-large to buy only those products bearing this label so as to enhance the economic position of organized labor.

Union organizer Member of a staff of a local union or international union whose main function is to recruit new members.

Union security clause A provision in a collective bargaining agreement designed to protect the institutional life of the union. *See* Agency shop, Closed shop, Maintenance-of-membership clause, Preferential hiring, and Union shop.

Union shop A bargaining unit covered by a union security clause stipulating that the employer may hire anyone he or she wants, but all workers must join the union within a specified period of time (by law, not less than 30 days) after being hired and retain membership as a condition of continuing employment. To be distinguished from closed shop.

Union steward *See* shop steward.

Unit determination The process of establishing a unit of appropriate job titles for the purpose of collective bargaining. The National Labor Relations Board and state labor relations agencies frequently use the following criteria when determining a bargaining unit: the desire of the employees, similarity of skills or occupations, collective bargaining history, and the organizational structure of the employer organization. Membership in a bargaining unit determines whether an employee may vote in a representation election; members of a bargaining unit are covered by the terms of subsequently negotiated collective bargaining agreement. *See* Certification.

United States Department of Labor (U.S. DOL) A unit of the executive branch of the federal government that administers some of the federal laws and regulations affecting labor relations. The U.S. DOL enforces ERISA, OSHA, and various employment standards. The department also oversees government training programs and gathers and publishes information dealing with labor issues. It was organized as a separate department in 1913. Before that time it was a division within the Department of Commerce and Labor.

Variable rate ranges A pay range for a particular classification or grade of jobs. Variable rate ranges have a minimum and maximum amount of pay for each range or pay grade. The exact amount of pay received by an employee whose job is classified in a particular range depends on the employee's experience, seniority, and quality of his or her job performance (merit).

Vesting The acquisition of pension rights that permit employees to terminate employment before attaining retirement age without forfeiting accrued pension benefits financed through employer contributions.

Vocational education A program of courses and training to provide skills and knowledge required for employment in a particular occupation, such as cosmetology and auto repair.

Vocational rehabilitation The process of returning individuals who are physically, mentally, or socially disabled to the mainstream of economic and social life. Often a vocational rehabilitation program retrains persons who are disabled and prepares them for new jobs.

Wagner Act National Labor Relations Act.

Walkout A strike, quickie strike, or wildcat strike.

Welfare fund A fund created through collective bargaining to provide welfare benefits for the employees of a number of employers. Under the terms of the Taft-Hartley Act, such funds are administered by trustees representing both employers and unions. Local building trades unions and the International Ladies' Garment Workers' Union are examples of unions with substantial welfare funds. Typically, welfare funds provide health and death benefits similar to those provided by welfare plans. A growing number also provide pension benefits.

Welfare plans Benefits plans for the employees of a single employer, providing for disability insurance, hospital, medical, and surgical protection, and life insurance. Welfare plans originally were financed almost entirely by joint employer-employee contributions. In recent years, the trend has been toward employer-financed plans. *See* Welfare fund.

Whipsaw strike A strike against only one employer of a group, typically the weakest, when the union could have struck them all. The union's purpose is to put great pressure on the struck employer, whose competitors remain open for business, in the hope that that employer will sign a contract favorable to the union and set a pattern for other employers, who would then be vulnerable to similar tactics unless they agreed to the same terms.

White-collar worker A nonmanual worker; for instance, a sales, supervisory, professional, or technical worker.

Wildcat strike A work stoppage violating the contract and not authorized by the union. Sometimes used interchangeably with quickie strike.

Worker Adjustment and Retraining Notification Act of 1988 (WARN) Requires that companies with more than 100 full-time employees give a 60-day notice of plant closings and mass layoffs.

Workers' compensation programs State-mandated insurance programs requiring the payment of benefits to workers suffering from occupational diseases or injuries sustained on the job. All 50 states have some type of employer-financed workers' compensation law. Federal government programs provide similar protection for federal employees, harbor workers, longshoremen, and employees of private concerns in the District of Columbia. There is considerable variation among the states in the amount of compensation and the duration of payments.

Work rules Regulations stipulating on-the-job conditions of work, usually incorporated in the collective bargaining agreement. Examples include: (1) limiting production work of supervisory personnel; (2) limiting the assignment of work outside an employee's classification; (3) requiring a minimum number of workers on a job; (4) limiting the use of labor-saving methods and equipment.

Work-to-rule A type of job action whereby employees perform only the minimum tasks required of them by official rules or regulations. Employees sometimes use the work-to-rule technique in an attempt to win concessions in those circumstances where a strike is illegal. Air traffic controllers, for example, have used this strategy successfully.

Yellow-dog contract An agreement, sometimes used in the past by employers to combat unions, in which a worker stated he or she was not then a member of a union and promised not to join a union so long as he or she worked for the particular company. The Norris-LaGuardia Act of 1932 nullified the yellow-dog contract by declaring it to be unenforceable in the courts.

Zipper clause A standard provision in a negotiated contract that attempts to preclude any negotiations of employment conditions during the life of the contract. The clause asserts that the agreement is the sole and complete instrument between the parties.

Adapted in part from Robert E. Doherty, *Industrial and Labor Relations Terms: A Glossary*, 5th ed. (Ithaca, New York: ILR Press, Cornell University, 1989). Reprinted with permission.

SUBJECT INDEX

A Behavioral Theory of Negotiations, 261
Acquired immune deficiency syndrome (AIDS), 571, 580–581, 586, 588–589
Affirmative action, 89, 227
Age Discrimination in Employment Act of 1967, 89, 92, 430, 458, 683
Agricultural workers, 67–68, 111
   state statutes, 111
   value-added criterion, 111
Airline Pilot, 191
Alcohol abuse, 600–602
Alter ego employer, 123
American Liberty League
   National Lawyer's Committee, 72
Americans with Disabilities Act of 1990, 576, 577
Anticipated animal exuberance, 345
Antiunion tactics, 64
Apprenticeship training, 208, 229
Arbitrability, 404, 409, 410–411
Arbitration, 397–443
   ad hoc, 401
   advisory, 668
   application of state and federal laws to, 409
   awards, 421–422
      and external law, 429
      factors affecting, 422–432
      reversal of, 404–405
      splitting of, 399
   binding, 10, 376
   briefs and transcripts, 421–422
   cancellation fees, 401
   case presentation, 414–415
      examination and cross examination, 416–418
      witnesses, role of, 416, 425–426
   civil rights cases, 408–409
   Code of Professional Responsibility for Arbitrators of Labor-Management Disputes, 434–443
   duty of fair representation, 408
   enforceability of, 403–404, 409
   errors in, 422
   evidence and exhibits, 418–421, 424–425
      admissability of, 418
      best, 420
      circumstantial, 419
      confessions, 419
      de minimus, 420
      direct, 419
      hearsay, 419
      new, 419
      parole, 420
   expedited, 391
   hearing, 412–422
   interest disputes, 398, 667–671
      conventional arbitration, 668
      final offer arbitration, 668–671
   legal status of, 402–410
   National Labor Relations Board, 408
   permanent, 401–402
   preparing a case for, 383–384, 411–412
   previous awards, impact of, 412, 431–432
   professional and ethical standards, 432, 434–443
   procedural issues in, 409
   quid pro quo, and, 403
   rights disputes, 398
   submission agreement, 413
   tribunals, 400–402
   tripartite, 402
Arbitrators
   ethical and professional standards, 398, 434–443
   selection of, 400–402
   qualifications of, 398–400
Attitudinal structuring, 263
Authorization cards, 147, 190
   showing of interest by employees, 158

Back pay, 72, 421, 487, 623
Bargaining order, 72
Bargaining power (*see* Collective bargaining, power)
Bargaining theory
   bargaining range theory, 258–260
   behavioral, 257, 261–262
   descriptive, 257–258
   Hick's bargaining model, 263–264
   key elements, 255
   mathematical/economic, 256–257
   role of, 255
   similarities among, 264–268
      communications issues, 267–268
      costs of agreeing and disagreeing, 265–266
      rationality assumption, 266
      settlement points and ranges, 264–265
      tactics and concessions, 268
      timing, 267
Bargaining unit, 6, 95–132
   accretions to, 121–122
   centralized, 114
   clarification petition, 121
   community of interest, 101, 102, 117, 121, 125
   composition of, 99
   confidential empoyees, 107
   craft, 96, 103–104, 114
   decentralized, 114
   dual-status employees, 112
   employee eligibility to vote in certification elections, 83
   employees entitled to separate units, 103–107
   excluded employees, 107–114
   health care institutions, 116, 124
   industrial, 114
   in expanding organizations, 121–124
   NLRB criteria, 57, 100–102
   part-time employees, 112
   plant guards and security personnel, 106–107

725

726 ▲ SUBJECT INDEX

Bargaining unit (*Continued*)
  presumptively appropriate units, 124–125
  professional employees, 104–106
    definition of, 105
  residual, 102
  seasonal employees, 112
  source of conflict, 323
  structures
    common forms, 114–121
    importance of, 98–100
    multi-employer, 101, 245, 323
    single employer, multi-location, 116–118
    single employer, single location, 115–116
  supervisors and managers, 107–110
    definition of, 108
  technical employees, 105
Blacklists, 43
Black Thursday, 44
Boston Herald, 642
Bumping, 568
Business agent (*see* Unions, local)
Business unionism, 25
Business Week, 681

Cash bonus plans, 232
Casual employees, 107
Certification election, 7, 57, 96, 158–164
  bargaining orders, 163–164
  captive-audience speeches before, 157–158
    24-hour rule, 157–158
  contract bar, 159, 165
  delays in certification, 159
  laboratory conditions, 166
  NLRB certification, 97
  post-election matters, 161–164
    challenged election ballots, 161–162
    resolving unfair labor practices, 162–164
  representation petition, 159
  runoff elections, 159, 161
  second-chance elections, 162
  12-month rule, 159, 161
  voter eligibility, 160
    economic strikers, 160
  voting area, 168
Checkoff provision, 69, 199, 583–584
Cherry picking, 144
Childcare programs, 525, 526
Child labor laws, 30, 37
Civil Service Reform Act of 1978, 91, 651, 652, 653
Civil rights
  equal employment opportunity, 89, 592, 593
  federal executive orders, 89
  movement, 637
  state laws, 89
Civil Rights Act of 1964
  Title VII, 89, 92, 362, 408, 430, 458, 485, 488, 489, 561, 683
Civil War, 35
Clayton Act, 44, 64
  labor-management cooperative programs, 693
Closed shop (*see* Union security)
Cold War, 216
Collective bargaining
  and the U.S. labor force, 12–13
  bargaining team members, 283–287
  caucuses, 308
  centralization of, 196
  concession bargaining, 215
  conduct during, 304–305
  cost-benefit approach, 263–264
  crisis (eleventh-hour), 312–316
  goals and priorities, 292–295
  good faith, 71, 75, 275, 298–303, 646
    employer's duty to furnish information, 299, 378
    mandatory bargaining subjects, 71, 216, 301–302
    illegal bargaining subjects, 301–302
    permissive (voluntary) subjects, 71, 216, 301–302
    "relevant and necessary" information, 71
    surface bargaining and dilatory tactics, 300
    "take-it-or-leave-it" posture, 71
    totality of conduct, 298–299
  impact on employees,17–18
  impact on employers, 18
  impact on society, 18–19
  impact on organizations and society, 15–19
  impasse, 302–303
  innovations in, 695–697
  laws governing institutional coverage, 59–60
  legal requirements, 297–303, 330
  management goals, 235–242
    compensation, 236–238
    employee benefits, 238–239
    factors affecting, 236–238
    nonwages issues, 239–241
    recent trends in, 241–242
  pattern, 99
  power, 57, 97, 242–244, 268–273, 275
    factors that dilute, 271–272
    sources of, 269–271
    types of, 272
  preparations, 280–296
  settlements, 273–274
  stages of, 280–281
  sticking points, 259–260, 292–295
  tactics and outcomes, 273–276, 285–286, 303–316, 324
  threats, use of, 268, 304–305
  types of, 217–218
  union goals in, 214–218
    determinants of, 215–217
  wages, 197
Collective bargaining agreement, 7
  accretion clause, 122
  ambiguous language, 367, 423–424
  compensation provisions, 450
  costing of provisions (*see* Labor costs)
  drafting provisions of, 284–285
  duration of, 239–240
  employee benefit provisions, 497–498
  group health insurance provisions, 508
  group life insurance provisions, 506
  health and safety, 571–572
  language of, 310–312
  local, 117
  management rights, 552–553
  master, 117, 118
  nonsuability clause, 350
  no-strike clause, 350, 410
  provisions of, 217–218
  ratification of, 217, 315–316
  zipper clauses, 553–554
Communists, 216
Company unions, 25, 43
Compensation, 447–495
  blue-circle rate, 467
  call-back pay, 367, 449, 450, 477
  cash bonuses, 476
  comparable worth, 485, 487–490
  contingent, 448
  cost-of-living adjustments, 241, 450, 454, 459, 479
  deferred, 448, 450, 478
  employee stock ownership plans, 483
  equal pay for equal work, 485, 486–487
  equity in, 455–456, 490
    external, 231, 455, 461, 469
    internal, 231, 455, 465–466, 469
    procedural, 456
  factors affecting, 450–460
  gold-circle rates, 476
  grievances over, 364
  hazardous work premiums, 449, 450

immediate, 448
impact of unions on, 458–460
Improshare, 485
incentive pay, 231, 449, 480–485, 491
  group, 449, 483–485
  individual, 449, 481–483
  piecework plan, 483
  restrictions on, 482–483
  standard hour plan, 483
  standards, 481–482
individual pay, 469
  merit and, 474, 475–476, 490
  seniority, and, 473–476, 490
job evaluation, 231, 456, 487, 491
  classification method, 494–495
  factor comparison method, 495
  major steps, 466–468
  point method, 471, 495
  ranking method, 494
laws affecting, 90–91, 456–458, 490
Lincoln Electric plan, 483, 485
lump-sum bonuses, 241
merit pay, 232
overtime pay, 450, 477
pay grades
  number of, 470–471
  overlap between, 472
  range of, 472
  rate ranges, 450
pay level, 455, 469
pay policy line, 468–470
pay structure, 455, 456, 465–468, 469
perquisites, 449
profit sharing plan, 483
red-circle rate, 467
re-openers, 450, 479
reporting pay, 449, 450, 477
Rucker plan, 485
salaries, 449
Scanlon plan, 483, 484–485
sex discrimination in, 485–490, 491
shift differentials, 449
silver-circle rates, 476
skill-based pay, 468
supplementary pay, 449, 450, 476–478
  "pyramiding" of, 478
surveys, wage and salary, 455, 461–465, 491
"taking wages out of competition," 459
travel expenses, 450
two-tier wages, 327, 450, 479–480
union-nonunion differentials, 232–233
wages, 449
Company unions, 69

Compulsory arbitration, 48
Confidential employees, 110–111
Conflict (*see* Labor-management conflict)
Consolidated Omnibus Budget Reconciliation Act of 1985 (COBRA), 430, 456
Conspiracy
  criminal, 29, 61
Consumer cooperatives, 37
Consumer Credit Protection Act, 430, 456
Consumer price index, 291, 458
Coordinated bargaining, 120–121
Construction industry, New York City, 212
Contract administration, 7, 9–11, 199, 360–396
  grievance procedures, 234, 361
  management responsibility for, 235
  public sector, 671
  role of, 361–362
Contract negotiations, 7–9
Convict labor, 30
Cooperative programs, labor and management (*see* Unions)
Corporate campaigns, 215–216
Cost-of-living adjustments (*see* Compensation)
Craft union (*see* Unions)

Davis-Bacon Act, 90, 45
Decertification
  campaigns, 99
  elections, 164–165
Democrats, 30, 183
Dependent unionism, 25
Depression Era, 44–45
Deregulation
  effect on unions, 681–683
Discipline and discharge of employees, 591–624
  arbitral criteria, 620–622
  arbitral remedies, 622–623
  burden of proof, 614
  causes of employee discipline problems, 597–598
  contractual employees
    explicit, 592
    implied, 596
  corrective disciplinary procedures, 617–620
    penalty structure, 619–620, 621
    seriousness of offenses, 617–618
  discharge, guidelines for, 616–617
  due process in, 614–615, 621
  equal protection, 615
  in contract administration, 363–364
  just cause, 9, 615
  malice and bad faith, 595

management's right to discharge, 592–597
  at-will employees, 593–596
  tenured employees, 593
  unionized employees, 596–597
mitigating (extenuating) circumstances, 621
public interest, contrary to, 594–595
reasonable rules and standards, 614
types of employee discipline problems, 598–614
  absenteeism and tardiness, 598–599
  carelessness and negligence, 613–614
  dishonesty, 603–606
  drug and alcohol abuse, 600–603
  horseplay, 613–614
  incompetency, 613–614
  insubordination and abusive behavior, 610–611
  off-duty misconduct, 606–610
  rule violations, 599–600
  USX-United Steelworkers procedure, 628–629
Distributive bargaining, 261
Drug abuse, 578, 602–603
Drug Free Workplace Act of 1988, 579
Drug testing, 578–580
Due process, 85
  procedural, 85

Eastern Europe, 51
EC'92, 689–690
Eight-hour day, 3
Eldercare programs, 525–526
Employee assistance programs, 526–527, 603
Employee associations, 636–637, 638
Employee benefits, 233, 496–548
  accidental death and dismemberment insurance, 497, 507
  childcare benefits, 525, 526
  eldercare benefits, 525–526
  government's role in, 500–504
  group health insurance
    Blue Cross/Blue Shield plans, 507
    cost containment measures, 242, 246, 496, 513–516
    deductible provisions, 509
    disability income insurance, 497, 511–513
    exclusions, 509
    major medical insurance, 508–509

Employee benefits (*Continued*)
  medical expense insurance, 507–510
  surgical insurance, 508
  group life insurance, 236, 497
  noncontributory plan, 506
  holidays, 524, 525
  hospital indemnity plans, 507
  income maintenance benefits, 522–523
  laws affecting 90–91
  paid holidays and vacations, 449
  prepaid legal plans, 528
  retirement programs, 449, 517–522
    concept of, 517–518
    contributory and noncontributory plans, 519
    defined contribution and defined benefit plans, 519
    eligibility standards, 519
    fiduciaries, 518, 521
    funding of, 520
    guaranteed benefit option, 518
    integrated plans, 521
    joint and survivor annuity, 518
    multi-employer plans, 521
    qualified and nonqualified plans, 521
    vesting provisions, 520
  role of, 498–499
  severance pay, 523
  sick leave, 525
  supplemental employment benefits, 522
  tuition-aid plans, 528
  unemployment compensation, 501–502
  vacations, 523, 523–524
  workers' compensation, 500–501
Employee involvement programs, 551
Employee ownership, 691–692
Employee Retirement Income Security Act of 1974, 90, 430, 456, 518–519, 683
Employee stock ownership plans (ESOPs), 232, 693
Employer associations (*see* Bargaining unit, structures)
Employment at will, 93, 234, 592, 59–596, 683
Equal Pay Act of 1963, 90, 430, 456, 485, 486, 487
Equity theory, 455
Erdman Act, 64
Exchange value, 451
Exclusive representation, doctrine of, 57, 96–98
Executive orders, federal
  Executive Order 10988 (1962), 637

Executive Order 11491 (1970), 651
Executive Order 11838 (1975), 651
equal employment opportunity, 89
Extortion, 211

Fair Labor Standards Act, 90, 430, 456, 477
  exempt and nonexempt employees, 477
  minimum wage, 179
Fair representation, union's duty of, 385–389, 392, 408
Federal Child Support Enforcement Program, 430, 456
Federal Employment Tax Act, 501
Federalists, 30
Flexible work schedules, 586
Food Stamp Act, 338
Free riders, 585, 638
Futility doctrine, 155

Gainsharing, 690, 694
General Schedule (GS) pay classifications, 494
Good-faith bargaining (*see* Collective bargaining, good-faith)
Government employees
  collective bargaining rights (*see* Public-sector collective bargaining)
Great Britain, 51
Greenbackism, 35
Grievance
  definition of, 370–371, 380–381
    closed definition, 371
    open definition, 371
  due process, 385
  evaluative criteria, 382–383
    allegations, 382
    assumptions, 382
    facts, 382
    opinions, 382
    quantum of proof, 383
    weighting, 383
  filing form, 379–380
  mediation of, 390–391
  merits of, 378, 384, 387–388
  moving party, 372, 381
  parties to, 369–370
  procedure, 9, 234, 289, 385
    abuse of, 384–385
    Boeing-IAM grievance procedure, 392–396
    criteria for evaluating, 389–391
    hearing, 381
    parties involved, 373–375, 414
    stages of, 377–384
    structure of, 370
    time limits, 373

representatives, union and management, 413
resolution of, 375–377, 383
  company-default provision, 372
  employee consent, 375
  theory of a case, 378, 384
Group health insurance, 507–517
Group life insurance, 505–506
Guaranteed annual income programs, 238
Guards and security personnel, 96

Harvard University, 642
Hatch Act, 635
Hawthorne studies, 20
Haymarket Square Riot, 32, 37
Health Maintenance Act, 430, 456, 511
Health Maintenance Organizations, 510–511
Health and safety, 571–582
  emerging issues, 578–582
  grievances over, 574–578
    employee physical or mental conditions, 576–577
    refusing to perform unsafe work, 574–576
    violation of plant safety rules, 577–578
Hobbs Act, 214
Holidays, paid, 524–525

Incentive pay (*see* Compensation)
Informal joint consultation, 7, 10–11
Immigrants, 28
Immigration Reform and Control Act, 430
Impasse, 8, 302–303, 329, 667–671
Incentive pay systems, 232–233
  group incentives, 232
  individual incentives, 232
Income
  monetary, 454
  real, 454
Independent contractors, 107, 113
Indentured servants, 28
Individual rights, 93
Industrial spies, 43
Industrial union (*see* Unions)
Instrumentality-expectancy theory, 455
Injunctions, 44
  equity court, 61
  conditions for obtaining, 61–6
  Pullman strike, 62
  uses and abuses of labor injunctions, 61–62
Institutionalist economists, 20
Insurance codes, 90
Integrative bargaining, 261–262
Interest dispute, 8

SUBJECT INDEX ▲ 727

SUBJECT INDEX ▲ 729

International Teamster, 191
Intraorganizational bargaining, 262, 292–295, 324–325

Japanese
  competition with U.S. industries, 689–690
  management, 562, 623, 690
Job (scarcity) conciousness, 26
Job enrichment, 14
Job posting and bidding, 452
Job security, 233–234, 243–244
  grievances over, 365–366
Journeyman, 229

Labor Arbitration Reports, 392, 432, 624
Labor costs, 238–239, 284, 289–291, 309–310, 533–548
Labor, demand for, 450–451
Labor force
  and collective bargaining, 12
  changes by the year 2000, 15
  early problems, 28–30
  illiteracy rate, 13
  median age, 14
  minorities, 14
  participation rate for females, 13
  percent of unionized employees, 13
  trends in U.S., 12–13
  underemployment, 14
Labor intensity, 452, 453
Labor Law Reform Act of 1977, 82, 94
Labor-management conflict, 321–328
  role of, 321–322
  sources of, 322–328
Labor-Management Reporting and Disclosure Act (*see* Landrum-Griffin Act)
Labor market
  conditions of, 327
  dual, 487–488
    primary segment, 488
    secondary segment, 488
  external, 450–451
  internal, 452
  real income, 327
  "tight" versus "loose," 327, 451
Labor mediation (*see* Mediation)
Labor mediator (*see* Mediation)
Labor movement
  definition, 24
  structure of, 177
  theory of, 24–25
  United States
    future of, 679–698
    major trends, 52–53
    since 1960, 50–51
Labor parties, 183

Labor relations
  academic foundation, 19–21
Labor relations law, 58–94
  historical roots, 60–61
  laissez faire economics, 63
  need for, 63–64
Labor Relations Reference Manual, 93
Labor spies, 64
Landrum-Griffin Act, 50, 84–88, 91, 92, 205, 227, 430, 582
  "Bill of Rights," 85–86
  control of trusteeships, 86–87
  criminal penalties, 88
  election of union officers, 86, 175, 192, 201
  enforcement of, 88
  fiduciary standards, 87
  historical background, 84–85
  labor-management cooperative programs, 692
  labor racketeering, 209
  provisions of, 85–88
Law of the shop, 361, 404, 427, 431, 615
Layoffs, 550, 566–568
Lloyd-LaFollette Act, 635
Lockout, 8, 351–353
  offensive, 352
  defensive, 351–352
Ludlow Massacre, 32

McClellan Committee, 50, 85, 86, 178
McNamara-O'Hara Act, 456
Management rights, 550–554, 586
  arbitration of, 554
  implied obligations, 551
  legal factors affecting, 553–554
  residualist rights, 551
Marginal revenue productivity theory, 451
May Day, 32
Mediation, 8, 314, 328–335
  effectiveness of, 334–335
  federal and state agencies, 329–330
  functions of, 330–334
    communications, 332–333
    procedural, 331–332
    substantive, 333–334
Medicare, 502, 532
Medicare Catastrophic Protection Act, 510
Memorial Day Massacre, 47
Molly Maguires, 32, 33
Multi-employer bargaining (*see* Bargaining-unit, structure)
Multilateral bargaining, 645–646, 648

National emergency disputes (*see* Taft-Hartley Act)
National Industrial Recovery Act, 46, 47, 64, 67
National Labor Relations Act (*see* Wagner Act)
New Deal, 67, 503
NLRA (*see* Wagner Act)
No-fault absenteeism programs, 599
No-raiding pacts, 49
Norma Rae, 143
Norris-LaGuardia Act, 44, 63, 65–66, 403, 430
  injunctions, 65–66
  yellow-dog contract, 63, 65–66

Occupational Safety and Health Act of 1970, 91, 430, 571, 572-574, 683
Occupational Safety and Health Administration, 91, 573
Open shop, 638
Organization campaigns, 133–158
  atmosphere of, 135
  factors affecting the outcome of
    personal and demographic factors, 139–141
    work environment, 138–139
  tactics used by employers, 148–158, 685–687
    antiunion statements, 155–156
    captive-audience speeches, 157–158
    misrepresentations of fact, 156–157
    proactive measures, 150, 151–152
    reactive measures, 151–158
    supervisory committees, 153
    threats, 154–155
    use consultants during, 135, 152–153
    vote-no committees, 152
  tactics used by unions, 142–148
    cherry picking, 144
    establishing organizational targets, 142
    making the initial advances, 143–146
    obtaining employee support, 146
    using pro-union employees
  unfair labor practices during, 155–158
Output restrictions, 73

Panic of 1837, 29
Past practices, 412
  conflicts over, 368
  role of, 426–429
Paternalism, 44
Pattern bargaining, 99

Pension programs (*see* Retirement programs)
Personnel/human resource management, 220–235
  compensation and employee benefits, 231–233
  differences between union and nonunion firms, 226–235
  employee discipline and control, 234
  employee performance appraisal, 229–230
    and merit systems, 230
    and seniority, 230
  functions of, 222–235
  management goals and strategies, 221–222
  recruitment and selection of employees, 226–227
  staffs, 197, 224, 225, 235, 243–244
  training and development of employees, 228–229
Philadelphia shoemakers, 28, 29
Picket lines
  staffing, 341
Picketing
  common-situs, 77
  extortionate, 87
  informational, 80
  organizational, 79–80
  primary, 77
  recognition, 79–80
  reserve gate, 77
  secondary 76–77
Plant closings, 215, 242, 550, 566–568, 683
Polygraph Protection Act of 1988, 605
Polygraph tests, 604–605
Postal Reorganization Act, 67, 653
Predatory unionism, 25
Preferential shop, 227
Pregnancy Discrimination Act, 510
Pre-hire agreements, 88
President's Commission on Organized Crime, 209, 211, 212, 213, 214, 219
Privatization, 672
Public Employee, 191
Public employment relations boards, 671–672
Public-sector collective bargaining, 91–92, 632–675
  budgeting issues, 646–649
  civil service model of, 635
  collective bargaining model of, 636
  differences from private-sector, 91–92, 633–635
  employee associations, 636–637, 638
  fact finding, 667–671
  federal employees, 651–653
  interest arbitration, 667–671
  mediation, 667
  military/public safety model of, 635
  multilateral bargaining, 645–646, 648
  organizational issues, 649–651
  patrician model of, 635
  patronage model of, 635
  sovereignty issue, 641–642
  state and local employees, 653–672
    bargaining rights, 653–654
    certification of unions, 656–657
    contract administration, 671
    employees covered, 655–656
    impasse resolution procedures, 667–671
    laws covering, 654–672, 671–672
    scope of bargaining, 657–659
    strikes and strike penalties, 662–667
    unfair labor practices, 659–662
  strikes, 329–330, 642–645
    arguments for and against, 644

Quality of Employment Survey, 210
Quality of worklife programs, 246

Racketeer Influenced and Corrupt Organizations Act (RICO), 347
Racketeering, labor, 179, 209–214
  effects of, 212–213
  government action against, 213–214
  magnitude of the problem, 209–212
Railway Labor Act, 64–65, 67, 91, 92, 579
Rehabilitation Act of 1973, 89, 430, 576, 577, 581
Representation election (*see* Certification election)
Representation petition, 80
Republicans, 183
Retirement programs, 236, 517–522
Revolutionary unionism, 25
Right-to-work laws, 216, 585, 586
Rights dispute, 9, 361
  sources of, 363–369
Roaring 1920s, 42–43
Robotics technology, 565–566
"Runaway" plant, 70

Sabotage, 346–347
Scabs, 29
Scientific management, 20, 481

Secondary boycott
  common-situs picketing, 77
  incidental effects, 77, 349
Self-managing work teams, 551
Seniority, 230, 325, 550, 567
  application of, 555–557
  benefit seniority, 230, 554
  calculating, 558
  competitive seniority, 230, 554
  discrimination in, 561–562
  effect of mergers and acquisitions on, 558–560
  promotions and transfers, 556–557
  superseniority, 375
Severance pay, 523
Sheet Metal Worker, 190
Sherman Antitrust Act, 43, 44, 92
  applied to the *Danbury Hatters* case, 62
  role in restraining the growth of unions, 62–63
  treble damages, 62
Shop floor, 243
Shop society, 200
Sick leave, paid, 525
Slavery, 28
Slowdowns, 73, 350–351
Smoking, workplace, 571, 581–582
Social Security, 502, 504, 532
Social Security Act, 90, 187, 430, 456
  benefits, 233
  Medicare, 187
Socialist party, 31
Sovereignty issue, 641–642
Soviet Union, 51, 207
Staggers Rail Act of 1980, 682
Steel industry, U.S., 245
Steelworkers Trilogy, 404–406, 411
Strikebreaking tactics, 43, 64
  Mohawk Valley Formula, 43
Strikes, 335–351
  costs of, 265–266, 334, 338–340
  economic, 8, 65, 337–347
    employee rights during, 343–345
    operations during, 275, 314–315, 340–341, 342
    permanent replacements for striking workers, 99, 275, 344
    strike funds, 196, 341
    violence during, 346–347
  impact of, 118, 328, 336–337
  insurance, 211, 212
  jurisdictional, 78
  Knights of Labor, 37
  management preparation for, 340–341, 342
  over unsafe working conditions, 349
  public sector, 329–330, 642–643, 662–667

SUBJECT INDEX ▲ 731

Pullman Company, 31, 40
sit down, 73
statistics on, 336–337
sympathy, 348–349
unfair labor practice, 347–348
union preparations for, 341
wildcat, 349–351
1946 strike wave, 48
Subcontracting, 550, 568–571
arbitral criteria, 570–571
Successorship employers, 121, 122–123, 559
Sunshine laws, 645–646
Superseniority, 373, 568
Supervisor, first-line, 199, 378
and grievances, 365
Supplemental unemployment benefits, 522
Sweatshops, 30
Sweetheart arrangements, 44, 69, 211

Taft-Hartley Act, 11, 49, 72–80, 92, 94, 188, 353, 375, 430, 585
labor-management cooperative programs, 692
national emergency disputes, 353–354
board of inquiry, 353
controversies surrounding, 353–354
injunction, 80-day, 353
provisions and coverage, 73–80, 91
reason for passage, 72–73
union unfair labor practices, 74–80
bad-faith bargaining, 75
excessive and discriminatory union dues and fees, 78–79
featherbedding, 79
hot-cargo agreements, 76
improper picketing, 79–80
jurisdictional disputes, 78
restraint and coercion of employees, 74
restraint and coercion of employers, 74–75
secondary boycotts, 76–77, 349
Tax Reform Act of 1986, 430, 456, 513, 520
Technological change, 240, 562–568, 586
collective bargaining agreement provisions pertaining to, 233–234
Tenure, 592, 593
Theft, employee, 604–606
antitheft policies, 605–606
Thurmond Act of 1979, 652
Two-tier wage plans (*see* Compensation)

Unemployment compensation, 430, 456, 501–502, 567
Union dues, 69, 78–79, 195, 199
Union label, 179
Unionization
"bread-and-butter," 40
labor supply, 229
professional employees, 50
threat effect of, 459
trends, 11–12
white-collar membership, 140
Unions
apprenticeship training, 208, 229
cooperative efforts with corporations, 245–249
conditions for success, 248–249
legal issues, 691–692
opportunities created by, 246–247
potential fears and drawbacks, 248
craft, 31
democracy in, 205–209
discipline of members, 200
employee interest in, 135–141
blue-collar employees, 137
white-collar employees, 137
impact on corporate mergers and buyouts, 204
industrial, 31
international, 176–177, 189–198
conventions, 191
finances, 195–196
functions, 190–191, 186–198
governance, 191–94
membership size, 189–190
officer salaries, 193–194
organizational structures, 194–195
local, 73, 176–177, 198–202
apprenticeship training, 200
business agent, 200, 201, 202, 243
craft, 200, 202
factory, 198
functions, 199–200
governance, 201–202
hiring halls, 199, 200, 583
industrial, 198
meetings, 200
nonfactory, 198, 199, 201
officers, 201–202, 243–244, 291
racial segregation in, 73, 208, 216
shop steward, 199, 243, 291, 371, 373, 378, 568
managements view of, 5–6
membership apathy, 205, 207
membership costs, 140
membership declines, 679–681

mergers between, 202–204
absorptions, 202
amalgamations, 202–203
merits of, 6
reason for existence, 4–5
relationship with management, 6–7, 7–11, 242–244
strategic management concepts, use of, 694–695
trusteeships, 86–87
Union security, 70, 188
agency shop, 583
arguments for and against, 584–585
checkoff, 583–584
closed shop, 227, 583
maintenance of membership shop, 583
modified union shop, 582–583
preferential shop, 227
pre-hire agreements, 88, 582
right-to-work laws, 585
union shop, 582
United States Bankruptcy Code, 275
Uplift unionism, 25
USA Today, 684
Utility functions, 256, 264

Vacations, paid, 523–524
Vietnam Era Veterans Readjustment Assistance Act of 1974, 89, 430
Violence
during strikes, 345–347
Greyhound strike, 274
in coal mining, 31–32, 346
on the railroads, 30–31
role in the labor movement, 33–34
roughshadowing, 43, 64
versus "anticipated animal exuberance", 345

Wages (*see* Compensation)
Wagner Act, 11, 47, 48, 52, 66–73, 83, 91, 92, 94, 110, 127, 150, 214, 298, 322, 324, 344, 406, 430, 553, 566, 569, 576, 581, 582, 583, 585, 593, 635, 649, 650, 652, 659, 683
certification election procedures, 147, 159, 165–166, 168
employer unfair labor practices, 68–71
discrimination against union supporters, 70–71
dominance or interference with unions, 69–70
bad-faith bargaining, 71
interference with section 7 rights, 68–69

Wagner Act (*Continued*)
   retaliation against persons filing unfair labor practice charges, 71
   excluded occupational groups, 67–68
   inadequacies of, 72–73
   labor-management cooperative programs, 692
   notification before modifying a collective bargaining agreement, 297–298, 330
   organizations and employees covered, 67–68
   results of, 72
   section 7, 68
Walking delegate, 29
Walsh-Healy Act, 90, 45
War Labor Disputes Act, 73
West Germany, 51, 689–690
Western Europe, 51, 97, 183, 185, 562, 689–690
Whipsawing, 351–352
Work assignments
   in jurisdictional disputes, 78
Work rules, 233–234, 563–565
   restrictions caused by, 229
   standardized, 27
Work sharing, 567
Worker Adjustment and Retraining Notification Act, 567
Workers' compensation, 430, 456, 500–501
Workingmen's parties, 30
World War I, 42, 52, 64, 67
World War II, 48–49, 52, 73, 196
Yellow-dog contracts, 43, 63
   in coal mining, 63
   Norris LaGuardia Act provisions, 63, 65–66
Zipper clauses, 553–554

NAME INDEX

Aaron, Benjamin, 636, 637, 638, 640, 642, 645, 646, 648, 649, 650, 653, 666, 669, 671
Abbasi, Sami M., 594
Abboushi, Suhail, 238
Abodeely, John E., 102
Aboud, Antone, 275, 568, 643
Abowd, John M., 337
Adams, Larry T., 203
Addison, John I., 337
Agnos, Art, 355, 356
Alexander, Kenneth O., 205
Alinsky, Saul, 32, 33, 45, 46
Allen, Harry E., 517
Allen, Steven G., 18, 222, 636
Ameci, Gina, 477
Ames, B. Charles, 686
Anderson, John C., 669
Anderson, Maureen, 355
Ansberry, Clare, 273
Anthony, Richard J., 528
Apcar, Leonard M., 563
Arshanapalli, Gangadha, 336
Arthur, Michael B., 224
Arvey, Richard D., 226
Ash, Philip, 369
Ashenfelter, Orley, 52, 460
Askin, Steve, 135
Atchison, Sandra D., 181, 573
Auster, Ellen R., 486
Avakian, Michael E., 684, 685
Axelrod, G.B., 593

Bacharach, Samuel B., 268, 269
Bacon, David L., 594
Bacon, Kenneth H., 516
Bahr, Morton, 133, 138
Bailyn, Lotte, 224
Bain, Trevor, 165, 424
Bakke, E. Wright, 636
Balkin, David B., 453, 466, 487
Bangs, Ruth, 599
Barlow, Wayne E., 123, 338
Barnard, Thomas H., 581
Barron, John M., 229

Bass, Bernard M., 228
Bazerman, Max H., 257
Beach, Dale S., 224
Bean, Ed., 605
Beary, Rodney P., 620
Beauvais, Laura, 135
Beeler, Duane, 377
Beggs, Steven D., 462
Begin, James P., 110
Belcher, D.W., 462
Bellace, Janice R., 85
Belous, 150
Belt, John, 224
Benedict, Mary Ellen, 667
Bennett, Amanda, 526
Bentsen, Lloyd, 183
Bequai, August, 604
Berg, N.R., 603
Bergman, Thomas J., 224, 487
Berkeley, Arthur Eliot, 258, 285, 646
Berkowitz, Alan D., 78, 85
Bernstein, Aaron, 14, 178, 181, 214, 454, 575, 688
Bernstein, Irving, 44
Bernstein, Jules, 152
Bertrand, Philip V., 337
Bieber, Owen, 83, 193
Biehl, Michael M., 515
Bigoness, William J., 165
Bills, David B., 452
Birdsall, William C., 503
Bishop, Robert L., 264
Black, Dan A., 556
Black, Henry Campbell, 386
Blackburn, Richard, 165
Blasi, Joseph, 693
Block, Richard N., 161
Bloom, David E., 400, 669
Bocher, Sheri L., 424
Bognanno, Mario, 264
Bok, Derek, 41, 343, 354, 564, 637
Bonaventura, Rich, 196
Boroson, Warren, 502
Boulware, Lemuel R., 300–301
Boyle, W.A. (Tony), 33, 192–193

Brankey, Edward, 227
Brett, Jeanne M., 137, 335, 391
Bridges, Harry, 207
Brief, Arthur P., 137
Briggs, Steven, 567
Brister, Jozell, 144
Britton, Raymond L., 411, 417, 418, 420, 429
Brody, David, 28, 45
Broehl, Wayne, Jr., 33
Brouwer, Paul J., 230
Brown, Bert R., 257
Brown, Charles, 481
Brown, James, 215
Brown, Thomas P. IV, 124
Buckley, John E., 475
Burcke, James M., 514
Burgoyne, Arthur C., 34
Burt, Robert E., 135
Burton, John F., Jr., 636, 637
Bush, George, 83, 687
Butler, Richard J., 670
Byrne, Dennis M., 349
Byrnes, Joseph F., 305, 307

Cain, Carol, 512
Cangemi, Joseph P., 604
Canoni, John D., 567
Capen, M., 501
Cappelli, Peter, 480
Card, David, 337
Carmell, William A., 408
Carnegie, Andrew, 34
Carnevale, Mary Lu, 340, 348
Carroll, Stephen J., 453, 517
Carter, Jimmy, 182
Cary, John, 196
Cathcart, D.A., 593
Cavanaugh, Christopher L., 400
Cerbone, Richard R., 556
Chaikin, Sol C., 183, 194, 459
Chaison, Gary N., 203, 204
Chalykoff, John, 148
Chamberlain, Neil W., 265, 269, 563, 642

733

NAME INDEX

Chapman, Fern Schumer, 525
Charlier, Marj, 340, 573
Chaubey, M.D., 668
Chavez, Cesar, 111, 193
Chelius, James R., 500
Chisholm, Rupert F., 140
Christiansen, Dorothy, 355
Christoperson, Susan, 562
Civiletti, Benjamin, 210
Cleveland, Grover, 31
Close, M. John, 224
Coddington, Alan, 256
Cohen, Sanford, 31, 35, 42
Cohen, Laurence J., 565
Cohn, E., 501
Coleman, Francis T., 164
Colosi, Thomas R., 258, 285, 646
Commons, John R., 20, 21, 26, 27, 269
Conant, John L., 203
Cook, James, 210
Cook, Karen, 196
Cook, Mary F., 525
Cooke, William N., 137, 153, 246, 247, 390
Coolidge, Calvin, 643
Cooper, Elizabeth A., 455
Costello, Cynthia B., 564
Crandall, Robert L., 682
Crino, Michael D., 222, 226, 228, 230, 231, 234, 238, 326, 475, 495, 573, 578, 582, 594, 619, 620
Cullen, Donald E., 323, 563
Cunningham, Daniel, 210
Curley, Michael A., 593
Currie, Janet, 670
Cutcher-Gershenfeld, Joel, 696

Daniels, Gene, 258, 292, 309
Dastmalchian, Ali, 369, 389
Davey, Harold W., 264
Davis, Marvin, 694
Davis, Mary F., 527
Day, Virgil B., 267
Debs, Eugene, 31, 40
DeCotiis, Thomas A., 137
Delaney, John Thomas, 184, 302, 659, 667, 668
Delaney, Meg, 509
DeNisi, Angelo S., 137
Dennis, Barbara, 246
Dennis, Rodney E., 390
Derber, Milton, 45, 645, 648, 649
Dereshinsky, Ralph, 78
Deshpande, Satish P., 137
Dichter, M.S., 593
Dickens, William T., 153
DiGiacomo, Gordon, 247
Dilts, David A., 337
DiLullo, Samuel, 77
Dobofsky, Melvin, 24, 41

Doherty, Robert E., 229, 230, 404
Donahue, Richard J., 510
Donahue, Thomas R., 193
Dotson, Donald, 686
Douglas, Paul W., 273
Doyel, Hoyt, 480
Drazin, Robert, 486
Drucker, Peter, 688–689, 698
Dubinsky, Frederick C., 694
Duffy, Henry, 193
Durtis, Carol, 602
Dukakis, Michael S., 183
Dunlop, John T., 41, 343, 354, 564, 637, 695
Dunn, Robert, 66
Durcan, James W., 269
Dyer, Lee 51
Dworkin, James B., 159, 165, 215

Eaton, Adrienne E., 249
Edmundson, Ray, 207
Edwards, P.K., 218
Edwards, Richard, 222
Ehrenberg, Ronald G., 453, 459, 460, 565, 670, 685
Ehrlich, Elizabeth, 14
Eisele, C. Frederick, 349
Elias, Christopher, 516
Elkouri, Edna Asper, 361, 373, 374, 384, 391, 399, 400, 405, 419, 422, 423, 424, 426, 429, 430, 552, 554, 559, 560, 570, 574, 620
Elkouri, Frank, 361, 373, 374, 384, 391, 399, 400, 405, 419, 422, 423, 424, 426, 429, 430, 552, 554, 559, 560, 570, 574, 620
Epp, David L., 671
Estenson, David L., 264
Estey, Martin, 176, 195, 231
Evansohn, John, 17
Ewing, David W., 226, 595, 624
Extejt, Marian, 165

Fain, James R., 159
Faley, Rober H., 226
Farber, Henry S., 137, 670
Feder, David L., 651
Feild, Hubert S., 226
Feinstein, Selwyn, 433
Feldacker, Bruce, 70, 97, 123, 345, 388
Feldman, Muriel N., 458
Feldman, Sidney P., 215
Ferris, N. Bruce, 462
Feuille, Peter, 659, 667, 668, 670
Fidandis, Nicholas A., 267, 329, 330, 331, 333
Finch, R.I., 34
Fink, Leon, 36, 37
Finney, Martha I., 326
Fiorito, Jack, 137, 141, 695

Flagler, John J., 426
Flaherty, Sean, 337
Flaim, Paul O., 567
Flanagan, Robert J., 153, 453, 459, 460, 565, 685
Fletcher, Meg, 501
Ford, Gerald, 651
Foulkes, Fred K., 221, 226, 232, 390
Franco, Joseph, 347
Frank, Jeff, 556
Frankfurter, Felix, 61
Freeman, Richard B., 137, 148, 210, 231, 232, 233, 455, 460, 554, 563, 636, 647, 648
Fryxell, Gerald E., 139
Fuess, Scott M., Jr., 229
Fullerton, Howard N., Jr., 13
Fulligar, Clive, 135, 137
Fulmer, William E., 141
Futrell, C., 482
Futrell, Mary Hatwood, 638

Gagla, Ken, 82, 136, 143, 258, 292, 309
Galenson, Walter, 52
Gallagher, Daniel G., 557, 647, 668
Gandz, Jeffrey, 369
Gannon, John A., 648–649
Garland, Susan B., 14, 454
Garraty, John A., 34
Gates, Conrad John, 371, 377, 381, 383, 384
Gatewood, Robert D., 226
Gershenfeld, Walter J., 408, 426, 606, 638, 663
Gersuny, Carl, 555
Getman, Julius, 137, 141
Gibbons, Muriel, 638, 663, 667, 669
Gifford, Courtney, 176, 189, 190, 640
Gilbreth, Frank, 20
Gilbreth, Lillian, 20
Ginger, Ray, 31
Glenn, Wayne, 343
Glick, Allen, 211
Glueck, William F., 116, 196
Goggin, Edward P., 374, 391, 399, 423, 553, 559, 574
Gold, Charlotte, 247, 248, 390
Gold, Michael Evan, 488
Goldberg, Stephen, 137, 335, 391
Goldfield, M., 164
Gomberg, William, 564
Gomez, Angel, III, 594
Gomez-Mejia, Luis R., 453, 487
Gompers, Samuel, 1, 38, 39, 52
Gordon, Michael E., 135, 137, 138
Gould, Jay, 34, 37
Gould, William B., 92
Goulden, Joseph C., 50
Graham, Joseph, III, 390

NAME INDEX ▲ 735

Gramm, Cynthia L., 337
Granoff, Michael H., 309, 535
Green, Nathan, 61
Green, William, 49
Greenberg, Jerald, 456
Grider, Doug, 488
Grigsby, David W., 269
Grimes, Gary R., 666
Grodin, Joseph R., 671
Grody, Donald, 415, 418
Groenveld, Judith, 603
Grossman, Jonathan, 51
Grubbs, Frank L., 38

Hackman, J.R., 455
Haggard, Thomas R., 345
Halbrecht, Herbert Z., 462
Hamburger, Paul M., 458
Hammer, Randi C., 102
Hammer, Richard, 347
Hammond, Doug, 334
Hamner, W. Clay, 137
Hankins, John L., 503
Harris, Frank, 32
Hatch, D. Diane, 123, 338
Hayford, Stephen L., 650
Haywood, "Big Bill," 33, 52
Hazelwood, Joseph, 601
Healy, R.J., 604
Heckscher, Charles C., 696
Helsby, Robert D., 638, 663, 667, 669
Henderson, Richard I., 453, 476
Hendricks, Wallece E., 337
Hendrix, William H., 151
Heneman, Herbert G., Jr., 603, 604
Heneman, Herbert G., III, 137, 143
Henry, Karen, 356
Herman, Jeanne, 137
Herrnstadt, Owen G., 93
Herzlinger, Regina E., 513
Hickman, Charles W., 195
Hicks, John R., 263–264
Hill, Marvin, Jr., 419, 421, 606
Hillman, Sidney, 6
Hills, Frederick S., 290, 291, 482, 483, 487
Hirsch, Barry T., 458
Hirsch, Werner, 672
Hobson, Charles J., 215
Hoerr, John, 246, 551, 594, 679, 681, 690, 691
Hoffa, Jimmy, 347
Hoffer, William, 578
Hoffman, Carl C., 488
Hoffman, Kathleen P., 488
Hoffman, Wilma, 246
Hoh, Ronald, 668
Holley, William H., Jr., 593
Hollman, Kenneth W., 594
Holzer, Harry J., 470

Holzinger, Albert G., 513
Hoover, Herbert, 635
Horton, Raymond D., 648
Howard, Sidney, 66
Hoxie, Robert F., 25
Hunsicker, J. Freedley, 68
Hunt, James W., 136, 156
Hunt, Janet C., 222
Hunt, Philip C., 498
Hutcheson, William, 46
Hyde, Alan, 403

Iacocca, Lee, 193, 215
Ichniowski, Casey, 212, 636, 638, 647, 654
Ihrig, Fritz, 282, 286
Imberman, Woodruf, 297
Irwin, Michael, 41
Issacson, W.J., 593
Ivancevich, John M., 501

Jackson, Tom, 224
Jacoby, Sanford M., 459
James, Frank E., 516
Janovsky, 561
Jarley, Paul, 215, 695
Jauch, Lawrence R., 116, 196
Jerdee, Thomas H., 519
Johnson, Lyndon B., 182
Johnson, Wayne, 673
Jones, Charles W., 680
Jones, Edgar A., Jr., 426

Kagel, Sam, 413
Kahn, Lawrence M., 337, 453, 459, 460, 556, 565, 685
Kahn, Mark, 562, 606
Kahn, Wendy L., 636, 641, 654, 656
Kandel, William L., 561
Kane, Jonathan A., 68
Kanin-Lovers, Jill, 468
Karim, Ahmad, 335
Karsh, Bernard, 137
Kaserman, David L., 203
Kashiro, Kazutoshi, 52
Katz, Harry C., 20, 52, 101, 115, 116, 122, 137, 203, 214, 217, 235, 248, 249, 276, 337, 390, 458, 459, 460, 670, 685, 691
Katzman, Marvin S., 528
Kaufman, Stuart Bruce, 38
Kaye, Beverly, 452
Keilin, Eugene J., 204
Kennedy, John F., 637, 651
Kennedy, Robert, 178
Kiker, B.F., 222
Kilgour, John G., 124, 140
Killingsworth, Charles C., 551
King, Randall H., 349
Kirk, J. Robert, 488
Kirkbride, Paul S., 269

Kirkland, Lane, 193, 684
Klein, Alfred, 518
Klein, Daniel L., 509
Klein, Janice A., 108
Klein, Katherine J., 483
Kleiner, Morris M., 148
Kleinmuntz, Benjamin, 605
Knight, Thomas R., 390
Kochan, Thomas A., 20, 51, 52, 101, 115, 116, 122, 137, 148, 203, 214, 217, 235, 248, 249, 276, 337, 390, 458, 459, 460, 645, 646, 659, 667, 668, 670, 685, 691
Komaroff, Michael I., 361
Kovner, Joseph, 200
Kramer, Andrew M., 314, 340, 342, 345, 346
Kramnick, Isaac, 643
Kressel, Kenneth, 667
Kroll, Mark J., 468
Krupman, William A., 178
Kuhn, James W., 265, 269
Kujawa, Tony, 349
Kuzmits, Frank E., 598, 599
Kymn, Kern O., 337

Laarman, Linda M., 515
Ladd, Robert T., 135
LaFollette, Robert, 39
Lagerfeld, Steve, 152, 153
Lahne, Herbert, 200
Landis, Brook I., 424, 425
Laski, Harold J., 642
Latham, Gary P., 228, 230
Lawler, Edward E., III, 468, 482, 484, 495
Lawler, Edward J., 268, 269
Lawler, John J., 148, 153, 157, 158, 164
Leap, Terry L., 150, 222, 226, 228, 230, 231, 234, 238, 269, 326, 425, 475, 495, 566, 573, 576, 578, 582, 594, 606, 619, 620
Ledford, Gerald E., Jr., 468
Ledoltes, Johannes, 519
Lee, Barbara A., 110, 124
Lee, Eleanor, 358
Lee, Rick, 515
Lefkowitz, Jerome, 638, 663, 667, 669
Leibig, Michael T., 636, 641, 654, 656
LeLouarn, Jean-Yves, 137
Lens, Sidney, 32
Lepore, Bruce A., 514
Lester, Richard A., 27, 669
Levin, Edward, 415, 418
Levine, Howard, 358
Levine, Marvin J., 166, 480
Levinson, Daniel J., 224
Levinson, Edward, 66

NAME INDEX

Levy, Peter B., 212
Lewicki, Roy J., 257
Lewin, David, 563, 659, 667, 668
Lewis, Drew, 340
Lewis, H. Gregg, 459
Lewis, John L., 1, 32, 33, 46, 47, 52, 207, 563
Lindbeck, Assar, 222
Lipset, Seymour Martin, 685
List, Jill Hauser, 620
List, Martin S., 581
Livernash, E. Robert, 369
Livesay, Harold G., 38
Locher, Mark, 357
Lodge, George C., 562
Loewenberg, J. Joseph, 642, 645
London, Jack, 137
Long, Larry E., 137
Lopez, Ed, 578
Lorber, Lawrence Z., 488
Lorenzo, Frank, 217, 340
Lorsch, J., 108
Loughran, Charles S., 258, 284, 285, 286, 287, 295, 309, 310, 312, 315, 316
Lowell, A. Lawrence, 643
Lublin, Joann S., 213
Lynch, Lisa M., 165
Lynn, Monty L., 144

Mace, Robert F., 123
McAdams, Jerry, 480
McCabe, Eileen, 515
McCann, Joseph E., 453
McLennan, Kenneth, 645
McConnell, Patrick L., 618
McCormick, Janice, 322
McCue, Lisa J., 605
McDermott, Thomas J., 390
McGrath, Paul, 336
McGuiness, Kevin, 605
McGuinn, John, 357
McKee, Kathryn, 452
McKelvey, Jean T., 385, 386, 592, 604, 615, 623
McKenna, Jack F., 455
McKersie, Robert B., 92, 148, 248, 249, 257, 260, 261, 262, 277, 685, 691, 696
McMasters, Scott, 196
McNamee, Mike, 514
McParland, James, 33
McPherson, Donald S., 371, 377, 381, 383, 384
MaCurdy, Thomas E., 256
Madigan, Kathleen, 514
Magee, John F., 689
Mahoney, Thomas A., 466, 489
Maranto, Cheryl L., 139, 141, 215
Martin, James E., 337
Marx, Gary S., 478

Marx, Karl, 24
Masi, Dale, 578
Masters, Marick F., 184, 637
Matell, Robin, 343
Matteson, Michael T., 501
Mayo, Elton, 20
Meany, George, 1, 49, 182
Medoff, James L., 137, 210, 231, 232, 233, 455, 460, 554, 563
Meyer, David, 390
Meyer, Herbert H., 232
Miernyk, William H., 563
Miles, Gregory L., 690
Milkovich, George T., 453, 461, 468
Miller, Edward B., 84
Miller, Norm, 178
Mills, Daniel Quinn, 92, 322, 556, 601
Miscimarra, Philip A., 78
Mitchell, Daniel J.B., 51, 222, 237, 459, 696, 697
Mittenthal, Richard, 427, 428
Mobley, William H., 137
Modic, Stanley J., 337
Moe, J.P., 603
Molleston, Julie L., 137
Montgomery, David, 52
Montgomery, Edward, 667
Montgomery, B. Ruth, 140
Moran, N.L., 593
Morgan, Chester A., 13, 25, 26, 31, 32, 35, 260
Morgan, Len, 555, 556, 559
Morgan, Richard L., 135
Morris, Charles G., 66, 110, 113, 119, 123, 299, 301, 302
Morton, John D., 461
Moskow, Michael H., 642, 645
Moye, William T., 51
Mulder, Frans, 599
Munzenrider, Robert F., 140
Murphy, Betty Southard, 123, 338
Murphy, Frank, 47
Murray, Joe H., 594
Murray, Michael L., 500
Murray, Philip, 47
Murrman, Kent, 153
Myers, D.W., 526

Najita, Joyce M., 636, 637, 638, 640, 642, 645, 646, 648, 649, 650, 653, 666, 669, 670
Naples, Michele I., 337
Nash, Al, 202
Nelson, Nels E., 399
Neufald, John I., 458
Newhams, Thomas H., 390
Newman, Harold R., 667
Newman, Jerry M., 453, 468
Ng, Ignace, 369, 389
Nixon, Richard M., 651

Norback, Craig T., 123, 400, 454, 510, 525
Northrup, Herbert R., 137, 301
Nussbaum, Bruce, 14

O'Brian, Bridget, 271
O'C. Hamilton, Joan, 517
Odewahn, Charles, 164
Olian, Judy, 517
Olson, Craig, 666, 669
Olson, Darrell, 599
O'Neil, John, 462
O'Reilly, James T., 299
Orkin, Neal, 80, 374
Osigweh, Chimezie A.B., 624

Palmer, Frank, 66
Palomba, Catherine, 337
Parker, Carlton, 27
Parker, Darrell, 556
Parker, Joan, 124
Patterson, Gregory A., 134, 516
Payson, M.F., 137
Peach, David, 369
Pegnetter, Richard, 335
Pencavel, John, 52, 256
Pennar, Karen, 14
Pepe, Stephen P., 593
Perkins, Robert E., 498
Perline, Martin M., 226
Perlman, Mark, 27
Perlman, Selig, 26–27
Perrucci, Carolyn C., 567
Perrucci, Robert, 567
Perry, Charles R., 215, 222, 314, 340, 342, 345, 346
Petertil, Jeffrey P., 509
Petersen, Paul F., 576
Peterson, Florence, 46
Peterson, William, 460
Phelan, Craig, 49
Philpot, John W., 135
Pierce, Ellen R., 165
Pigou, A.C., 258–260
Pizzolatto, Allayne Barrilleaux, 566
Porter, Andrew, 153
Porter, L.W., 455
Powderly, Terence V., 36, 52
Power, Mark L., 519
Poynter, David J., 226
Pranis, Robert, 369
Presser, Jackie, 193, 682
Preston, Anne, 212
Pulliam, Mark S., 275
Pullman, George, 31

Quaglieri, Philip L., 138, 159, 194, 459, 649, 682, 687

Radle, Janice A., 390
Ralston, August, 602

NAME INDEX ▲ 737

Ratacjczak, Donald, 679
Rayback, Joseph G., 36
Ready, Kathryn J., 458
Reagan, Ronald, 83, 340, 343, 686
Redeker, James R., 234, 598, 601, 612
Reed, Paul, 468
Reed, Thomas F., 143, 273
Rehmus, Charles M., 353, 669
Reichlin, Igor, 690
Rejda, George E., 503
Renshaw, Patrick, 41
Reuther, Walter, 6, 49
Reynolds, Lloyd, 29
Richards, Edward P., III, 501
Richardson, James, 224
Riley, Thomas, 480
Risher, Howard W., 453
Robertson, John D., 637
Rock, Robert H., 474
Rockefeller, John D., 34
Roderick, David, 237
Rogers, Kevin N., 371, 377, 381, 383, 384
Roman, Paul M., 601
Roomkin, Myron, 161
Roosevelt, Franklin D., 503, 635
Roosevelt, Theodore, 635
Rose, Joseph B., 245
Rose, Robert L., 350, 351, 451
Rosen, Benson, 489, 519
Rosenbloom, David H., 34
Rosow, Jerome M., 246
Ross, Arthur M. 27, 390
Ross, William H., Jr., 262, 334
Rowan, Richard L., 137
Ruben, George, 237, 273, 454, 643
Rubin, Jeffrey Z., 257
Rubin, George, 213
Rude, Dale E., 137
Rusen, Paul, 245
Rynes, Sara L., 461, 489

St. Antoine, Theodore J., 92, 404, 408
Saks, Daniel H., 137
Salim, Parvez, 565
Samuels, Stephen L., 488
Sandler, Andrew L., 102
Sandver, Marcus, 137, 143, 162, 165
Saunders, Debra J., 674
Scalise, Joseph, 245
Schares, Gail E., 690
Schecter, Jack H., 457
Scheinman, Martin F., 415, 418, 419
Scheuch, Richard, 229
Schiller, Zachary, 204
Schleger, Peter R., 528
Schlesinger, Lepnard A., 108
Schmertz, Eric J., 399
Schmoyer, Louise, 374
Schnake, Mel E., 227

Schneider, B.V.H., 642, 646, 653
Schneider, Thomas J., 314, 340, 342, 345, 346
Schneier, Craig Eric, 517
Schoen, Cathy, 514
Scholl, , Richard W., 455
Schriesheim, Chester A., 137
Schroeder, Michael, 454
Schuster, Michael, 246
Schwartz, Alvin, 5, 40, 47, 158, 193, 200, 201, 206, 334, 343, 348
Schwartz, Jeffrey, 513
Schwochau, Susan, 184, 670
Scott, Bruce R., 562
Scott, Clyde, 164, 424
Seaberry, Jane, 479
Sehgal, Ellen, 567
Seibert, W. Stanley, 337
Seidman, Joel, 63, 137, 207, 208, 209, 218
Serembus, John H., 686, 687
Sewell, Dan, 344
Sfiligoj, Mark, 244
Shain, Martin, 603
Shank, Mark A., 407
Shanker, Albert, 638
Shenon, Philip, 210
Shepard, Herbert A., 224
Shepard, I.M., 593
Sherer, Peter, 480
Shirai, Taishiro, 52
Shurdan, Mike, 488
Siegel, Boaz, 417
Siegel, Jay S., 338
Silvio, Conte, 567
Simkin, William E., 267, 329, 330–331, 333, 390
Simon, Bruce M., 205
Sinicropi, Anthony V., 419, 421, 650
Skeels, Jack W., 336
Slichter, Sumner, 269
Smith, A.W., 449
Smith, Adam, 24
Smith, Frank J., 137
Smith, Howard P., 230
Smith, Randall, 693, 694
Smith, Robert S., 453, 459, 460, 488, 500, 565, 685
Snower, Dennis J., 222
Snyder, Neil H., 196
Snyder, Wendy, 32
Sockell, Donna, 302
Solomon, Janet Stern, 564
Solomon, Jolie, 529, 607
Solon, G., 502
Somers, Gerald G., 562, 563
Sorrenson, Elaine, 488
Sovereign, Kenneth L., 594
Spellman, David J., III, 488
Spiller, William E., 135

Srb, Jozetta H., 519, 576
Stang, Harry R., 341
Staudohar, Paul D., 566, 567
Stephens, Uriah, 36
Stern, James L., 636, 637, 638, 639, 640, 642, 645, 648, 649, 650, 653, 666, 669, 670
Sterrett, Grace, 643
Stessin, Lawrence, 615
Steward, Ira, 35
Stewart, Potter, 637
Stieber, Jack, 92, 467, 562
Stipp, David, 504
Stiteler, Allen, 517
Stokes, J.B., 344
Stone, Irving, 31, 460
Storper, Michael, 562
Strasser, Adolph, 38
Sulkin, Howard Q., 369
Summers, Clyde W., 388–389, 403, 597
Sussman, John, 224
Swaim, Paul, 222
Swann, James P., Jr., 136
Swasy, Alecia, 178, 350, 565
Sweeny, John J., 687
Swenson, Leanne M., 407

Taft, Philip, 38, 39
Taft, William Howard, 635
Tang, Dena, 567
Tang, Harry, 567
Tannenbaum, Frank, 26
Tarnoff, Stephen, 500
Taylor, Benjamin, 60, 70, 101, 107, 163, 227, 275, 336, 350, 353, 386, 405, 585, 586, 653, 666
Taylor, Frederick, 20, 481
Taylor, G. Stephen, 151
Taylor, Robert R., 605
Taylor, William L., 604
Tener, Barbara Z., 638, 663, 667, 669
Thiebolt, Armand J., 345
Thomason, Terry, 636, 637
Thompson, Cynthia A., 135
Thornton, Robert J., 422
Tirone, Elizabeth, 80
Tomlins, Christopher L., 29
Tomsho, Robert, 344
Tracy, Joseph S., 337
Traynor, William J., 224
Treece, James B., 681, 690
Trice, Harrison M., 601
Trost, Cathy, 526
Trotta, Maurice S., 377, 381, 383

Ulman, Lloyd, 35
Upshaw, Gene, 343, 687–688
Ury, William L., 335, 391
Utgoff, Kathleen P., 521
Utz, John L., 526

NAME INDEX

Valente, Judith, 693
Valetta, Robert G., 648
Van Tine, Warren, 24
Varadarajan, P., 482
Vaughan, Emmett J., 512
Vaughan, James A., 228
Veglahn, Peter, 557
Verma, Anil, 222, 458
Vitberg, Alan, 224
Volz, Marlin M., 374, 391, 399, 423, 553, 559, 574
Voos, Paula B., 142, 247
Vroom, Victor H., 455

Wachter, Michael L., 222
Waldman, Seymour M., 386
Walesa, Lech, 52
Wallen, Saul, 424
Wallihan, James, 188, 194, 195, 196, 200
Walsh, Joseph, 556
Walsh, T.J., 604
Walther, Peter D., 68
Walton, Richard E., 257, 260, 261, 262, 277, 696

Ware, Norman, 36
Warner, Kenneth L., 140
Webb, Beatrice, 20, 25
Webb, Sidney, 20, 25
Wei, Zhu Z., 151
Weinberger, Theodore E., 462
Wellington, Harry H., 403
Wessel, David, 479, 514
West, Robin, 153, 157, 164
Westercamp, Patrick, 408
Wexley, Kenneth M., 228, 230
Whatlay, Arthur, 246
Wheeler, Charles, 682
Wheeler, Hoyt N., 645
Whitehead, J. David, 369
Whitney, James L., 490
Williams, C. Glyn, 222
Williams, John G., 356
Williams, Lynn, 680
Willig, Deborah R., 408
Wilson, Kinsey, 135
Wilson, Woodrow, 39
Wines, William A., 275
Winpisinger, William, 193
Winslow, Ron, 527
Wischmann, Lesley, 32

Witney, Fred, 60, 70, 101, 107, 163, 227, 275, 336, 350, 353, 386, 405, 585, 586, 653, 666
Wolf, Stephen M., 694
Wolkinson, Benjamin W., 407
Wolters, Roger S., 593
Work, Clemens P., 150
Workman, Douglas J., 196
Wren, Daniel, 481
Wynn, William H., 159, 193, 686

Yablonski, Joseph, 33, 192–193
Yoder, D., 603, 604
Young, Edwin, 45
Young, Oran R., 264
Youngblood, Stuart A., 137

Zack, Arnold M., 426, 427, 428, 467, 551, 597, 604, 615, 667, 669
Zalusky, John, 390, 391
Zax, Jeffrey S., 638, 647, 654, 672
Zellner, Wendy, 690
Zemke, Ron, 605
Zieger, Robert H., 46
Zirkel, Perry, 422
Zuckerman, Laurence, 210

CORPORATION, GOVERNMENT AGENCY, AND LABOR ORGANIZATION INDEX

▲ ▲

A. Philip Randolph Institute, 185
Adolph Coors Co., 181, 182
Aetna Life and Casualty Company, 530
Affiliated Hospitals of San Francisco, 355–356
AFL (*see* American Federation of Labor)
AFL-CIO (*see* American Federation of Labor and Congress of Industrial Organizations)
Agency for International Development, 184
Air California, 608
Air Line Pilots Association, 193, 216, 344, 350
Albertson's, Inc., 216
Allied Industrial Workers of America, 85, 210
Aluminum Workers International Union, 4
Amana Refrigeration, Inc., 552
Amalgamated Clothing and Textile Workers Union, 4, 216, 246, 273
Amalgamated Transit Union, 274, 344
American Airlines, 682
American Arbitration Association, 354, 399, 400, 401, 413, 421, 422, 434
American Association of Advertising Agencies, 357
American Association of University Professors, 639
American Civil LIberties Union, 605

American College of Life Underwriters, 512
American Compensation Association, 223
American Federation of Labor, 35, 38–40, 42, 45, 49, 52, 203
American Federation of Labor and Congress of Industrial Organizations, 5, 49–50, 51, 142, 176, 177, 178–189, 203, 215, 219, 516, 605, 683
  African-American Labor Center, 185
  American Institute for Free Labor Development, 185, 186
  Asian-American Free Labor Institute, 185
  associate memberships, 182
  Building and Construction Trades Department, 185
  civil rights, 185–186
  Civil Rights Committee, 185
  Committee on Political Education (COPE), 183
  community services, 184
  constitution of, 179
  constitutional departments, 179
  convention, 182
  Department of Civil Rights, 185
  Department of Community Services, 184
  Department of Economic Research, 187, 400
  Department of Education, 186
  Department of Housing and Urban Development, 184

Department of Information, 187
Department of International Affairs, 184
Department of Legislation, 182
Department of Occupational Safety, Health, and Social Security, 187
Department of Organization and Field Service, 181, 182
employment training and education, 186
Ethical Practices Codes, 178–179, 210
Executive Council, 179
financial aspects, 181
Free Trade Union Institute, 185
Free Trade Union News
General Board, 179, 183
George Meany Center for Labor Studies, 186
Human Resources Development Institute, 185, 186
international affairs, 184
Labor Institute of Public Affairs, 188
legislative concerns, 182–183
Office of Housing and Monetary Policy, 184
organizing nonunion workers, 181–182
Organizing Responsibilities Procedures System, 181
political and economic perspectives, 39–40, 181–189
political influence, 183–184

739

ORGANIZATION INDEX

American Federation of Labor and Congress of Industrial Organizations (*Continued*)
   structure of, 179–181
   unification of the AFL and CIO, 49–50
   worker well-being and social security, 186
American Federation of Government Employees, 640
American Federation of Musicians, 4, 206
American Federation of State, County, and Municipal Employees (AFSCME), 189, 489, 526, 639
American Federation of Teachers, 358, 638, 639
American Federation of Television and Radio Artists, 357
American Management Association, 578
American Medical Association, 605
American Postal Workers Union, 640
American Psychological Association, 605
American Railway Union, 31
American Society for Industrial Security, 223
American Society for Personnel Administration (Society for Human Resource Management)
American Society for Training and Development, 223
American Telephone & Telegraph Company (AT&T), 120, 526
American Watch Workers Union, 190
A.O. Smith Corporation, 691
ARA Services, 138
Armco Steel, 565
Armstrong Tire Company, 335
Assembly of Governmental Employees, 640
Associated Actors and Artistes of America, 192, 194–195
Association of National Advertising, 357
Association of Training and Employment Professionals, 223
A.T. Massey Coal Company, 346

Bakery and Confectionery Workers, 85
Baldwin-Felts Detective Agency, 32
Baltimore and Ohio Railroad, 30
Bell Atlantic Corp., 340
Bell of Pennsylvania, 348
Bethlehem Steel, 237, 273
Bituminous Coal Operators Association, 350
Blue Cross-Blue Shield, 182
Boeing Commercial Airplane Company, 10, 392, 454, 551
Borg-Warner Corporation, 516
Braniff International, 559
Brewery Workers, 203, 204
British Airways, 694
Brotherhood of Boilermakers, 203
Bureau of National Affairs, Inc., The, 392, 461, 624, 686
   bargaining information, 291
   surveys, 224, 241–242, 361, 401, 449–450, 471, 473, 474, 478, 481, 497, 506, 507, 511, 512, 513, 516, 521, 522, 523, 524, 525, 527, 552, 554, 559, 567, 569, 571, 583, 615

California Nurses Association, 355, 356
Canadian Labour Congress, 188
Cargill, Incorporated, 573
Carnegie Steel Works, 34
Carson Pirie Scott and Co., 515
Caterpillar Company, 551
CBS, 335
Central of Georgia Railroad Co., 523
Chamber of Commerce, U.S., 244, 578
Champion International, 551
Chrysler Motors Corporation, 8, 99, 193, 195, 215, 454, 458, 573
CIO (*see* Congress of Industrial Organizations)
Clergy Economic Foundation, 187
Coalition of Labor Union Women, 186
Collective Bargaining Forum, 690–691
Colorado Fuel and Iron Company, 32
Columbus Retail Merchants, 586
Communications Workers of America, 120, 138, 176, 348, 526
Community Hospital at Glen Cove, 128–131
Composers and Lyricists Guild of America, 190
Conair Corp., 169–171
Conference Board, 150
Congress of Industrial Organizations, 46–47, 48, 49, 52, 203
Consolidated Rail Corporation (CONRAIL), 116, 579
Continental Airlines, 682
Control Data Corporation, 515
Cooper Union, 126–128
Cooper Union Federation of College Teachers, 126
Culinary Workers and Bartenders Union, 167, 168
CWC Textron, 530

Days Inn of America, 605
Distillery, Rectifying, Wine, and Allied Workers' International Union, 176
District of Columbia Nurses Association, 7

Eastern Airlines, 3, 217, 271, 277, 340, 344, 355, 684, 693
Electronic Workers Union, 400
El Paso Natural Gas Company, 477

Federal Mediation and Conciliation Service (*see* United States, Federal Mediation and Conciliation Service)
Ford Motor Company, 99, 195, 332, 455, 458, 565
Fraternal Order of the Police, 640
Frontier Airlines, 216
Futuramik Industries, 130

General Dynamics Corp., 8
General Electric Company, 267, 300–301, 335
General Motors Corp., 47, 99, 122, 195, 455, 458
Gill Studios, Inc., 491–492
Goodyear Tire and Rubber Co., 324
Graphic Communications Union, 120
Greyhound Lines, 3, 274, 344

Harter Equipment, Inc., 337, 353
Hay Group, 461
Hewitt Associates, 529
Hospital and Health Care Workers Union, 516
Hotel Employees Restaurant Employees International Union, 210, 474

IBM (*see* International Business Machines)
IBP, Inc., 573
I.G. Metall, 690
Independent Guard Union, 693
Indiana General Corporation, 532
Industrial Workers Union, 339
Industrial Workers of the World, 40–41, 52
   political and economic perspectives, 40–41
   downfall of, 41
Institute of Social Research (*see* University of Michigan)
International Association of Fire Fighters, 640, 648
International Association of Machinists, 10, 11, 121, 176, 181–182, 193, 335, 344, 355, 393, 552, 693

ORGANIZATION INDEX ▲ 741

International Association of Personnel Women, 223
International Association of Sideographers, 190
International Brotherhood of Boilermakers, Iron Ship Builders, Blacksmiths, Forgers, and Helpers, 680
International Brotherhood of Electrical Workers, 120, 348, 365
International Brotherhood of Teamsters, 4, 50, 85, 121, 135, 176, 178, 181–182, 203, 204, 206, 210, 326, 681, 683
   Central States Pension Fund, 211
International Business Machines, 6, 232, 526
International Confederation of Free Trade Unions, 185
International Labor Communications Association, 188
International Labor Organization, 185
International Ladies' Garment Workers' Union, 169
International Longshoremen's and Warehousemen's Union, 207, 210, 565
International Molders' and Allied Workers' Union, 530
International Typographical Union, 203
International Union of Journeymen Horseshoers of the United States, 190

Jewish Labor Committee, 186
John Morrell & Co., 335
Johnson-Bateman Co., 579
Joint Council on Economic Education, 187
Jones & Laughlin Steel Company, 72
J.P. Stevens Company, 81, 216, 273

Kaiser Foundation, 87
Knights of Labor, Noble Order of, 32, 35, 36–40
   political and economic perspectives, 36–37
   rise and fall, 37–38

Labor, U.S. Department of (*see* United States, Department of Labor)
Labor Council for Latin American Advancement, 186
Laborers International Union, 210
Lamson & Sessions Co., 611
Los Angeles Unified School District, 672–673
Leadership Conference on Civil Rights, 185

Lockheed, 454
LTV Steel, 510

Maimonides Institute, 607
McCormick Harvester Machine Company, 32
McDonnell Douglas Corporation, 527
Metz Metallurgical Corp., 168–169
Mid Continent Airlines, 559
Midland Steel Products, 611
Milliken and Company, 81
Milwaukee Brewers, 427
Milwaukee Bucks, 427
Morgan Lewis, Githens & Ahn, 204
Motor Carrier Advisory Council, 245

National Academy of Arbitrators, 399, 434
National Association for the Advancement of Colored People, 186
National Association of Letter Carriers, 640
National Association of Manufacturers, 244, 246, 516
National Basketball Association, 427
National Basketball Players Association, 190
National Center for Employee Ownership, 693
National Education Association (NEA), 189, 192, 638, 639
National Football Players Association, 326, 343, 687
National Guard, 31, 47
National Gypsum Company, 352
National Hockey League Players Association, 190
National Labor Relations Board, 7, 10, 49, 67, 71, 81–84, 88, 94, 96, 116, 121, 122, 124–125, 147, 150, 274, 275, 329, 345, 352, 403, 406, 407, 566, 651, 652, 672, 687
   administrative law judges, 81
   appealing decisions to federal court, 81
   as a political, social, and economic force, 83–84, 686–687
   Board, 80, 83–84
   "C" cases, 80
   cease-and-desist orders, 81
   conducting certification elections, 82–83, 158–164, 165–166
   controversy surrounding, 83–84
   General Counsel, 80, 83
   private settlement of unfair labor practice cases, 82–83
   unfair labor practice charges, processing, 80–81
      deferral to arbitrators, 406–408

National Labor Union, 35–36
National Maritime Union of America, 178
National Mediation Board, 65, 329
National Railroad Adjustment Board, 65, 329
National Steel, 273, 454, 694
National Urban League, 185
National War Labor Board, 48, 67
New Jersey Bell, 348
New York Daily News, 340
New York University, 358–359
Newspaper Guild, 120
Nissan USA, 134, 166, 684
NLRB (*see* National Labor Relations Board)
Norfolk Southern Corp., 523
Northwest Airlines, 607
Nynex Corp., 340, 516

Ohio Civil Service Employees Association, 4
Operating Engineers, 85, 336, 353
Organization for Economic Cooperation & Development Trade Union Advisory Committee, 185
Orion Air, 340

Pacific Bell, 626
Pacific Maritime Association, 565
Pacific Telesis Group, 340
Pan American World Airways, 65
Parker Pen Company, 492
Pension Benefit Guaranty Corporation, 521
Personnel Accreditation Institute, 223
Phelps Dodge Magnet Wire Company, 400
Pinkerton's National Detective Agency, 33
Pittston Company, 273, 277, 340, 350, 355, 516, 565, 684
Potomac Electric Power Company, 608
Professional Air Traffic Controllers' Organization (PATCO), 340, 648
Pullman Company, 31

Quality Electric Steel Castings, Inc., 624

Rath Packing Company, 693
Red Cross, 185
Retail Clerks International Union, 4

Safeway Stores, 204
St. Louis Cardinals, 427

742 ▲ ORGANIZATION INDEX

Santa Fe Railway Company, 565
Screen Actors Guild, 357
Screen Extras Guild, 357
Seafirst Bank, 159
Service Employees International Union, 86, 121, 168, 176, 356, 640, 687
Six Hundred Superior Corporation, 474
Society for Human Resource Management, 223, 224, 461
Stephen F. Austin University, 138
Summit Timber Co., 339
Supreme Court, U.S. (*see* United States, Supreme Court)

Texas Air Corporation, 216, 340
Tobacco Workers International Union, 178
Trademark Society, Inc., 190
Trans World Airlines, 216
Transport Workers Union, 65
Transportation Communications International Union, 682
Trent Engineering Company, 492–493
Trucking Management, Inc., 245

Union Carbide, 573
United Airlines, 326, 694
United Auto Workers, 8, 11, 122, 134, 166, 192, 193, 195, 204, 246, 332, 335, 454, 458, 516, 521, 565, 611, 681, 684
 public review board, 203
United Cement, Lime, Gypsum, and Allied Workers International Union, 203
United Farm Workers, 193
United Food and Commercial Workers' Union, 159, 193, 204, 573, 681, 693

United Mine Workers, 33, 73, 114, 119, 178, 192–193, 204, 206, 207, 273, 277, 346, 349, 355, 516, 563, 565
United Motor Workers, Federal Labor Union, 532
United Rubber Workers, 326, 335, 493
United States
 Civil Rights Commission
 Department of Defense, 579
 Department of Justice, 214, 581
 Department of Labor, U.S., 87, 184, 193, 213, 214, 477, 56
  Bureau of Labor Statistics, 187, 291, 461
  enforcement of the Landrum-Griffin Act, 88
  Occupational Safety and Health Administration, 187, 431
  Office of Federal Contract Compliance Programs, 185
  Secretary of Labor, 88, 573, 698
 Department of State, 184
 Department of Transportation, 579
 Environmental Protection Agency, 187
 Equal Employment Opportunity Commission, 185, 408, 431, 458, 487, 591, 683
 Federal Aviation Administration, 350
 Federal Labor Relations Authority, 651
 Federal Mediation and Conciliation Service, 267, 297, 329, 330, 337, 353, 354, 355, 359, 399, 400, 401, 413, 421, 434, 653
 Federal Reserve, 653
 Federal Service Impasse Panel, 651, 653
 Immigration and Naturalization Service, 581
 Information Agency, 184

 Internal Revenue Service, 213
 Merit System Protection Board, 651
 Office of Personnel Management, 494, 651
 Postal Service, 653
 Senate Committee on Labor and Human Resources, 605
 Supreme Court, 81, 97, 107, 111, 122, 127, 371, 375, 388, 389, 402, 403, 404, 405, 486, 488, 489, 553, 569, 576, 579, 687
  writ of certiorari, 81
United States Steel Corp. (*see* USX)
United Steelworkers of America, 192, 203, 237, 245, 565, 628–629, 680
United Technologies Corp., 11
United Textile Workers, 50, 81, 85
United Transportation Union, 565
United Way, 184
University of California-Berkeley, 41
University of Michigan, 210
University of Pennsylvania, 388
University of Washington, 489
University of Wisconsin, 26, 27
Upholsterers International Union, 203
U.S. Pollution Control, Inc., 131–132
USX, 42, 237, 628–629, 691

Wabash Railroad, 37
Wall Street Journal, The, 349
War Labor Board, 42
Washington Hospital Center, 7
Weirton Steel, 693
Westwood Horizons Hotel, 167–168
Wheeling-Pittsburgh Steel Corp., 246
Wobblies, (*see* Industrial Workers of the World)
Writers Guild of America, 335

Xerox Corporation, 6, 246

CASE INDEX

Abood v. Detroit Board of Education, 95 LRRM 2411 (1977), 637
Adler v. Board of Education, 342 U.S. 485 (1952), 641
Air California, 63 LA 350 (1974), 608
Alameda Unified School District, 91 LA 60 (1988), 364
Ala Moana Volkswagen, 91 LA 1331 (1988), 366
Alexander v. Gardner Denver, 415 U.S. 36 (1974), 408, 409
Allen v. Prince George's County, 38 FEP Cases 1220 (1984), 561
American District Telegraph Company, 160 NLRB 1130 (1966), 107
American Federation of State, County, and Municipal Employees, AFL-CIO v. State of Washington, 38 FEP Cases 1353 (1985), 489
American Manufacturing Company, 363 U.S. 593 (1960), 404, 409
American Potash & Chemical Corp., 107 NLRB 1418 (1954), 104
American Ship Building Company v. NLRB, 380 U.S. 300 (1965), 352
Amoco Oil Co., 87 LA 232 (1986), 575
Ashland Oil, Inc., 59 LA 292 (1972), 602
Atlas Powder Co., 92 LA 17 (1988), 368

Babb Motors, 34 LRRM 1148 (1954), 124
Babcock & Wilcox, 73 LA 443 (1979), 600
Bard Manufacturing Co., 91 LA 193 (1988), 365
Baton Rouge Water Works, 103 LRRM 1056 (1979), 374
Bayside Enterprise, Inc., 94 LRRM 2199 (1977), 111

Beal v. Curtis, 37 FEP Cases 644 (1985), 487
Bell Aerospace Co., 219 NLRB 384 (1985), 566
Belnap Inc., v. Hale, 463 U.S. 591 (1983), 275, 348
Bendix Corp., 38 LA 909 (1962), 376
Bendix Corp., 94 LRRM 1596 (1977), 104
Berea Publishing Co., 52 LRRM 1051 (1963), 112
Beth Energy Mines, 87 LA 577 (1986), 575
Black Law Enforcement Officers v. City of Akron, 40 FEP Cases 322 (1986), 561
Boilermakers v. NLRB, CA DC. No 8-1189 (1988), 352
Bonanno Family Foods, Inc., 95 LRRM 1330 (1977), 112
Borden, Inc., Dairy Services Division, 196 NLRB 1170 (1973), 408
Bowen v. United States Postal Service, S. Ct. 112 LRRM 2281 (1983), 386, 389, 410
Boys Markets, Inc. v. Retail Clerks, Local 770, 398 U.S. 235 (1970), 410
Brennan v. Koch, 564 F. Supp. 322 (S.D.N.Y., 1983), 641
Budd Company, 75 LA 281 (1980), 611
Burns International Security Services, Inc., 74 LRRM 1098 (1970), 123

California Drilling and Blasting Company, 91 LA 66 (1988), 367
Calloway v. Westinghouse Electric Corp., 41 FEP Cases 1715 (1986), 561
Capital District Transportation Authority, 72 LA 1313 (1979), 612

Carbon Fuel v. United Mine Workers of America, 444 U.S. 212 (1979), 350
Carey v. Westinghouse, 55 LRRM 2042 (1964), 410
Central Illinois Public Service Company, 91 LA 127 (1988), 365
Champion International Corp., 91 LA 245 (1988), 365
Chicago Teachers Union, Local No. 1 v. Hudson, U.S. Sup. Ct., No. 84-1503, 1986), 583
Cities Services Co., 87 LA 1209 (1986), 373
City of Duluth, 91 LA 238 (1988), 367
City of El Paso, Texas, 76 LA 595 (1981), 9
City of Shawnee, Oklahoma, 91 LA 93 (1988), 363
Collyer Insulated Wire, 192 NLRB 837 (1971), 407, 410
Commonwealth v. Hunt, 4 Metcalf 3 (1842), 61
Commonwealth of Pennsylvania, 65 LA 280 (1975), 608
Consolidated Coal Co., 83 LA 1158 (1984), 423
Consolidated Edison Co., 48 LRRM 1539 (1961), 122
Consolidated Rail Corp. v. Railway Executives Association, U.S. Sup. Ct., No. 88-1 (June 19, 1989), 579
County of Ventura, 91 LA 107 (1988), 367
County of Washington v. Gunther, 25 FEP Cases 1521 (1981), 488
Crowley Constructors, 91 LA 32 (1988), 366
Curtis-Wright Corporation (1955), 425

Dairylea Coop., Inc., 219 NLRB 656 (1975), 373

743

744 ▲ CASE INDEX

Dayton Newspapers, 91 LA 201 (1988), 367
Del Casal v. Eastern Airlines, Inc., 106 LRRM 2276 (1981), 386
Di Giorgio Fruit Corp., 23 LRRM 1188 (1948), 111
Di Tomaso v. Electronic Data Systems, 3 IER Cases 1700 (1988), 579
Dixie Belle Mills, Inc., 51 LRRM 1344 (1962), 117
Dowd Box v. Courtney, 368 U.S. 502 (1962), 409

Eagle Discount, 120 LRRM 1047 (1985), 374
Eastern Coal Corp., 91 LA 245 (1988), 365
EEOC v. FLC & Brothers Rebel, Inc., 44 FEP Cases 362 (1987), 362
E.I. du Pont de Nemours & Co., 64 LRRM 1021 (1966), 103
Electrical Workers v. Foust, 101 LRRM 2365 (1979), 389
Elk Grove Firefighters Local 2340 v. Willis, 90 LRRM 2447 (1975), aff'd 93 LRRM 2019 (1976), 641
Elyria Board of Education, 86 LA 921 (1985), 607
Emporium Capwell Co. v. Western Addition Community Organization, 420 U.S. 50 (1975), 97
Ende v.Board of Regents of Regency Universities, 37 FEP Cases 575 (1985), 487
Enterprise Wheel & Car Corporation, 363 U.S. 593 (1960), 405, 409
EPE Inc., 125 LRRM 1166 (1987), 378
Essex Wire Corp., 47 LRRM 1369 (1961), 122
Excelsior Underwear, Inc., 156 NLRB 1236 (1962), 160

Fall River Dyeing v. NLRB, 107 S. Ct. 2225 (1987), 123, 559
Federal Correctional Institution, 75 LA 295 (1980), 611
Fibreboard Paper Products Corporation v. NLRB, 379 U.S. 203 (1964), 569
Firefighters Local 1784 v. Stotts, 34 FEP Cases 1702 (1984), 562
First National Maintenance Corp., 107 LRRM 2705 (1981), 553, 569
Food Employers Council, Inc., 87 LA 514 (1986), 372
Ford Motor Co. v. Huffman, 31 LRRM 2548 (1948), 385
Frankline, Inc., 127 LRRM 1132 (1988), 373

Gateway Coal Co. v. United Mine Workers, 85 LRRM 2049 (1974), 576
General Electric Co., 150 NLRB 192 (1964), 301
General Electric Co., 70 LA 1097 (1978), 606
General Knit of California, 239 NLRB No. 101 (1978), 157
General Motors Corp., Delco Moraine Division, 237 NLRB 167 (1978), 386
Goodman v. Lukens Steel Co., 39 FEP Cases 617 (1984), 561
Greater Harlem Nursing Home, 76 LA 680 (1981), 362
Greco v. Halliburton, 674 F. SUpp 1447 (1987), 579
Gulf & Western Manufacturing Co., 127 LRRM 1018 (1987), 339

Hall Industries Ltd., 126 LRRM 1162 (1987), 378
Hertz Corporation, 91 LA 261 (1988), 368
Hines v. Anchor Motor Freight, Inc., 91 LRRM 2481 (1976), 386, 388, 410, 604
Hitchman Coal Co., v. Mitchell, 245 U.S. 299 (1917), 63
H.K. Porter, Inc., 397 U.S. 99 (1970), 299
H-N Advertising and Display Company, 87 LA 776 (1986), 9
Hoffman v. Lozna, Inc., 108 LRRM 2772 (1981), 388
Hollywood Ceramics, 140 NLRB 221 (1962), 157
Holmberg, Inc., 64 LRRM 1025 (1966), 103
Holodnak v. Avco Corp., 90 LRRM 2614 (1975), 386
Hughes v. Teamsters Local 683, 95 LRRM 2652 (1977), 388

Indianapolis Power & Light Co., 87 LA 559 (1986), 575
Indianapolis Power & Light Co., 130 LRRM 1001 (1988), 349
Inland Steel Company, 77 NLRB 1, enforced 170 F. (2d) 247 (1948), cert. denied 336 U.S. 960 (1949), 498
Internal Revenue Service, 77 LA 19 (1981), 607
International Brotherhood of Teamsters v. United States, 97 S. Ct., 1843 (1977), 561

Jacobs Manufacturing Co., 28 LRRM 1162 (1951), aff'd, 196 F. 2d. 680 (CA 2, 1952), 553

John Wiley and Sons v. Livingston, 55 LRRM 2769 (1964), 409
Johnson-Bateman Co., 295 NLRB No. 26 (June 15, 1989), 579
Jones & Laughlin Steel Company, 301 U.S. 1 (1937), 72
J.P. Stevens v. NLRB, 441 F. (2d) 514 (CA 5, 1971), 163

Kansas State Meat Packers, 198 NLRB 543 (1972), 408
Kast Metals Corp., 65 LA 783 (1975), 602
Key v. Rutherford, 107 LRRM 2321 (1981), 641
Keyishian v. Board of Regents, 385 U.S. 589 (1967), 641
Kister Lumber Co., 37 LA 356 (1961), 375

Levitz Furniture, 92 LRRM 1069 (1976), 104
Lucky Stores, Inc., 83 LA 760 (1984), 9, 607
Luedtke v. Nabors Alaska Drilling (1989), 579

McAuliffe v. Mayor of New Bedford, 155 Mass. 216, 29 N.E. 517 (1892), 641
Mahoning Sparkle Markets, 91 LA 1366 (1988), 366
Maimonides Institute, 69 LA 876 (1977), 607
Mallinckrodt Chemical Works, 64 LRRM 1011 (1966), 103
Mantolete v. Bolger, 38 FEP Cases 1081 (1985), 577
Marin Honda, 91 LA 185 (1988), 364
Mead Paper, 91 LA 52 (1988), 363
Menzie Dairy Co., 45 LA 283 (1965), 607
Midland National Life Insurance Co., 263 NLRB No. 24 (1982), 157
Minneapolis Star Tribune, 295 NLRB No. 63 (June 15, 1989), 579
Minnesota Mining & Manufacturing Co., 85 LA 1179 (1985), 575
Moore Dry Dock, 92 NLRB 547 (1950), 77
Moore-McCormack Lines, Inc., 51 LRRM 1361 (1962), 124
Morton Thiokol, Inc., 88 LA 254 (1987), 575
Mountain State Construction Company, 203 NLRB 1085 (1973), 408

National Freight, Inc., 55 LRRM 1259 (1964), 113

CASE INDEX ▲ 745

National Tube Co., 76 NLRB 1199 (1948), 104
New York City Health and Hospital Corp., 76 LA 387 (1981), 609
NLRB v. Bell Aerospace Co., 416 U.S. 267 (1974), 109
NLRB v. Bildisco and Bildisco, 465 U.S. 513 (1984), 275
NLRB v. Borg-Warner, Wooster Div., 356 U.S. 342 (1958), 301
NLRB v. City Disposal Systems, Inc., 115 LRRM 3193 (1984), 576
NLRB v. Erie Resistor Corp., 373 U.S. 221 (1963), 345
NLRB v. General Electric Company, 418 F. (2d) 736 (1969), 300, 301
NLRB v. Georgia, Florida, and Alabama Transportation Co., 97 LRRM 2500 (1978), 112
NLRB v. Karl's Farm Dairy, Inc., 92 LRRM 1334 (1978), 111
NLRB v. Pinkerton's Inc., 74 LRRM 2355 (1970), 117
NLRB v. Plymouth Stamping Division, CA 6, No. 88–5469 (March 27, 1989), 569
NLRB v. Truck Drivers Local Union No. 449 et al. (Buffalo Linen Supply Company), 353 U.S. 85 (1956), 352
NLRB v. J. Weingarten, Inc., 88 LRRM 2689 (1975), 374
NLRB v. Truitt Manufacturing Co., 351 U.S. 149 (1956), 299
NLRB v. Yeshiva University, 103 LRRM 2526 (1980), 109, 127
Nolde Bros., Inc. v. Bakery and Confectionery Workers, Local 358 (1977), 409
North American Aviation, 16 LA 747 (1951), 361
Northwest Airlines, Inc., 53 LA 203 (1969), 607

OCAW Local 1–547 v. NLRB, 127 LRRM 3164 (1988), 349
Olin Corporation, 268 NLRB No. 86 (1984), 410
Operating Engineers, 68 LA 254 (1977), 608
Operating Engineers, Local 825 v. NLRB, CA 3, No. 86–3641 (1987), 336, 353
Otis Elevator Company, 116 LRRM 1075 (1984), 553, 569
Ozark Lead Co., 69 LA 1227 (1978), 613

Pacific Gas & Electric Co., 29 LRRM 1256 (1952), 124

Packinghouse Workers, Local 721 v. Needham Packing Company, 55 LRRM 2580 (1963), 409
Pargas of Cresent City, 78 LRRM 1712 (1971), 114
Pennsylvania Labor Relations Board v. State College Area School District, 337A .2d 285, Sup. Ct. of Pennsylvania (1975), 657
Police Associations Local 189 v. Barrett, 111 LRRM 2728 (1982), 641
Potomac Electric Power Co., 83 LA 449 (1984), 608

Raytheon Company, 140 NLRB 883 (1963)
Republic Steel Corp. v. Maddox, 58 LRRM 2193 (1965), 375
Retail Associates, Inc., 120 NLRB 395 (1958), 119
Retail Store Union v. NLRB, 66 LRRM (1967), 124
Riley v. Letter Carriers Local 380, 109 LRRM 2772 (1981), 388
Roemer Industries, 86 LA 232 (1986), 575
Russom v. Sears Roebuck and Company, 95 LRRM 2914 (1977), 388

Samuel Bingham Co., 67 LA 706 (1976), 577
San Antonio Portland Cement Company, 121 LRRM 1234 (1985), 374
Sargent Electric Co., 209 NLRB 630 (1974), 386
Schultz v. Wheaton Glass, 9 FEP Cases 502 (1970), 486
Scoa, Inc., 52 LRRM 1244 (1963), 112
Seng Company, 205 NLRB 200 (1973), 408
Shelton v. Tucker, 364 U.S. 479 (1960), 641
Shenango Valley Water Co., 53 LA 741 (1969), 570
Shopping Cart Food Market, Inc., 228 NLRB 190(1977), 157
Smith v. Evening News Association, 51 LRRM 2646 (1962), 410
Spaulding v. University of Washington, 35 FEP Cases 217 (1984), U.S. Sup. Ct., cert. denied, 36 FEP Cases 464 (1985), 489
Speilberg Manufacturing Company, 112 NLRB 1080 (1955), 406, 410
Steel v. Louisville and Nashville Railroad, 15 LRRM 708 (1944), 385

Steelworkers Local 2179 v. NLRB, 125 LRRM 3313 (1987), 569
St. Francis Hospital (II), 116 LRRM 1465, 130
St. Louis Post Dispatch, 92 LA 23 (1988), 364
Summer and Co., Linden Lumber Division v. NLRB, 419 U.S. 301 (1974), 163
Syres v. Oil Workers Union, 350 U.S. 892 (1955), 385

Taylor v. NLRB, 122 LRRM 2084 (1986), 407
Taracorp Industries, 117 LRRM 1497 (1984), 374
Teamsters, Local 174 v. Lucas Flour, 49 LRRM 2619 (1962), 409
Technocast, Inc., 91 LA 164 (1988), 364
Texas Employment Commission v. Hughes, 3 IER Cases 451 (1988), 579
Texlite, Inc., 46 LRRM 1014 (1960), 122
Textile Workers of America v. Lincoln Mills of Alabama, 353 U.S. 448 (1957), 403, 409
Todd Pacific Shipyards, 91 LA 30 (1988), 365
Trading Port, 219 NLRB 298 (1975), 164
Trans World Airlines v. Hardison, 97 S. Ct., 2275 (1977), 561
Tulsa-Whisenhunt Funeral Homes, 195 NLRB 106 (1972), 407

United Paperworkers v. Misco, Inc., 126 LRRM 3113 (1987), 406, 409
United Steelworkers v. Warrior & Gulf Navigation Company, 363 U.S. 574 (1960), 371, 427
United Technologies, 268 NLRB No. 83 (1984), 410
United Telephone Company of Ohio, 91 LA 245 (1988), 365
U.S. Army Armor Center & Fort Knox, 82 LA 464 (1984), 575
U.S. Postal Service, 85 LRRM 1212 (1974), 124

Vaca v. Sipes, 64 LRRM 2369 (1967), 386, 387, 410
Valmac Industries, Inc., 92 LRRM 1334 (1978), 111
Vulcan Asphalt Refining Company, 78 LA 1311 (1982), 608

Wallace Corp. v. NLRB, 323 U.S. 248 (1944), 385

Warrior & Gulf Navigation, 363 U.S. 574 (1960), 404, 409
Washington Hospital Center, 75 LA 32 (1980), 611
W.C. McQuaide, Inc., 220 NLRB 165 (1975), 345
Weis Markets, Inc., 39 LRRM 1465 (1956), 124
West Penn Power Co., 31 LA 297 (1958), 373

Whirlpool v. Marshall, 100 S. Ct. 883 (1980), 574
Whitehall-Copley School District, 76 LA 325 (1981), 611
W.R. Grace & Co. v. Rubber Workers Local 759, 113 LRRM 2641 (1983), 562
Wygant v. Jackson Board of Education, 40 FEP Cases 1321 (1986), 562

Yellow Bus Lines, Inc. v. Teamsters, 127 LRRM 2607 (1988), 347